CONSTITUTIONAL POLITICS

CONSTITUTIONAL POLITICS

The Political Behavior of Supreme Court Justices
and the Constitutional Policies That They Make

GLENDON A. SCHUBERT

Professor of Political Science
Michigan State University

HOLT, RINEHART AND WINSTON, INC. · NEW YORK

To Gus and Jim

Preface

THE SUPREME COURT of the United States is a unique political institution, and it certainly ranks second only to the Presidency as a distinctive American contribution to the policy science of governance. In the other Western democracies, one or a group of elderly statesmen who bear no direct political responsibility to the electorate may reign, but they do not rule. No other country in the world entrusts a group of men who are given the formal title of "Justice"—but who typically have had slight if any previous experience as judges—with the basic policy-making authority that is exercised by the Justices of the United States Supreme Court. It is of course true that not all of the decisions of the Supreme Court have important policy implications; but the same comment applies equally to decisions of the President and of the Congress, as students of the Presidency and of the national legislature constantly remind us. The point is that the American constitutional system is geared to the expectation that the Supreme Court frequently and continuously will make certain kinds of decisions, ranging from tentative to final and conclusive, that for political reasons cannot under existing institutional arrangements be made by other decision-making groups in our polity.

It is customary in textbooks and in casebooks in American constitutional law for the authors to focus their attention upon the substance of the Supreme Court's decisions, although incidental attention is always given, at least implicitly if not always systematically, to the political significance of the Court's role as an instrumentality or institution of government. Those who embrace this approach usually are led to attempt to present a more or less encyclopedic statement of constitutional law, which the authors define in terms of the meaning attributed to the Constitution by the Supreme Court in selected "leading" or "landmark" cases. This is a subject which certainly is not unworthy of study; and, no doubt, for the handful of lawyers who are able to make practice before the Supreme Court their principal stock in trade, this range of data and area of human knowledge are indispensable. And for the vast majority of lawyers, as for members of other professional and occupational groups, a selective knowledge of constitutional law in this sense (like a selective knowledge of congressional statutes and presidential and administrative orders and regulations and analogous sources of state policy directives) may indeed be important, at least from time to time. But it is doubtful that this lore is the most important universe of information about the Supreme Court, or that it is cast in a frame of reference that is likely to suggest the most significant insights, to students either of law or of political science.

In this book, it is assumed that a more relevant and a more fruitful approach consists of a focus upon the decision-making behavior of Supreme Court Justices, and upon the policy-making role, in selected major areas of substantive constitutional politics, of the Justices as a group and as the formal leaders of a governmental agency. Necessarily, this involves an examination of many of the same Supreme Court decisions that are included in casebooks organized in terms of more traditional approaches to constitutional law.[1] Indeed, this book contains as many or more cases than most of the other casebooks in constitutional law that have been published within the past decade. The difference in treatment lies not so much in the specific content as in the organization and analysis of the data, and the pedagogical goals that these cases are included to subserve. The focus in this book is upon how and why the Supreme Court makes certain decisions (i.e., chooses certain policy alternatives in preference to others), and with what consequences, although attention also is given to the substance of the decisions that the Court has made in various policy areas. No attempt is made, however, to present an emendated or annotated text of the Constitution; a number of satisfactory constitutional histories are available, and for an analytical approach keyed to the structure of the constitutional document, it seems unlikely that any other scholar will have much to add, at least for a time, to Professor Corwin's still recent and monumental compendium.[2]

It is customary when publishing a book for the author to give credit to those persons who have helped him to get the job done, and to claim in his own behalf personal responsibility for the inevitable errors of attention or judgment that appear in any work of substantial dimensions. I join in this quaint but gracious tradition. Errors may be inevitable, but they are best corrected; so I shall appreciate having readers call them to my attention. As for debts, undoubtedly my greatest intellectual obligation is to my friend and colleague, Robert G. Scigliano, who shared in the planning of the original outline and in the conceptualization of the work. It was intended that this book should be a joint

[1] Contrary to tradition, however, there is here no reprinting of the Constitution in an appendix. Certainly, this betokens a lack of neither interest in nor appreciation of the significance of the document as a document. The fact is, however, that only a small portion of the total text is relevant to the decision-making of the Supreme Court today; and those clauses that are germane have been quoted, usually, in the place in the text where a precise knowledge by the student of such language will be most useful. The complete text of the document is available in a wide variety of sources, such as the rear part of almost any text in American government, that will be convenient to most students.

[2] Edward S. Corwin (ed.), *The Constitution of the United States of America: Analysis and Interpretation*, 82d Congress, 2d Session, Senate Document No. 170 (Washington: G.P.O., 1953).

venture of his and mine; but, unfortunately, other commitments required him to be in Vietnam while I was on campus, and me to be in Norway after his return. As a consequence, we were half a world apart during the time when it was necessary to write and to publish the book, a responsibility which became exclusively my own. Sidney Ulmer, also my friend and colleague, has been most generous in giving of his time and advice in discussing a variety of problems relating to the writing and the content of the work. John R. Schmidhauser of the University of Iowa read the entire manuscript in an earlier draft, and Clement E. Vose of (Connecticut) Wesleyan University read Chapter Three, and their comments and suggestions were helpful to me. And Frank A. Pinner, Director of the Bureau of Social and Political Research at Michigan State University, has been most helpful in regard to and sympathetic toward the antecedent basic research carried out in recent years in conjunction with the Bureau; [3] and that research undoubtedly has exercised an important influence upon the selection and the shaping of materials for inclusion in this volume.

Although neither has had a direct hand in any aspect of the writing of this volume, except to the extent that I have referred to or quoted from their works in several places, I think that I should acknowledge the particular intellectual debt that I owe to two friends, and to part of their previously published work. I refer to Jack W. Peltason of the University of Illinois, and especially to his *Federal Courts in the Political Process;* [4] and to C. Herman Pritchett of the University of Chicago, and to his book *The Roosevelt Court: A Study in Judicial Politics and Values, 1937-1947.* [5] I wish also to express my particular appreciation to John R. Schmidhauser and to Clement E. Vose for their kind permission to quote extensively from several of their articles and papers. I have also relied indirectly, but I am sure significantly, upon the writings of Alpheus T. Mason of Princeton, and in particular upon his Bacon Lectures of a few years ago, *The Supreme Court: Vehicle of Revealed Truth or Power Group, 1930-1937.* [6]

Several of my former graduate assistants, but in particular Alvin Dozeman, Peter Sonnenfeld, and James Wresinski, performed indispensable functions in helping to assemble much of the data that has been used. Joyce Bell, Mary Vanden Berge, and Shirley M. Goodwin typed the original draft of the manuscript; and the Department of Political Science and the All-University Research Fund of Michigan State University assisted in providing physical facilities and funds without which the writing of the book would have been impossible. The index was prepared by Mrs. William H. Downey.

True to tradition, I reserve the best until last: the advice, comfort, and en-

[3] See Glendon A. Schubert, *Quantitative Analysis of Judicial Behavior* (Glencoe: The Free Press and the Michigan State University Bureau of Social and Political Research, 1959), and especially the set of "Working Papers in Research Methodology," cited therein at page 23.

[4] (Garden City: Doubleday Short Studies in Political Science [presently distributed by Random House], 1955).

[5] (New York: Macmillan, 1948).

[6] (Boston: Boston University, 1954).

couragement of my helpmeet. Only fellow-sufferers will truly appreciate the sympathy and forbearance required of a mother of five children who somehow manages to raise them in a domicile in which her husband is simultaneously engaged in the writing of a book. This particular work is dedicated to our two sons.

Glendon A. Schubert

Oslo, Norway
February, 1960

Contents

APPENDIXES   701

Figures and Tables

Introduction

IF THE ASSUMPTION is made that the Justices of the Supreme Court are a political group, it follows that the behavior of the Justices might be examined from the perspectives associated with various social-science approaches such as those denominated as "group theory," "role theory," "elite theory," and so forth. Few results of such research are reported in this volume, for a reason that is suggested in the following recent comment by a political scientist: [1]

> [I]t is somewhat disconcerting to find that C. Wright Mills' otherwise challenging analysis of the new American elite system [*The Power Elite*] virtually ignores the Court and its members as independent factors to be considered in determining the situs of political power and the nature of America's emerging political elite. Mills apparently disposed of this problem by simply overlooking the Court. Few would deny Mills' contention that "the center of initiative and decision has shifted from the Congress to the executive," but his failure to discuss the role of the court and the status (or lack of status) of Supreme Court members in the modern political elite is a serious omission.

The basic research in which modern social-science theories are applied to the behavior of the Supreme Court remains to be done. Legal scholars are sufficiently impressed with the importance of the Court's activities, but only during the past few years have they begun to explore the possibility of adapting social-science theories and research methods to the study of judicial decision-making. Social scientists, on the other hand, and with very few exceptions, have ignored the Su-

---

[1] John R. Schmidhauser, "The Justices of the Supreme Court: A Collective Portrait," *Midwest Journal of Political Science,* Vol. 3, pp. 3-4 (1959).

preme Court as an appropriate subject for political analysis. An attempt has been made to incorporate in this volume, however, examples typical of the limited volume of behavioral research in judicial decision-making that has taken place to the date of this writing. Conceptually this book owes much to such pioneering studies.

Part I attempts to establish a behavioral frame of reference for political analysis of the Supreme Court. This is accomplished primarily by analyses of (1) the reasons why the Court, because of its political role and function, is inescapably involved—at times more and at times less—in political controversy; [2] (2) the socio-economic-political backgrounds of the justices, and of the factors which affect the acquisition of and separation from office on the Supreme Court; and (3) the process by which the justices make decisions, in relationship to the other individuals and groups and institutional factors which affect Supreme Court decision-making. It is intended that these three chapters, plus chapter 4, will provide the conceptual tools which can then be applied to the study of the more substantively oriented materials in the remaining chapters in this book.

Part II deals with the interrelationships between the Supreme Court and the Congress, the Executive Branch, and the so-called "inferior" or lower courts, both federal and state. One of the Supreme Court's major functions is to arbitrate conflicts of interest among the three branches of the national government whose disparate activities reflect, very roughly and imperfectly, the "separation of powers" frequently attributed to the Constitution. An analysis of this subject need not be concerned with the historical quarrel whether (as most responsible scholars now agree) or not (as a minority voice proclaims from time to time—whenever the shoe begins to pinch) the "Fathers of the Constitution" intended the Supreme Court to exercise the power of judicial review. But very different is the question how and under what circumstances the Court ventures to veto policy decisions by what the Court itself terms the "political departments" of the government, and with what effect. It is equally important to know what kinds of restraints and controls the Congress and the President can exercise to overrule or to inhibit the Court's participation in the formulation of basic national policy. But it should not be assumed that such relationships are necessarily or usually one of conflict between branches which run around checking (if not checkmating) and balancing one another; mutual interdependence upon the reinforcing effects of the Court's sharing in national policy-making responsibilities may be a much more usual circumstance.

Part III is concerned with what is probably a more clearly indispensable function of the Court: the arbitration of conflicts of interest between the national government and the states. The "national government," in this sense, implies

[2] As Holmes once remarked of the Court, "We are very quiet there, but it is the quiet of a storm centre, as we all know." From his speech "Law and the Court," at a dinner of the Harvard Club in New York on February 15, 1913. Oliver Wendell Holmes, Jr., *Speeches* (Boston: Little, Brown, 1913), p. 98.

the policy norms which, by a complex antecedent political process, have received sufficient support to be cast in the form of "laws" such as acts of Congress, executive orders of the President or administrative regulations of subordinate administrative authority, or prior decisions of the Supreme Court or (sometimes) of lower federal courts. Similarly, by "states" we imply the analogous laws that embody policies resulting from the functioning of the political process within each state—by no means necessarily a less complex process of law-making than that which is associated with the national government. The "conflicts of interest" are therefore between the people who have induced governments at the two levels to establish policies which, at least in the special vocabulary of lawyers, can be said to be incompatible. From among a much larger universe of substantive policy areas in which there is coalescence of policy-making by the nation and the states, three have been selected as the most important to an understanding of the role played by the Supreme Court in providing a continuous, peaceful, and generally authoritative adjustment of the federal equilibrium in the American constitutional polity. Under historic practice and accepted constitutional practices, only the Supreme Court can and does perform this function except in times of great national crisis such as a major war; and under such circumstances, the constitutional system itself changes, with the political branches of the national government supplying initiative and political leadership that are beyond the capacity of the justices to provide.

Part IV focuses upon the Court's role in arbitrating interest conflicts between minorities and individuals, on the one hand, and the majority (or more cohesive and powerful minorities) who are able to speak through the agencies of organized government, on the other. In this, the area usually denoted as that of civil rights and liberties, there are two major policy strands which have figured most significantly in the work of the Court, whether measured in quantitative or in qualitative terms, during what is generally considered to be the modern period in the Court's jurisdiction: since 1925.[3] These relate to the freedoms of the First Amendment—speech, press, religion, assembly, and petition—and to the procedural and substantive rights of criminal defendants. During the 1950's, the constitutional policies appropriate to define the procedural rights of quasi defendants [4]—employees facing dismissal charges in loyalty hearings, hostile witnesses before legislative or judicial investigating committees,[5] aliens facing exclusion or deportation,

---

[3] For an explanation of why this date is chosen, see the section on "The Supreme Court's Jurisdiction" in chapter 3. Of course, when speaking not in terms of workload and discretionary control over jurisdiction but about the substantive constitutional policies that the Court supports, it would be more correct to say that the modern period dates from 1937, for reasons that are discussed in the concluding section of chapter 3.

[4] For this suggestive concept and term, which I have used freely in chapter 11, I am indebted to David Fellman's The Defendant's Rights (New York: Rinehart, 1958), especially his chapter 12.

[5] "Hostile" is used here in the technical, legal sense. From a political point of view, it would probably be more accurate to speak of "Witnesses before hostile legislative or judicial investigating committees."

passport applicants, and civilians being tried by courts-martial—were also among the most controversial issues upon which the Court acted. An understanding discussion of the Court's decisions affecting civil rights and liberties requires that some attention be given to legal conceptualism, particularly since the Constitution employs different language in postulating restraints upon the national and state governments, and federalism is an independent variable which intervenes, for many of the Justices, in policy choices affecting civil liberties.

Although the largest single class of data included in this book consists of edited abridgments of the official reports of formal decisions of the Supreme Court, it would have been impossible to explore the questions and the issues that had been defined as relevant if, as frequently is done, the nontextual material had been limited to Supreme Court cases. Consequently, numerous tables and charts, which combine economy in presentation with specific kinds of hypotheses about the behavior of the justices, have been utilized for the purpose of analyzing sets of related decisions. This kind of presentation makes possible an extension of the context and ramifications of the particular cases that are reprinted, in a way that should be much more meaningful and useful to the student than the usual legal "case note," which refers with brief or no comment to groups of related cases, somewhat after the fashion of a citator.

A not inconsiderable body of noncase writings also is included. Their incorporation within the book, in preference to more extensive bibliographic references, reflect the author's experience in teaching this and other related subjects in several universities and colleges, large and small. Basically, the justification is the same as that for reprinting Supreme Court cases instead of having students read the full text of the original reports in the library. Except for law libraries, even large universities frequently have but a single set of complete reports of the Supreme Court's decisions in the general library; and to turn a class of fifty students, or even one of half that size, loose to compete for access to the single volume in which each individual case is found results in mayhem to the reports and frustration for the class and their instructor. The same comment holds for bound periodicals and other sources in which relevant materials may be found. And, of course, many relevant materials are simply unavailable in the libraries of some smaller colleges. Consequently, it has been assumed that instead of a comprehensive (or even a select) bibliography that can and will be utilized effectively by only a small minority of students, it is preferable to incorporate readings, edited and abridged like the cases and selected for their specific utility as a complement to the cases, which will be available to all students in courses in which the book is used. Moreover, such incorporation makes possible a much closer degree of integration between textual matter, cases, and readings, both in terms of actual substance and in terms of student perception, than does a "list of readings" which the student pursues (in principle) in the library, frequently independently of both the cases and class discussion.

In editing the cases, an attempt has been made to adhere to certain criteria that ought to be observed, if there really is—as assumed here—a justification for employing the case method of instruction in preference to the greater economies that inhere in a textbook. The basic assumption is that students ought to be presented with what constitute, at least in one sense, the raw materials of a problem in policy-making, with consequent articulation of an interest conflict. By associating policy norms with a specific factual context, the abstractness of generalized statements about values can be reduced to more comprehensible terms, a reduction which is important since students, by and large, are not in a position to relate public policy norms to a body of personal experience. This objective implies that cases should be edited so as to retain an adequate statement of the facts upon which the questions for decision by the Court are premised. There are always alternatives of choice in the decisions of the Court, and if cases are to be used to present problems in public policy-making, students should be made aware of the alternatives as well as the choice of a majority of the Court. If they are to be aware, then concurring and dissenting opinions should be retained, at least to the extent that they focus upon questions germane to the policy issue to be exemplified by a case.

These points may seem so self-evident that mention of them is unnecessary; but it is not uncommon for casebooks to excise a few paragraphs from an opinion of the Court and to present these as a "case," as though the official rationale to support the Court's holding—the "rule of law" for which the case "stands"—were all that is really significant in a decision. The underlying assumption for the construction of such "cases" must be that the pedagogical objective is to string groups of them together like beads on a thread, so that the student can excogitate the "principle of law" which flows logically from a (chronological) series of related cases. This book is concerned with the rule of *stare decisis,* but not as the generating principle that accounts for a body of constitutional law that is a "seamless web." Indeed, it is doubtful that any serious student of the Court entertains such a notion today. Nevertheless, doctrinal analysis seems to be the major teaching objective for which many casebooks in constitutional laws are designed, if one is to judge from their organization and contents.

Of course, doctrinal analysis can also be used as an iconoclastic tool, to demonstrate the extent to which the Court fails to observe the rule of *stare decisis* in its decision-making.[6] But without more than this, one can conclude at the most that the Court is seldom inconsistent, or frequently inconsistent, or usually inconsistent, or always inconsistent. It is much more important to know how and why the Court makes changes in the constitutional policies that it announces, and with what consequences. This kind of understanding requires that relatively more attention be focused upon the behavior of the justices, of those persons who

---

[6] Cf. Victor G. Rosenblum, *Law As a Political Instrument* (Garden City: Doubleday Short Studies in Political Science, 1955).

share in the shaping of policy conflicts for their decision, of those persons responsible for the translation of the Court's mandates into specific human behaviors, and of those persons who are affected by, and who therefore respond to, the Court's decisions. Certainly not inattention, but correspondingly less emphasis upon the content of specific policy norms (i.e., "rules of law") is required, given the assumption that the major objective of studying constitutional law should not be to learn and to memorize what the Court has said, but rather should be to understand the ecological process by which decisions of the Court are made.

In addition to presenting the facts and the opinion of the Court and relevant concurring and dissenting opinions, and such usual indicia as the citation of the United States Reports,[7] other information has been associated systematically with the edited cases in this volume. When it is significant to know the time of decision more precisely than the year, this datum is included. If the dates of oral argument or reargument are important, they are included. If intervening personnel changes of the Court are relevant, they are noted. The lower court whose decision is being reviewed is always given, and also the process by which the Court made its jurisdictional decision in the case (usually certiorari or appeal or, in older cases, writ of error). A table accompanying the introduction to each case shows the voting and opinion-writing behavior of the justices in the decision, using the following standard symbols:

+ = voted with the majority who determined the disposition of the case
− = dissenting vote against the disposition made of the case
‘ ’ = wrote opinion
( ) = joined in the opinion of the Court
(= concurring opinion
) = dissenting opinion
NP = seated but not participating in this decision

Unless there is specific indication to the contrary, footnotes have been omitted from the opinions of the justices, and those few that have been retained have been renumbered. A similar practice has been followed in the editing of noncase materials which are quoted.

[7] The reporting of the decisions of the Court is explained in Appendix A.

A BEHAVIORAL
APPROACH TO THE
SUPREME COURT

A BEHAVIORAL APPROACH to the Supreme Court implies something more than logical analysis of the content of the Court's decisions, and of the opinions of the Court written in justification of the minority of decisions that the Court purports to decide "on the merits" of the issues presented. A behavioral approach implies at least this much:

1. A *political* approach to the Court views the justices as official decision-makers who are continuously engaged in the formulation and reformulation of public policy that results in a more or less authoritative reallocation of values, goods, and services within American political society. It requires investigation of the processes of persuasion by means of which persons and groups whose interests are affected by the Court's decisions attempt to influence the justices. This can be done by trying to prevent issues from reaching the Court for decision; by shaping the presentation of those issues that do reach the Court; by attempting to get the Court itself (or lower courts, or the Congress, or the Administration, etc.) to adhere to or to modify or revoke policies that the Court has announced; and so forth. A political approach also necessitates an analysis of the competence and effectiveness of the Court in making certain kinds of policy decisions in comparison to alternative decision-making agencies (such as lower courts, Congress, and the Presidency).

2. A *psychological* approach to decision-making by the Court makes an attempt to understand why the justices, as individual human beings, select some alternatives rather than others in their voting and opinion-writing behavior. Of course, negative action—which may take the form of refusing to participate in a decision, or of withholding one's vote until a later time, or of voting but refusing to accept any of the opinions written in a case—may in theory be just as significant as positive action, but it is much harder to study on the basis of the published official records of the Court's decision-making.

3. A *sociological* approach to the official actions of the justices views them as actors in a small, primary, elite group. Certain kinds of decisions are made by the individual justices, and other decisions are made for each of them by their administrative assistants, while still other decisions are made in the name of the whole Court by the Chief Justice. But the range of formal decision-making with which the Court is identified in public opinion involves group action of several stages: (a) consultation and voting on the "jurisdictional" decision; (b) the hearing of oral argument; (c) consultation and voting on the merits; and (d) announcement of the group decision and the reading of opinions authored by individuals

but representing views acceptable to the group as a whole, or to more-or-less stable subgroups, or to individual justices.

4. An *administrative* approach considers the Court to be a public agency whose decision-making processes can and should be investigated like those of other agencies of American government. Questions of hierarchy, span of control, formal and informal delegation of decision-making authority, staff and line relationships, and similar aspects of the organization of human beings and other resources, and of the processes through which they interact, are inescapably involved in the work of the Court. Questions of administrative efficiency are of vital concern to the justices themselves, and certainly are a relevant consideration to their decision-making.

5. A *quantitative* approach is necessary in order that systematic observation and measurement may be obtained of both the decisions of the Court as a group and the votes of the justices as individuals. The subjective evaluations of individual researchers are important, and in most respects it is not yet feasible to substitute quantitative indices for such qualitative judgments. But the insights of individual scholars are of uncertain validity and of limited reliability; and the creation of a scientific body of knowledge about the Court is largely a function of the development of standardized and transferable techniques of observation and measurement which facilitate systematic comparison of the voting behavior of the justices and of the decisions of the Court, and which minimize the subjective factors in the judgments of analysts. Moreover, quantitative analysis is a prerequisite to the examination of the total universe of the Court's decisions, which now includes approximately two thousand cases annually.

In the next three chapters, we shall attempt to establish a frame of reference consistent with the use of a combination of the behavioral approaches described above. In the first chapter we shall examine the ecological factors which make the Court's role, given the American constitutional policy, inherently political, and the Court's function necessarily controversial. In Chapter 2, attention is directed to the sociopolitical background of the individual justices who have been and who are members of the Court, in order to determine what kinds of values they can be expected to represent and what kinds of policies they can be expected to support. We must also look at the objectives and expectations of the Presidents who select men to be members of the Court, and similarly, we must examine the effect that senatorial concurrence has upon the selection process. The life term of the justices requires that we investigate the relationship between the age of the justices and their tenure and performance.

Chapter 3 focuses upon what might be termed the "natural history" of a case before the Court, tracing through the various steps involved in "consideration" by the "Court," from the agitation of selected issues by outside pressure groups (before a case is even initiated in the lower courts) to attempts to persuade the Court to reconsider decisions that it has formally made and announced. (As we pointed out in the Preface, much of Chapter 4 is closely related to this subject; and attempts to change the Court's decision by invoking the decision-making of other groups external to the Court are discussed in that chapter.) The materials examined in Chapter 3 strongly suggest that the kind of political and administrative experience that a justice has had *before* he joins the Court will have an extremely important influence upon the way in which he organizes and handles his work as a justice.

Any analysis of the voting and opinion-writing behavior of the justices that extends beyond mere counting must take into consideration the obvious fact that there are more-or-less stable subgroupings of the justices that reflect, it may be assumed, differences in their basic attitudes toward the policy issues raised for decision by cases, as well as their reactions to fact elements peculiar to each case. Such sociopsychological dimensions of the decision-making of the justices can be investigated, at least to some extent, by the use of certain methodological tools. In Chapter 3 and at appropriate points later in this volume, we shall employ bloc analysis, cumulative scaling, and some elementary concepts from game theory in order to extend our inquiry to relevant sociopsychological factors that otherwise would lie beyond the scope of our investigation.

It is hoped that Part I will provide both the concepts and an elementary understanding of the methodological tools which can then be used as a basis for class discussion and analysis of the materials in the chapters that follow in Parts II-IV.

1

The Supreme Court
in Political Context

SOME MEN worship icons, some worship spirits, and some worship judges. We are concerned in this book only with the latter form of reverence, and then only to the extent that it is a factor bearing upon political analysis of the Supreme Court. Some devotees of what the late Jerome Frank called "the cult of the robe" [1] would say, in effect, "My justices! May they always be right; but right or wrong, my justices!" [2] Others who are legal positivists take the position that the Supreme Court (like the Queen of England) can do no wrong, since the will of the Court *is* the law.[3] Whether by reason of faith or by reason of definition, in either case the Constitution means precisely what the justices say it means, neither more nor less. Those who are followers of this camp will doubtless be more shocked than amused by the following astringent piece of doggerel, which obviously dates from the days of the New Deal and the Court-packing episode:

Song of the Supreme Court [4]

We're nine judicial gentlemen who shun the common herd,
Nine official mental men who speak the final word.

[1] *Courts on Trial* (Princeton: Princeton University Press, 1949), chap. xviii.

[2] See the differing attitudes toward the Court expressed by federal and state judges, as reported in the *New York Times*, October 2, 1958, p. 20, col. 3.

[3] Such persons are fond of quoting the dar-ing remark by Charles Evans Hughes, uttered during the period between his two tenures on the Court, to the effect that "we are under a Constitution, but the Constitution is what the judges say it is."

[4] By Arthur L. Lippmann, in the former *Life Magazine*, Vol. 102, p. 7 (August, 1935).

11

We do not issue postage stamps or face the microphones,
Or osculate with infants, or preside at corner-stones.
But we're the court of last resort in litigation legal.
(See: Case of Brooklyn Chicken *versus* Washington Blue Eagle.)
We never heed the demagogues, their millions and their minions,
But use *this* handy yard-stick when in doubt about opinions:

Chorus
If it's In The Constitution, it's the law,
For The Constitution hasn't got a flaw.
If it's In The Constitution, it's okay,
Whether yesterday, tomorrow, or today—
Hooray!
If it's In The Constitution, it must stay!

Like oysters in our cloisters, we avoid the storm and strife.
Some President appoints us, and we're put away for life.
When Congress passes laws that lack historical foundation,
We hasten from a huddle and reverse the legislation.
The sainted Constitution, that great document for students,
Provides an air-tight alibi for all our jurisprudence.
So don't blame us if now and then we seem to act like bounders;
Blame Hamilton and Franklin and the patriotic founders.

Chorus
If it's In The Constitution, it's the law, *etc.*

Such sentiments are not only good-humored but also mild indeed by comparison to other charges that have been leveled against the justices, both before and since. The same comment applies to the substance of President Franklin Roosevelt's contemporaneous attack upon the Court—what Roosevelt said, and what he proposed, was relatively innocuous.[5] Yet there was an intense reaction to Roosevelt's proposals for the reorganization of the Court, which found most of the leaders of his own party as well as the opposition to the New Deal rallying to the support of the Court and the Constitution for which it stood. The tidal wave of political support that came to the temporary defense of the Court can be attributed, in part, to the anxieties engendered by the source of the attack; in part, to the skillful political leadership of Chief Justice Hughes in helping to or-

[5] In his message to the Congress, Roosevelt said that the justices of the middle 1930's were quite old men (which was true); that the justices could not keep up with their dockets (which was untrue then, but is true now); and that a group of younger assistant judges would help the Court to get its work done on time (which is doubtful). He later added that the values represented by a majority of the Court were those of the Republican Party, which the voters had recently and emphatically repudiated, not once but twice (which was true, but spoken too late).

ganize the opposition; and in part, to the strength of the "cult of the robe" as a political myth which most Americans believe and to which others ordinarily pay lip service.

The essence of New Deal criticism of the Court was that a majority of the justices refused to acquiesce—as they began to do immediately after the Roosevelt attack [6]—in the authority of the Presidency and the Congress to establish national policies that appeared to have widespread popular support. The Court won the logomachy, and was victorious in the war of symbols; but it was a Pyrrhic victory. The Court first reformed itself and ceased to oppose the policies and program of the New Deal. Immediately thereafter, the President began to pack the Court with a majority of justices of his own choice, a process that was completed within four years. It was sixteen years before the Supreme Court again interposed its authority to interfere in an important question of national policy; and that was in the Steel Seizure case of 1952,[7] when an outgoing President, who had lost control over Congress, presented the Court with an opportunity to choose between presidential and congressional policy alternatives.

By this time, both the "political departments" and the Court had changed so much that the shoe was on the other foot: once again liberal professors had begun to criticize the justices for their reactionary decisions.[8] At a time when Roosevelt appointees still constituted a majority of the Court—and four of them, Black, Reed, Frankfurter, and Douglas were (in that order) Roosevelt's initial choices to reform the Court—a Yale law professor was roundly berating Chief Justice Vinson and his brethren: [9]

> The Supreme Court of the United States today belies its awe-inspiring title. Degraded by President Truman's devil-may-care appointment of four justices whose work has ranged from mediocre to miserable, the Court has sunk to its lowest point in a hundred years.
>
> When Truman chose Harold H. Burton, Fred M. Vinson, Tom C. Clark and Sherman Minton, it was clear that their major qualification for the nation's top judicial jobs was that they were old cronies of the President. Today, it is clear that a nine-man Court weighed down by so sad a quartet either cannot or will not properly perform its high function.
>
> To say this is not to make a political judgment based on the undoubtedly rightist slant of all four Truman justices . . . [because] the Truman-Vinson Court, judged both by the quantity of work it takes on and by the quality of its work, has branded itself—conservatism aside—as incompetent, indolent and irresponsible. . . .

---

[6] See the concluding section of Chapter 3.
[7] *Youngstown Sheet and Tube Co.* v. *Sawyer*, 343 U.S. 579 (1952).
[8] See, e.g., Fowler V. Harper, and Alan S. Rosenthal, "What the Supreme Court Did Not Do in the 1949 Term—An Appraisal of Certiorari," *University of Pennsylvania Law Review*, Vol. 99, pp. 293-325 (1950).
[9] Fred Rodell, "Our Not So Supreme Supreme Court," *Look*, Vol. 15, No. 16, pp. 60, 63-64 (July 31, 1951). Copyright (c) 1951 by Cowles Magazines, Inc.

The Hughes Court in its heyday could have done all the work of this past term—beginning in October, when the court meets—and have been home with the term completed by Christmas.

Part of the difference is due to comparative incompetence and part to sheer laziness. Vinson's Court could not keep itself busy last term with the light work load it had undertaken. In the middle of winter, to the slight embarrassment of a couple of its more responsible members, it took off on a six-week vacation, simply for lack of anything much to do. . . .

The man most directly responsible for the Court's shoddy performance of late is, of course, its head, the Chief Justice . . . an old political pal of Truman's and allegedly his present choice for the White House if Truman himself does not run. . . . The talent that helped [Vinson] win the job of Chief Justice was his past-mastery of the political art of achieving compromise. He was supposed to heal the breach in the Court between a Black-Douglas faction and a Frankfurter-Jackson faction which had deepened from a liberal-against-conservative clash over issues into an open clash of personalities.

At this task, Vinson met with failure probably because the legal capacities of all four justices involved were superior to his. The intra-Court squabble has continued unabated, as witnessed by the undiminished flow of split decisions, bitter dissents, special concurring opinions and other evidences of disharmony.

. . . [But the] Court of the Nine Old Men, for all its conservatism, had the courage and integrity to take on the tough cases and meet squarely the important issues that elicited Holmes' and Brandeis' famous dissenting opinions. Vinson's Court, by contrast, has effectively muzzled [liberal justices] Black and Douglas whenever it has ducked a [segregated housing] case or a freedom-of-the-press case or any of scores of other cases where a probable conservative decision would doubtless have sparked a stinging dissent.

On the plain face of the record to date, the Truman-Vinson Court has not only carried its incompetence into irresponsibility but has also stretched its conservatism to the point of cowardice.

And if, as has been said, what Presidents do is often interred with their Administrations while it is their choice of Supreme Court Justices that lives after them, then Harry Truman may yet go down in history as the man who dishonored the Supreme Court of the United States.

Only six years later, however, the tide of political affairs had brought about another major change in the balance of political forces affecting the national government. By this time, four of the more conservative of the Roosevelt-Truman justices had departed from the bench, to be replaced by Eisenhower's appointees, including a new Chief Justice who was considered to be presidential timber. Now the Court was attacked on opposite grounds and from actors at the other extreme of the political spectrum. The justices were not too lazy; they were too zealous, and tried to decide too many cases. They were not incompetent; they refused to limit the sphere of their competence within reasonable bounds. They were not too conservative; they had become the vanguard of the radical proletarian groups that sought to subvert our free economy and the American way of life. As described by a friend of the Court, a different but also liberal Yale law professor: [10]

"Not since the Nine Old Men shot down Franklin Roosevelt's Blue Eagle in 1935 has the Supreme Court been the center of such general commotion. . . ." The reasons are plain. In the closing weeks of the October term, 1956, the Court handed down a spate of opinions boldly reasserting its authority to review and overturn federal and state action—judicial, legislative and executive—of the highest sensitivity. . . .

Strong courts provoke controversy, and the emergence, under Chief Justice Warren, of a "new" Court ready to exercise full judicial power has proved no exception to the rule. But more than mere controversy and "commotion" have been aroused. Today, regrettably, the Supreme Court is the object of a "wave of sometimes hysterical attack." The attack comes from many quarters, but is garbed in a rhetoric of tedious redundancy:

(1) Senator Byrd, for example, has found it appropriate to assail "the modern Thaddeus Stevens, now cloaked in the robes of the Chief Justice of the United States Supreme Court," who "has done and is doing more to destroy the form of government we have in this country than has any Chief Justice in the history of the United States"; whether the civil rights legislation over which the Senate battled this past summer reflected "any conspiracy between Chief Justice Warren and the NAACP," Senator Byrd "could not say."

(2) Senator Jenner has proposed to restrict the Court's appellate jurisdiction over cases relating to "subversion" or contempt of legislative bodies because the Court "is undermining efforts of the people's representatives at both the state and national levels to meet and master the Communist plot."

(3) Federal District Judge Timmerman has recently taken the justices to task for "reading meanings into the Constitution and out of it that discriminate against white citizens, especially those of the so-called Deep South," and for "construing the Constitution so as to make it a protective shield for the the criminally disposed and disloyal elements in our population." (Of course, to be fair to the jurist, Judge Timmerman was speaking "as a private citizen.")

(4) New Hampshire's Attorney General Louis C. Wyman, speaking as head of the National Association of Attorneys General, has charged that some of the Court's recent decisions constituted an attempt " 'by fiat of five justices' to substitute what he called a philosophy of government patently contrary to that contemplated by the Constitution's makers."

(5) The General Assembly of Georgia, by formal resolution of February 22, 1957, called for the impeachment and removal of the Chief Justice and

10 Louis H. Pollak, "The Supreme Court Under Fire," *Journal of Public Law*, Vol. 6, pp. 428-430 (1957).

Justices Black, Reed, Frankfurter, Douglas, and Clark, because they "are guilty of attempting to subvert the Constitution of the United States, and of high crimes and misdemeanors in office, and of giving aid or comfort to the enemies of the United States after taking an oath to support the Constitution. . . ."

The Yale professor of law thought that "Calumny of so gross a nature impels response"; and contrary to his colleague who had beleaguered the Court only a few years earlier, he devoted the remainder of his article to a scholarly defense of the justices. But in addition to the remarks of public officials, of which the professor quoted a representative sample, there were other hints that the justices were not only misguided but that at least several of them had become part of the Communist conspiracy to destroy America!

In a book bearing the provocative title *Nine Men Against America*, a spokesman for the free-enterprise-system point of view suggested that the justices had irresponsibly turned over their own constitutional responsibilities to a group of left-wing law-school graduates, and that a majority of the Court had conspired together to usurp the liberties of a free people.[11] The master mind behind this plot, according to Rosalie M. Gordon, was the new Chief Justice, former Governor Earl Warren of California. Although the judicial handwriting had been writ plainly on the wall during preceding terms, while the new Chief mustered his forces and gathered strength as more and more Eisenhower cronies took the place of Truman cronies, the day that would really live in infamy was one that "has come to be known as Red Monday, as well it might." [12] Caesar had his Brutus, Napoleon his Waterloo; and the American people, who might well profit from their example, now had the Supreme Court's decisions of June 17, 1957.[13]

According to this author's account, the conspiracy actually began well before Governor Warren became ensconced at the center of the Court. The ostensible reason for Eisenhower's appointment of Warren was, of course, that the new Chief Justice shared the political views of "modern Republicanism," which has been defined as "an elephant trying to make a jackass of himself." But the real reason, as revealed by Miss Gordon, was political in a more fundamental sense; "Earl Warren had delivered the California vote to Eisenhower at the 1952 Republican Convention. Now he had his reward." [14]

The Warren Court's left-wing law clerks were involved because of their influence in making recommendations to guide the votes of the justices in deciding

11 Rosalie M. Gordon, *Nine Men Against America: The Supreme Court and Its Attack on American Liberties* (New York: Devin-Adair, 1958), pp. 113-114, 128-131.

12 The obvious analogy is to May 27, 1935, dubbed "Black Monday" by liberals because of the spate of anti-New Deal decisions announced at that time by the "Nine Old Men."

13 Among the more notorious of these decisions were *Watkins* v. *United States*, 354 U.S. 178 (discussed in Chapter 11, *infra*); and *Yates* v. *United States*, 354 U.S. 298 (discussed in Chapter 10).

14 *Op. cit.*, p. 73. For the details of the alleged political deal, see Miss Gordon's account at pp. 73-74.

which cases, among the thousands that the Court is asked to review each term, should be heard and decided on the merits. A decade earlier, Rodell had castigated the Vinson Court for avoiding work; Gordon now railed against the Warren Court for trying to do too much. The zeal of the young socialists who assist the justices led them, consciously or otherwise, to induce the Warren Court to overcommit itself, thus falling further and further behind in its dockets: [15]

> . . . The thing that was causing the trouble was that the Court was agreeing to hear an unprecedented number of cases. In the 1956-1957 term, for instance, it agreed to hear 208 cases. From 1948 to 1955, the figure ran from eighty-eight to 162 cases per term. Legal experts familiar with the Court's work said it deserved no sympathy for the jam into which it had got itself. It was busy putting its "liberal" hand on a whole batch of lower court decisions on the assumption that these courts didn't know what they were doing. It would be interesting if we could have another survey of how much these bright young law clerks had to do with the high court's determination to make the lower courts truly "inferior.". . .

There are, hopefully, a number of remedies for "this great crisis in our history." As listed by Miss Gordon, these include:

1. Substituting appointment for fixed terms for the present life tenure of the justices.
2. A closely related suggestion that the justices undergo periodic reconfirmation by the Senate.
3. The requirement of substantial judicial experience as a condition to the appointment of at least half of the justices.
4. Substituting election by the Senate for the present system of presidential appointment of Supreme Court justices, subject to confirmation by the Senate.

As Miss Gordon points out, a major effect of at least three of these proposals would be to increase the influence of "the sovereign States" upon the selection, and presumably the decision-making behavior, of Supreme Court justices. In order to become effective, any of these proposals would require amendment of the Constitution.

A more basic reform, however, has been suggested by John T. Flynn, Miss Gordon's long-time associate and the person to whom her book is dedicated. Flynn's proposal must stand, for its stark and pristine simplicity, in a class by itself, like Khrushchev's U.N. speech of September 18, 1959, in which the Great Dict-nik proposed that the best way to reduce international tensions would be to have immediate, universal, and total disarmament. Miss Gordon, who thought

[15] *Ibid.*, p. 114.

that it "would seem to be a necessary prerequisite to all other reforms of the Court," described [16] the Flynn proposition as essentially

> that all decisions of the Supreme Court, from 1937 to the date of the adoption of the proposal, should be declared to have no force and effect as precedents in judicial or other proceedings in determining the meaning of the words, sections, and provisions of the Constitution.
>
> The purpose here is obvious. It is to enable all future Supreme Courts, no matter how otherwise reformed, to disregard the usurpations of the Court in the last twenty years. The justices would return to the body of law and precedents set up before the usurpations began in order to decide on all future cases that would come before them.

Whatever one may think of the merits of such proposals, they do testify to a deep concern for the kinds of policies sponsored by the Supreme Court. As we have seen, the pendulum of political critique of the Court completed two complete swings in only a generation: from left to right, back to the left, and then to the right again, reciprocally to the direction of movement of a majority of the Court. It would have been surprising had it been otherwise. Political criticism of the Supreme Court is neither unusual, unwise, nor—frequently—unwarranted. Certainly it is not "un-American." As Mr. Justice Brewer once put it,[17]

> It is a mistake to suppose that the Supreme Court is either honored or helped by being spoken of as beyond criticism. On the contrary, the life and character of its justices should be the objects of constant watchfulness by all, and its judgments subject to the freest criticism. . . . True, many criticisms may be, like their authors, devoid of good taste, but better all sorts of criticism than no criticism at all.

Constitutional historians, and readers of their works, are well aware of the fact that the United States Supreme Court has been "controversial," at times more so, and at times less so, throughout the history of the nation. So has the Presidency been controversial, and likewise the Congress, and for the same reason. Any group of men who have and who exercise the official power to make decisions that affect the lives and the interests of the American people is certain to become identified with policies which will be acceptable to some and will be opposed by other groupings of the citizenry.

To take a single but apt example, there was only one agency of the national government which, under existing institutional arrangements (viz., the Electoral College, and the rules of internal procedure of the United States Senate) could

16 *Ibid.*, p. 158.

17 From his address entitled "Government by Injunction," delivered on Lincoln Day, 1898, reprinted in 15 Nat. Corp. Rep. 849 (1898), and quoted in Frankfurter's *Mr. Justice Holmes and the Supreme Court* (1938), p. 94, n. 20; as quoted by Pollack, *op. cit.*, p. 431.

have established a national policy of racial integration. This agency was the Supreme Court. The fact that the Supreme Court is the least directly accountable of the three branches of the national government—or to put it more bluntly, the fact that of the three the Court is the most irresponsible politically—certainly does not argue against the legitimacy of criticism of the Court by those whose ox has been gored, nor of efforts on their part to bring about a revision of constitutional policy, by the Court itself or otherwise, in order to remold it more nearly in accordance with what they conceive to be their own self-interest or "the public interest," or closer to whatever other standard of value they may entertain. Congressmen and the President can be voted out of office, after a fashion, if enough of their fellow-countrymen consider them to be rascals. But what can the electorate do about a majority of Supreme Court justices who persist in supporting interpretations of the Constitution that are objected to by the kind of widespread political consensus among the voters which is necessary to deny a second term to an incumbent President or to unseat the veteran congressmen from one-party states or districts—men who, for the very reason of their single-party constituencies, dominate the committee chairmanships and other positions of power in both houses of Congress?

American political traditions reject certain alternatives that are not unknown among our good neighbors to the south; and others suggested in the proposals noted above have never attracted very much support in the past. The functioning of existing institutional restraints upon the justices is discussed in the next two chapters. The remaining restraint is that of public opinion; and we have now observed examples of several somewhat immoderate attempts to influence public attitudes toward the justices. The Georgia legislature does not seriously think—at least, not many of its members probably do—that the House will impeach and that the Senate will convict of "high crimes and misdemeanors" two-thirds of the incumbent members of the Supreme Court. It is even doubtful that Mr. Flynn believes it possible to expunge from the records substantial parts of over fifty volumes of the United States Reports, representing over twenty years of decision-making by the Court. It is enough for the propagandist if a number of Americans can be led to believe that several of the justices *ought* to be impeached, or that the contrariety of constitutional policies that the Court has made, unmade, and remade during the past generation *ought* somehow to be erased from the books.

Attacks from both the left and the right are the price that the Court must pay for being an important political institution. In order for the justices to be immune from dissent from the wings, they would first have to be stripped of effective political power; only then could the American people indulge in the luxury of worshiping the Court, in fact as well as fancy, as a symbol which bears no very meaningful relationship to the hard choices and regrettable conflicts of attitude and interest that characterize real life, including political life.

Legal analysis of the Court's opinions is, therefore, an incomplete and an inadequate basis for an understanding of American constitutional law. What is needed is more than a close reading of the announcements that emanate periodically from the Marble Palace, even if one's objective is to keep in line with the party line. In order to understand constitutional politics and the behavior of the justices, it is necessary to utilize political analysis. We shall begin by looking at the kind of men who become Supreme Court justices.

2

Staffing the Court

To the extent that it is possible to take public office "out of partisan politics," justices of the United States Supreme Court are, and have historically been, isolated from many direct influences of the American political-party system. The Constitution requires that a justice be nominated by the President of the United States; and if a nomination is concurred in by a majority of the Senate, in which all of the states are represented equally and all of the people are represented unequally, the President directs that a commission of appointment issue.[1] Once having taken the oath of office, a justice both literally and figuratively takes his seat[2] on the bench of the Supreme Court, either immediately or, if he should receive his appointment during the Court's summer recess, early in the following October. Once seated, a justice serves until he dies or resigns or retires.[3] His salary, as well as his tenure, is in effect guaranteed for life.

[1] There have been no instances in which an appointment was not offered to a nominee who received senatorial confirmation. See Cortez A. M. Ewing, *The Judges of the Supreme Court, 1789-1937* (Minneapolis: University of Minnesota, 1938), p. 15.

[2] The physical requirements both of sitting on the Court and of the individual justices are such that among the emoluments of office is an old-fashioned high-backed swivel chair designed, in each case, to facilitate the comfort and attentiveness of the occupant. Although the fitting of the chair to the man has been at times so harmonious that it is not unknown for elderly justices to have dozed during tedious and extended oral argument, there appears to be no place for such judicial behavior on the Court today.

[3] In principle, the justices can be removed by impeachment. However, there has been only one attempt—and that one unsuccessful —to remove a justice of the Supreme Court by this process; it occurred over a century and a half ago in the heat of an intense conflict between the two major political parties of the day. Federalist Mr. Justice Samuel Chase was impeached by the Republican House of Representatives for his partisan activities in carrying out his responsibilities for "riding circuit"—not for his actions on the Supreme Court per se—but he was acquitted after a trial by the Senate. We can safely conclude that the remote possibility of a successful impeachment has no significant impact upon the behavior of Supreme Court justices today. Resignation and retirement are discussed at a later point in this chapter.

The combined effect of these legal requisites is to define a milieu in which considerable judicial independence might be expected to thrive.

In this chapter, we are concerned with factors that relate to the staffing of the Supreme Court, and to the politics of the selection of the justices. What sort of men do Presidents nominate to Supreme Court justiceships, and why? How effective, in practice, is senatorial scrutiny of presidential nominations? To what extent does the behavior of the justices fulfill the expectations of the Presidents who appointed them? How, why, and under what circumstances do justices leave the Court? Obviously, the answers to such questions, though important to an understanding of the kind of decision-makers with whom we are concerned, adumbrate only in part the data necessary for a complete description and analysis of the social psychology of the Court. We are limited, however, by the available research, which only recently has begun to explore in any systematic way the hypotheses that bear upon many of the aspects of judicial "independence" that we have specified above.

The mere constitutional requirement that the justices be appointed by the President subject to senatorial confirmation tells us nothing, necessarily, about the extent to which either the Presidency or the Senate has considered the filling of Supreme Court vacancies to be important business. Several thousand positions in the federal executive field service, such as postmasterships, are filled by a process which is *legally* indistinguishable from that followed for Supreme Court appointments; neither the President personally nor the Senate as a whole is well informed about the qualifications of individual postmasters. On the other hand, most Presidents, most of the time, have taken considerable pains in making nominations to the Supreme Court. The point is that Presidents have considered appointments to the Court to be important not because of their constitutional obligations for "making" such appoinments; rather, it has been their recognition, at least since the days of John Adams, of the considerable power wielded by the justices collectively that accounts for the care given to such appointments. The substitution of one or two justices can result, and sometimes has resulted, in a sweeping change in the policies and decisions of the Court.

IS THE SUPREME COURT REPRESENTATIVE OF THE AMERICAN PEOPLE?

The author of a recent leading article has undertaken to examine systematically the social and economic background of all ninety-one justices appointed to the Supreme Court through 1957.[4] He quotes Professor Robert K. Carr,

[4] John R. Schmidhauser, "The Justices of the Supreme Court: A Collective Portrait," *Midwest Journal of Political Science,* Vol. 3, pp. 1-57 (1959). Selections and quotations from this work by permission of Wayne State University Press.

who pointed out somewhat earlier that "it is entirely possible that a careful examination of the personalities and the economic and social backgrounds of the . . . men who have served on the Supreme Court would prove to be as valuable an approach to the American Constitution as the more usual law school approach which lays so much emphasis upon the study of cases, the rule of *stare decisis,* and of fixed legal principles." [5] Among such socioeconomic background factors, "paternal occupation has been accepted as the most trustworthy clue to the determination of social origin." [6]

Occupational Heredity

Professor Schmidhauser divides the century and two-thirds since 1789 into six subperiods, as exemplified in two of his tables which we reproduce at a later point in this chapter. His first table analyzes the major nonpolitical occupations of the fathers of the Supreme Court justices.[7] The occupations are classified as of either "high" or "low" social status; and the high-status occupations are subdivided into merchants; manufacturers; bankers, bank officials, or financiers; plantation owners, wealthy farmers, or land speculators; and professional men, including lawyers, physicians, professors or college administrators, and clergymen. Low-status occupations include mechanics, laborers, and small farmers. If we accept the assumption that paternal occupation is the best criterion of social origin, Schmidhauser shows that at least half of the justices have always come from families identified with three high-status groups: merchants, wealthy farmers, and lawyers; during one period, that of the Taft Court (1920-1932), the proportion was as high as 86%; and the average for all six periods was 60%. On the other hand, the proportion for low-status occupational groups ranged from 0-21%, and the average for all six periods was less than 10%. In Schmidhauser's own words,[8]

> Throughout the entire history of the Supreme Court, only a handful of its members were of essentially humble origin. Nine individuals selected in widely scattered historical periods comprise the total. The remaining eighty-two (90%) were not only from families in comfortable economic circumstances, but were chosen overwhelmingly from the socially-prestigeful and politically-influential gentry class in the late eighteenth and early nineteenth century or the professionalized upper middle-class thereafter. A large number of justices (54, comprising 59% of the total) came from politically-active families. The politically-active families were essentially ones enjoying high social status (99% of the political activity was concentrated in high social status families).

5 *The Supreme Court and Judicial Review* (New York: Farrar and Rinehart, 1942), p. 235.

6 Schmidhauser, *op. cit.,* p. 6.
7 *Ibid.,* p. 7.
8 *Ibid.,* pp. 6, 9.

A concrete example of the effect of social background upon the political attitudes of a justice is found in the career of Samuel Freeman Miller, with whose appointment we shall deal in greater detail at a later point in this chapter. Mr. Justice Miller, of whom it has been said that he "made more constitutional law than the founding fathers," was by common acclaim the outstanding member of the Court during his period of service (1862-1890), and one of the greatest justices —and therefore one of the most important policy-makers—in American political history. It was at the close of this period, shortly after Miller's death, that the Supreme Court wrote laissez-faire into the Constitution.[9] According to Schmidhauser, "Of the sixteen justices chosen, only one man of humble origin, Samuel F. Miller, was appointed during this period [1862-1888], and he was destined to be the last until the selection of Pierce Butler in the 1920's." [10] As for Miller's political attitudes toward the rising tide of industrial giantism that came to dominate the Presidency and the Congress during most of Miller's service on the Court, his biographer has shown how faithful Miller remained, both in his life and in his judicial decisions and opinions, to the ethic of the lower middle class from which he came.

In a private letter written in 1878, Miller wrote: [11]

> I have met with but few things of a character affecting the public good of the whole country that has shaken my faith in human nature as much as the united vigorous, and selfish effort of the capitalists,—the class of men who as a distinct class are but recently known in this country—I mean those who live solely by interest and dividends. Prior to the late war they were not numerous. They had no interest separate from the balance of the community, because they could lend their money safely and at high rates of interest. But one of the effects of the war was greatly to reduce the rate of interest by reason of the great increase in the quantity of the circulating medium. Another was by the creation of a national funded debt, exempt from taxation, to provide a means for the investment of surplus capital. This resource for investment was quadrupled by the bonds issued by the States, by municipal corporations, and by Rail Road companies. The result has been the gradual formation of [a] new kind of wealth in this country, the income of which is the coupons of interest and stock dividends, and of a class whose only interest or stake in the country is the ownership of these bonds and stocks. They engage in no commerce, no trade, no manufactures, no agriculture. *They produce nothing.*

---

[9] See Benjamin R. Twiss, *Lawyers and the Constitution: How Laissez Faire Came to the Supreme Court* (Princeton: Princeton University Press, 1942), chap. vi; and cf. Clyde E. Jacobs, *Law Writers and the Courts* (Berkeley and Los Angeles: University of California, 1954), pp. 85-93.

[10] *Op. cit.*, p. 11.

[11] Quoted in Charles Fairman, "Justice Samuel F. Miller: A Study of a Judicial Statesman," *Political Science Quarterly*, Vol. 50, pp. 21-22 (March, 1935). Cf. Fairman's *Mr. Justice Miller and the Supreme Court, 1860-1890* (Cambridge: Harvard University Press, 1939).

"He opposed," says Professor Fairman, "that extension of judicial protection to property interests which made possible the 'era of acquisition and enjoyment.' . . . In a period when public virtue was no commonplace, Miller remained poor, honest, unwarped in sympathy or intellect. He lived as befitted his office, but his personal tastes were of the simplest. Congress, he felt, was generous in compensating the justices at $6,000, later $10,000, per annum. The Napoleonic maneuvers of railroad magnates might fascinate others, but on Miller's mind they produced only a sense of the hopelessness of protecting the public welfare. He was only amused at a proposal that he resign and accept retainers from such interests." [12] He was at the same time painfully aware of the fact that not all of his colleagues on the Court reacted as he did to the seductions, both direct and indirect, of the industrial entrepreneurs who constituted the ruling oligarchy of his day. At a time, it is important to note, when he was bitterly disappointed at having been passed over for filling the vacancy in the Chief Justiceship created by the death of Chase, and after thirteen years as an associate justice, Miller wrote, again in a private letter: [13]

If I had been made Chief Justice I think I should never have tired in this effort [to make and to keep our court what it should be]. And I may be more affected by the fact that I was not than I am conscious of. But I certainly strove very hard last term to have things go right and to get all the good out of our Chief and my brethren that could be had.

But I feel like taking it easy now. I cant make a silk purse out of a sows ear. I cant make a great Chief Justice out of a small man [Waite]. I cant make Clifford and Swayne, who are too old resign, nor keep the Chief Justice from giving them cases to write opinions in which their garrulity is often mixed with mischief. I cant hinder Davis from governing every act of his life by his hope of the Presidency, though I admit him to be as honest a man as I ever knew. But the best of us cannot prevent ardent wishes from coloring and warping our inner judgment.

It is in vain to contend with judges who have been at the bar advocates for forty years of rail road companies, and all the forms of associated capital, when they are called upon to decide cases where such interests are in contest. All their training, all their feelings are from the start in favor of those who need no such influence.

Thus far, we have *assumed* that a justice will tend to reflect the social ethic to which he was born and bred, and that the *Weltanschauung* that each justice brings with him to the Court will be a major factor affecting his decision-making. Schmidhauser has discussed this assumption of occupational "heredity," and in particular its relationship to familial political activism: [14]

[12] Fairman in *Political Science Quarterly*, Vol. 50, pp. 41, 43.

[13] Quoted in *ibid.*, pp. 42-43.

[14] This quotation, and the discussion which follows in the next several pages, including the two tables, are based directly upon or quoted from Schmidhauser, *op. cit.*, pp. 13-48 *passim*.

The social transmission of attitudes, beliefs, values and aspirations has as its most effective vehicle the family. Since political participation of a very advanced kind appears as a crucial ingredient in the life careers of all but one of the members of the Supreme Court, the nature and extent of family conditioning for such participation deserves special attention. . . . America's "political families" have been able to transmit . . . advantages [which] have included not only the prestige of possession of a "political" name and family connections in a local, state or even national political organization, but also a true political education which is derived from the practice and familiarity with political activity, the encouragement of political ambitions, expectations and perhaps a veritable sense of destiny respecting high political achievement.

Nearly two-thirds of the members of the Supreme Court were raised in this far from common-place type of American family. . . . To an even greater extent than the function of overall political participation, that of judicial service is exceedingly rare in America. Yet . . . thirty-one members of the Supreme Court (one-third) were related to jurists and intimately connected with families possessing a traditional of judicial service.

Ethnic Origins

Even more important than "occupational heredity," however, has been ethnic heredity as an unwritten but ironclad political qualification for office on the Supreme Court. The ethnic origins of every member of the Court, without a single exception, can be traced to Europe. Not a single African or Asian has even been nominated; and, of course, it does not appear that serious consideration has ever been given to the possibility of nominating a woman or a Negro. Indeed, 87% of the justices are derived from "sturdy Anglo-Saxon" stock, fifty-two of them having been English or Welsh and twenty-seven Scotch-Irish or Irish. This leaves only an even dozen, scattered throughout the Court's history, with ancestry from the Continent rather than from the British Isles. The short list includes four of French extraction (Jay, Duval, and the two Lamars); two of Dutch (W. Johnson and Van Devanter); one of Norwegian (Warren); four of Germanic (Catron, Miller, Brandeis, and Frankfurter); and one of Iberian (Cardozo). As Schmidhauser has pointed out, "Among the large ethnic groupings of European origin which have never been represented upon the Supreme Court are the Italians and Southern and Eastern Slavs." "The patterns of ethnic representation," he concludes, "are additional evidence of the virtual monopolization of Supreme Court appointments by the socially privileged segment of the population dubbed the 'old' Americans."

Religious Affiliation

Similarly, 70% of the justices have been affiliated with religious groups classified by Schmidhauser as enjoying high social status: Episcopalian, Presbyterian, Unitarian, Congregational, and in one case, French Calvinist. Another 18% include a scattering of justices affiliated with low social-status Protestant groups: Baptist, Methodist, Disciples of Christ, Lutheran, and Dutch Reformed. There was a single Quaker (Swayne), and fewer than 10% of the justices have been Roman Catholic or Jewish; with the exception of Taney, all of these latter have been appointed beginning in the 1890's. Schmidhauser concludes that, although four (Taney, White, McKenna, and Butler) of the six Catholics and two (Brandeis and Cardozo) of the three Jews were appointed prior to the advent of the New Deal, it was Franklin Roosevelt who first gave deliberate recognition to the claims in behalf of Catholic and Jewish "representation" on the Supreme Court, by his choice of Frank Murphy to succeed Pierce Butler and of Felix Frankfurter to replace Benjamin Cardozo. To the extent that it can be said that such a "custom" of providing representation to these minority faiths exists, it is a quite modern custom which goes back only two decades to the early days of the Roosevelt Court. President Truman deliberately ignored the "custom" when he choose Tom Clark, a Presbyterian, to replace Murphy. On the other hand, "President Eisenhower's selection of William Brennan, a Catholic, a New Jersey Democrat, and a state judge, again provided the Roman Catholic religious group representation on the Supreme Court, but it also fulfilled several other functions. Because the appointment was made just before the presidential election of 1956, some observers noted that it provided President Eisenhower an opportunity to demonstrate his peculiar ability for remaining 'above politics' while at the same time taking an action which might have considerable appeal among normally Democratic urban eastern Catholics." Frankfurter was still on the Court at the time Schmidhauser's article was published in 1959. In any event, Schmidhauser concluded, "The very controversy over the existence of the 'custom' has political significance, and it may be assumed that the religious representation, whether accepted or not, must play a part in subsequent presidential considerations of judicial selections."

The Profession of Law and Politics

LEGAL BACKGROUND OF THE JUSTICES

Schmidhauser's table which shows the kinds of legal education of Supreme Court justices is presented as Table 1, on page 28. During the first century of the Court's existence, a majority of the justices studied law by the apprenticeship system. Since 1889, a majority have attended law schools, and there have been only two justices appointed since the end of World War I who did not acquire

TABLE 1.

Legal Education of Members of the Supreme Court

	NUMBER OF JUSTICES						
TYPES OF EDUCATION	20 (100%) 1789-1828	14 (100%) 1829-1861	16 (100%) 1862-1888	18 (100%) 1889-1919	7 (100%) 1920-1932	17 (100%) 1933-1958	Totals 1789-1958
Law school of high standing in the period [a]	3 (15%)	2 (14%)	4 (26%)	8 (45%)	5 (72%)	11 (65%)	33 (36%)
Private apprenticeship and study under a prominent lawyer or judge	17 (85%)	12 (86%)	10 (61%)	4 (22%)	0	1 (6%)	44 (48%)
Law school of average standing in the period	0	0	1 (6%)	6 (33%)	1 (14%)	5 (29%)	13 (14%)
Self-taught	0	0	1 (6%)	0	1 (14%)	0	2 (2%)
No training in law	0	0	0	0	0	0	0

[a] This category includes colleges or universities which had law professorships but had not formally established law schools.

TABLE 2.

Kinds of Lawyers Appointed to the Supreme Court

TYPES	NUMBER OF JUSTICES							
	20 (100%) 1789-1828	14 (100%) 1829-1861	16 (100%) 1862-1888	18 (100%) 1889-1919	a7 (100%) 1920-1932	17 (100%) 1933-1958	Totals 1789-1958
Lawyers who were primarily politicians	17 (85%)	9 (63%)	5 (32%)	6 (33%)	2 (29%)	10 (59%)	49 (53%)
Lawyers who were primarily state or federal judges	3 (15%)	3 (21%)	7 (45%)	8 (45%)	2 (29%)	1 (6%)	24 (26%)
Corporation lawyers (primarily)	0	0	3 (19%)	4 (22%)	2 (29%)	3 (18%)	12 (13%)
Non-corporation lawyers (primarily)	0	2 (14%)	0	1 (6%)	0	0	3 (3%)
Lawyers by education who were primarily engaged in academic pursuits	0	0	0	0	1 (14%)	3 (18%)	4 (4%)

a Hughes was appointed a second time but is not included in the sample.

their legal education in a law school. No one without legal training has ever been appointed to the Supreme Court, although there is certainly no constitutional requirement that a justice be a lawyer. All except one of the justices practiced law at some stage of their careers; and law was the major *nonpolitical* occupation of all prior to their appointments. "One may conclude," says Schmidhauser, "that in the period before the full development of law schools, those members of the Supreme Court who were taught law by outstanding legal and political leaders gained incalculable educational and political advantages in the process. Throughout the history of the Supreme Court, the recruitment process has generally rewarded those whose educational backgrounds, both legal and non-legal, have comprised the rare combination of intellectual, social and political opportunities which have generally been available only to the economically comfortable and socially prominent segment of the American population."

Table 2, another of Schmidhauser's summaries, shows the kind of legal careers followed by the justices prior to appointment. A majority of the justices were lawyers who were primarily politicians; all of Truman's appointees, and most of Franklin Roosevelt's, fell into this category. About a fourth had pursued primarily judicial careers prior to their elevation to the Supreme Court; in 1956, William Brennan became the first appointee in this category in a quarter of a century. The next most numerous category—which includes three Eisenhower appointees who briefly filled lower federal judicial posts, also by his appointment, immediately prior to their promotions—had spent most of their adult careers as corporation lawyers. Only three of the justices were non-corporation lawyers (and primarily neither politicians nor judges); and four, all members of the Roosevelt Court, had been law-school professors or deans.

Politics as a Vocation

Apart from the fact that a majority had been active politicians, the universal orientation of Supreme Court justices towards legal training and practice is not without significant political implications:

> The very fact that all of the members of the Supreme Court were members of the legal profession in itself merits consideration as a conditioner of social, economic and political attitudes . . . [since] there has been rather general agreement that the influence of the bar in America has been essentially conservative. . . . There is considerable evidence to indicate that most lawyers on the high bench willingly espoused the sort of legal conservatism exemplified in the leadership and ideology of the American Bar Association.

The fact that 80% of the justices have been *either* active politicians or lower-court judges has implications of another sort, however, relating to the predictability of a nominee's behavior *after* his appointment to the Court. Frequently, discussions of judicial qualification have assumed that a political background was in diametrical opposition to a judicial background; and notwithstanding differences in the judgment of commentators as to *which* of these two career backgrounds was more appropriate for a Supreme Court justice, there appears to have been almost universal agreement that the propensities for the subsequent behavior on the Supreme Court of politician-justices and judge-justices were quite different, indeed, antithetical. One of Schmidhauser's most intriguing hypotheses is that a political and a judicial background function in *precisely the same way,* from the point of view of appointing authorities.

In discussing the relationship between political-party regularity and ideological constancy, Schmidhauser points out that:

> The choice of men ideologically committed or thought to be committed to the values of the President making the selection has been the policy most rigidly adhered to throughout American history. . . . The judicial selection process reveals rather convincingly that the selection of individuals of the president's political affiliation served not only as a method of rewarding political supporters, but also as one of several means of identification of a judicial candidate's ideology, although there has usually been strong pressure for both party and ideological consistency. . . . [With] only one exception, George Shiras [1892-1903], every member of the Supreme Court had actively participated in politics before his appointment to the nation's highest tribunal.

Of the 99% of the justices who held other political jobs before they joined the Supreme Court, 60% had filled federal offices, and 35% had been state officeholders, with the remaining 4% classified as political-party officeholders; there were none whose political careers were limited to local experience. The breakdown by branch of government is:

	Federal	*State*
Executive	34%	9%
Legislative	13	7
Judicial	13	19

Federal executice experience and state judicial experience have offered the most promising paths to Supreme Court appointment, and a majority of the justices have come to the Court from such wellsprings.

JUDGING AS A VOCATION

As for politico-judges or judicial-politicians, there has been more than usual propagandizing, in recent years, as exemplified by one of the proposals noted in the first chapter, in behalf of the establishment of a legal requirement that Supreme Court nominees have at least a minimum of prior judicial experience. Supporters of such proposals argue that such appointees will "follow precedent," ecshew social psychology as a source of law, and forego the temptations to indulge in judicial legislation. Some aid and comfort has been given to such partisans by President Eisenhower's penchant for choosing lower-court judges. Only his first appointment, of Warren to the Chief Justiceship, has been an exception to this rule; three of the next four were elevated from federal courts of appeals, and the other from a state supreme court. Schmidhauser, however, suggests that

> The contemporary advocacy of prior judicial experience as a prerequisite for Supreme Court appointment is only the most recent of the manifestations of the fact that advocacy of particular methods of judicial selection is inexorably related to desires for ideological control of the Court. . . . Well over fifty per cent of the justices had served in a judicial capacity at some time before appointment to the Supreme Court, but only slightly more than twenty-five per cent had had really extensive judicial careers. . . . [Moreover], the problem of political ambition whether directed toward the Presidency or, as is frequently overlooked, toward promotion to the Chief Justiceship, represents only one facet of a broader ideological problem. To put it bluntly, there is little evidence to support the view that individuals with primarily judicial careers before selection to the Supreme Court were more objective than those without such experience. And this was generally true whether they cherished political ambitions or not.
>
> There are several historical factors which support this conclusion. First, appointment to an inferior federal judgeship has generally been in the nature of a political reward for recognized partisans. The process of selection of inferior federal judges, which has always been essentially based on patronage, is hardly conducive to the choice of judges who are apt to be aloof to party or ideological issues . . . [and] generally speaking, high state judicial office has required party and ideological commitments whether the posts be appointive or elective. . . . Men like Justices Catron or Davis, despite the fact that they served in state judicial posts for much of their adult careers, were primarily political managers.
>
> Finally, the men chosen for the Supreme Court from the inferior federal bench or higher state courts have almost uniformly been strong ideological partisans. . . . The penchant for Presidents to appoint such men, especially during the periods 1862-1888 and 1889-1919 (when such appointees comprised 45% of the Supreme Court), reflected not a desire to choose men who were aloof, but rather a purposeful determination to select known ideological partisans. . . . [And] despite the examples of Holmes and Cardozo, some of the Supreme Court's most distinguished members, notably Marshall, Story, Taney, Curtis, Campbell, Miller, Bradley, Hughes, Brandeis, and Stone, were totally lacking in this experience before their appointments to the Supreme Court. . . .
>
> Although selection to the Supreme Court has not usually involved the

patronage considerations ordinarily associated with judicial appointment to the inferior federal courts, it has generally involved basically political considerations. Just as training in law has been a necessary educational step in the achievement of a Supreme Court appointment, so has political activism been a virtual precondition for such an appointment. The degree of political involvement of aspirants to the Supreme Court has, of course, varied considerably. In a large number of instances the justices, prior to their appointments, not only held high political office, but were deeply involved in party and campaign management and had close political associations and personal ties with the men who later nominated and appointed them. Thus political activism of a rather intense kind emerges as a necessary stage in career ascent to the Supreme Court.

Political involvement before Supreme Court appointment ordinarily serves as an effective medium for the identification of the political, social and economic values of prospective Court members by interest groups seeking to assure the ideological soundness of new appointees [and the] appointment of men with prior judicial experience, especially those with extensive careers in the inferior federal courts or the state courts, was of great importance in particular historical periods. These appointments frequently served the practical function of identifying ideological partisans as did selection from the ranks of the openly avowed political activists.

The picture that emerges in the pattern of recruitment of Supreme Court justices is one which emphasizes the intimacy of judicial and political affairs. Since the most important function of the Supreme Court is the settlement of fundamentally political issues through the medium of judicial review, the political background of the justices undoubtedly represents a very necessary and valuable source of experience and training.

A somewhat different view of this question is found in the more recent remarks of Felix Frankfurter. In his earlier professorial writings such as *Law and Politics*,[15] Frankfurter seems to agree with Schmidhauser that prior judicial experience *is* a useful index to a man's probable behavior as a justice; but Mr. Justice Frankfurter urges persuasively that service as a lower-court judge ought to be considered simply *irrelevant* to the choice of nominees to the Court. Thus, Schmidhauser's approach is realistic, because he purports to describe what is done and why; while the latter-day Frankfurter's approach is idealistic, because he addresses himself to the normative question of what ought to be recognized as relevant factors in choosing men for the Court who are likely to become recognized as great justices.[16] Frankfurter the judge wrote: [17]

---

[15] A. MacLeish and E. F. Prichard (ed.), *Law and Politics: Occasional Papers of Felix Frankfurter* (New York: Harcourt, 1939).

[16] Whether, indeed, the American polity would be better off if the Court were—as it never has been in the past—simultaneously populated primarily with great jurists like Marshall, Holmes, and Hughes, is at the very least an assumption that no doubt merits independent and critical examination. See John P. Frank, *The Marble Palace* (New York: Knopf, 1958), pp. 68-69.

[17] Felix Frankfurter, "The Supreme Court in the Mirror of Justices," *University of Pennsylvania Law Review*, Vol. 105, pp. 785, 787, 788, 795 (1957).

To an uncritical mind it ["judicial service"] carries emanations of relevance in that it implies that a man who sat on a lower court has qualifications for sitting on a higher court, or, conversely, that a man has not the qualifications for sitting on a higher court unless he has had the experience of having sat on a lower court, just as a man presumably cannot run a mile in less than four minutes unless he had already run it in six, or a player has not the aptitude or experience for a major league unless he has played in a minor league.

Need I say that judicial experience is not like that at all? For someone to have been a judge on some court for some time, having some kind of business resulting in some kind of experience, may have some abstract relation to the Supreme Court conceived of as an abstract judicial tribunal. The Supreme Court is a very special kind of court. "Judicial service" as such has no significant relation to the kinds of litigation that come before the Supreme Court, to the types of issues they raise, to qualities that these actualities require for wise decision. . . .

But, it may be suggested, if experience on a state court does not adequately prepare even the greatest of judges for the problems that are the main and certainly the most important business of the Supreme Court, judicial experience intrinsically fosters certain habits of mind and aloofness from daily influences, in short, educates and reinforces those moral qualities —disinterestedness and deep humility—which are indeed preconditions for the wise exercise of the judicial function on the Supreme Bench. Unhappily, history again disappoints such expectation. What is more inimical for good work on the Court than for a Justice to cherish political, and more particularly Presidential, ambition? . . . Sad and strange as it may be, the most numerous and in many ways the worst offenders in this regard have been men who came to the Court from state courts, in some instances with long service on such courts. Their temperamental partisanship and ambition were stronger than the disciplining sway supposedly exercised by the judiciary. . . . I think it is fair to say that fewer Justices who had had no prior judicial experience dallied with political ambition while on the Court than those who came there with it. . . .

Even though the history of the Court may demonstrate that judicial experience, whether on state or federal bench ought not to be deemed a prerequisite, what of the lower [federal] courts as a training ground for the Supreme Bench? The fact is that not one so trained emerges over a century and a half among the few towering figures of the Court. Oblivion has overtaken almost all of them. . . .

The search should be made among those men, inevitably very few at any time, who give the best promise of satisfying the intrinsic needs of the Court, no matter where they may be found, no matter in what professional way they have manifested the needed qualities. Of course these needs do not exclude prior judicial experience, but, no less surely, they do not call for judicial experience. One is entitled to say without qualification that the correlation between prior judicial experience and fitness for the functions of the Supreme Court is zero.

Frankfurter speaks with the authority of one who, for over half a century, has been widely recognized as one of the leading students of the United States Supreme Court, and one who also has had over two decades of direct experience as a member of that Court. He is, incidentally, to be numbered among those who came to the Court without any previous judicial service whatsoever.

THE COURT AS A STEPPINGSTONE

There are many examples of justices who harbored ambitions for the Chief Justiceship, or the Presidency, or both. Robert H. Jackson, for instance, was a presidential hopeful whose ambitions in this direction were foreclosed by F.D.R.'s third-term decision. His attention next focused upon the Chief Justiceship, for which he apparently believed he had some kind of commitment from Roosevelt; but the advent of World War II, in 1941, and Roosevelt's death, in 1945, caused the prize twice to elude his grasp. Jackson, as it was, took leave of the Court for a year in order to accept the political job of prosecutor at the Nuremberg "war crimes" trials.[18] His fellow New Dealer and colleague, James Byrnes, resigned from the Court in 1942, after only slightly more than a year of service as a justice, to take on the job of "Assistant President," as the press called it at the time. President Taft avowedly offered Hughes his first appointment to the Court with a quasi-promise, carefully hedged with a *rebus sic stantibus* clause, of the Chief Justiceship if it became vacant during Taft's Presidency. Taft apparently did this in order to eliminate a leading rival for the Republican nomination in 1912. The device worked, but only for a time; Hughes resigned from the Court in 1916 in order to accept the nomination of the Republican party as its presidential candidate. And, although Taft did not find it convenient to appoint Hughes to the vacancy in the Chief's chair brought about by Fuller's death (later in the same year that Hughes was appointed as an associate justice), Hughes eventually got that job, too. It is true that he did have to wait twenty years, and that, in a sense, Taft did eventually give it to him, since he replaced Taft as the Chief.

Lincoln appointed Salmon Portland Chase as Chief Justice in 1864, as a re-

---

[18] Chief Justice Stone, at least, was much opposed to Jackson's taking on this assignment, leaving the Court short-handed for an entire year, and involving a member of his Court in what he referred to in private correspondence, as Jackson's "high grade lynching party." See Alpheus Thomas Mason, "Extra-Judicial Work for Judges: The Views of Chief Justice Stone," *Harvard Law Review*, Vol. 67, pp. 209-213 (1953).

ward for campaign services rendered. Chase's presidential aspirations, while he was still a member of Lincoln's Cabinet, are well known. Indeed, "his ambitions were not stilled by his ascension to the bench, leading to the savage and probably accurate comment of Justice Miller: 'I doubt if for years before his death, his first thought in meeting any man of force, was not, invariably, how can I utilize him for my Presidential aspirations.' " [19] David Davis, Lincoln's 1860 convention campaign manager and the recipient, like Chase, of a seat on the Court in payment of a political debt—indeed, his appointment permitted Lincoln to pay off two debts with a single office [20]—also had the presidential bug, and he eventually ran as the candidate of a minor party.[21] Among other justices who notoriously campaigned for a presidential nomination without relinquishing their seats on the Court were Stephen J. Field [22] and John McLean. Of the latter, Professor John Frank says: [23]

> McLean, whose biographer has discerningly subtitled the book about him *A Politician on the United States Supreme Court,* went to the bench in 1829 and died there in 1861, having aspired to the Presidency at every four-year interval in the meantime. I have personally gone through the many boxes of McLean papers in the Library of Congress, and have found there substantially nothing on the business of being a judge, and an endless stream of observations on his candidacy. Appointed by President Jackson in 1829, he was one of the persons whom Lincoln had to shoulder aside for the Republican nomination in 1860. In the intervening years he attempted to win office with the supporters of John C. Calhoun, toyed with the possibility of joining the Antimasonic Party, and built himself up as a Whig. McLean's activities were so indiscreet that in 1849 there was a Congressional debate over whether the Supreme Court Justices should be allowed to send letters without postage, because McLean allegedly engaged in so much political correspondence. This perpetual candidate frequently discussed legal matters in public letters despite the fact that he might have to pass on the same questions from the bench.

There is nothing particularly surprising in the fact that a fairly substantial minority of the justices continued to entertain ambitions for higher office instead of viewing an associate justiceship as the pinnacle of their desires. After all, most of these men had been active politicians for the greater part of their adult lives. And there were very few who, like William Howard Taft, "loved judges" to the extent that they would consider the Presidency a less important job than that of being Chief Justice.[24]

[19] John P. Frank, *Marble Palace* (New York: Knopf, 1958), p. 274.

[20] *Ibid.,* pp. 57-58.

[21] *Ibid.,* p. 278.

[22] *Ibid.,* pp. 274-275.

[23] *Ibid.,* p. 273.

[24] See Daniel S. McHargue, "President Taft's Appointments to the Supreme Court," *Journal of Politics,* Vol. 12, p. 478 (1950). Taft is said to have declared: "I love judges and I love courts. They are my ideals on earth of what we shall meet afterward in

WHICH MEN DO PRESIDENTS NOMINATE TO THE COURT, AND WHY?

The Nominal vs the Real Politics of Candidates

Ninety-five appointments to the Supreme Court, involving ninety-two different individuals,[25] were made from 1789 to 1959. Since appointments to the Court have been motivated by partisan considerations not dissimilar, in many respects, to those that affect appointments to the President's Cabinet, it might, at first glance (Table 3), seem surprising that over 12% of the appointments to the Court have

TABLE 3.

Crossing Party Lines in Appointments to the Supreme Court

	President	Justice	Date of Appointment
1	Tyler (Whig)	Nelson (Dem.)	1845
2	Lincoln (Rep.)	Field (Dem.)	1863
3	Harrison (Rep.)	H. Jackson (Dem.)	1893
4	Taft (Rep.)	Lurton (Dem.)	1909
5	Taft (Rep.)	White (Dem.)	1910
6	Taft (Rep.)	J. Lamar (Dem.)	1910
7	Wilson (Dem.)	Brandeis (Rep.) [26]	1916
8	Harding (Rep.)	Butler (Dem.)	1922
9	Hoover (Rep.)	Cardozo (Dem.)	1932
10	F. Roosevelt (Dem.)	Stone (Rep.)	1941
11	Truman (Dem.)	Burton (Rep.)	1945
12	Eisenhower (Rep.)	Brennan (Dem.)	1956

involved the crossing of party lines. It would also appear that Republican Presidents have been more generous than their Democratic counterparts in bestowing largess upon the opposition party. It should be remembered, however, that dur-

Heaven under a just God." Taft is also reputed to have said, at the time he promoted White, "There is nothing I would have loved more than being chief justice of the United States. . . . I cannot help seeing the irony in the fact that I, who desired that office so much, should now be signing the commission of another man" (ibid., pp. 478-479, and cf. 491).

[25] Three men served both in the position of associate justice and Chief Justice, for which separate appointments (in each case, by a different President than the one who originally had placed the justice on the Court) were necessary.

[26] Although Brandeis campaigned actively for Wilson in 1912, he was registered as a Republican in Massachusetts at this time; cf. Joseph P. Harris, *The Advice and Consent of the Senate* (Los Angeles: University of California Press, 1953), p. 101; Alpheus T. Mason, *Brandeis: A Free Man's Life* (New York: Viking, 1946), p. 392. The objections of Massachusetts Democrats were apparently determinative in blocking Brandeis' nomination as Wilson's Attorney General in 1912 (Mason, *op. cit.*, pp. 393-394). Brandeis did not consider himself to be a "party man" (ibid., p. 376).

ing the two-thirds of a century that elapsed between the assassination of Lincoln and the inauguration of Franklin Roosevelt, twelve Republican Presidents served, and only two Democrats. It is more curious that Taft, a standpatter Republican, should have selected Southern Democrats for half of the appointments that he made to the Court; that the only two instances in which associate justices have been promoted to the Chief Justiceship (White and Stone) both involved crossing party lines; and that, of the nine justices professing Catholic or Jewish religious affiliation, four (White, Butler, Cardozo, and Brennan) received appointments as representatives of what was also the minority political faith, at the times of their appointments. Indeed, Edward White, who was elevated to the Chief Justiceship notwithstanding his Catholic and Southern Democratic affiliations, had a further disadvantage—he was a Confederate veteran, and his promotion came at a time when there was still substantial overlap in the membership of the G.O.P. and the G.A.R.; but none of these considerations were as important to President Taft as the fact that, as an associate justice, White had voted the right way in a case upholding the imposition of a military tariff in the Philippines under the authority of the then Governor, William Howard Taft.[27] He had demonstrated that his "real politics" were of the right sort.

Similarly, there is an explanation for each of these deviant appointments. To consider only the four most recent: (1) Cardozo, as the successor to Holmes, was virtually forced upon Hoover;[28] (2) Stone received preference over Robert Jackson, who in 1941 had the reputation of an ardent New Dealer, so that F.D.R. could create the aura of bipartisanship that he thought necessary for national unity upon the eve of American entrance into World War II; (3) Harold Burton was an old Senate crony of Harry Truman; and (4) as we have pointed out earlier in this chapter, the Brennan appointment on the eve of the 1956 presidential election made it possible for Eisenhower to continue to indulge in the posture of rising above politics while at the same time playing it very effectively by making a bid for the support of the many Catholic Democrats in the Eastern metropolitan urban complex. Certainly, the available evidence does not support any suggestion of either a custom or a trend toward disregarding political-party affiliation in making appointments to the Court. On the other hand, it does support our earlier hypothesis, that *either* party regularity *or* prior judicial experience is important, not in its own right, but because of the insight that both give into a prospective nominee's "real politics"—his expected voting behavior as a justice.

The scholar who has made the most careful study of appointments to the Court, covering the period 1789-1932, has stated as his conclusions:[29]

27 See William Howard Taft, *Our Chief Magistrate and His Powers* (New York: Columbia University Press, 1916), pp. 99-102. Cf. McHargue, *op. cit.* (in footnote 24, above), pp. 494-495.

28 Carl Brent Swisher, *American Constitu-* *tional Development* (Boston: Houghton, 1943), pp. 779-780.

29 Daniel S. McHargue, *Appointments to the Supreme Court, 1789-1932* (Unpublished Ph.D. dissertation, U.C.L.A., 1949), pp. 578, 593, 640-642.

. . . [The] President particularly, as the nominating authority, and only to a slightly lesser extent the Senate, as the confirming authority, have concerned themselves throughout our history with placing upon the Supreme Court only those men whose views were known and were acceptable. . . . Every president has sought to select individuals whose views—political, economic, and social—were such that they were not likely to impose a judicial veto upon the president's program and whose continued presence on the bench after the president's term was over would still be an influence directing constitutional interpretation in the "right" direction. . . .

In the normal course of events, and particularly during the earlier years of our history when party labels more accurately denoted a fundamental cleavage between the conservative or reactionary element on the one hand, and the liberal or radical on the other, the president would appoint only adherents of his party to places on the highest bench.[30] Nevertheless, President Taft, a Northerner, a Unitarian, and Republican elevated Edward D. White, a Southerner, Catholic, and Democrat to the chief justiceship because the latter's fundamental economic and political views were closely akin to his own.[31] The differences in section, religion, and party were felt to be distinctly secondary. It can hardly be overemphasized that identity of views of appointer and appointee was ordinarily a controlling factor, while co-membership in a political party was a usual but a subsidiary consideration.

But aside from the consideration mentioned above, there are numerous other factors that have played a part in determining the choice of justices. The importance of each factor necessarily varies according to the peculiar conditions and circumstances of the given moment. Among the considerations which have influenced appointments are the following: (1) It was to be expected that the president, as head of a political party, would bear in mind partisan considerations and would be tempted to satisfy poiltical obligations by rewarding his supporters with positions on the bench. The president naturally sought to reward those whose efforts brought about his nomination and election and to repay his most loyal friends. Many appointments were given to politically "doubtful" states or sections with a view to improving party strength therein. Most of the Supreme Court justices had held some kind of elective office before going on the bench. . . . (2) There was a geographical or sectional consideration to be taken into account, although this factor exerted far less influence after the justices ceased to perform regular

[30] For example: "On September 27, 1795, Washington wrote to Timothy Pickering, 'I shall not, whilst I have the honor to administer the government, bring a man into any office of consequence knowingly, whose political tenets are adverse to the measures which the general government are pursuing; for this, in my opinion, would be a sort of political suicide.' . . . President Madison nominated Levi Lincoln, Alexander Wolcott, and John Quincy Adams in the attempt to secure a New Englander whose views he considered proper. Their declinations and rejections forced him, as a fourth choice, to name Joseph Story, who, though a member of his own party, had not demonstrated a consistent loyalty to its program. Ex-President Jefferson had warned Madison that Story was a Tory, and Story's course on the bench proved that Jefferson's apprehensions were well founded." *Ibid.*, pp. 579, 580-581.

[31] Cf. McHargue, *op. cit.* (article; footnote 24, above), p. 478.

circuit duty. If the existing sectional representation of the personnel of the Supreme Court was considered equitable at the time a justice died, retired, or resigned, it was quite likely, other things being equal, that the President would seek to fill the vacancy from the section whose representation had been diminished. If some part of the country was without a representative on the bench, the president was subjected to severe pressure to remedy the deficiency. However, the low rank of sectional representation in the hierarchy of motives controlling appointments has been clearly shown by the over-representation of the South, New England, and later the Middle West at various times in our history. In addition the over-representation of "doubtful" and under-representation of "in the bag" states indicated that political considerations normally overrode those of equitable geographical representation. (3) It was often important to pay deference to the principle that it was not only important that justice be done, but also that it appeared to be done. To be more specific, religious groups were most anxious that their faith be represented on the bench. Thus, in recent years . . . the Catholics and Jews became more successful in making effective their demand for political recognition. . . . (4) It has generally been felt that not all of the justices should be members of the same political party.

Perhaps the best-known example of presidential discrimination between the formal political-party affiliation of a candidate and what the President perceived to be the prospect's basic political philosophy is found in a letter written by Theodore Roosevelt to Senator Henry Cabot Lodge. The prospect was Horace Lurton, an elderly federal judge with thirty years of experience on the bench, whose appointment was urged upon Roosevelt by his Secretary of War, William Howard Taft, and by Justice William Day, whom Roosevelt had appointed to the Court three years earlier. Although Lurton was (like White) a Southern Democrat and Confederate veteran, while both Taft and Day (like Roosevelt, of course) were Republicans, they had served as colleagues with Lurton on the Sixth Federal Circuit Court. William Moody, also referred to in the correspondence below, was a Republican and the incumbent Attorney General.

OYSTER BAY, N.Y., September 4, 1906

Personal

DEAR CABOT:

I knew how strongly Moody felt about Lurton. I did not know how you felt. I think you both are entirely in error. I say this frankly because I know you want me to talk frankly. Nothing has been so strongly borne in on me concerning lawyers on the bench as that the *nominal* politics of the man has nothing to do with his actions on the bench. His *real* politics are all important. [Roosevelt may well have been thinking of his disappointment in Oliver Wendell Holmes, which will be discussed below.] . . . [Lurton] is right on the negro question; he is right on the power of the Federal Government;

he is right on the insular business; he is right about corporations; and he is right about labor. On every question that would come before the bench he has so far shown himself to be in much closer touch with the policies in which you and I believe than even White, because he has been right about corporations, where White has been wrong. I have grown to feel most emphatically that the Supreme Court is a matter of too great importance for me to pay heed to where a man comes from. . . . I am tentatively taking into account the fact that if I appoint Lurton I *may* later be able to appoint Moody. . . .

Ever yours,
THEODORE ROOSEVELT

NAHANT, MASS., Sept. 10, 1906

Personal

DEAR THEODORE:

. . . I am glad that Lurton holds all the opinions that you say he does and that you are so familiar with his views. I need hardly say that those are the very questions on which I am just as anxious as you that judges should hold what we consider sound opinions, but I do not see why Republicans cannot be found who hold those opinions as well as Democrats. The fact that there have been one or two Republican disappointments does not seem to me to militate against the proposition. . . .

Of course you know my very high opinion of Moody, and that I should have been very glad to see him appointed some years ago. . . . Nothing would give me greater pleasure than to see him on the bench. . . .

Ever yrs,
H. C. LODGE [32]

In this case, politics appears to have triumphed over principle, because the appointment went to Moody. The very next vacancy, however, went to Lurton, who became the first of President Taft's six selections for the Court.

GEOPOLITICS AND AVAILABILITY: THE MILLER CASE

Although sectional considerations had become of lesser importance after the turn of the century, in no small measure because of the elimination of circuit-riding responsibilities for the justices, they were among the primary political factors which had to be balanced at the time, during the Civil War, when Samuel Freeman Miller joined the Court.[33] The extent to which sectional balance can now be disregarded is illustrated by the appointment of Cardozo, who became the third New Yorker to sit upon the Court during the period 1932-1938.

[32] Henry Cabot Lodge, *Selections from the Correspondence of Theodore Roosevelt and Henry Cabot Lodge, 1894-1918* (New York: Scribner, 1925), Vol. 2, pp. 228-231.

[33] For a detailed discussion of the representation of states and sections on the Court, see Ewing, *op. cit.,* chap. iii.

President Hoover, somewhat concerned about possible Senate reaction to the proposal to place another New Yorker on the bench alongside Stone and Hughes, raised the question with Senator Borah of Idaho, who had led the opposition to the Parker nomination only two years previously. Borah is reported to have replied, magnanimously, that Cardozo belonged as much to Idaho as to New York.[34] But in Miller's case and time, it was different: [35]

President Lincoln had asked Congress to rearrange the western circuits, and this it proceeded to do. It was slow work. One author wrote, ". . . the method of grouping the Western and Southwestern States became a subject of warm controversy in Congress; the House and the Senate adopted different plans; and it was not until the very end of the session, that on July 5, 1862, an agreement was reached and an Act passed reorganizing the Court." The reason for the delay was that the grouping of states into circuits would determine geographic availability of aspirants to the Court. Hence, ". . . while senators and congressmen talked geography, everyone was thinking of personalities." The extent to which the candidacies of aspirants for the Supreme Court were bound up with circuit reorganization is revealed in the following entry of March 26, 1862, in the diary of Attorney General Edward Bates;

Today, at my office—and tonight at my house, again had long talk, with Judge S[wayne] about the filling of the va[ca]nt seats on the Sup[rem]e bench. He thinks that a very strenuous effort is making to get C. B. Smith appointed, and that the effort is almost crowned with success—That there is a bill pending to gerry-mander the Circuits to suit—so as to give Smith a circuit without interferring [sic] with Browning—nobody it [I] think objects to Browning—He is a proper man—Note[.] I have warned the Prest to be on his guard.

In early June, 1862, Representative William Kellogg of Illinois stated to the House: "I fear that too many mantles for Supreme Court judges have already been cut out, and made up. If it were not for that, there would be little trouble in arranging the States in compact circuits."

Among the leading aspirants for the two existing vacancies on the bench were Senator Orville Browning, David Davis, and Thomas Drummond of Illinois, Secretary of the Interior Caleb Smith of Indiana, and Samuel F. Miller of Iowa. Miller's supporters knew he would have to compete with Browning, Davis, and Drummond if Iowa were placed in the same circuit with Illinois, hence Senator James Grimes and Representative James Wilson of Iowa fought a hard, and successful, ". . . legislative battle in order to force creation of a circuit composed of Iowa, Minnesota, Missouri, and Kansas." They and others had done much campaigning for Miller, and they felt he would be nominated if they could secure a trans-Mississippi circuit. . . .

[34] Frankfurter, "The Supreme Court in the Mirror of Justices," *University of Pennsylvania Law Review*, Vol. 105, p. 795 (1957).

[35] McHargue, *op. cit.* (dissertation; footnote 29, above), pp. 170-175. (Parts of two paragraphs of the original have been omitted, and the position of another paragraph has been changed, in the quotation here.)

Miller had been a physician in Kentucky, who had turned to law and passed the bar in 1849. His hatred of slavery induced him to move from Kentucky to Iowa in 1850. He had helped organize the Republican party in Iowa, and in 1861 he had been an unsuccessful candidate for nomination to the governorship. At the time of his appointment to the bench he was chairman of the district Republican committee at Keokuk, Iowa. He wanted the place on the bench intensely and mustered the forces in his behalf that waged the successful campaign. It has been said, "Laurels are seldom of spontaneous growth in our public life. They have generally been vigorously cultivated for years by the sweat of the brow which they at last adorn. It was plainly so in Miller's case." Governor Kirkwood of Iowa ". . . aided in securing Miller's appointment to the bench, and thus removed from the State a dangerous and powerful political rival." Miller had procured recommendations in his own behalf from the bars of Iowa, Kansas, Minnesota, and Wisconsin. He was so little known at the time that President Lincoln, who came from a neighboring state, had never heard of him and thought, until correctly informed, that the Miller being recommended was Daniel F. Miller, a former congressman from Iowa. But Miller had impressed Senators Harlan and Grimes of Iowa with his staunch Republicanism and ability as a lawyer, so they were anxious to further his cause. Besides they felt that at least one justice of the Supreme Court should be from west of the Mississippi. Miller not only had many of his friends personally solicit the place from President Lincoln but ". . . himself went to Washington to see that nothing was left undone."

Earlier President Lincoln had received many letters recommending Miller for the Court vacancy. On January 21, 1862, William B. Allison of Dubuque, Iowa, had suggested Miller's name and noted that, "The Bar of this State would be well pleased with this appointment." Miller's politically influential backers included Iowa's senators, representatives, governor, state legislators, and the governor of Colorado. Senators Grimes and Harlan persuaded most of the members of the Senate to sign a petition asking for Miller's nomination, and Congressman Wilson obtained the signatures of most of the House of Representatives on a similar memorial. . . .

The extensive congressional support for Miller added to the earlier support in his favor was sufficient to secure him a place on the bench. Only one day after he approved the reorganization of the circuits, Lincoln nominated Miller for the Court. In speaking of his nomination Miller wrote it was "confirmed in half an hour without reference to committee, a courtesy usually reserved for persons who have been members of that body [the Senate]."

Miller had only a local reputation, brief experience as an attorney, and no judicial experience whatsoever. But to Lincoln these were not disqualifications. He was looking for someone politically trustworthy, and Miller had changed residence because of his hatred of slavery and had helped organize the Republican party in his state. Miller was geographically "available" because of the new circuit arrangement. His recommendations, thanks largely to the work of Senators Harlan and Grimes, were almost unprecedentedly strong. "President Lincoln said that he had not known such a unanimous recommendation of any man for any office, and felt he could not err in making the appointment of a Federal Judge so generally approved by an intelligent bar, and, not less important in such a crisis, by a patriotic people."

THE SENATE, CONCURRING

Most Presidents have included their estimates of a candidate's acceptability to the Senate as a major factor to be weighed in making nominations. There are times, such as the Brandeis nomination in 1916, when the President's own chances for reelection were dependent upon his success in avoiding an open rejection, by the Senate, of his leadership; and although Wilson took the chance, most Presidents have felt that the wiser course lay in avoiding such risk-taking. The path of avoidance has lain in the selection of safe nominees, whose acceptability to the Senate was assured in advance. Senatorial confirmation has functioned, therefore, largely as a device to ensure that men whose views were considered to be deviant

TABLE 4.

Vetoing of Presidential Nominations to the Supreme Court (1789-1958) [36]

ACTION TAKEN	NOMINATED		
	86 (100%) 1789-1897	40 (100%) 1898-1958	126 (100%) Total
Rejected by the Senate [37]	22 (25.6%)	1 (2.5%)	23 (18.3%)
Confirmed by the Senate	64 (74.4%)	39 (97.5%)	103 (81.7%)
Decline appointment [38]	8 (9.3%)	0 (0.0%)	8 (6.3%)
Accepted appointment	56 (65.1%)	39 (97.5%)	95 (75.4%)
Total nominations vetoed (rejections plus declinations)	30 (34.9%)	1 (2.5%)	31 (24.6%)

[36] This table is based primarily upon data in Ewing, op. cit., p. 15 et seq., and Harris, op. cit., 303-305. Rutledge was nominated, confirmed, and appointed to the original Court in 1789, although he soon resigned; he was later given a recess appointment as Chief Justice in 1795, but rejected by the Senate. Taney and Matthews were initially rejected, but each received a subsequent nomination which was confirmed and resulted in appointment; White, Hughes, and Stone were each initially appointed as associate justice, and subsequently reappointed as Chief Justice. In each of these six cases, two separate nominations were made, and they have been so treated in the table. The total of 126 nominations relate, therefore, to 120 different persons.

[37] This category includes outright rejection, postponement of action and failure to act, and withdrawals.

[38] Included with these declinations is the one death before inauguration.

from those of the dominant political forces of the time would not receive serious consideration for appointment to the Court. Beyond this, there have been occasions when a lame-duck President, or one faced with a Senate controlled by the opposition party or faction, was denied the right to make any appointment to the Court, irrespective of the qualifications of his nominee. In addition, individual senators have at times been able to veto presidential nominations, through invocation of the rule of "senatorial courtesy"; it was because of this, for instance, that Cleveland was practically forced to select a senator (White) in 1894, after his first and second choices had been rejected because they were "personally obnoxious" to Senator Hill of New York.

In addition to those nominees who were rejected by the Senate, either directly by an unfavorable vote on a motion for confirmation or indirectly by the postponement of action or the failure to take action upon nominations, one President (Grant) withdrew two nominations in anticipation of outright Senate rejection. Particularly during the period before Jackson's administration, several persons declined to serve on the Court, even though they had received Senate confirmation and were offered commissions of appointment; at that time, service on the Supreme Court carried much less prestige than it does today. Lincoln's Secretary of War, Stanton, was confirmed by the Senate on the same day that it received his nomination by President Johnson, but Stanton died before taking the oath of office.

The most significant aspect of the data in Table 4 is the sharp drop in both rejections and declinations during the twentieth century. During the Federalist era and the nineteenth century, one-fourth of the presidential selections were rejected,[39] and in addition, eight of the sixty-four who were confirmed declined to serve. Over a third of the nominations to the Court were frustrated by the action of either the Senate or the nominees themselves during the first century of the history of the Court. In dramatic contrast, only one presidential nomination to the Court since the second administration of Grover Cleveland has failed to result in an appointment. This was the Parker case, which we shall discuss below. Indeed, there have been only five nominations during the modern period, including Parker's, which have encountered serious opposition in the Senate. Particularly during the past two decades, since the Court-packing episode of 1937, the consent of the Senate has become a *pro forma* matter, although it is difficult to say whether this should be interpreted to mean a trend toward abdication by the Senate of its constitutional responsibilities, or an indication of more careful presidential designation of nominees who were certain to be within the range of

[39] Rejections are scattered throughout the period, but with a concentration during the middle years from Jackson's inauguration in 1829 until Grant left office in 1877. Harris comments that "Few of the rejections of Supreme Court nominations in this period can be ascribed to any lack of qualifications on the part of the nominees; for the most part they were due to political differences between the President and a majority of the Senate" (*op. cit.*, p. 303).

choice acceptable to the Senate. In the aftermath of the School Segregation decision and in the face of an institutional milieu in which Southern Democrats are always powerful irrespective of party control of the Senate, Eisenhower's proclivity for appointing "experienced" judges may well be construed to lend support to the latter interpretation. The conclusion of a student of the Court, writing in 1941, that "the chief function of the confirmation process today is periodically to focus public attention on the Supreme Court" [40] should, perhaps, be accepted with reservations a generation later. Like the untimely intimations of the demise of Mark Twain, reports of the desuetude of the Senate's power of confirmation may yet prove to be somewhat exaggerated.

An alternative explanation for the manifest changes between the two periods is that the *criteria* upon which the Senate bases its confirmation decisions have shifted. Party regularity was the primary standard which guided the Senate during the early period; but during the present century, the Senate has attempted to apply the much more elusive test of the candidate's "political philosophy" as the basis for acceptability. It has proved to be a difficult criterion to enforce. According to Professor Frank,[41]

> The most significant feature of the Hughes, and in the same year [1930] the Parker, debates, was the emergence in complete form of the economic interpretation of the significance of the court. This trend toward economic consciousness [began] with the appointment of Matthews in 1881 and . . . gathered strength through the Twentieth Century. By the time of the Hughes and Parker appointments this concept was not only on the stage, as in Stone's case; it dominated the whole theater.

Professor Harris agrees, remarking that "the increasing role of the Supreme Court in passing upon social and economic measures has led to greater attention to the philosophy, record, and attitudes of nominees on such issues, and far less consideration than formerly to their party regularity. . . . In every case [provoking serious debate in the Senate since 1900] the opposition was due to the philosophy and supposed stand of the nominee on social and economic issues rather than to partisan considerations." [42]

THE CONFIRMATION OF BRANDEIS

The first case indicative of a changed Senate attitude was that of Brandeis, whose chances in the Senate were not enhanced by the fact that he was the first Jew to be nominated to the Court. Open discussion did not focus upon the candidate's religion, of course, and it is indisputable that the real basis for most objections to his appointment related to his progressive views and reputation. The

40 John P. Frank, "The Appointment of Supreme Court Justices: Prestige, Principles and Politics," *Wisconsin Law Review*, Vol. 16, p. 512 (1941).

41 *Ibid.*, p. 497.
42 Harris, *op. cit.*, p. 303.

controversy over the Brandeis nomination went on for months, and the ultimate decision was in substantial doubt during most of this time. As we pointed out earlier, the political life of the Wilson administration may well have hung in the balance. As the result of strong political pressure from both Wilson and Brandeis personally, among others, the Senate Judiciary Committee reported the nomination favorably to the floor of the Senate, by a straight party-line vote of 10 Democrats over 8 dissenting Republicans. Similarly, the final vote in the Senate, on June 1, 1916 (with the Democratic national convention only weeks away), was 47-22, with 44 Democrats and the 3 Progressives in the majority, and all 21 Republicans plus 1 Democrat in dissent. Under the circumstances, the generalization of Professor Harris, quoted above, should probably be understood to apply to the verbal behavior of the senators rather than to their voting behavior. It is undoubtedly true that the *debate* in the Senate revolved around what was alleged to be the candidate's "dangerous radicalism," but when the chips were down, the senators *voted* with eyes fixed upon the hustings, and their own individual political salvation, rather than upon the qualifications or probable voting behavior as a judge of a nominee widely and publicly branded as an "unscrupulous, muckraking socialist." The vote clearly was a function of party regularity.

The Rejection of Parker

The opposition to Stone, Hughes, and Parker came from the opposite quarter, with Senate liberals and progressives attacking these "reactionary" nominees. Typical was the comment, in regard to Hughes, made by Senator Norris: [43]

> [T]he man who has never felt the pinch of hunger and who has never known what it was to be cold, who has never been associated with those who have earned their bread by the sweat of their faces, but who has lived in luxury, who has never wanted for anything that money could buy, is not fit to sit in judgment in a contest between organized wealth and those who toil.

Subsequent events proved that the opposition was clearly wrong in the case of Stone, at least partially wrong regarding Hughes, and with a very high degree of probability, completely wrong about Parker. As related by McHargue: [44]

> Justice Sanford's death gave President Hoover a second opportunity to nominate a Supreme Court Justice. The president decided to name John J. Parker of North Carolina for the place and did so in spite of a warning given by Justice Stone. Parker had been Republican candidate for Congress in 1910, Republican nominee for governor of North Carolina in 1920, special assistant to the attorney general of the United States in 1923-1924, a member

---

[43] *Congressional Record,* Vol. 72, Part 4, p. 3566 (71st Cong., 2d Sess., Feb. 13, 1930), quoted in Harris, *op. cit.,* p. 115.

[44] *Op. cit.* (dissertation; footnote 29, above), pp. 475-478.

of the Republican national convention in 1924, and had been United States circuit judge for the fourth circuit since 1925. The reports of the motives which prompted President Hoover to select Parker are quite contradictory. One of the favorable accounts was as follows:

> The death of Mr. Justice Sanford of the Supreme Court of the United States created a vacancy in that tribunal. President Hoover was a close student of our form of government. No lawyer could have had a finer appreciation of the responsibility and power of a Federal judge and especially of a Supreme Court Justice. The Attorney General was asked to inquire into the qualifications of a number of lawyers and judges, including those from judicial circuits not then represented upon the Supreme Court. Among those inquired about was the United States Circuit Judge John J. Parker of the Fourth Circuit. The Attorney-General advised the President that Judge Parker was a very able, hard-working, fair-minded, impartial jurist with a thorough knowledge of the law, and of unquestionable integrity. This conclusion was based upon an inquiry which included an examination of something like 125 opinions which the Judge had written while sitting on the Court of Appeals. Justice Sanford had been from Tennessee. His death left Justice McReynolds the only member of the Court from the South. The Fourth Circuit had not been represented upon the Supreme Court for several decades. The personal character, professional standing and judicial qualifications of Judge Parker had been presented or vouched for by the most prominent citizens of his state (North Carolina) without reference to party, and from citizens from every walk of life. With scarcely an exception, every senator from the several states within his circuit had recommended or endorsed his appointment. Included among his endorsers were two United States Circuit Judges, ten United States District Judges, a large number of State judges, the president and five past-presidents of the American Bar Association, several presidents of State Bar Associations, and many other prominent members of the Bar from both political parties. The President decided to nominate Judge Parker, and did so. . . . [W. H. Myers and W. H. Newton, *The Hoover Administration* (1936), pp. 427-428.]

Other observers remarked, "In many ways Judge Parker was an ideal candidate since he fulfilled most of the requirements and conformed to the standards which normally govern such appointments. He was a Republican and a Southerner, he shared the conservative philosophy of Mr. Hoover and he represented the powerful 'lily white' faction which ruled the Republican party in the South." Another said, "The nomination was a natural one in succession to Justice Sanford, a Republican from a border state, Tennessee."

But the Senate did not take at all kindly to Parker's nomination. It was argued that Hoover nominated Parker simply for partisan reasons. To back up that claim a letter dated March 13, 1930, sent by James Dixon to Walter Newton, one of Hoover's secretaries, was quoted. It read in part:

> I speak as a native born North Carolina Republican. North Carolina gave President Hoover a 65,000 majority. In my judgment, it carries more hope of future permanent alignment with the Republican party than any other of the Southern states that broke from their political mooring last year. If the exigencies of the situ-

ation permit I believe the naming of Judge Parker to the Supreme Court would be a major political stroke.

In addition to the charge that the nomination was dictated by "political considerations," there were two other major charges brought against Parker: (1) as the Republican gubernatorial candidate in North Carolina in 1920, Parker had replied to Democratic claims that the Republicans intended to enfranchise Negroes in the state, stating that "the participation of the Negro in politics is a source of evil and danger to both races and is not desired by the wise men in either race or by the Republican party of North Carolina"; and (2) as a justice of the Fourth Circuit Court of Appeals, Parker had delivered the opinion of that court in the "Red Jacket" case in 1927, upholding the validity of a federal district court injunction which had been issued to enforce a yellow-dog contract, on the authority of and expressly following the decision of the United States Supreme Court in *Hitchman Coal and Coke Co.* v. *Mitchell*, 245 U.S. 229 (1917).

The consequent strong political pressure brought to bear by both organized Negro and organized labor groups was enough to ensure Parker's defeat. President Hoover's belated and indirect support of his nominee, and Parker's express disclaimers in his own behalf, were of no avail against the reiterated charges that he was antilabor and anti-Negro. In vain did Democratic Senator Overman of North Carolina, the chairman of the Senate subcommittee which supported Parker's confirmation, point out that the fourth federal circuit had not been represented on the Supreme Court "since the days of Iredell and Moore." The Senate Judiciary Committee divided 6 to 10, and filed an unfavorable report. It had become clear that the confirmation of Parker would be interpreted as a major defeat for labor and Negroes, and as a victory for the Hoover administration. It was a congressional election year (1930), and the final vote in the Senate was 39-41 against confirmation, with 17 Republicans voting in opposition. McHargue's summary of the result is that: [45]

> Most conservatives felt that in rejecting Parker the Senate had surrendered shamefully to the political pressure of minority factions, and in so doing had prevented a very able jurist from taking a place he would have filled with merit. Most liberals felt that at last the Senate had shown itself to be more liberal than the president by rejecting his illiberal nominee, and were happy that labor had scored a victory over the pro-corporation forces.

The defeat of Parker resulted in the appointment of Roberts, who was confirmed without fuss or fanfare. Professor Frank has commented that, "By the cosmic irony of such events, it was the Senate liberals who defeated Parker, and on the basis of the comparative careers of the two men, they would have been much better off if they had supported him." [46] In view of his background and rec-

45 *Ibid.*, p. 483.   46 *Marble Palace*, p. 48.

ord as a Republican Philadelphia lawyer who had primarily served wealthy clients, there was nothing at the time to indicate that Roberts would be a more liberal justice than Parker might have been; and although his role on the Court in the critical year of 1937 was an important one, he is not considered to have been one of the outstanding justices on the Court during the period of his tenure. Parker, on the other hand, ranked for the next quarter of a century at the top of his profession as one of the outstanding jurists in the country. As the chief judge of the Court of Appeals for the Fourth Circuit, it is ironic to note, Parker became a leading instrument in enforcing the legal right of Negroes to vote [47] and in racial integration cases arising in the aftermath of the School Segregation decision.[48] Professor Harris had concluded that "Parker [was] an able judge who would have honored the Court," and "the facts did not support the charges made against Judge Parker, and his record ever since has been that of an able, liberal judge." [49] But, as Swisher has noted, "Judge Parker himself had been only an incident in a controversy which went much deeper than the qualifications of any one man. The controversy rested upon a sharp divergence of economic and social philosophies which had revealed itself in the presidential campaign of 1924. . . ." [50]

Why Great Men Rarely Are Appointed to the Supreme Court

It was Parker's fortune to join the select group of lower-court judges, such as Learned Hand of the second federal circuit and Arthur Vanderbilt of New Jersey, whose pre-eminence as jurists was not enough—for reasons that we already have explained—to gain them a place on the Supreme Court.

If, however, the Parker rejection was essentially a question of timing (and he might well have been confirmed either a few years earlier or later—conceivably, even a few months later if someone else had been rejected in his place), it is equally true that the Brandeis confirmation was possible only by grace of fortuitous timing, without in any way discounting the prodigious efforts that were made both to support and to defeat his nomination. As Swisher has remarked, "If the nomination had been made in another year it is probable that it would have been defeated." [51] Thus, as with Parker's rejection, there is in Brandeis' confirmation an implication of importance that transcends the merits of the particular individual involved: [52]

The Brandeis confirmation case is one of the most significant in the history of the Senate. It brings into sharp focus several important aspects of

[47] See *Rice* v. *Elmore,* 165 F. 2d 387 (4 C.C.A., 1947), certiorari denied, 333 U.S. 875 (1948); and *Baskin* y. *Brown,* 174 F. 2d 391 (4 C.A., 1949).

[48] *Mayor and City Council of Baltimore* v. *Dawson,* 220 F. 2d 386 (4 C.A., 1955), affirmed, 350 U.S. 877 (1955); and *Fleming* v. *South Carolina Electric and Gas Co.,* 224 F. 2d 752 (4 C.A., 1955), appeal dismissed, 351 U.S. 901 (1956).

[49] *Op. cit.,* pp. 314, 305, and cf. pp. 218-219.

[50] *Op. cit.,* p. 778.

[51] *Ibid.,* p. 114.

[52] *Ibid.,* p. 113.

the process of senatorial confirmation—its strengths as well as its weaknesses. The case illustrates that a person who has played a leading role in civic and economic reform movements and has taken a definite stand on controversial public issues, particularly if he has incurred the hostility of powerful groups of society, will face strong opposition. Such a person can be confirmed only by the greatest effort, whereas a middle-of-the-road individual who has never participated in economic and social struggles or offended powerful groups is usually confirmed without opposition.

The process of confirmation by the Senate, therefore, tends to reinforce other political pressures focusing upon the Presidency, whose conjoint effect is to en-sure—with rare and scattered exceptions—that the justices of the Supreme Court will be considered to be political moderates at *the time of their appointments*.[53] This may well be for the best, but whether it is or not, it is a primary factor shaping the climate of opinion of the Supreme Court. Yet it is the occasional zealot of the left or of the right, the man who represents the values of a transient but revolutionary majority, who is most likely to be reckoned among the great justices of the Court. And, putting Marshall to one side, in order to have a Taney or Field or Brandeis or Black on the Court, there must first be a Jackson or Lincoln or Wilson or Franklin Roosevelt in the Presidency, which in turn re-quires the special kind of crisis in American politics that brought each of these great Presidents to power.

PRESIDENTIAL EXPECTATIONS AND JUDICIAL PERFORMANCE

We have seen that, as a general rule, most Presidents attempt, most of the time, to appoint justices whom they can expect to represent, in the decisions of the Court, the major political values accepted by the appointing President. It is well known that John Adams was eminently successful in doing precisely this, and that the Federalist party retained a citadel in the Supreme Court for decades after the party had disappeared as a significant factor in the control of the Presi-dency and the Congress. If all Presidents had been equally successful in packing the Court before themselves leaving office, the Supreme Court would necessarily have become, as it has sometimes been called, "the American House of Lords," a political institution condemned in perpetuity to the role of extending the grasp of the dead hand of the past. It is most doubtful, however, that such an institu-tion could have survived for a century and two-thirds and at the same time have

[53] Circumstances change, of course, and political society does not stand still. A justice who was a moderate at the time of his ap-pointment may appear to be a liberal or a conservative a generation later; and if he lives long enough, a liberal at the time of his appointment may be considered a conserva-tive as the end of his tenure draws near, or vice versa.

retained the capacity to function effectively as a branch of the government coordinate with the Presidency and the Congress. No House of Lords could have made, and made stick, such decisions as the Steel Seizure case or the School Segregation cases. Indeed, as we shall argue in a later chapter, the problem with the Court today is that on many issues it is the fulcrum of national policy-making, and a much more liberal force politically than either of the other two branches of the national government.

A partial explanation of the continuing vitality of the Court, therefore, lies in the fact that Presidents have frequently been quite unsuccessful in their efforts to place upon the Court delegates in whom will be reincarnated the spirit of administrations past. "Indeed," says Professor Frank,[54]

> its unpredictability is almost the clearest feature of the appointment process. Some Presidents have chosen Justices who thereafter performed just as the appointing Presidents expected they would. Chief Justice Marshall, chosen by the outgoing John Adams, impressed the Federalist spirit of Adams into the law for thirty-five years. On the Anti-Federalist side, Peter V. Daniel was chosen by the defeated Martin Van Buren only a few days before the latter went out of office. As Van Buren wrote his predecessor, Jackson, with some glee, he had left the Court with someone who had been a Democrat "ab ovo," or from the egg; and this is exactly what Daniel was. Harding's Butler, F.D.R.'s Black, and Jackson's Taney were just what those Presidents wanted.
>
> Nonetheless, the number of surprises is great, and no President can be sure of what he is getting. Wilson chose McReynolds, who proved to be the total antithesis of everything Wilson stood for and became the most fanatic and hard-bitten conservative extremist ever to grace the Court. Coolidge chose his own Attorney General, Harlan Stone, and Stone is commonly regarded as one of the great liberal Justices. Anti-Federalist Presidents sent Justice after Justice to the Court only to see them captivated by Marshall; among the more amusing stretches of American legal history are the papers flowing between Justice William Johnson, a Jefferson appointee [his first], and Jefferson as Johnson attempted to account for his deviations from good Jeffersonian faith.

There are, of course, many other examples which illustrate both the satisfaction and the frustration of presidential expectations. If Franklin Roosevelt got what he wanted in Black, his next appointment, Stanley Reed, must have occasioned some surprise; and it is reasonable to assume that Roosevelt would be disappointed to discover Felix Frankfurter, renowned as a liberal professor during the twenties and thirties, and picked for the Court with the expectation that he would bring "breadth of vision" to his brethren, leading the conservative wing of the Court in the fifties in a general opposition to Black that has persisted over the course of two decades.

[54] *Marble Palace,* p. 45.

Similarly, when Lincoln appointed his Secretary of the Treasury, Salmon Chase, as Chief Justice, he had every right to assume that here, at least, was one potential vote to uphold the constitutionality of the wartime issue of paper money. Although by no means an enthusiastic supporter of the greenback legislation, Chase had supported the bills as a wartime necessity; and as Secretary of the Treasury, he had administered the issuance of the "legal tender" currency. It is also true, of course, that Lincoln had put Chase on the Court for political reasons that were quite unrelated to his views, whatever they might be, on the Legal Tender controversy. But when the question reached the Supreme Court, Chief Justice Chase wrote for the majority in a 4-3 decision declaring the legislation unconstitutional.[55] There were two vacancies on the Court at this time; and on the very day that *Hepburn* v. *Griswold* was decided (February 7, 1870), President Grant sent to the Senate the nominations of William Strong and Joseph P. Bradley. The two new justices were confirmed and took their seats the following month; and two days later, Grant's Attorney General moved for reconsideration of the decision in *Hepburn* v. *Griswold*. Only a year later (on May 1, 1871), the three dissenters of the preceding year joined with Bradley in an opinion written by Justice Strong, overruling the Hepburn case and upholding the constitutionality of the Legal Tender acts; the former four-man majority of the latter case was now in dissent. There was, of course, a great outcry that Grant had deliberately packed the Court in order to force the Supreme Court to reverse itself so that he could get the decision he wanted. Grant is quoted as having later stated [56]

> that although he required no declaration from Judges Strong and Bradley on the constitutionality of the Legal Tender Act, he knew Judge Strong had on the Bench in Pennsylvania given a decision sustaining its Constitutionality, and he had reason to believe Judge Bradley's opinion tended in the same direction: that at the time he felt it important that the Constitutionality of the Law should be sustained, and while he would do nothing to exact anything like a pledge or expression of opinion from the parties he might appoint to the Bench, he had desired that the Constitutionality should be sustained by the Supreme Court; that he believed such had been the opinion of all his Cabinet at the time.

Grant received exactly what he expected to get out of the two appointments. And if President Grant was "guilty" of "Court-packing," his behavior differs only in degree, not in kind, from that of practically every other President, both before and since, who has attempted to appoint men with "the right sort" of views.

Theodore Roosevelt entertained precisely the same kind of motives as Grant, but was less successful in his choice of men. The case in which Roosevelt was interested was an antitrust prosecution of the Northern Securities Company, a

55 *Hepburn* v. *Griswold*, 8 Wall. 603 (1870).
56 Sidney Ratner, "Was the Supreme Court Packed by President Grant?" *Political Science Quarterly*, Vol. 50, p. 351 (1935).

holding company organized to control a majority of the stock of several competing railroads, including the Northern Pacific and the Great Northern companies. Behind the merger were such "malefactors of great wealth" as J. P. Morgan and James J. Hill. Roosevelt threw himself behind the prosecution with characteristic energy, and was determined to see it through to a successful conclusion, which would obviously entail a favorable decision by the Supreme Court. The President, who was later to remark that the constitutionality of a hypothesized steep federal tax law "would depend on whether a Judge of the Supreme Court came down heads or tails," [57] was well aware that a single replacement could reverse the favorable, but marginal, balance of a Court which frequently was closely divided in cases raising major questions of economic policy in the guise of constitutional interpretation.

While the case dragged on toward what ultimately became a favorable decision in the trial court, and argument was under way in the summer of 1902, Roosevelt was notified by Justice Horace Gray of his impending retirement. Gray, an appointee of President Arthur, was past seventy and rounding out two decades on the Court; he was resigning because of his failing health. In looking for a replacement for Gray, a former Chief Justice of Massachusetts, "it was congruous that Roosevelt should turn to another Chief Justice of the Massachusetts Supreme Court. That man proved to be Holmes. The President had been educated at Harvard, he was a close friend of Henry Cabot Lodge [the Senator from Massachusetts] and on terms of intimacy with many of the Back Bay aristocracy." [58] Although Oliver Wendell Holmes had the very qualifications that most appealed to Theodore Roosevelt—not the least of which was his war record as a thrice-wounded Union veteran—there remained a gnawing doubt whether Holmes adequately appreciated John Marshall. As on many other matters of the time, the President sought the advice of the Senator from Massachusetts: [59]

OYSTER BAY, N.Y., July 10, 1902

Personal

DEAR CABOT:

. . . Now as to Holmes: If it becomes necessary you can show him this letter. First of all, I wish to go over the reasons why I am in his favor. He possesses the high character and the high reputation both of which should if possible attach to any man who is to go upon the highest court of the entire civilized world. His father's name entitles the son to honor; and if the father had been an utterly unknown man the son would nevertheless now have won the highest honor. The position of Chief Justice of Massachusetts is in itself a guarantee of the highest professional standing. Moreover, Judge Holmes has behind him the kind of career and possesses the kind of personality which

---

[57] Silas Bent, *Justice Oliver Wendell Holmes* (Garden City: Vanguard Press, 1932), p. 252.

[58] *Ibid.*, p. 246.

[59] Lodge, *op. cit.*, Vol. 1, pp. 517-519. Emphasis supplied.

make a good American proud of him as a representative of our country. He has been a most gallant soldier, a most able and upright public servant, and in public and private life alike a citizen whom we like to think of as typical of the American character at its best. The labor decisions which have been criticized by some of the big railroad men and other members of large corporations constitute to my mind a strong point in Judge Holmes' favor. The ablest lawyers and greatest judges are men whose past has naturally brought them into close relationship with the wealthiest and most powerful clients, and I am glad when I can find a judge who has been able to preserve his aloofness of mind so as to keep his broad humanity of feeling and his sympathy for the class from which he has not drawn his clients. I think it eminently desirable that our Supreme Court should show in unmistakable fashion their entire sympathy with all proper effort to secure the most favorable possible consideration for the men who most need that consideration.

Finally, Judge Holmes' whole mental attitude, as shown for instance by his great Phi Beta Kappa speech at Harvard is such that I should naturally expect him to be in favor of those principles in which I so earnestly believe.

Now a word as to the other side. It may seem to be, but it is not really, a small matter that his speech on Marshall should be unworthy of the subject, and above all should show a total incapacity to grasp what Marshall did.[60] In the ordinary and low sense which we attach to the words "partisan" and "politician," a judge of the Supreme Court should be neither. But in the higher sense, in the proper sense, he is not in my judgment fitted for the position unless he is a party man, a constructive statesman, constantly keeping in mind his adherence to the principles and policies under which this nation has been built up and in accordance with which it must go on; and *keeping in mind also his relations with his fellow statesmen who in other branches of the government are striving in cooperation with him to advance the ends of government.* Marshall rendered such invaluable service because he was a statesman of the national type, like Adams who appointed him, like Washington whose mantle fell upon him. Taney was a curse to our national life because he belonged to the wrong party and faithfully carried out the criminal and foolish views of the party which stood for such a construction of the Constitution as would have rendered it impossible even to preserve the national life. The Supreme Court of the sixties was good exactly in so far as its members fitly represented the spirit of Lincoln.

This is true at the present day. *The majority of the present Court who have,* although without satisfactory unanimity, *upheld the policies of President McKinley and the Republican party in Congress, have rendered a great service to mankind* and to this nation. The minority—a minority so large as to lack but one vote of being a majority—have stood for such reactionary

<hr />

60 For an account of Holmes's remarks, uttered from the bench of the Massachusetts Supreme Court on February 4, 1901, the centennial of the day when Marshall joined the United States Supreme Court, see Bent, *op. cit.,* pp. 247-248.

folly as would have hampered well-nigh hopelessly this people in doing efficient and honorable work for the national welfare, and for the welfare of the islands themselves, in Porto Rico and the Philippines. No doubt they have possessed excellent motives and without doubt they are men of excellent personal character; but this no more excuses them than the same conditions excused the various upright and honorable men who took part in the wicked folly of secession in 1860 and 1861.

Now I should like to know that Judge Holmes was in entire sympathy with our views, that is with your views and mine and Judge Gray's, for instance, just as we know that ex-Attorney General Knowlton is, before I would feel justified in appointing him. Judge Gray has been one of the most valuable members of the Court. I should hold myself as guilty of an irreparable wrong to the nation if I should put in his place any man who was not absolutely sane and sound on the great national policies for which we stand in public life.

Faithfully yours,

THEODORE ROOSEVELT

Holmes received the appointment, but his joining the Court did very little to remold the justices in the spirit of Roosevelt. A five-man majority of the Court upheld, on March 14, 1904, the government's position in the Northern Securities case.[61] Holmes did not "cooperate," however, and his opinion in behalf of four dissenters, who would have upheld the railroad merger, was the first of what came in time to be his celebrated series of dissenting opinions. It was said at the time that "Justice Holmes, although he had previously called several times a week, had not been at the White House for some time." [62] At a much later time,[63]

> Holmes himself, to a friend, wrote of the curious doubt that troubled Roosevelt, as well as the circumstance that soon stirred his disappointment in Holmes: ". . . he was uneasy about appointing me because he thought I didn't appreciate Marshall. I thought it rather comic. I have no doubt that later he heartily repented over his choice when I didn't do what he wanted in the Northern Securities Case. . . . Long afterwards, at a dinner at the White House to some labor leaders, I said to one of them who had been spouting about the Judges: What you want is favor—not justice. But when I am on my job I don't care a damn what you want or what Mr. Roosevelt wants—and then repeated my remarks to him. You may think that a trifle crude—but I didn't like to say it behind his back and not to his face, and the fact had justified it—I thought and think" (Unpublished letter, dated April 1, 1928).

[61] *Northern Securities Co. v. United States,* 193 U.S. 197 (1904).

[62] Henry Pringle, *Theodore Roosevelt* (New York: Harcourt, 1931), p. 263.

[63] Quoted in Felix Frankfurter (Philip Elman, ed.), *Of Law and Men* (New York:

Harcourt, 1956), p. 172. Quoted from *Of Law and Men* by Felix Frankfurter, edited by Philip Elman, © 1956, by Felix Frankfurter. Reprinted by permission of Harcourt, Brace and Company, Inc.

THE PROBLEM OF JUDICIAL SUPERANNUATION

How Old Are the Justices?

Franklin Roosevelt's attack on the "Nine Old Men" [64] in 1937 served to dramatize what has been, and remains, a continuing problem of the Supreme Court. The problem is created by the constitutional guarantee of life tenure for the justices. It might be defined in terms of the implications for American political society of a system which places basic decisions of national policy in the hands of a small group of men—a group whose membership, at most times during our history, has included several very old men. A justice who resigned under the "Voluntary Retirement"—actually, voluntary resignation—Act of 1869,[65] after having attained the age of 70 with at least ten years of federal judicial service, received for life the same salary he was being paid at the time of his retirement, and he was free to engage in business or political pursuits. Roosevelt's "Court-packing" proposal, which we shall consider at greater length in the next chapter, provided in essence that Congress should enact legislation authorizing the President to appoint additional justices, up to a maximum of fifteen—one for each incumbent justice who had reached the age of 70 but refused to resign or retire. Congress rejected this proposal for the appointment of additional justices, but enacted legislation [66] which permitted justices to *retire*, subject to *ad hoc* assignment of temporary judicial duties in the circuits.[67] A retired justice thus would receive the benefit of any salary raises applicable to active justices.

If we classify the Court's history according to the periods used by Ewing, we find that there has been a gradual increase in the average age of justices *at the time of their appointment* until the most recent period. This is shown in Table 5.

No men who had reached the age of 60 were appointed until 1870, when Grant appointed Strong (62) and Bradley (67) in the midst of the Legal Tender

[64] See Drew Pearson and Robert S. Allen, *The Nine Old Men* (Garden City: Doubleday, 1936); also Alfred Haines Cope and Fred Krinsky, *Franklin D. Roosevelt and the Supreme Court* (Boston: Heath, 1952). The text of the President's Message to the Congress of February 5, 1937, is reprinted in *ibid.*, pp. 17-22; for the original, see *Congressional Record*, 75th Cong., 1st Sess., Vol. 81, Part 1, pp. 877-879.

[65] Act of April 10, 1869, 16 *Stat.* 44, effective the following December.

[66] Sumners-McCarran Act of March 1, 1937, 50 *Stat.* 24. The more recent Retirement Act of February 10, 1954, 68 Stat. 12-13, has had no apparent effect as yet upon the behavior of Supreme Court justices, except for Minton who retired at 65 in 1956 after 7 years' service. Its major provisions are to permit a justice to resign or retire at full pay at age 65 after 15 years of service, and to provide for disability retirement upon the filing of a certificate with the President. In the latter case, the age requirement for retirement is waived, and compensation depends upon length of service. Cf. 28 U.S.C.A. Sec. 371, 372.

[67] Justice Reed, who retired on October 16, 1956, and who sat with the Court of Claims during 1957 and 1958, was apparently the first justice to be assigned temporary judicial duties under the 1937 legislation, and two decades after its enactment, at that.

TABLE 5.

Average Age of Supreme Court Justices when Appointed

Period Number	Years	Average Age at Appointment
1	1789-1829	47.6
2	1829-1861	51.1
3	1861-1897	55.3
4	1897-1937	57.1
5	1937-1958	52.9

controversy, adding Hunt (62) two years later. Three other sexagenarians were added during the third period; and there were seven during the fourth period. Since 1937, there have been only two: Byrnes (62) and Warren (62); while Douglas (41) and Stewart (43) were the youngest men to be appointed to the Court in over a century. Obviously, one way to have a younger Court is to appoint younger men to the Court.

We can also approach the problem from the point of view of the average age of all of the sitting justices. In the graph (Figure 1, on page 59), this has been computed, by decades, to the nearest quarter of a year.[68]

This graph illustrates the fact that there was nothing spurious in the labeling of the Court of the early 1930's as that of the "Nine Old Men." The average age of the justices rose steadily, from a low of less than 52 in the decade in which the Court was deciding such cases as *McCulloch* v. *Maryland*, until an average of 64 was reached during the decade prior to the Civil War. The average, with slight fluctuations, remained about the same for seventy years, and was slightly less at the time of Wilson's Presidency than it had been in the days of Fillmore, Pierce, and Buchanan. But there was a sharp rise in the time of the Taft Court, which reached an all-time peak during the first half-dozen years after Hughes took over as Chief Justice. In fact, the actual peak was even higher than the graph (which is based on an average of years as well as of justices) reveals. In 1937, the year of the Court-packing attack, the average age of the Nine Old Men was *over* 72: Brandeis was 81; Van Devanter, 78; Hughes, Sutherland, and McReynolds, 75; Butler, 71; and only three members of the Court were under 70 (Cardozo was 67, Stone 65, and Roberts was a youngster of 62). As a result of Franklin Roosevelt's nine appointments, the average age of the justices dropped, during the following decade, to less than 60 for the first time in over a century. During the most recent decade (1948-1957), it has risen again, to an average of 62, which is still below any decade during the period 1850-1937. It appeared, at the end of the latest period covered by the graph and after Burton's retirement, that over half of the incumbent justices would exceed the retirement age during the decade 1958-

[68] For the period 1789-1937, the data is taken from Ewing, *op. cit.*, p. 72. We have calculated the data for the period since 1937.

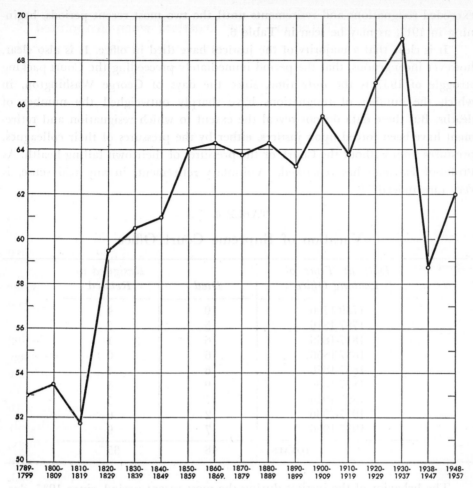

FIG. 1. *Average Age of Supreme Court Justices (by Decades) (1789-1957)*

1967 (Frankfurter and Black, who were already well beyond it, plus Warren, Douglas, and Clark); so the question whether the curve would continue to rise seemed to hinge upon the continued health of these five and the outcome of the presidential election of 1960.

Life Tenure in Action

We can also consider whether justices have tended to vacate their office by death, or by resignation (or retirement); and the relationship of either of these methods to age patterns. Except for the first few terms of the Court during Washington's administration, when several justices resigned at an early age in order to accept more important positions in state government, deaths consistently exceeded resignations and retirements until the two most recent periods, beginning in 1917, as may be seen in Table 6.

It is clear that a majority of the justices have died in office. It is also clear, however incongruous, that the period immediately preceeding the Court-packing struggle of 1937 is the *only* time, since the days of George Washington, in which the number of resignations have sharply outweighed the number of deaths. But these data do not reveal the extent to which resignation and retirement have been forced upon justices, either by the pressures of their colleagues, pressures from without the Court, or the pressures of their own failing health. As Professor Fairman has remarked, "Voluntary retirement, in any real sense, is very rare indeed." [69]

TABLE 6.

Vacation of Supreme Court Office

Date at Time of Leaving Office	Died	Resigned or Retired
1789-1796	0	4
1797-1816	5	2
1817-1836	6	1
1837-1856	6	0
1857-1876	6	4
1877-1896	9	4
1897-1916	7	5
1917-1936	2	6
1937-1956	7	9
TOTALS	48	35

The behavior of the justices during the most recent period, since 1937, does not appear to differ significantly from that of their predecessors. Of the nine appointees of Franklin Roosevelt: (a) four died in office—Stone having been 69 when Roosevelt elevated him to the Chief Justiceship, notwithstanding the President's vociferous compunctions, only four years earlier, about having "old men" dominating the work of the Court; (b) one resigned—Byrnes, to become "Assistant President"; (c) one retired; and (d) three, two of whom were by then septuagenarians, remained incumbents over two decades later, old men a generation removed from their patron's attack upon old men who refused to leave the Court. There were no resignations or retirements from the time of Roberts' resignation in 1945 until Reed retired in 1956 at the age of 72; and Reed was the first of the Roosevelt appointees to retire, which is a reflection of their relative youth at appointment (generally speaking).

[69] Charles Fairman, "The Retirement of Federal Judges," *Harvard Law Review*, Vol. 51, p. 430 (1938).

The graph (Figure 2, below) compares, at twenty-year intervals for the last century, the average age at time of death of Supreme Court justices who died in office, with average age at the time of retirement or resignation. Over the course of the past century, justices have been dying much younger, and retiring or

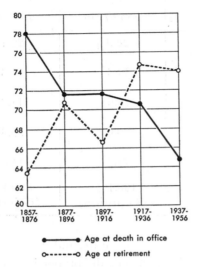

FIG. 2. *Vacation of Office by Supreme Court Justices (1857-1956)*

resigning much older. These two trends have tended to offset each other, however, so that the average age for separation from office (which we do not show on the graph) fluctuates within the much narrower range of 69.6–73.6, a difference of only 4 years. The average age of death, for the entire century, was 71.5, and of resignation and retirement, 70.6; the average age of separation from office during the past hundred years was 71.0.

It is also possible to make certain observations about the apparent effect of the retirement acts of 1869 and 1937 upon the behavior of the justices in leaving office. In Table 7, on page 62, we have classified separation from the Court into five categories: (A) Died *before* becoming eligible for resignation/retirement at full salary; (B) Resigned or retired *before* becoming eligible for resignation/retirement at full salary; (C) Died in office *after* having reached eligibility for resignation/retirement at full salary; (D) Resigned or retired at some time substantially *after* having reached eligibility for resignation/retirement; and (E) Resigned or retired promptly upon attaining eligibility for so doing with full salary. (In the period from 1789 to 1868, of course, there were only two possible categories: died in office, and resigned. Of the thirty-one justices who served during this early period, 71% died in office, and the remaining 29% resigned.) Since the period of time between the two statutes is three times as long as the period

TABLE 7.

When Justices Leave the Court
(In Relationship to Eligibility for Retirement with Pay)

CATEGORY	1869-1936	1937-1958	Total Number of Justices
A. Died before eligible	22.9%	29.4%	13
B. Resigned or retired before eligible	14.3	11.8	7
C. Died after eligible	28.6	11.8	12
D. Resigned or retired after eligible	20.0	35.3	13
E. Resigned or retired as soon as eligible	14.3	11.8	7
TOTALS	100.1% (35 justices)	100.1% (17 justices)	52

since the adoption of the more recent statute, and twice as many justices left office in the earlier period as in the later one, the proportion of justices falling in each category is given in percentages, for each period.

The only significant changes between the two periods involve the decrease in justices who died without having resigned after attaining eligibility (category C) and the increase in those who resigned or retired some time after having attained eligibility (category D). These two changes cancel each other out, however, since there is little difference between the total who stayed on after being eligible to retire on full salary in the earlier period (48.6%) and the equivalent total for the later period (47.1%). As the table shows, only slightly more than 10% of the justices chose to resign or retire at full salary as soon as they were eligible to do so during either period; and the adoption of the 1937 statute certainly has not, as yet, had any apparent greater effect in inducing justices to retire than did the 1869 act.

Almost half of the justices who have left office in the past ninety years stayed on beyond the time when they were eligible to resign or retire on full salary, thus falling in our categories C and D. We have also calculated (in Table 8, on page 63) how long, on the average, they remained on the Court after attaining eligibility for retirement.

Again, there are no important differences between the two periods. Of the 52 justices who have left office during the past ninety years, 38% died or retired before attaining eligibility under the statutes; generally speaking, this group constituted no problem from the point of view of superannuation. Another 13% retired as soon as they attained eligibility; this was the only group, apparently, whose behavior was adjusted to the intent of Congress in adopting the voluntary retirement legislation; and if we assume a point that may be debatable—that the retirement policy established by Congress is wise and appropriate—then this group, also, constituted no problem in terms of superannuation on the Court. But 48% of the justices did *not* retire in accordance with the congressional policy; and on the average, these justices stayed on the bench 6½ years beyond the time when they might have retired and when, it is to be presumed, most of them should have retired. It is this group, which constitutes half of the justices who have served on the Court since the end of the Civil War, that has constituted a superannuation problem.

TABLE 8.

Service Beyond Eligibility for Retirement with Pay

CATEGORY	1869-1936	1937-1958	Average for Both Periods Combined
C. After eligibility, died in:	5.2 yrs	3.5 yrs	4.9 yrs
D. After eligibility, retired in:	8.6 yrs	7.5 yrs	8.1 yrs
Average of C and D:	6.6 yrs	6.5 yrs	6.6 yrs

Why Judges Won't Quit

There are several reasons why superannuation has been a persistent problem, and remains an unsolved one, for the Supreme Court. Senility has not infrequently affected individual justices, either by rendering them physically incapable of carrying out their duties, or by putting them in their dotage.[70] Examples of physical incapacity are John McKinley, who was partially or completely absent from five of his last six terms on the Court until death terminated his tenure; Hunt, who was stricken speechless with paralysis and who did not participate in the work of the Court during his last four years of tenure; and Brown, who became almost totally blind, but remained on the Court for two more years until he was eligible to retire on a pension. The justices who were considered, by their own colleagues and contemporaries, to be feeble-minded, include Baldwin, Grier, Clifford, and Field.

It is possible, of course, to cite outstanding examples of justices who remained on the Court until they became octogenarians, with both physical and mental powers remarkably unimpaired. John Marshall died within three months of his eightieth birthday, after 34 years of service; Roger Taney died at 87, after 29 years; Brandeis retired at 82 after 23 years; and Holmes at 90, after 29 years on

[70] The discussion in this paragraph is based almost entirely upon the excellent ar- ticle by Professor Fairman. See *ibid.*, pp. 406, 407, 418-419, 421-422, 427, 439-440.

the United States Supreme Court and a combined total of over 48 years on the bench. In a very real sense, Holmes and Brandeis are the unique exceptions that prove the rule; and although Marshall and Taney are indisputably to be ranked among the greatest justices who have served on the Court, both lived beyond the time when the values which they represented were appropriate to the solutions of the political problems facing the country—and therefore the Court.[71]

Although Franklin Roosevelt's proposals for reorganization of the Court were couched, disingenuously, in terms of senility and consequent judicial inefficiency, everyone realized that the real basis for his criticism was premised on the argument that a majority of the Court in the middle 1930's were spokesmen for the policies and programs of the Coolidge and Hoover administrations,[72] and that it was politically irresponsible for such justices to checkmate New Deal legislation supported by large contemporary popular majorities. F.D.R.'s problem was not significantly different from that faced by Jefferson or Jackson or Lincoln; and as we shall see in a later chapter, his solution was basically the same as theirs.

Why do elderly justices cling to their offices? There are a variety of reasons. Many justices have hung on because they could not afford to resign. After 24 years on the Court, Justice Grier's salary was still only $6000; and the Act of 1869 was adopted, among other reasons, in order to make it possible for Grier to resign without having to give up his salary. At about the same time, the *Clerk* of the Supreme Court was receiving $30,000 a year in fees, making him, next to the President, the most highly compensated officer of the national government.[73] Even after the adoption of the 1869 statute, there were justices whose health would have impelled them to resign if they could have qualified for a pension. When Brown lost his vision at the age of 68 and after having completed more than the minimum of 10 years' service on the Court, he said: "Of course, I would resign if I could do so and draw my pay; but after nearly thirty years' service upon the Bench I do not feel called upon to do so when I am within a little over two years of completing my term." [74] Brown did resign as soon as he reached his seventieth birthday.

A frequent reason has been the desire to hold down a seat until one's replacement would be selected by a President representing the "right" political party. Taney came within a year of achieving his ambition to outlive Lincoln's Presidency and thus to prevent the nomination of a Republican Chief Justice as his successor. Republican Congressman Ben Wade is reputed to have remarked, "No man ever prayed as I did that Taney might outlive James Buchanan's term . . . but now I am afraid I have overdone it." [75] Democrat Clifford refused to enter the White House after the election of Rutherford B. Hayes, whom Clifford considered

---

71 *Ibid.*, p. 415.
72 Cope and Krinsky, *op. cit.*, pp. 73-74; Jack W. Peltason, *Federal Courts in the Political Process* (Garden City: Doubleday, 1955), p. 41.

73 Fairman, *op. cit.*, p. 419.
74 *Ibid.*, pp. 439-440.
75 Carl B. Swisher, *Roger B. Taney* (New York: Macmillan, 1935), p. 573; quoted in Peltason, *op. cit.*, p. 37.

to be a usurper; [76] and although he had been eligible to retire with a pension in 1873, he stayed on until his death in 1881. Clifford would have had to live another four years in order for a Democratic President (Cleveland) to pick his successor.

Chief Justice Taft, a man with decided views about the selection of Supreme Court justices, wrote to his brother in 1929: "I am older and slower and less acute and more confused. However, as long as things continue as they are, and I am able to answer in my place, I must stay on the court in order to prevent the Bolsheviki from getting control." [77] (Taft considered Hoover to be a dangerous progressive; shortly before his retirement in 1930, and almost on his deathbed, he had come to believe that "if a number of us died, Hoover would put in some rather extreme destroyers of the Constitution." [78] Twenty-seven years earlier, on the last day of his term as President, Taft had remarked to the press that of all the accomplishments of his administration, he was most proud of his six appointments to the Supreme Court; "'And I have said to them,' Taft chuckled, 'Damn you, if any of you die, I'll disown you.'") [79] During the second term of the Eisenhower Administration, the same sort of waiting game appeared to be being played by two of F.D.R.'s early appointees. In the summer of 1959, Black was 73 and Frankfurter 77; both had completed over two decades on the Supreme Court and were well beyond the retirement age; both could hope that, by hanging on for another year and a half, they could retire at a time when they might be replaced by a Democratic President. Conversely, of course, there have been pressures upon elderly justices to retire *before* a President of the opposition party should take office; but, as we have discussed earlier in this chapter, the Senate frequently has frustrated such schemes by refusing to confirm the nominations of lameduck Presidents.

Another reason that has been offered by some justices, although prior to the statutory change of 1937, is the perfectly understandable reluctance of a man who has led a busy and full life to stop working suddenly. Justice Miller, who at an earlier age had been quite critical of his elderly colleagues who refused to resign, discovered at the age of 70 that there were persuasive reasons why he should exempt himself from the advice that he had given others. "I do not believe," he wrote, "a healthy man of seventy years accustomed to any kind of work mental or physical, ought to quit it suddenly." [80] (Miller, it will be recalled, had been a physician in his youth.) Although, as his biographer tells us, "there should be no doubt that [Miller's] own mind retained its full vigor to the end," [81] the fact remains that he could not bring himself to quit when the appointed time came; and he died in the traces five years later. Indeed, Miller's death was apparently hastened, not by his labors in the Supreme Court, but in the execution

[76] Fairman, *op. cit.*, p. 422.

[77] Henry F. Pringle, *The Life and Times of William Howard Taft* (New York: Farrar & Rinehart, 1939), Vol. 2, p. 967; also quoted in Peltason, *op. cit.*, pp. 37-38.

[78] Alpheus T. Mason, *The Supreme Court from Taft to Warren* (Baton Rouge: Louisiana State University Press, 1958), p. 66.

[79] McHargue, *op. cit.* (article; footnote 24, above), p. 507.

[80] Fairman, *op. cit.*, p. 426.

[81] *Ibid.*

of his responsibility to ride circuit, a duty of which the justices were relieved shortly after Miller's death by the adoption of the Circuit Court of Appeals Act of 1891. With the abolition of circuit-riding, it has been argued that the physical and intellectual demands of a Supreme Court justiceship do not differ markedly from those made upon a university professor. As Professor Fairman has pointed out, however, the rule that was widely followed, even a generation ago, in the case of professors at most major universities, was compulsory retirement at age 65.[82]

At least in times past, and presumably at present too, there has been another reason why justices have been reluctant to resign, independently of the considerations already suggested. Female relatives have opposed the retirement of justices who were their fathers or brothers or husbands, because of the loss of social status in the nation's capital consequent upon retirement.

[82] *Ibid.*, pp. 432-433.

The Decision-Making Process

I N CHAPTER TWO, we examined the extent to which the Presidents and the Senate have been successful in their attempts to impose indirect control over the policy content of Supreme Court decisions by selecting the justices only from among those persons whose views on questions of political, economic, and social policy reflected the ideology prevailing at the time of their appointment. The unrepresentativeness, as a cross-section of American society, of the values entertained by the small group of justices who comprise at any given time the Supreme Court, is accentuated by the ravages of time; and the values of the Court are insulated against direct political adjustment, through the electoral process, by the constitutional guarantee of life tenure.

To say that the justices enjoy job security and legal independence from the power of direction and policy control of the President and the Congress is only the beginning rather than the end of significant inquiry into the meaning of judicial independence, however. The justices clearly are not independent from the legal profession; and guild restraints and distraints are a major channel of judicial responsibility. By this we mean that the justices normally retain active affiliation with bar associations; [1] they find that *noblesse oblige* requires, pretty much, that they make recurring guest appearances at the better-known law

[1] The resignation of Chief Justice Earl Warren from the American Bar Association after a membership of twenty years, early in 1959, in apparent anticipation of that organization's adoption two months later of resolutions critical of the Supreme Court's "softness" toward Communists, was highly unusual, and perhaps unprecedented. The precedent that he established was soon followed, however, by at least one justice of a state supreme court, Eugene F. Black of Michigan, who resigned from the A.B.A. on March 6, 1959, stating publicly that he was "ashamed of the A.B.A.'s attack on the U.S. Supreme Court and ashamed of my past membership."

67

schools; they write for and read the major law journals. Neither are the justices independent of the past, which surely includes, for each, the sociopsychological factors which have helped to shape his character and personality to say nothing of friendships which, not infrequently, survive a man's accession to the Court.[2] With the possible exception of occasional Olympians who eschew the reading of daily newspapers, the justices are aware of what is going on in the world; [3] and with different degrees of zest, they participate in the social life of official Washington. Moreover, the justices are not independent of each other, or of their clerks or other elements of the organization of which they are the formal leaders.[4] They are dependent, necessarily, upon many other human beings in order to do their work; and, being men with substantial experience in political affairs, they need not ask for whom the bell tolls—they know that it tolls for them together with the rest of humanity.

Traditional research in public law has not analyzed the independence of Supreme Court justices in terms of the variables that we have suggested. As Professor Jack W. Peltason has observed,[5]

> Studies that are primarily concerned with legal doctrines—tracing their historical development and discussing their desirability—or studies that deal with individual judges—examining the influences that molded their thoughts, discovering what they "really meant," applauding or criticizing their decisions —are very important. But these studies do not, except incidentally, provide a framework in which judicial activity can be related to the behavior of other branches of government. They still leave the judges outside the political process.

The result has been the neglect of much important and relevant political data. What would be the effect, asks Peltason, if we were to attempt to study the legislative process by the same methods that have, in the past, been considered adequate for a comprehension of judicial decision-making? [6]

> Biographies of leading congressmen would be the main staple of research. Discussion of statute-making would concentrate on activity within the legislative chamber. Legislators would be seen as an isolated group. A congressman's vote, say, for the Taft-Hartley Act would be explained as reflecting his

2 See, e.g., Mark DeWolfe Howe (ed.), *Holmes-Pollock Letters* (2 vols., 1946), *Holmes-Laski Letters,* (2 vols., 1953); both collections published at Cambridge: Harvard University.

3 See, e.g., Walter P. Armstrong, "What Do the Justices Read? Books of Interest to Supreme Court Members," *American Bar Association Journal,* Vol. 35, pp. 295-298 (1949).

4 For examples of such group interdependence, see Alexander M. Bickel, *The Unpublished Opinions of Mr. Justice Brandeis: The*

Supreme Court at Work (Cambridge: Harvard University, Belknap Press, 1957), *passim;* and Alan F. Westin, "Stephen J. Field and the Headnote to *O'Neil* v. *Vermont:* A Snapshot of the Fuller Court at Work," *Yale Law Journal,* Vol. 67, p. 363 (January, 1958).

5 *Federal Courts in the Political Process* (Garden City: Doubleday, 1955), p. 1. By Jack W. Peltason. © Copyright 1955 by Random House, Inc. Reprinted by permission.

6 *Ibid.,* pp. 1-2.

conviction that such a law was a reasonable regulation of commerce designed to promote the national interest. Studies of the legislative process would deal primarily with legislators' speeches and contain critical comments on their arguments. Attention would be focussed upon formal rules of procedure. Students in courses on legislation would be assigned readings from the *United States Code*. Little attention would be paid to the consequences of legislative decisions.

Even the neophyte student of government will recognize the sterility and inadequacy of such an approach to legislative decision-making. In this chapter, we shall examine the decision-making process of the Supreme Court as a significant aspect of the political process, and as a set of behaviors that can be studied by the use of methods similar to those customarily employed in the analysis of the decisions of other governmental officials.

LOBBYISTS BEFORE THE SUPREME COURT

The lobbying of interest groups with Congress and state legislatures is accepted today as a fundamental and desirable political process in a democratic polity. Administrative lobbying was less well understood, and certainly less generally accepted, a generation ago than it is today; and even now, there are many critics who insist that pressure politics has no legitimate role in relationship to certain kinds of administrative decision-making, such as government contracting or adjudication by regulatory commissions. When it comes to the judiciary, however, the norms of our society engender an attitude of open hostility toward lobbying tactics, most of which are generally considered to be invidious, unethical, and presumably illegal. Judges are not supposed to decide cases by succumbing to "outside" pressures and influences; the litigious model of Anglo-Saxon trial procedure retains clearly the vestigial traces of an enlightened age, now centuries past, when trial by battle displaced trial by ordeal and the compurgation oath as a path to truth and justice. It is considered unfair for third parties who are not "privy" to the conflict to enter the lists; rather, each party to the contest has his champion—an attorney—and judgment and justice alike are presumably forged in a crucible which is heated by the intensity of the conflicting interests. But the conflicting interests are those of the parties to the case, in the technical legal notion of party-litigant status; and even they articulate their interests, and exert pressure to evoke a favorable decision from the court, only through the mediatory role of official mouthpieces, who speak in a jargon which is shared by the only legitimate critics of the proceedings: other judges and other lawyers. Thus, group behaviors that are considered to be the very essence of the politics of democracy, when focused upon the Congress, are castigated as the antithesis of "a government of laws, not men" when the object of group pressures is the Supreme Court.

Nevertheless, lobbying with the Supreme Court has been going on for a long time, and ignoring its existence has not succeeded in eradicating it. As Twiss has shown, the now staid American Bar Association was originally formed, in 1878, as a national organization stemming from the Association of the Bar of the City of New York, which began in 1870. The latter association was organized "chiefly to combat the corruption of the judiciary by the Tweed Ring. At least in its early years it was a good example of how a bar association can be an important political pressure group." [7] During the first three decades of the present century, the National Consumers' League was particularly active in defending labor legislation from attack in the courts.[8] The League enlisted the services of such distinguished counsel as Louis Brandeis and Felix Frankfurter; and although its efforts met with greater success in the state courts than in the Supreme Court, a major change in the technique of persuasion before the Supreme Court resulted from the League's sponsorship of advocacy by means of the sociological or Brandeis brief. The purpose of such briefs, which were in essence compendious compilations of economic and social facts, with a minimum of emphasis upon the citation of legal precedents and doctrines which (then as now) made up the substance of conventional legal briefs, was to educate Supreme Court justices concerning the facts of industrial life in a changing world. Half a century ago, the novel sociological briefs met with just as severe criticism and resistance as has the Court's own reliance, in a more recent period, upon generalizations regarding human behavior based upon the research of social psychologists.

Three Tactics for Lobbying with the Supreme Court

The conventions surrounding judicial decision-making, at least as a formal process, stigmatize as illegal or unethical certain kinds of group-pressure activity. Thus, for instance, the picketing of federal courthouses is defined as a criminal act by congressional legislation; and the sending of mass petitions to the Supreme Court on behalf of condemned criminals has been condemned by the justices.[9] There are, however, a number of pressure tactics which have become increasingly common, including (1) the use of test cases; (2) building up a favorable professional climate of opinion in the law reviews; and (3) presenting the Court with a show of strength, by the temporary alliance of groups to support a formal party to a case through the *amicus curiae* device. We shall consider in turn each of these techniques for judicial lobbying.

[7] Benjamin R. Twiss, *Lawyers and the Constitution* (Princeton: Princeton University Press, 1942), pp. 145, 170.

[8] Clement E. Vose, "The National Consumers' League and the Brandeis Brief," *Midwest Journal of Political Science,* Vol. 1, 276-290 (November, 1957).

[9] Vose, "Litigation as a Form of Pressure Group Activity," *Annals of the American Academy of Political and Social Science,* Vol. 319, pp. 28-29 (September, 1958).

The Use of Test Cases

As Clement E. Vose, a leading student of interest group pressures on the judiciary, has explained: [10]

> Winning new constitutional protections for Negroes has depended on the development of individual test cases with a Negro as party in each. There is no chronicle of the human interest stories contained in the roles of Negroes in historic Supreme Court cases. But what is known reveals many difficulties to be inherent in improving the legal status of a group of fifteen million persons through individual court cases. In a suit by a single plaintiff, the case may become moot as the passage of time makes the remedy sought inapplicable. This danger, though avoided by the co-operation of state officials, was created in the Missouri Law School case of 1938 when the plaintiff, Lloyd Gaines, disappeared just as the case was completed. Also the concerted efforts of authorities to deny Negroes participation in the Texas white Democratic primary kept Dr. L. A. Nixon from voting even though he was the plaintiff in two Supreme Court victories. Furthermore there is always the temptation for compromise by the original plaintiff which would accomplish his narrow purpose but stop the litigation before the broad constitutional issue was before the appellate court.
>
> These dangers were largely overcome in the School Segregation Cases when federal court actions were instituted by individual plaintiffs both on their own behalf and on behalf of persons similarly situated. Since 1955, in the expanding litigation over race relations, the class action has become a procedural device of growing importance. Rule 23(a) of the Federal Rules of Civil Procedure provides under certain circumstances that

> if persons constituting a class are so numerous as to make it impracticable to bring them all before the court, such of them, one or more, as will fairly insure the adequate representation of all may, on behalf of all, sue or be sued.

> One authority has said that "school segregation is a group phenomenon which is peculiarly suited to resolution in a class action." As Negroes enter a new generation of litigation, their cases are apt increasingly to take the form of the class action.

The individuals whose cases reach the Supreme Court for decision are usually sponsored by or are merely fronts for organized groups with particular axes to grind: [11]

> Organizations support legal action because individuals lack the necessary time, money, and skill. With no delays a case takes an average of four years to pass through two lower courts to the Supreme Court of the United

---

10 *Ibid.*, pp. 23-24.   11 *Ibid.*, p. 22.

States. A series of cases on related questions affecting the permanent interest of a group may extend over two decades or more. The constant attention that litigation demands, especially when new arguments are being advanced, makes the employment of regular counsel economical. This may be supplemented by a legal staff of some size and by volunteer lawyers of distinction. Parties also pay court costs and meet the expense of printing the record and briefs. Organizations are better able to provide the continuity demanded in litigation than individuals. Some individuals do maintain responsibility for their own cases even at the Supreme Court level, but this is difficult under modern conditions.

The form of group participation in court cases is set by such factors as the type of proceeding, standing of the parties, legal or constitutional issues in dispute, the characteristics of the organization, and its interest in the outcome. Perhaps the most direct and open participation has been by organizations which have been obliged to protect their own rights and privileges.

Propaganda in Legal Periodicals

According to Chester Newland,[12]

Even the most casual perusal of the court reports will show that legal periodicals have been cited by the Supreme Court of the United States and by judges of some other courts in the past several years in proportions that are sharply increased over those of three decades ago. Most law schools now publish reviews; together with bar journals and related publications, their total number today is well over 100. Comment upon judicial decisions and critical inquiry into broader problems of the law have become generally accepted functions of these periodicals. Today, their critical role seems to be an almost inevitable element in the continuing process of fitting the law to the demands of society. It is commonly understood that legal counsel and judges regularly turn to the reviews as sources of information and analysis of legal problems. . . .

In 1931, Justice (then Chief Judge of the New York Court of Appeals) Benjamin N. Cardozo, in an introduction written for a compilation of articles on the law of contracts, called attention to the growth in respectability of law reviews as sources of legal "authority." Commenting on the reasons for the change in reliance on legal periodicals, Cardozo said "The leading cause . . . has been a dislocation of existing balances, a disturbance of the weights of authority and influence. Judges and advocates may not relish the admission, but the sobering truth is that leadership in the march of legal thought has been passing in our day from the benches of the courts to the chairs of the universities." Ten years after Cardozo wrote these words, Chief Justice

---

12 Chester A. Newland, "Legal Periodicals and the United States Supreme Court," *Midwest Journal of Political Science*, Vol. 3, pp. 58-59, 63, 64, 73 (February, 1959), reprinted by permission of the Wayne State University Press, publisher; and "Anti-trust Policy and the Influence of Legal Periodicals," a paper read by Professor Newland at the Annual Meeting of the Midwest Conference of Political Scientists (Ann Arbor, Michigan: April 25, 1958), p. 18, fn. 55.

Hughes characterized the law reviews as the "fourth estate" of the law. Hughes said: "It is not too much to say that, in confronting any serious problem, a wide-awake and careful judge will at once look to see if the subject has been discussed, or the authorities collated and analyzed, in a good law periodical." [And fifteen years later, Chief Justice Earl Warren, commenting at the dedication exercises commemorating the fiftieth anniversary of the Northwestern University Law Review, said: "Much of the finest legal thinking has been made available to us through leading law review articles. . . . Nor can it be doubted that the student writers . . . have themselves offered much that is constructive. Perhaps our sharpest critics, their disinterested inquiry is needed and appreciated."]

The clearest difference in reliance on legal periodicals among the justices, so far as group classification is concerned, appears to be related to the differences in their dispositions toward the changes in the law which accompanied the adoption in this country of the social welfare philosophy associated with the New Deal. The seven justices who most frequently cited legal periodicals, for example, were all Roosevelt appointees: Frankfurter, Douglas, Black, Jackson, Rutledge, Reed, and Murphy. The "dissenters" during the thirties—Justices Brandeis, Stone, and Cardozo—cited legal periodicals much more often than other members of the pre-Roosevelt Court, while the five justices who held out most firmly against the New Deal—McReynolds, Van Devanter, Butler, Sutherland, and Roberts—cited practically no law review writing. Later groupings of the justices according to divisions of opinions, however, reveal no marked differences in their reliance on law reviews. For example, Black, Douglas, Rutledge, and Murphy as a group did not differ much in the extent to which they relied on legal periodicals from Frankfurter, Jackson, and Reed as a group.

There is little evidence of a unique relationship between the fact that some justices were ex-law professors and the extent to which they cited law reviews or the particular periodicals which they cited . . . [although] Frankfurter and Douglas each cited the journals published by the schools with which they were earlier associated [Harvard and Yale, respectively] more frequently than they cited other law reviews.[13]

In most cases the law review articles which are cited are minor references in the justices' opinions. On the other hand, they are sometimes influential sources, as in *Erie Railroad* v. *Tompkins*. The justices differ in their manner of citing law reviews, and individual justices use these sources in a variety of ways in different opinions. Many of the references to frequently cited journals like the *Harvard Law Review* are inconsequential, whereas a single reference to a seldom-cited law review may be an influential source in an opinion.

By no means all observers share Professor Newland's dispassionate aplomb on this subject, however. Congressman Wright Patman of Texas, for instance, delivered a speech from the floor of the House on August 27, 1957. Patman entitled his

[13] For an amusing comment upon the reciprocal behavior of the justices' alma maters, see Peltason, *op. cit.*, p. 73, fn. 20.

speech, "Effect of Lobbyists' Propaganda upon Our Supreme Court," and said, in part: [14]

Today we are finding that an additional factor is creeping in to influence the thinking and action of the Supreme Court of the United States. That factor is the Court's consideration of unknown, unrecognized and nonauthoritative text books, Law Review articles, and other writings of propaganda artists and lobbyists. In some instances it appears that the Court has considered and adopted such questionable writings in an ex parte fashion because counsels' arguments and briefs made no reference thereto. Apparently therefore the Court itself uncovered and utilized the articles written by these lobbyists without having notified counsel of its intention so to do. If as indicated such a procedure was followed a situation would be presented wherein counsel would have enjoyed no opportunity to meet the arguments of these theorists and lobbyists. In adopting and relying upon such pseudo legalistic papers disseminated by the lobbyist-authors thereof the result is that the theories advanced by these pretended authorities were presented and received by the Court in an ex parte fashion.

In other cases however it appears that some of the articles written by the lobbyists were mentioned or cited in the brief by counsel for defendants and later cited in the Court's opinion. In such instances it seems to me that here again the Court has acted in an ex parte fashion unless it gave affirmative notice to opposing counsel that it intended to use and rely upon the miscellaneous nonauthoritative writings of the lobbyists and theorists referred to hereinabove. This is true, it seems to me, because counsel is entitled to assume that the Court will not pay attention to citations or writings not theretofore accepted by the Court as authoritative. The Law Review articles, treatises, and so forth, prepared and disseminated by the lobbyists command no respect, have no standing as legal authorities, and therefore warrant no consideration by opposing counsel. If the rule were otherwise counsel would be rendered helpless because their arguments would become diluted heavily with extraneous miscellaneous matter designed to overcome the various theories advanced by the lobbyists posing as legal authorities.

Perhaps many will be quite surprised to hear that the Supreme Court is being lobbied by persons who are partisan advocates. Moreso surprising is the fact that some of the partisan ex parte advocacy has had telling effect on decisions which vitally affect our people and which will continue to affect them adversely for years to come.

It has been noted hereinabove that the arguments of partisan theorists have been relied upon by the Supreme Court of the United States to sustain some of its most important recent decisions. That is true even though the arguments in question were received by the Court in the fashion described above which in turn means that the lobbyists in question have managed to

---

[14] *Congressional Record,* 85th Cong., 1st Sess., Vol. 103 Part 12, pp. 16160, 16162, 16169.

get the ear and reach the mind of the Justices of our great Supreme Court ex parte.

The procedure in question is something new in the long history of Anglo-Saxon jurisprudence. Never have the high courts of England resorted to such dubious conduct and until recently such was never done by the Supreme Court of the United States.

When and how did this new concept of relying upon such ex parte arguments creep into the decisions of the Supreme Court of the United States? It appears that it gained substantial acceptance when certain Justices of the Court commenced turning to the Harvard Law Review and other publications during about 1940 for advice on how the Supreme Court of the United States should decide antitrust cases. . . .

Much of the lobbying directed to the Supreme Court in recent years has taken the form of law review articles, pamphlets and books presented as if they were objective works of unbiased, unprejudiced, nonpartisan writers. Actually, many of them have been carefully planned and devised by opponents of our public policy against monopoly with a "view to formulate future antitrust policy."

Commenting specifically upon Congressman Patman's charges, Newland has remarked:[15]

In the light of the generality of reliance on legal periodicals by the courts and the bar today, the note of surprise at the Supreme Court's citation of such sources revealed some measure of naivete on Patman's part. However, his may not be the only conception of this aspect of the judicial process which is somewhat at variance with actuality. The law schools and their reviews have often been spoken of as wholly disinterested parties in the judicial process. And the ethical standards of the Bar still generally forbid comment by members while a case is *sub judice*. . . . The prejudice against law reviews has vanished so recently that views about their proper role in the judicial process are still in a formative state.

Since reliance on legal periodicals has become an accepted part of the judicial process in this country during the past 20 or 30 years, the power of law reviews to exert a formative influence on the law has increased. . . . Apparently this power of law reviews has not been overlooked by writers with axes to grind. Anniversary speeches honoring legal periodicals to the contrary, the torch held aloft by the law reviews does not radiate a wholly disinterested light. They are often vehicles for the expression of views on current policy issues. This seems essential if law reviews are not to limit their interests solely to the past. It is also reasonable to expect judges to be influenced by these publications of the legal profession. Critics may properly object that some views expressed in legal periodicals and adopted by the courts are contrary to policies which they deem desirable. But no greater unanimity of

15 Newland, *op. cit.* (article), pp. 73-74.

opinion usually exists among law faculties and reviews than exists on the Supreme Court. Legal periodicals appear to be "political" in somewhat the same way that the courts are.

Amici Curiae: Friends of the Court?

Professor Vose has explained that: [16]

The appearance of organizations as *amici curiae* has been the most noticed form of group representation in Supreme Court cases. This does not concern the technical office of *amicus curiae* for which an attorney is appointed to assist the court in deciding complex and technical problems. Today, the Supreme Court does sometimes, as in formulating its decree in the School Segregation Cases, issue a special invitation to the Solicitor General or to state Attorneys General to act as *amici curiae*. Of interest here is the rule under which individuals, organizations, and government attorneys have been permitted to file briefs and/or make oral argument in the Supreme Court. During the last decade *amici curiae* have submitted an average of sixty-six briefs and seven oral arguments in an average total of forty cases a term.

The frequent entrance of organizations into Supreme Court cases by means of the *amicus curiae* device has often given litigation the distinct flavor of group combat. This may be illustrated by the group representation in quite different cases. In 1943, when a member of the Jehovah's Witnesses challenged the constitutionality of a compulsory flag salute in the schools, his defense by counsel for the Watchtower Bible and Tract Society was supported by separate *amici curiae,* the American Civil Liberties Union and the Committee on the Bill of Rights of the American Bar Association. The appellant state board of education was supported by an *amicus curiae* brief filed by the American Legion. In 1951, in a case testing state resale price maintenance, the United States was an *amicus* against a Louisiana statute while the Commonwealth of Pennsylvania, the Louisiana State Pharmaceutical Association, American Booksellers, Inc., and the National Association of Retail Druggists entered *amici curiae* briefs in support of the statute.

Many *amici curiae* briefs are workmanlike and provide the Court with helpful legal argument and material. Yet writers who favor their use by organizations and recognize that "the *amicus curiae* has had a long and respected role in our own legal system and before that, in the Roman law" believe that many briefs in recent years display a "timewasting character." Another authority has said that after 1947 there were multiplying signs "that the brief *amicus curiae* had become essentially an instrumentality designed to exert extra-judicial pressure on judicial decisions." . . .

Supreme Court rules long provided that a "brief of an *amicus curiae* may be filed when accompanied by written consent of all parties to a case." Until 1949 permission was freely granted. In that year, the filing of briefs by forty

---

[16] Vose, *op. cit.* (in footnote 9, above), pp. 27-28, 29.30.

organizations in the case of the "Hollywood Ten" who had declined to testify before the House Un-American Activities Committee was widely regarded as an excessive use of the *amici curiae* procedure. The Supreme Court thereupon called attention to the "rule of consent" by elaborating the procedures and permitting persons denied consent by a party to seek leave from the Court itself to act as *amicus curiae*. The Solicitor General, as the legal representative of the United States in the Supreme Court, took the 1949 rule change to mean that he should exercise the "rule of consent" against persons or groups wishing to be *amici curiae* in all cases. Since the United States government is a party in approximately 50 per cent of all cases before the Supreme Court the universal refusal of consent cut the number of organizations filing *amici curiae* briefs rather drastically. This rigid policy was adhered to by a succession of Solicitors General until August 1952. Complaints by Justices Black and Frankfurter then led the Solicitor General to modify the practice and exercise administrative discretion in passing upon requests of organizations to file briefs *amici curiae*. This practice satisfied a majority of the Supreme Court for its 1949 rule change was incorporated into the full revision of the Court's rules which went into effect on July 1, 1954. However, Justice Black was still dissatisfied and, on adoption of the 1954 rules, declared:

> . . . I have never favored the almost insuperable obstacle our rules put in the way of briefs sought to be filed by persons other than the actual litigants. Most of the cases before this Court involve matters that affect far more than the immediate record parties. I think the public interest and judicial administration would be better served by relaxing rather than tightening the rule against *amicus curiae* briefs.

The standard governing grant or denial of consent to file *amicus curiae* briefs has been elaborated upon in a statement of policy issued by the Office of the Solicitor General. While espousing a liberal attitude, the Solicitor General frowns on applicants with "a general, abstract or academic interest" in a case and on "a brief which is 'a vehicle for propaganda efforts.'" Nor is a brief that merely repeats the arguments of the parties well regarded. On the other hand, consent is given "where the applicant has a concrete, substantial interest in the decision of the case, and the proposed brief would assist the Court by presenting relevant arguments or materials which would not otherwise be submitted." Furthermore, in recent years when the Solicitor General has refused consent, the Supreme Court in some cases has granted permission to an organization to file a brief *amicus curiae*.

Efforts to regulate the indiscriminate filing of *amici curiae* briefs prevent organizations on about ten occasions each term from participating in cases. For example, an American Legion post was refused consent to file an *amicus curiae* brief in the Steel Seizure Case while the Congress of Industrial Organizations was permitted to do so. The most active organizations in filing *amici curiae* briefs in recent years have been the American Civil Liberties Union, the American Federation of Labor-Congress of Industrial Organizations, the American Jewish Congress, and the National Lawyers Guild. Yet under the "rule of consent" by parties to the case each of these organizations has sometimes been denied leave to file briefs.

Is the *amicus curiae* brief incompatible with the dispensation of "dispassionate justice" in the Supreme Court? [17] Or is it a desirable device for extending the vision of the justices beyond the blinders imposed by the record of and the immediate interests of the direct parties to a case? The answers to these questions hinge, no doubt, upon the assumpton that most appropriately defines the modern role of the Court. If the justices sit as a "Supreme Tribunal of Errors and Appeals" to right every wrong in the lower courts, then the rights of the immediate parties are most important. But if the justices sit as major formulators of national policy, then it would seem desirable to encourage a broad proliferation of interest representation before the Court.

The NAACP as a Supreme Court Lobby

During the modern period, organizations prominent for their attempts to mold policy-making by the Supreme Court have included the American Liberty League of anti-New Deal fame; the Watch Tower Bible and Tract Society (Jehovah's Witnesses), which built up the imposing record of forty-four wins out of fifty-five cases in the Supreme Court, for a batting average of .800; and the National Association for the Advancement of Colored People, which won more than fifty Supreme Court cases in the half-century following its establishment.[18] The victories of the NAACP in the Supreme Court have had a tremendous impact upon our national policy, our political system, and our very way of life, so we shall use the lobbying activities of this group as a concrete example of the three lobbying tactics described above.

NAACP Strategy in the Restrictive Covenant Cases [19]

As a pressure group dealing mainly with the judiciary, the NAACP has developed many assets since its formation in 1909. It has had financial re-

[17] For an exceptionally pungent but well-written discussion of the *amicus* problem as seen by a Supreme Court justice, see Jackson's dissenting opinion in *Craig* v. *Harney*, 331 U.S. 367, 394 (1947). See also comments by Black and Frankfurter in *United States* v. *Lovknit*, 342 U.S. 915 (1952); *Lee* v. *United States*, 343 U.S. 924 (1952); and at 346 U.S. 947 (1954).

[18] Vose, *op. cit.* (in footnote 9, above), pp. 22, 24-25. For an extended discussion of group litigation in the Supreme Court, see Robert A. Horn, *Groups and the Constitution* (Stanford: Stanford University Press, 1956). For an excellent comparative analysis of the legal lobbying tactics of the American Civil Liberties Union and the American Jewish Congress as well as the NAACP, see the Note, "Private Attorneys-General: Group Action in the Fight for Civil Liberties," *Yale Law Journal*, Vol. 58, pp. 574-598 (1949).

[19] This selection is taken from "The Impact of Pressure Groups on Constitutional Interpretation," a paper read by Professor Vose at the Annual Convention of the American Political Science Association (Chicago, Illinois: September 8, 1954), pp. 1-4. For an extended development and documentation of these same points, see Vose, *Caucasians Only: The Supreme Court, the NAACP, and the Restrictive Covenant Cases* (Berkeley and Los Angeles: University of California Press, 1959).

sources. The [fifty-odd] Supreme Court victories of the Association have cost an enormous amount of money as $10,000 is the average expense for each case. For purposes of tax exemption and organization, the NAACP Legal and Educational Fund was incorporated primarily to sponsor and supervise court cases. Then in all major cities there were Negro attorneys bound together by the alumni ties of Howard University Law School and the mutual problems of racial discrimination. The presence of these devoted lawyers—the nucleus of the Association's National Legal Committee—at the local level, where po·tential Supreme Court cases began, has been of great strategic value. As cases moved from trial court to Supreme Court there was a healthy exchange of information between the volunteer attorneys in the field and the professionals in New York. National strategy meetings were held frequently as specific problems ripened into constitutional cases.

Scrutiny of the NAACP's part in the successful litigation which ended the court enforcement of racial restrictive convenants will indicate how the organization went about urging constitutional change. This was a long campaign from 1918, speeded up after 1945 and climaxed in 1948. Then, in *Shelley* v. *Kraemer,* the Supreme Court ruled that when a state court enjoins Negroes from taking restricted property it is state action in violation of the equal protection guarantee of the Fourteenth Amendment. In two cases from Washington, D.C., it was held contrary to the Civil Rights Act of 1866 and the nation's public policy for federal courts to use their equity powers to enforce racial restrictive covenants. [In 1953], in *Barrows* v. *Jackson,* the Supreme Court extended the doctrine by holding that a state court could not sanction a racial convenant by awarding damages in a suit at law.

Organized groups, not individuals, pressed conflicting constitutional claims upon the Supreme Court in each of the five restrictive covenant cases. In the *Shelley* case, for example, the Marcus Avenue Improvement Association of St. Louis was, in effect, the real party in interest, since Mrs. Fern Kraemer (the official plaintiff) had neither the time nor the resources to conduct the litigation. On the other side, an NAACP attorney, Mr. Loren Miller of Los Angeles, who handled the Association cause in *Barrows* v. *Jackson,* recently made this observation:

> . . . Supreme Court cases involving larger issues are contests between opposing forces rather than law suits between individuals. They are cast as individual pieces of litigation because the Constitution guarantees the rights of individuals rather than those of groups. However as a practical matter the individual is unable to pursue his rights to the ultimate and hence the job is done by groups of people who find themselves situated as the individual is situated and who secure their own rights by securing the rights of the similarly situated individual.

Since challenges to old interpretations of the Constitution must, under Article III, be presented in a "case or controversy" it is pertinent to observe the manner in which the NAACP dealt with this requirement. Then we may consider two other forms of attempted influence on the courts, creation of favorable legal opinion and the use of the amici curiae brief.

. . . It takes time for a group to persuade the Court to accept a case as a test. Through the years after 1926 when the judicial enforcement of a covenant was sanctioned by the Supreme Court the NAACP made five applications for writs of certiorari. In 1929 and 1937 these applications were denied outright. In 1940 the Court heard a case from Chicago and held the covenant unenforceable because of fraud so did not reach the constitutional issue. In 1945 the NAACP gained encouragement despite another denial of certiorari. Since only four votes are needed for certiorari to be issued the dissents of Justices Rutledge and Murphy in 1945 told the Association that its chances were improving.

[At a conference of primarily Negro attorneys convened in Washington, D. C.:]

It was pointed out that only Justices Murphy and Rutledge seemed to be anxious to have the court pass unequivocally upon restrictive covenants, and that the balance of the Court does not want to touch restrictive covenant cases at this time. Justice Burton is definitely opposed to our position and Justice Jackson is as yet uncommitted. Therefore, it is necessary that we provide JJ Murphy and Rutledge with leverage with which to bring two more Justices to their side in order to grant us certiorari. One attorney felt that it was important that we not build up a record of many applications for certiorari denied.

By 1945 potential test cases had begun in the trial courts of Los Angeles, Chicago, St. Louis, Columbus, Detroit, New York and Washington, D.C. The controversies grew out of Negro-white rivalry for homes with suits for injunction originating from the white side. Negroes in jeopardy turned naturally to the leading NAACP attorneys in their own city. As the cases progressed these lawyers shared notes at four conferences on racial covenants called by the national leaders of the Association. Careful work was done to establish a sound trial record in order to have the best possible vehicle available for the constitutional test because there was no way of knowing which cases would be accepted for review by the Court. In 1947 new writs of certiorari were applied for and granted in cases from St. Louis, Detroit and Washington, D.C.

Planning test cases is a necessity for any pressure group desiring a hearing before the Supreme Court for it is their primary means of access. The test case represents others which never advance to appellate courts. Quite clearly, the pressure group with continuity, central control and a far-flung network of alert attorneys is well-equipped to produce the necessary number of cases from which the Supreme Court may select a test.

. . . In addition [to] presenting a "case or controversy" to the Supreme Court—the one essential that any person or group must do to test a constitutional rule—other things will be attempted by a resourceful organization like the NAACP. Thus the campaign against racial covenants included an effort to influence legal opinion by publicizing a favorable innovation in constitutional theory. Scholars like Professor Robert Hale of Columbia had long stood for a broad view of state action when, in 1945, in the *California Law Review,* Professor D. O. McGovney offered a carefully prepared argument that the concept of state action should encompass the enforcement of racial restrictive covenants by state courts. This filled a serious gap in Negro legal theory. McGovney's argument was taken up in other law review articles and soon found its way into NAACP briefs.

The accumulated losses of thirty years standing as precedents against the NAACP led to reliance on sociological argument. In order to quote authority leaders of the Association arranged for publication of social and economic criticism of racial restrictive covenants. A coordinated effort was made to place articles in the law reviews. Spontaneity doubtless played its part to produce an impressive list of publications supporting the Negro position with only a single article in opposition.

Briefs filed with the Supreme Court relied heavily on the law review articles and thereby brought these constitutional and sociological points to the attention of the justices. In this way the NAACP sought again to bring a change in constitutional doctrine. If the bar and the law schools are regarded as part of the justices' professional constituency then it may not be the election returns but the law reviews that the Supreme Court follows.

. . . In the Shelley case nineteen briefs were filed by friends of the NAACP while five amici curiae briefs were entered by opposing groups. Since the parties permitted all interested groups to present briefs, a record number in a single Supreme Court case was established.

The NAACP had an impossible task of controlling the substance of these briefs as each organization had its own ideas of the best content. Some groups repeated the points of the main briefs without a line of novelty while others wrote briefs to distribute to its membership for propaganda purposes. Of course, each group opposed racial discrimination for its own private reasons. Jews, Indians and Japanese-Americans feared discrimination against themselves. Congregationalists and Unitarians preached the brotherhood of man while briefs of the A. F. of L. and C.I.O. protested that housing discrimination against Negroes nullified their economic gains as trade unionists. Civil liberties groups like the A.C.L.U. contended that restrictive covenants prevent the achievement of constitutional rights. The American Association for the United Nations pointed to the injury of United States prestige abroad. At times the NAACP feared that its friends would bore the Court with duplication of these and other arguments but no serious effort was made to eliminate briefs or fashion their content.

The reading of these briefs, and those filed in opposition by various neighborhood protection associations and the National Association of Real Estate Boards, shows the successful adjustment of numerous pressure groups to the judicial process. These amici curiae briefs provide a fascinating display of the accommodation of constitutional values to self-interest.

An amicus curiae brief by the Department of Justice in the *Shelley* case was another expression of interest group effort to influence the Court. Solicitor General Perlman has explained that he and the Attorney General, Tom Clark, were urged by organized groups to enter the case as a friend of the Negroes. The Department's action thus reflected pressures and added an official group to the Negro alliance. Since the United States appears as a party in controversy in [a majority] of the Court's cases, entering a case as a friend supplie[s] matchless prestige and expertness in preparing cases to the groups it favors.

"JUDGE AND COMPANY" AND THE SUPREME COURT

"The law is not made by judge alone," said Jeremy Bentham, "but by judge and company." [20] "Judge and company" include, from the point of view of the United States Supreme Court, at least three distinct categories of participants in the judicial decision-making process: (1) the judges of lower courts, and the counsel who represent the formal parties to a case; (2) the justices themselves, together with their administrative assistants (called "law clerks") and components of the immediate administrative bureaucracy under their direct control; and (3) the organized groups who sponsor litigation, form coalitions to support the litigious activities of other groups (as parties *amicus*), and propagandize with the objective of building a favorable climate of legal opinion. The latter we already have discussed; and the justices themselves we shall consider in the next section of this chapter. At this point we are concerned with the role of lower court judges, and counsel, as actors who exercise a predominant influence in shaping and defining questions for decision by the Supreme Court.

Groups may sponsor most of the litigation, and therefore the policy issues, that reach the Supreme Court for decision. Individual persons may often be the formal or nominal parties to cases, even when organized groups are the real parties at interest. But neither organized groups nor individual persons, as such, present their arguments and claims directly to the Supreme Court. It is true that justices of the Supreme Court frequently refer, in their opinions, to "the defendant" or "the petitioner" or "the appellant" as having done or failed to do thus-and-so, or as having asked the Court to do this-and-that, but unless the justice happens to be referring to some event that took place *before* the trial of the case, such references are almost invariably fictional. What the justice usually means is that the *attorney* for the defendant, etc., has "raised an insubstantial federal question," or asked the Court to distinguish a case decided at the previous term, or has argued that a particular state tax does (or does not) violate the due process clause, or the equal protection clause, or the commerce clause of the federal Constitution.

[20] As quoted in Paul A. Freund, *On Understanding the Supreme Court* (Boston: Little, 1951), p. 78.

The retained counsel of the parties to a case have a very substantial influence, therefore, in framing questions for decision by the Supreme Court. So, of course, do the judges of lower courts, who will have decided, in final form, almost all of the questions raised in any case, leaving only a minute proportion of the totality of decisions in a case open for reconsideration in the Supreme Court. It is customary to call the residue of questions left open in the Supreme Court the "most difficult" or the most "important" questions in the case; but this is probably not so, at least from the point of view of the parties to the case. Nor are the questions decided by the Supreme Court made the most difficult and important questions, simply because the Supreme Court has decided them. (Indeed, a law-school professor has argued, in a series of articles, that the Supreme Court consistently—and probably deliberately—avoids cases raising the most significant issues of public policy, in preference for more obscure and less controversial business.) [21]

Traditional theory has it that the lower courts spend their time applying "settled law," which represents in turn, and in substantial measure, earlier decisions of the Supreme Court which have, in due course, become understood and (of course) accepted by bench and bar. The Supreme Court addresses itself to the the novel questions which need authoritative resolution, and from time to time overhauls its outmoded precedents to keep them up to date—this is said to be proof of the "dynamic" nature of juridical or common (i.e., judge-made) law. It is at least dubious that such a simple explanation begins adequately to account for the functioning of an institution and set of behaviors as complex as those of the Supreme Court.

One alternative assumption might be that counsel, in both the trial and appellate courts, raise or sublimate issues, not in terms of what is perceived to be their abstract importance as public policy, but rather in terms of whether they are likely to help induce the most favorable response from the court. Except in what we earlier have described as test cases, both a party and his counsel are more likely to be interested in winning the decision than in winning points of law. But a large proportion of the cases we shall study in this book *were* test cases, in which the primary objective of the plaintiff was not the nominal object of the suit, but rather was to establish a particular policy norm in the form of a ruling by the Supreme Court. It is essential to emphasize this point, that the cases we shall study are *not* average, run-of-the-mill decisions of the Supreme Court. They are, to the contrary, the landmark cases, the turning points in the shaping of constitutional policy. It is inevitable, therefore, that they present a somewhat distorted view of the terrain of the substance of judicial policy-making—all peaks and no valleys or even plateaus—but in particular, they suggest a warped view of judicial behavior. Such cases do not constitute the best evidence to support a

---

21 Fowler V. Harper and Alan S. Rosenthal, "What the Supreme Court Did Not Do in the 1949 Term—An Appraisal of Certiorari," *University of Pennsylvania Law Review,* Vol. 99, pp. 293-325 (December, 1950); articles by Harper and various of his students, on the next three terms, appeared successively in Vols. 100-102.

theory of why and how cases reach the Court for decision, except for a small portion of the Court's work-load, at least until we have introduced other relevant factors than the actions of parties, their counsel, and lower courts.

A second question relates to the posture in which a case comes before the Court. Other things being substantially equal, the appellant or petitioner who asks the Supreme Court to reverse the decision of a lower court is less likely to evoke a favorable response from the Court, particularly on the jurisdictional decision but on the merits as well, than the party who has won in the lower court. Among the inequalities which make this generalization subject to qualification are (1) the kind of lower court from which the case comes; (2) the kind of jurisdictional and substantive policy issues raised by the case; and (3) whether there has been conflict in decision between two or more lower courts in the case. As an example of the first point, there is evidence which suggests that, when the Court agrees with the merits of the decision below, in cases raising on appeal identical questions for decision, it will summarily affirm on the merits the decision of a federal district court but dismiss for want of jurisdiction an appeal from a state court.[22] The other two points will be exemplified in a later section of this chapter, in which we discuss "The Certiorari Game."

A third question relates to the deference, or lack of deference, shown by the justices of the Supreme Court toward particular counsel and lower-court justices. We do not speak here of the deference generally shown by the Supreme Court to state courts as distinguished from federal courts; this is an *institutional* kind of deference, which springs from quite different considerations than those which underlie the *personal* deference with which we are presently concerned. It is simply one of the facts of life that the justices, like most other human beings, have their heroes (and villains); and the attitudes of Supreme Court justices toward counsel before them and toward the judge who wrote the opinion (or dissented) in the court below, not infrequently is an important consideration in the decision-making of the Court. This is a factor which, of course, is not important in every case; indeed, it probably is not significant in *most* cases decided by the Court, simply because the justices lack adequate information to have sharply defined attitudes toward all but a few of the many lawyers and judges with whom they deal. Moreover, it seems probable that deference is more frequently important as a positive (favorable) factor than as a negative one. A related but distinguishable factor is the deference accorded by the justices to the former "great" members of the Court; the effect of this kind of hero worship we shall consider in the next chapter as an aspect of *stare decisis*.

These propositions can be readily tested by the student himself in his study of the opinions in the chapters that follow, so we shall suggest, at this point, only a few characteristic examples. There are, of course, differences among individual

22 Note, "Supreme Court Per Curiam Practice: A Critique," *Harvard Law Review*, Vol. 69, pp. 712-713 (February, 1956).

justices in this regard, but the Supreme Court has frequently—and, indeed, very consistently, and for well over a century (at least since the days of Chancellor Kent, in fact)—reiterated the high respect in which it holds certain "strong" courts, among which both the New York State Court of Appeals and the federal Court of Appeals for the Second Circuit (which sits in New York City), are outstanding examples. "Only the other day," for instance (to use a favorite expression of the justice from whom we quote), Frankfurter remarked: [23]

> This court has often emphasized that in the exercise of our authority over state court decisions the Due Process Clause must not be construed in an abstract and doctrinaire way by disregarding local conditions. In considering the degree of respect to be given findings by the highest court of a State in cases involving the Due Process Clause, the course of decisions by that court should be taken into account. Particularly within the area of due process colloquially called "civil liberties," it is important whether such a course of decisions reflects a cavalier attitude toward civil liberties or real regard for them. Only unfamiliarity with its decisions and the outlook of its judges could generate a notion that the Court of Appeals of New York is inhospitable to claims of civil liberties or is wanting in respect for this Court's decisions in support of them. It is pertinent, therefore, to note that all members of the New York Court accepted the finding that [the defendant] was stopped [from making a public speech] not because the listeners or police officers disagreed with his views but because these officers were honestly concerned with preventing a breach of the peace. This unanimity is all the more persuasive since three members of the Court had dissented, only three months earlier, in favor of [another defendant in a different case], a man whose vituperative utterances must have been highly offensive to them.

Or, as Paul Freund has pointed out,[24]

> One may be permitted to wonder whether the decision in Betts v. Brady . . . would have been the same had the opinion of the Court below been written by someone less highly esteemed than Chief Judge Bond of Maryland, who is referred to by name in Mr. Justice Robert's opinion no less than fifteen times.

There are numerous instances in which various justices have shown deference to federal Circuit Judge Learned Hand, who undoubtedly enjoys higher esteem among members of the legal profession and the educated laity than most, certainly, of the members of the Supreme Court. And the expressions of such deference may serve a very functional purpose for the Court. In his opinion for the majority in the case upholding the convictions under the Smith Act of the leaders

[23] Concurring in *Niemotko* v. *Maryland*, 340 U.S. 268, 288 (1951).   [24] *Op. cit.*, p. 79.

of the Communist party, for instance, Chief Justice Vinson apparently sought to cash in on Learned Hand's reputation as a liberal judge, when he chose to *follow* Learned Hand on the most critical point of what is patently a most illiberal decision: [25]

> Chief Judge Learned Hand, writing for the majority below, interpreted the [clear and present danger] phrase as follows. . . . We adopt this statement of the rule. As articulated by Chief Judge Hand, it is as succinct and inclusive as any other we might devise at this time. It takes into consideration those factors which we deem relevant, and relates their significances. More we cannot expect from words.

As some indication of the practical impact upon Supreme Court decision-making of a lower-court judge who rates high with the Court, we might consider the record, in the Supreme Court, of Judge Henry W. Edgerton of the federal Court of Appeals for the District of Columbia. Judge Edgerton was formerly a professor of law at Cornell University, and his work has been particularly appreciated by the more liberal justices such as Rutledge and Douglas—both former law professors themselves—and Black and Murphy. Judge Edgerton's court is located, of course, only a few blocks from the Supreme Court building in Washington, so that the opportunity for personal contact between him and the Supreme Court justices also existed to a greater degree than would be true for a lower-court judge sitting elsewhere in the country. Edgerton anticipated, in his opinions, what later became the decisions of the Supreme Court (though in different cases) on a number of the most important policy issues of the last two decades, including the enforcibility of restrictive convenants, public school integration, the legality of the federal employee loyalty program, and the power of congressional investigatory committees to inquire into the political beliefs and attitudes of witnesses.[26] Of the cases in which Judge Edgerton wrote for the majority, and in which petitions for review by certiorari were filed in the Supreme Court, only 13% were granted; and having thus accepted jurisdiction in 9 out of 71 cases, the Court reversed and affirmed on the merits in about equal proportions.[27] This is about what we should expect to find, since the Court generally grants certiorari in only about 10% of the cases in which petitions are filed, and reverses and affirms certiorari cases formally in equal propositions.[28] But of the 37 decisions of the Court of Appeals of the District of Columbia, during this same period, in which Edgerton wrote dissenting opinions, the Supreme Court granted certiorari in 22 cases

[25] *Dennis* v. *United States*, 341 U.S. 494, 510 (1951). As for Hand's liberalism, see Irving Dilliard (ed.), *The Spirit of Liberty: Papers and Addresses of Learned Hand* (New York: Knopf, 1952).

[26] Peltason, *op. cit.*, p. 17.

[27] Simon Rosenzweig, "The Opinions of Judge Edgarton—A Study in the Judicial Process," *Cornell Law Quarterly*, Vol. 37, p. 164 (1952).

[28] Glendon A. Schubert, *Quantitative Analysis of Judicial Behavior* (Glencoe: The Free Press and the Michigan State University Bureau of Social and Political Research, 1959), pp. 43, 62.

(60%). Moreover, the Supreme Court agreed with Edgerton, and reversed the decision below, in 17 of these 22 cases (77%).[29] To put it somewhat differently, the Supreme Court upheld Edgerton in 94% (67 out of 71) of the cases in which he wrote for the majority in the court below; but even when Edgerton dissented, the Supreme Court upheld his views in almost half of the cases—46% (17 out of 37) in which its review was requested. (Whether we should properly count denials of certiorari as decisions *against* Edgerton in dissent, as we have, is a question to which we shall turn presently.)

There is, of course, evidence to indicate that the Supreme Court's deferential discriminations do not go unreciprocated.[30] Even a casual reading of the reports of state supreme courts, and even the daily press in many states, provides testimony of the generally negative deference accorded to incumbent justices by their counterparts in the state judiciary. Nor are such attitudes confined to state judges; the longtime Chief Judge of the federal Court of Appeals for the Fifth Circuit, Joseph C. Hutcheson, Jr., is quoted as having said that "the inferior courts, particularly the courts of appeals, have been in the Supreme Court doghouse, the administrators in the Supreme Court parlor eating bread and honey." [31]

"Of course we are aware," Paul Freund has said, "of the indebtedness of judges to the briefs and arguments of counsel in the preparation of opinions. Every schoolboy knows how large a part of Daniel Webster's arguments before the Supreme Court found their way into the opinions of Marshall." [32] Every schoolboy may be somewhat less aware, however, of the significance of the interplay between counsel and the justices at oral argument of cases, which often may have the effect of reinforcing the predispositions of the justices rather than that of persuading the Court to change either its precedents or the individual minds of its members.

John Frank has suggested that the really significant type of deference shown by the Court toward counsel is that which usually is paid to the professional expertise of the counsel for the government: [33]

---

[29] Rosenzweig, *op. cit.,* pp. 165-166.

[30] A federal district judge, writing on the subject "Augustus Noble Hand"—cousin and colleague on the Second Court of Appeals of Learned Hand—has stated: "The law clerk soon learns that cases from courts of co-ordinate authority are not equal in Judge Hand's eyes. He is interested not only in the name of the court but the name of the judges who sat and of the author of the opinion. . . . The judgment of a 'strong court' counts for more than the mere text of its opinion. . . . For Judge Hand, the strong courts include emphatically the New York Court of Appeals under Cardozo, the Supreme Court of the United States under Hughes, the Sixth Circuit Court of Appeals during most of the last half century, any court in which Judge Julian W. Mack sat and the English courts." Charles E. Wyzanski, Jr., "Augustus Noble Hand," *Harvard Law Review,* Vol. 61, p. 585 (April, 1948).

[31] Peltason, *op, cit.,* p. 16.

[32] *Op. cit.,* p. 79.

[33] John P. Frank, *Marble Palace* (New York: Knopf, 1958), pp. 94-95. For a contrary example, see Glendon A. Schubert, "The Steel Case: Presidential Responsibility and Judicial Irresponsibility," *Western Political Quarterly,* Vol. 6, p. 62 (March, 1953).

The ease of modern transportation coupled with the desire of individual lawyers to have the experience of appearing in the Supreme Court have almost totally destroyed the system of a Supreme Court bar, so that today a very small number of appearances makes a man an unusually experienced Supreme Court practitioner. The number of lawyers under the age of sixty engaged solely in private practice who have appeared before the Court a substantial number of times could be quickly counted. Today the lawyer from Little Rock takes in his own case, whereas in 1880 he would have retained A. H. Garland, who as Attorney General and private counsel argued 130 cases. Jeremiah Sullivan Black presented sixteen cases between 1861 and 1865 and won thirteen, including eight reversals of lower courts. Today a very experienced private practitioner may have argued five cases in a lifetime.

This is not true on the government side, and a very large proportion of the cases do involve the government. The office of Solicitor General is in charge of all government litigation in the Supreme Court, and the Solicitor General can either take the cases himself, parcel them out to his own small staff, or assign them to other government lawyers. This office has, from time to time, achieved considerable eminence. Among the great Solicitors General have been William Howard Taft, John W. Davis, and Thomas D. Thatcher, to name only those long gone [from the office]. As is the fate of government offices, it has also on occasion sunk to some amazing lows. Even at the lows, the office staff has usually been good. The citizen may be represented by a virtual novice in Supreme Court practice, the government by a pro who may do nothing else. As a result, the government has an immense edge in litigation.

This is true in the presentation of oral arguments, but it is even more true in the presentation of written briefs. In argument, the professional country bumpkin, than whom there is no slicker article, may quickly win the heart of the Court, which may be tired of the perpetual smoothness and finesse of the office of the Solicitor General. Once the Court begins sympathizing, it may also begin helping, and at that point alert Justices sometimes suggest by questions points that are better than those the counsel has brought with him.

In the briefs, which are the written detailed arguments of both sides submitted in advance of the oral argument, the difference can be enormous. In hundreds of cases each year the private litigant is represented by a lawyer whose brief reveals that he has no notion at all of the requisites of Supreme Court litigation or of what is and what is not persuasive to the Court to which the brief is addressed. These are the cases that never get to argument because by its preliminary order the Court disposes of them; and in such cases the government wins very frequently because of the weight of its experience.

THE SUPREME COURT'S JURISDICTION

Processes of Appellate Review

To understand the work of the Court, it is necessary to know something about the Court's jurisdiction, not so much as this is stated in the Constitution, but as it operates in practice. Article III, for instance, specifies the *original* jurisdiction of the Supreme Court, leaving to the Congress the definition of the *appellate* jurisdiction of the Court. In modern practice, considerably less than one case in a hundred decided by the Court arises in original jurisdiction, and the only original case which we shall study is *Marbury* v. *Madison,* in which the Court, technically, denied jurisdiction; so we shall study no original cases which the Court decided on the merits. All of the other cases decided by the Court are reviewed in appellate jurisdiction, under policies jointly established by the Congress and the Court itself.

Many of the older cases that we shall study (i.e., those which were decided prior to 1925) were reviewed by the Court under a process known as *writ of error.* This was a procedure which brought before the Supreme Court for consideration the entire record of the proceedings in a case in the lower courts, for the purpose of having the Supreme Court correct alleged "errors of law" committed by the lower court or courts. The writ of error was abolished in the 1920's by act of Congress; and for our purposes, it is enough to know that review by error was roughly comparable to the statutory procedure for review known as *appeal,* although not so discretionary as the latter process has, in practice, come to be. In addition to appeals, the Court today reviews decisions of lower courts by three other processes, those of review by extraordinary writ, by certification, and by certiorari.

The extraordinary writs of mandamus, prohibition, habeas corpus, and certiorari provide a possible but not very important process of appellate review. During the twelve terms of Court from 1945 to 1956, for instance, the Court granted precisely 5 out of a total of 1658 motions for such writs. The extraordinary writ of certiorari is not the same as the normal writ of certiorari under the Judges' Bill of 1925, which we shall discuss below. Certiorari as an extraordinary writ is almost never used; but certiorari under the 1925 statute is the most usual basis by far for establishing jurisdiction in the Supreme Court. The authors of the leading manual (for lawyers) on how to argue cases before the Court have explained that: [34]

Since the jurisdiction of the Court to issue an extraordinary writ is invoked as a means of correcting error in a lower court, the writs are an exercise

[34] Robert L. Stern and Eugene Gressman, *Supreme Court Practice* (Washington, D.C.: Published by Bureau of National Affairs, Inc., 1954, 2d ed.), pp. 276-277.

of the Supreme Court's appellate jurisdiction, not its original jurisdiction under Article III of the Constitution. But the application for the writ before the Supreme Court institutes a new case which has never been heard by a lower court even though its object is to correct error below. For that reason, the case in the Supreme Court is, in a sense, an original action, and was formerly covered by the same Rule that applied to original cases. . . . Indeed, until recent years, the extraordinary writ cases were placed on the Original Docket along with cases arising under the Court's original jurisdiction. Inasmuch as the constitutional and statutory bases for the issuance of the two types of cases are entirely different, the writs are now placed on the Court's Miscellaneous Docket. . . .

Certification cases, which are (like the extraordinary writ cases) even less frequent than original cases in the Supreme Court, are presented when the justices of the Court of Claims or one of the courts of appeal or district courts ask the Supreme Court to rule upon certain stipulated questions of law, the answers to which arise in a case held under advisement by the lower court and are, presumably, in substantial professional doubt. We shall encounter a few certification cases, but they fortuitously form a much higher proportion of the cases in this volume than they do in the work of the Court. Certification is neither a usual nor an important process of appellate review by the Supreme Court.

This leaves us with appeal and certiorari. Although the Supreme Court entertains occasional appeals from the federal courts of appeals, most appeals come either from (1) special three-judge federal district courts; or (2) the highest courts of states, or, to be more precise, the court of last resort in any particular case according to the state's system of appellate review for its own courts, since the state court of last resort in a given case is not necessarily the state supreme court. Generally speaking, cases from three-judge federal district courts can be appealed only when the lower court grants or denies an injunction in a civil action involving review of the orders of the Interstate Commerce Commission, or in suits to restrain the enforcement of a state or federal statute on grounds of unconstitutionality.[35] Cases can be appealed from state courts of last resort only when (1) the validity of a federal treaty or statute has been drawn in question and the state court has held it *invalid;* or (2) the validity of a state statute has been drawn in question and the state court has held it *valid.*

A three-judge district court is as large, of course, as the usual three-judge panel which hears and decides cases in the name of a federal court of appeals; indeed, a three-judge federal district court must include at least one circuit judge,

---

[35] There are other rarely used provisions for statutory appeal when an ordinary one-judge federal district court has held a federal statute unconstitutional, or has entered one of certain types of judgments adverse to the United States in criminal cases, or in a suit brought by the United States before any federal district court to enforce certain federal regulatory legislation; or when a federal court of appeals has held either a state or a federal statute unconstitutional.

and the three-judge panels of the courts of appeals not infrequently include a federal district judge who sits by special assignment. Hence, appeal from the three-judge district courts is directly to the Supreme Court rather than to a federal court of appeals; and in effect, the three-judge district courts are on the same level as the courts of appeals, from the point of view of the Supreme Court's appellate jurisdiction. The policy assumption underlying the convening of such special *ad hoc* tribunals, and the expedition of appeals from their decisions to the Supreme Court, is that the United States has a particular interest in any case that a three-judge district court is required to hear, as these are questions of policy in which there is a major public interest.

The assumption underlying the congressional policy governing appeals from state courts appears to involve an attribution of bias to the judges of state courts: that they are likely to uphold statutes enacted by their own legislature and to strike down acts of Congress, when confronted, in either case, with claims that the legislation violates the Constitution of the United States. The implication of the provision of appeal to the Supreme Court in such cases may be that the Court can be expected to bring a counteracting and opposite bias to the resolution of such questions.

Of the cases that the Supreme Court is asked to decide, 90 percent arise on petitions for review by the writ of certiorari. Of these certiorari cases that the Court is asked to review, the Court accepts jurisdiction in only about 10 percent. Nevertheless, the overwhelming majority of appellate cases that the Court reviews from lower federal courts are certiorari cases, and all but a handful of these come from the federal courts of appeals, the remainder coming from specialized federal courts like the Court of Claims. Well over a majority of the state cases reviewed by the Supreme Court are also certiorari rather than appeals cases.

Congress, in enacting the (Supreme Court) Judges' Bill of 1925, deliberately delegated to the Court the discretionary power to select those cases which, in the judgment of the justices, were of such fundamental importance from a public-policy point of view that they ought to command the time and attention of the Supreme Court. No longer was the Supreme Court to expend any substantial portion of its time and energies correcting errors of lower courts which affected, primarily, only the rights of the parties to the cases. In the words of the leading authority on this subject, Professor Frankfurter: [36]

At the heart of the proposal was the conservation of the Supreme Court as the arbiter of legal issues of national significance. But this object could hardly be attained so long as there persisted the obstinate conception that the Court was to be the vindicator of all federal rights. This conception the Judges' Bill completely overrode. Litigation which did not represent a wide public interest was left to state courts of last resort and to the circuit

[36] Felix Frankfurter and James M. Landis, *The Business of the Supreme Court* (New York: Macmillan, 1928), pp. 260-261.

courts of appeals, always reserving to the Supreme Court power to determine that some national interest justified invoking its jurisdiction.

Over two decades later, Chief Justice Vinson confirmed, in a speech to the American Bar Association, the opinion of Professor Frankfurter, at least in the sense that we can indeed say that this is now the orthodox theory which describes both what the Court *purports* to do, and what the Court is *supposed* to do, in its discretionary exercise of certiorari jurisdiction: [37]

> The Supreme Court is not, and never has been, primarily concerned with the correction of errors in lower court decisions. In almost all cases within the Court's appellate jurisdiction, the petitioner has already received one appellate review of his case. The debates in the Constitutional Convention make clear that the purpose of the establishment of one supreme national tribunal was, in the words of John Rutledge of South Carolina, "to secure the national rights & uniformity of Judgmts." The function of the Supreme Court is, therefore, to resolve conflicts of opinion on federal questions that have arisen among lower courts, to pass upon questions of wide import under the Constitution, laws, and treaties of the United States, and to exercise supervisory power over lower federal courts. If we took every case in which an interesting legal question is raised, or our *prima facie* impression is that the decision below is erroneous, we could not fulfill the Constitutional and statutory responsibilities placed upon the Court. To remain effective, the Supreme Court must continue to decide only those cases which present questions whose resolution will have immediate importance far beyond the particular facts and parties involved. Those of you whose petitions for certiorari are granted by the Supreme Court will know, therefore, that you are, in a sense, prosecuting or defending class actions; that you represent not only your clients, but tremendously important principles, upon which are based the plans, hopes, and aspirations of a great many people throughout the country. Lawyers might be well-advised, in preparing petitions for certiorari, to spend a little less time discussing the merits of their cases and a little more time demonstrating why it is important that the Court should hear them. By that I do not mean that the petition should paraphrase the standards set out in Rule 38 of the Supreme Court Rules, [28 U.S.C.A.], as so many petitions do now. What the Court is interested in is the actual, practical effect of the disputed decision—its consequences for other litigants and in other situations. A petition for certiorari should explain why it is vital that the question involved be decided finally by the Supreme Court.

[37] Fred M. Vinson, "Work of the Federal Courts," an address to the Assembly of the American Bar Association (St. Louis: September 9, 1944), published in *Supreme Court Reporter*, (St. Paul: West Publishing Co., 1949), Vol. 69, pp. vi-vii. Cf. Bennett Boskey, "The Mechanics of the Supreme Court's Certiorari Jurisdiction," *Columbia Law Review*, Vol. 46, pp. 255-265 (1946); and Robert L. Stern, "The Denial of Certiorari Despite a Conflict [Among the Circuits]," *Harvard Law Review*, Vol. 66, p. 469 (1953).

If it only succeeds in demonstrating that the decision below may be erroneous, it has not fulfilled its purpose.

The Judges' Bill was sponsored, drafted, and lobbied through the Congress by the then-incumbent justices of the Supreme Court, primarily under the impetus of Chief Justice Taft. After three decades of experience with the consequences of what was, and what was intended to be, a major change in the definition of the role of the Supreme Court as a decision-making agency, certain observations can be made. The bill certainly was successful in giving the Court the legal power and authority to control its own jurisdiction in all but a handful of the approximately two thousand cases which are docketed on the Court's calendars each term; indeed, the degree of discretion which the Court has come to exercise, in practice, has doubtless exceeded the most sanguine expectations of the Congress which enacted the 1925 statute, since the apparent assumption at that time was that the Court's jurisdiction over *appeals* would continue to be obligatory. In fact, however, the Court now dismisses appeals, and particularly those from state courts, in well over a majority of the cases in which appeals are filed, with the consequence that appeals jurisdiction is only somewhat less discretionary than certiorari jurisdiction. For most purposes and in most instances, the phrase "appeal dismissed for want of a substantial federal question" or "appeal dismissed for want of jurisdiction" connotes just as much, and just as little, as the more terse phrase "certiorari denied."

The bill was not successful, however, in reducing the work-load of the Court, so that the justices could (presumably) give more time and consideration to the "most important" cases. During the past three decades, the volume of the Court's total work-load has doubled, while the number of cases that the Court disposes of formally—after oral argument and with a signed opinion of the Court—is only half that which prevailed when the Judges' Bill was passed. Instead of devoting more attention to decisions on the merits of major cases, the Court increasingly spends more time disposing of jurisdictional decisions, and disposing of cases on the merits but summarily—without oral arguments or briefs on the merits, and by per curiam order or opinion.[38] During the 1957 Term, for instance, the Court decided 121 formal cases, of which 90 were split decisions; and there were 205 *per curiam* decisions, of which 53 were split decisions. It is true that the Court heard oral argument in some of these *per curiams,* and that 40 percent of these *per curiams* dealt, at least nominally, with procedural questions of jurisdiction; but the fact remains that the Court in this term decided almost as many cases on the merits summarily as formally, and in addition, made over fifteen hundred jurisdictional decisions, mostly by denial of certiorari.

[38] Note, "Supreme Court Per Curiam Practice: A Critique," *Harvard Law Review,* Vol. 69, pp. 707-725 (February, 1956); and Ernest J. Brown, "The Supreme Court, 1957 Term; Foreword: Process of Law," *Harvard Law Review,* Vol. 71, pp. 77-95 (November, 1958).

Since the focus of our attention, in the chapters that follow, will be upon formal decisions and opinions of the Court, it is important for the student to keep in mind the decision-making context from which such formal decisions and opinions emerge. The cases that we shall study certainly do not constitute a representative sample of the work of a Court which spends much, if not most, of its time deciding which cases it does not have time to decide.

Two procedural events of the last few years are symptomatic of the Court's trend toward more summary decision-making. On June 6, 1955, the Court announced that, beginning with the 1955 Term in the following October, the Court would meet in conference on Fridays. Saturday morning had been, for decades, the traditional time for conference, at which the Court discusses and votes upon cases which have been orally argued during the preceding week, and makes jurisdictional and summary decisions in other cases as well. The direct implication of shifting conference from Saturday to Friday was to reduce, by a fourth, the amount of time to be devoted by the Court to the hearing of oral argument and therefore, to the decision of formal cases. The other recent change occurred at the beginning of the 1957 Term, when the Reporter, acting under instructions of the Chief Justice, began for the first time to print all *per curiam* decisions in the front (i.e., prior to page 800 or 900) of the official volumes of the United States Reports. Prior to this time, the printing of *per curiam* opinions and orders was haphazard, according to the *ad hoc* decisions of the Chief Justice, with some going in the front of volumes among the formal cases, and others appearing in the back among the memorandum and other primarily jurisdictional and otherwise procedural decisions. Although one implication of printing all *per curiam* decisions among the formal cases was thus, obviously, to systematize what had theretofore been a most inconsistent practice, a much more important implication was that this step gave further prestige to *per curiam* decisions as a class, since thenceforth they appear in the same place and manner as the formal decisions of the Court.

Dockets and Procedural Precedence

The dockets of the Court have functional significance. There are three: the Original, Appellate, and Miscellaneous. Only the handful of cases in original jurisdiction are placed on the Original Docket; and these are not necessarily considered in the order of their docket sequence. Frequently, they are carried over for several terms, since there has been no previous trial in such cases; complex determination of detailed questions of fact usually is a prerequisite to their being heard by the Court; and the Court therefore appoints, and in each such case must await the report of, a "special master" who functions like a hearing examiner for an administrative regulatory commission, conducting a hearing, receiving and excluding evidence, and making recommendations to the Court for the disposition of the case.

All other cases that the Court decides formally must first be scheduled on the Appellate Docket. Prior to the 1956 Term, all of the appeals cases were placed upon this docket, in apparent recognition of the Court's statutory obligation to decide appeals cases on the merits. (As we pointed out earlier, in practice this is an obligation that is observed in the breach almost as frequently as in fulfillment.) Beginning in 1956, the Court established a new category of appeals *in forma pauperis,* which are placed on the Miscellaneous Docket and handled like the certiorari cases *in forma pauperis* that we shall discuss below. The other major category of cases on the Appellate Docket consists of certiorari cases. Slightly more than half of the total certiorari cases, and almost all of those that are not *in forma pauperis,* are placed on the Appellate Docket; the remainder are scheduled, at least initially, on the Miscellaneous Docket. In principle, there is an expectation that the Court will permit oral argument and dispose formally of Appellate Docket cases, unless—and the exception is a major one—the cases are dismissed on jurisdictional or other procedural grounds, as are over 75 percent of them. The occasional certification cases also are placed on the Appellate Docket; and any cases that originally have been put on the Miscellaneous Docket, including both appeals and certiorari cases *in forma pauperis* and all of the motions for extraordinary writs, must first be transferred to the Appellate Docket (with consequent assignment of new docket numbers) before the Court will order oral argument in them and proceed to a formal decision, usually on the merits.

The Miscellaneous Docket consists, therefore, of the appeals and certiorari cases *in forma pauperis* and motions for extraordinary writs. Only a handful of these cases get transferred to the Appellate Docket in any term; during the four recent terms 1953 through 1956, for instance, when the volume of Miscellaneous Docket cases ranged from 599 to 758 in a term, the proportion denied review was 100%, 99.4%, 98.7%, and 98.7%. The Miscellaneous Docket was first established in 1945, for reasons that relate primarily to certiorari petitions *in forma pauperis,* and the problems posed by the demands of a substantial segment of those persons, to whom Justice Jackson once referred as "our convict population," to be released from state prisons on the general claim that they were "railroaded" contrary to the due process of law guaranteed by the Fourteenth Amendment of the Constitution of the United States.

Special Problems of Certiorari Jurisdiction

The Jailhouse Lawyers [39]

The Court's *in forma* practice may be theoretically tied to the *in forma pauperis* statute, which gives every United States citizen a right to proceed in any federal court without payment of fees, upon his execution of a pauper's

[39] Edwin McElwain, "The Business of the Supreme Court as Conducted by Chief Justice Hughes," *Harvard Law Review,* Vol. 63, pp. 21-23 (1949). The next three footnotes are also taken from this article.

oath. But considerations of governmental accounting practice early made this statute unwieldy if not unworkable so far as Supreme Court cases were concerned. Accordingly, upon the original suggestion of Mr. Justice Brandeis, printing and other costs of cases where the parties were insolvent have long been paid out of a special fund administered by the Clerk and produced from such revenues as fees for admission to the bar, with the Court making its own rules, from case to case, as to when the fund should be drawn upon. By 1930, the *in forma* practice had developed to a point where every unprinted document addressed to the Court, whether typewritten or penciled in an illiterate scrawl, would be submitted to the Chief Justice in the first instance and would be reported upon by him at conference before any printing was done or other costs incurred. This placed a heavy burden on the Chief, but [Chief Justice Hughes's] capacity for making sense out of formless masses of paper made the task look easy.

In [Hughes's] time, the *in forma* cases fell into three general categories. There were first of all the applications filed by genuine adjudicated madmen, such for example as Clarence Brummett, who once asked the Court to assist him in a war of extermination he had vowed on the Kingdom of Turkey. Then there were penciled petitions coming from Alcatraz, Atlanta, Leavenworth [40] or some other large prison, which the Chief would dignify by the name of "applications for leave to file petitions for habeas corpus" and which the Court would ordinarily deny. The most difficult were genuine petitions for certiorari filed by a losing party himself without advice of counsel, without an adequate record and without anything approaching the standards set up for such petitions by the rules. In these cases, the Chief would often direct the Clerk to procure a proper record from the court below, and in general would perform for the petitioner the clerical work counsel normally perform.

There are two ways of approaching applications such as these. First, one might take the narrow view that the Supreme Court sits only to decide questions of large public importance presented by experienced counsel in accordance with the rules, and that lower courts and police courts can be counted upon to do justice in cases where the parties are too poor to print the record or to hire experienced counsel. Or, one can say that every man, however poor, should have access to the Supreme Court, and that the Court has a special and particular duty to guard against grave miscarriages of justice in the case of indigent persons, whom, for the most part, lower courts cannot be counted upon to protect. Hughes took a middle view. He had no wish to turn the Supreme Court into a police court. But he was more suspicious than some of his colleagues about the ability and even the desire of lower courts to protect indigent persons, particularly in cases involving civil

---

[40] It was then the rumor, and it probably was the fact, that there were prisoners in several of the big federal penitentiaries with enough legal training to be ranked by their associates as lawyers. For a carton of cigarettes, such "lawyers" would file any sort of paper for any prisoner in any court, completely without regard for the facts, the law, or any semblance of truth.

rights or racial minorities. Moreover, he thought it his firm duty to read with absolute care every paper which came before him no matter how it was written or composed. And so we find the master of complicated factual situations and masses of pieces of paper applying himself with his usual diligence to applications filed by madmen, thieves, bank robbers, and illiterate persons of every kind, and the results over a period of years have been quite astonishing.

One surprising result of the Chief's *in forma* activities (and perhaps not an altogether happy one) is to be found in the increase in the number of habeas corpus cases coming before the Court from the large state and federal prisons. In the years of the Taft Court and the first years of the Hughes Court, there were relatively few such applications, and indeed few *in forma* applications of any kind.[41] Beginning in 1937,[42] however, litigants began to win cases more and more frequently without high-priced counsel and sometimes merely by writing a letter to the Court. Such victories in the habeas corpus cases would usually be completely pyrrhic, for on remand to the courts below few prisoners would be actually released; but they nevertheless would be advertised to entire prison populations, each member of which would almost immediately seek a similar victory. And despite the absence of general jail deliveries, one case often did lead to another. By 1945, this snowballing had reached such proportions as to require the creation of a Miscellaneous Docket for *in forma* cases, and at the 1947 and 1948 terms, there were several hundred cases on this docket.

MINORITY POWER AND THE RULE OF FOUR

Most of the cases decided by the Court are disposed of under a rule of procedure which requires participation in decision by a quorum of the group (six to nine justices) and concurrence of a majority for decision. This practice affords significant opportunities for minority control, even in the disposition of formal cases. Only when there are no vacancies upon the Court and all members participate is an absolute majority of five justices required for decision; and even under these circumstances, the coalescence of shifting minorities may result in a decision to which clear majorities of the Court are opposed.[43] It happens not infrequently, however, that less than nine justices participate in decision; and a minority of the full Court often controls the disposition of such a case. Unless the Court is equally divided (in a 4-4, or a 3-3 decision), a minority of four can write an opinion of the Court (as in a 4-3 decision) laying down new substantive

[41] At October Term, 1928, there were only 19 *in forma cases* (counting miscellaneous applications as such cases), and none went to argument.

[42] This trend can be traced in very large part to the appearance of Justices Black and Frankfurter on the Court. They were more prone than the older judges to inquire into the facts of criminal cases, and they aided and abetted the Chief in every case where he thought he had smelled out a gross miscarriage of justice.

[43] See *National Mutual Insurance Co.* v. *Tidewater Transfer Co.,* 337 U.S. 582 (1949), and Chapter 5, below.

policy norms. Such norms are less obligatory under the principle of *stare decisis*, in the view of some justices, than are decisions joined in by a majority of five or more justices. But irrespective of whether this is so, minority opinions of the Court, or minority opinions "announcing the judgment of the Court" may nevertheless be of considerable political significance; not all members of the audience of the Court bother to make such fine distinctions as are suggested above.

A second example of minority power is found in the authority of a single justice to grant a writ of habeas corpus or a stay of execution. In legal theory, of course, such a power is exercised only for the purpose of maintaining the "status quo" until the Court can act; but in real life, of course, conditions never "remain the same," and such an order of an individual justice of the Supreme Court is itself an important and often catalytic event, at least from a political point of view. Chief Justice Taney's opinion in the Merryman case provides a well-known example.[44] More recent actions of this sort are exemplified by orders issued, in the early 1950's, by Justices Jackson and Douglas. Jackson granted a writ of habeas corpus to prevent the Immigration and Naturalization Service of the Department of Justice from deporting an alien who had been classified, with the then recent approval of the Supreme Court, as a security risk.[45] This occurred under quite dramatic circumstances; the alien already had been forced to board a waiting plane at Idlewild International Airport in New York, and word of Jackson's order was received by government officials there just minutes before the plane was to take off for Europe. Jackson's action was taken in order to permit the alien's attorney to perfect another application to the Supreme Court for appellate review of the decision of a lower federal court; and the Department of Justice appeared anxious, at the time, to frustrate the possibility of further Supreme Court action in the case.

Douglas issued a stay of execution in the literally world-renowned case of atomic spies Ethel and Julius Rosenberg. After having adjourned the 1952 Term earlier on the same day, the Court convened in Special Term on Monday, June 15, 1953, to hear argument on a motion for leave to file a petition for an extraordinary (called "original" by the official Reporter for the Court) writ of habeas corpus. Previous to this action in the case, the Court had denied certiorari on October 13, 1952; denied a petition for rehearing on November 17; denied certiorari again on May 25, 1953; the Chief Justice denied a stay of execution on May 26; Justice Jackson granted a stay order on June 12, with a recommendation that the Court hear oral argument on a motion relating to proposed petitions for review of other recent decisions of the Court of Appeals in the case; and on June 15, prior to the adjournment of the 1952 Term, the Court declined to hear oral argument and vacated the stay of execution granted by Justice Jackson. Meeting in Special Term, on the afternoon of June 15, the Court denied the motion for

---

[44] *Ex parte Merryman,* 17 Fed. Cas. 144 (C.Ct.Md., 1861), No. 9487.

[45] *In re Knauff,* 1 Ad.Law 2d 639 (1951).

leave to file a writ of habeas corpus. Later the same day, counsel for the Rosenbergs asked Justice Douglas to issue a stay; Douglas denied this request on the morning of Wednesday, June 17. But in the meantime, on June 16, counsel representing one Edelman, who described himself as "next friend" to the Rosenbergs, filed a separate petition with Justice Douglas, requesting both a writ of habeas corpus and a stay of execution. (All of the events of the week of June 15 transpired under the circumstance that the execution of both husband and wife had been scheduled for sometime during this week; indeed, the Court subsequently was to deny on Friday, June 19, a further and final request for stay of execution pending an application for executive clemency, with counsel alleging that execution was scheduled for 11:00 P.M. that night. Executive clemency was then denied by the President and the sentence of death was carried out.)

Later on Wednesday, June 17, Justice Douglas denied the writ of habeas corpus but granted the stay of execution requested by the *amicus* counsel. Douglas thought that the counsel for Edelman had raised a previously undecided and "substantial" question of statutory construction: that the Atomic Energy Act of 1946 had superseded the Espionage Act of 1917 and had rendered the district court without power to impose the death sentence. Douglas apparently relied primarily upon an article, published five years earlier in the *Yale Law Journal*, which argued that the judiciary eventually would have to reconcile the conflicting provisions of the two statutes. The Court met again in Special Term on Thursday, June 18, and vacated the stay ordered issued by Douglas. The Court ruled, with Justices Black and Frankfurter dissenting, that the question of statutory construction was not a "substantial" one, but that "Mr. Justice Douglas had power to issue the stay. No one has disputed this, and we think the proposition is indisputable." [46]

By far the most frequent instances of minority control on the Court occur, however, in relation to the Court's summary decision-making. As we have noted, the most numerous single category of cases docketed with the Court each term consists of certiorari petitions *in forma pauperis* on the Miscellaneous Docket. In practice, it appears that only the handful of these that are considered important by the Chief Justice (or, more likely, by his law clerks) are considered by the rest of the Court. In effect, the Court has delegated to a subcommittee of one justice its responsibilities for initial decision, which for well over 95 percent of the petitioners means *final* decision, in such cases; and the subcommittee has, in turn, subdelegated, at least in part, his responsibilities to his administrative subordinates. Similar structuring of decisional processes has, of course, frequently been observed and described in the Legislative and Executive branches of the government.

The next most numerous category is of considerably greater substantive im-

[46] *Rosenberg* v. *United States*, 346 U.S. 273, 285 (1953).

portance, in terms of the range of public-policy issues which it encompasses, than the certiorari cases on the Miscellaneous Docket. This is the system for minority control over the initial decisions regarding certiorari petitions on the Appellate Docket, a practice that usually is called "The Rule of Four." There are four sub-rules of procedure which, in effect, constitute the basic "rules of the game" for the grant or denial of Appellate Docket certiorari jurisdiction:

1. Irrespective of the number of justices (six to nine) participating in the initial decision regarding a particular certiorari petition, at least four justices must vote in favor of the scheduling of a case for oral argument and, as a normal consequence, disposition as a formal case. (All of the justices who have sat upon the Court during the past two decades appear to have accepted this rule, without question.)

2. The group of the Court which controls the grant of certiorari has the power to define which questions, among those raised by the petitioner or petitioners, the Court will accept for subsequent decision. (All of the justices appear to accept this rule.)

3. There is no rule of collective responsibility for decisions granting or denying certiorari; individual justices, or groups of justices, are free to express concurrence in or dissent from jurisdictional decisions of the Court, with or without an expression of opinion, as in the disposition of formal cases. (Justice Frankfurter frequently has reiterated his view that justices are free to express individual views only in decisions *granting* certiorari; his apparently unique position is that a justice has no right, or at least ought not to dissent from the *denial* of certiorari.)

4. After the Court has granted certiorari, all justices otherwise eligible to participate in the subsequent disposition of the case have an obligation to vote on the merits of the questions which the Court has accepted for decision by its grant of certiorari. (Only Justice Frankfurter appears to refuse to accept this rule; his stated position is that a justice who has dissented from a *grant* of certiorari has no obligation to participate in the Court's subsequent decision on the merits of the case, but to the contrary, such a justice remains free to dissent, either on the merits or from the Court's acceptance of jurisdiction, when the rest of the Court announces its decision on the merits.)

Frankfurter's rejection of the third and fourth rules appears to be unique; otherwise the Court, as constituted during the past two decades, appears to have been in agreement regarding these "rules of the game." These rules may be summarized as follows: a minority of four justices can force the Court as a whole to vote upon such questions (among those raised by the parties to the case) as have been approved for decision by the minority who control the grant of jurisdiction in certiorari cases on the Appellate Docket.[47] Of course, the grant of certiorari may be controlled by an absolute majority of the Court; and in such instances, it is even possible for a minority of four justices to be in the position of dissenting from a grant of certiorari by the minimum absolute majority consisting of the other five justices. It is also, of course, possible for four justices to vote to grant certiorari in a case, and to have the other five justices unpersuaded after oral argument, thus forcing the group granting certiorari into dissent in the decision on the merits.

Questions relating to both the practical and the theoretical implications of the Court's "Rule of Four," and of minority control of the Court's decision-making, are raised by the two selections which follow. The first selection consists of parts of the dissenting opinions in a case decided by the Court in 1957; the second selection represents an application of the theory of games to the political behavior of the justices, an application which was suggested to the author by the opinion of Justice Frankfurter in the case below.

FERGUSON v. MOORE-McCORMACK LINES

352 U.S. 521 (February 25, 1957)

Certiorari to the United States Court of Appeals for the Second Circuit.

Reversed.

5-3	
Douglas	('+'
Warren, C.J.	(+
Clark	(+
Brennan	(+
Burton	+
Reed	—
Frankfurter	'—')
Harlan	'—')
Black	NP[48]

This case was joined for decision with three cases arising under the Federal Employers' Liability Act. Technically, the Ferguson case arose under a different statute, the Jones Act which applied to injured seamen, while the other three cases involved railroad workers. The Court considered that all four cases raised the same legal question and policy issues. The discussion on the merits in the Douglas opinion, which also announced the judgment of the Court, is concerned with the sufficiency of the evidence in the record to support a jury verdict in favor of the employee, holding the employer liable for his injury. A majority of the Court decided in favor of the injured worker in the Ferguson case, and Frankfurter dissented on jurisdictional grounds and Harlan dissented on the merits.

[47] Mr. Justice Brennan recently has revealed that "the Rule of Four" applies also in the Court's consideration of appeals cases: "The Court's practice, when considering a jurisdictional statement whereby a litigant attempts to invoke the Court's jurisdiction on appeal, is quite similar to its well-known one on applications for writs of certiorari. That is, if four Justices or more are of opinion that the questions presented by the appeal should be briefed and argued orally, an order noting probable jurisdiction or

postponing further consideration of the jurisdictional questions to a hearing on the merits is entered. Even though this action is taken on the votes of only a minority of four of the Justices, the Court then approaches plenary consideration of the case anew as a Court. . . ." *Ohio ex rel. Eaton v. Price,* 360 U.S. 246 (June 8, 1959).

[48] The meaning of **the symbols** in these voting tables is **explained** in the Introduction, p. 6.

Black did not participate in the decision

Both Frankfurter and Harlan discussed the meaning, and the application to the decision of these cases, of the "Rule of Four."

MR. JUSTICE FRANKFURTER, dissenting.

*"The Federal Employers Liability Act gives to railroad employees a somewhat liberalized right of recovery for injuries on the job. A great number of cases under the Act have been brought to the Supreme Court, many of them cases in which the court of appeals had set aside, on the evidence, verdicts for the employees. Despite the human appeal of these cases, Brandeis never allowed himself to regard them as the proper business of the appellate jurisdiction of the Supreme Court."—*Paul A. Freund, The Liberalism of Justice Brandeis, address at a meeting of the American Historical Association in St. Louis, December 28, 1956.

In so discharging his judicial responsibility, Mr. Justice Brandeis did not disclose an idiosyncrasy in a great judge. His attitude expressed respect for the standards formulated by the Court in carrying out the mandate of Congress regarding this Court's appellate jurisdiction in cases arising under the Federal Employers' Liability Act. For he began his work on the Court just after Congress had passed the Act of September 6, 1916, 39 Stat. 726, relieving the Court of its obligatory jurisdiction over Federal Employers' Liability Act decisions by the highest state courts and the Circuit Courts of Appeals. Mr. Justice Brandeis' general outlook on the formulation by the Supreme Court of the public law appropriate for an evolving society has more and more prevailed; his concept of the role of the Supreme Court in our judicial system, and his consequent regard for the bearing on the judicial product of what business comes to the Court and how the Court deals with it, have often been neg-

lected in the name of "doing justice" in individual cases. To him these were not technicalities, in the derogatory sense, for the conduct of judicial business. He deemed wise decisions on substantive law within the indispensable area of the Court's jurisdiction dependent on a limited volume of business and on a truly deliberative process.

One field of conspicuous disregard of these vital considerations is that large mass of cases under the Federal Employers' Liability Act in which the sole issue is the sufficiency of the evidence for submission to the jury. For many years, I reluctantly voted on the merits of these negligence cases that had been granted review. In the last ten years, and more particularly within the past few years, as the Court has been granting more and more of these petitions, I have found it increasingly difficult to acquiesce in a practice that I regard as wholly incompatible with the certiorari policy embodied in the 1916 Act, the Judiciary Act of 1925, 43 Stat. 936, and the Rules formulated by the Court to govern certiorari jurisdiction for its own regulation and for the guidance of the bar. I have therefore felt compelled to vote to dismiss petitions for certiorari in such cases as improvidently granted without passing on the merits. In these cases I indicated briefly the reasons why I believed that this Court should not be reviewing decisions in which the sole issue is the sufficiency of the evidence for submission to the jury. In view of the increasing number of these cases that have been brought here for review—this dissent is to four decisions of the Court—and in view of the encouragement thereby given to continuing resort to this Court, I deem it necessary to enlarge upon the considerations that have guided me in the conviction that writs in this class of cases are "improvidently granted."

At the outset, however, I should deal

in the Ferguson case, although he appears to have participated in the decision of the three F.E.L.A. cases that were joined with Ferguson

for disposition and to which the Frankfurter and Harlan opinions also relate.

briefly with a preliminary problem. It is sometimes said that the "integrity of the certiorari process" as expressed in the "rule of four" (that is, this Court's practice of granting certiorari on the vote of four Justices) requires all the Justices to vote on the merits of a case when four Justices have voted to grant certiorari and no new factor emerges after argument and deliberation. There are two reasons why there can be no such requirement. Last Term, for example, the Court disposed of 1,361 petitions for certiorari. With such a volume of certiorari business, not to mention the remainder of the Court's business, the initial decision to grant a petition for certiorari must necessarily be based on a limited appreciation of the issues in a case, resting as it so largely does on the partisan claims in briefs of counsel. . . . The Court does not, indeed it cannot and should not try to, give to the initial question of granting or denying a petition the kind of attention that is demanded by a decision on the merits. The assumption that we know no more after hearing and deliberating on a case than after reading the petition for certiorari and the response is inadmissible in theory and not true in fact. Even an FELA case sometimes appears in quite a different light after argument than it appeared on the original papers. Surely this must be acknowledged regarding one of today's cases. . . . The course of argument and the briefs on the merits may disclose that a case appearing on the surface to warrant a writ of certiorari does not warrant it, . . . or may reveal more clearly that the only thing in controversy is an appraisal of facts on which this Court is being asked to make a second guess, to substitute its assessment of the testimony for that of the court below.

But there is a more basic reason why the "integrity of the certiorari process" does not require me to vote on the merits of these cases. The right of a Justice to dissent from an action of the Court is historic. Of course self-restraint should guide the expression of dissent. But dissent is essential to an effective judiciary in a democratic society, and especially for a tribunal exercising the powers of this Court. Not four, not eight, Justices can require another to decide a case that he regards as not properly before the Court. The failure of a Justice to persuade his colleagues does not require him to yield to their views, if he has a deep conviction that the issue is sufficiently important. Moreover, the Court operates ultimately by majority. Even though a minority may bring a case here for oral argument, that does not mean that the majority has given up its right to vote on the ultimate disposition of the case as conscience directs. This is not a novel doctrine. As a matter of practice, members of the Court have at various times exercised this right of refusing to pass on the merits of cases that in their view should not have been granted review.

This does not make the "rule of four" a hollow rule. I would not change the practice. No Justice is likely to vote to dismiss a writ of certiorari as improvidently granted after argument has been heard, even though he has not been convinced that the case is within the rules of the Court governing the granting of certiorari. In the usual instance, a doubting Justice respects the judgment of his brethren that the case does concern issues important enough for the Court's consideration and adjudication. But a different situation is presented when a class of cases is systematically taken for review. Then a Justice who believes that such cases raise insignificant and unimportant questions—insignificant and unimportant from the point of view of the Court's duties—and that an increasing amount of the Court's time is unduly drained by adjudication of these cases cannot forego his duty to voice his dissent to the Court's action.

The "rule of four" is not a command of Congress. It is a working rule devised by the Court as a practical mode of determining that a case is deserving of review, the theory being that if four Justices find that a legal question of general importance is raised, that is ample proof that the question has such importance. This is a fair enough rule of thumb on the assumption that four Justices find such importance on an individualized screening of the cases sought to be reviewed. The reason for deference to a minority view no longer holds when a class of litigation is given a special and privileged position. . . .

This is not the supreme court of review for every case decided "unjustly" by every court in the country. The Court's practice in taking these Federal Employers' Liability Act cases discriminates against other personal injury cases, for example those in the federal courts on diversity jurisdiction. Similar questions of negligence are involved there and the opportunity for swallowing up more of the Supreme Court's energy is very great indeed. While 1,332 cases were commenced under the Federal Employers' Liability Act in the Federal District Courts in the fiscal year 1956 and 2,392 cases under the Jones Act, 11,427 personal injury cases were begun under the diversity jurisdiction in the District Courts. Annual Report of the Director of the Administrative Office of the United States Courts—1956, pp. 52–53. The Court may well have had this discrimination in mind when it granted certiorari in the diversity case of *Gibson* v. *Phillips Petroleum Co.,* 352 U.S. 874, and decided it on the merits. A few more such decisions and a flood of petitions from this source may confidently be expected. Whether or not it be true that we are a litigious people, it is a matter of experience that clients, if not lawyers, have a strong urge to exhaust all possibility of further appeal, particularly when judicially encouraged to do so. Disappointed litigants and losing lawyers like to have another go at it, and why should they not try when certiorari was granted in cases like these?

It is not enough, however, to deal with this problem on an abstract, theoretical basis. The statistical history of the Federal Employers' Liability Act . . . gives concrete evidence of the recurring nature of the problem and the time-consuming nature of the litigation. In the early years of the Act, when review by this Court was on writ of error, there was a large number of cases in which sufficiency of evidence was at issue. Contrary to general belief, however, employees fared well in this type of case. Of the 42 cases decided by the Court raising that issue, a judgment for plaintiff was reversed for evidentiary reasons in only three cases and a judgment for the defendant railroad upheld in only seven. In the other 32 cases, judgments for plaintiffs were affirmed or judgments for defendants reversed.

Once easy access to this Court was shut off by the discretionary power of review over these cases that was given to the Court in 1916, few FELA decisions were rendered, and only four, of which one was on writ of error, dealing with the sufficiency of the evidence, in the five-year period covered by the 1918 through the 1922 Terms. During the next ten years, however, the Court concerned itself more and more with the Act, but during this era the railroads tended to prevail. Thirty-five decisions were rendered from the 1923 Term through the 1932 Term. In 27 of these a judgment for a plaintiff was reversed for evidentiary reasons; in another the Court affirmed the reversal of a judgment for a plaintiff; and in another the Court reversed the reversal of a directed verdict for a railroad. (For a review of certiorari policy under the FELA during this period, see Frankfurter and Landis, Business of the Supreme Court at October Term, 1931, 46 Harv. L. Rev. 226, 240-253.)

Thereafter, during the remaining eight Terms of Mr. Chief Justice Hughes, the number of sufficiency-of-the-evidence cases under the Act that were granted review fell off considerably. Only seven decisions were rendered during that period. The next nine-year period, however, saw a large increase again, with 27 decisions during the 1941 through 1949 Terms. Unlike the previous experience with the Act, it was not efforts of railroads seeking to reverse judgments in favor of injured workers that constituted the major portion of the business during this period, but rather efforts by injured workers to upset judgments for railroads. And they were successful. Judgments for railroads were sustained in only four cases. In all the others, the Court reversed a judgment of a lower court that either had reversed a jury verdict for a plaintiff or had affirmed a judgment for a railroad.

In the following four Terms, business again slackened and only two cases concerning sufficiency of the evidence were decided under the Act. We now seem to have entered again on a period of renewed activity by the Court in this field. Two decisions were rendered in the 1954 Term, three in the 1955 Term, four thus far this Term, and two additional petitions for certiorari have already been granted this Term.

A further indication of the tendency in recent Court decisions is provided by a study of petitions for certiorari in FELA cases from the 1938 through the 1954 Terms. This study disclosed that of the 260 petitions filed, sufficiency of the evidence of negligence or of causation for submission to the jury was the predominant question in 149. Seventy-eight of these petitions were filed by the employee and all of the 37 granted petitions were from this group, except one in which the writ was later dismissed as improvidently granted. . . .

These figures tell only a small part of the story. While this opinion concerns itself principally with cases under the Federal Employers' Liability Act, the same kind of question arises under many other statutes. . . . And experience leaves no doubt, though the fact cannot be established statistically, that by granting review in these cases, the Court encourages the filing of petitions for certiorari in other types of cases raising issues that likewise have no business to be brought here. Moreover, the considerations governing discharge of the Court's function involve only in part quantitative factors. Finally, and most important, granting review in one or two cases that present a compassionate appeal on this ground and one or two that present a compassionate appeal on that ground and one or two that present a compassionate appeal on a third ground inevitably makes that drain upon the available energy of the Court that is so inimical to the fullest investigation of, the amplest deliberation on, the most effective opinion-writing and the most critical examination of draft opinions in, the cases that have unquestioned claims upon the Court.

It is impossible to read the 106 written opinions of the Supreme Court dealing with this type of issue . . . without feeling that during different periods the Court, while using the same generalities in speaking about the relation of judge and jury to the cause of action for negligence, has applied those principles differently from time to time to the facts of different cases. The divided views on this Court today with respect to the application of those principles merely reflect the divided views of state and federal judges throughout the country on problems of negligence. As long as there is a division of functions between judge and jury, there will be division of opinion concerning the correctness of trial judges' actions in individual cases. But since the law obviously does not remain "settled" in this field very long, one does not have to be a prophet to be confident that the Court, if it continues its present certiorari policy, will one day return to its attitude of the

1920's in these individual cases. With a changed membership, the Court might tomorrow readily affirm all four of the cases that it decides today. There is nothing in the Federal Employers' Liability Act to say which view is correct. The Act expressed a social policy, and it expressed that policy in terms of a familiar, but elusively inapt, common-law cause of action. It is suggested in effect that the history of FELA litigation in this Court reveals a shift in mood, philosophy if one pleases, towards the Federal Employers' Liability Act—that at one time the chief concern may be lively regard for what are conceived to be unfair inroads upon the railroads' exchequer while at another period the preoccupation may be with protection of employees and their families, so far as money damages can do so, against the inherent hazards of their indispensable labor. Be that as it may, the desire to engraft a philosophy, either philosophy, upon an outmoded, unfair system of liability should not lead the Court to bend the rules by which it is governed in other cases in the exercise of its discretionary jurisdiction.

This unvarnished account of Federal Employers' Liability Act litigation in this Court relating to sufficiency of the evidence for submission of cases to the jury is surely not an exhilarating story. For the Supreme Court of the United States to spend two hours of solemn argument, plus countless other hours reading the briefs and record and writing opinions, to determine whether there was evidence to support an allegation that it could reasonably be foreseen that an ice-cream server on a ship would use a butcher's knife to scoop out ice cream that was too hard to be scooped with a regular scoop, is surely to misconceive the discretion that was entrusted to the wisdom of the Court for the control of its calendar. The Court may or may not be "doing justice" in the four insignificant cases it decides today; it certainly is doing injustice to the significant and important

cases on the calendar and to its own role as the supreme judicial body of the country.

It is, I believe, wholly accurate to say that the Court will be enabled to discharge adequately the vital, and I feel, the increasingly vital, responsibility it bears for the general welfare only if it restricts its reviewing power to the adjudication of constitutional issues or other questions of national importance, including therein settlement of conflict among the circuits. Surely it was this conviction, born of experience, that led the Court to ask of Congress that of the great mass of litigation in the state and federal courts only those cases should be allowed to be brought here that this Court deemed fit for review. Such was the jurisdictional policy accepted by Congress when it yielded to the Court's realization of the conditions necessary for its proper functioning.

For one thing, as the current United States Reports compared with those of even a generation ago amply prove, the type of cases now calling for decision to a considerable extent require investigation of voluminous literature far beyond the law reports and other legal writings. If it is to yield its proper significance, this vast mass of materials, often confused and conflicting, must be passed through the sieve of reflection. Judicial reflection is a process that requires time and freedom from the pressure of having more work to do than can be well done. It is not a bit of quixotism to believe that, of the 63 cases scheduled for argument during the remaining months of this Term, there are a half dozen that could alone easily absorb the entire thought of the Court for the rest of the Term.

The judgments of this Court are collective judgments. Such judgments are especially dependent on ample time for private study and reflection in preparation for discussion in Conference. Without adequate study, there cannot be adequate reflection; without adequate reflection, there cannot be adequate discussion; without adequate discussion, there cannot be that full and fruitful interchange of minds that is indispensable to wise decisions and persuasive opinions by the Court. Unless the Court vigorously enforces its own criteria for granting review of cases, it will inevitably face an accumulation of arrears or will dispose of its essential business in too hurried and therefore too shallow a way.

I would dismiss all four writs of certiorari as improvidently granted.

MR. JUSTICE HARLAN dissenting . . .

I.

I am in full agreement with what my Brother FRANKFURTER has written in criticism of the Court's recurring willingness to grant certiorari in cases of this type. For the reasons he has given, I think the Court should not have heard any of these four cases. Nevertheless, the cases having been taken, I have conceived it to be my duty to consider them on their merits, because I cannot reconcile voting to dismiss the writs as "improvidently granted" with the Court's "rule of four." In my opinion due adherence to that rule requires that once certiorari has been granted a case should be disposed of on the premise that it is properly here, in the absence of considerations appearing which were not manifest or fully apprehended at the time certiorari was granted. In these instances I am unable to say that such considerations exist, even though I do think that the arguments on the merits underscored the views of those of us who originally felt that the cases should not be taken because they involved only issues of fact, and presented nothing of sufficient general importance to warrant this substantial expenditure of the Court's time.

I do not think that, in the absence of the considerations mentioned, voting to dismiss a writ after it has been granted can be justified on the basis of an inherent right of dissent. In the case of a petition for certiorari that right, it seems to me—again without the presence of in-

tervening factors—is exhausted once the petition has been granted and the cause set for argument. Otherwise the "rule of four" surely becomes a meaningless thing in more than one respect. *First,* notwithstanding the "rule of four," five objecting Justices could undo the grant by voting, after the case has been heard, to dismiss the writ as improvidently granted—a course which would hardly be fair to litigants who have expended time, effort, and money on the assumption that their cases would be heard and decided on the merits. While in the nature of things litigants must assume the risk of "improvidently granted" dismissals because of factors not fully apprehended when the petition for certiorari was under consideration, short of that it seems to me that the Court would stultify its own rule if it were permissible for a writ of certiorari to be annulled by the later vote of five objecting Justices. Indeed, if that were proper, it would be preferable to have the vote of annulment come into play the moment after the petition for certiorari has been granted, since then at least the litigants would be spared useless effort in briefing and preparing for the argument of their cases. *Second,* permitting the grant of a writ to be thus undone would undermine the whole philosophy of the "rule of four," which is that any case warranting consideration in the opinion of such a substantial minority of the Court will be taken and disposed of. It appears to me that such a practice would accomplish just the contrary of what representatives of this Court stated to Congress as to the "rule of four" at the time the Court's certiorari jurisdiction was enlarged by the Judiciary Act of 1925. In effect the "rule of four" would, by indirection, become a "rule of five." *Third,* such a practice would, in my opinion, be inconsistent with the long-standing and desirable custom of not announcing the Conference vote on petitions for certiorari. For in the absence of the intervening circumstances which may cause a Justice to vote to dismiss a writ as improvidently granted, such a disposition of the case on his part is almost bound to be taken as reflecting his original Conference vote on the petition. And if such a practice is permissible, then by the same token I do not see how those who voted in favor of the petition can reasonably be expected to refrain from announcing their Conference votes at the time the petition is acted on.

My Brother FRANKFURTER states that the course he advocates will not result in making of the "rule of four" an empty thing, suggesting that in individual cases "a doubting Justice" will normally respect "the judgment of his brethren that the case does concern issues important enough for the Court's consideration and adjudication," and that it is only "when a class of cases is systematically taken for review" that such a Justice "cannot forego his duty to voice his dissent to the Court's action." However, it seems to me that it is precisely in that type of situation where the exercise of the right of dissent may well result in nullification of the "rule of four" by the action of five Justices. For differences of views as to the desirability of the Court's taking particular "classes" of cases—the situation we have here—are prone to lead to more or less definite lines of cleavage among the Justices, which past experience has shown may well involve an alignment of four Justices who favor granting certiorari in such cases and five who do not. If in such situations it becomes the duty of one Justice among the disagreeing five not to "forego" his right

to dissent, then I do not see why it is not equally the duty of the remaining four, resulting in the "rule of four" being set at naught. I thus see no basis in the circumstance that a case is an "individual" one rather than one of a "class" for distinctions in what may be done by an individual Justice who disapproves of the Court's action in granting certiorari.

Although I feel strongly that cases of this kind do not belong in this Court, I can see no other course, consistent with the "rule of four," but to continue our Conference debates, with the hope that persuasion or the mounting calendars of the Court will eventually bring our differing brethren to another point of view.

II.

Since I can find no intervening circumstances which would justify my voting now to dismiss the writs in these cases as improvidently granted, I turn to the merits of the four cases before us. . . . So far as I can see all this Court has done is to substitute its views on the evidence for those of the Missouri Supreme Court and the two Courts of Appeals, and that is my first reason for dissenting. . . .

MR. JUSTICE BURTON concurs in Part I of this opinion.

THE CHIEF JUSTICE, MR. JUSTICE BLACK, MR. JUSTICE DOUGLAS, MR. JUSTICE CLARK, and MR. JUSTICE BRENNAN concur in Part I of this opinion except insofar as it disapproves of the grant of the writ of certiorari in these cases.

The Certiorari Game [49]

Do Supreme Court justices combine into a bloc with the deliberate objective of forcing upon the rest of the Court the consideration of an issue which the bloc wants decided in a particular way? The data for the game

[49] Glendon A. Schubert, "The Study of Judicial Decision-Making as an Aspect of Political Behavior," *American Political Science Review*, Vol. 52, pp. 1023-1025 (December, 1958). For an extensive development of the game, see Schubert, *Quantitative Analysis of Judicial Behavior* (cited in footnote 28, above), pp. 214-254. For an extended discussion of game theory, written by mathematicians for a social-science audience, see R. Duncan Luce and Howard Raiffa, *Games and Decisions* (New York: Wiley, 1957).

consist of the decisions of the Supreme Court, both jurisdictional and on the merits, in Federal Employers' Liability Act evidentiary cases since 1942. The basic assumption is that a certiorari bloc was functioning throughout this period, although the number of justices affiliating with the bloc varied at different times and an antagonist player (Frankfurter) in opposition to the certiorari bloc entered the game (as such) only during the latter stages of the play. In order to simplify the discussion, let us confine our attention to the first period of the game, comprising the 1942-1948 Terms.

At that time, the certiorari bloc consisted of Murphy, Rutledge, Black, and Douglas. If we assume that the objective of the bloc was to maximize the number of decisions favorable to workmen's claims, game theory can prescribe how the bloc should behave rationally in order to accomplish this objective. Four justices are adequate to grant certiorari, but not (normally) to decide cases on the merits. It is assumed that, during this period, the remaining five justices had no fixed predisposition either toward or against the claimants. The only question in these cases is whether the trial court correctly evaluated the evidence; the cases turn, in other words, on questions of fact rather than law. Typically, they fall into two categories: (a) the trial court directs a judgment for the defendant railroad, on the ground that the evidence is insufficient for the case to go to a jury, or else the court directs a judgment for the defendant notwithstanding a jury verdict for the plaintiff; or (b) the trial judge enters a judgment for the plaintiff on the basis of a jury verdict. In either event, the decision of the trial court has been affirmed or reversed by a court of appeals, and either the plaintiff workman or the defendant railroad has petitioned the Supreme Court for certiorari. It is assumed that, since these cases turn only on the evaluation of evidence, there is an equal chance that any of the five uncommitted justices will vote either for or against a claimant if the court of appeals has disagreed with the trial court. Therefore, since the certiorari bloc needs to pick up only one additional favorable vote on the merits, the chances of its doing so should be 31/32, for the only permutation of the five uncommitted members on which the bloc could lose would be for all five of the other justices to vote against the claimant. The certiorari bloc has a pure strategy: never to vote in favor of petitions filed by railroads, always to vote to grant certiorari in cases in which review is sought by workers *and* in which an appellate court has reversed a judgment in favor of the plaintiff, and always to vote for the petitioner on the merits. *If* the certiorari bloc follows its pure strategy, the Court should decide 97 percent of the cases in favor of the claimants. If the bloc departs from its pure strategy, it can expect to win a smaller proportion of victories on the merits, because it has played irrationally.

As a matter of fact, the payoff to the certiorari bloc during this period was 92 percent (12 pro decisions and 1 con) in cases in which the bloc adhered to its pure strategy; of the 11 cases in which the bloc departed from its pure strategy by voting to grant certiorari for petitioners who had been two-time losers in the courts below, 8 were pro and 3 were con, for a payoff of only 73 percent. In later periods of the game, the bloc adhered much more closely to its pure strategy, and consequently enjoyed greater success. During the present period, the bloc consists of five justices, so the expected payoff is 100 percent. As a matter of fact, the bloc lost one of the fourteen cases decided on the merits during the 1956 and 1957 Terms, perhaps because the bloc, a little power drunk, became careless and granted certiorari in a case so frivolous that even the bloc members joined in the unanimous decision against the claimant. An alternative explanation for this deviant decision might be that the certiorari bloc was not being irrational, but rather that it *deliberately* accepted jurisdiction with the expectation that the decision would go unanimously against the workman, for the public relations objective of countering criticism that it *always* favored workmen.

THE SIGNIFICANCE OF THE DENIAL OF CERTIORARI

During the past decade, Mr. Justice Frankfurter has repeatedly written essays in the form of memorandum opinions, to accompany the otherwise cryptic orders of the Court denying certiorari. Over and over, Frankfurter, and Frankfurter alone, has felt it necessary to remind the bar and the bench that the Supreme Court's denial of petitions for the writ of certiorari have no substantive significance; all that such denial means, according to Frankfurter, is that less than four justices voted in favor of granting the writ.

The first of these memoranda appeared in *Maryland* v. *Baltimore Radio Show,* below. In this case, the Maryland Court of Appeals had reversed, in accordance with its understanding of recent Supreme Court decisions, a trial court's contempt conviction of radio-broadcasting officials and commentators for having interfered with a murder trial by making sensational charges against the defendant while the trial was in progress. Similarly, the notorious trial later in the decade of "Dr. Sam" Sheppard of Cleveland was luridly garnished with sensational exposures, both in and out of the courtroom, and review by certiorari of Sheppard's conviction was sought on the ground that in his case, trial by press had been substituted for trial by jury. In cases raising related issues that the Supreme Court has decided formally and on the merits, Frankfurter has voted consistently in favor of the orderly administration of criminal justice, including the authority of trial judges to enforce such order, and in preference to competing claims of freedom of the press.[50] Such an attitude should have logically led Justice Frankfurter to favor the *granting* of certiorari in both the Baltimore Radio Show and the Sheppard case.

Despite his frequent protestations that it has been his invariant practice never to note his own dissent to certiorari denials, the question arises why Justice Frankfurter has been such a persistent writer of these memoranda. Various

[50] See, e.g., Frankfurter, dissenting in *Bridges* v. *California,* 314 U.S. 252 (1941) and *Craig* v. *Harney,* 331 U.S. 367 (1947); and concurring in *Pennekamp* v. *Florida,* 328 U.S. 331 (1946) and *Shepherd* v. *Florida,* 341 U.S. 50 (1951).

other justices, and particularly Black and Douglas, have not hesitated to note their own dissent from certiorari denials. Is it possible that the Frankfurter memoranda are in effect a method by means of which Frankfurter is able to tip his hand while at the same time protesting that no justice, including himself, ought formally to note his dissent from negative certiorari jurisdictional decisions? Perhaps Frankfurter's failure to dissent from the denial of certiorari in these cases should not be construed to mean that he did not, in fact, dissent from such a disposition.

MARYLAND v. BALTIMORE RADIO SHOW

338 U.S. 912 (1950)

Petition for Writ of Certiorari to the Court of Appeals of Maryland.
Denied.

Opinion of MR. JUSTICE FRANKFURTER respecting the denial of the petition for writ of certiorari.

. . . The sole significance of . . . denial of a petition for writ of certiorari need not be elucidated to those versed in the Court's procedures. It simply means that fewer than four members of the Court deemed it desirable to review a decision of the lower court as a matter "of sound judicial discretion." . . . A variety of considerations underlie denials of the writ, and as to the same petition different reasons may lead different Justices to the same result. This is especially true of petitions for review on writ of certiorari to a State court. Narrowly technical reasons may lead to denials. Review may be sought too late; the judgment of the lower court may not be final; it may not be the judgment of a State court of last resort; the decision may be supportable as a matter of State law, not subject to review by this Court, even though the State court also passed on issues of federal law. A decision may satisfy all these technical requirements and yet may commend itself for review to fewer than four members of the Court. Pertinent considerations of judicial policy here come into play. A case

may raise an important question but the record may be cloudy. It may be desirable to have different aspects of an issue further illumined by the lower courts. Wise adjudication has its own time for ripening.

Since there are these conflicting and, to the uninformed, even confusing reasons for denying petitions for certiorari, it has been suggested from time to time that the Court indicate its reasons for denial. Practical considerations preclude. In order that the Court may be enabled to discharge its indispensable duties, Congress has placed the control of the Court's business, in effect, within the Court's discretion. . . . If the Court is to do its work it would not be feasible to give reasons, however brief, for refusing to take these cases. The time that would be required is prohibitive, apart from the fact as already indicated that different reasons not infrequently move different members of the Court in concluding that a particular case at a particular time makes review undesirable. It becomes relevant here to note that failure to record a dissent from a denial of a petition for writ of certiorari in nowise implies that only the member of the Court who notes his dissent thought the petition should be granted.

Inasmuch, therefore, as all that a denial of a petition for a writ of certiorari means is that fewer than four members of the Court thought it should be granted, this Court has rigorously insisted that such a denial carries with it no implication whatever regarding the Court's views on the merits of a case which it has declined to review. The Court has said this again and again; again and again the admonition has to be repeated. . . .

The issues considered by the Court of Appeals bear on some of the basic problems of a democratic society . . . that would have to be faced were we called upon to pass on the limits that the Fourteenth Amendment places upon the power of States to safeguard the fair administration of criminal justice by jury trial from mutilation or distortion by extraneous influences. These are issues that this Court has not yet adjudicated. It is not to be supposed that by implication it means to adjudicate them by refusing to adjudicate.

SHEPPARD v. OHIO
352 U.S. 910 (1956)

Petition for Writ of Certiorari to the Supreme Court of Ohio.
Denied.

[MR. JUSTICE BURTON took no part in the consideration or decision of this application.]

MR. JUSTICE FRANKFURTER.

The truth that education demands reiteration bears on the understanding, and not only by the laity, of the meaning of the denial of a petition for certiorari. Despite the Court's frequent exposition, misconception recurrently manifests itself regarding the exercise of our discretion in not bringing a case here for review. Appropriate occasions may therefore be utilized to make explicit what ought to be assumed. This is one.

The divided Supreme Court of Ohio sustained the conviction in a capital case the trial of which was enveloped in circumstances thus summarized in the opinion of that court:

"Murder and mystery, society, sex and suspense were combined in this case in such a manner as to intrigue and captivate the public fancy to a degree perhaps unparalleled in recent annals. Throughout the preindictment investigation, the subsequent legal skirmishes and the nine-week trial, circulation-conscious editors catered to the insatiable interest of the American public in the bizarre. Special seating facilities for reporters and columnists representing local papers and all major news services were installed in the courtroom. Special rooms in the Criminal Courts Building were equipped for broadcasters and telecasters. In this atmosphere of a 'Roman holiday' for the news media, Sam Sheppard stood trial for his life." 165 Ohio St. 293, 294, 135 N. E. 2d 340, 342.

The defendant claimed that a proceeding so infused and enveloped by the "atmosphere of a 'Roman Holiday' " precluded a fair trial and could not but deprive him of the due process of law guaranteed by the Fourteenth Amendment of the Constitution. The Supreme Court of Ohio rejected this claim and the defendant then invoked the discretionary power of this Court to review the correctness of its decision. This Court in turn now refuses the defendant the opportunity to bring the case here for review.

Such denial of his petition in no wise implies that this Court approves the decision of the Supreme Court of Ohio. It means and means only that for one reason or another this case did not commend itself to at least four members of the Court as falling within those considerations which should lead this Court to exercise its discretion in reviewing a lower court's decision. For reasons that have often been explained the Court does not give the grounds for denying the petitions for certiorari in the normally more than 1,000 cases each year in which petitions are denied. It has also been explained why not even the positions of the various Justices in such cases are matters of public record. The rare cases in which an individual position is noted leave unillumined the functioning of the certiorari system, and do not reveal the position of all the members of the Court. See *Maryland* v. *Baltimore Radio Show*, 338 U.S. 912.

BROWN v. ALLEN

344 U.S. 443, 542-543 (1953)

Certiorari to the United States Court of Appeals for the Fourth Circuit.

Affirmed.

	On the Merits	Jurisdictional question [a]
	6-3	4-5
Reed	('+')	+
Vinson, C.J.	(+)	+
Minton	(+)	+
Jackson	('+'	+
Burton	('+'	—
Clark	('+'	—
Black	'—')	—
Douglas	—)	—
Frankfurter	'—')	—

[a] For the vote tabulation on this question, + signifies that the justice was of the view that the previous denial of certiorari had substantive significance in this case, while — signifies the contrary (i.e., no substantive significance).

In 1953, the Court formally decided this case, in which the question of the significance of denial of certiorari was the critical point at issue. This was a complex case, in which the justices wrote five different opinions totaling 118 pages in the United States Reports. Having previously ruled that a state prisoner who sought habeas corpus in a state court must petition the Supreme Court for certiorari to review the state court's dismissal of habeas corpus, before a federal district court could entertain a writ of habeas corpus in his behalf, the Court was now asked to decide what effect the lower federal court should attribute to the denial of certiorari to the state court by the Supreme Court. In this case, the federal district court had treated the Supreme Court's denial of

certiorari to the state court as implying that the Supreme Court agreed on the merits with the state court's decision dismissing habeas corpus; and on this basis, the federal district court also dismissed the petition for a writ of habeas corpus. The federal Court of Appeals for the Fourth Circuit affirmed; and it was obvious that the Supreme Court had granted certiorari to that court, not because of the Court's concern whether this prisoner was detained (subject to execution of sentence of death) in violation of his constitutional rights, but rather in order to clarify the question of procedural law relating to the proper scope of discretion of federal district courts, in such cases, and the meaning of the previous denial of certiorari in this particular case. As it turned out, lack of consensus among the justices foreclosed the possibility of clarifying the law in this decision.

The justices divided into four different groups, with the consequence that one coalition controlled the disposition of this case on the merits—it was ruled by a vote of 6-3 that the federal district court's action in dismissing habeas corpus should be upheld—while a different coalition, dominated by the three justices who dissented on the merits, voted 5-4 that the Court's previous certiorari denial had no "legal significance"—the federal district judge should merely have noted that it happened, thus satisfying a procedural prerequisite to his own jurisdiction in such a case. Reed, Vinson, and Minton, who were the core of the majority on the merits, thought that the certiorari denial meant something, but not much; a trial court should "give consideration to the record of the prior certiorari in this Court and such weight to our denial as the District Court feels the record justifies" and should, if it so chooses, "consider relevant our denial of certiorari." Since, however, the Reed group were a minority of the Court on this point, they fell back to the position that, assuming that the trial court had committed error by giving weight to the previous certiorari denial, it was harmless error. Jackson agreed with the Reed group on both the procedural question and the merits; but he refused to admit that the federal district court had committed error, so he wrote a separate concurring opinion. Black and Douglas dissented on the merits, and agreed with the Frankfurter dissenting opinion which argued, of course, that certiorari denials meant nothing in general; and in particular, they meant nothing in in forma pauperis *cases such as this one: "The reasons why our denial of certiorari in the ordinary run of cases can be any number of things other than a decision on the merits are only multiplied by the circumstances of this class of petitions." The two switch voters, who supplied the support necessary to create both of the conflicting majorities, were Burton and Clark, who agreed with Frankfurter that certiorari denial was meaningless, and agreed with Reed that the federal district judge had committed only harmless error in having treated as meaningful the previous certiorari denial in this case.*

Only four of the justices participating in Brown v. Allen *remained on the Court six years later; and these four had all accepted the Frankfurter view of the procedural question. Nevertheless, as perhaps the strongest statement by a justice of the opposing point of view, a portion of Justice Jackson's opinion is not without interest.*

MR. JUSTICE JACKSON, concurring . . .

Darr v. *Burford* . . . as I understand it, held that in these circumstances the prisoner must apply to this Court for certiorari before he can go to any other federal court, because only by so doing could he exhaust his state remedy. Whatever one may think of that result, it does not seem logical to support it by asserting that this Court's certiorari power is any part of a state's remedy. An authority outside of the state imposes a duty upon the state to turn the case over to it, in a proceeding which makes the state virtually a defendant. To say that our command to certify the case to us is a state remedy is to indulge in fiction, and the difficulty with fictions is that those they are most apt to mislead are those who proclaim them.

But now it is proposed to neutralize the artificiality of the process and counterbalance the fiction that our certiorari is a state remedy by holding that this step which the prisoner must take means nothing to him or the state when it fails, as in most cases it does.

The Court is not quite of one mind on the subject. Some say denial means nothing, others says it means nothing much. Realistically, the first position is untenable and the second is unintelligible. How can we say that the prisoner must present his case to us and at the same time say that what we do with it means nothing to anybody. We might conceivably take either position but not, rationally, both, for the two will not only burden our own docket and harass the state authorities but it makes a prisoner's legitimate quest for federal justice an endurance contest.

True, neither those outside of the Court, nor on many occasions those inside of it, know just what reasons led six Justices to withhold consent to a certiorari. But all know that a majority, larger than can be mustered for a good many decisions, has found reason for not reviewing the case here. Because no one knows all that a denial means, does it mean that it means nothing?

Perhaps the profession could accept denial as meaningless before the custom was introduced of noting dissents from them. Lawyers and lower judges will not readily believe that Justices of this Court are taking the trouble to signal a meaningless division of opinion about a meaningless act. It is just one of the facts of life that today every lower court does attach importance to denials and to presence or absence of dissents from denials, as judicial opinions and lawyers' arguments show.

The fatal sentence that in real life writes *finis* to many causes cannot in legal theory be a complete blank.

DECISION-MAKING ON THE MERITS

How Formal Decisions Are Made

As many commentators have pointed out, and usually with pride, the conferences of the Supreme Court are secret, and much information that would need to be accessible, at least to researchers, for a rational comprehension of the Court's decision-making processes, remains enshrouded behind what Professor Fowler Harper has called "The Purple Curtain." No one is allowed in the conference room with the justices, which means that no systematic notes can be taken of their deliberations. If it is necessary for the justices to send out for references, or for their staff to get information in to them, the junior justice attends upon the door, somewhat after the fashion of Black Rod in the House of Commons. Thus, when Oliver Wendell Holmes joined the Court in 1902, already past his sixtieth birthday, he served as messenger boy for his senior colleagues.

Unlike other major national policy-makers, the justices hold no press conferences and rarely grant interviews to reporters. To a large extent, at least in the past, it has been necessary to rely upon the official reports of the Court's decisions and opinions, and the terse and cryptic information contained in the Court's journal and dockets, for our limited understanding of the Court's workways. It is true that copies of the record of *lower-court* proceedings (when printed), upon which it is presumed that the justices rely primarily for their own information about a particular case, are available in a limited number of depository libraries; and copies of briefs of counsel in cases docketed by the Court can usually be obtained by private request directed to the authors of the briefs, if one acts at or shortly after the time a case is under consideration by the Court. But there is not even a published record of oral argument before the Court.[51] This is a pity, since at most only a few dozen people who happen to be in Washington at the time a case is called for oral argument—in itself an event that is given no publicity—and who are successful in squeezing inside the main chamber of the Marble Palace can possibly have access to the occasionally fascinating interplay between counsel and the justices. Even those who are there may have difficulty in hearing what is being said, since our judicial Taj Mahal—as it is sometimes called by the irreverent—is notorious for its very bad acoustics; and, in any event, the room is apt to be filled with high school seniors and other casual tourists who descend upon the Nation's Capitol in cherry-blossom time, which happens to be the time of the year when the Court usually is making its most important decisions.

Judicial biographies and related types of historical research based upon the

[51] Portions of the oral argument in what the editors consider to be the more important cases are published, for the past couple of decades, in the Supreme Court Section of *United States Law Week* (Washington: Bureau of National Affairs); and the *New York Times* and other newspapers occasionally report parts of the oral argument in a case. See Appendix A.

private notes and papers of justices who have departed from the Court constitute the best source of published information, at the present time, concerning the major components of the decision-making process of the justices as a group. Concerning the processes by which any individual justice reaches his personal decision in a particular case, we know next to nothing, in any systematic way, although such sources as Holmes's letters and Brandeis' *unpublished* opinions provide insights, however fragmentary, of importance.[52]

A former clerk to Justice Black has described the milieu for interpersonal communication among the justices: [53]

> The Justices usually maintain houses in the Washington area, but these are scattered from Maryland to Virginia and great distances often separate them. The Justices have a certain amount of formal social exchange but no more personal intimacy than happens to appeal directly to any of them—commonly not much. Prior to the construction of the present Court building, the Justices frequently worked at their homes. Stone, for example, built himself a virtual palace of a workshop; and upon seeing the plans for the new Court building, with separate lavatory facilities in the office of each Justice, Holmes is perhaps apocryphally said to have observed that the abandonment of a common men's room meant that off the bench he would no longer see his brothers at all. The present building arrangement, in which each Justice has a suite of three rooms for himself and his clerks, secretary, and messenger, brought the Justices back together again. While doing their work they can now visit from office to office as freely as personal taste dictates, and, when they wish, can also use a common lunchroom reserved for them.
>
> The heart of the decision-making process has always been the conference. At the present time the Court hears cases for two weeks and then recesses for two weeks (except for one longer recess during the winter). During the two weeks of sittings, arguments are heard; during the two weeks of recess, opinions are prepared. At the end of each week of argument and at the end of the two-week recess, the judges gather to decide the matters that must be decided, to give final approval to opinions that have been generally agreed upon, and, in short, to transact the business of the Court. The conference is secret. No one other than the Justices is ever allowed in the room. A messenger sits outside the door, so that if some material is desired it can be sent for; and the junior Justice answers the door and receives from the messenger whatever he wishes to hand in. The Justices no longer confer in Washington boardinghouses, but meet in a grandly impressive room adjacent to the office of the Chief Justice, who presides at the head of a long table. . . .
>
> The two really meaningful functions of the Chief in relation to his

---

52 On the Holmes letters, see footnote 2, *supra;* on Brandeis' opinions, see Bickel, *op. cit.* (footnote 4, *supra*).

53 Frank, *The Marble Palace*, pp. 110-111, 75.

brethren are his chairmanship of the Court's own conference . . . and his assignment of the writing of opinions. When the judges gather in their conference room to decide the cases, the Chief, as chairman, opens the discussion by giving his own views on the questions at issue. The task of thus stating the case and indicating the questions to be decided is a genuine power, because in any discussion the first analysis of a problem will more often than not affect the analysis of everyone else. The man who selects the issues to be talked about very frequently dominates the end result.

A participant-observer of the Court's conferences has agreed that the role of the Chief is critical in the intra-group politics of the conference: [54]

> After everybody has had his say, beginning with the chief justice and following in order of seniority—and everybody can say whatever he wants to say—there is a formal vote. In order that the junior should not be influenced, everybody having already expressed his view, the formal voting begins with the junior. (How careful we are not to coerce anybody!) After conference, in cases in which the chief justice is with the majority, as he is in most instances, he designates the member of the Court who is to write the opinion. If he is in the minority, then the next senior justice of those in the majority does the assigning. So that in most of the cases the chief justice decides who is to speak for the Court. As for dissents and concurrences—that's for each member to choose for himself.
>
> You can see the important function that rests with the chief justice in determining who should be the spokesman of the Court in expressing the decision reached. The manner in which a case is stated, the grounds on which a decision is rested—one ground rather than another, or one ground rather than two grounds—how much is said and how it is said, what kind of phrasing will give least trouble in the future in a system of law in which as far as possible you are to decide the concrete issue and not embarrass the future too much —all these things matter a great deal. The deployment of his judicial force by the chief justice is his single most influential function. Some do it with ease. Some do it with great anguish. Some do it with great wisdom. Some have done it with less than great wisdom.
>
> No chief justice, I believe, equaled Chief Justice Hughes in the skill and wisdom and the disinterestedness with which he made his assignments. Some cases are more interesting than others, and it is the prerogative of the chief justice not only to be kindly and fair and generous in the distribution of cases, but also to appear to be so. The task calls for qualities of tact, understanding, and skill in the effective utilization of the particular qualities that are available. Should one man become a specialist in a subject? Or is it important not to place too much reliance on one man because he's a great

[54] Quoted from *Of Law and Men* by Felix Frankfurter, edited by Philip Elman, © 1956, by Felix Frankfurter. Pp. 136-137, 142. Reprinted by permission of Harcourt, Brace and Company, Inc.

authority in the field? Should you pick the man who will write the opinion in the narrowest possible way? Or should you take the chance of putting a few seeds in the earth for future flowering? Those are all very difficult, delicate, and responsible questions. . . . [Hughes's] governing consideration was what was best for the Court as to the particular case in the particular situation. That meant disregard of self but not of the importance of the chief justiceship as a symbol. For there are occasions when an opinion should carry the extra weight which pronouncement by the chief justice gives. . . . The grounds for assignment may not always be obvious to the outsider. Indeed, they are not always so to the members of the Court; the reasons normally remain within the breast of the chief justice. But these involve, if the duty is wisely discharged, perhaps the most delicate judgment demanded of the chief justice.

After the conference is over, and a decision has been reached,[55]

The opinions are announced orally from the bench. This is a remarkable proceeding; a busy institution interrupts pressing work in order to tell a handful of persons in the courtroom what everyone else in the country necessarily learns by reading. On opinion days, which during the regular term are commonly three Mondays in each month, from thirty minutes to four hours may sometimes be taken in making these announcements. In the extreme case this means that as much as twenty per cent of the courtroom time for a week may go into these statements, all of which would be as effective if the Justices simply handed them to the official reporter.

The Business of the Court as Conducted by Chief Justice Hughes

Perhaps the most extensive and detailed description that has been published, of the process by which the Court makes decisions, is the following somewhat eulogistic account, which was written by a former law clerk to the Chief Justice whose administrative work-ways are described.[56]

The distinctive atmosphere of the Hughes regime permeated to the regular conferences which convene Saturdays at high noon. Preparation for these conferences then began one week in advance when the Clerk would circulate all petitions for certiorari, jurisdictional statements and motions on the ready list. In the Chief's office, the arrival of this stack of papers always marked the beginning of a period of intense activity, for no matter the height of the stack (it was often four feet high) his law clerk was supposed to write a memorandum on each case by the following Thursday.

When they arrived at his desk, the Chief went after his clerk's memoranda and the records and briefs as though they were the books of one of

---

55 Frank, *op. cit.*, p. 121.
56 Edwin McElwain, "The Business of the Supreme Court as Conducted by Chief Jus- tice Hughes," *Harvard Law Review*, Vol. 63, pp. 6, 12-20 (1949). The next three footnotes are also taken from this article.

the absconding debtors he pursued in his early practice. He read rapidly but rarely consecutively through the briefs and records, inserting innumerable bookmarks and making occasional marginal checks and crosses. His emphasis, however, was on the record rather than the briefs, his instinct being to discover the facts for himself from original sources. Although at that stage the question before him was ordinarily whether certiorari should be granted or jurisdiction noted, he usually went into the merits of each case and often, it is believed, decided them then and there in his own mind.

The Chief had several purposes in going into the merits of a case on petition for certiorari or the jurisdictional statement. First, he was interested in preventing grave miscarriages of justice, and occasionally he would recommend the grant of certiorari in a case of no public importance whatever simply because the decision below was unjust, unreasonable, or plainly wrong. Second, he believed that by thorough initial consideration he could weed out a maximum of cases in which the Court's final decision could be foreseen with some certainty and in such cases he would often recommend that certiorari be granted and the judgment summarily reversed without argument. And third, he wished always to be ahead of the Court and at least abreast of counsel when the cases finally came on for argument. Indeed, his careful initial study of the merits was one of the main factors in the assurance with which he presided at arguments, the ease with which he led counsel in argument, and the facility with which he focused the Court's questions on essential points.

Having given the most thorough consideration imaginable to every case, the Chief would set out for Saturday conference with some very pronounced views on how each should be disposed of. And seated at the head of the conference table with records, briefs, and law books (all with innumerable bookmarks) piled high about him, he somehow exuded complete preparation and conveyed the impression that anyone who disagreed with him had better know *all* the facts and know them well. Under the circumstances, he was rarely challenged in the absence of a very complete preparation on the part of the challenger, and so it was that his own complete preparation raised by several notches the calibre of the entire Court's deliberations and decisions.

The regular conferences in those days ordinarily lasted from twelve noon on a Saturday until about five thirty in the afternoon, with half to three quarters of an hour for lunch. There would be on the average some thirty cases on the conference list, twenty of which would be before the Court on petitions for certiorari or jurisdictional statements, and the balance as argued cases. It was then the custom for the Chief Justice to begin the discussion of each case by stating it, after which comments would be made by the other Justices in order of seniority with a vote then taken in reverse order of seniority. The right to open discussion with a statement of the case the Chief viewed as very important, for it gave him the opportunity to fix the relative importance of the case against the perspective of the Court's entire deliberations, and to suggest (if not to determine) the amount of conference time which should be spent on each. He always had it in the back of his mind that on the average a petition for certiorari cannot be given more than 3½ minutes of conference time,[57] and he always remembered his experience as an Associate Justice on the White Court where the failure to limit discussion on certioraris and other preliminary motions often led to the neglect of the really important argued cases.

The Chief used to state the cases with great gusto and at a pace which would have shocked eminent counsel who often spent months in the preparation of one of them. In this connection, his performance at the conferences which immediately followed the summer recess was particularly noteworthy. There then would ordinarily be from two to three hundred petitions for certiorari, jurisdictional statements or motions upon the conference list, and most, if not all them, necessarily involved complicated issues simply by virtue of the fact that they had gone through one or more courts below. The task of stating even one Supreme Court case with clarity is a difficult one for most lawyers (as can any day be observed in the Court's bar), but by that time the Chief had so perfected the technique of going through briefs and records that three hundred seemed fairly easy. And so he would reel off the entire list using, but never reading, notes dictated by him for that purpose, and at a speed and with a spirit which kept the entire Court on its toes.

Immediately after a conference, the Chief would sit down with his law clerk to formulate the per curiam decisions and other orders to be handed down on the following Monday. Having voted on a case, the Court ordinarily left him a wide latitude as to the form of such decisions and orders, and the per curiams during the Chief's tenure of office are therefore almost pure Hughes. He attached great importance to the per curiams, for he believed that clear expression of the reasons for the Court's summary dismissals or affirmances would result in a reduction in the number of insubstantial cases brought before the Court. He used several more or less standard forms of per curiam with standard citations designed to cover particular categories of cases. And when a new pattern of insubstantial cases seemed to be emerging, he would write a "special" per curiam explaining the reasons for their insubstantial quality with the purpose of citing it in subsequent per curiams. First drafts of all per curiams were prepared by the Chief's law clerk on Sunday on the basis of the Chief's instructions given after the Saturday conference, and they would be submitted to him at 8:00 A.M. sharp, on Monday morning. At that time he used to check every citation and read every dictum page (at least when he did not know the citations and pages by heart) so as to be quite certain that a correct impression of the Court's decision was conveyed. Then

[57] In those days the Court used to sit from October through May, holding conferences three weeks out of four with perhaps three extra conferences at the opening of the term. That meant roughly 30 conferences a year with 5 hours to a conference. The Chief, however, always tried to devote the major part of a conference to the argued cases, and therefore considered as available for 1000-odd certioraris about 2 hours a conference for 30 conferences or 3600 conference minutes, 3.6 minutes each.

just before Court opened on Monday morning, he would proofread the entire decision list with Mr. Charles E. Cropley, the clerk, in order to make certain that not a period or a comma had been misplaced.

If a case survived its first conference and the following Monday's order list, it would soon come on for oral argument, at which, of course, the Chief would preside. This he did with an ease born of long experience and prompted by his sense of courtroom manners and the problems of counsel. It is unfortunately the fact that there is no real Supreme Court bar, and that except for the members of the Solicitor General's office and one or two senior partners of certain large firms, almost no single lawyer argues even one case a year on the average. This situation makes it inevitable that a large number of counsel will be unfamiliar with the special materials of the Court, and it is the basis for the statement, often attributed to Hughes, that many counsel lose but few win a Supreme Court case. The Chief was always conscious of the limitations of counsel, usually sizing them up a split second after the first word was uttered. Once conscious of such limitations, he would make every effort to keep counsel on the track and direct his attention to the important points at issue. From his study of the case on petition for certiorari or the jurisdictional statement, the Chief normally knew just as much if not more about the case than counsel, and it was not uncommon to hear him state the case, argue both sides of it, and then indicate his opinion in subtle fashion, all through a series of genial questions from the bench.

The Chief favored questions from the bench, believing that they tend to bring out the weak points of an argument, which are usually the important points in a case. Nothing irked him so much as the common answer that counsel would reach the point raised by the question at the appropriate point in his argument. When some other Justice received such an answer, one often would find the Chief boring in on counsel with the same question, in slightly different form, and it was not often that *he* failed to get an answer.

Although the Chief presided graciously and with good manners, he was in no way lax in the way he guided argument. Consider, for example, his timekeeping activities. The Chief was always extremely conscious of time, never arriving for an appointment or leaving a dinner either too early or too late. And in conducting the Court's open sessions, he was even more precise. Court opened at noon, not 11:59 A.M. or 12:01 P.M. When the hands of the Court clock were precisely together, the red drapes behind the bench would part, and there he would be. Down he would sit with his ancient gold watch (a present from a "quiz" class he taught at Columbia long before the turn of the century), and as counsel opened his mouth, he would be clocked. And come the end of the allotted time, he would inform counsel courteously but nonetheless firmly that it was time to sit down. It has been reported that on one occasion he called time on a leader of the New York Bar in the middle of the word "if." And once on being asked by the same gentleman how much time remained, he replied, with beard bristling, "14 seconds."

After argument, a case was always discussed and voted upon at the noon conference the following Saturday. In preparing for a discussion of argued cases, the Chief followed the practice he used in considering petitions for certiorari and jurisdictional statement: exhaustive study, many bookmarks, and notes dictated for the purpose of assisting him in stating the case to the conference. Again his preparation was so thorough as to discourage challenge without equal preparation by the challenger, and his very thoroughness resulted in his views being given great weight. He was, however, by no means insistent on those views when they were obviously in conflict with the views of the majority, and being always conscious of the time limitations upon the work of the Court, he would ordinarily merely record his minority views and vote, and then pass on to more fruitful subjects.

By custom of the Court, the Chief Justice assigns the opinions to be written amongst the Associate Justices, and that duty the Chief always regarded as one of the most important he had to perform. Immediately after each Saturday conference, he would sit down with his law clerk, pencil out the possible combinations with great care, and then come to a decision. In making assignments his first consideration naturally was to balance the work load amongst the Justices, to assign each his fair share of important cases, and generally to make the best possible disposition of the legal forces at hand. He considered the previous opinions of each Justice and quite often assigned a single line of cases to a single Justice, but that was by no means his invariable practice. He did not believe that the Court should be made up of tax experts, admiralty experts, patent experts, bankruptcy experts, or any other particular sort of expert, and so one will find each Associate Justice in his time writing on all or practically all subjects. In situations where the Court was divided, he would assign the case to the Justice nearest the center for the purpose of preventing any extreme opinions. This he did in the first AAA case, where the opinion was assigned to Mr. Justice Roberts, and the result was a very narrow decision which adopted the Hamilton-Story view of the general welfare clause though it struck down the particular tax as in substance a regulation of local affairs. Of particular interest is the way in which he would assign "liberal" opinions to "conservative" judges, and vice versa. For example, he assigned the decision against the constitutionality of the first Frazier-Lemke Farm Readjustment Act to Justice Brandeis, and the first *Scottsboro* case to Justice Sutherland (probably in the hope that he could bring over Justices Butler and McReynolds while some of the more "liberal" Justices could not). Finally there is the outstanding example of certain Southern civil rights cases. These he assigned to Mr. Justice Black with an eye to the unfortunate controversy which had enveloped Justice Black at the time of his appointment to the bench.

The writing and circulating [58] of opinions followed their assignment,

---

[58] The procedure was for each Justice to put his opinion in page proof and circulate it amongst the other Justices, who then would return the proof with a concurrence, with suggested changes, or perhaps with a wholly new opinion of their own suggested by way of substitution. When the views of every Justice on an opinion had been expressed in this fashion, the case would be called for the last time at Saturday conference, and the final majority opinion would be agreed upon.

and in this phase it was the Chief's purpose to secure as great a degree of unanimity as was possible without compromising the integrity of the majority opinion. He approached his own opinions with his usual meticulous care, turning out innumerable drafts in order to be certain of the most correct and precise language. But he had no particular pride of authorship, and if in order to secure a vote he was forced to put in some disconnected or disjointed thoughts or sentences, in they went and let the law schools concern themselves with what they meant. Similarly, when other Justices seemed fairly close together, he would try to save a dissent or a concurring opinion by suggesting the addition or subtraction of a paragraph here or a word there in one of the proposed opinions. In these endeavors he was highly successful because of the respect and admiration the other members of the Court had for his vast knowledge of the precedents and his thorough knowledge of the particular case. All were conscious of his absorption in the work of the Court and the high motives from which all suggestions came, and all accordingly paid more than merely courteous attention.

From the foregoing, it should not be inferred that the Chief made a fetish of unanimity. Nor did he go to extreme lengths in knocking heads together or in effecting meaningless compromises. While he rarely dissented himself,[59] he had a profound respect for the properly placed and timed dissent. . . .

The final step in the passage of a case through the Court is of course the delivery of the opinion. In some courts this is accomplished merely by filing the opinion with the clerk, but in the Supreme Court it has always been the practice to deliver opinions orally from the bench. This practice was continued and developed by Hughes, who saw in it an opportunity to make a public demonstration of the dignity and responsibility of the Court to the bar and to the thousands of visitors who came to the new Supreme Court Building during his regime. Before the Chief's time, it was a usual practice to read long opinions word for word, often in a low monotone, and opinion day came to be regarded by one and all as a waste of high-priced legal time. The Chief however encouraged (if he did not invent) the practice of summarizing opinions and delivering them in a forceful and easily understandable manner, and his own sonorous declamations impressed the visiting public, if not the bar, as possessing all the characteristics of *the* law. And with such declamations, there would come an end to cases which might have taken years to wind their way up through the lower courts, but which had had the going over of their lives in a few weeks' time at the hands of one of the most polished and efficient tribunals ever to sit as the highest court of this or any other land.

A generation ago, the accomplishments and the social and political costs of fascist totalitarianism were summarized in a slogan: "Mussolini made the trains

[59] He did not record a single dissenting vote at October Term, 1937. When he did, however, it was with emphasis and in cases where large issues were involved. See, e.g., Morehead v. New York *ex rel.* Tipaldo, 298 U.S. 587 (1936).

run on time." Should the judicial train run on time? in the United States Supreme Court? And, if so, at what cost? Hughes generally has been venerated as the greatest Chief Justice since Marshall; certainly, it is said, he and his predecessor Taft outshine any of the lesser administrators who preceded or followed them in office. In particular, White and Stone, who came before Taft and after Hughes, respectively, have been castigated for their inability or unwillingness to dominate their colleagues, in and out of the conference room, and for permitting too much discussion among the justices to take place. Stone's biographer, for instance, has written: [60]

> The bench Stone headed was the most frequently divided, the most openly quarrelsome in history. If success be measured by the Chief's ability to maintain the *appearance* of harmony, he certainly was a failure. There can be little doubt that his solid convictions [and, not infrequently, personal rancor toward his colleagues] handicapped him. He refused to use the high-pressure tactics of Taft and Hughes. Nor would he resort to ingenious reasoning, good fellowship, the caucus, or other familiar political devices useful in keeping the Court united; much less would he try to create that impression.

On the other hand, there has been at least one expression of dissent, from a law professor, concerning the consensus that Hughes was a great Chief and Stone was a less than mediocre one. This critic suggests that other criteria than business efficiency may be relevant to the administration of the conference: [61]

> I wonder whether the virtues of Hughes as a leader of the Court are not overstated; or whether some of the changes in the Court's behaviour [under Stone] were not changes for the better rather than for the worse. When Hughes was in the saddle the Court did, as you say, get through its Saturday conferences in four hours; and sometimes, under Stone, the conferences continued for four days. But I am not prepared to say that this was an undesirable development. I am shocked by the decisional process in the Supreme Court of the United States as it proceeded under Hughes. The judges heard arguments throughout the week on cases that had been for the most part carefully selected as the sort of cases that required the judgment of our highest Court. Few of the judges made any extensive notes about the cases they had heard; few of them made any careful study of the records or briefs of the cited authorities before they went to conference. Then in the space of four hours the Court decided not only the cases that it had heard, but also voted on the pending petitions for certiorari, jurisdictional statements, and other materials on the docket. This meant that the discussion in conference was perforce a statement of conclusions more than an exchange

[60] Alpheus Thomas Mason, *The Supreme Court from Taft to Warren* (Baton Rouge: Louisiana State University Press, 1958), pp. 154-155.

[61] John P. Frank, "Harlan Fiske Stone: An Estimate," *Stanford Law Review*, Vol. 9, p. 629n. (1957).

of mutually stimulating ideas. Some of the apparent unanimity in the Hughes Court derived, in my estimation, from the superficiality of the discussion which glossed over rather than illuminated difficulties in the path. If judging is as important a governmental task as we lawyers assert it to be, I am not at all inclined to say that extended conferences about the matters being judged should be viewed as a deficiency in a Court. . . . Hughes used to believe in the appearance of unanimity regardless of the reality. As a consequence of his policy, opinions were often published without the actual but with the apparent concurrence of the brethren. Hughes himself often switched his own vote in order to give a larger measure of apparent support to an opinion with which he did not in fact agree. I am dubious that this sort of intellectual flexibility is a sign of better judging than would be a more candid reflection of division when division exists.

Majority Opinions: The Least Common Denominator

All opinions written by Supreme Court justices are the product of a process of group compromise. This is true, to some extent, even of individual dissenting or concurring opinions, when the writing justice has failed to attract the support of even one other colleague. Although we deal with a complex social situation in which the vectors of pressure are of varying directions and magnitudes for each justice, the general thrust of the forces bearing upon most justices, most of the time, is toward consensus and conformity. Particularly does this become increasingly true as a justice's tenure on the Court increases, and he has to assume an ever-growing burden of commitments to the Court's past decisions, not just in terms of institutional loyalty and obligation, but in terms of *personal* commitment to his own previous votes and opinions as well. The normal aim of any justice assigned to write for the Court is to attract and to hold a majority of the Court; and beyond this basic precondition to the formation and retention of control over the disposition of the case and the policies for which it stands, there is usually a secondary objective to write in such a way that as large a majority as possible will be secured.

Orthodox theory holds that the opinion of the Court—joined in by at least a majority of the participating justices—is a product of group compromise. A related hypothesis that might be considered is that the extent of compromise which takes place in the writing of any opinion, majority or otherwise, is a function of several variables, of which the size of the group of justices who join in the opinion is a major one. Opinions of the Court are "more" a group product than are other opinions, not because they announce the judgment of the Court, but for two other reasons: (1) the size of groups joining in majority opinions (from four to nine) necessarily is larger than the size of groups joining in concurring or dissenting opinions (from one to four); and (2) rumors of dissension on the Court to the contrary notwithstanding, majority opinions are much more frequent than concurring or dissenting opinions—that is, there is more compromise in majority opinions than in dissenting or concurring opinions because there are more majority opinions. (When the Court divides 4-4 or 3-3, the decision of the court below is affirmed without an opinion of the Court, although concurring and dissenting opinions are sometimes written in such cases.) Independent of the size of group variable is the factor of *responsibility* as a felt obligation in opinion-writing. Presumably, those whose statements will have precedential effect, serving as norms to guide the subsequent decision-making of both lower courts and the Supreme Court itself, ought to feel a greater sense of caution in what they say than do those concurring or dissenting justices whose essential role is to function, in any given case, as public critics of the majority. Both of these factors, size of group and sense of responsibility, would tend to depersonalize majority opinions, and to make them, in the literal sense, the least common denominator of the majority group in any case.[62]

What has been said about majority opinions thus far has assumed that authorship of such an opinion is attributed to a single justice, who has been designated to write for the Court. All of these considerations apply with even greater force in the case of *per curiam* opinions, for which authorship is anonymous. Whether written by the Chief Justice or by an associate, their presumed function is to apply "settled law," and to do so more succinctly than frequently is true for signed opinions of the Court. If opinions of the Court are "more" a group product than concurring or dissenting opinions, then opinions *per curiam* are "most" so.

There is abundant evidence in the fourscore-odd published biographies of the justices to support the assumption that a great deal of give and take is involved in the forging of majority opinions, and especially in cases where the Court is, or threatens to become, divided in its vote. (In less decorous circles, this kind of interpersonal adjustment passes under more colorful terms, such as "horse-trading" or "logrolling.") The case below exemplifies the kinds of adjustments that frequently are made by the author of a majority opinion in order to satisfy, or to attempt to satisfy, the demands of his colleagues. Indeed, in this particular case, the justice writing for the Court changed not only language in his opinion; he was persuaded to reverse his own vote, the decision of the Court, and therefore the outcome of the case.[63]

Bullock v. *Florida,* 254 U.S. 513 (1921), was an undistinguished little case.

---

62 Robert H. Jackson, *The Supreme Court in the American System of Government,* (Cambridge: Harvard University Press, 1955), pp. 17-18.

63 For an example which involved the much less drastic circumstance of a change in the wording of a single sentence in an opinion, see Alan F. Westin, "Stephen J. Field and the Headnote to *O'Neil* v. *Ver-* mont: A Snapshot of the Fuller Court at Work," *Yale Law Journal,* Vol. 67, especially pp. 380-383 (1958). Curiously, the Field episode, relating to a detail of language, provoked rather acrimonious logomachy among several of the justices; while the Bullock case, involving major changes that are described in the text below, was disposed of by the Court most amicably.

Were it not for recent research of Alexander M. Bickel,[64] this case would doubtless have remained in the oblivion into which it lapsed almost immediately upon its having been decided. It involved a decree issued by a lower Florida court, authorizing the foreclosure sale of a bankrupt railroad to a purchaser who proposed to dismantle the railroad for scrap. The State of Florida obtained a writ of prohibition from the state supreme court, nullifying that part of the trial court's decree which had approved the dismantling of the railroad. The purchaser filed a petition for writ of certiorari and a writ of error in the United States Supreme Court, arguing that he had been denied due process of law under the Fourteenth Amendment by the decision of the Florida Supreme Court, since the effect of its decree was to force him to continue operation of the railroad at a loss. The United States Supreme Court reserved jurisdiction and heard argument, after which the conference voted to reverse the state supreme court, and the writing of the opinion of the Court was assigned to Holmes. Holmes wrote and circulated an opinion in which he argued that the purchaser succeeded to any right to discontinue operations that inhered in the bankrupt corporation; that such a right existed unless it had been waived under a contract, which did not appear to have been done in this case; and that the lower court's writ of prohibition should be reversed, thus reinstating the decree of the trial court which, notwithstanding its language, did not really confer a right to dismantle to the purchaser. The right to dismantle was the constitutional property right of the former operating company, which was transferred to the purchaser by the sale rather than by the trial court's decree.

At issue, of course, was the right of a public utility to discontinue its services, or to dispose of its equipment and facilities, without state permission. Brandeis raised a variety of doubts and questions in his return to Holmes's draft of the opinion of the Court; and he also wrote a dissenting opinion in which he argued that there was nothing that he could find in the federal Constitution which prevented a state from requiring a public utility to maintain its services to the public; that the policy announced by Holmes was contrary to the common law; and that the evidence in the case did not support the "prophecy" that the railroad could not be operated at a profit in the future. The making of such a prophecy was, Brandeis argued, the function of state courts, not of the United States Supreme Court. This dissent was written by Brandeis in longhand; and contrary to his usual practice, was not sent to the printer. Instead, he abandoned this initial draft in favor of a quite different approach, which was printed and, presumably, shown to Holmes. In this second draft, Brandeis dropped his attack on

[64] The discussion of *Bullock* v. *Florida* is based directly upon, and the quotations in this section are reprinted by permission of the publishers from, Alexander M. Bickel, *The Unpublished Opinions of Mr. Justice Brandeis* (Cambridge: Belknap Press of Harvard University Press, 1957; copyright, 1957, by the President and Fellows of Harvard College), chap. x, and especially pp. 235-236.

the policy issue of whether a railroad company had a federal constitutional right to cease operations without state consent. He retreated to the much narrower argument that the Supreme Court had no supervisory authority over state courts, and no power to reverse their decisions because it disagreed with the language in state-court opinions or the reasoning of state judges. The judgment of the Florida court should be *affirmed,* argued Brandeis, for the very reasons Holmes had stated in the draft of his opinion for the Court: because the trial court's decree could neither grant nor take away any constitutional rights of the purchaser. The state supreme court's writ of prohibition therefore affected only language in the trial court's decree which related to questions of local law, Brandeis concluded.

Although Brandeis could not persuade Holmes on the major policy question at issue, he did persuade Holmes that the logic of his own draft majority opinion pointed toward affirmance rather than reversal of the decree below. On Christmas Day, 1920, Holmes circulated a memorandum in which he said, in part, that

> Further reflection leads me to doubt the correctness of the opinion circulated. If it be plain, as there said, that the rights and only the rights of the mortgagor are transferred by the foreclosure and that those rights would be transferred without any language in the decree as to selling the road for one purpose or another, and equally would be transferred in the form prescribed by the [State] Supreme Court, how can it be said that any constitutional right is impaired? It is a mere fight about words. . . . [If] the higher Court says that the State should not be bound and that the decree was wrong, that is a local question of procedure, with which we have nothing to do, if I am right in thinking that the effect of the sale will be the same whichever form of words is employed.
>
> Please let me hear your views in time for action.

In the words of Professor Bickel:

> The problem now was to bring the Court around. A note from Holmes to Brandeis indicates that Holmes, at least, thought there was some chance that the case would be assigned to someone else, to be written in the sense in which Holmes had first done it. The note, which was dated January 4, 1921, accompanied a near-final draft of Holmes' changed opinion. ". . . I feel a little confused," Holmes said, "by my effort to avoid throwing the case on to someone else and don't feel satisfied—and yet hardly know what more to say or do."
>
> Holmes circulated to the rest of the Court as well as to Brandeis the draft which went with the note just quoted. Its last sentence read: "The result is that although the State Court acted on questionable or erroneous postulates there is nothing in its action that calls for a reversal of its judgment." This was a little too much for Brandeis. He inserted, "may have" after the

words, "State Court." His return read: "This is very good. Yes—but 'may have' should be inserted on p. 4. We have no right—as I see it—to express an opinion on that." Van Devanter returned: "Inclined to come in, but will wait to hear what others have to offer. A few feeble suggestions in the margin which are thought to be in keeping with your purpose." Van Devanter's suggestions may not have been momentous, but they were not feeble. This opinion was to strike neutral ground between opposite views, represented, no doubt, by himself on the one hand and Brandeis on the other; and Van Devanter, like Brandeis, had it in mind to make sure that the concluding— and decisive—sentences were truly neutral. Holmes suggested that the lower Florida court, whose decree the Florida Supreme Court had modified, had granted an authority to dismantle "more absolute than it could be in fact"— "considering the nature of the proceeding," Van Devanter inserted. Mc-Reynolds returned a bon mot: "This seems to save the substance to the mortgagee and the form to the [State] Supreme Court. I agree." Clarke agreed, but wished some of the statements in that part of the opinion which had remained unchanged might be shaved down a bit. "I fear," he said, "that, in its present form, [the opinion] may be seized upon as a justification for taking up temporarily unprofitable branch lines to the great inconvenience and loss of many communities."

On these returns, if Van Devanter and Brandeis could be held, there was a court. Holmes, custodian of the neutral ground, accepted the "may have" Brandeis asked for, and he took Van Devanter's suggestion. He ignored Clarke. The unchanged tone of the balance of the opinion presumably carried the day with the other brethren—or at least secured their silence.

The report of the case indicates that Holmes wrote for a unanimous Court.

The Critics of the Majority

The solitary dissenter or concurrer writes alone not through choice, but because his major premises (usually) or the version of the facts that he accepts (occasionally) are so different from those of his colleagues that they have failed to strike a balance among themselves that is also acceptable to the isolated justice; and he, in turn, has failed to exercise effective leadership in the instant case. As Justice Jackson has said,[65]

> The *right of dissent* is a valuable one. Wisely used on well-chosen occasions, it has been of great service to the profession and to the law. But there is nothing good, for either the Court or the dissenter, in dissenting per se. Each dissenting opinion is a confession of failure to convince the writer's

[65] *Op. cit.* (footnote 62, *supra*), p. 19. This quotation and the one below (from pp. 18-19 of the Jackson book) are reprinted by permission of the publishers, Harvard University Press; copyright, 1955, by William Eldred Jackson and G. Bowdoin Craighill, Executors.

colleagues, and the true test of a judge is his influence in leading, not in opposing, his court.

Of course, a dissent or concurrence may well be written with other objectives in view. The dissenter may be seeking to persuade groups *outside* rather than within the Court; or his opinion may force the Court or one of his colleagues to discuss matters that they would have preferred to leave unmentioned—indeed, the objective of the dissenter or concurrer may be to force the Court to take a *more* extreme rather than a less extreme position than would have been the case had he remained silent. Again, to quote Justice Jackson,

> There has been much undiscriminating eulogy of dissenting opinions. It is said they clarify the issues. Often they do the exact opposite. The technique of the dissenter often is to exaggerate the holding of the Court beyond the meaning of the majority and then to blast away at the excess. So the poor lawyer with a similar case does not know whether the majority opinion meant what it seemed to say or what the minority said it meant. Then, too, dissenters frequently force the majority to take positions more extreme than was originally intended. The classic example is the *Dred Scott Case,* in which Chief Justice Taney's extreme statements were absent in his original draft and were inserted only after Mr. Justice McLean, then a more than passive candidate for the presidency, raised the issue in dissent.

In view of the consensus that Chief Justice Hughes, like Taft before him, took unusual pains to "mass the Court" to present as much of a show of unanimity as possible and to discourage dissent, it is ironic that one of the most colorful and best-known defenses of dissenting opinions should have been written by Hughes. (Hughes' statement is quoted by Chief Justice Vinson, below.) Hughes wrote in 1928, however, two years *before* he became Chief Justice.[66] During seven terms as Chief (1931-1937), and before the new Roosevelt appointees began to take over control of the Court (as they did in the 1938 Term), Hughes dissented less often than any other of the justices: only 17 times in all, and only twice alone, according to Pritchett's count.[67] What a justice says, either in his opinions or in ex cathedra pronouncements such as Hughes', is not necessarily a reliable guide to his opinion-writing or voting behavior as a judge.

Chief Justice Vinson also dissented less frequently than any member of his court, except Clark. During the seven terms of his Chief Justiceship, however, Vinson dissented 90 times, including only one solo dissent, for an average of 13 dissents per term as compared to only 2 per term for Hughes for a similar period of time.[68] Vinson himself defended the use of dissenting opinions in a

---

[66] Charles Evans Hughes, *The Supreme Court in the United States* (New York: Columbia University Press, 1928), p. 68.

[67] C. Herman Pritchett, *The Roosevelt Court: A Study in Judicial Politics and*

Values, 1937-1947 (New York: Macmillan, 1948). See Pritchett's tables at pp. 32-36.

[68] Pritchett, *Civil Liberties and the Vinson Court* (Chicago: University of Chicago Press, 1954). See the tables at pp. 181 and 183.

speech to the American Bar Association, in what constitutes a characteristic example of orthodox thinking about dissenting judicial behavior: [69]

> I would not be understood as decrying the Supreme Court's dissenting opinions or minimizing their value. While it is true that division on the Court tends to break down what Chief Justice Stone has called "a much cherished illusion of certainty in the law and of infallibility of judges," my brother Douglas has pointed out, in a speech before the Section of Judicial Administration of the American Bar Association, that certainty and unanimity in the law are possible only under a fascist or communist system, where, indeed, they are indispensable. Democracy, in other words, must contemplate some division of opinion among judges as among lawyers and other human beings, for unvarying unanimity can result only from some power that directs the judges to decide cases one way rather than another.

> The dissenting opinion itself is of value in many different respects. For example, an opinion circulated to the Court as a dissent sometimes has so much in logic, reason, and authority to support it that it becomes the opinion of the Court. I must confess that the writer of the original Court opinion usually fails to see the error of his ways and turns his opinion into a dissent, so that the sum total of opinions is not reduced. But my point remains: A dissenting opinion may have immediate effect in the decision of cases.

> In the second place, the dissent gives assurance to counsel and to the public that the decision was reached only after much discussion, thought, and research—that it received full and complete consideration before being handed down.

> In the third place, a dissent may have far-reaching influence in bringing to public attention the ramifications of the Court's opinion and by sounding a warning note against further extension of legal doctrine, or the dissenter's conviction that existing doctrine has been unduly limited.

> And, finally, to quote Chief Justice Hughes, "A dissent in a court of last resort is an appeal to the brooding spirit of the law, to the intelligence of a future day, when a later decision may possibly correct the error into which the dissenting judge believes the court to have been betrayed."

> I do not mean by what I have said that unanimity is not desirable or that the Court does not seek long and earnestly to find it in every case. I believe, however, as Chief Justice Hughes also pointed out, that it is more important that the independence of the judges should be "maintained and recognized than that unanimity should be secured through its sacrifice."

The Vinson statement expresses the most obvious *justification* of dissenting opinions. It neglects completely, however, to focus attention upon the considerations of strategy and tactics that unquestionably enter into the real choices in decision-making of judicial politicians (or judicial "statesmen" to use the more common euphemism), which Supreme Court justices must of necessity be. In

[69] Vinson, *loc. cit.* (footnote 37, *supra*), pp. x-xi.

undertaking to examine the politics of dissent, perhaps it may be well to consider as an example, in addition to such nondissenting champions of the right to dissent as Hughes and Vinson, a justice who is renowned as one of the two or three "great dissenters" during the Court's entire history. Of course, Brandeis' reputation as a great dissenting judge rests more largely upon qualitative considerations than upon quantitative ones, and we shall turn to the former range of data presently; but it is not without interest to compare Brandeis' dissenting record with Hughes' during the terms in which they were colleagues on the Court.

There was a period of almost exactly nine years from the time when Hughes was seated as Chief Justice on February 24, 1930 until Brandeis' retirement on February 13, 1939; Hughes had resigned from his first term of service on the Court a few months before Brandeis was seated in 1916. During the seven terms from 1931 through 1937, while Hughes dissented 17 times, Brandeis dissented 62 times, including a single solo dissent.[70] Since the Brandeis total of 62 dissents in seven terms is substantially less than the Vinson total of 90 dissents in seven terms, it is obvious that the volume of a justice's dissent has significance only as a relational statistic, and is meaningful not in absolute terms but rather is relative to what is par for the course at the time when he is voting. Brandeis, with an average of 9 per term, was the second *most* frequent dissenter (after Stone), and Vinson, with an average of 13, was the second *least* frequent dissenter, during the respective periods covered.

There is another dimension that is important in the Hughes-Brandeis comparison, however. The difference in their respective dissenting activity was most acute during the 1931-1935 Terms, when Brandeis dissented 57 times and Hughes only 15. Table 9, on page 133, shows both the total of dissents for each justice and the number of times that any pair of justices dissented together (whether or not others joined them). Paired agreement of a justice with himself, indicated in parentheses along the diagonal, signifies solo dissents, of course. Hughes was weakly affiliated with a highly cohesive dissenting bloc of the left, of which Brandeis was a member; and the four right-wing justices formed a second but weakly cohesive dissenting bloc.

During the 1936 Term, when President Roosevelt made his Court-packing proposal, Brandeis dissented only five times and Hughes twice; we shall have more to say about this in "The Hughberts Game" later in this chapter, but it is pertinent to say now that it was in this term that the balance of dissent shifted from the left to the right wings of the Court, suggesting that effective power, in the sense of control over the decisions of the Court, had shifted in the opposite direction. With the Black appointment at the beginning of the 1937 Term, both Brandeis and Hughes were in the center of the Court, and in this term, Brandeis dissented only once and Hughes not at all. In the 1938 Term, it was Brandeis who was dead center on the Court and who voiced no dissents, while Hughes moved

[70] See footnote 67, *supra*.

further to the right and dissented five times. Brandeis retired in the middle of the 1938 Term, so the "great dissenter" ended his 22½ terms on the Court as the least dissenter during his final term, a center justice to whom all of the Court's decisions were acceptable. Hughes, to the contrary, moved further and further to the right of the Roosevelt justices during the two remaining terms before his own retirement. He dissented fourteen times in the 1939 Term, and twenty-four times—which was second high to Roberts—in the 1940 Term.[71]

TABLE 9.

Dissenting Blocs on the Hughes Court (1931-1935 Terms)[a]

1931-1935 TERMS	Stone	Cardozo	Brandeis	Hughes	Roberts	Van De- vanter	Suther- land	Butler	McRey- nolds
Total Dissents	67	55	57	15	15	17	23	36	33
Stone	(4)	51	53	12	6			1	
Cardozo	51	(3)	40	12	2	1		1	
Brandeis	53	40	(1)	10	8		1	3	
Hughes	12	12	10	(2)	1	1			
Roberts	6	2	8	1	(1)		5	7	3
Van Devanter		1		1		(1)	13	13	11
Sutherland			1		5	13	(1)	19	13
Butler	1	1	3		7	13	19	(5)	17
McReynolds					3	11	13	17	(13)

a This table is reproduced from Pritchett, *The Roosevelt Court,* p. 32, except that the designation of blocs has been added.

These data also suggest that dissenting behavior on the Court can be interpreted best in relational terms. Because of dynamic changes that were taking place within the group of justices who constituted the Court in the late 1930's, Hughes and Brandeis afford a study in contrasts. Chief Justice Hughes, the Great Administrator and seeker after unanimity, ended his career on the Court as a dissenting judge whose protests against the decisions of the Roosevelt majority exceeded even those of that confirmed and hard-bitten conservative James Clark McReynolds. And Brandeis, the alter ego of Holmes in dissent against the White and Taft Courts, ended his career as a middle-of-the-roader in perfect harmony with the dominant majority of the Court. Although, again, the difference is rela-

71 The figures on dissents in this paragraph are from *ibid.,* pp. 36-38.

tive, it might be said that the times finally had caught up with Brandeis, while passing Hughes by.

The recent study by Professor Bickel has shown that more may be learned about the politics of dissent, perhaps, by examining the circumstances under which dissents are *suppressed* than those in which they are uttered. Bickel has suggested a classic example of dissenting strategy in a case which involved, like *Bullock* v. *Florida,* an unpublished dissenting opinion of Mr. Justice Brandeis.

The Dissenter's Dilemma [72]

We know that in later years Brandeis at times suppressed his dissenting views on questions which he considered to be of no great consequence. As he said, apropos of a subsequent case that involved no jurisdictional question but dealt with a similar point on the merits, such cases were not important enough to warrant dissent. But it is equally true that Brandeis was very far from deeming the requirement that federal questions be timely brought to the attention of state courts a trivial one. From the first, and very consistently, he laid much stress on the scrupulous observance of all sorts of jurisdictional niceties. This was, for Brandeis, not a matter of *elegantia juris* but of first principles. Jurisdictional technicalities, as they might appear, in fact served ends of the greatest importance. Properly applied in a case such as this, they furthered the perfection of a balanced federal system by giving state courts a chance for voluntary compliance with federal law before they were coerced into obedience. Thus such "technicalities" tended to induce a responsible regard for federal law through the simple and courteous expedient of assuming respect for it whenever the contrary did not appear. On more than one occasion, Brandeis found the issue of the timely raising of federal questions in state courts to be decisive, and found it a worthy ground for dissent.

It may be that Brandeis' failure to register a dissent in [*St. Louis, Iron Mountain & Southern Ry.* v. *Starbird,* 243 U.S. 592 (1917)] is attributable to to the special circumstances of his first term of service on the Bench. At the time this case came down, Brandeis had not yet announced his first dissenting opinion. Doing that is, inevitably, an event in a judge's career; and in the perhaps somewhat anxious choice of the fitting occasion, he cannot help but have an eye for factors which may be irrelevant with respect to subsequent dissents. Brandeis had, in three earlier instances, joined in dissenting opinions written by others. In this case, neither Van Devanter nor anyone else presumably cared to write. And neither Van Devanter nor anyone else may have been prepared to join in a dissent by Brandeis. Brandeis may very well have felt that it would be unseemly to come forth, probably alone, with a first dissenting opinion pitched on what his senior colleagues con-

---

[72] This section is reprinted by permission from Bickel, *The Unpublished Opinions of*   *Mr. Justice Brandeis* (see footnote 64, above), pp. 28-30, 205-210.

sidered a side issue, in a case which otherwise involved only a minor statutory point. . . .

In discussing in a book published in 1937 the landmark case of *Pensacola Telegraph Co.* v. *Western Union Co.*, Felix Frankfurter, then Byrne Professor of Administrative Law at the Harvard Law School, remarked: "The scope of a Supreme Court decision is not infrequently revealed by the candor of dissent." This undoubted fact presents a Supreme Court judge with a subtle and recurring dilemma, which was present for Brandeis in the *Starbird* case. In the majority opinion in the *Pensacola* case, decided in 1877, the Court for the first time adumbrated the doctrine that a state might be without power to exclude corporations engaged in interstate commerce from doing business within its borders. But Chief Justice Waite, who wrote for the Court, "almost ostentatiously" avoided any explicit statement of the new doctrine. A dissent by Justice Field, however, addressed itself boldly to the implications of the Court's opinion. For that reason, as Professor Frankfurter pointed out, "the general emphasis which he [Field] placed upon the meaning of Waite's opinion in the *Pensacola* case is much more revealing of its dynamic significance than Waite's shrouded exposition."

Thus the dilemma. To remain silent, not drawing attention to a possibly nascent doctrine which one deems pernicious, not assisting, despite oneself, in its birth; or to speak out. Silence under such circumstances is a gamble taken in the hope of a stillbirth. The risk is that if the birth is successful, silence will handicap one's future opposition. For one is then chargeable with parenthood. Yet dissent may serve only to delineate clearly what the majority was diffident itself to say. Field in the *Pensacola* case made one choice. In years to come Brandeis was to face the dilemma more than once. Instinct, a craftsman's inarticulable feel, which must largely govern action in such a matter, dictated now one choice, now the other.

*　　*　　*

The *Southern Pacific* case concerned the Transportation Act of 1920. Congress had long since lodged comprehensive federal regulatory power over the nation's railroads in the Interstate Commerce Commission. By the 1920 Act, it had broadened that power still further. There was admittedly little room left for the states to make regulations of their own affecting interstate railroads. But, again admittedly and by specific proviso, there was some room left, so long as the I.C.C. did not assert its own jurisdiction. The issue in *Railroad Commission* v. *Southern Pacific Ry.* was how much is a little. . . .

California had ordered three interstate railroads coming into Los Angeles and maintaining separate terminals to build and use a single union station at a certain location, and while they were about it, to eliminate dangerous grade crossings within the city limits. The local interests that the order was aimed to promote are plain. The railroads maintained that they were being put to an expense of upwards of $25 million, and that only the

I.C.C., one of whose functions it was to try to keep the railroads solvent by controlling both their income and their outgo, had jurisdiction to make such an order. An opinion by McReynolds so held, and annulled the California order. The opinion consisted of a statement of facts, followed by four-and-a-half pages of straight quotation from the federal statute, followed by three paragraphs in which union terminals were characterized as "not a mere local facility," the breadth of the authority vested in the I.C.C. was emphasized, and the surmise was ventured that the I.C.C. could not perform its task "if the State Commissions may issue orders like the one here under consideration, where the subject matter is of general importance." There was a proviso in the federal statute saving some power to the states, to be sure, but it was "subordinate to the fundamental purposes of the Act and must be so construed."

McReynolds had dealt with the issue by blotting it out. He had said . . . that there was no regulatory function whatever preserved to the states. For it was the basic premise of the federal statute that interstate railroads and everything affecting them were "of general importance." The question was whether some matters, and which ones, also touched local interests so seriously that state regulation would, in the absence of supervening action by the I.C.C., be tolerable. Brandeis wrote the dissent printed below. It recited in detail the powers formerly exercised by the states, which the 1920 Act had now, by express provision, lodged exclusively in the federal Commission. The power to order the elimination of grade-crossings and the erection of terminals, previously conceded to the states, was not one of these. A specific statement by the chairman of the House Committee on Interstate and Foreign Commerce, who managed the bill, indicated that the omission was intentional. Of course, if the national interest was adversely affected, the I.C.C. could intervene, and its authority would then be paramount. But there had been no such intervention here.

SUPREME COURT OF THE UNITED STATES

Nos. 283, 284, 285.—October Term, 1923.

[283] *Railroad Commission of the State of California, Petitioner, vs. Southern Pacific Company and Southern Pacific Railroad Company.*

[284] *Railroad Commission of the State of California, Petitioner, vs. The Atchison, Topeka & Santa Fe Railway Company.*

[285] *Railroad Commission of the State of California, Petitioner, vs. Los Angeles & Salt Lake Railroad Company.*

On Writs of Certiorari to the Supreme Court of the State of California.

[January 7, 1924]

MR. JUSTICE BRANDEIS, dissenting.

Prior to Transportation Act 1920, the States could, in the exercise of the police power, require interstate railroads to eliminate dangerous grade crossings either by relocation of tracks or otherwise, *Erie Railroad Co. v. Public Utility Commissioners,* 254 U.S. 394 [1921]; and could, likewise, require them to provide adequate passenger stations. *Minneapolis & St. Louis R.R. Co. v. Minnesota,* 193 U.S.

53 [1904]. . . . That Act introduced limitations upon the States' police power. It set a limit upon requiring interstate railroads to make expenditures, by regulating the issue of securities. Section 20a. It set a limit upon requiring them to make low rates, by prohibiting any which would unduly discriminate against or burden interstate commerce. Section 15a. It prevents extensions or abandonment of lines by interstate carriers without first obtaining a certificate of convenience and necessity from the Interstate Commerce Commission. Paragraph 18 of Section 1. It conferred emergency powers over railroad property and routing. Paragraphs 15 and 16 of Section 1. But except for the control so provided, and the limitations resulting therefrom, the Act does not, in my opinion, affect the States' police power as applied either to grade crossings or to the furnishing of adequate terminals.

The Act contains no provision which deals specifically either with the elimination of grade crossings or with the establishment of terminals. Nor do I find a grant to the Interstate Commerce Commission of any power, general or special, which precludes the continued exercise of the States' police power over grade crossings and terminal facilities of interstate carriers, subject to the control above referred to. The relocation of tracks involved is obviously not an extension or abandonment of line within the meaning of Paragraph 18 of Section 1. See *Texas v. Eastern Texas R.R. Co.,* 258 U.S. 204 [1922]. The erection of the union station is not a joint use of terminals and tracks within the meaning of Paragraph 15 of Section 1. The great detail with which Transportation Act 1920 enumerates and describes every new or enlarged power conferred upon the Commission, prohibits our extending, by implication, its functions to other subjects. See *Peoria & Pekin Union Ry. Co. v. United States,* decided this day [263 U.S. 528 (1924)]. That Congress did not intend to take away the power of the States over depots was definitely stated by the Chairman of the Committee on Interstate and Foreign Commerce when explaining the bill to the House of Representatives. . . .

The new departure in policy inaugurated by Transportation Act 1920 . . . is the policy of ensuring adequacy in transportation service. It is not the policy of taking away the States' police power. That power was to be preserved unabridged in scope; but it was made subject to such control, by order of the Interstate Commerce Commission, as may be necessary to ensure adequate transportation service and otherwise to protect interstate commerce. . . .

In my opinion, Transportation Act 1920 affords no justification for judicial interference with the action of the state commission. The federal commission has made no order which can conceivably affect the matter here involved.

Nor does any fact appear, either by a finding of the lower court or otherwise, which would require the Interstate Commerce Commission to make any order, unless some carrier should seek to issue securities. It cannot be said, as a matter of law, that the erection of a union station at the cost of thirty million dollars will necessarily discriminate against or burden interstate commerce. For aught that appears, the carriers affected are prosperous, and the improvement directed by the state commission may afford the least expensive (if not the only appropriate) means of eliminating the dangerous grade crossings and of providing adequate terminals.

Speaking of the case later, Brandeis said that he had told Taft that he "couldn't stand for" McReynolds' opinion. There was too much in it that would "bother us in the future." Van Devanter, Brandeis went on to say, "worked with McReynolds and made changes, and the Chief asked me whether that will remove my sting. The corrections weren't adequate, and finally the Chief took over the opinion and put out what is now the Court's opinion and I suppressed my dissent, because, after all, it's merely a question of statutory construction and the worst things were removed by the Chief." (Even before Taft took over, Holmes had been uncertain whether it was worth dissenting in the case. He had returned to Brandeis' opinion: "I agree with this and only am not quite sure whether it is best to dissent." Holmes may have felt that dissent might unduly emphasize the case.)

Having . . . been delivered from rather than by McReynolds, the decision in *Southern Pacific* became a different matter. Taft's opinion trod carefully. Taft emphasized the expense involved, and the fact that relocation of main tracks and changes in the handling of interstate traffic would be necessary. He pointed out that building the new terminal was not necessarily tied in with elimination of the dangerous grade-crossings; a state order directed mainly at the grade-crossing problem might well be held valid. No doubt other functions were also saved to the states by the 1920 Act. In any event, the city of Los Angeles had in the meantime itself brought the dispute before the I.C.C. It would be best to let it run its course there. On these qualified grounds, Taft upset the California order.

Nevertheless, this was not one of Taft's most felicitious opinions, and events proved how much wiser it would have been to have accepted Brandeis' result and let the state order stand. As it was, it took a good many more years to straighten out the matter of the Los Angeles union terminal. In 1929, after proceedings before the I.C.C., Taft, again writing for a unanimous Court, held that the I.C.C. had no authority to compel erection of a union terminal. That had been the conclusion of the I.C.C. itself. It could only approve or disapprove such a project, the Commission had held, if the railroads themselves proposed it or the state ordered it. The state then made another order, which had I.C.C. approval, and Hughes in 1931 (McReynolds dissenting) held that the new state order as approved was unobjectionable [*Atchison, Topeka & Santa Fe Ry.* v. *Railroad Commission*, 283 U.S. 380 (1931)]. Thus, in 1931, an effort to obtain a union terminal which had been initiated in 1916 finally came to fruition. Brandeis' disposition in 1924 would have ensured the same outcome while avoiding several years' delay; although, to be sure, Taft's opinion made eventual erection of the union terminal possible at all without a new Act of Congress, which would have been necessary if McReynolds' opinion had prevailed in 1924.

Law Clerks: The Power Behind the Throne?

It is commonplace today for busy executives, in government as well as in business, to rely upon and to make extensive use of the services of administrative assistants. Whether or not they qualify as "executives" in the usual sense of that word, it is indisputable that Supreme Court justices are busy men who make many important decisions; and both individually and as a group, they need and make use of research assistance. But the responsibilities of judging, at least in the courts, have historically been conceived as peculiarly personal in nature, while the implications of the institutionalization of decision-making processes, with the normally consequent growth in the size and complexity of organization and administrative staff, are to depersonalize decision-making. Clearly, such changes have occurred, and in significant measure, in the Presidency and in the Congress, particularly within the last generation. There is no logical reason, and no reason in administrative organization theory, why such changes cannot come to the judiciary, including the Supreme Court, as well. The question is: Has the Supreme Court already become bureaucratized? And what are the implications, for both the authority and the responsibility of the Court, of bureaucratization?

The size of the Court itself, if we define "the Court" in terms of the number of justices, has remained unchanged for almost a century; while the size of the staff of the Court has increased several times over during the same period, and particularly during the past quarter of a century. The federal budget, for instance, lists the total personnel strength of the Supreme Court, at intervals of a decade, as follows: [73]

1927	52
1937	191
1947	181
1957	207

One need not subscribe to Parkinson's Law, even in modified form ("Work expands so as to fill the [space, rather than time] available for its completion") [74] in order to recognize that the Court's move in 1935 from extremely cramped quarters in the Capitol into the new Marble Palace may have had something to do with this increase in staff. We can compensate for the change in housing by subtracting from the total personnel assigned to the Supreme Court the number of custodial employees; and if we deduct also the nine justices, the remainder is equal to the administrative (professional-clerical-stenographic) personnel of the Court. The increase in administrative staff (including law clerks) has been:

1927	20
1937	30
1947	44
1957	63

Of course, the doubling in the volume of business on the Court's dockets during the same period is probably a much more important cause for the increase in administrative staff than the move into the new Supreme Court building; and this was a period of general growth in the size of government agencies. But even if we assume that the staff services provided by such administrative units as the

[73] *The Budget of the United States Government for the Fiscal Year Ending June 30 1929; ibid.,* 1939; 1949; 1959 (Appendix).

[74] C. Northcote Parkinson, *Parkinson's Law and Other Studies in Administration* (Boston: Houghton, 1957), p. 2.

offices of the Clerk, the Librarian, and the Reporter have a significant bearing upon the decision-making of the justices, it is likely that the most important organizational factor in the decision-making of any justice is that of his administrative assistants—his law clerks.

John Frank, who was clerk to Justice Black during the early forties, tells us that: [75]

> The practice of providing clerks for the Justices began in the late nineteenth century. Thereafter, for many years, each Justice had one clerk. Chief Justice Stone took two, and after World War II most of the rest of the Court followed suit. The number for Chief Justice Vinson was raised to three, and now usually the Chief has three clerks and the others [two], except Justice Douglas, who prefers one. These are almost always boys (or girls) recently out of law school who usually serve for one year, although some Justices have maintained permanent clerks. Justice Roberts, for example, had a husband-and-wife team as his permanent clerk and secretary. The selection of the clerks is the purely personal patronage of the Justices, who can make their choices on any basis. Harvard furnishes the clerks for Justice Frankfurter, Justice Black tries to get Southern boys—and tennis-players where possible— Justice Douglas chooses from the West Coast, and so on.

Some commentators have viewed this gradual increase in the number of clerks with something less than equanimity. But their criticism is only indirectly of the number of clerks—after all, the total has only doubled over a period of more than sixty years—but rather reflects the notion of the critics that these young men have the wrong kind of ideas, and that they therefore exert a bad influence upon the justices who, Heaven knows (as these critics would add), are in need of all the good influences that can be brought to bear, "consistent with our Republican system of Constitutional Government." The clerks are considered, as a group, to be starry-eyed young pinks, who leave the country's leading law schools —but especially Harvard and Yale—imbued with the "left-wing philosophy" of "New Dealism–Fair Dealism–Socialism." After all, it is a fact that before he himself joined the Court, Professor Felix Frankfurter had for over two decades sent a succession of his own bright students to the Court, where they became known, somewhat irreverently, as "Felix' Happy Hot Dogs." It is assumed that the clerks include—alas—no young Burkes or young Buckleys, although the first to break the seal of secrecy and raise this charge against the clerks as a group appears, by his own testimony, to be no left-winger. Indeed, the clerk in question, Mr. William H. Rehnquist, was employed by a conservative justice (Robert H. Jackson), published his remarks in a conservative magazine (David Lawrence's *U.S. News and World Report*), and provided the inspiration for an edi-

---

[75] *Marble Palace*, pp. 115-116.

torial, written by John T. Flynn's long-time research associate, for a conservative newsletter (*Human Events*).[76]

Rehnquist himself had rejected the notion that the clerks would be likely to attempt, or to succeed, in *deliberately* manipulating the decision-making of the justices for whom they work. But the question, he thought, was more subtle than this; there remained the possibility of the *"unconscious* slanting of material by clerks" in presenting their analyses and recommendations to the justices in handling the certiorari work. In his opinion,[77]

> The bias of the clerks . . . is not a random or hit-and-miss bias. From my observations of two sets of Court clerks during the 1951 and 1952 terms, the political and legal prejudices of the clerks were by no means representative of the country as a whole nor of the Court which they served.
>
> After conceding a wide diversity of opinion among the clerks themselves, and further conceding the difficulties and possible inaccuracies inherent in political cataloguing of people, it is nonetheless fair to say that the political cast of the clerks as a group was to the "left" of either the nation or the Court.
>
> Some of the tenets of the "liberal" point of view which commanded the sympathy of a majority of the clerks I knew were extreme solicitude for the claims of Communists and other criminal defendants, expansion of federal power at the expense of State power, great sympathy toward any government regulation of business—in short, the political philosophy now espoused by the Court under Chief Justice Earl Warren.

There seems to be a big jump from the advice of law clerks on certiorari petitions to the decisions on the merits and accompanying opinions of the Court in cases involving Communists, criminals, and businessmen. We know that at least two-thirds of the justices vote *against* the review of 90 percent of the certiorari petitions, so the argument must be that the Court ought not to review cases involving governmental regulation of Communists, criminals, and businessmen, unless there is some explicit way of bridging the gap between certiorari grants and policy decisions of the Court allowing Communists to receive passports and holding that organized boxing has functioned in restraint of interstate commerce. We have suggested one theory for bridging the gap in a particular set of cases in "The Certiorari Game"; but it seems unlikely that a clerk, no matter what his bias, could have disguised from his justice the policy issue underlying the

[76] Rosalie M. Gordon, "Behind the Black Robes; High Court Clerks: America's Hidden Lawmakers," *Human Events*, Vol. 15, No. 29, Article Section 1, p. 1 (July 21, 1958).

[77] William H. Rehnquist, "Who Writes Decisions of the Supreme Court?" Reprinted from *U.S. News and World Report,* an independent weekly news magazine published at Washington. Copyright 1957 United States News Publishing Corporation. Vol. 43, Part 2, p. 74-75 (December 13, 1957). See also William D. Rogers and William H. Rehnquist, "Do Law Clerks Wield Power in Supreme Court Cases?" *U.S. News and World Report*, Vol. 44, Part 1, pp. 114-116, (February 21, 1958).

F.E.L.A. evidentiary cases. In order to determine whether there is any other logical way to get from the imputed bias of the clerks to the substance of the Court's decisions and opinions, it is necessary to examine what role the clerks play both in jurisdictional decisions and in the writing of opinions. (We can disregard oral argument and the conference, because the clerks take no part in these formal rituals of the Court's decision-making process.)

The Clerks and Certiorari Petitions

"In respect to the more serious business of the Court," says John Frank, "some of the Justices use their clerks to summarize the petitions for certiorari, or the applications to be heard. Other Justices prefer to do this themselves." [78] Apparently, Mr. Frank's generalization is something of an understatement as applied to the Court today, and most of the justices do now rely upon their clerks for at least an initial sifting of the hundreds of Appellate Docket certiorari petitions. According to Rehnquist, in his article cited earlier,

> each clerk is in a position to offer only a worm's eye view of the Justice-clerk relation. He will know well the system used by the Justice for whom he works, but his knowledge about the use to which other Justices put their clerks will necessarily be sketchy. I commit my limited knowledge of the nonconfidential aspects of the system to public print because recent controversy about the Court's decisions may make it of general interest.
>
> During my tenure as law clerk for Justice Robert H. Jackson, from February, 1952, until June, 1953, he . . . had two law clerks. . . . Then, as now, there were two branches of the Court's business: first, choosing what cases it would decide, and, second, deciding them. . . .
>
> Each of [the] petitions for certiorari generally comprises a "brief" urging the Court to hear the case, another "brief" urging the Court not to hear the case, and an often lengthy record of all the proceedings in the lower courts. It is not surprising, therefore, that during my time the majority of Justices delegated substantial responsibilities to their clerks in the digesting of these petitions.
>
> In Justice Jackson's office, the petitions for certiorari which were scheduled to be discussed at the next conference of the Justices were split between the two clerks. Each clerk would then prepare memoranda on the petitions assigned to him. These would include the facts of the case, the law as declared by the lower courts, and a brief summary of previous cases involving the same point. They concluded with a recommendation by the clerk either that the petition be granted or that it be denied. Aided by this data, the Justice himself would then study the petitions in order to determine his vote. I believe that a procedure substantially similar to that just outlined was followed in the offices of a majority of the other Justices during the time that I was a clerk. . . .

[78] *Marble Palace,* p. 116.

Because of the great number of these petitions, sheer pressure of time often prevents a Justice from personally investigating every point involved. The clerk's memorandum is usually supposed not only to digest the relevant matter in the case which the Court is being asked to consider, but to summarize research of other cases on this point. Most of the Justices will base their vote in conference as to whether a petition should be granted at least in part on legal materials digested for him by a subordinate.

Obviously, if the clerk has erred in carrying out this digestive process, or if the clerk has consciously or unconsciously slanted the result of this process in a way different from the way the Justice himself might have done, the Justice may cast his vote in conference in a way different from that which he would have done if properly informed. I do not believe it can be denied that the possibility for influence by the clerks exists in this realm of the Court's activities.

The area in which it would be most likely, in other words, for a law clerk to influence a justice's voting behavior would be in the making of jurisdictional decisions, because the clerk has more and better information, about the decisions to be made, than does the Supreme Court justice for whom he works. It is elementary administrative theory that the control of decision-making is closely linked with the control over information relevant to the decisions to be made. It requires no knowledge of cybernetics to see that the law clerks necessarily are significant participants in the making of the jurisdictional decisions of the Supreme Court. But what about opinion-writing?

Ghost Writers on the Court?

Rehnquist continues:

The role of the clerks in the preparation of written opinions deciding cases in which the Court had already agreed to decide varied far more from Justice to Justice than did their role in the handling of petitions for certiorari. Likewise, where the end product was to be a written opinion carrying the name of a Justice as its author, rather than merely an oral vote in conference, individual clerks were rightly far more closemouthed in talking about procedure in their particular offices. . . .

Robert H. Jackson had one of the finest literary gifts in the history of the Supreme Court. Even a casual acquaintance with his opinions during the 13 years he served on the Court indicates that he neither needed nor used ghost writers. The great majority of opinions which he wrote were drafted originally by him and submitted to his clerks for their criticism and suggestions. Frequently such a draft would be batted back and forth between the Justice and the particular clerk working on it several times. The contributions of the clerk by way of research, organization and, to a lesser extent, method of approach, was often substantial. But the end product was unquestionably the Justice's own, both in form and in substance.

On a couple of occasions each term, Justice Jackson would ask each clerk to draft an opinion for him along lines which he suggested. If the clerk were reasonably faithful to his instructions and reasonably diligent in his work, the Justice could be quite charitable with his black pencil and paste pot. The result reached in these opinions was no less the product of Justice Jackson than those he drafted himself; in literary style, these opinions generally suffered by comparison with those which he had drafted.

The conclusions to be drawn from these observations as to the "influence" of the clerks on the work of the Court will necessarily suffer from the worm's-eye point of view referred to above; nonetheless, some tentative ones will be ventured.

The specter of the law clerk as a legal Rasputin, exerting an important influence on the cases actually decided by the Court, may be discarded at once. No published biographical materials dealing with any of the Justices suggest any such influence. I certainly learned of none during the time I spent as a clerk.

Granted that this is the sort of thing that biographers and commentators might not readily learn of, the complete absence of any known evidence of such influence is surely aided by the common-sense view of the relationship between Justice and clerk. It is unreasonable to suppose that a lawyer in middle age or older, of sufficient eminence in some walk of life to be appointed as one of nine judges of the world's most powerful court, would consciously abandon his own views as to what is right and what is wrong in the law because a stripling clerk just graduated from law school tells him to.

To Rehnquist's description of Jackson's work methods we can add the testimony of Brandeis' law clerk during the 1920 Term. Dean Acheson has said that: [79]

Generally I came down to the Justice's office on Sunday morning after a conference. [Saturday was the Court's conference day.] The Chief Justice's messenger brought around the assignment slips fairly early. These were printed slips bearing the names of the Justices with blank spaces to the right of them, into which the Chief Justice wrote the numbers of the cases which he had assigned to Justice Brandeis for opinion. The same was done with each of the Justices. Brandeis would instruct me to begin work on certain of the numbered cases and would say that others he would start on. At this time we rarely had much discussion about the cases or the opinion, although he would answer any questions or discuss any point which I wished to discuss with him. Usually, however, I knew very little about the case, except that it was to be affirmed, reversed or dismissed, and I would go to work on the record and briefs to find out about it. He did not look with

[79] As quoted by Bickel, *The Unpublished Opinions of Mr. Justice Brandeis*, p. 92.

much favor on his law clerks spending time in the court room listening to arguments, although on a case of outstanding interest he was broadminded on this.

My work usually was cast in the form of a draft opinion, since he found this the most helpful way to get it. When he finished his preliminary work on opinions which he took, he would give me the material to check, criticize, or rewrite, as I thought best. In those days he wanted a good deal more rigorous criticism from his law clerk than I think he regarded as necessary later in his judicial career. When I finished my work on a draft which had been assigned to me or got as far as I could, I gave it to him. As you know from the files, he tore it to pieces, sometimes using a little, sometimes none.

Bickel's study of Justice Brandeis' unpublished opinions suggests that the relationship between justice and clerk frequently was a happy symbiotic combination. The criticism and ideas of the clerk often were ventured with all the vigor and enthusiasm of youth; but they were considered, and accepted, or modified, or rejected by the experienced lawyer and judge, who indisputably decided what would be said, and how, and why, when the drafts of an opinion began to approach finished form. On one such occasion, a clerk (who later became a professor of law) erupted into three pages of incisive critique of a legal formula which Brandeis proposed to use in a commerce-clause case, and which the clerk considered to be "ridiculous" and "fallacious." Before Brandeis asked for his law clerk's comments, says Bickel, "he had considered more or less the line of argument [that the clerk] urged. And we know that he made no concessions to it—at this time, or in the future." [80] It does, in a way, strain the imagination to consider Oliver Wendell Holmes taking orders from his clerks, or having them write his opinions for him. He had joined the Court years before some of his latter-day clerks, whom he called indiscriminately "Sonny," had been born.

It is true that not all of the justices are Holmes or Brandeis, but Jackson and Black afford a fair sample, for recent years, of justices drawn from opposite poles of the Court; and John Frank indicates that Black's use of his clerks in opinion drafting during the early forties did not differ significantly from the practice of Brandeis in the early twenties, or from that of Jackson in the early fifties: [81]

In the early 1940's, at least, Justice Black wrote the first draft of all his opinions, except that toward the end of the year he would let the youngster try his hand at one first draft of something extremely unimportant. In my own case, the day of glory came when I did the first draft of a lone dissent on a minor point of statutory construction, which the Justice then revised and which no one has ever noticed since. Sometimes a Justice writes the first draft of one opinion while the clerk writes the first draft of another, and the

80 *Ibid.*, pp. 117-118.
81 This quotation, and the three immedi-   ately following, are from *Marble Palace*, pp. 116-119.

opinions are then exchanged and the clerk writes a second draft of his Justice's opinion while the Justice writes a second draft of the clerk's.

There are rumors, however, which Frank faithfully reports, to the effect that "Sometimes clerks are allowed to do the bulk of the serious writing for the Justice." This raises, he says, the whole problem of "ghost-writing" on the Court, and the use of clerks as ghosts for the justices, with Chief Justice Vinson constituting a notorious case in point. Frank went on to suggest that the problem of ghost-writing on the Court, to the extent that it exists, is essentially a sociological problem rather than an ethical one:

> The writing problem (which excludes the making of the ultimate decision but may include the making of a whole series of important intermediate decisions on details) raises a serious difficulty in the future of the Court. The Justices are very frequently chosen from other public offices. The complexities of the rest of government are such that the men who hold the great offices—Secretary of the Treasury, Senator from New York, or the Presidency itself—must be men who can delegate every function except decision-making. The jobs have become so big that even the very largest details cannot be handled by the leaders. Abraham Lincoln wrote almost all of his important state papers. If Franklin D. Roosevelt had done anything of the kind, he would have had no time left for anything else. We live in the age of the staff researcher, the ghost writer, the first-draft man; most important public officials must make use of them. We have developed a breed of men who work that way, and as a result we are filling the reservoir of public officials from which Supreme Court Justices are drawn with men who are able to handle broad responsibilities; Chief Justice Vinson, for example, was a superb holder of very important offices during the war. At the same time, we are developing men who are not at all cut out for traditional judicial responsibility.

Of course, the ghosting of opinions by clerks for justices could provide the missing link in the argument necessary to support Rehnquist's implications. But the only published discussions of the subject suggest only rumor and surmise, not evidence; and Frank himself has concluded that:

> Even on those rare occasions when the clerk does the writing, the judge does the deciding. The ultimate matters of yes or no, affirm or reverse, the judges invariably keep in their own hands; while the clerks may on rare occasions persuade, their influence in this regard is not really significant. Some newspaper talk to the contrary in the summer of 1957 was so much foolishness; in my own year as a law clerk, my Justice made approximately one thousand decisions, and I had precisely no influence on any of them.

Reconsideration

After the Court has announced its decision in a case and opinions (if any) have been read, there remains for the losing party the problem of how best to minimize or to overcome the effects of the decision. The possible strategies include the raising of a new case in the hope of persuading the Court to overrule or distinguish the undesirable decision, possibly with the help of intervening personnel changes among the justices; or efforts may be carried on in the executive or legislative branches, or at the state level, or in the lower federal courts, with the objective of frustrating the decision of the Court. Such maneuvers we place to one side for the present, because we shall consider them in some detail in the next chapter. But there is one other thing that a loser can attempt on the heels of the announcement of an unfavorable decision: he can ask the Court to change its mind.[82] To be more explicit, and changing the figure of speech from institutional to behavioral terms, the loser can hope to persuade one or more of the justices to switch his vote in the case.

The odds of succeeding in this sort of an appeal are never good, but lawyers are encouraged to make the attempt in most cases so that they cannot subsequently be entrapped in any nuance of the doctrine which requires a party to "exhaust" his remedies before seeking other relief, at least in the courts; and then, there is always the "long shot" possibility that some justice might change his vote. The Court denies most of these requests *pro forma,* with even less consideration than it gives to petitions on the Miscellaneous Docket.

It is also obvious that the chances of getting a decision reversed are directly related to the voting division of the Court in the case. The chances are best in cases where the Court is evenly divided (4-4 or 3-3) or where the majority has decided by a plurality of only one (5-4 or 4-3). They are least good when the decision has gone unanimously against a party.

The way in which a party asks the Court to reconsider a decision is by filing a petition or motion for rehearing; and if that is denied, it is still possible to file another motion for rehearing by giving it a different label, such as a "motion for recall of the judgment." Generally speaking, the probabilities for success with motions such as the latter are even less than those for timely petitions for rehearing. But both of these methods occasionally bear fruit; and when they do so, the resulting decisions usually afford an exceptionally fine opportunity for insight into the behavior of the justices.

Black and Jackson were antagonists in the celebrated Jewell Ridge case, in which the Court was asked, on motion for rehearing, to disqualify Justice Black from voting in the case, on grounds of bias. Black's former law partner was counsel for the winning party, and Black had voted with the majority in the 5-4 de-

---

[82] On the legal aspects of motions for rehearing, see generally Stern and Gressman, *op. cit.* (footnote 34, *supra*), chap. xii, especially p. 352.

cision of the Court. This motion caused great internal difficulties for the Court, as Stone's biographer has revealed; and it led more or less directly to Jackson's subsequent public attack on Black from Nuremburg.[83] The Court denied the motion for rehearing in the Jewell Ridge case, but Jackson and Frankfurter insisted that the following opinion be published following the curt order of denial by the Court:

No. 721. JEWELL RIDGE COAL CORPORATION v. LOCAL No. 6167, UNITED MINE WORKERS OF AMERICA.

[325 U.S. 897-898.] June 18, 1945.

Petition for rehearing denied.

MR. JUSTICE JACKSON, concurring.

Since announcement of a mere denial of this petition for rehearing might be interpreted to rest upon any one of several grounds, I consider it appropriate to disclose the limited grounds on which I concur.

The unusual feature of the petition in this case is that it suggests to the Court a question as to the qualification of one of the Justices to take part in the decision of the cause. This petition is addressed to all of the Court and must either be granted or denied in the name of the Court and on the responsibility of all the Justices. In my opinion the complaint is one which cannot properly be addressed to the Court as a whole and for that reason I concur in denying it.

No statute prescribes grounds upon which a Justice of this Court may be disqualified in any case. The Court itself has never undertaken by rule of Court or decision to formulate any uniform practice on the subject. Because of this lack of authoritative standards it appears always to have been considered the responsibility of each Justice to determine for himself the propriety of withdrawing in any particular circumstances. Practice of the Justices over the years has not been uniform, and the diversity of attitudes to the question doubtless leads to some confusion as to what the bar may expect and as to whether the action in any case is a matter of individual or collective responsibility.

There is no authority known to me under which a majority of this Court has power under any circumstances to exclude one of its duly commissioned Justices from sitting or voting in any case. As to the other and usual grounds, applications for rehearing in this Court, as in other bodies, are addressed to the majority which promulgated the decision. This is so formulated by our Rule 33. It is always obvious that unless one or more of them is willing to reconsider his position no good can come of reargument. Hence, being in dissent, I have no voice as to rehearing, except that I continue to adhere to the dissent.

Because of these considerations I concur in denial of the petition.

MR. JUSTICE FRANKFURTER concurs in this statement.

A more recent example, and one in which the motion for rehearing was successful, is provided by the *Reid* v. *Covert* and *Kinsella* v. *Krueger* cases. Both cases raised the same issue of constitutional policy, and they were together

[83] Alpheus T. Mason, *Harlan Fiske Stone: Pillar of the Law* (New York: Viking, 1956), pp. 640-645. On the public attack, see the *New York Times*, June 11, 1946, pp. 1-2; *United States News*, Vol. 20, June 21, 1946, pp. 15-16.

argued, decided, reargued, and decided again—but in a way opposite to the original decision. In each case, the civilian wife of a member of the United States armed services, stationed with her husband at an overseas base in a foreign country, shot and killed her spouse. Each widow was classified, by military law and act of Congress, as an accompanying dependent of a military person, and she was therefore subject to military trial. Both were tried by court-martial, convicted of murder, and returned to the United States for imprisonment. The alternatives to trial by court-martial would have been, in principle, trial in the civilian courts of the foreign country or trial by civil courts in the United States; but existing statutory and executive law at the time of the offenses made no provision for such alternative forms of trial. As a consequence, the real alternative to trial by court-martial was to permit the murderesses to go scot free—an event that might occasion some disquietude among married military personnel stationed with their wives at overseas bases.

In the case of Clarice Covert, which was before the Court on appeal, the lower federal court had reversed the court-martial conviction, on the ground that the section of the Uniform Military Code (a federal statute) authorizing the trial of accompanying civilian defendants in military courts was unconstitutional. In the other case, the Court granted certiorari to review the affirmance by a different federal court of the conviction of Dorothy Smith, who happened to be the daughter of General Walter Krueger of World War II fame.

The cases were argued together on May 3, 1956, and the 5-3 decision of the Court was announced only a month later, on June 11, 1956, at the close of the 1955 Term.[84] The constitutionality of the statute was upheld in an opinion for the Court delivered by Clark, in which Burton, Harlan, Minton, and Reed joined. Warren, Black, and Douglas dissented together, protesting that "we need more time than is available in these closing days of the Term in which to write our dissenting views. We will file our dissents during the next Term of Court." Frankfurter refused to vote and filed a "Reservation" in which he protested that the complexity of the issues raised by these cases precluded a snap decision: [85]

Time is required not only for the primary task of analyzing in detail the materials on which the Court relies. It is equally required for adequate reflection upon the meaning of these materials and their bearing on the issues now before the Court. Reflection is a slow process. Wisdom, like good wine, requires maturing.

Moreover, the judgments of this Court are collective judgments. They are neither solo performances nor debates between two sides, each of which has its mind quickly made up and then closed. The judgments of this Court presuppose full consideration and reconsideration by all of the reasoned views of each. Without adequate study there cannot be adequate reflection.

[84] *Kinsella* v. *Krueger,* 351 U.S. 470; *Reid* v. *Covert,* 351 U.S. 487.

[85] 351 U.S. 485. The Warren, Black, and Douglas dissent appears at 351 U.S. 486.

Without adequate reflection there cannot be adequate deliberation and discussion. And without these, there cannot be that full interchange of minds which is indispensable to wise decision and its persuasive formulation.

The circumstances being what they are, I am forced, deeply as I regret it, to reserve for a later date an expression of my views.

Normally, this would have been the end of the matter, except for the eventual filing of a dissenting opinion or opinions by the three libertarian justices. But this time it was different. Minton, who had been in the majority, retired on the following October 16; and on that same date, the appointment of William Brennan in his place was announced. Brennan had the reputation of a liberal judge on the New Jersey Supreme Court. The Solicitor General had filed motions for the rehearing of both cases during the summer, and the Court granted these motions on November 5, 1956.

It should be underscored that the government could not have expected the motions to be granted *because of* Brennan's replacement of Minton, and for two reasons. Not having participated in the original decision, Brennan was not eligible to participate in the decision of the motion for rehearing; and even if Frankfurter should have voted to grant rehearing, as he might logically have been expected to do, the Court would nevertheless have been deadlocked at 4-4, and the motion would be denied. As Jackson pointed out in his opinion in the Jewell Ridge case, the motion had no chance of success unless a member of the original majority were prepared to change his vote. Harlan did switch, and the motion for rehearing was granted by a 5-3 division, with the three libertarians plus Frankfurter and Harlan now in the majority, and with Clark, Burton, and Reed in dissent.

Reargument was held on February 27, 1957; and on June 11, 1957, almost a year to the day from the original decision on the merits, the Court reversed itself and now held that the statute was unconstitutional.[86] In the meantime, Reed had retired to be replaced by Whittaker, who was appointed after the reargument and therefore was ineligible to participate in the new decision on the merits. On the other hand, Brennan heard the reargument, and did participate. But the Court was unable to muster a majority who could agree upon a reason for declaring the statute unconstitutional. Black announced the judgment of the Court and delivered an opinion, in which Warren and Douglas and Brennan joined, which denounced in sweeping terms military trial of civilians. Frankfurter and Harlan preferred to justify their votes upon a much narrower (and the same) ground; each wrote a separate concurring opinion, and Harlan also felt obliged to explain, in his opinion, why he had changed his mind, and therefore his vote, in these cases. The only remaining members of the majority of the previous year were Clark and Burton; and they dissented together in an opinion written by

[86] *Reid* v. *Covert* and *Kinsella* v. *Krueger*, 354 U.S. 1.

Clark which restated, at somewhat greater length, the argument of the now expunged 1956 opinion of the Court.

We have dealt summarily in the preceding discussion with what is an important issue of constitutional policy, and we have gone into considerable detail regarding the voting position of the justices and the timing of the decisional process, because these cases illustrate very well the importance of the vote of a single justice to the establishment of public policy by the Court. Theodore Roosevelt knew whereof he spoke when he remarked, as we have noted earlier, that the success of a major program of his administration might well depend upon whether a single justice of the Supreme Court came up heads or tails. Moreover, the question of timing, in decision-making by the Supreme Court as in most other events in real life, is of critical importance. It is not usual for the Supreme Court to decide a case by a 5-3 vote in one term, and to reverse its own decision in the same case by a 2-6 vote in the next term. In these two cases, two personnel changes and a delayed vote contributed to the striking shift in the division of the Court, it is true. But the critical event, without which reconsideration and therefore a reversal of the decision in these cases would have been impossible, was the fact that a member of the original majority, Harlan, changed his mind during the summer of 1956. (For a graphic illustration of Harlan's central position in the disposition of these cases, see Table 10, page 152).

Our example of that most improbable event, a successful second motion for the rehearing of a case, is provided by a series of decisions in an F.E.L.A. evidentiary case in the 1955 Term. The case concerned the claim of a railroad brakeman. The employee, one Cahill, was injured by a truck while functioning as a watchman and flagging down traffic at a grade crossing. In the usual pattern of these cases, as described in "The Certiorari Game," Cahill sued the railroad for negligence, won a jury verdict of $90,000 and judgment in the trial court; this was reversed by a 2-1 decision of the federal Court of Appeals for the Second Circuit, and Cahill then carried his case by certiorari to the Supreme Court. The Supreme Court took its customary action under such circumstances; and announced its decision as follows: [87]

No. 436. CAHILL v. NEW YORK, NEW HAVEN & HARTFORD RAILROAD CO. On petition for writ of certiorari to the United States Court of Appeals for the Second Circuit. *Per Curiam:* The petition for writ of certiorari is granted and the judgment is reversed. MR. JUSTICE REED believes certiorari should have been denied and dissents from the judgment of reversal. MR. JUSTICE FRANKFURTER, MR. JUSTICE BURTON AND MR. JUSTICE HARLAN are of the opinion that the petition for writ of certiorari should have been denied. . . .

[87] 350 U.S. 898-899 (November 21, 1955).

TABLE 10.

The Three Decisions in the Covert-Krueger Cases
(1955 and 1956 Terms)

	Kinsella v. Krueger, 351 U.S. 470, and Reid v. Covert, 351 U.S. 487 (June 11, 1956)	Reid v. Covert, and Kinsella v. Krueger, 352 U.S. 901 (November 5, 1956) [On petition for rehearing]	Reid v. Covert, and Kinsella v. Krueger, 354 U.S. 1 (June 10, 1957) [On rehearing]
Black	'+')	+	('+'
Douglas	'+')	+	(+
Warren, C. J.	'+')	+	(+
Brennan	*	NP	(+
Frankfurter	R	+	('+'
Harlan	(−)	+	('+'
Minton	(−)	*	*
Reed	(−)	−	*
Burton	(−)	−	−)
Clark	('−')	−	'−')
Whittaker	*	*	NP
Voting Division	3-5 Con	5-3 Pro	6-2 Pro

LEGEND:

+	=	a vote in favor of the defendants
−	=	a vote against the defendants
' '	=	wrote opinion
( )	=	joined in the opinion of the Court
(	=	concurring opinion
)	=	dissenting opinion
*	=	not seated at the time of this decision
NP	=	seated but not participating in this decision
R	=	vote reserved until a later time

Obviously, the decision was 5-4 in favor of Cahill. The four members of the Certiorari Bloc—Brennan had not yet joined the Court—had played the odds successfully, and picked up the single additional vote—Minton's—that they needed in order to control disposition on the merits. Reed dissented on the merits and on jurisdictional grounds as well; and Burton and Harlan joined with Frankfurter in refusing to consider the merits and in limiting their dissent to the question of jurisdiction.

It should be noted that since this was a summary decision, made without benefit of oral argument, in which the jurisdictional decision and the decision on the merits were announced simultaneously, there was no previous opportunity for the minority to protest the grant of jurisdiction in this case. And the verbal conflict between Harlan and Frankfurter, concerning the obligation of all justices to vote on the merits, lay fifteen months in the future; apparently, Harlan had not thought through his position on this issue at this time. But there was nothing remarkable about the case. It was just like four others that the Court decided in the 1955 Term, or the ten others that the Court decided in the following term, including the Ferguson case.

The railroad filed a routine petition for rehearing, which the Supreme Court, in a correspondingly routine manner, denied on January 9, 1956.[88] The railroad then proceeded to pay the amount of the judgment to Cahill, after the district court denied its application for a stay of judgment; and the case soon received nationwide publicity as the result of what happened next in the Supreme Court.[89] After Cahill had been paid off, and (according to newspaper accounts) $20,000 of the money was spent to pay doctor and hospital bills and lawyers' fees, and another substantial part to buy a new home, counsel for the railroad filed in the Supreme Court "a petition for rehearing of a former petition for rehearing"—or, in plain English, a second motion for rehearing. This second petition alleged precisely what had been alleged in the first petition: that the railroad had appealed the district court judgment to the court of appeals on two distinct grounds; that the court of appeals, in reversing the district court, had explicitly based its decision on the first of these grounds, expressly stating that it was unnecessary for it to reach the other claim of error on the part of the trial judge; and finally, that as a consequence, the Supreme Court should not have simply *reversed* the decision below, thus reinstating the original judgment of the district court, but rather, the Supreme Court should have reversed and remanded the case to the court of appeals, so that that court might then consider the railroad's other claim of error.

This motion for re-hearing seemed to be explicitly barred by the Court's own Rule 58(4), which declared that: "Consecutive petitions for rehearings, and petitions for rehearing that are out of time under this rule, will not be received

---

88 350 U.S. 943 (January 9, 1956).
89 See, e.g., *New York Times*, May 15, 1956, 26:6; and May 16, 1956, 24:6.

[by the Clerk of the Court]." Nevertheless, the Court "received" it; and on May 14, 1956, it was announced in a brief *per curiam* opinion that the Court had decided to "recall" its prior judgment, and to remand the case to the court of appeals.[90] The new majority washed its hands of the problem of how Cahill might be able to repay a considerable sum of money that he had already spent, declaring majestically that "the problems that may arise from demand for repayment are not before us." The four members of the Certiorari Bloc dissented.

Since both the original decision and the later one were announced *per curiam*, no one wrote for the Court. Obviously some justice had changed his mind, since a 5-4 decision in favor of Cahill was reversed, after an interval of six months, by a 5-4 decision against him. Unlike Harlan in the Covert and Kinsella cases, the switch voter in the Cahill case enjoyed a certain amount of anonymity, but it was really not very much. Anybody who could subtract four from nine, twice, could determine that the justice who changed his vote must have been Sherman Minton. All eight of his colleagues dissented from one or the other of the two decisions, half from the original decision, and then his colleagues of that *ad hoc* majority dissented from the decision on re-rehearing.

The three jurisdictional dissents from the original decision—by Frankfurter, Burton, and Harlan—had been premised on the argument that the Court had no business deciding this case because the Court should devote its time to more important matters, and the like. These jurisdictional dissents were suddenly transformed into full-fledged votes for the railroad, on the merits. The explanation is self-evident. In the original decision, the jurisdictional dissenters knew that the case was decided against them anyhow, so it cost them nothing to indulge in the luxury of harassing the majority by protesting the decision on jurisdiction instead of the decision on the merits. But when Minton indicated his willingness to change, every other vote counted. There was a quorum of six participating in decision on the merits, even if Frankfurter-Burton-Harlan persisted in their jurisdictional dissent; but in that case, Cahill would still have won on the merits, on which the division of the Court would have been 4-2 with the Certiorari Bloc controlling disposition of the case over the Reed and Minton dissents on the merits. One might infer that since every vote counted, the jurisdictional dissenters forgot their scruples about how the Court ought to occupy its time and energies. Indeed, one might go further and infer from this example that votes to dismiss certiorari when cases are disposed of by the Court on the merits are simply an alternative means of expressing dissent *on the merits*, in cases that already have been lost or won irrespective of how the jurisdictional dissenter votes. This hypothesis finds some confirmation in the fact that an examination of the voting record of the principal practitioner reveals that Frankfurter has never voted to

90 351 U.S. 183. Upon remand the court of appeals affirmed *per curiam* the judgment of the trial court, citing with approval Black's *dissenting* opinion. 236 F. 2d 410 (August 22, 1956).

dismiss jurisdiction in an F.E.L.A. evidentiary decision on the merits when his vote could have changed the outcome.

Whether or not our interpretation of the tactics of jurisdictional dissents is correct, there is one qualification to our previous generalization that the Cahill case seems to suggest. A petition for rehearing has no chance unless at least one member of the former majority either leaves the Court or is willing to change his vote; but the rules of the Court do not necessarily stand in the way of obtaining such a rehearing, if a majority justice has been converted and the original decision was marginal.

BLOC BEHAVIOR

Libertarian Blocs

A *bloc* on the Court consists of three or more justices who manifest a relatively high degree of interagreement in their voting, whether in the majority or in dissent, over a period of at least a term. A bloc differs, therefore, from a *group* which consists of a temporary alignment of justices who vote together in a particular case or set of cases; a group lacks both the persistency and the consistency of a bloc.

Perhaps the best-known bloc which has functioned on the Court within recent years consists of those four justices whom Pritchett has labeled as the "Libertarian Activists." [91] This bloc consisted of Black, Douglas, Murphy, and Rutledge, and it was active from 1943 to 1949—six terms in all. The bloc was formed when Rutledge joined the Court in the middle of the 1942 Term, and it broke up when both Murphy and Rutledge died during the summer vacation between the 1948 and 1949 Terms.

Pritchett identified the Libertarian Activisits by examining the extent to which the justices who sat on the Vinson Court during the 1946-1952 terms favored libertarian claims in cases dealing with selected civil-liberties issues. (Murphy and Rutledge, of course, participated in such decisions only during the first three terms of this period.) He discovered that the average rate of support of the Court over all of these issues and cases was 35%; and that only five of the eleven justices who sat on the Court during this period had averages above this mean. Murphy was highest at 100%, followed by Rutledge (96%), Douglas (89%), Black (87%), and Frankfurter (61%). Pritchett next suggested that there were really two quite different factors which affected "libertarian activism": (1) "the direction and intensity of a justice's libertarian sympathies," and (2) whether a justice favored broad or narrow judicial review of the decisions of the other branches of the national government, and of the states. In order for a justice to

[91] Pritchett, *Civil Liberties and the Vinson Court*, chap. x, and especially pp. 190-192.

evince a really high level of support for civil liberties claims, said Pritchett, he would have to both be personally sympathetic to libertarian claims, and favor a broad scope of judicial review. On this basis, he decided that the top four justices were both "libertarian" and "activist," while Frankfurter was libertarian in his personal sympathies but a believer in and practitioner of judicial restraint. Pritchett referred somewhat euphemistically to the remaining justices, who ranked below the mean for the Court, as the "less libertarians."

It is convenient for some purposes to refer to the four justices, whom Pritchett termed libertarian activists, as the "libertarian bloc." There is ample evidence to support the designation of these four justices as a bloc. It has been suggested that one objective way of identifying blocs is to construct tables in which the paired voting agreement in split decisions is computed for each justice with every other, both in dissent, and for dissenting and assenting votes combined. When this is done, it is possible to measure the degree of cohesion of a bloc in dissent, and the degree of its interagreement when both majority and dissenting votes are combined.[92] Indices of cohesion of over .50, and of interagreement over .70, are considered to be high. Pritchett has published tables which show the paired voting agreement of the justices during the period that the Libertarian Activists were together on the Court; [93] and when these tables are measured by the indices, the results shown in Table 11, below, are obtained.

TABLE 11.

Cohesion and Interagreement Among the Libertarian Activists (1943-1948 Terms)

TERM	1943	1944	1945	1946-48 [a]
Index of Cohesion (over .50 is high)	.54	.44	.28	.62
Index of Interagreement (over .70 is high)	.78	.77	.65	.74

[a] Published data for the 1947 and 1948 Terms is not available except as combined with 1946 for the three-year period shown in the last column.

It is evident that the four Libertarian Activists may appropriately be termed a bloc of justices. They were high in their interagreement, in both assent and dissent, over a period of half a dozen terms, with the exception of their agreement in dissent in the 1945 Term. The exceptionally low cohesion of the libertarian bloc during that term is readily explained by the fact that only eight justices sat on the Court throughout this term; Jackson was away at Nuremberg.

92 See Schubert, *op. cit.* (footnote 49, *supra*), "The Study of Judicial Decision-Making," pp. 1011-1013; and *Quantitative Analysis of* *Judicial Behavior,* pp. 89-91.
93 *The Roosevelt Court,* pp. 41, 42, 43, 246, 247; *The Vinson Court,* pp. 181, 182.

There was little occasion for the libertarian bloc to be highly cohesive in dissent during this term, because the four other justices could not combine to form a majority to force the libertarian bloc into dissent. The very high cohesion of the libertarian bloc during the last three terms is readily explained by the fact that Jackson voted much more conservatively after his return from Nuremberg, and moved from the center to the right wing of the Court; and Vinson, who replaced Stone beginning in the 1946 Term, voted generally much more conservatively than had Stone.

The libertarian bloc of the forties is the best-known bloc on the Court in recent years, but it is by no means the only one. This bloc was replaced by another libertarian bloc beginning in the 1955 Term, when Warren joined the Court and affiliated with Black and Douglas; and the libertarians became again a bloc of four when Brennan was coopted following his appointment at the opening of the 1956 Term. This new libertarian bloc of four justices has functioned with high interagreement since that time. There have also been two different right blocs, one a successor to the other, which have been active on the Warren Court.[94] The first of these, composed of Minton, Reed, and Burton, functioned during the 1953-1955 Terms and broke up with the retirement of Minton and Reed; the second, composed of Burton, Frankfurter, and Harlan, formed in the 1955 Term, and coopted Whittaker upon his appointment to the Court in the middle of the 1956 Term. Thus, in the 1957 Term, the four-justice libertarian bloc was balanced by a four-justice right bloc (see Tables 12 and 13, on pages 158 and 159).

The remaining center justice, Clark, showed a definite leaning to the right, although the effect of considering him to be a member of the bloc is to cause both its cohesion in dissent and over-all interagreement to drop to a moderate level. Clark had been a center justice during the preceding four terms; and until Brennan had bumped him one position to the right in the 1956 Term, Clark had been closest to Warren, showing very high over-all agreement with the Chief Justice. Clark had also favored the libertarian bloc of three in dissent, particularly in 5-4 marginal dissents, when it was usually Clark who supplied the fourth dissenting vote. There was a sharp change in Clark's voting behavior in the 1957 Term, as the two tables below demonstrate. We might even infer that the polarization of the Court in this term into opposed blocs of four justices each had made Clark's position as a "neutral" or center justice untenable. Clark had been willing, during the four earlier terms, to join the libertarian bloc in dissent, but he had been much less willing to form majorities with these justices. Now that there were four of them, his consistent support would convert them into the dominant majority on the Court. (It will be recalled that this is precisely what Clark was doing, during the 1957 Term, in the F.E.L.A. cases discussed in "The Certiorari Game"; but on the other hand, Clark had joined the Certiorari Bloc

94 See Schubert, *Quantitative Analysis of Judicial Behavior*, pp. 111-116, 123.

TABLE 12.

Dissenting Blocs on the Warren Court (1957 Term)

1957 TERM	Douglas	Black	Warren	Brennan	Clark	Whittaker	Burton	Harlan	Frankfurter
Total Dissents	38	32	29	16	21	23	30	31	30
Douglas	(5)	29	26	15		1	2	1	2
Black	29		26	14	1	2	3		
Warren	26	26		12		2	1	1	
Brennan	15	14	12				2	2	2
Clark		1			(4)	7	13	9	6
Whittaker	1	2	2		7	(2)	14	14	11
Burton	2	3	1	2	13	14		18	12
Harlan	1		1	2	9	14	18		24
Frankfurter	2			2	6	11	12	24	(3)

Total Split Decisions: 90

INDICES OF COHESION

Left bloc = .71 (very high)
Right bloc = .55 (high)
Right bloc plus Clark = .47 (moderate)

From Schubert, *Quantitative Analysis of Judicial Behavior,* p. 148.

several years earlier, and *before* Brennan came to the Court. In any event, it appeared that Clark's affiliation with the libertarian bloc was highly selective, and had never extended over a broad enough range of issues to identify him as a member of the bloc, except in the marginal 5-4 decisions.) Faced with pressures from both the augmented libertarian bloc and the right bloc of four justices, and with his former close liaison with Warren broken up by the intervening presence of a new justice (Brennan), Clark began to move to the right, and to establish closer ties with the second John Marshall Harlan and with Burton. Indeed, Clark's relationship with Burton, his former colleague of the right bloc during the latter years of the Vinson Court, was reestablished just as soon as Brennan began to define his own position in the previous (1956) term.

TABLE 13.

Interagreement in Split Decisions of the Warren Court
(1957 Term—In Percentages)

1957 TERM	Douglas	Black	Warren	Brennan	Clark	Whit-taker	Burton	Harlan	Frank-furter
Percentage of Assent	69	73	75	87	82	81	75	74	75
Douglas		89	83	75	34	33	29	29	27
Black	89		92	79	41	41	36	33	31
Warren	83	92		79	46	43	34	34	31
Brennan	75	79	79		57	55	52	53	51
Clark	34	41	46	57		66	72	62	60
Whittaker	33	41	43	55	66		71	69	67
Burton	29	36	34	52	72	71		67	67
Harlan	29	33	34	53	62	69	67		87
Frankfurter	27	31	31	51	60	67	67	87	

Total Formal Decisions: 121   INDICES OF INTERAGREEMENT

Left bloc = .83 (very high)
Right bloc = .71 (high)
Right bloc plus Clark = .69 (marginally high)

From Schubert, *Quantitative Analysis of Judicial Behavior*, p. 163.

Political Stress and Judicial Strain: The 1936 Term

JUDICIAL BLOCS ON THE HUGHES COURT

Probably the most dramatic example of bloc behavior on the Supreme Court is found in the 1936 Term. It was early in this term that President Franklin Roosevelt presented his "Court-packing" message to Congress, advocating the re-organization of the Court and the appointment of additional justices who would presumably—although the President did not state this openly, at least at first—outvote the "Nine Old Men" who refused to retire. Roosevelt failed in his im-mediate objective of obtaining authority to appoint additional judges, although he was destined to make eight appointments to the Court before the expiration of his second term (which began less than three weeks before he made his speech), and four men of his choice had taken over control of the Court within two years of his attack on the judiciary. The assumption of control by the new Roosevelt justices came as an anticlimax, however, because the Court reformed itself during the late winter and spring months of the 1936 Term.

The celebrated "switch in time, that saved nine" can be demonstrated by bloc analysis, and also by game analysis; and we shall employ both of these tools in the discussion that follows. Assuming that a "switch" took place, the questions arise: Who switched? And why? The interpretation accepted by most scholars is that Mr. Justice Roberts switched, aided and abetted by Chief Justice Hughes. We shall take this view as our hypothesis for investigation.

Pritchett's tables [95] show that during the five years immediately preceding the Court-packing term, the justices were divided into two sharply defined and opposing blocs, with the Chief Justice and Roberts in the middle and less well integrated with either bloc than were their seven colleagues. (The personnel structure of the Court was unusually stable during this period, including 1936, of six terms; the only change came when Cardozo replaced Holmes in the middle of the first, the 1931 term.) The left bloc consisted of Stone, Cardozo, and Brandeis, who dissented frequently and with an extremely high Index of Cohesion of .80; it will be recalled that anything greater than .50 is considered to be high. The right bloc consisted of McReynolds, Butler, Sutherland, and Van Devanter, who dissented much less frequently than the left bloc, and whose cohesion as a bloc was high at .53. Both Hughes and Roberts dissented very infrequently, and only once together during the entire five years; but this is the extent of the similarity in their dissenting behavior. Hughes was affiliated, although at a much lower *level* of dissenting activity than the others, with the left bloc, for whom the Index of Cohesion, even including Hughes, was a very high .61. During this entire five-year period, Hughes joined Van Devanter (who was the member of the right bloc closest to the center of the table) in dissent just once, and the other members of the right bloc not at all. Clearly, when Hughes dissented, he did so with the left; and with the two exceptions noted, *only* with the left. But in view of his low rate of dissent, it is most accurate to say that Hughes was marginally affiliated with the left bloc in dissent. Roberts, however, distributed his few dissenting votes impartially between the two blocs; and it is clear that during the five years preceding the 1936 Term, he was independent of both the left and the right bloc—in dissent.

Hughes might dissent from time to time with the left bloc; and Roberts might do so on rare occasions; but since neither Hughes nor Roberts nor any member of the right bloc consistently joined *each other* in dissent with the left bloc, the best the left was able to do was to pick up a fourth dissenting vote in a small proportion of the cases in which the bloc was on the losing side of decisions.

95 Table 9, *supra,* p. 133, and *The Roosevelt Court,* p. 242.

The table of over-all interagreement, which takes into consideration majority (or assenting) votes as well as dissents, tells another story, however. As we have noted earlier in this chapter, dissenters and dissenting blocs lose decisions; and from the point of view of the effective exercise of power to control the decisions of the Court, it is the capacity to form majorities that counts most. The left bloc was very high in over-all interagreement, with an index of .84 (.70 or better being high for this index), which indicates that Stone, Cardozo, and Brandeis stuck together in assent as well as in dissent. The right bloc was also very high, with an index of .82. Hughes and Roberts showed consistently high-to-moderate over-all interagreement with all four members of the right bloc, while the interagreement of Hughes and Roberts with left bloc members was low. The Index of Interagreement for the right bloc plus Hughes and Roberts was a high .75, which indicates that both Hughes and Roberts should be considered to be members of the right bloc *in over-all interagreement*. In view of what we already know about the dissenting behavior of Hughes and Roberts, the inference is inescapable that both Hughes and Roberts were consistently forming majorities with the right bloc; and that the Court was dominated during the 1931-1935 terms by a six-man majority with Van Devanter and Sutherland in the middle, Hughes and Roberts arrayed to their left, and Butler and McReynolds on the extreme right wing. This was the situation as the Court entered the 1936 Term.

The Hughberts Game [96]

During the 1936 Term, the Court was divided between a three-justice liberal bloc and a four-justice conservative bloc, with Hughberts (Hughes and Roberts) in the middle. If we assume that, in the face of Roosevelt's attack upon the Court, the Chief Justice—with the support of Roberts—wished to maximize both his own authority within the Court and the degree of unanimity in the Court's decisions, while at the same time directing the Court to as liberal a course of decision as possible in order to forestall the possibility of the more drastic reforms proposed by the President, game theory can tell us how Hughberts should vote if he—I shall consider Hughes and Roberts to be a single player from now on—were to behave rationally in order to realize these objectives. A game must have a payoff which can be expressed in numerical terms, and for this purpose I have used the Shapley-Shubik empirical power index [97] in order to be able to compare the Court's actual voting behavior with the imputed utilities (*i.e.*, the payoff) postulated by the game model. Simply stated, the Shapley-Shubik index measures the extent

[96] Schubert, "The Study of Judicial Decision-Making," pp. 1022-1024. For a more detailed explanation and development of the game, see the same author's *Quantitative Analysis of Judicial Behavior*, chap. iv. Table 16 is taken from, and the accompanying discussion is based upon, pp. 208-210 of the same work.

[97] L. S. Shapley and Martin Shubik, "A Method for Evaluating the Distribution of Power in a Committee System," *American Political Science Review*, Vol. 48, pp. 791-792 (September, 1954).

TABLE 14.

Pay-off Matrix for the Hughberts Game

HUGHBERTS
(2 votes)

	+	−	
+	(3/9, 2/9, 4/9) [96] 2 (R) 1 (Bu, M) 1 (M) 1 (M)[St] 1 (Su)	(3/7, 0, 4/7) [0]	**+**
+	(3/5, 2/5, 0) [6] 1 [St, V]	(0, 1/3, 2/3) [4] 1 (H) 1 [St] 1 (R) 1 [Br, St]	**−**
−	(0, 1/3, 2/3) [5] 3 [St] 1 (Br) 1 (H, Br)[St]	(3/5, 2/5, 0) [8] 1 (M) 1 (V)[St]	**+**
−	(3/7, 0, 4/7) [0]	(3/9, 2/9, 4/9) [76] 2 (Bu, M) 1 (Bu) 1 (Br, R) 1 (M) 1 (M)[St]	**−**

THE LEFT (3 votes) — on the left; THE RIGHT (4 votes) — on the right.

Legend: The symbols + and − designate the players' strategies:
   + = voting for affirmance of the lower court's decision
   − = voting for reversal of the lower court's decision
The imputations for partitioning of the payoff among the players, according to the intersection of strategies, are given within parentheses at the top of each cell.
The number of decisions falling within each cell is given in brackets. The number of decisions, in each cell, in which there were deviations from the blocs, are itemized. Justices who defected from their respective blocs are shown in parentheses, and those who failed to participate in particular decisions are shown in brackets, according to the following key:

Br = Brandeis	H = Hughes	M = McReynolds
C = Cardozo	R = Roberts	Bu = Butler
St = Stone		Su = Sutherland
		V = Van Devanter

(Mr. Justice Cardozo did not deviate from the voting position attributed to the left bloc in any of the 195 decisions of the 1936 Term.)

TABLE 15.

Power Indices of Supreme Court Justices (1936 Term)

The Left		Hughberts		The Right	
Brandeis	.1312	Hughes	.1600	Van Devanter	.0957
Cardozo	.1264	Roberts	.1536	Sutherland	.0864
Stone	.1054			Butler	.0742
				McReynolds	.0672
Totals	.3630		.3136		.3235
Expected power:	.3333		.3333		.3333
Difference:	+ .0297		− .0197		− .0098

to which each justice shared in the power of decision, which is defined as the probability of his having been pivotal in the winning coalition.

The left bloc and the right bloc are each defined as players in the game, which is three-person and zero-sum. Hughberts has a pure strategy, which in essence requires that he form a coalition with the Left when possible, that he form a coalition with the Right when splintering or non-participation makes it impossible for him to form a winning coalition with the Left, and that he always join the coalition of the Left and the Right when the other players do not choose to adopt conflicting strategies. In fact, the voting behavior of Hughes and Roberts conforms very closely to the prescriptions of the game model [Table 14, on page 162].

In terms of the empirical payoff, the four-justice right bloc, the three-justice left bloc, and the two-justice center bloc are all approximately equal in power [as shown in Table 15].

It is easy to demonstrate that in a three-person simple majoritarian game, equality of power is imputed among the players. It is by no means a self-evident proposition, however, that among nine justices each casting a single and equal vote, two justices can be just as powerful as four justices.

It is also instructive to consider the question of side-payments in the Hughberts Game, and it is of particular interest to make an analysis of opinion assignment by Chief Justice Hughes since, as both McElwain and Frankfurter remarked, his assignment of the opinion of the Court was one of the distinguishing hallmarks of Hughes' greatness as a Chief Justice. One would suppose that the critical 1936 Term would have provided Hughes an exceptional opportunity for the exercise of his talents. It will be recalled, from earlier discussion in this chapter, that it is the custom of the Supreme Court for the Chief Justice to assign the writing of the opinion of the Court, when he is in the majority; otherwise, the senior justice in the majority does so. Since Hughes dissented only twice during the term, he assigned the majority opinion in 33 of these 35 split decisions;

and Van Devanter made the assignment in the other 2 cases, one to himself and the other to Roberts. The latter assignment is the only instance during the term in which a defector—a justice who split from his bloc in a given decision—was selected to write for the majority coalition. Opinions were assigned to individual justices, of course, but in the tabulation below (Table 16) we have combined the totals for justices according to the blocs which define the players in the Hughberts Game.

TABLE 16.

Opinion Assignment as a Form of Side Payment in the Hughberts Game

	COALITION				*Percentage of*
PLAYER	*L - HB - R*	*L - HB*	*HB - R*	*Totals*	*Total Cases*
The Left	7	4	0	11	35
Hughberts	3 [a]	8	3 [a]	14	45
The Right	2	0	4	6	20
Totals	12	12	7	31 [b]	100

[a] Includes one *per curiam* opinion, almost certainly written by Hughes.

[b] There were only 31 opinions for the 35 cases, because in two instances several cases were disposed of in a single opinion.

The pattern of Hughes's assignments is clear enough: when all three blocs combined in a near-unanimous decision, he usually assigned the opinion of the Court to a justice of the left; when Hughberts joined the left in a minimal winning coalition, he usually assigned the opinion to himself or to Roberts—the actual division was 5 to himself and 3 to Roberts; and only when Hughberts was forced to join with the right against the left did Hughes favor the right slightly in opinion assignments. On the average, justices of the left wrote 3.7 opinions each in the split decisions; those of the right wrote 1.5; and the average for Hughes and Roberts was 7.0 each. The totals certainly do not correspond to the size of the blocs—indeed, they are inversely related. But the ratios do correspond closely to the power rankings of the individual justices, as Table 17, on page 165, demonstrates.

The correlation between the ranking of the justices according to majority participation (power), and according to assignments to write for the Court, is not perfect, but it is obviously quite high; and all of the discrepancies between ranks occur within, not between, blocs. Hughes, the most powerful justice according to the index (and also, of course, the one who made the opinion assignments) personally wrote a fourth of the opinions, which decided a third of the cases, in these split decisions of the 1936 Term. It is not implausible to suggest,

TABLE 17.

Power Rankings of the Justices in Relation to Opinion Assignment in the Hughberts Game [a]

Power Rank	Justice	Power Index	Number of Opinions Written
1	Hughes	.1600	8
2	Roberts	.1536	6
5	Stone	.1054	5
4	Cardozo	.1264	4
3	Brandeis	.1312	2
7	Sutherland	.0864	2
8	Butler	.0742	2
6	Van Devanter	.0957	1
9	McReynolds	.0672	1

[a] The rank correlation coefficient (tau), for power rankings in comparison to rankings (as here) according to number of opinions written, is .86 at the 1% level of confidence.

on the basis of this evidence, that the assignment of the opinion of the Court could well have been a form of side-payment among the justices in the Hughberts Game.

A SWITCH IN TIME?

There certainly can be no doubt that the policy content of the Court's decisions changed, and changed drastically, in the 1936 Term. The questions that we raised initially, however, remain: Who switched? And why? The Hughberts Game has suggested one interpretation of the events, and one possible answer to the questions: that *both* Hughes and Roberts switched, in order to protect the institutional integrity and authority of the Supreme Court from the threatened much greater danger presented by the President's proposal to subject the Court to *external* political domination. It happens that these findings are confirmed by bloc analysis.

It will be observed in Table 18 (on page 166), which shows dissenting blocs for the 1936 Term, that the division of the Court was absolutely clear cut, with the right-bloc members dissenting only among themselves, and Hughes and Roberts dissenting only with the left bloc—never with each other. The index of cohesion for the right bloc is exceptionally high (.73), and it is very high for the left bloc alone (.60). Hughes and Roberts manifest a weak affiliation with the left bloc, and the index for all five of these justices drops to a moderate .40. Much more significant, however, are the respective levels of dissenting activity for the left bloc, Hughes and Roberts, and the right bloc, and particularly in comparison to the levels that obtained during the preceding five years (see Table 19, page 167).

TABLE 18.

Dissenting Blocs on the Hughes Court (1936 Term)[a]

1936 TERM	Stone	Cardozo	Brandeis	Hughes	Roberts	Van Devanter	Sutherland	Butler	McReynolds
Total Dissents	3	7	5	2	4	11	14	16	20
Stone		3	2	1	1				
Cardozo	3	(1)	4	2	1				
Brandeis	2	4		1	2				
Hughes	1	2	1						
Roberts	1	1	2		(2)				
Van Devanter							11	10	9
Sutherland						11	(1)	12	11
Butler						10	12	(1)	14
McReynolds						9	11	14	(6)

Total Split Decisions: 35   INDICES OF COHESION

Left bloc = .60 (very high)

Left bloc, plus Hughes and Roberts = .40 (moderate)

Right bloc = .73 (exceptionally high)

a This table has been reproduced from Pritchett, *The Roosevelt Court*, p. 34, except that the designation of blocs has been added.

Clearly, the level of dissenting activity by Hughes and Roberts is the same in 1936 as in the previous years. But the rate of dissent for members of the three-justice left bloc has been cut in half, while the members of the four-justice right bloc tripled their rate of dissent in the 1936 Term. The logical inference is that the balance of power on the Court has shifted from the right bloc (in 1931-1935) to the left bloc (in 1936). We should expect to find, therefore, that Hughes and Roberts shifted their allegiance *in assent* from the right to the left; and that instead of forming majorities with the right bloc, as they did most of the time in 1931-1935, they formed majorities in 1936 primarily with the left bloc. This is precisely what Table 20, which shows interagreement in the majority and in dissent combined, demonstrates.

Since we know that Hughes and Roberts never dissented with right-bloc members in the 1936 Term, the low indices of paired interagreement for Hughes and Roberts with justices to their right are attributable entirely to cases in which

TABLE 19.

Average Number of Dissents per Term per Bloc Member (1931-1936 Terms)[a]

| | BLOC | | |
TERMS	The Left	Hughes and Roberts	The Right
1931-1935	11.9	3.0	5.4
1936	5.0	3.0	15.2

a The computations for this table are based upon data reported by Pritchett. See Tables 9 and 18, *supra*.

Hughes and Roberts did join with the right to form majorities. We know from the Hughberts Game that in all except two such cases it was impossible for Hughes and Roberts to form a majority with the left bloc, so that the real choice they faced was joining the right bloc or going down to defeat in dissent with some portion of the left bloc. Left-bloc splintering was rare, however, and when it did happen, it was almost entirely due to Stone's illness and consequently high rate of

TABLE 20.

Interagreement in Split Decisions of the Hughes Court (1936 Term—In Percentages)[a]

	Cardozo	Stone	Brandeis	Hughes	Roberts	Van Devanter	Sutherland	Butler	McReynolds
Cardozo	—	100	90	84	71	40	32	26	13
Stone	100	—	91	91	78	39	35	26	17
Brandeis	90	91	—	83	83	45	37	30	17
Hughes	84	91	83	—	81	57	48	42	29
Roberts	71	78	83	81	—	50	42	35	23
Van Devanter	40	39	45	57	50	—	93	87	73
Sutherland	32	35	37	48	42	93	—	87	74
Butler	26	26	30	42	35	87	87	—	87
McReynolds	13	17	17	29	23	73	74	87	—

Total Opinions of the Court: 162

INDICES OF INTERAGREEMENT
Left-center bloc = .85 (very high)
Right bloc = .85 (very high)

a This table has been reproduced from Pritchett, *The Roosevelt Court*, p. 242, except that the designation of blocs has been added.

nonparticipation for the term. The Index of Interagreement does not take non-participation into account, but the high degree of over-all agreement among the members of the left bloc is evidenced by the unanimity between Cardozo and Stone and the almost as high index of .94 for the three members of the left bloc considered independently of Hughes and Roberts.

Hughes and Roberts did form in this term a bloc with the left in over-all interagreement, as the very high index of .85 for these five justices demonstrates. The index for the four-justice right bloc was an identical .85. The Court was divided, in the 1936 Term, into two highly cohesive blocs: a five-justice majority bloc of the center-left, and a four-justice minority bloc of the right. The finding supported by bloc analysis is that *both* Hughes and Roberts switched in the term of the Court-packing fight; and that by so doing, they converted a minority bloc of the left into a new and dominant—but *ad hoc* for the term—majority of the Court.

Not all observers would be prepared to accept either the interpretation or the conclusion presented above, however. Mr. Justice Frankfurter, for instance, recently has presented (below) Roberts' own explanation, in his own words, for his voting behavior in *West Coast Hotel Company* v. *Parrish,* which was one of the 35 cases that were the subject of the preceding game and bloc analysis. It is fair for the student to assume that the Frankfurter statement, and the Roberts memorandum that it includes, constitute a powerful rebuttal of the inferences supported by behavioral analysis of the Court. The student can decide for himself which kind of evidence, and which kind of approach to the comprehension of the Court's role in the Court-packing episode, appears to him to be the more persuasive.

Roberts' Switch: An Inside View [98]

It is one of the most ludicrous illustrations of the power of lazy repetition of uncritical talk that a judge with the character of Roberts should have attributed to him a change of judicial views out of deference to political considerations. One is more saddened than shocked that a high-minded and thoughtful United States Senator should assume it to be an established fact that it was by reason of "the famous switch of Mr. Justice Roberts" that legislation was constitutionally sustained after President Roosevelt's proposal for reconstructing the Court and because of it. The charge specifically relates to the fact that while Roberts was of the majority in *Morehead* v. *New York ex rel. Tipaldo,* 298 U.S. 587, decided June 1, 1936, in reaffirming *Adkins* v. *Children's Hospital,* 261 U.S. 525, and thereby invalidating the New York Minimum Wage Law, he was again with the majority in *West Coast Hotel Co.* v. *Parrish,* 300 U.S. 379, decided on March 29, 1937, overruling the

[98] This section, and the next two footnotes, are reprinted from Felix Frankfurter, "Mr. Justice Roberts," *University of Pennsylvania Law Review,* Vol. 104, pp. 313-316 (1955).

Adkins case and sustaining minimum wage legislation. Intellectual responsibility should, one would suppose, save a thoughtful man from the familiar trap of *post hoc ergo propter hoc*. Even those whose business it is to study the work of the Supreme Court have lent themselves to a charge which is refuted on the face of the Court records. It is refuted, that is, if consideration is given not only to opinions but to appropriate deductions drawn from data pertaining to the time when petitions for certiorari are granted, when cases are argued, when dispositions are, in normal course, made at conference, and when decisions are withheld because of absences and divisions on the Court.

It is time that this false charge against Roberts be dissipated by a recording of the indisputable facts. Disclosure of Court happenings not made public by the Court itself, in its opinions and orders, presents a ticklish problem. The secrecy that envelops the Court's work is not due to love of secrecy or want of responsible regard for the claims of a democratic society to know how it is governed. That the Supreme Court should not be amenable to the forces of publicity to which the Executive and the Congress are subjected is essential to the effective functioning of the Court. But the passage of time may enervate the reasons for this restriction, particularly if disclosure rests not an tittle-tattle or self-serving declarations. The more so is justification for thus lifting the veil of secrecy valid if thereby the conduct of a Justice whose intellectual morality has been impugned is vindicated.

The truth about the so-called "switch" of Roberts in connection with the *Minimum Wage* cases is that when the *Tipaldo* case was before the Court in the spring of 1936, he was prepared to overrule the *Adkins* decision. Since a majority could not be had for overruling it, he silently agreed with the Court in finding the New York statute under attack in the *Tipaldo* case not distinguishable from the statute which had been declared unconstitutional in the *Adkins* case. That such was his position an alert reader could find in the interstices of the United States Reports. It took not a little persuasion—so indifferent was Roberts to misrepresentation—to induce him to set forth what can be extracted from the Reports.[99] Here it is:

A petition for certiorari was filed in *Morehead v. Tipaldo,* 298 U.S. 587, on March 16, 1936. When the petition came to be acted upon, the Chief Justice spoke in favor of a grant, but several others spoke against it on the ground that the case was ruled by *Adkins v. Children's Hospital,* 261 U.S. 525. Justices Brandeis, Cardozo and Stone were in favor of a grant. They, with the Chief Justice, made up four votes for a grant.

When my turn came to speak I said I saw no reason to grant the writ unless the Court were prepared to re-examine and overrule the *Adkins* case. To this remark there was no response around the table, and the case was marked granted.

Both in the petition for certiorari, in the brief on the merits, and in oral

[99] Mr. Justice Roberts gave me this memorandum on November 9, 1945, after he had resigned from the bench. He left the occasion for using it to my discretion. For reasons indicated in the text, the present seems to me an appropriate time for making it public. [Frankfurter's note.]

argument, counsel for the State of New York took the position that it was unnecessary to overrule the *Adkins* case in order to sustain the position of the State of New York. It was urged that further data and experience and additional facts distinguished the case at bar from the *Adkins* case. The argument seemed to me to be disingenuous and born of timidity. I could find nothing in the record to substantiate the alleged distinction. At conference I so stated, and stated further that I was for taking the State of New York at its word. The State had not asked that the *Adkins* case be overruled but that it be distinguished. I said I was unwilling to put a decision on any such ground. The vote was five to four for affirmance, and the case was assigned to Justice Butler.

I stated to him that I would concur in any opinion which was based on the fact that the State had not asked us to re-examine or overrule *Adkins* and that, as we found no material difference in the facts of the two cases, we should therefore follow the *Adkins* case. The case was originally so written by Justice Butler, but after a dissent had been circulated he added matter to his opinion, seeking to sustain the *Adkins* case in principle. My proper course would have been to concur specially on the narrow ground I had taken. I did not do so. But at conference in the Court I said that I did not propose to review and re-examine the *Adkins* case until a case should come to the Court requiring that this should be done.

August 17, 1936, an appeal was filed in *West Coast Hotels* [sic] *Company v. Parrish*, 300 U.S. 379. The Court as usual met to consider applications in the week of Monday, October 5, 1936, and concluded its work by Saturday, October 10. During the conferences the jurisdictional statement in the *Parrish* case was considered and the question arose whether the appeal should be dismissed [100] on the authority of *Adkins* and *Morehead*. Four of those who had voted in the majority in the *Morehead* case voted to dismiss the appeal in the *Parrish* case. I stated that I would vote for the notation of probable jurisdiction. I am not sure that I gave my reason, but it was that in the appeal in the *Parrish* case the authority of *Adkins* was definitely assailed and the Court was asked to reconsider and overrule it. Thus, for the first time, I was confronted with the necessity of facing the soundness of the *Adkins* case. Those who were in the majority in the *Morehead* case expressed some surprise at my vote, and I heard one of the brethren ask another, "What is the matter with Roberts?"

Justice Stone was taken ill about October 14. The case was argued December 16 and 17, 1936, in the absence of Justice Stone, who at that time was lying in a comatose condition at his home. It came on for consideration at the conference on December 19. I voted for an affirmance. There were three other such votes, those of the Chief Justice, Justice Brandeis, and Justice Cardozo. The other four voted for a reversal.

If a decision had then been announced, the case would have been affirmed by a divided Court. It was thought that this would be an unfortunate outcome, as everyone on the Court knew Justice Stone's views. The case was, therefore, laid over for further consideration when Justice Stone should be able to participate. Justice Stone was convalescent during January and returned to the sessions of the Court on February 1, 1937. I believe that the *Parrish* case was

[100] Evidently he meant should be reversed summarily, since the Washington Supreme Court had sustained the status. [Frankfurter's note.]

taken up at the conference on February 6, 1937,[101] and Justice Stone then voted for affirmance. This made it possible to assign the case for an opinion, which was done. The decision affirming the lower court was announced March 29, 1937.

These facts make it evident that no action taken by the President in the interim had any causal relation to my action in the *Parrish* case.

More needs to be said for Roberts than he cared to say for himself. As a matter of history it is regrettable that Roberts' unconcern for his own record led him to abstain from stating his position. The occasions are not infrequent when the disfavor of separate opinions, on the part of the bar and to the extent that it prevails within the Court, should not be heeded. Such a situation was certainly presented when special circumstances made Roberts agree with a result but basically disagree with the opinion which announced it.

The crucial factor in the whole episode was the absence of Mr. Justice Stone from the bench, on account of illness, from October 14, 1936, to February 1, 1937. 299 U.S. at iii.

[101] This was the day *after* President Roosevelt submitted his Court-packing message to Congress.

II]

THE SEPARATED
POWERS

M ANY STUDENTS are preconditioned, by courses in American government or otherwise, to identify "judicial review" with decisions of the Supreme Court declaring acts of Congress to be unconstitutional. Moreover, there appears to be a widely entertained misapprehension that the "invalidation" of national statutes is the Court's major, if not its exclusive, function and preoccupation. Certainly such a notion is false by any conceivable criterion of quantitative measurement.

There have been only eighty-two cases in which the Supreme Court has declared acts of Congress, in whole or in part, to be unconstitutional.[1] During a total of ninety-nine years (1789-1864 and 1937-1959) which includes both the early and the most recent constitutional practice, the Court has invalidated federal statutes only once every dozen years or so, on the average. Or, to put it differently, during the past generation, approximately one out of every seven thousand cases docketed by the Court, and about one out of every four hundred in which oral argument is held and a formal decision announced, results in an exercise of judicial review adverse to an act of Congress.

Since 1936, the Court has invalidated executive orders and proclamations of the President in five decisions;[2] and there were exactly a dozen such cases from 1790 to 1936,[3] or a total of seventeen in all. In other words, the combined total of cases in which the Supreme Court has exercised judicial review adversely to either acts of the Congress or of the President, throughout the one hundred and seventy years since the establishment of the Supreme Court, has been less than a hundred.

The extent to which the Court has exercised judicial review *favorably* to presidential and congressional acts—that is, the number of decisions in which the

[1] In Wilfred C. Gilbert, *Provisions of Federal Law Held Unconstitutional by the Supreme Court of the United States* (Washington: G.P.O., 1936), a total of 76 cases are listed. Since this compilation, there have been six additional decisions through the 1958 Term of the Court: *Tot* v. *United States*, 319 U.S. 463 (1943); *United States* v. *Lovett*, 328 U.S. 303 (1946); *United States* v. *Cardiff*, 344 U.S. 174 (1952); *Toth* v. *Quarles*, 350 U.S. 11 (1955); *Reid* v. *Covert*, 354 U.S. 1 (1957); and *Trop* v. *Dulles*, 356 U.S. 86 (1958).

[2] *Duncan* v. *Kahanamoku*, 327 U.S. 304 (1946); *United States* ex rel. *Hirshberg* v. *Cooke*, 336 U.S. 210 (1949); *Youngstown Sheet and Tube Co.* v. *Sawyer*, 343 U.S. 579 (1952); *Cole* v. *Young*, 351 U.S. 536 (1956); and *Wiener* v. *United States*, 357 U.S. 349 (1958).

[3] Eleven decisions of the Supreme Court are listed in Appendix A to Glendon A. Schubert, *The Presidency in the Courts* (Minneapolis: University of Minnesota, 1957), to which should be added *Rathbun (Humphrey's Executor)* v. *United States*, 295 U.S. 602 (1935).

Court has ruled that Congress and the President have acted within the scope of their respective constitutional powers—is unknown; but without question, such a figure is many times greater than the ninety-nine adverse decisions that we have noted above.

Of course, it is true that such quantitative indices tell nothing of the relative importance of particular cases in which the Court undertakes to exercise a veto power over the decisions of the two "political" departments of the national government, irrespective of whether, to borrow Theodore Roosevelt's phrase, the Court "comes up heads or tails." The Dred Scott case [4] was a catalyst which helped to bring on the Civil War. On the other hand, most lawyers and political scientists (to say nothing of lay citizens) have never even heard of the Cardiff decision of 1952. The point is that decisions of the Court in which the justices judicially review decisions of the Executive and the Legislative departments constitute a very small part of the work of the Court; such decisions may, but do not necessarily, have important political significance and implications; and it is most misleading to overemphasize "judicial review," as is frequently done, as though this were the most important type of interrelationship between the Judicial department and the Legislative and Executive departments.

Particularly since 1937, there can hardly be any question that the Court's decisions in the civil liberties area, and particularly in their implications for the federal equilibrium between the nation and the states, have been much more important than the Court's "separation of powers" decisions. Moreover, constitutional interpretation (whether relating to the separation of powers, federalism, or civil liberties) is of lesser significance in the Court's total policy-making activity than two other types of decisions that the Court makes. Increasingly, the Court's work in "interpreting" federal statutes (which we discuss briefly in Chapter 4), and particularly its supervision of the decision-making of the lower federal courts —which, in turn, oversee administrative decision-making by federal agencies—in the area known as administrative law (which we do not discuss in this book), are each assuming greater significance than constitutional interpretation in the work of the Court. At least, this is so if we are to measure the importance of what the Court does in terms of its impact upon that composite of behaviors and activities that might be called the American way of life.

In the next three chapters, however, our concern is with an examination of the interrelationships of policy-making by the Supreme Court, the Congress, and the President. This involves an analysis of the circumstances under which the Court does, and also of those under which it does not, undertake to veto policy decisions of the other branches of the government. The reciprocal behavior of the Congress and of the President, in seeking to avoid (or to provoke) or to overcome (or to defend) particular decisions by the Court, is of course a factor that the justices must take into consideration in choosing between activism and

[4] *Dred Scott* v. *Sandford,* 19 How. 393 (1857).

restraint. This requires that we investigate not only the effect of judicial policy-making upon the Congress and the Presidency; we must also investigate the effect of legislative and executive policy-making upon the Supreme Court. There is also the question of the sharing of policy-making authority, by Congress and the Court, over the decision-making of lower federal courts.

4]

Judicial Policy-Making

A T THE close of Taft's administration as Chief Justice, an outspoken
liberal Senator, George Norris of Nebraska, remarked: [1]

> We have a legislative body, called the House of Representatives, of over
> 400 men. We have another legislative body, called the Senate, of less than
> a hundred men. We have, in reality, another legislative body, called the
> Supreme Court, of 9 men; and they are more powerful than all the others
> put together.

The purpose of this chapter is to examine the accuracy and the implications of
this charge.

Every American schoolboy learns at an early age that one of the most
fundamental—perhaps the most basic—postulate of our Constitution is the principle of the separation of powers. Reduced to its simplest terms, this means that the
"representatives of the people," in Congress assembled, make the laws; that the
President, who is the linear heir to the legal powers of the English crown—after
the Glorious Revolution, of course—is the immediate overseer of the Executive
Branch, under his obligation to see that the laws are faithfully executed; and
that the courts sit to protect the civil rights and liberties of the people; all to
the end that the government of the United States shall remain "a government of
laws, and not of men." Of course, there must be some lubricant to keep the
machinery of government running smoothly; and in the ultimate wisdom that

[1] *Congressional Record,* 71 Cong., 2d Sess.,
Vol. 72, Part 4, p. 3566 (February 13, 1930),
quoted in Alpheus T. Mason, *The Supreme*
Court from Taft to Warren (Baton Rouge:
Louisiana State University Press, 1958), p. 34.

conceived this beneficent scheme, the Founding Fathers made provision for certain "checks and balances," of which the power of judicial review was one. To those who cherish a deep and abiding faith in such a simple and yet majestic constitutional world, there is perhaps only one other creative act of comparable dimensions, motivated by a similar depth of vision of Man, living in Eden. But even Paradise was imperfect until God created woman; and the work of the Founding Fathers was incomplete until the Supreme Court discovered that it had the power to declare unconstitutional acts of the Congress and of the President. The rib of the Constitution was *Marbury* v. *Madison*.

JUDICIAL ACTIVISM

John Marshall's Fait Accompli

By any possible criterion, the most important decision that the Supreme Court has ever made was one of its earliest decisions. *Marbury* v. *Madison* was published in the first volume of Cranch, which is the fourth volume of the reports of the cases decided by the Court.[2] The decision was announced in 1803, only five years after the death of George Washington, and less than four years after the Eighteenth Century had passed into history. The principals in the case included a man who is on anybody's list of great Presidents: Thomas Jefferson; and the man who was to succeed Mr. Jefferson as President, one of our greatest Secretaries of State, and one who is known to history as the "Father of the Constitution," James Madison. Their antagonist, in fact though not in law, was not William Marbury, who was an obscure Federalist politician. The real antagonist of Jefferson and Madison was a worthy foe, the man who had been Madison's predecessor as Secretary of State, and the one upon whom has come to rest the consensual judgment of being "the Great Chief Justice," John Marshall. It is no exaggeration to say that these men were giants in their own day, as they would doubtless be in ours. In sharp contradistinction from most of the cases that we shall study in this book, *Marbury* v. *Madison* involved a battle of titans; and it is also an example of constitutional lawmaking at its very highest level of both doctrinal and political significance.

In the closing days of the Adams administration, a lameduck Congress, which had been repudiated at the polls almost four months earlier, bulled through an act to reorganize and to expand the federal judiciary. Technically, this legislation was an amendment to the Judiciary Act of 1789. Many of its provisions were highly desirable; for instance, one section of the statute would have established a group of permanent circuit courts, thus eliminating the circuit-riding responsibilities of Supreme Court justices. The subsequent repeal of this

---

2 For an explanation of how decisions of the Supreme Court are reported, see Appen-   dix A.

provision by the incoming Republican Congress resulted in a delay of almost a century in the establishment of a permanent system of intermediate-level federal appellate courts, and in the elimination of circuit-riding. Neither the enactment nor the repeal of this section of the 1801 statute were motivated by considerations of efficient judicial administration, however. The purpose of the circuit-court provision was to expand the number of federal judgeships; and all of these positions carried life tenure *except* the ones for the justices of the peace for the District of Columbia—which were authorized by a separate act of February 27, 1801, organizing a government for the new District. Having lost control over the "politically responsible" branches of the government—the Presidency and the Congress—the Federalists were determined to pack the federal judiciary, from which no turbulent popular majorities could dislodge the party while it rebuilt for the future and at the same time clung to a beachhead from which it could protect the values of the past.

The deserving Federalists who were chosen to fill these offices were the "Midnight Judges," so called because, according to tradition, President Adams stayed up long beyond the witching hour on the night of March 3, 1801—his last night in office—signing their commissions of appointment. His Secretary of State failed to complete the delivery of all these commissions before the Jefferson administration took over the reins of government on the following day; and it is certainly understandable that the commissions for a group of District of Columbia justices of the peace—at a time when the District was the nation's capital largely on paper only—should have been neglected in favor of the more important judgeships which carried life tenure. So some of the commissions were left behind in the office of outgoing Secretary of State John Marshall, where they presumably were found by the incoming Secretary, James Madison.

Notwithstanding the language in the opinion of the Court in this case, it is evident that the traditions of judicial independence and disinterestedness which we take for granted today were not the political norms of the eighteenth century. It would be unthinkable, in our times, for a Chief Justice of the Supreme Court to serve simultaneously as the Secretary of State, thus combining in one man the highest office in the Judicial Branch, and the second highest office in the Executive Branch. Yet, this was precisely John Marshall's status at the time of the events that led on to the Marbury case. It is equally unthinkable today for a justice of the Supreme Court to participate in the decision of a case in which he, personally, has a direct interest, having been a principal actor in the events leading to the dispute—to say nothing of his having been the protagonist. Yet, John Marshall delivered the opinion of the Court in this case in which he was the former Secretary of State who had been, at least initially, remiss in having failed to deliver to the claimant the commission of office that was the nominal object of the suit.

As we shall discuss presently, one of the basic rules of judicial restraint which the Court says that it follows is to decide jurisdictional questions *first*, and only if the Court finds that it "has" jurisdiction (and, as we should add today, only if the Court deems it wise to exercise jurisdiction) does it become necessary to reach the substantive questions, viz., to decide the case "on the merits." In reading the case below, the student should ask himself whether this is what Marshall did.

We shall also consider, at a later point in this chapter, the supposedly vital distinction between what is called the *"ratio decidendi"* and "obiter dicta" in an opinion of the Court. The first consists of the holding of the Court on points that are "necessary" for the Court to reach its decision; the latter, usually referred to by the shorthand term "dicta," consist of "extraneous" discussion of other points, relating to hypothetical fact situations or points *unnecessary* for the Court to have purported to rule upon in order to reach its decision. (We might observe, in passing, that in these terms, obiter dicta are by definition gratuitous judicial lawmaking.) Which would you consider Marshall's discussion below, of the Executive power of appointment and removal, to be—*ratio decidendi* or obiter dicta? (Jefferson referred to the opinion in this case as Marshall's "obiter dissertation.") Marshall's discussion of the appointment and removal power raises questions that we shall consider at some length in Chapter 6; and it bears, of course, upon the discussion of appointment and removal of the justices themselves in Chapter 2, *supra*.

A second major policy issue in the case relates to the legislative power to control the jurisdiction of the federal courts, which we shall consider at greater length in Chapter 5. Although Marshall interprets the intent of Congress, in the section of the Judiciary Act of 1789 which authorized the Supreme Court to issue the writ of mandamus, as being an attempt to augment the *original* jurisdiction of the Court, is this the only possible, or the most reasonable, interpretation of the statutory language? It was traditional for the English Court of King's Bench, which surely was the model from which the statute borrowed on this point, to issue various so-called extraordinary writs (including the writ of mandamus) as an aid to the enforcement of jurisdiction otherwise acquired. Could the Supreme Court, in Marbury's case, have avoided the constitutional issue (i.e., whether the Court had power to declare unconstitutional an act of Congress) simply by ruling that Congress had intended that the Court have authority to issue writs of mandamus only in appellate jurisdiction? Such a ruling would have achieved the same result for Marbury as the one that actually ensued: the Court would have ruled that Marbury asked the Court to do something that it had no power to do, and the case would have been dismissed for want of jurisdiction. After all, the Judiciary Act of 1789 was passed by the first session of the first Congress; and many of the members of the Federalist majority who voted for the bill were among the so-called Founding Fathers. James Madison, not John Marshall, was a member of this group. Presumably, such men would have been acutely cognizant of the "intent of the framers" of the judiciary article; and presumably, they would not have sought to usurp power in passing the act establishing the Supreme Court, nor would President Washington have given his approval to such an act.

Of course, if Marshall had decided the question of jurisdiction first, there could have been no sermon on the failure of Jefferson and Madison to live up to their constitutional oaths to execute faithfully the laws of the land. And if the Court had exercised judicial restraint in making the jurisdictional decision, and in interpreting the intent of Congress in the Judiciary Act of 1789, there would have been no occasion for the Court to stake out a claim of its right and duty to exercise the power of judicial review over acts of the other two branches of the government. But however legally correct such an approach might have been, it would have been pointless politically—and it cannot be overemphasized this was a political decision in a political case.

It ought also to be recognized that if the Court had ordered the writ of mandamus to issue, as was generally anticipated at the time, it is almost certain that the writ would have been ignored, and *Marbury* v. *Madison* would stand as a great precedent for the impotence of the Court to enforce its judgments against the will of a determined Executive.[3] Such a course of action would have had the result of strengthening the Presidency and weakening the Supreme Court as a political force. Marshall's solution to this dilemma was a stroke of political genius. He contrived a way out whereby the Court could both have its cake and eat it too, and all with no possible risk of having the judgment of the Court ignored. At one fell swoop, Marshall rejected the claims in behalf of Executive and Legislative power, and asserted in classic form the justification of ultimate judicial supremacy over the political branches of the government, casting the Supreme Court in the role of the protector of the legal rights of citizens in the face of Executive usurpation and tyranny.

MARBURY v. MADISON

1 Cranch 137 (February 24, 1803)

Ruling on a motion for an original writ of mandamus.

Motion dismissed.

6-0

Marshall, C.J.	('+')
Cushing	(+)
Paterson	(+)
Chase	(+)
Washington	(+)
Moore	(+)

Secretary of State James Madison refused, pursuant to the orders of President Thomas Jefferson, to surrender upon the demand of William Marbury and several others certain commissions of appointment to office as justice of the peace in the District of Columbia. These commissions had been signed by John Adams (then President), and John Marshall (then

[3] Cf. Jefferson's defeat of Marshall in the trial of Aaron Burr, in the federal circuit court for Virginia, over which the Chief Justice presided. *United States* v. *Burr*, 25 Fed. Cas. 187 (1807), No. 14,694. See also *Ex parte Bollman*, 4 Cranch 75 (1807), and the Appendix, notes (A) and (B) to volume 4 Cranch.

Secretary of State) had caused to be af-
fixed to them the Great Seal of the United
States. Upon Madison's refusal to deliver
the commissions, counsel for Marbury pe-
titioned the Supreme Court to issue a writ
of mandamus, ordering Secretary Madi-
son to transmit copies of the commissions
to the claimants.

CHIEF JUSTICE MARSHALL delivered the
opinion of the Court.

At the last term on the affidavits then
read and filed with the clerk, a rule
was granted in this case, requiring the
secretary of state to show cause why a
mandamus should not issue, directing
him to deliver to William Marbury his
commission as a justice of the peace for
the county of Washington, in the District
of Columbia.

No cause has been shown, and the
present motion is for a *mandamus*. . . .

In the order in which the court has
viewed this subject, the following questions have been considered and decided.

1st. Has the applicant a right to the
commission he demands?

2dly. If he has a right, and that right
has been violated, do the laws of his
country afford him a remedy?

3dly. If they do afford him a remedy,
is it a *mandamus* issuing from this court?

The first object of inquiry is,

1st. Has the applicant a right to the
commission he demands?

His right originates in an act of congress passed in February, 1801, concerning the District of Columbia.

After dividing the district into two
counties, the 11th section of this law
enacts, "that there shall be appointed in
and for each of the said counties, such
number of discreet persons to be justices
of the peace as the President of the
United States shall, from time to time
think expedient, to continue in office for
five years.

It appears, from the affidavits, that
in compliance with this law, a commission

for William Marbury, as a justice of
peace for the county of Washington, was
signed by John Adams, then President
of the United States, after which the seal
of the United States was affixed to it;
but the commission has never reached
the person for whom it was made out. . . .

The last act to be done by the president is the signature of the commission.
He has then acted on the advice and
consent of the senate to his own nomination. The time for deliberation has then
passed. He has decided. His judgment,
on the advice and consent of the senate
concurring with his nomination, has been
made, and the officer is appointed. . . .

The commission being signed, the subsequent duty of the secretary of state is prescribed by law, and not to be guided by
the will of the president. He is to affix
the seal of the United States to the commission, and is to record it.

This is not a proceeding which may be
varied, if the judgment of the executive
shall suggest one more eligible; but is a
precise course accurately marked out by
law, and is to be strictly pursued. It is
the duty of the secretary of state to conform to the law, and in this he is an
officer of the United States, bound to obey
the laws. He acts, in this respect, as has
been very properly stated at the bar,
under the authority of law, and not by
the instructions of the president. It is a
ministerial act which the law enjoins on a
particular officer for a particular purpose. . . .

It is, therefore, decidedly the opinion
of the court, that when a commission has
been signed by the president, the appointment is made; and that the commission
is complete when the seal of the United
States has been affixed to it by the secretary of state.

Where an officer is removable at the
will of the executive, the circumstance
which completes his appointment is of no
concern, because the act is at any time
revocable; and the commission may be
arrested, if still in the office. But when

the officer is not removable at the will of the executive, the appointment is not revocable, and cannot be annulled. It has conferred legal rights which cannot be resumed.

The discretion of the executive is to be exercised until the appointment has been made. But having once made the appointment, his power over the office is terminated in all cases where by law the officer is not revocable by him. The right to the office is then in the person appointed, and he has the absolute, unconditional power of accepting or rejecting it.

Mr. Marbury, then, since his commission was signed by the president and sealed by the secretary of state, was appointed; and as the law creating the office, gave the officer a right to hold for five years, independent of the executive, the appointment was not revocable, but vested in the officer legal rights, which are protected by the laws of his country.

To withhold his commission, therefore, is an act deemed by the court not warranted by law, but violative of a vested legal right.

This brings us to the second inquiry, which is,

2dly. If he has a right, and that right has been violated, do the laws of his country afford him a remedy?

The very essence of civil liberty certainly consists in the right of every individual to claim the protection of the laws whenever he receives an injury. One of the first duties of government is to afford that protection. . . .

The government of the United States has been emphatically termed a government of laws, and not of men. It will certainly cease to deserve this high appellation if the laws furnish no remedy for the violation of a vested legal right. . . .

By the constitution of the United States, the president is invested with certain important political powers, in the exercise of which he is to use his own discretion, and is accountable only to his country in

his political character, and to his own conscience. To aid him in the performance of these duties, he is authorized to appoint certain officers, who act by his authority and in conformity with his orders.

In such cases their acts are his acts; and whatever opinion may be entertained of the manner in which executive discretion may be used, still there exists, and can exist, no power to control that discretion. The subjects are political. They respect the nation, not individual rights, and being intrusted to the executive, the decision of the executive is conclusive. The application of this remark will be perceived by adverting to the act of congress for establishing the department of foreign affairs. This officer, as his duties were prescribed by that act, is to conform precisely to the will of the president. He is the mere organ by whom that will is communicated. The acts of such an officer, as an officer, can never be examinable by the courts.

But when the legislature proceeds to impose on that officer other duties; when he is directed peremptorily to perform certain acts; when the rights of individuals are dependent on the performance of those acts; he is so far the officer of the law; is amenable to the laws for his conduct; and cannot at his discretion sport away the vested rights of others.

The conclusion from this reasoning is, that where the heads of departments are the political or confidential agents of the executive, merely to execute the will of the president, or rather to act in cases in which the executive possesses a constitutional or legal discretion, nothing can be more perfectly clear than that their acts are only politically examinable. But where a specific duty is assigned by law, and individual rights depend upon the performance of that duty, it seems equally clear that the individual who considers himself injured, has a right to resort to the laws of his country for a remedy.

If this be the rule, let us inquire how

it applies to the case under the consideration of the court.

The power of nominating to the senate, and the power of appointing the person nominated, are political powers, to be exercised by the president according to his own discretion. When he has made an appointment, he has exercised his whole power, and his discretion has been completely applied to the case. If by law the officer be removable at the will of the president, then a new appointment may be immediately made, and the rights of the officer are terminated. But as a fact which has existed cannot be made never to have existed, the appointment cannot be annihilated; and, consequently, if the officer is by law not removable at the will of the president, the rights he has acquired are protected by the law, and are not resumable by the president. They cannot be extinguished by executive authority, and he has the privilege of asserting them in like manner as if they had been derived from any other source.

The question, whether a right has vested or not, is, in its nature, judicial, and must be tried by the judicial authority. . . .

It is then the opinion of the court,

1st. That by signing the commission of Mr. Marbury, the President of the United States appointed him a justice of peace for the county of Washington, in the District of Columbia; and that the seal of the United States, affixed thereto by the secretary of state, is conclusive testimony of the verity of the signature, and of the completion of the appointment; and that the appointment conferred on him a legal right to the office for the space of five years.

2dly. That, having this legal title to the office, he has a consequent right to the commission; a refusal to deliver which is a plain violation of that right, for which the laws of his country afford him a remedy.

It remains to be inquired whether,

3dly. He is entitled to the remedy for which he applies. This depends on,

1st. The nature of the writ applied for; and,

2dly. The power of this court.

1st. The nature of the writ.

Blackstone, in the 3d volume of his Commentaries, page 110, defines a *mandamus* to be "a command issuing in the king's name from the court of king's bench, and directed to any person, corporation, or inferior court of judicature within the king's dominions, requiring them to do some particular thing therein specified, which appertains to their office and duty, and which the court of king's bench has previously determined, or at least supposes, to be consonant to right and justice." . . .

[But] to render the *mandamus* a proper remedy, the officer to whom it is to be directed, must be one to whom, on legal principles, such writ may be directed; and the person applying for it must be without any other specific and legal remedy.

1st. With respect to the officer to whom it would be directed. The intimate political relation subsisting between the President of the United States and the heads of departments, necessarily renders any legal investigation of the acts of one of those high officers peculiarly irksome, as well as delicate; and excites some hesitation with respect to the propriety of entering into such investigation. Impressions are often received without much reflection or examination, and it is not wonderful that in such a case as this, the assertion, by an individual, of his legal claims in a court of justice, to which claims it is the duty of that court to attend, should at first view be considered by some as an attempt to intrude into the cabinet, and to intermeddle with the prerogatives of the executive.

It is scarcely necessary for the court to disclaim all pretensions to such a jurisdiction. An extravagance, so absurd and excessive, could not have been entertained for a moment. The province of the court is, solely, to decide on the rights of individuals, not to inquire how the executive, or executive officers, perform duties in which they have a discretion. Questions in their nature political, or which are, by the constitution and laws, submitted to the executive, can never be made in this court.

But, if this be not such a question; if, so far from being an intrusion into the secrets of the cabinet, it respects a paper which, according to law, is upon record, and to a copy of which the law gives a right, on the payment of ten cents; if it be no intermeddling with a subject over which the executive can be considered as having exercised any control; what is there in the exalted station of the officer which shall bar a citizen from asserting, in a court of justice, his legal rights, or shall forbid a court to listen to the claim, or to issue a *mandamus,* directing the performance of a duty, not depending on executive discretion, but on particular acts of congress, and the general principles of law?

If one of the heads of departments commits any illegal act, under color of his office, by which an individual sustains an injury, it cannot be pretended that his office alone exempts him from being sued in the ordinary mode of proceeding, and being compelled to obey the judgment of the law. How, then, can his office exempt him from this particular mode of deciding on the legality of his conduct, if the case be such a case as would, were any other individual the party complained of, authorize the process?

It is not by the office of the person to whom the writ is directed, but the nature of the thing to be done, that the propriety or impropriety of issuing a *mandamus* is to be determined. Where the head of a department acts in a case, in which executive discretion is to be exercised; in which he is the mere organ of executive will; it is again repeated, that any application to a court to control, in any respect, his conduct, would be rejected without hesitation.

But where he is directed by law to do a certain act affecting the absolute rights of individuals, in the performance of which he is not placed under the particular direction of the president, and the performance of which the president cannot lawfully forbid, and therefore is never presumed to have forbidden; as for example, to record a commission, or a patent for land, which has received all the legal solemnities; or to give a copy of such record; in such cases, it is not perceived on what ground the courts of the country are further excused from the duty of giving judgment that right be done to an injured individual, than if the same services were to be performed by a person not the head of a department. . . .

This, then, is a plain case for a *mandamus,* either to deliver the commission, or a copy of it from the record; and it only remains to be inquired,

Whether it can issue from this court.

The act to establish the judicial courts of the United States authorizes the supreme court "to issue writs of *mandamus,* in cases warranted by the principles and usages of law, to any courts appointed, or persons holding office, under the authority of the United States."

The secretary of state, being a person holding an office under the authority of the United States, is precisely within the letter of the description; and if this court is not authorized to issue a writ of *mandamus* to such an officer, it must be because the law is unconstitutional, and therefore absolutely incapable of conferring the authority, and assigning the duties which its words purport to confer and assign.

The constitution vests the whole judicial power of the United States in one supreme court, and such inferior courts as congress shall, from time to time, ordain and establish. This power is expressly extended to all cases arising under the laws of the United States; and consequently, in some form may be exercised over the present case, because the right claimed is given by a law of the United States.

In the distribution of this power it is declared that "the supreme court shall have original jurisdiction in all cases affecting ambassadors, other public ministers and consuls, and those in which a State shall be a party. In all other cases, the supreme court shall have appellate jurisdiction."

It has been insisted, at the bar, that as the original grant of jurisdiction, to the supreme and inferior courts, is general, and the clause assigning original jurisdiction to the supreme court, contains in negative or restrictive words, the power remains to the legislature to assign original jurisdiction to that court in other cases than those specified in the article which has been recited; provided those cases belong to the judicial power of the United States.

If it had been intended to leave it in the discretion of the legislature to apportion the judicial power between the supreme and inferior courts according to the will of that body, it would certainly have been useless to have proceeded further than to have defined the judicial power, and the tribunals in which it should be vested. The subsequent part of the section is mere surplusage, is entirely without meaning, if such is to be the construction. If congress remains at liberty to give this court appellate jurisdiction, where the constitution has declared their jurisdiction shall be original; and original jurisdiction where the constitution has declared it shall be appellate; the distribution of jurisdiction, made in the constitution, is form without substance. . . .

It cannot be presumed that any clause in the constitution is intended to be without effect; and, therefore, such a construction is inadmissible, unless the words require it. . . .

When an instrument organizing fundamentally a judicial system, divides it into one supreme, and so many inferior courts as the legislature may ordain and establish; then enumerates its powers, and proceeds so far to distribute them, as to define the jurisdiction of the supreme court by declaring the cases in which it shall take original jurisdiction, and that in others it shall take appellate jurisdiction; the plain import of the words seems to be, that in one class of cases its jurisdiction is original and not appellate; in the other it is appellate, and not original. If any other construction would render the clause inoperative, that is an additional reason for rejecting such other construction, and for adhering to their obvious meaning.

To enable this court, then, to issue a *mandamus*, it must be shown to be an exercise of appellate jurisdiction, or to be necessary to enable them to exercise appellate jurisdiction.

It has been stated at the bar that the appellate jurisdiction may be exercised in a variety of forms, and that if it be the will of the legislature that a *mandamus* should be used for that purpose, that will must be obeyed. This is true, yet the jurisdiction must be appellate, not original.

It is the essential criterion of appellate jurisdiction, that it revises and corrects the proceedings in a cause already instituted, and does not create that cause. Although, therefore, a *mandamus* may be directed to courts, yet to issue such a writ to an officer for the delivery of a paper, is in effect the same as to sustain an original action for that paper, and, therefore, seems not to belong to appellate, but to original jurisdiction. Neither is it necessary in such a case as this, to enable the court to exercise its appellate jurisdiction.

The authority, therefore, given to the supreme court, by the act establishing the judicial courts of the United States, to issue writs of *mandamus* to public officers, appears not to be warranted by the constitution; and it becomes necessary to inquire whether a jurisdiction so conferred can be exercised.

The question, whether an act repugnant

to the constitution can become the law of the land, is a question deeply interesting to the United States; but, happily, not of an intricacy proportioned to its interest. It seems only necessary to recognize certain principles, supposed to have been long and well established, to decide it.

That the people have an original right to establish, for their future government, such principles as, in their opinion, shall most conduce to their own happiness, is the basis on which the whole American fabric has been erected. The exercise of this original right is a very great exertion; nor can it nor ought it to be frequently repeated. The principles, therefore, so established, are deemed fundamental. And as the authority from which they proceed is supreme, and can seldom act, they are designed to be permanent.

This original and supreme will organizes the government, and assigns to different departments their respective powers. It may either stop here, or establish certain limits not to be transcended by those departments.

The government of the United States is of the latter description. The powers of the legislature are defined and limited; and that those limits may not be mistaken, or forgotten, the constitution is written. To what purpose are powers limited, and to what purpose is that limitation committed to writing, if these limits may, at any time, be passed by those intended to be restrained? The distinction between a government with limited and unlimited powers is abolished, if those limits do not confine the persons on whom they are imposed, and if acts prohibited and acts allowed, are of equal obligation. It is a proposition too plain to be contested, that the constitution controls any legislative act repugnant to it; or, that the legislature may alter the constitution by an ordinary act.

Between these alternatives there is no middle ground. The constitution is either a superior paramount law, unchangeable by ordinary means, or it is on a level with ordinary legislative acts, and, like other acts, is alterable when the legislature shall please to alter it.

If the former part of the alternative be true, then a legislative act contrary to the constitution, is not law; if the latter part be true, then written constitutions are absurd attempts, on the part of the people, to limit a power in its own nature illimitable.

Certainly all those who have framed written constitutions contemplate them as forming the fundamental and paramount law of the nation, and, consequently, the theory of every such government must be, that an act of the legislature, repugnant to the constitution, is void.

This theory is essentially attached to a written constitution, and is consequently to be considered, by this court, as one of the fundamental principles of our society. It is not, therefore, to be lost sight of in the further consideration of this subject.

If an act of the legislature, repugnant to the constitution, is void, does it, notwithstanding its invalidity, bind the courts, and oblige them to give it effect? Or, in other words, though it be not law, does it constitute a rule as operative as if it was a law? This would be to overthrow in fact what was established in theory; and would seem, at first view, an absurdity too gross to be insisted on. It shall, however, receive a more attentive consideration.

It is emphatically the province and duty of the judicial department to say what the law is. Those who apply the rule to particular cases, must of necessity expound and interpret that rule. If two laws conflict with each other, the courts must decide on the operation of each.

So if a law be in opposition to the constitution; if both the law and the constitution apply to a particular case, so that the court must either decide that case conformably to the law, disregarding the constitution, or conformably to the constitution, disregarding the law, the court must determine which of these conflicting rules governs the case. This is of the very essence of judicial duty.

If, then, the courts are to regard the constitution, and the constitution is superior to any ordinary act of the legislature, the constitution, and not such ordinary act, must govern the case to which they both apply.

. . . It is apparent that the framers of the constitution contemplated that instrument as a rule for the government of courts, as well as of the legislature.

Why otherwise does it direct the judges to take an oath to support it? This oath certainly applies in an especial manner to their conduct in their official character. How immoral to impose it on them, if they were to be used as the instruments, and the knowing instruments, for violating what they swear to support!

The oath of office, too, imposed by the legislature, is completely demonstrative of the legislative opinion on this subject. It is in these words: "I do solemnly swear that I will administer justice without respect to persons, and do equal right to the poor and to the rich; and that I will faithfully and impartially discharge all the duties incumbent on me as   , according to the best of my abilities and understanding, agreeably to the constitution and laws of the United States."

Why does a judge swear to discharge his duties agreeably to the constitution of the United States, if that constitution forms no rule for his government—if it is closed upon him, and cannot be inspected by him?

If such be the real state of things, this is worse than solemn mockery. To prescribe, or to take this oath, becomes equally a crime.

It is also not entirely unworthy of observation, that in declaring what shall be the supreme law of the land, the constitution itself is first mentioned; and not the laws of the United States generally, but those only which shall be made in pursuance of the constitution, have that rank.

Thus, the particular phraseology of the constitution of the United States confirms and strengthens the principle, supposed to be essential to all written constitutions, that a law repugnant to the constitution is void; and that courts, as well as other departments, are bound by that instrument.

The rule must be discharged.

The Theory and Practice of Judicial Review

"Judicial review," in the technical sense, takes place whenever the Court *considers,* on the merits, the question of whether an act of Congress should not be enforced by the courts because the statute conflicts with the Constitution; and in this sense, judicial review takes place irrespective of whether the Court upholds or strikes down the statute. Obviously, the Court has exercised judicial review in many more cases in which it has upheld congressional legislation than in cases in which it has ruled adversely; and this has been true even in the heyday of the Court's epochs of extreme judicial activism.

It is true that there is nowhere in the Constitution any *explicit* delegation of the power of judicial review to the Court. But the weight of the evidence seems to favor the view of most constitutional historians, which is that it is probable that many, if not most, of the leading Federalist sponsors of the Constitution expected that the Supreme Court would exercise such authority. In any event, the issue has been foreclosed by over a century and a half of practice. We simply note that the Court recognized its own implied power first in the Marbury case; some sixteen years later it attributed implied power to the Congress, in its decision in *McCulloch* v. *Maryland,* 4 Wheat 316 (1819); and it was not until the end of the century that the Court was willing, in *In re Neagle,* 135 U.S. 1 (1890), to make equivalent concessions to the Presidency—and then under most unusual circumstances.

During the century and a half that separates the decisions regarding the Secretaries of State of Jefferson and Eisenhower (*Marbury* v. *Madison,* and *Trop* v. *Dulles,* 356 U.S. 86 [March 31, 1958]), there were approximately eighty other decisions of the Supreme Court which declared acts of Congress to be unconstitutional either in whole or part. Only one other such decision, the disastrous Dred Scott case, came before the Civil War, so it is apparent that the Court exercised very considerable restraint in its use of the power to arrive at a decision of invalidation during the first seventy-four years of the Court's decisions (1791-1864). In sharp contrast to these first two decisions, one of which came at the beginning of Marshall's chief justiceship and the other, over a half-century later, near the close of the Taney regime, there were seventy-four decisions during the next seventy-two years (1865-1936)—an average of over a case each year. The expansion of the Court's power was steady during the latter third of the nineteenth century, but the floodgates really opened after the turn of the twentieth century. Judicial review became a two-edged sword for striking down the social and economic legislation of both the states and the national government, as the persistently conservative majority of the Court reflected, with perfect faithfulness, the values of interests that had been defeated at the polls and of the political generation that, for the time, had been most recently dead and buried.

The volume of Court decisions invalidating acts of both Congress and the President reached a peak during the first term of the Franklin Roosevelt administration, when the Hughes Court struck down New Deal statutes in twelve different cases within a four-year span, and three different presidential acts within a period of less than six months. This was, of course, the immediate cause of the Court-packing episode of the 1936 Term. There was an abrupt change thereafter, however, and during the next eighteen years, there were only three decisions—two of which were minor in significance—in which judicial review was exercised adversely. All three of these were civil-liberties cases, and thus differed sharply from the decisions of the New Deal era and the preceding half-century, during which the Court was declaring economic and social legislation to be unconstitutional. The Warren Court has added three more cases, all of which have dealt with civil-liberties problems relating to the exercise of military power and foreign relations.

Three principal conclusions may be inferred from these facts: (1) the Court was very parsimonious in its use of judicial review in the period before the Civil

War; and (2) from the end of the Civil War until 1937, the Court used judicial review primarily (and most of the time during this period of seven decades, exclusively) in order to protect property rights and to declare unconstitutional social and economic legislation; while (3) the Court has, since 1937, used considerably greater restraint and has invalidated congressional legislation, although with increasing frequency in recent years, only on civil-liberties grounds.

Judicial review by the Court is not limited to acts of Congress, of course. The Court is exercising the power of judicial review whenever it considers the constitutionality of state law; and it also uses judicial review, in the broadest sense of the words, when it exercises appellate jurisdiction over the decisions of lower courts or of administrative agencies. The acts of the President, too, have been subjected to judicial review by the Court on a basis that differs only in quantity from the Court's exercise of a censorial power over federal statutes. The seventeen cases in which the Supreme Court has held presidential orders and directives to be unconstitutional begin with *Little* v. *Barreme,* 2 Cranch 170 (1804), and extend through *Wiener* v. *United States,* 357 U.S. 349 (1958). The fact that there have been only a fifth as many Supreme Court decisions invalidating acts of the President as there have been declaring unconstitutional acts of Congress does not reflect, of course, the relative quantity of Executive rules and orders as compared to congressional statutes and resolutions. (The volume of presidential orders is much larger than that of acts of Congress.) Rather, the lesser number of antipresidential decisions of the Court is due to the greater procedural difficulties that arise when attempts are made to challenge presidential acts in a proceeding that the Court will accept as a "case of controversy." [4]

ARE JUDGES HUMAN?

From Marshall's opinion in the Marbury case to Warren's opinion in *Trop* v. *Dulles,* the official rationale relied upon by the Supreme Court's majorities as justification for their exercise of the power of judicial review over acts of the Congress has been an extreme form of analytical positivism which has been termed the "slot-machine theory of jurisprudence." However much the Court has admitted sociology and social psychology into opinions dealing with statutory interpretation and judicial review of state legislation, the theory under which the Court exercises a judicial veto power over national legislation remains today the same as in Marshall's day. The classic formulation of this doctrine is that of Mr. Justice Roberts in *United States* v. *Butler,* the decision which invalidated the first Agricultural Adjustment Act of the New Deal period: [5]

There should be no misunderstanding as to the function of this court in such a case. It is sometimes said that the court assumes a power to overrule

---

[4] Glendon A. Schubert, *The Presidency in the Courts* (Minneapolis: University of Minnesota Press, 1957), chap. xi.

[5] 297 U.S. 1, 62-63 (1936).

or control the action of the people's representatives. This is a misconception. The Constitution is the supreme law of the land ordained and established by the people. All legislation must conform to the principles it lays down. When an act of Congress is appropriately challenged in the courts as not conforming to the constitutional mandate the judicial branch of the Government has only one duty,—to lay the article of the Constitution which is invoked beside the statute which is challenged and to decide whether the latter squares with the former. All the court does, or can do, is to announce its considered judgment upon the question. The only power it has, if such it may be called, is the power of judgment. This court neither approves nor condemns any legislative policy. Its delicate and difficult office is to ascertain and declare whether the legislation is in accordance with, or in contravention of, the provisions of the Constitution; and, having done that, its duty ends.

More sophisticated observers like Justice Frankfurter, whose views may be considered to be representative of the sociological school of jurisprudence, have assured us, however, that: [6]

The answers that the Supreme Court is required to give are based on questions and on data that preclude automatic or even undoubting answers. If the materials on which judicial judgments must be based could be fed into a machine so as to produce ineluctable answers, if such were the nature of the problems that come before the Supreme Court and such were the answers expected, we would have IBM machines doing the work instead of judges.

On the other hand, spokesmen for the more extreme wing of the realist position in American jurisprudence recently have suggested that the time is at hand when the work of the Supreme Court might well be taken over, and perhaps done more efficiently, by a "bench of judicial robots." [7] Our immediate problem, however, is not whether an electronic brain—a judicial UNIVAC—might do a better job of constitutional policy-making than the Supreme Court; a more pressing question is whether the human justices who presently constitute the Court *behave* like robots (as Mr. Justice Roberts seems to have suggested) when they declare acts of Congress to be unconstitutional. Some light may be shed on this problem by undertaking a somewhat detailed examination of the Warren Court's decisions in *Trop* v. *Dulles* and some other recent and closely related cases.

[6] Quoted from *Of Law and Men,* by Felix Frankfurter, edited by Philip Elman, © 1956, by Felix Frankfurter. P. 42. Reprinted by permission of Harcourt, Brace and Company, Inc.

[7] See Chapter 11, footnote 27 and 28; and

Franklin M. Fisher, "The Mathematical Analysis of Supreme Court Decisions: The Use and Abuse of Quantitative Methods," *American Political Science Review,* Vol. 52, p. 321 (1958).

TROP v. DULLES

356 U.S. 86 (March 31, 1958)

Certiorari to the United States Court of Appeals for the Second Circuit.

Reversed.

5-4

Warren, C.J.	('+'
Black	('+'
Douglas	(+
Whittaker	(+
Brennan	('+'
Frankfurter	'—')
Burton	—)
Clark	—)
Harlan	—)

There was no opinion of the Court in this case, since there was full participation and only four justices joined in the opinion of the Chief Justice.

MR. CHIEF JUSTICE WARREN announced the judgment of the Court and delivered an opinion, in which MR. JUSTICE BLACK, MR. JUSTICE DOUGLAS, and MR. JUSTICE WHITTAKER join.

The petitioner in this case, a native-born American, is declared to have lost his United States citizenship and become stateless by reason of his conviction by court-martial for wartime desertion. As in *Perez* v. *Brownell, ante,* p. 44, the issue before us is whether this forfeiture of citizenship comports with the Constitution.

The facts are not in dispute. In 1944 petitioner was a private in the United States Army, serving in French Morocco. On May 22, he escaped from a stockade at Casablanca, where he had been confined following a previous breach of discipline. The next day petitioner and a companion were walking along a road towards Rabat, in the general direction back to Casablanca, when an Army truck approached and stopped. A witness testified that petitioner boarded the truck willingly and that no words were spoken. In Rabat petitioner was turned over to military police. Thus ended petitioner's "desertion." He had been gone less than a day and had willingly surrendered to an officer on an Army vehicle while he was walking back towards his base. He testified that at the time he and his companion were picked up by the Army truck, "we had decided to return to the stockade. The going was tough. We had no money to speak of, and at the time we were on foot and we were getting cold and hungry." A general court-martial convicted petitioner of desertion and sentenced him to three years at hard labor, forfeiture of all pay and allowances and a dishonorable discharge.

In 1952 petitioner applied for a passport. His application was denied on the ground that under the provisions of Section 401(g) of the Nationality Act of 1940, as amended, he had lost his citizenship by reason of his conviction and dishonorable discharge for wartime desertion. In 1955 petitioner commenced this action in the District Court, seeking a declaratory judgment that he is a citizen. The Government's motion for summary judgment was granted, and the Court of Appeals for the Second Circuit affirmed, Chief Judge Clark dissenting. . . .

Section 401(g), the statute that decrees the forfeiture of this petitioner's citizenship, is based directly on a Civil War statute, which provided that a deserter would lose his "rights of citizenship." The meaning of this phrase was not clear. When the 1940 codification and revision of the nationality laws was prepared, the Civil War statute was amended to make it certain that what a convicted deserter would lose was nationality itself. In 1944 the statute was further amended to provide that a convicted deserter would lose his citizenship only if he was dismissed from the service or dishonorably discharged. At the same time it was provided that citizenship could be regained if the deserter was restored to active duty in wartime with the permission of the military authorities.

Though these amendments were added to ameliorate the harshness of the statute, their combined effect produces a result that poses far graver problems than the ones that were sought to be solved. Section 401(g) as amended now gives the military authorities complete discretion to decide who among convicted deserters shall continue to be Americans and who shall be stateless. By deciding whether to issue and execute a dishonorable discharge and whether to allow a deserter to re-enter the armed forces, the military becomes the arbiter of citizenship. And the domain given to it by Congress is not as narrow as might be supposed. Though the crime of desertion is one of the most serious in military law, it is by no means a rare event for a soldier to be convicted of this crime. The elements of desertion are simply absence from duty plus the intention not to return. Into this category falls a great range of conduct, which may be prompted by a variety of motives—fear, laziness, hysteria or any emotional imbalance. The offense may occur not only in combat but also in training camps for draftees in this country. The Solicitor General informed the Court that during World War II, according to Army estimates, approximately 21,000 soldiers and airmen were convicted of desertion and given dishonorable discharges by the sentencing courts-martial and that about 7,000 of these were actually separated from the service and thus rendered stateless when the reviewing authorities refused to remit their dishonorable discharges. Over this group of men, enlarged by whatever the corresponding figures may be for the Navy and Marines, the military has been given the power to grant or withhold citizenship. And the number of youths subject to this power

could easily be enlarged simply by expanding the statute to cover crimes other than desertion. For instance, a dishonorable discharge itself might in the future be declared to be sufficient to justify forfeiture of citizenship. . . .

I.

In *Perez* v. *Brownell, supra,* I expressed the principles that I believe govern the constitutional status of United States citizenship. It is my conviction that citizenship is not subject to the general powers of the National Government and therefore cannot be divested in the exercise of those powers. The right may be voluntarily relinquished or abandoned either by express language or by language and conduct that show a renunciation of citizenship.

Under these principles, this petitioner has not lost his citizenship. Desertion in wartime, though it may merit the ultimate penalty, does not necessarily signify allegiance to a foreign state. Section 401(g) is not limited to cases of desertion to the enemy, and there is no such element in this case. This soldier committed a crime for which he should be and was punished, but he did not involve himself in any way with a foreign state. There was no dilution of his allegiance to this country. The fact that the desertion occurred on foreign soil is of no consequence. The Solicitor General acknowledged that forfeiture of citizenship would have occurred if the entire incident had transpired in this country.

Citizenship is not a license that expires upon misbehavior. The duties of citizenship are numerous, and the discharge of many of these obligations is essential to the security and well-being of the Nation. The citizen who fails to pay his taxes or to abide by the laws safeguarding the integrity of elections deals a dangerous blow to his country. But could a citizen be deprived of his nationality for evading these basic responsibilities of citizenship? In time of war the citizen's duties include not only the military defense of the Nation but also a full participation in the manifold activities of the civilian ranks. Failure to perform any of these obligations may cause the Nation serious injury, and, in appropriate circumstances, the punishing power is available to deal with derelictions of duty. But citizenship is not lost every time a duty of citizenship is shirked. And the deprivation of citizenship is not a weapon that the Government may use to express its displeasure at a citizen's conduct, however reprehensible that conduct may be. As long as a person does not voluntarily renounce or abandon his citizenship, and this petitioner has done neither, I believe his fundamental right of citizenship is secure. On this ground alone the judgment in this case should be reversed.

II.

Since a majority of the Court concluded in *Perez* v. *Brownell* that citizenship may be divested in the exercise of some governmental power, I deem it appropriate to state additionally why the action taken in this case exceeds constitutional limits, even under the majority's decision in *Perez*. The Court concluded in *Perez* that citizenship could be divested in the exercise of the foreign affairs power. In this case, it is urged that the war power is adequate to support the divestment of citizenship. But there is a vital difference between the two statutes that purport to implement these powers by decreeing loss of citizenship. The statute in *Perez* decreed loss of citizenship—so the majority concluded—to eliminate those international problems that were thought to arise by reason of a citizen's having voted in a foreign election. The statute in this case, however, is entirely different. Section 401(g) decrees loss of citizenship for those found guilty of the crime of desertion. It is essentially like Section 401(j) of the Nationality Act, decreeing loss of

citizenship for evading the draft by remaining outside the United States. This provision was also before the Court in *Perez,* but the majority declined to consider its validity. While Section 401(j) decrees loss of citizenship without providing any semblance of procedural due process whereby the guilt of the draft evader may be determined before the sanction is imposed, Section 401(g), the provision in this case, accords the accused deserter at least the safeguards of an adjudication of guilt by a court-martial.

The constitutional question posed by Section 401(g) would appear to be whether or not denationalization may be inflicted as a punishment, even assuming that citizenship may be divested pursuant to some governmental power. But the Government contends that this statute does not impose a penalty and that constitutional limitations on the power of Congress to punish are therefore inapplicable. We are told this is so because a committee of cabinet members, in recommending this legislation to the Congress, said it "technically is not a penal law." How simple would be the tasks of constitutional adjudication and of law generally if specific problems could be solved by inspection of the labels pasted on them! Manifestly the issue of whether Section 401(g) is a penal law cannot be thus determined. . . .

Plainly legislation prescribing imprisonment for the crime of desertion is penal in nature. If loss of citizenship is substituted for imprisonment, it cannot fairly be said that the use of this particular sanction transforms the fundamental nature of the statute. In fact, a dishonorable discharge with consequent loss of citizenship might be the only punishment meted out by a court-martial. . . .

Section 401(g) is a penal law, and we must face the question whether the Constitution permits the Congress to take away citizenship as a punishment for crime. If it is assumed that the power of Congress extends to divestment of citizenship, the problem still remains as to this statute whether denationalization is a cruel and unusual punishment within the meaning of the Eighth Amendment. Since wartime desertion is punishable by death, there can be no argument that the penalty of denationalization is excessive in relation to the gravity of the crime. The question is whether this penalty subjects the individual to a fate forbidden by the principle of civilized treatment guaranteed by the Eighth Amendment.

At the outset, let us put to one side the death penalty as an index of the constitutional limit on punishment. Whatever the arguments may be against capital punishment, both on moral grounds and in terms of accomplishing the purposes of punishment—and they are forceful, the death penalty has been employed throughout our history, and in a day when it is still widely accepted, it cannot be said to violate the constitutional concept of cruelty. But it is equally plain that the existence of the death penalty is not a license to the Government to devise any punishment short of death within the limit of its imagination.

The exact scope of the constitutional phrase "cruel and unusual" has not been detailed by this Court. But the basic policy reflected in these words is firmly established in the Anglo-American tradition of criminal justice. The phrase in our Constitution was taken directly from the English Declaration of Rights of 1688, and the principle it represents can be traced back to the Magna Carta. The basic concept underlying the Eighth Amendment is nothing less than the dignity of man. While the State has the power to punish, the Amendment stands to assure that this power be exercised within the limits of civilized standards. Fines, imprisonment and even execution may be imposed depending upon the enormity of the crime, but any technique outside the bounds of these traditional penalties is constitutionally suspect. This Court has had little occasion to give precise content to the Eighth Amendment, and in an enlightened democracy such as ours, this is not surprising. . . . The Amendment must draw its meaning from the evolving standards of decency that mark the progress of a maturing society.

We believe, as did Chief Judge Clark in the court below, that use of denationalization as a punishment is barred by the Eighth Amendment. There may be involved no physical mistreatment, no primitive torture. There is instead the total destruction of the individual's status in organized society. It is a form of punishment more primitive than torture, for it destroys for the individual the political existence that was centuries in the development. The punishment strips the citizen of his status in the national and international political community. His very existence is at the sufferance of the country in which he happens to find himself. While any one country may accord him some rights, and presumably as long as he remained in this country he would enjoy the limited rights of an alien, no country need do so because he is stateless. Furthermore, his enjoyment of even the limited rights of an alien might be subject to termination at any time by reason of deportation. In short, the expatriate has lost the right to have rights.

This punishment is offensive to cardinal principles for which the Constitution stands. It subjects the individual to a fate of ever-increasing fear and distress. He knows not what discriminations may be established against him, what proscriptions may be directed against him, and when and for what cause his existence in his native land may be terminated. He may be subject to banishment, a fate universally decried by civilized people. He is stateless, a condition deplored in the international community of democracies. It is no answer to suggest that all the disastrous consequences of this fate may not be brought to bear on a stateless person. The threat makes the punishment obnoxious.[8]

The civilized nations of the world are in virtual unanimity that statelessness is not to be imposed as punishment for crime. It is true that several countries prescribe expatriation in the event that their nationals engage in conduct in derogation of native allegiance. Even statutes of this sort are generally applicable primarily to naturalized citizens. But use of denationalization as punishment for crime is an entirely different matter. The United Nations' survey of the nationality laws of 84 nations of the world reveals that only two countries, the Philippines and Turkey, impose denationalization as a penalty for desertion. In this country the Eighth Amendment forbids this to be done.

In concluding as we do that the Eighth Amendment forbids Congress to punish by taking away citizenship, we are mindful of the gravity of the issue inevitably raised whenever the constitutionality of an Act of the National Legislature is challenged. No member of the Court believes that in this case the statute before us can be construed to avoid the issue of constitutionality. That issue confronts us, and the task of resolving it is inescapably ours. This task requires the exercise of judgment, not the reliance upon personal pref-

erences. Courts must not consider the wisdom of statutes but neither can they sanction as being merely unwise that which the Constitution forbids.

We are oath-bound to defend the Constitution. This obligation requires that congressional enactments be judged by the standards of the Constitution. The Judiciary has the duty of implementing the constitutional safeguards that protect individual rights. When the Government acts to take away the fundamental right of citizenship, the safeguards of the Constitution should be examined with special diligence.

The provisions of the Constitution are not time-worn adages or hollow shibboleths. They are vital, living principles that authorize and limit governmental powers in our nation. They are the rules of government. When the constitutionality of an Act of Congress is challenged in this Court, we must apply those rules. If we do not, the words of the Constitution become little more than good advice.

When it appears that an Act of Congress conflicts with one of these provisions, we have no choice but to enforce the paramount commands of the Constitution. We are sworn to do no less. We cannot push back the limits of the Constitution merely to accommodate challenged legislation. We must apply those limits as the Constitution prescribes them, bearing in mind both the broad scope of legislative discretion and the ultimate responsibility of constitutional adjudication. We do well to approach this task cautiously, as all our predecessors have counseled. But the ordeal of judgment cannot be shirked. In some 81 instances since this Court was established it has determined that congressional action exceeded the bounds of the Constitution. It is so in this case.

[8] The suggestion that judicial relief will be available to alleviate the potential rigors of statelessness assumes too much. Undermining such assumption is the still fresh memory of *Shaughnessy* v. *United States ex rel. Mezei*, 345 U.S. 206, where an alien, resident in this country for 25 years returned from a visit abroad to find himself barred from this country and from all others to which he turned. Summary imprisonment on Ellis Island was his fate, without any judicial examination of the grounds of his confinement. This Court denied relief, and the intolerable situation was remedied after four years' imprisonment only through executive action as a matter of grace. See N. Y. Times, Aug. 12, 1954, p. 10, col. 4. [Footnote by Chief Justice Warren.]

The judgment of the Court of Appeals for the Second Circuit is reversed and the cause is remanded to the District Court for appropriate proceedings.

Reversed and remanded.

MR. JUSTICE BRENNAN, concurring.

. . . Expatriation . . . constitutes an especially demoralizing sanction. The uncertainty, and the consequent psychological hurt, which must accompany one who becomes an outcast in his own land must be reckoned a substantial factor in the ultimate judgment. . . .

The novelty of expatriation as punishment does not alone demonstrate its inefficiency. In recent years we have seen such devices as indeterminate sentences and parole added to the traditional term of imprisonment. Such penal methods seek to achieve the end, at once more humane and effective, that society should make every effort to rehabilitate the offender and restore him as a useful member of that society as society's own best protection. Of course, rehabilitation is but one of the several purposes of the penal law. Among other purposes are deterrents of the wrongful act by the threat of punishment and insulation of society from dangerous individuals by imprisonment or execution. What then is the relationship of the punishment of expatriation to these ends of the penal law? It is perfectly obvious that it constitutes the very antithesis of rehabilitation, for instead of guiding the offender back into the useful paths of society it excommunicates him and makes him, literally, an outcast. I can think of no more certain way in which to make a man in whom, perhaps, rest the seeds of serious antisocial behavior, more likely to pursue further a career of unlawful activity than to place on him the stigma of the derelict, uncertain of many of his basic rights. Similarly, it must be questioned whether expatriation can really achieve the other effects sought by society in punitive devices. Certainly it will not insulate society from the deserter, for unless coupled with banishment the sanction leaves the offender at large. And as a deterrent device this sanction would appear of little effect, for the offender, if not deterred by thought of the specific penalties of long imprisonment or even death,

is not very likely to be swayed from his course by the prospect of expatriation. However insidious and demoralizing may be the actual experience of statelessness, its contemplation in advance seems unlikely to invoke serious misgiving, for none of us yet knows its ramifications.

In the light of these considerations, it is understandable that the Government has not pressed its case on the basis of expatriation of the deserter as punishment for his crime. Rather, the Government argues that the necessary nexus to the granted power is to be found in the idea that legislative withdrawal of citizenship is justified in this case because Trop's desertion constituted a refusal to perform one of the highest duties of American citizenship—the bearing of arms in a time of desperate national peril. It cannot be denied that there is implicit in this a certain rough justice. He who refuses to act as an American should no longer be an American—what could be fairer? But I cannot see that this is anything other than forcing retribution from the offender —naked vengeance. But many acts of desertion certainly fall far short of a "refusal to perform this highest duty of American citizenship." . . . Desertion is also committed where a soldier, without having received a regular discharge, re-enlists in the same or another service. The youngster, for example, restive at his assignment to a supply depot, who runs off to the front to be in the fight, subjects himself to the possibility of this sanction. Yet the statute imposes the penalty coextensive with the substantive crime. Since many acts of desertion thus certainly fall far short of a "refusal to perform this highest duty of American citizenship," it stretches the imagination excessively to establish a rational relation of mere retribution to the ends purported to be served by expatriation of the deserter. I simply cannot accept a judgment that Congress is free to adopt any measure at all to demonstrate its displeasure and exact its penalty from the offender against its laws.

It seems to me that nothing is solved by the uncritical reference to service in the armed forces as the "highest duty of American citizenship." Indeed, it is very difficult to imagine, on this theory of power, why Congress cannot impose expatriation as punishment for any crime at all—for tax evasion, for bank robbery, for narcotics offenses. As citizens we are also called upon to pay our taxes and to obey the laws, and these duties appear to me to be fully as related to the nature of our citizenship as our military obligations. But Congress' asserted power to expatriate the deserter bears to the war powers precisely the same relation as its power to expatriate the tax evader would bear to the taxing power.

I therefore must conclude that §401(g) is beyond the power of Congress to enact, [because] the requisite rational relation between this statute and the war power does not appear—for in this relation the statute is not "really calculated to effect any of the objects entrusted to the government * * *," M'Culloch v. Maryland, 4 Wheat. 316, 423—and therefore that §401 (g) falls beyond the domain of Congress.

Mr. Justice Frankfurter, whom Mr. Justice Burton, Mr. Justice Clark and Mr. Justice Harlan join, dissenting.

It is not easy to stand aloof and allow want of wisdom to prevail, to disregard one's own strongly held view of what is wise in the conduct of affairs. But it is not the business of this Court to pronounce policy. It must observe a fastidious regard for limitations on its own power, and this precludes the Court's giving effect to its own notions of what is wise or politic. That self-restraint is of the essence in the observance of the judicial oath, for the Constitution has not authorized the judges to sit in judgment on the wisdom of what Congress and the Executive Branch do. . . .

Possession by an American citizen of the rights and privileges that constitute citizenship imposes correlative obligations, of which the most indispensable may well be "to take his place in the ranks of the army of his country and risk the chance of being shot down in its defense," *Jacobson* v. *Massachusetts*, 197 U. S. 11, 29. Harsh as this may sound, it is no more so than the actualities to which it responds. Can it be said that there is no rational nexus between refusal to perform this ultimate duty of American citizenship and legislative withdrawal of that citizenship? Congress may well have thought that making loss of citizenship a consequence of wartime desertion would affect the ability of the military authorities to control the forces with which they were expected to fight and win a major world conflict. It is not for us to deny that Congress might reasonably have believed the morale and fighting efficiency of our troops would be impaired if our soldiers knew that their fellows who had abandoned them in their time of greatest need were to remain in the communion of our citizens.

Petitioner urges that imposing loss of citizenship as a "punishment" for wartime desertion is a violation of both the Due Process Clause of the Fifth Amendment and the Eighth Amendment. His objections are that there is no notice of expatriation as a consequence of desertion in the provision defining that offense, that loss of citizenship as a "punishment" is unconstitutionally disproportionate to the offense of desertion and that loss of citizenship constitutes "cruel and unusual punishment."

. . . However, like denaturalization, . . . expatriation under the Nationality Act of 1940 is not "punishment" in any valid constitutional sense. Cf. *Fong Yue Ting* v. *United States*, 149 U.S. 698, 730. Simply because denationalization was attached by Congress as a consequence of conduct that it had elsewhere made unlawful, it does not follow that denationalization is a "punishment," any more than it can be said that loss of civil rights as a result of conviction for a felony, see Gathings, Loss of Citizenship and Civil Rights for Conviction of Crime, 43 Am. Pol. Sci. Rev.

1228, 1233, is a "punishment" for any legally significant purposes. . . .

Even assuming, *arguendo,* that §401(g) can be said to impose "punishment," to insist that denationalization is "cruel and unusual punishment" is to stretch that concept beyond the breaking point. It seems scarcely arguable that loss of citizenship is within the Eighth Amendment's prohibition because disproportionate to an offense that is capital and has been so from the first year of Independence. . . . Is constitutional dialectic so empty of reason that it can be seriously urged that loss of citizenship is a fate worse than death? The seriousness of abandonding one's country when it is in the grip of mortal conflict precludes denial to Congress of the power to terminate citizenship here, unless that power is to be denied to Congress under any circumstance. . . .

Nor has Congress fallen afoul of that prohibition because a person's post-denationalization status has elements of unpredictability. Presumably a denationalized person becomes an alien *vis-à-vis* the United States. The very substantial rights and privileges that the alien in this country enjoys under the federal and state constitutions puts him in a very different condition from that of an outlaw in fifteenth-century England. . . .

This legislation is the result of an exercise by Congress of the legislative power vested in it by the Constitution and of an exercise by the President of his constitutional power in approving a bill and thereby making it "a law." To sustain it is to respect the actions of the two branches of our Government directly responsive to the will of the people and empowered under the Constitution to determine the wisdom of legislation. The awesome power of this Court to invalidate such legislation, because in practice it is bounded only by our own prudence in discerning the limits of the Court's constitutional function, must be exercised with the utmost restraint. . . . [The] power to invalidate legislation must not be exercised as if, either in constitutional theory or in the art of government, it stood as the sole bulwark against unwisdom or excesses of the moment.

THE EXPATRIATION CASES OF THE 1957 TERM

Two companion cases were decided on the same day as *Trop* v. *Dulles.* One of these, *Nishikawa* v. *Dulles,* 356 U.S. 129 (1958), concerned a native-born citizen of the United States of Japanese extraction who had visited Japan as a young man just prior to the outbreak of World War II and subsequently had served in the Japanese army, fighting against the United States in the Pacific. Without reaching any constitutional issues, a majority of the Court reversed two lower federal courts and made an independent judgment on the factual issue whether his military service for Japan had been involuntary, deciding that it had been such. The effect of the Court's decision was to restore Nishikawa's United States citizenship, which had been revoked for a period of almost twenty years by a combination of circumstances, including the events of the war years, administrative action by the Department of State, and the adverse decisions of the federal district court and court of appeals in his case.

The petitioner in the other case, *Perez* v. *Brownell,* 356 U.S. 44 (1958), was a native-born citizen of the United States of Mexican descent, whose parents removed him to Mexico when he was a child. He remained in Mexico as an adult and failed to register as a United States citizen for military service during World War II, although he knew of his obligation to do so. He did, however, make several temporary but illegal entries into the United States as an alien laborer during World War II, falsely representing himself to be a citizen of Mexico and not of the United States. He also voted in political elections in Mexico. When he applied, after the war, for admission as a citizen, the Immigration and Naturalization Service of the Department of Justice ruled that Perez had expatriated himself, and that his exclusion was required by the Nationality Act of 1940, since he had deliberately remained out of the country during wartime to evade his military obligations, and he also had voted in a foreign political election, either ground being sufficient to warrant his expatriation and exclusion. A majority of the Supreme Court upheld the constitutionality of the section of the act of Congress relating to voting in foreign elections, and affirmed the decisions of two lower federal courts approving the administrative determination of expatriation in Perez' case. The "important question" raised by the other section, which punished draft-dodgers who remained abroad, was expressly "reserved" by the majority (i.e., the Court refused to decide this question).

The voting division of the Supreme Court in the three cases is shown in Table 21, on page 201.

The outcome of the cases might well be considered to be in inverse relationship to the acts of disloyalty of the petitioners, all three of whom were native-born citizens of the United States. Nishikawa, whose admitted behavior fits precisely the constitutional definition of treason (which consists only "in levying War against [the United States], or in adhering to their Enemies, giving them Aid and Comfort") attracted the favorable votes of the largest number of justices— seven in all. Trop, a soldier who deserted in time of war (but whose specific actions consisted only of a few hours of walking around in a desert, far from the enemy and far from giving any effective aid to the enemy) was supported by a marginal majority who, in order to restore Trop's citizenship, went to the exceptional extreme of invalidating an act of Congress based upon the war power. But Perez, a citizen whose disloyalty consisted (so far as the decision of the Court was concerned) in his act of having voted in Mexican elections, was declared by a majority of the Court to have forfeited his right to United States citizenship. This somewhat topsy-turvy result is explicable only in terms of the fact that Brennan, unlike any of his colleagues, saw a critical difference—a constitutional difference— between the cases of Trop and Perez. (The favorable votes of Frankfurter and Burton in the Nishikawa case were explicitly based on a narrow issue of statutory construction.)

The consistent voting of five of the justices reflects the well-defined positions to which they adhered in all three cases. Warren, Black, and Douglas thought that Congress had *no* power to bring about the involuntary expatriation of citizens of the United States, irrespective of the circumstances. Citizenship, to these three

TABLE 21.

The Expatriation Cases of the 1957 Term

	Nishikawa (statutory interpretation and questions of fact)	Trop (constitutional interpretation and the war power)	Perez (constitutional interpretation and foreign-relations power)
Warren, C. J.	('+')	('+'	'+')
Black	('+'	('+'	+)
Douglas	(+)	(+	'+')
Whittaker	(+)	(+	'+')
Brennan	(+)	('+'	(−)
Frankfurter	('+'	'−')	('−')
Burton	(+	−).	(−)
Clark	−)	−)	(−)
Harlan	'−')	−)	(−)
Voting Division	7-2 Pro	5-4 Pro	4-5 Con

LEGEND:

+	=	a vote in favor of the retention of citizenship
−	=	a vote against the retention of citizenship
' '	=	wrote opinion
( )	=	joined in the opinion of the Court
(	=	concurring opinion
)	=	dissenting opinion

libertarians, was an absolute civil right beyond the constitutional power of the national government to abridge. Harlan and Clark, on the other hand, who voted against all three petitioners, obviously appeared to approve the wisdom of the expatriation policies established by Congress, and so they argued the virtues of judicial restraint in a democracy. Frankfurter and Burton joined forces with

Harlan and Clark as soon as the issue became one of constitutional rather than statutory construction. This left Whittaker and Brennan, both of whom entertained the same theory that there must be a "rational nexus" between expatriation for certain defined acts, and the power invoked by Congress to support its various policies of expatriation. Whittaker discovered no such rational relationship in either the Trop or Perez cases, although the latter was obviously marginal for him, and he might have voted differently if the majority had chosen to rule alternatively upon the other and reserved issue in the case [9] (i.e., expatriation for draft-dodgers abroad). Brennan, on the other hand, saw a rational relationship between expatriation and the foreign-relations power, but not between expatriation and the war power; and it was upon this distinction, reflecting the idiosyncratic views of a single justice who was at the time (generally speaking) the marginal member of the libertarian bloc of four, that "the Supreme Court" vetoed a constitutional policy that reflected the considered judgment of both of the political branches of the national government.

COURTS-MARTIAL AND THE WARREN COURT

In a concurring opinion in the Trop case, Black had announced for himself and Douglas that: [10]

> Even if citizenship could be involuntarily divested, I do not believe that the power to denationalize may be placed in the hands of military authorities. If desertion or other misconduct is to be a basis for forfeiting citizenship, guilt should be determined in a civilian court of justice where all the protections of the Bill of Rights guard the fairness of the outcome. Such forfeiture should not rest on the findings of a military tribunal. Military courts may try soldiers and punish them for military offense, but they should not have the last word on the soldier's right to citizenship. . . . Nothing in the Constitution or its history lends the slightest support for such military control over the right to be an American citizen.

Black's statement evokes another issue in the case: the authority of the military to exercise court-martial jurisdiction over civilians or over what are essentially nonmilitary rights or obligations. This has constituted one of the most important trends in Supreme Court decision-making in recent years. Of the six decisions, in the twenty-two years spanned by the 1937 and the 1958 Terms of the Court, in which acts of Congress were declared to be unconstitutional, the three most recent (at the time of this writing), came in the 1954, 1956, and 1957 terms; and these involved what at least several of the justices—and particularly libertarians Black and Douglas—perceived to be the fundamental constitutional question of military

---

[9] See Whittaker's memorandum of dissent, *Perez* v. *Brownell*, 356 U.S. 44, 84-85 (1958).

[10] *Trop.* v. *Dulles*, 356 U.S. 86, 104-105 (1958).

control over the civil rights and liberties of civilians, including rights of national citizenship.

Such issues are not new, as we shall observe in Chapter 6. But for the Supreme Court to crowd into a period of less than two and a half years three decisions adversely exercising judicial review over statutes that peculiarly involve the constitutional powers of both the Congress and the President—this is exceptional. Especially does it appear to be so in contrast to the preceding eighteen years, during which the Court disposed of the same number of cases exercising judicial review adversely, but with regard to diverse, scattered, and relatively insignificant issues.[11]

The 1955 decision was *Toth* v. *Quarles,* 350 U.S. 11 (November 8, 1955), in which the Court invalidated a section of the Uniform Code of Military Justice of 1950, which had extended court-martial jurisdiction to include offenses committed during a *prior* period of military service. Toth was a civilian working in a factory in Pittsburgh who was arrested by military police one day, whisked halfway across the world to Korea by military aircraft within a matter of hours, and then and there tried by court-martial for an offense which he had committed prior to his discharge from a period of military service. A majority of the Supreme Court reversed (in effect) his conviction, by directing a lower federal court to order his release on writ of habeas corpus.

The next case—actually two cases that were ultimately joined by the Court for common disposition—raised more complex problems for the Court. As defined by a majority of the Court, the issue for decision related to the constitutionality of a different section of the Uniform Code, which authorized trial by court-martial for offenses committed on certain overseas bases by dependent civilians who accompanied members of the armed services abroad. In one case, the civilian daughter of World War II hero General Walter Krueger shot and killed her officer husband, at an army base in Japan. In a second case, the wife of an air force sergeant shot and killed her husband at an army base in England. There was incipient conflict [12] among the circuits on the constitutional issue whether Congress could thus authorize military trial of civilians for civilian offenses, with one federal district court dismissing and another granting petitions for writs of habeas corpus for the release of these ladies from the custody of their respective jailers. After initially upholding the statute, the "Court" changed its mind (for reasons that are explained in detail in Chapter 3, *supra*) and by a 6-2 vote declared the relevant section of the Uniform Military Code to be unconstitutional, in *Reid* v. *Covert,* 354 U.S. 1 (June 10, 1957).

---

[11] The other three decisions include: *Tot* v. *United States,* 319 U.S. 463 (1943); *United States* v. *Lovett,* 328 U.S. 303 (1946); and *United States* v. *Cardiff,* 344 U.S. 174 (1952).

[12] Actual conflict, at the level of the courts of appeals, had not yet occurred. One case came to the Court on direct appeal from the District Court of the District of Columbia; and in the other, the Court granted certiorari while an appeal from a district court's decision was pending before the Court of Appeals for the Fourth Circuit.

Less than ten months later came the decision in *Trop* v. *Dulles,* with which we are already somewhat familiar. It will be recalled that Table 21 showed the Trop decision to be a marginal one on the issue of the congressional power of expatriation, hanging as it did upon Brennan's concurrence. Table 22 (page 205) suggests that, in relationship to the Toth and Reid cases which preceded it, the Trop decision was also a marginal one on the court-martial issue.

Brennan and Whittaker are generally considered to be more liberal, in their attitudes and voting behavior, than the justices whom they replaced, Minton and Reed. Assuming that this is correct, it might seem curious that, as Table 22 indicates, the Court mustered its largest favorable majority on the court-martial issue when Minton and Reed sat and dissented, while there was a smaller majority in the Trop decision, when Brennan and Whittaker both voted in the majority. But the table also suggests the answer to this paradox: the later cases required that a justice who would vote in behalf of the petitioners, and against the legislation, entertain an increasingly intense attitude of hostility to the military and correspondingly intense sympathy for civil rights.

Toth asked the Court to say that the military authorities could not shanghai a civilian and abduct him overseas for trial there by a military court, for an offense with which he was not charged while a member of the armed forces. Covert asked the Court to hold that the military could not try civilians who were already overseas, for crimes committed in places under military jurisdiction, and which apparently were not otherwise punishable under the laws of the United States.[13] This was too much for Clark, who started voting negatively at this point and wrote an opinion to explain why, although Brennan could accept such a policy result and join in an opinion written by Black, the member of the Court most hostile to military control over civilians. Trop asked the Court to say that the military could not inflict a punishment *less* than capital, as explicitly authorized by Congress, upon a soldier—not a civilian—who committed one of the most serious of *military* offenses, desertion in time of war—an offense that was concededly and constitutionally subject to capital punishment. Frankfurter and Harlan parted company with the majority at this point, and joined in an opinion explaining why.

It is most reasonable to assume that if another case should come along, asking the Court to support a libertarian claim more extreme than that of Trop, the liberal bloc might be hard pressed to keep Whittaker in the fold, or to attract Stewart, even assuming (as seems warranted) that Stewart's attitudes on this issue are likely to be more liberal than those of the man he replaced, who was the Court's anchor man in defense of the military. Indeed, the liberal bloc might well have to face up to the defection of Brennan, as in the Perez case. Even Warren

---

[13] The latter comment also applies to Toth; Reed noted in dissent that "the judgment just announced turns loose, without trial or possibility of trial, a man accused of murder." *Toth* v. *Quarles,* 350 U.S. 11, 24 (1955).

TABLE 22.

Decisions of the Warren Court Declaring Unconstitutional Acts of Congress Extending Court-Martial Jurisdiction over Civil Rights (1955-1957 Terms)

	Toth v. Quarles, 350 U.S. 11 (1955)	Reid v. Covert, 354 U.S. 1 (1957)	Trop v. Dulles, 356 U.S. 18 (1958)
Black	('+')	('+'	('+'
Warren, C. J.	(+)	(+	('+'
Douglas	(+)	(+	(+
Brennan	*	(+	('+'
Whittaker	*	NP	(+
Frankfurter	(+)	('+'	'−')
Harlan	(+)	('+'	−)
Clark	(+)	'−')	−)
Minton	−)	*	*
Reed	'−')	*	*
Burton	−)	−)	−)
Voting Division	6-3	6-2	5-4

LEGEND:

+	=	a vote in favor of holding the statute unconstitutional
−	=	a vote against holding the statute unconstitutional
' '	=	wrote opinion
( )	=	joined in the opinion of the Court
(	=	concurring opinion
)	=	dissenting opinion
*	=	not seated at the time of this decision
NP	=	seated but not participating in this decision

refused to associate himself with the Black-Douglas concurrence in Trop; and from all appearances, only those two justices considered the military-control-over-civilian-rights angle to bear a sufficiently important relationship to this case to justify discussion. It seemed most likely, on the basis of the data shown in Table 22, that the Court's trend toward curtailing military control over civil rights had come to an end, and that any case similiar to but less deprivational than Trop would find the libertarians, as on many other issues of constitutional policy that come before the Supreme Court for decision, exercising the traditional right of dissent.

JUDICIAL RESTRAINT

Not only does the Court uphold acts of the Congress and of the President in most of the cases in which it exercises judicial review; the Court also avoids the use of judicial review in many cases in which its decision is sought. There are three principal doctrines, above and beyond the obvious technique of refusing jurisdiction (which is probably the most important method of avoidance), by means of which the Court justifies its refusal to exercise judicial review. These are the doctrines of "case or controversy," judicial parsimony, and the "political question" concept. We shall discuss first the Court's own explanation of the three doctrines; and then we shall present a theory which purports to explain why and when they are invoked by the Court.

Cases and Controversies

The essence of the "case or controversy" notion is that neither the United States Supreme Court nor the lower federal courts (unlike some American state courts) will render advisory opinions. This "rule" of the Court is explained in various of its opinions, but perhaps most clearly in the otherwise insignificant case of *Muskrat* v. *United States,* 219 U.S. 346 (1911). In this case, Congress had approved by legislation a particular pattern of allotment of certain Indian tribal lands. Subsequently, Congress enacted amendatory legislation which had the effect of increasing the number of persons entitled to share in the allotment, thus infringing upon the prior rights of the original allottees. Reacting to the consequent pressures from both the original and the augmented groups of allottees, Congress decided to pass the problem on to the judiciary. Congress did this by enacting another statute, specially conferring jurisdiction upon the Court of Claims to hear a suit, to be brought by certain Indians (including one David Muskrat) who were named in the statute, and to be defended by the Attorney General, for the express purpose of testing the constitutionality of the allotment-amendment statute. A right to appeal to the Supreme Court the decision of the Court of

Claims was expressly provided for in the jurisdictional act. Without any question, the jurisdictional statute was an invitation to judicial review, by means of which Congress intended to hand over to the Supreme Court a political dispute that it was itself unwilling or unable to resolve.

The Court rejected this invitation in a unanimous decision, the effect of which was to exercise adversely the power of judicial review by declaring unconstitutional the jurisdictional statute, although the opinion of the Court is couched exclusively in terms of the Court's lack of power to render any decision in the case! The jurisdictional statute was unconstitutional, implied the Court, because its object was to induce from the Court an advisory opinion, while the Court was expressly limited by Article III to the decision of "cases" and "controversies." It may seem anomalous, at least to beginning students of constitutional law, that the Court should thus decide that an act of Congress was unconstitutional while at the same time protesting in its opinion that it had no constitutional power to decide the question of the constitutionality of a closely related act of Congress. (The experienced student of the Court grows hardened to such mysteries and learns to take them in his stride.) But even worldly-wise scholars may be somewhat perplexed by the result that the Court contrived: if we accept the Court's premise that the special jurisdictional statute was unconstitutional, whence came the power of the Court to acquire jurisdiction over the case so that it could exercise judicial review over the jurisdictional statute? The Court admittedly had no authority to exercise appellate review in this case other than under the "unconstitutional" jurisdictional statute.

Even if the Supreme Court, as an Article III court, had no jurisdiction to decide this case, the Court of Claims, as a so-called "legislative court," [14] was not limited to the decision of "cases and controversies." But the Court not only held unconstitutional that part of the jurisdictional statute that provided for an appeal to it from the Court of Claims; it went on to rule that the statute was not separable; it must all go, root and branch, for the pious reason that Congress would not have passed the statute in the first place except with the expectation that the Supreme Court, not the Court of Claims, would have the final say.[15]

Logically, the Supreme Court should have dismissed the case for lack of jurisdiction on its own part, instead of reversing the decision of the Court of Claims with directions to the lower court to dismiss the petitions for want of jurisdiction. But logic is rarely the primary consideration in the decisions in which the Court has exercised, or has refused to exercise, the power of judicial review.

The opinion of the Court in the Muskrat case declared that the Court was limited by Article III to the exercise of *judicial* power; and that even judicial

---

[14] For further discussion of the Supreme Court's distinction between "legislative" and "constitutional" courts, see Chapter 5. For present purposes, let us assume that a "legislative court" is one created by Congress on the basis of power other than that delegated to the Congress under Article III, to establish "inferior courts."

[15] *Muskrat* v. *United States,* 219 U.S. 346, 363 (1911).

power could be exercised only in a case or controversy. There were three elements essential to constitute a case or controversy: *first,* there must be a suit at law or in equity instituted according to the regular course of judicial procedure; *second,* the object of the suit must be either the protection or the enforcement of legal rights, or the prevention, redress, or punishment of wrongs; and *third,* there must be opposing parties with truly adverse interests, who have submitted their contentions to a court for adjudication. (We need not pause over any supposed difference between a "case" and a "controversy," and for two reasons: the words are as inseparably joined, in legal literature, as are Siamese twins in real life; and more importantly, there is no difference, or at least no difference of significance. According to the Court, "The term 'controversies,' if distinguishable at all from 'cases,' is so in that it is less comprehensive than the latter, and includes only suits of a civil nature.")

The adverse parties must, of course, possess the requisite "standing," or privity of interest, to have the courts recognize their right to raise a legal claim; without such privity of interest, they could not be admitted as parties to a case. This is very important. An altruistic desire to vindicate the public interest is not good enough—not good at all, in fact. In order for there to be a "case or controversy," there must be a "real, earnest, and vital controversy between *private individuals.*" It is no part of the constitutional function of the Supreme Court to decide cases in which merely the public interest is at stake.

Judicial Parsimony

The best-known statement of the policy norms which, presumably, guide the Court in the exercise of judicial parsimony are contained in a summary in a concurring opinion written by Justice Brandeis: [16]

> The Court [has] developed, for its own governance in the cases confessedly within its jurisdiction, a series of rules under which it has avoided passing upon a large part of all the constitutional questions pressed upon it for decision. They are:
>
> 1. The Court will not pass upon the constitutionality of legislation in a friendly, non-adversary, proceeding, declining because to decide such questions "is legitimate only in the last resort, and as a necessity in the determination of real, earnest and vital controversy between individuals. It never was thought that, by means of a friendly suit, a party beaten in the legislature could transfer to the courts an inquiry as to the constitutionality of the legislative act.". . .
>
> 2. The Court will not "anticipate a question of constitutional law in advance of the necessity of deciding it.". . .

[16] *Ashwander* v. *T.V.A.,* 297 U.S. 288, 346 ff. (1936).

3. The Court will not "formulate a rule of constitutional law broader than is required by the precise facts to which it is to be applied.". . .

4. The Court will not pass upon a constitutional question although properly presented by the record, if there is also present some other ground upon which the case may be disposed of. Thus, if a case can be decided on either of two grounds, one involving a constitutional question, the other a question of statutory construction or general law, the Court will decide only the latter. . . . Appeals from the highest court of a state challenging its decision of a question under the Federal Constitution are frequently dismissed because the judgment can be sustained on an independent state ground. . . .

5. The Court will not pass upon the validity of a statute upon complaint of one who fails to show that he is injured by its operation. . . . Among the many applications of this rule, none is more striking than the denial of the right of challenge to one who lacks a personal or property right. Thus, the challenge by a public official interested only in the performance of his official duty will not be entertained. . . .

6. The Court will not pass upon the constitutionality of a statute at the instance of one who has availed himself of its benefits. . . .

7. "When the validity of an act of the Congress is drawn in question, and even if a serious doubt of constitutionality is raised, it is a cardinal principle that this Court will first ascertain whether a construction of the statute is fairly possible by which the question may be avoided."

These so-called "Ashwander rules" are subject to at least two obvious qualifications. In the first place, they were enunciated in a concurring opinion that was accepted by a minority of only four justices: Brandeis, Stone, Roberts, and Cardozo. And secondly, the author of this opinion was, after all, Brandeis—the judge who, above all others who have sat upon the Court (to speak, as Frankfurter would say, only of the dead), was and is a symbol of expertise in the manipulation of technical rules of jurisdiction in order to restrain his colleagues and leave a large area for experimentation by legislative majorities, both state and national.[17] Brandeis' articulation of these norms to guide the Court, in February, 1936—less than a year before the eruption of the Court-packing fight—smacks at least as much of judicial gamesmanship as it does of a scholarly restatement of the law. The student can decide for himself the pertinency of this caveat by observing the extent to which the Court has, and has not, lived up to the "Ashwander rules," in the cases that we shall examine in the chapters that follow.

[17] Cf. the solution that Brandeis induced Holmes and the rest of the Court to accept in *Bullock* v. *Florida*, 254 U.S. 513 (1921), discussed in Chapter 3, *supra*, pp. 126-129.

Political Questions

COLEGROVE v. GREEN

328 U.S. 549 (June 10, 1946).

Appeal from the United States District Court for the Northern District of Illinois.

Affirmed.

4-3

Frankfurter	('+'
Reed	(+
Burton	(+
Rutledge	('+'
Black	'—')
Douglas	—)
Murphy	—)
Jackson	NP
Vacancies (C.J.)	1

Jackson was on leave at Nuremburg and Stone was dead at the time this case was decided, so only seven justices participated in the decision. The six Roosevelt appointees divided equally on the question whether the Court could and should order state officials to redistrict a state for purposes of congressional representation, so the deciding vote was cast by Burton, who was Truman's first appointee. Only three justices actually accepted the opinion announcing the judgment of the Court; Rutledge, whose concurring opinion is not reproduced below, agreed with the dissenters (i.e., the Black group) that the question presented was justiciable; but he voted (with the Frankfurter group) for dismissal on the grounds that, as a matter of "equitable discretion," jurisdiction was properly denied. As a consequence, it appears that a majority of the justices participating in the decision agreed with the views of the dissenting opinion on the merits of the question presented; but Rutledge's ambivalence and vote permitted the Frankfurter group to control disposition of the case. It will be observed that Rutledge plus the Black group comprise what we have earlier described as the "libertarian bloc"; and that the failure of this "bloc" to stick together in voting, when they were in agreement on the substance of the issues presented, is the more striking. Rutledge's defection from the bloc clearly cost the libertarians the power to control both the disposition of this particular case and the right to state the constitutional policy on the issues that it presented.

MR. JUSTICE FRANKFURTER announced the judgment of the Court and an opinion in which MR. JUSTICE REED and MR. JUSTICE BURTON concur.

This case is appropriately here . . . on direct review of a judgment of the District Court of the Nothern District of Illinois, composed of three judges, dismissing the complaint of the appellants. These are three qualified voters in Illinois districts which have much larger populations than other Illinois Congressional districts. They brought this suit against the Governor, the Secretary of State, and the Auditor of the State of Illinois, as members *ex officio* of the Illinois Primary Certifying Board, to restrain them, in effect, from taking proceedings for an election in November 1946, under the provisions of Illinois law governing Congressional districts. . . . Formally, the appellants asked for a decree, with its incidental relief, . . . declaring these provisions to be invalid because they violated various provisions of the United States Constitution and §3 of the Reapportionment Act of August 8, 1911 . . . in that by reason of subsequent changes in population the Congressional districts for the election of Representatives in the Congress created by the Illinois Laws of 1901 . . . lacked compactness of territory and approximate equality of population. . . .

We are of opinion that the appellants ask of this Court what is beyond its competence to grant. This is one of those demands on judicial power which cannot be met by verbal fencing about "jurisdiction." It must be resolved by considerations on the basis of which this Court, from time to time, has refused to intervene in controversies. It has refused to do so because due regard for the effective working of our Government revealed this issue to be of a peculiarly political nature and therefore not meet for judicial determination.

This is not an action to recover for damage because of the discriminatory exclusion of a plaintiff from rights enjoyed by other citizens. The basis for the suit is not a private wrong, but a wrong suffered by Illinois as a polity. . . . In effect this is an appeal to the federal courts to reconstruct the electoral process of Illinois in order that it may be adequately represented in the councils of the Nation. Because the Illinois legislature has failed to revise its Congressional Representative districts in order to reflect great changes, during more than a generation, in the distribution of its population, we are asked to do this, as it were, for Illinois.

Of course no court can affirmatively remap the Illinois districts so as to bring them more in conformity with the standards of fairness for a representative system. At best we could only declare the existing electoral system invalid. The result would be to leave Illinois undistricted and to bring into operation, if the Illinois legislature chose not to act, the choice of members for the House of Representatives on a state-wide ticket. The last stage may be worse than the first. The upshot of judicial action may defeat the vital political principle which led Congress, more than a hundred years ago, to require districting. . . . Assuming acquiescence on the part of the authorities of Illinois in the selection of its Representatives by a mode that defies the direction of Congress for selection by districts, the House of Representatives may not acquiesce. In the exercise of its power to judge the qualifi-

cations of its own members, the House may reject a delegation of Representatives-at-large. . . . Nothing is clearer than that this controversy concerns matters that bring courts into immediate and active relations with party contests. From the determination of such issues this Court has traditionally held aloof. It is hostile to a democratic system to involve the judiciary in the politics of the people. And it is not less pernicious if such judicial intervention in an essentially political contest be dressed up in the abstract phrases of the law.

The appellants urge with great zeal that the conditions of which they complain are grave evils and offend public morality. The Constitution of the United States gives ample power to provide against these evils. But due regard for the Constitution as a viable system precludes judicial correction. Authority for dealing with such problems resides elsewhere. Article I, §4 of the Constitution provides that "The Times, Places and Manner of holding Elections for . . . Representatives, shall be prescribed in each State by the Legislature thereof; but the Congress may at any time by Law make or alter such Regulations, . . ." The short of it is that the Constitution has conferred upon Congress exclusive authority to secure fair representation by the States in the popular House and left to that House determination whether States have fulfilled their responsibility. If Congress failed in exercising its powers, whereby standards of fairness are offended, the remedy ultimately lies with the people. Whether Congress faithfully discharges its duty or not, the subject has been committed to the exclusive control of Congress. An aspect of government from which the judiciary, in view of what is involved, has been excluded by the clear intention of the Constitution cannot be entered by the federal courts because Congress may have been in default in exacting from States obedience to its mandate.

The one stark fact that emerges from a

study of the history of Congressional apportionment is its embroilment in politics, in the sense of party contests and party interests. The Constitution enjoins upon Congress the duty of apportioning Representatives "among the several States . . . according to their respective Numbers, . . ." Article I, §2. Yet, Congress has at times been heedless of this command and not apportioned according to the requirements of the Census. It never occurred to anyone that this Court could issue mandamus to compel Congress to perform its mandatory duty to apportion. . . . Until 1842 there was the greatest diversity among the States in the manner of choosing Representatives because Congress had made no requirement for districting. . . . Congress then provided for the election of Representatives by districts. Strangely enough, the power to do so was seriously questioned; it was still doubted by a Committee of Congress as late as 1901. . . . In 1850 Congress dropped the requirement. . . . The Reapportionment Act of 1862 required that the districts be of contiguous territory. . . . In 1872 Congress added the requirement of substantial equality of inhabitants. . . . This was reinforced in 1911. . . . But the 1929 Act, as we have seen, dropped these requirements. . . . Throughout our history, whatever may have been the controlling Apportionment Act, the most glaring disparities have prevailed as to the contours and the population of districts. . . .

To sustain this action would cut very deep into the very being of Congress. Courts ought not to enter this political thicket. The remedy for unfairness in districting is to secure State legislatures that will apportion properly, or to invoke the ample powers of Congress. The Constitution has many commands that are not enforceable by courts because they clearly fall outside the conditions and purposes that circumscribe judicial action. Thus, "on Demand of the executive Authority," Art. IV, §2, of a State it is the duty of a sister State to deliver up a fugitive from

justice. But the fulfilment of this duty cannot be judicially enforced. *Kentucky* v. *Dennison,* 24 How. 66. The duty to see to it that the laws are faithfully executed cannot be brought under legal compulsion, *Mississippi* v. *Johnson,* 4 Wall. 475. Violation of the great guaranty of a republican form of government in States cannot be challenged in the courts. *Pacific Telephone Co.* v. *Oregon,* 223 U.S. 118. The Constitution has left the performance of many duties in our governmental scheme to depend on the fidelity of the executive and legislative action and, ultimately, on the viligance of the people in exercising their political rights.

Dismissal of the complaint is affirmed.

MR. JUSTICE BLACK, dissenting. . . .

It is difficult for me to see why the 1901 State Apportionment Act does not deny appellants equal protection of the laws. The failure of the Legislature to reapportion the congressional election districts for forty years, despite census figures indicating great changes in the distribution of the population, has resulted in election districts the populations of which range from 112,000 to 900,000. One of the appellants lives in a district of more than 900,000 people. His vote is consequently much less effective than that of each of the citizens living in the district of 112,000. And such a gross inequality in the voting power of citizens irrefutably demonstrates a complete lack of effort to make an equitable apportionment. The 1901 State Apportionment Act if applied to the next election would thus result in a wholly indefensible discrimination against appellants and all other voters in heavily populated districts. The equal protection clause of the Fourteenth Amendment forbids such discrimination. It does not permit the States to pick out certain qualified citizens or groups of citizens and deny them the right to vote at all. See *Nixon* v. *Herndon,* 273 U.S. 536, 541; *Nixon* v. *Condon,* 286 U.S. 73. No one would deny that the equal protection clause would also prohibit a law that would expressly give certain citizens a half-vote and others a full vote. The probable effect of the 1901 State Apportionment Act in the coming election will be that certain citizens, and among them the appellants, will in some instances have votes only one-ninth as effective in choosing representatives to Congress as the votes of other citizens. Such discriminatory legislation seems to me exactly the kind that the equal protection clause was intended to prohibit. . . .

Had Illinois passed an Act requiring that all of its twenty-six Congressmen be elected by the citizens of one county, it would clearly have amounted to a denial to the citizens of the other counties of their constitutionally guaranteed right to vote. And I cannot imagine that an Act that would have apportioned twenty-five Congressmen to the State's smallest county and one Congressman to all the others, would have been sustained by any court. . . .

. . . What is involved here is the right to vote guaranteed by the Federal Constitution. It has always been the rule that where a federally protected right has been invaded the federal courts will provide the remedy to rectify the wrong done. Federal courts have not hesitated to exercise their equity power in cases involving deprivation of property and liberty. . . . There is no reason why they should do so where the case involves the right to choose representatives that make laws affecting liberty and property.

. . . It is true that declaration of invalidity of the State Act and the enjoining of state officials would result in prohibiting the State from electing Congressmen under the system of the old congressional districts. But it would leave the State free to elect them from the State at large, which . . . is a manner authorized by the Constitution. It is said that it would be inconvenient for the State to conduct the election in this manner. But it has an element of virtue that the more convenient method does not have—namely, it does not discriminate against some groups to favor others, it gives all the people an equally effective voice in electing their representatives as is essential under a free government, and it is constitutional.

Mr. Justice Douglas and Mr. Justice Murphy join in this dissent.

A Strategy for Survival

Judicial Self-Restraint [18]

[A] pervasive tendency in the American political and constitutional tradition [is] directed towards taking the politics out of politics, and substituting some set of Platonic guardians for fallible politicians. . . . The rationale for this viewpoint is simple: "The people must be protected from themselves, and no institution is better fitted for the role of chaperone than the federal judiciary, dedicated as it is to the supremacy of the rule of law."

. . . The fact is that the United States Supreme Court, and the inferior federal courts under the oversight of the high Court, have enormous policy-making functions. Unlike their British and French counterparts, federal judges are not merely technicians who live in the shadow of a supreme legislature, but are fully equipped to intervene in the process of political decision-making. In theory, they are limited by the Constitution and the

18 John P. Roche, "Judicial Self-Restraint," *American Political Science Review,* Vol. 49, pp. 762-772 (1955).

jurisdiction it confers, but, in practice, it would be a clumsy judge indeed who could not, by a little skilful exegesis, adapt the Constitution to a necessary end. This statement is in no sense intended as a condemnation. . . .

Thus it is naive to assert that the Supreme Court is limited by the Constitution, and we must turn elsewhere for the sources of judicial restraint. The great power exercised by the Court has carried with it great risks, so it is not surprising that American political history has been sprinkled with demands that the judiciary be emasculated. The really startling thing is that, with the notable exception of the McCardle incident in 1869, the Supreme Court has emerged intact from each of these encounters. Despite the plenary power that Congress, under Article III of the Constitution, can exercise over the appellate jurisdiction of the high Court, the national legislature has never taken sustained and effective action against its House of Lords. . . .

TECHNIQUES OF JUDICIAL SELF-RESTRAINT

The major techniques of judicial self-restraint appear to fall under the two familiar rubrics: procedural and substantive. Under the former fall the various techniques by which the Court can avoid coming to grips with substantive issues, while under the latter would fall those methods by which the Court, in a substantive holding, finds that the matter at issue in the litigation is not properly one for judicial settlement. . . .

Procedural Self-Restraint. Since the passage of the Judiciary Act of 1925, the Supreme Court has had almost complete control over its business. . . . Furthermore, the Supreme Court can issue certiorari on its own terms. . . . Simple delay can be employed, perhaps in the spirit of the Croatian proverb that "delay is the handmaiden of justice." . . .

Substantive Self-Restraint. Once a case has come before the Court on its merits, the justices [usually] give some explanation for whatever action they may take. Here self-restraint can take many forms, notably, the doctrine of political questions, the operation of judicial parsimony, and—particularly with respect to the actions of administrative officers or agencies—the theory of judicial inexpertise.

The doctrine of political questions is too familiar to require much elaboration here. Suffice it to say that if the Court feels that a question before it, *e.g.,* the legitimacy of a state government, the validity of a legislative apportionment, or the correctness of executive action in the field of foreign relations, is one that is not properly amenable to judicial settlement, it will refer the plaintiff to the "political" organs of government for any possible relief. The extent to which this doctrine is applied seems to be a direct coefficient of judicial egotism, for the definition of a political question can be expanded or contracted in accordian-like fashion to meet the exigencies of the times. A juridical definition of the term is impossible, for at root the logic that supports it is circular: political questions are matters not soluble by the judicial process; matters not soluble by the judicial process are political questions. As an early dictionary explained, violins are small cellos, and cellos are large violins.

Nor do examples help much in definition. While it is certainly true that the Court cannot mandamus a legislature to apportion a state in equitable fashion, it seems equally true that the Court is without the authority to force state legislators to implement unsegregated public education. Yet in the former instance the Court genuflected to the "political" organs and took no action, while in the latter it struck down segregation as violative of the Constitution.

Judicial parsimony is another major technique of substantive self-restraint. In what is essentially a legal application of Occam's razor, the Court has held that it will not apply any more principles to the settlement of a case than are absolutely necessary, e.g., it will not discuss the constitutionality of a law if it can settle the instant case by statutory construction. Furthermore, if an action is found to rest on erroneous statutory construction, the review terminates at that point: the Court will not go on to discuss whether the statute, properly construed, would be constitutional. A variant form of this doctrine, and a most important one, employs the "case or controversy" approach, to wit, the Court, admitting the importance of the issue, inquires as to whether the litigant actually has standing to bring the matter up. . . .

A classic use of parsimony to escape from a dangerous situation occurred in connection with the evacuation of the Nisei from the West Coast in 1942. Gordon Hirabayashi, in an attempt to test the validity of the regulations clamped on the American-Japanese by the military, violated the curfew and refused to report to an evacuation center. He was convicted on both counts by the district court and sentenced to three months for each offense, the sentences to run *concurrently*. When the case came before the Supreme Court, the justices sustained his conviction for violating the *curfew*, but refused to examine the validity of the evacuation order on the ground that it would not make any difference to Hirabayashi anyway; he was in for ninety days no matter what the Court did with evacuation.

A third method of utilizing substantive self-restraint is particularly useful in connection with the activities of executive departments or regulatory agencies, both state and federal. I have entitled it the doctrine of judicial *inexpertise,* for it is founded on the unwillingness of the Court to revise the findings of experts. The earmarks of this form of restraint are great deference to the holdings of the expert agency usually coupled with such a statement as "It is not for the federal courts to supplant the [Texas Railroad] Commission's judgment even in the face of convincing proof that a different result would have been better." In this tradition, the Court has refused to question *some* exercises of discretion by the National Labor Relations Board, the Federal Trade Commission, and other federal and state agencies. But the emphasis on *some* gives the point away: in other cases, apparently on all fours with those in which it pleads its technical *inexpertise,* the Court feels free to assess evidence *de novo* and reach independent judgment on the technical issues involved. . . .

In short, with respect to expert agencies, the Court is equipped with both offensive and defensive gambits. If it chooses to intervene, one set of precedents is brought out, while if it decides to hold back, another set of equal validity is invoked. Perhaps the best summary of this point was made by Justice Harlan in 1910, when he stated bluntly that "the Courts have rarely, if ever, felt themselves so restrained by technical rules that they could not find some remedy, consistent with the law, for acts . . . that violated natural justice or were hostile to the fundamental principles devised for the protection of the essential rights of property." . . .

THE CONDITIONS OF JUDICIAL SELF-RESTRAINT

The power of the Supreme Court to invade the decision-making arena, I submit, is a consequence of that fragmentation of political power which is normal in the United States. No cohesive majority, such as normally exists in Britain, would permit a politically irresponsible judiciary to usurp decision-making functions, but, for complex social and institutional reasons, there are few issues in the United States on which cohesive majorities exist. The guerrilla warfare which usually rages between Congress and the President, as well as the internal civil wars which are endemic in both the legislature and the administration, give the judiciary considerable room for maneuver. If, for example, the Court strikes down a controversial decision of the Federal Power Commission, it will be supported by a substantial bloc of congressmen; if it supports the FPC's decision, it will also receive considerable congressional support. But the important point is that *either* way it decides the case, there is no possibility that Congress will exact any vengeance on the Court for its action. A disciplined majority would be necessary to clip the judicial wings, and such a majority does not exist on this issue.

On the other hand, when monolithic majorities do exist on issues, the Court is likely to resort to judicial self-restraint. A good case here is the current tidal wave of anti-communist legislation and administrative action, the latter particularly with regard to aliens, which the Court has treated most gingerly. About the only issues on which there can be found cohesive majorities are those relating to national defense, and the Court has, as Clinton Rossiter demonstrated in an incisive analysis, traditionally avoided problems arising in this area irrespective of their constitutional merits. . . . In short, judicial self-restraint and judicial power seem to be opposite sides of the same coin: it has been by judicious application of the former that the latter has been maintained. A tradition beginning with Marshall's *coup* in *Marbury* v. *Madison* and running through *Mississippi* v. *Johnson* and *Ex Parte Vallandigham* to *Dennis* v. *United States* suggests that the Court's power has been maintained by a wise refusal to employ it in unequal combat.

THE USE AND ABUSE OF PRECEDENTS

Following Precedents

> BASSANIO: . . . I beseech you,
> Wrest once the law to your authority.
> To do a great right, do a little wrong,
> And curb this cruel devil of his will.
>
> PORTIA: It must not be. There is no power in Venice
> Can alter a decree established.
> 'Twill be recorded for a precedent;
> And many an error by the same example
> Will rush into the state. It cannot be.
>
> SHAKESPEARE, *The Merchant of Venice,* IV:1:214-222

> "We worry ourselves overmuch about the enduring consequences of our errors. They may work a little confusion for a time. In the end, they will be modified or corrected or their teachings ignored. The future takes care of such things." CARDOZO, *The Nature of the Judicial Process,* p. 179

Shakespeare and Cardozo have thus articulated the polar positions around which the attitudes of Supreme Court justices, toward their obligation to follow past decisions of the Court, tend to gravitate. It would be misleading to assume, however, that justices can be neatly classified as either pro- or anti-*stare decisis* types. They all follow precedent under some circumstances; and they all refuse to follow precedent under other circumstances. Indeed, as we shall soon see, it is quite possible for opposing factions of the Court to proclaim, both sincerely and vociferously, that they are each the true followers of precedent in the case, while their opposing colleagues suffer temporarily from a curious perversion of vision.

Among the factors that affect a judge's attitudes toward *stare decisis,* length of tenure on the Court is undoubtedly one of the most important. A freshman justice is, at least potentially, a new broom. There are at least two reasons for this. For one thing, he has not yet developed alliances, entangling or otherwise, with his colleagues. Free for a time of the patterns of personal obligation and commitment that come, in time, to structure the interpersonal relationships within any small group, he is more flexible than a justice whose position on any controversial issue will necessarily induce echoes (even though they be inarticulate most of the time) of past battles, old scars, and former comradery and opposition. In the second place, a justice has two quite different kinds of obligation to the Court's earlier decisions. As a member of the Court, he has a quite rational and dispassionate responsibility to respect the judgment of former members of the institution of which he himself is for a time a part. Quite independent of this institutional loyalty is a justice's psychological need for consistency and self-respect, which is involved whenever the precedent in question is one that he helped personally to create.

Even within this last grouping, there are subcategories. A justice who had joined a majority opinion with which he really is in disagreement, preferring silent acquiescence to open dissent, may be only slightly embarrassed by the formal inconsistency between his presently articulated views and the views of another justice to which he had voiced no objection. This was one of the horns in the "Dissenter's Dilemma"—although in the case of "Roberts' switch," embarrassment was more than slight. But it takes an exceptional judge not to feel a compulsion to defend an earlier opinion of the Court, which he authored, when a new majority has found new light and is prepared to overrule or distinguish away the former guidepost. It is the latter kind of situation that tends to produce the most impassioned rhetoric in defense of "the principle of *stare decisis.*" Examples are Frankfurter's dissent in *West Virginia State Board of Education* v. *Barnette,* (Chapter 10, *infra*), which overruled the Gobitis case in which Frankfurter had written the opinion of the Court; and Robert's dissent in *Smith* v. *Allwright* (Chapter 9, *infra*), which overruled *Grovey* v. *Townsend* in which it was Roberts who spoke for the Court. This is, after all, an only too-human sort of reaction. It is behavior reciprocal to that equally human tendency expressed with such good humor in the topic sentence to the final paragraph of Robert Jackson's last writing. "Sometimes," said Justice Jackson, "one is tempted to quote his former self, not only to pay his respects to the author but to demonstrate the consistency of his views, if not their correctness." [19]

In this section, we shall discuss the role of *stare decisis* in the Supreme Court, in the view of a liberal justice; the relationship of *obiter dictum* to *stare decisis;* the alternative techniques of "distinguishing" cases, explicit overruling, and overruling *sub silentio;* and certain descriptive statistics about the overruling of its own earlier decisions by the Supreme Court. From these materials, the student should be in a position to form at least a preliminary judgment of his own about the extent to which *stare decisis* is a principle of law, or a tool of adjudication to support and lend authority to decisions arrived at on some *other* basis than respect for the obligation of precedents.

Stare Decisis [20]

We live in an age of doubt and confusion. Rules that once seemed fixed and certain today seem beclouded. Principles of law have been challenged and judges asked to refashion them. Many raised their voices in protest. Some were special pleaders with a stake in existing law. Others had a sincere belief

[19] Robert H. Jackson, *The Supreme Court in the American System of Government* (Cambridge: Harvard University Press, 1955), p. 82.

[20] William O. Douglas, "Stare Decisis," *Record of the Association of the Bar of the City of New York,* Vol. 4, pp. 152-179 (May, 1949).

that the foremost function of law in these days of stress and strain is to remain steady and stable so as to promote security. Thus judges have been admonished to hold steadfast to ancient precedents lest the courts themselves add fresh doubt, confusion, and concern over the strength of our institutions.

This search for a static security—in the law or elsewhere—is misguided. The fact is that security can only be achieved through constant change, through the wise discarding of old ideas that have outlived their usefulness, and through the adapting of others to current facts. There is only an illusion of safety in a Maginot Line. Social forces like armies can sweep around a fixed position and make it untenable. A position that can be shifted to meet such forces and at least partly absorb them alone gives hope of security. . . .

It is easy, however, to overemphasize *stare decisis* as a principle in the lives of men. Even for the experts law is only a prediction of what judges will do under a given set of facts—a prediction that makes rules of law and decisions not logical deductions but functions of human behavior. There are usually plenty of precedents to go around; and with the accumulation of decisions, it is no great problem for the lawyer to find legal authority for most propositions. The difficulty is to estimate what effect a slightly different shade of facts will have and to predict the speed of the current in a changing stream of the law. The predictions and prophecies that lawyers make are indeed appraisals of a host of imponderables. The decisions of yesterday or of the last century are only the starting points. . . .

The place of *stare decisis* in constitutional law is even more tenuous. A judge looking at a constitutional decision may have compulsions to revere past history and accept what was once written. But he remembers above all else that it is the Constitution which he swore to support and defend, not the gloss which his predecessors may have put on it. So he comes to formulate his own views, rejecting some earlier ones as false and embracing others. He cannot do otherwise unless he lets men long dead and unaware of the problems of the age in which he lives do his thinking for him.

This reexamination of precedent in constitutional law is a personal matter for each judge who comes along. When only one new judge is appointed during a short period, the unsettling effect in constitutional law may not be great. But when a majority of a Court is suddenly reconstituted, there is likely to be substantial unsettlement. There will be unsettlement until the new judges have taken their positions on constitutional doctrine. During that time—which may extend a decade or more—constitutional law will be in flux. That is the necessary consequence of our system and to my mind a healthy one. The alternative is to let the Constitution freeze in the pattern which one generation gave it. But the Constitution was designed for the vicissitudes of time. It must never become a code which carries the overtones of one period that may be hostile to another.

So far as constitutional law is concerned *stare decisis* must give way before the dynamic component of history. Once it does, the cycle starts again. Today's new and startling decision quickly becomes a coveted anchorage for new vested interests. The former proponents of change acquire an acute conservatism in their new *status quo*. It will then take an oncoming group from a new generation to catch the broader vision which may require an undoing of the work of our present and their past. . . .

I said that one measure of instability of the law is represented by the overruling of precedents. But the overruling itself is at times not the true measure of the change. Commonly the change extended over a long period; the erosion of a precedent was gradual. The overruling did not effect an abrupt change in the law; it rather recognized a *fait accompli.*

In other words the distinguishing of precedents is often a gradual and reluctant way of overruling cases. In modern times the House of Lords has rarely overruled a precedent. But . . . it has carried the technique of distinguishing precedents "to a very high pitch of ingenuity." And for us the process of distinguishing may indeed do service for overruling or have the same effect. . . .

Thus the actual overruling of cases is no true measure of the rate of change in the law. The overruling may come at the end of a cycle of change and not mark its commencement. It is this gradual process of erosion of constitutional doctrine that has the true unsettling effect. It is this which often breeds wasteful uncertainty. As the first landmark falls, the outsider may have few clues as to the importance of the shift. The overruling may and often does presage a sweeping change in constitutional doctrine. Years of litigation may be needed to rid the law of mischievous decisions which should have fallen with the first of the series to be overruled.

That is why it is my belief that it would be wise judicial administration when a landmark decision falls to overrule expressly all the cases in the same genus as the one which is repudiated, even though they are not before the Court. There is candor in that course. *Stare decisis* then is not used to breed the uncertainty which it is supposed to dispel. . . .

Much of the unsettling influence of the Court since 1937 has been in removing from constitutional doctrine excrescences produced early in the century. The tendency has been to return to older views of constitutional interpretation, and to sanction governmental power over social and economic affairs which the Court beginning in the '80's and particularly in the preceding ten to thirty years had denied. Only if this is understood can the work of the period be put into clear historical perspective. . . .

It is sometimes thought to be astute political management of a shift in position to proclaim that no change is under way. That is designed as a sedative to instill confidence and allay doubts. It has been a tool of judges as well as other officials. Precedents, though distinguished and qualified out of existence, apparently have been kept alive. The theory is that the outward appearance of stability is what is important.

The idea that any body of law, particularly public law, should appear to stay put and not be in flux is an interesting phenomenon that Frank has explored in *Law and the Modern Mind.* He points out how it is—in law and in other fields too—that men continue to chant of the immutability of a rule in order to "cover up the transformation, to deny the reality of change, to conceal the truth of adaptation behind a verbal disguise of fixity and universality." But the more blunt, open, and direct course is truer to democratic traditions. It reflects the candor of Cardozo. The principle of full disclosure has as much place in government as it does in the market place. A judiciary that discloses what it is doing and why it does it will breed understanding. And confidence based on understanding is more enduring than confidence based on awe. . . .

Obiter Dicta

"In the last analysis," said a federal district judge, "the Judges of the Supreme Court are the final arbiters as to what is or is not dicta in a previous opinion." [21] This is certainly true in fact, if not in theory. In theory, an "obiter dictum" is verbiage: language in an opinion unnecessary to the support the decision reached in a case. In practice, anything that a subsequent Court finds inconvenient or embarrassing, and that is not a part of the direct holding in the earlier case, may later be explained away as "only obiter" or as a "mere dictum." The difference, from this point of view, between the designation of dicta and the distinguishing (as it is called) of cases is this: When the Court wishes to avoid following the language of earlier opinions, it calls the language obiter dicta; when the Court wishes to avoid the "holding," or the rule of decision, of an earlier case, and without expressly overruling the case, it "distinguishes" between the "facts" of the two cases. We shall discuss distinguishment as a technique in the next subsection of this chapter.

A good example of the discretionary nature of dicta designation is found in a series of three cases, the first of which was *Ex Parte Bakelite Corporation*, 279 U.S. 438 (1929). In the Bakelite case, the Court decided, in a unanimous opinion written by Van Devanter, that it would not grant an extraordinary writ of prohibition to review a decision of the Court of Customs Appeals, since that court, being a "legislative court," was not limited by Article III to the decision of "cases or controversies." [22] But in the course of the opinion, the Court stated quite explicitly that *both* the Court of Claims and the superior courts of the District of Columbia were also legislative courts. Van Devanter's opinion argued by analogy from both the status of the Court of Claims and that of the District of Columbia courts in justifying his conclusion that the Court of Customs Appeals was a legislative court.

Only four years later, however, the Court ruled that that part of the Bakelite opinion which discussed the District of Columbia courts was nothing but obiter

---

[21] *Ochikubo* v. *Bonesteel*, 60 F. Supp. 916, 930 fn. 28 (1945).

[22] See page 206, *supra*, and page 285, *infra*.

dictum; while the language referring to the Court of Claims was an authoritative holding which the Court was now bound to follow under the principle of *stare decisis*. Let us see how this tour de force was accomplished.

O'Donoghue v. *United States*, 289 U.S. 516, and *Williams* v. *United States*, 289 U.S. 553, were companion cases, decided together on May 29, 1933. Sutherland wrote for the majority in both cases. O'Donoghue was a judge of a District of Columbia court, and Williams was a judge of the Court of Claims. The salary of each had been cut under an economy rider to a 1932 appropriation act, which authorized reductions to a fixed maximum in the salaries of all federal judges except those who were appointed to constitutional (i.e., Article III) courts. Acting in strict accord with the language in the Supreme Court's opinion in *Ex Parte Bakelite,* the Comptroller General had cut the salary of both O'Donoghue and Williams. Both brought claims, for payment of back salary, in the Court of Claims; that court certified both cases to the Supreme Court, thus inviting the Court, in effect, to reconsider what it had said in the Bakelite decision. Clearly, Williams' colleagues on the Court of Claims were interested parties, although not formally so of course, in this litigation.

The Supreme Court obliged by deciding that Williams and his colleagues had to accept the pay cut; while O'Donoghue was entitled to receive his full compensation, which could not be diminished during his (life) tenure of office. The reason for this was that, as the Court had said in the Bakelite case, the Court of Claims was a legislative court. The superior courts of the District of Columbia, it now appeared, however, were *both* constitutional and legislative courts. (We shall pass over, until the next chapter, the general implications of this chameleon-like status.) It is not without interest to note that Van Devanter, the author of the Bakelite opinion, dissented from the O'Donoghue decision (which "over-ruled" his "dictum" on the status of District of Columbia courts). He was joined by Hughes and Cardozo, who were not on the Court at the time of the Bakelite decision. But the decision in the Williams case, which *followed* Van Devanter's Bakelite dictum on the status of the Court of Claims, was unanimous.

As Sutherland explained, the language in the Bakelite decision referring to the District of Columbia courts was merely obiter dicta: [23]

> The government relies almost entirely upon the decision of this court in *Ex parte Bakelite Corp.*, 279 U.S. 438. In that case we held that the Court of Customs Appeals was a legislative court, not a constitutional court under Art. III of the Constitution. In the course of the opinion attention was called to the decisions in respect of the territorial courts, and it was said that a like view had been taken in respect of the status and jurisdiction of the courts provided by Congress for the District of Columbia. This observation, made incidentally, by way of illustration merely and without discussion or

[23] *O'Donoghue* v. *United States*, 289 U.S. 516, 550 (May 29, 1933).

elaboration, was not necessary to the decision, and is not in harmony with the views expressed in the present opinion. "It is a maxim, not to be disregarded," said Chief Justice Marshall in *Cohens* v. *Virginia,* 6 Wheat. 264, 399, "that general expressions, in every opinion, are to be taken in connection with the case in which those expressions are used. If they go beyond the case, they may be respected, but ought not to control the judgment in a subsequent suit when the very point is presented for decision. The reason of this maxim is obvious. The question actually before the Court is investigated with care, and considered in its full extent. Other principles which may serve to illustrate it, are considered in their relation to the case decided, but their possible bearing on all other cases is seldom completely investigated."

But the language in *Ex parte Bakelite* referring to the Court of Claims, although not strictly speaking a part of the *ratio decidendi,* was much more persuasive—indeed, almost authoritative—in character: [24]

It must be conceded at the threshold that this court in several cases has expressed, more or less irrelevantly, its opinion in the affirmative. Thus, in *United States* v. *Klein,* 13 Wall. 128, 145, after reference to the legislation with respect to the Court of Claims, the view is expressed that such court was thus constituted one of those inferior courts which Congress authorizes. In *United States* v. *Union Pacific R. Co.,* 98 U.S. 569, 603, it was said that under the authority of Art. III Congress had created the district courts, the circuit courts, and the Court of Claims, and vested each of them with a defined portion of the judicial power found in the Constitution. In *Minnesota* v. *Hitchcock,* 185 U.S. 373, 386, the court, after directing attention to the fact that the United States could not be sued without its consent, said that with its consent it might be sued, in which event the judicial power of the United States extended to such a controversy, and added, "Indeed, the whole jurisdiction of the Court of Claims rests upon this proposition." See also *Kansas* v. *United States,* 204 U.S. 331, 342; *United States* v. *Louisiana,* 123 U.S. 32, 35.

None of these cases involved the question now under consideration, and the expressions referred to were clearly *obiter dicta,* which, as said by Chief Justice Marshall in *Cohens* v. *Virginia,* 6 Wheat. 264, 399, "may be respected but ought not to control the judgment in a subsequent suit when the very point is presented for decision."

On the other hand, this court, in *Ex parte Bakelite Corp.,* 279 U.S. 438, in a fully considered opinion holding that the Court of Customs Appeals was a legislative court, definitely took the opposite view. The status of the Court of Claims is there discussed at length, and the conclusion reached that it likewise is a legislative court. . . .

It is true that the foregoing views expressed in the *Bakelite* case were likewise not strictly necessary to the decision; but unlike previous and con-

[24] *Williams* v. *United States,* 289 U.S. 553, 568, 570-571 (May 29, 1933).

trary expressions of opinion on the same subject, they are elucidated and fortified by reasoning and illustration, and, moreover, are the result of a careful review of the entire matter. It is also true that in the *O'Donoghue* case, *supra,* we have rejected the *dictum* in the *Bakelite* case as to the status of the Supreme Court and Court of Appeals of the District of Columbia, but a reference to the discussion in the *O'Donoghue* case will make apparent the difference in force between the *dictum* there involved and the one here involved. In addition to this, whatever may be said in respect of the *obiter* character of the opinion as to the Court of Claims, the status of the Court of Customs Appeals, as a purely legislative court, was definitely adjudged. And neither by brief nor in argument here is any serious attempt made to differentiate, in respect of the question now being considered, between the Court of Claims and the Court of Customs Appeals; and we have been unable to discover any ground for such a differentiation.

Further reflection tends only to confirm the views expressed in the *Bakelite* opinion as to the status of the Court of Customs Appeals, and we feel bound to reaffirm and apply them. And, giving these views due effect here, we see no escape from the conclusion that if the Court of Customs Appeals is a legislative court, so also is the Court of Claims.

Distinguishing Among Precedents

Among the more quaint euphemisms of the law is the notion that an earlier case becomes "distinguished" by being discarded as a precedent. The stereotype that usually is employed to describe this process is the assertion that the Court has "distinguished" a case "by confining it to its special facts." Of course, all facts are "special," and no two cases ever come to the Court with identical fact situations. The facts of each case are inherently unique. Supreme Court cases are not interchangeable parts in an assembly-line production process. Consequently, the technique of distinguishing precedents is another discretionary tool of adjudication that the Court can and does use to avoid following inconvenient precedents, and at the same time to avoid creating the impression that it is fomenting instability in the law by frequently overruling its own prior decisions.

The Court usually discards a precedent by "limiting it to its own special facts" instead of "forthrightly and artlessly overruling" it. A precedent about a generation old is perhaps the easiest to get around, no matter which technique of avoidance is relied upon. On the other hand, a really old precedent becomes enveloped in a mystique all of its own, and the Court generally is loath to tamper with it, either on the ground that it has been followed so much that to disturb it would involve revolutionary changes, or else on the ground that several generations of Supreme Court justices having refused to change it, it would be audacious of the incumbent justices to impute higher wisdom to themselves than to their predecessors. Whichever alternative is selected, some justices (such as

Frankfurter) will call the roll of the many distinguished former justices who have acquiesced in the hallowed precedent, which eventually becomes "almost as old as the Constitution itself." It is especially authoritative if it was a decision of the Marshall Court, in which event the odds would be excellent that the opinion was rendered by the Great Chief Justice himself. If the case was decided by the Taney Court, its authority is enhanced if the opinion of the Court was delivered by Justice Joseph Story. And so on.

But cases that have been recently decided present special problems, particularly if there have been intervening personnel changes on the Court. As we already have pointed out, the effect of such personnel changes is to increase the probabilities that a recent precedent will be rejected; but the freshness of the precedent is also a factor which militates against the likelihood that the Court will expressly overrule the recent decision. It is under these circumstances that the Court is most likely to resort to the technique of distinguishment. The Christoffel and Bryan cases, below, illustrate this process.

Less than a year separates the decisions in this pair of cases. Both raised the same question of law: could a witness testifying under compulsion of a subpoena, before a congressional committee, challenge, at the time of his trial for an offense committed before the committee, the legal competence of the committee at the time of his offense on the ground that a quorum of the committee was not present? In Christoffel, the Court answered "yes," in a marginal split decision; ten and a half months later, the Court added "and no," again by a bare majority of five justices. There were three intervening events of possible relevance to the Court's change of heart. In the first place, there was very severe criticism of the Christoffel decision in the law reviews and other publications; these commentators warned that the Court was opening Pandora's box when it opened the door leading to judicial supervision of the decision-making processes of the Congress. In the second place, two members of the five-man majority in the Christoffel case— Murphy and Rutledge—had died, to be replaced by Minton and Clark; so the group that controlled decision in the Christoffel case had lost their majority, unless they could coopt both Minton and Clark—an unlikely event. In the third place, Douglas had fallen off his horse, and the injuries that he suffered required his absence from the Court during most of the 1949 Term, and he was not able to participate in the decision in the Bryan case. This reduced the former five-justice majority to two. These were the two justices who dissented in the later case, although even then, one of the two—Frankfurter—changed his views on the merits of the question decided in the Christoffel case and dissented only on the basis of a different point that was raised only in the second case.

Both of these cases, as disposed of by the Supreme Court, raised only questions of statutory interpretation. Neither induced the Court to face the important constitutional questions, relating to the applicability of First Amendment rights to the testimony of witnesses before congressional committees, which were the really burning issues of the day. The Court generally refused to grant certiorari to review cases presenting such problems, although it was asked to do so; indeed, the Court did not decide such questions until another seven years had elapsed and Senator Joseph McCarthy was dead and buried. At this calmer time when McCarthyism already had been discredited politically, the Court handed down its decision in the Watkins case.[25]

CHRISTOFFEL v. UNITED STATES

338 U.S. 84 (June 27, 1949)

Certiorari to the Court of Appeals for the District of Columbia.

Reversed.

5-4

Murphy	('+')
Black	(+)
Frankfurter	(+)
Douglas	(+)
Rutledge	(+)
Jackson	'—')
Vinson, C.J.	—)
Reed	—)
Burton	—)

The libertarian bloc stuck together in this case, and were able to control the decision because of their success in co-opting Frankfurter. The Meyers case, discussed in the footnotes to this case, involved a businessman who had profiteered on government contracts during World War II. But it raised the same question of law about the necessity for a quorum on congressional committees as did Christoffel; and the lower court, which decided both cases, considered its prior Meyers decision to be a precedent for Christoffel. Since the libertarian bloc clearly had enough votes to have caused certiorari to be granted in the Meyers case, the question arises why they did not do so. Could it be because Christoffel, a labor leader,

presented a greater appeal to libertarian sympathies than did a businessman who had profiteered, through the connivance of an air force contracting officer, during World War II? Meyers was the officer, and he was accused of having perjured himself before a congressional committee in order to cover up "kickbacks" that he had illegally received.

MR. JUSTICE MURPHY delivered the opinion of the Court.

In March of 1947, the Committee on Education and Labor was, as it is now, a standing committee of the House of Representatives. During the first session of the 80th Congress it held frequent hearings on proposed amendments to the National Labor Relations Act. On March 1, 1947, petitioner appeared as a witness before the committee, under oath, and in the course of the proceedings was asked a series of questions directed to his political affiliations and associations. In his answers he unequivocally denied that he was a Communist or that he endorsed, supported or participated in Communist programs. As a result of these answers he was indicted for perjury under Title 22, § 2501 of the District of Columbia Code, and after a trial by jury was convicted. The Court of Appeals affirmed the conviction, 171 F. 2d 1004, and we granted certiorari to review its validity. . . .

No question is raised as to the relevancy or propriety of the questions asked. Petitioner's main contention is that the committee was not a "competent tribunal"

25 *Watkins* v. *United States,* 354 U.S. 178 (1957), discussed in Chapter 11, *infra.* Cf. C.

Herman Pritchett, *The American Constitution* (New York: McGraw, 1959), pp. 193-196.

within the meaning of the statute, in that a quorum of the committee was not present at the time of the incident on which the indictment was based. As to this, the record reveals the following: the Committee on Education and Labor consists of twenty-five members, of whom thirteen constitute a quorum. At the commencement of the afternoon session on Saturday, March 1, 1947, shortly after two o'clock, a roll call showed that fourteen members were present. Petitioner's testimony started some time after four o'clock. The responses said to constitute offenses were given just prior to five p. m.

Evidence was adduced at the trial from which a jury might have concluded that at the time of the allegedly perjurious answers less than a quorum—as few as six— of the committee were in attendance. Counsel for the petitioner contended vigorously at the trial, on appeal and in this Court that unless a quorum were found to be actually present when the crucial questions were asked, the statutory requirement of a competent tribunal was not met and that absent such a finding a verdict of acquittal should follow.

The trial court agreed that the presence of a quorum was an indispensable part of the offense charged, and instructed the jury that to find the defendant guilty they had to find beyond a reasonable doubt "That the defendant Christoffel appeared before a quorum of at least thirteen members of the said Committee," and "that at least that number must have been actually and physically present. . . . If such a Committee so met, that is, if thirteen members did meet at the beginning of the afternoon session of March 1, 1947, and thereafter during the progress of the hearing some of them left temporarily or otherwise and no question was raised as to the lack of a quorum, then the fact that the majority did not remain there would not affect, for the purposes of this case, the existence of that Committee as a competent tribunal provided that before the oath was ad-

ministered and before the testimony of the defendant was given there were present as many as 13 members of that Committee at the beginning of the afternoon session. . . ."

This charge is objected to insofar as it allows the jury to find a quorum present simply by finding that thirteen or more members were in attendance when the committee was convened, without reference to subsequent facts.

The Constitution of the United States provides that "Each House may determine the Rules of its Proceedings," Art. I, § 5, and we find that the subject of competency, both of the House as a whole and of its committees, has been a matter of careful consideration. Rule XI (2) (f) of the House of Representatives reads in part, "The Rules of the House are hereby made the rules of its standing committees so far as applicable. . . ." Rule XV of the House provides for a call of the House if a quorum is not present, and it has been held under this rule that such a call, or a motion to adjourn, is the only business that may be transacted in the absence of a quorum. IV Hind's Precedents 2950; IV *id.* 2988. See IV *id.* 2934, 2939; VI Cannon's Precedents 653; VI *id.* 680. It appears to us plain that even the most highly privileged business must be suspended in the absence of a quorum in the House itself.

A similar situation obtains in the committees.[26] The Legislative Reorganization Act of 1946, 60 Stat. 812, provides, referring to the standing committees, in § 133 (d), "No measure or recommenda-

---

26 There is some difference between procedure in the full House and in its committees. In the former, business is transacted on the assumption that a quorum is present at all times, unless a roll call or a division indicates the contrary. In committee meetings, however, the presence of a quorum must be affirmatively shown before the committee is deemed to be legally met. VIII Cannon's Precedents 2222. [This footnote and the next four are taken from the opinions in the Christoffel case, but are renumbered.]

tion shall be reported from any such committee unless a majority of the committee were actually present." The rule embodied in this subsection was effective as long ago as 1918 to keep off the floor of the House a bill from a committee attended by less than a quorum, even though no objection was raised in the committee meeting itself. It appeared that the situation in the committee was much like the one with which we are concerned, with members coming and going during the meeting. No point of no quorum was raised at the committee meeting. When the Chairman proposed in the House to bring up the bill considered in the meeting, the Speaker ruled, on objection being made from the floor, that in spite of the point's not having been raised in committee, the bill could not be reported. The absence of a quorum of the committee, though at the time unobjected to, had made effective action impossible. VIII Cannon's Precedents 2212. Witnesses in committee hearings cannot be required to be familiar with the complications of parliamentary practice. Even if they are, the power to raise a point of no quorum appears to be limited to members of the committee. We have no doubt that if a member of the committee had raised a point of no quorum and a count had revealed the presence of less than a majority, proceedings would have been suspended until the deficiency should be supplied. In a criminal case affecting the rights of one not a member, the occasion of trial is an appropriate one for petitioner to raise the question.

Congressional practice in the transaction of ordinary legislative business is of course none of our concern, and by the same token the considerations which may lead Congress as a matter of legislative practice to treat as valid the conduct of its committees do not control the issue before us. The question is neither what rules Congress may establish for its own governance, nor whether presumptions of continuity may protect the validity of its legislative conduct. The question is rather what rules the House has established and whether they have been followed. It of course has the power to define what tribunal is competent to exact testimony and the conditions that establish its competency to do so. The heart of this case is that by the charge that was given it the jury was allowed to assume that the conditions of competency were satisfied even though the basis in fact was not established and in face of a possible finding that the facts contradicted the assumption.

We are measuring a conviction of crime by the statute which defined it. As a consequence of this conviction, petitioner was sentenced to imprisonment for a term of from two to six years. An essential part of a procedure which can be said fairly to inflict such a punishment is that all the elements of the crime charged shall be proved beyond a reasonable doubt. An element of the crime charged in the instant indictment is the presence of a competent tribunal, and the trial court properly so instructed the jury. The House insists that to be such a tribunal a committee must consist of a quorum, and we agree with the trial court's charge that to convict, the jury had to be satisfied beyond a reasonable doubt that there were "actually physically present" a majority of the committee.[27]

Then to charge, however, that such re-

[27] In *Meyers* v. *United States*, 171 F. 2d 800, the appellant made contentions similar to those of petitioner. The Court of Appeals for the District of Columbia Circuit held the same view expressed here. "On October 6, 1947, however, only two senators were present at the hearing. Since they were a minority of the subcommittee, they could not legally function except to adjourn. For that reason, the testimony of Lamarre given on that day cannot be considered as perjury nor can appellant be convicted of suborning it." P. 811. The conviction was affirmed on the ground that all the perjurious statements alleged in the indictment were made on October 4, when a quorum was present. P. 812.

quirement is satisfied by a finding that there was a majority present two or three hours before the defendant offered his testimony, in the face of evidence indicating the contrary, is to rule as a matter of law that a quorum need not be present when the offense is committed. This not only seems to us contrary to the rules and practice of the Congress but denies petitioner a fundamental right. That right is that he be convicted of crime only on proof of all the elements of the crime charged against him. A tribunal that is not competent is no tribunal, and it is unthinkable that such a body can be the instrument of criminal conviction. The Court of Appeals erred in affirming so much of the instructions to the jury as allowed them to find a quorum present without reference to the facts at the time of the alleged perjurious testimony, and its judgment is reversed.

Reversed.

MR. JUSTICE JACKSON, dissenting.

THE CHIEF JUSTICE, MR. JUSTICE REED, MR. JUSTICE BURTON and I think the Court is denying to the records of the Congress and its committees the credit and effect to which they are entitled, quite contrary to all recognized parliamentary rules, our previous decisions, and the Constitution itself.

No one questions that the competency of a Committee of either House of Congress depends upon the action of the House in constituting the Committee, and in determining the rules governing its procedure. Nor does any one deny that each House has the power to provide expressly that a majority of the entire membership of any of its Committees shall constitute a quorum for certain purposes and that, for other purposes, a different number shall be sufficient. For example, either House may provide expressly that, for the purpose of convening a session of a Committee or of approving a report, a majority of the Committee's entire membership shall be necessary and that, for

the purpose of taking sworn testimony, one or more Committee members shall be sufficient to constitute a quorum. Similarly, each House may spell out a formal rule that a Committee shall constitute a competent tribunal to take sworn testimony if a majority of its members shall be present at the beginning of the session at which the testimony is taken and that such competency shall continue, although the attendance of Committee members may drop, during the Committee's session, to some smaller number. The reasonableness of such a rule is apparent because the value of the testimony taken by such a Committee is measured not so much by the number of people who hear it spoken at the session as it is by the number and identity of those who read it later.

But what Congress may do by express rule it may do also by its custom and practice. There is no requirement, constitutional or otherwise, that its body of parliamentary law must be recorded in order to be authoritative. In the absence of objection raised at the time, and in the absence of any showing of a rule, practice or custom to the contrary, this Court has the duty to presume that the conduct of a Congressional Committee, in its usual course of business, conforms to both the written and unwritten rules of the House which created it. "Each House may determine the Rules of its Proceedings, ..." Art. I, § 5, cl. 2. This Court accordingly can neither determine the rules for either House of Congress nor require those rules to be expressed with any degree of explicitness other than that chosen by the respective Houses.

The record shows a quorum of this committee present when the session began and neither Christoffel nor anyone else had raised the point of no quorum up to the time he gave false testimony. On trial for perjury he introduced oral testimony tending to show that, at the moment he so testified, less than a quorum were actually present. The trial court charged that, in the absence of challenge or proof to the contrary, the quorum established at the beginning of the session is presumed to continue and the jury could find Christoffel guilty of perjury if he gave false testimony before such a body. He was found guilty. The Court now holds the charge was erroneous and that if the Government cannot show positively that there was a quorum present when he falsified, the committee was not a "competent tribunal" within the Perjury Statute of the District and his conviction thereunder is invalid.

Thus the issue is not whether a quorum is required in order for the committee to be a competent tribunal, but whether committee rules, practices and records, and congressional rules, practices and records in analogous situations, are subject to attack by later oral testimony and to invalidation by the courts.

All the parliamentary authorities, including those cited by the Court, agree that a quorum is required for action, other than adjournment, by any parliamentary body; and they agree that the customary law of such bodies is that, the presence of a quorum having been ascertained and recorded at the beginning of a session, that record stands unless and until the point of no quorum is raised. This is the universal practice. If it were otherwise, repeated useless roll calls would be necessary before every action.

In this case, therefore, the record on the subject of quorum was entitled to full credit. Christoffel himself did not, during his testimony, raise the question of no quorum. Whether one not a member of the body would have been permitted to do so and what effect it would have, had he been refused, we need not decide. The fact is, he made no effort to raise the point. To have then even suggested the objection would have given opportunity to the Committee to correct it. And if there were not enough committee members present to make a legal body, he would be at liberty, if his objection

were overruled, to walk out. Instead, he chose to falsify to the committee and now says that, despite the record, he should be allowed to prove that not enough members were present for his lie to be legal perjury. The Court agrees and holds that the House Rules requiring a quorum for action require this result. Since the constitutional provision governing the House itself also requires a quorum before that body can do business, this raises the question whether the decision now announced will also apply to the House itself. If it does, it could have the effect of invalidating any action taken or legislation passed without a record vote, which represents a large proportion of the business done by both House and Senate. The effect is illustrated by noting that such a rule would make possible the invalidation of not only this conviction for perjury, but the Perjury Act [28] itself, as well as the Judicial Code [29] which is now the source of this Court's authority to review the conviction. Moreover, this rule is in direct contravention of the Constitution which does not require either House or Senate, much less a committee, to take a record vote except "at the Desire of one fifth of those Present." Art. I, § 5, cl. 3.

The Court significantly omits citation of any prior decision in support of its present conclusion.[30] The reason is fairly

[28] Passed without record vote by the Senate, 34 Cong. Rec., Pt. 4, pp. 3496-97, and by the House without a record vote, 34 Cong. Rec., Pt. 4, p. 3586.

[29] Passed by the Senate without a record vote, 94 Cong. Rec., Pt. 7, p. 7930, and motion to reconsider withdrawn, 94 Cong. Rec., Pt. 7, p. 8297. Passed by the House without a record vote, 94 Cong. Rec., Pt. 7, p. 8501.

[30] This is not because others have not tried to raise the issue. In *Meyers* v. *United States*, 171 F. 2d 800, certiorari denied 336 U.S. 912, the petitioner was convicted of subornation of perjury committed before a committee of Congress on two separate days —October 4 and October 6. The conviction was allowed to stand despite a charge to the jury that the quorum on October 4 was presumed to continue unless and until a committee member raised the point of no quo-

clear—the others are inconsistent with this one. For example, in *United States* v. *Ballin*, 144 U.S. 1, we held it to be within the competency of the House to prescribe any method reasonably certain to ascertain the fact of a quorum; that the courts are not concerned with the wisdom or advantages of any such rule—"with the courts the question is only one of power."

rum, and that false testimony given before the point is raised is perjurious under this same statute. That charge is practically identical with the charge given in this case, of which this Court now says "The heart of this case is that by the charge that was given it the jury was allowed to assume that the conditions of competency were satisfied even though the basis in fact was not established and in face of a possible finding that the facts contradicted the assumption." This perfectly describes the *Meyers* case, considering only the October 4th testimony, on which it is said the conviction rested. Considering only that part of each count, Meyers was convicted and is now imprisoned for suborning perjury given under identical conditions as did Christoffel; and Meyers' guilt was determined by a jury which received the same ruling the Court now holds to be error as applied to Christoffel. Yet the Meyers conviction was affirmed and we denied his plea for review. Such a denial here of course does not imply approval of the law announced below but, on the undisputed facts, Meyers' conviction rests on a basis which this Court says is "unthinkable" as to Christoffel whose conviction is reversed.

Moreover, the Meyers jury was permitted to convict partly at least on the basis of testimony given before a Committee on October 6 when the *committee records showed, and the Government admits, that no quorum was present at any time.* Today's opinion is diametrically opposed to the Meyers conviction based on the October 4th testimony alone, but the Meyers conviction also rests in part on testimony before a body which demonstrably and admittedly *never* amounted to a quorum, while Christoffel's is reversed merely because the charge permitted the jury to ignore oral testimony "indicating" that a quorum once admittedly established may have evaporated. I do not see how the Court can justify such discrimination. The court below evidently could not, for it relied on the *Meyers* case as a precedent for affirming the conviction of Christoffel on this identical issue. 171 F. 2d 1004, 1005, n. 1.

The House has adopted the rule and practice that a quorum once established is presumed to continue unless and until a point of no quorum is raised. By this decision, the Court, in effect, invalidates that rule despite the limitations consistently imposed upon courts where such an issue is tendered. . . .

We do not think we should devise a new rule for this particular case to extend aid to one who did not raise his objection when it could be met and who has been prejudiced by absence of a quorum only if we assume that, although he told a falsehood to eleven Congressmen, he would have been honest if two more had been present. But in no event should we put out a doctrine by which every Congressional Act or Committee action, and perhaps every judgment here, can be overturned on oral testimony of interested parties.

We should affirm the conviction.

UNITED STATES v. BRYAN

339 U.S. 323 (May 8, 1950)

Certiorari to the Court of Appeals for the District of Columbia.

Reversed.

5-2

Vinson, C.J.	('+')
Reed	(+)
Burton	(+)
Minton	(+)
Jackson	('+'
Frankfurter	'—')
Black	'—')
Douglas	NP
Clark	NP

It is probable that if they had participated, Clark would have joined the majority and Douglas would have dissented. If this had happened, the result would have remained unchanged, although there might then have been five justices who clearly accepted the opinion of the Court —as there is not, since Jackson concurred in the result only and Frankfurter, while agreeing with the majority on the quorum question, dissented on other grounds. In the vernacular of legislative voting behavior, Douglas and Clark were in effect "paired," although there was, of course, no formal or informal voting contract between them. Their reasons for not participating were independent and unrelated. The justice who was physically absent from the Court on June 27, 1949, the date of the Christoffel decision, was Douglas; Jackson comments upon the absence, in his concurring opinion, but does not reveal the identity of the absentee.

MR. CHIEF JUSTICE VINSON delivered the opinion of the Court.

Respondent is the executive secretary of an organization known as the Joint Anti-Fascist Refugee Committee (hereinafter referred to as the association) and as such has custody of its records. Prior to April 4, 1946, the Committee on Un-American Activities of the House of Representatives, which was conducting an investigation into the activities of the association, had attempted without success to procure these records from respondent and from the chairman of the association's executive board, Dr. Edward K. Barsky. On March 29, 1946, the Committee issued subpoenas to each of the known members of the executive board summoning them to appear in the Committee's room on April 4, 1946, at 10 a.m., to testify and produce certain specified records of the association, and an identical subpoena directed to the association by name was served upon respondent Bryan in her official capacity.

Bryan and the members of the executive board appeared before the Committee at the date and time set out in the subpoenas and in response thereto. Each person so summoned failed to produce any of the records specified in the sub-

poenas. The members of the executive board made identical statements in which each declared that he or she did not have possession, custody or control of the records; that Miss Bryan, the executive secretary, did. Respondent admitted that the records were in her possession but refused to comply with the subpoena because "after consulting with counsel [she] came to the conclusion that the subpoena was not valid" because the Committee had no consitutional right to demand the books and records. Asked whether the executive board supported her action, she refused to answer because she did not think the question pertinent.

The Committee on Un-American Activities then submitted its report and resolution to the House. Setting out at length the Committee's attempts to procure the records of the association, the report concludes: "The willful and deliberate refusal of Helen R. Bryan and the members of the executive board of the Joint Anti-Fascist Refugee Committee as named herein to produce the books, papers, and records called for in the subpoenas deprives your committee of evidence necessary in the conduct of its investigation of the Joint Anti-Fascist Refugee Committee, which evidence is pertinent to the said investigation and places the said persons in contempt of the House of Representatives of the United States."

The resolution directing the Speaker to certify the Committee's report to the United States Attorney for the District of Columbia for legal action was approved by the full House after debate.

Respondent was indicted for violation of R.S. § 102, in that she had failed to produce the records called for in the subpoenas and had thereby wilfully made default. At the trial she contended, *inter alia*, that she was not guilty of wilful default because a quorum of the Committee on Un-American Activities had not been present when she appeared on the return day. However, the trial court withdrew that issue from the jury's consideration by instructing the jury "as a matter of law, that the Committee on Un-American Activities of the House of Representatives was a validly constituted committee of the Congress, and was at the time of the defendant's appearance." Respondent was found guilty, 72 F.Supp. 58, but the Court of Appeals for the District of Columbia, one judge dissenting, reversed the judgment on the ground that the presence of a quorum of the Committee at the hearing on April 4, 1946, was a material question of fact in the alleged offense and should have been submitted to the jury. . . . We granted a writ of certiorari . . . to consider this important question affecting the procedures of congressional committees.

First. R.S. § 102 was enacted in 1857. Its purpose, as stated by its sponsors, was to avoid the procedural difficulties which had been experienced by the House of Representatives when persons cited for contempt of the House were brought before its bar to show cause why they should not be committed, and, more important, to permit the imprisonment of a contemnor beyond the expiration of the current session of Congress. Transmission of the fact of the commission of a contempt to the prosecuting authority is made under the Seal of the House or Senate by the Speaker or President of the Senate. The judicial proceedings are intended as an alternative method of vindicating the authority of Congress to compel the disclosure of facts which are needed in the fulfillment of the legislative function. . . .

"Default" is, of course, a failure to comply with the summons. In this case we may assume, without deciding, that the subpoena served on respondent required her to produce the records of the association before the Committee on Un-American Activities, sitting as a committee. Upon that assumption, respondent takes the position that, absent a quorum, the Committee was without power to receive

the records on the return day; that she cannot be guilty of a default in failing to produce papers before an "agency organizationally defective," which, for that reason, "cannot be obstructed." Respondent does not and cannot, in view of the jury's verdict, contest the finding that she deliberately and intentionally refused to produce the papers called for in the subpoena. Her contention is that a quorum of the Committee was required to meet to witness her refusal. Reliance is placed upon certain precedents of the House of Representatives, which hold that a committee report may be challenged in the House on the ground that a quorum of the committee was not present when the report was approved, and upon this Court's recent decision in Christoffel v. United States, 1949, 338 U.S. 84. . . .

The Christoffel case in inapposite. For that decision, which involved a prosecution for perjury before a congressional committee, rests in part upon the proposition that the applicable perjury statute requires that a "competent tribunal" be present when the false statement is made. There is no such requirement in R.S. § 102. It does not contemplate some affirmative act which is made punishable only if performed before a competent tribunal, but an intentional failure to testify or produce papers, however the contumacy is manifested. Respondent attempts to equate R.S. § 102 with the perjury statute considered in the Christoffel case by contending that it applies only to the refusal to testify or produce papers before a committee—*i.e.*, in the presence of a quorum of the committee. But the statute is not so limited. In the first place, it refers to the wilful failure by any person "to give testimony or to produce papers *upon any matter under inquiry* before * * * any committee of either House of Congress," not to the failure to testify before a congressional Committee. And the fact that appearance before a committee is not an essential element of the offense is further emphasized by additional language in the statute, which, after defining wilful default in the terms set out above, continues, "or who, *having appeared,* refuses to answer any question pertinent to the question under inquiry, shall be deemed guilty of a misdemeanor, * * *." (Emphasis supplied.)

It is clear that R.S. § 102 is designed to punish the obstruction of inquiries in which the Houses of Congress or their committees are engaged. If it is shown that such an inquiry is, in fact, obstructed by the intentional withholding of documents, it is unimportant whether the subpoenaed person proclaims his refusal to respond before the full committee, sends a telegram to the chairman, or simply stays away from the hearing on the return day. His statements or actions are merely evidence from which a jury might infer an intent to default. A proclaimed refusal to respond, as in this case, makes that intent plain. But it would hardly be less plain if the witness embarked on a voyage to Europe on the day before his scheduled appearance before the committee. . . .

Second. It is argued, however, that even if the Government is not required to prove presence of a quorum affirmatively, lack of a quorum is a defense raising material questions of fact which should have been submitted to the jury. The theory is that if the subpoena required production of the records before the Committee on Un-American Activities *qua* committee, respondent could not have complied with the subpoena in the absence of a quorum had she wished to do so, and therefore her default is not wilful, albeit deliberate and intentional. While she did not introduce any direct evidence at the trial, respondent appropriately raised the defense by cross-examination and by her motions, requests and objections. . . .

Every exemption from testifying or producing records . . . presupposes a very real interest to be protected. If a privilege based upon that interest is asserted its validity must be assessed. Since we assume in this case that the subpoenas refer to the production of papers before the Committee *qua* committee, we agree that respondent could rightfully have demanded attendance of a quorum of the Committee and declined to testify or to produce documents so long as a quorum was not present. But the courts need not treat as important that which the witness obviously regarded as unimportant.[31] Testimonial compulsion is an intensely practical matter. If, therefore, a witness seeks to excuse a default on grounds of inability to comply with the subpoena, we think the defense must fail in the absence of even a modicum of good faith in responding to the subpoena. That such was the situation in this case does not admit of doubt.

In the first place, if respondent had legitimate reasons for failing to produce the records of the association, a decent respect for the House of Representatives, by whose authority the subpoenas issued, would have required that she state her reasons for noncompliance upon the return of the writ. At the time and place specified in the subpoenas the Chairman of the Committee and a number of other members—whether or not a quorum was present at any time is not clear from the

[31] It is, of course, clear that respondent's "inability" to comply with the subpoena because a quorum of the Committee was not present amounts to no more than the claim that she is excused from doing so. The jury found that she had power to produce the papers. The question therefore arises as to what possible prejudice respondent might have suffered if she had turned over the records to less than a quorum of the Committee. In the case of oral testimony, a witness might well desire to appear only if a quorum was present because of a feeling that some committee members, unrestrained by presence of a majority, might exceed proper bounds of inquiry. But that consideration is obviously inapplicable to the production of papers and is irrelevant here in any event since respondent testified. [This footnote is taken from the opinion of the Court.]

record—presented themselves for the taking of testimony and receipt of papers. The defect in composition of the Committee, if any, was one which could easily have been remedied. But the Committee was not informed until the trial, two years after the refusal to produce the records, that respondent sought to excuse her noncompliance on the ground that a quorum of the Committee had not been present. For two years, now grown to four, the Committee's investigation was obstructed by an objection which, so far as we are informed, could have been rectified in a few minutes.

Such a patent evasion of the duty of one summoned to produce papers before a congressional committee cannot be condoned. . . .

In the second place, the fact that the alleged defect upon which respondent now insists is, in her own estimation, an immaterial one, is clearly shown by her reliance before the Committee upon other grounds for failing to produce the records. She does not deny, and the transcript of the hearing makes it perfectly clear, that she would not have complied with the subpoenas no matter how the Committee had been constituted at the time. . . .

We hold that the Government is not required to prove that a quorum of the Committee was present when the default occurred, and that under the circumstances disclosed by this record a defense of lack of a quorum was not open to respondents. . . .

Reversed

MR. JUSTICE FRANKFURTER agrees with this opinion except as to the portion marked *Third*, [omitted here] . . . which requires him to dissent from the judgment of reversal.

MR. JUSTICE BLACK wrote a dissenting opinion.

MR. JUSTICE DOUGLAS and MR. JUSTICE CLARK took no part in the consideration or decision of this case.

MR. JUSTICE JACKSON, concurring.

With the result I am in agreement, but I do not see how this decision and that in the Christoffel case . . . can coexist.

The Court is agreed that this defendant could rightly demand attendance of a quorum of the Committee and decline to testify or to produce documents so long as a quorum was not present. Therefore the real question here is whether, without making any demand, the issue may be raised for the first time long afterwards in a trial for contempt.

This case is the duplicate of Christoffel in this respect: in both cases defendants have sought to raise the question of no quorum for the first time in court, when they are on trial for an offense, without having raised it in any manner before the Committee while there was time to remedy it. The Court is now saying, quite properly I think, that this question must be raised at the time when it can be corrected, and proper records made, and cannot be kept as an ace up the sleeve to be produced years later at a trial. But in Christoffel, the majority took the opposite view and said, "In a criminal case affecting the rights of one not a member, the occasion of a trial is an appropriate one for petitioner to raise the question." . . . If this statement of the law is to be left standing, I do not see how we can say that what was timely for Christoffel is too late for Bryan. It is plain we are not following the Christoffel decision and so I think we should candidly overrule it.

The practice of withholding all objection until time of trial is not helpful in protecting a witness' right to a valid Committee. It prevents correction of any error in that respect and profits only the witness who seeks a concealed defect to exploit. Congressional custom, whether written or not, has established that Committee Members may indulge in temporary absences, unless there is objection, without disabling those remaining from continuing work as a Committee. Members may step out to interview constituents, consult members of their staffs, confer with each other, dictate a letter, or visit a washroom, without putting an end to the Committee—but always subject to call whenever the point of no quorum is raised; that is notice that someone deems their personal presence important. This is the custom Christoffel, in effect, denied to members of Congress. A Member now steps out of a committee room at risk of nullifying the whole proceeding.

It is ironic that this interference with legislative procedures was promulgated by exercise within the Court of the very right of absentee participation denied to Congressmen. Examination of our journal on the day Christoffel was handed down shows only eight Justices present and that four Justices dissented in that case. The prevailing opinion does not expressly indicate the Justices who joined in it, but only four nondissenting Justices were present to do so. On the record this would show only an equally divided Court, which would affirm the judgment below. The only way the four who were present and for a reversal could have prevailed was by counting for it one shown by the record to be absent. There is not even any public record to show that *in absentia* he joined the decision, or approved the final opinion, or considered the matter after the dissent was circulated; nor is there any written rule or law which permitted him to do so.

I want to make it clear that I am not criticizing any Justice or suggesting the slightest irregularity in what was done. I have no doubt that authorization to include the absent Justice was given; and I know that to vote and be counted *in absentia* has been sanctioned by practice and was without objection by anyone. It is the fact that it is strictly regular and customary, according to our unwritten practice, to count as present for purposes of Court action one physically absent that makes the denial of a comparable practice in Congress so anomalous. Of course, there is this difference: The absent Congressman was only necessary to a quorum; the absent Justice was necessary to a decision. No Committee action was dependent upon the Representatives presumed to be absent in the Christoffel case. All they could have done if present was to listen. In our own case, personal judgment and affirmative action of the absent member was necessary to make the Christoffel opinion a decision of the Court.

The ruling of the Court today seems irreconcilable with the Court's decision in that case. True, the ink on Christoffel is hardly dry. But the principle of *stare decisis,* which I think should be the normal principle of judicial action, is not well served by failing to make explicit an overruling which is implicit in a later decision. Unless we really accede to its authority, it were far better to undo Christoffel before it becomes embedded in the law as a misleading influence with the profession. Of course, it is embarrassing to confess a blunder; it may prove more embarrassing to adhere to it. In view of the holding today, I think that the decision in the Christoffel case should be forthrightly and artlessly overruled.

The Overruling of Precedents

Not infrequently, the Supreme Court overrules its precedents *sub silentio,* which in plain English means that the Court, without referring to or discussing an earlier decision, makes a later decision that so directly contradicts the earlier holding that the only logical inference is that the Court has rejected the rule of policy associated with the prior decision. The Court may also, in effect, do the same thing even though it discusses the older case in the later opinion. But the Court also explicitly overrules its precedents, as it has done upon at least 70 occasions, in addition to which there were 20 other instances which, in the opinion of the authors of a recent study,[32] obviously constituted overrulings. Of this total of 90 cases, 60 dealt with questions of constitutional law. The fundamental significance of the 1936 Term is again underscored when one considers that over half of the total overrulings have taken place since then. There were 43 cases during the century and a half from 1789 up to, but not including, the decision in *West Coast Hotel Co.* v. *Parrish,* 300 U.S. 379, which was announced on March 29, 1937.[33] Beginning with that case, there were 47 overruling cases through the 1956 Term—a period of only 20 years. According to Pritchett's tally, 32 of these 47 cases came during the first decade following the Court-packing episode, and were decisions of the Roosevelt Court.[34]

The first of these overruling cases was *Hudson* v. *Guestier,* 6 Cranch 281 (1810), which expressly overruled the decision, only two years previously, in *Rose* v. *Himely,* 4 Cranch 241 (1808). Marshall, who had written for the Court in *Rose* v. *Himely,* dissented alone in *Hudson* v. *Guestier. Hylton* v. *United States,* 3 Dallas 171 (1796), was the earliest decision of the Court to be overruled; but although it stood for ninety-nine years, it was not the oldest precedent to be overruled. The oldest precedent was *City of New York* v. *Miln,* 11 Peters 102, decided in 1837 and overruled 104 years later by *Edwards* v. *California,* 314 U.S. 160 (1941). The quickest "overruling," according to the authors of this study, came in *Jones* v. *Opelika,* 316 U.S. 584 (1942) and 319 U.S. 103 (1943), where the interval between decisions was only eleven months.[35] Technically, the first decision in *Jones* v. *Opelika* was vacated by the second decision after rehearing, and strictly speaking ought to be classified with the Cahill case discussed in the previous chapter rather than considered an example of overruling. We shall, however, discuss below *Jones* v. *Opelika* because of its relationship to one of the most celebrated instances in which the Court did overrule itself within a very short time: the flag-salute cases.

One of the early decisions of the Roosevelt Court was *Erie Railroad Co.* v. *Tompkins,* 304 U.S. 64 (1938), which overruled *Swift* v. *Tyson,* 16 Peters 1 (1842), which had established the policy that the federal courts were to develop their own body of case law in diversity of citizenship cases, rather than (as had been true for the first fifty years under the Constitution, and as has been the practice since 1938) to follow the substantive decisional law of the states in which the federal trial courts sit. Justice Brandeis, who wrote for the Court in the Erie case, remarked that "the doctrine of Swift v. Tyson is, as Mr. Justice Holmes said, 'an

---

[32] Albert P. Blaustein and Andrew H. Field, " 'Overruling' Opinions in the Supreme Court," *Michigan Law Review,* Vol. 57, pp. 152-155 (1958).

[33] *Ibid.,* pp. 161, 184-194.

[34] Pritchett, *The Roosevelt Court,* pp. 300-301.

[35] Blaustein and Field, *op. cit.,* pp. 159-160.

unconstitutional assumption of powers by courts of the United States which no lapse of time or respectable array of opinion should make us hesitate to correct.' " [36] Taking this statement at face value, it took the Court almost a hundred years to correct its own earlier "unconstitutional" decision.

Brandeis, Holmes, and Stone were the most frequent dissenters in cases that were subsequently overruled.[37] In other words, these liberal justices advocated, time and again in dissent, policy alternatives that later were accepted by a majority of the Court as being correct. On the other hand, there have been other justices who have been conspicuous for their frequent dissent in *overruling* cases, which means, of course, that they argued in behalf of *stare decisis* and the retention of old precedents. A sociologist has suggested that judicial liberalism/conservatism be defined as: [38]

> LIBERALISM: a state of *readiness* to accept "new" constitutional
> interpretations;
> CONSERVATISM: a state of *reluctance* to accept "new" constitutional interpretations.

If these definitions are appropriate, then it necessarily follows that these latter justices are the leading conservatives who have sat upon the Court. They include Frankfurter, Reed, McReynolds, Roberts, and Robert Jackson.

Two comments upon this conclusion seem in order. In the first place, the concentration of overruling cases during the decade of the Roosevelt Court (1937-1946), in combination with the fact that over a fifth of the overruled cases (26 of 122) were decided by the Taft and Hughes Courts (1921-1936), means that earlier justices had less of an opportunity to establish a record in either category, measured by this criterion. Consequently, we should qualify our conclusion by stating that these were the liberal and conservative justices of the past forty years. Secondly, it should be observed that, although there would be consensus that the three justices who are liberals by this test are recognized as being liberal in their sociopolitical philosophy, there would be no such consensus regarding the five justices whom we have designated as conservatives. Only McReynolds would be recognized as a philosophical conservative [39] by most students of the Court, who would consider Frankfurter, Reed, Roberts, and Jackson to be middle-of-the-roaders.

THE FLAG-SALUTE CASES

On June 3, 1940, the Supreme Court decided, in an opinion delivered by Frankfurter in *Minersville School District* v. *Gobitis,* 310 U.S. 586, that public

36 304 U.S. 64, 79.
37 Blaustein and Field, *op. cit.,* p. 161.
38 Eloise C. Snyder, "The Supreme Court as a Small Group," *Social Forces,* Vol. 36, p. 234 (1958).

39 Cf. the definition of conservatism in Robert G. McCloskey, *American Conservatism in the Age of Enterprise* (Cambridge: Harvard University Press, 1951), pp. 22-23.

school children could be compelled to salute the national flag, notwithstanding defendants' claim that to do so violated their religious freedom and liberty of conscience under the Fourteenth Amendment. Chief Justice Hughes, Roberts, Reed, and "libertarians" Black, Douglas, and Murphy joined in the decision and opinion of the Court. McReynolds concurred in the result; and only Justice Stone dissented. Three years and eleven days later, the Court announced, in *West Virginia State Board of Education* v. *Barnette*,[40] that "the decision of this Court in *Minersville School District* v. *Gobitis* and the holdings of those few *per curiam* decisions which preceded and foreshadowed it are overruled. . . ." The decision in the Barnette case was 6-3, with Frankfurter, who had written for the Court in the Gobitis case, writing a passionate dissent in defense of the Gobitis decision. What had happened to the Court in the space of three years to convert a majority of eight into a minority of three, and to create a new majority which felt strongly enough about the issue to risk the criticism certain to follow the overruling of such a recent and well-publicized precedent? And this apart from the fact that the Barnette case, which held that school children could not constitutionally be required to indulge in the patriotic gesture of saluting the symbol of national unity, was decided in the middle of World War II; or that Jackson, who spoke for the majority in that case ranks generally as a *stare decisis* conservative who dissented (like Frankfurter) *against* overruling cases rather than helping to create them.

Both the Gobitis and Barnette cases involved defendants who were members of the Jehovah's Witnesses sect, as did a number of other cases that the Court decided during the early 1940's. One such case concerned the quite different question of the applicability to the Witnesses, who distributed and sold religious literature from door to door, of a municipal license tax on peddlers. The Witnesses lost *Jones* v. *Opelika* by a 5-4 vote, but Black, Douglas, and Murphy dissented together—Stone dissented independently—in an opinion which constituted an open invitation to the Witnesses to bring up another flag-salute case for the purpose of challenging the Gobitis decision: [41]

> The opinion of the Court sanctions a device which in our opinion suppresses or tends to suppress the free exercise of a religion practiced by a minority group. This is but another step in the direction which *Minersville School District* v. *Gobitis,* 310 U.S. 586, took against the same religious minority, and is a logical extension of the principles upon which that decision rested. Since we joined in the opinion in the Gobitis case, we think this is an appropriate occasion to state that we now believe that it also was wrongly decided.

This somewhat extraordinary confession and solicitation assured the Witnesses of the four votes necessary to grant certiorari; and either a change in personnel

---

40 319 U.S. 624, 642 (June 14, 1943). See also Chapter 10, below.

41 *Jones* v. *Opelika,* 316 U.S. 584, 623-624 (June 8, 1942).

among the other justices or the conversion of one of them was all that would be needed to create a new and favorable majority. Naturally, the Witnesses responded and the Barnette case was duly docketed on the following December 16, although it came to the Court on appeal rather than certiorari. As it happened, both possibilities for picking up the necessary additional vote were realized, so that the majority became one of six rather than five. Jackson, who generally was quite hostile to the Witnesses both before and after the Barnette decision, became a temporary and quite articulate convert to the support of the Witnesses' litigious activities. And Byrnes (who had replaced McReynolds) resigned, to be replaced himself on February 15, 1943, by Rutledge, who promptly aligned himself with the Black group. The remaining four justices stuck to their guns: Stone voted consistently in favor of the Witnesses in Gobitis, both Opelika decisions, and Barnette; and Frankfurter, Roberts, and Reed voted against them in all four decisions. (See Table 23, on page 241.)

The Opelika decision itself—actually a group of cases from three different states—was reversed upon rehearing, a month earlier than the Barnette decision, in a brief *per curiam* opinion that was announced by Douglas.[42] The voting division here was 5-4, with Jackson in dissent, voting his usual anti-Witness views.

In summary, Gobitis was overruled by Barnette for two reasons: two justices of the Gobitis majority (Hughes and McReynolds) retired, and they were replaced by Jackson and Rutledge, who voted the opposite way on the flag-salute issue; and three justices not only changed their minds but publicly requested an opportunity to change their votes. It is the latter circumstance that was really unusual. Normally, overrulings can be accounted for by changes in the personnel of the Court.

JUDICIAL LEGISLATION

Statutory Interpretation

THE PSYCHOANALYSIS OF CONGRESS

It is very easy to develop an exaggerated notion of the relative importance of constitutional and statutory interpretation in the work of the Supreme Court. The lay impression undoubtedly is that the Court spends its time—its entire time —deciding cases in which it explains the meaning of the Constitution. Such misapprehensions can be readily corrected by the examination of any of the annual reports for the past two decades of the Director of the Administrative Office of United States Courts. These reports analyze the work-load of the Court by substantive as well as procedural case categories; and it is apparent that the Court devotes most of its time to the interpretation of federal statutes. Even in qualitative terms, it is possible that the most important part of the Court's policy-making

---

42 *Jones* v. *Opelika*, 319 U.S. 103, 104 (May 3, 1943).

TABLE 23.

The Overruling of the Flag-Salute Precedent
(1939-1942 Terms)

	Minersville School District v. Gobitis, 310 U.S. 586 (June 3, 1940)	Jones v. Opelika, 316 U.S. 584 (June 8, 1942)	Jones v. Opelika [on rehearing], 319 U.S. 103 (May 3, 1943) a	West Virginia Board of Education v. Barnette, 319 U.S. 624 (June 14, 1943)
Stone	'+')	'+')	(+)	(+)
Rutledge	*	*	(+)	(+)
Murphy	(−)	'+')	(+)	('+'
Douglas	(−)	'+')	(+)	('+'
Black	(−)	'+')	(+)	('+'
Jackson	*	(−)	'−')	('+')
Hughes	(−)	*	*	*
McReynolds	−	*	*	*
Byrnes	*	(−)	*	*
Roberts	(−)	(−)	−)	−
Reed	(−)	('−')	'−')	−
Frankfurter	('−')	(−)	'−')	'−')
Voting Division	1-8	4-5	5-4	6-3

LEGEND:

+ = a vote in favor of the Jehovah's Witness claimant
− = a vote against the Jehovah's Witness claimant
‘ ’ = wrote opinion
( ) = joined in the opinion of the Court
(= concurring opinion
) = dissenting opinion
* = not seated at the time of this decision

a The *per curiam* opinion in *Jones v. Opelika,* 319 U.S. 103, was announced by Mr. Justice Douglas.

is done in the reformulation of statutory rather than of constitutional norms. Theories of legal positivism, stemming from the Austinian and Kelsenian schools of jurisprudence, have posited a hierarchical model of legal systems in which the Constitution is, by definition, "higher" and "superior to" other formal processes for the articulation of public policy. Such thinking has conditioned the perceptions of constitutional-law scholars to the extent that they customarily ignore the bulk of even the formal portion of the Court's decision-making.

We shall present in this volume primarily cases that deal with issues of constitutional policy, but with the caveat that such an emphasis necessarily suggests a distorted view of the decision-making behavior of the justices. As the fourth and seventh of the "Ashwander rules" suggest, the Court usually (but by no means consistently, let alone invariably) disposes of cases which seek to challenge the constitutionality of federal statutes by reformulating—i.e., "interpreting"—not the Constitution, but the statute that is being attacked. By reading the statute to mean something different than the Administration or one of the parties urges, the Court manages to "avoid" having to face the constitutional question. Taking the statements of the Court on this point at face value, however, it is clear that the interpretation of a statute is an alternative tool or technique to the interpretation of the Constitution. Under such circumstances, a federal statute and a clause of the Constitution provide alternative pegs upon which the Court can hang a decision. And the remaking of constitutional policy and the remaking of statutory policy are equally processes of judicial policy-making.

There are two different techniques of statutory interpretation in common use in American courts, and neither the Supreme Court nor its individual justices consistently follow either one. The first is to infer meaning from the "literal text," and to read "the face of the statute." This is the so-called "plain meaning" rule. The opinions of the Court tend to agree that this is the rule that English courts follow today and that the Supreme Court used to follow. The alternative technique is to look behind the literal language that was enacted and to examine various materials of "legislative history" in order that the Court may understand the "spirit of the act," or in other words, what the legislature *really* meant—as distinguished from what the statute says. It was such a quest for legislative intent, which necessitates evaluation by the Court of a complex hodgepodge of political data, that once led Justice Cardozo to observe that "the process of psychoanalysis has spread to unaccustomed fields." [43]

Frequently these materials—excerpts from the *Congressional Record,* not excluding the Appendix thereto; self-serving and biased assertions of committee majority reports, or of minority reports; statements to press conferences by committee chairmen; the published or quoted views of the sponsor of a bill as to what *he* intended—have been neither briefed nor argued before the Court. Thus, decision by the Court may hinge upon the Court's understanding of evidence not

[43] Dissenting, in *United States* v. *Constantine,* 296 U.S. 287, 298-299 (1936).

of record, which never has been submitted to examination, to say nothing of cross-examination, by either party to the case. The reliability of such data is certainly no higher than that of the contents of an unevaluated F.B.I. file. The assumption that congressmen behave like judges are supposed to behave just isn't supported by the available research findings, notwithstanding the fact that the highest title that one can bestow upon a member of the national legislature is to call him—even is he was only a justice of the peace once forty years earlier—not "Senator," but "Judge." Such admiration is reciprocated by the majority of Supreme Court justices who have had no congressional experience and who exhibit the greatest confidence in their capacity for the divination of legislative intent through the study of legislative history.

The ambiguity of judicial choice in statutory interpretation is guaranteed by "the law" on this point. It is said to be hornbook law that courts do not interpret statutes unless the statutory language is doubtful. If the language is clear, it is simply read: effect is given to the plain, literal meaning. If it is unclear, it then becomes necessary to interpret the language: this is done by discovering the intent that is presumed to underlie the language used. Except to those utterly without sophistication in the use of language, such a formulation of the decision-making situation almost always lends itself to a choice between the two techniques.

Justice Frankfurter is among the leading exponents of the divination of legislative intent by the examination of legislative history. He has pointed out in an article that this was the practice of the English courts in the sixteenth century.[44] The reason underlying English adherence to the literal-text rule in more recent times is the fiction that the Sovereign, in giving her assent, is not privy to the legislative history of bills; and it is the Queen who is making the law. Frankfurter quotes Lord Haldane,[45] who in turn quoted Willes J.[46] as having laid down in 1769 the principle of construction that has not been seriously challenged since then: "The sense and meaning of an Act of Parliament must be collected from what it says when passed into a law; and not from the history of changes it underwent in the house where it took its rise. That history is not known to the other house or to the sovereign."

Frankfurter explained what he described as the practice of the Supreme Court today, as follows: [47]

> Courts examine the forms rejected in favor of the words chosen. They look at later statutes "considered to throw a cross light" upon an earlier enactment. The consistent construction by an administrative agency charged with effectuating the policy of an enactment carries very considerable weight. While assertion of authority does not demonstrate its existence, long-con-

44 *Of Law and Men*, pp. 63-64.
45 *Viscountess Rhondda's Claim* [1922] 2 A.C. 339, 383.
46 *Millar* v. *Taylor* 4 Burr. 2332 (1769).
47 Quoted from *Of Law and Men*, by Felix

Frankfurter, edited by Philip Elman, © 1956, by Felix Frankfurter. Pp. 66-67. Reprinted by permission of Harcourt, Brace and Company, Inc.

tinued, uncontested assertion is at least evidence that the legislature conveyed the authority. Similarly, while authority conferred does not atrophy by disuse, failure over an extended period to exercise it is some proof that it was not given. And since "a page of history is worth a volume of logic," courts have looked into the background of statutes, the mischief to be checked and the good that was designed, looking sometimes afield and taking notice also as judges of what is generally known by men. . . . A painstaking, detailed report by a Senate Committee bearing directly on the immediate question may settle the matter. A loose statement even by a chairman of a committee, made impromptu in the heat of debate, less informing in cold type than when heard on the floor, will hardly be accorded the weight of an encyclical.

Spurious use of legislative history must not swallow the legislation so as to give point to the quip that only when legislative history is doubtful do you go to the statute. While courts are no longer confined to the language, they are still confined by it.

Several of the cases that follow will afford the student an opportunity to check the accuracy of both the propositions that we have advanced and of the assertions of Justice Frankfurter.

PROFESSIONAL AND JUDICIAL SPORTS

The application of the Sherman Anti-Trust Act of 1890 to organized commercial sports provides a good example of policy-making by the Court by statutory interpretation. The sports that have thus far figured in the Court's decisions are major-league baseball and football, and championship boxing matches. It would belabor the obvious to demonstrate to an American college student that the management of these sports is "big business" in the United States. To take baseball and football first, the similarities in the organization and practices in the management of these two sports far outweigh their differences. Clubs stage local exhibitions, but this almost always entails interstate travel by one of the clubs competing in a given match, since the home stadia of the clubs are widely scattered among large cities in states throughout the eastern, midwestern, and far western sections of the country. Each club is an integrated business enterprise, corporate in form, with subsidiary producers ("farm clubs") and exclusive rights to the services of performers (whose contracts may be bought, traded, etc.).[48] Prospective recruits for the major football league are apportioned among the clubs by a system of preferential choice intended to stabilize the relative prowess of the various member clubs; and recruits normally undergo a period of apprenticeship in the minor leagues, which are controlled by the clubs of the major league. Statistics on the results of competition among the clubs are reported in

---

[48] For additional information about the "big business" aspects of baseball, see the concurring opinion of Mr. Justice Burton in *Toolson* v. *New York Yankees, Inc.*, 346 U.S. 356, 357-359 (1953).

copious detail and with the same faithfulness with which the machinations of the stock markets are recorded. "Star" performers are rewarded for their services with compensation equivalent to that received by big-business executives.

There can be no doubt, however, that Congress had no intent to control organized sports when it adopted the Sherman Act. That statute, adopted in the year normally taken as roughly fixing the closing of the western frontier in America, was designed for the great industrial trusts of the day. No one suggested that it was needed, or should be used, to curb the highly competitive entrepreneurial practices then prevalent in baseball and boxing; and professional football did not even exist. These were the days of the iron man and the flying wedge, when the conception of the forward pass still lay a quarter of a century in the future, dormant in the womb of time.

The Supreme Court was first asked to extend the Sherman Act to include professional sports in 1922. The Federal Baseball Club of Baltimore claimed that the National and American Leagues had together conspired to destroy the then-competing Federal League and the business of the Baltimore Club, and the club sued and won a verdict for triple damages against these perpetrators of monopolistic practices in interstate commerce. The reversal of this decision by a federal circuit court of appeals was affirmed in an unanimous opinion of the Supreme Court. Speaking through Mr. Justice Holmes, the Court held that baseball was merely an exhibition—a "purely state affair." The players were "free persons" who were induced, of their own volition, to cross state lines in order to compete in games. The transportation of players across state lines for the purpose of playing games was "incidental," not "essential" to the purposes of the clubs. "Personal effort, not related to production," announced Holmes, "is not a subject of commerce." From these articulate major premises, it was not difficult for the Court to conclude that the reserve-clause restrictions in players' contracts were "not an interference with commerce among the States." [49]

This decision certainly was not out of line with the restrictive interpretation generally given to the commerce clause in Court decisions of the time. In effect, however, the Court did much more than simply rule that Congress had not intended to have the Sherman Act apply to organized baseball. Such a decision would have left Congress free to extend the act to organized baseball, if—and the assumption is really quite preposterous—it so chose. But the Court decided that baseball was not "in" interstate commerce, with the clear implication that any statute that purported to put it there would doubtless be unconstitutional. Thus, we have an example of the close relationship in practice between constitutional and statutory interpretation. This opinion written by Holmes and joined in by Brandeis, the two great exponents of deference to legislative majorities, is hardly an example of the fourth and seventh "Ashwander rules" in practice, however. Instead of interpreting the statute in order to avoid a constitutional question,

[49] *Federal Baseball Club of Baltimore* v. *National League,* 259 U.S. 200, 208-209 (1922).

the Court, in effect, interpreted the Constitution to avoid having to interpret the statute. If the Court had approached the question by deciding that Congress had not meant the Sherman Act to apply to baseball, whether baseball was in or out of interstate commerce would have been quite irrelevant.

The question did not arise again for over three decades, and all subsequent decisions on this subject have been those of the Warren Court. In the meantime, various bills both to extend the Sherman Act to organized sports and to exempt them from it have failed of enactment; and they have continued so to fail to the time of this writing. In a brief *per curiam* opinion,[50] the Warren Court was careful to construe its precedent in such a way as to sublimate its constitutional implications and exaggerate its significance as merely an interpretation of the statute. Such a rendition of the earlier ruling had the effect, of course, of reopening the door for congressional regulation, which would clearly be permissible in the light of the latitudinarian construction of the commerce clause indulged by the Court since 1937:

> In *Federal Baseball Club of Baltimore* v. *National League of Professional Baseball Clubs,* 259 U.S. 200 (1922), this Court held that the business of providing public baseball games for profit between clubs of professional baseball players was not within the scope of the federal antitrust laws. Congress has had the ruling under consideration but has not seen fit to bring such business under these laws by legislation having prospective effect. The business has thus been left for thirty years to develop, on the understanding that it was not subject to existing antitrust legislation. The present cases ask us to overrule the prior decision and, with retrospective effect, hold the legislation applicable. We think that if there are evils in this field which now warrant application to it of the antitrust laws it should be by legislation. Without re-examination of the underlying issues, the judgments below are affirmed on the authority of *Federal Baseball Club of Baltimore* v. *National League of Professional Baseball Clubs, supra,* so far as that decision determines that Congress had no intention of including the business of baseball within the scope of the federal antitrust laws.

This opinion appears to show considerably more deference to Congress than did the Holmes opinion for the Taft Court. That precedent was "followed," but at the same time it was carefully confined and distinguished. Burton and Reed dissented together in an opinion in which they reported data to support their conclusion that baseball was, *in fact,* in interstate commerce in 1953. (It will be observed that this *approach* is identical to that of the Taft Court in 1922; only the conclusion is different.) Therefore, argued these two judicial activists, the Sherman Act applied to organized baseball; if there were to be an exemption of baseball from the general language of the Sherman Act, which was plain enough

---

[50] *Toolson v. New York Yankees, Inc.,* 346 U.S. 356-357 (1953).

on its face, it was the responsibility of the Congress, not the Supreme Court, to carve out a special and privileged exemption from the law for baseball monopolists.

This chicken came home to roost in a series of cases within the next few terms, in which the Court was asked to apply the Toolson "precedent" to theatrical enterprises, boxing, and football. The Toolson decision proved to be an inconvenient, but not insuperable, barrier, as the Court found that all three of these latter activities were within the scope of the Sherman Act. In the case of the theatrical enterprises, an assist must be credited to a favorable precedent which was just as good—indeed, better than—the Federal Baseball case. In 1923, the year after the Federal Baseball decision, the Court, again speaking unanimously through Justice Holmes, had ruled that the Sherman Act did apply to vaudeville, at least to the extent that the case should go to trial, on the ground that "in the transportation of vaudeville acts the apparatus sometimes is more important than the performers." [51] (Whether this was meant to imply that the game could go on without baseballs, mitts, and bats is not clear.) The attempt of the present defendants, the Shubert enterprises, to hide behind the Toolson decision was misguided because, as Chief Justice Warren explained,[52]

> Toolson was a narrow application of the rule of *stare decisis*. The defendants would have us convert this narrow application of the rule into a sweeping grant of immunity to every business based on the live presentation of local exhibitions, regardless of how extensive its interstate phases may be. We cannot do so. If the *Toolson* holding is to be expanded—or contracted—the appropriate remedy lies with Congress. See *United States* v. *South-Eastern Underwriters Assn.*, 322 U.S. 533, 561.

This is precisely the argument that Burton and Reed had used, in dissent in the Toolson case, against the use of Federal Baseball as a precedent. Since Toolson was decided 7-2 in favor of baseball, and the next case to come along—*United States* v. *International Boxing Club of New York*—was decided only two years later by a vote of 7-2 *against* boxing, what had happened to the Court in this short interval? Or was there really a difference in the (necessarily, inarticulate) intent of Congress with regard to these two sports? Or were they significantly different in regard to either the kinds of monopolistic practices that prevailed or their relationship to interstate commerce?

Four justices voted consistently as between baseball and boxing. Burton and Reed, who had dissented in the Toolson case, now concurred. They thought that all nationally organized professional sports were subject to the literal language of the Sherman Act, and that was that. Frankfurter and Minton, who were in the

---

[51] *Hart* v. *B. F. Keith Vaudeville Exchange*, 262 U.S. 271, 273 (1923); cf. *United States* v. *Shubert*, 348 U.S. 222, 229 (1955).

[52] *United States* v. *Shubert*, 348 U.S. 222, 230 (1955).

Toolson majority, now dissented, but for somewhat different reasons. Minton followed the substance of Holmes's opinion in the Federal Baseball case, announcing that, as he (Minton) saw it, "boxing is not trade of commerce. There can be no monopoly or restraint of nonexistent commerce or trade." [53] Frankfurter, however, followed the rule of *stare decisis:* since there were really no tenable differences between boxing and baseball, it followed that if baseball was exempt, then boxing must be also. The "unsavory elements" said to be associated with the boxing game were hardly relevant, in Frankfurter's opinion, unless it could be supposed "that this Court gave a preferred position to baseball because it is the great American sport." [54]

The other five members of the majority in the International Boxing case consisted of Harlan, who had replaced Jackson since the Toolson decision, and four justices who switched their positions as between the two cases: Warren, Black, Douglas, and Clark. Here was an instance where what was sauce for the goose was *not* sauce for the gander. Like Frankfurter, the Warren majority claimed to follow *stare decisis* in this case although, oddly enough, it led them to an opposite result. Federal Baseball, after all, had dealt with *baseball,* not *boxing;* so it applied only to baseball cases. Neither Federal Baseball nor Toolson, on this reasoning, was a precedent for the application of the antitrust laws to boxing. Moreover, the majority continued, it was their *duty* to apply the antitrust laws as the Congress had written them; any *additional* exemptions were up to Congress. And thus, the logic of the dissent in the Toolson case became that of the majority in International Boxing: [55]

> It follows that *stare decisis* cannot help the defendants here; for, contrary to their argument, *Federal Baseball* did not hold that all businesses based on professional sports were outside the scope of the antitrust laws. The issue confronting us is, therefore, not whether a previously granted exemption should continue, but whether an exemption should be granted in the first instance. And that issue is for Congress to resolve, not this Court. See *United States* v. *South-Eastern Underwriters Assn.,* 322 U.S. 533, 561.

The South-Eastern Underwriters case, which was cited in the same way in the Shubert case, is a decision based upon the interpretation of the Constitution rather than federal legislation. In South-Eastern Underwriters, decided in 1944, the Court overruled a seventy-five-year-old precedent to declare that the insurance business was in interstate commerce, after all, and that it was therefore subject to the Sherman Act. Congress, which was preoccupied with the prosecution of a war at the time, quickly adopted "remedial" legislation, the effect of which was

[53] *United States* v. *International Boxing Club of New York, Inc.,* 348 U.S. 236, 253 (1955).

[54] *Ibid.,* p. 249.

[55] *Ibid.,* p. 243. A civil antitrust decree for the government was subsequently affirmed by the Court on the merits. *International Boxing Club* v. *United States,* 358 U.S. 242 (January 12, 1959).

explicitly to exempt the insurance business from the antitrust laws and to re-linquish national regulatory jurisdiction over insurance underwriting and sales in favor of a continuance of the existing pattern of state controls. In effect, the Supreme Court was now saying: if the Congress does not like our legislation, let it overrule us, as it has done before.

Football came to the Court two years later, in the 1956 Term; [56] and football, it developed, was more like boxing than like baseball. This was a 6-3 decision, and there were only minor changes in the voting alignment in this case from that of International Boxing. Clark, instead of Warren, wrote for the majority. Burton and Reed, apparently satisfied that they had made the point of their Toolson dissent, joined in the majority opinion instead of concurring. Brennan replaced Minton, and voted for football just as Minton had voted for boxing. Only Harlan switched his vote, for reasons that will be stated below.

Of course, by this time, the Court had precedents pointing in both directions. It was possible to argue, as the majority did, that bringing football under the Sherman Act was merely to show deference to the will of Congress; after all, the Sherman Act said what it said, and if Congress disagreed with the Court, Congress could always overrule the Court. (Obviously, this was the same logic employed in the Toolson dissent and the International Boxing majority opinion.) But it was also possible to argue, as the dissenters did, that congressional silence implied congressional consent; and that the way to show deference to Congress was to leave it to Congress to extend the antitrust acts to football, if Congress should choose to do so. Both groups of justices could, and did, claim that they were the true devotees of the principle of *stare decisis;* both groups could, and did, claim that it was they who were exercising judicial restraint and leaving the political solution to the problem of the legislature.

Clark, speaking for the majority, explained away the Toolson ruling on the ground that "the Court did this because it was concluded that more harm would be done in overruling *Federal Baseball* than in upholding a ruling *which was at best of dubious validity.*" [57] Moreover, he added,[58]

> If this ruling is unrealistic, inconsistent, or illogical, it is sufficient to answer, aside from the distinctions between the businesses, that were we considering the question of baseball for the first time upon a clean slate we would have no doubts. But *Federal Baseball* held the business of baseball outside the scope of the Act. No other business claiming the coverage of those cases [i.e., Federal Baseball and Toolson] has such an adjudication. We, therefore, conclude that the orderly way to eliminate error or discrimination, if any there be, is by legislation and not by court decision. . . . Of course, the doctrine of *Toolson* and *Federal Baseball* must yield to any congressional action and continues only at its sufferance.

[56] *Radovich* v. *National Football League,* 352 U.S. 345 (1957).

[57] *Ibid.,* p. 450. Italics supplied.
[58] *Ibid.,* p. 452.

Frankfurter, dissenting alone, thought that by this time, the real problems evoked by the Radovich case related not to "Sherman Law" which was, "after all, a question for judicial determination"; [59] the serious question, rather, pertained to the application of the principle of *stare decisis* in these circumstances. In the end, he concluded that since only two years had elapsed since the decision in International Boxing, "respect for the doctrine of *stare decisis* does not yet require me to disrespect the views I expressed in the *Boxing* case." [60] In other words, Frankfurter adhered to his dissent in International Boxing, to the effect that Federal Baseball had exempted all professional sports from the antitrust laws, unless and until Congress should act to bring them under the legislation.

Harlan confessed that he had not really understood, at the time, the implications of his joining with the majority in the boxing case. These implications were made crystal clear for him by the present football case: football organization and practices were obviously very similar to those of baseball and very dissimilar to those of boxing. Yet the majority was assimilating football to the legal status of boxing rather than baseball. How could such a result be defended as equitable? Was naked precedent enough to justify the retention of a privileged position in the law for baseball alone among American professional sports? Harlan thought not: [61]

> What was foreshadowed by *United States* v. *International Boxing Club*, 348 U.S. 236, has now come to pass. The Court, in holding that professional football is subject to the antitrust laws, now says in effect that professional baseball is *sui generis* so far as those laws are concerned, and that therefore *Federal Baseball Club* v. *National League*, 259 U.S. 200, and *Toolson* v. *New York Yankees, Inc.*, 346 U.S. 356, do not control football by reason of *stare decisis*. Since I am unable to distinguish football from baseball under the rationale of *Federal Baseball* and *Toolson*, and can find no basis for attributing to Congress a purpose to put baseball in a class by itself, I would adhere to the rule of *stare decisis* and affirm the judgment below.
>
> If the situation resulting from the baseball decisions is to be changed, I think it far better to leave it to be dealt with by Congress than for this Court to becloud the situation further, either by making untenable distinctions between baseball and other professional sports, or by discriminatory fiat in favor of baseball.

The answer to Harlan's decisional dilemma is found, no doubt, in the incompetence of the judicial policy-making process to provide adequate solutions to socioeconomic problems as complex as those involved in these professional sports cases. The Court contributed to its own ultimate difficulties when it gratuitously purported to exclude a possible change in congressional policy by basing the Federal Baseball decision in 1922 upon the nature of baseball as an

[59] *Ibid.*, p. 455.
[60] *Ibid.*, p. 456.

[61] *Ibid.*

enterprise instead of upon an attribution of congressional intent. Thirty years later, the Court compounded its difficulties by attempting to make the decision that should have been made in 1922, instead of establishing a general policy that it was prepared to maintain. And by the time a majority of the Court had arrived at a policy that they were prepared to maintain, it was too late to have a general policy. The result appeared to be two policies, equally the product of "statutory interpretation": one policy for baseball, and a different policy for all other professional sports. (Or was there, as some suggested, one policy for "good, clean" sports like baseball, and another policy for "dirty" or "rough" sports like boxing and football? If such distinctions were to be made, it was argued, they might better be made by the Congress than by the Supreme Court.) The only thing that was absolutely certain was that national antitrust policy for organized sports had been made, for the past four decades, by the United States Supreme Court.

The Supreme Court's Rule-Making Authority

The Supreme Court exercises policy-making power in at least three different senses. In the first place, the Court formulates substantive policy norms in the opinions accompanying its formal decisions. Secondly, and particularly since the inauguration of the annual Conference of Senior Circuit Court Justices—now termed the Judicial Conference of the United States—was begun under the leadership of Chief Justice Taft in the early 1920's, the Supreme Court has promulgated, subject to congressional disallowance, written rules of procedure to govern the trial of both civil and criminal cases in the federal district courts. The third sense in which the Court makes policies is by decisional law, in the exercise of the Court's supervisory authority over the decision-making of lower federal courts.

The McNabb decision, below, is the earliest clear articulation of the premises on the basis of which the Court purports to act when laying down procedural norms for the lower federal courts through the exercise of the authority to review their decisions. As we shall see in Chapter 11, the Court has reinterpreted some of its earlier decisions and opinions, with the benefit of the hindsight afforded by the McNabb opinion, to attribute to these earlier cases a meaning and significance that apparently escaped the justices of the Supreme Court who actually participated in these decisions and wrote the opinions. Frankfurter wrote the opinion of the Court in the McNabb case; and Frankfurter's opinion *Wolf* v. *Colorado,* 338 U.S. 25 (1949), which as interpreted by Black reconstructed the rationale of *Weeks* v. *United States,* 232 U.S. 383 (1914), is an excellent example of the revisionist uses to which the McNabb decision has been put.

The function served by such revision is to limit the application of certain precedents to the federal courts. The reason is this: if such precedents were construed to establish policies resulting from the interpretation of the Constitution, some of the justices would take the position that such policies ought to be applied in both federal and state cases. But the same justices would agree that the Supreme Court has no supervisory authority over state courts, and therefore no discretionary power to direct what procedures—beyond those "required" by the Constitution—they must follow. Hence, if the Court's decisions in cases originating in federal courts are construed to have involved "merely" the exercise of the Court's supervisory authority rather than the interpretation of the Constitution, their precedential effect can be confined to other federal cases.

McNABB v. UNITED STATES

318 U.S. 332 (1943)

Certiorari to the Circuit Court of Appeals for the Sixth Circuit.

Reversed.

7-1	
Frankfurter	('+')
Stone, C.J.	(+)
Roberts	(+)
Black	(+)
Douglas	(+)
Murphy	(+)
Jackson	(+)
Reed	('—')
Rutledge	NP

MR. JUSTICE FRANKFURTER delivered the opinion of the Court.

The petitioners are under sentence of imprisonment for forty-five years for the murder of an officer of the Alcohol Tax Unit of the Bureau of Internal Revenue engaged in the performance of his official duties. They were convicted of second-degree murder in the District Court for the Eastern District of Tennessee, and on appeal to the Circuit Court of Appeals for the Sixth Circuit the convictions were sustained. We brought the case here because the petition for certiorari presented serious questions in the administration of federal criminal justice. . . . Determination of these questions turns upon the circumstances relating to the admission in evidence of incriminating statements made by the petitioners.

On the afternoon of Wednesday, July 31, 1940, information was received at the Chattanooga office of the Alcoholic Tax Unit that several members of the McNabb family were planning to sell that night whiskey on which federal taxes had not been paid. The McNabbs were a clan of Tennessee mountaineers living about twelve miles from Chattanooga in a section known as the McNabb Settlement. Plans were made to apprehend the McNabbs while actually engaged in their illicit enterprise. That evening four revenue agents, accompanied by the Government's informers, drove to the McNabb Settlement. When they approached the rendezvous arranged between the McNabbs and the informers, the officers got out of the car. The informers drove on and met five of the McNabbs, of whom three—the twin brothers Freeman and Raymond, and their cousin Benjamin—are the petitioners here. (The two others, Emuil and Barney McNabb, were acquitted at the direction of the trial court.) The group proceeded to a spot near the family cemetery where the liquor was hidden. While cans containing whiskey were being loaded into the car, one of the informers flashed a prearranged signal to the officers who thereupon came running. One of these called out, "All right, boys, federal officers!", and the McNabbs took flight.

Instead of pursuing the McNabbs, the officers began to empty the cans. They heard noises coming from the direction of the cemetery, and after a short while a large rock landed at their feet. An officer named Leeper ran into the cemetery. He looked about with his flashlight but discovered no one. Noticing a couple of whiskey cans there, he began to pour out their contents. Shortly afterwards the other officers heard a shot; running into the cemetery they found Leeper on the ground, fatally wounded. A few minutes later—at about ten o'clock—he died without having identified his assailant. A second shot slightly wounded another officer. A search of the cemetery proved futile, and the officers left.

About three or four hours later—between one and two o'clock Thursday morning—federal officers went to the home of Freeman, Raymond, and Emuil McNabb and there placed them under arrest. Freeman and Raymond were twenty-five years old. Both had lived in the Settlement all their lives; neither had gone beyond the fourth grade in school; neither had ever been farther from his home than Jasper, twenty-one miles away. Emuil was twenty-two years old. He, too, had lived in the Settlement all his life, and had not gone beyond the second grade.

Immediately upon arrest, Freeman, Raymond, and Emuil were taken directly to the Federal Building at Chattanooga. They were not brought before a United States commissioner or a judge. Instead, they were placed in a detention room (where there was nothing they could sit or lie down on, except the floor), and kept there for about fourteen hours, from three o'clock Thursday morning until five o'clock that afternoon. They were given some sandwiches. They were not permitted to see relatives and friends who attempted to visit them. They had no lawyer. There is no evidence that they requested the assistance of counsel, or that they were told that they were entitled to such assistance.

Barney McNabb, who had been arrested early Thursday morning by the local police, was handed over to the federal authorities about nine or ten o'clock that morning. He was twenty-eight years old; like the other McNabbs he had spent his entire life in the Settlement, had never gone beyond Jasper, and his schooling stopped at the third grade. Barney was placed in a separate room in the Federal Building where he was questioned for a short period. The officers then took him to the scene of the killing, brought him back to the Federal Building, questioned him further for about an hour, and finally removed him to the county jail three blocks away.

In the meantime, direction of the investigation had been assumed by H. B. Taylor, district supervisor of the Alcohol Tax Unit, with headquarters at Louisville, Kentucky. Taylor was the Government's chief witness on the central issue of the admissibility of the statements made by the McNabbs. Arriving in Chattanooga early Thursday morning, he spent the day in study of the case before beginning his interrogation of the prisoners. Freeman, Raymond, and Emuil, who had been taken to the county jail about five o'clock Thursday afternoon, were brought back to the Federal Building early that evening. According to Taylor, his questioning of them began at nine o'clock. Other officers set the hour earlier. . . .

Benjamin McNabb, the third of the petitioners, came to the office of the Alcohol Tax Unit about eight or nine o'clock Friday morning and voluntarily surrendered. Benjamin was twenty years old, had never been arrested before, had lived in the McNabb Settlement all his life, and had not got beyond the fourth grade in school. He told the officers that he had heard that they were looking for him but that he was entirely innocent of any connection with the crime. The officers made him take his clothes off for a few minutes because, so he testified, "they wanted to look at me. This scared me pretty much." He was not taken before a United States Commissioner or a judge. Instead, the officers questioned him for about five or six hours. When finally in the afternoon he was confronted with the statement that the others accused him of having fired both shots, Benjamin said, "If they are going to accuse me of that, I will tell the whole truth; you may get your pencil and paper and write it down." He then confessed that he had fired the first shot, but denied that he had also fired the second.

Because there were "certain discrepancies in their stories, and we were anxious to straighten them out," the defendants were brought to the Federal Building from the jail between nine and ten o'clock Friday night. They were again questioned, sometimes separately, sometimes together. Taylor testified that "We had Freeman McNabb on the night of the second [Friday] for about three and one-half hours. I don't remember the time but I remember him particularly because he certainly was hard to get anything out of. He would admit he lied before, and then tell it all over again. I knew some of the things about the whole truth and it took about three and one-half hours before he would say it was the truth, and I finally got him to tell a story which he said was true and which certainly fit better with the physical facts and circumstances than any other story he had told. It took me three and one-half hours to get a story that was satisfactory or that I believed was nearer the truth than when we started."

The questioning of the defendants continued until about two o'clock Saturday morning, when the officers finally "got all the discrepancies straightened out." Benjamin did not change his story that he had fired only the first shot. Freeman and Raymond admitted that they were present when the shooting occurred, but denied Benjamin's charge that they had urged him to shoot. Barney and Emuil, who were acquitted at the direction of the trial court, made no incriminating admissions.

Concededly, the admissions made by Freeman, Raymond and Benjamin con-

stituted the crux of the Government's case against them, and the convictions cannot stand if such evidence be excluded. Accordingly, the question for our decision is whether these incriminating statements, made under the circumstances we have summarized, were properly admitted. Relying upon the guarantees of the Fifth Amendment that no person "shall be compelled in any criminal case to be a witness against himself, nor be deprived of life, liberty, or property, without due process of law," the petitioners contend that the Constitution itself forbade the use of this evidence against them. The Government counters by urging that the Constitution proscribes only "involuntary" confessions, and that judged by appropriate criteria of "voluntariness" the petitioners' admissions were voluntary and hence admissible.

It is true, as the petitioners assert, that a conviction in the federal courts, the foundation of which is evidence obtained in disregard of liberties deemed fundamental by the Constitution, cannot stand. . . .

In the view we take of the case, however, it becomes unnecessary to reach the Constitutional issue pressed upon us. For, while the power of this Court to undo convictions in state courts is limited to the enforcement of those "fundamental principles of liberty and justice," which are secured by the Fourteenth Amendment, the scope of our reviewing power over convictions brought here from the federal courts is not confined to ascertainment of Constitutional validity. Judicial supervision of the administration of criminal justice in the federal courts implies the duty of establishing and maintaining civilized standards of procedure and evidence. Such standards are not satisfied merely by observance of those minimal historic safeguards for securing trial by reason which are summarized as "due process of law" and below which we reach what is really trial by force. Moreover, review by this Court of state action expressing its notion of what will best further its own security in the administration of criminal justice demands appropriate respect for the deliberative judgment of a state in so basic an exercise of its jurisdiction. Considerations of large policy in making the necessary accommodations in our federal system are wholly irrelevant to the formulation and application of proper standards for the enforcement of the federal criminal law in the federal courts.

The principles governing the admissibility of evidence in federal criminal trials have not been restricted, therefore, to those derived solely from the Constitution. In the exercise of its supervisory authority over the administration of criminal justice in the federal courts, see *Nardone* v. *United States,* 308 U.S. 338, 341-42, this Court has, from the very beginning of its history, formulated rules of evidence to be applied in federal criminal prosecutions. *E.g., Ex parte Bollman & Swartwout,* 4 Cranch 75, 130-31 [1807]. . . . And in formulating such rules of evidence for federal criminal trials the Court has been guided by considerations of justice not limited to the strict canons of evidentiary relevance.

Quite apart from the Constitution, therefore, we are constrained to hold that the evidence elicited from the petitioners in the circumstances disclosed here must be excluded. . . .

The circumstances in which the statements admitted in evidence against the petitioners were secured reveal a plain disregard of the duty enjoined by Congress upon federal law officers. Freeman and Raymond McNabb were arrested in the middle of the night at their home. Instead of being brought before a United States commissioner or a judicial officer, as the law requires, in order to determine the sufficiency of the justification for their detention, they were put in a barren cell and kept there for fourteen hours. For two days they were subjected to unremitting questioning by numerous officers. Benjamin's confession was secured by detaining him unlawfully and questioning him

continuously for five or six hours. The McNabbs had to submit to all this without the aid of friends or the benefit of counsel. The record leaves no room for doubt that the questioning of the petitioners took place while they were in the custody of the arresting officers and before any order of commitment was made. Plainly, a conviction resting on evidence secured through such a flagrant disregard of the procedure which Congress has commanded cannot be allowed to stand without making the courts themselves accomplices in willful disobedience of law. Congress has not explicitly forbidden the use of evidence so procured. But to permit such evidence to be made the basis of a conviction in the federal courts would stultify the policy which Congress has enacted into law.

Unlike England, where the Judges of the King's Bench have prescribed rules for the interrogation of prisoners while in the custody of police officers, we have no specific provisions of law governing federal law enforcement officers in procuring evidence from persons held in custody. But the absence of specific restraints going beyond the legislation to which we have referred does not imply that the circumstances under which evidence was secured are irrelevant in ascertaining its admissibility. The mere fact that a confession was made while in the custody of the police does not render it inadmissible. . . . But where in the course of a criminal trial in the federal courts it appears that evidence has been obtained in such violation of legal rights as this case discloses, it is the duty of the trial court to entertain a motion for the exclusion of such evidence and to hold a hearing, as was done here, to determine whether such motion should be granted or denied. . . .

In holding that the petitioners' admissions were improperly received in evidence against them, and that having been based on this evidence their convictions cannot stand, we confine ourselves to our limited function as the court of ultimate review of the standards formulated and applied by federal courts in the trial of criminal cases. We are not concerned with law enforcement practices except in so far as courts themselves become instruments of law enforcement. We hold only that a decent regard for the duty of courts as agencies of justice and custodians of liberty forbids that men should be convicted upon evidence secured under the circumstances revealed here. In so doing, we respect the policy which underlies Congressional legislation. The history of liberty has largely been the history of observance of procedural safeguards. And the effective administration of criminal justice hardly requires disregard of fair procedures imposed by law.

Reversed.

MR. JUSTICE RUTLEDGE took no part in the consideration or decision of this case.

MR. JUSTICE REED, dissenting:

I find myself unable to agree with the opinion of the Court in this case. An officer of the United States was killed while in the performance of his duties. From the circumstances detailed in the Court's opinion, there was obvious reason to suspect that the petitioners here were implicated in firing the fatal shot from the dark. The arrests followed. As the guilty parties were known only to the McNabbs who took part in the assault at the burying ground, it was natural and proper that the officers would question them as to their actions. . . .

Were the Court today saying merely that in its judgment the confessions of the McNabbs were not voluntary, there would be no occasion for this single protest. A notation of dissent would suffice. The opinion, however, does more. Involuntary confessions are not constitutionally admissible because violative of the provision of self-incrimination in the Bill of Rights. Now the Court leaves undecided whether the present confessions are voluntary or involuntary and declares that the confessions must be excluded because in addition to questioning the petitioners, the arresting officers failed promptly to take them before a committing magistrate. The Court finds a basis for the declaration of this new rule of evidence in its supervisory authority over the administration of criminal justice. I question whether this offers to the trial courts and the peace officers a rule of admissibility as clear as the test of the voluntary character of the confession. I am opposed to broadening the possibilities of defendants escaping punishment by these more rigorous technical requirements in the administration of justice. If these confessions are otherwise voluntary, civilized standards, in my opinion, are not advanced by setting aside these judgments. . . .

THE FINALITY OF SUPREME COURT DECISIONS

The decisions of the Supreme Court almost always have some effect; but the effect is not necessarily acquiescence in, submission to, and compliance with, the Court's orders. Persons and groups who have made the investment in time and money to see a case through a decision by the Court do not always stop in their tracks simply because the Court has spoken. They may, and not infrequently do, carry on their suits, either by a continuation of legal or by other means. The decision of the Court is usually only one stage in a complex sequence of decisions and other events. The Court's decision in 1952 that President Truman had neither constitutional nor statutory power to authorize government control of the major steel mills did not solve the then-current labor-management dispute, and neither did it insure an adequate supply of steel for the armed forces; to the contrary, the Court's decision precipitated a major strike. The Court's decisions in the "white primary" cases did not end discrimination against Negro voting. The School Segregation decision did not integrate the schools in Little Rock. The South-Eastern Underwriters Association case did not bring about national regulation of the insurance business; nor did the Tidelands Oil cases result in national control over the exploitation of the mineral resources under the marginal seas.

Questioning whether the Constitution is "what the judges say it is," Professor Jack W. Peltason has concluded that: [62]

> In almost every decision in which judges have imposed a check upon Congress in the name of the Constitution, in *one way or another* Congress eventually has done what the judges at first said it should not and could not do. . . . In fact, it is difficult to find a major decision denying Congress authority to do something which it does not do today.

Peltason suggested five methods commonly used to circumvent Supreme Court decisions, by parties who seek to overcome or to minimize the effects of an adverse decision by the Court.[63] In somewhat modified form, these techniques of circumvention are summarized below.

Five Ways of Nullifying a Supreme Court Decision

1. *The Supreme Court can be persuaded to overrule itself.* We have presented a number of examples of this in the preceding sections of this chapter, and in Chapter 3.

2. *Congress can be persuaded to overrule the Supreme Court, even in "constitutional" cases.* In legal theory, Congress can always overrule the Court's interpretation of federal statutes, at least prospectively. This is the official view frequently touted by the Court itself. Of course, it is utterly unrealistic. Decisions of the Court are themselves political data, and they provide strong ammunition for congressmen who would defend the status quo—as defined by the Court, of course—against proposals for legislative change. To this must be added the immense inertia that must be overcome to force controversial bills through the Congress, apart from the implications of a recent Court decision adverse to such a bill. Many congressmen are lawyers; and the argument that proponents of the

amendatory bill are showing disrespect for the highest court in the land is an effective one. We do not mean to suggest that Congress cannot, and does not, overrule the Court. But we do suggest that the blithe notion that Congress can readily change its mind, and disagree with the Court in cases that involve "merely" statutory interpretation, is politically naive. It is much more accurate to say that: (a) the Supreme Court's decisions interpreting federal statutes are, from a practical point of view, hardly less "final" than the Court's decisions interpreting the Constitution; and, conversely, (b) the Congress can, and does, overrule the Court on constitutional points only somewhat less frequently than on statutory points.

3. *Lower courts may decide in favor of a party, notwithstanding an adverse and intervening decision of the Supreme Court.* Few cases are disposed of, in the technical sense, by a Supreme Court decision. The usual thing is for one or a few out of many questions in a case to be brought before the Court; and the Court's decision may leave a large number of other questions in the case still to be resolved by the lower courts. The Supreme Court may reverse a court of appeals affirmance of the refusal of a federal district judge to permit an F.E.L.A. case to go to a jury, on insufficiency-of-evidence grounds; but this does not mean that the claimant can collect his money. All that it means is that a trial may take place. He may or may not win a jury verdict; the trial court may or may not accept such a verdict; the court of appeals may or may not agree with the trial court; and if the two lower courts agree, he may or may not succeed in getting the Supreme Court to grant certiorari—such a case is a poor risk, in terms of the analysis of the Certiorari Game. Or, to take a different example, a state convict may be released from the penitentiary—or more likely, held in a local jail pending a new trial— because the Supreme Court has said that his original conviction violates the Fourteenth Amendment. After a new trial and a proper conviction, the convict is returned to the penitentiary. Consider the following postscript to *Moore* v. *Michigan,* 355 U.S. 155 (December 9, 1957): an Associated Press dispatch, under the Kalamazoo dateline of June 6, 1958, reads:

> Willie B. Moore, 38 of Kalamazoo, today was sentenced to 24 to 40 years in prison for second degree murder and told 19½ years already served for the same crime will not count toward parole or as time served. Moore was convicted by a circuit court jury last week in a re-trial for the rape-slaying of Mrs. Josie Zeedyke, 68-year-old Kalamazoo woman, in 1938. Moore pleaded guilty to first degree murder at his original trial in 1938 and was sentenced to life imprisonment. He won a re-trial order from the U.S. supreme court, claiming he pleaded guilty to first degree murder under threat of mob violence. . . Moore's attorney said he would move for a new trial on grounds Judge Mosier erred in admitting Moore's original confession as evidence in the re-trial.

4. The decision can be ignored or its enforcement opposed by force. It is likely that a great many of the Court's decisions are ignored. Certainly this is true of many of the Court's pronouncements relating to municipal police powers, such as the regulation of peddlers, or access to municipal parks by minority religious groups, or the released time decisions relating to the integration of church and school. Direct opposition by force is less common since the Civil War; but this has certainly been part of the response of segregationists to the Court's School Segregation decisions.

5. If necessary, the Constitution may be amended to overrule the Supreme Court. This was attempted in the instance of national regulation of child labor; the effort was dropped because the goal was achieved by other means. The Eleventh, Thirteenth, Fourteenth, and Sixteenth Amendments were proposed and adopted for the express purpose of overruling specific and contrary decisions of the Supreme Court. This is, nevertheless, an ultimate political weapon that is rarely successfully employed, and can hope to succeed only when the Court has undertaken to block goals that are sought by cohesive, persistent, and widespread national coalitions of groups—not necessarily national "majorities," however.

The first four of these methods, as we have listed them, are undoubtedly the most important ways to get around a decision of the Court. We have already considered several examples of the first method; and we shall consider an example of the second in the next chapter.[64] We present below examples of the third and fourth points: further recourse to state courts, and simple disregard of the Constitution as interpreted by the Supreme Court.

STATE COURT EVASION OF SUPREME COURT MANDATES

Two notes in the *Harvard Law Review* have examined litigation subsequent to Supreme Court reversals over a twenty-year period to determine how much discretion the state courts still retain, and to ascertain to what extent this discretion is inconsistent with the decisions of the Supreme Court in these state cases. As the author of the first note pointed out: [65]

> The most significant characteristic of Supreme Court review of state court decisions is the fact that the Court has no power to make a final determination of any case. Its sole function is to decide the federal issue in a case, and then send it back to the state court to render final judgment. Therefore, the state courts may have the opportunity to mitigate or nullify the effects of the reversal. . . . The opportunity for the use of discretion arises from

[64] Cf. Note, "Congressional Reversal of Supreme Court Decisions, 1945-1957," *Harvard Law Review,* Vol. 71, pp. 1324-1337 (1958).
[65] "Final Disposition of State Court Decisions Reversed and Remanded by the Supreme Court, October Term 1931 to October Term, 1940," *Harvard Law Review,* Vol. 55, p. 1357 (1942).

the power in the state courts to raise new issues after remand. It is obvious that once new issues are raised, the final result of the litigation can go either way.

As a matter of fact, decisions of the state courts do go "either way" when they reconsider cases remanded to them by the Supreme Court. Of 187 state court cases reversed by the Supreme Court during the decade spanning the 1931-1940 terms, there were 34 cases in which new issues were raised. In only 9 of these 34 cases—slightly over one-fourth—did the state court render judgment for the same party who was favored by the decision of the Supreme Court. In the remaining 25 cases, state courts either modified their judgments in order to bring them into formal compliance with the Supreme Court mandate, or else considered new issues—in either event with the result that the decisions reached were identical with those reached before the Supreme Court reversals in these cases.[66]

During the more recent period of the 1941-1951 terms, there were 175 cases remanded to state courts for further proceedings. Of the 46 in which there was further litigation, slightly less than half of the parties who won in the Supreme Court lost in the state courts when the ultimate judgments went into effect.[67] There were, for instance, two cases raising quite different issues that were decided by the Supreme Court at about the same time and returned to the Supreme Court of Nebraska. In *Radio Station WOW, Inc.* v. *Johnson*,[68] the United States Supreme Court decided a question of federal law which the Nebraska court reexamined, upon remand, and decided in the opposite way in order to reaffirm its own earlier judgment. In *Hawk* v. *Olsen*,[69] the Supreme Court ruled that the defendant in a criminal case was entitled to a hearing on the merits of his claim of denial, during his trial, of due process under the Fourteenth Amendment. But the Nebraska supreme court adhered to its original decision, stating that the prisoner had sought the wrong remedy to raise such a question (i.e., he should have asked for a writ of *coram nobis* rather than a writ of habeas corpus); and this procedural matter was exclusively a question of state law which was therefore beyond the authority or competence of the Supreme Court to decide.

The evasive tactics resorted to by the Nebraska state court in these cases were somewhat extreme, but the clear finding of these studies is that during a recent period of twenty-one years, state courts adhered to the results obtained by their own original decisions in a substantial minority of the state cases that were "reversed" by the United States Supreme Court.

[66] *Ibid.*, p. 1357, 1359-1360.
[67] "Evasion of Supreme Court Mandates in Cases Remanded to State Courts Since 1941," *Harvard Law Review*, Vol. 67, p. 1251 (1954).

[68] Reversed, 326 U.S. 120 (1945); on remand, 146 Neb. 429 (1945).
[69] Reversed, 326 U.S. 271 (1945); on remand, 146 Neb. 875 (1945).

The Sociopolitical Impact of a Supreme Court Decision [70]

In 1948 the United States Supreme Court decided the case of *Illinois ex rel. McCollum* v. *Board of Education* [333 U.S. 203 (1948); and see Chapter 10, *infra*] holding that the use of public school facilities by religious organizations to give religious instruction to school children violated the no-establishment-of-religion clause of the First Amendment. This study is an attempt to detail some of the empirical consequences of that decision. . . .

McCollum grew out of the system of weekday religious education in operation in some of the public schools of Illinois. Similar programs had been developed in communities of all sizes in various parts of the nation. These programs were generally sponsored and conducted by pastors and church leaders at the community level. School-age youngsters, whose parents had given permission, were enrolled in religion classes conducted during school hours and, in some communities, conducted also in school buildings. Such a program was in operation in a school district in the city of Champaign, Illinois, in 1945. At that time, Mrs. Vashti McCollum, a resident taxpayer, brought an action in a court in Champaign County seeking a mandamus to end weekday religious instruction in that community. The writ was refused. On appeal a unanimous Illinois Supreme Court affirmed the decision of the trial court.

On March 8, 1948, in an eight-to-one decision, the United States Supreme Court reversed the state court. . . .

McCollum was remanded to the Illinois Supreme Court and ultimately a writ of mandamus was served on Champaign School Board Number 71. . . .

The weekday religious education program in Champaign ended, but the Protestant pastors who had sponsored it substituted another. Their new program was established after school hours on public school property. The supporters of this new program paid the local school officials a rental fee and went ahead with the new arrangement. This was much less successful than the first Champaign plan. It faltered and was dissolved in 1950. Enrollments had lagged, attendance had fallen off, and the sponsors of the program had difficulties in getting instructors. But these local developments were only one small part of the pattern of compliance which evolved from the *McCollum* decision. . . .

In Illinois and elsewhere the *McCollum* decision was viewed differently and put into effect in different ways. In a great number of instances, it led to the termination or extensive modification of weekday programs held during school hours in school buildings. In many others, it was considered as not pertaining to programs using public school time only. In a few other cases, no change was made in weekday programs regardless of their status with reference to public school time and property. But, generally speaking, the weekday programs which entailed the simultaneous use of public school

[70] Gordon Patric, "The Impact of a Court Decision: Aftermath of the McCollum Case," *Journal of Public Law*, Vol. 6, pp. 455-463 (1957).

time and property were the only ones either severely modified or completely abolished.

A large number of weekday programs were terminated as a result of the Court's holding in *McCollum*. Some were closed down immediately. Some continued for weeks or even until the end of the school year the following June. In some of these cases, the initiative for ending the programs was supplied by school or other public officials; in others, churchmen supplied the initiative. In the cities of Elgin and Rockford, programs which had provided weekday religious instruction to about thirty-seven hundred school children were ended. The Elgin program was completely terminated—after eleven years of operation. On March 9, 1948, the day after the Supreme Court of the United States reversed the courts of Illinois, Rockford school authorities expressed unwillingness to break up their on-premises plan prior to a directive from the Illinois Superintendent of Public Instruction. The sponsoring churchmen, on the other hand, were certain that their weekday classes would have to be withdrawn from public school buildings. This was done; plans were considered for a substitute weekday program, but failed to materialize. . . .

On the other hand, no changes were made as a result of the decision in some of the communities which had programs of religious instruction held in school buildings during classroom time. For example, no changes whatsoever were made in the northern Illinois communities of Zion and Polo. . . .

In Indiana, Minnesota and California, where legislation had been passed before *McCollum* which permitted religious instruction for public school pupils during school hours, the attorneys general ruled that no action in compliance with the decision was necessary. Moreover, in these states it was a rare occurrence for a program involving only public school time to be discontinued as a result of the decision in *McCollum*. . . .

Thus, indications are that in those states where legislators favored religious instruction on public school time before *McCollum,* and where state officials did not view it as unconstitutional after the decision, changes in weekday programs were unlikely to occur because of the decision. . . .

Finally . . . there were the opponents of weekday religion in New York City who interpreted the *McCollum* decision quite broadly as meaning that all weekday religion which in any way impinged upon the public schools was unconstitutional. However, the *McCollum* decision was not put into effect in any manner in New York City. The public school authorities there simply continued to release youngsters from portions of their public school schedules for weekday religious education in local churches and elsewhere. Seeing this, opponents of weekday religion later supported the suit brought by Mrs. Zorach [*Zorach* v. *Clauson,* 343 U.S. 306 (1952); and see particularly footnote 51 to Chapter 10, *infra*]. . . .

But when it came to putting the Court's decision into effect, which people were most influential? In most instances, decisions were made by state governmental officials (principally attorneys general and public education authorities), local public school officials, Protestant churchmen, and other religious groups. These, of course, were the people most closely associated with weekday religion programs. It had been through their efforts that the programs, whether on-premises or not, had been started in the first place. After the decision, these same people interpreted the Court's ruling and were usually responsible for putting it into effect—particularly where there was no local pressure for maximum compliance. In general, the advocates of weekday religion and those who neither favored the decision nor sought compliance with it were most influential in determining the pattern of compliance. On the other hand, the groups which supported the Court's ruling exercised much less influence. In only a few instances (e.g., St. Louis, Missouri and Portland, Oregon), were local opponents of religious instruction able to secure enforcement of the *McCollum* decision with regard to other than on-premises programs.

The Court's Role as a National Policy-Maker

Decision-Making in a Democracy: The Role of the Supreme Court [71]

It is to be expected . . . that the Court is least likely to be successful in blocking a determined and persistent lawmaking majority on a major policy and most likely to succeed against a "weak" majority; e.g., a dead one, a transient one, a fragile one, or one weakly united upon a policy of subordinate importance. An examination of the cases in which the Court has held federal legislation unconstitutional confirms, on the whole, our expectations. Over the whole history of the Court, about half the decisions have been rendered more than four years after the legislation was passed. . . . It is illuminating to examine the cases where the Court has acted on legislation within four years after enactment—where the presumption is, that is to say, that the lawmaking majority is not necessarily a dead one. Of the twelve New Deal cases, two were, from a policy point of view, trivial; and two, although perhaps not trivial, were of minor importance to the New Deal program. A fifth involved the NRA, which was to expire within three weeks of the decision. . . . As to the seven other cases . . . in a few years most of the constitutional interpretation on which the decisions rested had been unceremoniously swept under the rug. . . . Thus a lawmaking majority with major policy objectives in mind usually has an opportunity to seek for ways of overcoming the Court's veto. . . . Congress and the President do generally succeed in overcoming a hostile Court on major policy issues. . . .

Second, the elaborate "democratic" rationalizations of the Court's defenders and the hostility of its "democratic" critics are largely irrelevant, for lawmaking majorities generally have had their way . . . [and] although the Court seems never to have succeeded in holding out indefinitely, in a very

[71] Robert A. Dahl, "Decision-Making in a Democracy: The Role of the Supreme Court as a National Policy-Maker," *Journal of*   *Public Law,* Vol. 6, pp. 286, 287, 288, 291, 292-294 (1957).

small number of important cases it has delayed the application of policy up to as much as twenty-five years. . . .

[Third.] In the entire history of the Court there is not one case arising under the First Amendment in which the Court has held federal legislation unconstitutional. If we turn from these fundamental liberties of religion, speech, press and assembly, we do find a handful of cases—something less than ten—arising under Amendments Four to Seven in which the Court has declared acts unconstitutional that might properly be regarded as involving basic liberties . . . [although] it is doubtful that the fundamental conditions of liberty in this country have been altered by more than a hair's breadth as a result of these decisions. . . . Over against these decisions we must put the fifteen or so cases in which the Court used the protections of the Fifth, Thirteenth, Fourteenth and Fifteenth Amendments to preserve the rights and liberties of a relatively privileged group at the expense of the rights and liberties of a submerged group: chiefly slaveholders at the expense of slaves, white people at the expense of colored people, and property holders at the expense of wage earners and other groups. These cases, unlike the relatively innocuous ones of the preceding set, all involved liberties of genuinely fundamental importance, where an opposite policy would have meant thoroughly basic shifts in the distribution of rights, liberties, and opportunities in the United States—where, moreover, the policies sustained by the Court's action have since been repudiated in every civilized nation of the Western world, including our own. Yet, if our earlier argument is correct, it is futile —precisely because the basic distribution of privilege was at issue—to suppose that the Court could have possibly acted much differently in these areas of policy from the way in which it did in fact act. . . .

[Fourth.] Except for short-lived transitional periods when the old alliance is disintegrating and the new one is struggling to take control of political institutions, the Supreme Court is inevitably a part of the dominant national alliance. As an element in the political leadership of the dominant alliance, the Court of course supports the major policies of the alliance. By itself, the Court is almost powerless to affect the course of national policy. In the absence of substantial agreement within the alliance, an attempt by the Court to make national policy is likely to lead to disaster, as the *Dred Scott* decision and the early New Deal cases demonstrate. [And the School Segregation cases?] . . . [However, the] Supreme Court . . . is an essential part of the political leadership and possesses some bases of power of its own, the most important of which is the unique legitimacy attributed to its interpretations of the Constitution . . . [so] within the somewhat narrow limits set by the basic policy goals of the dominant alliance, the Court *can* make national policy. Its discretion, then, is not unlike that of a powerful committee chairman in Congress who cannot, generally speaking, nullify the basic policies substantially agreed on by the rest of the dominant leadership, but who can, within these limits, often determine important questions of timing, effectiveness, and subordinate policy. Thus the Court is least effective against a current lawmaking majority—and evidently least inclined to act. It is most effective when it sets the bound of policy for officials, agencies, state governments or even regions, a task that has come to occupy a very large part of the Court's business.

Few of the Court's policy decisions can be interpreted sensibly in terms of a "majority" versus a "minority." In this respect the Court is no different from the rest of the political leadership. Generally speaking, policy at the national level is the outcome of conflict, bargaining, and agreement among minorities; the process is neither minority rule nor majority rule but what might better be called *minorities* rule, where one aggregation of minorities achieves policies opposed by another aggregation.

The main objective of presidential leadership is to build a stable and dominant aggregation of minorities with a high probability of winning the presidency and one or both houses of Congress. The main task of the Court is to confer legitimacy on the fundamental policies of the successful coalition.

5

Congressional Policy-Making

WITH THE EXCEPTION OF the original jurisdiction of the Supreme Court, and the guarantee of tenure and salary for federal judges of the so-called constitutional (or "Article III") courts, the organization and jurisdiction and procedure of all adjudicatory agencies of the national government is defined, directly or indirectly, by statute. It is true that Section 2 of Article III of the Constitution defines "the judicial power" in terms of broad categories of subjects and parties; and Section 1 of the same article states that "The judicial Power of the United States shall be vested in one Supreme Court, and in such inferior Courts as the Congress may from time to time ordain and establish." But the Supreme Court's appellate jurisdiction—which constitutes in excess of 99 percent of its current business—is expressly made subject to "such Exceptions, and under such Regulations as the Congress shall make." And in practice, the jurisdiction of the inferior federal courts is defined, both positively and negatively, by Title 28 of the United States Code, which is a codification of federal statutes beginning with the Judiciary Act of 1789. In addition, the rules of procedure for the federal courts are defined partly by statute, and partly by regulations that have been adopted by the Supreme Court under delegated statutory authority, and partly (as we observed in Chapter 4) by Supreme Court decisional law under claim of its implied power to supervise the decision-making of inferior federal courts (and also, indirectly, the activities of federal law-enforcement agencies.) There is no question that the organization of all federal courts, including the places where they are located and the number of judges, is a question left to the discretion of the "political branches" of the national government.

However value judgments may differ as to the wisdom of either Franklin

Roosevelt's "Court-packing" proposal of 1937, or segregationist proposals of a generation later to curtail the appellate jurisdiction of the Supreme Court, only those ignorant of American constitutional history could sincerely argue that such political changes would have been or would be "unconstitutional." The size of the Supreme Court, for instance, was changed no less than seven times during the first eighty years under the Constitution—an average of almost once every decade. All of these changes were made for one of three partisan, political reasons: (1) to make it possible for an incumbent President to pack the Court more rapidly than might have been possible if he waited for vacancies to occur through death and retirement; (2) to prevent an incumbent President from making any appointments to the Court, by abolishing positions as they should become vacant; or (3) to give representation on the Court to new states and regions as the frontier receded to the West during most of the nineteenth century. Franklin Roosevelt's reason for wanting to pack the Court in 1937 was the first of the three purposes listed above.

The Judiciary Act of 1789 provided for a Chief Justice and five associate justices—six in all. A lameduck Federalist Congress reduced the size of the Court to five in 1801, with the objective of preventing Jefferson from appointing any Republicans to the Court. The Republican majority in Congress changed it back to six in 1802, and added another justice in 1807 in order to give representation to Kentucky, Tennessee, and Ohio. The fourth change came in 1837, when the Democrats increased the size of the Court from seven to nine, in order "to insure a majority in that tribunal favorable to State Banks and negro slavery." [1] The Court reached its largest size in 1863, when Lincoln was given an additional appointment—he already had appointed three justices—to make certain that a majority of the Court would uphold the constitutionality of the war measures undertaken by the President and the Congress. Only three years later, however, the Congress passed over the veto of President Johnson a bill which required the next three vacancies on the Court to remain unfilled, until the size was reduced to seven. The obvious reason for this was the distrust of Johnson by the Radical Republican majority of the Congress, and the fear—doubtless well justified—that Johnson appointees would have voted against the constitutionality of the Reconstruction legislation. The final change came another three years later, in 1869, when the size of the Court was again upped to nine. Grant was the President by this time; and the men whom he appointed to the two positions created by the 1869 statute were Justices Strong and Bradley, who promptly joined with what had been the minority of the Court in order to overrule the Court's recent decision in the first Legal Tender case and restore to constitutionality the greenback legislation.

[1] W. A. Sutherland, "Politics and the Supreme Court," *American Law Review*, Vol. 48, p. 395 (1914); quoted in Daniel S. McHargue, *Appointments to the Supreme Court of the United States* (unpublished doctoral dissertation, U.C.L.A., 1949), p. 595.

Against such a background, the power of Congress to manipulate the size of the Court would seem to be well established. The practice was engaged in by Federalist, Democratic-Republican, Democratic, and Republican Congresses,[2] for the benefit of Presidents including Jefferson and Lincoln; and it was acquiesced in by the Great Chief Justice John Marshall. On the other hand, the size of the Court has remained stable at nine since 1837, with the exception of the half-dozen years from 1863 to 1869; and the political tradition of over a century, reinforced by the nominal defeat of Roosevelt on this issue, doubtless is strong enough to forestall any further change in the size of the Supreme Court, at least until a really extraordinary political crisis makes such action both necessary and possible. Our point is that this is a political question, not a question of the constitutional power of the Congress.

The size of the lower federal courts has increased constantly, of course, paralleling the growth in the area and population of the country and the consequent increase in litigation in the federal courts. At present, there are over ninety federal district courts and eleven federal courts of appeals. These courts are staffed with approximately three hundred federal judges. Each state has at least one federal district court; the larger and more populous states have as many as four. Anywhere from one to as many as sixteen judges may be assigned to a single district court; but in most cases, a single judge presides over trials in the federal district courts. The size of the courts of appeals ranges from three to nine, and these courts normally hear appeals by panels of three justices. The federal district courts and the courts of appeals are courts of general jurisdiction. In addition, there are federal district courts located in certain of the territories (Puerto Rico, Guam, the Virgin Islands, and the Canal Zone), and there are federal courts of specialized jurisdiction, such as the Court of Claims, the Court of Customs and Patent Appeals, the Tax Court of the United States, and the Court of Military Appeals.[3]

In this chapter, we are concerned with two major questions of legislative policy-making. One of these concerns the extent to which the Supreme Court has acquiesced in Congress' own interpretation of the scope of the national legislature's constitutional discretion to make policy regarding subjects other than those specifically mentioned in the text of the Constitution, and to delegate policy-making authority and responsibility to other decision-making agencies of the national government. The other question involves the power and practice of Congress in regulating the appellate jurisdiction of the Supreme Court, and in

---

[2] Cf. Appendix C.

[3] For a discussion of the history of federal judicial organization, see Frankfurter and Landis, *The Business of the Supreme Court* (New York: Macmillan, 1928). For a more detailed description of the contemporary organization of the federal courts, see any of the following: C. Herman Pritchett, *The American Constitution* (New York: McGraw, 1959), chap. vii; Jack W. Peltason, *Federal Courts in the Political Process* (Garden City: Doubleday, 1955), pp. 13-17; Lewis Mayers, *The American Legal System* (New York: Harper, 1955), pp. 80-89.

establishing and defining the jurisdiction of the inferior federal courts. Since the national legislature and the Supreme Court each claim an interest, based upon direct constitutional responsibility, in the answers to all of these questions, these are always matters of at least potential conflict between Congress and the Court.

Such competition and overlapping of jurisdiction between the two branches of government is a normal characteristic of the American constitutional polity, the so-called principle of separation of powers to the contrary notwithstanding. The discussion below analyzes a few of the salients, some on the part of the Court and some on the part of Congress, that each has ventured from time to time into the fairly extensive no man's land which separates several of the larger areas of legislative and judicial condominium.

THE IMPLIED POWERS OF CONGRESS

McCULLOCH v. MARYLAND

4 Wheaton 316 (1819)

Error to the court of appeals of the State of Maryland.

Reversed.

6-0	
Marshall, C.J.	('+')
Washington	(+)
Johnson	(+)
Livingston	(+)
Duvall	(+)
Story	(+)
Todd	NP

Having claimed for itself the implied power of judicial review, in the opinion in Marbury v. Madison *in 1803, the Court next attributed similar authority, beyond the literal language of the Constitution, to the Congress. If* Marbury v. Madison *is, as we have suggested, the most important decision in American constitutional law, then* McCulloch v. Maryland *is certainly the next most important case. The question with which it dealt—whether Congress could charter a national bank which* would be more powerful than, and would compete with, state banks—was a major public-policy issue of the time, and one which divided the political parties. The first United States Bank was chartered by the Federalists, and allowed to expire by the Democratic-Republicans, only to be revived when necessity made it a virtue during the financial crisis following the War of 1812. The second United States Bank, which was chartered in 1816, was sponsored by Democrats and opposed, though unsuccessfully, by the remnants of the Federalist party. It was later attacked by western Democrats, led by President Andrew Jackson; and the present system of national banks was inaugurated as a war measure during the Civil War. Certainly, the authority for the Federal Reserve System in effect today stems directly from the interpretation of the Constitution approved by John Marshall in 1819 in McCulloch v. Maryland.

The opinion below deletes the Court's extended discussion of a second question, the power of a state to tax such a Bank of the United States. The reason for omitting this portion of Marshall's opinion is that the doctrine of reciprocal tax immunity, though important to the relations between the national and state governments for over a hundred years, is now significant primarily as a phase of constitutional history. The doctrine was specifically overruled by the Roosevelt Court a generation ago; and Marshall's famous dictum— that "the power to tax is the power to destroy"—has in effect been qualified out of existence by the general acceptance of the retort, originally uttered in dissent, of Mr. Justice Holmes: "The power to tax is not the power to destroy while this Court sits." Faith in the Court has replaced what was, for Marshall, the logic of an argument pushed to its extreme.

This was an action of debt, brought by the defendant in error, John James, who sued as well for himself as for the State of Maryland, in the county court of Baltimore county, in the said State, against the plaintiff in error, McCulloch, to recover certain penalties under the act of the legislature of Maryland, hereafter mentioned. Judgment being rendered against the plaintiff in error, upon the following statement of facts, agreed and submitted to the court by the parties, was affirmed by the court of appeals of the State of Maryland, the highest court of law of said State, and the cause was brought, by writ of error, to this court.

It is admitted by the parties in this cause, by their counsel, that there was passed, on the 10th day of April, 1816, by the congress of the United States, an act, entitled, "An act to incorporate the subscribers to the Bank of the United States"; and that there was passed, on the 11th day of February, 1818, by the general assembly of Maryland, an act, entitled, "An act to impose a tax on all banks, or branches thereof, in the State of Maryland, not chartered by the legislature." . . .

The question submitted to the court for their decision in this case, is as to the validity of the said act of the general assembly of Maryland, on the ground of its being repugnant to the constitution of the United States, and the act of congress. . . .

MARSHALL, C. J., delivered the opinion of the court.

In the case now to be determined, the defendant, a sovereign state, denies the obligation of a law enacted by the legislature of the Union; and the plaintiff, on his part, contests the validity of an act which has been passed by the legislature of that State. The constitution of our country, in its most interesting and vital parts, is to be considered; the conflicting powers of the government of the Union and of its members, as marked in that constitution, are to be discussed; and an opinion given, which may essentially influence the great operations of the government. No tribunal can approach such a question without a deep sense of its importance, and of the awful responsibility involved in its decision. But it must be decided peacefully, or remain a source of hostile legislation, perhaps of hostility of a still more serious nature; and if it is to be so decided, by this tribunal alone can the decision be made. On the supreme court of the United States has the constitution of our country devolved this important duty.

The first question made in the cause is, has congress power to incorporate a bank?

It has been truly said, that this can scarcely be considered as an open question, entirely unprejudiced by the former proceedings of the nation respecting it. The principle now contested was introduced at a very early period of our history, has been recognized by many successive legislatures, and has been acted upon by the judicial department, in cases of peculiar delicacy, as a law of undoubted obligation.

It will not be denied, that a bold and daring usurpation might be resisted, after an acquiescence still longer and more complete than this. But it is conceived that a doubtful question, one on which human reason may pause, and the human judgment be suspended, in the decision of which the great principles of liberty are not concerned, but the respective powers of those who are equally the representatives of the people, are to be adjusted; if not put at rest by the practice of the government, ought to receive a considerable impression from that practice. An exposition of the constitution, deliberately established by legislative acts, on the faith of which an immense property has been advanced, ought not to be lightly disregarded.

The power now contested was exercised by the first congress elected under the present constitution. The bill for incorporating the Bank of the United States did not steal upon an unsuspecting legislature, and pass unobserved. Its principle was completely understood, and was opposed with equal zeal and ability. After being resisted, first in the fair and open field of debate, and afterwards in the executive cabinet, with as much persevering talent as any measure has ever experienced, and being supported by arguments which convinced minds as pure and as intelligent as this country can boast, it became a law. The original act was permitted to expire; but a short experience of the embarrassments to which the refusal to revive it exposed the government, convinced those who were most prejudiced against the measure of its necessity, and induced the passage of the present law. It would require no ordinary share of intrepidity to assert, that a measure adopted under these circumstances, was a bold and plain usurpation, to which the constitution gave no countenance. . . .

This government is acknowledged by all to be one of enumerated powers. The principle, that it can exercise only the powers granted to it, would seem too apparent to have required to be enforced by all those arguments which its enlightened friends, while it was depending before the people, found it necessary to urge. That principle is now universally admitted. But the question respecting the extent of the powers actually granted, is perpetually arising, and will probably continue to arise, as long as our system shall exist.

In discussing these questions, the conflicting powers of the general and State governments must be brought into view, and the supremacy of their respective laws, when they are in opposition, must be settled.

If any one proposition could command the universal assent of mankind, we might expect it would be this: that the government of the Union, though limited in its powers, is supreme within its sphere of action. This would seem to result necessarily from its nature. It is the government of all; its powers are delegated by all; it represents all, and acts for all. Though any one State may be willing to control its operations, no State is willing to allow others to control them. The nation, on those subjects on which it can act, must necessarily bind its component parts. But this question is not left to mere reason: the people have, in express terms, decided it, by saying, "this constitution, and the laws of the United States, which shall be made in pursuance thereof," "shall be the supreme law of the land," and by requiring that the members of the State legislatures, and the officers of the executive and judicial departments of the States, shall take the oath of fidelity to it.

The government of the United States, then, though limited in its powers, is supreme; and its laws, when made in pursuance of the constitution, form the supreme law of the land, "any thing in the constitution or laws of any State, to the contrary notwithstanding."

Among the enumerated powers, we do not find that of establishing a bank or creating a corporation. But there is no phrase in the instrument which, like the articles of confederation, excludes incidental or implied powers; and which requires that every thing granted shall be expressly and minutely described. Even the 10th amendment, which was framed for the purpose of quieting the excessive jealousies which had been excited, omits the word "expressly," and declares only that the powers "not delegated to the United States, nor prohibited to the States, are reserved to the States or to the people"; thus leaving the question, whether the particular power which may become the subject of contest, has been delegated to the one government, or prohibited to the other, to depend on a fair construction of the whole instrument. The men who drew and adopted this amendment, had experienced the embarrassments resulting from the insertion of this word in the articles of confederation, and probably omitted it to avoid those embarrassments. A constitution, to contain an accurate detail of all the subdivisions of which its great powers will admit, and of all the means by which they may be carried into execution, would partake of the prolixity of a legal code, and could scarcely be embraced by the human mind. It would probably never be understood by the public. Its nature, therefore, requires, that only its great outlines should be marked, its important objects designated, and the minor ingredients which compose those objects be deduced from the nature of the objects themselves. That this idea was entertained by the framers of the American constitution, is not only to be inferred from the nature of the instrument, but from the language. Why else were some of the limitations, found in the 9th section of the 1st article, introduced? It is also, in some degree, warranted by their having omitted to use any restrictive term which might prevent its receiving a fair and just interpretation. In considering this question, then, we must never forget, that it is a constitution we are expounding.

Although, among the enumerated powers of government, we do not find the word "bank," or "incorporation," we find the great powers to lay and collect taxes; to borrow money; to regulate commerce; to declare and conduct a war; and to raise and support armies and navies. The sword and the purse, all the external relations, and no inconsiderable portion of the industry of the nation, are intrusted to its government. It can never be pretended that these vast powers draw after them others of inferior importance, merely because they are inferior. Such an idea can never be advanced. But it may, with great reason, be contended, that a government, intrusted with such ample powers, on the due execution of which the happiness and prosperity of the nation so vitally depends, must also be intrusted with ample means for their execution. The power being given, it is the interest of the nation to facilitate its execution. It can never be their interest, and cannot be presumed to have been their intention, to clog and embarrass its execution by withholding the most appropriate means. . . .

The power of creating a corporation, though appertaining to sovereignty, is not, like the power of making war, or levying taxes, or of regulating commerce, a great substantive and independent power, which cannot be implied as incidental to other powers, or used as a means of executing them. It is never the end for which other powers are exercised, but a means by which other objects are accomplished. No contributions are made to charity for the sake of an incorporation, but a corporation is created to administer the charity; no seminary of learning is instituted in order to be incorporated, but the corporate character is conferred to subserve the purposes of education. No city was ever built with the sole object of being incorporated, but is incorporated as affording the best means of being well governed. The power of creating a corporation is never used for its own sake, but for the purpose of effecting something else. No sufficient reason is, therefore, perceived, why it may not pass as incidental to those powers which are expressly given, if it be a direct mode of executing them.

But the constitution of the United States has not left the right of congress to employ the necessary means, for the execution of the powers conferred on the government, to general reasoning. To its enumeration of powers is added that of making "all laws which shall be necessary and proper, for carrying into execution the foregoing powers, and all other powers vested by this constitution, in the government of the United States, or in any department thereof."

The counsel for the State of Maryland have urged various arguments, to prove that this clause, though in terms a grant of power, is not so in effect. . . .

But the argument on which most reliance is placed, is drawn from the peculiar language of this clause. Congress is not empowered by it to make all laws, which may have relation to the powers conferred on the government, but such only as may be "necessary and proper" for carrying them into execution. The word "necessary" is considered as controlling the whole sentence, and as limiting the right to pass laws for the execution of the granted powers, to such as are indispensable, and without which the power would be nugatory. That it excludes the choice of means, and leaves to congress, in each case, that only which is most direct and simple. . . .

[But had] the intention been to make this clause restrictive, it would unquestionably have been so in form as well as in effect.

The result of the most careful and attentive consideration bestowed upon this clause is, that if it does not enlarge, it cannot be construed to restrain the powers of congress, or to impair the right of the legislature to exercise its best judgment in the selection of measures, to carry into execution the constitutional powers of the government. If no other motive for its insertion can be suggested, a sufficient one is found in the desire to remove all doubts respecting the right to legislate on that vast mass of incidental powers which must be involved in the constitution, if that instrument be not a splendid bauble.

We admit, as all must admit, that the powers of the government are limited, and that its limits are not to be transcended. But we think the sound construction of the constitution must allow to the national legislature that discretion, with respect to the means by which the powers it confers are to be carried into execution, which will enable that body to perform the high duties assigned to it, in the manner most beneficial to the people. Let the end be legitimate, let it be within the scope of the constitution, and all means which are appropriate, which are plainly adapted to that end, which are not prohibited, but consist with the letter and spirit of the constitution, are constitutional.

That a corporation must be considered as a means not less usual, not of higher dignity, not more requiring a particular specification than other means, has been sufficiently proved. If we look to the origin of corporations, to the manner in which they have been framed in that government, from which we have derived most of our legal principles and ideas, or to the uses to which they have been applied, we find no reason to suppose that a constitution, omitting, and wisely omitting, to enumerate all the means for carrying into execution the great powers vested in government, ought to have specified this. Had it been intended to grant this power as one which should be distinct and independent, to be exercised in any case whatever, it would have found a place among the enumerated powers of the government. But being considered merely as a means, to be employed only for the purpose of carrying into execution the given powers, there could be no motive for particularly mentioning it. . . .

If a corporation may be employed indiscriminately with other means to carry into execution the powers of the government, no particular reason can be assigned for excluding the use of a bank, if required for its fiscal operations. To use one, must be within the discretion of congress, if it be an appropriate mode of executing the powers of government. That it is a convenient, a useful, and essential instrument in the prosecution of its fiscal operations, is not now a subject of controversy. All those who have been concerned in the administration of our finances, have concurred in representing its importance and necessity; and so strongly have they been felt, that statesmen of the first class, whose previous opinions against it had been confirmed by every circumstance which can fix the human judgment, have yielded those opinions to the exigencies of the nation. Under the confederation, congress justifying the measure by its necessity, transcended, perhaps, its powers to obtain the advantage of a bank; and our own legislation attests the universal conviction of the utility of this measure. The time has passed away when it can be necessary to enter into any discussion in order to prove the importance of this instrument, as a means to effect the legitimate objects of the government.

But were its necessity less apparent, none can deny its being an appropriate measure; and if it is, the degree of its necessity, as has been very justly observed, is to be discussed in another place. Should congress, in the execution of its powers, adopt measures which are prohibited by the constitution; or should congress, under the pretext of executing its powers, pass laws for the accomplishment of objects not intrusted to the government, it would become the painful duty of this tribunal, should a case requiring such a decision come before it, to say that such an act was not the law of the land. But where the law is not prohibited, and is really calculated to effect any of the objects intrusted to the government, to undertake here to inquire into the degree of its necessity, would be to pass the line which circumscribes the judicial department, and to tread on legislative ground.

This court disclaims all pretensions to such a power. . . .

After the most deliberate consideration, it is the unanimous and decided opinion of this court, that the act to incorporate the Bank of the United States is a law made in pursuance of the constitution, and is a part of the supreme law of the land.

The branches, proceeding from the same stock, and being conducive to the complete accomplishment of the object, are equally constitutional. . . .

It being the opinion of the court, that the act incorporating the bank is constitutional; and that the power of establishing a branch in the State of Maryland might be properly exercised by the bank itself, we proceed to inquire:—

2. Whether the State of Maryland may, without violating the constitution, tax that branch?

. . . The court has bestowed on this subject its most deliberate consideration. The result is a conviction that the States have no power, by taxation or otherwise, to retard, impede, burden, or in any manner control, the operations of the constitutional laws enacted by congress to carry into execution the powers vested in the general government. This is, we think, the unavoidable consequence of that supremacy which the constitution has declared.

We are unanimously of opinion that the law passed by the legislature of Maryland, imposing a tax on the Bank of the United States, is unconstitutional and void.

. . . It is therefore adjudged and ordered, that the . . . judgment of the . . . court of appeals of the State of Maryland, in this case, be, and the same hereby is, reversed and annulled . . . and that judgment be entered in the Baltimore county court for . . . James W. McCulloch.

Reversed.

THE DELEGATION OF LEGISLATIVE POWER

On January 7, 1935, the Supreme Court announced its decision in *Panama Refining Co.* v. *Ryan,* 293 U.S. 388, the so-called "Hot Oil" case (or, in the alternative, the "Hip Pocket" case). Less than five months later came the decision in *Schechter Poultry Corp.* v. *United States,* 295 U.S. 495, more familiarly known to its contemporaries as the "Sick Chicken" case. How and why these cases acquired their nicknames need not detain us; the story is readily accessible to students of constitutional history.[4] The importance of the cases to constitutional politics is that these two decisions, coming together near the crest of the flood tide by means of which the "Nine Old Men" sought to wash away the political sins of the New Deal, constitute the only instances in which the Supreme Court has ever declared an act of Congress to be unconstitutional on the grounds that an unlawful delegation of legislative power to the President had been attempted.[5] Both cases involved different sections of the same statute—the National Industrial Recovery Act of 1933, which was due to expire by its own terms, in any event, within a few weeks of the decision in the Schechter case. But the Schechter decision added nothing to the constitutional theory suggested in the Court's opinion in the Panama Refining case; instead, it purported to be an application of the principles of the earlier case to a different situation (i.e., to other sections of the same statute).

In order for a delegation of legislative power to the President to be lawful, said Hughes, at least three criteria must be met:

1. The "policy" must be clearly declared in the language of the statute, and not left to the discretion of the "grantee"—i.e., the recipient of the delegated power, who acts as the agent of the Congress.

2. The statute must pronounce "standards" to guide the executory behavior of the President (or whomever else Congress might select as its subordinate administrator); presumably, (although Hughes did not mention this) such standards would also have the virtue of giving the Court something to sink its teeth into, in exercising judicial review to ascertain whether the subordinate administrative action was *ultra vires* the statute.

3. Formal "findings" by the President would be a condition precedent to a valid exercise of his delegated authority, assuming that the statute satisfied the above "policy" and "standards" criteria; or in other words, the President must specify in his order the facts and circumstances that justified

---

[4] See Louis Jaffe, "An Essay on Delegation of Legislative Power," *Columbia Law Review,* Vol. 47, pp. 359, 561 (1947).

[5] In *Carter* v. *Carter Coal Co.,* 298 U.S. 238 (1936), the Court held unconstitutional a delegation of statutory authority to what it considered to be a private rather than a public administrative agency.

the action that he purported to take under the statute delegating to him his authority to act.

Since this novel constitutional policy was given retroactive effect at the time it was first announced by the Court, it is not surprising that the prior acts of the Congress and the President, during 1933 and 1934, failed to pass muster under the new requirements. The surprising thing is that the three criteria for the lawful delegation of legislative power passed so quickly from view, below the judicial horizon. They have rarely been invoked, and never as the basis for a determination of unconstitutionality, in subsequent decisions of the Court.[6] Certainly this is not because the delegations of legislative power to the President during and subsequent to World War II have been less broad than the statutory grants of discretion of the New Deal era.

During the century and a half of constitutional history that preceded these New Deal cases, there had been many other attempts to invoke the maxim *delegata potestas non potest delegari,* and they had always failed.[7] In the autumn of 1934 when the Panama case was being briefed and argued, no one suspected that the basic policy of the common law of agency lay dormant in the "faithful execution" clause of Article II of the Constitution, or wherever else in the Constitution it may have been that the Court discovered the wellsprings for the theory of nondelegation that was subsequently articulated in the Court's opinion. One can only speculate as to the sources, in terms of the language of the Constitution, upon which the Court relied for justification of the policy it pronounced; there is no reference, in Hughes's opinion for the Court, to any particular constitutional clauses which were thought to be transgressed; and as for previous holdings of the Court, the Panama decision was quite literally unprecedented.

The Supreme Court had upheld the delegation of power to the President to suspend and to revive the effectiveness of neutrality and embargo statutes as early as 1813; [8] and in 1825, John Marshall himself had upheld a congressional statute which delegated to the federal courts the legislative power to make procedural rules of law.[9] Indeed, the first session of the First Congress had enacted the Judiciary Act of 1789, Section 17 of which provided: "That all the said courts shall have power . . . to make and establish all necessary rules for the orderly conducting business in the said courts, provided such rules are not repugnant to the laws of the United States." All three of the criteria announced by Hughes in

---

[6] An attempt to challenge a delegation to the President in the field of foreign policy was sharply rebuffed in the following year, by the Court's decision in the Curtiss-Wright case (see Chapter 6); and similar attempts to challenge wartime rationing programs failed in *Yakus* v. *United States,* 321 U.S. 414 (1944), and *Bowles* v. *Willingham,* 321 U.S. 503 (1944). See particularly the dissenting opinions in these cases by Mr. Justice Roberts,

who concluded that there was no doubt that the Schechter decision had been "now overruled."

[7] Glendon A. Schubert, "The Executive Rule-Making Power: Hart and Comer Revisited," *Journal of Public Law,* Vol. 4, pp. 376-389 (1955).

[8] *The Brig Aurora,* 7 Cranch 382 (1813).

[9] *Wayman* v. *Southard* 10 Wheaton 1 (1825).

the Panama decision are conspicuous by their total absence from this enactment, which had been approved by a Congress which included a goodly number of the Founding Fathers, and of course, by President George Washington, too.

As Comer explained the practice during the century preceding the New Deal: [10]

> In its attempt to "put over," by means of symbols, the general character-istic of that legislation which may not be delegated, as well as that which may, the Judiciary since 1825 has failed to make very great progress in set-ting limitations. Only in the steady accumulation of examples has there been a contribution. In Wayman v. Southard [10 Wheat. 1 (1825)], Chief Justice Marshall used the terms "general principles," "great outlines," "important outlines" to express that part of legislation which, in his opinion, could not be delegated. Later the terms "purpose," "criterion," "general provisions," "general rules," "terms of the statute," "predicate of the Act," "congressional intention," "purely legislative power," "legal principles that control," "policy of the law," "objects of the law," "vital provisions," "general scheme," "pri-mary standard," merely variations of the original expressions have been used to express the same idea. . . . Perhaps the Court in Wayman v. Southard thought the expressions used in indicating what legislation could be dele-gated would give more definite content to the essential duties of the law-making body, thereby suggesting limitations upon delegation. At all events, "subjects of less interest," "filling up the details," "minor regulations" were expressions used to define legislative delegation. Consciously or not, later attempts on the part of the courts failed to find better language with which to express the same idea. "Administration," "mere details," "supplementary rules," "mere administrative rules," "power to apply general rules," "rules fulfilling the objects of the statute," "subordinate and supplemental details," "aids or adjuncts," "the determination of some fact or state of things," are some of the terms later used.

Necessity is also the mother of constitutional invention, in the form of con-stitutional practices. A large measure of discretion on the part of the other two branches of government, to make specific policies within (presumably) the general framework of norms enacted in statutes, always has been necessary. As the Ameri-can national government has grown larger and more complex, and as the policy questions facing the Congress for decision have become more diverse and techni-cal, more and more delegation of the authority to make national policy has taken place. Congress is limited in time, in the information available to it, and in the individual and collective competence of its members. Congress has, for instance, largely turned over to the Supreme Court the function of making the procedural rules for the federal courts; and during the past several decades, the Court has in

[10] John Preston Comer, *Legislative Func-tions of National Administrative Authorities* (New York: Columbia University Press, 1927), pp. 123-125.

effect subdelegated much of its responsibilities in this regard to various advisory groups, who "assist" the justices in the periodic revision of the federal rules of criminal procedure, and of civil procedure, for example. No one has questioned the constitutionality of this practice; and few would argue that Congress would perform this function either more wisely or more responsibly. Similarly, the President and higher administrative officials of the Executive Branch must subdelegate much of their authority to subordinates; [11] as the federal Second (and then, Circuit) Court of Appeals remarked, "in the nature of things the President cannot personally exercise the least fraction of the manifold powers of every description which are granted to him—more truly, which are imposed upon him. If he may not depute their exercise, they are sterile as stones." [12]

There are no cases in which the Supreme Court has declared unconstitutional congressional delegation of legislative power to the federal courts or public administrative officers or agencies or to the federal regulatory commissions. During the quarter of a century that has elapsed since the spring of 1935, the Supreme Court has discovered no further instances of unconstitutional delegation of legislative power to the President. To the contrary: [13]

> The courts have upheld such variable standards as "the law of war," and "military equipment or supplies" to be subject to export controls, War Food Regulations establishing a control system for milk handlers were viewed as a kind of "fact-finding" and the mere "filling in of the details" of the statutory mandate, and it was announced that a regulation "within the sphere of foreign relations . . . is thus free from the limitations imposed on delegated authority." The most forthright statement, however, was that of the Second Circuit Court of Appeals, which blandly remarked:
>
>> It is true that the section [5(b)] gives the President an unrestricted power to be exercised at his discretion and without any standard except that he shall act through "rules and regulations." The only objection to this which can be raised is that it disturbs the constitutional "separation of powers" . . . [which] is in the end a matter of degree anyway. Indeed, the power conferred upon the President in Section 7(c) of the Trading with the Enemy Act is without condition; and, so far as concerns unconstitutional delegation, it makes no difference that it is limited to enemy property.
>
> It is difficult to understand how the valid phrases "the law of war" and "rules and regulations" provide any more rational standards than invalid phrases such as "housing" and "unfair trade practices." The explanation lies in the seeming inconsistency and aberration of [these] decisions of the New Deal period, in comparison with the trend of judicial opinion, both before and since, throughout the nation's history.

11 See Glendon A. Schubert, "The Presidential Subdelegation Act of 1950," *Journal of Politics,* Vol. 13, pp. 647-674 (1951).

12 *Silesian-American Corp.* v. *Markham,* 156 F. 2d 793, 796 (1947); affirmed in *Silesian-American Corp.* v. *Clark,* 332 U.S. 469 (1947).

13 Schubert, *op. cit.* (footnote 7, *supra*), p. 390.

CONGRESSIONAL REGULATION OF THE
SUPREME COURT'S APPELLATE REVIEW

One reaction to the School Segregation cases and to other libertarian decisions of the Warren Court was the introduction in Congress, during the middle and late fifties, of a series of bills designed to curtail the appellate jurisdiction of the Court. This was, without doubt, the most serious and sustained attack of this sort upon the Court since the early days of Reconstruction, when the Court itself contributed to the establishment of a precedent which demonstrates the extremes to which a determined congressional majority can go in shielding controversial legislation from judicial review by the Court.

The precedent, *Ex parte McCardle,* was decided under circumstances that are unique in American history. There are no higher stakes in constitutional politics than those at issue when the McCardle case was before the Court. Congress had passed a statute on February 5, 1867, which authorized all federal judges and justices to issue writs of habeas corpus in all cases where persons were restrained in violation of the Constitution and national law, excepting military prisoners charged with violations of military law. The act was intended to protect officials of the national government and loyalists against retribution from sympathizers of the Confederacy in the southern states. It provided, also, for a special right of appeal to the Supreme Court from decisions of circuit courts in such cases. The procedure of the act was invoked, however, by one McCardle, a newspaperman who was held for trial by a military commission on orders of the military commander in charge of the Reconstruction government in Mississippi. McCardle, who had criticized in his paper certain acts and policies of the military occupation forces from the North, was charged with disturbance of the public peace; inciting to insurrection, disorder, and violence; libel; and impeding Reconstruction. His petition for release on habeas corpus was denied, after a hearing, by the local federal circuit court, from whose decision he appealed to the Supreme Court.

Counsel for the government filed a motion to dismiss the appeal for want of jurisdiction, arguing that the recently enacted habeas corpus statute did not apply to this case, because that statute was intended to apply to prisoners of *state* officials; McCardle had committed a "military offence," and therefore fell within the express exception of Section 2 of the statute; and that, in any event, the Supreme Court's own appellate jurisdiction was limited to the review of cases that the circuit courts heard on appeal, not cases that originated in the circuit courts. And if the 1867 statute did not apply, it was argued, the Court had no jurisdiction otherwise to review the case, since no such appellate authority was conferred by the Judiciary Act of 1789. In *Ex parte McCardle,* 6 Wallace 318, 324 (1868), the Court unanimously denied the motion to dismiss, in a brief opinion by the Chief Justice. In addition to ruling that it did have jurisdiction under the 1867 statute, Chief Justice Chase undertook to refute the claim that, in the absence of that statute, the Court would have had no power to review the case:

> Prior to the passage of that act this court exercised appellate jurisdiction over the action of inferior courts by *habeas corpus*. In the case of *Burford* [3 Cranch 449, 453 (1806)], this court, by *habeas corpus*, aided by a writ of *certiorari*, reviewed and reversed the judgment of the Circuit Court of the District of Columbia. In that case a prisoner brought before the Circuit Court by the writ had been remanded, but was discharged upon the *habeas corpus* issued out of this court.
>
> By the writ of *habeas corpus* also, aided by a *certiorari*, this court, in the case of *Bollman* and *Swartwout* [4 Cranch 75 (1807)], again revised a commitment of the Circuit Court of the District. The prisoners had been committed on a charge of treason by order of the Circuit Court, and on their petition this court issued the two writs, and, the prisoners having been produced, it was ordered that they should be discharged on the ground that the commitment of the Circuit Court was not warranted by law.
>
> But, though the exercise of appellate jurisdiction over judgments of inferior tribunals was not unknown to the practice of this court before the act of 1867, it was attended by some inconvenience and embarrassment. It was necessary to use the writ of *certiorari* in addition to the writ of *habeas corpus,* and there was no regulated and established practice for the guidance of parties invoking the jurisdiction.

So the case was set down for argument; and at the very time that counsel were pressing their claims on the merits before the Supreme Court, impeachment charges against the President of the United States were filed in the House of Representatives. One reason for the impeachment of Johnson was his having vetoed a number of the Reconstruction bills on constitutional grounds; and although these were passed over his veto, the majority in Congress wanted to avoid having the Supreme Court brand the legislation as unconstitutional. Amid widespread speculation as to the decision that the Court would make in the McCardle case—because it could have been easily used as a vehicle for declaring unconstitutional the entire Reconstruction program—there were persistent rumors that the Court, though divided, had decided to rule against the Radical Republicans and order the release of McCardle. Under these circumstances, Congress enacted, over the veto of President Johnson, the act of March 27, 1868, which repealed that part of the habeas corpus act of February 5, 1867, which authorized appeals to the Supreme Court from decisions of the circuit courts.

Although the case had been fully argued and, in all probability, decided on the merits, counsel moved for permission to have the case reheard, so that the Court could consider the effect of the repealer statute upon its jurisdiction. This circumstance, in combination with the absence from the Court of Chief Justice

Chase, who was presiding over the impeachment trial of the President in the Senate, induced the Court to postpone the McCardle case until the next (i.e., December 1868) term. Justices Grier and Field filed a bitter public protest against this procedure, accusing their colleagues of evading their constitutional responsibilities and indulging in deliberate procrastination so that a decision on the merits of the case might be avoided.[14] As Carl Brent Swisher has remarked, "The Supreme Court seems to have acted on the principle that discretion was the better part of valor." [15] Certainly, the Court's handling of this case exemplifies Roche's comment that "simple delay can be employed, perhaps in the spirit of the Croatian proverb that 'delay is the handmaiden of justice.' " [16]

EX PARTE McCARDLE

7 Wallace 506 (1869)

Appeal from the Circuit Court for the Southern District of Mississippi.

Dismissed.

8-0

Chase, C.J.	('+')
Nelson	(+)
Grier	(+)
Clifford	(+)
Swayne	(+)
Miller	(+)
Davis	(+)
Field	(+)
Vacancies	1

The case was this:

The Constitution of the United States ordains as follows:

"§ 1. The judicial power of the United States shall be vested *in one Supreme Court,* and in such inferior courts as the Congress may from time to time ordain and establish.

"§ 2. The judicial power shall extend to all cases in law or equity arising *under this Constitution, the laws of the United States,"* &c.

And in these last cases the Constitution ordains that,

"The Supreme Court shall have appellate jurisdiction, both as to law and fact, *with such exceptions, and under such regulations, as the Congress shall make."*

With these constitutional provisions in existence, Congress, on the 5th February, 1867, by "An act to amend an act to establish the judicial courts of the United States, approved September 24, 1789," provided that the several courts of the United States, and the several justices and judges of such courts, within their respective jurisdiction, in addition to the authority already conferred by law, should have power to grant writs of *habeas corpus* in all cases where any person may be restrained of his or her liberty in violation of the Constitution, or of any treaty or law of the United States. And that, from the final decision of any judge, justice, or court inferior to the Circuit Court, appeal might be taken to the Circuit Court of the United States for the district in which the cause was heard, and *from the judgment of the said Circuit Court to the Supreme Court of the United States.*

This statute being in force, one McCardle, alleging unlawful restraint by

---

[14] For a detailed account of the Grier-Field dissent and of the background of the case generally, see Charles Warren, *The Supreme Court in United States History* (Boston: Little, 1928), Vol. 2, pp. 465, 473-474, 480-484, 487-488.

[15] *American Constitutional Development* (Boston: Houghton, 1943 ed.), p. 326.

[16] John P. Roche, "Judicial Self-Restraint," quoted in Chapter 4, *infra.*

military force, preferred a petition in the court below, for the writ of *habeas corpus.*

The writ was issued, and a return was made by the military commander, admitting the restraint, but denying that it was unlawful.

It appeared that the petitioner was not in the military service of the United States, but was held in custody by military authority for trial before a military commission, upon charges founded upon the publication of articles alleged to be incendiary and libellous, in a newspaper of which he was editor. The custody was alleged to be under the authority of certain acts of Congress.

Upon the hearing, the petitioner was remanded to the military custody; but, upon his prayer, an appeal was allowed him to this court, and upon filing the usual appeal-bond, for costs, he was admitted to bail upon recognizance, with sureties, conditioned for his future appearance in the Circuit Court, to abide by and perform the final judgment of this court. The appeal was taken under the above-mentioned act of February 5, 1867.

A motion to dismiss this appeal was made at the last term, and, after argument, was denied.

Subsequently, on the 2d, 3d, 4th, and 9th March, the case was argued very thoroughly and ably upon the merits, and was taken under advisement. While it was thus held, and before conference in regard to the decision proper to be made, an act was passed by Congress, returned with objections by the President, and, on the 27th March, repassed by the constitutional majority, the second section of which was as follows:

"*And be it further enacted,* That so much of the act approved February 5, 1867, entitled 'An act to amend an act to establish the judicial courts of the United States, approved September 24, 1789,' as authorized an appeal from the judgment of the Circuit Court to the Su-

preme Court of the United States, or the exercise of any such jurisdiction by said Supreme Court, on appeals which have been, or may hereafter be taken, be, and the same is hereby repealed."

The attention of the court was directed to this statute at the last term, but counsel having expressed a desire to be heard in argument upon its effect, and the Chief Justice being detained from his place here, by his duties in the Court of Impeachment, the cause was continued under advisement. Argument was now heard upon the effect of the repealing act.

The CHIEF JUSTICE delivered the opinion of the court.

The first question necessarily is that of jurisdiction; for, if the act of March, 1868, takes away the jurisdiction defined by the act of February, 1867, it is useless, if not improper, to enter into any discussion of other questions.

It is quite true, as was argued by the counsel for the petitioner, that the appellate jurisdiction of this court is not derived from acts of Congress. It is, strictly speaking, conferred by the Constitution. But it is conferred "with such exceptions and under such regulations as Congress shall make."

It is unnecessary to consider whether, if Congress had made no exceptions and no regulations, this court might not have exercised general appellate jurisdiction under rules prescribed by itself. For among the earliest acts of the first Congress, at its first session, was the act of September 24th, 1789, to establish the judicial courts of the United States. That act provided for the organization of this court, and prescribed regulations for the exercise of its jurisdiction.

The source of that jurisdiction, and the limitations of it by the Constitution and by statute, have been on several occasions subjects of consideration here. . . . [The] whole matter was carefully examined, and the court held, that while "the appellate powers of this court are not given by the judicial act, but are given by the Constitution," they are, nevertheless, "limited and regulated by that act, and by such other acts as have been passed on the subject." The court said, further, that the judicial act was an exercise of the power given by the Constitution to Congress "of making exceptions to the appellate jurisdiction of the Supreme Court." "They have described affirmatively," said the court, "its jurisdiction, and this affirmative description has been understood to imply a negation of the exercise of such appellate power as is not comprehended within it."

The principle that the affirmation of appellate jurisdiction implies the negation of all such jurisdiction not affirmed having been thus established, it was an almost necessary consequence that acts of Congress, providing for the exercise of jurisdiction, should come to be spoken of as acts granting jurisdiction, and not as acts making exceptions to the constitutional grant of it.

The exception to appellate jurisdiction in the case before us, however, is not an inference from the affirmation of other appellate jurisdiction. It is made in terms. The provision of the act of 1867, affirming the appellate jurisdiction of this court in cases of *habeas corpus* is expressly repealed. It is hardly possible to imagine a plainer instance of positive exception.

We are not at liberty to inquire into the motives of the legislature. We can only examine into its power under the Constitution; and the power to make exceptions to the appellate jurisdiction of this court is given by express words.

What, then, is the effect of the repealing act upon the case before us? We cannot doubt as to this. Without jurisdiction the court cannot proceed at all in any cause. Jurisdiction is power to declare the law, and when it ceases to exist, the only function remaining to the court is that of announcing the fact and dismissing

the cause. And this is not less clear upon authority than upon principle.

. . . The general rule . . . is, that "when an act of the legislature is repealed, it must be considered, except as to transactions past and closed, as if it never existed." And the effect of repealing acts upon suits under acts repealed, has been determined by the adjudications of this court . . . [and] it was held that no judgment could be rendered in a suit after the repeal of the act under which it was brought and prosecuted.

It is quite clear, therefore, that this court cannot proceed to pronounce judgment in this case, for it has no longer jurisdiction of the appeal; and judicial duty is not less fitly performed by declining ungranted jurisdiction than in exercising firmly that which the Constitution and the laws confer.

Counsel seem to have supposed, if effect be given to the repealing act in question, that the whole appellate power of the court, in cases of *habeas corpus*, is denied. But this is an error. The act of 1868 does not except from that jurisdiction any cases but appeals from Circuit Courts under the act of 1867. It does not affect the jurisdiction which was previously exercised.[17]

The appeal of the petitioner in this case must be

Dismissed for want of jurisdiction.

[17] *Ex parte McCardle,* 6 Wallace, 324. [This footnote by the Court is a citation to the language from the 1868 decision that we have quoted, above, to the effect that the Court had jurisdiction, *independent of* the habeas corpus act of 1867, to review lower-court decisions in cases of this sort by invoking the extraordinary (or "common law") writ of certiorari, in combination with an application directly to itself for a writ of habeas corpus. The implication of this footnote seems to be that the Court did not lack power to decide this case, unless its jurisdiction were confined to the 1867 statute. Did counsel for McCardle miss a bet by failing to press for a further hearing, asking the Court to exercise its discretion to accept jurisdiction on this alternative ground?]

CONGRESSIONAL CONTROL OVER
INFERIOR FEDERAL COURTS

If all power, like all of Gaul, is divided into three parts, certain theoretical problems arise when attempts are made to relate theory to the actual practices involved in the administration of a system of governance. To put the matter in a slightly different way: if the Constitution presumes that there will be three, and only three, branches of the government—legislative, executive, and judicial—does it follow that there are three, and only three, kinds of governmental power? In the classic formulation of Article XXX of the Massachusetts Constitution of 1780, and in the words of John Adams:

> In the government of this commonwealth, the legislative department shall never exercise the executive and judicial powers, or either of them; the executive shall never exercise the legislative and judicial powers, or either of them; the judicial shall never exercise the legislative and executive powers, or either of them; to the end that it may be a government of laws and not of men.

We have seen that one such problem clusters about what is called "the delegation of legislative power"; and we have also observed that the principle of the separation of powers has had slight effect in impeding such delegation. Another facet of the same basic concept relates to the exercise of judicial power.

If "judicial power" describes the authority for everything that judges do, then the pristine simplicity of the principle of separation can be preserved, because it no longer has meaning except as a description of whatever happens, at a particular time, to be the status quo. But if "judicial power" refers to a particular type of decision-making process, then the principle of separation is difficult to maintain, except as an unattainable ideal, because officials in all branches of the government exercise judicial power in this sense. Persons called "judges" who wear robes and work for agencies called "courts" exercise judicial power; but so do persons called "commissioners" or "hearing officers" or "trial examiners" who are assigned to administrative agencies; and so do congressmen sitting on committees and subcommittees of the houses of Congress. And so do many other officials of the Executive Branch, including both those in civilian and those in military capacity.

Although, for a time, there were attempts to "soften . . . by a *quasi*" [18] the frank recognition of this dispersion of judicial power throughout the government, the Supreme Court has come in time to accept, at least in part, the realities of the situation. [19] Such recognition has brought with it, however, other

[18] Holmes, dissenting in *Springer* v. *Philippine Islands*, 277 U.S. 189, 210 (1928).

[19] Of course, there is a similar dispersion of legislative and executive power among all three branches of the government, and there is an equal reluctance to accommodate constitutional theory to governmental practices in this regard as well.

problems in semantic adjustment. Are there lower federal courts, other than the "inferior courts" referred to in Article III? If so, what kind of "judicial power" is exercised by such non-Article III courts, and what is its source? Can a given court be both an Article III and a non-Article III court, at the same time and sitting in the same place? Can the Supreme Court draw upon Article III judicial power in order to review the exercise of some other kind of judicial power by these non-Article III courts? Can Article III judges sit, by temporary assignment, upon non-Article III courts, and vice versa? Is there a process of metamorphosis by means of which an administrative agency can be converted into a non-Article III court, and perhaps ultimately, like a worm turning into a butterfly, become a genuine Article III court? And, by no means least, is it possible for Congress to confer both kinds of judicial power upon the Article III courts?

Not all of these questions have been answered by the Supreme Court, but a number of them were raised in a series of cases that came to the Court at the same time that the Great Depression visited the nation. The first of these cases was the one below.

EX PARTE BAKELITE
CORPORATION

279 U.S. 438 (1929)

Original petition for a writ of prohibition to the Court of Customs Appeals.

Denied.

9-0

VanDevanter	('+')
Taft, C.J.	(+)
Holmes	(+)
McReynolds	(+)
Brandeis	(+)
Sutherland	(+)
Butler	(+)
Sanford	(+)
Stone	(+)

As we pointed out in Chapter 3, the Court would now consider such a case as this to be on the Miscellaneous Docket as a case in appellate jurisdiction, rather than as a case in original jurisdiction. By the time this case was decided, the Court of Customs Appeals had already been converted into the Court of Customs and Patent Appeals, with jurisdiction

jointly over appeals from the Customs Court (the decisions of robe-wearing judges) and from the Commissioner of Patents (indisputably a robeless administrative official). The hybrid jurisdiction of the Court of Customs and Patent Appeals is of interest, because decisions of the C.C.P.A. are, in turn, subject to review by certiorari by the Supreme Court. Indeed, in this very case, a subsequent petition for certiorari was denied, sub. nom. Frischer & Co. v. Tariff Commission, *282 U.S. 852 (1930).*

MR. JUSTICE VAN DEVANTER delivered the opinion of the Court.

This is a petition for a writ of prohibition to the Court of Customs Appeals prohibiting it from entertaining an appeal from findings of the Tariff Commission in a proceeding begun and conducted under § 316 of the Tariff Act of 1922.... A rule to show cause was issued; return was made to the rule; and a hearing has been had on the petition and return.

Section 316 of the Tariff Act is long and not happily drafted. A summary of it will suffice for present purposes. It is designed to protect domestic industry and trade against "unfair methods of competition and unfair acts" in the importation of articles into the United States and in their sale after importation. To that end it empowers the President, whenever the existence of any such unfair methods or acts is established to his satisfaction, to deal with them by fixing an additional duty upon the importation of the articles to which the unfair practice relates, or, if he is satisfied the unfairness is extreme, by directing that the articles be excluded from entry.

The section provides that, "to assist the President" in making decisions thereunder, the Tariff Commission shall investigate allegations of unfair practice, conduct hearings, receive evidence, and make findings and recommendations, subject to a right in the importer or consignee, if the findings be against him, to appeal to the Court of Customs Appeals on questions of law affecting the findings. There is also a provision purporting to subject the decision of that court to review by this Court upon certiorari. Ultimately the commission is required to transmit its findings and recommendations, with a transcript of the evidence, to the President so that he may consider the matter and act thereon.

A further provision declares that "any additional duty or any refusal of entry under this section shall continue in effect until the President shall find and instruct the Secretary of the Treasury that the conditions which led to the assessment of such additional duty or refusal of entry no longer exist."

The present petitioner, the Bakelite Corporation, desiring to invoke action under that section, filed with the Tariff Commission a sworn complaint charging unfair methods and acts in the importation and subsequent sale of certain articles and alleging a resulting injury to its domestic business of manufacturing and selling similar articles. The commission entertained the complaint, gave public notice thereof and conducted a hearing, in which interested importers appeared and presented evidence claimed to be in refutation of the charge. The commission made findings sustaining the charge and recommended that the articles to which the unfair practice related be excluded from entry. The importers appealed to the Court of Customs Appeals, where the Bakelite Corporation challenged the court's jurisdiction on constitutional grounds. The court upheld its jurisdiction and announced its purpose to entertain the appeal. Thereupon the Bakelite Corporation presented to this Court its petition for a writ of prohibition. Pending a decision on the petition further proceedings on the appeal have been suspended.

The grounds on which the jurisdiction of the Court of Customs Appeals was challenged in that court, and on which a writ of prohibition is sought here, are:

1. That the Court of Customs Appeals is an inferior court created by Congress under section 1 of Article III of the Constitution, and as such it can have no jurisdiction of any proceeding which is not a case or controversy within the meaning of section 2 of the same Article.

2. That the proceeding presented by the appeal from the Tariff Commission is not a case or controversy in the sense of that section, but is merely an advisory proceeding in aid of executive action.

The Court of Customs Appeals considered these grounds in the order just stated and by its ruling sustained the first and rejected the second.

In this Court counsel have addressed arguments not only to the two questions bearing on the jurisdiction of the Court of Customs Appeals, but also to the question whether, if that court be exceeding its jurisdiction, this Court has power to issue to it a writ of prohibition to arrest the unauthorized proceedings.

The power of this Court to issue writs of prohibition never has been clearly defined by statute or by decisions. And the existence of the power in a situation like the present is not free from doubt. But the doubt need not be resolved now, for, assuming that the power exists, there is here, as will appear later on, no tenable basis for exercising it. In such a case it is admissible, and is common practice, to pass the question of power and to deny the writ because without warrant in other respects.

While Article III of the Constitution declares, in section 1, that the judicial power of the United States shall be vested in one Supreme Court and in "such inferior courts as the Congress may from time to time ordain and establish," and prescribes, in section 2, that this power shall extend to cases and controversies of certain enumerated classes, it long has been settled that Article III does not express the full authority of Congress to create courts, and that other Articles invest Congress with powers in the exertion of which it may create inferior courts and clothe them with functions deemed essential or helpful in carrying those powers into execution. But there is a difference between the two classes of courts. Those established under the specific power given in section 2 of Article III are called constitutional courts. They share in the exercise of the judicial power defined in that section, can be invested with no other jurisdiction, and have judges who hold office during good behavior, with no power in Congress to provide otherwise. On the other hand, those created by Congress in the exertion of other powers are called legislative courts. Their functions always are directed to the execution of one or more of such powers and are prescribed by Congress independently of section 2 of Article III; and their judges hold for such term as Congress prescribes, whether it be a fixed period of years or during good behavior.

The first pronouncement on the subject by this Court was in *American Insurance Co. v. Canter,* 1 Pet. 511 [1828], where the status and jurisdiction of courts created by Congress for the Territory of Florida were drawn in question. Chief Justice Marshall, speaking for the court,

said, p. 546: "These Courts, then, are not constitutional Courts, in which the judicial power conferred by the Constitution on the general government can be deposited. They are incapable of receiving it. They are legislative Courts, created in virtue of the general right of sovereignty which exists in the government, or in virtue of that clause which enables Congress to make all needful rules and regulations respecting the territory belonging to the United States. The jurisdiction with which they are invested, is not a part of that judicial power which is defined in the 3d article of the Constitution, but is conferred by Congress, in the execution of those general powers which that body possesses over the territories of the United States."

That ruling has been accepted and applied from that time to the present in cases relating to territorial courts.

A like view has been taken of the status and jurisdiction of the courts provided by Congress for the District of Columbia. These courts, this Court has held, are created in virtue of the power of Congress "to exercise exclusive legislation" over the district made the seat of the government of the United States, are legislative rather than constitutional courts, and may be clothed with the authority and charged with the duty of giving advisory decisions in proceedings which are not cases or controversies within the meaning of Article III, but are merely in aid of legislative or executive action, and therefore outside the admissible jurisdiction of courts established under that Article. . . .

Legislative courts also may be created as special tribunals to examine and determine various matters, arising between the government and others, which from their nature do not require judicial determination and yet are susceptible of it. The mode of determining matters of this class is completely within congressional control. Congress may reserve to itself the power to decide, may delegate that power to executive officers, or may commit it to judicial tribunals.

Conspicuous among such matters are claims against the United States. These may arise in many ways and may be for money, lands or other things. They all admit of legislative or executive determination, and yet from their nature are susceptible of determination by courts; but no court can have cognizance of them except as Congress makes specific provision therefor. Nor do claimants have any right to sue on them unless Congress consents; and Congress may attach to its consent such conditions as it deems proper, even to requiring that the suits be brought in a legislative court specially created to consider them.

The Court of Claims is such a court. It was created, and has been maintained, as a special tribunal to examine and determine claims for money against the United States. This is a function which belongs primarily to Congress as an incident of its power to pay the debts of the United States. But the function is one which Congress has a discretion either to exercise directly or to delegate to other agencies.

For sixty-five years following the adoption of the Constitution Congress made it a practice not only to determine various claims itself but also to commit the determination of many to the executive departments. In time, as claims multiplied, that practice subjected Congress and those departments to a heavy burden. To lessen that burden Congress created the Court of Claims and delegated to it the examination and determination of all claims within stated classes. Other claims have since been included in the delegation and some have been excluded. But the court is still what Congress at the outset declared it should be—"a court for the investigation of claims against the United States." The matters made cognizable therein include nothing which inherently or necessarily requires judicial determination. On the contrary, all are matters which are susceptible of legislative or executive determination and can have no other save under and in conformity with permissive legislation by Congress. . . .

While what has been said of the creation and special function of the [Court of Claims] definitely reflects its status as a legislative court, there is propriety in mentioning the fact that Congress always has treated it as having that status. From the outset Congress has required it to give merely advisory decisions on many matters. Under the act creating it all of its decisions were to be of that nature. Afterwards some were to have effect as binding judgments, but others were still to be merely advisory. This is true at the present time. A duty to give decisions which are advisory only, and so without force as judicial judgments, may be laid on a legislative court, but not on a constitutional court established under Article III. . . .

Without doubt that court is a court of the United States within the meaning of § 375 of Title 28, U. S. C., just as the superior courts of the District of Columbia are; but this does not make it a constitutional court. . . .

Before we turn to the status of the Court of Customs Appeals it will be helpful to refer briefly to the Customs Court. Formerly it was the Board of General Appraisers. Congress assumed to make the board a court by changing its name. There was no change in powers, duties, or personnel.[20] The board was an executive agency charged with the duty of reviewing acts of appraisers and collectors in appraising and classifying imports and in liquidating and collecting customs duties. But its functions, although mostly quasi-judicial, were all susceptible of performance by executive officers and had been performed by such officers in earlier times.

The Court of Customs Appeals was created by Congress in virtue of its power

20 Act May 28, 1926, c. 411, 44 Stat. 669. [Footnote by the Court.]

to lay and collect duties on imports and to adopt any appropriate means of carrying that power into execution. The full province of the court under the act creating it is that of determining matters arising between the Government and others in the executive administration and application of the customs laws. These matters are brought before it by appeals from decisions of the Customs Court, formerly called the Board of General Appraisers. The appeals include nothing which inherently or necessarily requires judicial determination, but only matters the determination of which may be, and at times has been, committed exclusively to executive officers. True, the provisions of the customs laws requiring duties to be paid and turned into the Treasury promptly, without awaiting disposal of protests against rulings of appraisers and collectors, operate in many instances to convert the protests into applications to refund part or all of the money paid; but this does not make the matters involved in the protests any the less susceptible of determination by executive officers. In fact their final determination has been at times confided to the Secretary of the Treasury, with no recourse to judicial proceedings.

This summary of the court's province as a special tribunal, of the matters subjected to its revisory authority, and of its relation to the executive administration of the customs laws, shows very plainly that it is a legislative and not a constitutional court. . . .

A feature much stressed is the absence of any provision respecting the tenure of the judges. From this it is argued that Congress intended the court to be a constitutional one, the judges of which would hold their offices during good behavior. And in support of the argument it is said that in creating courts Congress has made it a practice to distinguish between those intended to be constitutional and those intended to be legislative by making no provision respecting the tenure of judges

of the former and expressly fixing the tenure of judges of the latter. But the argument is fallacious. *It mistakenly assumes that whether a court is of one class or the other depends on the intention of Congress,*[21] whereas the true test lies in the power under which the court was created and in the jurisdiction conferred. Nor has there been any settled practice on the part of Congress which gives special significance to the absence or presence of a provision respecting the tenure of judges. This may be illustrated by two citations. The same Congress that created the Court of Customs Appeals made provision for five additional circuit judges and declared that they should hold their offices during good behavior; and yet the status of the judges was the same as it would have been had that declaration been omitted. In creating courts for some of the Territories Congress failed to include a provision fixing the tenure of the judges; but the courts became legislative courts just as if such a provision had been included.

Another feature much stressed is a provision purporting to authorize temporary assignments of circuit and district judges to the Court of Customs Appeals when vacancies occur in its membership or when any of its members are disqualified or otherwise unable to act. This it is said shows that Congress intended the Court to be a constitutional one, for otherwise such assignments would be inadmissible under the Constitution. But if there be constitutional obstacles to assigning judges of constitutional courts to legislative courts, the provision cited is for that reason invalid and cannot be saved on the theory that Congress intended the court to be in one class when under the Constitution it belongs in another. Besides, the inference sought to be drawn from that provision is effectually refuted by two later enactments—one permitting judges of that court to be assigned from time to

21 Emphasis added.

time to the superior courts of the District of Columbia, which are legislative courts, and the other transferring to that court the advisory jurisdiction in respect of appeals from the Patent Office which formerly was vested in the Court of Appeals of the District of Columbia [by the Act of March 2, 1929]. . . .

As it is plain that the Court of Customs Appeals is a legislative and not a constitutional court, there is no need for now inquiring whether the proceeding under § 316 of the Tariff Act of 1922, now pending before it, is a case or controversy within the meaning of section 2 of Article III of the Constitution, for this section applies only to constitutional courts. Even if the proceeding is not such a case or controversy, the Court of Customs Appeals, being a legislative court, may be invested with jurisdiction of it, as is done by § 316.

Of course, a writ of prohibition does not lie to a court which is proceeding within the limits of its jurisdction, as the Court of Customs Appeals appears to be doing in this instance.

Prohibition denied.

Ex parte Bakelite was followed by two cases which raised the question of the power of the Supreme Court to exercise judicial review of the decisions of the Court of Appeals for the District of Columbia, when that court was adjudicating in its capacity as a legislative court. *Federal Radio Commission* v. *General Electric Co.,* 281 U.S. 464 (1930), held that the Supreme Court could not review decisions of the Court of Appeals for the District in appeals from licensing decisions of the Federal Radio Commission, because the statutory discretion of the Court of Appeals was so broad that that Court's function was administrative and "the proceeding in that court was not a case or controversy in the sense of the judiciary article." Congress promptly amended the Radio Act of 1927, by the Act of July 1, 1930, to limit the scope of review by the Court of Appeals to questions of law, for the express purpose of ensuring review of the decisions of the Court of Appeals by the Supreme Court. In *Federal Radio Commission* v. *Nelson Bros.,* 289 U.S. 266 (1933), the Supreme Court held that this function of the Court of Appeals was no longer administrative, and that judicial review of its decisions by the Supreme Court was now possible.

Two companion cases, O'Donoghue and Williams, also were decided in 1933. As we noted in Chapter 4, in each of these cases a federal judge sued for back salary in the Court of Claims on the ground that, as a judge of a constitutional court, his salary could not legally be reduced during his (life) tenure. In *O'Donoghue* v. *United States,* 289 U.S. 516, 546, the Court upheld the claims of judges of the superior courts of the District of Columbia, having changed its mind in the four years since the Bakelite case was decided. The Court now decided, by a 6-3 vote, that the District of Columbia courts were *both* constitutional and legislative courts:

If, in creating and defining the jurisdiction of the courts of the District, Congress were limited to Art. III, as it is in dealing with the other federal courts, the administrative and other jurisdiction spoken of could not be conferred upon the former. But the clause giving plenary power of legislation over the District enables Congress to confer such jurisdiction in addition to the federal jurisdiction which the District courts exercise under Art. III, notwithstanding that they are recipients of the judicial power of the United States under, and are constituted in virtue of, that article.

Rejecting its own precedents stretching back over half a century, the Court followed instead the recent dictum of *Ex parte Bakelite*, and ruled that judges of the Court of Claims belonged to a legislative court. This decision was not based upon statutory interpretation or the intent of Congress, but was said to be an inescapable result of the application of the principle of the separation of powers. It is worth repeating that this was 1933, and the Court managed to discover a host of mysterious emanations from the principle of separation of powers during the period 1925-1936. Among the Court's most enthusiastic interpreters of Montesquieu was Justice Sutherland, who delivered the unanimous opinion of the Court in *Williams* v. *United States*, 289 U.S. 553:

> . . . The Court of Claims, originally nothing more than an administrative or advisory body, was converted into a court, in fact as well as in name, and given jurisdiction over controversies which were susceptible of judicial cognizance. It is only in that view that the appellate jurisdiction of this court in respect of the judgments of that court could be sustained, or *concurrent* jurisdiction appropriately be conferred upon the federal district courts. The Court of Claims, therefore, undoubtedly, in entertaining and deciding these controversies, exercises judicial power, but the question still remains—and is the vital question—whether it is the judicial power defined by Art. III of the Constitution.
>
> . . . [Where] a controversy is of such a character as to require the exercise of the judicial power *defined by Art. III,* jurisdiction thereof can be conferred only on courts established in virtue of that article, and . . . Congress is without power to vest *that* judicial power in any other judicial tribunal, or, of course, in an executive officer, or administrative or executive board, since, to repeat the language of Chief Justice Marshall in *American Insurance Co.* v. *Canter, supra,* "they are incapable of receiving it." . . . [But the] view under discussion—that Congress having consented that the United States may be sued, the judicial power defined in Art. III at once attaches to the court authorized to hear and determine the suits—must, then, be rejected, for the further reason, or, perhaps, what comes to the same reason differently stated, that it cannot be reconciled with the limitation fundamentally implicit in the constitutional separation of the powers, namely, that a power definitely assigned by the Constitution to one department can neither be surrendered nor delegated by that department, nor vested by *statute* in another department or agency. Compare *Springer* v. *Philippine Islands,* 277 U.S. 189, 201-202. And since Congress, whenever it thinks proper, undoubtedly may,

without infringing the Constitution, confer upon an executive officer or administrative board, or an existing or specially constituted court, or retain for itself, the power to hear and determine controversies respecting claims against the United States, it follows indubitably that such power, in whatever guise or by whatever agency exercised, is no part of the judicial power vested in the constitutional courts by the third article. That is to say, a power which may be developed, at the will of Congress, upon any of the three departments plainly is not within the doctrine of the separation and independent exercise of governmental powers contemplated by the tripartite distribution of such powers. . . .

From whatever point of view the question be regarded, the conclusion is inevitable that the Court of Claims receives no authority and its judges no rights from the judicial article of the Constitution, but that the court derives its being and its powers and the judges their rights from the acts of Congress passed in pursuance of other and distinct constitutional provisions.

Twenty years after the Williams decision, Congress enacted Public Law 158 (83rd Cong., 1st. Sess., approved July 28, 1953), which amended Section 71 of Title 28 of the United States Code, relating to the Court of Claims, by adding the following sentence: "Such court is hereby declared to be a court established under Article III of the Constitution of the United States." There is no doubt that the Congress intended, by this act, to overrule the decision of the Supreme Court in the Williams case of 1933. The bill originated in the House of Representatives, and was reported out favorably by the House Judiciary Committee with an accompanying committee report which explained that:

The principal purpose of this bill is to declare the United States Court of Claims to be a court established under article III of the Constitution. . . . By Congress declaring unequivocally—as this bill proposes—that the Court of Claims was in fact established as, and continues to be, a constitutional court, this measure not only will protect the independence of the bench of the Court of Claims, but also will remove any doubt as to the power of Congress to authorize the Chief Justice of the United States to assign district and circuit judges to assist the judges of the Court of Claims whenever such action is considered necessary or expedient. Authority for such assignments of judges is conferred by sections 2 and 3 of the bill.

The first section of the bill declares the Court of Claims to be a court established under article III of the Constitution, i.e., a "constitutional court." Need for this declaration arises from the decision of the Supreme Court in 1933 in the case of Williams v. United States . . . which held that the Court of Claims was not one of the inferior courts established by Congress under article III of the Constitution, but rather was created by Congress as a "legislative court" in the exercise of congressional power, under article I, to pay the debts of the United States. Section 1 of the bill should remove any doubt that the Court of Claims is a constitutional court.

Congress was possessed of two powers under which it might have created the Court of Claims, and it would seem appropriate for it to say which of the powers it was intending to exercise. The Williams case held that in the creation of the Court of Claims Congress was exercising the power granted by article I to pay the debts of the United States. On the other hand, article III provides that—"The judicial Power of the United States shall extend . . . to Controversies to which the United States shall be a Party. . . ." The United States is a party in all cases in the Court of Claims. It would seem, therefore, that the Court of Claims exercises the judicial power thus defined in article III and is one of the inferior courts which Congress is empowered to create under that article.

It seems certain that Congress, when it established the Court of Claims in 1854, intended to create a court under article III. . . .

It appears also that at least until 1929, the Supreme Court of the United States was of the opinion that the Court of Claims was an article III court. . . .

It soon was apparent that the congressional overruling of the Williams case was no isolated event. Congress followed it up with two more identical clauses relating to the Customs Court and the Court of Customs and Patent Appeals. Public Law 703 (84th Cong., 2d Sess., approved July 14, 1956) declared that the Customs Court was (and had been) established under Article III; and Public Law 755 (85th Cong., 2d Sess., approved August 25, 1958) did the same for the Court of Customs and Patent Appeals. The effect of these two statutes was to overrule *Ex parte Bakelite* as well. Thus, three different and successive Congresses formally and by official action expressed their disagreement with the Supreme Court's interpretation both of earlier statutes and of the judiciary article of the Constitution (viz., "they [the Court of Claims, etc.] are incapable of receiving it [Article III judicial power]"). Moreover, Congress further formalized its obvious intention of asserting its own constitutional power to "ordain and establish" inferior federal courts by directing that the United States Code publish the codified statutes governing the organization and jurisdiction of the Court of Claims, the Customs Court, and the Court of Customs and Patent Appeals in the same part of Title 28 and immediately following the provisions for the Courts of Appeals and the District Courts; other federal courts are dealt with elsewhere in the code.

The Supreme Court appeared to acquiesce in this congressional action when retired Supreme Court Justices Minton and Reed were assigned to temporary duty with the Court of Claims, Minton in 1957 and Reed in both 1957 and 1958.[22] These assignments were made under Section 294 (a) of Title 28 of the United States Code, which authorizes the assignment, with his consent, of a retired Supreme Court justice to "judicial duties in any circuit." Section 291 (b) of the same title authorizes the assignment of retired federal *circuit* judges to the Court of Claims, and other sections authorize similar assignments to the Customs

[22] See 354 U.S. 944 and 355 U.S. 860, 880, 886 (1957); 357 U.S. 901 (1958).

Court and to the Court of Customs and Patent Appeals. But the absence of any explicit authority for the assignment of retired Supreme Court justices to any of the latter three courts suggests that the assignments of Minton and Reed by Chief Justice Warren constituted at least an implicit recognition that the Court of Claims (and presumably the other two courts as well) is a "constitutional court," and that the statutes declaring these three courts to be established under Article III are considered by the Court to be constitutional.

Irrespective of whether the Court should eventually overrule explicitly the Bakelite, Williams, and—perhaps—O'Donoghue cases, or as seems more likely, leave them to rest in peace, acquiescence by the Court would serve to strengthen the hand of Congress in exercising discretion to select the necessary and proper means —i.e., by invoking its power under either Article III or Article I, or perhaps both— to delegate judicial power to the inferior courts that it has chosen to establish.

NATIONAL MUTUAL INSURANCE CO. v. TIDEWATER TRANSFER CO.

337 U.S. 582 (1949)

Certiorari to the United States Court of Appeals for the Fourth Circuit.

Reversed.

5-4

Jackson	('+'
Black	(+
Burton	(+
Rutledge	('+'
Murphy	(+
Vinson, C.J.	'—')
Douglas	—)
Frankfurter	'—')
Reed	—)

The 5-4 vote in this case relates only to the decision of the Court that a 1940 act of Congress, extending the diversity jurisdiction of federal district courts to include residents of the District of Columbia, was constitutional. There were two independent grounds on which the validity of the statute could be upheld, and the Court voted 3-6 against the first ground, and 2-7 against the second ground. Nevertheless, a vote to sustain

the statute, on either ground, was a vote to reverse the decision below holding the act to be unconstitutional; so the two minorities of the Court combined to form a majority that controlled disposition of the case. It may be helpful to present the voting pattern in the form of a matrix, as in Table 24 (below), with attitudes toward the policy issues shown as the strategy alternatives, and the intersection of strategies in the cells defining the positions of the justices. Ground 1 we shall define as the belief that Congress can delegate non-Article III judicial power to constitutional courts. Ground 2 is the view that the District of Columbia should be considered to be a "State" within the meaning of the diversity clause of Article III. A plus sign means to favor, and a minus sign to oppose, either proposition.

Obviously, such a definition of the question for decision favors Congress, since votes in any of three of the cells are votes in favor of the constitutionality of the statute; while only votes in the remaining fourth cell, opposition on both grounds, count against the statute. (In this particular case, the upper left cell is blank, because none of the justices thought that this statute could be upheld on both grounds.)

Under the circumstances, there was a

TABLE 24.

Voting Matrix for the National Mutual Insurance Case

		Ground 1		
		+	−	Total
Ground 2	+	0	2 Rut, M	2
	−	3 J, Bl, Bu	4 V, D, F, Re	7
	Total	3	6	9

judgment, but no opinion, of the Court.[23] Although the case, as presented below, is long, it was nevertheless necessary to excise extended portions of the opinions as originally reported. Two observations, with reference to deleted material, are particularly pertinent. Justice Jackson was careful to point out, for instance, that Congress, in the Tort Claims Act of 1946, had delegated concurrent jurisdiction to the federal district (constitutional) courts and to the Court of Claims (which Jackson assumed to be a legislative court). What Jackson failed to mention was that the same statute also delegated concurrent adjudicatory power and jurisdiction, limited only as to amount, to several executive departments and administrative agencies, authorizing them to make precisely the same kind of judgments as might be made, alternatively, by the Court of Claims or the regular federal courts. Given this additional fact, it would appear that Jackson's argument would support not only the indiscriminate placement of "Article I" judicial power as between constitutional and legislative

23 For a discussion of the significance of this type of decision, see "Supreme Court No-Clear Majority Decisions; A Study in *Stare Decisis*," *University of Chicago Law Review*, Vol. 24, pp. 99-156 (1956).

courts, but as between either of them and administrative agencies, as well.

The omitted portion of the Vinson opinion argues forcefully for a rigid separation between constitutional and legislative courts, with constitutional courts exercising exclusively Article III judicial power, and legislative courts exercising exclusively Article I judicial power, although "legislative courts created by Congress also can and do decide questions arising under the Constitution and laws of the United States (and, in the case of territorial courts, other types of jurisdiction enumerated in Art. 3, sec. 2 as well)." The Chief Justice did not carry his argument through to its logical conclusion, however. If the Supreme Court exercises only Article III judicial power, and legislative courts, such as (Vinson assumed) the Court of Customs and Patent Appeals, exercise only Article I judicial power, how can the decisions of the latter be reviewed directly by the Supreme Court in appellate jurisdiction? Perhaps the Court was correct in docketing the petition for a writ of prohibition in Ex parte Bakelite as a case of original jurisdiction. Would not such a petition, whether for prohibition or certiorari, present an original case or controversy, from the point of view of the initial invocation of Article III judicial power?

These questions are suggested, not because it is thought that answers to them will change either the tendency of Congress to disperse adjudicatory functions widely throughout the government or the frequent desire of Congress to give the Supreme Court the final say, at least in principle, over the decision-making of subordinate adjudicators. Rather, the questions suggest some of the difficulties implicit in the attempts of the Supreme Court to cling to John Marshall's solution, adequate as it was for the problem of supporting in 1828 the authority of the courts of the Territory of Florida. It is most doubtful that Marshall himself would be impressed that his reasoning *then would be either a necessary or a proper means of dealing with the quite different and vastly more complex problems of administrative law and judicial administration in mid-twentieth-century America. (And neither, it might be added, would Marshall necessarily think that, because it was appropriate not to conceptualize a plot of largely uninhabited swampland as a "State" in 1804, it might not have become appropriate so to analogize the metropolis that served as the nation's capital a century and a half later.)*

MR. JUSTICE JACKSON announced the judgment of the Court and an opinion in which MR. JUSTICE BLACK and MR. JUSTICE BURTON join.

This case calls up for review a holding that it is unconstitutional for Congress to open federal courts in the several states to action by a citizen of the District of Columbia against a citizen of one of the states. The petitioner, as plaintiff, commenced in the United States District Court for Maryland an action for money judgment on a claim arising out of an insurance contract. No cause of action under the laws or Constitution of the United States was pleaded, jurisdiction being predicated only upon an allegation of diverse citizenship. The diversity set fourth was that plaintiff is a corporation created by District of Columbia law, while the defendant is a corporation chartered by Virginia, amenable to suit in Maryland by virtue of a license to do business there. The learned District Judge concluded that, while this diversity met jurisdictional requirements under the Act of Congress, it did not comply with diversity requirements of the Constitution as to federal jurisdiction, and so dismissed. The Court of Appeals, by a divided court, affirmed.[24] Of twelve district courts that had considered the question up to the time review in this Court was sought, all except three had held the enabling Act

[24] Chief Judge John J. Parker dissented.

unconstitutional and the two Courts of Appeals which had spoken on the subject agreed with that conclusion. The controversy obviously was an appropriate one for review here and writ of certiorari issued in the case.

The history of the controversy begins with that of the Republic. In defining the cases and controversies to which the judicial power of the United States could extend, the Constitution included those "between Citizens of different States." In the Judiciary Act of 1789, Congress created a system of federal courts of first instance and gave them jurisdiction of suits "between a citizen of the State where the suit is brought, and a citizen of another State." In 1804, the Supreme Court, through Chief Justice Marshall, held that a citizen of the District of Columbia was not a citizen of a State within the meaning and intendment of this Act.[25] This decision closed federal courts in the states to citizens of the District of Columbia in diversity cases, and for 136 years they remained closed. In 1940 Congress enacted the statute challenged here. It confers on such courts jurisdiction if the action "Is between citizens of different States, or citizens of the District of Columbia, the Territory of Hawaii, or Alaska, and any State or Territory." . . .

This constitutional issue affects only the mechanics of administering justice in our federation. It does not involve an extension or a denial of any fundamental right or immunity which goes to make up our freedoms. Those rights and freedoms do not include immunity from suit by a citizen of Columbia or exemption from process of the federal courts. Defendant concedes that it can presently be sued in some court of law, if not this one, and it grants that Congress may make it suable at plaintiff's complaint in some, if not this, federal court. Defendant's contention only amounts to this: that it cannot be made to answer this plaintiff in the

[25] *Hepburn & Dundas* v. *Ellzey*, 2 Cranch 445. [Footnote by Justice Jackson.]

particular court which Congress has decided is the just and convenient forum.

The considerations which bid us strictly to apply the Constitution to congressional enactments which invade fundamental freedoms or which reach for powers that would substantially disturb the balance between the Union and its component states, are not present here. In mere mechanics of government and administration we should, so far as the language of the great Charter fairly will permit, give Congress freedom to adapt its machinery to the needs of changing times. In no case could the admonition of the great Chief Justice be more appropriately heeded—". . . we must never forget, that it is *a constitution* we are expounding."

Our first inquiry is whether, under the third, or Judiciary, Article of the Constitution, extending the judicial power of the United States to cases or controversies "between Citizens of different States," a citizen of the District of Columbia has the standing of a citizen of one of the states of the Union. This is the question which the opinion of Chief Justice Marshall answered in the negative, by way of dicta if not of actual decision. *Hepburn & Dundas v. Ellzey,* 2 Cranch 445. To be sure, nothing was before that Court except interpretation of a statute which conferred jurisdiction substantially in the words of the Constitution with nothing in the text or context to show that Congress intended to regard the District as a state. But Marshall resolved the statutory question by invoking the analogy of the constitutional provisions of the same tenor and reasoned that the District was not a state for purposes of the Constitution and, hence, was not for purposes of the Act. The opinion summarily disposed of arguments to the contrary. . . .

To now overrule this early decision of the Court on this point and hold that the District of Columbia is a state would, as that opinion pointed out, give to the word "state" a meaning in the Article which sets up the judicial establishment quite different from that which it carries in those Articles which set up the political departments and in other Articles of the instrument. While the word is one which can contain many meanings, such inconsistency in a single instrument is to be implied only where the context clearly requires it. There is no evidence that the Founders, pressed by more general and immediate anxieties, thought of the special problems of the District of Columbia in connection with the judiciary. This is not strange, for the District was then only a contemplated entity. But had they thought of it, there is nothing to indicate that it would have been referred to as a state and much to indicate that it would have required special provisions to fit its anomalous relationship into the new judicial system, just as it did to fit it into the new political system.

In referring to the "States" in the fateful instrument which amalgamated them into the "United States," the Founders obviously were not speaking of states in the abstract. They referred to those concrete organized societies which were thereby contributing to the federation by delegating some part of their sovereign powers and to those that should later be organized and admitted to the partnership in the method prescribed. They obviously did not contemplate unorganized and dependent spaces as states. The District of Columbia being nonexistent in any form, much less as a state, at the time of the compact, certainly was not taken into the Union of states by it, nor has it since been admitted as a new state is required to be admitted.

We therefore decline to overrule the opinion of Chief Justice Marshall, and we hold that the District of Columbia is not a state within Article III of the Constitution. In other words, cases between citizens of the District and those of the states were not included in the catalogue of controversies over which the Congress could give jurisdiction to the federal courts by virtue of Art. III.

This conclusion does not, however, determine that Congress lacks power under other provisions of the Constitution to enact this legislation. Congress, by the Act in question, sought not to challenge or disagree with the decision of Chief Justice Marshall that the District of Columbia is not a state for such purposes. It was careful to avoid conflict with that decision by basing the new legislation on powers that had not been relied upon by the First Congress in passing the Act of 1789.

The Judiciary Committee of the House of Representatives recommended the Act of April 20, 1940, as "a reasonable exercise of the constitutional power of Congress to legislate for the District of Columbia and for the Territories." This power the Constitution confers in broad terms. . . . The Congress has acted on the belief that it possesses that power. We believe their conclusion is well founded. . . .

However, it is contended that Congress may not combine this function, under Art. I with those under Art. III in district courts of the United States. Two objections are urged to this. One is that no jurisdiction other than specified in Art. III can be imposed on courts that exercise the judicial power of the United States thereunder. The other is that Art. I powers over the District of Columbia must be exercised solely within that geographic area.

Of course there are limits to the nature of duties which Congress may impose on the constitutional courts vested with the federal judicial power. The doctrine of separation of powers is fundamental in our system. It arises, however, not from Art. III nor any other single provision of the Constitution. . . .

This statute . . . does not authorize or require either the district courts or this Court to participate in any legislative, administrative, political or other nonjudicial function or to render any advisory opinion. The jurisdiction conferred is limited to controversies of a justiciable nature, the sole feature disinguishing them from countless other controversies handled by the same courts being the fact that one party is a District citizen. Nor has the Congress by this statute attempted to usurp any judicial power. It has deliberately chosen the district courts as the appropriate instrumentality through which to exercise part of the judicial functions incidental to exertion of sovereignty over the District and its citizens.

Unless we are to deny to Congress the same choice of means through which to govern the District of Columbia that we have held it to have in exercising other legislative powers enumerated in the same Article, we cannot hold that Congress lacked the power it sought to exercise in the Act before us.

It is too late to hold that judicial functions incidental to Art. I powers of Congress cannot be conferred on courts existing under Art. III for it has been done with this Court's approval. *O'Donoghue* v. *United States*, 289 US 516. In that case it was held that, although District of Columbia courts are Art. III courts, they can also exercise judicial power conferred by Congress pursuant to Art. I. The fact that District of Columbia courts, as local courts, can also be given administrative or legislative functions which other Art. III courts cannot exercise, does but emphasize the fact that, although the latter are limited to the exercise of judicial power, it may constitutionally be received from either Art. III, or Art. I, and that congressional power over the District, flowing from Art. I, is plenary in every respect.

It is likewise too late to say that we should reach this result by overruling Chief Justice Marshall's view, unless we are prepared also to overrule much more, including some of our own very recent utterances.

. . . We have held unanimously that congressional authority under Art. I, not the Art. III jurisdiction over suits to which the United States is a party, is the sole source of power to establish the Court of Claims and of the judicial power which that court exercises. *Williams* v. *United States,* 289 U.S. 553. In that decision we also noted that it is this same Art. I power that is conferred on district courts by the Tucker Act which authorizes them to hear and determine such claims in limited amounts. Since a legislative court such as the Court of Claims is "incapable of receiving" Art. III judicial power, *American Insurance Co.* v. *Canter,* 1 Pet. 511, 546, it is clear that the power thus exercised by that court and concurrently by the district courts flows from Art. I, not Art. III. Indeed, more recently and again unanimously, this Court has said that by the Tucker Act the Congress authorized the district courts to sit as a court of claims [26] exercising the same but no more judicial power. *United States* v. *Sherwood,* 312 U.S. 584, 591. And but a few terms ago, in considering an Act by which Congress directed rehearing of a rejected claim and its redetermination in conformity with directions given in the Act, Chief Justice Stone, with the concurrence of all sitting colleagues, reasoned that "The problem presented here is no different than if Congress had given a like direction to any district court to be followed as in other Tucker Act cases." *Pope* v. *United States,* 323 U.S. 1, 14. Congress has taken us at our word and recently conferred on the district courts exclusive jurisdiction of tort claims cognizable under the Federal Tort Claims Act, 60 Stat. 842, 843, also enacted pursuant to Art. I powers. . . .

Congress also is given power in Art. I to make uniform laws on the subject of bankruptcies. That this, and not the judicial power under Art. III, is the source of our system of reorganizations and bankruptcy is obvious. . . . Not only may the district courts be required to handle these proceedings, but Congress may add to their

[26] This concurrent jurisdiction of the district courts has frequently been referred to in opinions of this Court with no indication that it presented any constitutional problem with respect to the jurisdiction of either the district courts or this Court. [Footnote by Justice Jackson.]

jurisdiction cases between the trustee and others that, but for the bankruptcy powers, would be beyond their jurisdiction because of lack of diversity required under Art. III. . . .

Unless we are to deny the jurisdiction in such cases which has consistently been upheld, we must rely on the Art. I powers of the Congress. We have been cited to no holding that such jurisdiction cannot spring from that Article. Under Art. I the Congress has given the district courts not only jurisdiction over cases arising under the bankruptcy law but also judicial power over nondiversity cases which do not arise under that or any other federal law. And this Court has upheld the latter grant.

Consequently, we can deny validity to this present Act of Congress, only by saying that the power over the District given by Art. I is somehow less ample than that over bankruptcy given by the same Article. If Congress could require this district court to decide this very case if it were brought by a trustee, it is hard to see why it may not require its decision for a solvent claimant when done in pursuance of other Art. I powers.

We conclude that where Congress in the exercise of its powers under Art. I finds it necessary to provide those on whom its power is exerted with access to some kind of court or tribunal for determination of controversies that are within the traditional concept of the justiciable, it may open the regular federal courts to them regardless of lack of diversity of citizenship. . . .

We therefore hold that Congress may exert its power to govern the District of Columbia by imposing the judicial function of adjudicating justiciable controversies on the regular federal courts which under the Constitution it has the power to ordain and establish and which it may invest with jurisdiction and from which it may withhold jurisdiction "in the exact degrees and character which to Congress may seem proper for the public good." . . .

The Act before us, as we see it, is not a resort by Congress to these means to reach forbidden ends. Rather, Congress is reaching permissible ends by a choice of means which certainly are not expressly forbidden by the Constitution. No good reason is advanced for the Court to deny them by implication. In no matter should we pay more deference to the opinions of Congress than in its choice of instrumentalities to perform a function that is within its power. To put federally administered justice within the reach of District citizens, in claims against citizens of another state, is an object which Congress has a right to accomplish. Its own carefully considered view that it has the power and that it is necessary and proper to utilize United States District Courts as means to this end, is entitled to great respect. Our own ideas as to the wisdom or desirability of such a statute or the constitutional provision authorizing it are totally irrelevant. Such a law of Congress should be stricken down only on a clear showing that it transgresses constitutional limitations. We think no such showing has been made. The Act is valid.

The judgment is

Reversed.

Mr. Justice Rutledge, with whom Mr. Justice Murphy agrees, concurring.

I join in the Court's judgment. But I strongly dissent from the reasons assigned to support it in the opinion of Mr. Justice Jackson.

While giving lip service to the venerable decision in *Hepburn & Dundas* v. *Ellzey,* 2 Cranch 445, and purporting to distinguish it, that opinion ignores nearly a century and a half of subsequent consistent construction. In all practical consequence, it would overrule that decision with its later reaffirmations. . . .

However, nothing but naked precedent, the great age of the *Hepburn* ruling, and the prestige of Marshall's name, supports such a result. It is doubtful whether anyone could be found who now would write

into the Constitution such an unjust and discriminatory exclusion of District citizens from the federal courts. All of the reasons of justice, convenience, and practicality which have been set forth for allowing District citizens a furtive access to federal courts, point to the conclusion that they should enter freely and fully as other citizens and even aliens do.

Precedent of course is not lightly to be disregarded, even in the greater fluidity of decision which the process of constitutional adjudication concededly affords. And Marshall's sponsorship in such matters always is weighty. But when long experience has disclosed the fallacy of a ruling, time has shown its injustice, and nothing remains but a technicality the only effect of which is to perpetuate inequity, hardship and wrong, those are the circumstances which this Court repeatedly has said call for reexamination of prior decisions. If those conditions are fulfilled in any case, they are in this one.

The *Hepburn* decision was made before time, through later decisions here, had destroyed its basic premise and at the beginning of Marshall's judicial career, when he had hardly started upon his great work of expounding the Constitution. The very brevity of the opinion and its groundings, especially in their ambiguity, show that the master hand which later made his work immortal faltered. . . .

I cannot believe that the Framers intended to impose so purposeless and indefensible a discrimination, although they may have been guilty of understandable oversight in not providing explicitly against it. Despite its great age and subsequent acceptance, I think the *Hepburn* decision was ill-considered and wrongly decided. Nothing hangs on it now except the continuance or removal of a gross and wholly anomalous inequality applied against a substantial group of American citizens, not in relation to their substantive rights, but in respect to the forums available for their determination. This Court has not hesitated to override even long-standing decisions when much more by way of substantial change was involved and the action taken was much less clearly justified than in this case, a most pertinent instance being *Erie R. Co. v. Tompkins*. . . .

That course should be followed here. It should be followed directly, not deviously. Although I agree with the Court's judgment, I think it overrules the *Hepburn* decision in all practical effect. With that I am in accord. But I am not in accord with the proposed extension of "legislative" jurisdiction under Article I for the first time to the federal district courts outside the District of Columbia organized pursuant to Article III, and the consequent impairment of the latter Article's limitations upon judicial power; and I would dissent from such a holding even more strongly than I would from a decision today reaffirming the *Hepburn* ruling. That extension, in my opinion, would be the most important part of today's decision, were it accepted by a majority of the Court. It is a dangerous doctrine which would return to plague both the district courts and ourselves in the future, to what extent it is impossible to say. The *O'Donoghue* and *Williams* decisions would then take on an importance they have never before had and were never considered likely to attain.

MR. CHIEF JUSTICE VINSON, with whom MR. JUSTICE DOUGLAS joins, dissenting.

. . . I agree with the views expressed by MR. JUSTICE FRANKFURTER and MR. JUSTICE RUTLEDGE which relate to the power of Congress under Art. I of the Constitution to vest federal district courts with jurisdiction over suits between citizens of States and the District of Columbia, and with the views of MR. JUSTICE FRANKFURTER and MR. JUSTICE JACKSON as to the proper interpretation of the word "States" in the diversity clause of Art. III. . . .

I hardly need add that I consider a finding of unconstitutionality of a statute a matter of grave concern. Nevertheless, Congress cannot do that which the Constitution specifically forbids. I think that it has attempted to do so here.

MR. JUSTICE FRANKFURTER, with whom MR. JUSTICE REED concurs, dissenting.

No provisions of the Constitution, barring only those that draw on arithmetic, as in prescribing the qualifying age for a President and members of a Congress or the length of their tenure of office, are more explicit and specific than those pertaining to courts established under Article III. "The judicial power" which is "vested" in these tribunals and the safeguards under which their judges function are enumerated with particularity. Their tenure and compensation, the controversies which may be brought before them, and the distribution of original and appellate jurisdiction among these tribunals are defined and circumscribed, not left at large by vague and elastic phrasing. The precision which characterizes these portions of Article III is in striking contrast to the imprecision of so many other provisions of the Constitution dealing with other very vital aspects of government. This was not due to chance or ineptitude on the part of the Framers. The differences in subject-matter account for the drastic differences in treatment. Great concepts like "Commerce . . . among the several States," "due process of law," "liberty," "property" were purposely left to gather meaning from experience. For they relate to the whole domain of social and economic fact, and the statesmen who founded this Nation knew too well that only a stagnant society remains unchanged. But when the Constitution in turn gives strict definition of power or specific limitations upon it we cannot extend the definition or remove the translation. Precisely because "it is *a constitution* we are expounding," *M'Culloch v. Maryland,* 4 Wheat (U.S.) 316, 407, we ought not to take liberties with it.

There was a deep distrust of a federal judicial system, as against the State judiciaries, in the Constitutional Convention. This distrust was reflected in the evolution of Article III. Moreover, when they dealt with the distribution of judicial power as between the courts of the States and the courts of the United States, the Framers were dealing with a technical subject in a professional way. More than that, since the judges of the courts for which Article III made provision not only had the last word (apart from amending the Constitution) but also enjoyed life tenure, it was an essential safeguard against control by the judiciary of its own jurisdiction, to define the jurisdiction of those courts with particularity. The Framers guarded against the self-will of the courts as well as against the will of Congress by marking with exactitude the outer limits of federal judicial power.

According to Article III only "judicial power" can be "vested" in the courts established under it. At least this limitation, which has been the law of the land since 1792, *Hayburn's Case,* 2 Dall (U.S.) 409, is not yet called into question. And so the President could not today elicit this Court's views on ticklish problems of international law any more than Washington was able to do in 1793. . . .

To find a source for "the judicial Power," therefore, which may be exercised by courts established under Article III of the Constitution outside that Article would be to disregard the distribution of powers made by the Constitution. The other alternative—to expand "the judicial Power" of Article III to include a controversy between a citizen of the District of Columbia and a citizen of one of the States by virtue of the provision extending "the judicial Power" to controversies "between Citizens of different States"—would disregard an explicit limitation of Article III. For a hundred and fifty years "States" as there used meant "States"—the political organizations that form the Union and alone have power to amend the Constitution. The word did not cover the district which was to become "the Seat of the Gov-ernment of the United States," nor the "Territory" belonging to the United States, both of which the Constitution dealt with in differentiation from the States. A decent respect for unbroken history since the country's foundation, for contemporaneous interpretation by those best qualified to make it, for the capacity of the distinguished lawyers among the Framers to express themselves with precision when dealing with technical matters, unite to admonish against disregarding the explicit language of Article III extending the diversity jurisdiction of the federal courts "to Controversies . . . between Citizens of different States," not to controversies between "Citizens of different States, including the District and the Territory of the United States."

The Framers, in making provision in regard to "States," meant the States which sent them as delegates to the Philadelphia Convention and the States which were to be admitted later. It was not contemplated that the district which was to become the seat of government could ever become a State. Marshall had no mean share in securing adoption of the Constitution and took special interest in the Judiciary Article. He merely gave expression to the common understanding—the best test of the meaning of words—when he rejected summarily the notion that the Citizens of the District are included among Citizens of "States." . . .

Of course every indulgence must be entertained in favor of constitutionality when legislation of Congress can fairly be deemed an exercise of the discretion, in the formulation of policy, given to Congress by the Constitution. But the cases to which jurisdiction may be extended under Article III to the courts established under it preclude any claim of discretionary authority to add to the cases listed by Article III or to change the distribution as between original and appellate jurisdiction made by that Article. Congress need not establish inferior courts; Congress need not grant the full scope of jurisdiction which it is empowered to vest in them; Congress need not give this Court any appellate power; it may withdraw appellate jurisdiction once conferred and it may do so even while a case is *sub judice. Ex parte McCardle*, 7 Wall. 506. But when the Constitution defined the ultimate limits of judicial power exercisable by courts which derive their sole authority from Article III, it is beyond the power of Congress to extend those limits. If there is one subject as to which this Court ought not to feel inhibited in passing on the validity of legislation by doubts of its own competence to judge what Congress has done, it is legislation affecting the jurisdiction

of the federal courts. When Congress on a rare occasion through inadvertence or generosity exceeds those limitations, this Court should not good-naturedly ignore such a transgression of congressional powers.

A substantial majority of the Court agrees that each of the two grounds urged in support of the attempt by Congress to extend diversity jurisdiction to cases involving citizens of the District of Columbia must be rejected—but not the same majority. And so, conflicting minorities in combination bring to pass a result—paradoxical as it may appear—which differing majorities of the Court find insupportable.

6

Presidential Policy-Making

THE AMERICAN PRESIDENCY is a prime force in the making of national policies in the United States. Although there is variance depending upon the times and upon the individual who is President, the Chief Executive always plays a major role; and in times of crisis, his role is pre-eminent. Of course it is true that the basic restraints upon presidential decision-making are political rather than legal; but judicial review *is* a political check, and it therefore becomes relevant to ask how, and how well, judicial review has functioned as a check upon the Chief Executive.

We put to one side the whole vast area of judicial review of the decision-making of subordinate officials of the Executive Branch and of the so-called "independent federal regulatory commissions"; this subject provides the content for what is traditionally known as administrative law. The source of legal authority of such subordinate administrators is a complex mesh of delegated statutory and subdelegated presidential (and, at lower echelons, higher administrative) powers; and the role of the courts in this context is one of interpreting congressional, executive, and administrative legislation supplemented by judicial and administrative adjudication. It may well be that in terms of actual impact upon American society, such an inquiry into the interrelationship between judicial and administrative decision-making is more important than our present investigation of the interrelationship among the Judicial, Legislative, and Executive branches of the national government; but the subject lies beyond the scope of the present volume. Judicial review of administrative action can usually involve questions of constitutional interpretation only to the extent that such cases also evoke consideration of the constitutional authority of the Congress and the President.

We already have questioned, in Chapter 4, the effectiveness of judicial review of acts of either the Congress or the President, if we take into consideration the available means of circumventing the Court's decisions and the capacity of the so-called political branches *ultimately* to insist that their policies shall prevail. But the capacity of the political branches to countermand the Court, and their willingness to engage in such a struggle, are quite different matters. The Supreme Court has one tremendous political advantage—an extra ace of spades up the sleeves of its judicial robes, as it were. Most of the time and on most issues, the Court has a corner on the market of the ultimate symbols of legitimacy. Manipulating, as it does, a process that has been termed "a mystery wrapped in an enigma," neither the Court's decisions, nor the rationales that are employed to support them, are comprehensible to the "average" citizen who may at the same time consider himself to be an authority upon nuclear disarmament, the appropriate level of the national debt, and the exploration of outer space. The Court's authority rests, therefore, upon the blind but devout faith of a public that attributes to it the unique faculty of revealing the true meaning of the Constitution. Part of that function is to make pronouncements, from time to time, upon the correlative authority of the Legislative and Executive departments of the government.

The Court, in other words, is the overseer of the no man's land of the Constitution; it is the arbiter of the "great silences" of that document which demark the boundaries which, at least in traditional theory, separate the component parts of government in the United States. In thus arbitrating between the Congress and the President, the Court in effect picks a side to support; and even on the same issue, sometimes the Court favors the President, and sometimes it is the Congress upon whom the Court smiles. It is rare that the odd branch—the one, that is, whose acts have been branded by the Court as unconstitutional—can hope to overcome successfully the combined political strength of the Supreme Court plus the other branch with which the Court has allied itself. Therefore, where there is genuine conflict between policy goals favored by the President and the Congress, the Supreme Court may well have an opportunity to have the determinative say by throwing its weight in support of either of the two contestants. This is a real power, and it is important.

On the other hand, the Court should, logically, abstain from pitting itself against the combined strength of the Presidency and the Congress at the behest of third parties who claim that fraternization between the Executive and the legislature has become too intimate. We already have observed that, with a single exception, the Court has refused to interfere with the "delegation of legislative power" to other officials of the government. And the exception, in 1935, led directly to an attack upon the Court which resulted in a revolutionary recasting of the Court's own personnel and policies. We shall see, below, that the Court's reluctance is intensified when Legislative-Executive liaison relates not to domestic policies but to relations with other nations, either in peace or war. Moreover, on those rare occasions when either the President or the Congress has temporarily assumed dictatorial powers, and is both sufficiently strong and sufficiently ruthless to overcome the potential combined opposition of the other branch *plus* the Court, it is futile to expect the Supreme Court "to uphold the Constitution."

The 1860's afford examples of both situations, with a military regime replacing, throughout much of the country during the entire decade, the civil processes of government "guaranteed" by the Constitution. During the period of actual hostilities, the Presidency was ascendant, and the military took its orders from Lincoln; after the war, the Presidency sank to its lowest estate, and the military took its orders from Congress. It was during the latter period that a President was impeached, for the only time in American history, for attempting to uphold what the Supreme Court later—over half a century later—declared to have been his indisputable powers and responsibility under the Constitution. (The impeachment of Johnson posed an infinitely greater threat to the separation of powers than has any decision ever rendered by the Supreme Court.)

It was at this same time that the Court refused to intervene in what was without question a direct and major conflict over policy between the Presidency and the Congress. *Mississippi* v. *Johnson,* 4 Wallace 475 (1867), is the exception to our rule, with the Court refusing to exercise an arbitral function, because to have upheld Congress would have resulted in adding an aura of legitimacy and respectability to what was probably unwise as well as unconstitutional legislation; while to have upheld the President and to have defied the Congress would have invited drastic retribution and the possibility of a crippling blow at the Court's own status and survival as an institution. A Congress that was prepared to impeach the President would not have been likely to hesitate in impeaching Supreme Court justices, should that have proved necessary. The McCardle case is testimony of the extremes to which both Congress and the Court were willing to go, under such circumstances.

THE FAITHFUL EXECUTION OF THE LAWS

Administrators in the American national government live in a world of pluralistic responsibilities. In part, they are responsible to the Congress; in part, to the President; in part, to the courts; and in part, to higher administrative authority. At subordinate administrative levels, responsibility to higher administrative authority is in effect all-embracing; and responsibility to the Congress, to the President, or to the Supreme Court is almost always indirect. But at the level of federal department, bureau, and independent-agency heads, competition between the Congress and the President for policy direction over administrative functions is pervasive and persistent; and judicial direction of administrative action, not infrequently, is a third vector of fundamental importance. Indeed, for some agencies—the "independent federal regulatory commissions" such as the Federal Trade Commission—judicial control may in practice be more important than either congressional or presidential control. The latter situation, however, falls within the scope of what is considered to be administrative law, so we shall confine our consideration, below, to two aspects of the Court's arbitration between Congress and the President, in their competition for determinative control over administrative policy and action.

Presidential Legislation

Although the Court gave early and explicit recognition, in its decisions, to the invocation of implied (as well as enumerated) powers by both the Court itself and the Congress, the Court has never articulated an equivalent general theory of implied presidential powers. There is no such counterpart, in the Court's decisions, to *Marbury* v. *Madison* (1803) or *McCulloch* v. *Maryland* (1819). This is not to say, however, that such a theory has not been advanced and frequently relied upon in practice. Every one of the Presidents whom historians have designated as "great" has conspicuously urged and acted under some variant form of expression of the notion that the President is not limited to the letter of the Constitution, and particularly, not in times of crisis. The Court itself has advocated such theories, but only selectively, and not as a general principle. Several of the cases that we shall examine in this chapter involve the Court's articulation and support of selective theories of implied presidential powers.

The advocacy of the general theory has been confined, in the decisions of the Court, to concurring and dissenting opinions. An apt and recent example of the latter genre is found in the separate concurring opinion of Mr. Justice Clark in the Steel Seizure case, in which he said:

> The limits of presidential power are obscure. However, Article II, no less than Article I, is part of "a constitution intended to endure for ages to come, and, consequently, to be adapted to the various crises of human affairs." Some of our Presidents, such as Lincoln, "felt that measures otherwise unconstitutional might become lawful by becoming indispensable to the preservation of the nation." Others, such as Theodore Roosevelt, thought the President to be capable, as a "steward" of the people, of exerting all power save that which is specifically prohibited by the Constitution or the Congress. In my view—taught me not only by the decision of Chief Justice Marshall in *Little* v. *Barreme,* but also by a score of other pronouncements of distinguished members of this bench—the Constitution does grant to the President extensive authority in times of grave and imperative national emergency. In fact, to my thinking, such a grant may well be necessary to the very existence of the Constitution itself. . . . In describing this authority I

care not whether one calls it "residual," "inherent," "moral," "implied," "aggregate," "emergency," or otherwise. I am of the conviction that those who have had the gratifying experience of being the President's lawyer have used one or more of these adjectives only with the utmost of sincerity and the highest of purpose.

The significant fact remains, nevertheless, that neither in *Little* v. *Bareme*, 2 Cranch 170 (1804)—in which the decision was *against* the legality of military orders of President Adams—nor at any time during the subsequent century and a half has the Supreme Court seen fit to satisfy the logical hiatus in the symmetry of the principle of separation of powers by according to the President a constitutional status equivalent to that which it has claimed for itself or approved for the Congress. The reason has not been the lack of occasions suitable for such a pronouncement.

CUNNINGHAM v. NEAGLE
(In re NEAGLE)

135 U.S. 1 (1890)

Appeal from the United States Circuit Court for the Northern District of California.

Affirmed.

6-2

Miller	('+')
Bradley	(+)
Harlan	(+)
Gray	(+)
Blatchford	(+)
Brewer	(+)
Lamar	'—')
Fuller, C.J.	—)
Field	NP

The Neagle *case raised the question whether the President has implied power, under circumstances that made it most difficult for the Supreme Court to disagree. To have disagreed, the Court would have had to rule that the President had no constitutional power to authorize the assignment of bodyguards to protect Supreme Court justices from being murdered while carrying out their official duties in riding circuit.*

The case is without parallel in American constitutional history, and a similar set of circumstances is not likely to recur. For one thing, the circuit-riding responsibilities of the justices were abolished by act of Congress only a couple of years after this decision was announced. But the underlying policy issue with which the case is concerned—the scope of the President's constitutional authority to act in the public interest even in the absence of explicit statutory delegation of power—is a recurring and frequently critical question in American constitutional politics.

Stephen J. Field, the justice who required a bodyguard, had been appointed by Lincoln, and had served on the Court for over a quarter of a century at the time of the events related in the case. Field was by then a septuagenarian, and his enforced (by his colleagues) retirement for senility was to occur less than a decade later. Field's antagonist and assailant, Terry, was a former Chief Justice of the California Supreme Court—a position that Field himself had filled earlier. Field had been a controversial figure in California, his adopted state, before his elevation to the Supreme Court; and he remained controversial twenty-six years later, not least because of his decisions and opinions both on the Supreme Court and on Circuit in California. The Neagle case stemmed directly from a litigation over which Field had presided in circuit.

MILLER, J. This is an appeal by Cunningham, sheriff of the county of San Joaquin, in the state of California, from a judgment of the circuit court of the United States for the northern district of California, discharging David Neagle from the custody of said sheriff, who held him a prisoner on a charge of murder. . . .

If it be true, as stated in this order of the court discharging the prisoner, that he was held "in custody for an act done in pursuance of a law of the United States, and in custody in violation of the constitution and laws of the United States," there does not seem to be any doubt that, under the statute on that subject, he was properly discharged by the circuit court. . . .

By the law, as it existed at the time of the enactment of the Revised Statutes, an appeal could be taken to the circuit court from any court of justice or judge inferior to the circuit court in a certain class of *habeas corpus* cases. But there was no appeal to the supreme court in any case except where the prisoner was the subject or citizen of a foreign state, and was committed or confined under the authority or law of the United States, or of any state, on account of any act done or omitted to be done under the commission or authority of a foreign state, the validity of which depended upon the law of nations.[1] But afterwards, by the act of congress of March 3, 1885, (23 St. 437,) this was extended by amendment as follows: "That section seven hundred and sixty-four of the Revised Statutes be amended so that the same shall read as follows: 'From the final decision of such circuit court an appeal may be taken to the supreme court in the cases described in the preceding section.' " The preceding section here referred to is sec-

tion 763 [2] and is the one on which the prisoner relies for his discharge from custody in this case. It will be observed that in both the provisions of the Revised Statutes and of this latter act of congress the mode of review, whether by the circuit court of the judgment of an inferior court or justice or judge, or by this court of the judgment of a circuit court, the word "appeal," and not "writ of error," is used; and, as congress had always used these words with a clear understanding of what is meant by them, namely, that by a writ of error only questions of law are brought up for review, as in actions at common law, while by an appeal, except when specially provided otherwise, the entire case, on both law and facts, is to be reconsidered, there seems to be little doubt that, so far as it is essential to a proper decision of this case, the appeal requires us to examine into the evidence brought to sustain or defeat the right of the petitioner to his discharge.

The history of the incidents which led to the tragic event of the killing of Terry by the prisoner, Neagle, had its origin in a suit brought by William Sharon, of Nevada, in the circuit court of the United States for the district of California, against Sarah Althea Hill, alleged to be a citizen of California, for the purpose of obtaining a decree adjudging a certain instrument in writing possessed and exhibited by her, purporting to be a declaration of marriage between them under the Code of California, to be a forgery, and to have it set aside and annulled. This suit, which was commenced October 3, 1883, was finally heard before Judge SAWYER, the circuit judge for that circuit, and Judge DEADY, United States district judge for Oregon, who had been duly appointed to assist in holding the circuit court for the district

[1] Cf. *Ex parte McCardle.*

[2] Section 763 provides, among other cases, for the issuing of writs of *habeas corpus* by the circuit courts on petition of persons alleged to be restrained of their liberty in violation of the constitution or laws of the United States. [Footnote by the Court.]

of California. The hearing was on September 29, 1885, and on the 15th of January, 1886, a decree was rendered granting the prayer of the bill. . . .

Nothing was done under this decree. The defendant, Sarah Althea Hill, did not deliver up the instrument to the clerk to be canceled, but she continued to insist upon its use in the state court. Under these circumstances, Frederick W. Sharon, as the executor of the will of his father, William Sharon, filed in the circuit court for the northern district of California, on March 12, 1888, a bill of revivor, stating the circumstances of the decree, the death of his father, and that the decree had not been performed; alleging, also, the intermarriage of Miss Hill with David S. Terry, of the city of Stockton, in California, and making the said Terry and wife parties to this bill of revivor. . . .

This case was argued in the circuit court before FIELD, circuit justice, SAWYER, circuit judge, and SABIN, district judge. While the matter was held under advisement, Judge SAWYER, on returning from Los Angeles, in the southern district of California, where he had been holding court, found himself on the train as it left Fresno, which is understood to have been the residence of Terry and wife, in a car in which he noticed that Mr. and Mrs. Terry were in a section behind him, on the same side. On this trip from Fresno to San Francisco, Mrs. Terry grossly insulted Judge SAWYER, and had her husband change seats so as to sit directly in front of the judge, while she passed him with insolent remarks, and pulled his hair with a vicious jerk, and then, in an excited manner, taking her seat by her husband's side, said: "I will give him a taste of what he will get by and by. Let him render this decision if he dares,"—the decision being the one already mentioned, then under advisement. Terry then made some remark about too many witnesses being in the car, adding that "the best thing to do with him would be to take him out into the bay, and drown

him." These incidents were witnessed by two gentlemen who knew all the parties, and whose testimony is found in the record before us. This was August 14, 1888. On the 3d of September the court rendered its decision granting the prayer of the bill of revivor in the name of Frederick W. Sharon and against Sarah Althea Terry and her husband, David S. Terry. The opinion was delivered by Mr. Justice FIELD, and during its delivery a scene of great violence occurred in the court-room. It appears that shortly before the court opened on that day, both the defendants in the case came into the court-room and took seats within the bar at the table next the clerk's desk, and almost immediately in front of the judges. Besides Mr. Justice FIELD, there were present on the bench Judge SAWYER and Judge SABIN, of the district court of the United States for the district of Nevada. The defendants had denied the jurisdiction of the court originally to render the decree sought to be revived, and the opinion of the court necessarily discussed this question, without reaching the merits of the controversy. When allusion was made to this question, Mrs. Terry arose from her seat, and, addressing the justice who was delivering the opinion, asked, in an excited manner, whether he was going to order her to give up the marriage contract to be canceled. Mr. Justice FIELD said: "Be seated, madam." She repeated the question, and was again told to be seated. She then said, in a very excited and violent manner, that Justice FIELD had been bought, and wanted to know the price he had sold himself for; that he had got Newland's money for it, and everybody knew that he had got it, or words to that effect. Mr. Justice FIELD then directed the marshal to remove her from the court-room. She asserted that she would not go from the room, and that no one could take her from it. Marshal Franks proceeded to carry out the order of the court by attempting to compel her to leave, when Terry, her husband, arose from his seat under great excitement, exclaiming that no man living should touch his wife, and struck the marshal a blow in his face so violent as to knock out a tooth. He then unbuttoned his coat, thrust his hand under his vest, apparently for the purpose of drawing a bowie-knife, when he was seized by persons present, and forced down on his back. In the meantime Mrs. Terry was removed from the court-room by the marshal, and Terry was allowed to rise, and was accompanied by officers to the door leading to the marshal's office. As he was about leaving the room, or immediately after being out of it, he succeeded in drawing a bowie-knife, when his arms were seized by a deputy-marshal and others present to prevent him from using it; and they were able to wrench it from him only after a severe struggle. The most prominent person engaged in wresting the knife from Terry was Neagle, the prisoner now in court. For this conduct both Terry and his wife were sentenced by the court to imprisonment for contempt,—Mrs. Terry for one month, and Terry for six months; and these sentences were immediately carried into effect. Both the judgment of the court on the petition for the revival of the decree in the case of Sharon against Hill, and the judgment of the circuit court imprisoning Terry and wife for contempt, have been brought to this court for review; and in both cases the judgments have been affirmed. . . .

Terry and Mrs. Terry were separately indicted by the grand jury of the circuit court of the United States, during the same term, for their part in these transactions; and the cases were pending in said court at the time of Terry's death. It also appears that Mrs. Terry, during her part of this altercation in the court room, was making efforts to open a small satchel which she had with her, but through her excitement she failed. This satchel, which was taken from her, was found to have in it a revolving pistol.

From that time until his death the de-nunciations by Terry and his wife of Mr. Justice FIELD were open, frequent, and of the most vindictive and malevolent character. While being transported from San Francisco to Alameda, where they were imprisoned, Mrs. Terry repeated a number of times that she would kill both Judge FIELD and Judge SAWYER. Terry, who was present, said nothing to restrain her, but added that he was not through with Judge FIELD yet; and, while in jail at Alameda, Terry said that after he got out of jail he would horsewhip Judge FIELD, and that he did not believe he would ever return to California, but this earth was not large enough to keep him from finding Judge FIELD and horsewhipping him; and, in reply to a remark that this would be a dangerous thing to do, and that Judge FIELD would resent it, he said: "If Judge FIELD resents it, I will kill him." . . . [The] evidence is abundant that both Terry and wife contemplated some attack upon Judge FIELD during his official visit to California in the summer of 1889, which they intended should result in his death. Many of these matters were published in the newspapers, and the press of California was filled with the conjectures of a probable attack by Terry on Justice FIELD as soon as it became known that he was going to attend the circuit court in that year.

So much impressed were the friends of Judge FIELD, and of public justice, both in California and in Washington, with the fear that he would fall a sacrifice to the resentment of Terry and his wife, that application was made to the attorney general of the United States suggesting the propriety of his furnishing some protection to the judge while in California. This resulted in a correspondence between the attorney general of the United States, the district attorney, and the marshal of the northern district of California on that subject. . . .

"Department of Justice, Washington, D. C., May 27, 1889. J. C. Franks, Esq., United States Marshal, San Francisco,

Cal.—Sir: Referring to former correspondence of the department relating to a possible disorder in the session of the approaching term of court, owing to the small number of bailiffs under your control to preserve order, you are directed to employ certain special deputies at a *per diem* of five dollars, payable out of the appropriation for fees and expenses of marshals, to be submitted to the court, as a separate account from your other accounts against the government, for approval, under section 846, Revised Statutes, as an extraordinary expense, that the same may be forwarded to this department in order to secure executive action and approval. Very respectfully, W. H. H. MILLER, Attorney General."

The result of this correspondence was that Marshal Franks appointed Mr. Neagle a deputy-marshal for the northern district of California, and gave him special instructions to attend upon Judge FIELD both in court and while going from one court to another, and protect him from any assault that might be attempted upon him by Terry and wife. Accordingly, when Judge FIELD went from San Francisco to Los Angeles, to hold the circuit court of the United States at that place, Mr. Neagle accompanied him, remained with him for the few days that he was engaged in the business of that court, and returned with him to San Francisco. It appears from the uncontradicted evidence in the case that, while the sleeping car in which were Justice FIELD and Mr. Neagle stopped a moment, in the early morning, at Fresno, Terry and his wife got on the train. The fact that they were on the train became known to Neagle, and he held a conversation with the conductor as to what peace-officers could be found at Lathrop, where the train stopped for breakfast; and the conductor was requested to telegraph to the proper officers of that place to have a constable or some peace-officer on the ground when the train should arrive, anticipating that there might be violence attempted by Terry

upon Judge FIELD. It is sufficient to say that this resulted in no available aid to assist in keeping the peace. When the train arrived, Neagle informed Judge FIELD of the presence of Terry on the train, and advised him to remain, and take his breakfast in the car. This the judge refused to do, and he and Neagle got out of the car, and went into the dining-room, and took seats beside each other in the place assigned them by the person in charge of the breakfast-room; and very shortly after this Terry and wife came into the room, and Mrs. Terry, recognizing Judge FIELD, turned and left in great haste, while Terry passed beyond where Judge FIELD and Neagle were, and took his seat at another table. It was afterwards ascertained that Mrs. Terry went to the car, and took from it a satchel in which was a revolver. Before she returned to the eating-room, Terry arose from his seat, and, passing around the table in such a way as brought him behind Judge FIELD, who did not see him or notice him, came up where he was sitting with his feet under the table, and struck him a blow on the side of his face, which was repeated on the other side. He also had his arm drawn back and his fist doubled up, apparently to strike a third blow, when Neagle, who had been observing him all this time, arose from his seat with his revolver in his hand, and in a very loud voice shouted out: "Stop! stop! I am an officer!" Upon this Terry turned his attention to Neagle, and, as Neagle testifies, seemed to recognize him, and immediately turned his hand to thrust it in his bosom, as Neagle felt sure, with the purpose of drawing a bowie-knife. At this instant Neagle fired two shots from his revolver into the body of Terry, who immediately sank down, and died in a few minutes. Mrs. Terry entered the room, with the satchel in her hand, just after Terry sank to the floor. She rushed up to the place where he was, threw herself upon his body, made loud exclamations and moans, and commenced inviting the spectators to avenge her wrong upon FIELD and Neagle. She appeared to be carried away by passion, and in a very earnest manner charged that Field and Neagle had murdered her husband intentionally; and shortly afterwards she appealed to the persons present to examine the body of Terry to see that he had no weapons. This she did once or twice. The satchel which she had, being taken from her, was found to contain a revolver. . . .

[A] justification would be a proper subject for consideration on a trial of the case for murder in the courts of the state of California; and there exists no authority in the courts of the United States to discharge the prisoner while held in custody by the state authorities for this offense, unless there be found in aid of the defense of the prisoner some element of power and authority asserted under the government of the United States. This element is said to be found in the facts that Mr. Justice FIELD, when attacked, was in the immediate discharge of his duty as judge of the circuit courts of the United States within California. . . .

Mr. Justice FIELD was a member of the supreme court of the United States, and had been a member of that court for over a quarter of a century, during which he had become venerable for his age and for his long and valuable service in that court. The business of the supreme court has become so exacting that for many years past the justices of it have been compelled to remain for the larger part of the year in Washington city, from whatever part of the country they may have been appointed. The term for each year, including the necessary travel and preparations to attend at its beginning, has generally lasted from eight to nine months. But the justices of this court have imposed upon them other duties, the most important of which arise out of the fact that they are also judges of the circuit courts of the United States. Of these circuits there are nine, to each one of which a justice of the supreme court is allotted, under section 606 of the Revised Statutes, the provision of which is as follows: "The chief justice and associate justices of the supreme court shall be allotted among the circuits by an order of the court; and a new allotment shall be made whenever it becomes necessary or convenient, by reason of the alteration of any circuit, or of the new appointment of a chief justice or associate justice, or otherwise." Section 610 declares that it "shall be the duty of the chief justice and of each justice of the supreme court to attend at least one term of the circuit court in each district of the circuit to which he is allotted during every period of two years." Although this enactment does not require, in terms, that the justices shall go to their circuits more than once in two years, the effect of it is to compel most of them to do this, because there are so many districts in many of the circuits that it is impossible for the circuit justice to reach them all in one year; and the result of this is that he goes to some of them in one year, and to others in the next year, thus requiring an attendance in the circuit every year. The justices of the supreme court have been members of the circuit courts of the United States ever since the organization of the government; and their attendance on the circuit, and appearance at the places where the courts are held, has always been thought to be a matter of importance. In order to enable him to perform this duty, Mr. Justice FIELD had to travel each year from Washington city, near the Atlantic coast, to San Francisco, on the Pacific coast. In doing this, he was as much in the discharge of a duty imposed upon him by law as he was while sitting in court and trying causes. There are many duties which the judge performs outside of the court-room where he sits to pronounce judgment or to preside over a trial. The statutes of the United States, and the established practice of the courts, require that the judge perform a very large share of his judicial labors at what is called "chambers." This chamber work is as important, as necessary, as much a discharge of his official duty, as that performed in the court-house. Important cases are often argued before the judge at any place convenient to the parties concerned, and a decision of the judge is arrived at by investigations made in his own room, wherever he may be; and it is idle to say that this is not as much the performance of judicial duty as the filing of the judgment with the clerk, and the announcement of the result in open court. So it is impossible for a justice of the supreme court of the United States, who is compelled by the obligations of duty to be so much in Washington city, to discharge his duties of attendance on the circuit courts, as prescribed by section 610, without traveling, in the usual and most convenient modes of doing it, to the place where the court is to be held. This duty is as much an obligation imposed by the law as if it had said in words: "The justices of the supreme court shall go from Washington city to the place where their terms are held every year." Justice FIELD had not only left Washington, and traveled the 3,000 miles or more which was necessary to reach his circuit, but he had entered upon the duties of that circuit, had held the court at San Francisco for some time, and, taking a short leave of that court, had gone down to Los Angeles, another place where a court was to be held, and sat as a judge there for several days, hearing cases and rendering decisions. It was in the necessary act of returning from Los Angeles to San Francisco, by the usual mode of travel between the two places, where his court was still in session, and where he was required to be, that he was assaulted by Terry in the manner which we have already described.

The occurrence which we are called upon to consider was of so extraordinary a character that it is not to be expected that many cases can be found to cite as authority upon the subject. . . . [but we] have no doubt that Mr. Justice FIELD, when attacked by Terry, was engaged in the discharge of his duties as circuit justice of the ninth circuit, and was entitled to all the protection, under those circumstances, which the law could give him.

It is urged, however, that there exists no statute authorizing any such protection as that which Neagle was instructed to give Judge FIELD in the present case, and, indeed, no protection whatever against a vindictive or malicious assault growing out of the faithful discharge of his official duties; and that the language of section 753 of the Revised Statutes, that the party seeking the benefit of the writ of *habeas corpus* must, in this connection, show that he is "in custody for an act done or omitted in pursuance of a law of the United States," makes it necessary that upon this occasion it should be shown that the act for which Neagle is imprisoned was done by virtue of an act of congress. It is not supposed that any special act of congress exists which authorizes the marshals or deputy-marshals of the United States, in express terms, to accompany the judges of the supreme court through their circuits, and act as a bodyguard to them, to defend them against malicious assaults against their persons. But we are of opinion that this view of the statute is an unwarranted restriction of the meaning of a law designed to extend in a liberal manner the benefit of the writ of *habeas corpus* to persons imprisoned for the performance of their duty; and we are satisfied that, if it was the duty of Neagle, under the circumstances—a duty which could only arise under the laws of the United States,—to defend Mr. Justice FIELD from a murderous attack upon him, he brings himself within the meaning of the section we have recited. . . . In the view we take of the constitution of the United States, any obligation fairly and properly inferable from that instrument, or any duty of the marshal to be derived from the general scope of his duties under the laws of the United States, is a "law," within the meaning of this phrase. It would be a great reproach to the system of government of the United States, declared to be within its sphere sovereign and supreme, if there is to be found within the domain of its powers no means of protecting the judges, in the conscientious and faithful discharge of their duties, from the malice and hatred of those upon whom their judgments may operate unfavorably. It has in modern times become apparent that the physical health of the community is more efficiently promoted by hygienic and preventive means than by the skill which is applied to the cure of disease after it has become fully developed. So, also, the law, which is intended to prevent crime, in its general spread among the community, by regulations, police organization, and otherwise, which are adapted for the protection of the lives and property of citizens, for the dispersion of mobs, for the arrest of thieves and assassins, for the watch which is kept over the community, as well as over this class of people, is more efficient than punishment of crimes after they have been committeed. If a person in the situation of Judge FIELD could have no other guaranty of his personal safety while engaged in the conscientious discharge of a disagreeable duty than the fact that, if he was murdered, his murderer would be subject to the laws of a state, and by those laws could be punished, the security would be very insufficient. . . . We do not believe that the government of the United States is thus inefficient, or that its constitution and laws have left the high officers of the government so defenseless and unprotected. . . .

We cannot doubt the power of the president to take measures for the protection of a judge of one of the courts of the United States who, while in the discharge of the duties of his office, is threatened with a personal attack which may probably result in his death; and we think it clear that where this protection is to be afforded through the civil power, the department of justice is the proper one to set in motion the necessary means of pro-

tection. The correspondence between the marshal of the northern district of California and the attorney general and the district attorney of the United States for that district, although prescribing no very specific mode of affording this protection by the attorney general, is sufficient, we think, to warrant the marshal in taking the steps which he did take, in making the provisions which he did make, for the protection and defense of Mr. Justice FIELD.

But there is positive law investing the marshals and their deputies with powers which not only justify what Marshal Neagle did in this matter, but which imposed it upon him as a duty. In chapter 14, title 13, of the Revised Statutes of the United States, which is devoted to the appointment and duties of the district attorneys, marshals, and clerks of the courts of the United States, section 788 declares: "The marshals and their deputies shall have, in each state, the same powers in executing the laws of the United States as the sheriffs and their deputies in such state may have, by law, in executing the laws thereof." If, therefore, a sheriff of the state of California was authorized to do in regard to the laws of California what Neagle did, —that is, if he was authorized to keep the peace, to protect a judge from assault and murder,—then Neagle was authorized to do the same thing in reference to the laws of the United States. . . . That there is a peace of the United States; that a man assaulting a judge of the United States while in the discharge of his duties violates that peace; that in such case the marshal of the United States stands in the same relation to the peace of the United States which the sheriff of the county does to the peace of the state of California,—are questions too clear to need argument to prove them. That it would be the duty of a sheriff, if one had been present at this assault by Terry upon Judge FIELD, to prevent this breach of the peace, to prevent this assault, to prevent the murder which was contemplated by it, cannot be doubted. . . . So the marshal of the United States, charged with the duty of protecting and guarding the judge of the United States court against this special assault upon his person and his life, being present at the critical moment, when prompt action was necessary, found it to be his duty—a duty which he had no liberty to refuse to perform—to take the steps which resulted in Terry's death. This duty was imposed on him by the section of the Revised Statutes which we have recited, in connection with the powers conferred by the state of California upon its peace officers, which become, by this statute, in proper cases, transferred as duties to the marshals of the United States. . . . The result at which we have arrived is that . . . in taking the life of Terry, under the circumstances, he was acting under the authority of the law of the United States, and was justified in so doing; and that he is not liable to answer in the courts of California on account of his part in that transaction. We therefore affirm the judgment of the circuit court authorizing his discharge from the custody of the sheriff of San Joaquin county.

Affirmed.

FIELD, J., did not sit at the hearing of this case, and took no part in its decision.

[LUCIUS Q. C.] LAMAR, J., (*dissenting.*) The chief justice and myself are unable to assent to the conclusion reached by the majority of the court. Our dissent is not based on any conviction as to the guilt or innocence of the appellee. The view which we take renders that question immaterial to the inquiry presented by this appeal. That inquiry is whether the appellee, Neagle, shall in this *ex parte* proceeding be discharged and delivered from any trial or further inquiry in any court, state or federal, for what he has been accused of in the forms prescribed by the constitution and laws of the state in which the act in question was committed. . . . In [the national constitution] is found not only the answer to the gen-

eral line of argument pursued in this case, but also to the specific question propounded by the attorney general in respect to the president's oath and its implications. The president is sworn to "preserve, protect, and defend the constitution." That oath has great significance. The sections which follow that prescribing the oath (sections 2 and 3 of article 2) prescribe the duties and fix the powers of the president. But one very prominent feature of the constitution which he is sworn to preserve, and which the whole body of the judiciary are bound to enforce, is the closing paragraph of section 8, art. 1, in which it is declared that "the congress shall have power * * * to make all laws which shall be necessary and proper for carrying into execution the foregoing powers, and all other powers vested by this constitution in the government of the United States, or in any department or officer thereof." This clause is that which contains the germ of all the implication of powers under the constitution. It is that which has built up the congress of the United States into the most august and imposing legislative assembly in the world, and which has secured vigor to the practical operations of the government, and at the same time tended largely to preserve the equilibrium of its various powers among its co-ordinate departments, as partitioned by that instrument. And that clause alone conclusively refutes the assertion of the attorney general that it was "the duty of the executive department of the United States to guard and protect at any hazard the life of Mr. Justice FIELD in the discharge of his duty, because such protection is essential to the existence of the government." Waiving the question of the essentiality of any such protection to the existence of the government, the manifest answer is that the protecion needed and to be given must proceed not from the president, but primarily from congress. Again, while it is the president's duty to take care that the laws be faithfully executed, it is not his duty to make laws or a law of the

United States. The laws he is to see executed are manifestly those contained in the constitution and those enacted by congress, whose duty it is to make all laws necessary and proper for carrying into execution the powers of those tribunals. In fact, for the president to have undertaken to make any law of the United States pertinent to this matter would have been to invade the domain of power expressly committed by the constitution exclusively to congress. That body was perfectly able to pass such laws as it should deem expedient in reference to such matter. Indeed, it has passed such laws in reference to elections, expressly directing the United States marshals to attend places of election, to act as peace-officers, to arrest with and without process, and to protect the supervisors of election in the discharge of their duties; and there was not the slightest legal necessity out of which to imply any such power in the president. For these reasons the letters of the attorney general to Marshal Franks, granting that they did import what is claimed, and granting that the attorney general was to all intents and purposes, *pro hac vice,* the president, invested Neagle with no special powers whatever. They were, if so construed, without authority of law; and Neagle was then and there a simple deputy-marshal,—no more and no less.

It is claimed that the law needed for appellee's case can be found in section 788 of the Revised Statutes. . . . It is then argued that by the Code of California the sheriff has extensive powers as a conservator of the peace, the statutes to that effect being quoted *in extenso;* that he also has certain additional common-law powers and obligations to protect the judges, and to personally attend them on their visits to that state; that, therefore, no statutory authority of the United States for the attendance on Mr. Justice FIELD by Neagle, and for Neagle's personal presence on the scene, was necessary; and that that statute constituted Neagle a peace-officer to keep the peace of the

United States. This line of argument seems to us wholly untenable. . . .

We are not unmindful of the fact that in the foregoing remarks we have not discussed the bearings of this decision upon the autonomy of the states, in divesting them of what was once regarded as their exclusive jurisdiction over crimes committed within their own territory, against their own laws, and in enabling a federal judge or court, by an order in a *habeas corpus* proceeding, to deprive a state of its power to maintain its own public order, or to protect the security of society and the lives of its own citizens, whenever the amenability to its courts of a federal officer or employe or agent is sought to be enforced. We have not entered upon that question because, as arising here, its suggestion is sufficient, and its consideration might involve the extent to which legislation in that direction may constitutionally go, which could only be properly determined when directly presented by the record in a case before the court for adjudication.

UNITED STATES v. MIDWEST OIL CO.

236 U.S. 459 (Argued January 9 and 19, 1914. Ordered for reargument before a full bench April 20, 1914. Reargued May 7, 1914. Decided February 23, 1915).

Certificate from the United States Circuit Court for the Eighth Circuit.

Remanded with directions to reverse.

5-3	
Lamar	('+')
White, C.J.	(+)
Holmes	(+)
Hughes	(+)
Pitney	(+)
Day	'—')
McKenna	—)
VanDevanter	—)
McReynolds	NP

The conservation of national resources raised major policy issues for the Theodore Roosevelt and William Howard Taft administrations. Illustrative of the explosive propensities of conservation policy as a political issue is the Glavis-Ballinger dispute, which was a contributory factor leading to Taft's defeat at the polls in 1912.[3]

Although it was Roosevelt rather than Taft who championed the "Stewardship Theory" of presidential prerogative which was argued, and successfully, by the Solicitor General in this case, it was Taft who signed the presidential proclamation that was at issue. Of the Stewardship Theory, private citizen Taft later remarked, in a lecture delivered in the same year as this decision, that ". . . the view of . . . Mr. Roosevelt, ascribing an undefined residuum of power to the President is an unsafe doctrine and . . . it might lead under emergencies to results of an arbitrary character, doing irremediable injustice to private right. The mainspring of such a view is that the Executive is charged with responsibility for the welfare of all the people in a general way, that he is to play the part of a Universal Providence and set all things right, and that anything that in his judgment will help the people he ought to do, unless he is expressly forbidden not to do it." [4]

The Solicitor General at the time of this case was John W. Davis, who was later to be Ambassador to Great Britain, Democratic candidate for the Presidency of the United States (1924), president of the American Bar Association, and an eminently successful corporation lawyer and distinguished defender of conservative causes generally (including the civil liberties of the "Big Steel" corporations, and

of white supremacists in South Carolina, both of which he represented before the Supreme Court in the argument of the Steel Seizure and School Segregation cases nearly forty years later—see pages 324 and 494, below). Davis' brief for the government in the Midwest Oil case included the following statement: [5]

Ours is a self-sufficient Government within its sphere. (Ex parte Siebold, 100 U.S., 371, 395; In re Debs, 158 U.S., 564, 568.) "Its means are adequate to its ends" (McCulloch v. Maryland, 4 Wheat., 316, 424), and it is rational to assume that its active forces will be found equal in most things to the emergencies that confront it. While perfect flexibility is not to be expected in a Government of divided powers, and while division of power is one of the principal features of the Constitution, it is the plain duty of those who are called upon to draw the dividing lines to ascertain the essential, recognize the practical, and avoid a slavish formalism which can only serve to ossify the Government and reduce its efficiency without any compensating good. The function of making laws is peculiar to Congress, and the Executive can not exercise that function to any degree. But this is not to say that all of the *subjects* concerning which laws might be made are perforce removed from the possibility of Executive influence. The Executive may act upon things and upon men in many relations which have not, though they might have, been actually regulated by Congress. In other words, just as there are fields which are peculiar to Congress and fields which are peculiar to the Executive, so there are fields which are common to both, in the sense that the Executive may move within them until they shall have been occupied by legislative action. These are not the fields of legislative prerogative, but fields within which the lawmaking power may enter and dominate whatever it chooses. This situation results from the fact that *the President is the ac-*

---

[3] See, e.g., Alpheus T. Mason, *Bureaucracy Convicts Itself* (New York: Viking, 1941); and Winifred McCulloch, *The Glavis-Ballinger Dispute* (New York: Inter-University Case Series No. 4, 1952).

[4] William Howard Taft, *Our Chief Magistrate and His Powers* (New York: Columbia University Press, 1916), p. 144.

[5] Emphasis added.

tive agent, not of Congress, but of the Nation. As such he performs the duties which the Constitution lays upon him immediately, and as such, also, he executes the laws and regulations adopted by Congress. *He is the agent of the people of the United States, deriving all his powers from them and responsible directly to them.* In no sense is he the agent of Congress. He obeys and executes the laws of Congress, not because Congress is enthroned in authority over him, but because the Constitution directs him to do so.

MR. JUSTICE [JOSEPH R.] LAMAR delivered the opinion of the court:

All public lands containing petroleum or other mineral oils, and chiefly valuable therefor, have been declared by Congress to be "free and open to occupation, exploration, and purchase by citizens of the United States . . . under regulations prescribed by law." Act of February 11, 1897. . . .

As these regulations permitted exploration and location without the payment of any sum, and as title could be obtained for a merely nominal amount, many persons availed themselves of the provisions of the statute. Large areas in California were explored; and petroleum having been found, locations were made, not only by the discoverer, but by others on adjoining land. And, as the flow through the well on one lot might exhaust the oil under the adjacent land, the interest of each operator was to extract the oil as soon as possible, so as to share what would otherwise be taken by the owners of nearby wells.

The result was that oil was so rapidly extracted that on September 17, 1909, the Director of the Geological Survey made a report to the Secretary of the Interior which, with inclosures, called attention to the fact that, while there was a limited supply of coal on the Pacific coast, and the value of oil as a fuel had been fully demonstrated, yet, at the rate at which oil lands in California were being patented

by private parties, it would "be impossible for the people of the United States to continue ownership of oil lands for more than a few months. After that the government will be obliged to repurchase the very oil that it has practically given away. . . ." "In view of the increasing use of fuel by the American Navy there would appear to be an immediate necessity for assuring the conservation of a proper supply of petroleum for the government's own use . . ." and "pending the enactment of adequate legislation on this subject, the filing of claims to oil lands in the state of California should be suspended."

This recommendation was approved by the Secretary of the Interior. Shortly afterwards he brought the matter to the attention of the President, who on September 27, 1909, issued the following proclamation:

Temporary Petroleum Withdrawal No. 5

In aid of proposed legislation affecting the use and disposition of the petroleum deposits on the public domain, all public lands in the accompanying lists are hereby temporarily withdrawn from all forms of location, settlement, selection, filing, entry, or disposal under the mineral or nonmineral public-land laws. All locations or claims existing and valid on this date may proceed to entry in the usual manner after filing, investigation, and examination.

The list attached described an area aggregating 3,041,000 acres in California and Wyoming. . . .[6]

On March 27, 1910, six months after the publication of the proclamation, William T. Henshaw and others entered upon a quarter section of this public land in Wyoming, so withdrawn. They made ex-

[6] These were the same lands that subsequently figured in the Teapot Dome Scandal after an Executive Order signed by President Harding had reversed, in effect, the Taft proclamation in this case. See *United States v. Pan-American Petroleum Co.,* 55 F. 2d 753, 769 (1932), certiorari denied 287 U.S. 612 (1932); *Mammoth Oil Co.* v. *United States,* 275 U.S. 13, 31 (1927).

plorations, bored a well, discovered oil, and thereafter assigned their interest to the appellees, who took possession and extracted large quantities of oil. On May 4, 1910, they filed a location certificate.

As the explorations by the original claimants, and the subsequent operation of the well, were both long after the date of the President's proclamation, the government filed, in the district court of the United States for the district of Wyoming, a bill in equity against the Midwest Oil Company and the other appellees, seeking to recover the land and to obtain an accounting for 50,000 barrels of oil alleged to have been illegally extracted. The court sustained the defendant's demurrer and dismissed the bill. Thereupon the government took the case to the circuit court of appeals of the eighth circuit, which rendered no decision, but certified certain questions to this court. . . .

Both parties, as well as other persons interested in oil lands similarly affected, have submitted lengthy and elaborate briefs on the single and controlling question as to the validity of the withdrawal order. On the part of the government it is urged that the President, as Commander in Chief of the Army and Navy, had power to make the order for the purpose of retaining and preserving a source of supply of fuel for the Navy, instead of allowing the oil land to be taken up for a nominal sum, the government being then obliged to purchase at a great cost what it had previously owned. It is argued that the President, charged with the care of the public domain, could, by virtue of the executive power vested in him by the Constitution (art. 2, § 1), and also in conformity with the tacit consent of Congress, withdraw, in the public interest, any public land from entry or location by private parties.

The appellees, on the other hand, insist that there is no dispensing power in the Executive, and that he could not suspend a statute or withdraw from entry or location any land which Congress had affirmatively declared should be free and open to acquisition by citizens of the United States. They further insist that the withdrawal order is absolutely void, since it appears on its face to be a mere attempt to suspend a statute—supposed to be unwise—in order to allow Congress to pass another more in accordance with what the Executive thought to be in the public interest.

1. We need not consider whether, as an original question, the President could have withdrawn from private acquisition what Congress had made free and open to occupation and purchase. The case can be determined on other grounds and in the light of the legal consequences flowing from a long-continued practice to make orders like the one here involved. For the President's proclamation of September 27, 1909, is by no means the first instance in which the Executive, by a special order, has withdrawn lands which Congress, by general statute, had thrown open to acquisition by citizens. And while it is not known when the first of these orders was made, it is certain that "the practice dates from an early period in the history of the government." Grisar v. McDowell, 6 Wall. 381. Scores and hundreds of these orders have been made; and treating them as they must be (Wolsey v. Chapman, 101 U.S. 769), as the act of the President, an examination of official publications will show that (excluding those made by virtue of special congressional action, Donnelly v. United States, 228 U.S. 255), he has, during the past eighty years, without express statutory,—but under the claim of power so to do,—made a multitude of Executive orders which operated to withdraw public land that would otherwise have been open to private acquisition. They affected every kind of land—mineral and nonmineral. The size of the tracts varied from a few square rods to many square miles, and the amount withdrawn has aggregated millions of acres. The number of such instances cannot, of course, be accurately given, but the extent of the

practice can best be appreciated by a consideration of what is believed to be a correct enumeration of such Executive orders mentioned in public documents.

They show that prior to the year 1910 there had been issued

  99 Executive orders establishing or enlarging Indian reservations;
109 Executive orders establishing or enlarging military reservations and setting apart land for water, timber, fuel, hay, signal stations, target ranges, and rights of way for use in connection with military reservations;
  44 Executive orders establishing bird reserves.

In the sense that these lands may have been intended for public use, they were reserved for a public purpose. But they were not reserved in pursuance of law, or by virtue of any general or special statutory authority. For it is to be specially noted that there was no act of Congress providing for bird reserves or for these Indian reservations. There was no law for the establishment of these military reservations or defining their size or location. There was no statute empowering the President to withdraw any of these lands from settlement, or to reserve them for any of the purposes indicated.

But when it appeared that the public interest would be served by withdrawing or reserving parts of the public domain, nothing was more natural than to retain what the government already owned. And in making such orders, which were thus useful to the public, no private interest was injured. For, prior to the initiation of some right given by law, the citizen had no enforceable interest in the public statute, and no private right in land which was the property of the people. The President was in a position to know when the public interest required particular portions of the people's lands to be withdrawn from entry or location; his action inflicted no wrong upon any private citizen, and being subject to disaffirmance by Congress,

could occasion no harm to the interest of the public at large. Congress did not repudiate the power claimed or the withdrawal orders made. On the contrary, it uniformly and repeatedly asquiesced in the practice, and, as shown by these records, there had been, prior to 1910, at least 252 Executive orders making reservations for useful, though nonstatutory, purposes.

This right of the President to make reservations—and thus withdraw land from private acquisition—was expressly recognized in Grisar v. McDowell, 6 Wall. 364, where (1867) it was said that "from an early period in the history of the government it has been the practice of the President to order from time to time, as the exigencies of the public service required, parcels of land belonging to the United States, to be reserved from sale and set apart for public uses." . . .

2. It may be argued that while these facts and rulings prove a usage, they do not establish its validity. But Government is a practical affair, intended for practical men. Both officers, lawmakers, and citizens naturally adjust themselves to any long-continued action of the Executive Department, on the presumption that unauthorized acts would not have been allowed to be so often repeated as to crystallize into a regular practice. . . .

The Executive, as agent, was in charge of the public domain; by a multitude of orders extending over a long period of time, and affecting vast bodies of land, in many states and territories, he withdrew large areas in the public interest. These orders were known to Congress, as principal, and in not a single instance was the act of the agent disapproved. Its acquiescence all the more readily operated as an implied grant of power in view of the fact that its exercise was not only useful to the public, but did not interfere with any vested right of the citizen. . . .

6. Nor is the position of the appellees strengthened by the act of June 25, 1910 . . . to authorize the President to make

withdrawals of public lands, and requiring a list of the same to be filed with Congress. . . .

The legislative history of the statute shows that there was no such intent and no purpose to make the act retroactive, or to disaffirm what the agent in charge had already done. The proclamation of September 27, 1909, withdrawing oil lands from private acquisition, was of far-reaching consequence both to individuals and to the public. It gave rise to much discussion, and the old question as to the authority of the President to make these orders was again raised. Various bills were introduced on the subject, and the President himself sent a message to Congress, calling attention to the existence of the doubt, and suggesting the desirability of legislation to expressly grant the power and ratify what had been done. A bill passed the House, containing such ratification and authorizing future withdrawals. When the bill came to the Senate it was referred to a committee, and, as its members did not agree in their view of the law, two reports were made. The majority, after a review of the practice of the Department, the acquiescence of Congress in the practice, and the decisions of the courts, reported that the President already had a general power of withdrawal, and recommended the passage of the pending bill, inasmuch as it operated to restrict the greater power already possessed. Sen. Rep. 171 (61st Cong. 2d Session). . . .

Congress, by this statute, did not legislate against the public and validate what was then an invalid location. The act left the rights of parties in the position of these appellees, to be determined by the state of the law when the proclamation was issued. As heretofore pointed out, the long-continued practice, the acquiescence of Congress, as well as the decisions of the courts, all show that the President had the power to make the order. . . . The case is therefore remanded to the District Court with directions that the decree dismissing the bill be reversed.

[*Reversed.*]

MR. JUSTICE DAY, with whom concurred MR. JUSTICE McKENNA and MR. JUSTICE VAN DEVANTER, dissenting: . . .

The constitutional authority of the President of the United States (art. 2, § § 1, 3) includes the executive power of the nation and the duty to see that the laws are faithfully executed. "The President 'shall take care that the laws be faithfully executed.' Under this clause his duty is not limited to the enforcement of acts of Congress according to their express terms. It includes 'the rights and obligations growing out of the Constitution itself, our international relations, and all the protection implied by the nature of the government under the Constitution.'" Cooley, Const. Law, p. 121; Re Neagle, 135 U.S. 1. The Constitution does not confer upon him any power to enact laws or to suspend or repeal such as the Congress enacts. Kendall v. United States, 12 Pet. 524, 613. The President's powers are defined by the Constitution of the United States, and the government does not contend that he has any general authority in the disposition of the public land which the Constitution has committed to Congress, and freely concedes the general proposition as to the lack of authority in the President to deal with the laws otherwise than to see that they are faithfully executed. . . .

It is to be noted that the act of June 25, 1910, conferred specific authority for the future upon the President, but gave no approval to the withdrawal of September 27, 1909, containing instead an express provision that the act should not be construed as a recognition, abridgment, or enlargement of any asserted rights or claims initiated upon any oil or gas bearing lands after the withdrawal of such lands, made prior to the passage of the act. While the order of September 27, 1909, withdrew the lands from all form of settlement, location, sale, entry, or disposal under the mineral or nonmineral public land laws, the act of June 25, 1910, excepts from the power of withdrawal conferred upon the President lands embraced in any lawful homestead or desert-land entry theretofore made or upon which any valid settlement had been made and was being maintained and perfected pursuant to law. Furthermore, the act provides that the rights of a bona fide occupant or claimant of oil or gas bearing lands, complying with the provisions of the statute relating thereto, shall not be affected or impaired by a subsequent order of withdrawal. In this statute there certainly is no congressional assent to the Executive withdrawal of September 27, 1909. The validation or ratification asked in the President's message was withheld, and only restricted authority for the future was granted in the act of June 25, 1910; not only so, but the rights of the locators involved in this case were preserved to whatever extent they existed in the absence of a ratification of the withdrawal. When express ratification is thus asked and refused, in our view no power by implication can be fairly inferred. . . . The act of June 25, 1910, neither ratified the withdrawal of September 27, 1909, nor empowered the President so to do by his order of July 2, 1910.

The government of the United States is one of limited powers. The three co-ordinate branches of the government are vested with certain authority, definite and limited, in the Constitution. . . .

These principles ought not to be departed from in the judicial determinations of this court, and their enforcement is essential to the administration of the govern-ment, as created and defined by the Constitution. The grant of authority to the Executive, as to other departments of the government, ought not to be amplified by judicial decisions. The Constitution is the legitimate source of authority of all who exercise power under its sanction, and its provisions are equally binding upon every officer of the government, from the highest to the lowest. It is one of the great functions of this court to keep, so far as judicial decisions can subserve that purpose, each branch of the government within the sphere of its legitimate action, and to prevent encroachments of one branch upon the authority of another.

In our opinion, the action of the Executive Department in this case, originating in the expressed view of a subordinate official of the Interior Department as to the desirability of a different system of public land disposal than that contained in the lawful enactments of Congress, did not justify the President in withdrawing this large body of land from the operation of the law, and virtually suspending, as he necessarily did, the operation of that law, at least until a different view expressed by him could be considered by Congress. This conclusion is reinforced in this particular instance by the refusal of Congress to ratify the action of the President, and the enactment of a new statute authorizing the disposition of the public lands by a method essentially different from that proposed by the Executive.

Two generations and three wars separate Taft's Administration from that of President Truman, and Midwest Oil from the Steel Seizure case. Politically, socially, economically, and psychologically, the cases belong to different centuries, with the Midwest Oil case typifying the problems arising from the exploitation of the commonwealth and the closing of the western frontier, and Steel Seizure exemplifying the three-cornered struggles of a mature industrial society among giant capitalism, giant labor, and a government that was not big enough to solve the problem. The breakdown of government witnessed by this case can be attributed in part to the presidential policy of drift and muddle-along; to the congressional policy of do-nothing in an election year; and to the Supreme Court's reaction to one of the most vitriolic national press campaigns that the country has ever witnessed.

As we have noted, a major participant in the Steel Seizure case—as chief of counsel for the plaintiff steel companies—was none other than John W. Davis, who had argued the other side of the case for the government in Midwest Oil, over thirty-seven years earlier.

YOUNGSTOWN SHEET & TUBE CO. v. SAWYER
(The Steel Seizure Case)

343 U.S 579 (June 2, 1952).

Certiorari to the United States Court of Appeals for the District of Columbia.

Reversed (i.e., judgment of the District Court *affirmed*).

6-3

Black	('+')
Frankfurter	('+'
Douglas	('+'
Jackson	('+'
Burton	('+'
Clark	('+'
Vinson, C.J.	'—')
Reed	—)
Minton	—)

The labor-management dispute which resulted in presidential seizure of the steel mills was a domestic incident of the Korean War, which began on June 25, 1950. Later in the same summer, the Congress enacted the Defense Production Act of 1950; and on December 16, 1950, President Truman declared the existence of a national emergency. The impasse in the renegotiation of a nationwide collective-bargaining contract for the "Big Steel" industry came just a year later; and after more months of futile efforts on the part of the Administration to mediate the conflict, President Truman ordered his Secretary of Commerce to assume legal control over the major steel mills. Executive Order

No. 10340, dated April 9, 1952 and issued just a few hours before a strike deadline called by the union, explicitly referred to the President's prior declaration of a national emergency and to the military hostilities in which American armed forces were then engaged in Korea.[7]

But the Court's major premise (inarticulate) was the assumption that the United States was at peace during the Korean War; while the articulate minor premise was the principle of separation of powers. Although the six justices comprising the majority wrote individual opinions detailing their views, the Black opinion was the lowest common denominator, and was joined in by five justices, with Clark concurring in the judgment only.

It is of interest to note that, although a clear majority of the Court disapproved the invocation of implied presidential powers in the circumstances of this case, only two justices (Black and Douglas) rejected the principle of implied presidential powers. On the other hand, a clear majority of the Court—the three dissenters plus Clark and Jackson—gave their express and unambiguous approval to the exercise of implied presidential powers in the absence of a clear and con-

[7] For more extended discussions of the background of the controversy, see Grant McConnell, *The Steel Seizure of 1952* (New York: Inter-University Case Program, 1958); and Alan Westin, *The Anatomy of a Constitutional Law Case* (New York: Macmillan, 1958). Among the many articles which discuss the case, perhaps the best is Edward S. Corwin, "The Steel Seizure Case: A Judicial Brick without Straw," *Columbia Law Review*, Vol. 53, p. 1 (1953).

tradictory congressional policy and action; while the remaining two justices (Frankfurter and Burton) expressly reserved the general question of the nature and scope of implied presidential powers. Only time will tell, therefore, whether the case was important primarily as a political rebuff to an unpopular and lameduck President, or whether its significance will be as a precedent which an activist Court will follow to restrain the Presidency in future times of crisis and national emergency.

MR. JUSTICE BLACK delivered the opinion of the Court.

We are asked to decide whether the President was acting within his constitutional power when he issued an order directing the Secretary of Commerce to take possession of and operate most of the Nation's steel mills. The mill owners argue that the President's order amounts to lawmaking, a legislative function which the Constitution has expressly confided to the Congress and not to the President. The Government's position is that the order was made on findings of the President that his action was necessary to avert a national catastrophe which would inevitably result from a stoppage of steel production, and that in meeting this grave emergency the President was acting within the aggregate of his constitutional powers as the Nation's Chief Executive and the Commander in Chief of the Armed Forces of the United States. The issue emerges here from the following series of events:

In the latter part of 1951, a dispute arose between the steel companies and their employees over terms and conditions that should be included in new collective bargaining agreements. Long-continued conferences failed to resolve the dispute. On December 18, 1951, the employees' representative, United Steelworkers of America, C.I.O., gave notice of an intention to strike when the existing bargaining agreements expired on December 31. The Federal Mediation and Conciliation Service then intervened in an effort to get labor and management to agree. This failing, the President on December 22, 1951, referred the dispute to the Federal Wage Stabilization Board to investigate and make recommendations for fair and equitable terms of settlement. This Board's report resulted in no settlement. On April 4, 1952, the Union gave notice of a nationwide strike called to begin at 12:01 A.M. April 9. The indispensability of steel as a component of substantially all weapons and other war materials led the President to believe that the proposed work stoppage would immediately jeopardize our national defense and that governmental seizure of the steel mills was necessary in order to assure the continued availability of steel. Reciting these considerations for his action, the President, a few hours before the strike was to begin, issued Executive Order 10340. . . . The order directed the Secretary of Commerce to take possession of most of the steel mills and keep them running. The Secretary immediately issued his own possessory orders, calling upon the presidents of the various seized companies to serve as operating managers for the United States. They were directed to carry on their activities in accordance with regulations and directions of the Secretary. The next morning the President sent a message to Congress reporting his action. Cong. Rec., April 9, 1952, p. 3962. Twelve days later he sent a second message. Cong. Rec., April 21, 1952, p. 4192. Congress has taken no action.

Obeying the Secretary's orders under protest, the companies brought proceedings against him in the District Court. Their complaints charged that the seizure was not authorized by an act of Congress or by any constitutional provisions. The District Court was asked to declare the orders of the President and the Secretary invalid and to issue preliminary and permanent injunctions restraining their enforcement. Opposing the motion for preliminary injunction, the United States asserted that a strike disrupting steel production for even a brief period would so endanger the well-being and safety of the Nation that the President had "inherent power" to do what he had done—power "supported by the Constitution, by historical precedent, and by court decisions." The Government also contended that in any event no preliminary injunction should be issued because the companies had made no showing that their available legal remedies were inadequate or that their injuries from seizure would be irreparable. Holding against the Government on all points, the District Court on April 30 issued a preliminary injunction restraining the Secretary from "continuing the seizure and possession of the plant . . . and from acting under the purported authority of Executive Order No. 10340." 103 F. Supp. 569. On the same day the Court of Appeals stayed the District Court's injunction. 197 F. 2d 582. Deeming it best that the issues raised be promptly decided by this Court, we granted certiorari on May 3 and set the cause for argument on May 12. . . .

The President's power, if any, to issue the order must stem either from an act of Congress or from the Constitution itself. There is no statute that expressly authorizes the President to take possession of property as he did here. Nor is there any act of Congress to which our attention has been directed from which such a power can fairly be implied. Indeed, we do not understand the Government to rely on statutory authorization for this seizure. There are two statutes which do authorize the President to take both personal and real property under certain conditions. However, the Government admits that these conditions were not met and that the President's order was not rooted in either of the statutes. The Government refers to the seizure provisions of one of these statutes (sec. 201 (b) of the Defense Production Act) as "much too cumbersome, involved, and time-consuming for the crisis which was at hand."

Moreover, the use of the seizure technique to solve labor disputes in order to prevent work stoppages was not only unauthorized by any congressional enactment; prior to this controversy, Congress had refused to adopt that method of settling labor disputes. When the Taft-Hartley Act was under consideration in 1947, Congress rejected an amendment which would have authorized such governmental seizures in cases of emergency. Apparently it was thought that the technique of seizure, like that of compulsory arbitration, would interfere with the process of collective bargaining. Consequently, the plan Congress adopted in that Act did not provide for seizure under any circumstances. Instead, the plan sought to bring about settlements by use of the customary devices of mediation, conciliation, investigation by boards of inquiry, and public reports. In some instances temporary injunctions were authorized to provide cooling-off periods. All this failing, the unions were left free to strike if the majority of the employees, by secret ballot, expressed a desire to do so.

It is clear that if the President had authority to issue the order he did, it must be found in some provisions of the Constitution. And it is not claimed that express constitutional language grants this power to the President. The contention is that presidential power should be implied from the aggregate of his powers under the Constitution. Particular reliance is placed on provisions in Article II which say that "the executive Power shall be vested in a President . . ."; that "he shall take Care that the Laws be faithfully executed"; and that he "shall be Commander in Chief of the Army and Navy of the United States."

The order cannot properly be sustained as an exercise of the President's military power as Commander in Chief of the Armed Forces. The Government attempts to do so by citing a number of cases upholding broad powers in military commanders engaged in day-to-day fighting in a theater of war. Such cases need not concern us here. Even though "theater of war" be an expanding concept, we cannot with faithfulness to our constitutional system hold that the Commander in Chief of the Armed Forces has the ultimate power as such to take possession of private property in order to keep labor disputes from stopping production. This is a job for the Nation's lawmakers, not for its military authorities.

Nor can the seizure order be sustained because of the several constitutional provisions that grant executive power to the President. In the framework of our Constitution, the President's power to see that the laws are faithfully executed refutes the idea that he is to be a lawmaker. The Constitution limits his functions in the law-making process to the recommending of laws he thinks wise and the vetoing of laws he thinks bad. And the Constitution is neither silent nor equivocal about who shall make laws which the President is to execute. The first section of the first article says that "All legislative Powers herein granted shall be vested in a Congress of the United States. . . ." After granting many powers to the Congress, Article I goes on to provide that Congress may "make all Laws which shall be necessary and proper for carrying into Execution the foregoing Powers and all other Powers vested by this Constitution in the Government of the United States, or in any Department or Officer thereof."

The President's order does not direct that a congressional policy be executed in a manner prescribed by the President. The preamble of the order itself, like that of many statutes, sets out reasons why the President believes certain policies should be adopted, proclaims these policies as rules of conduct to be followed, and again, like a statute, authorizes a government official to promulgate additional rules and regulations consistent with the policy proclaimed and needed to carry that policy into execution. The power of Congress to adopt such public policies as those proclaimed by the order is beyond question. It can authorize the taking of private property for public use. It can make laws regulating the relationships between employers and employees, prescribing rules designed to settle labor disputes, and fixing wages and working conditions in certain fields of our economy. The Constitution does not subject this lawmaking power of Congress to presidential or military supervision or control.

It is said that other Presidents without congressional authority have taken possession of private business enterprises in order to settle labor disputes. But even if this be true, Congress has not thereby lost its exclusive constitutional authority to make laws necessary and proper to carry out the powers vested by the Constitution "in the Government of the United States, or any Department or Officer thereof."

The Founders of this Nation entrusted the lawmaking power to the Congress alone in both good and bad times. It would do no good to recall the historical events, the fears of power and the hopes for freedom that lay behind their choice. Such a review would but confirm our holding that this seizure order cannot stand.

The judgment of the District Court is
Affirmed.

Mr. Justice Frankfurter, concurring. . . .

The Framers . . . did not make the judiciary the overseer of our government. They were familiar with the revisory functions entrusted to judges in a few of the States and refused to lodge such powers in this Court. Judicial power can be exercised only as to matters that were the traditional concern of the courts at Westminster, and only if they arise in ways that to the expert feel of lawyers constitute "Cases" or "Controversies." Even as to questions that were the staple of judicial business, it is not for the courts to pass upon them unless they are indispensably involved in a conventional litigation—and then, only to the extent that they are so involved. Rigorous adherence to the narrow scope of the judicial function is especially demanded in controversies that arouse appeals to the Constitution. The attitude with which this Court must approach its duty when confronted with such issues is precisely the opposite of that normally manifested by the general public. So-called constitutional questions seem to exercise a mesmeric influence over the popular mind. This eagerness to settle—preferably forever—a specific problem on the basis of the broadest possible constitutional pronouncements may not unfairly be called one of our minor national traits. An English observer of our scene has acutely described it: "At the first sound of a new argument over the United States Constitution and its interpretation the hearts of Americans leap with a fearful joy. The blood stirs powerfully in their veins and a new lustre brightens their eyes. Like King Harry's men before Harfleur, they stand like greyhounds in the slips, straining upon the start." The Economist, May 10, 1952, p. 370.

The path of duty for this Court, it bears repetition, lies in the opposite direction. Due regard for the implications of the distribution of powers in our Constitution and for the nature of the judicial process as the ultimate authority in interpreting the Constitution, has not only confined the Court within the narrow domain of appropriate adjudication. It has also led to "a series or rules under which it has avoided passing upon a large part of all the constitutional questions pressed upon it for decision." Brandeis, J., in *Ashwander* v. *Tennessee Valley Authority*, 297 U.S. 288, 341, 346. A basic rule is the duty of the Court not to pass on a constitutional issue at all, however narrowly it may be confined, if the case may, as a matter of intellectual honesty, be decided without even considering delicate problems of power under the Constitution. It ought to be, but apparently is not, a matter of common understanding that clashes between different branches of the government should be avoided if a legal ground

of less explosive potentialities is properly available. Constitutional adjudications are apt by exposing differences to exacerbate them. . . .

To be sure, the content of the three authorities of government is not to be derived from an abstract analysis. The areas are partly interacting, not wholly disjointed. The Constitution is a framework for government. Therefore the way the framework has consistently operated fairly establishes that it has operated according to its true nature. Deeply embedded traditional ways of conducting government cannot supplant the Constitution or legislation, but they give meaning to the words of a text or supply them. It is an inadmissibly narrow conception of American constitutional law to confine it to the words of the Constitution and to disregard the gloss which life has written upon them. In short, a systematic, unbroken, executive practice, long pursued to the knowledge of the Congress and never before questioned, engaged in by Presidents who have also sworn to uphold the Constitution, making as it were such exercise of power part of the structure of our government, may be treated as a gloss on "executive Power" vested in the President by § 1 of Art. II.

Such was the case of *United States* v. *Midwest Oil Co.*, 236 U.S. 459. The contrast between the circumstances of that case and this one helps to draw a clear line between authority not explicitly conferred yet authorized to be exercised by the President and the denial of such authority. In both instances it was the concern of Congress under express constitutional grant to make rules and regulations for the problems with which the President dealt. In the one case he was dealing with the protection of property belonging to the United States in the other with the enforcement of the Commerce Clause and with raising and supporting armies and maintaining the Navy. In the *Midwest Oil* case lands which Congress had opened for entry were, over a period of 80 years and in 252 instances and by Presidents learned and unlearned in the law, temporarily withdrawn from entry so as to enable Congress to deal with such withdrawals. No remotely comparable practice can be vouched for executive seizure of property at a time when this country was not at war, in the only constitutional way in which it can be at war. It would pursue the irrelevant to reopen the controversy over the constitutionality of some acts of Lincoln during the Civil War. See J. G. Randall, Constitutional Problems under Lincoln (Revised ed. 1951). Suffice it to say that he seized railroads in territory where armed hostilities had already interrupted the movement of troops to the beleaguered Capitol, and his order was ratified by the Congress.

The only other instances of seizures are those during the periods of the first and second World Wars. In his eleven seizures of industrial facilities, President Wilson acted, or at least purported to act, under authority granted by Congress. Thus his seizures cannot be adduced as interpretations by a President of his own powers in the absence of statute.

Down to the World War II period, then, the record is barren of instances comparable to the one before us. Of twelve seizures by President Roosevelt prior to the enactment of the War Labor Disputes Act in June, 1943, three were sanctioned by existing law, and six others were effected after Congress, on December 8, 1941, had declared the existence of a state of war. In this case, reliance on the powers that flow from declared war has been commendably disclaimed by the Solicitor General. Thus the list of executive assertions of the power of seizure in circumstances comparable to the present reduces to three in the six-month period from June to December of 1941. We need not split hairs in comparing those actions to the one before us, though much might be said by way of differentiation. Without passing on their validity, as we are not called upon to do so, it suffices to say that

these three isolated instances do not add up, either in number, scope, duration or contemporaneous legal justification, to the kind of executive construction of the Constitution revealed in the *Midwest Oil* case. Nor do they come to us sanctioned by long-continued acquiescence of Congress giving decisive weight to a construction by the Executive of its powers.

MR. JUSTICE JACKSON, concurring in the judgment and opinion of the Court.

That comprehensive and undefined presidential powers hold both practical advantages and grave dangers for the country will impress anyone who has served as legal adviser to a President in time of transition and public anxiety. While an interval of detached reflection may temper teachings of that experience, they probably are a more realistic influence on my views than the conventional materials of judicial decision which seem unduly to accentuate doctrine and legal fiction. But as we approach the question of presidential power, we half overcome mental hazards by recognizing them. The opinions of judges, no less than executives and publicists, often suffer the infirmity of confusing the issue of a power's validity with the cause it is invoked to promote, of confounding the permanent executive office with its temporary occupant. The tendency is strong to emphasize transient results upon policies—such as wages or stabilization—and lose sight of enduring consequences upon the balanced power structure of our Republic.

A judge, like an executive advisor, may be surprised at the poverty of really useful and unambiguous authority applicable to concrete problems of executive power as they actually present themselves. Just what our forefathers did envision, or would have envisioned had they foreseen modern conditions, must be divined from materials almost as engimatic as the dreams Joseph was called upon to interpret for Pharaoh. A century and a half of partisan debate and scholarly speculation yields no net result but only supplies more or less apt quotations from respected sources on each side of any question. They largely cancel each other.[8] And court decisions are indecisive because of the judicial practice of dealing with the largest questions in the most narrow way.

The actual art of governing under our Constitution does not and cannot conform to judicial definitions of the power of any of its branches based on isolated clauses or even single Articles torn from context. While the Constitution diffuses power the better to secure liberty, it also contemplates that practice will integrate the dispersed powers into a workable government. It enjoins upon its branches separateness but interdependence, autonomy but reciprocity. Presidential powers are not fixed but fluctuate, depending upon their disjunction or conjunction with those of Congress. We may well begin by a somewhat oversimplified grouping of practical situations in which a President may doubt, or others may challenge, his powers, and by distinguishing roughly the legal consequences of this factor of relativity.

1. When the President acts pursuant to an express or implied authorization of Congress, his authority is at its maximum, for it includes all that he possesses in his own right plus all that Congress can delegate. In these circumstances, and in these only, may he be said (for what it may be worth), to personify the federal sovereignty. If his act is held unconstitutional

under these circumstances, it usually means that the Federal Government as an undivided whole lacks power. A seizure executed by the President pursuant to an Act of Congress would be supported by the strongest of presumptions and the widest latitude of judicial interpretation, and the burden of persuasion would rest heavily upon any who might attack it.

2. When the President acts in absence of either a congressional grant or denial of authority, he can only rely upon his own independent powers, but there is a zone of twilight in which he and Congress may have concurrent authority, or in which its distribution is uncertain. Therefore, congressional inertia, indifference or quiescence may sometimes, at least as a practical matter, enable, if not invite, measures on independent presidential responsibility. In this area, any actual test of power is likely to depend on the imperatives of events and contemporary imponderables rather than on abstract theories of law.

3. When the President takes measures incompatible with the expressed or implied will of Congress, his power is at its lowest ebb, for then he can rely only upon his own constitutional powers minus any constitutional powers of Congress over the matter. Courts can sustain exclusive Presidential control in such a case only by disabling the Congress from acting upon the subject. Presidental claim to a power at once so conclusive and preclusive must be scrutinized with caution, for what is at stake is the equilibrium established by our constitutional system.

Into which of these classifications does this executive seizure of the steel industry fit? It is eliminated from the first by admission, for it is conceded that no congressional authorization exists for this seizure. That takes away also the support of the many precedents and declarations which were made in relation, and must be confined, to this category.

Can it then be defended under flexible tests available to the second category? It

[8] A Hamilton may be matched against a Madison. 7 The Works of Alexander Hamilton, 76-117; 1 Madison, Letters and Other Writings, 611-654. Professor Taft is counterbalanced by Theodore Roosevelt. Taft, Our Chief Magistrate and His Powers, 139-140; Theodore Roosevelt, Autobiography, 388-389. It even seems that President Taft cancels out Professor Taft. Compare his "Temporary Petroleum Withdrawal No. 5" of September 27, 1909, United States v. Midwest Oil Co., 236 U.S. 459, 467, 468, with his appraisal of executive power in "Our Chief Magistrate and His Powers" 139-140. [Footnote by Justice Jackson.]

seems clearly eliminated from that class because Congress has not left seizure of private property an open field but has covered it by three statutory policies inconsistent with this seizure. In cases where the purpose is to supply needs of the Government itself, two courses are provided: one, seizure of a plant which fails to comply with obligatory orders placed by the Government, another, condemnation of facilities, including temporary use under the power of eminent domain. The third is applicable where it is the general economy of the country that is to be protected rather than exclusive governmental interests. None of these were invoked. In choosing a different and inconsistent way of his own, the President cannot claim that it is necessitated or invited by failure of Congress to legislate upon the occasions, grounds and methods for seizure of industrial properties.

This leaves the current seizure to be justified only by the severe tests under the third grouping, where it can be supported only by any remainder of executive power after subtraction of such powers as Congress may have over the subject. In short, we can sustain the President only by holding that seizure of such strike-bound industries is within his domain and beyond control by Congress. Thus, this Court's first review of such seizures occurs under circumstances which leave Presidential power most vulnerable to attack and in the least favorable of possible constitutional postures.

. . . I cannot be brought to believe that this country will suffer if the Court refuses further to aggrandize the presidential office, already so potent and so relatively immune from judicial review, at the expense of Congress.

But I have no illusion that any decision by this Court can keep power in the hands of Congress if it is not wise and timely in meeting its problems. A crisis that challenges the President equally, or perhaps primarily, challenges Congress. If not good law, there was worldly wisdom in the maxim attributed to Napoleon that "The tools belong to the man who can use them." We may say that power to legislate for emergencies belongs in the hands of Congress, but only Congress itself can prevent power from slipping through its fingers.

The essence of our free Government is "leave to live by no man's leave, underneath the law"—to be governed by those impersonal forces which we call law. Our Government is fashioned to fulfill this concept so far as humanly possible. The Executive, except for recommendation and veto, has no legislative power. The executive action we have here originates in the individual will of the President and represents an exercise of authority without law. No one, perhaps not even the President, knows the limits of the power he may seek to exert in this instance and the parties affected cannot learn the limit of their rights. We do not know today what powers over labor or property would be claimed to flow from Government possession if we should legalize it, what rights to compensation would be claimed or recognized, or on what contingency it would end. With all its defects, delays and inconveniences, men have discovered no technique for long preserving free government except that the Executive be under the law, and that the law be made by parliamentary deliberations.

Such institutions may be destined to pass away. But it is the duty of the Court to be last, not first, to give them up.

MR. CHIEF JUSTICE VINSON, with whom MR. JUSTICE REED and MR. JUSTICE MINTON join, dissenting.

. . . It is those who assert the invalidity of the Executive Order who seek to amend the Constitution in this case.

A review of executive action demonstrates that our Presidents have on many occasions exhibited the leadership contemplated by the Framers when they made the President Commander in Chief, and imposed upon him the trust to "take

Care that the Laws be faithfully executed." With or without explicit statutory authorization, Presidents have at such times dealt with national emergencies by acting promptly and resolutely to enforce legislative programs, at least to save those programs until Congress could act. Congress and the courts have responded to such executive initiative with consistent approval.

. . . In his autobiography, President [Theodore] Roosevelt expounded the "Stewardship Theory" of Presidential power, stating that "the executive is subject only to the people, and, under the Constitution, bound to serve the people affirmatively in cases where the Constitution does not explicitly forbid him to render the service." . . . In [Our Chief Magistrate and His Powers (1916), 139-147], President Taft agreed that such powers of the President as the duty "to take care that the laws be faithfully executed" could not be confined to "express Congressional statutes." *In re Neagle* . . . and *In re Debs* . . . were cited as conforming with Taft's concept of the office, *id.*, at pp. 88-94, as they were later to be cited with approval in his opinion as Chief Justice in *Myers* v. *United States,* 272 U.S. 52, 133 (1926).

In 1909, President Taft was informed that government owned oil lands were being patented by private parties at such a rate that public oil lands would be depleted in a matter of months. Although Congress had explicitly provided that these lands were open to purchase by United States citizens, 29 Stat. 526 (1897), the President nevertheless ordered the lands withdrawn from sale "[in] aid of proposed legislation." In *United States* v. *Midwest Oil Co.,* 236 U.S. 459 (1915), the President's action was sustained as consistent with executive practice throughout our history. . . .

The President reported to Congress the morning after the seizure that he acted because a work stoppage in steel production would immediately imperil the safety of the Nation by preventing execution of the legislative programs for procurement of military equipment. And, while a shutdown could be averted by granting the price concessions requested by plaintiffs, granting such concessions would disrupt the price stabilization program also enacted by Congress. Rather than fail to execute either legislative program, the President acted to execute both.

Much of the argument in this case has been directed at straw men. We do not now have before us the case of a President acting solely on the basis of his own notions of the public welfare. Nor is there any question of unlimited executive power in this case. The President himself closed the door to any such claim when he sent his Message to Congress stating his purpose to abide by any action of Congress, whether approving or disapproving his seizure action. Here, the President immediately made sure that Congress was fully informed of the temporary action he had taken only to preserve the legislative programs from destruction until Congress could act.

The absence of a specific statute authorizing seizure of the steel mills as a mode of executing the laws—both the military procurement program and the anti-inflation program—has not until today been thought to prevent the President from executing the laws. Unlike an administrative commission confined to the enforcement of the statute under which it was created, or the head of a department when administering a particular statute, the President is a constitutional officer charged with taking care that a "mass of legislation" be executed. Flexibility as to mode of execution to meet critical situations is a matter of practical necessity. This practical construction of the "Take Care" clause, advocated by John Marshall, was adopted by this Court in *In re Neagle, In re Debs* and other cases cited *supra*. See also *Ex Parte Quirin,* 317 U.S. 1, 26 (1942). Although more restrictive views of executive power, advocated in dissenting opinions of Justices Holmes, McReynolds, and Brandeis, were emphatically rejected by this Court in *Myers* v. *United States, supra,* members of today's majority treat these dissenting views as authoritative.

There is no statute prohibiting seizure as a method of enforcing legislative programs. Congress has in no wise indicated that its legislation is not to be executed by the taking of private property (subject of course to the payment of just compensation) if its legislation cannot otherwise be executed. . . .

Whatever the extent of Presidential power on more tranquil occasions, and whatever the right of the President to execute legislative programs as he sees fit without reporting the mode of execution to Congress, the single Presidential purpose disclosed on this record is to faithfully execute the laws by acting in an emergency to maintain the status quo, thereby preventing collapse of the legislative programs until Congress could act. The President's action served the same purposes as a judicial stay entered to maintain the status quo in order to preserve the jurisdiction of a court. In his Message to Congress immediately following the seizure, the President explained the necessity of his action in executing the military procurement and anti-inflation legislative programs and expressed his desire to cooperate with any legislative proposals approving, regulating or rejecting the seizure of the steel mills. Consequently, there is no evidence whatever of any Presidential purpose to defy Congress or act in any way inconsistent with the legislative will.

In *United States* v. *Midwest Oil Co., supra,* this Court approved executive action where, as here, the President acted to preserve an important matter until Congress could act—even though his action in that case was contrary to an express statute. In this case, there is no statute prohibiting the action taken by the President in a matter not merely important

but threatening the very safety of the Nation. Executive inaction in such a situation, courting national disaster, is foreign to the concept of energy and initiative in the Executive as created by the Founding Fathers. The Constitution was itself "adopted in a period of grave emergency. . . . While emergency does not create power, emergency may furnish the occasion for the exercise of power." The Framers know, as we should know in these times of peril, that there is real danger in Executive weakness. There is no cause to fear Executive tyranny so long as the laws of Congress are being faithfully executed. Certainly there is no basis for fear of dictatorship when the Executive acts, as he did in this case, only to save the situation until Congress could act. . . .

When the President acted on April 8, he had exhausted the procedures for settlement available to him. Taft-Hartley was a route parallel to, not connected with, the WSB procedure. The strike had been delayed 99 days as contrasted with the maximum delay of 80 days under Taft-Hartley. There had been a hearing on the issues in dispute and bargaining which promised settlement up to the very hour before seizure had broken down. Faced with immediate national peril through stoppage in steel production on the one hand and faced with destruction of the wage and price legislative programs on the other, the President took temporary possession of the steel mills as the only course open to him consistent with his duty to take care that the laws be faithfully executed. . . .

The diversity of views expressed in the six opinions of the majority, the lack of reference to authoritative precedent, the repeated reliance upon prior dissenting opinions, the complete disregard of the uncontroverted facts showing the gravity of the emergency and the temporary nature of the taking all serve to demonstrate how far afield one must go to affirm the order of the District Court.

The broad executive power granted by Article II to an officer on duty 365 days a year cannot, it is said, be invoked to avert disaster. Instead, the President must confine himself to sending a message to Congress recommending action. Under this messenger-boy concept of the Office, the President cannot even act to preserve legislative programs from destruction so that Congress will have something left to act upon. There is no judicial finding that the executive action was unwarranted because there was in fact no basis for the President's finding of the existence of an emergency for, under this view, the gravity of the emergency and the immediacy of the threatened disaster are considered irrelevant as a matter of law. . . . No basis for claims of arbitrary action, unlimited powers or dictatorial usurpation of congressional power appears from the facts of this case. On the contrary, judicial, legislative and executive precedents throughout our history demonstrate that in this case the President acted in full conformity with his duties under the Constitution. Accordingly, we would reverse the order of the District Court.

The Executive Removal Power

The question of the President's power of appointment was one of the first great issues of constitutional policy to reach the Supreme Court, in *Marbury* v. *Madison;* but the Court avoided any full-dress consideration of the presidential removal power until after World War I. When the question did reach the Court, it was in the form of the same issue that led to the impeachment of Johnson: could Congress limit the President's discretion by statute, by providing that the Chief Executive could remove certain officers only with the consent of the Senate? At stake in the controversy, as the events surrounding the Johnson impeachment clearly showed, was the control of the Executive Department of the government.

The Philadelphia Convention had compromised the issue by saying nothing, explicitly, in the text of the Constitution, thus leaving the question to be resolved by the practice of future generations. It came up before the House of Representatives in the first session of the first Congress; and as James Hart has described in detail,[9] a majority led by Madison upheld the direct constitutional authority of the President to remove at his discretion members of his cabinet. Chief Justice Marshall upheld the same position, in a dictum in *Marbury* v. *Madison*. This became the settled practice of the government, until the controversy between Johnson and the Radical Republicans over Reconstruction policy led to the enactment of the first of a series of tenure-of-office acts. But Johnson's acquittal had the effect of reaffirming the traditional view, at least with regard to the removal of members of the President's cabinet.

Shortly after Reconstruction ended, however, the Congress enacted the Pendleton Act establishing a classified executive civil service; and the effect of this and subsequent statutes, together with implementing executive orders, was to make the vast majority of federal officials and employees subject to administra-

[9] *The American Presidency in Action: 1789* (New York: Macmillan, 1948), pp. 155-214.

tive removal rather than to direct removal by the President. Subject to presidential appointment, and therefore—in some manner—subject to presidential removal, were occupants of patronage positions, primarily in the federal field service, and the heads of major administrative agencies, including (in addition to the handful of department heads who sat in the Cabinet) bureau chiefs, other senior officials at the "departmental level," and heads of a host of nondepartmentalized (or "independent") agencies. Moreover, it was less than a decade after the passing of the Pendleton Act that the Congress established the Interstate Commerce Commission, the first of a series of agencies with important economic regulatory functions that Congress intended to have establish policies independently of the political direction of the incumbent Administration. And finally, there were, of course, presidential appointees to judicial positions, who were presumed to be removable only by the Congress through the impeachment process.

It is more than likely that the first major decision of the Court on this subject was a major decision because the incumbent Chief Justice wanted to have the Court settle this issue—his way, of course—for once and for all. Taft, the only Chief Justice who had been President, had pronounced views on the question of the scope of the presidential power of removal. It is true that in his Blumenthal Lectures, delivered at Columbia University a decade before the decision in the Myers case, Taft had criticized Theodore Roosevelt's Stewardship Theory, as a general proposition; but this did not mean that he favored weakening the President's administrative control over his subordinates, and especially in deference to the Senate. Elsewhere in the same lectures, Taft remarked: [10]

> It was settled, as long ago as the first Congress . . . that even where the advice and consent of the Senate was necessary to the appointment of an officer, the President had the absolute power to remove him without consulting the Senate. This was on the principle that the power of removal was incident to the Executive power and must be untrammeled. . . . [The tenure of office act] never came before the courts directly in such a way as to invite a decision on its validity, but there are intimations in the opinions of the Supreme Court that in the tenure of office act Congress exceeded its legislative discretion.

The intimations became more pronounced in a case that was first argued only two years after President Taft entered upon his duties as Chief Justice.

[10] *Our Chief Magistrate and His Powers,* pp. 56-57.

MYERS v. UNITED STATES

272 U.S. 52 (Argued December 5, 1923; reargued April 13, 14, 1925; decided October 25, 1926).

Appeal from the Court of Claims.

Affirmed.

6-3

Taft, C.J.	('+')
VanDevanter	(+)
Sutherland	(+)
Butler	(+)
Sanford	(+)
Stone	(+)
Holmes	'—')
McReynolds	'—')
Brandeis	'—')

President Wilson appointed F. S. Myers as postmaster of Portland, Oregon, in 1917; and Wilson removed Myers in 1920, before the expiration of the statutory term of the office. Myers died while asserting a claim for back salary, and his wife and administratrix appealed an adverse decision of the Court of Claims. After a year had passed since the initial argument, the Court ordered reargument of the case and invited Senator George Wharton Pepper to argue in defense of the Senate's interests (i.e., in behalf of the constitutionality of the statute defining Myers' rights of tenure, and against the President's claim of power to remove him).

It should be noted that the Supreme Court could have avoided the constitutional issues by simply affirming the decision of the lower court, which was based upon nonconstitutional, procedural grounds. Instead, Taft chose to plunge into the whole issue, not only as it related to the facts of the case, but in its broadest and most sweeping terms. Both the liberal Brandeis and the conservative McReynolds dissented (as did Holmes) against the extremity of Taft's opinion, even though it upheld an exercise of authority by the President who had appointed them

to the Court. The opinions that follow— an abridgement of the 243 pages that the case occupies in the United States Reports—*open with an extract from the brief submitted by Solicitor General Beck, in defense of the implied powers of the President:*

There may be a middle ground between absolute power in the President to remove and absolute power in Congress to control removal. The power of removal may be subject to such general laws as do not destroy the exercise by the President of his power of removal, but allow its exercise subject to standards of public service. If this "middle ground" does not commend itself to the Court, then the broader question becomes whether the power of removal is a constitutional prerogative of the President and, as such, can not be regulated by Congress.

On this theory, Congress may undoubtedly control the power to regulate the removal, when exercised *by any other official,* to whom the power of appointment has been delegated (for they owe their power of appointment solely to Congress,) and unquestionably the Congress can grant to other officials—such as the heads of departments—the power of appointment upon any conditions as to the power of removal by them that it thinks proper. The power of the President, however, is not *statutory,* but *constitutional.* As it is indisputable that the removal of a civil servant is essentially an executive power, it must follow that, as executive power is vested in a President, the power of removal inheres in him as a part of his prerogative, except where such power is expressly limited by the Constitution. It cannot now be seriously contended that the removal by the President of civil officers, who are his subordinates, must await the slow process of impeachment.

From the beginning of the Government removal has been recognized as essentially an executive function. In no sense is it either judicial or legislative. . . .

MR. CHIEF JUSTICE TAFT delivered the opinion of the Court.

This case presents the question whether under the Constitution the President has the exclusive power of removing executive officers of the United States whom he has appointed by and with the advice and consent of the Senate.

Myers, appellant's intestate, was on July 21, 1917, appointed by the President, by and with the advice and consent of the Senate, to be a postmaster of the first class at Portland, Oregon, for a term of four years. On January 20, 1920, Myers' resignation was demanded. He refused the demand. On February 2, 1920, he was removed from office by order of the Postmaster General, acting by direction of the President. February 10th, Myers sent a petition to the President and another to the Senate Committee on Post Offices, asking to be heard, if any charges were filed. He protested to the Department against his removal, and continued to do so until the end of his term. He pursued no other occupation and drew compensation for no other service during the interval. On April 21, 1921, he brought this suit in the Court of Claims for his salary from the date of his removal, which, as claimed by supplemental petition filed after July 21, 1921, the end of his term, amounted to $8,838.71. In August, 1920, the President made a recess appointment of one Jones, who took office September 19, 1920. . . .

By the 6th section of the Act of Congress of July 12, 1876, 19 Stat. 80, 81, c. 179, under which Myers was appointed with the advice and consent of the Senate as a first-class postmaster, it is provided that

> Postmasters of the first, second and third classes shall be appointed and may be removed by the President by and with the advice and consent of the Senate and shall hold their offices for four years unless sooner removed or suspended according to law.

The Senate did not consent to the President's removal of Myers during his term. If this statute, in its requirement that his term should be four years unless sooner removed by the President by and with the consent of the Senate, is valid, the appellant, Myers' administratrix, is entitled to recover his unpaid salary for his full term, and the judgment of the Court of Claims must be reversed. The Government maintains that the requirement is invalid, for the reason that under Article II of the Constitution the President's power of removal of executive officers appointed by him with the advice and consent of the Senate is full and complete without consent of the Senate. If this view is sound, the removal of Myers by the President without the Senate's consent was legal and the judgment of the Court of Claims against the appellant was correct and must be affirmed. . . .

The vesting of the executive power in the President was essentially a grant of the power to execute the laws. But the President alone and unaided could not execute the laws. He must execute them by the assistance of subordinates. This view has since been repeatedly affirmed by this Court. . . . *Cunningham* v. *Neagle,* 135 U.S. 1, 63. . . . As he is charged specifically to take care that they be faithfully executed, the reasonable implication, even in the absence of express words, was that as part of his executive power he should select those who were to act for him under his direction in the execution of the laws. The further implication must be, in the absence of any express limitation respecting removals, that as his selection of administrative officers is essential to the execution of the laws by him, so must be his power of removing those for whom he can not continue to be responsible.

It was pointed out in [the] great debate [of 1789, in the House of Representatives] that the power of removal, though equally essential to the executive power, is different in its nature from that of appointment. . . . A veto by the Senate—a part of the legislative branch of the Government—upon removals is a much greater limitation upon the executive branch and a much more serious blending of the legislative with the executive than a rejection of a proposed appointment. It is not to be implied. The rejection of a nominee of the President for a particular office does not greatly embarrass him in the conscientious discharge of his high duties in the selection of those who are to aid him, because the President usually has an ample field from which to select for office, according to his preference, competent and capable men. The Senate has full power to reject newly proposed appointees whenever the President shall remove the incumbents. Such a check enables the Senate to prevent the filling of offices with bad or incompetent men or with those against whom there is tenable objection.

The power to prevent the removal of an officer who has served under the President is different from the authority to consent to or reject his appointment. When a nomination is made, it may be presumed that the Senate is, or may become, as well advised as to the fitness of the nominee as the President, but in the nature of things the defects in ability or intelligence or loyalty in the administration of the laws of one who has served as an officer under the President, are facts as to which the President, or his trusted subordinates, must be better informed than the Senate, and the power to remove him may, therefore, be regarded as confined, for very sound and practical reasons, to the governmental authority which has administrative control. The power of removal is incident to the power of appointment, not to the power of advising and consenting to appointment, and when the grant of the executive power is enforced by the express mandate to take care that the laws be faithfully executed, it emphasizes the necessity for including

within the executive power as conferred the exclusive power of removal. . . .

In the discussion in the First Congress fear was expressed that such a constitutional rule of construction as was involved in the passage of the bill would expose the country to tyranny through the abuse of the exercise of the power of removal by the President. Underlying such fears was the fundamental misconception that the President's attitude in his exercise of power is one of opposition to the people, while the Congress is their only defender in the Government, and such a misconception may be noted in the discussions had before this Court. . . . The President is a representative of the people just as the members of the Senate and of the House are, and it may be, at some times, on some subjects, that the President elected by all the people is rather more representative of them all than are the members of either body of the Legislature whose constituencies are local and not countrywide; and, as the President is elected for four years, with the mandate of the people to exercise his executive power under the Constitution, there would seem to be no reason for construing that instrument in such a way as to limit and hamper that power beyond the limitations of it, expressed or fairly implied. . . .

The possible extent of the field of the President's political executive power may be judged by the fact that the quasi-civil governments of Cuba, Porto Rico and the Philippines, in the silence of Congress, had to be carried on for several years solely under his direction as commander in chief.

In all such cases, the discretion to be exercised is that of the President in determining the national public interest and in directing the action to be taken by his executive subordinates to protect it. In this field his cabinet officers must do his will. He must place in each member of his official family, and his chief executive subordinates, implicit faith The moment that he loses confidence in the intelligence, ability, judgment or loyalty of any one of them, he must have the power to remove him without delay. To require him to file charges and submit them to the consideration of the Senate might make impossible that unity and co-ordination in executive administration essential to effective action.

The duties of the heads of departments and bureaus in which the discretion of the President is exercised and which we have described, are the most important in the whole field of executive action of the Government. There is nothing in the Constitution which permits a distinction between the removal of the head of a department or a bureau, when he discharges a political duty of the President or exercises his discretion, and the removal of executive officers engaged in the discharge of their other normal duties. The imperative reasons requiring an unrestricted power to remove the most important of his subordinates in their most important duties must, therefore, control the interpretation of the Constitution as to all appointed by him.

But this is not to say that there are not strong reasons why the President should have a like power to remove his appointees charged with other duties than those above described. The ordinary duties of officers prescribed by statute come under the general administrative control of the President by virtue of the general grant to him of the executive power, and he may properly supervise and guide their construction of the statutes under which they act in order to secure that unitary and uniform execution of the laws which Article II of the Constitution evidently contemplated in vesting general executive power in the President alone. Laws are often passed with specific provision for the adoption of regulations by a department or bureau head to make the law workable and effective. The ability and judgment manifested by the official thus empowered, as well as

his energy and stimulation of his subordinates, are subjects which the President must consider and supervise in his administrative control. Finding such officers to be negligent and inefficient, the President should have the power to remove them. Of course there may be duties so peculiarly and specifically committed to the discretion of a particular officer as to raise a question whether the President may overrule or revise the officer's interpretation of his statutory duty in a particular instance. Then there may be duties of a quasi-judicial character imposed on executive officers and members of executive tribunals whose decisions after hearing affect interests of individuals, the discharge of which the President can not in a particular case properly influence or control. But even in such a case he may consider the decision after its rendition as a reason for removing the officer, on the ground that the discretion regularly entrusted to that officer by statute has not been on the whole intelligently or wisely exercised. Otherwise he does not discharge his own constitutional duty of seeing that the laws be faithfully executed. . . .

The power to remove inferior executive officers, like that to remove superior executive officers, is an incident of the power to appoint them, and is in its nature an executive power. The authority of Congress given by the excepting clause to vest the appointment of such inferior officers in the heads of departments carries with it authority incidentally to invest the heads of departments with power to remove. It has been the practice of Congress to do so and this Court has recognized that power. The Court also has recognized . . . that Congress, in committing the appointment of such inferior officers to the heads of departments, may prescribe incidental regulations controlling and restricting the latter in the exercise of the power of removal. But the Court never has held, nor reasonably could hold, although it is argued to the contrary on behalf of the appellant, that the excepting clause enables Congress to draw to itself, or to either branch of it, the power to remove or the right to participate in the exercise of that power. To do this would be to go beyond the words and implications of that clause and to infringe the constitutional principle of the separation of governmental powers.

. . . It is true that the remedy for the evil of political executive removals of inferior offices is with Congress by a simple expedient, but it includes a change of the power of appointment from the President with the consent of the Senate. Congress must determine first that the office is inferior, and second that it is willing that the office shall be filled by appointment by some other authority than the President with the consent of the Senate. . . .

For the reasons given, we must therefore hold that the provision of the law of 1876, by which the unrestricted power of removal of first class postmasters is denied to the President, is in violation of the Constitution, and invalid. This leads to an affirmance of the judgment of the Court of Claims. . . .

Judgment affirmed.

MR. JUSTICE HOLMES, dissenting. . . .

We have to deal with an office that owes its existence to Congress and that Congress may abolish tomorrow. Its duration and the pay attached to it while it lasts depend on Congress alone. Congress alone confers on the President the power to appoint to it and at any time may transfer the power to other hands. With such power over its own creation, I have no more trouble in believing that Congress has power to prescribe a term of life for it free from any interference than I have in accepting the undoubted power of Congress to decree its end. I have equally little trouble in accepting its power to prolong the tenure of an incumbent until Congress or the Senate shall have assented to his removal. The duty of the President to see that the laws

be executed is a duty that does not go beyond the laws or require him to achieve more than Congress sees fit to leave within his power.

MR. JUSTICE McREYNOLDS, dissenting.

The long struggle for civil service reform and the legislation designed to insure some security of official tenure ought not to be forgotten. Again and again Congress has enacted statutes prescribing restrictions on removals and by approving them many Presidents have affirmed its power therein. . . .

Nothing short of language clear beyond serious disputation should be held to clothe the President with authority wholly beyond congressional control arbitrarily to dismiss every officer whom he appoints except a few judges. There are no such words in the Constitution, and the asserted inference conflicts with the heretofore accepted theory that this government is one of carefully enumerated powers under an intelligible charter. . . .

If the phrase "executive power" infolds the one now claimed, many others heretofore totally unsuspected may lie there awaiting future supposed necessity; and no human intelligence can define the field of the President's permissible activities. "A masked battery of constructive powers would complete the destruction of liberty."

. . . We have no such thing as three totally distinct and independent departments; the others must look to the legislative for direction and support. . . .

We are asked by the United States to treat the definite holding in *Marbury* v. *Madison* that the plaintiff was not subject to removal by the President at will as mere *dictum*—to disregard it. But a solemn adjudication by this Court may not be so lightly treated. For a hundred and twenty years that case has been regarded as among the most important ever decided. It lies at the very foundation of our jurisprudence. Every point determined was deemed essential, and the suggestion of *dictum,* either idle or partisan exhortation, ought not to be tolerated. The point here involved was directly passed upon by the great Chief Justice, and we must accept the result unless prepared to express direct disapproval and exercise the transient power which we possess to overrule our great predecessors —the opinion cannot be shunted.

MR. JUSTICE BRANDEIS, dissenting. . . .

The separation of the powers of government did not make each branch completely autonomous. It left each, in some measure, dependent upon the others, as it left to each power to exercise, in some respects, functions in their nature executive, legislative and judicial. Obviously the President cannot secure full execution of the laws, if Congress denies to him adequate means of doing so. Full execution may be defeated because Congress declines to create offices indispensable for that purpose. Or, because Congress, having created the office, declines to make the indispensable appropriation. Or, because Congress, having both created the office and made the appropriation, prevents, by restrictions which it imposes, the appointment of officials who in quality and character are indispensable to the efficient execution of the law. If, in any such way, adequate means are denied to the President, the fault will lie with Congress. The President performs his full constitutional duty, if, with the means and instruments provided by Congress and within the limitations prescribed by it, he uses his best endeavors to secure the faithful execution of the laws enacted. Compare *Kendall* v. *United States*, 12 Pet. 524, 613, 626. . . .

RATHBUN (HUMPHREY'S EXECUTOR) v. UNITED STATES

295 U.S. 602 (May 27, 1935).

Certificate from the Court of Claims.

Questions answered.

9-0	
Sutherland	('+')
Hughes, C.J.	(+)
VanDevanter	(+)
Brandeis	(+)
Butler	(+)
Stone	(+)
Roberts	(+)
Cardozo	(+)
McReynolds	+

William Humphrey, the chairman and most conservative member of the Federal Trade Commission in the spring of 1933, still had four years remaining of the seven-year term to which he had been reappointed by President Hoover. But he had less than a year left to live, as it turned out, when F.D.R. removed him to make way for a good New Dealer. Consequently, it was Humphrey's executor, like Myers', who was left to press his claim for back salary in the Court of Claims and, eventually, in the Supreme Court. But the issue this time, as defined by the Court, was different. Humphrey raised again the question of the "middle ground" that Solicitor General Beck had urged upon the Court a decade earlier, only to have Taft at that time brush aside such an obvious compromise on an issue regarding which, in Taft's judgment, compromise was neither necessary nor desirable. (Granting that the Senate could not participate in the decision to remove an official appointed by the President, could not the Congress, by statute, specify the grounds on which the President might remove, at least for certain positions?)

The Chief Justice at this time was not a former President, but rather he was a man who had just missed becoming President. Five of the justices had acquiesced in Taft's dictum to the contrary in his Myers opinion, but they now rejected that dictum in favor of the compromise that had not seemed necessary in the earlier case. McReynolds adhered to his dissenting views in Myers, which led him, of course, to concur in the decision of the Court in this case, but not in what was otherwise the unanimous opinion of the Court. It should be noted that the Court was forced into the compromise position that it now accepted, at least in part by the extremity of the argument offered by the government. (A similar circumstance occurred, at least before the trial court, in the Steel Seizure case.) Solicitor General (later Mr. Justice) Stanley Reed "conceded," during oral argument of Humphrey's case before the Court, that the logic of his argument in behalf of a presidential power to remove Federal Trade Commissioners would require the Court also to approve presidential removal of the judges of the Court of Claims, possibly for their disagreement in this very case! Naturally, the Court was unprepared to approve of presidential power to remove judges, even though no President ever had claimed such authority. Certainly, Taft would have rejected such a claim, for his views on the independence of judges were much stronger than his views on the executive removal power.

President Roosevelt's reply to the Court's decision in this case was twofold. In the following year, his Committee on Administrative Management branded the federal regulatory commissions, declared to be "independent" by the Court in the Humphrey case, a "headless fourth branch of the government," and recommended that their "executive" and "legislative" functions be taken away, departmentalized, and thus placed under the presidential power of policy direction and control. The stripped-down commissions would have been left with "quasi-judicial" functions, which they presumably would exercise subject to the policy direction of the Supreme Court, through its power to review their decisions. These recommendations were realized only in part—a portion of the "executive function" part— through the adoption at a later time of a series of reorganization plans sponsored by Presidents Truman and Eisenhower.

The second part of Roosevelt's reply to the Court came in February, 1937, when he presented his "Court-packing" proposals.

The extracts here begin with a portion of Solicitor General Reed's statement of the Administration's position:

It is true, as the legislative history of the Act indicates, that the Commission was intended to be or to become an experienced and informed body, free from certain of the handicaps that were deemed to inhere in departmental organization. But there is nothing in the language or the legislative history of the Act to suggest that these purposes were thought to require a limitation of the removal power to the causes named. . . .

The independence which Congress sought for the Federal Trade Commission does not depend upon an implied limitation of the removal power such as that contended for by the plaintiff. The Commission was left free from the continuing supervision of a departmental head; its membership was required to represent more than one political party; and the terms of its members were arranged to expire at different times. In later Acts creating similar commissions, these factors alone have apparently been deemed sufficient to secure the objective of an independent body. Compare, for example, the Acts creating the United States Employees' Compensation Commission . . . ; the Federal Radio Commission . . . ; the Federal Power Commission . . . ; The Federal Home Loan Bank Board . . . ; the Securities and Exchange Commission . . . ; and the Federal Communications Commission. . . . Each of these Acts provides that not more than a bare majority of the members of the Commission shall have overlapping terms. In none of these Acts did Congress impose any limitation on removal. The effect of this omission is that the power of removal is unrestricted, since the power to remove, at least in the absence of constitutional or statutory provision, is an incident of the power to appoint. . . .

Faithful execution of the laws may require more than freedom from inefficiency, neglect of duty, or malfeasance in office. Particularly in the case of those officers entrusted with the task of enforcing new legislation, such as the Securities Act of 1933, which embodies new concepts of federal regulation in the public interest, faithful execution of the laws may presuppose wholehearted sympathy with the purposes and policy of the law, and energy and resourcefulness beyond that of the ordinarily efficient public servant. The President should be free to judge in what measure these qualities are possessed and to act upon that judgment. *Myers* v. *United States*, 272 U.S. 52, 135.

The so-called legislative functions performed by the Federal Trade Commission do not differ in nature from those performed by the regular executive departments. Reports to Congress on special topics are made by the Commission; but such reports are likewise made by the heads of departments.

The Federal Trade Commission is not a judicial tribunal. . . .

The so-called quasi-judicial functions of the Commission are not different from those regularly committed to the executive departments. Functions so committed include the determination of a wide range of controversies respecting such important matters as immigration, . . . internal revenue and customs duties, . . . public-land claims, . . . pension claims, . . . use of the mails, . . . practices at stockyards, . . . [and] trading in grain futures. . . .

It cannot be questioned that the head of a department, however numerous or important may be his functions of this kind, is subject to removal by the President without limitation by Congress, under the decision in the *Myers* case, *supra*. An attempt to distinguish, in respect of the President's removal power, between various administrative agencies would logically require distinctions also between the same agency at different times.

MR. JUSTICE SUTHERLAND delivered the opinion of the Court.

Plaintiff brought suit in the Court of Claims against the United States to recover a sum of money alleged to be due the deceased for salary as a Federal Trade Commissioner from October 8, 1933, when the President undertook to remove him from office, to the time of his death on February 14, 1934. The court below has certified to this court two questions . . . in respect of the power of the President to make the removal. The material facts which give rise to the questions are as follows:

William E. Humphrey, the decedent, on December 10, 1931, was nominated by President Hoover to succeed himself as a member of the Federal Trade Commission, and was confirmed by the United States Senate. He was duly commissioned for a term of seven years expiring September 25, 1938; and, after taking the required oath of office, entered upon his duties. On July 25, 1933, President Roosevelt addressed a letter to the commissioner asking for his resignation, on the ground "that the aims and purposes of the Administration with respect to the work of the Commission can be carried out most effectively with personnel of my own selection," but disclaiming any reflection upon the commisisoner personally or upon his services. The commissioner replied, asking time to consult his friends. After some further correspondence upon the subject, the President on August 31, 1933, wrote the commissioner expressing the hope that the resignation would be forthcoming and saying:

> You will, I know, realize that I do not feel that your mind and my mind go along together on either the policies or the administering of the Federal Trade Commission, and, frankly, I think it is best for the people of this country that I should have a full confidence.

The commissioner declined to resign; and on October 7, 1933, the President wrote him:

> Effective as of this date you are hereby removed from the office of Commissioner of the Federal Trade Commission.

Humphrey never acquiesced in this action, but continued thereafter to insist that he was still a member of the commission, entitled to perform its duties and receive the compensation provided by law at the rate of $10,000 per annum. Upon these and other facts set forth in the certificate . . . the following questions are certified:

> 1. Do the provisions of section 1 of the Federal Trade Commission Act, stating that "any commissioner may be removed by the President for inefficiency, neglect of duty, or malfeasance in office," restrict or limit the power of the President to remove a commissioner except upon one or more of the causes named?

If the foregoing question is answered in the affirmative, then—

> 2. If the power of the President to remove a commissioner is restricted or limited as shown by the foregoing interrogatory and the answer made thereto, is such a restriction or limitation valid under the Constitution of the United States?

The Federal Trade Commission Act [of 1914] creates a commission of five members to be appointed by the President by and with the advice and consent of the Senate, and § 1 provides:

> Not more than three of the commissioners shall be members of the same political party. . . . The commission shall choose a chairman from its own membership. . . . Any commissioner may be removed by the President for inefficiency, neglect of duty, or malfeasance in office. . . .

First. The question first to be considered is whether, by the provisions of § 1 of the Federal Trade Commission Act already quoted, the President's power is limited to removal for the specific causes enumerated therein. . . .

The commission is to be non-partisan; and it must, from the very nature of its duties, act with entire impartiality. It is charged with the enforcement of no policy except the policy of the law. Its duties are neither political nor executive, but predominantly quasi-judicial and quasi-legislative. Like the Interstate Commerce Commission, its members are called upon to exercise the trained judgment of a body of experts "appointed by law and informed by experience." . . .

The debates in both houses demonstrate that the prevailing view was that the commission was not to be "subject to anybody in the government but . . . only to the people of the United States"; free from "political domination or control" or the "probability or possibility of such a thing"; to be "separate and apart from any existing department of the government—not subject to the orders of the President." . . .

Thus, the language of the act, the legislative reports, and the general purposes of the legislation as reflected by the debates, all combine to demonstrate the Congressional intent to create a body of experts who shall gain experience by length of service—a body which shall be independent of executive authority, *except in its selection,* and free to exercise its judgment without the leave or hindrance of any other official or any department of the government. To the accomplishment of these purposes, it is clear that Congress was of opinion that length and certainty of tenure would vitally contribute. And to hold that, nevertheless, the members of the commission continue in office at the mere will of the President, might be to thwart, in large measure, the very ends which Congress sought to realize by definitely fixing the term of office.

We conclude that the intent of the act is to limit the executive power of removal to the causes enumerated, the existence of none of which is claimed here; and we pass to the second question.

Second. To support its contention that the removal provision of § 1, as we have just construed it, is an unconstitutional interference with the executive power of the President, the government's chief reliance is *Myers* v. *United States,* 272 U.S. 52. . . . Nevertheless, the narrow point actually decided was only that the President had power to remove a postmaster of the first class, without the advice and consent of the Senate as required by act of Congress. In the course of the opinion of the court, expressions occur which tend to sustain the government's contention, but these are beyond the point involved and, therefore, do not come within the rule of *stare decisis.* In so far as they are out of harmony with the views here set forth, these expressions are disapproved.

The office of a postmaster is so essentially unlike the office now involved that the decision in the *Myers* case cannot be accepted as controlling our decision here. A postmaster is an executive officer restricted to the performance of executive functions. He is charged with no duty at all related to either the legislative or judicial power. The actual decision in the *Myers* case finds support in the theory that such an officer is merely one of the units in the executive department and, hence, inherently subject to the exclusive and illimitable power of removal by the Chief Executive, whose subordinate and aid he is. Putting aside *dicta,* which may be followed if sufficiently persuasive but which are not controlling, the necessary reach of the decision goes far enough to include all purely executive officers. It goes no farther;—much less does it include an officer who occupies no place in the executive department and who exercises no part of the executive power vested by the Constitution in the President.

The Federal Trade Commission is an administrative body created by Congress to carry into effect legislative policies embodied in the statute in accordance with the legislative standard therein prescribed, and to perform other specified duties as a legislative or as a judicial aid. Such a body cannot in any proper sense be characterized as an arm or an eye of the executive. Its duties are performed without executive leave and, in the contemplation of the statute, must be free from executive control. In administering the provisions of the statute in respect of "unfair methods of competition"—that is to say in filling in and administering the details embodied by that general standard—the commission acts in part quasi-legislatively and in part quasi-judicially. In making investigations and reports thereon for the information of Congress under § 6, in aid of the legislative power, it acts as a legislative agency. Under § 7, which authorizes the commission to act as a master in chancery under rules prescribed by the court, it acts as an agency of the judiciary. To the extent that it exercises any executive function—as distinguished from executive power in the constitutional sense—it does so in the discharge and effectuation of its quasi-legislative or quasi-judicial powers, or as an agency of the legislative or judicial departments of the government.

If Congress is without authority to prescribe causes for removal of members of the trade commission and limit executive power of removal accordingly, that power at once becomes practically all-inclusive in respect of civil officers with the exception of the judiciary provided for by the Constitution. The Solicitor General, at the bar, apparently recognizing this to be true, with commendable candor, agreed that his view in respect of the removability of members of the Federal Trade Commission necessitated a like view in respect of the Interstate Commerce Commission and the Court of Claims. We are thus confronted with the serious question whether not only the members of these quasi-legislative and quasi-judicial bodies, but the judges of the legislative Court of Claims, exercising judicial power (*Williams* v. *United States*, 289 U. S. 553, 565-567), continue in office only at the pleasure of the President.

We think it plain under the Constitution that illimitable power of removal is not possessed by the President in respect of officers of the character of those just named. The authority of Congress, in creating quasi-legislative or quasi-judicial agencies, to require them to act in discharge of their duties independently of executive control cannot well be doubted; and that authority includes, as an appropriate incident, power to fix the period during which they shall continue in office, and to forbid their removal except for cause in the meantime. For it is quite evident that one who holds his office only during the pleasure of another, cannot be depended upon to maintain an attitude of independence against the latter's will.

The fundamental necessity of maintaining each of the three general departments of government entirely free from the control or coercive influence, direct or indirect, of either of the others, has often been stressed and is hardly open to serious question. So much is implied in the very fact of the separation of the powers of these departments by the Constitution; and in the rule which recognizes their essential coequality. The sound application of a principle that makes one master in his own house precludes him from imposing his control in the house of another who is master there. . . .[11]

The power of removal here claimed for the President falls within this principle, since its coercive influence threatens the independence of a commission, which is not only wholly disconnected from the executive department, but which, as already fully appears, was created by Congress as a means of carrying into operation legislative and judicial powers, and as an agency of the legislative and judicial departments.

In the light of the question now under consideration, we have reëxamined the precedents referred to in the *Myers* case, and find nothing in them to justify a conclusion contrary to that which we have reached. . . .

In *Marbury* v. *Madison*, [at] pp. 162, 165-166, it is made clear that Chief Justice Marshall was of opinion that a justice of the peace for the District of Columbia was not removable at the will of the President; and that there was a distinction between such an officer and officers appointed to aid the President in the performance of his constitutional duties. In the latter case, the distinction he saw was that "their acts are his acts" and his will, therefore, controls; and, by way of illustration, he adverted to the act establishing the Department of Foreign Affairs, which was the subject of the "decision of 1789."

The result of what we now have said is this: Whether the power of the President to remove an officer shall prevail over the authority of Congress to condition the power by fixing a definite term and precluding a removal except for cause, will depend upon the character of the office; the *Myers* decision, affirming the power of the President alone to make the removal, is confined to purely executive officers; and as to officers of the kind here under consideration, we hold that no removal can be made during the prescribed term for which the officer is appointed, except for one or more of the causes named in the applicable statute.

To the extent that, between the decision in the *Myers* case, which sustains the unrestrictable power of the President to remove purely executive officers, and our present decision that such power does not extend to an office such as that here in-

11 And who is master in the mansions of the F.T.C.? the commissioners themselves? Congress? the Supreme Court? "the American people"?

volved, there shall remain a field of doubt, we leave such cases as may fall within it for future consideration and determination as they may arise.

In accordance with the foregoing, the questions submitted are answered.

Question No. 1, Yes.
Question No. 2, Yes.

There has been remarkably little probing of the indeterminate zone, the metes and bounds of which were demarked by the Myers and the Humphrey decisions. One can only speculate as to whether senior politicians, noting certain morbid similarities between the two earlier cases, tended to prefer involuntary retirement to the prosecution of suits for back pay by their heirs-at-law. A few years after the Humphrey case, a federal circuit court of appeals upheld President Roosevelt's removal of the chairman of the board of the Tennessee Valley Authority, who had become conspicuously involved in an intra-agency political squabble over policy issues. Although the authorizing statute provided for presidential removal only in cases involving violation of the merit principle in dealing with TVA personnel, reserving to the Congress a general power of removal by concurrent resolution,[12] the lower federal court decided that TVA came under the rule of the Myers case as an "executive or administrative agency," and therefore was properly subject to the presidential power of administrative direction and control; and the Supreme Court denied certiorari to review the case.[13]

On the other hand, President Eisenhower's removal of a member of the board of a temporary agency, the War Claims Commission, for partisan reasons that were identical to those motivating Franklin Roosevelt twenty years earlier, was branded as unconstitutional by the unanimous decision of the Warren Court in *Wiener* v. *United States*, 357 U.S. 349 (1958). There was no carryover between the personnel of the Courts that decided the Humprey and Wiener cases. There was, however, at least one obvious difference between the two decisions. Franklin Roosevelt could and did fight back against the Court's rebuff. But it was a sure bet that the aging and tired Eisenhower would acquiesce without a murmur of protest. Wiener, in other words, was a "safe" decision for the Court to make: the President no longer cared, the Democratic majority in Congress would applaud, and no major interest group would be adversely affected by the result. The decision served the function of expanding further the power and status of the Court itself, and of weakening somewhat further a Presidency whose powers had been flowing, for almost a decade, in ebb tide. This was no time for judicial restraint.

The complete silence of the authorizing statute regarding any process for

[12] For a discussion of the constitutional problems implicit in such a use of concurrent resolutions, see William E. Rhode, *Congressional Review of Administrative Decision-Making by Committee Clearance and Resolutions* (East Lansing: Michigan State University, Ph.D. dissertation, 1958), ch. IX.

[13] *Morgan* v. *T.V.A.*, 115 F.2d 990 (1940), certiorari denied, 312 U.S. 701 (1941).

removing War Claims Commissioners made no difference, said the Court, since this commission was an "adjudicatory body," and therefore was governed by the "philosophy of *Humphrey's Executor,* in its explicit language as well as its implications." Actually, the Wiener decision went considerably beyond the policy of the Humphrey case. In the latter, the Supreme Court had arbitrated a direct conflict between a policy established by Congress and action taken by the President; but the "implied constitutional" limitation against the President's right to remove Commissioner Wiener was declared not by Congress but by the Supreme Court.

The Court's Aristotelian claim to the right to discriminate between constitutional and unconstitutional exercise of the presidential removal power, according to the "nature" of the office at issue, evokes another range of problems, however, closely akin to those that we examined in the preceding chapter affecting the chameleon-like "legislative" courts. Frankfurter spoke for the unanimous Court in the Wiener case when he asserted that Congress might well have delegated to the regular federal courts precisely the same function that was vested, in the event, in the War Claims Commission. But six members of the Court, including Frankfurter himself, had disputed this possibility less than a decade earlier in the Tidewater decision, arguing then that Article III judicial power could not be vested in non-Article III courts—and this rule certainly would include administrative commissions—and that Article I judicial power could not be vested in Article III courts. Once again, the logic of the principle of separation of powers, in combination with the peculiar limitations of the case method as a policy-making process, appears to have led the Court into a blind alley.

SOME POLITICAL QUESTIONS

When the Court considers national survival to be at stake, neither the principle of separation of powers, nor the federal division of powers between the nation and the states, nor claims of individual civil rights and liberties are allowed to interfere with the prophylactic measures deemed necessary by the political and military leaders of the country. Especially is this true when the President and the Congress act conjointly to present, as it were, a massive show of force; but an equivalent result can also be achieved when constitutional imbalance is so great that either the President or, more rarely, the Congress has established for itself a clear (if temporary) position of dominance. We should not anticipate, nor do we find, interference by the Court in circumstances that the justices *recognize* as those of genuine crisis. But it is precisely those occasions, infrequent though they be, when the justices attempt to assay an independent judgment concerning the seriousness of the national emergency, that lead to domestic constitutional crises. Examples are provided by the Panama Refining and Steel Seizure cases. A conclusion about the seriousness and probable consequences of a major economic depression or a "shooting war" involves the exercise of political, not judicial, judgment. This is normally the Court's position; and it has led to the virtual abdication, by the Court, of the power of judicial review over the conduct of foreign relations or the prosecution of war.

Foreign Affairs

Statutes are made by the Congress, subject to the veto of the President which can be, and occasionally is, overridden by extraordinary majorities in both houses of the Congress. Treaties, however, are made by the President, subject to the veto power of a minority of the upper chamber alone. Of course, many treaties are not self-executing but require implementing legislation to provide funds and administrative machinery for enforcement, which gives the House an effective though indirect voice in this as well as other aspects of the conduct of foreign relations. But it remains true that a treaty is in essence a form of presidential ordinance, and it is the President rather than the Congress who has the primary voice in this form of national policy-making. To the extent that the Constitution provides no substantive limitations upon the scope of treaty-making, this provides an important source of implied Executive power. The Supremacy Clause (Article VI, Section 2) of the Constitution states that all statutes that are made in "pursuance" of the Constitution "shall be the supreme law of the land"; but it requires of treaties only that they be made "under the authority of the United States." This suggests that the national government might be able to establish policies by treaty that would be unconstitutional, as an invasion of states' rights, if formulated by act of Congress. And this was precisely the holding of *Missouri v. Holland,* below. In any event, the Supreme Court never has held either a treaty or an executive agreement to be unconstitutional.[14]

There certainly has been no systematic attempt to exploit such propensities of the treaty power, either before or after the decision in this case; but the possibility was one of the major concerns of the "Brickerites," who in the early 1950's constituted a loose coalition of midwest isolationist and "states' rights" groups and conservatives generally, whose political leadership was centered in the American Bar Association. One of the key sections of the constitutional amendment proposed by Senator Bricker provided that "a treaty shall become effective as internal law in the United States only through legislation which would be valid in the absence of treaty." This provision was specifically intended to overrule the decision in *Missouri v. Holland,* and it failed by a single vote of passing the Senate on February 26, 1954, although after this defeat support for the proposed amendment became dissipated.[15]

---

[14] For a discussion of the constitutionality of executive agreements, see Glendon A. Schubert, *The Presidency in the Courts* (Minneapolis: University of Minnesota Press, 1957), pp. 103-107.

[15] For a case history of the Bricker Amendment, see Schubert, "Politics and the Constitution: The Bricker Amendment During 1953," *Journal of Politics,* Vol. 16, pp. 257-298 (1954).

MISSOURI v. HOLLAND,
U.S. GAME WARDEN

252 U.S. 416 (1920).

Appeal from the United States District Court for the Western District of Missouri.

Affirmed.

7-2

Holmes	('+')
White, C.J.	(+)
McKenna	(+)
Day	(+)
McReynolds	(+)
Brandeis	(+)
Clarke	(+)
VanDevanter	—
Pitney	—

Since the precise object of the treaty at issue in Missouri v. *Holland, together with the implementing statute and administrative regulations, was to provide for cooperative international control of the hunting of migratory game birds, one might wonder about the nature of the "national interest of very nearly the first magnitude" referred to in the concluding paragraph of the opinion of the Court. The explanation is found in the Malthusian major premise upon which Mr. Justice Holmes relied. The hunting regulations were a necessary and proper means of protecting the national food supply; and in their absence, the man-made destruction of nature's balance could be expected to result in famine and pestilence.*

MR. JUSTICE HOLMES delivered the opinion of the Court.

This is a bill in equity brought by the State of Missouri to prevent a game warden of the United States from attempting to enforce the Migratory Bird Treaty Act of July 3, 1918 . . . and the regulations made by the Secretary of Agriculture in pursuance of the same. The ground of the bill is that the statute is an unconstitutional interference with the rights reserved to the States by the Tenth Amendment, and that the acts of the defendant done and threatened under that authority invade the sovereign right of the State and contravene its will manifested in statutes. The State also alleges a pecuniary interest, as owner of the wild birds within its borders and otherwise, admitted by the Government to be sufficient, but it is enough that the bill is a reasonable and proper means to assert the alleged quasi sovereign rights of a State. . . . A motion to dismiss was sustained by the District Court on the ground that the Act of Congress is constitutional. . . .

On December 8, 1916, a treaty between the United States and Great Britain was proclaimed by the President. It recited that many species of birds in their annual migrations traversed many parts of the United States and of Canada, that they were of great value as a source of food and in destroying insects injurious to vegetation, but were in danger of extermination through lack of adequate protection. It therefore provided for specified closed seasons and protection in other forms, and agreed that the two powers would take or propose to their lawmaking bodies the necessary measures for carrying the treaty out. . . . The above mentioned act of July 3, 1918, entitled an act to give effect to the convention, prohibited the killing, capturing or selling any of the migratory birds included in the terms of the treaty except as permitted by regulations compatible with those terms, to be made by the Secretary of Agriculture. Regulations were proclaimed on July 31, and October 25, 1918. . . . It is unnecessary to go into any details, because, as we have said, the question raised is the general one whether the treaty and statute are void as an interference with the rights reserved to the States.

To answer this question it is not enough to refer to the Tenth Amendment, reserving the powers not delegated to the United

States, because by Article 2, Section 2, the power to make treaties is delegated expressly, and by Article 6 treaties made under the authority of the United States, along with the Constitution and laws of the United States made in pursuance thereof, are declared the supreme law of the land. If the treaty is valid there can be no dispute about the validity of the statute under Article 1, Section 8, as a necessary and proper means to execute the powers of the Government. The language of the Constitution as to the supremacy of treaties being general, the question before us is narrowed to an inquiry into the ground upon which the present supposed exception is placed.

It is said that a treaty cannot be valid if it infringes the Constitution, that there are limits, therefore, to the treaty-making power, and that one such limit is that what an act of Congress could not do unaided, in derogation of the powers reserved to the States, a treaty cannot do. An earlier act of Congress that attempted by itself and not in pursuance of a treaty to regulate the killing of migratory birds within the States had been held bad in the District Court. United States v. Shauver, 214 Fed. 154. United States v. McCullagh, 221 Fed. 288. Those decisions were supported by arguments that migratory birds were owned by the States in their sovereign capacity for the benefit of their people, and that . . . this control was one that Congress had no power to displace. The same argument is supposed to apply now with equal force.

Whether the two cases cited were decided rightly or not they cannot be accepted as a test of the treaty power. Acts of Congress are the supreme law of the land only when made in pursuance of the Constitution, while treaties are declared to be so when made under the authority of the United States. It is open to question whether the authority of the United States means more than the formal acts prescribed to make the convention. We do not mean to imply that there are no quali-

fications to the treaty-making power; but they must be ascertained in a different way. It is obvious that there may be matters of the sharpest exigency for the national well being that an act of Congress could not deal with but that a treaty followed by such an act could, and it is not lightly to be assumed that, in matters requiring national action, "a power which must belong to and somewhere reside in every civilized government" is not to be found.

. . . [When] we are dealing with words that also are a constituent act, like the Constitution of the United States, we must realize that they have called into life a being the development of which could not have been foreseen completely by the most gifted of its begetters. It was enough for them to realize or to hope that they had created an organism; it has taken a century and has cost their successors much sweat and blood to prove that they created a nation. The case before us must be considered in the light of our whole experience and not merely in that of what was said a hundred years ago. The treaty in question does not contravene any prohibitory words to be found in the Constitution. The only question is whether it is forbidden by some invisible radiation from the general terms of the Tenth Amendment. We must consider what this country has become in deciding what that amendment has reserved.

The State as we have intimated founds its claim of exclusive authority upon an assertion of title to migratory birds, an assertion that is embodied in statute. No doubt it is true that as between a State and its inhabitants the State may regulate the killing and sale of such birds, but it does not follow that its authority is exclusive of paramount powers. To put the claim of the State upon title is to lean upon a slender reed. Wild birds are not in the possession of anyone; and possession is the beginning of ownership. The whole foundation of the State's rights is the presence within their jurisdiction of birds that yesterday had not arrived, tomorrow may be in another State and in a week a thousand miles away. If we are to be accurate we cannot put the case of the State upon higher ground than that the treaty deals with creatures that for the moment are within the state borders, that it must be carried out by officers of the United States within the same territory, and that but for the treaty the State would be free to regulate this subject itself.

As most of the laws of the United States are carried out within the States and as many of them deal with matters which in the silence of such laws the State might regulate, such general grounds are not enough to support Missouri's claim. Valid treaties of course "are as binding within the territorial limits of the States as they are elsewhere throughout the dominion of the United States." . . . No doubt the great body of private relations usually fall within the control of the State, but a treaty may override its power. We do not have to invoke the later developments of constitutional law for this proposition; it was recognized . . . by Chief Justice Marshall. . . .

Here a national interest of very nearly the first magnitude is involved. It can be protected only by national action in concert with that of another power. The subject matter is only transitorily within the State and has no permanent habitat therein. But for the treaty and the statute there soon may be no birds for any powers to deal with. We see nothing in the Constitution that compels the Government to sit by while a food supply is cut off and the protectors of our forests and our crops are destroyed. It is not sufficient to rely upon the States. The reliance is vain, and were it otherwise, the question is whether the United States is forbidden to act. We are of opinion that the treaty and statute must be upheld. . . .

Decree affirmed.

There are few opinions of the Supreme Court that constitute more unblushing paeans to the prerogatives of the Presidency than does that of Justice Sutherland in *United States* v. *Curtiss-Wright Export Corporation.* In one sense, this almost unanimous ode to the Executive, coming as it did on the heels of the "Hot Oil" and "Sick Chicken" decisions, at a time when the Nine Old Men were still riding high in the flush of their "victory" over the New Deal, and less than two months before the Court-packing proposal, was nothing less than remarkable. The Court was even favored with a decision and opinion of the trial court that was exceptionally hostile to the government, sustaining a demurrer to an indictment on the ground that the joint resolution of Congress, defining the crime with which the corporation was charged, constituted an unconstitutional attempt to delegate legislative power to the President.

But George Sutherland's views on the question at issue had crystallized long before the New Deal period; indeed, they were formed long before he joined the Supreme Court. Over a quarter of a century earlier, Senator Sutherland, then a member of the United States Senate Committee on the Judiciary, set forth his views in an article entitled "The Internal and External Powers of the National Government." We present a few sentences from this twelve-page article, so that the reader can compare them with the language and general argument of the opinion below in the Curtiss-Wright case. According to Senator Sutherland,[16]

> Much of the confusion [concerning the character and authority of the Government of the United States] has resulted from a failure to distinguish between our internal and our external relations—a failure to recognize the difference which, from the structure and character of the American dual political system, must of necessity exist between the federal powers of the General Government which are exerted in its dealings with the several States and their people and the national powers which are exerted in its dealings with the outside world. Among ourselves we are many governments and many peoples—to others we are one government and one people. . . . And . . . national sovereignty inhered in the United States from the beginning. Neither the Colonies nor the States which succeeded them ever separately exercised authority over foreign affairs. . . . [The] powers of external sovereignty passed from the Kingdom of Great Britain [to *one sovereign nation*]. These powers were never delegated by the States; they were never possessed by the States, and the States could not delegate something which they did not have. . . . [The] denial *to* the General Government of any necessary power over national affairs . . . [is] subversive of the spirit of the Constitution, which is the paramount law of State and nation alike.

The circumstance suggests that, as with Taft and the Myers case, neither the specific facts nor the argument of counsel was determinative of the outcome of the Curtiss-Wright case. What was important was that one member of the Court had strong personal views on the subject, reflecting attitudes that were formed quite independently of the Supreme Court and its decisional processes; and this strongly committed justice was able to persuade a majority of his colleagues to let him have his say. Of course, there is at least one important difference between the two cases. Taft gained only the *ad hoc* acquiescence of his Court, as the defection of five members of his majority, less than a decade later in the Humphrey case, conclusively demonstrates. The Curtiss-Wright decision, to the contrary, has been neither watered down nor distinguished away during the past two decades. Instead, the Roosevelt, Vinson, and Warren Courts have made it the cornerstone of a massive edifice of Executive discretion in the conduct of foreign affairs. As the Chief of State, the President's fiat has become absolute law, beyond effective challenge in the courts, because in this area he does not share constitutional power as an equal of the Congress, as he does in the case of the war power

---

16 *Senate Document No. 417,* 61st Cong., 2d Sess., (March 8, 1910), pp. 1-2, 3, 4, 12. Emphasis in the original. Cf. Senator Sutherland's lectures on the Blumenthal Foundation, *Constitutional Power and World Af-* *fairs* (New York: Columbia University Press, 1919), pp. 47ff, cited by Foster H. Sherwood, "Foreign Relations and the Constitution," *Western Political Quarterly,* Vol. 1, p. 393 (1948).

of the national government. In the making of foreign policy, the President is either the primary or else the exclusive organ of governmental power. As Congressman John Marshall said, shortly before he became Chief Justice, "The President is the *sole* organ of the nation in its external relations."

UNITED STATES v. CURTISS-WRIGHT EXPORT CORP.

299 U.S. 304 (December 21, 1936)

Appeal from the United States District Court for the Southern District of New York.

Reversed.

7-1

Sutherland	('+')
Hughes, C.J.	(+)
VanDevanter	(+)
Brandeis	(+)
Butler	(+)
Roberts	(+)
Cardozo	(+)
McReynolds	—
Stone	NP

In response to a presidential request, Congress had adopted the Joint Resolution of May 28, 1934; and on the same day the President promulgated a proclamation placing an embargo on the shipment of arms and munitions to Bolivia and Paraguay. These Latin American Good Neighbors were, at the time, engaged in the Gran Chaco War. At the expiration of the war eighteen months later, President Roosevelt revoked his embargo, except that liability for violations committed while the proclamation was in effect were to remain subject to prosecution. The Curtiss-Wright Export Corporation was so indicted for the offense of having conspired to sell fifteen aircraft machine guns to one of the combatants.

MR. JUSTICE SUTHERLAND delivered the opinion of the Court. . . .

It is contended that by the Joint Resolution, the going into effect and continued operation of the resolution was conditioned (a) upon the President's judgment as to its beneficial effect upon the reëstablishment of peace between the countries engaged in armed conflict in the Chaco; (b) upon the making of a proclamation, which was left to his unfettered discretion, thus constituting an attempted substitution of the President's will for that of Congress; (c) upon the making of a proclamation putting an end to the operation of the resolution, which again was left to the President's unfettered discretion; and (d) further, that the extent of its operation in particular cases was subject to limitation and exception by the President, controlled by no standard. In each of these particulars, appellees urge that Congress abdicated its essential functions and delegated them to the Executive.

Whether, if the Joint Resolution had related solely to internal affairs it would be open to the challenge that it constituted an unlawful delegation of legislative power to the Executive, we find it unnecessary to determine. The whole aim of the resolution is to affect a situation entirely external to the United States, and falling within the category of foreign affairs. The determination which we are called to make, therefore, is whether the Joint Resolution, as applied to that situation, is vulnerable to attack under the rule that forbids a delegation of the law-making power. In other words, assuming (but not deciding) that the challenged delegation, if it were confined to internal affairs, would be invalid, may it nevertheless be sustained on the ground that its exclusive aim is to afford a remedy for a hurtful condition within foreign territory?

It will contribute to the elucidation of the question if we first consider the differences between the powers of the federal government in respect of foreign or external affairs and those in respect of domestic or internal affairs. That there are differences between them, and that these differences are fundamental, may not be doubted.

The two classes of powers are different, both in respect of their origin and their nature. The broad statement that the federal government can exercise no powers except those specifically enumerated in the Constitution, and such implied powers as are necessary and proper to carry into effect the enumerated powers, is categorically true only in respect of our internal affairs. In that field, the primary purpose of the Constitution was to carve from the general mass of legislative powers *then possessed by the states* such portions as it was thought desirable to vest in the federal government, leaving those not included in the enumeration still in the states. . . . That this doctrine applies only to powers which the states had, is self evident. And since the states severally never possessed international powers, such powers could not have been carved from the mass of state powers but obviously were transmitted to the United States from some other source. . . .

As a result of the separation from Great Britain by the colonies acting as a unit, the powers of external sovereignty passed from the Crown not to the colonies severally, but to the colonies in their collective and corporate capacity as the United States of America. Even before the Declaration, the colonies were a unit in foreign affairs, acting through a common agency— namely the Continental Congress, composed of delegates from the thirteen colonies. That agency exercised the powers of war and peace, raised an army, created a navy, and finally adopted the Declaration of Independence. Rulers come and go; governments end and forms of government change; but sovereignty survives. A

political society cannot endure without a supreme will somewhere. Sovereignty is never held in suspense. When, therefore, the external sovereignty of Great Britain in respect of the colonies ceased, it immediately passed to the Union. . . .

The Union existed before the Constitution, which was ordained and established among other things to form "a more perfect Union." Prior to that event, it is clear that the Union, declared by the Articles of Confederation to be "perpetual," was the sole possessor of external sovereignty and in the Union it remained without change save in so far as the Constitution in express terms qualified its exercise. The Framers' Convention was called and exerted its powers upon the irrefutable postulate that though the states were several their people in respect of foreign affairs were one. . . .

It results that the investment of the federal government with the powers of external sovereignty did not depend upon the affirmative grants of the Constitution. The powers to declare and wage war, to conclude peace, to make treaties, to maintain diplomatic relations with other sovereignties, if they had never been mentioned in the Constitution, would have vested in the federal government as necessary concomitants of nationality. . . .

Not only, as we have shown, is the federal power over external affairs in origin and essential character different from that over internal affairs, but participation in the exercise of the power is significantly limited. In this vast external realm, with its important, complicated, delicate and manifold problems, the President alone has the power to speak or listen as a representative of the nation. He *makes* treaties with the advice and consent of the Senate; but he alone negotiates. Into the field of negotiation the Senate cannot intrude; and Congress itself is powerless to invade it. As Marshall said in his great argument of March 7, 1800, in the House of Representatives, "The President is the sole organ of the nation in its external relations, and its sole representative with foreign nations." Annals, 6th Cong., col. 613. . . .

It is important to bear in mind that we are here dealing not alone with an authority vested in the President by an exertion of legislative power, but with such an authority plus the very delicate, plenary and exclusive power of the President as the sole organ of the federal government in the field of international relations—a power which does not require as a basis for its exercise an act of Congress, but which, of course, like every other governmental power, must be exercised in subordination to the applicable provisions of the Constitution. It is quite apparent that if, in the maintenance of our international relations, embarrassment—perhaps serious embarrassment—is to be avoided and success for our aims achieved, congressional legislation which is to be made effective through negotiation and inquiry within the international field must often accord to the President a degree of discretion and freedom from statutory restriction which would not be admissible were domestic affairs alone involved. Moreover, he, not Congress, has the better opportunity of knowing the conditions which prevail in foreign countries, and especially is this true in time of war. He has his confidential sources of information. He has his agents in the form of diplomatic, consular and other officials. Secrecy in respect of information gathered by them may be highly necessary, and the premature disclosure of it productive of harmful results. Indeed, so clearly is this true that the first President refused to accede to a request to lay before the House of Representatives the instructions, correspondence and documents relating to the negotiation of the Jay Treaty—a refusal the wisdom of which was recognized by the House itself and has never since been doubted. . . .

When the President is to be authorized by legislation to act in respect of a matter intended to affect a situation in foreign territory, the legislator properly bears in mind the important consideration that the form of the President's action—or, indeed, whether he shall act at all—may well depend, among other things, upon the nature of the confidential information which he has or may thereafter receive, or upon the effect which his action may have upon our foreign relations. This consideration, in connection with what we have already said on the subject, discloses the unwisdom of requiring Congress in this field of governmental power to lay down narrowly definite standards by which the President is to be governed. . . .

In the light of the foregoing observations, it is evident that this court should not be in haste to apply a general rule which will have the effect of condemning legislation like that under review as constituting an unlawful delegation of legislative power. The principles which justify such legislation find overwhelming support in the unbroken legislative practice which has prevailed almost from the inception of the national government to the present day. . . .

Practically every volume of the United States Statutes contains one or more acts or joint resolutions of Congress authorizing action by the President in respect of subjects affecting foreign relations, which either leave the exercise of the power to his unrestricted judgment, or provide a standard far more general than that which has always been considered requisite with regard to domestic affairs. . . .

The result of holding that the joint resolution here under attack is void and unenforceable as constituting an unlawful delegation of legislative power would be to stamp this multitude of comparable acts and resolutions as likewise invalid. And while this court may not, and should not, hesitate to declare acts of Congress, however many times repeated, to be unconstitutional if beyond all rational doubt it finds them to be so, an impressive array of legislation such as we have just set forth, enacted by nearly every Congress from the beginning of our national existence to the present day, must be given unusual weight in the process of reaching a correct determination of the problem. A legislative practice such as we have here, evidenced not by only occasional instances, but marked by the movement of a steady stream for a century and a half of time, goes a long way in the direction of proving the presence of unassailable ground for the constitutionality of the practice, to be found in the origin and history of the power involved, or in its nature, or in both combined. . . .

The judgment of the court below must be reversed and the cause remanded for further proceedings in accordance with the foregoing opinion.

Reversed.

The War Power

"The power to wage war," observed Charles Evans Hughes during the interval between his terms of service on the Court, "is the power to wage war successfully"; and he concluded his speech to the American Bar Association with the reminder that "we have a *fighting* constitution." Of course, Hughes spoke on September 5, 1917, shortly after the United States formally entered World War I; and we might dismiss the remark—notwithstanding the eminence of the speaker— as the hyperbole of a patriotic speech were it not for the fact that Hughes' dictum has since become the official dogma of the Supreme Court. The unmistakable trend during the period between the two world wars was to define the war power of the national government in terms of the illimitable boundaries of military necessity; and this tendency has been accentuated by the decisions since Pearl Harbor. As Mr. Justice Jackson said, in his dissent from a decision of the Court which upheld the detention of thousands of American citizens in protective custody in concentration camps for the duration of the war: [17]

A military order, however unconstitutional, is not apt to last longer than the military emergency. Even during that period a succeeding commander may revoke it all. But once a judicial opinion rationalizes such an order to show that it conforms to the Constitution, or rather rationalizes the Constitution to show that the Constitution sanctions such an order, the Court for all time has validated the principle of racial discrimination in criminal procedure and of transplanting American citizens. The principle then lies about like a loaded weapon ready for the hand of any authority that can bring forward a plausible claim of an urgent need. Every repetition imbeds that principle more deeply in our law and thinking and expands it to new purposes. All who observe the work of courts are familiar with what Judge Cardozo described as "the tendency of a principle to expand itself to the limit of its logic." A military commander may overstep the bounds of constitutionality, and it is an incident. But if we review and approve, that passing incident becomes the doctrine of the Constitution. There it has a generative power of its own, and all that it creates will be in its own image. . . .

[17] *Korematsu v. United States*, 323 U.S. 214, 248 (1944).

Of course the existence of a military power resting on force, so vagrant, so centralized, so necessarily heedless of the individual, is an inherent threat to liberty. But I would not lead people to rely on this Court for a review that seems to me wholly delusive. . . . If the people ever let command of the war power fall into irresponsible and unscrupulous hands, the courts wield no power equal to its restraint. The chief restraint upon those who command the physical forces of the country, in the future as in the past, must be their responsibility to the political judgments of their contemporaries and to the moral judgments of history.

The difficulties involved in attempts to challenge exercises of the war power are compounded by procedural technicalities. Generally speaking, this means that a person who seeks to challenge the constitutionality of acts of the President and the Congress under the war power must first violate the law, and then attempt to raise the question of constitutionality in defense to criminal prosecution, as in *Korematsu* v. *United States*. Even this approach may not be open, as the Yakus case exemplifies.[18] World War II price- and rent-control legislation could be challenged only after an administrative appeal, followed by an appeal to a special federal Court of Emergency Appeals, whose decision the Supreme Court could be asked to review by certiorari. As was the case in President Johnson's day, attempts following World War II to challenge the postwar military reconstruction (and the military trial of war criminals) by petitioning the Supreme Court for leave to file writs of habeas corpus were uniformly unsuccessful.[19] Neither has it proved possible to restrain the President, whether in his capacity as the Commander in Chief or otherwise, from proceeding "faithfully to execute" allegedly unconstitutional legislation. This was most clearly demonstrated in the unsuccessful attempt of the State of Mississippi to enjoin Andrew Johnson from carrying out a program which was described to the Supreme Court, by Mississippi's counsel, in the following terms: [20]

According to the President's own opinion, as expressed in his veto messages, the Constitution of the United States is, by the Reconstruction Acts, subverted and overthrown, and a military despotism is erected upon

18 Cf. *Yakus* v. *United States*, 321 U.S. 414 (1944), especially the dissenting opinion of Mr. Justice Rutledge.

19 See, e.g., *Everett* v. *Truman, Commander in Chief of the Armed Forces of the United States*, 334 U.S. 824 (1948); *In re Yamashita*, 327 U.S. 1 (1946); and *Hirota* v. *MacArthur*, 335 U.S. 876 (1948). Cf. the trial of Lincoln's assassins, recounted in Clinton Rossiter, *The Supreme Court and the Commander in Chief* (Ithaca: Cornell University Press, 1951), pp. 110-112. Such cases as *Ex parte Milligan*, 4 Wall. 2 (1866), and *Duncan* v. *Kahanamoku*, 327 U.S. 304 (1946), may seem to be excep-

tions to the generalization in the text, but both of these cases were postwar decisions which ruled against the trial of civilians for civil offenses by military courts during wartime; neither had the slightest effect upon the prosecution of either the Civil War or World War II. The situation would be quite different if the Court had pronounced—as it could have—the doctrine of Milligan in *Ex parte Vallandigham*, 1 Wall. 243 (1864), or the doctrine of *Duncan* v. *Kahanamoku* in *Hirabayashi* v. *United States*, 320 U.S. 81 (1943).

20 *Mississippi* v. *Johnson*, 4 Wall. 475, 497 (1867).

its ruins. Ten States are to be expelled from the Union; ten millions of people are to be deprived of all the benefits of the Constitution; deprived of the right of trial by jury. These ten States are cut up into five military districts; people are to be tried outside of their States for offences unknown and undefined, merely at the will of a military officer; deprived of the right of trial by jury; all this in time of profound peace, when Congress itself, speaking, as it has done in several acts, of "States lately in rebellion," admits that there is no rebellion in the land; deprived of their rights and privileges of American citizens. So far as constitutional liberty is concerned, they might as well be living under a Czar . . . as in this free country. Life, liberty, and property may be taken from them without due process of law.

A unanimous Court, speaking through Chief Justice Chase, ruled that the suit must be dismissed, since the Supreme Court had "no jurisdiction of a bill to enjoin the President in the performance of his official duties."

Ironically enough, the President's principal subordinate in the enforcement of the Reconstruction program, the Secretary of War, was not following the orders of his Commander in Chief at this time, receiving his directions instead from congressional committees; but no matter, it was no more possible to enjoin the Secretary of War than the Commander in Chief, as *Georgia* v. *Stanton,* 6 Wall. 50 (1868), soon demonstrated.

The lower courts have taken their cue from the Supreme Court, which in more recent decades has conceptualized the fusion of the power of Congress, to declare war formally, with the status of the President as the Commander in Chief of the Armed Forces. The result of this merger has been to make the principle of separation of powers largely irrelevant; to the extent that the Court does not know and cannot tell which quantum of the war power constitutionally inheres in the Congress, and which quantum is constitutionally invested in the President, either the Congress or the President may individually or conjointly exercise any authority attributable to the United States as a "sovereign state" at war, or more broadly, *not* at peace. To an increasing extent, the Court has also come to consider "war" to be synonymous with "national emergency"—the Steel Seizure case being an obvious and important exception. There has been a continuous presidentially declared national emergency (of one sort or another) for over two decades beginning on September 8, 1939. In the words of a federal district judge,[21]

It is to be noted with emphasis that the matter of a national emergency is, and always has been, left to the judgment of the President. This has been expressly and repeatedly confirmed in many statutes giving the President varied powers whenever in his judgment a National Emergency exists. . . . In these statutes . . . the following phrases are used synonymously, "During the existence of war or of a national emergency"; "During time of war or

[21] *Brown* v. *Bernstein,* 49 F.Supp. 728, 731-732 (M.D.Pa., 1943).

during any other period of national emergency"; "In time of war or threatened war"; "In time of war or when the President shall so direct."

The various Acts of Congress authorizing the President to take action
in the event of a National Emergency show that congress throughout the
years made little or no distinction between a State of National Emergency
and a State of War.

The result of the coalescence of the powers of the President with those of
Congress to create the hybrid "war power," in combination with the blurring by
the Court of the distinction between war and peace, is to make the "fighting Constitution" always potentially available to support the exigencies of the indeterminate national emergency. There may be limits when the President and Congress
disagree, as the Steel Seizure case demonstrates, but what may be the limits when
the Executive and the Legislature join forces is impredictable and uncertain.
The virtual abdication of the Court from the adverse exercise of judicial review
in this area of constitutional policy has been well summarized by a leading
student of the Presidency, Clinton Rossiter:

The Supreme Court and the Commander in Chief [22]

. . . [The] Court . . . has fixed neither the outer boundaries nor the inner
divisions of the President's martial authority, and has failed completely to
draw the line between his powers and those of Congress . . . [and] the Court's
estimate of its ability to intervene in an improper exercise of the war powers
has been one thing at one time, another at another. Often in one period, or
even in one case, its attitude has been quite ambivalent. Counsel for injured
interests can always quote an overpowering and apparently conclusive array
of decisions and dicta proving that the Court will actively defend the Constitution against the havoc of war; but the government's lawyers can come
right back with an equally impressive array, plucked in many instances from
the very same cases, proving the incapacity of the Court to put a bridle on the
war powers. Of course, by now almost all great constitutional problems have
respectable lines of precedents on both sides, as the present Court reminds
us repeatedly with its split decisions. Yet in this area of the war powers it is
particularly striking how unsure the Court has been about its real or nominal
authority to substitute its judgment for that of Congress, the President, or
his military subordinates. . . . [Moreover, the Court's] preference for statutory over constitutional authority actually works to the President's advantage, for the merger of his military powers with those of Congress
produces something known simply but grandly as "the war powers of the
United States," under which just about any presidential wartime action can be
brought within the limits of the Constitution. Both President and Congress
have constitutional powers of their own in military and foreign affairs;

[22] Rossiter, *op. cit.* (footnote 19, *supra*), pp. 5-7, 126-131.

when these powers are merged they are virtually irresistible, at least in the courts. . . .

The total performance of the Court in and after our three great wars leads to these observations concerning judicial review and control of the President's actions as commander in chief:

First . . . the Court has been asked to examine only a tiny fraction of his significant deeds and decisions as commander in chief. . . .

Second . . . The Army and the government lawyers apparently have no scruples about staving off an unpredictable judicial pronouncement, for we know that they will release interned prisoners and hand back seized factories the day before attorneys for these injured interests are to begin arguments in Washington. The Court in its turn will gladly agree that the case is moot, or it will seize with relief upon a technicality preventing it from taking jurisdiction, or, if forced to speak, it will decide the issue on the narrowest possible grounds. . . .

Third, whatever limits the Court has set upon the employment of the war powers have been largely theoretical, rarely practical. . . . Lincoln . . . and Roosevelt . . . were long dead, Wilson but three days from the end of his term, when the great limiting decision of each one's particular war was announced by a stern-visaged Court. . . .

Fourth . . . [there is a] predictable pattern of wartime judicial review . . . all pointing to *power*. . . . *Post bellum* we will hear about *limitations*. . . . There do indeed seem to be two Constitutions—one for peace, the other for war.

Fifth, the Court has had little success in preventing the precedents of war from becoming precedents of peace. . . . [The] Court has made a positive contribution to the permanent peacetime weakening of the separation of powers, the principle of non-delegation, the Fifth Amendment, and the necessary and proper clause as applicable limits to governmental power. . . .

Sixth . . . Increasingly the justices are speaking and interpreting in terms of "the *fighting* Constitution." . . .

Seventh . . . The "allowable limits of military discretion" that the Court will tolerate are those that a reasonable man would have determined in the circumstances. . . . This, of course, is a formula of practically no value for judicial review of executive-military action. . . .

Finally . . . As in the past, so in the future, President and Congress will fight our wars with little or no thought about a reckoning with the Supreme Court.

III

THE NATION
AND THE STATES

I N PART II, we examined the role of the Supreme Court as an arbiter in certain cases of real or supposed conflict between the Congress and the Presidency, and between either or both of the so-called "political branches" of the national government and the Court itself. We examined some of the consequences, both for the effective and responsible making of national policy and for the Court's survival as an institution, of the assumption by the justices of an activist role as national policy-makers. The materials presented strongly suggest that the Court is in no position to dictate the terms and conditions of interaction among the major organizational subdivisions of the national government. But the Court can and does function as a major factor in the realignment and readjustment of governmental agencies and governmental policies to fundamental shifts in the direction and in the intensity of political forces in American society. It is in this sense that the Supreme Court confirms the Dooley dictum that "th' supreme coort follows th' iliction returns." [1]

As an arbiter between the national and the state governments, however, the Supreme Court has played a much more pre-eminent role, and particularly during the last hundred years since the Civil War settled the political question of the ultimate enforceability upon the states of national policy. There are essentially two reasons for this. The structure of the American political-party system, in relationship to the Electoral College and to the internal organization and rules of procedure of the Congress, is such that the President and the Congress (and particularly the latter) are generally impotent to take an effective stand against the disparate, parochial interests that control them—except in periods of national crisis. There is therefore what Charles A. Beard once termed a "sphere of anarchy," or to use Roche's phrase, a "political vacuum," into which the Court has the capability of moving precisely because the justices are not directly and personally accountable at the hustings for their decisions. The Court's political irresponsibility is thus a major source of its political power. (This does not speak to the enforceability of decisions resting only on the Court's authority; we are referring at the moment only to the capacity to make and to announce the formal decisions.)

The second reason is that the Court is an agency of the *national* government. It is true that variation in the attitudes of the individual justices, or of the dominant majority among them, has been considerable; a nationalist like Marshall has been followed by a states' rightist like Taney, or a nationalist like Black has sat as a colleague of a decentralizationist like Frankfurter. But whatever the variation at any particular time, the general, the over-all, the long-range impact of

[1] Peter Finley Dunne, "The Supreme Court's Decisions" in *Mr. Dooley's Opinions* (New York: Russell, 1901), p. 26.

the decisions of the Court affecting national-state conflict clearly has been pro-national. This is seen most clearly by contrasting the decisions of the Supreme Court, at any given time, with corresponding decisions emanating from the highest courts of the states. Although this is by no means either a sufficient or a complete explanation, one reason has been the fact that the organizational and institutional loyalties of Supreme Court justices have been national in their orientation, more so than those of the lower federal judiciary (generally speaking), and certainly more so than those of the state judiciaries. In an oft-quoted statement, a Civil War veteran and former state judge remarked, after several years of experience on the Supreme Court: [2]

> I do not think the United States would come to an end if we lost our power to declare an Act of Congress void. I do think the Union would be imperiled if we could not make that declaration as to the laws of the several States. For one in my place sees how often a local policy prevails with those who are not trained to national views and how often action is taken that embodies what the Commerce Clause was meant to end.

In Part III of this volume, we shall examine three major areas in which the Supreme Court has functioned, if not as "the sole organ of the nation," at least as the principal agency for national policy-making in the adjustment of actual or potential conflict between the interests of nationally organized groups and those who have been successful in establishing their policies within single states or groups of states. These next three chapters deal with the Court's own policy-making vis-à-vis the regulation of commerce by both the national and state governments; primarily state legislation regulating economic enterprise; and both national and state action relating to the race problem in the United States.

[2] Oliver Wendell Holmes, *Collected Legal Papers* (New York: Harcourt, 1920), pp. 295-296.

7

The Regulation of Commerce

THERE CAN BE NO DOUBT that one of the primary objects of the sponsors of the Constitution of the United States was to eliminate state interference with trade and commercial intercourse, as between one state and another and as between any state and foreign countries. Indeed, the interference of Great Britain with the trade of the colonies had been perhaps the most important factor leading to and precipitating the Revolutionary War. The intent of the framers is reflected in the explicit language of the Constitution, which specifically authorizes national regulation of commerce. Although there are other relevant provisions, the three clauses of the Constitution most germane to the discussion in this chapter, which happen also to be the most important clauses, are:

The Commerce Clause (Article I, Section 8, Clause 3):
The Congress shall have power . . . To regulate Commerce with foreign Nations, and among the several States, and with the Indian Tribes.

The Elastic Clause (Article I, Section 8, Clause 18):
The Congress shall have power . . . To make all Laws which shall be necessary and proper for carrying into Execution the foregoing Powers.

The Supremacy Clause (Article VI, Section 2):
This Constitution, and the Laws of the United States which shall be made in Pursuance thereof . . . shall be the Supreme Law of the Land; and the Judges in every State shall be bound thereby, any Thing in the Constitution or Laws of any State to the Contrary notwithstanding.

The cases which we shall examine in this chapter deal with two broad questions: (1) the commerce clause in combination with the supremacy clause as a *limitation* upon the reserved powers of the states; and (2) the commerce clause in combination with the elastic clause as a *source* of national regulatory power over economic enterprise. Our objective in presenting these six cases, selected out of the hundreds of commerce-clause decisions of the Supreme Court, is to focus attention upon the critical significance of the Court's function as a policy-maker in this key area where the relationships between state and nation, and between free enterprise and positive government, are inextricably fused. Our purpose is not, most assuredly, to present an exegesis on the Law of the Commerce Clause. As the late and great Harvard professor of constitutional law, Thomas Reed Powell, is reputed to have remarked, it is not difficult to summarize that law. According to Paul A. Freund,[1] Professor Powell suggested the following Restatement (as such summaries are called in legal jargon) of the commerce clause:

CONGRESS MAY REGULATE INTERSTATE COMMERCE. *The states may also regulate interstate commerce, but not too much.* (How much is too much is beyond the scope of this Restatement.)

We shall be concerned only with the Court's making of constitutional policy relating to commerce "among the several States." The Court has generally considered that the regulation of foreign commerce raises questions that are intimately related to the conduct of foreign affairs, which in turn has induced the Court to use great restraint in interfering with such political judgments of the President and the Congress, as we observed in Chapter 6. Contrary to the historic trends of legislative activity of the national and state governments relating to interstate commerce, the national government has always assumed primary responsibility for the regulation of foreign commerce, and state regulation of foreign commerce has usually been the incidental effect of legislation adopted for other purposes (such as raising revenue, health and safety inspection, etc.). Questions of state regulation of foreign commerce have not assumed great importance in the work of the Court; and when they have arisen, they have generally been disposed of by the invocation of the commerce and supremacy clauses.[2] Similarly, the regulation of trade with the Indian tribes was of importance primarily in the national territories as the frontier receded to the West; the states were in no position to exercise effective control over commerce that generally took place outside of the territorial jurisdiction of any state; and the

---

1 Professor Freund tells the story in his Foreword to Powell's posthumously published Carpentier Lectures, *Vagaries and Varieties in Constitutional Interpretation* (New York: Columbia University Press, 1956),

p. ix.

2 E.g., *Brown* v. *Maryland*, 12 Wheaton 419 (1827); for a modern exception, see *Bob-Lo Excursion Co.* v. *Michigan*, 333 U.S. 28 (1947).

problems of civil-military relationships posed by national regulation of the Indian trade are today of only historic significance.

STATE CONTROL OVER INTERSTATE COMMERCE

The Court's first opinion interpreting the commerce clause was one of the few really popular decisions, at least among his contemporaries, delivered by John Marshall. The problem to which it related was by no means confined to the single steamship route between Elizabethtown, New Jersey, and New York City. According to Swisher, "At the time of the decision, the controversies between the several states over the control of steamboat navigation had provoked hostility similar to that which prevailed prior to the adoption of the Constitution." [3] The direct consequence of this political controversy was the decision below and the first opinion of the Court to interpret the commerce clause.

GIBBONS v. OGDEN

9 Wheaton 1 (February Term, 1824)

Error to the Court for the Trial of Impeachments and Correction of Errors of the State of New York.

Reversed.

	6-0
Marshall, C.J.	('+')
Washington	(+)
Todd	(+)
Duvall	(+)
Story	(+)
Johnson	('+'
Thompson	NP

The invention of Robert Fulton's steamboat had been spurred by an offer from the New York legislature, twice renewed, of exclusive navigation rights on New York territorial waters if he and his partner, Livingston, were successful. Once the commercial feasibility of the invention was established, however, rivals who were

[3] Carl Brent Swisher, *American Constitutional Development* (Boston: Houghton, 1943 ed.), p. 193.

not licensed by Fulton and Livingston sought to establish interstate routes in competition with licensees such as Aaron Ogden, the respondent in this case.

Daniel Webster, who argued Gibbons' cause before the Supreme Court, urged that the commerce clause be interpreted as having established a constitutional policy of exclusive national jurisdiction over interstate commerce. This was good Federalist doctrine, but such a ruling would certainly have antagonized the Democrats; and it is ironic that the only justice to accept this argument was William Johnson, Jefferson's first appointee to the Court. New York's Chancellor Kent, on the other hand, had ruled in the trial court that the states exercised exclusive jurisdiction over their own territorial waters and internal commerce, and counsel for Ogden asserted before the Court that the states retained concurrent jurisdiction over interstate commerce, which was limited to the exchange of commodities and did not include navigation (i.e., the instrumentalities by means of which commerce was carried on.)

Marshall could have accepted Webster's argument and disposed of the case by ruling that the New York state statute granting the steamboat monopoly was in direct conflict with the commerce clause itself—this was Johnson's position in concurrence. Such a ruling would have denied any power to the states to regulate interstate commerce. Instead, Marshall chose to steer a middle course, and base the decision of the Court on the conflict between the state statute and a federal statute, thus making the supremacy clause decisive of the issue. And thus Marshall laid the cornerstone for the process of compromise that has characterized commerce-clause decisions from his day to our own. National regulation of interstate commerce, to the extent that it was established by positive enactments of Congress, was to be upheld over conflicting state regulation; but left open was the question whether states could regulate interstate commerce in the absence of a positive national policy. Neither did Marshall purport to decide whether the New York statute, which logically should have been held valid if there had been no conflicting act of Congress, was based upon the general powers reserved to the states under the Tenth Amendment (i.e., the "police power") or a concurrent state power to regulate interstate commerce (implied from the states' reserved power to regulate intrastate commerce). Having disposed of the case on the basis of the commerce and supremacy clauses, Marshall announced that it was unnecessary for the Court to consider appellant Gibbons' other claim, that the New York "patent" also was in conflict with the exclusive authority of the Congress to grant patents and copyrights (I, 8:8).

Aaron Ogden filed his bill in the court of chancery of [New York], against Thomas Gibbons, setting forth the several acts of the legislature thereof, enacted for the purpose of securing to Robert R. Livingston and Robert Fulton, the exclusive navigation of all the waters within the jurisdiction of that State, with boats moved by fire or steam, for a term of years which has not yet expired; and authorizing the chancellor to award an injunction, restraining any person whatever from navigating those waters with boats of that description. The bill stated an assignment from Livingston and Fulton to one John R. Livingston, and from him to the complainant, Ogden, of the right to navigate the waters between Elizabethtown, and other places in New Jersey, and the city of New York; and that Gibbons, the defendant below, was in possession of two steamboats, called The Stoudinger and The Bellona, which were actually employed in running between New York and Elizabethtown, in violation of the exclusive privilege conferred on the complainant, and praying an injunction to restrain the said Gibbons from using the said boats, or any other propelled by fire or steam, in navigating the waters within the territory of New York. The injunction having been awarded, the answer of Gibbons was filed, in which he stated that the boats employed by him were duly enrolled and licensed, to be employed in carrying on the coasting trade, under the act of congress, passed the 18th of February, 1793, c. 8, (1 Stats. at Large, 305,) entitled, "An act for enrolling and licensing ships and vessels to be employed in the coasting trade and fisheries, and for regulating the same." And the defendant insisted on his right, in virtue of such licenses, to navigate the waters between Elizabethtown and the city of New York, the said acts of the legislature of the State of New York to the contrary notwithstanding. At the hearing, the chancellor perpetuated the injunction, being of the opinion that the said acts were not repugnant to the constitution and laws of the United States, and were valid. This decree was affirmed in the court for the trial of impeachments and correction of errors, which is the highest court of law and equity in the State, before which the cause could be carried, and it was thereupon brought to this court by writ of error.

MARSHALL, C. J., delivered the opinion of the court, and, after stating the case, proceeded as follows:—

The appellant contends that this decree is erroneous, because the laws which purport to give the exclusive privilege it sustains, are repugnant to the constitution and laws of the United States.

They are said to be repugnant—

1. To that clause in the constitution which authorizes congress to regulate commerce. . . .

The State of New York maintains the constitutionality of these laws; and their legislature, their council of revision, and their judges, have repeatedly concurred in this opinion. It is supported by great names—by names which have all the titles to consideration that virtue, intelligence, and office, can bestow. No tribunal can approach the decision of this question, without feeling a just and real respect for that opinion which is sustained by such authority; but it is the province of this court, while it respects, not to bow to it implicitly; and the judges must exercise, in the examination of the subject, that understanding which Providence has bestowed upon them, with that independence which the people of the United States expect from this department of the government.

As preliminary to the very able discussions of the constitution which we have heard from the bar, and as having some influence on its construction, reference has been made to the political situation of these states, anterior to its formation. It has been said that they were sovereign, were completely independent, and were connected with each other only by a league. This is true. But, when these allied sovereigns converted their league into a government, when they converted their congress of ambassadors, deputed to deliberate on their common concerns, and to recommend measures of general utility, into a legislature, empowered to enact laws on the most interesting subjects, the whole character in which the States appear underwent a change, the extent of which must be determined by a fair consideration of the instrument by which that change was effected.

This instrument contains an enumeration of powers expressly granted by the people to their government. . . . We know of no rule for construing the extent of such powers, other than is given by the language of the instrument which confers them, taken in connection with the purposes for which they were conferred. . . .

The word used in the constitution . . . comprehends, and has been always understood to comprehend, navigation, within its meaning; and a power to regulate navigation is as expressly granted as if that term had been added to the word "commerce."

To what commerce does this power extend? The constitution informs us, to commerce "with foreign nations, and among the several States, and with the Indian tribes." . . .

Comprehensive as the word "among" is, it may very properly be restricted to that commerce which concerns more States than one. The phrase is not one which would probably have been selected to indicate the completely interior traffic of a State, because it is not an apt phrase for that purpose; and the enumeration of the particular classes of commerce to which the power was to be extended, would not have been made, had the intention been to extend the power to every description. The enumeration presupposes something not enumerated; and that something, if we regard the language, or the subject of the sentence, must be the exclusively internal commerce of a State. The genius and character of the whole government seem to be, that its action is to be applied to all the external concerns of the nation, and to those internal concerns which affect the States generally; but not to those which are completely within a particular State, which do not affect other States, and with which it is not necessary to interfere, for the purpose of executing some of the general powers of the government. The completely internal commerce of a State, then, may be considered as reserved for the State itself.

But, in regulating commerce with foreign nations, the power of congress does not stop at the jurisdictional lines of the several States. It would be a very useless power, if it could not pass those lines. The commerce of the United States with foreign nations, is that of the whole United States. Every district has a right to participate in it. The deep streams which penetrate our country in every direction, pass through the interior of almost every State in the Union, and furnish the means of exercising this right. If congress has the power to regulate it, that power must be exercised whenever the subject exists. If it exists within the States, if a foreign voyage may commence or terminate at a port within a State, then the power of congress may be exercised within a State.

This principle is, if possible, still more clear, when applied to commerce "among the several States." . . .

We are now arrived at the inquiry—what is this power?

It is the power to regulate; that is, to prescribe the rule by which commerce is to be governed. This power, like all others vested in congress, is complete in itself, may be exercised to its utmost extent, and acknowledges no limitations other than are prescribed in the constitution. These are expressed in plain terms, and do not affect the questions which arise in this case, or which have been discussed at the bar. If, as has always been understood, the sovereignty of congress, though limited to specified objects, is plenary as to those objects, the power over commerce with foreign nations, and among the several States, is vested in congress as absolutely as it would be in a single govern-

ment, having in its constitution the same restrictions on the exercise of the power as are found in the constitution of the United States. The wisdom and the discretion of congress, their identity with the people, and the influence which their constituents possess at elections, are, in this, as in many other instances, as that, for example, of declaring war, the sole restraints on which they have relied, to secure them from its abuse. They are the restraints on which the people must often rely solely, in all representative governments.

The power of congress, then, comprehends navigation within the limits of every State in the Union, so far as that navigation may be, in any manner, connected with "commerce with foreign nations, or among the several States, or with the Indian tribes." It may, of consequence, pass the jurisdictional line of New York, and act upon the very waters to which the prohibition now under consideration applies. . . .

That inspection laws may have a remote and considerable influence on commerce will not be denied; but that a power to regulate commerce is the source from which the right to pass them is derived, cannot be admitted. The object of inspection laws is to improve the quality of articles produced by the labor of a country; to fit them for exportation; or it may be, for domestic use. They act upon the subject before it becomes an article of foreign commerce, or of commerce among the States, and prepare it for that purpose. They form a portion of that immense mass of legislation, which embraces every thing within the territory of a State, not surrendered to a general government; all which can be most advantageously exercised by the States themselves. Inspection laws, quarantine laws, health laws of every description, as well as laws for regulating the internal commerce of a State, and those which respect turnpike roads, ferries, &c., are component parts of this mass.

No direct general power over these objects is granted to congress; and, consequently, they remain subject to state legislation. If the legislative power of the Union can reach them, it must be for national purposes; it must be where the power is expressly given for a special purpose, or is clearly incidental to some power which is expressly given. It is obvious that the government of the Union, in the exercise of its express powers, that, for example, of regulating commerce with foreign nations and among the States, may use means that may also be employed by a State, in the exercise of its acknowledged powers; that, for example, of regulating commerce within the State. . . .

In our complex system, presenting the rare and difficult scheme of one general government, whose action extends over the whole, but which possesses only certain enumerated powers; and of numerous state governments, which retain and exercise all powers not delegated to the Union, contests respecting power must arise. Were it even otherwise, the measures taken by the respective governments to execute their acknowledged powers, would often be of the same description, and might, sometimes, interfere. This, however, does not prove that the one is exercising, or has a right to exercise, the powers of the other. . . .

Since, however, in exercising the power of regulating their own purely internal affairs, whether of trading or police, the States may sometimes enact laws, the validity of which depends on their interfering with, and being contrary to, an act of congress passed in pursuance of the constitution, the court will enter upon the inquiry, whether the laws of New York, as expounded by the highest tribunal of that State, have, in their application to this case, come into collision with an act of congress, and deprived a citizen of a right to which that act entitles him. Should this collision exist, it will be im-

material whether those laws were passed in virtue of a concurrent power "to regulate commerce with foreign nations and among the several States," or, in virtue of a power to regulate their domestic trade and police. In one case and the other, the acts of New York must yield to the law of congress; and the decision sustaining the privilege they confer, against a right given by a law of the Union, must be erroneous.

This opinion has been frequently expressed in this court, and is founded as well on the nature of the government as on the words of the constitution. In argument, however, it has been contended that, if a law passed by a State, in the exercise of its acknowledged sovereignty, comes into conflict with a law passed by congress in pursuance of the constitution, they affect the subject, and each other, like equal opposing powers.

But the framers of our constitution foresaw this state of things, and provided for it by declaring the supremacy not only of itself, but of the laws made in pursuance of it. The nullity of any act, inconsistent with the constitution, is produced by the declaration that the constitution is the supreme law. The appropriate application of that part of the clause which confers the same supremacy on laws and treaties, is to such acts of the state legislatures as do not transcend their powers, but, though enacted in the execution of acknowledged state powers, interfere with, or are contrary to the laws of congress, made in pursuance of the constitution, or some treaty made under the authority of the United States. In every such case, the act of congress, or the treaty, is supreme; and the law of the State, though enacted in the exercise of powers not controverted, must yield to it.

In pursuing this inquiry at the bar, it has been said that the constitution does not confer the right of intercourse between State and State. That right derives its source from those laws whose authority is acknowledged by civilized man through-out the world. This is true. The constitution found it an existing right, and gave to congress the power to regulate it. In the exercise of this power, congress passed "an act for enrolling or licensing ships or vessels to be employed in the coasting trade and fisheries, and for regulating the same." The counsel for the respondent contend, that this act does not give the right to sail from port to port, but confines itself to regulating a preëxisting right, so far only as to confer certain privileges on enrolled and licensed vessels, in its exercise.

. . . [But to] the court it seems very clear that the whole act on the subject of the coasting trade, according to those principles which govern the construction of statutes, implies, unequivocally, an authority to licensed vessels to carry on the coasting trade. . . .

The real and sole question seems to be, whether a steam machine, in actual use, deprives a vessel of the privileges conferred by a license. . . .

But all inquiry into this subject seems to the court to be put completely at rest, by the act already mentioned, entitled, "An act for the enrolling and licensing of steam-boats." . . .

This act demonstrates the opinion of congress, that steam-boats may be enrolled and licensed, in common with vessels using sails. They are, of course, entitled to the same privileges, and can no more be restrained from navigating waters, and entering ports which are free to such vessels, than if they were wafted on their voyage by the winds, instead of being propelled by the agency of fire. The one element may be as legitimately used as the other, for every commercial purpose authorized by the laws of the Union; and the act of a State inhibiting the use of either to any vessel having a license under the act of congress, comes, we think, in direct collision with that act. . . .

Reversed.

JOHNSON, J. The judgment entered by the court in this cause, has my entire approbation; but having adopted my conclusions on views of the subject materially different from those of my brethren, I feel it incumbent on me to exhibit those views. I have, also, another inducement; in questions of great importance and great delicacy, I feel my duty to the public best discharged, by an attempt to maintain my opinions in my own way. . . .[4]

It is impossible, with the views which I entertain of the principle on which the commercial privileges of the people of the United States among themselves rests, to concur in the view which this court takes of the effect of the coasting license in this cause. I do not regard it as the foundation of the right set up in behalf of the appellant. If there was any one object riding over every other in the adoption of the constitution, it was to keep the commercial intercourse among the States free from all invidious and partial restraints. And I cannot overcome the conviction, that if the licensing act was repealed to-morrow, the rights of the appellant to a reversal of the decision complained of, would be as strong as it is under this license. One half the doubts in life arise from the defects of language; and if this instrument had been called an exemption instead of a license, it would have given a better idea of its character. Licensing acts, in fact, in legislation, are universally restraining acts; as, for example, acts licensing gaming houses, retailers of spirituous liquors, &c. The act, in this instance, is distinctly of that character, and forms part of an extensive system, the object of which is to encourage American shipping, and place them on an equal footing with the shipping of other nations. Almost every commercial nation reserves to its own subjects a monopoly of its coasting trade; and a countervailing

4 Cf. Donald G. Morgan, *Justice William Johnson, The First Dissenter* (Columbia: University of South Carolina Press, 1954), Chap. x: "The Origin of Dissent."

privilege in favor of American shipping is contemplated in the whole legislation of the United States on this subject. It is not to give the vessel an American character, that the license is granted; that effect has been correctly attributed to the act of her enrolment. But it is to confer on her American privileges, as contradistinguished from foreign; and to preserve the government from fraud by foreigners, in surreptitiously intruding themselves into the American commercial marine, as well as frauds upon the revenue in the trade coastwise, that this whole system is projected. Many duties and formalities are necessarily imposed upon the American foreign commerce, which would be burdensome in the active coasting trade of the States, and can be dispensed with. A higher rate of tonnage also is imposed, and this license entitles the vessels that take it to those exemptions, but to nothing more. . . . I consider the license, therefore, as nothing more than what it purports to be, according to the 1st section of this act, conferring on the licensed vessel certain privileges in that trade, not conferred on other vessels; but the abstract right of commercial intercourse, stripped of those privileges, is common to all.

The next commerce case to reach the Court was *Brown* v. *Maryland,* 12 Wheaton 419 (1827), which was concerned with state taxation of foreign commerce, and was disposed of primarily on the basis of the explicit constitutional prohibition of state impost duties (I, 10:2). But two years later, Marshall announced the unanimous opinion of the Court in *Willson* v. *Blackbird Creek Marsh Company,* 2 Peters 245 (1829), upholding a state statute even though it was in seeming conflict with the identical act of Congress that had been held decisive in *Gibbons* v. *Ogden.* An act of the New Jersey legislature had authorized the construction of a dam by the plaintiff company, for the purpose of draining the marsh. Although the reclaimed land would have enhanced commercial value, draining the swamp also subserved the public health. The defendant, who held a coasting license under the act of Congress of 1789, had smashed his sloop through the dam in order to continue navigation of the stream. As in *Gibbons* v. *Ogden,* Marshall's decision in *Willson* v. *Blackbird Creek Marsh Company,* appears to have been the "just" result that was in the public interest; but in order to reach it, he had to ignore Willson's license and treat the case as though there were no conflict with the federal statute. Once having done this, Marshall was able to rule that there was no conflict between the New Jersey act and the commerce clause, since the state statute was based on the state's "police power" rather than upon a concurrent power to regulate interstate commerce.

Thus, one of the two major questions left open by *Gibbons* v. *Ogden* was resolved, at least for the time being. The other undecided question, which Marshall managed to avoid throughout his long tenure on the Court, was whether the states could exercise concurrent power to regulate interstate commerce if there was no conflicting national policy. This was the question decided by the Court in the Cooley case.

COOLEY v. BOARD OF WARDENS OF PORT OF PHILADELPHIA

12 Howard 299 (1851)

Error to the Supreme Court of Pennsylvania

Affirmed.

7-2

Curtis	('+')
Taney, C.J.	(+)
Catron	(+)
McKinley	(+)
Nelson	(+)
Grier	(+)
Daniel	('+'
McLean	'—')
Wayne	—)

In the Cooley case, the relevant act of Congress, far from conflicting with the state legislation, had expressly authorized the states to continue in effect their pre-existing regulations of the pilots who guided vessels through the local waterways of the nation's seaports. Otherwise, there was no national regulation of pilotage, even though sixty years had elapsed since the enactment of the first Congress delegating such authority to the states. Under these circumstances, it was certainly reasonable for the Court to uphold the local pilotage regulations, many of which antedated the Constitution itself, since Congress had expressly acquiesced in this system and there was no alternative policy for national regulation. And as Marshall had done before, the Court chose to avoid the extremes of inherent and independent state power (argued by Daniel's concurrence) and of exclusive national power over commerce (stated by the McLean dissent, in the tradition of William Johnson and Daniel Webster). Mediating these absolutist arguments, the Court defined a verbal formula which could be used in the future either to accept or to reject state claims of concurrent power to regulate interstate commerce, depending upon the facts in particular cases. Subjects (like pilotage) that related to local problems of interstate or foreign commerce could be regulated by the states, in the absence of a contradictory national policy; if the subject were of such a nature as to require national regulation, or if there were conflict between national and state policies, then state regulation would be invalid. It would be up to the Supreme Court, of course, to decide which subjects were "local" and which were "national" in character; and thus armed with the policy of national supremacy (established in Gibbons) and the policy of selective state regulation (established in Cooley), the Court was prepared to undertake the arbitration of the conflict between the public policies of the states and the claims to freedom of enterprise (including the "freedom of commerce") of an emergent capitalism in a country whose industrial revolution was almost at hand.

CURTIS, J., delivered the opinion of the court.

These cases are brought here by writs of error to the supreme court of the commonwealth of Pennsylvania.

They are actions to recover half-pilotage fees under the 29th section of the act of the legislature of Pennsylvania, passed on the second day of March, 1803. The plaintiff in error alleges that the highest court of the State has decided against a right claimed by him under the constitution of the United States. That right is, to be exempted from the payment of the sums of money, demanded pursuant to the state law above referred to, because that law contravenes several provisions of the constitution of the United States. . . .

That the power to regulate commerce includes the regulation of navigation, we consider settled. And when we look to the nature of the service performed by pilots, to the relations which that service and its compensations bear to navigation between the several States, and between the ports of the United States and foreign countries, we are brought to the conclusion, that the regulation of the qualifications of pilots, of the modes and times of offering and rendering their services, of the responsibilities which shall rest upon them, of the powers they shall possess, of the compensation they may demand, and of the penalties by which their rights and duties may be enforced, do constitute regulations of navigation, and consequently of commerce, within the just meaning of this clause of the constitution. . . .

Now, a pilot, so far as respects the navigation of the vessel in that part of the voyage which is his pilotage-ground, is the temporary master charged with the safety of the vessel and cargo, and of the lives of those on board, and intrusted with the command of the crew. He is not only one of the persons engaged in navigation, but he occupies a most important and responsible place among those thus engaged. And if congress has power to regulate the seamen who assist the pilot in the management of the vessel, a power never denied, we can perceive no valid reason why the pilot should be beyond the reach of the same power. It is true that, according to the usages of modern commerce on the ocean, the pilot is on board only during a part of the voyage between ports of different States, or between ports of the United States and foreign countries; but if he is on board for such a purpose and during so much of the voyage as to be engaged in navigation, the power to regulate navigation extends to him while thus engaged, as clearly as it would if he were to remain on board throughout the whole passage, from port to port. For it is a power which extends to every part of the voyage, and may regulate those who conduct or assist in conducting navigation in one part of a voyage as much as in another part, or during the whole voyage.

Nor should it be lost sight of, that this subject of the regulation of pilots and pilotage has an intimate connection with, and an important relation to, the general subject of commerce with foreign nations and among the several States, over which it was one main object of the constitution to create a national control. Conflicts between the laws of neighboring States, and discriminations favorable or adverse to commerce with particular foreign nations, might be created by state laws regulating pilotage, deeply affecting that equality of commercial rights, and that freedom from state interference, which those who formed the constitution were so anxious to secure, and which the experience of more than half a century has taught us to value so highly. The apprehension of this danger is not speculative merely. For, in 1837, congress actually interposed to relieve the commerce of the country from serious embarrassment, arising from the laws of different States, situate upon waters which are the boundary between them. This was done by an enactment of the 2d of March, 1837, in the following words:—

"Be it enacted, that it shall and may be lawful for the master or commander of any vessel coming into or going out of any port situate upon waters which are the boundary between two States, to employ any pilot duly licensed or authorized by the laws of either of the States bounded on the said waters, to pilot said vessel to or from said port, any law, usage, or custom to the contrary notwithstanding."

The act of 1789, 1 Stats. at Large, 54 . . . contains a clear legislative exposition of the constitution by the first congress, to the effect that the power to regulate pilots was conferred on congress by the constitution; as does also the act of March the 2d, 1837, the terms of which have just been given. . . . And a majority of the court are of opinion, that a regulation of pilots is a regulation of commerce, within the grant to congress of the commercial power, contained in the third clause of the eighth section of the first article of the constitution.

It becomes necessary, therefore, to consider whether this law of Pennsylvania, being a regulation of commerce, is valid.

. . . If it were conceded on the one side, that the nature of this power, like that to legislate for the District of Columbia, is absolutely and totally repugnant to the existence of similar power in the States, probably no one would deny that the grant of the power to congress, as effectually and perfectly excludes the States from all future legislation on the subject, as if express words had been used to exclude them. And on the other hand, if it were admitted that the existence of this power in congress, like the power of taxation, is compatible with the existence of a similar power in the States, then it would be in conformity with the contemporary exposition of the constitution, (Federalist, No. 32,) and with the judicial construction, given from time to time by this court, after the most deliberate consideration, to hold that the mere grant of such a power to congress, did not imply a prohibition on the States to exercise the same power; that it is not the mere existence of such a power, but its exercise by congress, which may be incompatible with the exercise of the same power by the States, and that the States may legislate in the absence of congressional regulations. Sturges *v.* Crowninshield, 4 Wheat. 193; Houston *v.* Moore, 5 Wheat. 1; Wilson [sic: Willson] *v.* Blackbird Creek Co. 2 Pet. 251.

. . . Now, the power to regulate commerce, embraces a vast field, containing not only many, but exceedingly various subjects, quite unlike in their nature; some imperatively demanding a single uniform rule, operating equally on the commerce of the United States in every port; and some, like the subject now in question, as imperatively demanding that diversity, which alone can meet the local necessities of navigation.

Either absolutely to affirm, or deny that the nature of this power requires exclusive legislation by congress, is to lose sight of the nature of the subjects of this power, and to assert concerning all of them, what is really applicable but to a part. Whatever subjects of this power are in their nature national, or admit only of one uniform system, a plan of regulation, may justly be said to be of such a nature as to require exclusive legislation by congress. That this cannot be affirmed of laws for the regulation of pilots and pilotage, is plain. The act of 1789 contains a clear and authoritative declaration by the first congress, that the nature of this subject is such, that until congress should find it necessary to exert its power, it should be left to the legislation of the States; that it is local and not national; that it is likely to be the best provided for, not by one system, or plan of regulations, but by as many as the legislative discretion of the several States should deem applicable to the local peculiarities of the ports within their limits. . . .

It is the opinion of a majority of the court that the mere grant to congress of the power to regulate commerce, did not deprive the States of power to regulate pilots, and that although congress has legislated on this subject, its legislation manifests an intention, with a single exception, not to regulate this subject, but to leave its regulation to the several States. To these precise questions, which are all we are called on to decide, this opinion must be understood to be confined. It does not extend to the question what other subjects, under the commercial power, are within the exclusive control of congress, or may be regulated by the States in the absence of all congressional legislation; nor to the general question, how far any regulation of a subject by congress, may be deemed to operate as an exclusion of all legislation by the States upon the same subject. We decide the precise questions before us, upon what we deem sound principles, applicable to this particular subject in the State in which the legislation of congress has left it. We go no further. . . .

We are of opinion that this state law was enacted by virtue of a power, residing in the State to legislate, that it is not in conflict with any law of congress; that it does not interfere with any system which congress has established by making regulations, or by intentionally leaving individuals to their own unrestricted action; that this law is therefore valid, and the judgment of the supreme court of Pennsylvania in each case must be affirmed.

[*Affirmed.*]

M'LEAN, J., and WAYNE, J., dissented; and DANIEL, J., although he concurred in the judgment of the court, yet dissented from its reasoning.

M'LEAN, J. It is with regret that I feel myself obliged to dissent from the opinion of a majority of my brethren in this case. . . .

Congress adopted the pilot laws of the States, because it was well understood, they could have had no force, as regulations of foreign commerce or of commerce among the States, if not so adopted. By their adoption they were made acts of congress, and ever since they have been so considered and enforced.

Each State regulates the commerce within its limits; which is not within the range of federal powers. So far, and no further, could effect have been given to the pilot laws of the States, under the constitution. But those laws were only adopted "until further legislative provisions shall be made by congress."

This shows that congress claimed the whole commercial power on this subject, by adopting the pilot laws of the States, making them acts of congress; and also by declaring that the adoption was only until some further legislative provision could be made by congress. . . .

That a State may regulate foreign commerce, or commerce among the States, is a doctrine which has been advanced by individual judges of this court; but never before, I believe, has such a power been sanctioned by the decision of this court. In this case, the power to regulate pilots is admitted to belong to the commercial power of congress; and yet it is held, that a State, by virtue of its inherent power, may regulate the subject, until such regulation shall be annulled by congress. This is the principle established by this decision. Its language is guarded, in order to apply the decision only to the case before the court. But such restrictions can never operate so as to render the principle inapplicable to other cases. And it is in this light that the decision is chiefly to be regretted. The power is recognized in the State, because the subject is more appropriate for state than federal action; and consequently, it must be presumed the constitution cannot have intended to inhibit state action. This is not a rule by which the constitution is to be construed. It can receive but little support from the discussions which took place on the adoption of the constitution, and none at all from the earlier decisions of this court. . . .

I think the charge of half pilotage is correct under the circumstances, and I only object to the power of the State to pass the law. Congress, to whom the subject peculiarly belongs, should have been applied to, and no doubt it would have adopted the act of the State.

DANIEL, J. I agree with the majority in their decision, that the judgments of the supreme court of Pennsylvania in these cases should be affirmed, though I cannot go with them in the process or argument by which their conclusion has been reached. The power and the practice of enacting pilot laws, which has been exercised by the States from the very origin of their existence, although it is one in some degree connected with commercial intercourse, does not come essentially and regularly within that power of commercial regulation vested by the constitution in congress. . . .

This is a power which is deemed indispensable to the safety and existence of every community. It may well be made a question, therefore, whether it could, under any circumstances, be surrendered; but certainly it is one which cannot be supposed to have been given by mere implication, and as incidental to another, to the exercise of which it is not indispensable. It is not just nor philosophical to argue from the possibility of abuse against the rightful existence of this power in the States; such an argument would, if permitted, go to the overthrow of all power in either the States or in the federal government, since there is no power which may not be abused. The true ques-

tion here is, whether the power to enact pilot laws is appropriate and necessary, or rather most appropriate and necessary to the state or the federal governments. It being conceded that this power has been exercised by the States from their very dawn of existence; that it can be practically and beneficially applied by the local authorities only; it being conceded, as it must be, that the power to pass pilot laws, as such, has not been in any express terms delegated to congress, and does not necessarily conflict with the right to establish commercial regulations, I am forced to conclude that this is an original and inherent power in the States, and not one to be merely tolerated, or held subject to the sanction of the federal government.

Rarely was there conflict between state and national legislation during the second half of the nineteenth century following the Cooley decision. The principal reason for this was that Congress made no serious or sustained attempt to invoke its powers to regulate interstate commerce until the first century of our constitutional history drew to a close. (The kind of federal legislation that was at issue in the cases we have examined thus far, licensing vessels or delegating power to the states, is very different from the vast programs for regulating the national economy which Congress today bases upon the commerce clause.) Consequently, it is usually argued that at least until the present century, the real choice facing the Court in cases which challenged state legislation on the ground that it attempted to regulate interstate commerce was between state regulation and complete laissez faire. *Paul* v. *Virginia,* 8 Wallace 168 (1869), in which the Court upheld state regulation of insurance against the claim that insurance sales were in interstate commerce and therefore beyond the power of the states to control, is a case in point.

It is certainly doubtful whether the Congress would have established a national program for insurance regulation in the year following President Johnson's impeachment, when the Congress remained preoccupied with the problems of Reconstruction; indeed, it is doubtful that it would be politically possible for the Congress to establish such a program today. But one very important reason why this would be politically difficult was the Supreme Court's decision of ninety years ago that the insurance business was not in interstate commerce, and was an appropriate subject for state rather than national regulation. Decisions such as *Paul* v. *Virginia* inevitably were used as a two-edged sword; the *intent* may have been to uphold state regulation, but the incidental *effect* of the decision was to prejudice the political feasibility of national regulation at a later time.

Paul v. Virginia was overruled, at least on the point whether the insurance business is in interstate commerce, by *United States* v. *South-Eastern Underwriters Assn.*, 322 U.S. 533 (1944), in which the Court upheld the Sherman Act prosecution of an insurance holding corporation. The decision, coming as it did in the middle of World War II, did not induce a Congress that was preoccupied with the problems of the war to adopt basic national legislation regulating the conduct of the insurance business, although the three dissenters in the 4-3 decision in South-Eastern Underwriters bewailed that this was what Congress would have to do, since all state legislation regulating insurance was unconstitutional now that insurance had become a part of interstate commerce in law as well as in fact. These three dissenters were arguing, of course, the old Webster doctrine that the exclusive regulatory power of Congress over interstate commerce precluded state regulation; but this notion had never been accepted by a majority of the Court. The most plausible explanation of these dissents, therefore, is that they were an exhibition of gamesmanship, employed for purposes of political strategy rather than being seriously offered as descriptions of the effect of the Court's previous decisions regarding the power of the states to regulate interstate commerce. Especially does this seem so, since the opinion of the Court in South-Eastern Underwriters expressly disclaimed any intention of invalidating state regulation of insurance: [5]

> It is settled that, for Constitutional purposes, certain activities of a business may be intrastate and therefore subject to state control, while other activities of the same business may be interstate and therefore subject to federal regulation. And there is a wide range of business and other activities which, though subject to federal regulation, are so intimately related to local welfare that in the absence of Congressional action, they may be regulated or taxed by the states. In marking out these activities the primary test applied by the Court is not the mechanical one of whether the particular activity affected by the state regulation is part of interstate commerce, but rather whether, in each case, the competing demands of the state and national interests involved can be accommodated.

The majority, therefore, upheld *both* national and state regulation; while the dissenters argued that the price of upholding national antitrust regulation was to relinquish the general control exercised in the past by the states.

Congress, out of abundant caution, and doubtless unnecessarily, promptly passed the McCarran Act, which, like the act of the first Congress regarding state pilotage laws, recognized the legitimacy of the existing general programs for

[5] 322 U.S. 533, 548 (1944).

insurance regulation carried on by the states. The McCarran Act, in turn, was upheld by the Court in *Prudential Insurance Co.* v. *Benjamin,* 328 U.S. 408 (1946).

The vast increase during the twentieth century in national regulatory legislation based upon the commerce clause has necessarily multiplied the possibilities
for direct conflict between state and national legislation. Most of the Court's decisions, however, have dealt with situations where there was no direct conflict; the
"direct conflict" cases were not so likely to reach the Court, since they were readily
covered by the policy of *Gibbons* v. *Ogden.* But the Court decided many cases that
spawned a variety of "doctrines" and "tests" to supplement the so-called "Cooley
rule." For over a century, the Court purported to define the limits of state taxing
power in terms of whether or not goods that moved in interstate commerce were
still in their "original packages," or whether the "seal" had been broken, thus permitting the goods to merge with the communality of property subject to the state's
fiscal and other powers. An *ad hoc* rule of judicial policy that made good sense in
the case for which it was contrived—*Brown* v. *Maryland,* 12 Wheaton 419 (1827),
involving state taxation of imports in foreign commerce—led to ridiculous definitions of "original package" in some later cases.

Similarly, the "Silence of Congress Doctrine" and the "Pre-emption Doctrine" led to inconsistent and undesirable results when mechanically applied, as
they sometimes were. Neither of these so-called doctrines embodies very high-level
intellectual processes; and they could hardly be expected to be of much use in
the determination of complex social, economic, and political issues. The Silence of
Congress Doctrine (if Congress has failed to regulate a subject over which it has
clear authority, the inference is that Congress has intended to permit state regulation of the subject) says little more than the homily, frequently invoked in regard
to other interpersonal relationships, that "silence means consent." And the
Pre-emption Doctrine (if Congress has legislated at all upon a given subject, the
inference is that Congress has intended to "occupy the field" and foreclose *any*
state regulation of the same subject) differs little from the adage, "If you give him
an inch, he'll take a mile." The problems of divination of congressional intent
implicit in the use of these formulae are similar to those that we discussed in
Chapter 4 in regard to statutory interpretation. Such doctrines may have been
useful to the Court, to the extent that they permitted the Court to attribute to
Congress responsibility for policies that the Court was in the process of formulating and announcing; [6] but they could not have been of much value in deciding

[6] A recent example would be *Pennsylvania* v. *Nelson,* 350 U.S. 497 (1956), in which the Court borrowed the Pre-emption Doctrine from the commerce cases in order to strike down a state anti-sedition law, on the ground that Congress had intended to "occupy the field" of combating Communism when it passed the Smith Act of 1940. There was almost no evidence that Congress had any such intent; and bills were introduced in Congress to overrule the Court. The issue became obfuscated when the Department of Justice argued that the more general of the bills, which attempted to overrule not merely the Nelson decision but the Pre-emption Doctrine as well, would lead to immense confusion in the regulation of interstate commerce; and the Senate then defeated both bills by the margin of a single vote. See C. Herman Pritchett, *The American Constitution* (New York: McGraw, 1959), pp. 65-66.

whether state legislation regulating or taxing interstate commerce should or should not have been upheld, unless the doctrines were applied mechanically, in which case they would have become substitutes for thought and judgment.

These doctrines, together with such "tests" as the Burden Test (Does state regulation or taxation obstruct or place an "undue" or "unreasonable" burden upon interstate commerce?), or the corresponding Affectation Test for national regulation of commerce (activities which "directly" affect interstate commerce are subject to national control; those which affect it "indirectly" are subject to state control) are terms of art, of course. We mention them, not in criticism of the Court, but because they are apt to be confusing to students. And the commerce-clause opinions of the Court prior to two decades ago are generally cast in a frame of reference of such formulae. It was perhaps natural for justices who accepted Austinian jurisprudence to express themselves in these terms. But the decided trend, beginning with the commerce opinions of the Roosevelt Court, has been to define the Court's role forthrightly as being that of striking a satisfactory accommodation of, and appropriate balance among, the interests represented by the national and state governments. This recasting of the issues in commerce-clause cases, and of the Court's role in their resolution, doubtless reflects the pervasive influence of more modern theories of sociological and realist jurisprudence among the justices who have sat upon the Court during the recent past. It is exemplified in the opinions of Chief Justice Stone in both the *Parker* v. *Brown* and Southern Pacific cases. In *Parker* v. *Brown*, for instance, Stone spoke for a unanimous Court (including, therefore, Justice Black), when he said: [7]

> When Congress has not exerted its power under the Commerce Clause, and state regulation of matters of local concern is so related to interstate commerce that it also operates as a regulation of that commerce, the reconciliation of the power thus granted with that reserved to the state is to be attained by the accommodation of the competing demands of the state and national interests involved.

Accommodation by the United States Supreme Court, of course. And at a later point in the same opinion, Stone described the Supreme Court's function in the decision of this case as that of "comparing the relative weights of the conflicting local and national interests involved."

Such a frank acknowledgment that the Court "weighs" and "balances" the interests in conflict puts the Court, it might be said, in the role of a "super-legislature," as Mr. Justice Black argues in his dissent in the Southern Pacific case, below.[8] But this has always been the Court's real function in the state commerce-clause cases. Particularly in this area, the Court's decisions have been pragmatic, with a strong orientation "towards concreteness and adequacy, to-

[7] 317 U.S. 341, 362 (1943).

[8] But compare Justice Black's own formulation of the role of the Court in his opinion in South-Eastern Underwriters, quoted above in the text at footnote 5—which seems to be identical with that stated by Stone!

wards facts, towards action and towards power." [9] The Court's new definition of its role does not mean that the Court's function has changed; all that it signifies is that legal theory has caught up with the historic practice of the Court.

SOUTHERN PACIFIC CO. v. ARIZONA

325 U.S. 761 (June 18, 1945)

Appeal from the Supreme Court of Arizona.

Reversed.

7-2

Stone, C.J.	('+')
Roberts	(+)
Reed	(+)
Frankfurter	(+)
Murphy	(+)
Jackson	(+)
Rutledge	+
Black	'—')
Douglas	'—')

MR. CHIEF JUSTICE STONE delivered the opinion of the Court.

The Arizona Train Limit Law of May 16, 1912 . . . makes it unlawful for any person or corporation to operate within the state a railroad train of more than fourteen passenger or seventy freight cars, and authorizes the state to recover a money penalty for each violation of the Act. The questions for decision are . . . whether the statute contravenes the commerce clause of the Federal Constitution.

In 1940 the State of Arizona brought suit in the Arizona Superior Court against appellant, the Southern Pacific Company, to recover the statutory penalties for operating within the state two interstate trains, one a passenger train of more than fourteen cars, and one a freight train of more than seventy cars. Appellant answered, admitting the train operations,

[9] William James, *Essays in Pragmatism* (New York: Hafner, 1948), pp. 144-145.

but defended on the ground that the statute offends against the commerce clause and the due process clause of the Fourteenth Amendment and conflicts with federal legislation. After an extended trial, without a jury, the court made detailed findings of fact on the basis of which it gave judgment for the railroad company. The Supreme Court of Arizona reversed and directed judgment for the state. . . .

The Supreme Court left undisturbed the findings of the trial court and made no new findings. It held that the power of the state to regulate the length of interstate trains had not been restricted by Congressional action. It sustained the Act as a safety measure to reduce the number of accidents attributed to the operation of trains of more than the statutory maximum length, enacted by the state legislature in the exercise of its "police power." This power the court held extended to the regulation of the operations of interstate commerce in the interests of local health, safety and well-being. It thought that a state statute, enacted in the exercise of the police power, and bearing some reasonable relation to the health, safety and well-being of the people of the state, of which the state legislature is the judge, was not to be judicially overturned, notwithstanding its admittedly adverse effect on the operation of interstate trains. . . .

For a hundred years it has been accepted constitutional doctrine that the commerce clause, without the aid of Congressional legislation . . . affords some protection from state legislation inimical to the national commerce, and that in such cases, where Congress has not acted, this Court, and not the state legislature, is under the commerce clause the final arbiter of the competing demands of state and national interests. *Cooley* v. *Board of Wardens.* . . .

Congress has undoubted power to redefine the distribution of power over interstate commerce. It may either permit the states to regulate the commerce in a manner which would otherwise not be permissible, . . . or exclude state regulation even of matters of peculiarly local concern which nevertheless affect interstate commerce. . . .

But in general Congress has left it to the courts to formulate the rules thus interpreting the commerce clause in its application, doubtless because it has appreciated the destructive consequences to the commerce of the nation if their protection were withdrawn, . . . and has been aware that in their application state laws will not be invalidated without the support of relevant factual material which will "afford a sure basis" for an informed judgment. . . . Meanwhile, Congress has accommodated its legislation, as have the states, to these rules as an established feature of our constitutional system. There has thus been left to the states wide scope for the regulation of matters of local state concern, even though it in some measure affects the commerce, provided it does not materially restrict the free flow of commerce across state lines, or interfere with it in matters with respect to which uniformity of regulation is of predominant national concern.

Hence the matters for ultimate determination here are the nature and extent of the burden which the state regulation of interstate trains, adopted as a safety measure, imposes on interstate commerce. . . .

The unchallenged findings leave no doubt that the Arizona Train Limit Law imposes a serious burden on the interstate commerce conducted by appellant. It materially impedes the movement of appellant's interstate trains through that state and interposes a substantial obstruction to the national policy proclaimed by Congress, to promote adequate, economical and efficient railway transportation service. Interstate Commerce Act, preceding § 1, 54 Stat. 899. Enforcement of the law in Arizona, while train lengths remain unregulated or are regulated by varying standards in other states, must inevitably result in an impairment of uniformity of efficient railroad operation because the railroads are subjected to regulation which is not uniform in its application. Compliance with a state statute limiting train lengths requires interstate trains of a length lawful in other states to be broken up and reconstituted as they enter each state according as it may impose varying limitations upon train lengths. The alternative is for the carrier to conform to the lowest train limit restriction of any of the states through which its trains pass, whose laws thus control the carriers' operations both within and without the regulating state.

Although the seventy car maximum for freight trains is the limitation which has been most commonly proposed, various bills introduced in the state legislatures provided for maximum freight train lengths of from fifty to one hundred and twenty-five cars, and maximum passenger train lengths of from ten to eighteen cars. With such laws in force in states which are interspersed with those having no limit on train lengths, the confusion and difficulty with which interstate operations would be burdened under the varied system of state regulation and the unsatisfied need for uniformity in such regulation, if any, are evident.

At present the seventy freight car laws are enforced only in Arizona and Oklahoma, with a fourteen car passenger car limit in Arizona. The record here shows that the enforcement of the Arizona statute results in freight trains being broken up and reformed at the California border and in New Mexico, some distance from the Arizona line. Frequently it is not feasible to operate a newly assembled train from the New Mexico yard nearest to Arizona, with the result that the Arizona limitation governs the flow of traffic as far east as El Paso, Texas. For similar reasons the Arizona law often controls the length of passenger trains all the way from Los Angeles to El Paso.

If one state may regulate train lengths, so may all the others, and they need not prescribe the same maximum limitation. The practical effect of such regulation is to control train operations beyond the boundaries of the state exacting it because of the necessity of breaking up and reassembling long trains at the nearest terminal points before entering and after leaving the regulating state. The serious impediment to the free flow of commerce by the local regulation of train lengths and the practical necessity that such regulation, if any, must be prescribed by a single body having a nation-wide authority are apparent.

The trial court found that the Arizona law had no reasonable relation to safety, and made train operation more dangerous. Examination of the evidence and the detailed findings makes it clear that this conclusion was rested on facts found which indicate that such increased danger of accident and personal injury as may result from the greater length of trains is more than offset by the increase in the number of accidents resulting from the larger number of trains when train lengths are reduced. . . .

Examination of all the relevant factors makes it plain that the state interest is outweighed by the interest of the nation in an adequate, economical and efficient railway transportation service, which must prevail.

Reversed.

MR. JUSTICE BLACK, dissenting. . . .

In the state court a rather extraordinary "trial" took place. Charged with violating the law, the railroad admitted the charge. It alleged that the law was unconstitutional, however, and sought a trial of facts on that issue. The essence of its charge of unconstitutionality rested on one of these two grounds: (1) the legislature and people of Arizona erred in 1912 in determin-

ing that the running of long trains was dangerous; or (2) railroad conditions had so improved since 1912 that previous dangers did not exist to the same extent, and that the statute should be stricken down either because it cast an undue burden on interstate commerce by reason of the added cost, or because the changed conditions had rendered the Act "arbitrary and unreasonable." Thus, the issue which the court "tried" was not whether the railroad was guilty of violating the law, but whether the law was unconstitutional either because the legislature had been guilty of misjudging the facts concerning the degree of the danger of long trains, or because the 1912 conditions of danger no longer existed.

Before the state trial court finally determined that the dangers found by the legislature in 1912 no longer existed, it heard evidence over a period of 5½ months which appears in about 3,000 pages of the printed record before us. It then adopted findings of fact submitted to it by the railroad, which cover 148 printed pages, and conclusions of law which cover 5 pages. We can best understand the nature of this "trial" by analogizing the same procedure to a defendant charged with violating a state or national safety appliance act, where the defendant comes into court and admits violation of the act. In such cases, the ordinary procedure would be for the court to pass upon the constitutionality of the act, and either discharge or convict the defendants. The procedure here, however would justify quite a different trial method. Under it, a defendant is permitted to offer voluminous evidence to show that a legislative body has erroneously resolved disputed facts in finding a danger great enough to justify the passage of the law. This new pattern of trial procedure makes it necessary for a judge to hear all the evidence offered as to why a legislature passed a law and to make findings of fact as to the validity of those reasons. If under today's ruling a court does make findings, as to a danger contrary to the findings of the legislature, and the evidence heard "lends support" to those findings, a court can then invalidate the law. In this respect, the Arizona County Court acted, and this Court today is acting as a "super-legislature."

Even if this method of invalidating legislative acts is a correct one, I still think that the "findings" of the state court do not authorize today's decision. That court did not find that there is no unusual danger from slack movements in long trains. It did decide on disputed evidence that the long train "slack movement" dangers were more than offset by prospective dangers as a result of running a larger number of short trains, since many people might be hurt at grade crossings. There was undoubtedly some evidence before the state court from which it could have reached such a conclusion. There was undoubtedly as much evidence before it which would have justified a different conclusion.

Under those circumstances, the determination of whether it is in the interest of society for the length of trains to be governmentally regulated is a matter of public policy. Someone must fix that policy—either the Congress, or the state, or the courts. A century and a half of constitutional history and government admonishes this Court to leave that choice to the elected legislative representatives of the people themselves, where it properly belongs both on democratic principles and the requirements of efficient government.

I think that legislatures, to the exclusion of courts, have the constitutional power to enact laws limiting train lengths, for the purpose of reducing injuries brought about by "slack movements." Their power is not less because a requirement of short trains might increase grade crossing accidents. This latter fact raises an entirely different element of danger which is itself subject to legislative regulation. For legislatures may, if necessary, require railroads to take appropriate steps to reduce the likelihood of injuries at grade crossings. . . . And the fact that grade crossing improvements may be expensive is no sufficient reason to say that an unconstitutional "burden" is put upon a railroad even though it be an interstate road. . . .

There have been many sharp divisions of this Court concerning its authority, in the absence of congressional enactment, to invalidate state laws as violating the Commerce Clause. . . . That discussion need not be renewed here, because even the broadest exponents of judicial power in this field have not heretofore expressed doubt as to a state's power, absent a paramount congressional declaration, to regulate interstate trains in the interest of safety. . . .

This record in its entirety leaves me with no doubt whatever that many employees have been seriously injured and killed in the past, and that many more are likely to be so in the future, because of "slack movement" in trains. Everyday knowledge as well as direct evidence presented at the various hearings, substantiates the report of the Senate Committee that the danger from slack movement is greater in long trains than in short trains. It may be that offsetting dangers are possible in the operation of short trains. The balancing of these probabilities, however, is not in my judgment a matter for judicial determination, but one which calls for legislative consideration. Representatives elected by the people to make their laws, rather than judges appointed to interpret those laws, can best determine the policies which govern the people. That at least is the basic principle on which our democratic society rests. I would affirm the judgment of the Supreme Court of Arizona.

NATIONAL REGULATION OF
INTERSTATE COMMERCE

Although the Supreme Court has functioned, throughout our history, as the national censor of state legislation affecting the national economy, the Court has ventured to exercise a veto power over national legislation based upon the commerce clause only during a period of approximately half a century, extending roughly from 1890 to 1937. One reason for the Court's inactivity during the first century of our constitutional history was that Congress made little attempt to use the commerce clause as a basis for programs of social and economic reforms until the nineteenth century drew to a close. And after 1936, the Court abdicated its power of censorship at least to the extent that no acts of Congress regulating inter-state commerce have been declared unconstitutional since then except for a minor provision of the Federal Firearms Act, which was invalidated on Fifth Amend-ment due-process grounds: *Tot* v. *United States,* 319 U.S. 463 (1943).

Congress began to enact programs of national economic regulation based upon the commerce and elastic clauses at the very time when the political power of railroad, industrial, and other corporate interests was at its zenith. No doubt there were other more basic political forces, such as the Granger movement and the rise of the Populist party and the progressive movement within the two major parties, which account for the inception of such congressional restraints upon what had become free enterprise, free competition, and freedom of commerce. Certainly the Supreme Court did little to aid or abet such activities of the Con-gress, although the Court did serve as a catalyst to bring about the enactment of the first great national regulatory statute.

When organized farmers pushed through state legislatures, during the 1870's and 1880's, the so-called Granger acts which provided for state control over railroad rates and operations, the Supreme Court struck them down in *Wabash, St. L. & P. Ry. Co.* v. *Illinois,* 118 U.S. 557 (1886). It is true that these state measures had proved to be only partially effective at best; and the Court applied the Cooley policy, declaring that only Congress had authority to regulate inter-state railroad operations. Within four months, Congress passed the Interstate Commerce Act, establishing the first of the federal regulatory commissions and the rudiments of a system for national control over the railroads. Three years later came the Sherman Anti-Trust Act, also based upon the commerce clause, and in-tended to control monopolistic corporate organization and practices. From this time on, such legislation came with increasing frequency, although this was par-ticularly true of the first term of the Wilson Administration and the first two terms of Franklin Roosevelt's Presidency.

A conservative majority dominated the Supreme Court throughout the fifty years between the establishment of the Interstate Commerce Commission in 1887 and President Roosevelt's Court-packing message in 1937; and during this period, the Court occasionally invalidated national regulation under the commerce clause, on the ground that it "invaded the reserved powers of the states," or used a legitimate means for an illicit purpose, or attempted to control activities within the states that had only an "indirect" effect upon interstate commerce. Much more commonly, the Court accomplished the same result of nullifying acts of Congress by interpreting them in order to "save" them from the fate of judicial review; this permitted the Court, as a favor to the Congress, to reinterpret congressional intent so that the policies of the statutes were acceptable to a majority of the Court. This was the early fate of the Sherman Anti-Trust Act, in decisions such as that of the Fuller Court in *United States* v. *E. C. Knight Co.* (the Sugar Trust case), 156 U.S. 1 (1895), quashing the prosecution of a corporate syndicate that controlled 95 percent of the sugar manufactured, and therefore distributed, in the United States. Surely, remarked Chief Justice Fuller for all members of his Court except the senior Harlan, "Congress did not attempt . . . to limit and restrict the rights of corporations created by the states or the citizens of the states in the acquisition, control, or disposition of property; or to regulate or prescribe the price or prices at which such property or the products thereof should be sold." The fact that "trade or commerce might be indirectly affected" by the manufacturing monopoly "was not enough to entitle complainants to a decree." In a word, manufacturing was manufacturing, not commerce. Equally characteristic of this period was the Court's decision, almost a quarter of a century later, in the first Child Labor case. Although, as we shall see in the next chapter, there were other constitutional clauses under which laissez-faire economics masqueraded as constitutional principle, "freedom of commerce" was one of its most active aliases at this time.

HAMMER v. DAGENHART

247 U.S. 251 (1918)

Appeal from the United States District Court for the Western District of North Carolina.

Affirmed.

5-4

Day	('+')
White, C.J.	(+)
VanDevanter	(+)
Pitney	(+)
McReynolds	(+)
Holmes	'—')
McKenna	—)
Brandeis	—)
Clarke	—)

MR. JUSTICE DAY delivered the opinion of the Court.

A bill was filed in the United States District Court for the Western District of North Carolina by a father in his own behalf and as next friend of his two minor sons, one under the age of fourteen years and the other between the ages of fourteen and sixteen years, employés in a cotton mill at Charlotte, North Carolina, to enjoin the enforcement of the act of Congress intended to prevent interstate commerce in the products of child labor. Act Sept. 1, 1916, 39 Stat. 675. . . .

The District Court held the act unconstitutional and entered a decree enjoining its enforcement. . . .

The attack upon the act rests upon three propositions: First: It is not a regulation of interstate and foreign commerce; second: It contravenes the Tenth Amendment to the Constitution; third: It conflicts with the Fifth Amendment to the Constitution.

The controlling question for decision is: Is it within the authority of Congress in regulating commerce among the states to prohibit the transportation in interstate commerce of manufactured goods, the product of a factory in which, within thirty days prior to their removal therefrom, children under the age of fourteen have been employed or permitted to work, or children between the ages of fourteen and sixteen years have been employed or permitted to work more than eight hours in any day, or more than six days in any week, or after the hour of 7 o'clock P.M., or before the hour of 6 o'clock A.M.?

The power essential to the passage of this act, the government contends, is found in the commerce clause of the Constitution which authorizes Congress to regulate commerce with foreign nations and among the states.

In Gibbons v. Ogden, 9 Wheat. 1, Chief Justice Marshall speaking for this court, and defining the extent and nature of the commerce power, said, "It is the power to regulate; that is, to prescribe the rule by which commerce is to be governed." In other words, the power is one to control the means by which commerce is carried on, which is directly the contrary of the assumed right to forbid commerce from moving and thus destroying it as to particular commodities. But it is insisted that adjudged cases in this court establish the doctrine that the power to regulate given to Congress incidentally includes the authority to prohibit the movement of ordinary commodities and therefore that the subject is not open for discussion. The cases demonstrate the contrary. They rest upon the character of the particular subjects dealt with and the fact that the scope of governmental authority, state or national, possessed over them is such that the authority to prohibit is as to them but the

exertion of the power to regulate. . . .

In each of these instances the use of interstate transportation was necessary to the accomplishment of harmful results. In other words, although the power over interstate transportation was to regulate, that could only be accomplished by prohibiting the use of the facilities of interstate commerce to effect the evil intended.

This element is wanting in the present case. The thing intended to be accomplished by this statute is the denial of the facilities of interstate commerce to those manufacturers in the states who employ children within the prohibited ages. The act in its effect does not regulate transportation among the states, but aims to standardize the ages at which children may be employed in mining and manufacturing within the states. The goods shipped are of themselves harmless. The act permits them to be freely shipped after thirty days from the time of their removal from the factory. When offered for shipment, and before transportation begins, the labor of their production is over, and the mere fact that they were intended for interstate commerce transportation does not make their production subject to federal control under the commerce power.

Commerce "consists of intercourse and traffic * * * and includes the transportation of persons and property, as well as the purchase, sale and exchange of commodities." The making of goods and the mining of coal are not commerce, nor does the fact that these things are to be afterwards shipped, or used in interstate commerce, make their production a part thereof. . . .

Over interstate transportation, or its incidents, the regulatory power of Congress is ample, but the production of articles, intended for interstate commerce, is a matter of local regulation. . . . If it were otherwise, all manufacture intended for interstate shipment would be brought under federal control to the practical exclusion of the authority of the states, a result certainly not contemplated by the framers of the Constitution when they vested in Congress the authority to regulate commerce among the States. . . .

It is further contended that the authority of Congress may be exerted to control interstate commerce in the shipment of child-made goods because of the effect of the circulation of such goods in other states where the evil of this class of labor has been recognized by local legislation, and the right to thus employ child labor has been more rigorously restrained than in the state of production. In other words, that the unfair competition, thus engendered, may be controlled by closing the channels of interstate commerce to manufacturers in those states where the local laws do not meet what Congress deems to be the more just standard of other states.

There is no power vested in Congress to require the states to exercise their police power so as to prevent possible unfair competition. Many causes may co-operate to give one state, by reason of local laws or conditions, an economic advantage over others. The commerce clause was not intended to give to Congress a general authority to equalize such conditions. In some of the states laws have been passed fixing minimum wages for women, in others the local law regulates the hours of labor of women in various employments. Business done in such states may be at an economic disadvantage when compared with states which have no such regulations; surely, this fact does not give Congress the power to deny transportation in interstate commerce to those who carry on business where the hours of labor and the rate of compensation for women have not been fixed by a standard in use in other states and approved by Congress.

The grant of power to Congress over the subject of interstate commerce was to enable it to regulate such commerce, and not to give it authority to control the states in their exercise of the police power over local trade and manufacture.

The grant of authority over a purely federal matter was not intended to destroy the local power always existing and carefully reserved to the states in the Tenth Amendment to the Constitution.

Police regulations relating to the internal trade and affairs of the states have been uniformly recognized as within such control.

That there should be limitations upon the right to employ children in mines and factories in the interest of their own and the public welfare, all will admit. That such employment is generally deemed to require regulation is shown by the fact that the brief of counsel states that every state in the Union has a law upon the subject, limiting the right to thus employ children. In North Carolina, the state wherein is located the factory in which the employment was had in the present case, no child under twelve years of age is permitted to work.

It may be desirable that such laws be uniform, but our federal government is one of enumerated powers; "this principle," declared Chief Justice Marshall in McCulloch v. Maryland, 4 Wheat. 316, "is universally admitted."

A statute must be judged by its natural and reasonable effect. . . . The control by Congress over interstate commerce cannot authorize the exercise of authority not entrusted to it by the Constitution. . . . The maintenance of the authority of the states over matters purely local is as essential to the preservation of our institutions as is the conservation of the supremacy of the federal power in all matters entrusted to the nation by the federal Constitution.

In interpreting the Constitution it must never be forgotten that the nation is made up of states to which are entrusted the powers of local government. And to them and to the people the powers not expressly delegated to the national government are reserved. . . . The power of the states to regulate their purely internal affairs by such laws as seem wise to the local authority is inherent and has never been surrendered to the general government. New York v. Miln, 11 Pet. 102,

139 . . . Slaughter House Cases, 16 Wall. 36, 63. . . . To sustain this statute would not be in our judgment a recognition of the lawful exertion of congressional authority over interstate commerce, but would sanction an invasion by the federal power of the control of a matter purely local in its character, and over which no authority has been delegated to Congress in conferring the power to regulate commerce among the states.

We have neither authority nor disposition to question the motives of Congress in enacting this legislation. The purposes intended must be attained consistently with constitutional limitations and not by an invasion of the powers of the states. This court has no more important function than that which devolves upon it the obligation to preserve inviolate the constitutional limitations upon the exercise of authority federal and state to the end that each may coninue to discharge, harmoniously with the other, the duties entrusted to it by the Constitution.

In our view the necessary effect of this act is, by means of a prohibition against the movement in interstate commerce of ordinary commercial commodities to regulate the hours of labor of children in factories and mines within the states, a purely state authority. Thus the act in a two-fold sense is repugnant to the Constitution. It not only transcends the authority delegated to Congress over commerce but also exerts a power as to a purely local matter to which the federal authority does not extend. The far reaching result of upholding the act cannot be more plainly indicated than by pointing out that if Congress can thus regulate matters entrusted to local authority by prohibition of the movement of commodities in interstate commerce, all freedom of commerce will be at an end, and the power of the states over local matters may be eliminated, and thus our system of government be practically destroyed.

For these reasons we hold that this law exceeds the constitutional authority of Congress. It follows that the decree of the District Court must be

Affirmed.

MR. JUSTICE HOLMES, dissenting.

The single question in this case is whether Congress has power to prohibit the shipment in interstate or foreign commerce of any product of a cotton mill situated in the United States, in which within thirty days before the removal of the product children under fourteen have been employed, or children between fourteen and sixteen have been employed more than eight hours in a day, or more than six days in any week, or between seven in the evening and six in the morning. The objection urged against the power is that the States have exclusive control over their methods of production and that Congress cannot meddle with them, and taking the proposition in the sense of direct intermeddling I agree to it and suppose that no one denies it. But if an act is within the powers specifically conferred upon Congress, it seems to me that it is not made any less constitutional because of the indirect effects that it may have, however obvious it may be that it will have those effects, and that we are not at liberty upon such grounds to hold it void.

The first step in my argument is to make plain what no one is likely to dispute—that the statute in question is within the power expressly given to Congress if considered only as to its immediate effects and that if invalid it is so only upon some collateral ground. The statute confines itself to prohibiting the carriage of certain goods in interstate or foreign commerce. Congress is given power to regulate such commerce in unqualified terms. It would not be argued today that the power to regulate does not include the power to prohibit. Regulation means the prohibition of something, and when interstate commerce is the matter to be regulated I cannot doubt that the regulation may prohibit any part of such commerce that Congress sees fit to forbid. At all events it is established by the Lottery Case and others that have followed it that a law is not beyond the regulative power of Congress merely because it prohibits certain transportation out and out. Champion v. Ames, 188 U.S. 321. . . . So I repeat that this statute in its immediate operation is clearly within the Congress's constitutional power.

The question then is narrowed to whether the exercise of its otherwise constitutional power by Congress can be pronounced unconstitutional because of its possible reaction upon the conduct of the States in a matter upon which I have admitted that they are free from direct control. I should have thought that that matter had been disposed of so fully as to leave no room for doubt. I should have thought that the most conspicuous decisions of this Court had made it clear that the power to regulate commerce and other constitutional powers could not be cut down or qualified by the fact that it might interfere with the carrying out of the domestic policy of any State.

The manufacture of oleomargarine is as much a matter of State regulation as the manufacture of cotton cloth. Congress levied a tax upon the compound when colored so as to resemble butter that was so great as obviously to prohibit the manufacture and sale. In a very elaborate discussion the present Chief Justice excluded any inquiry into the purpose of an act which apart from that purpose was within the power of Congress. McCray v. United States, 195 U.S. 27. . . . Fifty years ago a tax on state banks, the obvious purpose and actual effect of which was to drive them, or at least their circulation, out of existence, was sustained, although the result was one that Congress had no constitutional power to require. The Court made short work of the argument as to the purpose of the Act. "The Judicial cannot prescribe to the Legislative Departments of the Government limitations upon the exercise of its acknowledged

powers." Veazie Bank v. Fenno, 8 Wall. 533. . . . And to come to cases upon interstate commerce notwithstanding United States v. E. C. Knight Co., 156 U.S. 1, the Sherman Act (Act July 2, 1890, c. 647, 26 Stat. 209) has been made an instrument for the breaking up of combinations in restraint of trade and monopolies, using the power to regulate commerce as a foothold, but not proceeding because that commerce was the end actually in mind. The objection that the control of the States over production was interfered with was urged again and again but always in vain. Standard Oil Co. v. United States, 221 U.S. 1, 68, 69, United States v. American Tobacco Co., 221 U.S. 106, 184. . . .

The notion that prohibition is any less prohibition when applied to things now thought evil I do not understand. But if there is any matter upon which civilized countries have agreed—far more unanimously than they have with regard to intoxicants and some other matters over which this country is now emotionally aroused—it is the evil of premature and excessive child labor. I should have thought that if we were to introduce our own moral conceptions where in my opinion they do not belong, this was preeminently a case for upholding the exercise of all its powers by the United States.

But I had thought that the propriety of the exercise of a power admitted to exist in some cases was for the consideration of Congress alone and that this Court always had disavowed the right to intrude its judgment upon questions of policy or morals. It is not for this Court to pronounce when prohibition is necessary to regulation if it ever may be necessary—to say that it is permissible as against strong drink but not as against the product of ruined lives.

The Act does not meddle with anything belonging to the States. They may regulate their internal affairs and their domestic commerce as they like. But when they seek to send their products across the State line they are no longer within their rights. If there were no Constitution and no Congress their power to cross the line would depend upon their neighbors. Under the Constitution such commerce belongs not to the States but to Congress to regulate. It may carry out its views of public policy whatever indirect effect they may have upon the activities of the States. Instead of being encountered by a prohibitive tariff at her boundaries the State encoun-

ters the public policy of the United States which it is for Congress to express. The public policy of the United States is shaped with a view to the benefit of the nation as a whole. . . . The national welfare as understood by Congress may require a different attitude within its sphere from that of some self-seeking State. It seems to me entirely constitutional for Congress to enforce its understanding by all the means at its command.

Congress tried again in the following year, this time attempting to base child-labor regulation on its taxing power. And once again, the Supreme Court invalidated the effort, this time in *Bailey* v. *Drexel Furniture Co.,* 259 U.S. 20 (1922). Proponents of national regulation of child labor then turned to a proposed constitutional amendment, which the Court refused to invalidate in *Coleman* v. *Miller,* 307 U.S. 433 (1939), invoking instead the "political question" doctrine. But by this time, the objective had already been achieved without constitutional amendment by the adoption of the Fair Labor Standards Act of 1938, which the Court upheld in *United States* v. *Darby,* 312 U.S. 100 (1941). It is not inaccurate to say, however, that the Supreme Court had succeeded, by its decisions in *Hammer* v. *Dagenhart* and in the Bailey case, in delaying for a generation the implementation of a national program for child-labor regulation.

On the other hand, it would be misleading to imply that the Court did not uphold, at least as reinterpreted by the justices, most national regulatory legislation based upon the commerce clause, during the early decades of the twentieth century. But the Court's support of national regulation, like the Court's support of state regulation, was selective. For example, in the Shreveport case (*Houston, E. & W. Texas Ry. Co.* v. *United States,* 234 U.S. 342 [1914]), the Court upheld an order of the Interstate Commerce Commission changing railroad shipping rates between points all in the same state from the levels that had been established by a state commission. It was accepted that this was "local" or intrastate commerce; but the Court agreed with the Interstate Commerce Commission that sharp rate differentials had the effect of diverting traffic from interstate commerce (i.e., from various shipping points in Texas to Shreveport, Louisiana) to intrastate commerce (i.e., to other Texas cities instead). This, said the Court, was an obstruction to interstate commerce. Of course, this obstacle could have been removed just as well by ordering the I.C.C. to lower the interstate rates, instead of approving the I.C.C.'s order raising the intrastate rates; but the Court chose the latter course.

The Court also upheld the constitutionality of the Packers and Stockyards Act of 1921 in *Stafford* v. *Wallace,* 258 U.S. 495 (1922), although it should be noted that another two decades were to pass before the Court finally gave its approval to administrative enforcement of the statute in the Morgan cases.[10] In *Stafford* v. *Wallace,* the Court supported national regulation of the major livestock markets with the "throat of commerce" concept, the notion being that livestock were only temporarily at rest in the stockyards, having traveled in interstate commerce in order to get there, and traveling again (in whatever form) in interstate commerce after they left the stockyards. Hence, the stockyard activities were but a temporary interruption in a continuous stream of commerce. The Court could visualize the hogs going into the slaughterhouses, and everything (as it is said) except the squeal emerging to continue its journey; Congress could therefore regulate both phases of the travel plus the intervening metamorphosis.

It developed that this was as far as the Court was prepared to go in upholding national regulation, however, at least until the end of the era. In the Sugar Trust case and in *Hammer* v. *Dagenhart,* the Court had refused to approve a concept of interstate commerce that included the processing of commodities antecedent to their actual shipment. The policy grounds for this refusal were clearly articulated by Chief Justice Fuller in his opinion for the Court in the Sugar Trust case: [11]

> Slight reflection will show that, if the national power extends to all contracts and combinations in manufacture, agriculture, mining, and other productive industries, whose ultimate result may affect external commerce, comparatively little of business operations and affairs would be left for state control.

In *Schechter Poultry Corp.* v. *United States,* 295 U.S. 495 (1935), the Court took the position that what happened to commodities after shipment had ended was no part of interstate commerce, either. Like *Stafford* v. *Wallace,* the *Schechter* case involved slaughterhouse operations, with what for the Court was the critical difference that the product, after processing, moved into local rather than a continuance of interstate commerce. Under such circumstances, said Chief Justice Hughes, commerce was over. It had come to an end. Of course, the major economic problem of the depression which had led to the statute at issue, the National Industrial Recovery Act, was that of glutted markets: an oversupply of goods that could not be sold. Hence, a major objective of the New Deal was to raise prices by controlling distribution processes and the capacity to consume. But the Court could see at best only an indirect relationship between goods moving in interstate commerce and the necessity for a market to attract the movement of the goods. Not even Brandeis, not even Stone, not even Cardozo, was willing to vote that the national government possessed powers under the Constitution adequate to cope with a really serious economic crisis. And since the

10 *Morgan* v. *United States,* 298 U.S. 468 (1936); *Morgan* v. *United States,* 304 U.S. 1 (1938); *United States* v. *Morgan,* 307 U.S. 183 (1939); *United States* v. *Morgan,* 313 U.S. 409 (1941).

11 *United States* v. *E. C. Knight Co.,* 156 U.S. 1, 16 (1895).

states certainly could not hope to cope with the depression—they had tried and failed during the four years of the Hoover administration—the implication of the decision was that Nature, having visited the depression upon the country, would have to provide its own cure, in its own way. Thus the Court struck another blow in behalf of laissez faire,[12] but it was destined to be one of the last such blows that the Court would strike, at least for some time to come.

Even more extreme than the Schechter case was the Court's decision in the following year in *Carter* v. *Carter Coal Co.,* 298 U.S. 238 (1936). In the Bituminous Coal Conservation Act of 1935, Congress had established a special code authority to fix minimum prices for soft coal moving in interstate commerce; and a special board in the Department of Labor was given jurisdiction over wages-and-hours disputes between labor and management in the industry. This was patently a non-adversary suit which failed to meet "case or controversy" jurisdictional requirements, with a group of stockholders suing the president of the Carter Coal Company to prevent him from complying with the provisions of the statute, which were alleged to be unconstitutional. The Court brushed aside such jurisdictional considerations, and chose also to ignore a specific separability provision of the statute in which Congress declared that if any part of the act should be held invalid, the rest should stand. Sutherland, writing for the majority, found that the labor provisions of the statute were unconstitutional, even though they had not yet gone into effect; and he then declared that the price-fixing provisions would have to go too, since the Court could not believe that Congress meant what it said in the separability clause! The price-fixing and labor provisions were dealt with in separate titles of the statute; they were administered by different administrative agencies; Congress had explicitly declared that they were intended to function independently of each other; but "the conclusion is unavoidable," said Sutherland, "that the price-fixing provisions of the code are so related to and dependent upon the labor provisions as conditions, considerations or compensations, as to make it clearly probable that the latter being held bad, the former would not have been passed. The fall of the latter, therefore, carries down with it the former." [13]

The grounds for invalidation were similar to those in the Schechter case: unlawful delegation of legislative power, and attempted invasion of the reserved powers of the states under the purported regulation of interstate commerce. But there were some differences. The unlawful delegation of power in Schechter was

---

12 Actually, the decision of the Court in the Schechter case had little effect upon the National Recovery Administration as an experiment in economic regulation. Whatever for good or ill was to be done in the name of the Blue Eagle already had been wrought; the Administration was anxious to dump the makeshift code authorities in favor of other more permanent programs—although the Attorney General and the President undoubtedly wanted to win this test case which the government had chosen for its legal defense of the N.R.A.; and the National Industry Recovery Act was scheduled to expire on June 16—slightly less than three weeks after the Schechter decision was announced.

13 298 U.S. 238, 316 (1936).

to the President; in Carter, it was an unlawful delegation to "private persons" to fix the maximum hours of labor in the industry. In Schechter, Congress was attempting to regulate business practices that took place after interstate commerce had ended; in Carter, Congress was attempting to regulate business practices before interstate commerce began. The effect of such practices was "indirect," in Carter as in Schechter; but Sutherland, unlike Hughes, attempted to define "direct" and "indirect," although the definition took the form of an exercise in logic. Such nuances aside, the really important difference between the two cases is that the liberal bloc—Stone, Brandeis, and Cardozo—dissented in Carter on the ground that the price-fixing provisions were clearly within the scope of the power of Congress to regulate interstate commerce; and Chief Justice Hughes, in a separate opinion, agreed with the majority that the labor provisions were unconstitutional, agreed with the dissenters that the price-fixing provisions were valid, and argued that the majority should have respected the congressional declaration of separability of the statute.

The Carter decision came at the close of the 1935 Term. The 1936 Term began inauspiciously, and was progressing normally when the President presented his proposals for the reorganization of the Court in his message of February 5, 1937.[14] Ten weeks later, at the height of the ensuing controversy, the Court announced its decision in six major labor cases, which challenged the constitutionality of the National Labor Relations Act of 1935 on commerce-clause and other grounds. It was anticipated that the Court would come forth with another decision like Schechter and Carter, denouncing once again the New Deal's persistent attempts to pervert the commerce clause and defy the Tenth Amendment. Instead, Hughes and Roberts joined with the three liberals, as they had done on March 1 in *Holyoke Water Power Co.* v. *American Writing Paper Co.,* 300 U.S. 324, and on March 29 in *West Coast Hotel Co.* v. *Parrish,* 300 U.S. 379, to form a majority favorable to the constitutionality of the new national labor policy. Chief Justice Hughes wrote for the Court, as he had done in Schechter; and he even found it possible to cite and to quote with approval from his opinion in the Schechter case. It was an act of consummate judicial statesmanship.

NATIONAL LABOR RELATIONS BOARD v. JONES & LAUGHLIN STEEL CORP.

301 U.S. 1 (April 12, 1937)

Certiorari to the United States Circuit Court of Appeals for the Fifth Circuit.

Reversed.

[14] See the section on "Judicial Blocs on the Hughes Court" in Chapter 3; and see particularly the Hughberts Game described therein.

5-4

Hughes, C.J.	('+')
Brandeis	(+)
Stone	(+)
Roberts	(+)
Cardozo	(+)
McReynolds	'—')
VanDevanter	—)
Sutherland	—)
Butler	—)

MR. CHIEF JUSTICE HUGHES delivered the opinion of the Court.

In a proceeding under the National Labor Relations Act of 1935, the National Labor Relations Board found that the respondent, Jones & Laughlin Steel Corporation, had violated the Act by engaging in unfair labor practices affecting commerce. The proceeding was instituted by the Beaver Valley Lodge No. 200, affiliated with the Amalgamated Association of Iron, Steel and Tin Workers of America, a labor organization. The unfair labor practices charged were that the corporation was discriminating against members of the union with regard to hire and tenure of employment, and was coercing and intimidating its employees in order to interfere with their self-organization. The discriminatory and coercive action alleged was the discharge of certain employees.

The National Labor Relations Board, sustaining the charge, ordered the corporation to cease and desist from such discrimination and coercion, to offer reinstatement to ten of the employees named, to make good their losses in pay, and to post for thirty days notices that the corporation would not discharge or discriminate against members, or those desiring to become members, of the labor union. As the corporation failed to comply, the Board petitioned the Circuit Court of Appeals to enforce the order. The court denied the petition, holding that the order lay beyond the range of federal power. . . .

The procedure in the instant case followed the statute. The labor union filed with the Board its verified charge. . . .

Contesting the ruling of the Board, the respondent argues (1) that the Act is in reality a regulation of labor relations and not of interstate commerce; (2) that the Act can have no application to the respondent's relations with its production employees because they are not subject to regulation by the federal government. . . .

The corporation is organized under the laws of Pennsylvania and has its principal office at Pittsburgh. It is engaged in the business of manufacturing iron and steel in plants situated in Pittsburgh and nearby Aliquippa, Pennsylvania. It manufactures and distributes a widely diversified line of steel and pig iron, being the fourth largest producer of steel in the United States. With its subsidiaries—nineteen in number—it is a completely integrated enterprise, owning and operating ore, coal and limestone properties, lake and river transportation facilities and terminal railroads located at its manufacturing plants. It owns or controls mines in Michigan and Minnesota. It operates four ore steamships on the Great Lakes, used in the transportation of ore to its factories. It owns coal mines in Pennsylvania. It operates towboats and steam barges used in carrying coal to its factories. It owns limestone properties in various places in Pennsylvania and West Virginia. It owns the Monongahela connecting railroad which connects the plants of the Pittsburgh works and forms an interconnection with the Pennsylvania, New York Central and Baltimore and Ohio Railroad systems. It owns the Aliquippa and Southern Railroad Company which connects the Aliquippa works with the Pittsburgh and Lake Erie, part of the New York Central system. Much of its product is shipped to its warehouses in Chicago, Detroit, Cincinnati and Memphis,—to the last two places by means of its own barges and transportation equipment. In Long Island City, New York, and in New Orleans it operates structural steel fabricating shops in connection with the warehousing of semi-finished materials sent from its works. Through one of its wholly-owned subsidiaries its owns, leases and operates stores, warehouses and yards for the distribution of equipment and supplies for drilling and operating oil and gas wells and for pipe lines, refineries and pumping stations. It has sales offices in twenty cities in the United States and a wholly-owned subsidiary which is devoted exclusively to distributing its product in Canada. Approximately 75 per cent of its product is shipped out of Pennsylvania.

Summarizing these operations, the Labor Board concluded that the works in Pittsburgh and Aliquippa "might be likened to the heart of a self-contained, highly integrated body. They draw in the raw materials from Michigan, Minnesota, West Virginia, Pennsylvania in part through arteries and by means controlled by the respondent; they transform the materials and then pump them out to all parts of the nation through the vast mechanism which the respondent has elaborated."

To carry on the activities of the entire steel industry, 33,000 men mine ore, 44,000 men mine coal, 4,000 men quarry limestone, 16,000 men manufacture coke, 343,-000 men manufacture steel, and 83,000 men transport its product. Respondent has about 10,000 employees in its Aliquippa plant, which is located in a community of about 30,000 persons.

Respondent points to evidence that the Aliquippa plant, in which the discharged men were employed, contains complete facilities for the production of finished and semi-finished iron and steel products from raw materials; that its works consist primarily of a by-product coke plant for the production of coke; blast furnaces for the production of pig iron; open hearth furnaces and Bessemer converters for the production of steel; blooming mills for the reduction of steel ingots into smaller shapes; and a number of finishing mills such as structural mills, rod mills, wire mills and the like. In addition there are other buildings, structures and equipment, storage yards, docks and an intra-plant storage system. Respondent's operations at these works are carried on in two distinct stages, the first being the conversion of raw materials into pig iron and the second being the manufacture of semi-finished and finished iron and steel products; and in both cases the operations result in substantially changing the character, util-ity and value of the materials wrought upon. . . .

Practically all the factual evidence in the case, except that which dealt with the nature of respondent's business, concerned its relations with the employees in the Aliquippa plant whose discharge was the subject of the complaint. These employees were active leaders in the labor union. Several were officers and others were leaders of particular groups. Two of the employees were motor inspectors; one was a tractor driver; three were crane operators; one was a washer in the coke plant; and three were laborers. . . . The evidence supports the findings of the Board that respondent discharged these men "because of their union activity and for the purpose of discouraging membership in the union." We turn to the questions of law which respondent urges in contesting the validity and application of the Act.

First. The scope of the Act.—The Act is challenged in its entirety as an attempt to regulate all industry, thus invading the reserved powers of the States over their local concerns. It is asserted that the references in the Act to interstate and foreign commerce are colorable at best; that the Act is not a true regulation of such commerce or of matters which directly affect it but on the contrary has the fundamental object of placing under the compulsory supervision of the federal government all industrial labor relations within the nation. . . .

If this conception of terms, intent and consequent inseparability were sound, the Act would necessarily fall by reason of the limitation upon the federal power which inheres in the constitutional grant, as well as because of the explicit reservation of the Tenth Amendment. *Schechter Corp. v. United States*, 295 U.S. 495, 549, 550, 554. The authority of the federal government may not be pushed to such an extreme as to destroy the distinction, which the commerce clause itself establishes, between commerce "among the several States" and the internal concerns of a

State. That distinction between what is national and what is local in the activities of commerce is vital to the maintenance of our federal system. *Id.*

But we are not at liberty to deny effect to specific provisions, which Congress has constitutional power to enact, by superimposing upon them inferences from general legislative declarations of an ambiguous character, even if found in the same statute. The cardinal principle of statutory construction is to save and not to destroy. We have repeatedly held that as between two possible interpretations of a statute, by one of which it would be unconstitutional and by the other valid, our plain duty is to adopt that which will save the act. Even to avoid a serious doubt the rule is the same. . . .

We think it clear that the National Labor Relations Act may be construed so as to operate within the sphere of constitutional authority. . . . Whether or not particular action does affect commerce in such a close and intimate fashion as to be subject to federal control, and hence to lie within the authority conferred upon the Board, is left by the statute to be determined as individual cases arise. We are thus to inquire whether in the instant case the constitutional boundary has been passed.

Second. The unfair labor practices in question.—The unfair labor practices found by the Board are those defined in § 8, subdivisions (1) and (3). These provide:

Sec. 8. It shall be an unfair labor practice for an employer—
(1) To interfere with, restrain, or coerce employees in the exercise of the rights guaranteed in section 7.
(3) By discrimination in regard to hire or tenure of employment or any term or condition of employment to encourage or discourage membership in any labor organization: . . .

Third . . . The fact that the employees here concerned were engaged in production is not determinative. The question remains as to the effect upon interstate commerce of the labor practice involved. In the *Schechter* case, *supra*, we found that the effect there was so remote as to be beyond the federal power. To find "immediacy or directness" there was to find it "almost everywhere," a result inconsistent with the maintenance of our federal system. In the *Carter* case, . . . the Court was of the opinion that the provisions of the statute relating to production were invalid upon several grounds,—that there was improper delegation of legislative power, and that the requirements not only went beyond any sustainable measure of protection of interstate commerce but were also inconsistent with due process. These cases are not controlling here.

Fourth. Effects of the unfair labor practice in respondent's enterprise.—Giving full weight to respondent's contention with respect to a break in the complete continuity of the "stream of commerce" by reason of respondent's manufacturing operations, the fact remains that the stoppage of those operations by industrial strife would have a most serious effect upon interstate commerce. In view of respondent's far-flung activities, it is idle to say that the effect would be indirect or remote. It is obvious that it would be immediate and might be catastrophic. We are asked to shut our eyes to the plainest facts of our national life and to deal with the question of direct and indirect effects in an intellectual vacuum. Because there may be but indirect and remote effects upon interstate commerce in connection with a host of local enterprises throughout the country, it does not follow that other industrial activities do not have such a close and intimate relation to interstate commerce as to make the presence of industrial strife a matter of the most urgent national concern. When industries organize themselves on a national scale, making their relation to interstate commerce the dominant factor in their activities, how can it be maintained that their industrial labor relations constitute a forbidden field into which Congress may not enter when it is necessary to protect interstate commerce from the paralyzing consequences of industrial war? We have often said that interstate commerce itself is a practical conception. It is equally true that interferences with that commerce must be appraised by a judgment that does not ignore actual experience.

. . . The steel industry is one of the great basic industries of the United States, with ramifying activities affecting interstate commerce at every point. The Government aptly refers to the steel strike of 1919-1920 with its far-reaching consequences. The fact that there appears to have been no major disturbance in that industry in the more recent period did not dispose of the possibilities of future and like dangers to interstate commerce which Congress was entitled to foresee and to exercise its protective power to forestall. It is not necessary again to detail the facts as to respondent's enterprise. Instead of being beyond the pale, we think that it presents in a most striking way the close and intimate relation which a manufacturing industry may have to interstate commerce and we have no doubt that Congress had constitutional authority to safeguard the right of respondent's employees to self-organization and freedom in the choice of representatives for collective bargaining. . . .

Our conclusion is that the order of the Board was within its competency and that the Act is valid as here applied.

Reversed.

MR. JUSTICE MCREYNOLDS delivered the following dissenting opinion in the cases preceding:

MR. JUSTICE VAN DEVANTER, MR. JUSTICE SUTHERLAND, MR. JUSTICE BUTLER and I are unable to agree with the decisions just announced.

We conclude that these causes were rightly decided by the three Circuit Courts of Appeals and that their judgments should be affirmed. The opinions there given without dissent are terse, well-considered and sound. They disclose the meaning ascribed by experienced judges to what this Court has often declared. . . .

Consider the far-reaching import of these decisions, the departure from what we understand has been consistently ruled here, and the extraordinary power confirmed to a Board of three, the obligation to present our views becomes plain.

The Court, as we think, departs from well-established principles followed in *Schechter Corp.* v. *United States,* 295 U.S. 495 (May, 1935) and *Carter* v. *Carter Coal Co.,* 298 U.S. 238 (May, 1936). Upon the authority of those decisions, the Circuit Courts of Appeals of the Fifth, Sixth and Second Circuits in the causes now before us have held the power of Congress under the commerce clause does not extent to relations between employers and their employees engaged in manufacture, and therefore the Act conferred upon the National Labor Relations Board no authority in respect of matters covered by the questioned orders. . . . [The] Circuit Court of Appeals, Fourth Circuit, held the Act inapplicable to manufacture and expressed the view that if so extended it would be invalid. Six district courts, on the authority of *Schechter's* and *Carter's* cases, have held that the Board has no authority to regulate relations between employers and employees engaged in local production. No decision or judicial opinion to the contrary has been cited, and we find none. Every consideration brought forward to uphold the Act before us was applicable to support the Acts held unconstitutional in causes decided within two years. And the lower courts rightly deemed them controlling. . . .

The three respondents happen to be manufacturing concerns—one large, two relatively small. The Act is now applied to each upon grounds common to all. Obviously what is determined as to these concerns may gravely affect a multitude of employers who engage in a great variety of private enterprises—mercantile, manufacturing, publishing, stock-raising, mining, etc. It puts into the hands of a Board power of control over purely local industry beyond anything heretofore deemed permissible. . . . In No. 419 ten men out of ten thousand were discharged; in the other cases only a few. The immediate effect in the factory may be to create discontent among all those employed and a strike may follow, which, in turn, may result in reducing production, which ultimately may reduce the volume of goods moving in interstate commerce. By this chain of indirect and progressively remote events we finally reach the evil with which it is said the legislation under consideration undertakes to deal. A more remote and indirect interference with interstate commerce or a more definite invasion of the powers reserved to the states is difficult, if not impossible, to imagine.

The Constitution still recognizes the existence of states with indestructible powers; the Tenth Amendment was sup-

posed to put them beyond controversy.

. . . It is unreasonable and unprecedented to say the commerce clause confers upon Congress power to govern relations between employers and employees in these local activities. . . . In *Schechter's* case we condemned as unauthorized by the commerce clause assertion of federal power in respect of commodities which had come to rest after interstate transportation. And, in *Carter's* case, we held Congress lacked power to regulate labor relations in respect of commodities before interstate commerce has begun. . . .

That Congress has power by appropriate means, not prohibited by the Constitution, to prevent direct and material interference with the conduct of interstate commerce is settled doctrine. But the interference struck at must be direct and material, not some mere possibility contingent on wholly uncertain events; and there must be no impairment of rights guaranteed. . . .

The floodgates were down, and the next few years witnessed a wholesale overturning of many of the Court's outstanding policies, in the commerce area as in others. Some of these policy reversals involved what were technically overrulings of earlier decisions, and others did not. *Mulford* v. *Smith*, 307 U.S. 38 (1939), for instance, did not technically overrule such decisions as *United States* v. *Butler*, 297 U.S. 1 (1936), in which the Court had invalidated the Agricultural Adjustment Act of 1935 on Tenth Amendment grounds; nor did it technically overrule commerce-clause decisions such as the Sugar Trust and Carter cases, which had declared the policy that the processing of commodities prior to shipment was not subject to regulation as a part of interstate commerce. But *Mulford* v. *Smith* did uphold the constitutionality of the Agricultural Adjustment Act of 1938, which established a system of production quotas, under penalty, for the marketing of tobacco and other farm crops. The A.A.A. of 1938 was clearly unconstitutional if the Court were to follow its precedents; but Roberts wrote for a majority of seven which had made a clean break with the past; and only Butler and McReynolds, the two remaining members of what had been the conservative bloc of the Court, joined in dissent against the New Order. *United States* v. *Darby*, 312 U.S. 100 (1941), on the other hand, which upheld the constitutionality of the Fair Labor Standards Act of 1938 as a proper regulation of wages and hours (including child labor) under the commerce clause, explicitly overruled *Hammer*

v. *Dagenhart*. The Carter case, however, was "limited in principle" instead of being overruled, presumably to soothe the feelings of Mr. Justice Roberts and of Chief Justice Hughes, both of whom had joined in the majority in Carter on this point and who now acquiesced silently in the unanimous opinion of the Court in the Darby case. As we observed in Chapter 4, it is easier for the Court to over-rule the decisions of dead justices than of those who are still around to voice a protest against the Court's disregard of the principle of *stare decisis*.

The case that has frequently been described as having upheld the most extreme exertion of the commerce power is *Wickard* v. *Filburn* (below). *Wickard* v. *Filburn* was extreme, at least as compared to the commerce-clause decisions prior to 1937, in one sense. This decision extended the concept of interstate commerce to include a crop, grown for consumption on a farm, which never left the farm. The only link between such production and interstate commerce was statistical. Perhaps more picturesque, if not more extreme—technically the issue was one of statutory rather than constitutional construction—was the subsequent decision of the Court holding that elevator operators who traveled only vertically at the same spot on Manhattan Island were also a part of interstate commerce and subject to the regulatory power of Congress.[15]

WICKARD, SECRETARY OF AGRICULTURE v. FILBURN

317 U.S. 111 (Argued May 4, 1942; re-argued October 13, 1942; decided, November 9, 1942.)

Appeal from the United States District Court for the Southern District of Ohio.

Reversed.

	8-0
Jackson	('+')
Stone, C.J.	(+)
Roberts	(+)
Black	(+)
Reed	(+)
Frankfurter	(+)
Douglas	(+)
Murphy	(+)
Vacancies	1

Mr. Justice Byrnes resigned on October 3, 1942, before the case was reargued; and

[15] *Borden* v. *Bordella*, 325 U.S. 679 (1945); but see also *10 East 40th Street Bldg.* v. *Callus*, 325 U.S. 578 (1945).

his seat remained vacant at the time of decision. Trial was held before a three-judge district court, which granted a permanent injunction against Secretary Wickard, forbidding enforcement of the statute and administrative regulations establishing a quota for wheat production on Filburn's farm.

MR. JUSTICE JACKSON delivered the opinion of the Court.

The appellee filed his complaint against the Secretary of Agriculture of the United States, three members of the County Agricultural Conservation Committee for Montgomery County, Ohio, and a member of the State Agricultural Conservation Committee for Ohio. He sought to enjoin enforcement against himself of the marketing penalty imposed by the amendment of May 26, 1941, to the Agricultural Adjustment Act of 1938, upon that part of his 1941 wheat crop which was available for marketing in excess of the marketing quota established for his farm. He also sought a declaratory judgment that the wheat marketing quota provisions of the Act as amended and applicable to him were unconstitutional because not sustainable under the Commerce Clause or consistent with the Due Process Clause of the Fifth Amendment. . . .

The appellee for many years past has owned and operated a small farm in Montgomery County, Ohio, maintaining a herd of dairy cattle, selling milk, raising poultry, and selling poultry and eggs. It has been his practice to raise a small acreage of winter wheat, sown in the Fall and harvested in the following July; to sell a portion of the crop; to feed part to poultry and livestock on the farm, some of which is sold; to use some in making flour for home consumption; and to keep the rest for the following seeding. The intended disposition of the crop here involved has not been expressly stated.

In July of 1940, pursuant to the Agricultural Adjustment Act of 1938, as then amended, there were established for the appellee's 1941 crop a wheat acreage allotment of 11.1 acres and a normal yield of 20.1 bushels of wheat an acre. He was given notice of such allotment in July of 1940, before the Fall planting of his 1941 crop of wheat, and again in July of 1941, before it was harvested. He sowed, however, 23 acres, and harvested from his 11.9 acres of excess acreage 239 bushels, which under the terms of the Act as amended on May 26, 1941, constituted farm marketing excess, subject to a penalty of 49 cents a bushel, or $117.11 in all. The appellee has not paid the penalty and he has not postponed or avoided it by storing the excess under regulations of the Secretary of Agriculture, or by delivering it up to the Secretary. The Committee, therefore, refused him a marketing card, which was, under the terms of Regulations promulgated by the Secretary, necessary to protect a buyer from liability to the penalty and upon its protecting lien.

The general scheme of the Agricultural Adjustment Act of 1938 as related to wheat is to control the volume moving in interstate and foreign commerce in order to avoid surpluses and shortages and the consequent abnormally low or high wheat prices and obstructions to commerce. Within prescribed limits and by prescribed standards the Secretary of Agriculture is directed to ascertain and proclaim each year a national acreage allotment for the next crop of wheat, which is then apportioned to the states and their counties, and is eventually broken up into allotments for individual farms. . . .

It is urged that under the Commerce Clause of the Constitution, Article I, § 8, clause 3, Congress does not possess the power it has in this instance sought to exercise. The question would merit little consideration since our decision in *United States* v. *Darby,* 312 U.S. 100, sustaining the federal power to regulate production of goods for commerce, except for the fact that this Act extends federal regulation to production not intended in any part for commerce but wholly for consumption on the farm. The Act includes a definition of "market" and its derivatives, so that as related to wheat, in addition to its conventional meaning, it also means to dispose of "by feeding (in any form) to poultry or livestock which, or the products of which, are sold, bartered, or exchanged, or to be so disposed of." Hence, marketing quotas not only embrace all that may be sold without penalty but also what may be consumed on the premises. Wheat produced on excess acreage is designated as "available for marketing" as so defined, and the penalty is imposed thereon. Penalties do not depend upon whether any part of the wheat, either within or without the quota, is sold or intended to be sold. The sum of this is that the Federal Government fixes a quota including all that the farmer may harvest for sale or for his own farm needs, and declares that wheat produced on excess acreage may neither be disposed of nor used except upon payment of the penalty, or except it is stored as required by the Act or delivered to the Secretary of Agriculture.

Appellee says that this is a regulation of production and consumption of wheat. Such activities are, he urges, beyond the reach of Congressional power under the Commerce Clause, since they are local in character, and their effects upon interstate commerce are at most "indirect." In answer the Government argues that the statute regulates neither production nor consumption, but only marketing; and, in the alternative, that if the Act does go beyond the regulation of marketing it is sustainable as a "necessary and proper" implementation of the power of Congress over interstate commerce.

The Government's concern lest the Act be held to be a regulation of production or consumption, rather than of marketing, is attributable to a few dicta and decisions of this Court which might be understood to lay it down that activities such as "production," "manufacturing," and "mining" are strictly "local" and, except in special circumstances which are not present here, cannot be regulated under the commerce power because their effects upon interstate commerce are, as matter of law, only "indirect." Even today, when this power has been held to have great latitude, there is no decision of this Court that such activities may be regulated where no part of the product is intended for interstate commerce or intermingled with the subjects thereof. We believe that a review of the course of decision under the Commerce Clause will make plain, however, that questions of the power of Congress are not to be decided by reference to any formula which would give controlling force to nomenclature such as "production" and "indirect" and foreclose consideration of the actual effects of the activity in question upon interstate commerce.

At the beginning Chief Justice Marshall described the federal commerce power with a breadth never yet exceeded. *Gibbons* v. *Ogden,* 9 Wheat. 1, 194-195. He made emphatic the embracing and penetrating nature of this power by warning that effective restraints on its exercise must proceed from political rather than from judicial processes. *Id.* at 197.

For nearly a century, however, decisions of this Court under the Commerce Clause dealt rarely with questions of what Congress might do in the exercise of its granted power under the Clause, and almost entirely with the permissibility of state activity which it was claimed discriminated against or burdened interstate commerce. During this period there was perhaps little occasion for the affirmative exercise of the commerce power, and the influence of the Clause on American life and law was a negative one, resulting almost wholly from its operation as a restraint upon the powers of the states. In discussion and decision the point of reference, instead of being what was "necessary and proper" to the exercise by Congress of its granted power, was often some concept of sovereignty thought to be implicit in the status of statehood. Certain activities such as "production," "manufacturing," and "mining" were occasionally said to be within the province of state governments and beyond the power of Congress under the Commerce Clause. . . . But even if appellee's activity be local and though it may not be regarded as commerce, it may still, whatever its nature, be reached by Congress if it exerts a substantial economic effect on interstate commerce, and this irrespective of whether such effect is what might at some earlier time have been defined as "direct" or "indirect."

The parties have stipulated a summary of the economics of the wheat industry. Commerce among the states in wheat is large and important. Although wheat is raised in every state but one, production in most states is not equal to consumption. Sixteen states on average have had a surplus of wheat above their own requirements for feed, seed, and food. Thirty-two states and the District of Columbia, where production has been below consumption, have looked to these surplus-producing states for their supply as well as for wheat for export and carry-over.

The wheat industry has been a problem industry for some years. Largely as a result of increased foreign production and import restrictions, annual exports of wheat and flour from the United States during the ten-year period ending in 1940 averaged less than 10 per cent of total production, while during the 1920's they averaged more than 25 per cent. The decline in the export trade has left a large surplus in production which, in connection with an abnormally large supply of wheat and other grains in recent years, caused congestion in a number of markets; tied up railroad cars; and caused elevators in some instances to turn away grains, and railroads to institute embargoes to prevent further congestion. . . .

The effect of consumption of home-grown wheat on interstate commerce is due to the fact that it constitutes the most variable factor in the disappearance of the wheat crop. Consumption on the farm where grown appears to vary in an amount greater than 20 per cent of average production. The total amount of wheat consumed as food varies but relatively little, and use as seed is relatively constant.

The maintenance by government regulation of a price for wheat undoubtedly can be accomplished as effectively by sustaining or increasing the demand as by limiting the supply. The effect of the statute before us is to restrict the amount which may be produced for market and the extent as well to which one may forestall resort to the market by producing to meet his own needs. That appellee's own contribution to the demand for wheat may be trivial by itself is not enough to remove him from the scope of federal regulation where, as here, his contribution, taken together with that of many others similarly situated, is far from trivial. . . .

It is well established by decisions of this Court that the power to regulate commerce includes the power to regulate the prices at which commodities in that commerce are dealt in and practices affecting such prices. One of the primary purposes of the Act in question was to increase the market price of wheat, and to that end to limit the volume thereof that could affect the market. It can hardly be denied that a factor of such volume and variability as home-consumed wheat would have a substantial influence on price and market conditions. This may arise because being in marketable condition such wheat overhangs the market and, if induced by rising prices, tends to flow into the market and check price increases. But if we assume that it is never marketed, it supplies a need of the man who grew it which would otherwise be reflected by purchases in the open market. Home-grown wheat in this sense competes with wheat in commerce. The stimulation of commerce is a use of the regulatory function quite as definitely as prohibitions or restrictions thereon. This record leaves us in no doubt that Congress may properly have considered that wheat consumed on the farm where grown, if wholly outside the scheme of regulation, would have a substantial effect in defeating and obstructing its purpose to stimulate trade therein at increased prices.

It is said, however, that this Act, forcing some farmers into the market to buy what they could provide for themselves, is an unfair promotion of the markets and prices of specializing wheat growers. It is of the essence of regulation that it lays a restraining hand on the self-interest of the regulated and that advantages from the regulation commonly fall to others. The conflicts of economic interest between the regulated and those who advantage by it are wisely left under our system to resolution by the Congress under its more flexible and responsible legislative process. Such conflicts rarely lend themselves to judicial determination. And with the wisdom, workability, or fairness, of the plan of regulation we have nothing to do.

Reversed.

A footnote to *Wickard* v. *Filburn* came sixteen years later. One Stanley Yankus, a Dowagiac, Michigan, chicken farmer, expatriated himself to live under what he described as the "free enterprise" economy of the Australian government, in protest against precisely the same quota provisions that Farmer Filburn had protested in vain. Yankus was fined $5,070 for growing too much (i.e., non-quota) wheat to feed his chickens. After an exploratory flying trip to visit the land of the free, financed by an ultraconservative Chicago newspaper, Yankus returned to Michigan, sold his farm, and sailed with his family from San Francisco on May 18, 1959, to begin a new life where (he hoped) there would be no wheat controls for chicken farmers. A bill to amend the federal agricultural marketing act was introduced by one of Michigan's Democratic Senators, and received prompt approval of the Senate by a voice vote only five days after Yankus' embarkation. The bill was reputed to be favored by Eisenhower's Secretary of Agriculture Ezra Taft Benson. It appeared as though Congress might be persuaded to reverse itself by political action, almost a generation after an appeal to the Supreme Court had failed. But most importantly, it seemed to be generally agreed by this time that the issue was one to be appropriately settled by a political decision of Congress, rather than to ask the Supreme Court to dispose of it as a question of constitutional policy.

8

Liberty and Property

A S WE HAVE SEEN, the commerce clause has served the Court, during the present century, as a Janus-like instrumentality: it has functioned both as the major source for broad programs of socioeconomic regulation by the national government, and it has also operated, throughout most of our constitutional history, as a limitation upon the regulatory powers of both the nation and the states. It is no coincidence that at the very time that the Court was discovering the potentialities of the commerce clause as a restriction upon national power to regulate the economy, the justices also found an equivalent restraint upon state regulatory power, hidden within the interstices of the Fourteenth Amendment. The important differences between the commerce clause and the Fourteenth Amendment are that the latter has functioned as a limitation upon the national government only indirectly, and by means of a process of judicial legerdemain which we shall call "reverse incorporation," and define below; and secondly, that the Court never has supported the use of the Fourteenth Amendment as a source of power for either the Congress or the states. The important similarity is that the Court has used the Fourteenth Amendment, like the commerce clause, as the basis for defining a broad area of power and discretion *for the judiciary,* as the justices have defined their own role as being that of Philosopher Kings who, as an agency of the national government and in the name of "the sovereign people of the United States," will decide which social and economic policies of the states are wise, good, and in the ultimate public interest.

As was true of the Court's use of the commerce clause, time has been a dimension of critical significance in the judicial revelation of the secrets locked

408

within the language of the Fourteenth Amendment. The Amendment itself did not become a part of the Constitution, of course, until after the Civil War had settled what had been the major issue of constitutional policy prior to 1860: whether political supremacy belonged to the nation or to the states. The amendment may properly be viewed as the constitutional imprimatur of the terms of peace imposed by the victor upon the vanquished. The Court's initial reaction, however, was to reject the revolutionary implications of the postwar amendments, and to throw its weight in the scales of the federal balance behind the "sovereign" states, thus restoring, in substantial measure, the judicial image of the Constitution to its *prewar* legal equilibrium. (Parallel political changes were taking place within the party system and the Congress.) It was only after thirty years of repetitious importunities by advocates for the dominant industrial corporate class that the Court finally, at the close of the century, was prepared to use the amendment for revolutionary purposes—but purposes that were quite different from those for which the Civil War had been fought. For a period of precisely forty years, from 1897 to 1937, the Court used the post-Civil War amendments as a shield for the rights of property against the "tyrannical" control of state legislative majorities. And, although the basis for conceptual change was laid a decade earlier, it has been only since 1937 that the Court has used the Fourteenth and Fifteenth Amendments to insulate personal civil rights and liberties from the "invasions" of these rights authorized by popular majorities in the states.

In this chapter, we are concerned with the evolution of judicial policy regarding property rights under the Fourteenth Amendment, and the Court's arbitration of state social and economic policies affecting business enterprise and, in particular, labor relations. The last case with which we deal was decided in 1937, because the Court has for all practical purposes renounced its arbitral function in this area since that date. In the following chapter, we shall consider the civil rights of racial minorities under the Fourteenth and Fifteenth Amendments; and most of the cases that we shall present in Chapter 9 have been decided since 1937, reflecting the basic shift in the Court's policies referred to above. But there has been no basic shift in the Court's *role* since 1937; in supporting the rights of property from the turn of the century up to that date, and in supporting personal rights since that date, the Court has equally invoked the post-Civil War amendments as the source of its own power to censor the socioeconomic policies of the states.

There are two different concepts of liberalism relevant to the definition of the Court's role in relationship to the Fourteenth Amendment. Under the older concept that prevailed until 1897, "liberalism" for the Court consisted in deference to state legislative majorities, which should be permitted considerable leeway for experimentation as quasi-autonomous entities within the American federal system. Mistakes there might be, but they should be corrected by political rather than judicial action (which was, of course, viewed as nonpolitical); and their effect would be confined, in any event, to the "insulated chambers" of individual states. Thus would a free people grow in political wisdom. Courts should interfere with state policies only in "extreme" instances, when no rational basis could be adduced in support of the decisions of state legislative majorities, or when *specific* limitations of the Constitution upon state power were violated. This was the brand of liberalism espoused by Holmes and Brandeis during the early decades of the present century, at a time when the Court's majorities had accepted a different and contradictory concept of "liberalism." Logically, the older view of liberalism implied a policy of judicial restraint, irrespective of whether the Court was asked to strike down state legislation in the name of property rights or personal rights.

The alternative concept of liberalism defines the justices' role in terms of judicial activism, to support whatever values are postulated as subserving the common weal of the "community" at a given time. In accordance with such a definition, it was "liberal" for the Court to uphold the rights of property during the early decades of this century, because in doing so the justices were protecting the Good Life for all—to the best of their own lights and understanding. It was equally consistent with this definition for the justices of the Roosevelt Court to uphold personal rights, given their disparate major premise that it was the market place in ideas, not the market place in goods and commodities, that demanded protection from state interference; for after the New Deal, the justices could infer that "community ideals" had substituted the gospel of social egalitarianism for the gospel of wealth. Thus the "liberals" of the Roosevelt Court poured new wine into the bottles of the "liberals" of the Taft Court.

Of course, the proponents of judicial activism in behalf of *personal* rights do not consider judicial activism in support of *property* rights to be a hallmark of liberalism; to the contrary, the latter is considered to be conservatism. And fashions in language change, so that property-right judicial activists today accept the label of conservatism, and look upon personal-right judicial activists not as "liberals" but as "libertarians." Such semantic nuances to one side, it is indisputable that the Court pursued a policy of judicial restraint in its use of the Fourteenth Amendment from 1868 to 1897; and that the policy of the Court since 1897 has been one of judicial activism, in behalf of property rights until 1937 and in behalf of personal rights since that date.

From the point of view of a longer-range time perspective, the Court's activism during the twentieth century was not novel, but marked a return to the aggressive nationalism of the Marshall Court. Although in Marshall's time there was no Fourteenth Amendment, Marshall found a functional equivalent for the Fourteenth Amendment in the contract clause of Section 10 of Article I of the Constitution. In decisions such as *Fletcher* v. *Peck,* 6 Cranch 87 (1810), and *Trustees of Dartmouth College* v. *Woodward,* 4 Wheaton 518 (1819), the Court declared state legislation unconstitutional for violation of "vested" rights of property. For a time, the Court converted the liberty of contract into a natural right, based upon a "higher law" [1] that was both anterior and superior to the regulatory powers of state governments under the Constitution. This particular development was truncated by the rise of Jacksonian democracy, and the replacement of Marshall by Taney and a Court majority sympathetic to theories of states' rights. Marshall himself had referred to "that immense mass of legislation which embraces everything within the territory of a State not surrendered to the general government; all which can be most advantageously exercised by the States themselves. Inspection laws, quarantine laws, health laws of every description, as well as laws for regulating the internal commerce of a state, and those which respect turnpike-roads, ferries, etc., are component parts of this mass." [2] The Taney Court gave a name to such "regulations of police": the police power; and Taney had hardly joined the Court before he delivered the opinion in *Charles River Bridge* v. *Warren Bridge*, 11 Peters 420 (1837), upholding as a legitimate exercise of the police power state legislation challenged under the contract clause. "While the rights of private property are sacredly guarded," Taney remarked, "we must not forget that the community also have rights, and that the happiness and well being of every citizen depends on their faithful preservation." [3] The contract clause continued to function, during the next half-century, as the major basis upon which the Court relied for the invalidation of state legislation; but the period generally was one of restraint rather than activism in judicial review of state economic regulation. And by the end of the nineteenth century, the contract clause fell into desuetude, having been replaced by a much more dynamic instrument for judicial activism.

When the Supreme Court began to interpret the Fourteenth Amendment, in the Slaughter-House cases in 1873, it was by no means clear which, if any, of the clauses of that amendment might serve as the successor to the contract clause, as a vehicle for the translation of theories of natural law and natural rights into specific constitutional policies enunciated by the Court. In this case primeval, the justices were asked to strike down a butchers' monopoly as being contrary to any or all of the three major clauses of the amendment: privileges and immunities, due process, and equal protection. In its pristine form, Section 1 of the amendment gives no hint as to which, if any, of the clauses is the more important. It decrees that:

[1] Edward S. Corwin, "The 'Higher Law' Background of American Constitutional Law," *Harvard Law Review*, Vol. 42, pp. 149, 365 (1928-29); Charles G. Haines, *The Revival of Natural Law Concepts* (Cambridge: Harvard University Press, 1930); J. A. C. Grant, "Natural Law Background of Due Process of Law," *Columbia Law Review*, Vol. 31 p. 56 (1931), and "The 'Higher Law' Background of the Law of Eminent Domain," *Wisconsin Law Review*, Vol. 6, p. 67 (1931).

[2] *Gibbons* v. *Ogden*, 9 Wheaton 1, 203 (1824).

[3] 11 Peters 420, 548.

No State shall make or enforce any law which shall abridge the privileges or immunities of citizens of the United States; nor shall any State deprive any person of life, liberty, or property, without due process of law; nor deny to any person within its jurisdiction the equal protection of the laws.

As it happened, the privileges and immunities clause was quickly and firmly interred; and it has since remained a dead-letter clause of the Constitution. The privileges and immunities of citizens of the United States have remained neither more nor less than they were prior to the adoption of the Fourteenth Amendment, the language of Section 1 to the seeming contrary notwithstanding. The equal-protection clause was the first of the three to be used to strike down state legislation, in a case involving racial discrimination; but equal protection played a secondary role as a limitation upon state economic regulation, and at that primarily during the 1920's and 1930's. It was the due-process clause that the Court ultimately selected for gilding; and through the word-magic of an adjective— "*substantive* due process"—a legal concept that had historically stood for fair and orderly procedure in *making* decisions was transformed into a Pandora's box of "liberties," some (such as "liberty of contract") excogitated from mysteries of natural law, and others (such as "freedom of speech") being borrowed from the first eight amendments to the Constitution.

The latter borrowing process has been important primarily with regard to personal rather than property rights, and we shall examine this question in greater detail in Chapters 10 and 11. To the extent that the Court has thus nationalized First Amendment rights by reading them into the due-process clause of the Fourteenth Amendment, it is sometimes said that the Court has "incorporated" the First Amendment into the concept of substantive due process of the Fourteenth. This has been a two-way street for the Court, however, and the justices have resorted to borrowing from the Fourteenth Amendment in order to create substance for the due-process clause of the Fifth Amendment as well.

Like direct incorporation, reverse incorporation involves the transubstantiation of both natural and positive rights. In *Adkins* v. *Childrens' Hospital*, below, the Court read the natural "liberty of contract" into the due-process clause of the Fifth Amendment, borrowing from the substantive content that the Court had supplied to the Fourteenth Amendment's due-process clause a generation earlier. And possibly in *Hurd* v. *Hodge* and certainly in *Bolling* v. *Sharpe* (two cases that we shall examine in the next chapter), the Court read the equal-protection clause of the Fourteenth Amendment into the substance of the due-process clause of the Fifth Amendment. Neither the contract clause of Article I, Section 10, nor the equal-protection clause of the Fourteenth Amendment purport to limit the national government. Both the contract clause and the equal-protection clause are prefaced by the words, "No *State* shall. . . ." Of course, it is also true that the First Amendment begins with the words, "*Congress* shall make no law . . ."; yet it is specifically the First Amendment rights that the Court has chosen to "incorporate" into the substance of the due-process clause of the Fourteenth Amendment, as limitations upon the constitutional power of the states.

It is noteworthy, perhaps, that all three of the reverse incorporation cases that we shall examine in this and in the following chapter relate specifically to the District of Columbia, where Congress has legislated for a local area rather than to establish a national policy which would apply, under the supremacy clause, throughout the states. And the policy issues to which these cases relate were in each instance considered, at least at the time of the Court's decision, to be characteristically questions of state rather than of national competence and authority. Consequently, the Court was extending to the District, rather than to the country as a whole, the policies that it had established for the states generally under the aegis of the Fourteenth Amendment.

The fact remains, however, that with regard to both due-process clauses and to the definition of their substantive content, the Supreme Court has not permitted the letter of the Constitution to stand in the way of the establishment of constitutional policies that a majority of the justices deemed wise. And it has made no difference whether the substance to be supplied related to property or to personal rights; or whether the source of such rights could be traced to positive language somewhere in the Constitution or was to be attributed to the so-called natural law. The only important difference has been that property rights captured the support of a majority of the justices until the year of the Court-packing episode; and personal rights have commanded the support of a majority since that time.

THE LAW OF THE LAND, ANTE BELLUM

A full century before the shift from a substantive due process of property rights to one of personal liberty, the Court was asked, for the first time, to nationalize the Fifth Amendment, by declaring it binding upon the states as well as the national government. Specifically at issue was the right to just compensation for property alleged to have been taken for a public purpose by an instrumentality of a state government. But the aging Marshall, rounding out his years on the Court, thought that such a question was preposterous. The whole Court considered the answer to be so obvious that the Chief Justice cut off the oral argument of the man who was to be his successor, Roger Brooke Taney (who was counsel for the City of Baltimore in opposition to the claim); there was no need to argue further a closed issue of settled constitutional policy.

BARRON v. BALTIMORE

7 Peters 243 (1833)

Error to the Court of Appeals of the western shore of the State of Maryland.

Dismissed for want of jurisdiction.

6-0	
Marshall, C.J.	('+')
Johnson	(+)
Duvall	(+)
Story	(+)
Thompson	(+)
McLean	(+)
Baldwin	NP

Case by the plaintiff in error against the city of Baltimore, to recover damages for injuries to the wharf-property of the plaintiff, arising from the acts of the corporation.

The city, in the asserted exercise of its corporate authority over the harbor, the paving of streets, and regulating grades for paving, and over the health of Baltimore, diverted from their accustomed and natural course, certain streams of water, which flow from the range of hills bordering the city, and diverted them, so that they made deposits of sand and gravel near the plaintiff's wharf, and thereby rendered the water shallow, and prevented the access of vessels.

The decision of Baltimore county court was against the defendants, and a verdict for $4,500 was rendered for the plaintiff. The court of appeals reversed the judgment of Baltimore county court, and did not remand the case to that court for a further trial. From this judgment the defendant in the court of appeals, prosecuted a writ of error to this court.

MARSHALL, C. J., delivered the opinion of the court.

The judgment brought up by this writ of error having been rendered by the court of a State, this tribunal can exercise no jurisdiction over it, unless it be shown to come within the provisions of the 25th section of the Judicial Act [of 1789].

The plaintiff in error contends that it comes within that clause in the 5th amendment to the constitution, which inhibits the taking of private property for public use, without just compensation. He insists that this amendment, being in favor of the liberty of the citizen, ought to be so construed as to restrain the legislative power of a State, as well as that of the United States. If this proposition be untrue, the court can take no jurisdiction of the cause.

The question thus presented is, we think, of great importance, but not of much difficulty.

The constitution was ordained and established by the people of the United States for themselves, for their own government and not for the government of the individual States. Each State established a constitution for itself, and, in that constitution, provided such limitations and restrictions on the powers of its particular government as its judgment dictated. The people of the United States framed such a government for the United States as they supposed best adapted to their situation, and best calculated to promote their interests. The powers they conferred on this government were to be exercised by itself; and the limitations on power, if expressed in general terms, are naturally, and, we think, necessarily applicable to the government created by the instrument. They are limitations of power granted in the instrument itself; not of distinct governments, framed by different persons and for different purposes.

If these propositions be correct, the 5th amendment must be understood as restraining the power of the general government, not as applicable to the States. In their several constitutions they have imposed such restrictions on their respective governments as their own wisdom suggested; such as they deemed most proper for themselves. It is a subject on which they judge exclusively, and with which others interfere no further than they are supposed to have a common interest.

The counsel for the plaintiff in error insists that the constitution was intended to secure the people of the several States against he undue exercise of power by their respective state governments; as well as against that which might be attempted by their general government. In support of this argument he relies on the inhibitions contained in the 10th section of the 1st article.

We think that section affords a strong if not a conclusive argument in support of the opinion already indicated by the court. . . .

The 9th section having enumerated, in the nature of a bill of rights, the limitations intended to be imposed on the powers of the general government, the 10th proceeds to enumerate those which were to operate on the state legislatures. These restrictions are brought together in the same section, and are by express words applied to the States. "No State shall enter into any treaty," &c. Perceiving that in a constitution framed by the people of the United States for the government of all, no limitation of the action of government on the people would apply to the state government, unless expressed in terms; the restrictions contained in the 10th section are in direct words so applied to the States.

It is worthy of remark, too, that these inhibitions generally restrain state legislation on subjects intrusted to the general government, or in which the people of all the States feel an interest.

A State is forbidden to enter into any treaty, alliance, or confederation. If these compacts are with foreign nations, they interfere with the treaty-making power, which is conferred entirely on the general government; if with each other, for political purposes, they can scarcely fail to interfere with the general purpose and intent of the constitution. To grant letters of marque and reprisal, would lead directly to war; the power of declaring

which is expressly given to congress. To coin money is also the exercise of a power conferred on congress. It would be tedious to recapitulate the several limitations on the powers of the States which are contained in this section. They will be found, generally, to restrain state legislation on subjects intrusted to the government of the Union, in which the citizens of all the States are interested. In these alone were the whole people concerned. The question of their application to States is not left to construction. It is averred in positive words.

If the original constitution, in the 9th and 10th sections of the 1st article, draws this plain and marked line of discrimination between the limitations it imposes on the powers of the general government, and on those of the States; if in every inhibition intended to act on state power, words are employed which directly express that intent; some strong reason must be assigned for departing from this safe and judicious course in framing the amendments, before that departure can be assumed.

We search in vain for that reason.

Had the people of the several States, or any of them, required changes in their constitutions; had they required additional safeguards to liberty from the apprehended encroachments of their particular governments; the remedy was in their own hands, and would have been applied by themselves. A convention would have been assembled by the discontented State, and the required improvements would have been made by itself. The unwieldy and cumbrous machinery of procuring a recommendation from two thirds of congress, and the assent of three fourths of their sister States, could never have occurred to any human being as a mode of doing that which might be effected by the State itself. Had the framers of these amendments intended them to be limitations on the powers of the state governments, they would have imitated the framers of the original constitution, and have expressed that intention. Had congress engaged in the extraordinary occupation of improving the constitutions of the several States by affording the people additional protection from the exercise of power by their own governments in matters which concerned themselves alone, they would have declared this purpose in plain and intelligible language.

But it is universally understood, it is a part of the history of the day, that the great revolution which established the constitution of the United States, was not effected without immense opposition. Serious fears were extensively entertained that those powers which the patriot statesmen, who then watched over the interests of our country, deemed essential to union, and to the attainment of those invaluable objects for which union was sought, might be exercised in a manner dangerous to liberty. In almost every convention by which the constitution was adopted, amendments to guard against the abuse of power were recommended. These amendments demanded security against the apprehended encroachments

of the general government, not against those of the local governments.

In compliance with a sentiment thus generally expressed to quiet fears thus extensively entertained, amendments were proposed by the required majority in congress, and adopted by the States. These amendments contain no expression indicating an intention to apply them to the state governments. This court cannot so apply them.

We are of opinion that the provision in the 5th amendment to the constitution, declaring that private property shall not be taken for public use without just compensation, is intended solely as a limitation on the exercise of power by the government of the United States, and is not applicable to the legislation of the States. We are therefore of opinion, that there is no repugnancy between the several acts of the general assembly of Maryland, given in evidence by the defendants at the trial of this cause, in the court of that State, and the constitution of the United States. This court, therefore, has no jurisdiction of the cause; and it is dismissed.

Barron v. *Baltimore* expresses the traditional view, not only of the intent of the framers toward the scope and applicability of the Bill of Rights, but toward the basic nature of the federal union, as well. Political relationships that were to develop within forty, even within thirty years, were unthinkable in 1833. Indeed, after the passing of another generation subsequent to the decision in *Barron* v. *Baltimore,* it remained true that: [4]

The Supreme Court Justices of 1853 were bound by the traditions and experience with the earliest days of the Republic. With Taney as Chief Justice, the Court included in order of seniority, McLean, Wayne, Catron, McKinley, Daniel, Nelson, Grier, and Curtis. Only Curtis was born in the Nineteenth Century. Taney was only a year younger than the Declaration of Independence and four other Justices were older than the Constitution which they expounded. All of them could remember when there was not a state west of the Mississippi and few west of the Alleghanies. They had known invasion of the United States by a foreign power. Their thinking was conditioned by their intellectual development at a time when slavery was

4 John P. Frank, "The Appointment of Supreme Court Justices: Prestige, Principles and Politics," *Wisconsin Law Review,* Vol. 16, pp. 173-174 (1941).

thought of only casually as an evil, and they could remember when Garrison and the abolitionists were considered troublemakers and radicals.

Within the lifetime of these Justices the Supreme Court had played its important part in establishing a strong central government and an economic system which served the commercial interests of the country. It had survived the attacks of the Jeffersonian Republicans and had gained a fair amount of national prestige.

Within ten years of 1853 the Court was to lose its prestige almost entirely by running counter to a powerful drift of popular opinion in the *Dred Scott* case; within the same period it was almost entirely reconstituted. After 1853, and more particularly after 1860, the men who came to the Court faced two major problems: first, how to meet the political conditions which arose from the war; and second, how to adapt the Constitution to the needs of post-war capitalist expansion.

A DEAD-LETTER CLAUSE OF THE FOURTEENTH AMENDMENT

The Path of Due Process: I [5]

It all began quietly enough. The phrase "due process of law" is of ancient lineage. For a long time it had been an authoritative term for the established ways of justice. An injunction that "no person" shall "be deprived of life, liberty, or property without due process of law" had for decades reposed quietly within the Fifth Amendment. It served a necessary purpose in preventing arbitrary imprisonments, in forbidding seizures of possessions, in compelling resort to ordinary procedures, and in restraining public officials from acting without legal warrant. But in all the years that stretched away from the early days of the Constitution to the close of the Civil War, it was not an invitation to those who found Acts of Congress distasteful to appeal to the judiciary for relief. . . . If there was a higher law in whose name legislation might be struck down by a court, it was elsewhere in the Constitution or in the great unchartered domain of natural rights. In reputable opinion due process of law was firmly fixed within the ancient domain of procedure.

It was the Civil War which disturbed the verbal calm. The course of events made the emancipation of the slaves a military and political necessity. The ways of thought again became receptive to the philosophy of Mr. Jefferson, and to the self-evident truths of the Declaration of Independence. The rights "to life, liberty, and the pursuit of happiness"—already inalienable within an order of nature—were written into the constitutions of several of the conquered Southern States. An injunction in perpetuity against slavery and involuntary servitude was made a part of the supreme law of the land,

[5] Walton H. Hamilton, "The Path of Due Process of Law," in Conyers Read, *The Constitution Reconsidered* (New York: Columbia University Press, 1938), pp. 168-175.

and a correlative amendment undertook to safeguard the rights of the newly enfranchised blacks. It began with the novel declaration that "all persons born or naturalized in the United States, and subject to the jurisdiction thereof, are citizens of the United States and of the state wherein they reside." Then, in words whose revolutionary character could be appreciated only by men of the age who had been steeped in an older political philosophy, it was provided that "no State shall make or enforce any law which shall abridge the privileges or immunities of citizens of the United States; nor shall any State deprive any person of life, liberty, or property without due process of law; nor deny to any person within its jurisdiction the equal protection of the laws." A number of other provisions, all relating to matters growing out of the late rebellion, were followed by a final section which granted, not to the courts, but "to the Congress," "power to enforce, by appropriate legislation, the provisions of this article." A little later the Constitution was made further to stipulate that "the right of citizens of the United States to vote shall not be denied or abridged by the United States or by any state on account of race, color, or previous condition of servitude." In occasion, ideology, and intent the Fourteenth Amendment seems clearly of a piece with the Thirteenth and the Fifteenth.

Yet high authority would dismiss context as irrelevance and would have construction accept "the plain and obvious meaning of the words." The bother is that the language is general and abstract. The clauses are filled with verbal symbols quite receptive to a content strong enough to possess them; not one single concretion is to be found to suggest interpretation or to point direction. . . .

II

If words are in want of definition, the proper appeal is to the law. And it was hardly half a decade after the amendment had been adopted before the meaning of its high-sounding phrases became the concern of the United States Supreme Court. . . . The men who had taken part in the late rebellion had been disenfranchised; the reconstruction program of the Black Republican Congress was in full swing; and in the states which had made up the Confederacy, the legislatures had fallen into the hands of freedmen of color and carpetbaggers. A flood of reckless legislation ensued; some marked by social vision, some savoring strongly of privilege and corruption, all anathema to the white aristocracy which before the war had been in the saddle. The old South had lost in war and at the polls. But someone within its defeated ranks had the vague idea that an appeal to the courts might yet save the situation. Whose idea it was is lost to history. But an adage was current—"Leave it to God and Mr. Campbell"—and presently the Hon. John Archibald Campbell [6] was putting his ex-judicial mind to a difficult problem.

[6] John Archibald Campbell was born in 1811 and died in 1889. He became a justice of the United States Supreme Court in 1853 and resigned in 1861, when his state, Alabama, left the Union. Upon his judicial appointment he freed his slaves. In the Dred

Who chose the particular statute which in single combat was to stand for hundreds of its kind has escaped the record. But whether choice fell to an unknown, to Mr. Campbell, or to a group, a more strategic selection could not have been made. An act of the legislature of Louisiana had granted to a corporation of seventeen persons for a period of twenty-five years an exclusive franchise in respect to the slaughtering of animals for meat in the parish of New Orleans and the two next adjacent. . . .

The situation clearly invited a challenge of the statute in the name of the higher law. But to Mr. Campbell no ready-made formula was at hand. . . . His strategy had the audacity of an ex-member pleading before his old court, of an ex-rebel confronting his victorious enemies. He abandoned the older parts of the Constitution, whose well-litigated clauses did not point his way, and took his stand upon an article which as yet had drawn forth no judicial utterance. He decided to add another to the many paradoxes with which the history of legal doctrine is strewn. The Fourteenth Amendment was intended to secure the rights of the recently emancipated blacks against their former masters. The ink upon the fresh constitutional entry was hardly dry; yet he proposed to use the self-same article to guard the rights of the Southern whites against the political power of the newly liberated Negroes.

. . . The Thirteenth Amendment ended not only slavery but involuntary servitude in every degree and form; it made forever unlawful throughout the whole land a servitude for a year, for an hour, or even for an occasion. A master could no longer command a servant to dance, to frolic, or to make merry before him.

But the impulse of a mighty revolution was not spent in a single enactment. In the Fourteenth Amendment all ranks were leveled, all marks and perquisites of social status were obliterated. All classes, whatever had been their previous conditions, were made a single people. "The law of citizenship became as broad as the law of freedom"; and every person became the equal of every other person before the legislature and at law. In respect to "conscience, speech, publication, security, occupation, freedom, and whatever else is essential to liberty or is proper as an attribute of citizenship," every man became equal to every other man. The amendment—a political as well as a social revolution—"brought the federal government into immediate contact with every person and gave to every citizen a claim upon its protecting power." The natural rights of men, "life, liberty, property, protection, privilege, and immunity"—their reiterated beat falls upon page after page [of his brief]—are "the sacred inheritance of the people." The Fourteenth Amendment "was designed to afford a permanent and powerful guarantee to them." They are to be recognized as "the assured estate of population"; the mandate to the states is, not "to abridge or destroy," but "to

Scott Case he concurred in the judgment of the court in a separate opinion. After the war he resumed the practice of law and frequently argued constitutional cases before the court of which he had once been a member. [Footnote in the original.]

maintain and preserve them." In respect to these rights, inalienable and indefeasible, the federal government becomes every man's guardian.

With such a philosophic start it was easy to get down to constitutional concretions. . . . Mr. Campbell converts an abstract right to work into the worker's vested interest in his occupation. Every trade must—in an order of nature to which the Constitution has come into accord—be open to all who choose to take its chances; and "no kind of occupation, employment or trade can be imposed upon" the workingman "or prohibited to him so as to avoid election on his part." Here, then, in tangible and specific terms is a con- stitutional right, a privilege and an immunity of citizenship, a liberty and a property, a claim to the equal protection of the laws, which the national government must under solemn mandate maintain against a state legislature gone astray.

And, having given concretion to his absolutes, with telling strokes the attorney drove the argument home. He had no quarrel with the state in its exercise of the police power; its right to promote by legislation "salubrity, security, and order" is not challenged; but the statute on trial is not a health measure. Instead "the recitals of concern for the general welfare," the "de- lusive and deceitful promises of public good," the "expression of an unusual benevolence for the domestic comfort or the sanitary care of a neglected community" are sheer pretense. The statute emerges from "no proper legis- lative procedure"; it serves no motive—note the usage of the time—"of the public utility." On the contrary its one characteristic, its sole import, is to create a private corporation and to grant to a favored group of seventeen the exclusive privilege of an ordinary occupation. The ordinance was a return to the age of feudalism; it had created a banality in favor of a single firm; Louisiana had, in defiance of the federal Constitution, become "enthralled ground." There is at issue not one jot or tittle of regulation by the state which those who are pressing the suits wish to avoid. Instead a monopoly— under the ban of the common law, intolerable in a democracy, forbidden by the Fourteenth Amendment—has been created at the expense of men who have made "an ancient trade the business of their lives." The Louisiana statute abridges the privileges and immunities of citizens of the United States; it denies to persons life, liberty, and property without due process of law; it takes from them the equal protection of the laws. Liberty and property were before there was law. The rights of man, which belong to the order of nature, are above "the chartered rights" of a corporation. The cause is that of the workingman, of the community, and of the Constitution.

THE SLAUGHTER-HOUSE CASES

(Butchers' Benevolent Association of New Orleans v. Crescent City Live-Stock Landing and Slaughter-House Company)

16 Wallace 36 (Argued January 11, 1872; reargued February 3-5, 1873; decided April 14, 1873)

Error to the Supreme Court of Louisiana.

Affirmed.

5-4

Miller	('+')
Clifford	(+)
Davis	(+)
Strong	(+)
Hunt	(+)
Field	'—')
Chase, C.J.	—)
Bradley	'—')
Swayne	'—')

MR. JUSTICE MILLER . . . delivered the opinion of the court.

The statute . . . assailed as unconstitutional was passed March 8th, 1869, and is entitled "An act to protect the health of the city of New Orleans, to locate the stock-landings and slaughter-houses, and to incorporate the Crescent City Live-Stock Landing and Slaughter-House Company." . . .

This statute is denounced not only as creating a monopoly and conferring odious and exclusive privileges upon a small number of persons at the expense of the great body of the community of New Orleans, but it is asserted that it deprives a large and meritorious class of citizens—the whole of the butchers of the city—of the right to exercise their trade, the business to which they have been trained and on which they depend for the support of themselves and their families;

and that the unrestricted exercise of the business of butchering is necessary to the daily subsistence of the population of the city.

But a critical examination of the act hardly justifies these assertions.

It is true that it grants, for a period of twenty-five years, exclusive privileges. And whether those privileges are at the expense of the community in the sense of a curtailment of any of their fundamental rights, or even in the sense of doing them an injury, is a question open to considerations to be hereafter stated. But it is not true that it deprives the butchers of the right to exercise their trade, or imposes upon them any restriction incompatible with its successful pursuit, or furnishing the people of the city with the necessary daily supply of animal food.

The act divides itself into two main grants of privilege,—the one in reference to stock-landings and stock-yards, and the other to slaughter-houses. That the landing of live-stock in large droves, from steamboats on the bank of the river, and from railroad trains, should, for the safety and comfort of the people and the care of the animals, be limited to proper places, and those not numerous, it needs no argument to prove. Nor can it be injurious to the general community that while the duty of making ample preparation for this is imposed upon a few men, or a corporation, they should, to enable them to do it successfully, have the exclusive right of providing such landing-places, and receiving a fair compensation for the service.

It is, however, the slaughter-house privilege, which is mainly relied on to justify the charges of gross injustice to the public, and invasion of private right.

It is not, and cannot be successfully controverted, that it is both the right and the duty of the legislative body—the supreme power of the State or municipality—to prescribe and determine the localities where the business of slaughtering for a great city may be conducted. To do this effectively it is indispensable that all persons who slaughter animals for food shall do it in those places *and nowhere else.*

The statute under consideration defines these localities and forbids slaughtering in any other. It does not, as has been asserted, prevent the butcher from doing his own slaughtering. On the contrary, the Slaughter-House Company is required, under a heavy penalty, to permit any person who wishes to do so, to slaughter in their houses; and they are bound to make ample provision for the convenience of all the slaughtering for the entire city. The butcher then is still permitted to slaughter, to prepare, and to sell his own meats; but he is required to slaughter at a specified place and to pay a reasonable compensation for the use of the accommodations furnished him at that place.

The wisdom of the monopoly granted by the legislature may be open to question, but it is difficult to see a justification for the assertion that the butchers are deprived of the right to labor in their occupation, or the people of their daily service in preparing food, or how this statute, with the duties and guards imposed upon the company, can be said to destroy the business of the butcher, or seriously interfere with its pursuit.

The power here exercised by the legislature of Louisiana is, in its essential nature, one which has been, up to the present period in the constitutional history of this country, always conceded to belong to the States, however it may *now* be questioned in some of its details. . . .

The regulation of the place and manner of conducting the slaughtering of animals, and the business of butchering within a city, and the inspection of the animals to be killed for meat, and of the meat afterwards, are among the most necessary and frequent exercises of this power. . . . [And] we think it may be safely affirmed, that the Parliament of Great Britain, representing the people in their legislative functions, and the legislative bodies of this country,

have from time immemorial to the present day, continued to grant to persons and corporations exclusive privileges—privileges denied to other citizens—privileges which come within any just definition of the word monopoly, as much as those now under consideration; and that the power to do this has never been questioned or denied. Nor can it be truthfully denied, that some of the most useful and beneficial enterprises set on foot for the general good, have been made successful by means of these exclusive rights, and could only have been conducted to success in that way.

It may, therefore, be considered as established, that the authority of the legislature of Louisiana to pass the present statute is ample, unless some restraint in the exercise of that power be found in the constitution of that State or in the amendments to the Constitution of the United States, adopted since the date of the decisions we have already cited.

If any such restraint is supposed to exist in the constitution of the State, the Supreme Court of Louisiana having necessarily passed on that question, it would not be open to review in this court.

The plaintiffs in error accepting this issue, allege that the statute is a violation of the Constitution of the United States in these several particulars:

That it creates an involuntary servitude forbidden by the thirteenth article of amendment;

That it abridges the privileges and immunities of citizens of the United States;

That it denies to the plaintiffs the equal protection of the laws; and,

That it deprives them of their property without due process of law; contrary to the provisions of the first section of the fourteenth article of amendment.

This court is thus called upon for the first time to give construction to these articles.

We do not conceal from ourselves the great responsibility which this duty devolves upon us. No questions so far-reaching and pervading in their consequences, so profoundly interesting to the people of this country, and so important in their bearing upon the relations of the United States, and of the several States to each other and to the citizens of the States and of the United States, have been before this court during the official life of any of its present members. We have given every opportunity for a full hearing at the bar; we have discussed it freely and compared views among ourselves; we have taken ample time for careful deliberation, and we now propose to announce the judgments which we have formed in the construction of those articles, so far as we have found them necessary to the decision of the cases before us, and beyond that we have neither the inclination nor the right to go.

Twelve articles of amendment were added to the Federal Constitution soon after the original organization of the government under it in 1789. Of these all but the last were adoped so soon aferwards as to justify the statement that they were practically contemporaneous with the adoption of the original; and the twelfth, adopted in eighteen hundred and three, was so nearly so as to have become, like all the others, historical and of another age. But within the last eight years three other articles of amendment of vast importance have been added by the voice of the people to that now venerable instrument.

The most cursory glance at these articles discloses a unity of purpose, when taken in connection with the history of the times, which cannot fail to have an important bearing on any question of doubt concerning their true meaning.

. . . A few years' experience satisfied the thoughtful men who had been the authors of the other two amendments that, notwithstanding the restraints of those articles on the States, and the laws passed under the additional powers granted to Congress, these were inadequate for the protection of life, liberty, and property,

without which freedom to the slave was no boon. They were in all those States denied the right of suffrage. The laws were administered by the white man alone. It was urged that a race of men distinctively marked as was the Negro, living in the midst of another and dominant race, could never be fully secured in their person and their property without the right of suffrage.

Hence the fifteenth amendment, which declares that "the right of a citizen of the United States to vote shall not be denied or abridged by any States on account of race, color, or previous condition of servitude." The Negro having, by the fourteenth amendment, been declared to be a citizen of the United States, is thus made a voter in every State of the Union.

We repeat, then, in the light of . . . events, almost too recent to be called history, but which are familiar to us all; and on the most casual examination of the language of these amendments, no one can fail to be impressed with the one pervading purpose found in them all, lying at the foundation of each, and without which none of them would have been even suggested; we mean the freedom of the slave race, the security and firm establishment of that freedom, and the protection of the newly-made freeman and citizen from the oppressions of those who had formerly exercised unlimited dominion over him.

. . . Not only may a man be a citizen of the United States without being a citizen of a State, but an important element is necessary to convert the former into the latter. He must reside within the State to make him a citizen of it, but it is only necessary that he should be born or naturalized in the United States to be a citizen of the Union.

It is quite clear, then, that there is a citizenship of the United States, and a citizenship of a State, which are distinct from each other, and which depend upon different characteristics or circumstances in the individual.

We think this distinction and its explicit recognition in this amendment of great weight in this argument, because the next paragraph of this same section, which is the one mainly relied on by the plaintiffs in error, speaks only of privileges and immunities of citizens of the United States, and does not speak of those of citizens of the several States. The argument, however, in favor of the plaintiffs rests wholly on the assumption that the citizenship is the same, and the privileges and immunities guaranteed by the clause are the same. . . .

Was it the purpose of the fourteenth amendment, by the simple declaration that no State should make or enforce any law which shall abridge the privileges and immunities of *citizens of the United States,* to transfer the security and protection of all the civil rights which we have mentioned, from the States to the Federal government? And where it is declared that Congress shall have the power to enforce that article, was it intended to bring within the power of Congress the entire domain of civil rights heretofore belonging exclusively to the States?

All this and more must follow, if the proposition of the plaintiffs in error be sound. For not only are these rights subject to the control of Congress whenever in its discretion any of them are supposed to be abridged by State legislation, but that body may also pass laws in advance, limiting and restricting the exercise of legislative power by the States, in their most ordinary and usual functions, as in its judgment it may think proper on all such subjects. And still further, such a construction followed by the reversal of the judgments of the Supreme Court of Louisiana in these cases, would constitute this court a perpetual censor upon all legislation of the States, on the civil rights of their own citizens, with authority to nullify such as it did not approve as consistent with those rights, as they existed at the time of the adoption of this amendment. The argument we admit is not always the most conclusive which is drawn from the consequences urged against the adoption of a particular construction of an instrument. But when, as in the case before us, these consequences are so serious, so far-reaching and pervading, so great a departure from the structure and spirit of our institutions; when the effect is to fetter and degrade the State governments by subjecting them to the control of Congress, in the exercise of powers heretofore universally conceded to them of the most ordinary and fundamental character; when in fact it radically changes the whole theory of the relations of the State and Federal governments to each other and of both these governments to the people; the argument has a force that is irresistible, in the absence of language which expresses such a purpose too clearly to admit of doubt.

We are convinced that no such results were intended by the Congress which proposed these amendments, nor by the legislatures of the States which ratified them.

Having shown that the privileges and immunities relied on in the argument are those which belong to citizens of the States as such, and that they are left to the State governments for security and protection, and not by this article placed under the special care of the Federal government, we may hold ourselves excused from defining the privileges and immunities of citizens of the United States which no State can abridge, until some case involving those privileges may make it necessary to do so.

But lest it should be said that no such privileges and immunities are to be found if those we have been considering are excluded, we venture to suggest some which owe their existence to the Federal government, its National character, its Constitution, or its laws.

One of these is well described in the case of *Crandall* v. *Nevada* [6 Wallace 35 (1868)]. It is said to be the right of the citizen of this great country, protected by implied guarantees of its Constitution, "to come to the seat of government to assert any claim he may have upon that government, to transact any business he may have with it, to seek its protection, to share its offices, to engage in administering its functions. He has the right of free access to its seaports, through which all operations of foreign commerce are conducted, to the sub-treasuries, land offices, and courts of justice in the several States." . . .

Another privilege of a citizen of the United States is to demand the care and protection of the Federal government over his life, liberty, and property when on the high seas or within the jurisdiction of a foreign government. Of this there can be no doubt, nor that the right depends upon his character as a citizen of the United States. The right to peaceably assemble and petition for redress of grievances, the privilege of the writ of *habeas corpus,* are rights of the citizen guaranteed by the Federal Constitution. The right to use the navigable waters of the United States, however they may penetrate the territory of the several States, all rights secured to our citizens by treaties with foreign nations, are dependent upon citizenship of the United States, and not citizenship of a State. One of these privileges is conferred by the very article under consideration. It is that a citizen of the United States can, of his own volition, become a citizen of any State of the Union by a *bona fide* residence therein, with the same rights as other citizens of that State. To these may be added the rights secured by the thirteenth and fifteenth articles of amendment, and by the other clause of the fourteenth, next to be considered.

But it is useless to pursue this branch of the inquiry, since we are of opinion that the rights claimed by these plaintiffs in error, if they have any existence, are not privileges and immunities of citizens of the United States within the meaning of the clause of the fourteenth amendment under consideration. . . .

The argument has not been much pressed in these cases that the defendant's charter deprives the plaintiffs of their property without due process of law, or that it denies to them the equal protection of the law. The first of these paragraphs has been in the Constitution since the adoption of the fifth amendment, as a restraint upon the Federal power. It is also to be found in some form of expression in the constitutions of nearly all the States, as a restraint upon the power of the States. This law, then, has practically been the same as it now is during the existence of the government, except so far as the present amendment may place the restraining power over the States in this matter in the hands of the Federal government.

We are not without judicial interpretation, therefore, both State and National, of the meaning of this clause. And it is sufficient to say that under no construction of that provision that we have ever seen, or any that we deem admissible, can the restraint imposed by the State of Louisiana upon the exercise of their trade by the butchers of New Orleans be held to be a deprivation of property within the meaning of that provision.

"Nor shall any State deny to any person within its jurisdiction the equal protection of the laws."

In the light of the history of these amendments, and the pervading purpose of them, which we have already discussed, it is not difficult to give a meaning to this clause. The existence of laws in the States where the newly emancipated negroes resided, which discriminated with gross injustice and hardship against them as a class, was the evil to be remedied by this clause, and by it such laws are forbidden.

If, however, the States did not conform their laws to its requirements, then by the fifth section of the article of amendment Congress was authorized to enforce it by suitable legislation. We doubt very much whether any action of a State not directed by way of discrimination against the negroes as a class, or on account of their race, will ever be held to come within the purview of this provision. It is so clearly a provision for that race and that emergency, that a strong case would be necessary for its application to any other. . . . We find no such case in the one before us, and do not deem it necessary to go over the argument again, as it may have relation to this particular clause of the amendment.

In the early history of the organization of the government, its statesmen seem to have divided on the line which should separate the powers of the National government from those of the State governments, and though this line has never been very well defined in public opinion, such a division has continued from that day to this.

The adoption of the first eleven amendments to the Constitution so soon after the original instrument was accepted, shows a prevailing sense of danger at that time from the Federal power. And it cannot be denied that such a jealousy continued to exist with many patriotic men until the breaking out of the late civil war. It was then discovered that the true danger to the perpetuity of the Union was in the capacity of the State organizations to combine and concentrate all the powers of the State, and of contiguous States, for a determined resistance to the General Government.

Unquestionably this has given great force to the argument, and added largely to the number of those who believe in the necessity of a strong National government.

But, however pervading this sentiment, and however it may have contributed to the adoption of the amendments we have been considering, we do not see in those amendments any purpose to destroy the main features of the general system. Under the pressure of all the excited feeling growing out of the war, our statesmen have still believed that the existence of the States with powers for domestic and local government, including the regulation of civil rights—the rights of person and of property—was essential to the perfect working of our complex form of government, though they have thought proper to impose additional limitations on the States, and to confer additional power on that of the Nation.

But whatever fluctuations may be seen in the history of public opinion on this subject during the period of our national existence, we think it will be found that this court, so far as its functions required, has always held with a steady and an even hand the balance between State and Federal power, and we trust that such may continue to be the history of its relation to that subject so long as it shall have duties to perform which demand of it a construction of the Constitution, or of any of its parts.

The judgments of the Supreme Court of Louisiana in these cases are

Affirmed.

MR. JUSTICE FIELD, dissenting: . . .

The first clause of the fourteenth amendment changes this whole subject, and removes it from the region of discussion and doubt. It recognizes in express terms, if it does not create, citizens of the United States, and it makes their citizenship dependent upon the place of their birth, or the fact of their adoption, and not upon the constitution or laws of any State or the condition of their ancestry. A citizen of a State is now only a citizen of the United States residing in that State. The fundamental rights, privileges, and immunities which belong to him as a free man and a free citizen, now belong to him as a citizen of the United States, and are not dependent upon his citizenship of any State. The exercise of these rights and privileges, and the degree of enjoyment received from such exercise, are always more or less affected by the condition and the local institutions of the State, or city, or town where he resides. They are thus affected in a State by the wisdom of its laws, the ability of its officers, the efficiency of its magistrates, the education and morals of its people, and by many other considerations. This is a result which follows from the constitution of society, and can never be avoided, but in no other way can they be affected by the action of the State, or by the residence of the citizen therein. They do not derive their existence from its legislation, and cannot be destroyed by its power.

The amendment does not attempt to confer any new privileges or immunities upon citizens, or to enumerate or define those already existing. It assumes that there are such privileges and immunities which belong of right to citizens as such, and ordains that they shall not be abridged by State legislation. If this inhibition has no reference to privileges and immunities of this character, but only refers, as held by the majority of the court in their opinion, to such privileges and immunities as were before its adoption specially designated in the Constitution or necessarily implied as belonging to citizens of the United States, it was a vain and idle enactment, which accomplished nothing, and most unnecessarily excited Congress and the people on its passage. With privileges and immunities thus designated or implied no State could ever have interfered by its laws, and no new constitutional provision was required to inhibit such interference. The supremacy of the Constitution and the laws of the United States always controlled any State legislation of that character. But if the amendment refers to the natural and inalienable rights which belong to all citizens, the inhibition has a profound significance and consequence.

What, then, are the privileges and immunities which are secured against abridgment by State legislation?

. . . The privileges and immunities designated are those *which of right belong to the citizens of all free governments.* Clearly among these must be placed the right to pursue a lawful employment in a lawful manner, without other restraint than such as equally affects all persons. . . .

This equality of right, with exemption from all disparaging and partial enactments, in the lawful pursuits of life, throughout the whole country, is the distinguishing privilege of citizens of the United States. To them, everywhere, all pursuits, all professions, all avocations are open without other restrictions than such as are imposed equally upon all others of the same age, sex, and condition. The State may prescribe such regulations for every pursuit and calling of life as will promote the public health, secure the good order and advance the general prosperity of society, but when once prescribed, the pursuit or calling must be free to be followed by every citizen who is within the conditions designated, and will conform to the regulations. This is the fundamental idea upon which our institutions rest, and unless adhered to in the legislation of the country our government will be a republic only in name. The fourteenth amendment, in my judgment, makes it essential to the validity of the legislation of every State that this equality of right should be respected. How widely this equality has been departed from, how entirely rejected and trampled upon by the act of Louisiana, I have already shown. And it is to me a matter of profound regret that its validity is recognized by a majority of this court, for by it the right of free labor, one of the most sacred and imprescriptible rights of man, is violated. . . .

Mr. Justice Bradley, also dissenting: . . .

If my views are correct with regard to what are the privileges and immunities of citizens, it follows conclusively that any law which establishes a sheer monopoly, depriving a large class of citizens of the privilege of pursuing a lawful employment, does abridge the privileges of those citizens.

The amendment also prohibits any State from depriving any person (citizen or otherwise) of life, liberty, or property, without due process of law.

In my view, a law which prohibits a large class of citizens from adopting a lawful employment, or from following a lawful employment previously adopted, does deprive them of liberty as well as property, without due process of law. Their right of choice is a portion of their liberty; their occupation is their property. Such a law also deprives those citizens of the equal protection of the laws, contrary to the last clause of the section. . . .

It is futile to argue that none but persons of the African race are intended to be benefited by this amendment. They may have been the primary cause of the amendment, but its language is general, embracing all citizens, and I think it was purposely so expressed.

The mischief to be remedied was not merely slavery and its incidents and consequences; but that spirit of insubordination and disloyalty to the National government which had troubled the country for so many years in some of the States, and that intolerance of free speech and free discussion which often rendered life and property insecure, and led to much unequal legislation. The amendment was an attempt to give voice to the strong National yearning for that time and that condition of things, in which American citizenship should be a sure guaranty of safety, and in which every citizen of the United States might stand erect on every portion of its soil, in the full enjoyment of every right and privilege belonging to a freeman, without fear of violence or molestation. . . .

MR. JUSTICE SWAYNE, dissenting: . . .

Labor is property, and as such merits protection. The right to make it available is next in importance to the rights of life and liberty. It lies to a large extent at the foundation of most other forms of property, and of all solid individual and national prosperity. "Due process of law" is the application of the law as it exists in the fair and regular course of administrative procedure. "The equal protection of the laws" places all upon a footing of legal equality and gives the same protection to all for the preservation of life, liberty, and property, and the pursuit of happiness. . . .

The Path of Due Process: II [7]

It was a powerful—even if not quite successful—appeal. In the decision all the justices who spoke for the court or in dissent addressed themselves to Mr. Campbell's argument. At its judicial début four out of nine were converted to a novel constitutional doctrine and the majority of five found it hard going to contrive a dialectical answer. Chance got in its deft stroke and shaped the course of constitutional events by a single vote. As Mr. ex-Justice Campbell, the Southerner, argued for national sovereignty, Mr. Justice Miller, the Northerner, denied it. As the native of Georgia argued that all citizens were one people in an indivisible union, the unionist from Iowa refused to curb the authority of the states. As the ex-Confederate asserted that whites and blacks were equal before the Constitution, the abolitionist on the bench refused to erase the color line. There was, according to the court, a citizenship of the United States, but Mr. Justice Miller neglected to remove it from the realm of the abstract, to define its terms or to endow it

7 Hamilton, *loc. cit.*, pp. 175-176.

with substantive rights. The Fourteenth was an addendum to the Thirteenth Amendment; it had been designed to make secure the rights of the blacks. But white men, though industrious artisans, were without benefit of its coverage. The legislature had passed the statute as a health measure, and with the act of a sovereign state the Court would not interfere.

It was, however, only as a judgment to go at that. Mr. Justice Field boldly spread upon the record a powerful dissent. The court, like lost sheep, had gone astray; he with three of his colleagues—especially he—was sound in a just-discovered faith. There was a citizenship of the United States, whose privileges and immunities had by the Constitution been put beyond the reach of the state, and that citizenship knew neither race nor color. The rhetoric was the rhetoric of Field, but the ideas were visible imports from the Campbell briefs. A milder echo of the same argument reappeared as the opinion of Mr. Justice Bradley. In the midst of a paragraph toward the end— as if it were a passing thought—he set it down that a possible mandate with which to curb the power of the legislature might be found in "due process of law." So the cause was lost.[8] The "privileges and immunities of citizenship" disappeared from constitutional law. . . .

In the very year that the Fourteenth Amendment was adopted, the Court had decided that a Nevada statute placing a special tax upon all persons leaving the state by railroad, stage, or coach was unconstitutional, because it interfered with the right of national citizenship to move freely from state to state. (The measure was intended to inhibit emigration.) It is true that the case was decided a few months too soon for the Fourteenth Amendment to have entered into the decision; but the holding was perfectly explicit that the right of free ingress and free egress was a right of national citizenship. Two justices concurred in *Crandall v. Nevada,* 6 Wall. 35 (1868), arguing that the Court should have based its decision on the commerce clause, since the Nevada statute clearly was an unreasonable burden upon interstate commerce.

In 1935, Hughes and Roberts and the four more conservative justices of the right wing, grasping for straws, briefly flirted with an extension of the privileges-and-immunities clause to include the freedom of business enterprise and to strike down a state income-tax statute; [9] but this experiment was nipped in the bud by

---

[8] Having lost the decision in this case, the butchers continued their political action to overthrow the monopoly; and with the restoration of the suffrage, the Reconstruction legislature was turned out of office, and the statute unsuccessfully challenged in the Slaughter-House cases was repealed. "This time," as Walton Hamilton has said, "it was the Crescent City Company which refused to accept the voice of the people and girded itself for judicial combat. As the situation demanded, the two combatants exchanged positions, legal weapons, and arguments. The monopoly hurled at the Court the Campbell brief done up in fresh verbiage." *Loc. cit.,* p. 177. The repealing amendment to the state constitution, it was now claimed, violated the due process of law. But Mr. Justice Miller again wrote for the Court, upholding the power of the state and rejecting the due-process claim, in *Butchers' Union Slaughter-House* v. *Crescent City Live-Stock Landing Co.,* 111 U.S. 746 (1884).

[9] *Colgate* v. *Harvey,* 296 U.S. 404 (1935).

an overruling decision of the Roosevelt Court in 1940.[10] It was against this background that the case below came to the Court, in the following year.

EDWARDS v. CALIFORNIA

314 U.S. 160 (1941)

Appeal from the Superior Court for Yuba County, State of California.

Reversed.

9-0

Byrnes	('+')
Stone, C.J.	(+)
Roberts	(+)
Reed	(+)
Frankfurter	(+)
Douglas	('+'
Black	(+
Murphy	(+
Jackson	('+'

The 9-0 voting division applies, of course, to the vote on the disposition of the case; on the question of the appropriate grounds for decision, and the issue with which we presently are concerned, the Court was split 5-4. The case was originally argued on April 28-29, 1941; and after Byrnes and Jackson replaced Hughes and McReynolds, who had retired, the case was reargued on October 21, 1941, and was decided on November 24, 1941. Four justices—Douglas, Black, Murphy, and Jackson—concurred in the judgment only, arguing that, as the Court had specifically ruled in Crandall v. Nevada, *the privileges and immunities of national citizenship included at least the right to emigrate from one state to another. The importance of timing, in decisions of the Supreme Court as in other human events, is underscored by the fact that the case would in all likelihood have been decided differently if it had come up only eighteen months later, when Rutledge took Byrnes' place on the Court. If this had happened,*

the concurring four would almost certainly have become a majority of five (including Rutledge); and the privileges-and-immunities clause would very likely have been discovered in the future to subsume other civil rights and liberties, in addition to the right of ingress and egress among the states. Lacking the critical fifth vote, the Edwards case instead marks the requiescat in pace of the privileges-and-immunities clause.*

MR. JUSTICE BYRNES delivered the opinion of the Court.

The facts of this case are simple and are not disputed. Appellant is a citizen of the United States and a resident of California. In December, 1939, he left his home in Marysville, California, for Spur, Texas, with the intention of bringing back to Marysville his wife's brother, Frank Duncan, a citizen of the United States and a resident of Texas. When he arrived in Texas, appellant learned that Duncan had last been employed by the Works Progress Administration. Appellant thus became aware of the fact that Duncan was an indigent person and he continued to be aware of it throughout the period involved in this case. The two men agreed that appellant should transport Duncan from Texas to Marysville in appellant's automobile. Accordingly, they left Spur on January 1, 1940, entered California by way of Arizona on January 3, and reached Marysville on January 5. When he left Texas, Duncan had about $20. It had all been spent by the time he reached Marysville. He lived with appellant for about ten days until he obtained financial assistance from the Farm Security Administration. During the ten day interval, he had no employment.

In Justice Court a complaint was filed against appellant under § 2615 of the Welfare and Institutions Code of California,

---

[10] *Madden* v. *Kentucky,* 309 U.S. 83 (1940).

which provides: "Every person, firm or corporation or officer or agent thereof that brings or assists in bringing into the State any indigent person who is not a resident of the State, knowing him to be an indigent person, is guilty of a misdemeanor." On demurrer to the complaint, appellant urged that the Section violated several provisions of the Federal Constitution. The demurrer was overruled, the cause was tried, appellant was convicted and sentenced to six months imprisonment in the county jail, and sentence was suspended.

On appeal to the Superior Court of Yuba County, the facts as stated above were stipulated. The Superior Court, although regarding as "close" the question of the validity of the Section, felt "constrained to uphold the statute as a valid exercise of the police power of the State of California." Consequently, the conviction was affirmed. No appeal to a higher state court was open to appellant. . . .

At the threshold of our inquiry a question arises with respect to the interpretation of § 2615. On reargument, the Attorney General of California has submitted an exposition of the history of the Section, which reveals that statutes similar, though not identical, to it have been in effect in California since 1860. . . . Neither under these forerunners nor under § 2615 itself does the term "indigent person" seem to have been accorded an authoritative interpretation by the California courts. The appellee claims for the Section a very limited scope. It urges that the term "indigent person" must be taken to include only persons who are presently destitute of property and without resources to obtain the necessities of life, and who have no relatives or friends able and willing to support them. It is conceded, however, that the term is not confined to those who are physically or mentally incapacitated. While the generality of the language of the Section contains no hint of these limitations, we are content to assign to the term this narrow meaning.

Article I, § 8 of the Constitution delegates to the Congress the authority to regulate interstate commerce. And it is settled beyond question that the transportation of persons is "commerce," within the meaning of that provision. It is nevertheless true, that the States are not wholly precluded from exercising their police power in matters of local concern even though they may thereby affect interstate commerce. . . . The issue presented in this case, therefore, is whether the prohibition embodied in § 2615 against the "bringing" or transportation of indigent persons into California is within the police power of that State. We think that it is not, and hold that it is an unconstitutional barrier to interstate commerce.

The grave and perplexing social and economic dislocation which this statute reflects is a matter of common knowledge and concern. We are not unmindful of it. We appreciate that the spectacle of large segments of our population constantly on the move has given rise to urgent demands upon the ingenuity of government. Both the brief of the Attorney General of California and that of the Chairman of the Select Committee of the House of Representatives of the United States, as *amicus curiae,* have sharpened this appreciation. The State asserts that the huge influx of migrants into California in recent years has resulted in problems of health, morals, and especially finance, the proportions of which are staggering. It is not for us to say that this is not true. We have repeatedly and recently affirmed, and we now reaffirm, that we do not conceive it our function to pass upon "the wisdom, need, or appropriateness" of the legislative efforts of the States to solve such difficulties. . . .

But this does not mean that there are no boundaries to the permissible area of State legislative activity. There are. And none is more certain than the prohibition against attempts on the part of any single State to isolate itself from difficulties common to all of them by restraining the transportation of persons and property across its borders. It is frequently the case that a State might gain a momentary respite from the pressure of events by the simple expedient of shutting its gates to the outside world. But, in the words of Mr. Justice Cardozo: "The Constitution was framed under the dominion of a political philosophy less parochial in range. It was framed upon the theory that the peoples of the several States must sink or swim together, and that in the long run prosperity and salvation are in union and not division." *Baldwin* v. *Seelig,* 294 U.S. 511, 523.

It is difficult to conceive of a statute more squarely in conflict with this theory than the Section challenged here. Its express purpose and inevitable effect is to prohibit the transportation of indigent persons across the California border. The burden upon interstate commerce is intended and immediate; it is the plain and sole function of the statute. Moreover, the indigent non-residents who are the real victims of the statute are deprived of the opportunity to exert political pressure upon the California legislature in order to obtain a change in policy. *South Carolina Highway Dept.* v. *Barnwell Bros.,* 303 U.S. 177, 185, n. 2. We think this statute must fail under any known test of the validity of State interference with interstate commerce. . . .

Whether an able-bodied but unemployed person like Duncan is a "pauper" within the historical meaning of the term is open to considerable doubt. . . . But assuming that the term is applicable to him and to persons similarly situated, we do not consider ourselves bound by the language [of] *City of New York* v. *Miln* [which] was decided in 1837. Whatever may have been the notion then prevailing, we do not think that it will now be seriously contended that because a person is without employment and without funds he constitutes a "moral pestilence." Poverty and immorality are not synonymous. We are of the opinion that § 2615 is

not a valid exercise of the police power of California; that it imposes an unconstitutional burden upon interstate commerce, and that the conviction under it cannot be sustained. In the view we have taken it is unnecessary to decide whether the Section is repugnant to other provisions of the Constitution.

Reversed.

MR. JUSTICE DOUGLAS, concurring:

I express no view on whether or not the statute here in question runs afoul of Art. I, § 8 of the Constitution granting to Congress the power "to regulate Commerce with foreign Nations, and among the several States." But I am of the opinion that the right of persons to move freely from State to State occupies a more protected position in our constitutional system than does the movement of cattle, fruit, steel and coal across state lines. While the opinion of the Court expresses no view on that issue, the right involved is so fundamental that I deem it appropriate to indicate the reach of the constitutional question which is present.

The right to move freely from State to State is an incident of *national* citizenship protected by the privileges and immunities clause of the Fourteenth Amendment against state interference. Mr. Justice Moody in *Twining* v. *New Jersey,* 211 U.S. 78, 97, stated, "Privileges and immunities of citizens of the United States . . . are only such as arise out of the nature and essential character of the National Government, or are specifically granted or secured to all citizens or persons by the Constitution of the United States." And he went on to state that one of those rights of *national* citizenship was "the right to pass freely from State to State." *Id.,* p. 97. Now it is apparent that this right is not specifically granted by the Constitution. Yet before the Fourteenth Amendment it was recognized as a right fundamental to the national character of our Federal government. It was so decided in 1867 by *Crandall* v. *Nevada,* 6 Wall. 35. In that case this Court struck down a Nevada tax "upon every person leaving the State" by common carrier. Mr. Justice Miller writing for the Court held that the right to move freely throughout the nation was a right of *national* citizenship. That the right was implied did not make it any the less "guaranteed" by the Constitution. *Id.,* p. 47. To be sure, he emphasized that the Nevada statute would obstruct the right of a citizen to travel to the seat of his national government or its offices throughout the country. . . . But there is not a shred of evidence in the record of the *Crandall* case that the persons there involved were en route on any such mission any more than it appears in this case that Duncan entered California to interview some federal agency. The point which Mr. Justice Miller made was merely in illustration of the damage and havoc which would ensue if the States had the power to prevent the free movement of citizens from one State to another. . . .

So, when the Fourteenth Amendment was adopted in 1868, it had been squarely and authoritatively settled that the right to move freely from State to State was a right of *national* citizenship. As such it was protected by the privileges and immunities clause of the Fourteenth Amendment against state interference. . . .

MR. JUSTICE JACKSON, concurring.

. . . [The] migrations of a human being, of whom it is charged that he possesses nothing that can be sold and has no wherewithal to buy, do not fit easily into my notions as to what is commerce. To hold that the measure of his rights is the commerce clause is likely to result eventually either in distorting the commercial law or in denaturing human rights. I turn, therefore, away from principles by which commerce is regulated to that clause of the Constitution by virtue of which Duncan is a citizen of the United States and which forbids any State to abridge his privileges or immunities as such.

This clause was adopted to make United States citizenship the dominant and paramount allegiance among us. The return which the law had long associated with allegiance was protection. The power of citizenship as a shield against oppression was widely known from the example of Paul's Roman citizenship, which sent the centurion scurrying to his higher-ups with the message: "Take heed what thou doest: for this man is a Roman." I suppose none of us doubts that the hope of imparting to American citizenship some of this vitality was the purpose of declaring in the Fourteenth Amendment: "All persons born or naturalized in the United States, and subject to the jurisdiction thereof, are citizens of the United States and of the State wherein they reside. No State shall make or enforce any law which shall abridge the privileges or immunities of citizens of the United States . . ."

But the hope proclaimed in such generality soon shriveled in the process of judicial interpretation. For nearly three-quarters of a century this Court rejected every plea to the privileges and immunities clause. The judicial history of this clause and the very real difficulties in the way of its practical application to specific cases have been too well and recently reviewed to warrant repetition.[11]

While instances of valid "privileges or immunities" must be but few, I am convinced that this is one. I do not ignore or belittle the difficulties of what has been characterized by this Court as an "almost forgotten" clause. But the difficulty of the task does not excuse us from giving these general and abstract words whatever of specific content and concreteness they will bear as we mark out their application, case by case. That is the method of the common law, and it has been the method of this Court with other no less general statements in our fundamental law. This Court has not been timorous about giving concrete meaning to such obscure and

[11] See dissenting opinion of Mr. Justice Stone in *Colgate* v. *Harvey,* 296 U.S. 404, 436 *et. seq.* [Footnote by Mr. Justice Jackson.]

vagrant phrases as "due process," "general welfare," "equal protection," or even "commerce among the several States." But it has always hesitated to give any real meaning to the privileges and immunities clause lest it improvidently give too much.

This Court should, however, hold squarely that it is a privilege of citizenship of the United States, protected from state abridgment, to enter any state of the Union, either for temporary sojourn or for the establishment of permanent residence therein and for gaining resultant citizenship thereof. If national citizenship means less than this, it means nothing.

The language of the Fourteenth Amendment declaring two kinds of citizenship is discriminating. It is: "All persons born or naturalized in the United States, and subject to the jurisdiction thereof, are citizens of the United States and of the State wherein they reside." While it thus establishes national citizenship from the mere circumstance of birth within the territory and jurisdiction of the United States, birth within a state does not establish citizenship thereof. State citizenship is ephemeral. It results only from residence and is gained or lost therewith. That choice of residence was subject to local approval is contrary to the inescapable implications of the westward movement of our civilization.

Even as to an alien who had "been admitted to the United States under the Federal law," this Court, through Mr. Justice Hughes, declared that "He was thus admitted with the privilege of entering and abiding in the United States, and hence of entering and abiding in any State in the Union." *Truax* v. *Raich*, 239 U.S. 33, 39. Why we should hesitate to hold that federal citizenship implies rights to enter and abide in any state of the Union at least equal to those possessed by aliens passes my understanding. The world is even more upside down than I had supposed it to be, if California must accept aliens in deference to their federal privileges but is free to turn back citizens of

the United States unless we treat them as subjects of commerce.

The right of the citizen to migrate from state to state which, I agree with MR. JUSTICE DOUGLAS, is shown by our precedents to be one of national citizenship, is not, however, an unlimited one. In addition to being subject to all constitutional limitations imposed by the federal government, such citizen is subject to some control by state governments. He may not, if a fugitive from justice, claim freedom to migrate unmolested, nor may he endanger others by carrying contagion about. These causes, and perhaps others that do not occur to me now, warrant any public authority in stopping a man where it finds him and arresting his progress across a state line quite as much as from place to place within the state.

It is here that we meet the real crux of this case. Does "indigence" as defined by the application of the California statute constitute a basis for restricting the freedom of a citizen, as crime or contagion warrants its restriction? We should say now, and in no uncertain terms, that a man's mere property status, without more, cannot be used by a state to test, qualify, or limit his rights as a citizen of the United States. "Indigence" in itself is neither a source of rights nor a basis for denying them. The mere state of being without funds is a neutral fact—constitutionally an irrelevance, like race, creed, or color. I agree with what I understand to be the holding of the Court that cases which may indicate the contrary are overruled.

Any measure which would divide our citizenry on the basis of property into one class free to move from state to state and another class that is poverty-bound to the place where it has suffered misfortune is not only at war with the habit and custom by which our country has expanded, but is also a short-sighted blow at the security of property itself. Property can have no more dangerous, even if unwitting, enemy than one who would make its possession a pretext for unequal or exclusive civil rights. Where those rights are derived from national citizenship no State may impose such a test, and whether the Congress could do so we are not called upon to inquire.

I think California had no right to make the condition of Duncan's purse, with no evidence of violation by him of any law or social policy which caused it, the basis of excluding him or of punishing one who extended him aid.

If I doubted whether his federal citizenship alone were enough to open the gates of California to Duncan, my doubt would disappear on consideration of the obligations of such citizenship. Duncan owes a duty to render military service, and this Court has said that this duty is the result of his citizenship. Mr. Chief Justice White declared in the *Selective Draft Law Cases,* 245 U.S. 366, 378: "It may not be doubted that the very conception of a just government and its duty to the citizen includes the reciprocal obligation of the citizen to render military service in case of need and the right to compel it." A contention that a citizen's duty to render military service is suspended by "indigence" would meet with little favor. Rich or penniless, Duncan's citizenship under the Constitution pledges his strength to the defense of California as a part of the United States, and his right to migrate to any part of the land he must defend is something she must respect under the same instrument. Unless this Court is willing to say that citizenship of the United States means at least this much to the citizen, then our heritage of constitutional privileges and immunities is only a promise to the ear to be broken to the hope, a teasing illusion like a munificent bequest in a pauper's will.[12]

HOW LAISSEZ FAIRE CAME TO THE CONSTITUTION

The Path of Due Process: III [13]

After two decisive defeats,[14] the Fourteenth Amendment came quietly into constitutional law. The pomp and circumstance which had attended the

[12] The right to travel *within* the United States was recognized, at least as a dictum, as a privilege and immunity of national citizenship for almost three-quarters of a century—from 1868 to 1941. But what of the logical extension of that "right": the right to travel *outside* of the United States, including the right to leave the country? This question has not been controversial until quite recently, the period of the Cold War subsequent to World War II, to be specific. Prior to that time, passport controls were enforced only in time of war, when various other abridgments of the rights of citizens also were considered necessary and were imposed. When the question of the right to travel abroad and to leave the country reached the Warren Court, in what the majority obviously considered to be peacetime, it came as what lawyers call a case of "first impression." The Court responded by reading into the due-process clause of the Fifth Amendment, as a form of personal liberty, what might have been but never quite became the content of the privileges-and-immunities clause of the Fourteenth Amendment. Douglas, writing for the majority in *Kent* v. *Dulles,* 357 U.S. 116 (1958), cited the Edwards case along with Crandall as though the concurrers in Edwards had written the opinion of the Court. So the right of external travel became a "liberty" of national citizenship by grace of the increasingly expansive due-process clause of the Fifth Amendment; while the right of internal travel appeared to remain, however incongruously, a function of the commerce clause.

[13] Hamilton, *loc. cit.,* pp. 178-184, 185-187.

[14] The Slaughter-House decision of 1873; and *Davidson* v. *New Orleans,* 96 U.S. 97 (1878), in which a unanimous Court defined the Fourteenth Amendment due-process clause in procedural terms, as applied to the facts of the case, while conceding in a dictum the *principle* of substantive due process.

previous causes was absent. A municipal ordinance in California had made a pretty verbal display to the effect that laundries carried on in brick buildings were within the law; but if they were housed in wooden structures, the authorities must be satisfied that the chance of fire was not a hazard to public safety. In obvious intent and in administration it said that the trade was open to the whites but that Orientals were to be subjected to the closest scrutiny before admission to so exclusive a club. Yick Wo, denied the right to work at his chosen trade, essayed judicial combat, had syllogisms broken in his behalf, and came away with the signal victory of the highest court in the land. His right to his trade was as good as that of any other man. The victory was scored, not by a recently emancipated black, not by a Southern white whose pride in race did not forbid the use of the Negro's legal protection, but by a yellow man from China. Against the arbitrary act of the state, "equal protection of the laws" came into constitutional law where "privileges and immunities" and "due process" had been denied admission. And the new doctrine had been accepted by the Court without a single vote in dissent.

The breath of life had been breathed into the Fourteenth Amendment. The right to work at one's chosen occupation had at last become a part of the supreme law of the land. The substance to which "equal protection" gave a verbal home could pass on by contagion into a liberty and a property fortified by "due process." Eighteen years had passed since the amendment was adopted and fourteen since Mr. Campbell had blazed the path for a novel doctrine. But at last, in 1886, even against the action of the state, the rights of man had been accorded the protection of the Constitution.

III

Yet long before this decision another course of events was under way. The Campbell arguments were much too useful to be left to butchers, bakers, and laundry workers. At the bar, and at least before the bench, we find them presently clad in the livery of an alien master. In his briefs—with all their concern for the liberties of the workingman—ex-Justice Campbell could not leave the word "property" alone. He made the right to work a property; and somewhat abstractly, on his own and within quotation marks, he declared the idea that property derives from the state to be the most revolutionary of notions; for, "if the state creates, the state can destroy." As with the individual, so with the nation-on-the-make, no clean-cut line was to be drawn; liberty was the liberty to acquire property. To Mr. Justice Field, rounding out his decades on the high judicial bench, liberty and property came to be a single word with a constant shift of accent to the right. . . . And, long before Yick Wo won his legal tilt against Hopkins and California, attorneys for corporations as plaintiffs in error were presenting in brief and oration a round of exquisite variations on a theme of Campbell.

Although lawyers were admonished for pleading reasons that had been rejected, the recitation went on. In the challenge to the regulation of grain elevators, to the railway legislation of Granger days, to legislative attempts to abate or to subdue the trade in alcoholic beverages, the theme was omnipresent. It was always put forward as a defense of the frontiers of business enterprise against legislative attack. If invariably it fell before the police powers of the state, it acquired momentum and an enhancing repute in the opinions in dissent. As the decade of the eighties moved along, general admissions that legislation must meet the standards of due process were wrung from the Court, while it was still loath to apply the doctrine in the instant case. It was, however, not until the nineties that the personnel of the bench became radical enough to give effect to novel doctrine. Then, by judicial surgery, the Interstate Commerce Act was stripped of its sting and the Sherman Anti-Trust Act limited to an innocuous domain. Although the first real program of national regulation was rendered impotent rather than declared invalid, and the Fourteenth Amendment was not called into service, a judicial opinion had come to prevail in which a due process, fitted out with substance, might by the Court be thrown as a buttress about corporate interest.

The first decisive commitments came—if not off stage—at least in the realm of dicta. In arguing a case of tax avoidance for a railway company, Mr. Roscoe Conkling attempted to use a humble confession to advance the cause of his client. He hinted that the Fourteenth Amendment was the result of a conspiracy between politicians and industrialists; and admitted that, in Congressional committee, the word "person" had been chosen instead of "citizen" to extend the protection of the due process clause to the corporation. His prestige at the bar was at its height; he had refused the high office then held by Mr. Chief Justice Waite and the hardly less honored seat then occupied by Mr. Justice Blatchford. He quoted at some length from the minutes of the Congressional committee; and although the record had not been published and he did not produce it, his remarks made quite an impression. They left no decisive imprint in the reports; for although the Court found it easy to listen to elaborate constitutional argument, it found it difficult to resolve the issue. As the months passed without result, a motion to dismiss was allowed on the ground that the question had become moot, and the issue was left in abeyance. It was long afterward that the minutes of the committee were made available and it was discovered that Conkling had taken excerpts from their context, tempered entries to his cause and reshaped quotations to serve his argumentative purpose.

But decades before historical research was to reveal a deliberate indulgence in historical error, his confidential knowledge had had its effect. Four years later, in 1886, an attorney for the same railroad, in another case of tax avoidance, proposed to argue the same issue. He was stopped by Mr. Chief Justice Waite, who announced that the Court was prepared to admit, without argument, that a corporation was a person within the intendment of the equal protection clause. Again a case, elaborately argued on constitutional grounds, was disposed of without recourse to constitutional doctrine; and the elevation of the corporation to the protective eminence of a person remained a dictum. But the dictum was set down in the reports; and, oblivious to its lack of authority, it began presently to assert its claim as a holding.

The eighties gave way to the more receptive attitude of the nineties. Courts must awaist their causes; and from the play of minds upon issues which are potential the law takes its course. A simple case from Minnesota concerned with the regulation of railroad rates touched off a conflict of values and quickened the germs of doctrine into life. A state commission, acting in pursuance of statute, had fixed rates for milk moving within the boundaries of the commonwealth. No notice had been given, no hearing held, no opportunity accorded for the presentation of evidence. A railroad company, denied an opportunity to present witnesses, regarded the act of the commission as "unjust, unreasonable, and confiscatory" and appealed to the judiciary. To minds steeped in the requisites of criminal process such behavior was most irregular, and the majority of the Court chose to find a procedural issue. The Act deprived "the Company of its right to a judicial investigation, by due process of law, under the forms and with the machinery provided by the wisdom of successive ages for the investigation judicially of the truth of a matter in controversy." It "substitutes as an absolute finality the action of the Railroad Commission" which "cannot be regarded as clothed with judicial function or possessing the machinery of a court of justice." As a result—with an easy transition from procedure to substance— if "without a judicial investigation" the company "is deprived of the power of charging reasonable rates," it is "deprived of the lawful use of its property and thus, in substance and effect, of the property itself." Thus the ancient right of access to the court, with little bother as to what is a proper cause of action, is used to proclaim a judicial overlordship over what had up to the moment been set down as the province of the legislature. . . .

Another six years passed. A number of significant causes came and went, stamped with the attitude of the changing bench. But not until 1897— and then only through a reaching out toward issues that need not have been raised—did an opportunity come for a better fitting of due process to the current temper of the Court [in *Allgeyer* v. *Louisiana*, 165 U.S. 578]. A Louisiana statute had prescribed a regulation of insurance companies within the state; the officials had attempted to bring under its penal provisions a firm which had contracted for marine insurance upon shipments of cotton with a New York company. It seems to have been admitted by all concerned that the contracts had been made in New York and that in the instant case the only matter of local concern was the notices sent of shipments upon which the insurance was to take effect. It was easy enough for the Court to waive so incidental a part of the transaction out from under the Act. That done, the decision of the case demanded no more than the simple comment that an act of Louisiana had no application to a matter beyond the jurisdiction of the state. It might even have been declared null and void as an interference with commerce among the several states. But so obvious a disposition was not for the new blood within the Court. Mr. Justice Peckham, a fresh recruit, had the zeal of the reformer and a faith in the enlightened opinion of his own day untroubled by doubt. The holding depends upon the way the question is put; and he chose—with the consent of his brethren—to view the Act as a "real" interference with "the liberty of the defendants to place insurance on property of their own" where they pleased. Thus the issue became larger, more general, and more significant than the unresolved query in the litigation. As thus stated no question of the right of the Court to review the matter was raised by any of the nine justices. That hurdle had been got over by a succession of rhetorical yieldings in a number of important cases—helped along by the high vault in the Minneosta milk rate case. As formulated by the spokesman for the Court, business privilege was squarely opposed to state regulation with "due process of law" as the arbiter.

It is idle to argue that he went out of his way to do it; for, to the individualistic mind of Mr. Justice Peckham, his was the only way. It was a superb opportunity to bring the orthodoxy of classical economics into the higher law and he was not going to allow it to pass. In a rhetoric which is strangely familiar the dissent of yesterday becomes the opinion of the Court. He quotes Mr. Justice Bradley in the Crescent City Case as if he had been the spokesman for the Court; and the familiar arguments, even the illustrations of the Campbell brief, are repeated. The "inalienable rights" of the Declaration of Independence; the pursuit of happiness; the right of the butcher, the baker, and the candlestick-maker are all there. . . .

[But in] the Allgeyer case "the police power" remained in the background. The cause had little concern with human rights; a trio of judicial bows acknowledged an abstract authority to regulate; and judicial silence prevented a conflict between an upstart due process and the more venerable doctrine . . . and it was only in 1905 that due process first won in a clean-cut combat with the police power. A statute of New York had limited the hours of employees in bakeshops to ten in any one day or sixty in any one week; and, because of his lack of workaday respect for the Act, the People of New York were at odds with a certain Mr. Lochner. The judgment of the Supreme Court—one of the habitual five to four variety—was again delivered by the learned jurist and sound economist, Mr. Justice Peckham. He had only to elaborate his former argument, now fortified by the official citation of *Allgeyer* v. *Louisiana*. Freedom of contract, in respect to trade or employment, was an aspect of the liberty and property which a state might not abridge without due process of law. The challenge of the police power was met by a formidable parade of personal and common-sense opinion that the hours of bakers had little or no relation to the public health.

Again the distinguished jurist made the question before the Court far broader than the issue which the case presented. . . . The opinion of the Court was intended to be an apostolic letter to the many legislatures in the land, appointing limits to their police power and laying a ban upon social legislation.

So it might have become but for the dissent. Mr. Justice Harlan objected that the question of the relation of hours to health was one of fact; that as reasonable men, members of the legislature were entitled to their opinion; and that "there are few, if any, questions in political economy about which entire certainty can be predicted." With him White and Day, JJ., concurred. A youngster of sixty-four, newly come to the Court [Mr. Justice Holmes], seized his chance and scribbled the most famous dissent in all legal history. . . . It is common for latter-day liberals to set this down as the first blast of the trumpet in behalf of a social oversight of human rights; but the historian is more likely to view it as a lance worthily broken in behalf of an ancient cause now in retreat.

LOCHNER v. NEW YORK

198 U.S. 45 (April 17, 1905)

Error to the Oneida County Court of the State of New York.

Reversed.[15]

5-4

Peckham	('+')
Fuller, C.J.	(+)
Brewer	(+)
Brown	(+)
McKenna	(+)
Holmes	('—')
Harlan	('—')
White	—)
Day	—)

---

[15] Half a century later, when the Lochner case remained a subject of scholarly disputation in the pages of professional journals, a commentator noted that "the papers of Justice John Marshall Harlan, which are currently in this writer's possession for the preparation of a biography, indicate that the Court originally voted 5-4 to *sustain* the New York bakers law. Justice Harlan wrote his opinion [given below, following Justice Peckham's] as a majority statement, only to find that one Justice had changed his mind between the time of the original conference and the final vote. Harlan made only minor changes in his draft and submitted it as the dissent of Harlan, White and Day." Alan F.

Statement by MR. JUSTICE PECKHAM:

This is a writ of error to the county court of Oneida county, in the state of New York (to which court the record had been remitted), to review the judgment of the court of appeals of that state, affirming the judgment of the supreme court, which itself affirmed the judgment of the county court, convicting the defendant of a misdemeanor on an indictment under a statute of that state, known, by its short title, as the labor law. . . .

The indictment averred that the defendant "wrongfully and unlawfully required and permitted an employee working for him in his biscuit, bread, and cake bakery and confectionery establishment, at the city of Utica, in this county, to work more than sixty hours in one week," after having been theretofore convicted of a violation of the same act; and therefore, as

Westin, "The Supreme Court and Group Conflict: Thoughts or Seeing Burke Put Through the Mill," *American Political Science Review,* Vol. 52, p. 667n. (1958). It may not be irrelevant to note that the events to which this case relates transpired in what might be characterized as the home constituency of the justice who *did* write for the majority. Mr. Justice Peckham's ancestral homestead (to which he repaired as his own labors came to an end less than five years later) was located at Altamont in the Mohawk Valley in central New York, only a couple score miles or so from the Lochner Bakery in Utica. See 215 U.S. v.

averred, he committed the crime of misdemeanor, second offense. The plaintiff in error demurred to the indictment on several grounds, one of which was that the facts stated did not constitute a crime. The demurrer was overruled, and, the plaintiff in error having refused to plead further, a plea of not guilty was entered by order of the court and the trial commenced, and he was convicted of misdemeanor, second offense, as indicted, and sentenced to pay a fine of $50, and to stand committed until paid, not to exceed fifty days in the Oneida county jail.

MR. JUSTICE PECKHAM, after making the foregoing statement of the facts, delivered the opinion of the court:

. . . The mandate of the statute, that "no employee shall be required or permitted to work," is the substantial equivalent of an enactment that "no employee shall contract or agree to work," more than ten hours per day; and, as there is no provision for special emergencies, the statute is mandatory in all cases. It is not an act merely fixing the number of hours which shall constitute a legal day's work, but an absolute prohibition upon the employer permitting, under any circumstances, more than ten hours' work to be done in his establishment. The employee may desire to earn the extra money which would arise from his working more than the prescribed time, but this statute forbids the employer from permitting the employee to earn it.

The statute necessarily interferes with the right of contract between the employer and employees concerning the number of hours in which the latter may labor in the bakery of the employer. The general right to make a contract in relation to his business is part of the liberty of the individual protected by the 14th Amendment of the Federal Constitution. *Allgeyer* v. *Louisiana,* 165 U.S. 578. Under that provision no state can deprive any person of life, liberty, or property without due process of law. The right to purchase or to sell labor is part of the liberty protected by this amendment, unless there are circumstances which exclude the right. There are, however, certain powers, existing in the sovereignty of each state in the Union, somewhat vaguely termed police powers, the exact description and limitation of which have not been attempted by the courts. Those powers, broadly stated, and without, at present, any attempt at a more specific limitation, relate to the safety, health, morals, and general welfare of the public. Both property and liberty are held on such reasonable conditions as may be imposed by the governing power of the state in the exercise of those powers, and with such conditions the 14th Amendment was not designed to interfere. . . .

The state, therefore, has power to prevent the individual from making certain kinds of contracts, and in regard to them the Federal Constitution offers no protection. If the contract be one which the state, in the legitimate exercise of its police power, has the right to prohibit, it is not prevented from prohibiting it by the 14th Amendment. Contracts in violation of a statute, either of the Federal or state government, or a contract to let one's property for immoral purposes, or to do any other unlawful act, could obtain no protection from the Federal Constitution, as coming under the liberty of person or of free contract. Therefore, when the state, by its legislature, in the assumed exercise of its police powers, has passed an act which seriously limits the right to labor or the right of contract in regard to their means of livelihood between persons who are *sui juris* (both employer and employee), it becomes of great importance to determine which shall prevail,—the right of the individual to labor for such time as he may choose, or the right of the state to prevent the individual from laboring, or from entering into any contract to labor, beyond a certain time prescribed by the state.

This court has recognized the existence and upheld the exercise of the police powers of the states in many cases which might fairly be considered as border ones, and it has, in the course of its determination of questions regarding the asserted invalidity of such statutes, on the ground of their violation of the rights secured by the Federal Constitution, been guided by rules of a very liberal nature, the application of which has resulted, in numerous instances, in upholding the validity of state statutes thus assailed....

[But it] must, of course, be conceded that there is a limit to the valid exercise of the police power by the state. There is no dispute concerning this general proposition. Otherwise the 14th Amendment would have no efficacy and the legislatures of the states would have unbounded power, and it would be enough to say that any piece of legislation was enacted to conserve the morals, the health, or the safety of the people; such legislation would be valid, no matter how absolutely without foundation the claim might be. The claim of the police power would be a mere pretext,—become another and delusive name for the supreme sovereignty of the state to be exercised free from constitutional restraint. This is not contended for. In every case that comes before this court, therefore, where legislation of this character is concerned, and where the protection of the Federal Constitution is sought, the question necessarily arises: Is this a fair, reasonable, and appropriate exercise of the police power of the state, or is it an unreasonable, unnecessary, and arbitrary interference with the right of the individual to his personal liberty, or to enter into those contracts in relation to labor which may seem to him appropriate or necessary for the support of himself and his family? Of course the liberty of contract relating to labor includes both parties to it. The one has as much right to purchase as the other to sell labor.

This is not a question of substituting the judgment of the court for that of the legislature. If the act be within the power of the state it is valid, although the judgment of the court might be totally opposed to the enactment of such a law. But the question would still remain: Is it within the police power of the state? and that question must be answered by the court.

The question whether this act is valid as a labor law, pure and simple, may be dismissed in a few words. There is no reasonable ground for interfering with the liberty of person or the right of free contract, by determining the hours of labor, in the occupation of a baker. There is no contention that bakers as a class are not equal in intelligence and capacity to men in other trades or manual occupations, or that they are not able to assert their rights and care for themselves without the protecting arm of the state, interfering with their independence of judgment and of action. They are in no sense wards of the state. Viewed in the light of a purely labor law, with no reference whatever to the question of health, we think that a law like the one before us involves neither the safety, the morals, nor the welfare, of the public, and that the interest of the public is not in the slightest degree affected by such an act. The law must be upheld, if at all, as a law pertaining to the health of the individual engaged in the occupation of a baker. It does not affect any other portion of the public than those who are engaged in that occupation. Clean and wholesome bread does not depend upon whether the baker works but ten hours per day or only sixty hours a week. The limitation of the hours of labor does not come within the police power on that ground.

It is a question of which of two powers or rights shall prevail,—the power of the state to legislate or the right of the individual to liberty of person and freedom of contract. The mere assertion that the subject relates, though but in a remote degree, to the public health, does not necessarily render the enactment valid. The act must have a more direct relation, as a means to an end, and the end itself must be appropriate and legitimate, before an act can be held to be valid which interferes with the general right of an individual to be free in his person and in his power to contract in relation to his own labor. . . .

We think the limit of the police power has been reached and passed in this case. There is, in our judgment, no reasonable foundation for holding this to be necessary or appropriate as a health law to safeguard the public health, or the health of the individuals who are following the trade of a baker. If this statute be valid, and if, therefore, a proper case is made out in which to deny the right of an individual, *sui juris,* as employer or employee, to make contracts for the labor of the latter under the protection of the provisions of the Federal Constitution, there would seem to be no length to which legislation of this nature might not go. . . .

We think that there can be no fair doubt that the trade of a baker, in and of itself, is not an unhealthy one to that degree which would authorize the legislature to interfere with the right to labor, and with the right of free contract on the part of the individual, either as employer or employee. In looking through statistics regarding all trades and occupations, it may be true that the trade of a baker does not appear to be as healthy as some other trades, and is also vastly more healthy than still others. To the common understanding the trade of a baker has never been regarded as an unhealthy one. Very likely physicians would not recommend the exercise of that or of any other trade as a remedy for ill health. . . . It is unfortunately true that labor, even in any department, may possibly carry with it the seeds of unhealthiness. But are we all, on that account, at the mercy of legislative majorities? A printer, a tinsmith, a locksmith, a carpenter, a cabinetmaker, a dry goods clerk, a bank's, a law-

yer's, or a physician's clerk, or a clerk in almost any kind of business, would all come under the power of the legislature, on this assumption. No trade, no occupation, no mode of earning one's living, could escape this all-pervading power, and the acts of the legislature in limiting the hours of labor in all employments would be valid, although such limitation might seriously cripple the ability of the laborer to support himself and his family. . . .

We do not believe in the soundness of the views which uphold this law. On the contrary, we think that such a law as this, although passed in the assumed exercise of the police power, and as relating to the public health, or the health of the employees named, is not within that power, and is invalid. The act is not, within any fair meaning of the term, a health law, but is an illegal interference with the rights of individuals, both employers and employees, to make contracts regarding labor upon such terms as they may think best, or which they may agree upon with the other parties to such contracts. Statutes of the nature of that under review, limiting the hours in which grown and intelligent men may labor to earn their living, are mere meddlesome interferences with the rights of the individual, and they are not saved from condemnation by the claim that they are passed in the exercise of the police power . . . [and] a prohibition to enter into any contract of labor in a bakery for more than a certain number of hours a week is, in our judgment, so wholly beside the matter of a proper, reasonable, and fair provision as to run counter to that liberty of person and of free contract provided for in the Federal Constitution.

This interference on the part of the legislatures of the several states with the ordinary trades and occupations of the people seems to be on the increase. . . .

It is impossible for us to shut our eyes to the fact that many of the laws of this character, while passed under what is claimed to be the police power for the purpose of protecting the public health or welfare, are, in reality, passed from other motives. We are justified in saying so when, from the character of the law and the subject upon which it legislates, it is apparent that the public health or welfare bears but the most remote relation to the law. The purpose of a statute must be determined from the natural and legal effect of the language employed; and whether it is or is not repugnant to the Constitution of the United States must be determined from the natural effect of such statutes when put into operation, and not from their proclaimed purpose. . . . It seems to us that the real object and purpose were simply to regulate the hours of labor between the master and his employees (all being men, *sui juris*), in a private business, not dangerous in any degree to morals, or in any real and substantial degree to the health of the employees. Under such circumstances the freedom of master and employee to contract with each other in relation to their employment, and in defining the same, cannot be prohibited or interfered with, without violating the Federal Constitution. . . .

Reversed.

MR. JUSTICE HARLAN (with whom MR. JUSTICE WHITE and MR. JUSTICE DAY concurred) dissenting: . . .

It is plain that this statute was enacted in order to protect the physical well-being of those who work in bakery and confectionary establishments. It may be that the statute had its origin, in part, in the belief that employers and employees in such establishments were not upon an equal footing, and that the necessities of the latter often compelled them to submit to such exactions as unduly taxed their strength. Be this as it may, the statute must be taken as expressing the belief of the people of New York that, as a general rule, and in the case of the average man, labor in excess of sixty hours during

a week in such establishments may endanger the health of those who thus labor. Whether or not this be wise legislation it is not the province of the court to inquire. Under our systems of government the courts are not concerned with the wisdom or policy of legislation. So that, in determining the question of power to interfere with liberty of contract, the court may inquire whether the means devised by the state are germane to an end which may be lawfully accomplished and have a real or substantial relation to the protection of health, as involved in the daily work of the persons, male and female, engaged in bakery and confectionery establishments. But when this inquiry is entered upon I find it impossible, in view of common experience, to say that there is here no real or substantial relation between the means employed by the state and the end sought to be accomplished by its legislation. . . . Still less can I say that the statute is, beyond question, a plain, palpable invasion of rights secured by the fundamental law. . . . Therefore I submit that this court will transcend its functions if it assumes to annul the statute of New York. It must be remembered that this statute does not apply to all kinds of business. It applies only to work in bakery and confectionery establishments, in which, as all know, the air constantly breathed by workmen is not as pure and healthful as that to be found in some other establishments or out of doors.

Statistics show that the average daily working time among workingmen in different countries is, in Australia, eight hours; in Great Britain, nine; in the United States, nine and three-quarters; in Denmark, nine and three-quarters; in Norway, ten; Sweden, France, and Switzerland, ten and one-half; Germany, ten and one-quarter; Belgium, Italy, and Austria, eleven; and in Russia, twelve hours.

We judicially know that the question of the number of hours during which a workman should continuously labor has been, for a long period, and is yet, a subject of serious consideration among civilized peoples, and by those having special knowledge of the laws of health. Suppose the statute prohibited labor in bakery and confectionery establishments in excess of eighteen hours each day. No one, I take it, could dispute the power of the state to enact such a statute. But the statute before us does not embrace extreme or exceptional cases. It may be said to occupy a middle ground in respect of the hours of labor. . . .

We also judicially know that the number of hours that should constitute a day's labor in particular occupations involving the physical strength and safety of workmen has been the subject of enactments by Congress and by nearly all of the states. Many, if not most, of those enactments fix eight hours as the proper basis of a day's labor. . . . We cannot say that the state has acted without reason, nor ought we to proceed upon the theory that its action is a mere sham. Our duty, I submit, is to sustain the statute as not being in conflict with the Federal Constitution, for the reason—and such is an all-sufficient reason—it is not shown to be plainly and palpably inconsistent with that instrument. Let the state alone in the management of its purely domestic affairs, so long as it does not appear beyond all question that it has violated the Federal Constitution. This view necessarily results from the principle that the health and safety of the people of a state are primarily for the state to guard and protect.

I take leave to say that the New York statute, in the particulars here involved, cannot be held to be in conflict with the 14th Amendment, without enlarging the scope of the amendment far beyond its original purpose, and without bringing under the supervision of this court matters which have been supposed to belong exclusively to the legislative departments of the several states. . . .

MR. JUSTICE HOLMES dissenting: . . .

This case is decided upon an economic theory which a large part of the country does not entertain. If it were a question whether I agreed with that theory, I should desire to study it further and long before making up my mind. But I do not conceive that to be my duty, because I strongly believe that my agreement or disagreement has nothing to do with the right of a majority to embody their opinions in law. It is settled by various decisions of this court that state constitutions and state laws may regulate life in many ways which we as legislators might think as injudicious, or if you like as tyrannical, as this, and which, equally with this, interfere with the liberty to contract. Sunday laws and usury laws are ancient examples. A more modern one is the prohibition of lotteries. The liberty of the citizen to do as he likes so long as he does not interfere with the liberty of others to do the same, which has been a shibboleth for some well-known writers, is interfered with by school laws, by the Postoffice, by every state or municipal institution which takes his money for purposes thought desirable, whether he likes it or not. The 14th Amendment does not enact Mr. Herbert Spencer's Social Statics. . . . Some . . . laws embody convictions or prejudices which judges are likely to share. Some may not. But a Constitution is not intended to embody a particular economic theory, whether of paternalism and the organic relation of the citizen to the state or of *laissez faire*. It is made for people of fundamentally differing views, and the accident of our finding certain opinions natural and familiar, or novel, and even shocking, ought not to conclude our judgment upon the question whether statutes embodying them conflict with the Constitution of the United States.

General propositions do not decide concrete cases. The decision will depend on a judgment or intuition more subtle than any articulate major premise. But I think that the proposition just stated, if it is accepted, will carry us far toward the end. Every opinion tends to become a law. I think that the word "liberty," in the 14th Amendment, is perverted when it is held to prevent the natural outcome of a dominant opinion, unless it can be said that a rational and fair man necessarily would admit that the statute proposed would infringe fundamental principles as they have been understood by the tradi-tions of our people and our law. It does not need research to show that no such sweeping condemnation can be passed upon the statute before us. A reasonable man might think it a proper measure on the score of health. Men whom I certainly would not pronounce unreasonable would uphold it as a first instalment of a general regulation of the hours of work. Whether in the latter aspect it would be open to the charge of inequality I think it unnecessary to discuss.

The Path of Due Process: IV [16]

[The] four dissenters saw as clearly as the five—who, by the virtue of being one more, were the Court—that the challenged act might be "the first installment of a general regulation of the hours of work"; and they wished to keep the way open. It was probably too late for Harlan, J., or even for Holmes, J., to argue that in such matters the legislature was the sole and exclusive judge and that the Court had no rightful power of review; at least such an argument was not attempted. The all-but-equal vote led to an even balance of doctrines. Neither the police power nor due process was to be preferred; in an even-handed formula, liberty and property are to be set against public policy; as case follows case, these concepts are to be filled with the values of life, a balance is to be struck, and a judgment rendered. An engaging number of rules for the game of review have come and gone; the decisions of the Court have with the circumstances, its personnel, and the temper of the times swung now toward one side, now toward the other. But the balance of values recorded in *Lochner* v. *the People of New York* has endured as the judicial formula for the ultimate judgment upon legislation designed to promote the public interest. . . . For in respect to the public control of business, the Constitution of the United States dates, not from 1787, nor from 1868, but from 1905.

IV

. . . If in the Slaughter House Cases, the Campbell argument had commanded just one vote more, what difference would it have made? We would doubtless by now possess an august corpus on the privileges and immunities of citizenship, and the entries under due process would be correspondingly thin. But would the hypothetical domain be a great and humane code concerned with the rights of man? Or would the corporation, which became a person, just as easily have passed into the protected position of a citizen of the United States? And, in such an event, would the only change be that all

16 Hamilton, *loc. cit.*, pp. 187-190.

that is now written down as liberty and property would be entered as the privileges of citizenship?

Or was the logic of the commitment inevitable—and the specific legal doctrine by which business enterprise sought immunity from regulation a mere rhetorical device? Due process was fashioned from the most respectable ideological stuff of the later nineteenth century. The ideas out of which it was shaped were in full accord with the dominant thought of the age. They were an aspect of common sense, a standard of economic orthodoxy, a test of straight thinking and sound opinion. In the domain of thought their general attitude was omnipresent. In philosophy it was individualism, in government laissez faire, in economics the natural law of supply and demand, in law the freedom of contract. The system of thought had possessed every other discipline; it had in many a domain reshaped the law to its teachings. A respect for the obligations of contract had been set down in the Constitution in 1787; the "ancient maxim" *caveat emptor* had become dominant in the law of sales by the forties; an individual responsibility for industrial accidents was definitely established in torts shortly after the middle of the century. An impact that had been irresistible elsewhere should surely have won its way into constitutional law. Its coming seemed inevitable; the constitutional concept which it made its domicile was a mere matter of doctrinal accident. Words on parchment could not be adamant before so powerful a thrust; privileges and immunities, due process, equal protection, were all available; and, had there been no Fourteenth Amendment, "the obligations" might have been made to encompass "the freedom" of contract; or as a last resort, a vague "natural rights" as a higher law might have been found to permeate the whole Constitution.

The wonder is, not that laissez faire made its entrance, but that it found so insecure a lodgment within the Constitution. Ex-Justice Campbell had a superb case, his strategy was adroit, he suited his arguments to a state of mind which it took a civil war to produce—yet he could not quite command a majority of the Court. It was nearly twenty years before even as a dictum the protection of the Fourteenth Amendment was accorded to a corporation and it was nearly twenty more before the first installment in a program of social legislation was struck down by the Court. Even when it was at last accorded constitutional standing, its victories were often obtained by the narrow margin of five to four. Its triumph did not come until half a decade after the turn of the century, when it had ceased to be common sense, when legislators were forsaking its precepts, and when in philosophy, economics, and government it was on the way out. Even then its victory was inconclusive; it could never claim the faith of the full bench, and it had to share its sovereignty with the antithetical doctrine of the police power.

Freedom of contract took up its abode within "due process of law" too late for easy and secure lodgment. Its legal insecurity may rest upon personnel; a change of a justice here and there would have affected mightily the course of judicial events. It seems strange that so many jurists stood steadfast against the seductions of laissez faire; history, political science, and economics can boast no such record. Or it may be due to the older and established doctrine that the state might intervene with regulation to promote public safety, public health, public morals, and public welfare—against which the cause of the independence of the business system could achieve only a partial success. Or does the whole story, in irony, paradox, and compromise, derive from the innate conservatism of the law—a rock of ages which even the untamed strength of laissez faire could move but could not blast?

Only three years after the Lochner decision, the Court decided *Muller* v. *Oregon,* 208 U.S. 412 (1908), unanimously upholding an Oregon statute establishing the ten-hour day for female factory and laundry employees. In so far as state maximum-hour legislation in relationship to the Fourteenth Amendment was concerned, it appeared that the Court recognized a constitutional difference between men and women. It has been said that: [17]

> One can distinguish *Muller* v. *Oregon* from *Lochner* by seeing the controversy in *Muller* as politically unimportant because involving a fringe group of the economy. In *Muller* the matter was a moral one, involving the special protection of women. The Court clearly considered the care of women to be a matter of special concern and attention for the community. Their weaker physical nature justified their exemption from the ordinary organizational struggles of society. The Court evidenced the emotion with which it viewed legislative protection of women when it said in *Muller,* "As healthy mothers are essential to vigorous offspring, the physical well-being of women becomes an object of public interest and care in order to preserve the strength and vigor of the race. . . . The limitations which this statute places upon her contractual powers, upon her right to agree with her employer as to the time she shall labor, are not imposed solely for her benefit, but also for the benefit of all." Justices who were in the majority in the *Lochner* case voted in unanimity with their colleagues in *Muller.* [But between] *Muller* and *Adkins* v. *Children's Hospital* [below], half a generation and the culmination of the movement for women's suffrage in the passage of the Nineteenth Amendment intervened.

Muller v. *Oregon* is noteworthy, apart from the decision of the Court, as the first of a series of cases in which Louis D. Brandeis argued before the Court in support of labor legislation which was being defended by the National Consumers' League.[18] Brandeis created something of a sensation in the Muller case by filing with the Court "a brief of one hundred and thirteen pages, of which only two

[17] Albert A. Mavrinac, "From *Lochner* to *Brown* v. *Topeka:* The Court and Conflicting Concepts of the Political Process," *American Political Science Review,* Vol. 52, p. 647 (1958).

[18] Clement E. Vose, "The National Consumers' League and the Brandeis Brief," *Midwest Journal of Political Science,* Vol. 1, pp. 276-277 (1957).

pages could be construed as a strictly legal argument." [19] The purpose of such a "sociological" or "scientific" brief was to educate the justices, and to demonstrate that there was a sufficient basis in *fact* (or rather, in what was accepted at the time as being "facts") to support the legislative policy, so that the Court could *not* say that the legislative decision was "arbitrary" or "unreasonable." In the hands of Brandeis (and his associate and successor in this role, Felix Frankfurter), the objective of such briefs was not to prove to the Court that the legislature had made the "right" or "correct" or proper decision; it was rather to prove that there was substantial factual evidence upon which the legislature might reasonably have relied in establishing the socioeconomic policy under attack in the Court. Such an approach provided strong support, of course, for the Holmes position: the Court had no right to pass upon the wisdom of state legislation, and it ought to uphold statutes that could pass the scrutiny of his fictional but symbolic "reasonable man," who articulated the common sense of the community.

ADKINS v. CHILDREN'S HOSPITAL

261 U.S. 925 (1923)

Appeal from the United States Court of Appeals for the District of Columbia.

Affirmed.

5-3

Sutherland	('+')
McKenna	(+)
VanDevanter	(+)
McReynolds	(+)
Butler	(+)
Taft, C.J.	'—')
Sanford	—)
Holmes	'—')
Brandeis	NP

The "Brandeis brief" (as such socioeconomic "fact" briefs have come to be called) played a significant, if not quite successful, role in the Adkins case. "Felix Frankfurter and Miss [Mary W.] Dewson prepared the brief which the National Consumers' League provided for the Minimum Wage Commission of the District of Columbia. At a short

meeting in New York, Frankfurter asked Miss Dewson to collect a great quantity of factual data supporting the reasonableness of the minimum-wage law for women, which was under attack. Frankfurter believed that a bulky brief would by sheer size impress Chief Justice Taft. It apparently did. At any rate, the brief of 1,138 pages was the largest produced by the League; and Taft, in dissent, did adopt its position." [20] Brandeis' nonparticipation can be attributed, no doubt, to his close relationship with the League prior to his appointment to the Court in 1916; there can be no doubt, however, that he would have joined the dissenters had he considered himself qualified to participate. The majority of five consisted of McKenna, whose position remained consistent with his vote in the Lochner case, and the four justices whom we designated in Chapter 3 as the conservative bloc of the 1936 Term. Technically, of course, the statute under attack in Adkins was an act of Congress, so the due-process clause to be invoked was that of the Fifth rather than the Fourteenth Amendment. But the issue was one of local policy in the District of Columbia, not a matter of national policy which would apply in all of the

[19] *Ibid.,* p. 278, quoting *The Outlook,* March 21, 1908.

[20] *Ibid.,* pp. 280-281.

states; and the majority, undisturbed by any technical or historical differences between the two amendments, had no difficulty in reading the "liberty of contract," which the Court by now considered to be firmly established in the Fourteenth Amendment's due-process clause, into the due-process clause of the Fifth Amendment.

MR. JUSTICE SUTHERLAND delivered the opinion of the Court.

The question presented for determination by these appeals is the constitutionality of the Act of September 19, 1918, providing for the fixing of minimum wages for women and children in the District of Columbia. . . . [The] purposes of the act are—"to protect the women and minors of the District from conditions detrimental to their health and morals, resulting from wages which are inadequate to maintain decent standards of living; and the act in each of its provisions and in its entirety shall be interpreted to effectuate these purposes."

The appellee in the first case is a corporation maintaining a hospital for children in the District. It employs a large number of women in various capacities, with whom it had agreed upon rates of wages and compensation satisfactory to such employees, but which in some instances were less than the minimum wage fixed by an order of the board made in pursuance of the act. The women with whom appellee had so contracted were all of full age and under no legal disability. The instant suit was brought by the appellee in the Supreme Court of the District to restrain the board from enforcing or attempting to enforce its order on the ground that the same was in contravention of the Constitution, and particularly the due process clause of the Fifth Amendment. . . .

The Supreme Court of the District denied the injunction and dismissed the bill . . . [but] the Court of Appeals . . . held the act in question to be unconstitu-

tional and reversed the decrees of the trial court. . . .

The statute now under consideration is attacked upon the ground that it authorizes an unconstitutional interference with the freedom of contract included within the guaranties of the due process clause of the Fifth Amendment. That the right to contract about one's affairs is a part of the liberty of the individual protected by this clause is settled by the decisions of this court and is no longer open to question. Allgeyer v. Louisiana, 165 U.S. 578, 591. . . . Within this liberty are contracts of employment of labor. In making such contracts, generally speaking, the parties have an equal right to obtain from each other the best terms they can as the result of private bargaining. . . .

The law takes account of the necessities of only one party to the contract. It ignores the necessities of the employer by compelling him to pay not less than a certain sum, not only whether the employee is capable of earning it, but irrespective of the ability of his business to sustain the burden, generously leaving him, of course, the privilege of abandoning his business as an alternative for going on at a loss. Within the limits of the minimum sum, he is precluded, under penalty of fine and imprisonment, from adjusting compensation to the differing merits of his employees. It compels him to pay at least the sum fixed in any event, because the employee needs it, but requires no service of equivalent value from the employee. It therefore undertakes to solve but one-half of the problem. The other half is the establishment of a corresponding standard of efficiency, and this forms no part of the policy of the legislation, although in practice the former half without the latter must lead to ultimate failure, in accordance with the inexorable law that no one can continue indefinitely to take out more than he puts in without ultimately exhausting the supply. The law is not confined to the great and powerful employers but embraces those whose bargaining power may be as weak as that of the employee. It takes no account of periods of stress and business depression, of crippling losses, which may leave the employer himself without adequate means of livelihood. To the extent that the sum fixed exceeds the fair value of the services rendered, it amounts to a compulsory exaction from the employer for the support of a partially indigent person, for whose condition there rests upon him no peculiar responsibility, and therefore, in effect, arbitrarily shifts to his shoulders a burden which, if it belongs to anybody, belongs to society as a whole.

The feature of this statute, which perhaps more than any other, puts upon it the stamp of invalidity, is that it exacts from the employer an arbitrary payment for a purpose and upon a basis having no causal connection with his business, or the contract or the work the employee engages to do. The declared basis, as already pointed out, is not the value of the service rendered, but the extraneous circumstance that the employee needs to get a prescribed sum of money to insure her subsistence, health, and morals. . . . A statute requiring an employer to pay in money, to pay at prescribed and regular intervals, to pay the value of the services rendered, even to pay with fair relation to the extent of the benefit obtained from the service, would be understandable. But a statute which prescribes payment without regard to any of these things, and solely with relation to circumstances apart from the contract of employment, the business affected by it, and the work done under it, is so clearly the product of a naked, arbitrary exercise of power that it cannot be allowed to stand under the Constitution of the United States.

We are asked, upon the one hand, to consider the fact that several states have adopted similar statutes, and we are invited, upon the other hand, to give weight to the fact that three times as many states, presumably as well informed and as anxious to promote the health and morals of their people, have refrained from enacting such legislation. We have also been furnished with a large number of printed opinions approving the policy of the minimum wage, and our own reading has disclosed a large number to the contrary. These are all proper enough for the consideration of the lawmaking bodies, since their tendency is to establish the desirability or undesirability of the legislation; but they reflect no legitimate light upon the question of its validity, and that is what we are called upon to decide. The elucidation of that question cannot be aided by counting heads.

It is said that great benefits have resulted from the operation of such statutes, not alone in the District of Columbia but in the several states where they have been in force. A mass of reports, opinions of special observers and students of the subject, and the like, has been brought before us in support of this statement, all of which we have found interesting, but only mildly persuasive. That the earnings of women are now greater than they were formerly, and that conditions affecting women have become better in other respects, may be conceded; but convincing indications of the logical relation of these desirable changes to the law in question are significantly lacking. They may be, and quite probably are, due to other causes. . . . No real test of the economic value of the law can be had during periods of maximum employment, when general causes keep wages up to or above the minimum; that will come in periods of depression and struggle for employment, when the efficient will be employed at the minimum rate, while the less capable may not be employed at all. . . .

It has been said that legislation of the kind now under review is required in the interest of social justice, for whose ends freedom of contract may lawfully be subjected to restraint. The liberty of the individual to do as he pleases, even in innocent matters, is not absolute. It must frequently yield to the common good, and the line beyond which the power of interference may not be pressed is neither definite nor unalterable, but may be made to move, within limits not well defined, with changing need and circumstance. Any attempt to fix a rigid boundary would be unwise as well as futile. But, nevertheless, there are limits to the power, and, when these have been passed, it becomes the plain duty of the courts in the proper exercise of their authority to so declare. To sustain the individual freedom of action contemplated by the Constitution is not to strike down the common good, but to exalt it; for surely the good of society as a whole cannot be better served than by the preservation against arbitrary restraint of the liberties of its constituent members.

It follows, from what has been said, that the act in question passes the limit prescribed by the Constitution, and accordingly the decrees of the court below are

Affirmed.

MR. CHIEF JUSTICE TAFT, dissenting.

I regret much to differ from the court in these cases.

The boundary of the police power beyond which its exercise becomes an invasion of the guaranty of liberty under the Fifth and Fourteenth Amendments to the Constitution is not easy to mark. Our court has been laboriously engaged in pricking out a line in successive cases. We must be careful, it seems to me, to follow that line as well as we can, and not to depart from it by suggesting a distinction that is formal rather than real.

Legislatures in limiting freedom of contract between employee and employer by a minimum wage proceed on the assumption that employees, in the class receiving least pay, are not upon a full level of equality of choice with their employer and in their necessitous circumstances are prone to accept pretty much anything that is offered. They are peculiarly subject to

the overreaching of the harsh and greedy employer. The evils of the sweating system and of the long hours and low wages which are characteristic of it are well known. Now, I agree that it is a disputable question in the field of political economy how far a statutory requirement of maximum hours or minimum wages may be a useful remedy for these evils, and whether it may not make the case of the oppressed employee worse than it was before. But it is not the function of this court to hold congressional acts invalid simply because they are passed to carry out economic views which the court believes to be unwise or unsound.

Legislatures which adopt a requirement of maximum hours or minimum wages may be presumed to believe that when sweating employers are prevented from paying unduly low wages by positive law they will continue their business, abating that part of their profits, which were wrung from the necessities of their employees, and will concede the better terms required by the law, and that while in individual cases, hardship may result, the restriction will inure to the benefit of the general class of employees in whose interest the law is passed, and so to that of the community at large. . . .

If it be said that long hours of labor have a more direct effect upon the health of the employee than the low wage, there is very respectable authority from close observers, disclosed in the record and in the literature on the subject quoted at length in the briefs that they are equally harmful in this regard. Congress took this view and we cannot say it was not warranted in so doing. . . .

MR. JUSTICE HOLMES, dissenting.

The question in this case is the broad one, Whether Congress can establish minimum rates of wages for women in the District of Columbia with due provision for special circumstances, or whether we must say that Congress had no power to meddle with the matter at all. To me, notwithstanding the deference due to the prevailing judgment of the Court, the power of Congress seems absolutely free from doubt. The end, to remove conditions leading to ill health, immorality and the deterioration of the race, no one would deny to be within the scope of constitutional legislation. The means are means that have the approval of Congress, of many States, and of those governments from which we have learned our greatest lessons. When so many intelligent persons, who have studied the matter more than any of us can, have thought that the means are effective and are worth the price it seems to me impossible to deny that the belief reasonably may be held by reasonable men. . . . But in the present instance the only objection that can be urged is found within the vague contours of the Fifth Amendment, prohibiting the depriving any person of liberty or property without due process of law. To that I turn.

The earlier decisions upon the same words in the Fourteenth Amendment began within our memory and went no farther than an unpretentious assertion of the liberty to follow the ordinary callings. Later that innocuous generality was ex-

panded into the dogma, Liberty of Contract. Contract is not specially mentioned in the text that we have to construe. It is merely an example of doing what you want to do, embodied in the word liberty. But pretty much all law consists in forbidding men to do some things that they want to do, and contract is no more exempt from law than other acts. . . .

I confess that I do not understand the principle on which the power to fix a minimum for the wages of women can be denied by those who admit the power to fix a maximum for their hours of work. I fully assent to the proposition that here as elsewhere the distinctions of the law are distinctions of degree, but I perceive no difference in the kind or degree of interference with liberty, the only matter with which we have any concern, between the one case and the other. The bargain is equally affected whichever half you regulate. Muller v. Oregon, I take it, is as good law today as it was in 1908. It will need more than the Nineteenth Amendment to convince me that there are no differences between men and women, or that legislation cannot take those differences into account.

THE COUNTERREVOLUTION OF 1937

The Adkins decision was typical of the Court's attitude toward and disposition of cases which challenged state legislation that tampered with the liberty and vested rights of property, during the forty years from the Allgeyer decision to the presentation of President Roosevelt's proposals for the reform of the Supreme Court. It would be more tedious and redundant than enlightening to recount the details. Characteristically the decisions were 5-4, but the liberals were never able to attract the sustained support of a fifth justice, which would have been necessary in order to establish, as a matter of constitutional policy, the liberty of the states to function as laboratories for social and economic experimentation and the right of state legislative majorities to pursue programs that might be considered to be unwise by majorities of the United States Supreme Court. Not that all, or even most, attempts to challenge such legislation before the Supreme Court were successful; of course, the Court upheld, or refused to consider, the constitutionality of more state regulatory laws than it invalidated even during this era of judicial activism. But a majority of the justices frequently reminded the representatives of the "Bolsheviki" (as Chief Justice Taft called them in 1929) that the Supreme Court sat to uphold the Constitution and the fundamental liberties therein enshrined, of which none were more sacred than the rights of property.

The Court's basic tool of adjudication was the Fourteenth Amendment, as in the Lochner and Adkins cases, and primary (although not exclusive) reliance was placed upon the due-process clause. But sometimes the Court chose the equal-protection clause as its grounds for invalidation; and occasionally, the Court would invoke both the due-process clause and, for good measure, the equal-protection clause as well, as in *Truax* v. *Corrigan,* 257 U.S. 321 (1921), in which a five-justice majority headed by Chief Justice Taft rode roughshod over a state supreme court decision to strike down a state statute protecting peaceful picketing. Denouncing the union behavior as a "conspiracy" and a "direct invasion of . . . ordinary business and property rights," Taft proclaimed that "The Constitution was intended—its very purpose was—to prevent experimentation with the fundamental rights of the individual."

As recently as June 1, 1936, the Court invalidated a New York minimum-wage law for women and children, in *Morehead* v. *New York ex rel. Tipaldo,* 298 U.S. 587, with Hughes joining the three liberals in dissent against a five-justice majority consisting of Roberts and the conservative bloc. How much longer liberty of contract might have remained a dominant constitutional policy, if Roosevelt had chosen to wait a bit longer for vacancies instead of attacking the Court, is a moot question; the answer would have depended upon the fortuity of the longevity of individual justices. It seems most likely, viewing the matter from the perspective of two decades, that vacancies would have made possible the appointment of a liberal majority before the expiration of Roosevelt's second term. But the President did not wait; and in the considered judgment of most informed observers, the decision below, reflecting a change that took place within the Court—with no change in its personnel—was a function of the President's impatience and the immediately consequent events.

WEST COAST HOTEL CO. v. PARRISH

300 U.S. 379 (Argued Dec. 16, 17, 1936; decided March 29, 1937)

Appeal from the Supreme Court of Washington.

Affirmed.

5-4

Hughes, C.J.	('+')
Brandeis	(+)
Stone	(+)
Roberts	(+)
Cardozo	(+)
Sutherland	'—')
VanDevanter	—)
McReynolds	—)
Butler	—)

This was the case in which, it has been widely assumed, Roberts' switch in time saved nine. (See Chapter 3 for a discussion of "Roberts' switch.") The four dissenters in this case had comprised, with McKenna, the majority of thirteen years earlier in the Adkins decision; none of the majority in West Coast Hotel had participated in the decision in Adkins.

MR. CHIEF JUSTICE HUGHES delivered the opinion of the Court.

This case presents the question of the constitutional validity of the minimum wage law of the State of Washington.

The Act, entitled "Miminum Wages for Women," authorizes the fixing of minimum wages for women and minors. . . . It provides:

"SECTION 1. The welfare of the State of Washington demands that women and minors be protected from conditions of labor which have a pernicious effect on their health and morals. The State of Washington, therefore, exercising herein its police and sovereign power declares that inadequate wages and unsanitary con-

ditions of labor exert such pernicious effect. . . ."

The appellant conducts a hotel. The appellee Elsie Parrish was employed as a chambermaid and (with her husband) brought this suit to recover the difference between the wages paid her and the minimum wage fixed pursuant to the state law. The minimum wage was $14.50 per week of 48 hours. The appellant challenged the act as repugnant to the due process clause of the Fourteenth Amendment of the Constitution of the United States. The Supreme Court of the State, reversing the trial court, sustained the statute and directed judgment for the plaintiffs. *Parrish v. West Coast Hotel Co.,* 185 Wash. 581; 55 P. (2d) 1083. The case is here on appeal.

The appellant relies upon the decision of this Court in *Adkins* v. *Children's Hospital,* 261 U.S. 525, which held invalid the District of Columbia Minimum Wage Act, which was attacked under the due process clause of the Fifth Amendment.

. . . The state court has refused to regard the decision in the *Adkins* case as determinative and has pointed to our decisions both before and since that case as justifying its position. We are of the opinion that this ruling of the state court demands on our part a reëxamination of the *Adkins* case. The importance of the question, in which many States having similar laws are concerned, the close division by which the decision in the *Adkins* case was reached, and the economic conditions which have supervened, and in the light of which the reasonableness of the exercise of the protective power of the State must be considered, make it not only appropriate, but we think imperative, that in deciding the present case the subject should receive fresh consideration.

The history of the litigation of this question may be briefly stated. The minimum wage statute of Washington was enacted over twenty-three years ago. Prior to the decision in the instant case it had twice been held valid by the Supreme Court of the State. . . . The Washington statute is essentially the same as that enacted in Oregon in the same year. . . . The validity of the latter act was sustained by the Supreme Court of Oregon in *Stettler* v. *O'Hara,* 69 Ore. 519; 139 Pac. 743, and *Simpson* v. *O'Hara,* 70 Ore. 261; 141 Pac. 158. These cases, after reargument, were affirmed here by an equally divided court, in 1917. 243 U.S. 629. The law of Oregon thus continued in effect. . . .

The principle which must control our decision is not in doubt. The constitutional provision invoked is the due process clause of the Fourteenth Amendment governing the States, as the due process clause invoked in the *Adkins* case governed Congress. In each case the violation alleged by those attacking minimum wage regulation for women is deprivation of freedom of contract. What is this freedom? The Constitution does not speak of freedom of contract. It speaks of liberty and prohibits the deprivation of liberty without due process of law. In prohibiting that deprivation the Constitution does not recognize an absolute and uncontrollable liberty. Liberty in each of its phases has its history and connotation. But the liberty safeguarded is liberty in a social organization which requires the protection of law against the evils which menace the health, safety, morals and welfare of the people. Liberty under the Constitution is thus necessarily subject to the restraints of due process, and regulation which is reasonable in relation to its subject and is adopted in the interests of the community is due process. . . .

We think . . . that the decision in the *Adkins* case was a departure from the true application of the principles governing the regulation by the State of the relation of employer and employed. . . . What can be closer to the public interest than the health of women and their protection from unscrupulous and overreaching employers? And if the protection of women is a legitimate end of the exercise of state power, how can it be said that the require-

ment of the payment of a minimum wage fairly fixed in order to meet the very necessities of existence is not an admissible means to that end? The legislature of the State was clearly entitled to consider the situation of women in employment, the fact that they are in the class receiving the least pay, that their bargaining power is relatively weak, and that they are the ready victims of those who would take advantage of their necessitous circumstances. The legislature was entitled to adopt measures to reduce the evils of the "sweating system," the exploiting of workers at wages so low as to be insufficient to meet the bare cost of living, thus making their very helplessness the occasion of a most injurious competition. The legislature had the right to consider that its minimum wage requirements would be an important aid in carrying out its policy of protection. The adoption of similar requirements by many States evidences a deepseated conviction both as to the presence of the evil and as to the means adapted to check it. Legislative response to that conviction cannot be regarded as arbitrary or capricious, and that is all we have to decide. Even if the wisdom of the policy be regarded as debatable and its effects uncertain, still the legislature is entitled to its judgment.

There is an additional and compelling consideration which recent economic experience has brought into a strong light. The exploitation of a class of workers who are in an unequal position with respect to bargaining power and are thus relatively defenceless against the denial of a living wage is not only detrimental to their health and well being but casts a direct burden for their support upon the community. What these workers lose in wages the taxpayers are called upon to pay. The bare cost of living must be met. We may take judicial notice of the unparalleled demands for relief which arose during the recent period of depression and still continue to an alarming extent despite the degree of economic recovery which has been achieved. It is unnecessary to cite official statistics to establish what is of common knowledge through the length and breadth of the land. While in the instant case no factual brief has been presented, there is no reason to doubt that the State of Washington has encountered the same social problem that is present elsewhere. The community is not bound to provide what is in effect a subsidy for unconscionable employers. The community may direct its law-making power to correct the abuse which springs from their selfish disregard of the public interest. The argument that the legislation in question constitutes an arbitrary discrimination, because it does not extend to men, is unavailing. This Court has frequently held that the legislative authority, acting within its proper field, is not bound to extend its regulation to all cases which it might possibly reach. . . . This familiar principle has repeatedly been applied to legislation which singles out women, and particular classes of women, in the exercise of the State's protective power. . . . Their relative need in the presence of the evil, no less than the existence of the evil itself, is a matter for the legislative judgment.

Our conclusion is that the case of *Adkins* v. *Children's Hospital, supra,* should be, and it is, overruled. The judgment of the Supreme Court of the State of Washington is

Affirmed.

9

Equal Protection and Racial Discrimination

WITH REGARD TO STATE REGULATION of economic enterprise, subsequent to the adoption of the Civil War amendments, we found that the Court was permissive during the quarter-century from 1873-1897; for the next four decades, from 1897 to 1937, a majority of the Court were activist defenders of the rights of business enterprise and a laissez-faire economy against "meddling interference" by the states; and since 1937, the Court has returned to a permissive role, deferring to the judgment of state legislative majorities in questions of political economy. Consequently, all except one of the cases that we studied in the preceding chapter were decided in or before 1937.

In this chapter, all except one of the seven cases that we shall examine were decided *after* 1937. Judicial review by the Supreme Court of state economic regulation has been a static and passive area of constitutional politics for over two decades; but the Court's policy-making in relationship to the states, with regard to the race problem in the United States, has emerged as the Court's most controversial and most important activity during the period 1944-1959. The trends of judicial activism and restraint regarding state policies toward racial segregation are almost reciprocal to those regarding state economic regulation, although there has been a basic shift in the *direction* of the Court's activism during the ninety years that have elapsed since the adoption of the Fourteenth and Fifteenth Amendments (in 1868 and 1870).

During the Reconstruction period, the Court was activist, striking down pro-integration legislation of the states on commerce-clause grounds, and of Con-

458

gress as a violation of the Tenth Amendment. In so doing, the Court was acting to restore the prewar federal balance of authority between the nation and the states; but the effect of the Court's decisions was also to uphold the values of segregation. After the end of Reconstruction, pro-integration legislation by either the Congress or the states of the South (where the race problem is felt most acutely) became politically infeasible. During the past three-quarters of a cen-tury, the Court has been faced with the opposite question—whether it should uphold the constitutionality of pro-segregation legislation. Until 1937, the Court vacillated, generally applying the "separate but equal" doctrine established in 1896 in *Plessy* v. *Ferguson* (below); and as a consequence, state legislation requiring racial discrimination and the unequal protection of the laws was usually upheld. It was not the South, but the Constitution, of which the Court demanded flexibility and conformity to the prevailing mores of the age. There were some exceptions in cases involving the political right to vote that was explicitly and specially "guaranteed" by the Fifteenth Amendment; [1] but none of these decisions of the Court had any significant effect upon Negro suffrage, either in the states to which they related or elsewhere in the country. It has been only since 1937 that the Court has consistently pursued a strongly activist policy in behalf of racial integration. The result has been twofold: undoubtedly, the Court's decisions of the past two decades have had a dramatic and dynamic effect upon the relationship between whites and Negroes throughout the nation; and equally without question, the Court's decisions have been primarily responsible for the most serious and widespread friction, between the national government and the dominant groups in a substantial minority of the states, that has existed since the days of Reconstruction. Both results testify to the importance of the Supreme Court as a national policy-maker. It is doubtful whether either the President or the Congress, or both together, could have established the national policy of public school integration announced by the Court in *Brown* v. *Board of Education* (the School Segregation Cases; below). Whether the Court, having done so, can make its policy stick remains to be seen.

Any issue of constitutional policy of the magnitude of the race problem in the United States has many dimensions. Obviously, we could approach the question from the point of view of the civil rights of a minority group in relationship to the governmental authority through which, in terms of somewhat oversimplified democratic theory, the majority speak. We have assumed, however, that the problems of racial integration differ both quantitatively and qualitatively from the civil-liberties problems with which we deal in Part IV of this volume. None of the latter proximately involves, as does the race problem, the fundamental political relationship between the nation and the states, nor the underlying status

[1] "Section 1. The right of citizens of the United States to vote shall not be denied or abridged by the United States or by any State on account of race, color, or previous condition of servitude. Section 2. The Congress shall have power to enforce this article by appropriate legislation."

and prestige of the Court itself. The Supreme Court took an immense and calculated risk, both for itself and for the nation as a whole, when it announced its decision in the School Segregation Cases in 1954. We believe that this necessitates our approaching this issue of constitutional policy primarily as an aspect of American federalism.

FEDERAL PROTECTION OF CIVIL RIGHTS[2]

The Congress enacted a series of "civil rights acts" during the decade 1866-1875, some preceding and some following the adoption of the Fourteenth and Fifteenth Amendments. Of these statutes, only a few brief paragraphs survived into the twentieth century.[3] The remainder were either repealed by later Congresses, or else were declared unconstitutional by the Supreme Court. The Court did uphold provisions of the civil rights acts which defined interference with participation in federal elections as a crime;[4] but the Court emasculated the civil rights acts by establishing a strict and narrow concept of "state action" in its decision in the *Civil Rights Cases,* 109 U.S. 3 (1883). Under this view, most forms of racial discrimination were beyond the jurisdiction of the national government; and even in cases where equal rights under the United States Constitution clearly were denied, their vindication was left to the judges and courts of states which, by and large, were aggressive sponsors of the very policies which had resulted in the denial of federal rights. This general state of affairs persisted for over half a century following the decision of the *Civil Rights Cases.*

It was not until 1939 that a Civil Rights Section was established, by administrative action, in the Department of Justice. The policy of Congress was to starve this unit by refusing to support its activities with adequate funds, adequate personnel, or any statutory authority additional to that of the surviving sections from the Reconstruction era civil rights acts. Consequently, the Civil Rights Section (later Division) has labored under severe legal and administrative handicaps during the past two decades. Nevertheless, the Section had a significant impact upon the Court's decisions abolishing the white primary, which we discuss in a later section of this chapter. Major responsibility for bringing the restrictive covenant and public-education cases (also discussed below) before the Court must be attributed, however, not to the Department of Justice but to the National

[2] The best general discussion of this subject is Robert K. Carr, *Federal Protection of Civil Rights: Quest for a Sword* (Ithaca: Cornell University Press, 1947); and for the more recent period, including a summary of the Civil Rights Act of 1957, see C. Herman Pritchett, *The American Constitution* (New York: McGraw, 1959), chap. xxxiv.

[3] See *United States Code,* Title 18, Sections 241 and 242; and Title 42, Sections 1981-1994, to which a new section regarding summary punishment of criminal contempt of court was added as No. 1995 by the Civil Rights Act of September 9, 1957. See also Appendix 2 to Carr, *op. cit.,* which collects the relevant statutes.

[4] *Ex parte Siebold,* 100 U.S. 371 (1880); *Ex parte Yarbrough,* 110 U.S. 651 (1884).

Association for the Advancement of Colored People. (Some of the lobbying tactics of the N.A.A.C.P. are discussed in Chapter 3.) It remains correct to say that during the past two decades, national policy regarding racial segregation has been made primarily by the Supreme Court; only to a much lesser extent by the Presidency; and almost not at all by the Congress. In a sense, the Court had come full circle: having frustrated a congressional policy of integration at a time when the reaction to the excesses of Reconstruction was running at full tide, the Court found itself, during the middle decades of the twentieth century, the only major decision-making agency of the national government with the political capacity to recast the pro-segregation policies which the Court itself had written into the Constitution in decisions such as the *Civil Rights Cases* and *Plessy* v. *Ferguson*. The Roosevelt and Vinson and Warren Courts have reacted to the pro-integration pressures of nationally organized interests and groups, just as the Courts presided over by Chief Justices Waite and Fuller established diametrically opposed constitutional policies, in response to the dominant political pressures—and state of judicial knowledge—of an earlier age.

THE SEPARATE AND UNEQUAL REGULATION OF COMMERCE

Among the more intriguing facets of the Court's decisions affecting racial discrimination has been the interplay of the commerce and the equal-protection clauses of the Constitution, as these relate to state regulation of segregation in transportation, and state regulation of public schools.[5] State authority to regulate segregation in either transportation or education stems, from the point of view of the Supreme Court, from the state's "police power," that undefined (in the United States Constitution) residuum of governmental authority, under the Tenth Amendment, to act in the "public interest." A conspicuous example of the loose use of principle and precedent characteristic of the Court's decisions in this area occurred in the case below, *Plessy* v. *Ferguson,* in which the majority cite a pre-Civil War decision of a state court, upholding various kinds of segregation (i.e., by age, sex, and race) in public schools, as persuasive authority for the Supreme Court's interpretation of the equal-protection clause to countenance racial segregation in intrastate transportation. *Plessy* v. *Ferguson,* in turn, became recognized as the leading authority for the proposition that "separate but equal" schools for Negro and white children were not a denial of the rights of either under the Fourteenth Amendment.

The initial challenges to state legislation regulating segregation in transportation were raised under the commerce clause, not under the Fourteenth Amendment. In *Hall* v. *De Cuir,* 95 U.S. 485 (1878), a Louisiana statute *prohibit-*

---

[5] See Victor G. Rosenblum, *Law as a Political Instrument* (Garden City: Doubleday, 1955), chaps. iii and iv.

ing segregation on common carriers within the state, which had been upheld by the two lower (state) courts, was declared by the Supreme Court to be an unconstitutional "direct burden" upon interstate commerce. But twelve years later, in *Louisville, New Orleans, and Texas Railway Co.* v. *Mississippi*, 133 U.S. 587 (1890), the Supreme Court upheld a Mississippi statute *requiring* segregation on common carriers within the state. To require railroads to provide duplicate facilities for white and Negro passengers did not burden interstate commerce; to require railroads to provide the same facilities for any of its passengers did burden interstate commerce. Students unfamiliar with the processes of legal reasoning may experience some initial difficulty in grasping the logical consistency of these two decisions of the Court, in relation either to each other or to the "facts" which are supposed to play such an important part in commerce-clause decisions.

Plessy v. *Ferguson* was concerned with a similar statute of Louisiana, with the claim of unconstitutionality now based upon the equal-protection rather than the commerce clause. But the Fourteenth Amendment, announced the Court, was not intended to redress the inequalities of nature by an artificial and enforced fraternization, contrary to "racial instincts" and "distinctions based upon physical differences" between the two races. To require "separate" but "equal" facilities was not unreasonable, said the Court, and therefore it was not contrary to the equal-protection clause of the Fourteenth Amendment.

PLESSY v. FERGUSON

163 U.S. 537 (May 18, 1896)

Error to the Supreme Court of Louisiana.

Affirmed.

7-1

Brown	('+')
Fuller, C.J.	(+)
Field	(+)
Gray	(+)
Shiras	(+)
White	(+)
Peckham	(+)
Harlan	'—')
Brewer	NP

MR. JUSTICE BROWN . . . delivered the opinion of the court.

This case turns upon the constitutionality of an act of the general assembly of the state of Louisiana, passed in 1890, providing for separate railway carriages for the white and colored races. . . .

The first section of the statute enacts "that all railway companies carrying passengers in their coaches in this state, shall provide equal but separate accommodations for the white, and colored races, by providing two or more passenger coaches for each passenger train, or by dividing the passenger coaches by a partition so as to secure separate accommodations: provided, that this section shall not be construed to apply to street railroads. No person or persons shall be permitted to occupy seats in coaches, other than the ones assigned to them, on account of the race they belong to."

By the second section it was enacted "that the officers of such passenger trains shall have power and are hereby required to assign each passenger to the coach or compartment used for the race to which such passenger belongs; any passenger insisting on going into a coach or compartment to which by race he does not belong, shall be liable to a fine of twenty-five dollars, or in lieu thereof to imprisonment for a period of not more than twenty days in the parish prison, and any officer of any railroad insisting on assigning a passenger to a coach or compartment other than the one set aside for the race to which said passenger belongs, shall be liable to a fine of twenty-five dollars, or in lieu thereof to imprisonment for a period of not more than twenty days in the parish prison; and should any passenger refuse to occupy the coach or compartment to which he or she is assigned by the officer of such railway, said officer shall have power to refuse to carry such passenger on his train, and for such refusal neither he nor the railway company which he represents shall be liable for damages in any of the courts of this state."

The third section provides penalties for the refusal or neglect of the officers, directors, conductors, and employés of railway companies to comply with the act, with a proviso that "nothing in this act shall be construed as applying to nurses attending children of the other race." The fourth section is immaterial.

The information filed in the criminal district court charged, in substance, that Plessy, being a passenger between two stations within the state of Louisiana, was assigned by officers of the company to the coach used for the race to which he belonged, but he insisted upon going into a coach used by the race to which he did not belong. Neither in the information nor plea was his particular race or color averred.

The petition for the writ of prohibition averred that petitioner was seven-eighths Caucasian and one-eighth African blood; that the mixture of colored blood was not discernible in him; and that he was entitled to every right, privilege, and immunity secured to citizens of the United States of the white race; and that, upon such theory, he took possession of a vacant seat in a coach where passengers of the white race were accommodated, and was ordered by the conductor to vacate said coach, and take a seat in another, assigned to persons of the colored race, and, having refused to comply with such demand, he was forcibly ejected, with the aid of a police officer, and imprisoned in the parish jail to answer a charge of having violated the above act.

The constitutionality of this act is attacked upon the ground that it conflicts both with the thirteenth amendment of the constitution, abolishing slavery, and the fourteenth amendment, which prohibits certain restrictve legislation on the part of the states.

That it does not conflict with the thirteenth amendment, which abolished slavery and involuntary servitude, except as a punishment for crime, is too clear for argument. Slavery implies involuntary servitude,—a state of bondage; the ownership of mankind as a chattel, or, at least, the control of the labor and services of one man for the benefit of another, and the absence of a legal right to the disposal of his own person, property, and services. . . .

A statute which implies merely a legal distinction between the white and colored races—a distinction which is founded in the color of the two races, and which must always exist so long as white men are distinguished from the other race by color— has no tendency to destroy the legal equality of the two races, or re-establish a state of involuntary servitude. . . .

The object of the [Fourteenth] amendment was undoubtedly to enforce the absolute equality of the two races before the law, but, in the nature of things, it could not have been intended to abolish distinctions based upon color, or to enforce social, as distinguished from political, equality, or a commingling of the two races upon terms unsatisfactory to either. Laws permitting, and even requiring, their separation, in places where they are liable to be brought into contact, do not necessarily imply the inferiority of either race to the other, and have been generally, if not universally, recognized as within the competency of the state legislatures in the exercise of their police power. The most common instance of this is connected with the establishment of separate schools for white and colored children, which have been held to be a valid exercise of the legislative power even by courts of states where the political rights of the colored race have been longest and most earnestly enforced.

One of the earliest of these cases is that of Roberts v. City of Boston, 5 Cush. 198, in which the supreme judicial court of Massachusetts held that the general school committee of Boston had power to make provision for the instruction of colored children in separate schools established exclusively for them, and to prohibit their attendance upon the other schools. "The great principle," said Chief Justice Shaw, "advanced by the learned and eloquent advocate for the plaintiff [Mr. Charles Sumner], is that, by the constitution and laws of Massachusetts, all persons, without distinction of age or sex, birth or color, origin or condition, are equal before the law. * * * But, when this great principle comes to be applied to the actual and various conditions of persons in society, it will not warrant the assertion that men and women are legally clothed with the same civil and political powers, and that children and adults are legally to have the same functions and be subject to the same treatment; but only that the rights of all, as they are settled and regulated by law, are equally entitled to the paternal consideration and protection of the law for their maintenance and security." It was held that the powers of the committee extended to the establishment of separate schools for children of different ages, sexes and colors, and that they might also establish special schools for poor and neglected children, who have become too old to attend the primary school, and yet have not acquired the rudiments of learning, to enable them to enter the ordinary schools. Similar laws have been enacted by con-

gress under its general power of legislation over the District of Columbia . . . as well as by the legislatures of many of the states, and have been generally, if not uniformly, sustained by the courts. . . .

Laws forbidding the intermarriage of the two races may be said in a technical sense to interfere with the freedom of contract, and yet have been universally recognized as within the police power of the state. . . .

The distinction between laws interfering with the political equality of the Negro and those requiring the separation of the two races in schools, theaters, and railway carriages has been frequently drawn by this court. Thus, in Strauder v. West Virginia, 100 U.S. 303, it was held that a law of West Virginia limiting to white male persons 21 years of age, and citizens of the state, the right to sit upon juries, was a discrimination which implied a legal inferiority in civil society, which lessened the security of the right of the colored race, and was a step towards reducing them to a condition of servility. Indeed, the right of a colored man that, in the selection of jurors to pass upon his life, liberty, and property, there shall be no exclusion of his race, and no discrimination against them because of color, has been asserted in a number of cases. . . .

Upon the other hand, where a statute of Louisiana required those engaged in the transporation of passengers among the states to give to all persons traveling within that state, upon vessels employed in that business, equal rights and privileges in all parts of the vessel, without distinction on account of race or color, and subjected to an action for damages the owner of such a vessel who excluded colored passengers on account of their color from the cabin set aside by him for the use of whites, it was held to be, so far as it applied to interstate commerce, unconstitutional and void. Hall v. De Cuir, 95 U.S. 485. The court in this case, however, expressly disclaimed that it had anything whatever to do with the statute as a regulation of internal commerce, or affecting anything else than commerce among the states. . . .

Much nearer, and, indeed, almost directly in point, is the case of the Louisville, N. O. & T. Ry. Co. v. State, 133 U.S. 587, wherein the railway company was indicted for a violation of a statute of Mississippi, enacting that all railroads carrying passengers should provide equal, but separate, accommodations for the white and colored races, by providing two or more passenger cars for each passenger train, or by dividing the passenger cars by a partition, so as to secure separate accommodations. The case was presented in a different aspect from the one under consideration, inasmuch as it was an indictment against the railway company for failing to provide the separate accommodations, but the question considered was the constitutionality of the law. In that case, the supreme court of Missisisippi . . . had held that the statute applied solely to commerce within the state, and, that being the construction of the state statute by its highest court, was accepted as conclusive. "If it be a matter," said the court (page 591, 133 U.S.), "respecting commerce wholly within a state, and not interfering with commerce between the states, then, obviously, there is no violation of the commerce clause of the federal constitution. * * * No question arises under this section as to the power of the state to separate in different compartments interstate passengers, or affect, in any manner, the privileges and rights of such passengers. All that we can consider is whether the state has the power to require that railroad trains within her limits shall have separate accommodations for the two races. That affecting only commerce within the state is no invasion of the power given to congress by the commerce clause."

A like course of reasoning applies to the case under consideration, since the supreme court of Louisiana, in the case of State v. Judge . . . held that the statute

in question did not apply to interstate passengers, but was confined in its application to passengers traveling exclusively within the borders of the state. The case was decided largely upon the authority of Louisville, N. O. & T. Ry. Co. v. State. . . . In the present case no question of interference with interstate commerce can possibly arise, since the East Louisiana Railway appears to have been purely a local line, with both its termini within the state of Louisiana . . . [and] we think the enforced separation of the races, as applied to the internal commerce of the state, neither abridges the privileges or immunities of the colored man, deprives him of his property without due process of law, nor denies him the equal protection of the laws, within the meaning of the fourteenth amendment. . . .

. . . [It] is also suggested by the learned counsel for the plaintiff in error that the same argument that will justify the state legislature in requiring railways to provide separate accommodations for the two races will also authorize them to require separate cars to be provided for people whose hair is of a certain color, or who are aliens, or who belong to certain nationalities, or to enact laws requiring colored people to walk upon one side of the street, and white people upon the other, or requiring white men's houses to be painted white, and colored men's black, or their vehicles or business signs to be of different colors, upon the theory that one side of the street is as good as the other, or that a house or vehicle of one color is as good as one of another color. The reply to all this is that every exercise of the police power must be reasonable, and extend only to such laws as are enacted in good faith for the promotion of the public good, and not for the annoyance or oppression of a particular class. . . .

So far, then, as a conflict with the fourteenth amendment is concerned, the case reduces itself to the question whether the statute of Louisiana is a reasonable regulation, and with respect to this there must necessarily be a large discretion on the part of the legislature. In determining the question of reasonableness, it is at liberty to act with reference to the established usages, customs, and traditions of the people, and with a view to the promotion of their comfort, and the preservation of the public peace and good order. Gauged by this standard, we cannot say that a law which authorizes or even requires the separation of the two races in public conveyances is unreasonable, or more obnoxious to the fourteenth amendment than the acts of congress requiring separate schools for colored children in the District of Columbia, the constitutionality of which does not seem to have been questioned, or the corresponding acts of state legislatures.

We consider the underlying fallacy of the plaintiff's argument to consist in the assumption that the enforced separation of the two races stamps the colored race with a badge of inferiority. If this be so, it is not by reason of anything found in the act, but solely because the colored race chooses to put that construction upon it. The argument necessarily assumes that if, as has been more than once the case, and is not unlikely to be so again, the colored race should become the dominant power in the state legislature, and should enact a law in precisely similar terms, it would thereby relegate the white race to an inferior position. We imagine that the white race, at least, would not acquiesce in this assumption. The argument also assumes that social prejudices may be overcome by legislation, and that equal rights cannot be secured to the negro except by an enforced commingling of the two races. We cannot accept this proposition. If the two races are to meet upon terms of social equality, it must be the result of natural affinities, a mutual appreciation of each other's merits, and a voluntary consent of individuals. . . . Legislation is powerless to eradicate racial instincts, or to abolish distinctions based upon physical differences, and the attempt to do so can only result in accentuating the difficulties of the present situation. If the civil and political rights of both races be equal, one cannot be inferior to the other civilly or politically. If one race be inferior to the other socially, the constitution of the United States cannot put them upon the same plane. . . .

The judgment of the court below is therefore affirmed.

MR. JUSTICE HARLAN, dissenting. . . .

In respect of civil rights, common to all citizens, the constitution of the United States does not, I think, permit any public authority to know the race of those entitled to be protected in the enjoyment of such rights. Every true man has pride of race, and under appropriate circumstances, when the rights of others, his equals before the law, are not to be affected, it is his privilege to express such pride and to take such action based upon it as to him seems proper. But I deny that any legislative body or judicial tribunal may have regard to the race of citizens when the civil rights of those citizens are involved. Indeed, such legislation as that here in question is inconsistent not only with that equality of rights which pertains to citizenship, national and state, but with the personal liberty enjoyed by every one within the United States.

The thirteenth amendment does not permit the withholding or the deprivation of any right necessarily inhering in freedom. It not only struck down the institution of slavery as previously existing in the United States, but it prevents the imposition of any burdens or disabilities that constitute badges of slavery or servitude. It decreed universal civil freedom in this country. This court has so adjudged. But, that amendment having been found inadequate to the protection of the rights of those who had been in slavery, it was followed by the fourteenth amendment, which added greatly to the dignity and glory of American citizenship, and to the security of personal liberty.... These two amendments, if enforced according to their true intent and meaning, will protect all the civil rights that pertain to freedom and citizenship. Finally, and to the end that no citizen should be denied, on account of his race, the privilege of participating in the political control of his country, it was declared by the fifteenth amendment that "the right of citizens of the United States to vote shall not be denied or abridged by the United States or by any state on account of race, color or previous condition of servitude."

These notable additions to the fundamental law were welcomed by the friends of liberty throughout the world. They removed the race line from our governmental systems. They had, as this court has said, a common purpose, namely, to secure "to a race recently emancipated, a race that through many generations have been held in slavery, all the civil rights that the superior race enjoy." They declared, in legal effect, this court has further said, "that the law in the states shall be the same for the black as for the white; that all persons, whether colored or white, shall stand equal before the laws of the states; and in regard to the colored race, for whose protection the amendment was primarily designed, that no discrimination shall be made against them by law because of their color." We also said: "The words of the amendment, it is true, are prohibitory, but they contain a necessary implication of a positive immunity or right, most valuable to the colored race,—the right to exemption from unfriendly legislation against them distinctively as colored; exemption from legal discriminations, implying inferiority in civil socety, lessening the security of their enjoyment of the rights which others enjoy; and discriminations which are steps towards reducing them to the condition of a subject race." . . .

It was said in argument that the statute of Louisiana does not discriminate against either race, but prescribes a rule applicable alike to white and colored citizens. But this argument does not meet the difficulty. Every one knows that the statute in question had its origin in the purpose, not so much to exclude white persons from railroad cars occupied by blacks, as to exclude colored people from coaches occupied by or assigned to white persons. Railroad corporations of Louisiana did not make discrimination among whites in the matter of accommodation for travelers. The thing to accomplish was, under the guise of giving equal accommodation for whites and blacks, to compel the latter to keep to themselves while traveling in railroad passenger coaches. No one would be so wanting in candor as to assert the contrary.

. . . [If] this statute of Louisiana is consistent with the personal liberty of citizens, why may not the state require the separation in railroad coaches of native and naturalized citizens of the United States, or of Protestants and Roman Catholics?

The answer given at the argument to these questions was that regulations of the kind they suggest would be unreasonable, and could not, therefore, stand before the law. Is it meant that the determination of questions of legislative power depends upon the inquiry whether the statute whose validity is questioned is, in the judgment of the courts, a reasonable one, taking all the circumstances into consideration? A statute may be unreasonable merely because a sound public policy forbade its enactment. But I do not understand that the courts have anything to do with the policy or expediency of legislation. A statute may be valid, and yet, upon grounds of public policy, may well be characterized as unreasonable. Mr. Sedgwick correctly states the rule when he says that, the legislative intention being clearly ascertained, "the courts have no other duty to perform than to execute the legislative will, without any regard to their views as to the wisdom or justice of the particular enactment." Sedg. St. & Const. Law, 324. There is a dangerous tendency in these latter days to enlarge the functions of the courts, by means of judicial interference with the will of the people as expressed by the legislature. Our institutions have the distinguishing characteristic that the three departments of government are co-ordinate and separate. Each must keep within the limits defined by the constitution. And the courts best discharge their duty by executing the will of the law-making power, constitutionally expressed, leaving the results of legislation to be dealt with by the people through their representatives. . . .

The white race deems itself to be the dominant race in this country. And so it is, in prestige, in achievements, in education, in wealth, and in power. So, I doubt not, it will continue to be for all time, if it remains true to its great heritage, and holds fast to the principles of constitutional liberty. But in view of the constitution, in the eye of the law, there is in this country no superior, dominant, ruling class of citizens. There is no caste here. Our constitution is color-blind, and neither knows nor tolerates classes among citizens. In respect of civil rights, all citizens are equal before the law. The humblest is the peer of the most powerful. The law regards man as man, and takes no account of his surroundings or of his color when his civil rights as guaranteed by the supreme law of the land are involved. It is therefore to be regretted that this high tribunal, the final expositor of the fundamental law of the land, has reached the conclusion that it is competent for a state to regulate the enjoyment by citizens of their civil rights solely upon the basis of race.

In my opinion, the judgment this day rendered will, in time, prove to be quite as pernicious as the decision made by this tribunal in the Dred Scott Case.

It was adjudged in that case that the descendants of Africans who were imported into this country, and sold as slaves, were not included nor intended to be included under the word "citizens" in the constitution, and could not claim any of the rights and privileges which that instrument provided for and secured to citizens of the United States; that, at the time of the adoption of the constitution, they were "considered as a subordinate and inferior class of beings, who had been subjugated by the dominant race, and, whether emancipated or not, yet remained subject to their authority, and had no rights or privileges but such as those who held the power and the government might choose to grant them." 17 How. 393, 404. The recent amendments of the constitution, it was supposed, had eradicated these principles from our institutions. But it seems that we have yet, in some of the states, a dominant race,— a superior class of citizens,—which assumes to regulate the enjoyment of civil rights, common to all citizens, upon the basis of race. The present decision, it may well be apprehended, will not only stimulate aggressions, more or less brutal and irritating, upon the admitted rights of colored citizens, but will encourage the belief that it is possible, by means of state enactments, to defeat the beneficent purposes which the people of the United States had in view when they adopted the recent amendments of the constitution, by one of which the blacks of this country were made citizens of the United States and of the states in which they respectively reside, and whose privileges and immunities, as citizens, the states are forbidden to abridge. Sixty millions of whites are in no danger from the presence here of eight millions of blacks. The destinies of the two races, in this country, are indissolubly linked together, and the interests of both require that the common government of all shall not permit the seeds of race hate to be planted under the sanction of law. What can more certainly arouse race hate, what more certainly create and perpetuate a feeling of distrust between these races, than state, enactments which, in fact, proceed on the ground that colored citizens are so inferior and degraded that they cannot be allowed to sit in public coaches occupied by white citizens? That, as all will admit, is the real meaning of such legislation as was enacted in Louisiana.

The sure guaranty of the peace and security of each race is the clear, distinct, unconditional recognition by our governments, national and state, of every right that inheres in civil freedom, and of the equality before the law of all citizens of the United States, without regard to race. State enactments regulating the enjoyment of civil rights upon the basis of race, and cunningly devised to defeat legitimate results of the war, under the pretense of recognizing equality of rights, can have no other result than to render permanent peace impossible, and to keep alive a conflict of races, the continuance of which must do harm to all concerned. This question is not met by the suggestion that social equality cannot exist between the white and black races in this country. That argument, if it can be properly regarded as one, is scarcely worthy of consideration; for social equality no more exists between two races when traveling in a passenger coach or a public highway than when members of the same races sit by each other in a street car or in the jury box, or stand or sit with each other in a political assembly, or when they use in common the streets of a city or town, or when they are in the same room for the purpose of having their names placed on the registry of voters, or when they approach the ballot box in order to exercise the high privilege of voting. . . .

The arbitrary separation of citizens, on the basis of race, while they are on a public highway, is a badge of servitude wholly inconsistent with the civil freedom and the equality before the law established by the constitution. It cannot be justified upon any legal grounds.

If evils will result from the commingling of the two races upon public highways established for the benefit of all, they will be infinitely less than those that will surely come from state legislation regulating the enjoyment of civil rights upon the basis of race. We boast of the freedom enjoyed by our people above all other peoples. But it is difficult to reconcile that boast with a state of the law which, practically, puts the brand of servitude and degradation upon a large class of our fellow citizens,—our equals before the law. The thin disguise of "equal" accommodations for passengers in railroad coaches will not mislead any one, nor atone for the wrong this day done. . . .

I do not deem it necessary to review the decisions of state courts to which reference was made in argument. Some, and the most important, of them, are wholly inapplicable, because rendered prior to the adoption of the last amendments of the constitution, when colored people had very few rights which the dominant race felt obliged to respect. Others were made at a time when public opinion, in many localities, was dominated by the institution of slavery; when it would not have been safe to do justice to the black man; and when, so far as the rights of blacks were concerned, race prejudice was, practically, the supreme law of the land. Those decisions cannot be guides in the era introduced by the recent amendments of the supreme law, which established universal civil freedom, gave citizenship to all born or naturalized in the United States, and residing here, obliterated the race line from our systems of governments, national and state, and placed our free institutions upon the broad and sure foundation of the equality of all men before the law.

I am of opinion that the statute of Louisiana is inconsistent with the personal liberty of citizens, white and black, in that state, and hostile to both the spirit and letter of the constitution of the United States. . . .

For a long time, there was no serious attempt to challenge the so-called separate-but-equal doctrine. Instead, efforts were directed, though without success, to ensure that Negroes would be provided with facilities that were equal in fact in public education [6] or in interstate transportation.[7] And a child of Chinese ancestry, it developed, was not denied the equal protection of the laws by being required to attend Mississippi's public schools for Negroes and being denied admission to the white public schools.[8] The basic difference, it appeared, was not between whites and Negroes, but between purebred Caucasians and persons who were "colored"—brown, yellow, black, or—as alleged in *Hurd* v. *Hodge*, below, or as in *Rice* v. *Sioux City Memorial Park Cemetery Corp.*, 348 U.S. 880 (1954) and 349 U.S. 70 (1955)—red. The Constitution may have been color-blind, as the elder John Marshall Harlan suggested, but the justices were not.

The partial breakdown of the separate-but-equal doctrine in the field of transportation did not begin until after the Roosevelt appointees had established firm control of the Court. But in 1941, a ruling of the Interstate Commerce Commission, upholding the denial, to a Negro member of the United States House of Representatives, of Pullman accommodations while his train passed through segregated Arkansas, was reversed by the Court—because Congressman Mitchell had been denied "separate and equal" facilities.[9] (Mitchell would have been permitted, under existing I.C.C. regulations, to have traveled in the Pullman car if a drawing room had been vacant, because in that case, none of the other passengers could have seen him and thus, presumably, been embarrassed by his presence.) And in 1946, a Virginia statute requiring racial segregation on buses within the state—whites and Negroes could ride in the same bus, providing whites rode in the front seats and Negroes in the rear—was declared by the Court to be an unconstitutional burden upon interstate commerce.[10] This left open the possibility, at least in theory, that if Congress were to establish the "uniform, national rule" that the Court said the subject required, it could just as well be a rule of segregation as of integration. Also curious was the Court's failure to discuss its 1890 decision upholding the Mississippi statute identical to the Virginia statute now struck down. The best guess was that *Louisville, New Orleans and Texas Railway Co.* v. *Mississippi* had been overruled *sub silentio*—but it was only a guess.

In 1948, the Court upheld the Michigan Civil Rights Act, which had been applied to prohibit discrimination on an excursion ship which traveled in foreign commerce to an amusement park in Canadian waters.[11] Such compulsory integration might seem to be just as much a burden upon foreign commerce as the Louisiana statute that was struck down as a burden upon interstate commerce in

[6] *Cumming* v. *County Board of Education*, 175 U.S. 528 (1899).

[7] *McCabe* v. *Atchison, Topeka & Santa Fe Railway Co.*, 235 U.S. 151 (1914).

[8] *Gong Lum* v. *Rice*, 275 U.S. 78 (1927).

[9] *Mitchell* v. *United States*, 313 U.S. 80 (1941).

[10] *Morgan* v. *Virginia*, 328 U.S. 373 (1946).

[11] *Bob-Lo Excursion Co.* v. *Michigan*, 333 U.S. 28 (1948).

Hall v. *De Cuir,* but it did not appear so to a majority of the Court, who distinguished *Hall* v. *De Cuir* rather than to overrule it. And in 1950, the Court reversed another ruling of the I.C.C., this time, in effect, postulating an economically infeasible standard for equality in the separate service of Negroes in Pullman dining cars.[12] An unattainable standard of "separate equality" implied, no doubt, the Court's disagreement with the policy announced in *Plessy* v. *Ferguson,* but this has remained a matter for surmise. The Court has not yet declared that segregation in interstate transportation violates the equal-protection clause of the Fourteenth Amendment. It has not yet declared—as it has for public education—that segregated transportation facilities are inherently unequal. Nor has *Plessy* v. *Ferguson* been overruled. Even in the School Segregation decision in 1954, the most that the Court was prepared to say was that modern psychological knowledge supported a finding that segregated education could not be equal education for Negro children; and "any language in *Plessy* v. *Ferguson* contrary to this finding is rejected." The rejection of Mr. Justice Brown's social psychology is a far cry from the overruling of *Plessy* v. *Ferguson* as a precedent. In view of the profligacy with which the Court has abandoned precedents with considerably more in both logic and utility to commend them than *Hall* v. *De Cuir,* or the Louisville railway case, or *Plessy* v. *Ferguson* (see Chapter 4 as to the overruling of precedents), the Court has shown an unusual reluctance to overrule a set of decisions that stand for the opposite of the rule of constitutional policy it appears to favor today. The Court's reluctance is curious, since the forthright proscription of segregation in transportation would have been much easier to enforce and would have aroused less antagonism among white supremacists and the spokesmen for states' rights than did integration in public education, the issue on which the Court chose to take its stand.

THE WHITE PRIMARY

At least in theory, no right in a democracy is more fundamental than the right to vote. During the Reconstruction period and under the protection of the Union army, the freedmen of the South voted and were elected to public office, gaining control for a brief time of the governments of most of the states of the former Confederacy. This was possible in large measure because, at this same time, the white citizens of the South who had been loyal to the Confederacy were being *denied* the right to vote. But with the restoration of white suffrage in the South as Reconstruction drew to a close and the armies of the Union were withdrawn,

---

12 This decision, *Henderson* v. *United States,* 339 U.S. 816, was announced on June 5, 1950, the same day on which the Court also announced its decision in *Sweatt* v. *Painter,* 339 U.S. 629, and employed a similar technique by positing unattainable standards of equality for separate law schools for Negroes.

the right of Negroes to vote was correspondingly eliminated. We have seen the results of such changes in voting participation, in the two Louisiana statutes at issue in the Slaughter-House cases, the first (in 1869) establishing, and the later one (in the 1870's) repealing, the butchers' monopoly; and in the two Louisiana statutes discussed in the preceding section of this chapter, the earlier (1869) forbidding, and the later (1890) requiring, segregation on common carriers within the state.

A variety of devices have been relied upon to disenfranchise Negro citizens of the United States, the Fifteenth Amendment to the contrary notwithstanding. Some of these, such as the Grandfather Clauses, were intended to be of temporary duration, and were declared unconstitutional by the Supreme Court [13]—although not until after they had largely succeeded in accomplishing their purpose of permitting otherwise legally disqualified white citizens to get their names upon the permanent registration lists. But with a single exception, the other devices relied upon to keep Negroes from the polls in the South—violence and intimidation, inequitable administration of "literacy" tests, the poll tax, unequal and inferior educational and economic opportunities—remain in effect, although to a lesser extent, to this day, irrespective of whether they received the disapprobation or the approval of the Supreme Court. Generally speaking, the Court disapproved of the terrorism of the Ku Klux Klan, but found no infringement of the Fifteenth Amendment in more sophisticated techniques of disenfranchisement such as the poll tax,[14] or literacy tests [15] in which white grammar-school graduates solemnly declared that Negro college graduates could not "understand" the state constitution—a document generally comprehensible only among lawyers, in any event.

The exception was the white primary. Since the South is largely, and has been until recently to an even greater extent, a one-party region, disenfranchisement from participation in the Democratic party primary elections is tantamount to exclusion from any effective voice in the general election that follows. So when the Court ruled in *Newberry* v. *United States,* 256 U.S. 232 (1921), an election fraud case that had nothing to do with racial discrimination, that Congress had no power (or at best, dubious power) to regulate primary elections in the states, the white primary seemed to offer a perfectly legal device for disenfranchising Negroes. We say "dubious power" because the Court's decision was 5-4, and one of the majority justices thought that the result should have been different if the act of Congress regulating primaries had been passed *after* the adoption of the Seventeenth Amendment, since the Newberry case dealt with a contested election to the United States Senate.

Two years after the Supreme Court's decision in the Newberry case, the legis-

---

[13] *Guinn* v. *United States,* 238 U.S. 347 (1915); and *Lane* v. *Wilson,* 307 U.S. 268 (1939).
[14] *Breedlove* v. *Suttles,* 302 U.S. 277 (1937).

[15] *Williams* v. *Mississippi,* 170 U.S. 213 (1898); but cf. *Schnell* v. *Davis,* 336 U.S. 933 (1949).

lature of the State of Texas enacted a statute which directly forbade Negro participation in the state's Democratic party primary election. The ensuing litigation, sponsored for a time by Dr. Charles Nixon, a Negro dentist from Houston, was spread over the next two decades, and is summarized in the opinion of the Court in the case below. It should be noted that the Fifteenth Amendment explicitly prohibits racial discrimination by states in their regulation of elections, while the Fourteenth Amendment does this in more general terms by the equal-protection clause. Historically, indeed, the Fifteenth Amendment was adopted in order to make perfectly specific the meaning of equal protection as applied to voting. We have, then, another example of the Court's peculiar reluctance to give the most obvious interpretation to the Civil War amendments. Nixon won his cases, but on the basis of the Fourteenth, not the Fifteenth Amendment. It was not until after 1937 and the decision below in *Smith* v. *Allwright* that a majority of the Court was willing to apply the Fifteenth Amendment to the white primary.

SMITH v. ALLWRIGHT

321 U.S. 649 (Argued November 10, 12, 1943; reargued January 12, 1944; decided April 3, 1944)

Certiorari to the United States Circuit Court of Appeals for the Fifth Circuit.

Reversed.

8-1

Reed	('+')
Stone, C.J.	(+)
Black	(+)
Douglas	(+)
Murphy	(+)
Jackson	(+)
Rutledge	(+)
Frankfurter	+
Roberts	'—')

We have mentioned, in Chapter 4, the Roberts dissent in this case, as an example of the personal (as distinguished from institutional) loyalty of the justices to the precedents of the Court. The author of the opinion of the Court in the overruled precedent, Grovey v. Townsend *was, of course, Mr. Justice Roberts.*

MR. JUSTICE REED delivered the opinion of the Court.

This writ of certiorari brings here for review a claim for damages in the sum of $5,000 on the part of petitioner, a Negro citizen of the 48th precinct of Harris County, Texas, for the refusal of respondents, election and associate election judges respectively of that precinct, to give petitioner a ballot or to permit him to cast a ballot in the primary election of July 27, 1940, for the nomination of Democratic candidates for the United States Senate and House of Representatives, and Governor and other state officers. The refusal is alleged to have been solely because of the race and color of the proposed voter.

The actions of respondents are said to violate § § 31 and 43 of Title 8 [16] of the

---

[16] U.S.C. § 31: "All citizens of the United States who are otherwise qualified by law to vote at any election by the people in any State, Territory, district, county, city, parish, township, school district, municipality, or other territorial subdivision, shall be entitled and allowed to vote at all such elections, without distinction of race, color, or previous condition of servitude; any constitution, law, custom, usage, or regulation of any State or Territory, or by or under its authority, to the contrary notwithstanding." § 43: "Every person who, under color of any statute, ordinance, regulation, custom, or usage, of any State or Territory, subjects, or causes to be subjected, any citizen of the

United States Code in that petitioner was deprived of rights secured by § § 2 and 4 of Article I and the Fourteenth, Fifteenth and Seventeenth Amendments to the United States Constitution. . . .

The District Court denied the relief sought and the Circuit Court of Appeals quite properly affirmed its action on the authority of *Grovey* v. *Townsend,* 295 U.S. 45. We granted the petition for certiorari to resolve a claimed inconsistency between the decision in the *Grovey* case and that of *United States* v. *Classic,* 313 U.S. 299. . . .

The State of Texas by its Constitution and statutes provides that every person, if certain other requirements are met which are not here in issue, qualified by residence in the district or county "shall be deemed a qualified elector." . . . [The] Democratic party was required to hold the primary which was the occasion of the alleged wrong to petitioner. . . .

The Democratic party on May 24, 1932, in a state convention adopted the following resolution, which has not since been "amended, abrogated, annulled or avoided": "Be it resolved that all white citizens of the State of Texas who are qualified to vote under the Constitution and laws of the State shall be eligible to membership in the Democratic party and, as such, entitled to participate in its deliberations." It was by virtue of this resolution that the respondents refused to permit the petitioner to vote.

Texas is free to conduct her elections and limit her electorate as she may deem wise, save only as her action may be affected by the prohibitions of the United States Constitution or in conflict with powers delegated to and exercised by the National Government. The Fourteenth

United States or other person within the jurisdiction thereof to the deprivation of any rights, privileges, or immunities secured by the Constitution and laws, shall be liable to the party injured in an action at law, suit in equity, or other proper proceeding for redress." [Footnote by the Court.]

Amendment forbids a State from making or enforcing any law which abridges the privileges or immunities of citizens of the United States and the Fifteenth Amendment specifically interdicts any denial or abridgement by a State of the right of citizens to vote on account of color. Respondents appeared in the District Court and the Circuit Court of Appeals and defended on the ground that the Democratic party of Texas is a voluntary organization with members banded together for the purpose of selecting individuals of the group representing the common political beliefs as candidates in the general election. As such a voluntary organization, it was claimed, the Democratic party is free to select its own membership and limit to whites participation in the party primary. Such action, the answer asserted, does not violate the Fourteenth, Fifteenth or Seventeenth Amendment as officers of government cannot be chosen at primaries and the Amendments are applicable only to general elections where governmental officers are actually elected. Primaries, it is said, are political party affairs, handled by party, not governmental, officers. . . .

The right of a Negro to vote in the Texas primary has been considered heretofore by this Court. The first case was *Nixon* v. *Herndon,* 273 U.S. 536. At that time, 1924, the Texas statute . . . declared "in no event shall a Negro be eligible to participate in a Democratic Party primary election in the State of Texas." Nixon was refused the right to vote in a Democratic primary and brought a suit for damages against the election officers. . . . It was urged to this Court that the denial of the franchise to Nixon violated his Constitutional rights under the Fourteenth and Fifteenth Amendments. Without consideration of the Fifteenth, this Court held that the action of Texas in denying the ballot to Negroes by statute was in violation of the equal protection clause of the Fourteenth Amendment and reversed the dismissal of the suit.

The legislature of Texas reenacted the article but gave the State Executive Committee of a party the power to prescribe the qualifications of its members for voting or other participation. This article remains in the statutes. The State Executive Committee of the Democratic party adopted a resolution that white Democrats and none other might participate in the primaries of that party. Nixon was refused again the privilege of voting in a primary and again brought suit for damages. . . . This Court again reversed the dismissal of the suit for the reason that the Committee action was deemed to be state action and invalid as discriminatory under the Fourteenth Amendment. The test was said to be whether the Committee operated as representative of the State in the discharge of the State's authority. *Nixon* v. *Condon,* 286 U.S. 73. The question of the inherent power of a political party in Texas "without restraint by any law to determine its own membership" was left open. *Id.,* 84-85.

In *Grovey* v. *Townsend,* 295 U.S. 45, this Court had before it another suit for damages for the refusal in a primary of a county clerk, a Texas officer with only public functions to perform, to furnish petitioner, a Negro, an absentee ballot. The refusal was solely on the ground of race. This case differed from *Nixon* v. *Condon, supra,* in that a state convention of the Democratic party had passed the resolution of May 24, 1932, hereinbefore quoted. It was decided that the determination by the state convention of the membership of the Democratic party made a significant change from a determination by the Executive Committee. The former was party action, voluntary in character. The latter, as had been held in the *Condon* case, was action by authority of the State. The managers of the primary election were therefore declared not to be state officials in such sense that their action was state action. A state convention of a party was said not to be an organ of the State. This Court went on to announce that to deny a vote in a primary was a mere refusal of party membership with which "the State need have no concern," *loc. cit.* at 55, while for a State to deny a vote in a general election on the ground of race or color violated the Constitution. Consequently, there was found no ground for holding that the county clerk's refusal of a ballot because of racial ineligibility for party membership denied the petitioner any right under the Fourteenth or Fifteenth Amendment.

Since *Grovey* v. *Townsend* and prior to the present suit, no case from Texas involving primary elections has been before this Court. We did decide, however, *United States* v. *Classic,* 313 U.S. 299. We there held that § 4 of Article I of the Constitution authorized Congress to regulate primary as well as general elections, . . . "where the primary is by law made an integral part of the election machinery." . . . Consequently, in the *Classic* case, we upheld the applicability to frauds in a Louisiana primary of §§ 19 and 20 of the Criminal Code. Thereby corrupt acts of election officers were subjected to Congressional sanctions because that body had power to protect rights of federal suffrage secured by the Constitution in primary as in general elections. . . . This decision depended, too, on the determination that under the Louisiana statutes the primary was a part of the procedure for choice of federal officials. By this decision the doubt as to whether or not such primaries were a part of "elections" subject to federal control, which had remained unanswered since *Newberry* v. *United States,* 256 U.S. 232, was erased. The *Nixon Cases* were decided under the equal protection clause of the Fourteenth Amendment without a determination of the status of the primary as a part of the electoral process. The exclusion of Negroes from the primaries by action of the State was held invalid under that Amendment. The fusing by the *Classic* case of the primary and general elections into a single instrumentality for choice of officers has a definite bearing on the permissibility under the Constitution of excluding Negroes from primaries. This is not to say that the *Classic* case cuts directly into the rationale of *Grovey* v. *Townsend*. This latter case was not mentioned in the opinion. *Classic* bears upon *Grovey* v. *Townsend* not because exclusion of Negroes from primaries is any more or less state action by reason of the unitary character of the electoral process but because the recognition of the place of the primary in the electoral scheme makes clear that state delegation to a party of the power to fix the qualifications of primary elections is delegation of a state function that may make the party's action the action of the State. When *Grovey* v. *Townsend* was written, the Court looked upon the denial of a vote in a primary as a mere refusal by a party of party membership. . . . As the Louisiana statutes for holding primaries are similar to those of Texas, our ruling in *Classic* as to the unitary character of the electoral process calls for a reexamination as to whether or not the exclusion of Negroes from a Texas party primary was state action.

The statutes of Texas relating to primaries and the resolution of the Democratic party of Texas extending the privileges of membership to white citizens only are the same in substance and effect today as they were when *Grovey* v. *Townsend* was decided by a unanimous Court. The question as to whether the exclusionary action of the party was the action of the State persists as the determinative factor. In again entering upon consideration of the inference to be drawn as to state action from a substantially similar factual situation, it should be noted that *Grovey* v. *Townsend* upheld exclusion of Negroes from primaries through the denial of party membership by a party convention. A few years before, this Court refused approval of exclusion by the State Executive Committee of the party. A dif-

ferent result was reached on the theory that the Committee action was state authorized and the Convention action was unfettered by statutory control. Such a variation in the result from so slight a change in form influences us to consider anew the legal validity of the distinction which has resulted in barring Negroes from participating in the nominations of candidates of the Democratic party in Texas. . . .

It may now be taken as a postulate that the right to vote in such a primary for the nomination of candidates without discrimination by the State, like the right to vote in a general election, is a right secured by the Constitution. *United States* v. *Classic,* 313 U.S. at 314. . . . By the terms of the Fifteenth Amendment that right may not be abridged by any State on account of race. Under our Constitution the great privilege of the ballot may not be denied a man by the State because of his color.

We are thus brought to an examination of the qualifications for Democratic primary electors in Texas, to determine whether state action or private action has excluded Negroes from participation. Despite Texas' decision that the exclusion is produced by private or party action, . . . federal courts must for themselves appraise the facts leading to that conclusion. It is only by the performance of this obligation that a final and uniform interpretation can be given to the Constitution, the "supreme Law of the Land." Texas requires electors in a primary to pay a poll tax. Every person who does so pay and who has the qualifications of age and residence is an acceptable voter for the primary. . . . Texas . . . directs the selection of all party officers.

Primary elections are conducted by the party under state statutory authority. . . . We think that this statutory system for the selection of party nominees for inclusion on the general election ballot makes the party which is required to follow these legislative directions an agency of the State in so far as it determines the participants in a primary election. The party takes its character as a state agency from the duties imposed upon it by state statutes; the duties do not become matters of private law because they are performed by a political party. . . . When primaries become a part of the machinery for choosing officials, state and national, as they have here, the same tests to determine the character of discrimination or abridgement should be applied to the primary as are applied to the general election. If the State requires a certain electoral procedure, prescribes a general election ballot made up of party nominees so chosen and limits the choice of the electorate in general elections for state offices, practically speaking, to those whose names appear on such a ballot, it endorses, adopts and enforces the discrimination against Negroes, practiced by a party entrusted by Texas law with the determination of the qualifications of participants in the primary. This is state action within the meaning of the Fifteenth Amendment. *Guinn* v. *United States*, 238 U.S. 347, 362.

The United States is a constitutional democracy. Its organic law grants to all citizens a right to participate in the choice of elected officials without restriction by any State because of race. This grant to the people of the opportunity for choice is not to be nullified by a State through casting its electoral process in a form which permits a private organization to practice racial discrimination in the election. Constitutional rights would be of little value if they could be thus indirectly denied. . . .

The privilege of membership in a party may be, as this Court said in *Grovey* v. *Townsend*, 295 U.S. 45, 55, no concern of a State. But when, as here, that privilege is also the essential qualification for voting in a primary to select nominees for a general election, the State makes the action of the party the action of the State.

In reaching this conclusion we are not unmindful of the desirability of continuity of decision in constitutional questions. However, when convinced of former error, this Court has never felt constrained to follow precedent. In constitutional questions, where correction depends upon amendment and not upon legislative action this Court throughout its history has freely exercised its power to reexamine the basis of its constitutional decisions. This has long been accepted practice, and this practice has continued to this day. This is particularly true when the decision believed erroneous is the application of a constitutional principle rather than an interpretation of the Constitution to extract the principle itself. Here we are applying, contrary to the recent decision in *Grovey* v. *Townsend*, the well-established principle of the Fifteenth Amendment, forbidding the abridgement by a State of a citizen's right to vote. *Grovey* v. *Townsend* is overruled.

Judgment reversed.

Mr. Justice Roberts:

. . . I have expressed my views with respect to the present policy of the court freely to disregard and to overrule considered decisions and the rules of law announced in them. This tendency, it seems to me, indicates an intolerance for what those who have composed this court in the past have conscientiously and deliberately concluded, and involves an assumption that knowledge and wisdom reside in us which was denied to our predecessors. I shall not repeat what I there said for I consider it fully applicable to the instant decision, which but points the moral anew. . . .

I believe it will not be gainsaid [that *Grovey* v. *Townsend,* 295 U.S. 45 (1935)] received the attention and consideration which the questions involved demanded and the opinion represented the views of all the justices. It appears that those views do not now commend themselves to the court. I shall not restate them. They are exposed in the opinion and must stand or fall on their merits. Their soundness, however, is not a matter which presently concerns me.

The reason for my concern is that the instant decision, overruling that announced about nine years ago, tends to bring adjudications of this tribunal into the same class as a restricted railroad ticket, good for this day and train only. I have no assurance, in view of current decisions, that the opinion announced today may not shortly be repudiated and overruled by justices who deem they have new light on the subject. In the present term the court has overruled three cases. . . .

It is regrettable that in an era marked by doubt and confusion, an era whose greatest need is steadfastness of thought and purpose, this court, which has been looked to as exhibiting consistency in adjudication, and a steadiness which would hold the balance even in the face of temporary ebbs and flows of opinion, should now itself become the breeder of fresh doubt and confusion in the public mind as to the stability of our institutions.

Smith v. *Allwright* had a direct and significant impact upon Negro voting, especially in the larger cities of the South. South Carolina promptly repealed all of its statutes regulating primary elections in the state, in an obvious attempt to evade the decision in *Smith* v. *Allwright* under the legal fiction that the Democratic party was thenceforth merely a private club, and its primary elections were no longer "state action" within the meaning of the Fourteenth and Fifteenth Amendments. This maneuver was invalidated by the Fourth Circuit Court of Appeals in *Rice* v. *Elmore*, 165 F.2d 387 (1947), with the Supreme Court denying certiorari to review the case. Following this decision, the Democratic party of South Carolina adopted rules under which control of the primaries in that state was delegated to "local clubs," which in turn exacted, as a condition of participation in the clubs' primary elections, an oath from prospective voters, stipulating that they believed in the "social and educational separation of the races" and were opposed to "the proposed Federal so-called F.E.P.C. law." Again, the Court of Appeals for the Fourth Circuit ruled against this attempt to disenfranchise Negro citizens, in *Baskin* v. *Brown*, 174 F.2d 391 (1949). In both the Rice and Baskin cases, the unanimous opinion of the federal court of appeals was written by Chief Judge John J. Parker, the man whose nomination to the Supreme Court was rejected by the Senate in 1930, in no small measure because of N.A.A.C.P. opposition to Parker's reputed race prejudice.

The Supreme Court itself invoked the Fifteenth Amendment, the Allwright precedent, and the decisions of Judge Parker's court as authority for proscribing a somewhat similar Texas political club, in *Terry* v. *Adams*, 345 U.S. 461 (1953). The principal differences between the Texas and the South Carolina clubs were that the Jaybird party of Fort Bend County (Texas) was organized in 1889, rather than as a reaction to the Allwright decision; and the operation of the system was confined to a single county. For over sixty years the Jaybirds had conducted a preprimary election, which selected the candidates who were then successfully sponsored by the Jaybirds in the regular Democratic primary election. Only Justice Minton, who had been a leading New Dealer in his days as a United States Senator, dissented from the Court's extension of "state action" to include the political activities of the Jaybirds.

RESTRICTIVE COVENANTS AND PRIVATE HOUSING

Although the legal right to political participation on a basis of equality with other citizens of the United States was indisputably a major policy goal of organized Negro groups during the 1930's and 1940's, equality of economic opportunity emerged as a problem of at least as great importance to Negroes during this same period. In particular, the migration of hundreds of thousands of Negroes from rural areas in the South to the metropolitan complexes of the North led to insistent pressures by Negroes for access to housing in a market that was critically undersupplied—apart from the race question—as the result of other circumstances incident to the Second World War. At this time, the courts were functioning in effect as enforcement agencies to support a widespread system of private zoning whereby access to most urban residential housing was denied to the "non-Caucasian" members of several racial minority groups. In this economy of scarcity, the Caucasians—the "neighborhood improvement associations" and realtors' organizations—fought to maintain property values and to hold the color line in segregated residential housing against the encroachments and infiltration of Negroes, "orientals," and other "undesirables."

One important difference between the political struggles over Negro voting participation and segregated residential housing was that the question of electoral right was primarily—like that of segregated public education—a problem in the South; while the question of equality of access to housing was most critical (as a political, economic, social, and legal problem) in the North. We have already discussed in Chapter 3, in the section on "NAACP Strategy in the Restrictive Covenant Cases," the political background of the two cases presented below.

SHELLEY v. KRAEMER

334 U.S. 1 (May 3, 1948).

Certiorari to the Supreme Court of Missouri; together with *McGhee* v. *Sipes,* certiorari to the Supreme Court of Michigan.

Both *reversed.*

6-0

Vinson, C.J.	('+')
Black	(+)
Frankfurter	(+)
Douglas	(+)
Murphy	(+)
Burton	(+)
Reed	NP
Jackson	NP
Rutledge	NP

MR. CHIEF JUSTICE VINSON delivered the opinion of the Court.

These cases present for our consideration questions relating to the validity of court enforcement of private agreements, generally described as restrictive covenants, which have as their purpose the exclusion of persons of designated race or color from the ownership or occupancy of real property. Basic constitutional issues of obvious importance have been raised.

The first of these cases comes to this Court on certiorari to the Supreme Court of Missouri. On February 16, 1911, thirty out of a total of thirty-nine owners of property fronting both sides of Labadie Avenue between Taylor Avenue and Cora Avenue in the city of St. Louis, signed an agreement, which was subsequently recorded, providing in part: ". . . the said property is hereby restricted to the use and occupancy for the term of Fifty (50) years from this date, so that it shall be a condition all the time and whether recited and referred to as [*sic*] not in subsequent conveyances and shall attach to the land as a condition precedent to the

sale of the same, that hereafter no part of said property or any portion thereof shall be, for said term of Fifty-years, occupied by any person not of the Caucasian race, it being intended hereby to restrict the use of said property for said period of time against the occupancy as owners or tenants of any portion of said property for resident or other purpose by people of the Negro or Mongolian Race."

The entire district described in the agreement included fifty-seven parcels of land. The thirty owners who signed the agreement held title to forty-seven parcels, including the particular parcel involved in this case. At the time the agreement was signed, five of the parcels in the district were owned by Negroes. One of those had been occupied by Negro families since 1882, nearly thirty years before the restrictive agreement was executed. The trial court found that owners of seven out of nine homes on the south side of Labadie Avenue, within the restricted district and "in the immediate vicinity" of the premises in question, had failed to sign the restrictive agreement in 1911. At the time this action was brought, four of the premises were occupied by Negroes, and had been so occupied for periods ranging from twenty-three to sixty-three years. A fifth parcel had been occupied by Negroes until a year before this suit was instituted.

On August 11, 1945, pursuant to a contract of sale, petitioners Shelley, who are Negroes, for valuable consideration received from one Fitzgerald a warranty deed to the parcel in question.[17] The trial court found that petitioners had no actual knowledge of the restrictive agreement at the time of the purchase.

On October 9, 1945, respondents, as

[17] The trial court found that title to the property which petitioners Shelley sought to purchase was held by one Bishop, a real estate dealer, who placed the property in the name of Josephine Fitzgerald. Bishop, who acted as agent for petitioners in the purchase, concealed the fact of his ownership. [Footnote by the Court.]

owners of other property subject to the terms of the restrictive covenant, brought suit in the Circuit Court of the city of St. Louis praying that petitioners Shelley be restrained from taking possession of the property and that judgment be entered divesting title out of petitioners Shelley and revesting title in the immediate grantor or in such other person as the court should direct. The trial court denied the requested relief on the ground that the restrictive agreement, upon which respondents based their action, had never become final and complete because it was the intention of the parties to that agreement that it was not to become effective until signed by all property owners in the district, and signatures of all the owners had never been obtained.

The Supreme Court of Missouri sitting *en banc* reversed and directed the trial court to grant the relief for which respondents had prayed. That court held the agreement effective and concluded that enforcement of its provisions violated no rights guaranteed to petitioners by the Federal Constitution. At the time the court rendered its decision, petitioners were occupying the property in question.

The second of the cases under consideration comes to this Court from the Supreme Court of Michigan. The circumstances presented do not differ materially from the Missouri case. . . .

[The] petitioners urge that they have been denied the equal protection of the laws, deprived of property without due process of law, and have been denied privileges and immunities of citizens of the United States. We pass to a consideration of those issues.

I.

Whether the equal protection clause of the Fourteenth Amendment inhibits judicial enforcement by state courts of restrictive covenants based on race or color is a question which this Court has not heretofore been called upon to consider. . . .

It should be observed that these covenants do not seek to proscribe any particular use of the affected properties. Use of the properties for residential occupancy, as such, is not forbidden. The restrictions of these agreements, rather, are directed toward a designated class of persons and seek to determine who may and who may not own or make use of the properties for residential purposes. The excluded class is defined wholly in terms of race or color; "simply that and nothing more."

It cannot be doubted that among the civil rights intended to be protected from discriminatory state action by the Fourteenth Amendment are the rights to acquire, enjoy, own and dispose of property. Equality in the enjoyment of property rights was regarded by the framers of that Amendment as an essential pre-condition to the realization of other basic civil rights and liberties which the Amendment was intended to guarantee. Thus, § 1978 of the Revised Statutes, derived from § 1 of the Civil Rights Act of 1866 which was enacted by Congress while the Fourteenth Amendment was also under consideration,[18] provides: "All citizens of the United States shall have the same right, in every State and Territory, as is enjoyed by white citizens thereof to inherit, purchase, lease, sell, hold, and convey real and personal property." This Court has given specific recognition to the same principle. *Buchanan* v. *Warley*, 245 U.S. 60 (1917).

It is likewise clear that restrictions on the right of occupancy of the sort sought to be created by the private agreements in these cases could not be squared with the requirements of the Fourteenth Amendment if imposed by state statute or local ordinance. We do not understand

[18] . . . The Civil Rights Act of 1866 was reenacted in § 18 of the Act of May 31, 1870, subsequent to the adoption of the Fourteenth Amendment. . . . [Footnote by the Court. This section is now codified as 42 U.S.C. § 1982.]

respondents to urge the contrary. In the case of *Buchanan* v. *Warley, supra,* a unanimous Court declared unconstitutional the provisions of a city ordinance which denied to colored persons the right to occupy houses in blocks in which the greater number of houses were occupied by white persons, and imposed similar restrictions on white persons with respect to blocks in which the greater number of houses were occupied by colored persons. . . .

But the present cases, unlike [that] just discussed, do not involve action by state legislatures or city councils. Here the particular patterns of discrimination and the areas in which the restrictions are to operate, are determined, in the first instance, by the terms of agreements among private individuals. Participation of the State consists in the enforcement of the restrictions so defined. The crucial issue with which we are here confronted is whether this distinction removes these cases from the operation of the prohibitory provisions of the Fourteenth Amendment.

Since the decision of this Court in the *Civil Rights Cases,* 109 U.S. 3 (1883), the principle has become firmly embedded in our constitutional law that the action inhibited by the first section of the Fourteenth Amendment is only such action as may fairly be said to be that of the States. That Amendment erects no shield against merely private conduct, however discriminatory or wrongful.

We conclude, therefore, that the restrictive agreements standing alone cannot be regarded as violative of any rights guaranteed to petitioners by the Fourteenth Amendment. So long as the purposes of those agreements are effectuated by voluntary adherence to their terms, it would appear clear that there has been no action by the State and the provisions of the Amendment have not been violated. Cf. *Corrigan* v. *Buckley,* [271 U.S. 323 (1926).]

But here there was more. These are cases in which the purposes of the agreements were secured only by judicial enforcement by state courts of the restrictive terms of the agreements. The respondents urge that judicial enforcement of private agreements does not amount to state action; or, in any event, the participation of the State is so attenuated in character as not to amount to state action within the meaning of the Fourteenth Amendment. Finally, it is suggested, even if the States in these cases may be deemed to have acted in the constitutional sense, their action did not deprive petitioners of rights guaranteed by the Fourteenth Amendment. We move to a consideration of these matters.

II.

That the action of state courts and judicial officers in their official capacities is to be regarded as action of the State within the meaning of the Fourteenth Amendment, is a proposition which has long been established by decisions of this Court. That principle was given expression in the earliest cases involving the construction of the terms of the Fourteenth Amendment. Thus, in *Virginia* v. *Rives,* 100 U.S. 313, 318 (1880), this Court stated: "It is doubtless true that a State may act through different agencies,— either by its legislative, its executive, or its judicial authorities; and the prohibitions of the amendment extend to all action of the State denying equal protection of the laws, whether it be action by one of these agencies or by another." . . . In the *Civil Rights Cases,* 109 U.S. 3, 11, 17 (1883), this Court pointed out that the Amendment makes void "State action of every kind" which is inconsistent with the guaranties therein contained, and extends to manifestations of "State authority in the shape of laws, customs, or judicial or executive proceedings." . . .

We have no doubt that there has been state action in these cases in the full and complete sense of the phrase. The undisputed facts disclose that petitioners were willing purchasers of properties upon which they desired to establish homes. The owners of the properties were willing sellers; and contracts of sale were accordingly consummated. It is clear that but for the active intervention of the state courts, supported by the full panoply of state power, petitioners would have been free to occupy the properties in question without restraint.

These are not cases, as has been suggested, in which the States have merely abstained from action, leaving private individuals free to impose such discriminations as they see fit. Rather, these are cases in which the States have made available to such individuals the full coercive power of government to deny to petitioners, on the grounds of race or color, the enjoyment of property rights in premises which petitioners are willing and financially able to acquire and which the grantors are willing to sell. The difference between judicial enforcement and non-enforcement of the restrictive covenants is the difference to petitioners between being denied rights of property available to other members of the community and being accorded full enjoyment of those rights on an equal footing.

The enforcement of the restrictive agreements by the state courts in these cases was directed pursuant to the common-law policy of the States as formulated by those courts in earlier decisions. In the Missouri case, enforcement of the covenant was directed in the first instance by the highest court of the State after the trial court had determined the agreement to be invalid for want of the requisite number of signatures. In the Michigan case, the order of enforcement by the trial court was affirmed by the highest state court. The judicial action in each case bears the clear and unmistakable imprimatur of the State. We have noted that previous decisions of this Court have established the proposition that judicial action is not immunized from the operation of the Fourteenth Amendment sim-

ply because it is taken pursuant to the state's common-law policy. Nor is the Amendment ineffective simply because the particular pattern of discrimination, which the State has enforced, was defined initially by the terms of a private agreement. State action, as that phrase is understood for the purposes of the Fourteenth Amendment, refers to exertions of state power in all forms. And when the effect of that action is to deny rights subject to the protection of the Fourteenth Amendment, it is the obligation of this Court to enforce the constitutional commands.

We hold that in granting judicial enforcement of the restrictive agreements in these cases, the States have denied petitioners the equal protection of the laws and that, therefore, the action of the state courts cannot stand. We have noted that freedom from discrimination by the States in the enjoyment of property rights was among the basic objectives sought to be effectuated by the framers of the Fourteenth Amendment. That such discrimination has occurred in these cases is clear. Because of the race or color of these petitioners they have been denied rights of ownership or occupancy enjoyed as a matter of course by other citizens of different race or color. . . .

The task of determining whether the action of a State offends constitutional provisions is one which may not be undertaken lightly. Where, however, it is clear that the action of the State violates the terms of the fundamental charter, it is the obligation of this Court so to declare.

The historical context in which the Fourteenth Amendment became a part of the Constitution should not be forgotten. Whatever else the framers sought to achieve, it is clear that the matter of primary concern was the establishment of equality in the enjoyment of basic civil and political rights and the preservation of those rights from discriminatory action on the part of the States based on considerations of race or color. Seventy-five years ago this Court announced that the provisions of the Amendment are to be construed with this fundamental purpose in mind.[19] Upon full consideration, we have concluded that in these cases the States have acted to deny petitioners the equal protection of the laws guaranteed by the Fourteenth Amendment. Having so decided, we find it unnecessary to consider whether petitioners have also been deprived of property without due process of law or denied privileges and immunities of citizens of the United States.

For the reasons stated, the judgment of the Supreme Court of Missouri and the judgment of the Supreme Court of Michigan must be reversed.

Reversed.

HURD v. HODGE

334 U.S. 24 (May 3, 1948)

Certiorari to the United States Court of Appeals for the District of Columbia.

Reversed.

6-0

Vinson, C.J.	('+')
Black	(+)
Douglas	(+)
Murphy	(+)
Burton	(+)
Frankfurter	('+'
Reed	NP
Jackson	NP
Rutledge	NP

Newspaper speculation at the time was that Reed, Jackson, and Rutledge disqualified themselves [20] from participation

[19] *Slaughter-House Cases*, 16 Wall. 36, 81 (1873) . . . [Footnote by the Court.]

[20] It is somewhat unusual for as many as three justices to disqualify themselves in the same decision, and particularly when all parties to the cases, as in *Shelley* v. *Kraemer* and *Hurd* v. *Hodge*, are private persons. However, when the national government is a party to litigation before the Supreme Court,

in the decision of the Restrictive Covenant cases because of their personal ownership of property in the Washington area subject to restrictive covenants—which, if true, would have made the justices concerned signatories of such agreements. But we cannot be certain of their grounds for nonparticipation, for reasons that have already been explained in the Jackson-Frankfurter opinion in the Jewell Ridge rehearing decision, in Chapter 3 at p. 148.

MR. CHIEF JUSTICE VINSON delivered the opinion of the Court.

These are companion cases to *Shelley* v. *Kraemer* and *McGhee* v. *Sipes, ante*, p. 1, and come to this Court on certiorari to the United States Court of Appeals for the District of Columbia.

In 1906, twenty of thirty-one lots in the 100 block of Bryant Street, Northwest, in the City of Washington, were sold subject to the following covenant: ". . . that said lot shall never be rented, leased, sold, transferred or conveyed unto any Negro or colored person, under a penalty of Two Thousand Dollars ($2,000), which shall be a lien against said property." The covenant imposes no time limitation on the restriction.

Prior to the sales which gave rise to these cases, the twenty lots which are subject to the covenants were at all times owned and occupied by white persons, except for a brief period when three of the houses were occupied by Negroes who were eventually induced to move

former service as Attorney General or as Solicitor General may pose difficult problems of multiple-disqualification of the justices, since some anti-trust suits may result in the official involvement of the Department of Justice for over a decade; indeed, during the World War II period, the Court was unable to decide some cases because of the simultaneous self-disqualification of Stone, Reed, Murphy, and Jackson, and the consequent lack of the statutory quorum of six. In such cases, Congress has provided that the decision of the relevant federal Court of Appeals shall be final.

without legal action. The remaining eleven lots in the same block, however, are not subject to a restrictive agreement and, as found by the District Court, were occupied by Negroes for the twenty years prior to the institution of this litigation.

These cases involve seven of the twenty lots which are subject to the terms of the restrictive covenants. In No. 290, petitioners Hurd, found by the trial court to be Negroes,[21] purchased one of the restricted properties from the white owners. In No. 291, petitioner Urciolo, a white real estate dealer, sold and conveyed three of the restricted properties to the Negro petitioners Rowe, Savage, and Stewart. Petitioner Urciolo also owns three other lots in the block subject to the covenants. In both cases, the Negro petitioners are presently occupying as homes the respective properties which have been conveyed to them.

Suits were instituted in the District Court by respondents, who own other property in the block subject to the terms of the covenants, praying for injunctive relief to enforce the terms of the restrictive agreement. The cases were consolidated for trial, and after a hearing, the court entered a judgment declaring null and void the deeds of the Negro petitioners; enjoining petitioner Urciolo and one Ryan, the white property owners who had sold the houses to the Negro petitioners, from leasing, selling or conveying the properties to any Negro or colored person; enjoining the Negro petitioners from leasing or conveying the properties and directing those petitioners "to remove themselves and all of their personal belongings" from the premises within sixty days.

The United States Court of Appeals for the District of Columbia, with one justice dissenting, affirmed the judgment of the District Court. The majority of the court was of the opinion that the action of the District Court was consistent with earlier decisions of the Court of Appeals and that those decisions should be held determinative in these cases.

Petitioners have attacked the judicial enforcement of the restrictive covenants in these cases on a wide variety of grounds. Primary reliance, however, is placed on the contention that such governmental action on the part of the courts of the District of Columbia is forbidden by the due process clause of the Fifth Amendment of the Federal Constitution.

Whether judicial enforcement of racial restrictive agreements by the federal courts of the District of Columbia violates the Fifth Amendment has never been adjudicated by this Court. In *Corrigan* v. *Buckley,* 271 U.S. 323 (1926), an appeal was taken to this Court from a judgment of the United States Court of Appeals for the District of Columbia which had affirmed an order of the lower court granting enforcement to a restrictive covenant. But . . . the only constitutional issue which had been raised in the lower courts in the *Corrigan* case and, consequently, the only constitutional question before this Court on appeal, related to the validity of the private agreements as such. . . .

Petitioners urge that judicial enforcement of the restrictive covenants by courts of the District of Columbia should . . . be held to deny rights of white sellers and Negro purchasers of property, guaranteed by the due process clause of the Fifth Amendment. . . .

Upon full consideration, however, we have found it unnecessary to resolve the constitutional issue which petitioners advance; for we have concluded that judicial enforcement of restrictive covenants by the courts of the District of Columbia is improper for other reasons. . . .

[The] explicit language employed by Congress [in Section 1 of the Civil Rights Act of 1866, now 42 U.S.C. sec. 1982] to effectuate its purposes leaves no doubt that judicial enforcement of the restric-

---

21 Petitioner James M. Hurd maintained that he is not a Negro but a Mohawk Indian. [Footnote by the Court.]

tive covenants by the courts of the District of Columbia is prohibited by the Civil Rights Act. That statute, by its terms, requires that all citizens of the United States shall have the same right "as is enjoyed by white citizens . . . to inherit, purchase, lease, sell, hold, and convey real and personal property." That the Negro petitioners have been denied that right by virtue of the action of the federal courts of the District is clear. The Negro petitioners entered into contracts of sale with willing sellers for the purchase of properties upon which they desired to establish homes. Solely because of their race and color they are confronted with orders of court divesting their titles in the properties and ordering that the premises be vacated. White sellers, one of whom is a petitioner here, have been enjoined from selling the properties to any Negro or colored person. Under such circumstances, to suggest that the Negro petitioners have been accorded the same rights as white citizens to purchase, hold, and convey real property is to reject the plain meaning of language. We hold that the action of the District Court directed against the Negro purchasers and the white sellers denies rights intended by Congress to be protected by the Civil Rights Act and that, consequently, the action cannot stand.

But even in the absence of the statute, there are other considerations which would indicate that enforcement of restrictive covenants in these cases is judicial action contrary to the public policy of the United States, and as such should be corrected by this Court in the exercise of its supervisory powers over the courts of the District of Columbia. The power of the federal courts to enforce the terms of private agreements is at all times exercised subject to the restrictions and limitations of the public policy of the United States as manifested in the Constitution, treaties, federal statutes, and applicable legal precedents. Where the enforcement of private agreements would be violative of that policy, it is the obligation of courts to refrain from such exertions of judicial power.

We are here concerned with action of federal courts of such a nature that if taken by the courts of a State would violate the prohibitory provisions of the Fourteenth Amendment. *Shelley* v. *Kraemer, supra*. It is not consistent with the public policy of the United States to permit federal courts in the Nation's capital to exercise general equitable powers to compel action denied the state courts where such state action has been held to be violative of the guaranty of the equal protection of the laws. We cannot presume that the public policy of the United States manifests a lesser concern for the protection of such basic rights against discriminatory action of federal courts than against such action taken by the courts of the States.

Reversed.

It is clear that in *Shelley* v. *Kraemer,* the Court established the policy that state courts cannot order specific performance on restrictive racial covenants (i.e., the state courts cannot utilize their equity powers to force parties to such contracts to live up to their agreements) because such action by state judges would be "state action" which would deny the equal protection of the laws to members of proscribed minority groups, such as Negroes. It is equally clear that there is no equal-protection clause, applicable to the national government, in the Constitution. What the Court did in *Hurd* v. *Hodge* was to impute the more specific limitations upon state action, provided by the equal-protection clause of the Fourteenth Amendment, to be a limitation upon the national government as well, by defining the prohibition against enforcement of restrictive covenants as contrary to the public policy which the Supreme Court establishes through its supervisory responsibilities over adjudication by the lower federal courts. In so doing, the Supreme Court partially nationalized the equal-protection clause, by attributing to it the same meaning as a limitation upon both the national and state governments, with uniform effect throughout the nation. As we shall see, below, the Court recently has further nationalized the equal-protection clause in relationship to racial segregation in public education.

The intermeshing of federal and state precedents makes for a subtle interplay in the evolution of the Court's policy-making. The next restrictive covenant case to arise, for instance, was one in which a white covenantor was sued for damages by her white neighbors, for having agreed to sell her property to a "non-Caucasian." But no "non-Caucasians" were parties to *Barrows* v. *Jackson,* 346 U.S. 249 (1953), and their legal rights were involved only indirectly (although certainly, vitally) in the suit. Nevertheless, six justices ruled that the courts of California could not penalize the breach of a contract that could not be enforced in equity by the state courts or incorporated into a statutory policy because of the Fourteenth Amendment, and more importantly, that would be *contrary to public policy* and would therefore be unenforceable in any form in the *federal* courts. Thus, a policy that the Court could establish because of its supervisory authority over the *federal* courts became binding upon state courts as well, now in the form of the *constitutional* policy of equal protection of the Fourteenth Amendment. This occurred notwithstanding the presumed deference that the Supreme Court owes to state courts (as the agents of the states in our federal system of government), and over whom it therefore supposedly exercises no general supervisory authority. Consistent with their nonparticipation in *Shelley* v. *Kraemer* and *Hurd* v. *Hodge,* Reed and Jackson did not participate in the decision of *Barrows* v. *Jackson;* and Chief Justice Vinson, who had written the opinion of the Court in the Shelley and Hurd cases, made this the occasion for his only solo dissent as a member of the Supreme Court.[22]

THE DESEGREGATION OF PUBLIC EDUCATION

The Break-Through in Higher Education

The most controversial, and probably the most important, decision that the Supreme Court has made in the twentieth century was in the School Segregation Cases, in 1954. In that decision, the Court declared that the public educational systems of over a third of the states of the United States unconstitutionally

[22] C. Herman Pritchett, *Civil Liberties and the Vinson Court* (Chicago: University of Chicago Press, 1954), p. 143.

discriminated against Negro children by requiring that they attend inferior schools separate from those for white children. The decision should not have come as a surprise, however, for it was the climax of an evolutionary process of Court policy-making regarding segregated public education that has extended over two full decades.

The first of the Court's decisions that resulted in the eventual repudiation of the separate-but-equal doctrine in the field of education came in the year following the crucial changes of the 1936 Term. In *Missouri ex rel. Gaines* v. *Canada,* 305 U.S. 337 (1938), an admittedly qualified Negro student, Lloyd Gaines, sued the registrar of the University of Missouri to compel his admission to the law school of the university. The law school had admitted only white students in the past; but since Missouri maintained no separate Negro law school and the university was a state-supported institution, there was an arrangement under which otherwise qualified Negro applicants could attend the law school of any neighboring state to which they might gain admission, with the State of Missouri paying the tuition. Since, in the opinion of the Court, there would be special advantages, for one who wanted to practice law in Missouri, to study law in that state rather than another, irrespective of any other qualitative differentials that might distinguish legal training in neighboring states as compared to that offered at the law school of the University of Missouri, Lloyd Gaines was denied the equal protection of the laws.

Chief Justice Hughes, who had written for the Court a quarter of a century earlier in *McCabe* v. *Atchison, Topeka & Santa Fe Railway Co.,* 235 U.S. 151 (1914), cited that case in his opinion for the Court in the Gaines case. It was "commendable," he said, that Missouri had pioneered in the establishment of "a separate university for negroes on the same basis as the state university for white students." Nevertheless, Lincoln University did not offer instruction in law; and the fact that there appeared to have been limited Negro demand for legal training was no more relevant than had been the limited demand of Negroes, at the time of the McCabe decision, for Pullman accommodations. But Hughes also explicitly stated that Missouri could have fulfilled its obligation for providing legal instruction to Negroes "by furnishing equal facilities in separate schools, a method the validity of which has been sustained by our decisions"—citing the Plessy, McCabe, Gong Lum, and Cumming cases. What the Constitution guaranteed to Gaines was not admission to the law school of the University of Missouri, but a legal education in Missouri. Clearly, the Court at this time considered that it was following and applying the separate-but-equal policy of the Plessy decision.

The remaining two members of the conservative bloc of the preceding terms—McReynolds and Butler—dissented together, expressing the view that if Missouri should choose to admit Gaines to the university law school instead of establishing a separate-but-equal school for Negroes, the result would be to "damnify both races." Missouri chose to set up a law school for Negroes at Lincoln University;

but Lloyd Gaines disappeared [23] shortly before the Court's decision was announced, before he ever attended any law school.

A similar question had been raised two years earlier before the Court of Appeals of the State of Maryland; [24] and the state court's decision, which was cited by Hughes, differed from that of the Supreme Court in the Gaines case in two important respects. The Maryland court agreed that the out-of-state tuition arrangement for Negro law students denied them equal protection, and for the same reasons that subsequently were accepted by the Supreme Court; but the Court of Appeals ordered that the petitioner be immediately admitted to the University of Maryland Law School, and explicitly rejected the alternative remedy of ordering or allowing the establishment of a separate Maryland law school for Negroes. And what is more, this petitioner *did* enter and in due course graduate from the University of Maryland Law School.[25] So even in 1938, the Supreme Court's first step in the direction of changing the separate-but-equal doctrine was a faltering and hesitating one, in a decision that was considerably less libertarian than the almost contemporaneous decision of the highest court of one of the border states.

It is probably no accident that not only these two cases but three of the next four higher-education cases to be decided by the Supreme Court also related to *legal* education. This was the one field of education for which "Brandeis briefs" would be unnecessary to supplement the direct knowledge and experience of the justices themselves. The only justice who participated in these higher-education cases (and the only one who has been a member of the Court since 1933) who has not been a law-school graduate was Robert H. Jackson; and even he had a year at the Albany Law School. All were lawyers; and all understood the importance to a young lawyer just getting started in his profession of both such tangible factors as the size and quality of a law school's library, and of such intangible factors as the prestige of his alma mater. On the basis of his own personal experience, each justice could bring to bear an off-the-record criterion of the implications of "equality" in judging whether a substitute for a state's university law school denied a qualified Negro resident and applicant the equal protection of the laws.

After the Gaines decision, a decade elapsed before the Court accepted jurisdiction in a similar case. Having done so, the Court disposed of the case, *Sipuel* v. *Oklahoma,* 332 U.S. 631 (1948), by reversing the state court in a brief *per curiam* opinion which cited the Gaines case but failed to specify what action the state should take, stating cryptically that "the petitioner is entitled to secure legal education afforded by a state institution." The state courts decided that the Negro applicant, Miss Ada Lois Sipuel, was entitled to immediate enrollment in the

[23] Albert P. Blaustein and Clarence Ferguson, *Desegregation and the Law* (New Brunswick: Rutgers University Press, 1957), p. 107.

[24] *Pearson* v. *Murray,* 169 Md. 478 (1936).
[25] Blaustein and Ferguson, *op. cit.,* p. 107.

University of Oklahoma Law School, unless the university were to suspend all enrollment of entering students, until such time as the state should establish a separate law school for Negroes. Miss Sipuel, who in the interim had become Mrs. Fisher, asked the Supreme Court to rule that the action of the state courts did not satisfy the Court's Delphic mandate in the primary decision in her case; but the Court responded with another *per curiam* opinion, 333 U.S. 147 (February 16, 1948), announcing in *Fisher* v. *Hurst* that she had no standing to challenge the separate-but-equal "doctrine," and apparently no basis for complaint if she were admitted and then subsequently evicted from the University of Oklahoma Law School so long as other arrangements were then made for her legal education in a state-sponsored law school for Negroes.

Against this background, the shift in the Court's policy that was announced only a year later was the more dramatic. Moreover, Murphy and Rutledge had participated in the Sipuel-Fisher decisions, dissenting in the latter, and by 1950 had been replaced by justices whose voting behavior was generally considerably less sympathetic to civil-liberties claims than that of the two libertarians. Nevertheless, the Court took a giant stride toward paving the way for the School Segregation Cases in two decisions that were announced on June 5, 1950. In each case, Chief Justice Vinson delivered the unanimous opinion of the Court.

In the first, *Sweatt* v. *Painter*, 339 U.S. 629, 634, the Court posited what amounted to unattainable requisites of equality for separate law schools for Negroes. Texas had established such a separate law school, in apparent good-faith reliance upon the Court's decision in the Gaines case. Heman Sweatt, a Negro applicant to the University of Texas Law School, argued that the new law school at the Texas State University for Negroes was inferior to that of the University of Texas. (And, of course, it was; indeed, *any* law school which has been hastily set up a year or two earlier, whether segregated or not, would necessarily have been inferior to the established institution at the major university in the state, and would have remained so for a long time to come.) The Court could, of course, have stopped after cataloguing the obvious physical differences between the old and the new law schools; these adequately demonstrated the lack of equality between the two, at least to support the Court's decision which, unlike the mandate in the earlier cases of Gaines and Sipuel-Fisher, ordered that Sweatt "be admitted to the University of Texas Law School," as a requirement of "the Equal Protection Clause of the Fourteenth Amendment." But Vinson went further:

> What is more important, the University of Texas Law School possesses to a far greater degree those qualities which are incapable of objective measurement but which make for greatness in a law school. Such qualities, to name but a few, include reputation of the faculty, experience of the administration, position and influence of the alumni, standing in the community, traditions and prestige. It is difficult to believe that one who had a free choice between these law schools would consider the question close.

Moreover, although the law is a highly learned profession, we are well aware that it is an intensely practical one. The law school, the proving ground for legal learning and practice, cannot be effective in isolation from the individuals and institutions with which the law interacts. Few students and no one who has practiced law would choose to study in an academic vacuum, removed from the interplay of ideas and the exchange of views with which the law is concerned. The law school to which Texas is willing to admit petitioner excludes from its student body members of the racial groups which number 85% of the population of the State and include most of the lawyers, witnesses, jurors, judges and other officials with whom petitioner will inevitably be dealing when he becomes a member of the Texas Bar. With such a substantial and significant segment of society excluded, we cannot conclude that the education offered petitioner is substantially equal to that which he would receive if admitted to the University of Texas Law School.

Such intangible considerations were the most conspicuous element of the facts in the other case. G. W. McLaurin, a Negro citizen of Oklahoma who had already acquired a master's degree, had applied for admission to the University of Oklahoma as a doctoral candidate in the field of education. Notwithstanding the Gaines case, McLaurin was denied admission because of his race; and there was no Negro institution of higher learning within the state which granted the degree of Doctor of Education. A federal district court ruled that the state statutes, under which it would have been a crime for the University of Oklahoma authorities to have admitted McLaurin, were unconstitutional; and the trial court purported to "follow"—actually, it seemed to be somewhat in advance of— the Supreme Court's decisions in the Gaines and Sipuel cases. The state legislature responded with a new statute which authorized the admission of qualified Negroes to white colleges, when the state's Negro institutions did not offer a program leading to the degree for which application was made. The instruction of any Negroes so admitted to institutions of higher learning intended for the "white race" was explicitly required to be on a "segregated basis," which was defined to mean "classroom instruction given in separate classrooms, or at separate times."

McLaurin was the only Negro pursuing the doctorate of education at the University of Oklahoma at the time of his admission. Rather than establish separate classes for him alone, the authorities of the state university—persons who, generally speaking, try to cooperate with the state legislatures whence cometh university money—tried to comply with the statute by "segregating" McLaurin. At the time his case was under consideration by the Court, the Acme Newsphoto service distributed a nationally published photograph which showed George McLaurin, a mild-looking Negro professor who wore spectacles and appeared to be approaching middle age, seated in the hall outside an open classroom door.[26]

26 See, e.g., *United States News and World Report,* Vol. 28, Part 1, February 17, 1950, p. 22; and Part 2, June 16, 1950, p. 18.

He could see the instructor and the instructor could see him, but the rest of the class, presumably persons of tender years and lesser fortitude, were spared the possible anguish and embarrassment of openly sharing the room with McLaurin, who was hidden in his vestibule from the view of most of his fellow students.

According to the opinion of the Court: [27]

. . . He was required to sit apart at a designated desk in an anteroom adjoining the classroom; to sit at a designated desk on the mezzanine floor of the library, but not to use the desks in the regular reading room; and to sit at a designated table and to eat at a different time from the other students in the school cafeteria. . . . For some time, the section of the classroom in which appellant sat was surrounded by a rail on which there was a sign stating, "Reserved For Colored," but these have been removed. He is now assigned to a seat in the classroom in a row specified for colored students. . . .

These restrictions were obviously imposed in order to comply, as nearly as could be, with the statutory requirements of Oklahoma. But they signify that the State, in administering the facilities it affords for professional and graduate study, sets McLaurin apart from the other students. The result is that appellant is handicapped in his pursuit of effective graduate instruction. Such restrictions impair and inhibit his ability to study, to engage in discussions and exchange views with other students, and, in general, to learn his profession.

Our society grows increasingly complex, and our need for trained leaders increases correspondingly. Appellant's case represents, perhaps, the epitome of that need, for he is attempting to obtain an advanced degree in education, to become, by definition, a leader and trainer of others. Those who will come under his guidance and influence must be directly affected by the education he receives. Their own education and development will necessarily suffer to the extent that his training is unequal to that of his classmates. State-imposed restrictions which produce such inequalities cannot be sustained. . . .

There is a vast difference—a Constitutional difference—between restrictions imposed by the state which prohibit the intellectual commingling of students, and the refusal of individuals to commingle where the state presents no such bar. . . . Appellant, having been admitted to a state-supported graduate school, must receive the same treatment at the hands of the state as students of other races.

The decisions in the Sweatt and McLaurin cases signified a general, although not immediate, breakdown of segregation in public higher education in the states of the South. Almost a decade later, in 1959, the public colleges and universities of four states remained closed to Negroes. These four states were the heart of the

27 *McLaurin* v. *Oklahoma State Regents*, 339 U.S. 637, 640-642 (1950).

"blackbelt" (i.e., the states containing the most counties in which Negroes comprised a majority of the population),[28] and included Mississippi, Alabama, Georgia, and South Carolina. In the middle of the 1955-1956 academic year, the University of Alabama admitted Autherine Lucy under the coercion of an order of the United States Supreme Court;[29] but Miss Lucy's brief presence on campus was attended by riots and threats of open violence. The local federal district court upheld her subsequent expulsion by university authorities, on the ground that she (i.e., the local N.A.A.C.P. attorney) had made "baseless" charges against officials of the university, accusing them of complicity in the riots that had driven her from the campus.[30] Soon thereafter, Miss Lucy married and moved with her husband to Texas, where both were admitted to public colleges.

In Florida, Virgil D. Hawkins was in and out of the courts for almost a decade, as he unsuccessfully sought admission to the University of Florida Law School. The United States Supreme Court ruled, shortly after the Lucy fiasco, that Hawkins should be admitted,[31] but the Florida Supreme Court resorted to evasive action, and a subsequent attempt to get the United States Supreme Court to involve itself in the enforcement problem failed, as the Court denied certiorari, suggesting that Hawkins try the local federal district court instead.[32] Less than a year later, however, George Henry Starke, Jr., was admitted to the university law school as the first Negro to enter a public institution of higher learning in Florida, and others followed in his wake. It was estimated early in 1957 that over half of the 208 publicly supported colleges and universities in the South had adopted policies under which Negroes as well as whites could be accepted; and that approximately two thousand Negroes were actually in attendance in about ninety percent of these institutions.[33]

The School Segregation Cases

Of even greater importance, perhaps, than the opening to Negroes of the tax-supported colleges and universities of the South, was the significance of the Sweatt and McLaurin precedents in paving the way for the decision in the School Segregation Cases. Much of the criticism of the Court's opinion in the latter cases has been directed at Footnote 11 of Warren's opinion, the so-called "sociological footnote," in which the Court cited several books and articles authored by sociologists, social psychologists, and educational psychologists.[34] It has been widely

---

28 V. O. Key, Jr. *Southern Politics* (New York: Knopf, 1949), pp. 5-6.

29 *Lucy* v. *Adams*, 350 U.S. 1 (October 10, 1955); and cf. *Adams* v. *Lucy*, 228 F.2d 619 (December 30, 1955), certiorari denied, 351 U.S. 931 (May 14, 1956).

30 *Race Relations Law Reporter*, Vol. 1, pp. 456, 894 (1956).

31 *Florida ex rel. Hawkins* v. *Board of*

Control, 350 U.S. 413 (March 12, 1956).

32 *Ibid.*, 355 U.S. 839 (October 14, 1957).

33 *Southern School News*, Vol. 3, No. 8 (February, 1957), pp. 1-3.

34 For an excellent discussion of this issue, see Herbert Garfinkel, "Social Science Evidence and the School Segregation Cases," *Journal of Politics*, Vol. 21, pp. 37-59 (February, 1959).

charged that the Court's decision was premised upon the assumption that the research findings reported in the studies by these social scientists is valid scientific knowledge. By exposing error in the research techniques or findings, critics have sought to demonstrate that Warren's Court relied upon a social psychology to which little greater reliability can be imputed than the folklore with which Brown adorned his opinion in *Plessy* v. *Ferguson.*

Such criticism misses the main point, and probably does so deliberately. What Warren says (in his opinion below) is that "Whatever may have been the extent of psychological knowledge at the time of *Plessy* v. *Ferguson,* this finding [i.e., that the segregation of white and Negro children in public schools has a detrimental educational effect upon Negro children] is amply supported by modern authority." Whether or not the social scientists cited by the Court are right is irrelevant; they do articulate the consensus of modern authorities, and this *is* what they say. In any event, it is unlikely that the justices would have accepted the views of the social scientists as authoritative, were it not for the critical circumstance that such views corresponded closely to the personal experiences of the justices, learned in the field of education that they knew best. Such nonprofessional psychological conclusions, reflecting the justices' own estimation of the importance of "intangible factors" in legal education, played a key role in Vinson's opinions in the Sweatt and McLaurin cases, which in turn provide the precedents upon which the Court places principal reliance in the opinion and decision below.

THE PRIMARY DECISION IN THE STATE CASES

The principal decision and opinion of the Court came in the group of four state cases which share the title: *Brown* v. *Board of Education.* A federal case from the District of Columbia was disposed of independently as *Bolling* v. *Sharpe;* and all five cases were joined for common disposition a year later in the "mandate" decision under the same title as the primary decision in the state cases. *Bolling* v. *Sharpe* is presented and the mandate decision is discussed below, following the principal decision.

BROWN v. BOARD OF EDUCATION

[*Brown* v. *Board of Education of Topeka; Briggs* v. *Elliott; Davis* v. *County School Board of Prince Edward County, Virginia;* and *Gebhart* v. *Belton*]

347 U.S. 483 (Argued December 9-11, 1952; reargued December 7-9, 1953; decided May 17, 1954)

Appeals from the United States District Courts for the District of Kansas, the Eastern District of South Carolina, the Eastern District of Virginia; and certiorari to the Supreme Court of Delaware.

Decrees withheld and cases restored to the docket for further argument.

9-0

Warren, C.J.	('+')
Black	(+)
Reed	(+)
Frankfurter	(+)
Douglas	(+)
Jackson	(+)
Burton	(+)
Clark	(+)
Minton	(+)

In the Kansas case, *Brown* v. *Board of Education,* the plaintiffs are Negro children of elementary school age residing in Topeka. They brought this action in the United States District Court for the District of Kansas to enjoin enforcement of a Kansas statute which permits, but does not require, cities of more than 15,000 population to maintain separate school facilities for Negro and white students. . . . Pursuant to that authority, the Topeka Board of Education elected to establish segregated elementary schools. Other public schools in the community, however, are operated on a nonsegregated basis. The three-judge District Court . . . found that segregation in public education has a detrimental effect upon Negro children, but denied relief on the ground that the Negro and white schools were substantially equal with respect to buildings, transportation, curricula, and educational qualifications of teachers. . . .

In the South Carolina case, *Briggs* v. *Elliott,* the plaintiffs are Negro children of both elementary and high school age residing in Clarendon County. They brought this action in the United States District Court for the Eastern District of South Carolina to enjoin enforcement of provisions in the state constitution and statutory code which require the segregation of Negroes and whites in public schools. . . . The three-judge District Court . . . denied the requested relief. The court found that the Negro schools were inferior to the white schools and

ordered the defendants to begin immediately to equalize the facilities. But the court sustained the validity of the contested provisions and denied the plaintiffs admission to the white schools during the equalization program. 98 F. Supp. 529. This Court vacated the District Court's judgment and remanded the case for the purpose of obtaining the court's views on a report filed by the defendants concerning the progress made in the equalization program. 342 U.S. 350. On remand, the District Court found that substantial equality had been achieved except for buildings and that the defendants were proceeding to rectify this inequality as well. 103 F. Supp. 920. The case is again here on direct appeal. . . .

In the Virginia case, *Davis* v. *County School Board,* the plaintiffs are Negro children of high school age residing in Prince Edward County. They brought this action in the United States District Court for the Eastern District of Virginia to enjoin enforcement of provisions in the state constitution and statutory code which require the segregation of Negroes and whites in public schools. . . . The three-judge District Court . . . denied the requested relief. The court found the Negro school inferior in physical plant, curricula, and transportation, and ordered the defendants forthwith to provide substantially equal curricula and transportation and to "proceed with all reasonable diligence and dispatch to remove" the inequality in physical plant. But, as in the South Carolina case, the court sustained the validity of the contested provisions and denied the plaintiffs admission to the white schools during the equalization program. 103 F. Supp. 337. The case is here on direct appeal. . . .

In the Delaware case, *Gebhart* v. *Belton,* the plaintiffs are Negro children of both elementary and high school age residing in New Castle County. They brought this action in the Delaware Court of Chancery to enjoin enforcement of provisions in the state constitution and statutory code which require the segregation of Negroes and whites in public schools. . . . The Chancellor gave judgment for the plaintiffs and ordered their immediate admission to schools previously attended only by white children, on the ground that the Negro schools were inferior with respect to teacher training, pupil-teacher ratio, extracurricular activities, physcial plant, and time and distance involved in travel. 87 A. 2d 862. The Chancellor also found that segregation itself results in an inferior education for Negro children . . . but did not rest his decision on that ground. *Id.*, at 865. The Chancellor's decree was affirmed by the Supreme Court of Delaware, which intimated, however, that the defendants might be able to obtain a modification of the decree after equalization of the Negro and white schools had been accomplished. 91 A. 2d 137, 152. The defendants, contending only that the Delaware courts had erred in ordering the immediate admission of the Negro plaintiffs to the white schools, applied to this Court for certiorari. . . .[35]

MR. CHIEF JUSTICE WARREN delivered the opinion of the Court.

These cases come to us from the States of Kansas, South Carolina, Virginia, and Delaware. They are premised on different facts and different local conditions, but a common legal question justifies their consideration together in this consolidated opinion.

In each of the cases, minors of the Negro race, through their legal representatives, seek the aid of the courts in obtaining admission to the public schools of their community on a nonsegregated basis. In each instance, they had been denied admission to schools attended by white children under laws requiring or permitting segregation according to race. This segregation was alleged to deprive

[35] This statement of the facts is taken from footnote 1 to the opinion of the Court, 347 U.S. 483, 486-488.

the plaintiffs of the equal protection of the laws under the Fourteenth Amendment. In each of the cases other than the Delaware case, a three-judge federal district court denied relief to the plaintiffs on the so-called "separate but equal" doctrine announced by this Court in *Plessy* v. *Ferguson*, 163 U.S. 537. Under that doctrine, equality of treatment is accorded when the races are provided substantially equal facilities, even though these facilities be separate. In the Delaware case, the Supreme Court of Delaware adhered to that doctrine, but ordered that the plaintiffs be admitted to the white schools because of their superiority to the Negro schools.

The plaintiffs contend that segregated public schools are not "equal" and cannot be made "equal," and that hence they are deprived of the equal protection of the laws. Because of the obvious importance of the question presented, the Court took jurisdiction. Argument was heard in the 1952 Term, and reargument was heard this Term on certain questions propounded by the Court.

Reargument was largely devoted to the circumstances surrounding the adoption of the Fourteenth Amendment in 1868. It covered exhaustively consideration of the Amendment in Congress, ratification by the states, then existing practices in racial segregation, and the views of proponents and opponents of the Amendment. This discussion and our own investigation convince us that, although these sources cast some light, it is not enough to resolve the problem with which we are faced. At best, they are inconclusive. The most avid proponents of the post-War Amendments undoubtedly intended them to remove all legal distinctions among "all persons born or naturalized in the United States." Their opponents, just as certainly, were antagonistic to both the letter and the spirit of the Amendments and wished them to have the most limited effect. What others in Congress and the state legislatures had in mind cannot be determined with any degree of certainty.

An additional reason for the inconclusive nature of the Amendment's history, with respect to segregated schools, is the status of public education at that time. In the South, the movement toward free common schools, supported by general taxation, had not yet taken hold. Education of white children was largely in the hands of private groups. Education of Negroes was almost nonexistent, and practically all of the race were illiterate. In fact, any education of Negroes was forbidden by law in some states. Today, in contrast, many Negroes have achieved outstanding success in the arts and sciences as well as in the business and professional world. It is true that public school education at the time of the Amendment had advanced further in the North, but the effect of the Amendment on Northern States was generally ignored in the congressional debates. Even in the North, the conditions of public education did not approximate those existing today. The curriculum was usually rudimentary; ungraded schools were common in rural areas; the school term was but three months a year in many states; and compulsory school attendance was virtually unknown. As a consequence, it is not surprising that there should be so little in the history of the Fourteenth Amendment relating to its intended effect on public education.

In the first cases in this Court construing the Fourteenth Amendment, decided shortly after its adoption, the Court interpreted it as proscribing all state-imposed discriminations against the Negro race.[36] The doctrine of "separate but equal" did not make its appearance in this Court until 1896 in the case of *Plessy* v. *Ferguson, supra,* involving not

36 *Slaughter-House Cases,* 16 Wall. 36, 67-72 (1873); *Strauder* v. *West Virginia,* 100 U.S. 303, 307-308 (1880) . . . [Footnote by the Court.]

education but transportation.[37] American courts have since labored with the doctrine for over half a century. In this Court, there have been six cases involving the "separate but equal" doctrine in the field of public education. In *Cumming* v. *County Board of Education,* 175 U.S. 528, and *Gong Lum* v. *Rice,* 275 U.S. 78, the validity of the doctrine itself was not challenged.[38] In more recent cases, all on the graduate school level, inequality was found in that specific benefits enjoyed by white students were denied to Negro students of the same educational qualifications. *Missouri ex rel. Gaines* v. *Canada,* 305 U.S. 337; *Sipuel* v. *Oklahoma,* 332 U.S. 631; *Sweatt* v. *Painter,* 339 U.S. 629; *McLaurin* v. *Oklahoma State Regents,* 339 U.S. 637. In none of these cases was it necessary to re-examine the doctrine to grant relief to the Negro plaintiff. And in *Sweatt* v. *Painter, supra,* the Court expressly reserved decision on the question whether *Plessy* v. *Ferguson* should be held inapplicable to public education.

In the instant cases, that question is directly presented. Here, unlike *Sweatt* v. *Painter,* there are findings below that

37 The doctrine apparently originated in *Roberts* v. *City of Boston,* 59 Mass. 198, 206 (1850), upholding school segregation against attack as being violative of a state constitutional guarantee of equality. Segregation in Boston public schools was eliminated in 1855. Mass. Acts 1855, c. 256. But elsewhere in the North segregation in public education has persisted in some communities until recent years. It is apparent that such segregation has long been a nationwide problem, not merely one of sectional concern. [Footnote by the Court.]

38 In the *Cumming* case, Negro taxpayers sought an injunction requiring the defendant school board to discontinue the operation of a high school for white children until the board resumed operation of a high school for Negro children. Similarly, in the *Gong Lum* case, the plaintiff, a child of Chinese descent, contended only that state authorities had misapplied the doctrine by classifying him with Negro children and requiring him to attend a Negro school. [Footnote by the Court.]

the Negro and white schools involved have been equalized, or are being equalized, with respect to buildings, curricula, qualifications and salaries of teachers, and other "tangible" factors. Our decision, therefore, cannot turn on merely a comparison of these tangible factors in the Negro and white schools involved in each of the cases. We must look instead to the effect of segregation itself on public education.

In approaching this problem, we cannot turn the clock back to 1868 when the Amendment was adopted, or even to 1896 when *Plessy* v. *Ferguson* was written. We must consider public education in the light of its full development and its present place in American life throughout the Nation. Only in this way can it be determined if segregation in public schools deprives these plaintiffs of the equal protection of the laws.

Today, education is perhaps the most important function of state and local governments. Compulsory school attendance laws and the great expenditures for education both demonstrate our recognition of the importance of education to our democratic society. It is required in the performance of our most basic public responsibilities, even service in the armed forces. It is the very foundation of good citizenship. Today it is a principal instrument in awakening the child to cultural values, in preparing him for later professional training, and in helping him to adjust normally to his environment. In these days, it is doubtful that any child may reasonably be expected to succeed in life if he is denied the opportunity of an education. Such an opportunity, where the state has undertaken to provide it, is a right which must be made available to all on equal terms.

We come then to the question presented: Does segregation of children in public schools solely on the basis of race, even though the physical facilities and other "tangible" factors may be equal, deprive the children of the minority group of equal educational opportunities? We believe that it does.

In *Sweatt* v. *Painter, supra,* in finding that a segregated law school for Negroes could not provide them equal educational opportunities, this Court relied in large part on "those qualities which are incapable of objective measurement but which make for greatness in a law school." In *McLaurin* v. *Oklahoma State Regents, supra,* the Court, in requiring that a Negro admitted to a white graduate school be treated like all other students, again resorted to intangible considerations: ". . . his ability to study, to engage in discussions and exchange views with other students, and, in general, to learn his profession." Such considerations apply with added force to children in grade and high schools. To separate them from others of similar age and qualifications solely because of their race generates a feeling of inferiority as to their status in the community that may affect their hearts and minds in a way unlikely ever to be undone. The effect of this separation on their educational opportunities was well stated by a finding in the Kansas case by a court which nevertheless felt compelled to rule against the Negro plaintiffs: "Segregation of white and colored children in public schools has a detrimental effect upon the colored children. The impact is greater when it has the sanction of the law; for the policy of separating the races is usually interpreted as denoting the inferiority of the negro group. A sense of inferiority affects the motivation of a child to learn. Segregation with the sanction of law, therefore, has a tendency to [retard] the educational and mental development of negro children and to deprive them of some of the benefits they would receive in a racial[ly] integrated school system." Whatever may have been the extent of psychological knowledge at the time of

Plessy v. *Ferguson,* this finding is amply supported by modern authority.[39] Any language in *Plessy* v. *Ferguson* contrary to this finding is rejected.

We conclude that in the field of public education the doctrine of "separate but equal" has no place. Separate educational facilities are inherently unequal. Therefore, we hold that the plaintiffs and others similarly situated for whom the actions have been brought are, by reason of the segregation complained of, deprived of the equal protection of the laws guaranteed by the Fourteenth Amendment. This disposition makes unnecessary any discussion whether such segregation also violates the Due Process Clause of the Fourteenth Amendment. . . .

THE FEDERAL CASE

In *Hurd* v. *Hodge* and *Barrows* v. *Jackson,* the Court had nationalized the unenforceability of restrictive convenants under the equal protection clause of the Fourteenth Amendment by invoking its supervisory powers over the federal courts. In *Bolling* v. *Sharpe,* below, the Court now nationalized the unconstitutionality of segregated public school education under the equal-protection clause of the Fourteenth Amendment by invoking the right, against the national government, to be free from the deprivation of liberty without due process of law, under the Fifth Amendment. Such "incorporation" of a civil right of the Fourteenth Amendment into the substance of the due process of the Fifth Amendment is the reverse of the more generally recognized process that we shall discuss in the next chapter, by means of which the First Amendment's restrictions upon the national government have become nationalized as the result of the Court's incorporation of them into Fourteenth Amendment due process. In order for rights to become "nationalized," in accordance with our definition, it is essential that the Court consider its decisions to be interchangeable as precedents, irrespective of whether the cases relate to action by the national or by state governments. We have observed that this condition holds for the Restrictive Covenant Cases, and *Bolling* v. *Sharpe* demonstrates that it holds also for the School Segregation Cases. In this regard, it is significant that the state cases and the federal case, referring now to the governments to which they relate rather than the lower courts in which they were tried, although separated for purposes of the Court's primary decision, were joined for common disposition in the mandate decision, which came a year later and is also discussed below.

The footnote in *Bolling* v. *Sharpe* to *Hurd* v. *Hodge* raises the question whether the Court may not re-evaluate the latter case, and decide that the unen-

[39] K. B. Clark, Effect of Prejudice and Discrimination on Personality Development (Midcentury White House Conference on Children and Youth, 1950); Witmer and Kotinsky, Personality in the Making (1952), c.VI; Deutscher and Chein, The Psychological Effects of Enforced Segregation: A Survey of Social Science Opinion, 26 J. Psychol. 259 (1948); Chein, What are the Psychological Effects of Segregation Under Conditions of Equal Facilities?, 3 Int. J. Opinion and Attitude Res. 229 (1949); Brameld, Educational Costs, in Discrimination and National Welfare (MacIver, ed., 1949), 44-48; Frazier, The Negro in the United States (1949), 674-681. And see generally Myrdal, An American Dilemma (1944). [Footnote by the Court. This is the celebrated "social science" footnote.]

forceability of restrictive covenants in federal courts rests upon Fifth Amendment due process, rather than upon the Court's supervisory authority. Such a recasting of the rationale of Hurd would provide a less questionable major premise for Barrows; and the "reinterpretation" of cases is by no means unknown, at least in reciprocal form. As we shall see in Chapter 11, *Weeks* v. *United States,* 232 U.S. 383 (1914), states that the decision is based upon the Fourth Amendment; but thirty-five years later, a subsequent generation of justices implied in *Wolf* v. *Colorado,* 338 U.S. 25 (1949), that the so-called "Weeks rule" was really based upon the Supreme Court's supervisory powers over lower federal courts.[40]

BOLLING v. SHARPE

347 U.S. 497 (May 17, 1954)

Certiorari to the Court of Appeals for the District of Columbia.

Decree withheld and case restored to the docket for further argument.

9-0

Warren, C.J.	('+')
Black	(+)
Reed	(+)
Frankfurter	(+)
Douglas	(+)
Jackson	(+)
Burton	(+)
Clark	(+)
Minton	(+)

MR. CHIEF JUSTICE WARREN delivered the opinion of the Court.

This case challenges the validity of segregation in the public schools of the District of Columbia. The petitioners, minors of the Negro race, allege that such segregation deprives them of due process of law under the Fifth Amendment. They were refused admission to a public school attended by white children solely because of their race. They sought the aid of the District Court for the District of Columbia in obtaining

[40] See particularly Mr. Justice Black's concurring opinion in *Wolf* v. *Colorado,* which makes this point explicitly.

admission. That court dismissed their complaint. The Court granted a writ of certiorari before judgment in the Court of Appeals because of the importance of the constitutional question presented. 344 U.S. 873.

We have this day held that the Equal Protection Clause of the Fourteenth Amendment prohibits the states from maintaining racially segregated public schools. The legal problem in the District of Columbia is somewhat different, however. The Fifth Amendment, which is applicable in the District of Columbia, does not contain an equal protection clause as does the Fourteenth Amendment which applies only to the states. But the concepts of equal protection and due process, both stemming from our American ideal of fairness, are not mutually exclusive. The "equal protection of the laws" is a more explicit safeguard of prohibited unfairness than "due process of law," and, therefore, we do not imply that the two are always interchangeable phrases. But, as this Court has recognized, discrimination may be so unjustifiable as to be violative of due process.

Classifications based solely upon race must be scrutinized with particular care, since they are contrary to our traditions and hence constitutionally suspect. As long ago as 1896, this Court declared the principle "that the Constitution of the United States, in its present form, forbids, so far as civil and political rights are concerned, discrimination by the General Government, or by the States, against any citizen because of his race." And in *Buchanan* v. *Warley,* 245 U.S. 60, the Court held that a statute which limited the right of a property owner to convey his property to a person of another race was, as an unreasonable discrimination, a denial of due process of law.

Although the Court has not assumed to define "liberty" with any great precision, that term is not confined to mere freedom from bodily restraint. Liberty under law extends to the full range of conduct which the individual is free to pursue, and it cannot be restricted except for a proper governmental objective. Segregation in public education is not reasonably related to any proper governmental objective, and thus it imposes on Negro children of the District of Columbia a burden that constitutes an arbitrary deprivation of their liberty in violation of the Due Process Clause.

In view of our decision that the Constitution prohibits the states from maintaining racially segregated public schools, it would be unthinkable that the same Constitution would impose a lesser duty on the Federal Government.[41] We hold that racial segregation in the public schools of the District of Columbia is a denial of the due process of law guaranteed by the Fifth Amendment to the Constitution.

[41] Cf. *Hurd* v. *Hodge,* 334 U.S. 24. [Footnote by the Court.]

The Enforcement Problem

Reargument in all five cases was held in April 1955; and slightly over a year later than the primary decisions, the Court announced its "mandate" decision, 349 U.S. 294 (May 31, 1955). Chief Justice Warren wrote for a unanimous Court in reversing the decisions below in all of the cases except the appeal from the Supreme Court of Delaware, which had ordered immediate integration of the Negro plaintiffs in white schools; *Gebhart* v. *Belton* was affirmed and remanded. By this time, Justice Jackson had died, and his place had been taken by the younger John Marshall Harlan (grandson of the dissenter in *Plessy* v. *Ferguson*— surely a symbolic presidential choice, under the circumstances!); otherwise, the composition of the Court was the same as in the primary decision of the preceding year.

It takes two full pages of the *United States Reports,* 349 U.S. 296-297, just to list the many counsel—for the parties, the *amici curiae,* and (by invitation of the Court) the Solicitor General of the United States and several state attorneys general—who filed briefs and participated in the oral reargument, which occupied fourteen hours and the greater part of a week of the Court's time. It was very unusual for the Court to allow such extended oral argument, and it was also unusual for the Court to extend special invitations for the participation of state attorneys general. Obviously, the Court was well aware of the significance of these cases and of the policy decision that it had made in them in 1954.

But having wrestled with the problem of enforcement for over a year, and after having listened to lengthy advice in court (and presumably, out of court as well), the justices ultimately decided to buck the issue back down to the trial courts. It appeared to be impossible to formulate a rule for school integration throughout the country that would be uniform and at the same time politically feasible. Thus the Court was able, for a time, to avoid the general problem of enforcement, leaving the door open for intervention in specific instances in which the justices might choose to accept appellate jurisdiction. The Supreme Court's mandate to the lower courts—that they oversee the transition to a racially non-discriminatory system of admission to public schools "with all deliberate speed" —appeared also to describe aptly the tempo of the Court's own role in overseeing the work of the federal courts of appeal and state supreme courts, who in turn were to monitor the activities of the trial courts, among whom the federal district courts were particularly important. It was the latter corps of judges who served in the front-line trenches in the battle over integration.

For the next several years, attempts to invoke the Court's appellate jurisdiction in segregation cases were carefully disposed of by summary rather than by formal decision-making. Among a host of cases in the lower courts, the reports of which fill the initial volumes of the newly established *Race Relations Law Reporter,* there were a few which evoked significant (if laconic) responses from the Supreme Court, in addition to the higher-education cases such as *Hawkins* and *Lucy* which we discussed earlier in this chapter.[42] On November 7, 1955, the Court affirmed *per curiam,* in *Mayor and City Council of Baltimore City* v. *Dawson,* 350 U.S. 877, a decision of Judge Parker and the United States Court of Appeals for the Fourth Circuit ordering desegregation of municipal bathing beaches. On the same day, the Court reversed *per curiam,* in *Holmes* v. *City of Atlanta,* 350 U.S. 879, a decision of the federal Court of Appeals for the Fifth Circuit; the effect of the Court's reversal was to order the immediate desegregation of the municipality's public golf courses. A year later, on November 13, 1956, the Court unanimously affirmed, and again *per curiam,* a federal district-court decision which invalidated state statutes requiring racial segregation of municipal buses in Montgomery, Alabama, in *Gayle* v. *Browder,* 352 U.S. 903.

At the same time, the Court assiduously avoided the decision of cases that would have required the justices either openly to disagree with or else to approve the slowdown in public school integration, in the deliberate accomplishment of which many lower courts and local school boards were cooperating.[43] Neither did the Court permit itself to become embroiled in the attempts of several states to fabricate a legal facade under which their public school systems would masquerade as "private" schools; [44] such evasive "state action" appeared to be clearly unconstitutional, if the precedents established in the Court's white-primary deci-

---

[42] For a more detailed account of the aftermath of the Court's decision in the School Segregation cases, see Blaustein and Ferguson, *op. cit.* footnote 23, *supra,* chaps. xi-xv.

[43] See, e.g., *Shuttlesworth* v. *Birmingham Board of Education,* 358 U.S. 101 (1958); and *Slade* v. *Board of Education of Hartford*

County, 357 U.S. 906 (1958).

[44] *Pennsylvania* v. *Board of Directors of City Trusts of City of Philadelphia* (the Girard College case), 357 U.S. 570 (1958); and see Arthur S. Miller, *Racial Discrimination and Private Education* (Chapel Hill: University of North Carolina Press, 1957).

sions were to be followed. But eventually the whole integration issue came to a head, and the attention not merely of the nation but of much of the world as well came to a focus upon Little Rock, Arkansas, and the open defiance of the Supreme Court's decision by a southern governor who ordered soldiers to prevent the enforcement of the constitutional policy announced in the School Segregation Cases. The Court could avoid the issue no longer; and the result was the decision below.

COOPER v. AARON

358 U.S. 1 (Argued August 28, 1958, and September 11, 1958; judgment *per curiam* announced September 12, 1958; Opinion of the Court delivered September 29, 1958; and concurring opinion of Mr. Justice Frankfurter filed October 6, 1958)

Certiorari to the United States Court of Appeals for the Eighth Circuit.

Affirmed.

9-0

Warren, C.J.	('+')
Black	('+')
Douglas	('+')
Burton	('+')
Clark	('+')
Harlan	('+')
Brennan	('+')
Whittaker	('+')
Frankfurter	('+'

Little Rock, Arkansas, became a test case for the enforcement of the Court's decree, with Arkansas Governor Faubus emerging as both a symbol and a leader of public school segregation. When events reached a crisis and Governor Faubus ordered the Arkansas National Guard to prevent integration of Little Rock's Central High School, in direct and deliberate defiance of the Court's decision in Brown v. Board of Education, President Eisenhower was forced to take the ultimate action of ordering the regular army into action to uphold the authority of the fed-

eral district court for the Eastern District of Arkansas. The superior force of the national government prevailed, at least in the immediate issue. No more dramatic clash between the national and a state government has occurred in the United States during the twentieth century.

Cooper v. Aaron presented the Court with the concrete kind of enforcement issue that the Court had avoided deciding three years earlier in Brown v. Topeka and its companion cases. The petitioners were William G. Cooper and other members of the Board of Directors of the Independent School District of Little Rock, Arkansas, and Superintendent of Schools Virgil T. Blossom. The respondent and plaintiff in the trial court was John Aaron, a Negro parent. The Court convened in special term in order to hear argument and dispose of this case before the scheduled opening of the Little Rock public schools in September, 1958. The joint authorship of the opinion of the Court—instead of the more usual (and anonymous) per curiam opinion—was intended, no doubt, to emphasize the unanimity, indeed, the solidarity, of the justices on this policy issue. If such was the Court's intent, as language at the close of the opinion suggests, this show of force was marred by the scholarly Frankfurter's not unusual insistence upon appending an independent statement of his own views. The only effect that any independent opinion could have, under the circumstances, would be to weaken the authority of the opinion of the Court.

Opinion of the Court by THE CHIEF JUSTICE, MR. JUSTICE BLACK, MR. JUS-

TICE FRANKFURTER, MR. JUSTICE DOUG-
LAS, MR. JUSTICE BURTON, MR. JUSTICE
CLARK, MR. JUSTICE HARLAN, MR. JUS-
TICE BRENNAN, and MR. JUSTICE WHIT-
TAKER.

As this case reaches us it raises questions of the highest importance to the
maintenance of our federal system of
government. It necessarily involves a
claim by the Governor and Legislature of a State that there is no duty on
state officials to obey federal court orders
resting on this Court's considered interpretation of the United States Constitution. Specifically it involves actions by the
Governor and Legislature of Arkansas
upon the premise that they are not bound
by our holding in *Brown* v. *Board of
Education,* 347 U.S. 483. That holding
was that the Fourteenth Amendment forbids States to use their governmental
powers to bar children on racial grounds
from attending schools where there is
state participation through any arrangement, management, funds or property.
We are urged to uphold a suspension
of the Little Rock School Board's plan
to do away with segregated public schools
in Little Rock until state laws and efforts
to upset and nullify our holding in *Brown*
v. *Board of Education* have been further
challenged and tested in the courts. We
reject these contentions.

The case was argued before us on September 11, 1958. On the following day
we unanimously affirmed the judgment
of the Court of Appeals for the Eighth
Circuit, 257 F. 2d 33, which had reversed
a judgment of the District Court for the
Eastern District of Arkansas, 163 F. Supp.
13. The District Court had granted the
application of the petitioners, the Little
Rock School Board and School Superintendent, to suspend for two and one-
half years the operation of the School
Board's court-approved desegregation program. In order that the School Board
might know, without doubt, its duty in
this regard before the opening of school,

which had been set for the following
Monday, September 15, 1958, we immediately issued the judgment, reserving the
expression of our supporting views to a
later date. This opinion of all of the
members of the Court embodies those
views.

[In *Brown* v. *Board of Education,* 349
U.S. 294] the District Courts were directed to require "a prompt and reasonable start toward full compliance," and
to take such action as was necessary to
bring about the end of racial segregation in the public schools "with all deliberate speed." *Ibid.* Of course, in many
locations, obedience to the duty of desegregation would require the immediate
general admission of Negro children, otherwise qualified as students for their appropriate classes, at particular schools. On
the other hand, a District Court, after
analysis of the relevant factors (which,
of course, excludes hostility to racial desegregation), might conclude that justification existed for not requiring the
present nonsegregated admission of all
qualified Negro children. In such circumstances, however, the courts should scru-
tinize the program of the school authorities to make sure that they had developed
arrangements pointed toward the earliest
practicable completion of desegregation,
and had taken appropriate steps to put
their program into effective operation.
It was made plain that delay in any
guise in order to deny the constitutional
rights of Negro children could not be
countenanced, and that only a prompt
start, diligently and earnestly pursued, to
eliminate racial segregation from the public schools could constitute good faith
compliance. State authorities were thus
duty bound to devote every effort toward
initiating desegregation and bringing
about the elimination of racial discrimination in the public school system.

On May 20, 1954, three days after the
first *Brown* opinion, the Little Rock District School Board adopted, and on May
23, 1954, made public, a statement of

policy entitled "Supreme Court Decision—Segregation in Public Schools." In this statement the Board recognized that "It is our responsibility to comply with Federal Constitutional Requirements and we intend to do so when the Supreme Court of the United States outlines the method to be followed."

Thereafter the Board undertook studies of the administrative problems confronting the transition to a desegregated public school system at Little Rock. It instructed the Superintendent of Schools to prepare a plan for desegregation, and approved such a plan on May 24, 1955, seven days before the second *Brown* opinion. The plan provided for desegregation at the senior high school level (grades 10 through 12) as the first stage. Desegregation at the junior high and elementary levels was to follow. It was contemplated that desegregation at the high school level would commence in the fall of 1957, and the expectation was that complete desegregation of the school system would be accomplished by 1963. Following the adoption of this plan, the Superintendent of Schools discussed it with a large number of citizen groups in the city. As a result of these discussions, the Board reached the conclusion that "a large majority of the residents" of Little Rock were of "the belief . . . that the Plan, although objectionable in principle," from the point of view of those supporting segregated schools, "was still the best for the interests of all pupils in the District."

Upon challenge by a group of Negro plaintiffs desiring more rapid completion of the desegregation process, the District Court upheld the School Board's plan, *Aaron* v. *Cooper*, 143 F. Supp. 855. The Court of Appeals affirmed. 243 F. 2d 361. Review of that judgment was not sought here.

While the School Board was thus going forward with its preparation for desegregating the Little Rock school system, other state authorities, in contrast, were actively pursuing a program designed to perpetuate in Arkansas the system of racial segregation which this Court had held violated the Fourteenth Amendment. First came, in November 1956, an amendment to the State Constitution flatly commanding the Arkansas General Assembly to oppose "in every Constitutional manner the Un-constitutional desegregation decisions of May 17, 1954 and May 31, 1955 of the United States Supreme Court," Ark. Const. Amend. 44, and, through the initiative, a pupil assignment law, Ark. Stat. 80–1519 to 80–1524. Pursuant to this state constitutional command, a law relieving school children from compulsory attendance at racially mixed schools, Ark. Stat. 80–1525. and a law establishing a State Sovereignty Commission, Ark. Stat. 6–801 to 6–824, were enacted by the General Assembly in February 1957.

The School Board and the Superintendent of Schools nevertheless continued with preparations to carry out the first stage of the desegregation program. Nine Negro children were scheduled for admission in September 1957 to Central High School, which has more than two thousand students. Various administrative measures, designed to assure the smooth transition of this first stage of desegregation, were undertaken.

On September 2, 1957, the day before these Negro students were to enter Central High, the school authorities were met with drastic opposing action on the part of the Governor of Arkansas who dispatched units of the Arkansas National Guard to the Central High School grounds, and placed the school "off limits" to colored students. As found by the District Court in subsequent proceedings, the Governor's action had not been requested by the school authorities, and was entirely unheralded. The findings were these: "Up to this time [September 2], no crowds had gathered about Central High School and no acts of violence or threats of violence in connection with the carrying out of the plan had occurred. Nevertheless, out of an abundance of caution, the school authorities had frequently conferred with the Mayor and Chief of Police of Little Rock about taking appropriate steps by the Little Rock police to prevent any possible disturbances or acts of violence in connection with the attendance of the 9 colored students at Central High School. The Mayor considered that the Little Rock police force could adequately cope with any incidents which might arise at the opening of school. The Mayor, the Chief of Police, and the school authorities made no request to the Governor or any representative of his for State assistance in maintaining peace and order at Central High School. Neither the Governor nor any other official of the State government consulted with the Little Rock authorities about whether the Little Rock police were prepared to cope with any incidents which might arise at the school, about any need for State assistance in maintaining peace and order, or about stationing the Arkansas National Guard at Central High School." *Aaron* v. *Cooper,* 156 F. Supp. 220, 225.

The Board's petition for postponement in this proceeding states: "The effect of that action [of the Governor] was to harden the core of opposition to the Plan and cause many persons who theretofore had reluctantly accepted the Plan to believe that there was some power in the State of Arkansas which, when exerted, could nullify the Federal law and permit disobedience of the decree of this [District] Court, and from that date hostility to the Plan was increased and criticism of the officials of the [School] District has become more bitter and unrestrained." The Governor's action caused the School Board to request the Negro students on September 2 not to attend the high school "until the legal dilemma was solved." The next day, September 3, 1957, the Board petitioned the District Court for instructions,

and the court, after a hearing, found that the Board's request of the Negro students to stay away from the high school had been made because of the stationing of the military guards by the state authorities. The court determined that this was not a reason for departing from the approved plan, and ordered the School Board and Superintendent to proceed with it.

On the morning of the next day, September 4, 1957, the Negro children attempted to enter the high school but, as the District Court later found, units of the Arkansas National Guard "acting pursuant to the Governor's order, stood shoulder to shoulder at the school grounds and thereby forcibly prevented the 9 Negro students . . . from entering," as they continued to do every school day during the following three weeks. 156 F. Supp., at 225.

That same day, September 4, 1957, the United States Attorney for the Eastern District of Arkansas was requested by the District Court to begin an immediate investigation in order to fix responsibility for the interference with the orderly implementation of the District Court's direction to carry out the desegregation program. Three days later, September 7, the District Court denied a petition of the School Board and the Superintendent of Schools for an order temporarily suspending continuance of the program.

Upon completion of the United States Attorney's investigation, he and the Attorney General of the United States, at the District Court's request, entered the proceedings and filed a petition on behalf of the United States, as *amicus curiae,* to enjoin the Governor of Arkansas and officers of the Arkansas National Guard from further attempts to prevent obedience to the court's order. After hearings on the petition, the District Court found that the School Board's plan had been obstructed by the Governor through the use of National Guard troops, and granted a preliminary injunction on September 20, 1957, enjoining the Governor and the officers of the Guard from preventing the attendance of Negro children at Central High School, and from otherwise obstructing or interfering with the orders of the court in connection with the plan. 156 F. Supp. 220, affirmed, *Faubus* v. *United States*, 254 F. 2d 797. The National Guard was then withdrawn from the school.

The next school day was Monday, September 23, 1957. The Negro children entered the high school that morning under the protection of the Little Rock Police Department and members of the Arkansas State Police. But the officers caused the children to be removed from the school during the morning because they had difficulty controlling a large and demonstrating crowd which had gathered at the high school. 163 F. Supp., at 16. On September 25, however, the President of the United States dispatched federal troops to Central High School and admission of the Negro students to the school was thereby effected. Regular army troops continued at the high school until November 27, 1957. They were then replaced by federalized National Guardsmen who remained throughout the balance of the school year. Eight of the Negro students remained in attendance at the school throughout the school year.

We come now to the aspect of the proceedings presently before us. On February 20, 1958, the School Board and the Superintendent of Schools filed a petition in the District Court seeking a postponement of their program for desegregation. Their position in essence was that because of extreme public hostility, which they stated had been engendered largely by the official attitudes and actions of the Governor and the Legislature, the maintenance of a sound educational program at Central High School, with the Negro students in attendance, would be impossible. The Board therefore proposed that the Negro students already admitted to the school be withdrawn and sent to segregated schools, and that all further steps to carry out the Board's desegregation program be postponed for a period later suggested by the Board to be two and one-half years.

After a hearing the District Court granted the relief requested by the Board. Among other things the court found that the past year at Central High School had been attended by conditions of "chaos, bedlam, and turmoil"; that there were "repeated incidents of more or less serious violence directed against the Negro students and their property"; that there was "tension and unrest among the school administrators, the class-room teachers, the pupils, and the latters' parents, which inevitably had an adverse effect upon the educational program"; that a school official was threatened with violence; that a "serious financial burden" had been cast on the School District; that the education of the students had suffered "and under existing conditions will continue to suffer"; that the Board would continue to need "military assistance or its equivalent"; that the local police department would not be able "to detail enough men to afford the necessary protection"; and that the situation was "intolerable." 163 F. Supp., at 20–25.

The District Court's judgment was dated June 20, 1958. The Negro respondents appealed to the Court of Appeals for the Eighth Circuit and also sought there a stay of the District Court's judgment. . . . The Court of Appeals did not act on the petition for a stay but on August 18, 1958, after convening in special session on August 4 and hearing the appeal, reversed the District Court, 257 F. 2d 33. . . .

In affirming the judgment of the Court of Appeals which reversed the District Court we have accepted without reservation the position of the School Board, the Superintendent of Schools, and their counsel that they displayed entire good faith in the conduct of these proceedings and in dealing with the unfortunate and distressing sequence of events which has been outlined. We likewise have accepted the findings of the District Court as to the conditions at Central High School during the 1957–1958 school year, and also the findings that the educational progress of all the students, white and colored, of that school has suffered and will continue to suffer if the conditions which prevailed last year are permitted to continue.

The significance of these findings, however, is to be considered in light of the fact, indisputably revealed by the record before us, that the conditions they depict are directly traceable to the actions of legislators and executive officials of the State of Arkansas, taken in their official capacities, which reflect their own determination to resist this Court's decision in the *Brown* case and which have brought about violent resistance to that decision in Arkansas. . . .

One may well sympathize with the position of the Board in the face of the frustrating conditions which have confronted it, but, regardless of the Board's good faith, the actions of the other state agencies responsible for those conditions compel us to reject the Board's legal position. Had Central High School been under the direct management of the State itself, it could hardly be suggested that those immediately in charge of the school should be heard to assert their own good faith as a legal excuse for delay in implementing the constitutional rights of these respondents, when vindication of those rights was rendered difficult or impossible by the actions of other state officials. The situation here is in no different posture because the members of the School Board and the Superintendent of Schools are local officials; from the point of view of the Fourteenth Amendment, they stand in this litigation as the agents of the State.

The constitutional rights of respondents are not to be sacrificed or yielded to the violence and disorder which have followed upon the actions of the Governor and Legislature. As this Court said some 41 years ago in a unanimous opinion in a case involving another aspect of racial segregation: "It is urged that this proposed segregation will promote the public peace by preventing race conflicts. Desirable as this is, and important as is the preservation of the public peace, this aim cannot be accomplished by laws or ordinances which deny rights created or protected by the Federal Constitution." *Buchanan* v. *Warley*, 245 U.S. 60, 81. Thus law and order are not here to be preserved by depriving the Negro children of their constitutional rights. The record before us clearly establishes that the growth of the Board's difficulties to a magnitude beyond its unaided power to control is the product of state action. Those difficulties, as counsel for the Board forthrightly conceded on the oral argument in this Court, can also be brought under control by state action.

The controlling legal principles are plain. The command of the Fourteenth Amendment is that no "State" shall deny to any person within its jurisdiction the equal protection of the laws. "A State acts by its legislative, its executive, or its judicial authorities. It can act in no other way. The constitutional provision, therefore, must mean that no agency of the State, or of the officers or agents by whom its powers are exerted, shall deny to any person within its jurisdiction the equal protection of the laws. Whoever, by virtue of public position under a State government . . . denies or takes away the equal protection of the laws, violates the constitutional inhibition; and as he acts in the name and for the State, and is clothed with the State's power, his act is that of the State. This must be so, or the constitutional prohibition has no meaning." *Ex parte Virginia*, 100 U.S. 339, 347.

Thus the prohibitions of the Fourteenth Amendment extend to all action of the State denying equal protection of the laws; whatever the agency or the State taking the action. . . . In short, the constitutional rights of children not to be discriminated against in school admission on grounds of race or color declared by this Court in the *Brown* case can neither be nullified openly and directly by state legislators or state executive or judicial officers, nor nullified indirectly by them through evasive schemes for segregation whether attempted "ingeniously or ingenuously." . . .

What has been said, in the light of the facts developed, is enough to dispose of the case. However, we should answer the premise of the actions of the Governor and Legislature that they are not bound by our holding in the *Brown* case. It is necessary only to recall some basic constitutional propositions which are settled doctrine.

Article VI of the Constitution makes the Constitution the "supreme Law of the Land." In 1803, Chief Justice Marshall, speaking for a unanimous Court, referring to the Constitution as "the fundamental and paramount law of the nation," declared in the notable case of *Marbury* v. *Madison,* 1 Cranch 137, 177, that "It is emphatically the province and duty of the judicial department to say what the law is." This decision declared the basic principle that the federal judiciary is supreme in the exposition of the law of the Constitution, and that principle has ever since been respected by this Court and the Country as a permanent and indispensable feature of our constitutional system. It follows that the interpretation of the Fourteenth Amendment enunciated by this Court in the *Brown* case is the supreme law of the land, and Art. VI of the Constitution makes it of binding effect on the States "any Thing in the Constitution or Laws of any State to the Contrary notwithstanding." Every state legislator and executive and judicial officer is solemnly committed by oath taken pursuant to Art. VI, ¶3 "to support this Constitution." Chief Justice Taney, speaking for a unanimous Court in 1859, said that this requirement reflected the framers' "anxiety to preserve it [the Constitution] in full force, in all its powers, and to guard against resistance to or evasion of its authority, on the part of a State. . . ." *Ableman* v. *Booth,* 21 How. 506, 524.

No state legislator or executive or judicial officer can war against the Constitution without violating his undertaking to support it. Chief Justice Marshall spoke for a unanimous Court in saying that: "If the legislatures of the several states may, at will, annul the judgments of the courts of the United States, and destroy the rights acquired under those judgments, the constitution itself becomes a solemn mockery. . . ." *United States* v. *Peters,* 5 Cranch 115, 136. A Governor who asserts a power to nullify a federal court order is similarly restrained. If he had such power, said Chief Justice Hughes, in 1932, also for a unanimous Court, "it is manifest that the fiat of a state Governor, and not the Constitution of the United States, would be the supreme law of the land; that the restrictions of the Federal Constitution upon the exercise of state power would be but impotent phrases. . . ." *Sterling* v. *Constantin,* 287 U.S. 378, 397-398.

It is, of course, quite true that the responsibility for public education is primarily the concern of the States, but it is equally true that such responsibilities, like all other state activity, must be exercised consistently with federal constitutional requirements as they apply to state action. The Constitution created a government dedicated to equal justice under law. The Fourteenth Amendment embodied and emphasized that ideal. State support of segregated schools through any arrangement, management, funds, or property cannot be squared with the Amendment's command that no State shall deny to any person within its jurisdiction the equal protection of the laws. The right of a student not to be segregated on racial grounds in schools so maintained is indeed so fundamental and pervasive that it is embraced in the concept of due process of law. *Bolling* v. *Sharpe, 347* U.S. 497. The basic decision in *Brown* was unanimously reached by this Court only after the case had been briefed and twice argued and the issues had been given the most serious consideration. Since the first *Brown* opinion three new Justices have come to the Court. They are at one with the Justices still on the Court who participated in that basic decision as to its correctness, and that decision is now unanimously reaffirmed. The principles announced in that decision and the obedience of the States to them, according to the command of the Constitution, are indispensable for the protection of the freedoms guaranteed by our fundamental charter for all of us. Our constitutional ideal of equal justice under law is thus made a living truth.

Concurring opinion of MR. JUSTICE FRANKFURTER.

While unreservedly participating with my brethren in our joint opinion, I deem it appropriate also to deal individually with the great issue here at stake. . . .

On the few tragic occasions in the history of the Nation, North and South, when law was forcibly resisted or systematically evaded, it has signalled the breakdown of constitutional processes of government on which ultimately rest the liberties of all. . . . Our kind of society cannot endure if the controlling authority of the Law as derived from the Constitution is not to be the tribunal specially charged with the duty of ascertaining and declaring what is "the supreme Law of the Land." . . . Particularly is this so where the declaration of what "the supreme Law" commands on an underlying moral issue is not the dubious pronouncement of a gravely divided Court but is the unanimous conclusion of a long-matured deliberative process. . . .

. . . Compliance with decisions of this Court, as the constitutional organ of the supreme Law of the Land, has often, throughout our history, depended on active support by state and local authorities. It presupposes such support. To withhold it, and indeed to use political power to try to paralyze the supreme Law, precludes the maintenance of our federal system as we have known and cherished it for one hundred and seventy years. . . .

Cooper v. *Aaron* did not mean, however, that the Court had changed, or expected the lower courts to change, the previously announced constitutional policy of "all *deliberate* speed" for the enforcement of public school integration. And the American federal system of government, including the federal system of courts, provided ample opportunity for the fulfillment of the prophecy that *Brown* v. *Board of Education* would beget, as progeny, "a generation of litigation." Indeed, at the very close of the 1958 Term to which *Cooper* v. *Aaron* had served as the prelude, the Court itself appeared to make a positive contribution to the slow-down in integration enforcement by reversing a federal district court which had enjoined a Virginia "barratry" statute that was part of the state's "massive resistance" program against desegregation of the public schools. In *Harrison* v. *N.A.A.C.P., 360* U.S. 167 (June 8, 1959), a majority of six justices (including Black, and over the dissents of Warren, Brennan, and Douglas) ruled that federal courts should stay their hand, in questions such as this, until the state statutes first had been "interpreted" by the state's own courts. Apart from its obvious tactical significance, the Harrison decision seemed to underscore the extent to which not merely Frankfurter but a majority of the Court viewed public school integration, not primarily in civil-libertarian dimensions, but rather as essentially a basic political issue of American federalism.

IV

CIVIL LIBERTY AND GOVERNMENTAL AUTHORITY

I N DISCUSSING NATIONAL JUDICIAL POLICY toward racial integration, we suggested that there were a variety of perspectives from which we might reasonably undertake to view selected dimensions of a complex political issue. Two major perspectives relevant to racial integration are those of federalism and civil liberties. We selected federalism as the primary basis from which we would view the Supreme Court's role in the development of national policy regarding the race problem, because of the political importance of the implications of the Court's decision-making in this area for the balance of power between the nation and the states. The evidence that we examined suggests that the Court has functioned, in regard to racial segregation, as a constitutional balance wheel: when Congress has been strongly pronationalist (as in the 1860's and 1870's), the Court has served as an equipoise and sought to restore the ante bellum constitutional powers of the states; and when the Congress has been dominated by a states'-right dynasty who hold the key positions of internal power in both houses (as in the 1940's and 1950's), the Supreme Court has been the political dynamo through which interest-group pressures have been transformed into an activist policy of nationalism.

This is not to say that the question of whether Negroes should receive equality of treatment under the law with other citizens of the United States is "less important" than the question of whether it is possible in the American constitutional system to establish national policies on social issues. Our objective is not to provide the "right" answers to the ultimate questions of political, legal, and social valuation such as these. Rather, our purpose is to analyze and to assess the way in which the Supreme Court has reacted to such questions.

In Part IV, we turn to a range of issues in which the Court has given consideration to questions of minority rights to nonconformance with the public-policy norms established by political majorities for the time being. In other words, in the next three chapters, we deal with issues of fundamental political freedom, civil right, and personal liberty. In each case, there is the correlative question of governmental authority, the democratic principle of majority rule, and civic obligation. A majority of the Court has defined for itself the same kind of arbitral role here as we have observed in other areas of the Court's work. The model to describe its decision-making function in civil-liberties cases, as suggested by the Court itself, is that of the seesaw or simple mechanical balance. In a recent decision, for instance, the majority remarked: "We conclude that the balance between the individual and the governmental interests here at stake must be struck in favor of the latter, and that therefore the provisions of the First Amendment have not been offended." [1]

[1] *Barenblatt* v. *United States,* 360 U.S. 109, 134 (June 8, 1959). Cf. the opening paragraphs of Warren's dissent in *Barr* v. *Matteo,* 360 U.S. 564 (June 29, 1959).

We shall examine in Chapter 11 a procedure which has been proposed for weighing various factors in a set of cases that deal with a common problem. The notion underlying this procedure is similar to that articulated in the quotation above. It is certainly doubtful, however, whether the Court's decision-making which affects civil liberties can adequately be symbolized by either scales or a simple continuum which demarks the range of conflict, within which choice for the Court may roam, for the opposing extremes of governmental authority (on the one side) and civil liberty (on the other). Even though for most of the justices in most of these cases the dominant variable is considered to be a complex of minority/majority (or freedom/authority) issues, secondary variables are always present too, either explicitly or implicitly.

Justice Frankfurter, for instance, has articulated in the following chapters the primary significance of the Federalism variable in most of the state cases in which he participated—and if he participated, he generally wrote an opinion. The characteristic line of argument pursued by Frankfurter, as we shall see, has been that he personally happens as an individual to believe strongly in libertarian values; as a justice, however, his primary obligation is to uphold the principle of majority rule, which means deference to Congress and the President in federal cases (the Separation of Powers variable) and, alternatively, deference to state legislative majorities in state cases (the Federalism variable). Since any case that the Court decides involving civil-liberties problems is either a federal or a state case, such a formula, followed consistently to its logical extreme, would mean that Frankfurter would never vote to uphold the position of civil-liberties claimants. Indeed, it could be argued that whatever the form of words, in articulating the deference owed by the Court to Congress or to the states, in effect Frankfurter—like his colleagues—is rationalizing a choice in behalf of governmental authority (majority rule) rather than individual right. To the extent, however, that Frankfurter—or other justices—perceive differences in the degree of deference that the Court ought to show to Congress or the President, on the one hand, and to state legislatures or constitution-makers, on the other hand, the Federalism variable assumes significance. Perhaps the best way to explain the relative effect of Separation of Powers and Federalism as intervening variables is to say that for a justice who is not a libertarian activist, the considerations pointing toward judicial restraint that are evoked when an act of the national government is challenged for infringing civil liberties are reinforced when state action is at issue.

Such fundamental orientations of the basic political attitudes of the justices doubtless are of much greater importance in the making of the Court's "civil liberties" decisions than whether the language of the Constitution is specific or vague, and whether a subject is explicitly mentioned in the document or supplied by judicial implication. Neither the presence nor the absence of particular words in the Constitution has ever been an insurmountable obstacle for the "sense of justice" with which the members of the Court, individually and collectively, have been imbued. Consequently, the technical discussion about phrases and formulae that frequently appear to divide the justices in the cases that we shall examine in the chapters below should not be allowed to obscure the point that their disagreement is only relative, and as to any issue is a matter of more or less.

Black may castigate some of his colleagues for their invocation of natural-law ideals (which he considers to be "bad" and they consider to be "good"); and Frankfurter may reply that Black, in advocating that the Court read the entire Bill of Rights into some part or other of the Fourteenth Amendment, is trying to put twentieth-century human liberty into an eighteenth-century straitjacket. Yet both may agree that it is not contrary to the Constitution for local police officials to seize illegally a doctor's patient book and use it as evidence to convict the doctor of a serious crime, although both are also agreed that such evidence would be inadmissible in a federal court. Black may argue vociferously that the states are "bound" by the Fourth Amendment, and Frankfurter may deny that this is so; yet Frankfurter may be, of all the justices during the past two decades, the most sympathetic and consistent supporter of search-and-seizure claims, for which Black may manifest a peculiar blind spot in his voting behavior. Black, who was once affiliated with the Ku Klux Klan, may demonstrate strong and consistent support in his voting for rigid observance of the technicalities of procedure to ensure fair trials of criminal defendants by the states; while Frankfurter, the defender of Sacco and Vanzetti, may urge the Court to acquiesce in such unfairness (i.e., deprivations of the right to counsel and tolerance of third-degree methods of police investigation) as commends itself to a reasonable portion of the organized English-speaking political societies of the world. Such differences among the justices are neither to be mapped nor explained by the language of the Bill of Rights or the Fourteenth Amendment; nor is it likely that the talk in judicial opinions about "the preferred-position doctrine" or "the incorporation of the Bill of Rights" really helps very much to explain the underlying differentials in attitude among the justices, nor the consequent variations in their voting behavior.

The language of the opinions of the justices, like that of other political documents, may be of great importance because of its effect upon the behavior of other people, such as lower-court judges, lawyers generally, and the public at large. It may serve as a factor which, under the expected obligations associated with the principle of *stare decisis,* conditions the range of decision-making discretion of the justices of the Court in the future. But such verbal behavior of the justices is only suggestive of the underlying attitudes which also find expression in judicial votes in particular cases; and the votes are probably a more accurate clue to such attitudes than the words which the Court offers in their justification.

From this point of view, Black is right when he charges Frankfurter with voting his "personal predelictions" in the guise of the "ideals of a civilized society"; but Frankfurter is also right when he replies that the justices are the product of a professional discipline, who work within the confines of a set of institutional traditions and both substantive and procedural norms that bring to a narrow focus the range of judicial discretion. Any man who can gain appointment to the Court, even under the somewhat extraordinary circumstances that made both the Black and Frankfurter appointments possible, is confined—to use the Holmesian phrase—from "molar to molecular motions." So the limits of feasible choice, for the Court, are narrow, and occupy a miniscule zone on the continuum representing the social and political values recognized in the United States, to say nothing of the English-speaking or non-English-speaking parts of the rest of the world. Only within this narrow zone is choice possible for Supreme Court justices; and within this zone they agree (most of the time) and disagree. We emphasize the essential homogeneity of the attitudes and voting behavior of the justices, because it is most misleading to assume that they are in general conflict and disagreement with each other about most civil-liberties questions that arise before the Court for decision. Such a false impression might be conveyed, however, from the cases that we present, which focus precisely upon examples in which groups of the justices are in disagreement, and have articulated sharply the reasons—appropriate for public consumption—that they advance in explanation and justification for their differences.

None of the cases in the remaining three chapters were decided before World War I. The clustering of decisions within the last two generations, and particularly in the period since the 1936 Term, reflects the fact that the arbitration of civil-liberties problems did not bulk large in the work of the Court during the first century and a half of its existence. Following *Barron* v. *Baltimore* (Chapter 8, *supra*) it was not until after the adoption of the Fourteenth Amendment that it appeared possible to invoke the Constitution in support of civil-liberties claims against alleged infringement by states. As we have seen, there was a thirty-year lag between the adoption of the amendment and the Court's acceptance of substantive due process as a property right; it took another thirty years before the Court gave similar recognition to the substantive due process of personal liberty in a decision *upholding* such a claim under the Fourteenth Amendment. Personal liberty was read into the Fourteenth Amendment by the Court at the very time that liberty of property was on the verge of being read out by a new generation of justices; the 1936 Term is both convenient and accurate as a point demarking the end of the Court's use of the Fourteenth Amendment as a shield for property rights against state regulation, and the essential beginning of the Court's shift to the use of the same amendment to uphold claims of personal liberty against state infringement.

Actually, the change did not take place in a single term, of course. The first decision upholding a personal-liberty claim under the Fourteenth Amendment came a decade earlier in a freedom-of-speech case, *Fiske* v. *Kansas*, 274 U.S. 380, decided in 1927. Similarly, a claim of freedom of the press was upheld by the

Court in *Near* v. *Minnesota,* 283 U.S. 697 (1931), and a claim of right to a fair trial in *Powell* v. *Alabama,* 287 U.S. 45 (1932). Indeed, the Court had asserted that the First Amendment rights of freedom of assembly and petition were protected by the Fourteenth Amendment as early as 1873, in a dictum in the majority opinion in the Slaughter-House Cases (Chapter 8, *supra*). At the time of the Slaughter-House decision, however, it was by no means clear whether or how the Fourteenth Amendment might become a vehicle for subsuming the Bill of Rights, either in whole or in part.

In 1873, there were at least three different clauses of the Fourteenth Amendment that might have been adapted for such a purpose; and in his argument in behalf of liberty of contract in the Slaughter-House Cases, Campbell gave primary emphasis to the privileges-and-immunities clause, in the apparent assumption that that clause was a more likely candidate for the infusion of natural rights than the equal-protection or due-process clauses. This turned out to be a poor prediction of the Court's eventual behavior. The equal-protection clause, as we saw in Chapter 9, was not used by the Court as an important restraint upon state action until the 1930's; and then essentially in independence of personal liberties postulated in the Bill of Rights. Instead of the first eight amendments providing a content for the equal-protection clause, it was the equal-protection clause which came to furnish a basis for supplying policy norms for the Fifth Amendment, in *Bolling* v. *Sharpe* in 1953. And to this day, the Court has not yet been willing to attribute any significance to the privileges-and-immunities clause. Instead, the Court has made the due-process clause of the Fourteenth Amendment the primary vessel for the embodiment of the civil rights and liberties which are the counterpart, more or less, of some of the clauses of the first eight amendments. The relevant language is simple: "nor shall any State deprive any person of life, liberty, or property, without due process of law."

The specific issue in *Barron* v. *Baltimore,* it will be recalled, was a claim—prior to the Fourteenth Amendment—of the right to just compensation; and the Court had ruled in 1833 that nothing in the Constitution of the United States prevented a state from depriving a person of his property without the payment of just compensation. But in 1897, in *Chicago, B. & Q. R. Co.* v. *Chicago,* 166 U.S. 226, the Court declared that to take private property for public use without just compensation was forbidden by the Fourteenth Amendment; it was a deprivation of property by a state without due process of law. For the next forty years, the Court used the due-process clause of the Fourteenth Amendment to protect property rights against state interference. Only during the last of these four decades (i.e., 1927-1937) did the Court begin, in its decisions, to uphold the rights of life and personal liberty, under the due-process clause of the Fourteenth Amendment, against abridgement by the states. Since 1937, property rights under the due-process clause have fallen into the same kind of oblivion that enshrouded personal liberties prior to 1927; and the Court has converted the right to personal liberty under the due-process clause into an even more important limitation upon the states, at least in terms of the number of decisions, than that of the equal-protection clause, during the same period.

The cases that we shall examine in the following three chapters are not limited, however, to claims under the Fourteenth Amendment against state infringement of civil liberties. We shall also be concerned with claims against the national government based directly upon various parts of the Bill of Rights. In particular, we shall be concerned with the question of whether the Court has attributed the same meaning and effect to claims of civil liberty against the states as to equivalent claims made against the national government.

10

First-Amendment Freedoms

T HE FIRST AMENDMENT PROCLAIMS THAT *"Congress* shall make no law respecting an establishment of religion, or prohibiting the free exercise thereof; or abridging the freedom of speech, or of the press; or the right of the people peaceably to assemble and to petition the Government for a redress of grievances." In effect, the Supreme Court has amended the Constitution by "interpreting" it as though the First Amendment read: "Neither Congress nor any State shall make any law, etc." But like laissez faire in the 1880's and 1890's, civil liberty came to the Constitution in the 1920's and 1930's slowly, quietly, and by grace of the Court's decisions in a succession of individual cases.

With the exception of the Alien and Sedition Acts of 1798 and certain acts of executive and congressional legislation during the Civil War, there were until World War I relatively few acts of the national government that could have given a basis for raising before the Supreme Court claims under the First Amendment; and throughout this period, it was generally assumed that the First Amendment had no application to the states. Justices Harlan and Field had argued the contrary, but in dissent. But in 1907, Mr. Justice Holmes remarked for the Court: "We leave undecided the question whether there is to be found in the Fourteenth Amendment a prohibition similar to that in the First . . . [i.e.,] to assume that freedom of speech and freedom of the press were protected from abridgment on the part not only of the United States but also of the States. . . ."[1] And in 1919, the Court decided the first of a series of cases challenging (though unsuccessfully) the power of Congress to suppress political dissent in time of war. The war was followed by the "Red scare," and the twenties produced a series of cases

[1] *Patterson* v. *Colorado,* 205 U.S. 454, 462 (1907).

concerned with the suppression by the states of political expression and dissent. It is from this period that we date the formulation of the Court's constitutional policies governing the right to dissent in the American democracy.

FREEDOM OF POLITICAL EXPRESSION

Comprehension of the Court's decision-making in this area may possibly entail, and an understanding of the literature in the field certainly requires, some knowledge of certain legal concepts which purport to describe the Court's policies (or "doctrines") relating to the First Amendment rights. Among these legal concepts, perhaps the most important are: (1) "the clear-and-present-danger test"; (2) the "incorporation of the First Amendment with the Fourteenth"; and (3) the "preferred-position doctrine." We shall discuss the first two of these concepts below, and the third in a later section of this chapter.

The Birth of a Dogma: Clear and Present Danger

Whatever Mr. Justice Holmes may have meant at the time he uttered one of his more celebrated dicta in *Schenck* v. *United States*,[2] it is clear that other persons both on and off the Court have converted the so-called "clear-and-present-danger test" into a dogma. Schenck's case was decided by the Court in 1919, less than four months after the armistice and long before the Treaty of Versailles was signed. Schenck was a criminal defendant. He was also a national leader of the Socialist party, and a militant pacifist. He was convicted by a jury of having committed a political crime: that of open dissent against the war policy, by distributing printed leaflets urging draftees to exercise their constitutional rights by refusing to acquiesce in an unlawful war; and all of this during open hostilities in World War I. Of course, it could be and was argued that the First Amendment should be construed to apply in war as well as in peace; and that the words "Congress shall make no law . . . abridging the freedom . . . of the press; or the right of the people . . . to petition the Government for a redress of grievances" applied precisely to the facts of this case. There was no proof that Schenck had in fact succeeded in obstructing the draft; he was tried on a conspiracy charge. But such details were pushed to one side by the thrice-wounded Civil War veteran who announced the decision of the Court.

It seems warranted to restate, as we have just done, facts that are also clearly stated in the opinion of the Court, because of the heroic proportions to which the Holmes legend has grown. So many students of the Court have identified with Mr. Justice Holmes that it is not easy, at least for the beginning student, to divorce himself from the almost unimpeachable prima-facie assumption that any

2 249 U.S. 47 (March 3, 1919).

opinion written by Holmes was a great blow on behalf of civil liberty. Such an attitude of piety, we might add, is the very negation of the approach that attracted Holmes's own skeptical and pragmatic mind throughout his long lifetime. Holmes would have been the last person likely to subscribe either to the Holmes legend or to the latter-day formulations of the clear-and-present-danger test.

The Schenck decision was an illiberal one, at least in terms of present-day standards of liberalism on the Supreme Court. But it was perfectly consistent with the Supreme Court's wartime decisions, in both earlier and later wars. There was no clear and present danger that Schenck would obstruct the draft; there did not need to be. Holmes's opinion for the unanimous Court applied the common-law rule in deciding that the natural tendency of the leaflets, and the intent that Schenck must have had in mind in sending them, was to obstruct the draft. The jury, said Holmes, might reasonably conclude (as they did) that Schenck's leaflets must have had such a bad tendency—irrespective of whether or not they had any effect in fact; and "if the act, (speaking, or circulating a paper,) its tendency and the intent with which it is done are the same, we perceive no ground for saying that success alone warrants making the act a crime." The so-called "bad-tendency" test usually is associated with Sanford's opinion in the Gitlow case (below), apparently because Holmes dissented in that case and argued the contrary. But it is indisputable that the Court based its decision in the Schenck case directly upon an application of the constitutional policy that has since come to be known as the "bad-tendency"test.

All of the talk about clear and present danger in the Schenck opinion is pure obiter dictum. Holmes does not present it as anything else. It has been suggested, says Holmes, that Schenck's publication is protected by the First Amendment. Holmes then says that whether or not one would have a right, under the First Amendment, to attempt to persuade others not to submit to compulsory military service is a relative matter. In "many places" and in "ordinary times" (i.e., in time of peace), the First Amendment would have protected Schenck; but not "so long as men fight." This discussion is pure obiter, because Schenck's offense did take place in time of war while other men fought in defense of the country; it was Gitlow, not Schenck, who invoked First Amendment claims under other circumstances in time of peace. And Gitlow's offense was against the state of New York, not against the United States of America. Continuing his dictum in Schenck, Holmes next asserted that "the question in every case is whether the words used are used in such circumstances and are of such a nature as to create a clear and present danger that they will bring about the substantive evils that Congress has a right to prevent." But this is not the criterion that the Court used to uphold Schenck's conviction. If it had been, the Court would have reversed the conviction, because there was no evidence that Schenck's publication had created a clear and present danger of obstruction of the draft. The Court admitted that "in form at least" the document "confined itself to peaceful measures such as a petition for the repeal of the act"; nor was there any evidence that, *in fact,* the document had had the effect of inducing that or any other behavior in those who read it.

As so frequently is true of seminal cases,[3] the opinion of the Court in Schenck contained the wellsprings for equal and opposing policies—in this case, for *both* the bad-tendency and the clear-and-present-danger tests. Holmes himself emphasized first one, and then the other, of the two conflicting strands of the Schenck opinion—the holding and the dictum—in other decisions of the Court later in the same year. In the Frohwerk and Debs cases [4] (which also involved defendants who had engaged in political expression against the war effort), Holmes applied the bad-tendency test in speaking again for a unanimous Court to uphold the convictions. But in the Abrams and Schaefer cases,[5] Holmes and Brandeis dissented together against the rest of the Court, arguing in the latter (in an opinion written by *Brandeis*) that the Court should apply the clear-and-present-danger dictum of the Schenck opinion. Such voting and opinion-writing behavior, on the part of Holmes and Brandeis, is perfectly consistent with our suggestion (in the introduction to Part IV) about differentials in the underlying attitudes of individual justices. Holmes and Brandeis would vote to uphold the convictions of wartime dissenters—up to a point; and after that point was reached, they would vote to reverse, because in the total circumstances of decision (including, perhaps, the fact that Abrams was decided in November, 1919, and Schaefer in March, 1920; while Schenck, Frohwerk, and Debs were decided in March, 1919), they were convinced that it was more important to re-establish the constitutional milieu of peacetime rights of political expression than to perpetuate the repressions of civil liberties that were a part of the many necessary sacrifices in order to win the war. Such an attitude is markedly similar to that expressed by Lincoln as the Civil War drew to a close. It happened that Holmes and Brandeis shared the same turning point in these cases; but we hypothesize that other points existed, at least potentially, for their colleagues as well.

It should be noted that Holmes's opinion in Schenck makes no differentiation between freedom of the press and freedom of speech. The behaviors involved and circumstances normally attendant upon speechmaking and publication are by no means identical; and it is not inconceivable that the Court might adapt, to the differing characteristics of speech and of publication as forms of political behavior, the constitutional policies that it would approve. The common law certainly distinguished between slander and libel, for instance. But this is not what the Court has chosen to do; to the contrary, the Court has generally followed

---

[3] Cf. *Powell* v. *Alabama* 287 U.S. 45 (1932), in which the opinion of the Court sows the seeds for both the "capital offense" and the "fair trial" rules, which constitute competing norms in subsequently decided right-to-counsel cases. See also Chapter 11.

[4] *Frohwerk* v. *United States,* 249 U.S. 204 (March 10, 1919); *Debs* v. *United States,* 249 U.S. 211 (March 10, 1919).

[5] *Abrams* v. *United States,* 250 U.S. 616 (November 10, 1919); *Schaefer* v. *United States,* 251 U.S. 466 (March 1, 1920).

the example of Holmes's opinion in Schenck, referring indiscriminately to freedom of speech when the issue, on the facts, is one of freedom of the press, and coalescing its precedents that relate to one or the other kind of behavior.

It should also be noted that there is a position beyond the bad-tendency and the clear-and-present-danger tests, as we suggested at the beginning of this chapter. It is at least logically possible that the Court might have read "Congress shall make no law" to mean just what it says: *no law,* in war as in peace, in bad times as in good; but such an extreme view has never attracted the support of a majority of the Supreme Court. As articulated by Holmes, the clear-and-present-danger test was doubtless a more liberal principle than the common-law bad-tendency policy, for it required at least that there be a reasonable relationship between the political expression of the defendant and the consequences flowing from his acts. But the clear-and-present-danger formula was far less libertarian than the literal words of the First Amendment; and it is worth noting that in practice, the clear-and-present-danger formula has been useful principally as a device for providing a pragmatic sanction for convicting defendants for having expressed their political views in public.[6] It is no accident that the Supreme Court discusses the clear-and-present-danger test in each of the four cases that we shall examine in this section, and that the Court also upheld the convictions of all four of these defendants. And at least three of these four cases are, by any of the conventional criteria of relevance and significance, the "leading cases" among the Supreme Court's decisions on this subject.

SCHENCK v. UNITED STATES

249 U.S. 47 (March 3, 1919)

Error to United States District Court for the Eastern District of Pennsylvania.

Affirmed.

9-0

Holmes	('+')
White, C.J.	(+)
McKenna	(+)
Day	(+)
VanDevanter	(+)
Pitney	(+)
McReynolds	(+)
Brandeis	(+)
Clarke	(+)

MR. JUSTICE HOLMES delivered the opinion of the Court.

This is an indictment in three counts. The first charges a conspiracy to violate the Espionage Act of June 15, 1917, . . . by causing and attempting to cause insubordination, &c., in the military and naval forces of the United States, and to obstruct the recruiting and enlistment service of the United States, when the United States was at war with the German Empire, to-wit, that the defendant wilfully conspired to have printed and circulated to men who had been called and accepted for military service under the Act of May 18, 1917, . . . a document set forth and alleged to be calculated to cause such insubordination and obstruction. . . . The defendants were found guilty. . . . They set up the First Amendment to the Constitution forbidding Congress to make

6 Cf. Walter Berns, *Freedom, Virtue, and The First Amendment* (Baton Rouge: Louisi-ana State University Press, 1957), chap. iv, and especially pp. 55-56.

any law abridging the freedom of speech, or of the press, and bringing the case here on that ground have argued some other points also of which we must dispose.

It is argued that the evidence, if admissible, was not sufficient to prove that the defendant Schenck was concerned in sending the documents. According to the testimony Schenck said he was general secretary of the Socialist party and had charge of the Socialist headquarters from which the documents were sent. He identified a book found there as the minutes of the Executive Committee of the party. The book showed a resolution of August 13, 1917, that 15,000 leaflets should be printed on the other side of one of them in use, to be mailed to men who had passed exemption boards, and for distribution. Schenck personally attended to the printing. On August 20 the general secretary's report said "Obtained new leaflets from printer and started work addressing envelopes" &c.; and there was a resolve that Comrade Schenck be allowed $125 for sending leaflets through the mail. He said that he had about fifteen or sixteen thousand printed. There were files of the circular in question in the inner office which he said were printed on the other side of the one sided circular and were there for distribution. Other copies were proved to have been sent through the mails to drafted men. Without going into confirmatory details that were proved, no reasonable man could doubt that the defendant Schenck was largely instrumental in sending the circulars about. . . .

The document in question upon its first printed side recited the first section of the Thirteenth Amendment, said that the idea embodied in it was violated by the conscription act and that a conscript is little better than a convict. In impassioned language it intimated that conscription was despotism in its worst form and a monstrous wrong against humanity in the interest of Wall Street's chosen few.

It said, "Do not submit to intimidation," but in form at least confined itself to peaceful measures such as a petition for the repeal of the act. The other and later printed side of the sheet was headed "Assert Your Rights." It stated reasons for alleging that any one violated the Constitution when he refused to recognize "your right to assert your opposition to the draft," and went on, "If you do not assert and support your rights, you are helping to deny or disparage rights which it is the solemn duty of all citizens and residents of the United States to retain." It described the arguments on the other side as coming from cunning politicians and a mercenary capitalist press, and even silent consent to the conscription law as helping to support an infamous conspiracy. It denied the power to send our citizens away to foreign shores to shoot up the people of other lands, and added that words could not express the condemnation such cold-blooded ruthlessness deserves, &c., &c., winding up, "You must do your share to maintain, support and uphold the rights of the people of this country." Of course the document would not have been sent unless it had been intended to have some effect, and we do not see what effect it could be expected to have upon persons subject to the draft except to influence them to obstruct the carrying of it out. The defendants do not deny that the jury might find against them on this point.

But it is said, suppose that that was the tendency of this circular, it is protected by the First Amendment to the Constitution. Two of the strongest expressions are said to be quoted respectively from well-known public men. It well may be that the prohibition of laws abridging the freedom of speech is not confined to previous restraints, although to prevent them may have been the main purpose. . . . We admit that in many places and in ordinary times the defendants in saying all that was said in the circular would have been within their constitutional rights. But the character of every act depends upon the circumstances in which it is done. . . . The most stringent protection of free speech would not protect a man in falsely shouting fire in a theatre and causing a panic. It does not even protect a man from an injunction against uttering words that may have all the effect of force. . . . The question in every case is whether the words used are used in such circumstances and are of such a nature as to create a clear and present danger that they will bring about the substantive evils that Congress has a right to prevent. It is a question of proximity and degree. When a nation is at war many things that might be said in time of peace are such a hindrance to its effort that their utterance will not be endured so long as men fight and that no Court could regard them as protected by any constitutional right. It seems to be admitted that if an actual obstruction of the recruiting service were proved, liability for words that produced that effect might be enforced. The statute of 1917 . . . punishes conspiracies to obstruct as well as actual obstruction. If the act, (speaking, or circulating a paper,) its tendency and the intent with which it is done are the same, we perceive no ground for saying that success alone warrants making the act a crime. . . .

Judgments affirmed.

Subsequently in dissent, however, Holmes argued that logical supposition was not enough, and that convictions for political expression must be supported by some evidence of the consequences of the speech or publication; he also enunciated a laissez-faire theory of free speech that came very close to providing intellectual support for an absolutist interpretation of the First Amendment. In his dissent in the Abrams case, Holmes said: [7]

Persecution for the expression of opinions seems to me perfectly logical. If you have no doubt of your premises or your power and want a certain result with all your heart you naturally express your wishes in law and sweep away all opposition. To allow opposition by speech seems to indicate that you think the speech impotent. . . . But when men have realized that time has upset many fighting faiths, they may come to believe even more than they believe the very foundations of their own conduct that the ultimate good desired is better reached by free trade in ideas—that the best test of truth is the power of the thought to get itself accepted in the competition of the market, and that truth is the only ground upon which their wishes safely can be carried out. That at any rate is the theory of our Constitution.

Holmes's later dissent in the Gitlow case (below) is essentially a variation upon this same theme of the virtues of the market place in ideas. To modern social scientists, at least, there may appear to be naïve optimism in Holmes's expressed faith that "truth" will necessarily triumph over error when they grapple for control over the allegiance of men, with no holds barred. Perhaps the proliferation of the *ersatz* values which Madison Avenue has peddled so successfully and so profitably during the past generation has made it difficult for students today to accept a theory of political communication premised upon a *Weltanschauung*

[7] 250 U.S. 616, 630.

derived from the teachings of Adam Smith, David Hume, and Charles Darwin. Holmes was a product of the nineteenth century, who by the accident of exceptional longevity lived on through the first third of the twentieth century. He was almost an octogenarian when he wrote his Abrams dissent; and he was eighty-four when he repeated the argument, in the Gitlow case. The values that Holmes espouses in these dissents are appropriate for philosophers; certainly they are not appropriate for the rational, ordinary citizens who are supposed to serve as jurors; and obviously they have been considered inappropriate by the justices comprising a majority of the Supreme Court, in Holmes' day as in our own. Even with Senator Joseph McCarthy safely interred, it is certainly doubtful how many Americans would agree with the proposition that Communists should be allowed without restraint to propagandize for the establishment of the "dictatorship of the proletariat" which would result in the destruction of the freedom of political expression for all—including Communists. Yet this is the conclusion to which logic inexorably drives Holmes and Brandeis in their dissenting opinion in Gitlow. Whether they would reach the same conclusion today is, of course, also dubious. Holmes wrote in the days of the New Economic Policy, when liberals foresaw the rise of a new and shining civilization in a Russia that would be a land of liberty, equality, and brotherhood; the purges, a Big Brother called Steel, and the Cold War remained secrets locked in the womb of time when Benjamin Gitlow's case reached the Supreme Court.

The Incorporation of the First Amendment

As corporations achieved the constitutional status of "persons" under the Fourteenth Amendment casually, by grace of an oral "admission" announced by Chief Justice Fuller in behalf of the whole Court, so the marriage of the First and Fourteenth Amendments began inauspiciously and unobtrusively in a case in which the Supreme Court approved the conviction of another left-wing radical, Benjamin Gitlow, who had been found by a New York jury to be a "criminal anarchist." Not infrequently, the Court "assumes" the hypothetical existence of either a state of facts or a proposition of law (i.e., a proposed policy norm), and almost always for the purpose of knocking down the straw man. The defendant argues (the Court will say) that A is true, and that consequently we should hold thus and so. Let us assume, for the sake of argument (the Court continues), that A *were* true; so what? We still would have to conclude this and that rather than thus and so, as the defendant suggests. It was in this manner that freedom of speech and of the press was first recognized by a majority of the Court as a fundamental personal right which was part of the liberty included in the due-process clause of the Fourteenth Amendment.

In our earlier discussion of the "reverse incorporation" of the equal-protection clause of the Fourteenth Amendment into the liberty included in the due-process clause of the Fifth Amendment, we suggested that precision of analysis would be enhanced if certain minimal criteria were established for use of the concept "nationalization." There is much loose talk, both on and off the Court, about the "incorporation" of the Sixth Amendment or the Fourth Amendment in addition to the First Amendment, or of the Bill of Rights as a whole. We prefer the term "nationalization," because what is functionally significant is whether the Court interprets the Constitution to postulate the same range of liberty or right, irrespective of whether restraint emanates from the national or a state government. If the Constitution is interpreted to mean the same thing throughout the country, and as applied to any source of governmental authority in the United States, then it is appropriate to say that the Court has "nationalized" such a right. There are two criteria that ought to be met before one recognizes a right as having been nationalized: (1) the Court should consider its precedents to be interchangeable, citing cases decided directly under a different section of the Constitution as authority for a subsequent decision under one of the due-process clauses; and (2) the Court should discuss, in its opinions in cases arising under a due-process clause, the right that has been "nationalized" as though the relevant substantive clause bore directly upon the case being decided. In other words, in a freedom-of-speech case arising in a state court under the due-process clause of the Fourteenth Amendment, the Court should cite (indiscriminately) as precedents cases which arose in federal courts involving action by the national government directly under the First Amendment; and the opinion of the Court should discuss the defendant's rights as being under the First Amendment, thus ignoring the intermediary and catalytic role played, in theory, by the due-process clause of the Fourteenth Amendment. As we shall see in the cases presented in this and the next two chapters, only the First Amendment has been nationalized by marriage with the due-process clause of the Fourteenth, in terms of the suggested criteria.

On the other hand, we observed in Chapter 9 that the equal-protection clause of the Fourteenth Amendment has (more recently) been nationalized by assimilation with the due-process clause of the Fifth Amendment. Another reason why we prefer the term "nationalized" is that it is broad enough to include such action as the Court took in *Hurd* v. *Hodge,* in which the Court merged the equal-protection clause not with Fifth Amendment due process but rather with the equally vague and undefined supervisory powers of the Court over adjudication in the lower federal courts. The latter kind of nationalization has different logical implications when there is a "feedback" such as occurred when *Hurd* v. *Hodge* was cited as a precedent for *Barrows* v. *Jackson,* because then the Court is in effect extending its supervisory authority to include adjudication in the state courts—for which there is no support in present constitutional theory. But even if the theoretical pedigree is more legitimate, as when the Court "incorporates" freedom of speech into the Fourteenth Amendment, it is still possible to argue (as Frankfurter and Jackson and other justices have argued) that the Court *in effect* is extending its supervisory authority over state court adjudication, by insisting that the states observe the same policy norms that the Court has pronounced for trials in the federal courts involving the national government.

Holmes and Brandeis, in their dissenting opinion below, appear to argue that personal liberty under the Fourteenth Amendment includes the "general principle of free speech," but that the Court ought to attribute greater power to the states to restrain such free speech than it attributes to the national government. Like the powers of restraint of the national government in war and in peace, this is a relative matter, of course. Specifically, they interject the caveat that Fourteenth Amendment personal liberty "may be accepted with a somewhat larger latitude of interpretation [i.e., permissible restraint of free speech by the states] than is allowed to Congress by the sweeping language that governs or ought to govern the laws of the United States." The libertarian dissenters of a generation later went considerably beyond Holmes and Brandeis; they advocated equivalence of restraint against both the national and state governments. One perhaps unanticipated cost of their success, which was achieved at least for First Amendment liberties, was that the *illiberal* decisions (which considerably outnumbered in volume the liberal ones) under the First Amendment then provided the policy norms for decisions under the Fourteenth Amendment, and vice versa. There is no particular extension of human liberty if the Court admits that the states must recognize freedom of speceh to the same extent as the national government—and then concludes that neither must give too much recognition to the right of freedom of speech when anything of political importance is being discussed. This, in effect, is what the Court ruled in the decision below.

GITLOW v. NEW YORK

268 U.S. 652 (1925)

Error to the Supreme Court of the State of New York.

Affirmed.

6-2

Sanford	('+')
Taft, C.J.	(+)
VanDevanter	(+)
McReynolds	(+)
Sutherland	(+)
Butler	(+)
Holmes	'—')
Brandeis	—)
Stone	NP[8]

---

[8] Alpheus T. Mason, *Harlan Fiske Stone: Pillar of the Law* (New York: Viking, 1956), p. 518.

MR. JUSTICE SANFORD delivered the opinion of the Court.

Benjamin Gitlow was indicted in the Supreme Court of New York, with three others, for the statutory crime of criminal anarchy. New York Penal Law, §§ 160, 161.[9] He was separately tried, convicted, and sentenced to imprisonment. The judgment was affirmed by the Appellate Division and by the Court of Appeals. . . .

The contention here is that the statute, by its terms and as applied in this case, is repugnant to the due process clause of the Fourteenth Amendment. Its material provisions are:

"Sec. 160. *Criminal Anarchy Defined.* Criminal anarchy is the doctrine that organized government should be over-

[9] This statute was originally enacted in 1902. [Footnote by the Court.]

thrown by force or violence, or by assassination of the executive head or of any of the executive officials of government, or by any unlawful means. The advocacy of such doctrine either by word of mouth or writing is a felony.

"Sec. 161. *Advocacy of Criminal Anarchy*. Any person who:

"1. By word of mouth or writing advocates, advises or teaches the duty, necessity or propriety of overthrowing or overturning organized government by force or violence, or by assassination of the executive head or of any of the executive officials of government, or by any unlawful means; or,

"2. Prints, publishes, edits, issues or knowingly circulates, sells, distributes or publicly displays any book, paper, document, or written or printed matter in any form, containing or advocating, advising or teaching the doctrine that organized government should be overthrown by force, violence or any unlawful means,

* * *

"Is guilty of a felony and punishable," by imprisonment or fine, or both.

The indictment was in two counts. The first charged that the defendant had advocated, advised and taught the duty, necessity and propriety of overthrowing and overturning organized government by force, violence and unlawful means, by certain writings therein set forth entitled "The Left Wing Manifesto"; the second that he had printed, published and knowingly circulated and distributed a certain paper called "The Revolutionary Age," containing the writings set forth in the first count advocating, advising and teaching the doctrine that organized government should be overthrown by force, violence and unlawful means.

The following facts were established on the trial by undisputed evidence and admissions: The defendant is a member of the Left Wing Section of the Socialist Party, a dissenting branch or faction of that party formed in opposition to its dominant policy of "moderate Socialism." Membership in both is open to aliens as well as citizens. The Left Wing Section was organized nationally at a conference in New York City in June, 1919, attended by ninety delegates from twenty different States. The conference elected a National Council, of which the defendant was a member, and left to it the adoption of a "Manifesto." This was published in The Revolutionary Age, the official organ of the Left Wing. The defendant was on the board of managers of the paper and was its business manager. He arranged for the printing of the paper and took to the printer the manuscript of the first issue which contained the Left Wing Manifesto, and also a Communist Program and a Program of the Left Wing that had been adopted by the conference. Sixteen thousand copies were printed, which were delivered at the premises in New York City used as the office of the Revolutionary Age and the headquarters of the Left Wing, and occupied by the defendant and other officials. These copies were paid for by the defendant, as business manager of the paper. Employees at this office wrapped and mailed out copies of the paper under the defendant's direction; and copies were sold from this office. It was admitted that the defendant signed a card subscribing to the Manifesto and Program of the Left Wing, which all applicants were required to sign before being admitted to membership; that he went to different parts of the State to speak to branches of the Socialist Party about the principles of the Left Wing and advocated their adoption; and that he was responsible for the Manifesto as it appeared. . . .

There was no evidence of any effect resulting from the publication and circulation of the Manifesto. . . .

[The] Manifesto . . . condemned the dominant "moderate Socialism" for its recognition of the necessity of the democratic parliamentary state; repudiated its policy of introducing Socialism by legislative measures; and advocated, in plain and unequivocal language, the necessity of accomplishing the "Communist Revolution" by a militant and "revolutionary Socialism," based on "the class struggle" and mobilizing the "power of the proletariat in action," through mass industrial revolts developing into mass political strikes and "revolutionary mass action," for the purpose of conquering and destroying the parliamentary state and establishing in its place, through a "revolutionary dictatorship of the proletariat," the system of Communist Socialism. . . .

The sole contention here is, essentially, that as there was no evidence of any concrete result flowing from the publication of the Manifesto or of circumstances showing the likelihood of such result, the statute as construed and applied by the trial court penalizes the mere utterance, as such, of "doctrine" having no quality of incitement, without regard either to the circumstances of its utterance or to the likelihood of unlawful sequences; and that, as the exercise of the right of free expression with relation to government is only punishable "in circumstances involving likelihood of substantive evil," the statute contravenes the due process clause of the Fourteenth Amendment. The argument in support of this contention rests primarily upon the following propositions: 1st. That the "liberty" protected by the Fourteenth Amendment includes the liberty of speech and of the press; and 2d, That while liberty of expression "is not absolute," it may be restrained "only in circumstances where its exercise bears a causal relation with some substantive evil, consummated, attempted or likely," and as the statute "takes no account of circumstances," it unduly restrains this liberty and is therefore unconstitutional.

The precise question presented, and the only question which we can consider under this writ of error, then is, whether the statute, as construed and applied in this case by the State courts, deprived the defendant of his liberty of expression in violation of the due process clause of the Fourteenth Amendment.

The statute does not penalize the utterance or publication of abstract "doctrine" or academic discussion having no quality of incitement to any concrete action. It is not aimed against mere historical or philosophical essays. It does not restrain the advocacy of changes in the form of government by constitutional and lawful means. What it prohibits is language advocating, advising or teaching the overthrow of organized government by unlawful means. These words imply urging to action. Advocacy is defined in the Century Dictionary as: "1. The act of pleading for, supporting, or recommending; active espousal." It is not the abstract "doctrine" of overthrowing organized government by unlawful means which is denounced by the statute, but the advocacy of action for the accomplishment of that purpose. It was so construed and applied by the trial judge, who specifically charged the jury that: "A mere grouping of historical events and a prophetic deduction from them would neither constitute advocacy, advice or teaching of a doctrine for the overthrow of government by force, violence or unlawful means. [And] if it were a mere essay on the subject, as suggested by counsel, based upon deductions from alleged historical events, with no teaching, advice or advocacy of action, it would not constitute a violation of the statute. * * *"

The Manifesto, plainly, is neither the statement of abstract doctrine nor, as suggested by counsel, mere prediction that industrial disturbances and revolutionary mass strikes will result spontaneously in an inevitable process of evolution in the economic system. It advocates and urges in fervent language mass action which shall progressively foment industrial disturbances and through political mass strikes and revolutionary mass action overthrow and destroy organized parliamentary government. It concludes with a call to action in these words: "The proletariat revolution and the Communist reconstruction of society—*the struggle for these*—is now indispensable. * * * The Communist International calls the proletariat of the world to the final struggle!"

This is not the expression of philosophical abstraction, the mere prediction of future events; it is the language of direct incitement.

The means advocated for bringing about the destruction of organized parliamentary government, namely, mass industrial revolts usurping the functions of municipal government, political mass strikes directed against the parliamentary state, and revolutionary mass action for its final destruction, necessarily imply the use of force and violence, and in their essential nature are inherently unlawful in a constitutional government of law and order. That the jury were warranted in finding that the Manifesto advocated not merely the abstract doctrine of overthrowing organized government by force, violence and unlawful means, but action to that end, is clear.

For present purposes we may and do assume that freedom of speech and of the press—which are protected by the First Amendment from abridgment by Congress—are among the fundamental personal rights and "liberties" protected by the due process clause of the Fourteenth Amendment from impairment by the States. . . .

It is a fundamental principle, long established, that the freedom of speech and of the press which is secured by the Constitution, does not confer an absolute right to speak or publish, without responsibility, whatever one may choose, or an unrestricted and unbridled license that gives immunity for every possible use of language and prevents the punishment of those who abuse this freedom. . . .

That a State in the exercise of its police power may punish those who abuse this freedom by utterances inimical to the public welfare, tending to corrupt public morals, incite to crime, or disturb the public peace, is not open to question. . . . And . . . a State may punish utterances endangering the foundations of organized government and threatening its overthrow by unlawful means. These imperil its own existence as a constitutional State. Freedom of speech and press . . . does not protect publications prompting the overthrow of government by force; the punishment of those who publish articles which tend to destroy organized society being essential to the security of freedom and the stability of the state. . . . And a State may penalize utterances which openly advocate the overthrow of the representative and constitutional form of government of the United States and the several States, by violence or other unlawful means. . . . In short this freedom does not deprive a State of the primary and essential right of self preservation; which, so long as human governments endure, they cannot be denied. . . .

That utterances inciting to the overthrow of organized government by unlawful means, present sufficient danger of substantive evil to bring their punishment within the range of legislative discretion, is clear. Such utterances, by their very nature, involve danger to the public peace and to the security of the State. They threaten breaches of the peace and ultimate revolution. And the immediate danger is none the less real and substantial, because the effect of a given utterance cannot be accurately foreseen. The State cannot reasonably be required to measure the danger from every such utterance in the nice balance of a jeweler's scale. A single revolutionary spark may kindle a fire that, smouldering for a time, may burst into a sweeping and destructive conflagration. It cannot be said that the State is acting arbitrarily or unreasonably when in the exercise of its judgment as to the measures necessary to protect the public peace and safety, it seeks to extinguish the spark without waiting until it has enkindled the flame or blazed into the conflagration. It cannot reasonably be required to defer the adoption of measures for its own peace and safety until the revolutionary utterances lead to actual disturbances of the public peace or imminent and immediate danger of its own destruction; but it may, in the exercise of its judgment, suppress the threatened danger in its incipiency. . . .

We cannot hold that the present statute is an arbitrary or unreasonable exercise of the police power of the State unwarrantably infringing the freedom of speech or press; and we must and do sustain its constitutionality.

This being so it may be applied to every utterance—not too trivial to be beneath the notice of the law—which is of such a character and used with such intent and purpose as to bring it within the prohibition of the statute. . . . In other words, when the legislative body has determined generally, in the consitutional exercise of its discretion, that utterances of a certain kind involve such danger of substantive evil that they may be punished, the question whether any specific utterance coming within the prohibited class is likely, in and of itself, to bring about the substantive evil, is not open to consideration. It is sufficient that the statute itself be constitutional and that the use of the language comes within its prohibition.

It is clear that the question in such cases is entirely different from that involved in those cases where the statute merely prohibits certain acts involving the danger of substantive evil, without any reference to language itself, and it is sought to apply its provisions to language used by the defendant for the purpose of bringing about the prohibited results. There, if it be contended that the statute cannot be applied to the language used by the defendant because of its protection by the freedom of speech or press, it must necessarily be found, as an original question, without any previous determination by the legislative body, whether the specific language used involved such likelihood of bringing about the substantive evil as to deprive it of the constitutional protection. In such case it has been held that the general provisions of the statute may be constitutionally applied to the specific utterance of the defendant if its natural tendency and probable effect was to bring about the substantive evil which the legislative body might prevent. Schenck v. United States, [249 U.S. 47], p. 51; Debs v. United States, 249 U.S. 211 (1919), pp. 215, 216. And the general statement in the Schenck Case, p. 52, that the "question in every case is whether the words used are used in such circumstances and are of such a nature as to create a clear and present danger that they will bring about the substantive evils,"—upon which great reliance is placed in the defendant's argument—was manifestly intended, as shown by the context, to apply only in cases of this class, and has no application to those like the present, where the legislative body itself has previously determined the danger of substantive evil arising from utterances of a specified character.

. . . It was not necessary, within the meaning of the statute, that the defendant should have advocated "some definite or immediate act or acts" of force, violence or unlawfulness. It was sufficient if such acts were advocated in general terms; and it was not essential that their immediate execution should have been advocated. Nor was it necessary that the language should have been "reasonably and ordinarily calculated to incite certain persons" to acts of force, violence or unlawfulness. The advocacy need not be addressed to specific persons. . . .

And finding, for the reasons stated, that the statute is not in itself unconstitutional, and that it has not been applied in the present case in derogation of any constitutional right, the judgment of the Court of Appeals is

Affirmed.

MR. JUSTICE HOLMES (dissenting).

MR. JUSTICE BRANDEIS and I are of opinion that this judgment should be reversed. The general principle of free speech, it seems to me, must be taken to be included in the Fourteenth Amendment, in view of the scope that has been given to the word "liberty" as there used, although perhaps it may be accepted with a somewhat larger latitude of interpretation than is allowed to Congress by the sweeping language that governs or ought to govern the laws of the United States. If I am right then I think that the criterion sanctioned by the full Court in Schenck v. United States, 249 U.S. 47, 52 [1919], applies: "The question in every case is whether the words used are used in such circumstances and are of such a nature as to create a clear and present danger that they will bring about the substantive evils that [the State] has a right to prevent."

It is true that in my opinion this criterion was departed from in Abrams v. United States, 250 U.S. 616 [1919], but the convictions that I expressed in that case are too deep for it to be possible for me as yet to believe that it and Schaefer v. United States, 251 U.S. 466 [1920], have settled the law. If what I think the correct test is applied it is manifest that there was no present danger of an attempt to overthrown the government by force on the part of the admittedly small minority who shared the defendant's views. It is said that this manifesto was more than a theory, that it was an incitement. Every idea is an incitement. It offers itself for belief and if believed it is acted on unless some other belief outweighs it or some failure of energy stifles the movement at its birth. The only difference between the expression of an opinion and an incitement in the narrower sense is the speaker's enthusiasm for the result. Eloquence may set fire to reason. But whatever may be thought of the redundant discourse before us it had no chance of starting a present conflagration. If in the long run the beliefs expressed in proletarian dictatorship are destined to be accepted by the dominant forces of the community, the only meaning of free speech is that they should be given their chance and have their way. . . .

The Classic Case: The Soap-Box Orator

Schenck had been a national leader of the Socialist party, and Gitlow a national leader of the faction of that party that split off to form the Communist party. Eugene Dennis, in the fourth case in this group, was the national executive secretary of the Communist party at the time he was tried with the other national officers of the party. But Irving Feiner was a youth, considered to be callow by at least several of his professors at Syracuse University, who made a speech in the streets to a local crowd, on a subject of local political interest. The purpose of Feiner's *ad hoc* remarks was to protest the cancellation of an address by an official of the Independent Progressive party, which had run Henry Wallace as its presidential candidate only four months previously and had attracted the political support of several hundred thousand non-Communist voters. Originally an address by O. John Rogge, a former United States Assistant Attorney General, had been scheduled for Lincoln Auditorium in Central High School; this was a facility frequently used for public meetings in the city. When school authorities revoked permission to use the auditorium, on the eve of the appointed time for the meeting, the sponsoring groups, the Young Progressives of America, and the

American Labor party (which elected candidates to Congress in New York), hired a hall in the leading local hotel. Whether or not the Young Progressives were a "Communist group" or "Communist-dominated" as many persons alleged, the events described above—for a political organization to hire a hall to hear a speaker of their choice talk on a political subject—would appear to be in the best tradition of American political democracy, and in precise accord with the Holmesian "market place" theory of free speech. These happenings provide the background, however, rather than the specific events at issue in the Feiner case.

The facts of the Feiner case are adequately described in the opinions below. But it is also relevant to note that less than two years earlier the Court had flaunted the "normal" requirements of judicial restraint; and on the pretext of a dubious point of procedure, it had reversed the conviction for breach of the peace of Arthur Terminiello. The procedural question had been neither claimed nor argued by the parties in the Supreme Court or in any of the three state courts below; and according to the Chief Justice, it had been "ferretted out by the independent research of the Court [i.e., Douglas]." Father Terminiello was a henchman of Gerald L. K. Smith, who in turn was a leading spokesman for native American fascism. As described in the various opinions of the justices in the two cases, Feiner's little fracas was a pink tea party in more senses than one in comparison to Father Terminiello's ugly racist provocations to open and immediate mob violence.[10] Yet, because Clark and Reed shifted position in the two cases, the Court voted 5-4 to uphold (in effect) Terminiello's right to indulge in free speech of the most vituperative character, while rejecting by a vote of 3-6 Feiner's claim of right to engage in the pale pyrotechnics of adolescent forensics. At the time of their respective offenses, Terminiello was no boy, and Feiner was no man, as any reader can judge from the facts of official record in the two cases. But Feiner was a "pink," a "left-winger," maybe even a young Communist; while Arthur Terminiello was merely a fascist. Whatever the Court's intent, the two cases in close juxtaposition logically raised the question whether the Constitution of the United States guaranteed freedom of speech for fascists, but not for Communists. If Irving Feiner's speech went beyond the bounds of liberty protected by the Fourteenth Amendment (i.e., by the Supreme Court), it is difficult to imagine what kind of political discussion *is* within the "legitimate" scope of free speech—unless the American political system can be assumed to avoid the dangers implicit in "democratic centralism" (as it is called in the U.S.S.R.) by a tolerance of political discussion in public places that is confined to such questions as sewers, schools, and garbage collection.

10 For details, consult Mr. Justice Jackson's concurring opinion in *Terminiello* v. *Chicago,* 337 U.S. 1, 13 (1949).

FEINER v. NEW YORK

340 U.S. 315 (1951)

Certiorari to the New York Court of Appeals.

Affirmed.

6-3

Vinson, C.J.	('+')
Reed	(+)
Jackson	(+)
Burton	(+)
Clark	(+)
Frankfurter	('+'
Black	'—')
Douglas	'—')
Minton	—)

MR. CHIEF JUSTICE VINSON delivered the opinion of the Court.

Petitioner was convicted of the offense of disorderly conduct, a misdemeanor under the New York penal laws, in the Court of Special Sessions of the City of Syracuse and was sentenced to thirty days in the county penitentiary. The conviction was affirmed by the Onondaga County Court and the New York Court of Appeals. . . . The case is here on certiorari, . . . petitioner having claimed that the conviction is in violation of his right of free speech under the Fourteenth Amendment.

In the review of state decisions where First Amendment rights are drawn in question, we of course make an examination of the evidence to ascertain independently whether the right has been violated. Here, the trial judge, who heard the case without a jury, rendered an oral decision at the end of the trial, setting forth his determination of the facts upon which he found the petitioner guilty. His decision indicated generally that he believed the state's witnesses, and his summation of the testimony was used by the two New York courts on review in stating the facts. Our appraisal of the facts is, therefore, based upon the uncontroverted facts and, where controversy exists, upon that testimony which the trial judge did reasonably conclude to be true.

On the evening of March 8, 1949, petitioner Irving Feiner was addressing an open-air meeting at the corner of South McBride and Harrison Streets in the City of Syracuse. At approximately 6:30 P.M., the police received a telephone complaint concerning the meeting, and two officers were detailed to investigate. One of these officers went to the scene immediately, the other arriving some twelve minutes later. They found a crowd of about seventy-five or eighty people, both Negro and white, filling the sidewalk and spreading out into the street. Petitioner, standing on a large wooden box on the sidewalk, was addressing the crowd through a loud-speaker system attached to an automobile. Although the purpose of his speech was to urge his listeners to attend a meeting to be held that night in the Syracuse Hotel, in its course he was making derogatory remarks concerning President Truman, the American Legion, the Mayor of Syracuse, and other local political officials.

The police officers made no effort to interfere with petitioner's speech, but were first concerned with the effect of the crowd on both pedestrian and vehicular traffic. They observed the situation from the opposite side of the street, noting that some pedestrians were forced to walk in the street to avoid the crowd. Since traffic was passing at the time, the officers attempted to get the people listening to petitioner back on the sidewalk. The crowd was restless and there was some pushing, shoving and milling around. One of the officers telephoned the police station from a nearby store, and then both policemen crossed the street and mingled with the crowd without any intention of arresting the speaker.

At this time, petitioner was speaking in a "loud, high-pitched voice." He gave the impression that he was endeavoring to arouse the Negro people against the whites, urging that they rise up in arms and fight for equal rights. The statements before such a mixed audience "stirred up a little excitement." Some of the onlookers made remarks to the police about their inability to handle the crowd and at least one threatened violence if the police did not act. There were others who appeared to be favoring petitioner's arguments. Because of the feeling that existed in the crowd both for and against the speaker, the officers finally "stepped in to prevent it from resulting in a fight." One of the officers approached the petitioner, not for the purpose of arresting him, but to get him to break up the crowd. He asked petitioner to get down off the box, but the latter refused to accede to his request and continued talking. The officer waited for a minute and then demanded that he cease talking. Although the officer had thus twice requested petitioner to stop over the course of several minutes, petitioner not only ignored him but continued talking. During all this time, the crowd was pressing closer around petitioner and the officer. Finally, the officer told petitioner he was under arrest and ordered him to get down from the box, reaching up to grab him. Petitioner stepped down, announcing over the microphone that "the law has arrived, and I suppose they will take over now." In all, the officer had asked petitioner to get down off the box three times over a space of four or five minutes. Petitioner had been speaking for over a half hour.

On these facts, petitioner was specifically charged with violation of § 722 of the Penal Law of New York.[11] . . . The

bill of particulars, demanded by petitioner and furnished by the State, gave in detail the facts upon which the prosecution relied to support the charge of disorderly conduct. Paragraph C is particularly pertinent here: "By ignoring and refusing to heed and obey reasonable police orders issued at the time and place mentioned in the Information to regulate and control said crowd and to prevent a breach or breaches of the peace and to prevent injury to pedestrians attempting to use said walk, and being forced into the highway adjacent to the place in question, and prevent injury to the public generally."

We are not faced here with blind condonation by a state court of arbitrary police action. Petitioner was accorded a full, fair trial. The trial judge heard testimony supporting and contradicting the judgment of the police officers that a clear danger of disorder was threatened. After weighing this contradictory evidence, the trial judge reached the conclusion that the police officers were justified in taking action to prevent a breach of the peace. The exercise of the police officers' proper discretionary power to prevent a breach of the peace was thus approved by the trial court and later by two courts on review. The courts below recognized petitioner's right to hold a street meeting at this locality, to make use of loud-speaking equipment in giving his speech, and to make derogatory remarks concerning public officials and the American Legion. They found that the officers in making the arrest were motivated solely by a proper concern for the preservation of order and protection of the general welfare, and that there was no evidence which could lend color to a claim that the acts of the police were a cover for suppression of petitioner's views and opinions. Petitioner was thus neither arrested nor convicted for the making or the content

11 "§722. Any person who with intent to provoke a breach of the peace, or whereby a breach of the peace may be occasioned, commits any of the following acts shall be deemed to have committed the offense of disorderly conduct: 1. Uses offensive, disorderly, threatening, abusive or insulting language, conduct or behavior; 2. Acts in such a manner as to annoy, disturb, interfere with, obstruct, or be offensive to others; 3. Congre-

gates with others on a public street and refuses to move on when ordered by the police; . . ." [Footnote by the Court.]

of his speech. Rather, it was the reaction which it actually engendered. . . .

We are well aware that the ordinary murmurings and objections of a hostile audience cannot be allowed to silence a speaker, and are also mindful of the possible danger of giving overzealous police officials complete discretion to break up otherwise lawful public meetings. . . . But we are not faced here with such a situation. It is one thing to say that the police cannot be used as an instrument for the suppression of unpopular views, and another to say that, when as here the speaker passes the bounds of argument or persuasion and undertakes incitement to riot, they are powerless to prevent a breach of the peace. . . . The findings of the state courts as to the existing situation and the imminence of greater disorder coupled with petitioner's deliberate defiance of the police officers convince us that we should not reverse this conviction in the name of free speech.

Affirmed.

MR. JUSTICE DOUGLAS, with whom MR. JUSTICE MINTON concurs, dissenting.

Feiner, a university student, made a speech on a street corner in Syracuse, New York, on March 8, 1949. The purpose of the speech was to publicize a meeting of the Young Progressives of America to be held that evening. A permit authorizing the meeting to be held in a public school auditorium had been revoked and the meeting shifted to a local hotel.

Feiner delivered his speech in a small shopping area in a predominantly colored residential section of Syracuse. . . .

The speech was mainly devoted to publicizing the evening's meeting and protesting the revocation of the permit. It also touched on various public issues. The following are the only excerpts revealed by the record:

"Mayor Costello (of Syracuse) is a champagne-sipping bum; he does not speak for the negro people."

"The 15th Ward is run by corrupt politicians, and there are horse rooms operating there."

"President Truman is a bum."

"Mayor O'Dwyer is a bum."

"The American Legion is a Nazi Gestapo."

"The negroes don't have equal rights; they should rise up in arms and fight for their rights."

There was some pushing and shoving in the crowd and some angry muttering. That is the testimony of the police. But there were no fights and no "disorder" even by the standards of the police. There was not even any heckling of the speaker.

But after Feiner had been speaking about 20 minutes a man said to the police officers, "If you don't get that son of a bitch off, I will go over and get him off there myself." It was then that the police ordered Feiner to stop speaking; when he refused, they arrested him.

Public assemblies and public speech occupy an important role in American life. One high function of the police is to protect these lawful gatherings so that the speakers may exercise their constitutional rights. When unpopular causes are sponsored from the public platform there will commonly be mutterings and unrest and heckling from the crowd. When a speaker mounts a platform it is not unusual to find him resorting to exaggeration, to vilification of ideas and men, to the making of false charges. . . .

A speaker may not, of course, incite a riot any more than he may invite a breach of the peace by the use of "fighting words." See *Chaplinsky* v. *New Hampshire*, 315 U.S. 568. But this record shows no such extremes. It shows an unsympathetic audience and the threat of one man to haul the speaker from the stage. It is against that kind of threat that speakers need police protection. If they do not receive it and instead the police throw their weight on the side of those who would break up the meetings, the police become the new censors of speech.

MR. JUSTICE BLACK, dissenting.

The record before us convinces me that petitioner, a young college student, has been sentenced to the penitentiary for the unpopular views he expressed on matters of public interest while lawfully making a street-corner speech in Syracuse, New York.[12] Today's decision, however, indicates that we must blind ourselves to this fact because the trial judge fully accepted the testimony of the prosecution witnesses on all important points.[13] Many

times in the past this Court has said that despite findings below, we will examine the evidence for ourselves to ascertain whether federally protected rights have been denied; otherwise review here would fail of its purpose in safeguarding constitutional guarantees. Even a partial abandonment of this rule marks a dark day for civil liberties in our Nation.

But still more has been lost today. Even accepting every "finding of fact" below, I think this conviction makes a mockery of the free speech guarantees of the First and Fourteenth Amendments. The end result of the affirmance here is to approve a simple and readily available technique by which cities and states can with impunity subject all speeches, political or otherwise, on streets or elsewhere, to the supervision and censorship of the local police. I will have no part or parcel in this holding which I view as a long step toward totalitarian authority. . . .

The Court's opinion apparently rests on this reasoning: The policeman, under the circumstances detailed, could reasonably conclude that serious fighting or even riot was imminent; therefore he could stop petitioner's speech to prevent a breach of peace; accordingly, it was "disorderly conduct" for petitioner to continue speaking in disobedience of the officer's request. As to the existence of a dangerous situation on the street corner, it seems far-fetched to suggest that the "facts" show any imminent threat of riot or uncontrollable disorder. It is neither unusual nor unexpected that some people at public street meetings mutter, mill about, push, shove, or disagree, even violently, with the speaker. Indeed, it is rare where controversial topics are discussed that an outdoor crowd does not do some or all of these things. Nor does one isolated threat to assault the speaker forebode disorder. Especially should the danger be discounted where, as here, the person threatening was a man whose wife and two small children accompanied him

---

[12] There was no charge that any city or state law prohibited such a meeting at the place or time it was held. Evidence showed that it was customary to hold public gatherings on that same corner every Friday night, and the trial judge who convicted petitioner admitted that he understood the meeting was a lawful one. Nor did the judge treat the lawful meeting as unlawful because a crowd congregated on the sidewalk. Consequently, any discussion of disrupted pedestrian and vehicular traffic, while suggestive coloration, is immaterial under the charge and conviction here.

It is implied in a concurring opinion that the use of sound amplifiers in some way caused the meeting to become less lawful. This fact, however, had nothing to do with the conviction of petitioner. In sentencing him the trial court said: "You had a perfect right to appear there and to use that implement, the loud speaker. You had a right to have it in the street." . . . [Footnote by Justice Black.]

[13] . . . I believe the record demonstrates rather conclusively that petitioner did not use the phrase "in arms" in the manner testified to by the officers. Reliable witnesses swore that petitioner's statement was that his listeners "could rise up and fight for their rights by going arm in arm to the Hotel Syracuse, black and white alike, to hear John Rogge." The testimony of neither of the two officers contained the phrase "in arms" when they first testified on this subject; they added it only after counsel for the prosecution was permitted by the court, over petitioner's objection, to propound leading and suggestive questions. In any event, the statement ascribed to petitioner by the officers seems clearly rhetorical when read in context. [Footnote by Justice Black.]

and who, so far as the record shows, was never close enough to petitioner to carry out the threat.

Moreover, assuming that the "facts" did indicate a critical situation, I reject the implication of the Court's opinion that the police had no obligaton to protect petitioner's constitutional right to talk. The police of course have power to prevent breaches of the peace. But if, in the name of preserving order, they ever can interfere with a lawful public speaker, they first must make all reasonable efforts to protect him. Here the policemen did not even pretend to try to protect petitioner. According to the officers' testimony, the crowd was restless but there is no showing of any attempt to quiet it; pedestrians were forced to walk into the street, but there was no effort to clear a path on the sidewalk; one person threatened to assault petitioner but the officers did nothing to discourage this when even a word might have sufficed. Their duty was to protect petioner's right to talk, even to the extent of arresting the man who threatened to interfere. Instead, they shirked that duty and acted only to suppress the right to speak.

Finally, I cannot agree with the Court's statement that petitioner's disregard of the policeman's unexplained request amounted to such "deliberate defiance" as would justify an arrest or conviction for disorderly conduct. On the contrary, I think that the policeman's action was a "deliberate defiance" of ordinary official duty as well as of the constitutional right of free speech. For at least where time allows, courtesy and explanation of commands are basic elements of good official conduct in a democratic society. Here petitioner was "asked" then "told" then "commanded" to stop speaking, but a man making a lawful address is certainly not required to be silent merely because an officer directs it. Petitioner was entitled to know why he should cease doing a lawful act. Not once was he told. I understand that people in authoritarian countries must obey arbitrary orders. I had hoped that there was no such duty in the United States. . . .

MR. JUSTICE FRANKFURTER, concurring.

. . . Feiner forced pedestrians to walk in the street by collecting a crowd on the public sidewalk, he attracted additional attention by using sound amplifiers, he indulged in name-calling, he told part of his audience that it should rise up in arms. In the crowd of 75 to 80 persons, there was angry muttering and pushing. Under these circumstances, and in order to prevent a disturbance of the peace, an officer asked Feiner to stop speaking. When he had twice ignored the request, Feiner was arrested. The trial judge concluded that "the officers were fully justified in feeling that a situation was developing which could very, very easily result in a serious disorder." His view was sustained by an intermediate appellate court and by a unanimous decision of the New York Court of Appeals. . . . The estimate of a particular local situation thus comes here with the momentum of the weightiest judicial authority of New York.

This Court has often emphasized that in the exercise of our authority over state court decisions the Due Process Clause must not be construed in an abstract and doctrinaire way by disregarding local conditions. In considering the degree of respect to be given findings by the highest court of a State in cases involving the Due Process Clause, the course of decisions by that court should be taken into account. Particularly within the area of due process colloquially called "civil liberties," it is important whether such a course of decisions reflects a cavalier attitude toward civil liberties or real regard for them. Only unfamiliarity with its decisions and the outlook of its judges could generate a notion that the Court of Appeals of New York is inhospitable to claims of civil liberties or is wanting in respect for this Court's decisions in support of them. It is pertinent, therefore, to note that all members of the New York Court accepted the finding that Feiner was stopped not because the listeners or police officers disagreed with his views but because these officers were honestly concerned with preventing a breach of the peace. . . . Where conduct is within the allowable limits of free speech, the police are peace officers for the speaker as well as for his hearers. But the power effectively to preserve order cannot be displaced by giving a speaker complete immunity. Here, there were two police officers present for 20 minutes. They interfered only when they apprehended imminence of violence. It is not a constitutional principle that, in acting to preserve order, the police must proceed against the crowd, whatever its size and temper, and not against the speaker. . . .

The Communist Conspiracy

Less than six months after the Feiner decision, and in the same term, the Court disposed of the Dennis case, which involved the conviction, for conspiracy to organize the American Communist party and to teach and advocate the overthrow of the government by force and violence, of the eleven top Communist party leaders, whose trial had begun three years earlier. Superficially, at least, there were important differences between the two cases. Feiner was charged with disorderly conduct, not with an attempt to bring about the dictatorship of the proletariat. He was tried for a petty offense against a municipal ordinance, and in a state court; while Dennis and his cohorts were considered to be the most dangerous men in the United States, and were tried in a federal court for violation of an act of Congress. Few Americans heard of Irving Feiner, either before or after his case was disposed of by the Supreme Court; while the prosecution of the Communist party leaders was front-page news for over a year, not only throughout the United States but also throughout much of the world. The name of the municipal judge who presided over Feiner's trial is unknown except to legal scholars who bother to dig it out of the record in the case (or the files of *The New York Times*); while Federal District Judge Harold Medina became something of a national hero. Books were written about Medina; he became widely recognized as an oracle of patriotic wisdom and a paragon of judicial virtue; and he was promptly promoted to a position on the bench of the United States Court of Appeals for the Second Circuit. But these seeming differences had little effect upon the Supreme Court's voting behavior.

Justice Jackson, for instance, expressly remarks in his concurring opinion in the Dennis case that he would reserve the clear-and-present-danger test for use in the kind of case for which it was devised by Holmes and Brandeis; and he offers, as an example of such a case, one in which "the issue is criminality of a hot-headed speech on a street corner"—with the clear implication, in context, that the public interest in free political discussion ought to outweigh the slight inconvenience to local traffic and public order that the delivery of such a speech might entail. "The formula in such cases," he says, "favors freedoms that are vital to our society, and, even if sometimes applied too generously, the consequences cannot be grave." But if Feiner's behavior did not constitute "a harmless letting off of steam," what would? Jackson voted to uphold Feiner's conviction just as he voted to uphold Eugene Dennis'. The only differences in the voting behavior of the justices in the two cases were: (1) Clark disqualified himself in Dennis because of his previous relationship to the case as the Attorney General under whom the prosecution was begun; without any question whatsoever, if Clark had participated, he would have voted to uphold Dennis' conviction, as he did vote to affirm in Feiner's case; and (2) Minton, who had dissented in Feiner, voted to affirm in Dennis. Thus, only Minton, of all the justices, saw enough difference in the two cases to warrant a change in his vote.

The main focus of discussion in most of the opinions in the case is upon the question whether the judiciary could and should substitute their own judgment for that of Congress concerning the probability of success of "the Communist conspiracy." Essentially three different positions are argued. Frankfurter and Jackson urge that judicial restraint should preclude the Court from reconsidering the expressed judgment of Congress and the President that the Communist party was a criminal conspiracy against the security of the United States. Under this view, the clear-and-present-danger test was irrelevant to the Court's decision. Four of the justices joined in an opinion by Vinson which did reconsider the congressional judgment, arriving at the conclusion that the Communist party did, in fact, constitute a clear and present danger to national security; therefore, the party leaders were properly convicted under the statute, and the statute was constitutional. Black and Douglas thought that the statute was unconstitutional on its face and as applied to these defendants, since there was no evidence in the record to support the conclusion that their organizing, teaching, and advocacy of Communist doctrine had as yet resulted in any "substantive evil" that Congress had a right to prevent.

It is true that the clear-and-present-danger formula *could* have been used, as the dissenters argued in Gitlow and Feiner, to support the reversal of convictions, without deciding the constitutional question—under the *Fourteenth* Amendment —of legislative power to punish seditious utterance. But the formula could have been used to achieve such a result only by the state courts, because only they could interpret the legislation at issue as not having been intended to apply to such events as Gitlow's Manifesto or Feiner's harangue. For under the Court's own (Federalism variable) policies for deference to state courts, the Supreme Court is supposed to be bound by state judicial interpretation of the meaning of state law. Consequently, the only alternative open to the Supreme Court in the Gitlow and Feiner cases was to affirm or else to declare the relevant state legislation to be unconstitutional under the Fourteenth Amendment. Vinson's opinion in Dennis makes this point explicit. In Dennis, therefore, the Court had, as in Schenck, an additional alternative: that of interpreting the Smith Act in such a way as to make it inapplicable to the specific behaviors of the defendants. Such a course would have avoided the constitutional question, but it did not appear to commend itself to any of the justices in the Dennis decision. Once this alternative was rejected, the Court was left with a choice among the three positions argued by the justices in their opinions in the case, neither of which was able to attract the support of a majority. And once it was agreed that the Smith Act did apply to the behaviors upon which prosecution was based, the question before the Court—given the intervening "incorporation of the First and Fourteenth Amendments" —was the same as it had been in Gitlow: does a sedition statute violate the First Amendment? The majority answered in the negative, paying lip service to the clear-and-present-danger test but invoking the bad-tendency test as the basis for decision. In so doing, they were merely following the trail that had been blazed by their predecessors in the Gitlow decision and—with a unanimous Court speaking through Mr. Justice Holmes—in the Schenck case.

DENNIS v. UNITED STATES

341 U.S. 494 (June 4, 1951)

Certiorari to the United States Court of Appeals for the Second Circuit.

Affirmed.

6-2

Vinson, C.J.	('+'
Reed	(+
Burton	(+
Minton	(+
Frankfurter	('+'
Jackson	('+'
Black	'—')
Douglas	'—')
Clark	NP

MR. CHIEF JUSTICE VINSON announced the judgment of the Court and an opinion in which MR. JUSTICE REED, MR. JUSTICE BURTON, and MR. JUSTICE MINTON join. . . .

The indictment charged the petitioners with wilfully and knowingly conspiring (1) to organize as the Communist Party of the United States of America a society, group and assembly of persons who teach and advocate the overthrow and destruction of the Government of the United States by force and violence, and (2) knowingly and wilfully to advocate and teach the duty and necessity of overthrowing and destroying the Government of the United States by force and violence. . . .

The trial of the case extended over nine months, six of which were devoted to the taking of evidence, resulting in a record of 16,000 pages. Our limited grant of the writ of certiorari has removed from our consideration any question as to the sufficiency of the evidence to support the jury's determination that petitioners are guilty of the offense charged. Whether on this record petitioners did in fact advocate the overthrow of the Government by force and violence is not before us, and we must base any discussion of this point upon the conclusions stated in the opinion of the Court of Appeals, which treated the issue in great detail. That court held that the record in this case amply supports the necessary finding of the jury that petitioners, the leaders of the Communist Party in this country, were unwilling to work within our framework of democracy, but intended to initiate a violent revolution whenever the propitious occasion appeared. Petitioners dispute the meaning to be drawn from the evidence, contending that the Marxist-Leninist doctrine they advocated taught that force and violence to achieve a Communist form of government in an existing democratic state would be necessary only because the ruling classes of that state would never permit the transformation to be accomplished peacefully, but would use force and violence to defeat any peaceful political and economic gain the Communists could achieve. But the Court of Appeals held that the record supports the following broad conclusions: By virtue of their control over the political apparatus of the Communist Political Association, petitioners were able to transform that organization into the Communist Party; that the policies of the Association were changed from peaceful cooperation with the United States and its economic and political structure to a policy which had existed before the United States and the Soviet Union were fighting a common enemy, namely, a policy which worked for the overthrow of the Government by force and violence; that the Communist Party is a highly disciplined organization, adept at infiltration into strategic positions, use of aliases, and double-meaning language; that the Party is rigidly controlled; that Communists, unlike other political parties, tolerate no dissension from the policy laid down by the guiding forces, but that the approved program is slavishly followed by the members of the Party; that the literature of the Party and the statements and activities of its leaders, petitioners here, advocate, and the general goal of the Party was, during the period in question, to achieve a successful overthrow of the existing order by force and violence.

. . . This is a federal statute which we must interpret as well as judge. Herein lies the fallacy of reliance upon the manner in which this Court has treated judgments of state courts. Where the statute as construed by the state court transgressed the First Amendment, we could not but invalidate the judgments of conviction.

The very language of the Smith Act negates the interpretation which petitioners would have us impose on that Act. It is directed at advocacy, not discussion. Thus, the trial judge properly charged the jury that they could not convict if they found that petitioners did "no more than pursue peaceful studies and discussions or teaching and advocacy in the realm of ideas." He further charged that it was not unlawful "to conduct in an American college or university a course explaining the philosophical theories set forth in the books which have been placed in evidence." Such a charge is in strict accord with the statutory language, and illustrates the meaning to be placed on those words. Congress did not intend to eradicate the free discussion of political theories, to destroy the traditional rights of Americans to discuss and evaluate ideas without fear of governmental sanction. Rather Congress was concerned with the very kind of activity in which the evidence showed these petitioners engaged.

. . . [The] basis of the First Amendment is the hypothesis that speech can rebut speech, propaganda will answer propaganda, free debate of ideas will result in the wisest governmental policies. It is for this reason that this Court has recognized the inherent value of free discourse. An analysis of the leading cases in this Court which have involved direct limitations on speech, however, will demonstrate that both the majority of the Court and the dissenters in particular cases have recognized that this is not an unlimited, unqualified right, but that the societal value of speech must, on occasion, be subordinated to other values and considerations.

No important case involving free speech was decided by this Court prior to *Schenck* v. *United States,* 249 U.S. 47

(1919). Indeed, the summary treatment accorded an argument based upon an individual's claim that the First Amendment protected certain utterances indicates that the Court at earlier dates placed no unique emphasis upon that right. It was not until the classic dictum of Justice Holmes in the *Schenck* case that speech *per se* received that emphasis in a majority opinion. . . . [But] neither Justice Holmes nor Justice Brandeis ever envisioned that a shorthand phrase should be crystallized into a rigid rule to be applied inflexibly without regard to the circumstances of each case. Speech is not an absolute, above and beyond control by the legislature when its judgment, subject to review here, is that certain kinds of speech are so undesirable as to warrant criminal sanction. Nothing is more certain in modern society than the principle that there are no absolutes, that a name, a phrase, a standard has meaning only when associated with the considerations which gave birth to the nomenclature. . . . To those who would paralyze our Government in the face of impending threat by encasing it in a semantic straitjacket we must reply that all concepts are relative.

In this case we are squarely presented with the application of the "clear and present danger" test, and must decide what that phrase imports. We first note that many of the cases in which this Court has reversed convictions by use of this or similar tests have been based on the fact that the interest which the State was attempting to protect was itself too insubstantial to warrant restriction of speech. In this category we may put such cases as . . . *West Virginia Board of Education* v. *Barnette,* 319 U.S. 624 (1943); [and] *Thomas* v. *Collins,* 323 U.S. 516 (1945). . . . Overthrow of the Government by force and violence is certainly a substantial enough interest for the Government to limit speech. Indeed, this is the ultimate value of any society, for if a society cannot protect its very structure from armed internal attack, it must follow that no subordinate value can be protected. If, then, this interest may be protected, the literal problem which is presented is what has been meant by the use of the phrase "clear and present danger" of the utterances bringing about the evil within the power of Congress to punish.

Obviously, the words cannot mean that before the Government may act, it must wait until the *putsch* is about to be executed, the plans have been laid and the signal is awaited. If Government is aware that a group aiming at its overthrow is attempting to indoctrinate its members and to commit them to a course whereby they will strike when the leaders feel the circumstances permit, action by the Government is required. The argument that there is no need for Government to concern itself, for Government is stong, it possesses ample powers to put down a rebellion, it may defeat the revolution with ease needs no answer. For that is not the question. Certainly an attempt to overthrow the Government by force, even though doomed from the outset because of inadequate numbers or power of the revolutionists, is a sufficient evil for Congress to prevent. The damage which such attempts create both physically and politically to a nation makes it impossible to measure the validity in terms of the probability of success, or the immediacy of a successful attempt. . . . We must therefore reject the contention that success or probability of success is the criterion.

The situation with which Justices Holmes and Brandeis were concerned in *Gitlow* was a comparatively isolated event, bearing little relation in their minds to any substantial threat to the safety of the community. . . .

Chief Judge Learned Hand, writing for the majority below, interpreted the phrase as follows: "In each case [courts] must ask whether the gravity of the 'evil,' discounted by its improbability, justifies such invasion of free speech as is necessary to avoid the danger." 183 F. 2d at 212. We adopt this statement of the rule. As articulated by Chief Judge Hand, it is as succinct and inclusive as any other we might devise at this time. It takes into consideration those factors which we deem relevant, and relates their significances. More we cannot expect from words.

Likewise, we are in accord with the court below, which affirmed the trial court's finding that the requisite danger existed. . . .

We hold that . . . the Smith Act [does] not inherently, or as construed or applied in the instant case, violate the First Amendment and other provisions of the Bill of Rights, or the First and Fifth Amendments because of indefiniteness. Petitioners intended to overthrow the Government of the United States as speedily as the circumstances would permit. Their conspiracy to organize the Communist Party and to teach and advocate the overthrow of the Government of the United States by force and violence created a "clear and present danger" of an attempt to overthrow the Government by force and violence. They were properly and constitutionally convicted for violation of the Smith Act. The judgments of conviction are

Affirmed.

MR. JUSTICE JACKSON, concurring. . . .

The "clear and present danger" test was an innovation by Mr. Justice Holmes in the *Schenck* case, reiterated and refined by him and Mr. Justice Brandeis in later cases, all arising before the era of World War II revealed the subtlety and efficacy of modernized revolutionary techniques used by totalitarian parties. In those cases, they were faced with convictions under so-called criminal syndicalism statutes aimed at anarchists but which, loosely construed, had been applied to punish socialism, pacifism, and left-wing ideologies, the charges often resting on far-fetched inferences which, if true,

would established only technical or trivial violations. They proposed "clear and present danger" as a test for the sufficiency of evidence in particular cases.

I would save it, unmodified, for application as a "rule of reason" in the kind of case for which it was devised. When the issue is criminality of a hot-headed speech on a street corner, or circulation of a few incendiary pamphlets, or parading by some zealots behind a red flag, or refusal of a handful of school children to salute our flag, it is not beyond the capacity of the judicial process to gather, comprehend, and weigh the necessary materials for decision whether it is a clear and present danger of substantive evil or a harmless letting off of steam. It is not a prophecy, for the danger in such cases has matured by the time of trial or it was never present. The test applies and has meaning where a conviction is sought to be based on a speech or writing which does not directly or explicitly advocate a crime but to which such tendency is sought to be attributed by construction or by implication from external circumstances. The formula in such cases favors freedoms that are vital to our society, and, even if sometimes applied too generously, the consequences cannot be grave. . . .

If we must decide that this Act and its application are constitutional only if we are convinced that petitioner's conduct creates a "clear and present danger" of violent overthrow, we must appraise imponderables, including international and national phenomena which baffle the best informed foreign offices and our most experienced politicians. We would have to foresee and predict the effectiveness of Communist propaganda, opportunities for infiltration, whether, and when, a time will come that they consider propitious for action, and whether and how fast our existing government will deteriorate. And we would have to speculate as to whether an approaching Communist *coup* would not be anticipated by a nationalistic fascist movement. No doctrine can be sound whose application requires us to make a prophecy of that sort in the guise of a legal decision. The judicial process simply is not adequate to a trial of such far-flung issues. The answers given would reflect our own political predilections and nothing more.

The authors of the clear and present danger test never applied it to a case like this, nor would I. If applied as it is proposed here, it means that the Communist plotting is protected during its period of incubation; its preliminary stages of organization and preparation are immune from the law; the Government can move only after imminent action is manifest, when it would, of course, be too late. . . .

What really is under review here is a conviction of conspiracy, after a trial for conspiracy, on an indictment charging conspiracy, brought under a statute outlawing conspiracy. With due respect to my colleagues, they seem to me to discuss anything under the sun except the law of conspiracy. One of the dissenting opinions even appears to chide me for "invoking the law of conspiracy." As that is the case before us, it may be more amazing that its reversal can be proposed without even considering the law of conspiracy.

The Constitution does not make conspiracy a civil right. . . .

MR. JUSTICE BLACK, dissenting.

. . . These petitioners were not charged with an attempt to overthrow the Government. They were not charged with overt acts of any kind designed to overthrow the Government. They were not even charged with saying anything or writing anything designed to overthrow the Government. The charge was that they agreed to assemble and to talk and publish certain ideas at a later date: The indictment is that they conspired to organize the Communist Party and to use speech or newspapers and other publica-

tions in the future to teach and advocate the forcible overthrow of the Government. No matter how it is worded, this is a virulent form of prior censorship of speech and press, which I believe the First Amendment forbids. I would hold § 3 of the Smith Act authorizing this prior restraint unconstitutional on its face and as applied. . . .

MR. JUSTICE DOUGLAS, dissenting. . . .

So far as the present record is concerned, what petitioners did was to organize people to teach and themselves teach the Marxist-Leninist doctrine contained chiefly in four books: Stalin, Foundations of Leninism (1924); Marx and Engels, Manifesto of the Communist Party (1848); Lenin, The State and Revolution (1917); History of the Communist Party of the Soviet Union (B.) (1939).

Those books are to Soviet Communism what Mein Kampf was to Nazism. . . .

We might as well say that the speech of petitioners is outlawed because Soviet Russia and her Red Army are a threat to world peace. . . . [But if] we are to take judicial notice of the threat of Communists within the nation, it should not be difficult to conclude that as a political party they are of little consequence. Communists in this country have never made a respectable or serious showing in any election. I would doubt that there is a village, let alone a city or county or state, which the Communists could carry. Communism in the world scene is no bogeyman; but Communism as a political faction or party in this country plainly is. Communism has been so thoroughly exposed in this country that it has been crippled as a political force. Free speech has destroyed it as an effective political party. . . .

How it can be said that there is a clear and present danger that this advocacy will succeed is, therefore, a mystery. Some nations less resilient than the United States, where illiteracy is high and where democratic traditions are only budding, might have to take drastic steps and jail these men for merely speaking their creed. But in America they are miserable merchants of unwanted ideas; their wares remain unsold. The fact that their ideas are abhorrent does not make them powerful. . . .

The First Amendment provides that "Congress shall make no law . . . abridging the freedom of speech." The Constitution provides no exception. . . . The First Amendment makes confidence in the common sense of our people and in their maturity of judgment the great postulate of our democracy. Its philosophy is that violence is rarely, if ever, stopped by denying civil liberties to those advocating resort to force. . . . The political

censor has no place in our public debates. Unless and until extreme and necessitous circumstances are shown, our aim should be to keep speech unfettered and to allow the processes of law to be invoked only when the provocateurs among us move from speech to action.

Vishinsky wrote in 1938 in The Law of the Soviet State, "In our state, naturally, there is and can be no place for freedom of speech, press, and so on for the foes of socialism."

Our concern should be that we accept no such standard for the United States. Our faith should be that our people will never give support to these advocates of revolution, so long as we remain loyal to the purposes for which our Nation was founded.

Once the convictions of the national leaders of the Communist party had been upheld by the Supreme Court, the Department of Justice began the prosecution of the "second string" or state leaders of the party. Conceivably, if these convictions had been upheld, it would have been legally possible to prosecute every individual member of the Communist party, under the Smith Act, upon the theory that all were parties to the same grand conspiracy to overthrow the government by force and violence, at the first opportune moment that might be presented. But it took another six years for the first of these cases involving the state leaders to reach the Supreme Court; and by that time, changes of considerable moment had taken place, both in the Court itself and in the country at large. McCarthyism had by this time been largely discredited and repudiated; and the climate of opinion that had supported such decisions as Feiner and Dennis was no more. The vote in Dennis had been 6-2 to uphold the convictions; in Yates v. United States, 354 U.S. 298 (1957), the vote in favor of upholding the convictions of the second-string Communists was only 1-6. The six-man majority of Dennis had disappeared completely in only six years: two were dead (Vinson and Jackson) and two retired (Reed and Minton), while the remaining two (Frankfurter and Burton) switched position as between the two cases. Clark, the lone dissenter in Yates from the reversal of the convictions,[14] voted consistently with the way he would have voted if he had participated in Dennis; and

[14] Technically, the majority in Yates ordered, in reversing the convictions of the defendants, that the indictments be dismissed with regard to five, while new trials be granted to the nine others. Black and Douglas concurred in the judgment of the Court respecting the five acquittals, but dissented from the remand directing a new trial for the others; these two justices thought that all of the defendants should have been acquitted. Clark, on the other hand, dissented because he believed that the convictions of all fourteen defendants should have been affirmed by the Court.

the votes of Black and Douglas remained consistent. Of the four justices who had come to the Court in the interim, two (Warren and Harlan) joined with Frankfurter, Burton, Black, and Douglas to form the new six-man majority; while the remaining two (Brennan and Whittaker) had joined the Court too late to participate in the decision.

As we pointed out earlier, the Court could have avoided the constitutional issues in the Dennis case by interpretation of the Smith Act; but at that time a majority wanted to place the imprimatur of the Court upon the Smith Act and the Medina trial. In Yates, however, the new majority chose to avoid resting its decision upon constitutional grounds; the Smith Act had been upheld in Dennis, and the Court announced that it was now following that precedent. In so doing, the new majority (speaking through Harlan) contrived the tour de force of quoting repeatedly from the opinions in Dennis in order to support an opposite decision on the merits. Lower federal courts and the Department of Justice, it now appeared, had not understood the underlying significance of the Dennis decision. For one thing, it appeared that when the word "organize" was used in the Smith Act, it referred to a single creative act, like Athena springing from the brow of Zeus with a mighty war cry and in complete armor, or like the transformation of Eve from Adam's rib. The Smith Act, as now construed by the Court, did not contemplate the continuing kind of politico-administrative activity essential to the survival of organizations in real life. Therefore, these second-string Communists were wrongfully convicted of having helped to "organize" the Communist party, since the party was "organized" in 1945 (replacing the Communist Political Association, which functioned during the era of good feeling between Uncle Joe and Uncle Sam, during World War II); and since the indictment was not filed until 1951, the defendants were protected against the "organizing" charge by the three-year federal statute of limitations.

An additional ground for reversal was that the trial judge had failed, in his charge to the jury, to emphasize sufficiently the difference between the mere "teaching" and the "advocacy" of Communist doctrine, the intent to incite being an essential element of the latter behavior. It is not without significance, in view of the fact that these convictions were reversed, that the Court did not rely upon the clear-and-present-danger test for its solution to the problems raised by this case; "clear and present danger" was relegated to a footnote, which merely announced that the Court found it unnecessary to give any consideration to what effect, if any, this dogma might have upon the case. To some observers, it looked as though the demise of the clear-and-present-danger rule was an essential precondition to the establishment by the Court of a constitutional policy of freedom of political expression.

A year earlier, the Court had taken a long step in the direction of the new policy of free political expression by striking down the state sedition acts, under which many state leaders of the Communist party were being prosecuted in proceedings parallel to, and based upon grounds identical to, those of the federal prosecutions which were the follow-up to the Dennis decision. In *Pennsylvania v. Nelson*, 350 U.S. 497 (1956), the Court gave an unusual twist to its commerce-clause precedents by following a few well-selected ones and voting 6-3 to invalidate the Pennsylvania Sedition Act, on the ground that Congress had *occupied the field* of extirpating Communists. The dominant interest of the national government in punishing "the knowing advocacy of the overthrow of the Government of the United States by force and violence," manifested in the Smith Act and subsequent amendatory acts of Congress, precluded (said the Court) the "intervention" and "interference" of the states with this federal program. The Court's decision was facilitated by the fact that the Pennsylvania Supreme Court had reached the same decision first, and had ruled against the state statute, so that the United States Supreme Court was able to affirm, instead of having to reverse, the decision below.

The combined result of Nelson and Yates, however, was essentially to negate the possibility of state prosecution of sedition, and to cause a drastic drop in the probability of successful federal prosecutions. Gitlow and Dennis had been overruled in effect, though not, of course, in form; few precedents would be likely to survive the kind of bear hug visited upon Dennis by Yates. Under the leadership of a libertarian Chief Justice and a reformed libertarian bloc, the Supreme Court appeared to be moving into a new era in which it would support free political expression as a civil liberty under the First and Fourteenth Amendments, at least to a greater extent than had been true in the past.

FREEDOM AND VIRTUE

The relativistic implications of the First Amendment for freedom of political expression hold also for the Court's vacillating policies in the area of aesthetic expression and appreciation. The Court has approved considerable intolerance of serious political debate under the assumption that the political security of the nation is a higher good that ought to be preferred. But what of public morality? If society has an important stake in a virtuous citizenry, does it follow that public morality can best be assured by "a bevy of Platonic Guardians," to use Learned Hand's phrase? It was for crimes against public morality that Socrates was forced to drink the hemlock, but there are important differences between the constitutional democracies of the Athenian city-state and the United States. If national security in the American polity is primarily a responsibility of the national government, is public morality primarily a responsibility of the states? Such premises argue against the use of the Fourteenth Amendment as a vehicle for striking down, in the name of personal aesthetic liberty, state legislation regulating public morals, and in favor of what lawyers call a strict construction of the limitations placed upon the national government by the First Amendment.

In practice, the Supreme Court manifested considerable tolerance of state regulation of morality until the 1940's, and had little or no occasion to consider congressional regulation, which arises primarily in conjunction with the regulation of interstate and foreign commerce and the use of the mails. In 1946, however, the Court reversed a decision of the Postmaster General, denying second-class mailing privileges to *Esquire* magazine on the ground that it failed to "contribute to the public good and the public welfare." The Court announced that *Esquire* did include some material that might be characterized as the "smoking room type of humor"—the choice of language implies good, clean, male fun— but that Congress had not intended to confer power on the Postmaster General to censor the mails, excepting, of course, matter that was legally obscene. And two years later, the Court invalidated a New York statute that penalized the distribution of magazines made up principally of stories of deeds of bloodshed, lust, or crime.[15] But shortly thereafter, the Court upheld New York's ban on the sale and distribution of *Memoirs of Hecate County,* whose author was Edmund Wilson, generally acclaimed as America's most distinguished literary critic.[16] Commenting upon this untoward result, under the caption "Depravity, Yes—Obscenity, No," Walter Berns has remarked: [17]

> . . . Surely if the Supreme Court justices were asked to determine the more vulgar, if not the more obscene, of the two publications, there would be unanimous agreement on *Headquarters Detective.* Surely if the Court were asked which publication constituted the greater threat to decency as this is understood in ordinary speech, *Headquarters Detective* would be the answer. Surely if the Court were asked which publication's clientele was more in need of paternal guidance by the State of New York, it could find a majority at least in favor of guidance for the readers of *Headquarters Detective.* On the basis of circulation alone [the first printing of the novel was 10,000 copies; the Hillman Detective group sells 675,000 copies monthly], *Headquarters Detective* is the more objectionable, since its stories reach a much larger audience. By whatever argument censorship is justified, it would seem that this magazine is more censorable than this novel.

With such seemingly incongruous decisions emanating from the Court in the same term, it seems warranted to ask what standards, beyond their individual

---

15 *Winters* v. *New York,* 333 U.S. 507 (1948). The decision was 6-3, with Frankfurter, Jackson, and Burton in dissent.

16 *Doubleday* v. *New York,* 335 U.S. 848 (1948). The judgment of the New York Court of Appeals was affirmed by an equally divided Supreme Court, with Justice Frankfurter not participating. Presumably, the

Libertarian Four (Murphy, Rutledge, Black, and Douglas) voted for reversal; so the two justices who voted differently in *Doubleday* than in *Winters* were Vinson and Reed.

17 *Op. cit.,* p. 41. For a thoughtful discussion of the Court's policies and decisions affecting censorship and morality, see *ibid.,* chaps. i and iii.

"prepossessions," guide the decision-making of the justices in the formulation of constitutional policy regarding aesthetic freedom?

In a subsequent decision, in 1952, the Court established the policy that "expression by means of motion pictures is included within the free speech and free press guaranty of the First and Fourteenth Amendments." [18] This overruled, in effect, a 1915 precedent of the Court which had ruled to the contrary. At the point in the Court's opinion in which the precedent was rejected, there is a footnote which suggests that "It is not without significance that talking pictures were first produced in 1926, eleven years after the [earlier] decision." The clear implication here is that the exhibition of silent movies did not qualify for constitutional protection because they involved only claims of freedom of the press; while talkies merited (after a hiatus of twenty-six years) recognition as a form of liberty under the Fourteenth Amendment because they are the technological analogue of *both* freedom of speech and freedom of the press. Such niceties contrast strangely with the Court's general reluctance to make any distinction between freedom of speech and freedom of the press, treating the twin concepts as isotopes. A policy in which constitutional rights hinge upon engineering developments places certain communicative acts and processes in the lap of chance,[19] as the decision of a federal district court demonstrates.[20]

The Court's more usual practice, of completely ignoring any differences in constitutional policy that might reasonably be called for by the differences between speaking and writing as forms of human behavior, is illustrated by Frankfurter's unanimous opinion for the Court in *Butler* v. *Michigan,* 352 U.S. 380 (1957). A Detroit newsdealer was convicted for the violation of a 116-year-old Michigan statute intended to protect the morals of school children; the defendant had sold to a police officer a paperback novel, *The Devil Rides Outside* by John Howard Griffin. According to an executive of the publisher (Pocket Books), this was a deliberate test case. The novel is concerned with the spiritual and earthly struggles of a young musician who, after experiencing the peace and solace of "the cloister within" the walls of a monastery, ultimately rejects the "concupiscent flesh" of the outer world—where the Devil rides.[21]

[18] *Burstyn* v. *Wilson,* 343 U.S. 495, 502 (1952).

[19] Compare the Supreme Court's fumbling treatment of such a technologically simple problem as audio amplification in the two sound-truck cases, *Saia* v. *New York,* 334 U.S. 558 (1948), and *Kovacs* v. *Cooper,* 336 U.S. 77 (1949).

[20] Elizabeth Bentley, while she was being interviewed on the "Meet the Press" television show, accused of having been a Communist, the late William Remington, whose legal right to recover damages depended upon whether the law of slander or the law of libel applied. A federal district court decided that Mrs. Bentley's remarks were "slanderous *per se*," since television was more like radio (slander) than moving pictures (libel). *Remington* v. *Bentley,* 88 F. Supp. 166, 169 (S.D.N.Y., 1949). Presumably, if the telecast had been filmed, the outcome might have been different since, logically, the law of libel should apply (under the distinction made by the court) to filmed telecasts, and the law of slander to "live" shows. But how, pray tell, would the courts decide to analogize "taped" telecasts?

[21] The publishers' estimate of the general interests of readers of this story is suggested by the titles of the three books advertised

According to the opinion of the Court, the defense rested specifically on the proposition that the Michigan statutes "unduly restricted freedom of *speech* as protected by the Due Process Clause of the Fourteenth Amendment." But there was no speech involved in this case; and the Michigan statute clearly applied to materials that were written, printed, or photographed—not to oral communication. The Supreme Court agreed with the defendant, however, remarking that "The incidence of this enactment is to reduce the adult population of Michigan to reading only what is fit for children." And so the constitutional right (of freedom of speech?) to read Mickey Spillane as well as John Howard Griffin became "one of those liberties of the individual, now enshrined in the Due Process Clause of the Fourteenth Amendment, that history has attested as the indispensable conditions for the maintenance and progress of a free society."

But there had to be some limits, and they appeared in three decisions that were announced only five months later. A majority of the justices who had participated in the Court's 1948 decision, which affirmed New York's ban on Edmund Wilson's novel, had by this time been replaced by others; but as Chapter 2 demonstrates, the new justices were the products of the same basic socioeconomic background as those who had departed from the Court in the interim. The inarticulate standard which justified the approval of *Headquarters Detective* and *The Devil Rides Outside* and the disapproval of *Memoirs of Hecate County* became explicit in the three decisions of June, 1957. An unwholesome interest in or portrayal of sex was contrary to public morality, and therefore "beyond the scope" of the freedom protected by the First Amendment (i.e., by the Supreme Court).[22] It is true that the legal term for this subject is "obscenity" rather than "sex"; but a reading of judicial opinions which interpret "obscenity" as a statutory term makes it clear that the social values and human behaviors that judges generally, and a majority of the Supreme Court specifically, associate with "a wholesome interest in sex" are those reported by Louisa May Allcott, not the late Dr. Kinsey. Here, at least, is an area where the research of social psychologists has not unduly swayed the judgment of the Court.

It is also true that the "Miracle" case in 1952, extending the freedom of the First Amendment to include (talking) moving pictures, dealt on its facts with what some considered to be a sexual theme (seduction and consequent childbirth out of wedlock) and was exhibited as part of a trilogy entitled *Ways of Love*; but the specific charge against the film was that it was "sacrilegious." The Court agreed unanimously that "sacrilegious" was too vague a standard to meet the requirements of due process as a standard for censorship; but the opinion of the majority took pains to point out that "it is not necessary for us to decide . . . whether a state may censor motion pictures under a clearly drawn statute designed and applied to prevent the showing of obscene films." A similar dictum

---

on the inside of the rear cover: *The Confessions of Saint Augustine, The Cardinal,* and

Napoleon.
[22] Cf. Berns, *op. cit.,* p. 41.

had appeared in a contemporaneous case, in which the Court had justified the exclusion of libelous speech from the protection of the Fourteenth Amendment on the ground that libel, like obscenity, is "no essential part of any exposition of ideas, and [is] of such slight social value as a step to truth that any benefit that may be derived . . . is clearly outweighed by the social interest in order and morality." [23] As we shall see, in the cases presented below, the Court developed the same kind of inter-dictum feedback that had been employed, at an earlier time, to justify a constitutional policy of racial segregation. Segregated transportation was justified because segregated public education was widespread; later, segregated public education was justified because segregation in transportation was constitutional. Similarly, libel was not a protected form of communicative behavior because obscenity was not; later, there was no necessity for proof that an obscene publication had in fact stimulated antisocial conduct on the part of its readers, because the clear-and-present-danger test was irrelevant in the case of *libelous* utterances.

In *Kingsley Books* v. *Brown*, 354 U.S. 436 (1957), the Court upheld by a 5-4 vote the decision of a New York state judge, sitting without a jury, that some paperback booklets entitled *Nights of Horror* were clearly obscene. Although obscenity, unlike sacrilege, is a legal term with a well-understood technical legal meaning, the trial judge explained what he meant by invoking the amplifying phrase that is so frequently employed in judicial opinions which undertake to explicate the term: "dirt for dirt's sake." But the major concern of the Supreme Court in this case was not with whether obscenity was sufficiently precise to meet due-process requirements—this was taken for granted—but rather was with the New York procedure which put on trial the book instead of its distributor.

Two other cases decided on the same day were joined for common disposition. As we pointed out in regard to the mandate decision in the School Segregation Cases, such a procedure has interesting implications, since one of the cases challenged a federal statute and the other was a state case. Their combination for joint decision certainly suggests that the Court considered to be identical the relevant policy norms associated, respectively, with the First and Fourteenth Amendments. Particularly does this comment seem justified in view of the fact that one of the justices argues vigorously and (though not so, obviously, to his colleagues) persuasively that the federal case and the state case ought to be judged by different standards, and decided oppositely. The Court's joinder of the two cases for common decision and the same disposition in the face of this argument is further evidence of the extent to which the First Amendment has become nationalized and incorporated as a part of the Fourteenth.

23 *Beauharnais* v. *Illinois,* 343 U.S. 250, 257 (1952).

ROTH v. UNITED STATES
(No. 582)
ALBERTS v. CALIFORNIA
(No. 61)

354 U.S. 476 (June 24, 1957).

Certiorari to the United States Court of Appeals for the Second Circuit, and on appeal from the Superior Court of Los Angeles County, Appellate Department, State of California.

Both *affirmed*.

	Roth: 6-3	Alberts: 7-2
Brennan	('+')	('+')
Frankfurter	(+)	(+)
Burton	(+)	(+)
Clark	(+)	(+)
Whittaker	(+)	(+)
Warren, C.J.	('+'	('+'
Harlan	'—')	('+'
Douglas	'—')	'—')
Black	—)	—)

MR. JUSTICE BRENNAN delivered the opinion of the Court.

The constitutionality of a criminal obscenity statute is the question in each of these cases. In *Roth,* the primary constitutional question is whether the federal obscenity statute violates the provision of the First Amendment that "Congress shall make no law . . . abridging the freedom of speech, or of the press. . . ." In *Alberts,* the primary constitutional question is whether the obscenity provisions of the California Penal Code invade the freedoms of speech and press as they may be incorporated in the liberty protected from state action by the Due Process Clause of the Fourteenth Amendment. . . .

Roth conducted a business in New York in the publication and sale of books, photographs and magazines. He used circulars and advertising matter to solicit sales. He was convicted by a jury in the District Court for the Southern District of New York upon 4 counts of a 26-count indictment charging him with mailing obscene circulars and advertising, and an obscene book, in violaton of the federal obscenity statute. . . .

Alberts conducted a mail-order business from Los Angeles. He was convicted by the Judge of the Municipal Court of the Beverly Hills Judicial District (having waived a jury trial) under a misdemeanor complaint which charged him with lewdly keeping for sale obscene and indecent books, and with writing, composing and publishing an obscene advertisement of them, in violation of the California Penal Code. . . .

The dispositive question is whether obscenity is utterance within the area of protected speech and press.[24] Although this is the first time the question has been squarely presented to this Court, either under the First Amendment or under the Fourteenth Amendment, expressions found in numerous opinions indicate that this Court has always assumed that obscenity is not protected by the freedoms of speech and press. . . .

The protection given speech and press was fashioned to assure unfettered interchange of ideas for the bringing about of political and social changes desired by the people. . . .

All ideas having even the slightest redeeming social importance—unorthodox ideas, controversial ideas, even ideas hateful to the prevailing climate of opinion—have the full protection of the guaranties, unless excludable because they encroach upon the limited area of more important interests. But implicit in the history of the First Amendment is the rejection of obscenity as utterly without redeeming social importance. . . . We hold that obscenity is not within the

[24] No issue is presented in either case concerning the obscenity of the material involved. [Footnote by the Court.]

area of constitutionally protected speech or press.

It is strenuously urged that these obscenity statutes offend the constitutional guaranties because they punish incitation to impure sexual *thoughts,* not shown to be related to any overt antisocial conduct which is or may be incited in the persons stimulated to such *thoughts.* In *Roth,* the trial judge instructed the jury: "The words 'obscene, lewd and lascivious' as used in the law, signify that form of immorality which has relation to sexual impurity and has a tendency to excite lustful *thoughts.*" (Emphasis added.) In *Alberts,* the trial judge applied the test . . . whether the material has "a substantial tendency to deprave or corrupt its readers by inciting lascivious *thoughts* or arousing lustful desires." (Emphasis added.) It is insisted that the constitutional guaranties are violated because convictions may be had without proof either that obscene material will perceptibly create a clear and present danger of antisocial conduct, or will probably induce its recipients to such conduct.[25] But, in light of our holding that obscenity is not protected speech, the complete answer to this argument is in the holding of this Court in *Beauharnais* v. *Illinois, supra,* at 266:

> "Libelous utterances not being within the area of constitutionally protected speech, it is unnecessary, either for us or for the State courts, to consider the issues behind the phrase 'clear and present danger.' Certainly no one would contend that obscene speech, for example, may be punished only upon a showing of such circumstances. Libel, as we have seen, is in the same class."

However, sex and obscenity are not synonymous. Obscene material is material which deals with sex in a manner

[25] *Dennis* v. *United States,* 341 U.S. 494. . . . [Footnote by the Court.]

appealing to prurient interest.[26] The portrayal of sex, *e. g.,* in art, literature and scientific works, is not itself sufficient reason to deny material the constitutional protection of freedom of speech and press. Sex, a great and mysterious motive force in human life, has indisputably been a subject of absorbing interest to mankind through the ages; it is one of the vital problems of human interest and public concern. . . .

In summary, then, we hold that these statutes, applied according to the proper standard for judging obscenity, do not offend constitutional safeguards against convictions based upon protected material, or fail to give men in acting adequate notice of what is prohibited.

Roth's argument that the federal obscenity statute unconstitutionally encroaches upon the powers reserved by the Ninth and Tenth Amendments to the States and to the people to punish speech and press where offensive to decency and morality is hinged upon his contention that obscenity is expression not excepted from the sweep of the provision of the First Amendment that "*Congress shall* make *no law* . . . abridging the freedom of speech, or of the press. . . ." (Emphasis added.) That argument falls in light

[26] I.e., material having a tendency to excite lustful thoughts. Webster's New International Dictionary (Unabridged, 2d ed., 1949) defines *prurient,* in pertinent part, as follows: ". . . Itching; longing; uneasy with desire or longing; of persons having itching, morbid, or lascivious longings; of desire, curiosity, or propensity, lewd. . . ."
Pruriency is defined, in pertinent part, as follows: ". . . Quality of being prurient; lascivious desire or thought. . . ." . . . We perceive no significant difference between the meaning of obscenity developed in the case law and the definition of the A.L.I., Model Penal Code . . . :
". . . A thing is obscene if, considered as a whole, its predominant appeal is to prurient interest, i.e., a shameful or morbid interest in nudity, sex, or excretion, and if it goes substantially beyond customary limits of candor in description or representation of such matters. . . ." [Footnote by the Court.]

of our holding that obscenity is not expression protected by the First Amendment.[27] . . .

The judgments are

Affirmed.

MR. CHIEF JUSTICE WARREN, concurring in the result. . . .

The line dividing the salacious or pornographic from literature or science is not straight and unwavering. Present laws depend largely upon the effect that the materials may have upon those who receive them. It is manifest that the same object may have a different impact, varying according to the part of the community it reached. But there is more to these cases. It is not the book that is on trial; it is a person. The conduct of the defendant is the central issue, not the obscenity of a book or picture. The nature of the materials is, of course, relevant as an attribute of the defendant's conduct, but the materials are thus placed in context from which they draw color and character. A wholly different result might be reached in a different setting.

The personal element in these cases is seen most strongly in the requirement of *scienter.* Under the California law, the prohibited activity must be done "wilfully and lewdly." The federal statute limits the crime to acts done "knowingly." In his charge to the jury, the district judge stated that the matter must be "calculated" to corrupt or debauch. The defendants in both cases were engaged in the business of purveying textual or graphic matter openly advertised to appeal to the erotic interest of their customers. They were plainly engaged in the commercial exploitation of the morbid and shameful craving for materials

27 For the same reason, we reject, in this case, the argument that there is greater latitude for state action under the word "liberty" under the Fourteenth Amendment than is allowed to Congress by the language of the First Amendment. [Footnote by the Court.]

with prurient effect. I believe that the State and Federal Governments can constitutionally punish such conduct. That is all that these cases present to us, and that is all we need to decide.

MR. JUSTICE HARLAN, concurring in the result in No. 61, and dissenting in No. 582. . . .

In judging the constitutionality of this conviction, we should remember that our function in reviewing state judgments under the Fourteenth Amendment is a narrow one. We do not decide whether the policy of the State is wise, or whether it is based on assumptions scientifically substantiated. We can inquire only whether the state action so subverts the fundamental liberties implicit in the Due Process Clause that it cannot be sustained as a rational exercise of power. See Jackson, J., dissenting in *Beauharnais* v. *Illinois,* 343 U.S. 250, 287. The States' power to make printed words criminal is, of course, confined by the Fourteenth Amendment, but only insofar as such power is inconsistent with our concepts of "ordered liberty." *Palko* v. *Connecticut,* 302 U.S. 319, 324-325.

What, then, is the purpose of this California statute? Clearly the state legislature has made the judgment that printed words *can* "deprave or corrupt" the reader—that words can incite to antisocial or immoral action. The assumption seems to be that the distribution of certain types of literature will induce criminal or immoral sexual conduct. It is well known, of course, that the validity of this assumption is a matter of dispute among critics, sociologists, psychiatrists, and penologists. There is a large school of thought, particularly in the scientific community, which denies any causal connection between the reading of pornography and immorality, crime, or delinquency. Others disagree. Clearly it is not our function to decide this question. That function belongs to the state legislature. Nothing in the Constitution requires California to accept as truth the most advanced and sophisticated psychiatric opinion. It seems to me clear that it is not irrational, in our present state of knowledge, to consider that pornography can induce a type of sexual conduct which a State may deem obnoxious to the moral fabric of society. In fact the very division of opinion on the subject counsels us to respect the choice made by the State.

Furthermore, even assuming that pornography cannot be deemed ever to cause, in an immediate sense, criminal sexual conduct, other interests within the proper cognizance of the States may be protected by the prohibition placed on such materials. The State can reasonably draw the inference that over a long period of time the indiscriminate dissemination of materials, the essential character of which is to degrade sex, will have an eroding effect on moral standards. And the State has a legitimate interest in protecting the privacy of the home against invasion of unsolicited obscenity.

Above all stands the realization that we deal here with an area where knowledge is small, data are insufficient, and experts are divided. Since the domain of sexual morality is pre-eminently a matter of state concern, this Court should be slow to interfere with state legislation calculated to protect that morality. It seems to me that nothing in the broad and flexible command of the Due Process Clause forbids California to prosecute one who sells books whose dominant tendency might be to "deprave or corrupt" a reader. I agree with the Court, of course, that the books must be judged as a whole and in relation to the normal adult reader.

What has been said, however, does not dispose of the case. It still remains for us to decide whether the state court's determination that this material should be suppressed is consistent with the Fourteenth Amendment; and that, of course, presents a federal question as to which we, and not the state court, have the ulti-

mate responsibility. And so, in the final analysis, I concur in the judgment because, upon an independent perusal of the material involved, and in light of the considerations discussed above, I cannot say that its suppression would so interfere with the communication of "ideas" in any proper sense of that term that it would offend the Due Process Clause. I therefore agree with the Court that appellant's conviction must be affirmed.

I dissent in . . . *Roth* v. *United States.*

We are faced here with the question whether the federal obscenity statute, as construed and applied in this case, violates the First Amendment to the Constitution. To me, this question is of quite a different order than one where we are dealing with state legislation under the Fourteenth Amendment. I do not think it follows that state and federal powers in this area are the same, and that just because the State may suppress a particular utterance, it is automatically permissible for the Federal Government to do the same. I agree with Mr. Justice Jackson that the historical evidence does not bear out the claim that the Fourteenth Amendment "incorporates" the First in any literal sense. See *Beauharnais* v. *Illinois, supra.*[28] But laying aside any con-

[28] "The assumption of other dissents is that the 'liberty' which the Due Process Clause of the Fourteenth Amendment protects against denial by the States is the literal and identical 'freedom of speech or of the press' which the First Amendment forbids only Congress to abridge. The history of criminal libel in America convinces me that the Fourteenth Amendment did not 'incorporate' the First, that the powers of Congress and of the States over this subject are not of the same dimensions, and that because Congress probably could not enact this law it does not follow that the States may not. . . . The inappropriateness of a single standard for restricting State and Nation is indicated by the disparity between their functions and duties in relation to those freedoms. Criminality of defamation is predicated upon power either to protect the private right to enjoy integrity of reputation or the public

sequences which might flow from that conclusion, cf. Mr. Justice Holmes in *Gitlow* v. *New York,* 268 U.S. 652, 672,[29] I prefer to rest my views about this case on broader and less abstract grounds.

The Constitution differentiates between those areas of human conduct subject to the regulation of the States and those subject to the powers of the Federal Government. The substantive powers of the two governments, in many instances, are distinct. And in every case where we are called upon to balance the interest in free expression against other interests, it seems to me important that we should keep in the forefront the question of whether those other interests are state or federal. Since under our constitutional scheme the two are not necessarily equivalent, the balancing process must needs often produce different results. Whether a particular limitation on speech or press is to be upheld because it subserves a paramount governmental interest must, to a large extent, I think, de-

right to tranquility. Neither of these are objects of federal cognizance except when necessary to the accomplishment of some delegated power, such as protection of interstate commerce. When the Federal Government puts liberty of press in one scale, it has a very limited duty to personal reputation or local tranquillity to weigh against it in the other. But state action affecting speech or press can and should be weighed against and reconciled with these conflicting social interests. For these reasons I should not, unless clearly required, confirm to the Federal Government such latitude as I think a State reasonably may require for orderly government of its manifold concerns. The converse of the proposition is that I would not limit the power of the State with the severity appropriately prescribed for federal power." 343 U.S. 250, 288, 294-295 (1952).

29 "The general principle of free speech, it seems to me, must be taken to be included in the Fourteenth Amendment, in view of the scope that has been given to the word 'liberty' as there used, although perhaps it may be accepted with a somewhat larger latitude of interpretation than is allowed to Congress by the sweeping language that governs or ought to govern the laws of the United States."

pend on whether that government has, under the Constitution, a direct substantive interest, that is, the power to act, in the particular area involved.

The Federal Government has, for example, power to restrict seditious speech directed against it, because that Government certainly has the substantive authority to protect itself against revolution. Cf. *Pennsylvania* v. *Nelson,* 350 U.S. 497. But in dealing with obscenity we are faced with the converse situation, for the interests which obscenity statutes purportedly protect are primarily entrusted to the care, not of the Federal Government, but of the States. Congress has no substantive power over sexual morality. Such powers as the Federal Government has in this field are but incidental to its other powers, here the postal power, and are not of the same nature as those possessed by the States, which bear direct responsibility for the protection of the local moral fabric. . . .

MR. JUSTICE DOUGLAS, with whom MR. JUSTICE BLACK concurs, dissenting. . . .

The tests by which these convictions were obtained require only the arousing of sexual thoughts. Yet the arousing of sexual thoughts and desires happens every day in normal life in dozens of ways. Nearly 30 years ago a questionnaire sent to college and normal school women graduates asked what things were most stimulating sexually. Of 409 replies, 9 said "music"; 18 said "pictures"; 29 said "dancing"; 40 said "drama"; 95 said "books"; and 218 said "man." Alpert, Judicial Censorship of Obscene Literature, 52 Harv. L. Rev. 40, 73. . . .

The absence of dependable information on the effect of obscene literature on human conduct should make us wary. It should put us on the side of protecting society's interest in literature, except and unless it can be said that the particular publication has an impact on action that the government can control.

As noted, the trial judge in the *Roth*

case charged the jury in the alternative that the federal obscenity statute outlaws literature dealing with sex which offends "the common conscience of the community." That standard is, in my view, more inimical still to freedom of expression.

The standard of what offends "the common conscience of the community" conflicts, in my judgment, with the command of the First Amendment that "Congress shall make no law . . . abridging the freedom of speech, or of the press." Certainly that standard would not be an acceptable one if religion, economics, politics or philosophy were involved. How does it become a constitutional standard when literature treating with sex is concerned?

Any test that turns on what is offensive to the community's standards is too loose, too capricious, too destructive of freedom of expression to be squared with the First Amendment. Under that test, juries can censor, suppress, and punish what they don't like, provided the matter relates to "sexual impurity" or has a tendency "to excite lustful thoughts." This is community censorship in one of its worst forms.

It creates a regime where in the battle between the literati and the Philistines, the Philistines are certain to win. If experience in this field teaches anything, it is that "censorship of obscenity has almost always been both irrational and indiscriminate."

. . . I reject too the implication that problems of freedom of speech and of the press are to be resolved by weighing against the values of free expression, the judgment of the Court that a particular form of that expression has "no redeeming social importance." The First Amendment, its prohibition in terms absolute, was designed to preclude courts as well as legislatures from weighing the values of speech against silence. The First Amendment puts free speech in the preferred position. . . .

I would give the broad sweep of the First Amendment full support. I have the same confidence in the ability of our people to reject noxious literature as I have in their capacity to sort out the true from the false in theology, economics, politics, or any other field.

Two years later, however, the Court unanimously indicated that it was only obscenity—"hard-core pornography"—that was "beyond the scope of the protection" of the First and Fourteenth Amendments. The New York courts had upheld the denial of a license for the exhibition of *Lady Chatterley's Lover,* a film based upon the by now almost classic novel by D. H. Lawrence, a book which has been read by several generations of undergraduates in college courses in English literature. The New York Court of Appeals "unanimously and explicitly rejected any notion that the film is obscene"; but agreed (4-3) that the movie was "immoral," not because of the three isolated scenes to which the licensing authority had objected but rather because the picture as a whole "alluringly portrays adultery as proper behavior." A majority consisting of the four libertarians plus Potter Stewart joined in an opinion written by the freshman justice which invalidated the state statute, on the explicit authority of *Burstyn* v. *Wilson.*[30] There were also four concurring opinions, of which the principal one (by Har-

[30] *Kingsley International Pictures Corp.* v. *Regents of the University of the State of New York,* 360 U.S. 684 (June 29, 1959). As was becoming increasingly usual, a group of senators (this time, five Democrats) at once sponsored a proposed constitutional amendment to overrule the decision.

lan,[31] Frankfurter, and Whittaker) argued that the Court should have reversed the application of the statute to this particular movie rather than declaring the statute to be unconstitutional.

Frankfurter also penned an individual concurrence, in which he noted: [32]

> As one whose taste in art and literature hardly qualified him for the *avant-garde*, I am more than surprised, after viewing the picture, that the New York authorities should have banned "Lady Chatterley's Lover." To assume that this motion picture would have offended Victorian moral sensibilities is to rely only on the stuffiest of Victorian conventions. . . .

He added that D. H. Lawrence himself had advocated the censorship of genuine pornography, the author of *Love Among the Haystacks* remarking of "feelthy peetchur" post cards that: "Ugly and cheap they make the human nudity, ugly and degraded they make the sexual act, trivial and cheap and nasty."

Black rejoined that, unlike his colleagues, he had not seen the picture because he agreed with Douglas that prior censorship of moving pictures was unconstitutional on its face as a form of previous restraint. As for the case-by-case approach advocated by the right-wing triumvirate, under which the Supreme Court would decide for itself, after viewing a film, whether it was "immoral," "obscene," "appealing to the prurient interest," sexy in an "unwholesome" way, "art for art's sake," or "dirt for money's sake," Black concluded that [33]

> The different standards which different people may use to decide about the badness of pictures are well illustrated by the contrasting standards mentioned in the opinion of the New York Court of Appeals and the concurring opinion of Mr. Justice Frankfurter here. As I read the New York court's opinion this movie was held immoral and banned because it makes adultery too alluring. Mr. Justice Frankfurter quotes Mr. Lawrence, author of the book from which the movie was made, as believing censorship should be applied only to publications that make sex look ugly, that is, as I understand it, less alluring.
>
> In my judgment, this Court should not permit itself to get into the very center of such policy controversies, which have so little in common with lawsuits.

It seems unlikely, however, that a majority of the Court will agree to the libertarian constitutional policy of aesthetic freedom advocated by Black and Douglas. The alternative would be the case-by-case approach, leaving the Court

---

[31] In concurring, Harlan seemed to disregard his own recent dictum in the Roth case, in which he ventured to remark that "if the people of one State, through their legislature, decide that 'Lady Chatterley's Lover' goes so far beyond the acceptable standards of candor that it will be deemed offensive and non-sellable, . . . the State next door is still free to make its own choice. . . . The fact that the people of one State cannot read some of the works of D. H. Lawrence seems to me, if not wise or desirable, at least acceptable." 354 U.S. 476, 506 (1957).

[32] *Ibid.*, pp. 691-692.

[33] *Ibid.*, p. 691.

free to choose appropriate cases, as substantial minorities of four (or more) jus, tices might see fit, from among the abundant variety docketed each term. Almost contemporaneous with the announcement of the Court's decision upholding the Lady Chatterley *movie,* for instance, Postmaster General Summerfield announced that he was banning the *book* from the mails, having come to the conclusion that the unexpurgated version of Lawrence's literary classic was obscene. In the following month, however, the federal district court in New York City granted an injunction against the enforcement of the postal ban on the novel. As the direct result of all of this priceless publicity, sales of several unexpurgated editions of the novel—hardbound and paperback—zoomed to unprecedented heights.

In the same week as the Court's decision regarding the Lady Chatterley movie, the Mayor of Chicago announced that as the result of his own viewing of the premiere of another much-publicized moving picture (complete with sound), he was going to take steps to have the film banned in his city as obscene. This movie was based upon Robert Traver's best-selling novel, *Anatomy of a Murder,* which included frank courtroom discussion of testimony and other evidence bearing upon the rape and murder which jointly provide the background for the trial with which the book is concerned. It was also well-known that "Robert Traver" was the nom de plume of John D. Voelker, a justice of the Michigan Supreme Court.

It was tempting to speculate what the United States Supreme Court would do if it were presented simultaneously with one case involving federal censorship on obscenity grounds of a book, the movie version of which already had received the *non obstante* of the Court; and with a second case involving state censorship of a movie based upon a book written by a state supreme court justice upon a subject—a trial at law—that Supreme Court justices would be likely to consider (like legal education) peculiarly within the area of their own sociopsychological *expertise.* Surely, neither of these works could be considered "hard-core pornography." But would the Court say that either the book, *Lady Chatterley's Lover,* or the movie, *Anatomy of a Murder,* appealed to the "prurient interest"? If so, to whose prurient interest would the work have appealed?

THE PREFERRED POSITION OF
FIRST-CLASS RIGHTS

From the appointment of Wiley Rutledge on February 15, 1943, until the death of Chief Justice Harlan Stone on April 22, 1946, there were five libertarians on the Court: Rutledge, Murphy, Stone, Black, and Douglas. During, and only during, this fleeting three-year period, the libertarian bloc commanded an absolute majority of votes on the Court, for the first and only time in American political history. It happened that these were years in which the nation was engaged in a great war, which is significant to note because of the customary repression of civil liberties in wartime. And during this three-year period, the Court applied in a few of its decisions a constitutional policy that has come to be known as the "preferred-position doctrine." Apologists of the left frequently argue that the policy was in effect for a longer period of time than we have specified; and critics of the right sometimes deny that the policy ever was in effect, in the sense that it commanded the support of a clear majority of the justices. With all due respect for the views of a trained and experienced participant-observer in the events,[34] it must be said that the facts support the position of neither friends nor foes of the doctrine. It was the policy of the Court, and for a very brief time only.

Simply stated, the essence of the preferred-position doctrine was that legislation—whether by Congress or a state was immaterial—was more likely to be declared unconstitutional by the Court if it affected the exercise of First Amendment freedoms. Ordinarily, according to the Court, the so-called burden of proof is upon one who invokes a claim of constitutional right as the basis for asking the Court to invalidate a statute, because the judiciary must always presume that a co-ordinate branch of the government (or in the alternative, the duly elected representatives of the people of the states in a federal system) has acted within the scope of its legitimate authority. But when the civil-liberty claim was based upon a First Amendment freedom, then there was a shifting of the burden of proof from the claimant *toward* the government. This is not quite the same thing as to say that "legislation touching First Amendment rights is presumed to be unconstitutional." Unquestionably, some among the many justices who at one time or another associated themselves with some form of preferred-position statement meant that such a presumption ought to apply; but most of them probably meant considerably less than that. Why should it be assumed, as it is in most discussions of the subject, that the policy necessarily meant the same thing at all times to all of the justices? It is much more likely that the doctrine never implied quite the same thing to any two of the justices at any one time, and that it meant different things to each individual justice at different times. We think the most accurate form of statement is to say that for a short time a majority of the justices felt more strongly than has been customary for the Court that First Amendment freedoms are more fundamental than other civil liberties and ought, therefore, to be enforced more strictly.

If the result of the policy was to convert First Amendment freedoms into "first-class" rights, and consequently to relegate other civil liberties to the status of "second-class" or "third-class" rights,[35] it may be that the Court was articulat-

---

[34] Mr. Justice Frankfurter, concurring in *Kovacs* v. *Cooper*, 336, U.S. 77 (1949).

[35] Mr. Justice Jackson, dissenting in *Brinegar* v. *United States*, 338 U.S. 160, 180 (1949): "We cannot give some constitutional rights a preferred position without relegating others to a deferred position. We can establish no firsts without thereby establishing seconds. Indications are not wanting that Fourth Amendment freedoms are tacitly marked as secondary rights. . . ."

ing and stating as a general policy something that each individual justice does anyhow. It is very easy to demonstrate, by scalogram analysis and other research techniques,[36] that each justice individually, and the Court collectively, has a hierarchy of values which affect the responses of the justices (i.e., their voting behavior) to the cases that confront them for decision. Such hierarchies may shift through time, for the Court as a group as well as for individual justices. Therefore, at any point in time for the Court, there is always a set of gradations which reflect the relative enthusiasm with which the justices will support specific civil liberties, ranging from Class 1 through classes 2, 3, 4, . . . n. During the period 1943 through 1946, First Amendment freedoms were in Class 1 for a majority of the justices.

One other comment seems warranted before we turn to the rise and fall of the doctrine. Obviously, the notion of First Amendment incorporation was a necessary condition precedent to the preferred-position doctrine. The indiscriminate talk about *First Amendment* freedoms in opinions that discuss the preferred-position doctrine could be misleading to one who did not realize that the doctrine was *never* applied to acts of Congress during World War II. It was invoked only in state cases; and it must, in candor, be recorded that the triumphs of the policy were without exception over relatively unimportant local matters: whether school children could be coerced to salute the flag, whether peddlers of religious literature could be forced to submit to municipal licensing systems, whether a visiting labor leader could be required to apply for a permit before making a speech in which he invited workingmen to join the union. This was the heyday of the Jehovah's Witnesses litigious activities, and many of the cases involved the activities of this evangelistic sect. The offenses at issue generally involved misdemeanors, not serious crimes.

As usually is the case, the preferred-position policy began in dicta and ended in dissent and occasional lip service by the majority. Its origins are usually associated with Mr. Justice Cardozo's opinion for a unanimous Court in *Palko* v. *Connecticut,* 302 U.S. 319 (1937). The question in that case (which is presented in Chapter 11) related to the double-jeopardy clause of the Fifth Amendment, which the Court decided was not a fundamental element of due process. By way of contrast, Cardozo remarked that "we reach a different plane of social and moral values when we pass to . . . freedom of thought and speech . . . [which] is the matrix, the indispensable condition, of nearly every other form of freedom." [37] And only four months later in the same term, Hughes, Roberts, and Brandeis joined in an opinion by Stone which included, in a case otherwise concerned with federal regulation of milk adulteration under the commerce clause, the following footnote: [38]

[36] See Glendon A. Schubert, *Quantitative Analysis of Judicial Behavior* (Glencoe: The Free Press, 1959), chap. v.

[37] 302 U.S. 326-327.

[38] *United States* v. *Carolene Products Co.,* 304 U.S. 144, 152-153 fn. 4 (1938).

There may be narrower scope for operation of the presumption of constitutionality when legislation appears on its face to be within a specific prohibition of the Constitution, such as those of the first ten amendments, which are deemed equally specific when held to be embraced within the Fourteenth. . . .

It is unnecessary to consider now whether legislation which restricts those political processes which can ordinarily be expected to bring about repeal of undesirable legislation, is to be subjected to more exacting judicial scrutiny under the general prohibitions of the Fourteenth Amendment than are most other types of legislation. . . .

Nor need we enquire whether similar considerations enter into the review of statutes directed at particular religious . . . or national . . . or racial minorities . . . : whether prejudice against discrete and insular minorities may be a special condition, which tends seriously to curtail the operation of those political processes ordinarily to be relied upon to protect minorities, and which may call for a correspondingly more searching judicial inquiry. . . .

Cardozo, who (it may reasonably be assumed) would have agreed with the opinion and the footnote, was absent from the Court due to fatal illness, and did not participate in the decision. Black, whose first-term behavior was somewhat deviant from what subsequently became his defined position, accepted all of the opinion *except* the part that included the footnote. But the footnote was, in any event, merely a dictum, introduced (according to *post hoc* testimony) by Louis Lusky, who was Stone's law clerk at the time.[39]

Jackson's opinion in *West Virginia State Board of Education* v. *Barnette*, 319 U.S. 624 (1943), is doubtless the most eloquent, but the Rutledge opinion for the Court in *Thomas* v. *Collins*, 323 U.S. 516 (1945), is generally considered to be the most extreme statement in support of the preferred-position doctrine. The Libertarian Four lost Chief Justice Stone's vote in the latter case, but Jackson concurred and supplied the decisive vote in the 5-4 decision. "The case," said Rutledge,[40]

confronts us again with the duty our system places on this Court to say where the individual's freedom ends and the State's power begins. Choice on that border, now as always delicate, is perhaps more so where the usual presumption supporting legislation is balanced by the preferred place given in our scheme to the great, the indispensable democratic freedoms secured by the First Amendment. . . . That priority gives these liberties a sanctity and a sanction not permitting dubious intrusions. And it is the character of the right, not of the limitations, which determines what standard governs the choice. Compare *United States* v. *Carolene Products Co.*, 304 U.S. 144, 152-153.

---

39 Mason, *op. cit.*, p. 513.   40 323 U.S. 516, 529-530, 540.

For these reasons any attempt to restrict those liberties must be justified by clear public interest, threatened not doubtfully or remotely, but by clear and present danger. The rational connection between the remedy provided and the evil to be curbed, which in other contexts might support legislation against attack on due process grounds, will not suffice. These rights rest on firmer foundation. Accordingly, whatever occasion would restrain orderly discussion and persuasion, at appropriate time and place, must have clear support in public danger, actual or impending. Only the gravest abuses, endangering paramount interests, give occasion for permissible limitation. . . . We think a requirement that one must register before he undertakes to make a public speech to enlist support for a lawful movement is quite incompatible with the requirements of the First Amendment.

As we shall see again shortly in Jackson's opinion in the Barnette case, the clear-and-present-danger doctrine, incorporation theory, and the preferred-position doctrine have coalesced in Rutledge's opinion to supply the presumption against the validity of legislation that Frankfurter later said, in his concurrence in *Kovacs* v. *Cooper,* "has never commended itself to a majority of this Court." [41] However tenuous may have been the majority in *Thomas* v. *Collins,* an absolutely clear-cut majority of six justices accepted the preferred position in the Barnette case.[42]

FREEDOM OF RELIGION

There is no constitutional guarantee of "freedom of belief," as such. What the First Amendment says is that "Congress shall make no law respecting an establishment of religion, or prohibiting the free exercise thereof. . . ." Assuming the nationalization of the First Amendment that we already have discovered in the freedom of speech-and-press cases, there would appear to be two quite different issues of constitutional policy for the Court to resolve:

1. What degree of integration between church and state constitutes "establishment"?

2. How much nonconformity should be tolerated in the name of the "free exercise" of religion?

We shall deal with these two questions in reverse order, as that is the sequence in which the Court developed policies.

Obviously, there must be some limits to the kinds of religious behaviors to

41 336 U.S. 77, 95 (1949).

42 Black and Douglas did concur in a separate opinion rather than join in Jackson's opinion for the Court, but certainly not on the ground that they rejected the preferred-position doctrine. They chose to emphasize the absence of a clear and present danger to national security in the Barnette case, and considered the occasion appropriate to make a brief statement of the reasons for their change of view (and votes) since Gobitis.

which a majority of the Court can be expected to accord constitutional "protection." We need no test cases to know that the Supreme Court of the United States, as constituted now or at any time in the past, is not going to approve the blood sacrifice of either comely virgins or first-born sons under the guise—however sincere—of the free exercise of religion. But the aggressive evangelism of the Jehovah's Witnesses sect provided the Court with many opportunities, during the late 1930's and the 1940's, to consider how far short of direct physical violence the right to proselyte should extend. There have also been a few cases in which the shoe has been worn on the other foot, and the question has been how far adherents to minority faiths should be required to act contrary to their beliefs.

Perhaps the most extreme example of Court approval of the right to proselyte occurred on May 3, 1943, only two and one-half months after Wiley Rutledge joined the justices, when a newly formed libertarian majority upheld 5-4 the right of a Jehovah's Witness task force to descend upon a slumbering factory town early on Palm Sunday morning, setting up a command post in a filling station just beyond the city limits, and desecrating the Sabbath of the residents in the name of the free exercise of their own fighting faith. (For details of the "invasion," see the opinion of Justice Jackson in *Douglas* v. *Jeannette,* 319 U.S. 157, 166.) [43] According to Justice Douglas, who spoke for the five libertarians, "This form of religious activity occupies the same high estate under the First Amendment as do worship in the churches and preaching from the pulpits. It has the same claim to protection as the more orthodox and conventional exercises of religion. It also has the same claim as the others to the guarantees of freedom of speech and freedom of the press." Moreover, he added, "Freedom of press, freedom of speech, freedom of religion are in a preferred position."

Freedom of Belief

In the month after the Jeannette decision came the opinion in the Barnette case (below), which is probably the most extreme example of Court protection of minority nonconformity because of religious belief. For reasons already explained, it was no accident that what may fairly be described as the limits of the Court's tolerance of the free exercise of religion, in both active and passive form, should have been reached at this particular time. What was surprising was that Jackson, only six weeks after his caustic criticism of the Witnesses in the

[43] In a connected case, *Martin* v. *Struthers,* 319 U.S. 141, decided at the same time, Black remarked for the libertarian majority: "The authors of the First Amendment knew that novel and unconventional ideas might disturb the complacent, but they chose to encourage a freedom which they believed essential if vigorous enlightenment was ever to triumph over slothful ignorance." Jackson dissented in behalf of the rights of the majority, replying: "I doubt if only the slothfully ignorant wish repose in their homes, or that the forefathers intended to open the door to such forced 'enlightenment' as we have here."

Jeannette case, joined forces with the libertarians to provide a superfluous but doubtless welcome sixth vote. Jackson's switch is perhaps best explained in terms of the sharp distinction he drew between *active* and *passive* exercise of the freedom of religion. Although generally opposed to activist claims of freedom of religion, Jackson was the most fervent advocate on the Court in defense of the passive right of freedom of belief in the intransitive sense.[44] It is the more interesting that, under these circumstances, Chief Justice Stone assigned the writing of the opinion of the Court to Jackson rather than to himself or to one of the "Libertarian Four," to use Pritchett's phrase once more. In any event, the result of Jackson's temporary defection and of the Chief Justice's choice of spokesman was the passionate opinion of the Court in the case below, which ranks with the Holmes-Brandeis dissent in Gitlow and Harlan's dissent in the Plessy case—among the few really great essays on human liberty to be found in the literature of the Supreme Court.

WEST VIRGINIA STATE
BOARD OF EDUCATION v.
BARNETTE

319 U.S. 624 (June 14, 1943)

Appeals from the United States District Court for the Southern District of West Virginia.

Affirmed.

6-3

Jackson	('+')
Stone, C.J.	(+)
Rutledge	(+)
Murphy	('+'
Black	('+'
Douglas	('+'
Roberts	—
Reed	—
Frankfurter	'—')

---

44 For example, see *United States* v. *Ballard,* 322 U.S. 78 (1944), a "free exercise" case involving the federal mail-fraud trial of several "I Am" cultists, who apparently were associates both spiritual and in a more worldly way of faith-healer "Guy W. Ballard, now deceased, alias Saint Germain, Jesus, George Washington, and Godfre Ray King." Jackson dissented because the Libertarian Four—who were temporarily augmented by Reed—refused to go as far as Jackson in ex-

The decision in the Gobitis case had been 8-1, with Stone the solitary dissenter. But Murphy, Black, and Douglas had made a public confession of error in their dissent from the initial decision in Jones v. Opelika, 316 U.S. 584, 623-624 (June 8, 1942), *in which they openly declared that they were now convinced that the Gobitis case "was wrongly decided" (see Chapter 4). Rutledge's appointment in the middle of the 1942 Term gave the libertarians the necessary fifth vote to overrule Gobitis at the first opportunity to present itself in response to their solicitation.*

The opinion of the Court in the Gobitis case to which Mr. Justice Jackson

tirpating the "business of judicially examining other people's faiths"; obviously, under these circumstances, the libertarian bloc could have adopted the more extreme position Jackson urged in this case—they could have formed a majority with him instead of Reed, had they chosen to do so. Perhaps the sharpest articulation of Jackson's position is found in his dissent against the Court's decision upholding the disclaimer-oath section of the Taft-Hartley Act, in *American Communications Assn.* v. *Douds,* 339 U.S. 382, 444 (1950): "I think that under our system, it is time enough for the law to lay hold of the citizen when he acts illegally, or in some rare circumstances when his thoughts are given illegal utterance. I think we must let his mind alone."

refers below was authored, needless to say, by Mr. Justice Frankfurter, whose dissent in this case should be compared with Roberts' dissent in Smith v. Allwright *(see Chapter 9). Frankfurter's views regarding the obligations of stare decisis, expressed in his opinion below, contrast sharply with the remarks he offered in concurrence a few years later in* Kovacs v. Cooper, *336 U.S. 77, 89 (1949), a decision with which Frankfurter agreed and which in effect overruled a seven-month old precedent against which he had dissented.*

MR. JUSTICE JACKSON delivered the opinion of the Court.

Following the decision by this Court on June 3, 1940, in *Minersville School District* v. *Gobitis,* 310 U.S. 586, the West Virginia legislature amended its statutes to require all schools therein to conduct courses of instruction in history, civics, and in the Constitutions of the United States and of the State "for the purpose of teaching, fostering and perpetuating the ideals, principles and spirit of Americanism, and increasing the knowledge of the organization and machinery of the government." Appellant Board of Education was directed, with advice of the State Superintendent of Schools, to "prescribe the courses of study covering these subjects" for public schools. The Act made it the duty of private, parochial and denominational schools to prescribe courses of study "similar to those required for the public schools."

The Board of Education on January 9, 1942, adopted a resolution containing recitals taken largely from the Court's *Gobitis* opinion and ordering that the salute to the flag become "a regular part of the program of activities in the public schools," that all teachers and pupils "shall be required to participate in the salute honoring the Nation represented by the Flag; provided, however, that refusal to salute the Flag be regarded as an act of insubordination, and shall be dealt with accordingly."

The resolution originally required the "commonly accepted salute to the Flag" which it defined. Objections to the salute as "being too much like Hitler's" were raised by the Parent and Teachers Association, the Boy and Girl Scouts, the Red Cross, and the Federation of Women's Clubs. Some modification appears to have been made in deference to these objections, but no concession was made to Jehovah's Witnesses.[45] What is now required is the "stiff-arm" salute, the saluter to keep the right hand raised with palm turned up while the following is repeated: "I pledge allegiance to the Flag of the United States of America and to the Republic for which it stands; one Nation, indivisible, with liberty and justice for all."

Failure to conform is "insubordination" dealt with by expulsion. Readmission is denied by statute until compliance. Meanwhile the expelled child is "unlawfully absent" and may be proceeded against as a delinquent. His parents or guardians are liable to prosecution, and if convicted are subject to fine not exceeding $50 and jail term not exceeding thirty days.

Appellees, citizens of the United States and of West Virginia, brought suit in the United States District Court for themselves and others similarly situated asking its injunction to restrain enforcement of these laws and regulations against Jehovah's Witnesses. The Witnesses are an unincorporated body teaching that the obligation imposed by law of God is superior to that of laws enacted by temporal government. Their religious beliefs include

45 They have offered in lieu of participating in the flag salute ceremony "periodically and publicly" to give the following pledge: "I have pledged my unqualified allegiance and devotion to Jehovah, the Almighty God, and to His Kingdom, for which Jesus commands all Christians to pray. I respect the flag of the United States and acknowledge it as a symbol of freedom and justice to all. I pledge allegiance and obedience to all the laws of the United States that are consistent with God's law, as set forth in the Bible." [Footnote by the Court.]

a literal version of Exodus, Chapter 20, verses 4 and 5, which says: "Thou shalt not make unto thee any graven image, or any likeness of anything that is in heaven above, or that is in the earth beneath, or that is in the water under the earth; thou shalt not bow down thyself to them nor serve them." They consider that the flag is an "image" within this command. For this reason they refuse to salute it. . . .

There is no doubt that, in connection with the pledges, the flag salute is a form of utterance. Symbolism is a primitive but effective way of communicating ideas. The use of an emblem or flag to symbolize some system, idea, institution, or personality, is a short cut from mind to mind. Causes and nations, political parties, lodges and ecclesiastical groups seek to knit the loyalty of their followings to a flag or banner, a color or design. The State announces rank, function, and authority through crowns and maces, uniforms and black robes; the church speaks through the Cross, the Crucifix, the altar and shrine, and clerical raiment. Symbols of State often convey political ideas just as religious symbols come to convey theological ones. Associated with many of these symbols are appropriate gestures of acceptance or respect: a salute, a bowed or bared head, a bended knee. A person gets from a symbol the meaning he puts into it, and what is one man's comfort and inspiration is another's jest and scorn.[46]

Over a decade ago Chief Justice Hughes led this Court in holding that the display of a red flag as a symbol of opposition by peaceful and legal means to organized government was protected by the free speech guaranties of the Constitution.

[46] "Some who profess belief in the Bible read literally what others read as allegory or metaphor, as they read Aesops' fables. Religious symbolism is even used by some with the same mental reservations one has in teaching of Santa Claus or Uncle Sam or Easter bunnies or dispassionate judges." Jackson, dissenting in *United States* v. *Ballard,* 322 U.S. 78, 94 (1944).

Stromberg v. *California,* 283 U.S. 359. Here it is the State that employs a flag as a symbol of adherence to government as presently organized. It requires the individual to communicate by word and sign his acceptance of the political ideas it thus bespeaks. Objection to this form of communication when coerced is an old one, well known to the framers of the Bill of Rights.

It is also to be noted that the compulsory flag salute and pledge requires affirmation of a belief and an attitude of mind. It is not clear whether the regulation contemplates that pupils forego any contrary convictions of their own and become unwilling converts to the prescribed ceremony or whether it will be acceptable if they simulate assent by words without belief and by a gesture barren of meaning. It is now a commonplace that censorship or suppression of expression of opinion is tolerated by our Constitution only when the expression presents a clear and present danger of action of a kind the State is empowered to prevent and punish. It would seem that involuntary affirmation could be commanded only on even more immediate and urgent grounds than silence. . . . [Many] citizens who do not share [appellees'] religious views hold such a compulsory rite to infringe constitutional liberty of the individual.[47] It is

[47] Cushman, Constitutional Law in 1939-40, 35 American Political Science Review 250, 271, observes: "All of the eloquence by which the majority extol the ceremony of flag saluting as a free expression of patriotism turns sour when used to describe the brutal compulsion which requires a sensitive and conscientious child to stultify himself in public." For further criticism of the opinion in the *Gobitis* case by persons who do not share the faith of the Witnesses see: Powell, Conscience and the Constitution, in Democracy and National Unity (University of Chicago Press, 1941) 1; Wilkinson, Some Aspects of the Constitutional Guarantees of Civil Liberty, 11 Fordham Law Review 50; Fennell, The "Reconstructed Court" and Religious Freedom: The Gobitis Case in Retrospect, 19 New York University Law Quarterly Review 31; Green, Liberty under the Fourteenth

not necessary to inquire whether non-conformist beliefs will exempt from the duty to salute unless we first find power to make the salute a legal duty.

The *Gobitis* decision, however, *assumed,* as did the argument in that case and in this, that power exists in the State to impose the flag salute discipline upon school children in general. The Court only examined and rejected a claim based on religious beliefs of immunity from an unquestioned general rule. The question which underlies the flag salute controversy is whether such a ceremony so touching matters of opinion and political attitude may be imposed upon the individual by official authority under powers committed to any political organization under our Constitution. We examine rather than assume existence of this power and, against this broader definition of issues in this case, reëxamine specific grounds assigned for the *Gobitis* decision.

1. It was said that the flag-salute controversy confronted the Court with "the problem . . . which Lincoln cast in memorable dilemma: 'Must a government of necessity be too *strong* for the liberties of its people, or too *weak* to maintain its own existence?' " and that the answer must be in favor of strength. *Minersville School District* v. *Gobitis, supra,* at 596. . . .

It may be doubted whether Mr. Lincoln would have thought that the strength of government to maintain itself would be impressively vindicated by our confirming power of the State to expel a handful of children from school. . . . Free public education, if faithful to the ideal of secular instruction and political neutrality, will not be partisan or enemy of any class, creed, party, or faction. If it is to impose any ideological discipline, however, each party or denomination must seek to con-

Amendment, 27 Washington University Law Quarterly 497; 9 International Juridical Association Bulletin 1; 39 Michigan Law Review 149; 15 St. John's Law Review 95. [Footnote by the Court.]

trol, or failing that, to weaken the influence of the educational system. Observance of the limitations of the Constitution will not weaken government in the field appropriate for its exercise.

2. It was also considered in the *Gobitis* case that functions of educational officers in States, counties, and school districts were such that to interfere with their authority "would in effect make us the school board for the country." *Id.* at 598.

The Fourteenth Amendment, as now applied to the States, protects the citizen against the State itself and all of its creatures—Boards of Education not excepted. These have, of course, important, delicate, and highly discretionary functions, but none that they may not perform within the limits of the Bill of Rights. That they are educating the young for citizenship is reason for scrupulous protection of Constitutional freedoms of the individual, if we are not to strangle the free mind at its source and teach youth to discount important principles of our government as mere platitudes.

Such Boards are numerous and their territorial jurisdiction often small. But small and local authority may feel less sense of responsibility to the Constitution, and agencies of publicity may be less vigilant in calling it to account. The action of Congress in making flag observance voluntary and respecting the conscience of the objector in a matter so vital as raising the Army contrasts sharply with these local regulations in matters relatively trivial to the welfare of the nation. There are village tyrants as well as village Hampdens, but none who acts under color of law is beyond reach of the Constitution.

3. The *Gobitis* opinion reasoned that this is a field "where courts possess no marked and certainly no controlling competence," that it is committed to the legislatures as well as the courts to guard cherished liberties and that it is constitutionally appropriate to "fight out the wise use of legislative authority in the forum

of public opinion and before legislative assemblies rather than to transfer such a contest to the judicial arena," since all the "effective means of inducing political changes are left free." *Id.* at 597-598, 600.

The very purpose of a Bill of Rights was to withdraw certain subjects from the vicissitudes of political controversy, to place them beyond the reach of majorities and officials and to establish them as legal principles to be applied by the courts. One's right to life, liberty, and property, to free speech, a free press, freedom of worship and assembly, and other fundamental rights may not be submitted to vote; they depend on the outcome of no elections.

In weighing arguments of the parties it is important to distinguish between the due process clause of the Fourteenth Amendment as an instrument for transmitting the principles of the First Amendment and those cases in which it is applied for its own sake. The test of legislation which collides with the Fourteenth Amendment, because it also collides with the principles of the First, is much more definite than the test when only the Fourteenth is involved. Much of the vagueness of the due process clause disappears when the specific prohibitions of the First become its standard. The right of a State to regulate, for example, a public utility may well include, so far as the due process test is concerned, power to impose all of the restrictions which a legislature may have a "rational basis" for adopting. But freedoms of speech and of press, of assembly, and of worship may not be infringed on such slender grounds. They are susceptible of restriction only to prevent grave and immediate danger to interests which the State may lawfully protect. It is important to note that while it is the Fourteenth Amendment which bears directly upon the State it is the more specific limiting principles of the First Amendment that finally govern this case.

Nor does our duty to apply the Bill of Rights to assertions of official authority depend upon our possession of marked competence in the field where the invasion of rights occurs. True, the task of translating the majestic generalities of the Bill of Rights, conceived as part of the pattern of liberal government in the eighteenth century, into concrete restraints on officials dealing with the problems of the twentieth century, is one to disturb self-confidence. These principles grew in soil which also produced a philosophy that the individual was the center of society, that his liberty was attainable through mere absence of governmental restraints, and that government should be entrusted with few controls and only the mildest supervision over men's affairs. We must transplant these rights to a soil in which the *laissez-faire* concept or principle of non-interference has withered at least as to economic affairs, and social advancements are increasingly sought through closer integration of society and through expanded and strengthened governmental controls. These changed conditions often deprive precedents of reliability and cast us more than we could choose upon our own judgment. But we act in these matters not by authority of our competence but by force of our commissions. We cannot, because of modest estimates of our competence in such specialties as public education, withhold the judgment that history authenticates as the function of this Court when liberty is infringed.

4. Lastly, and this is the very heart of the *Gobitis* opinion, it reasons that "National unity is the basis of national security," that the authorities have "the right to select appropriate means for its attainment," and hence reaches the conclusion that such compulsory measures toward "national unity" are constitutional. *Id.* at 595. Upon the verity of this assumption depends our answer in this case.

National unity as an end which officials may foster by persuasion and example is not in question. The problem is whether under our Constitution compulsion as here employed is a permissible means for its achievement.

Struggles to coerce uniformity of sentiment in support of some end thought essential to their time and country have been waged by many good as well as by evil men. Nationalism is a relatively recent phenomenon but at other times and places the ends have been racial or territorial security, support of a dynasty or regime, and particular plans for saving souls. As first and moderate methods to attain unity have failed, those bent on its accomplishment must resort to an ever-increasing severity. As governmental pressure toward unity becomes greater, so strife becomes more bitter as to whose unity it shall be. Probably no deeper division of our people could proceed from any provocation than from finding it necessary to choose what doctrine and whose program public educational officials shall compel youth to unite in embracing. Ultimate futility of such attempts to compel coherence is the lesson of every such effort from the Roman drive to stamp out Christianity as a disturber of its pagan unity, the Inquisition, as a means to religious and dynastic unity, the Siberian exiles as a means to Russian unity, down to the fast failing efforts of our present totalitarian enemies. Those who begin coercive elimination of dissent soon find themselves exterminating dissenters. Compulsory unification of opinion achieves only the unanimity of the graveyard.

It seems trite but necessary to say that the First Amendment to our Constitution was designed to avoid these ends by avoiding these beginnings. There is no mysticism in the American concept of the State or of the nature or origin of its authority. We set up government by consent of the governed, and the Bill of Rights denies those in power any legal opportunity to coerce that consent. Authority here is to be controlled by public opinion, not public opinion by authority.

The case is made difficult not because the principles of its decision are obscure but because the flag involved is our own. Nevertheless, we apply the limitations of the Constitution with no fear that freedom to be intellectually and spiritually diverse or even contrary will disintegrate the social organization. To believe that patriotism will not flourish if patriotic ceremonies are voluntary and spontaneous instead of a compulsory routine is to make an unflattering estimate of the appeal of our institutions to free minds. We can have intellectual individualism and the rich cultural diversities that we owe to exceptional minds only at the price of occasional eccentricity and abnormal attitudes. When they are so harmless to others or to the State as those we deal with here, the price is not too great. But freedom to differ is not limited to things that do not matter much. That would be a mere shadow of freedom. The test of its substance is the right to differ as to things that touch the heart of the existing order.

If there is any fixed star in our constitutional constellation, it is that no official, high or petty, can prescribe what shall be orthodox in politics, nationalism, religion, or other matters of opinion or force citizens to confess by word or act their faith therein. If there are any circumstances which permit an exception, they do not now occur to us.

We think the action of the local authorities in compelling the flag salute and pledge transcends constitutional limitations on their power and invades the sphere of intellect and spirit which it is the purpose of the First Amendment to our Constitution to reserve from all official control.

The decision of this Court in *Minersville School District* v. *Gobitis* and the holdings of those few *per curiam* decisions which preceded and foreshadowed it are overruled, and the judgment enjoining enforcement of the West Virginia Regulation is

Affirmed.

MR. JUSTICE FRANKFURTER, dissenting:

One who belongs to the most vilified and persecuted minority in history is not likely to be insensible to the freedoms guaranteed by our Constitution. Were my purely personal attitude relevant I should wholeheartedly associate myself with the general libertarian views in the Court's opinion, representing as they do the thought and action of a lifetime. But as judges we are neither Jew nor Gentile, neither Catholic nor agnostic. We owe equal attachment to the Constitution and are equally bound by our judicial obligations whether we derive our citizenship from the earliest or the latest immigrants to these shores. As a member of this Court I am not justified in writing my private notions of policy into the Constitution, no matter how deeply I may cherish them or how mischievous I may deem their disregard. The duty of a judge who must decide which of two claims before the Court shall prevail, that of a State to enact and enforce laws within its general competence or that of an individual to refuse obedience because of the demands of his conscience, is not that of the ordinary person. It can never be emphasized too much that one's own opinion about the wisdom or evil of a law should be excluded altogether when one is doing one's duty on the bench. The only opinion of our own even looking in that direction that is material is our opinion whether legislators could in reason have enacted such a law. In the light of all the circumstances, including the history of this question in this Court, it would require more daring than I possess to deny that reasonable legislators could have taken the action which is before us for review. Most unwillingly, therefore, I must differ from my brethren with regard to legislation like this. I cannot bring my mind to believe that the "liberty" secured by the Due Process Clause gives this Court authority to deny to the State of West Virginia the attainment of that which we all recognize as a legitimate legislative end, namely, the promotion of good citizenship, by employment of the means here chosen.

Not so long ago we were admonished that "the only check upon our own exercise of power is our own sense of self-restraint. For the removal of unwise laws from the statute book appeal lies not to the courts but to the ballot and to the processes of democratic government." *United States* v. *Butler,* 297 U.S. 1, 79 (dissent). . . .

The admonition that judicial self-restraint alone limits arbitrary exercise of our authority is relevant every time we are asked to nullify legislation. The Constitution does not give us greater veto power when dealing with one phase of "liberty" than with another. . . . [Our] function [is not] comparable to that of a legislator [nor] are we free to act as though we were a super-legislature. Judicial self-restraint is equally necessary whenever an exercise of political or legislative power is challenged. There is no warrant in the constitutional basis of this Court's authority for attributing different rôles to it depending upon the nature of the challenge to the legislation. Our power does not vary according to the particular provision of the Bill of Rights which is invoked. The right not to have property taken without just compensation has, so far as the scope of judicial power is concerned, the same constitutional dignity as the right to be protected against unreasonable searches and seizures, and the latter has no less claim than freedom of the press or freedom of speech or religious freedom. In no instance is this Court the primary protector of the particular liberty that is invoked. This Court has recognized, what hardly could be denied, that all the provisions of the first ten Amendments are "specific" prohibitions, *United States* v. *Carolene Products Co.,* 304 U.S. 144, 152, n. 4. But each specific Amendment, in so far as embraced within the Fourteenth Amendment, must be equally respected, and the function of this Court does not differ in passing on the constitutionality of legislation challenged under different Amendments.

When Mr. Justice Holmes, speaking for this Court, wrote that "it must be remembered that legislatures are ultimate guardians of the liberties and welfare of the people in quite as great a degree as the courts," . . . he went to the very essence of our constitutional system and the democratic conception of our society. He did not mean that for only some phases of civil government this Court was not to supplant legislatures and sit in judgment upon the right or wrong of a challenged measure. He was stating the comprehensive judicial duty and rôle of this Court in our constitutional scheme whenever legislation is sought to be nullified on any ground, namely, that responsibility for legislation lies with legislatures, answerable as they are directly to the people, and this Court's only and very narrow function is to determine whether within the broad grant of authority vested in legislatures they have exercised a judgment for which reasonable justification can be offered.

. . . It is, of course, beyond our power to rewrite the State's requirement, by providing exemptions for those who do not wish to participate in the flag salute or by making some other accommodations to meet their scruples. That wisdom might suggest the making of such accommodations and that school administration would not find it too difficult to make them and yet maintain the ceremony for those not refusing to conform, is outside our province to suggest. . . . [The] real question is, who is to make such accommodations, the courts or the legislature?

This is no dry, technical matter. It cuts deep into one's conception of the democratic process—it concerns no less the practical differences between the means for making these accommodations that are open to courts and to legislatures. A court can only strike down. It can only say "This or that law is void." It cannot modify or qualify, it cannot make exceptions to a general requirement. And it strikes down not merely for a day. At least the finding of unconstitutionality ought not to have ephemeral significance unless the Constitution is to be reduced to the fugitive importance of mere legislation. When we are dealing with the Constitution of the United States, and more particularly with the great safeguards of the Bill of Rights, we are dealing with principles of liberty and justice "so rooted in the traditions and conscience of our people as to be ranked as fundamental"—something without which "a fair and enlightened system of justice would be impossible." *Palko* v. *Connecticut*, 302 U.S. 319, 325; *Hurtado* v. *California*, 110 U.S. 516, 530, 531. If the function of this Court is to be essentially no different from that of a legislature, if the considerations governing constitutional construction are to be substantially those that underlie legislation, then indeed judges should not have life tenure and they should be made directly responsible to the electorate. There have been many but unsuccessful proposals in the last sixty years to amend the Constitution to that end. . . .

Conscientious scruples, all would admit, cannot stand against every legislative compulsion to do positive acts in conflict with such scruples. We have been told that such compulsions override religious scruples only as to major concerns of the state. But the determination of what is major and what is minor itself raises questions of policy. For the way in which men equally guided by reason appraise importance goes to the very heart of policy. Judges should be very diffident in setting their judgment against that of a state in determining what is and what is not a major concern, what means are appropriate to proper ends, and what is the total social cost in striking the balance of imponderables. . . .

I am fortified in my view of this case by the history of the flag salute controversy in this Court. Five times has the precise question now before us been adjudicated. Four times the Court unanimously found that the requirement of such a school exercise was not beyond the powers of the states. Indeed in the first three cases to come before the Court the constitutional claim now sustained was deemed so clearly unmeritorious that this Court dismissed the appeals for want of a substantial federal question. . . . In the fourth case the judgment of the district court upholding the state law was summarily affirmed on the authority of the earlier cases. . . . The fifth case, *Minersville District* v. *Gobitis,* 310 U.S. 586, was brought here because the decision of the Circuit Court of Appeals for the Third Circuit ran counter to our rulings. They were reaffirmed after full consideration, with one Justice dissenting.

What may be even more significant than this uniform recognition of state authority is the fact that every Justice—thirteen in all—who has hitherto participated in judging this matter has at one or more times found no constitutional infirmity in what is now condemned.[48] Only the two

Justices sitting for the first time on this matter have not heretofore found this legislation inoffensive to the "liberty" guaranteed by the Constitution. And among the Justices who sustained this measure were outstanding judicial leaders in the zealous enforcement of constitutional safeguards of civil liberties—men like Chief Justice Hughes, Mr. Justice Brandeis, and Mr. Justice Cardozo, to mention only those no longer on the Court.

One's conception of the Constitution cannot be severed from one's conception of a judge's function in applying it. The Court has no reason for existence if it merely reflects the pressures of the day. Our system is built on the faith that men set apart for this special function, freed from the influences of immediacy and from the deflections of worldly ambition, will become able to take a view of longer range than the period of responsibility entrusted to Congress and legislatures. We are dealing with matters as to which legislators and voters have conflicting views. Are we as judges to impose our strong convictions on where wisdom lies? That which three years ago had seemed to five successive Courts to lie within permissible areas of legislation is now outlawed by the deciding shift of opinion of two Justices.[49] What reason is there to believe that they or their successors may not have another view a few years hence? Is that which was deemed to be of so fundamental a nature as to be written into the Constitution to endure for all times to be the sport of

[48] There are interesting implications to Justice Frankfurter's statistical inferences. Among the thirteen justices who, according to Frankfurter, "found no constitutional infirmity in what is now condemned" were two (Sutherland and Cardozo) who participated only in the first and a third justice (Brandeis) who participated only in the first two of the *per curiam* decisions, which dismissed appeals "for want of a substantial federal question." (Incidentally, the third *per curiam*—the Gabrielli case—was dismissed "for want of jurisdiction," not "for want of a substantial federal question.") According to the Court's own theory, the justices do *not* pass upon the merits of a question when they dismiss an appeal; such a decision is jurisdictional, and as Frankfurter himself has insisted with regard to denials of certiorari, may be based upon all sorts of technical and

other considerations completely unrelated to the views of individual justices, to say nothing of the Court as a whole, upon the merits of the constitutional questions sought to be raised by an appellee. Does Frankfurter's statement constitute an inadvertent confirmation of the suggestion in Chapter 3 that both dismissals of appeals and denials of certiorari frequently have substantive significance?

[49] Frankfurter's statement is ambiguous, but it is clear that three justices shifted their votes between the Gobitis and Barnette decisions: Murphy, Black, and Douglas.

shifting winds of doctrine? Of course, judicial opinions, even as to questions of constitutionality, are not immutable. As has been true in the past, the Court will from time to time reverse its position. But I believe that never before these Jehovah's Witnesses cases . . . has this Court overruled decisions so as to restrict the powers of democratic government. . . .

Of course patriotism can not be enforced by the flag salute. But neither can the liberal spirit be enforced by judicial invalidation of illiberal legislation. Our constant preoccupation with the constitutionality of legislation rather than with its wisdom tends to preoccupation of the American mind with a false value. The tendency of focussing attention on constitutionality is to make constitutionality synonymous with wisdom, to regard a law as all right if it is constitutional. Such an attitude is a great enemy of liberalism. Particularly in legislation affecting freedom of thought and freedom of speech much which should offend a free-spirited society is constitutional. Reliance for the most precious interests of civilization, therefore, must be found outside of their vindication in courts of law. Only a persistent positive translation of the faith of a free society into the convictions and habits and actions of a community is the ultimate reliance against unabated temptations to fetter the human spirit.

The Wall of Separation

The Supreme Court's three most important decisions dealing with the issue of religious-educational integration all clustered, as it happened, within a period of less than half a dozen years; and all were decisions of the Vinson Court. The "libertarian" and "conservative" labels that we have associated with other issues of constitutional policy that we have discussed do not apply in the cases relating to the present question; both wings of the Court splintered in the two (of the three) cases that we shall present below, with Rutledge in opposition to the other members of the "Libertarian Four" in the Everson case, and Black and Douglas divided in the Zorach case. Similarly, Reed voted consistently in favor of the integration of religion and education in all three cases (Everson, McCollum, and Zorach), while Frankfurter and Jackson were just as consistent in voting for segregation; indeed, these three were the only justices to vote consistently in all three cases. The other four justices who participated in all three decisions shifted from one side to the other of the underlying issue of constitutional policy, a practice which became so conspicuous that some critics suggested that the members of the Court were building not a wall of separation but rather a welter of confusion in their efforts to demark the disparate spheres of influence of ecclesiastical and civil authorities.

EVERSON v. BOARD OF
EDUCATION

330 U.S. 1 (1947)

Appeal from the Court of Errors and
Appeals of New Jersey.

Affirmed.

5-4

Black	('+')
Vinson, C.J.	(+)
Reed	(+)
Douglas	(+)
Murphy	(+)
Jackson	'—')
Frankfurter	—)
Rutledge	'—')
Burton	—)

---

*This was the first case under the Four-
teenth Amendment in which the Supreme
Court interpreted the establishment clause
of the First Amendment. Both the libertarians and the conservative wing of the
Court were split by this issue, with Rutledge writing a long historical analysis
of the intent of the framers of the First
Amendment (largely omitted from the
abridged version below) and arguing in
favor of a strict constitutional policy of
separation between church and school as
well as between church and state. Vinson
and Reed joined with the remaining
libertarians to form a majority which
argued that to enforce a policy of separation in this case would discriminate
against the free exercise of religion by
Catholics. The decision, in any event, was
warmly applauded by Catholic spokesmen, and roundly denounced by leading
Protestant clergymen.*

MR. JUSTICE BLACK delivered the opinion of the Court.

A New Jersey statute authorizes its
local school districts to make rules and
contracts for the transportation of children to and from schools. The appellee,
a township board of education, acting
pursuant to this statute, authorized reimbursement to parents of money expended
by them for the bus transportation of
their children on regular busses operated
by the public transportation system. Part
of this money was for the payment of
transportation of some children in the
community to Catholic parochial schools.
These church schools give their students,
in addition to secular education, regular
religious instruction conforming to the
religious tenets and modes of worship of
the Catholic Faith. The superintendent
of these schools is a Catholic priest.

The appellant, in his capacity as a
district taxpayer, filed suit in a state
court challenging the right of the Board
to reimburse parents of parochial school
students. He contended that the statute
and the resolution passed pursuant to it
violated both the State and the Federal
Constitutions. That court held that the
legislature was without power to authorize
such payment under the state constitution. . . . The New Jersey Court of Errors
and Appeals reversed, holding that
neither the statute nor the resolution
passed pursuant to it was in conflict with
the State constitution or the provisions of
the Federal Constitution in issue. . . .

Since there has been no attack on the
statute on the ground that a part of its
language excludes children attending private schools operated for profit from enjoying State payment for their transportation, we need not consider this
exclusionary language; it has no relevancy to any constitutional question here
presented.[50] Furthermore, if the exclusion

[50] Appellant does not challenge the New
Jersey statute or the resolution on the
ground that either violates the equal protection clause of the Fourteenth Amendment
by excluding payment for the transportation
of any pupil who attends a "private school
run for profit." Although the township resolution authorized reimbursement only for
parents of public and Catholic school pupils,
appellant does not allege, nor is there anything in the record which would offer the
slightest support to an allegation, that there

clause had been properly challenged, we do not know whether New Jersey's highest court would construe its statutes as precluding payment of the school transportation of any group of pupils, even those of a private school run for profit. Consequently, we put to one side the question as to the validity of the statute against the claim that it does not authorize payment for the transportation generally of school children in New Jersey.

The only contention here is that the state statute and the resolution, insofar as they authorized reimbursement to parents of children attending parochial schools, violate the Federal Constitution [in that the] . . . statute and the resolution forced inhabitants to pay taxes to help support and maintain schools which are dedicated to, and which regularly teach, the Catholic Faith. This is alleged to be a use of state power to support church schools contrary to the prohibition of the First Amendment which the Fourteenth Amendment made applicable to the states. . . .

Prior to the adoption of the Fourteenth Amendment, the First Amendment did not apply as a restraint against the states. Most of them did soon provide similar constitutional protections for religious liberty. But some states persisted for about half a century in imposing restraints upon the free exercise of religion and in discriminating against particular religious groups. In recent years, so far as the provision against the establishment of a religion is concerned, the question has most frequently arisen in connection with proposed state aid to church schools and efforts to carry on religious teachings in the public schools in accordance with the tenets of a particular sect. Some churches have either sought or accepted state financial support for their schools. Here again the efforts to obtain state aid or acceptance of it have not been limited to any one particular faith. The state courts, in the main, have remained faithful to the language of their own constitutional provisions designed to protect religious freedom and to separate religions and governments. Their decisions, however, show the difficulty in drawing the line between tax legislation which provides funds for the welfare of the general public and that which is designed to support institutions which teach religion.

The meaning and scope of the First Amendment, preventing establishment of religion or prohibiting the free exercise thereof, in the light of its history and the evils it was designed forever to suppress, have been several times elaborated by the decisions of this Court prior to the application of the First Amendment to the states by the Fourteenth. The broad meaning given the Amendment by these earlier cases has been accepted by this Court in its decisions concerning an individual's religious freedom rendered since the Fourteenth Amendment was interpreted to make the prohibitions of the First applicable to state action abridging religious freedom. There is every reason to give the same application and broad interpretation to the "establishment of religion" clause. . . .

The "establishment of religion" clause of the First Amendment means at least this: Neither a state nor the Federal Government can set up a church. Neither can pass laws which aid one religion, aid all religions, or prefer one religion over

_____

were any children in the township who attended or would have attended, but for want of transportation, any but public and Catholic schools. It will be appropriate to consider the exclusion of students of private schools operated for profit when and if it is proved to have occurred, is made the basis of a suit by one in a position to challenge it, and New Jersey's highest court has ruled adversely to the challenger. Striking down a state law is not a matter of such light moment that it should be done by a federal court *ex mero motu* on a postulate neither charged nor proved, but which rests on nothing but a possibility. . . . [Footnote by the Court.]

another. Neither can force nor influence a person to go to or to remain away from church against his will or force him to profess a belief or disbelief in any religion. No person can be punished for entertaining or professing religious beliefs or disbeliefs, for church attendance or non-attendance. No tax in any amount, large or small, can be levied to support any religious activities or institutions, whatever they may be called, or whatever form they may adopt to teach or practice religion. Neither a state nor the Federal Government can, openly or secretly, participate in the affairs of any religious organizations or groups and *vice versa*. In the words of Jefferson, the clause against establishment of religion by law was intended to erect "a wall of separation between church and State." . . .

We must consider the New Jersey statute in accordance with the foregoing limitations imposed by the First Amendment. But we must not strike that state statute down if it is within the State's constitutional power even though it approaches the verge of that power. . . . New Jersey cannot consistently with the "establishment of religion" clause of the First Amendment contribute tax-raised funds to the support of an institution which teaches the tenets and faith of any church. On the other hand, other language of the amendment commands that New Jersey cannot hamper its citizens in the free exercise of their own religion. Consequently, it cannot exclude individual Catholics, Lutherans, Mohammedans, Baptists, Jews, Methodists, Non-believers, Presbyterians, or the members of any other faith, *because of their faith, or lack of it,* from receiving the benefits of public welfare legislation. While we do not mean to intimate that a state could not provide transportation only to children attending public schools, we must be careful, in protecting the citizens of New Jersey against state-established churches, to be sure that we do not inadvertently prohibit New Jersey from extending its general state law benefits to all citizens without regard to their religious belief.

Measured by these standards, we cannot say that the First Amendment prohibits New Jersey from spending tax-raised funds to pay the bus fares of parochial school pupils as a part of a general program under which it pays the fares of pupils attending public and other schools. It is undoubtedly true that children are helped to get to church schools. There is even a possibility that some of the children might not be sent to the church schools if the parents were compelled to pay their children's bus fares out of their own pockets when transportation to a public school would have been paid for by the State. The same possibility exists where the state requires a local transit company to provide reduced fares to school children including those attending parochial schools, or where a municipally owned transportation system undertakes to carry all school children free of charge. Moreover, state-paid policemen, detailed to protect children going to and from church schools from the very real hazards of traffic, would serve much the same purpose and accomplish much the same result as state provisions intended to guarantee free transportation of a kind which the state deems to be best for the school children's welfare. And parents might refuse to risk their children to the serious danger of traffic accidents going to and from parochial schools, the approaches to which were not protected by policemen. Similarly, parents might be reluctant to permit their children to attend schools which the state had cut off from such general government services as ordinary police and fire protection, connections for sewage disposal, public highways and sidewalks. Of course, cutting off church schools from these services, so separate and so indisputably marked off from the religious function, would make it far more difficult for the schools to operate. But such is obviously not the purpose of the First Amendment. That Amendment requires the state to be a neutral in its relations with groups of religious believers and non-believers; it does not require the state to be their adversary. State power is no more to be used so as to handicap religions than it is to favor them.

This Court has said that parents may, in the discharge of their duty under state compulsory education laws, send their children to a religious rather than a public school if the school meets the secular educational requirements which the state has power to impose. See *Pierce* v. *Society of Sisters*, 268 U.S. 510. It appears that these parochial schools meet New Jersey's requirements. The State contributes no money to the schools. It does not support them. Its legislation, as applied, does no more than provide a general program to help parents get their children, regardless of their religion, safely and expeditiously to and from accredited schools.

The First Amendment has erected a wall between church and state. That wall must be kept high and impregnable. We could not approve the slightest breach. New Jersey has not breached it here.

Affirmed.

MR. JUSTICE JACKSON, dissenting.

I find myself, contrary to first impressions, unable to join in this decision. I have a sympathy, though it is not ideological, with Catholic citizens who are compelled by law to pay taxes for public schools, and also feel constrained by conscience and discipline to support other schools for their own children. Such relief to them as this case involves is not in itself a serious burden to taxpayers and I had assumed it to be as little serious in principle. Study of this case convinces me otherwise. The Court's opinion marshals every argument in favor of state aid and puts the case in its most favorable light, but much of its reasoning confirms my conclusions that there are no good

grounds upon which to support the present legislation. In fact, the undertones of the opinion, advocating complete and uncompromising separation of Church from State, seem utterly discordant with its conclusion yielding support to their commingling in educational matters. The case which irresistibly comes to mind as the most fitting precedent is that of Julia who, according to Byron's reports, "whispering 'I will ne'er consent.'—consented."

I.

The Court sustains this legislation by assuming two deviations from the facts of this particular case; first, it assumes a state of facts the record does not support, and secondly, it refuses to consider facts which are inescapable on the record.

The Court concludes that this "legislation, as applied, does no more than provide a general program to help parents get their children, regardless of their religion, safely and expeditiously to and from accredited schools," and it draws a comparison between "state provisions intended to guarantee free transportation" for school children with services such as police and fire protection, and implies that we are here dealing with "laws authorizing new types of public services. . . ." This hypothesis permeates the opinion. The facts will not bear that construction.

The Township of Ewing is not furnishing transportation to the children in any form; it is not operating school busses itself or contracting for their operation; and it is not performing any public service of any kind with this taxpayer's money. All school children are left to ride as ordinary paying passengers on the regular busses operated by the public transportation system. What the Township does, and what the taxpayer complains of, is at stated intervals to reimburse parents for the fares paid, provided the children attend either public schools or Catholic Church schools. This expenditure of tax funds has no possible effect on the child's safety or expedition in transit. As passengers on the public busses they travel as fast and no faster, and are as safe and no safer, since their parents are reimbursed as before.

In addition to thus assuming a type of service that does not exist, the Court also insists that we must close our eyes to a discrimination which does exist. The resolution which authorizes disbursement of this taxpayer's money limits reimbursement to those who attend public schools and Catholic schools. That is the way the Act is applied to this taxpayer.

The New Jersey Act in question makes the character of the school, not the needs of the children, determine the eligibility of parents to reimbursement. The Act permits payment for transportation to parochial schools or public schools but prohibits it to private schools operated in whole or in part for profit. Children often are sent to private schools because their parents feel that they require more individual instruction than public schools can provide, or because they are backward or defective and need special attention. If all children of the state were objects of impartial solicitude, no reason is obvious for denying transportation reimbursement to students of this class, for these often are as needy and as worthy as those who go to public or parochial schools. Refusal to reimburse those who attend such schools is understandable only in the light of a purpose to aid the schools, because the state might well abstain from aiding a profit-making private enterprise. Thus, under the Act and resolution brought to us by this case, children are classified according to the schools they attend and are to be aided if they attend the public schools or private Catholic schools, and they are not allowed to be aided if they attend private secular schools or private religious schools of other faiths.

Of course, this case is not one of a Baptist or a Jew or an Episcopalian or a pupil of a private school complaining of discrimination. It is one of a taxpayer urging that he is being taxed for an unconstitutional purpose. I think he is entitled to have us consider the Act just as it is written. . . . As applied to this taxpayer by the action he complains of, certainly the Act does not authorize reimbursement to those who choose any alternative to the public school except Catholic Church schools.

If we are to decide this case on the facts before us, our question is simply this: Is it constitutional to tax this complainant to pay the cost of carrying pupils to Church schools of one specified denomination?

II.

Whether the taxpayer constitutionally can be made to contribute aid to parents of students because of their attendance at parochial schools depends upon the nature of those schools and their relation to the Church. . . .

I should be surprised if any Catholic would deny that the parochial school is a vital, if not the most vital, part of the Roman Catholic Church. If put to the choice, that venerable institution, I should expect, would forego its whole service for mature persons before it would give up education of the young, and it would be a wise choice. Its growth and cohesion, discipline and loyalty, spring from its schools. Catholic education is the rock on which the whole structure rests, and to render tax aid to its Church school is indistinguishable to me from rendering the same aid to the Church itself.

III.

It is of no importance in this situation whether the beneficiary of this expenditure of tax-raised funds is primarily the parochial school and incidentally the pupil, or whether the aid is directly bestowed on the pupil with indirect benefits to the school. The state cannot maintain a Church and it can no more tax its citizens to furnish free carriage to those who attend a Church. The prohibition against establishment of religion cannot be circumvented by a subsidy, bonus or reimbursement of expense to individuals for receiving religious instruction and indoctrination. . . .

MR. JUSTICE RUTLEDGE, dissenting. . . .

No one conscious of religious values can be unsympathetic toward the burden which our constitutional separation puts on parents who desire religious instruction mixed with secular for their children. They pay taxes for others' children's education, at the same time the added cost of instruction for their own. Nor can one happily see benefits denied to children which others receive, because in conscience they or their parents for them desire a different kind of training others do not demand.

But if those feelings should prevail, there would be an end to our historic constitutional policy and command. No more unjust or discriminatory in fact is it to deny attendants at religious schools the cost of their transportation than it is to deny them tuitions, sustenance for their teachers, or any other educational expense which others receive at public cost. Hardship in fact there is which none can blink. But, for assuring to those who undergo it the greater, the most comprehensive freedom, it is one written by design and firm intent into our basic law.

Of course discrimination in the legal sense does not exist. The child attending the religious school has the same right as any other to attend the public school. But he foregoes exercising it because the same guaranty which assures this freedom forbids the public school or any agency of the state to give or aid him in securing the religious instruction he seeks.

Were he to accept the common school, he would be the first to protest the teaching there of any creed or faith not his own. And it is precisely for the reason that their atmosphere is wholly secular that children are not sent to public schools under the *Pierce* doctrine. But that is a constitutional necessity, because we have staked the very existence of our country on the faith that complete separation between the state and religion is best for the state and best for religion. . . .

That policy necessarily entails hardship upon persons who forego the right to educational advantages the state can supply in order to secure others it is precluded from giving. Indeed this may hamper the parent and the child forced by conscience to that choice. But it does not make the state unneutral to withhold what the Constitution forbids it to give. On the contrary it is only by observing the prohibition rigidly that the state can maintain its neutrality and avoid partisanship in the dissensions inevitable when sect opposes sect over demands for public moneys to further religious education, teaching or training in any form or degree, directly or indirectly. Like St. Paul's freedom, religious liberty with a great price must be bought. And for those who exercise it most fully, by insisting upon religious education for their children mixed with secular, by the terms of our Constitution the price is greater than for others.

The problem then cannot be cast in terms of legal discrimination or its absence. This would be true, even though the state in giving aid should treat all religious instruction alike. . . .

Two great drives are constantly in motion to abridge, in the name of education, the complete division of religion and civil authority which our forefathers made. One is to introduce religious education and observances into the public schools. The other, to obtain public funds for the aid and support of various private religious schools. . . . In my opinion both avenues were closed by the Constitution. Neither should be opened by this Court. The matter is not one of quantity, to be measured by the amount of money expended. Now as in Madison's day it is one of principle, to keep separate the separate spheres as the First Amendment drew them; to prevent the first experiment upon our liberties; and to keep the question from becoming entangled in corrosive precedents. We should not be less strict to keep strong and untarnished the one side of the shield of religious freedom than we have been of the other. The judgment should be reversed.

As Justice Rutledge pointed out, in addition to the efforts of private religious groups to obtain public funds for their aid and support, their other great drive is to introduce religious education and observances into the public schools. This observation was supported by subsequent events in New Jersey, the state in which the Everson case originated. In *Doremus v. Board of Education*, 5 N.J. 435 (1950), the state supreme court unanimously ruled that the Old Testament is not a "sectarian" book, and that the required daily reading of verses from the Old Testament books of the Bible, in the New Jersey public schools, did not violate the establishment clauses of either the state constitution or the Fourteenth Amendment. The United States Supreme Court avoided this issue, dismissing an appeal in the case on jurisdictional grounds, 342 U.S. 429 (1952). In the following year, however, the New Jersey Supreme Court decided that it was contrary to the Fourteenth Amendment to permit the public schools to cooperate with the Gideons International, a Protestant group, in making a free distribution of the King James Bible to school children whose parents approved their receiving the gift. Unlike the Old Testament, the King James version was a "sectarian" book. It may not be irrelevant to note that Jewish and Catholic spokesmen strongly supported the state court's decision, and that various social scientists (i.e., educational psychologists) testified at the trial as to the harmful effects that Bible distribution would have upon the mental health and social well-being of school children. (Organized Catholics and Jews traditionally have exercised considerable political influence in the State of New Jersey.) The state supreme court also refused to follow what it considered to be the policy implications of the majority opinion of the United States Supreme Court in the case below, which had been decided in the preceding year.

ZORACH v. CLAUSON

343 U.S. 306 (1952)

Appeal from the Court of Appeals of New York.

Affirmed.

As in the Everson case, the libertarians were split by the policy issue in this case, which related to the extent to which the public schools could be used to help administer a municipal program of religious

6-3

Douglas	('+')
Vinson, C.J.	(+)
Reed	(+)
Burton	(+)
Clark	(+)
Minton	(+)
Black	'—')
Frankfurter	'—')
Jackson	'—')

education. *Murphy and Rutledge were gone by now, and Warren did not join the Court until the following year; so the only libertarians on the Court were Douglas and Black, who divided. The conservatives were also split, although most of them joined the majority which upheld the New York system of "released time." Four years earlier, following shortly after Everson, the Court had decided 8-1 against the constitutionality of the Champaign, Illinois, released-time system, under which classes in religion were conducted by clergymen in the public-school classrooms. Only Reed dissented; and the majority were not even dissuaded by the fact that the plaintiff in the case (a Mrs. Vashti McCollum) was an avowed athiest who objected to the Christian indoctrination of her child or, in the alternative, to the discrimination and social stigma that were the consequence of nonparticipation in religious instruction. (The aftermath of the McCollum decision is discussed in the concluding section of Chapter 4, at p. 261).*[51]

Justice Douglas' opinion for the majority in the case below is noteworthy for the emphasis it places upon the identity of meaning of the establishment clause as a constitutional policy under either the First or the Fourteenth Amendment. Douglas refers to the First Amendment ten times, generally as though it were directly applicable to state public-school policies (as the equal-protection clause is); while he mentions the Fourteenth Amendment only once, and parenthetically at that.

MR. JUSTICE DOUGLAS delivered the opinion of the Court.

New York City has a program which permits its public schools to release students during the school day so that they may leave the school buildings and school

51 Cf. Frank J. Sorauf, *"Zorach* v. *Clauson:* The Impact of a Supreme Court Decision," *American Political Science Review,* Vol. 53, pp. 777–791 (September, 1959).

grounds and go to religious centers for religious instruction or devotional exercises. A student is released on written request of his parents. Those not released stay in the classrooms. The churches make weekly reports to the schools, sending a list of children who have been released from public school but who have not reported for religious instruction.

This "released time" program involves neither religious instruction in public school classrooms nor the expenditure of public funds. All costs, including the application blanks, are paid by the religious organizations. The case is therefore unlike *McCollum* v. *Board of Education,* 333 U.S. 203, which involved a "released time" program from Illinois. In that case the classrooms were turned over to religious instructors. We accordingly held that the program violated the First Amendment which (by reason of the Fourteenth Amendment) prohibits the states from establishing religion or prohibiting its free exercise.

Appellants, who are taxpayers and residents of New York City and whose children attend its public schools, challenge the present law, contending it is in essence not different from the one involved in the *McCollum* case. Their argument, stated elaborately in various ways, reduces itself to this: the weight and influence of the school is put behind a program for religious instruction; public school teachers police it, keeping tab on students who are released; the classroom activities come to a halt while the students who are released for religious instruction are on leave; the school is a crutch on which the churches are leaning for support in their religious training; without the cooperation of the schools this "released time" program, like the one in the *McCollum* case, would be futile and ineffective. The New York Court of Appeals sustained the law against this claim of unconstitutionality. . . .

The briefs and arguments are replete with data bearing on the merits of this type of "released time" program. Views *pro* and *con* are expressed, based on practical experience with these programs and with their implications. We do not stop to summarize these materials nor to burden the opinion with an analysis of them. For they involve considerations not germane to the narrow constitutional issue presented. They largely concern the wisdom of the system, its efficiency from an educational point of view, and the political considerations which have motivated its adoption or rejection in some communities. Those matters are of no concern here, since our problem reduces itself to whether New York by this system has either prohibited the "free exercise" of religion or has made a law "respecting an establishment of religion" within the meaning of the First Amendment.

It takes obtuse reasoning to inject any issue of the "free exercise" of religion into the present case. No one is forced to go to the religious classroom and no religious exercise or instruction is brought to the classrooms of the public schools. A student need not take religious instruction. He is left to his own desires as to the manner or time of his religious devotions, if any.

There is a suggestion that the system involves the use of coercion to get public school students into religious classrooms. There is no evidence in the record before us that supports that conclusion.[52] The present record indeed tells us that the school authorities are neutral in this regard and do no more than release students whose parents so request. If in fact coercion were used, if it were established that any one or more teachers were using their office to persuade or force students to take the religious instruction, a wholly

different case would be presented.[53] Hence we put aside that claim of coercion both as respects the "free exercise" of religion and "an establishment of religion" within the meaning of the First Amendment.

Moreover, apart from that claim of coercion, we do not see how New York by this type of "released time" program has made a law respecting an establishment of religion within the meaning of the First Amendment. There is much talk of the separation of Church and State in the history of the Bill of Rights and in the decisions clustering around the First Amendment. See *Everson* v. *Board of Education,* 330 U.S. 1; *McCollum* v. *Board of Education, supra.* There cannot be the slightest doubt that the First Amendment reflects the philosophy that Church and State should be separated. And so far as interference with the "free exercise" of religion and an "establishment" of religion are concerned, the separation must be complete and unequivocal. The First Amendment within the scope of its coverage permits no exception; the prohibition is absolute. The First Amendment, however, does not say that in every and all respects there shall be a separation of Church and State. Rather, it studiously defines the manner, the specific ways, in which there shall be no concert or union or dependency one on the other. That is the common sense of the matter. Otherwise the state and religion would be aliens to each other—hostile, suspicious, and even unfriendly. Churches could not be required to pay even property taxes. Municipalities would not be permitted to render police or fire protection to religious groups. Policemen who helped parishioners into their places of worship would violate the Con-

---

[52] Nor is there any indication that the public schools enforce attendance at religious schools by punishing absentees from the released time programs for truancy. [Footnote by the Court.]

[53] Appellants contend that they should have been allowed to prove that the system is in fact administered in a coercive manner. The New York Court of Appeals declined to grant a trial on this issue, noting *inter alia,* that appellants had not properly raised their claim in the manner required by state practice. . . . [Footnote by the Court.]

stitution. Prayers in our legislative halls; the appeals to the Almighty in the messages of the Chief Executive; the proclamations making Thanksgiving Day a holiday; "so help me God" in our courtroom oaths—these and all other references to the Almighty that run through our laws, our public rituals, our ceremonies would be flouting the First Amendment. A fastidious atheist or agnostic could even object to the supplication with which the Court opens each session: "God save the United States and this Honorable Court."

We would have to press the concept of separation of Church and State to these extremes to condemn the present law on constitutional grounds. . . .

We are a religious people whose institutions presuppose a Supreme Being. We guarantee the freedom to worship as one chooses. We make room for as wide a variety of beliefs and creeds as the spiritual needs of man deem necessary. We sponsor an attitude on the part of government that shows no partiality to any one group and that lets each flourish according to the zeal of its adherents and the appeal of its dogma. When the state encourages religious instruction or cooperates with religious authorities by adjusting the schedule of public events to sectarian needs, it follows the best of our traditions. For it then respects the religious nature of our people and accommodates the public service to their spiritual needs. To hold that it may not would be to find in the Constitution a requirement that the government show a callous indifference to religious groups. That would be preferring those who believe in no religion over those who do believe. Government may not finance religious groups nor undertake religious instruction nor blend secular and sectarian education nor use secular institutions to force one or some religion on any person. But we find no constitutional requirement which makes it necessary for government to be hostile to religion and to

throw its weight against efforts to widen the effective scope of religious influence. The government must be neutral when it comes to competition between sects. It may not thrust any sect on any person. It may not make a religious observance compulsory. It may not coerce anyone to attend church, to observe a religious holiday, or to take religious instruction. But it can close its doors or suspend its operations as to those who want to repair to their religious sanctuary for worship or instruction. No more than that is undertaken here.

This program may be unwise and improvident from an educational or a community viewpoint. That appeal is made to us on a theory, previously advanced, that each case must be decided on the basis of "our own prepossessions." See *McCollum* v. *Board of Education, supra,* p. 238. Our individual preferences, however, are not the constitutional standard. The constitutional standard is the separation of Church and State. The problem, like many problems in constitutional law, is one of degree. See *McCollum* v. *Board of Education, supra,* p. 231.

In the *McCollum* case the classrooms were used for religious instruction and the force of the public school was used to promote that instruction. Here, as we have said, the public schools do no more than accommodate their schedules to a program of outside religious instruction. We follow the *McCollum* case. But we cannot expand it to cover the present released time program unless separation of Church and State means that public institutions can make no adjustments of their schedules to accommodate the religious needs of the people. We cannot read into the Bill of Rights such a philosophy of hostility to religion.

Affirmed.

MR. JUSTICE BLACK, dissenting.

Illinois ex rel. McCollum v. *Board of Education,* 333 U.S. 203, held invalid as an "establishment of religion" an Illinois system under which school children, compelled by law to go to public schools, were freed from some hours of required school work on condition that they attend special religious classes held in the school buildings. Although the classes were taught by sectarian teachers neither employed nor paid by the state, the state did use its power to further the program by releasing some of the children from regular class work, insisting that those released attend the religious classes, and requiring that those who remained behind do some kind of academic work while the others received their religious training. We said this about the Illinois system: "Pupils compelled by law to go to school for secular education are released in part from their legal duty upon the condition that they attend the religious classes. This is beyond all question a utilization of the tax-established and tax-supported public school system to aid religious groups to spread their faith. And it falls squarely under the ban of the First Amendment. . . ." *McCollum* v. *Board of Education, supra,* at pp. 209-210.

I see no significant difference between the invalid Illinois system and that of New York here sustained. Except for the use of the school buildings in Illinois, there is no difference between the systems which I consider even worthy of mention. In the New York program, as in that of Illinois, the school authorities release some of the children on the condition that they attend the religious classes, get reports on whether they attend, and hold the other children in the school building until the religious hour is over. As we attempted to make categorically clear, the *McCollum* decision would have been the same if the religious classes had not been held in the school buildings. We said: "Here *not only* are the State's tax-supported public school buildings used for the dissemination of religious doctrines. The State *also* affords sectarian groups an invaluable aid in that it helps to provide pupils for their

religious classes through use of the State's compulsory public school machinery. *This* is not separation of Church and State." (Emphasis supplied.) *McCollum* v. *Board of Education, supra,* at p. 212. *McCollum* thus held that Illinois could not constitutionally manipulate the compelled classroom hours of its compulsory school machinery so as to channel children into sectarian classes. Yet that is exactly what the Court holds New York can do.

I am aware that our *McCollum* decision on separation of Church and State has been subjected to a most searching examination throughout the country. Probably few opinions from this Court in recent years have attracted more attention or stirred wider debate. Our insistence on "a wall between Church and State which must be kept high and impregnable" has seemed to some a correct exposition of the philosophy and a true interpretation of the language of the First Amendment to which we should strictly adhere.[54] With equal conviction and sincerity, others have thought the *McCollum* decision fundamentally wrong[55] and have pledged continuous warfare against it. The opinions in the court below and the briefs here reflect these diverse viewpoints. In dissenting today, I mean to do more than give routine approval to our *McCollum* decision. I mean also to reaffirm my faith in the fundamental philosophy expressed in *McCollum* and *Everson.* . . .

[54] See, e.g., Newman, The Sectarian Invasion of Our Public Schools; Moehlman, The Wall of Separation between Church and State; Thayer, The Attack upon the American Secular School, pp. 179-199; Butts, The American Tradition in Religion and Education, pp. 201-208. See also Symposium on Religion and the State, 14 Law & Contemp. Prob. 1-159. [Footnote by Justice Black.]

[55] See, e.g., O'Neill, Religion and Education Under the Constitution, pp. 219-253; Parsons, The First Freedom, pp. 158-178; Van Dusen, God in Education. See also Symposium on Religion and the State, *supra.* [Footnote by Justice Black.]

MR. JUSTICE JACKSON, dissenting.

This released time program is founded upon a use of the State's power of coercion, which, for me, determines its unconstitutionality. Stripped to its essentials, the plan has two stages: first, that the State compel each student to yield a large part of his time for public secular education; and, second, that some of it be "released" to him on condition that he devote it to sectarian religious purposes.

No one suggests that the Constitution would permit the State directly to require this "released" time to be spent "under the control of a duly constituted religious body." This program accomplishes that forbidden result by indirection. If public education were taking so much of the pupils' time as to injure the public or the students' welfare by encroaching upon their religious opportunity, simply shortening everyone's school day would facilitate voluntary and optional attendance at Church classes. But that suggestion is rejected upon the ground that if they are made free many students will not go to the Church. Hence, they must be deprived of freedom for this period, with Church attendance put to them as one of the two permissible ways of using it.

The greater effectiveness of this system over voluntary attendance after school hours is due to the truant officer who, if the youngster fails to go to the Church school, dogs him back to the public schoolroom. Here schooling is more or less suspended during the "released time" so the nonreligious attendants will not forge ahead of the churchgoing absentees. But it serves as a temporary jail for a pupil who will not go to Church. It takes more subtlety of mind than I possess to deny that this is governmental constraint in support of religion. It is as unconstitutional, in my view, when exerted by indirection as when exercised forthrightly.

As one whose children, as a matter of free choice, have been sent to privately supported Church schools, I may challenge the Court's suggestion that opposition to this plan can only be antireligious, atheistic, or agnostic. My evangelistic brethren confuse an objection to compulsion with an objection to religion. It is possible to hold a faith with enough confidence to believe that what should be rendered to God does not need to be decided and collected by Caesar.

The day that this country ceases to be free for irreligion it will cease to be free for religion—except for the sect that can win political power. The same epithetical jurisprudence used by the Court today to beat down those who oppose pressuring children into some religion can devise as good epithets tomorrow against those who object to pressuring them into a favored religion. And, after all, if we concede to the State power and wisdom to single out "duly constituted religious" bodies as exclusive alternatives for compulsory secular instruction, it would be logical to also uphold the power and wisdom to choose the true faith among those "duly constituted." We start down a rough road when we begin to mix compulsory public education with compulsory godliness.

A number of Justices just short of a majority of the majority that promulgates today's passionate dialectics joined in answering them in *Illinois ex rel. McCollum* v. *Board of Education,* 333 U.S. 203. The distinction attempted between that case and this is trivial, almost to the point of cynicism, magnifying its nonessential details and disparaging compulsion which was the underlying reason for invalidity. A reading of the Court's opinion in that case along with its opinion in this case will show such difference of overtones and undertones as to make clear that the *McCollum* case has passed like a storm in a teacup. The wall which the Court was professing to erect between Church and State has become even more warped and twisted than I expected.

Today's judgment will be more interesting to students of psychology and of the judicial processes than to students of constitutional law.

The combination of Everson and Zorach, coming within a few years of each other, made it clear that the Court had established a new constitutional policy of tolerance toward the integration of religion and the public schools. School monies could be used to help defray the costs of sending children to parochial schools, and school authorities could assist in the administration of programs of religious instruction. Perhaps the basic difficulty, of which the unusual voting combinations of the justices in these two cases may have been symptomatic, has been best articulated by Justice Jackson in his concurrence in the McCollum case: [56]

> It is idle to pretend that this task is one for which we can find in the Constitution one word to help us as judges to decide where the secular ends and the sectarian begins in education. Nor can we find guidance in any other legal source. It is a matter on which we can find no law but our own prepossessions. If with no surer legal guidance we are to take up and decide every variation of this controversy . . . we are likely to have much business of this sort. And, more importantly, we are likely to make the legal "wall of separation between church and state" as winding as the famous serpentine wall designed by Mr. Jefferson for the University he founded.

[56] *McCollum* v. *Board of Education,* 333 U.S. 203, 237-238 (1948).

11

Procedural Due Process

A s we have seen in Chapter 10, the Constitution was interpreted, for a century and a third, to mean that freedom of speech, press, religion, assembly, and petition could be restrained by the states, subject only to the guarantees of civil rights and liberties contained in the states' own constitutions. Eighty-one years after the Philadelphia Convention adjourned, the Fourteenth Amendment was added to the Constitution; but in spite of the revolutionary potentialities, for the federal balance of power, incipient in the egalitarian goals posited by the great constitutional change of the nineteenth century, another fifty-nine years elapsed before the Fourteenth Amendment began to subsume the content and meaning of the First Amendment. Both before and since the "incorporation" of the First Amendment, the Court has been asked to nationalize other of the civil rights and liberties of the Bill of Rights— the Fourth through the Eighth amendments. Apart from an occasional dictum, and the advocacy of concurrence and dissent, the Court has consistently rejected the suggestion that it should read the entire Bill of Rights into some part of the Fourteenth Amendment.

The reasons for the Court's reluctance to nationalize the Bill of Rights are various. In one sense, the most fundamental reason is that five justices who believed strongly in the desirability of such a constitutional policy have never sat upon the Court at the same time. The strongest verbal support that such a proposed policy change ever has attracted was in *Adamson* v. *California* (below), which was decided at the end of the 1946 Term, when the "Libertarian Four" dissented against the majority's refusal to incorporate the Fifth Amendment (in part). The deaths of Murphy and Rutledge reduced the advocates of such a policy to two; although the decisions of the 1956-58 terms made it clear that Chief Justice Warren had aligned himself with Black and Douglas to increase to three the size of the "full incorporation" minority.[1] And Brennan [2] and Whittaker [3] (and later Stewart) seemed to be possible candidates for future conversion to the cause.

THE SECOND-CLASS RIGHTS OF CRIMINAL DEFENDANTS

Why would a majority not support the policy of full incorporation? There appear to be two primary reasons.

In the first place, the notions associated with the "freedoms" of the First Amendment are sufficiently broad and vacuous that the Court retains—as we observed in the preceding chapter—considerable room for maneuver in relating them to the diverse fact situations of particular cases arising at different points in time. Freedom of speech, thought, and belief—all these are essentially political rights, not legal rights in any narrow or technical sense. The right to be tried by a jury of twelve men good and true, and to suffer the pains and penalties consequent upon conviction only if all jurors agree adversely to the defendant (together with a host of ancillary policies) is relatively much more precise as a norm for the Court to apply. The basic policy is the fruit, moreover, of the experience of another people, living in another land, at another and much earlier time. Consequently (the argument of the Court's majority runs) it would be unwise to "freeze" into the Constitution specific rules of procedure that happened to seem beneficial to English colonists in the eighteenth century. Such policies might be inappropriate today, or tomorrow; and conversely, other needed procedural innovations to protect civil liberties might be more difficult to establish as norms of national constitutional policy if the Fourteenth Amendment were equated with the federal Bill of Rights. These latter objections would apply to the Bill of Rights in relationship to the national government as well, of course; and it is generally agreed that the Bill of Rights is "frozen" in this application. Even so, there is a loophole; the Court increasingly is coming to rely upon its broad "supervisory responsibilities for the administration of justice in the federal courts" as a source of authority for the establishment of procedural rules which define, in effect, civil rights and liberties in addition to those specified in the Bill of Rights.

The libertarian justices have tended to argue this position in rebuttal: the

[1] See, e.g., *Bartkus* v. *Illinois,* 359 U.S. 121 (March 30, 1959).

[2] See *Frank* v. *Maryland,* 359 U.S. 360 (May 4, 1959), in which Brennan joined in the dissenting opinion; and cf. Brennan's

dissenting opinion in *Bartkus* v. *Illinois,* 359 U.S. 121, 164 (1959).

[3] See Whittaker's concurring opinion in *Frank* v. *Maryland,* 359 U.S. 360, 373 (1959).

Court should indeed insist upon strict observance of the Bill of Rights in application to the national government, and the Court very properly has invoked its supervisory powers to upgrade the standards for the administration of justice in the federal courts. But in addition, as the Supreme Court of the *entire* United States, the Court ought to nationalize the entire Bill of Rights to establish a national *minimum* of civil rights and liberties throughout the country, in relationship to any level or source of governmental authority. Moreover, the establishment of such a set of minimal guarantees should not inhibit the Court from using the language of the due-proess, equal-protection, and the privileges-and-immunities clauses of the Fourteenth Amendment as the basis for the recognition of such modern civil rights and liberties as that of workingmen to organize in labor unions and to picket employers or to go on strike, or the right of members of an organized group to be free from defamation and recrimination (such as the loss of public or private employment) because of their association with the group.

In the second place, the libertarian position is tenable only to the extent that the justices who accept it are willing to sublimate the values clustered in the other two major variables inescapably present in civil-liberties litigation. If the question at issue relates to a criminal trial in the federal courts, for instance, it generally evokes the scope of the authority of investigatory officials of the Executive Branch, whose claim of power is based, directly or indirectly, upon congressional legislation. For example, the Court cannot decide, as it recently did,[4] that the "right to confrontation" (established by the Court under its supervisory power rather than the Fifth Amendment) bars the reception as testimony in a federal court of confidential F.B.I. reports, without at the same time nullifying a consistent administrative-judicial practice of the past two decades which has unquestionably received the wholehearted support and approval of the Presidency and the Congress throughout this period. In order to uphold the claim of civil right, the Court had to challenge both political branches of the government on an issue that was inescapably political as well as legal, with the elected representatives of the people publicly declaring that the Court's decision would endanger the security of the nation. In thus vetoing J. Edgar Hoover, the Court had made a political decision that no President in recent years would have felt politically strong enough to risk.[5]

To restate this point, for some justices the considerations of judicial restraint that are evoked when a policy issue is defined primarily in terms of the separation-of-powers variable take precedence over claims of civil right in cases where libertarian justices consider the civil-right issue to be the paramount value at stake and the one which the Court ought to uphold. Choice is never a simple

[4] *Jencks* v. *United States,* 353 U.S. 657 (1957).

[5] Cf. Joseph F. Marsh, Jr., "The F.B.I. Retirement Bill," in Harold Stein (ed.), *Public Administration and Policy Development* (New York: Harcourt, 1952), pp. 650-660.

matter of preferring either "governmental authority," on the one hand, or a claim of civil right, on the other hand, except for justices who are willing to put on judicial blinders and redefine all cases involving libertarian claims in terms of a single dominant variable.

The most persistent intervening variable, as we have pointed out earlier, is that of federalism. For the Court to uphold a claim of federal constitutional right in a state criminal case, it is necessary for the Court to hold some form of state action to be unconstitutional. When this is recognized, it is understandable that for some justices, such a case typically evokes considerations of judicial restraint keyed to federal balance, the deference due to state judges who are *not* (in theory) subject to the "supervisory power" of the Supreme Court, *plus* the separation-of-powers value of deference to experimentation by popular majorities, either in state legislatures or constituent assemblies or as expressed in direct referenda.

The Deferred Position of the Fifth Amendment

As early as 1884, the Court was asked to rule that the due-process clause of the then recently adopted Fourteenth Amendment prohibited the states from inflicting capital punishment upon a convicted defendant who had been brought to trial, not on the basis of a grand jury indictment, but rather (as authorized by California law) by an information filed against him by the prosecuting attorney. After thorough consideration of the issue, including many of the considerations (such as the evolving-standards-of-civilized-decency versus a constitutional "strait-jacket" argument) to which we have alluded above, the Court rejected the suggestion that the states were confined, in their administration of criminal justice, by the same specific procedural limitations that the middle articles of the Bill of Rights (*viz.*, Amendments IV-VIII) made applicable to the national government. The decision in *Hurtado* v. *California,* 110 U.S. 516 (1884), against which the senior Harlan dissented alone, was hardly surprising; it was to be yet another fifteen years before the Court would apply the due-process clause of the Fourteenth Amendment to protect *property* rights against claims of state abridgement.

Hurtado was followed by other decisions in which the Court rejected the policy of Fourteenth Amendment incorporation of federal procedural rights, on either a full or a selective basis. The most important of these decisions, prior to the post-World War II period, were *Maxwell* v. *Dow,* 176 U.S. 581 (1900), *Twining* v. *New Jersey,* 211 U.S. 78 (1908), and *Palko* v. *Connecticut,* 302 U.S. 319 (1937). All three cases were decided, like Hurtado, by decisive majorities of 8-1. A quarter of a century separates Hurtado and Twining; but the senior John Marshall Harlan stuck to his guns, and reiterated in the Maxwell and Twining cases substantially the same argument he had advanced in Hurtado. (In Palko, Mr. Justice Butler dissented without opinion.) In all three cases, the defendant attempted to persuade the Court to read Fifth or Sixth Amendment rights into either the due-process clause, or alternatively, the privileges-and-immunities clause of the Fourteenth Amendment.[6] The Court's pattern of response varied significantly through time, however.

In 1884, discussion had been limited to the due-process clause. In 1900, the defendant placed primary reliance upon his privileges-and-immunities claim, and only secondary reliance upon the due-process claim. This was certainly a reasonable tactic at the time. Allgeyer had just been decided, and Lochner remained inchoate in an unforeseen future; so the imminent victory of the rights of *property* to substantive due process was not as apparent to Charles Maxwell's counsel as it is to those who can view the question with the benefit of hindsight. The Court responded with a lengthy discussion of the privileges-and-immunities question, and an almost cursory dismissal of the due-process claim. In 1908, the major policy issues of both Hurtado and Maxwell were thrashed over once again, Mr. Justice Moody's opinion for the Court in Twining and Harlan's dissent alike giving roughly equivalent space and consideration to both the privileges-and-immunities and the due-process issues.[7]

As we learned in Chapter 10, however, the Court had invented and had begun to contrive a content for the concept of substantive due process as a *personal* right during the dozen years preceding the Palko case; and at the time Palko was decided, it was not yet clear that substantive due process as a *property* right was on the threshold of disappearing from the Court's jurisprudence. It is not surprising, therefore, that Cardozo's opinion in Palko should focus upon the due-process issue, dismissing the privileges-and-immunities issue with a curt citation of Maxwell. Thus the logomachy had come full circle; and this helps to explain why Palko, reconsidering the same fundamental policy issue as Hurtado after a hiatus of half a century, differs considerably in perspective and in its implications from the earlier decision.

[6] The specific issues in Maxwell were (as in Hurtado) the Fifth Amendment right to indictment by a grand jury, and the Sixth Amendment right to trial by a petit jury according to the common law. In Twining, the specific claim was to the Fifth Amendment privilege against testimonial compulsion (i.e., self-incrimination).

[7] Twining illustrates also another dilemma of judicial restraint: whether to decide first the federal constitutional question (as Moody did), out of deference to the decision of a state court on a question of state law; or whether to decide first (as Harlan urged) whether the privilege of self-incrimination had in fact been violated, because if there were no violation, it would be improper for the Court to decide the constitutional issue as a question of abstract doctrine.

PALKO v. CONNECTICUT

302 U.S. 319 (December 6, 1937)

Appeal from the Supreme Court of Errors of Connecticut.

Affirmed.

8-1

Cardozo	('+')
Hughes, C.J.	(+)
McReynolds	(+)
Brandeis	(+)
Sutherland	(+)
Stone	(+)
Roberts	(+)
Black	(+)
Butler	—

MR. JUSTICE CARDOZO delivered the opinion of the Court.

Appellant was indicted in Fairfield County, Conn., for the crime of murder in the first degree. A jury found him guilty of murder in the second degree, and he was sentenced to confinement in the state prison for life. Thereafter the State of Connecticut, with the permission of the judge presiding at the trial, gave notice of appeal to the Supreme Court of Errors. This it did pursuant to an act adopted in 1886. . . . Upon such appeal, the Supreme Court of Errors reversed the judgment and ordered a new trial. . . . It found that there had been error of law to the prejudice of the state (1) in excluding testimony as to a confession by defendant; (2) in excluding testimony upon cross-examination of defendant to impeach his credibility; and (3) in the instructions to the jury as to the difference between first and second degree murder.

Pursuant to the mandate of the Supreme Court of Errors, defendant was brought to trial again. Before a jury was impaneled, and also at later stages of the case, he made the objection that the effect of the new trial was to place him twice in jeopardy for the same offense, and in so doing to violate the Fourteenth Amendment of the Constitution of the United States. Upon the overruling of the objection the trial proceeded. The jury returned a verdict of murder in the first degree, and the court sentenced the defendant to the punishment of death. The Supreme Court of Errors affirmed the judgment of conviction. . . .

1. The execution of the sentence will not deprive appellant of his life without the process of law assured to him by the Fourteenth Amendment of the Federal Constitution.

The argument for appellant is that whatever is forbidden by the Fifth Amendment is forbidden by the Fourteenth also. The Fifth Amendment, which is not directed to the States, but solely to the federal government, creates immunity from double jeopardy. No person shall be "subject for the same offense to be twice put in jeopardy of life or limb." The Fourteenth Amendment ordains, "nor shall any State deprive any person of life, liberty, or property, without due process of law." To retry a defendant, though under one indictment and only one, subjects him, it is said, to double jeopardy in violation of the Fifth Amendment, if the prosecution is one on behalf of the United States. From this the consequence is said to follow that there is a denial of life or liberty without due process of law, if the prosecution is one on behalf of the people of a state. . . .

We do not find it profitable to mark the precise limits of the prohibition of double jeopardy in federal prosecutions. The subject was much considered in Kepner v. United States, 195 U.S. 100, . . . decided in 1904 by a closely divided court. The view was there expressed for a majority of the court that the prohibition was not confined to jeopardy in a new and independent case. It forbade jeopardy in the same case if the new trial was at the instance of the government and not upon defendant's motion. . . . All this may be assumed for the purpose of the case at hand, though the dissenting opinions . . . show how much was to be said in favor of a different ruling. Right-minded men, as we learn from those opinions, could reasonably, even if mistakenly, believe that a second trial was lawful in prosecutions subject to the Fifth Amendment, if it was all in the same case. Even more plainly, right-minded men could reasonably believe that in espousing that conclusion they were not favoring a practice repugnant to the conscience of mankind. Is double jeopardy in such circumstances, if double jeopardy it must be called, a denial of due process forbidden to the States? The tyranny of labels . . . must not lead us to leap to a conclusion that a word which in one set of facts may stand for oppression or enormity is of like effect in every other.

We have said that in appellant's view the Fourteenth Amendment is to be taken as embodying the prohibitions of the Fifth. His thesis is even broader. Whatever would be a violation of the original bill of rights (Amendments 1 to 8) if done by the federal government is now equally unlawful by force of the Fourteenth Amendment if done by a state. There is no such general rule.

The Fifth Amendment provides, among other things, that no person shall be held to answer for a capital or otherwise infamous crime unless on presentment or indictment of a grand jury. This court has held that, in prosecutions by a state, presentment or indictment by a grand jury may give way to informations at the instance of a public officer. Hurtado v. California, 110 U.S. 516. . . .

The Fifth Amendment provides also that no person shall be compelled in any criminal case to be a witness against himself. This court has said that, in prosecutions by a state, the exemption will fail if the state elects to end it. Twining v. New Jersey, 211 U.S. 78, 106, 111, 112. . . . The Sixth Amendment calls for a jury trial in criminal cases and the Seventh for a jury trial in civil cases at common law where the value in controversy shall exceed $20. This court has ruled that consistently with those amendments trial by jury may be modified by a state or abolished altogether. Walker v. Sauvinet, 92 U.S. 90 . . . Maxwell v. Dow, 176 U.S. 581. . . . As to the Fourth Amendment, one should refer to Weeks v. United States, 232 U.S. 383, 398. . . .

On the other hand, the due process clause of the Fourteenth Amendment may make it unlawful for a state to abridge by its statutes the freedom of speech which the First Amendment safeguards against encroachment by the Congress (De Jonge v. Oregon, 299 U.S. 353, 364, . . . Herndon v. Lowry, 301 U.S. 242, 259) . . . or the like freedom of the press (Grosjean v. American Press Co., 297 U.S. 233, . . . Near v. Minnesota, 283 U.S. 697, 707) . . . or the free exercise of religion (Hamilton v. Regents of University, 293 U.S. 245, 262) . . . or the right of peaceable assembly, without which speech would be unduly trammeled (De Jonge v. Oregon, supra; Herndon v. Lowry, supra), or the right of one accused of crime to the benefit of counsel (Powell v. Alabama, 287 U.S. 45). . . . In these and other situations immunities that are valid as against the federal government by force of the specific pledges of particular amendments have been found to be implicit in the concept of ordered liberty, and thus, through the Fourteenth Amendment, become valid as against the states.

The line of division may seem to be wavering and broken if there is a hasty catalogue of the cases on the one side and the other. Reflection and analysis will induce a different view. There emerges the perception of a rationalizing principle which gives to discrete instances a proper order and coherence. The right to trial by jury and the immunity from prosecution except as the result of an indictment may have value and importance. Even so, they are not of the very essence of a scheme of ordered liberty. To abolish them is not to violate a "principle of justice so rooted in the traditions and conscience of our people as to be ranked as fundamental." . . . Few would be so narrow or provincial as to maintain that a fair and enlightened system of justice would be impossible without them. What is true of jury trials and indictments is true also, as the cases show, of the immunity from compulsory self-incrimination. Twining v. New Jersey, supra. This too might be lost, and justice still be done. Indeed, today as in the past there are students of our penal system who look upon the immunity as a mischief rather than a benefit, and who would limit its scope, or destroy it altogether. No doubt there would remain the need to give protection against torture, physical or mental.

. . . Justice, however, would not perish if the accused were subject to a duty to respond to orderly inquiry. The exclusion of these immunities and privileges from the privileges and immunities protected against the action of the States has not been arbitrary or casual. It has been dictated by a study and appreciation of the meaning, the essential implications, of liberty itself.

We reach a different plane of social and moral values when we pass to the privileges and immunities that have been taken over from the earlier articles of the Federal Bill of Rights and brought within the Fourteenth Amendment by a process of absorption. These in their origin were effective against the federal government alone. If the Fourteenth Amendment has absorbed them, the process of absorption has had its source in the belief that neither liberty nor justice would exist if they were sacrificed. Twining v. New Jersey, . . . 211 U.S. 78 at page 99.[8] . . . This is true,

for illustration, of freedom of thought and speech. Of that freedom one may say that it is the matrix, the indispensable condition, of nearly every other form of freedom. With rare aberrations a pervasive recognition of that truth can be traced in our history, political and legal. So it has come about that the domain of liberty, withdrawn by the Fourteenth Amendment from encroachment by the states, has been enlarged by latter-day judgments to include liberty of the mind as well as liberty of action. The extension became, indeed, a logical imperative when once it was recognized, as long ago it was, that liberty is something more than exemption from physical restraint, and that even in the field of substantive rights and duties the legislative judgment, if oppressive and arbitrary, may be overridden by the courts. . . . Fundamental too in the concept of due process, and so in that of liberty, is the thought that condemnation shall be rendered only after trial. . . . The hearing, moreover, must be a real one, not a sham or a pretense. . . . For that reason, ignorant defendants in a capital case were held to have been condemned unlawfully when in truth, though not in form, they were refused the aid of counsel. Powell v. Alabama, supra, 287 U.S. 45, at pages 67, 68. . . . *The decision did not turn upon the fact that the benefit of counsel would have been guaranteed to the defendants by the provisions of the Sixth Amendment if they had been prosecuted in a federal court. The decision turned upon the fact that in the particular situation laid before us in the evidence the benefit of counsel was essential to the substance of a hearing.*[9]

Our survey of the cases serves, we think, to justify the statement that the dividing line between them, if not unfaltering

8 "It is possible that some of the personal rights safeguarded by the first eight Amendments against national action may also be safeguarded against state action, because a denial of them would be a denial of due process of law. . . . If this is so, it is not because those rights are enumerated in the

first eight Amendments, but because they are of such a nature that they are included in the conception of due process of law." [Footnote by the Court.]

9 Emphasis added. See the further discussion of the Powell case in the right-to-counsel section of this chapter.

throughout its course, has been true for the most part to a unifying principle. On which side of the line the case made out by the appellant has appropriate location must be the next inquiry and the final one. Is that kind of double jeopardy to which the statute has subjected him a hardship so acute and shocking that our polity will not endure it? Does it violate those "fundamental principles of liberty and justice which lie at the base of all our civil and political institutions"? . . . The answer surely must be "no." What the answer would have to be if the state were permitted after a trial free from error to try the accused over again or to bring another case against him, we have no occasion to consider. We deal with the statute before us and no other. The state is not attempting to wear the accused out by a multitude of cases with accumulated trials. It asks no more than this, that the case against him shall go on until there shall be a trial free from the corrosion of substantial legal error. . . . This is not cruelty

at all, nor even vexation in any immoderate degree. If the trial had been infected with error adverse to the accused, there might have been review at his instance, and as often as necessary to purge the vicious taint. A reciprocal privilege, subject at all times to the discretion of the presiding judge . . . has now been granted to the state. There is here no seismic innovation. The edifice of justice stands, its symmetry, to many, greater than before.

2. The conviction of appellant is not in derogation of any privileges or immunities that belong to him as a citizen of the United States.

There is argument in his behalf that the privileges and immunities clause of the Fourteenth Amendment as well as the due process clause has been flouted by the judgment.

Maxwell v. Dow, supra, 176 U.S. 581, at page 584, [1900] . . . gives all the answer that is necessary.

The judgment is affirmed.

The Palko case was decided late in the year of the Court-packing episode, and at the beginning of what has become known as the period of the Roosevelt Court. Only one of the justices who participated in Palko was a Roosevelt appointee, and Black joined in the opinion of the Court; Butler alone dissented, and for what reasons we may never know, since he wrote no opinion. When the issue was raised again a decade later, it was nearing the end of the Roosevelt Court era, even though seven of the justices who participated in the Adamson case (below) were the choices of F.D.R. Perhaps if the question had been faced only fifteen months earlier, when Stone was Chief Justice and Jackson was in Nuremberg, the decision might have been different. Probably not, however, since Stone (like Frankfurter) was clearly identified with the sociological-jurisprudence school of legal philosophy, for which Cardozo was a leading spokesman and of which the Palko opinion is an excellent example. In any event, Adamson became the case in which the pro-incorporation libertarian minority bloc made their strongest argument in behalf of what has always been a losing cause.

ADAMSON v. CALIFORNIA

332 U.S. 46 (1947)

Appeal from the Supreme Court of California.

Affirmed.

5-4

Reed	('+')
Vinson, C.J.	(+)
Jackson	(+)
Burton	(+)
Frankfurter	('+'
Black	'—')
Douglas	—)
Murphy	'—')
Rutledge	—)

MR. JUSTICE REED delivered the opinion of the Court.

The appellant, Adamson, a citizen of the United States, was convicted, without recommendation for mercy, by a jury in a Superior Court of the State of California of murder in the first degree. After considering the same objections to the conviction that are pressed here, the sentence of death was affirmed by the Supreme Court of the state. . . . The provisions of California law which were challenged in the state proceedings as invalid under the Fourteenth Amendment to the Federal Constitution . . . permit the failure of a defendant to explain or to deny evidence against him to be commented upon by court and by counsel and to be considered by court and jury. The defendant did not testify. . . .

The appellant was charged in the information with former convictions for burglary, larceny and robbery and . . . answered that he had suffered the previous convictions. This answer barred allusion to these charges of convictions on the trial. Under California's interpretation . . . of the Penal Code and . . . of the Code of Civil Procedure, however, if the defendant, after answering affirmatively charges alleging prior convictions, takes the witness stand to deny or explain away other evidence that has been introduced "the commission of these crimes could have been revealed to the jury on cross-examination to impeach his testimony." . . . This forces an accused who is a repeated offender to choose between the risk of having his prior offenses disclosed to the jury or of having it draw harmful inferences from uncontradicted evidence that can only be denied or explained by the defendant.

In the first place, appellant urges that the provision of the Fifth Amendment that no person "shall be compelled in any criminal case to be a witness against himself" is a fundamental national privilege or immunity protected against state abridgment by the Fourteenth Amendment or a privilege or immunity secured, through the Fourteenth Amendment, against deprivation by state action because it is a personal right, enumerated in the federal Bill of Rights. . . .

We shall assume, but without any intention thereby of ruling upon the issue, that permission by law to the court, counsel and jury to comment upon and consider the failure of defendant "to explain or to deny by his testimony any evidence or facts in the case against him" would infringe defendant's privilege against self-incrimination under the Fifth Amendment if this were a trial in a court of the United States under a similar law. Such an assumption does not determine appellant's rights under the Fourteenth Amendment. It is settled law that the clause of the Fifth Amendment, protecting a person against being compelled to be a witness against himself, is not made effective by the Fourteenth Amendment as a protection against state action on the ground that freedom from testimonial compulsion is a right of national citizenship, or because it is a personal privilege or immunity secured by the Federal Constitution as one of the rights of man that are listed in the Bill of Rights. . . .

Appellant . . . contends that if the privilege against self-incrimination is not a right protected by the privileges and immunities clause of the Fourteenth Amendment against state action, this privilege, to its full scope under the Fifth Amendment, inheres in the right to a fair trial. A right to a fair trial is a right admittedly protected by the due process clause of the Fourteenth Amendment. Therefore, appellant argues, the due process clause of the Fourteenth Amendment protects his privilege against self-incrimination. The due process clause of the Fourteenth Amendment, however, does not draw all the rights of the federal Bill of Rights under its protection. That contention was made and rejected in *Palko* v. *Connecticut,* 302 U.S. 319, 323. . . . Nothing has been called to our attention that either the framers of the Fourteenth Amendment or the states that adopted intended its due process clause to draw within its scope the earlier amendments to the Constitution. *Palko* held that such provisions of the Bill of Rights as were "implicit in the concept of ordered liberty," p. 325, became secure from state interference by the clause. But it held nothing more.

Specifically, the due process clause does not protect, by virtue of its mere existence, the accused's freedom from giving testimony by compulsion in state trials that is secured to him against federal interference by the Fifth Amendment. *Twining* v. *New Jersey,* 211 U.S. 78, 99-114; *Palko* v. *Connecticut, supra,* p. 323. For a state to require testimony from an accused is not necessarily a breach of a state's obligation to give a fair trial. Therefore, we must examine the effect of the California law applied in this trial to see whether the comment on failure to testify violates the protection against state action that the due process clause does grant to an accused. . . .

However sound may be the legislative

conclusion that an accused should not be compelled in any criminal case to be a witness against himself, we see no reason why comment should not be made upon his silence. It seems quite natural that when a defendant has opportunity to deny or explain facts and determines not to do so, the prosecution should bring out the strength of the evidence by commenting upon defendant's failure to explain or deny it. The prosecution evidence may be of facts that may be beyond the knowledge of the accused. If so, his failure to testify would have little if any weight. But the facts may be such as are necessarily in the knowledge of the accused. In that case a failure to explain would point to an inability to explain.

Appellant sets out the circumstances of this case, however, to show coercion and unfairness in permitting comment. The guilty person was not seen at the place and time of the crime. There was evidence, however, that entrance to the place or room where the crime was committed might have been obtained through a small door. It was freshly broken. Evidence showed that six fingerprints on the door were petitioner's. Certain diamond rings were missing from the deceased's possession. There was evidence that appellant, sometime after the crime, asked an unidentified person whether the latter would be interested in purchasing a diamond ring. As has been stated, the information charged other crimes to appellant and he admitted them. His argument here is that he could not take the stand to deny the evidence against him because he would be subjected to a cross-examination as to former crimes to impeach his veracity and the evidence so produced might well bring about his conviction. Such cross-examination is allowable in California. . . . Therefore, appellant contends the California statute permitting comment denies him due process.

It is true that if comment were forbidden, an accused in this situation could remain silent and avoid evidence of former crimes and comment upon his failure to testify. We are of the view, however, that a state may control such a situation in accordance with its own ideas of the most efficient administration of criminal justice. The purpose of due process is not to protect an accused against a proper conviction but against an unfair conviction. When evidence is before a jury that threatens conviction, it does not seem unfair to require him to choose between leaving the adverse evidence unexplained and subjecting himself to impeachment through disclosure of former crimes. Indeed, this is a dilemma with which any defendant may be faced. If facts, adverse to the defendant, are proven by the prosecution, there may be no way to explain them favorably to the accused except by a witness who may be vulnerable to impeachment on cross-examination. The defendant must then decide whether or not to use such a witness. The fact that the witness may also be the defendant makes the choice more difficult but a denial of due process does not emerge from the circumstance. . . .

We find no other error that gives ground for our intervention in California's administration of criminal justice.

Affirmed.

MR. JUSTICE FRANKFURTER, concurring.

. . . When, as in a case like the present, a conviction in a State court is here for review under a claim that a right protected by the Due Process Clause of the Fourteenth Amendment has been denied, the issue is not whether an infraction of one of the specific provisions of the first eight Amendments is disclosed by the record. The relevant question is whether the criminal proceedings which resulted in conviction deprived the accused of the due process of law to which the United States Constitution entitled him. Judicial review of that guaranty of the Fourteenth Amendment inescapably im-

poses upon this Court an exercise of judgment upon the whole course of the proceedings in order to ascertain whether they offend those canons of decency and fairness which express the notions of justice of English-speaking peoples even toward those charged with the most heinous offenses. These standards of justice are not authoritatively formulated anywhere as though they were prescriptions in a pharmacopoeia. But neither does the application of the Due Process Clause imply that judges are wholly at large. The judicial judgment in applying the Due Process Clause must move within the limits of accepted notions of justice and is not to be based upon the idiosyncrasies of a merely personal judgment. The fact that judges among themselves may differ whether in a particular case a trial offends accepted notions of justice is not disproof that general rather than idiosyncratic standards are applied. An important safeguard against such merely individual judgment is an alert deference to the judgment of the State court under review.

MR. JUSTICE BLACK, dissenting.

. . . The appellant's contention in the state court and here has been that the statute denies him a right guaranteed by the Federal Constitution. The argument is that (1) permitting comment upon his failure to testify has the effect of compelling him to testify so as to violate that provision of the Bill of Rights contained in the Fifth Amendment that "No person . . . shall be compelled in any criminal case to be a witness against himself"; and (2) although this provision of the Fifth Amendment originally applied only as a restraint upon federal courts, *Barron* v. *Baltimore*, 7 Pet. 243, the Fourteenth Amendment was intended to, and did, make the prohibition against compelled testimony applicable to trials in state courts.

The Court refuses to meet and decide the appellant's first contention. But while the Court's opinion, as I read it, strongly implies that the Fifth Amendment does not, of itself, bar comment upon failure to testify in federal courts, the Court nevertheless assumes that it does in order to reach the second constitutional question involved in appellant's case. I must consider the case on the same assumption that the Court does. For the discussion of the second contention turns out to be a decision which reaches far beyond the relatively narrow issues on which this case might have turned.[10]

This decision reasserts a constitutional theory spelled out in *Twining* v. *New Jersey*, 211 U.S. 78, that this Court is endowed by the Constitution with boundless power under "natural law" periodically to expand and contract constitutional standards to conform to the Court's conception of what at a particular time constitutes "civilized decency" and "fundamental liberty and justice." Invoking this *Twining* rule, the Court concludes that although comment upon testimony in a federal court would violate the Fifth Amendment, identical comment in a state court does not violate today's fashion in civilized decency and fundamentals and is therefore not prohibited by the Federal Constitution as amended.

The *Twining* case was the first, as it is the only, decision of this Court which has squarely held that states were free, notwithstanding the Fifth and Fourteenth Amendments, to extort evidence from one accused of crime. I agree that if *Twining* be reaffirmed, the result reached might appropriately follow. But I would not

10 In other words, Black is saying that if the majority had been willing to decide whether the California statute in fact compelled the defendant to be a witness against himself within the meaning of the Fifth Amendment, and had decided that question in the negative, he (Black) might have voted with the majority. In any event, such a procedure would have made it possible, Black says, to avoid the showdown on the issue of full incorporation. Cf. Black's vote and opinion in *Wolf* v. *Colorado*, below; and cf. also footnote 7, above.

reaffirm the *Twining* decision. I think that decision and the "natural law" theory of the Constitution upon which it relies degrade the constitutional safeguards of the Bill of Rights and simultaneously appropriate for this Court a broad power which we are not authorized by the Constitution to exercise. . . .

My study of the historical events that culminated in the Fourteenth Amendment, and the expressions of those who sponsored and favored, as well as those who opposed its submission and passage, persuades me that one of the chief objects that the provisions of the Amendment's first section, separately, and as a whole, were intended to accomplish was to make the Bill of Rights, applicable to the states. With full knowledge of the import of the *Barron* decision, the framers and backers of the Fourteenth Amendment proclaimed its purpose to be to overturn the constitutional rule that case had announced. This historical purpose has never received full consideration or exposition in any opinion of this Court interpreting the Amendment.

. . . And I further contend that the "natural law" formula which the Court uses to reach its conclusion in this case should be abandoned as an incongruous excrescence on our Constitution. I believe that formula to be itself a violation of our Constitution, in that it subtly conveys to courts, at the expense of legislatures, ultimate power over public policies in fields where no specific provision of the Constitution limits legislative power. And my belief seems to be in accord with the views expressed by this Court, at least for the first two decades after the Fourteenth Amendment was adopted.

. . . In my judgment the people of no nation can lose their liberty so long as a Bill of Rights like ours survives and its basic purposes are conscientiously interpreted, enforced and respected so as to afford continuous protection against old, as well as new, devices and practices which might thwart those purposes. I fear to see the consequences of the Court's practice of substituting its own concepts of decency and fundamental justice for the language of the Bill of Rights as its point of departure in interpreting and enforcing that Bill of Rights. If the choice must be between the selective process of the *Palko* decision applying some of the Bill of Rights to the States, or the *Twining* rule applying none of them, I would choose the *Palko* selective process. But rather than accept either of these choices, I would follow what I believe was the original purpose of the Fourteenth Amendment—to extend to all the people of the nation the complete protection of the Bill of Rights. To hold that this Court can determine what, if any, provisions of the Bill of Rights will be enforced, and if so to what degree, is to frustrate the great design of a written Constitution.

Conceding the possibility that this Court is now wise enough to improve on the Bill of Rights by substituting natural law concepts for the Bill of Rights, I think the possibility is entirely too speculative to agree to take that course. I would therefore hold in this case that the full protection of the Fifth Amendment's proscription against compelled testimony must be afforded by California. This I would do because of reliance upon the original purpose of the Fourteenth Amendment.

It is an illusory apprehension that literal application of some or all of the provisions of the Bill of Rights to the States would unwisely increase the sum total of the powers of this Court to invalidate state legislation. The Federal Government has not been harmfully burdened by the requirement that enforcement of federal laws affecting civil liberty conform literally to the Bill of Rights. Who would advocate its repeal? It must be conceded, of course, that the natural-law-due-process formula, which the Court today reaffirms, has been interpreted to limit substantially this Court's power to prevent state violations of the individual civil liberties guaranteed by the Bill of Rights. But this formula also has been used in the past, and can be used in the future, to license this Court, in considering regulatory legislation, to roam at large in the broad expanses of policy and morals and to trespass, all too freely, on the legislative domain of the States as well as the Federal Government. . . .

Mr. Justice Murphy, dissenting. . . .

I agree that the specific guarantees of the Bill of Rights should be carried over intact into the first section of the Fourteenth Amendment. But I am not prepared to say that the latter is entirely and necessarily limited by the Bill of Rights. Occasions may arise where a proceeding falls so far short of conforming to fundamental standards of procedure as to warrant constitutional condemnation in terms of a lack of due process despite the absence of a specific provision in the Bill of Rights.

That point, however, need not be pursued here inasmuch as the Fifth Amendment is explicit in its provision that no person shall be compelled in any criminal case to be a witness against himself. That provision, as Mr. Justice Black demonstrates, is a constituent part of the Fourteenth Amendment. . . .

DOUBLE JEOPARDY IN THE WARREN COURT

The extent to which the Supreme Court in the late 1950's was a more liberal group than the Court of a generation earlier is suggested by a comparison of the division of votes in the Palko case, and in the series of recent double-jeopardy cases presented in Table 25, on page 608. Black is the only justice whose tenure spans the twenty-one years separating Palko from the later cases; and he joined the other members of the liberal bloc of 1937—Stone, Brandeis, and Cardozo—in denying to a state defendant the immunity from double jeopardy to which, as Cardozo assumed, he would have been entitled as a defendant in a federal criminal trial. But Black explicitly recanted his vote in Palko, some twenty years after the event.[11] In the more recent cases, the division of the Court was much closer, although this increase in liberal sentiment had little effect upon the parties defendant to these cases. Only one of them, a federal defendant, obtained a reversal of his conviction; the other six suffered a form of double jeopardy that is not forbidden by the Fifth or Fourteenth Amendments to the Constitution, according to the Court's majorities.

The rules of constitutional policy that these seven cases established were as follows:

1. The Fifth Amendment prohibits a federal court from retrying under a first-degree murder charge (punishable by death) a defendant who was acquitted, *sub silentio*, of a first-degree charge at an earlier trial, the defendant having been granted a new trial when he appealed his conviction on an alternative charge of second-degree murder. *Green* v. *United States*, 355 U.S. 184 (December 16, 1957).

2. The Fourteenth Amendment does not prevent a state from subjecting a defendant, who had been acquitted in a single trial of the offenses charged in three indictments, to a second trial resulting in conviction, under a fourth and subsequent indictment based upon the same event (the robbery of several different persons at the same time). *Hoag* v. *New Jersey*, 356 U.S. 464 (May 19, 1958).

3. The Fourteenth Amendment does not prevent a state from subjecting a defendant, who has been convicted and sentenced to imprisonment in two previous trials for first-degree murder, to a third trial resulting in a sentence of the death penalty (also for conviction of first-degree murder), the three murders having occurred (together with a fourth murder for which the defendant did not stand trial) at the same time and place. *Ciucci* v. *Illinois*, 356 U.S. 571 (May 19, 1958).

4. The Fifth Amendment does not prevent the trial and conviction of a federal defendant under three different statutes defining various crimes to arise as the consequence of a single event (a sale of narcotics). *Gore* v. *United States*, 357 U.S. 386 (June 30, 1958).

5. Neither the Fifth nor the Fourteenth Amendments prevent cooperation between the law-enforcement officials of the nation and of the states, or the conviction of a defendant in a state court through the use of the same evidence on the basis of which he previously had been acquitted in a federal court trial

---

11 *Hoag* v. *New Jersey*, 356 U.S. 464, 480 fn. 5 (1958).

for an analogous offense. *Bartkus* v. *Illinois,* 359 U.S. 121 (March 30, 1959).

6. The Fifth Amendment does not prevent the trial and conviction of a federal defendant for an offense flowing from the same acts for which he had been previously tried and convicted in a state court for a violation of state law. *Abbate* v. *United States,* 359 U.S. 187 (March 30, 1959).

7. The Fourteenth Amendment does not prevent a state from inflicting capital punishment upon a defendant who pleaded guilty to kidnapping, the defendant having previously been sentenced to life imprisonment upon his plea of guilty to a charge of murder, when the kidnapping and murder related to the same victim. *Williams* v. *Oklahoma,* 358 U.S. 576 (February 24, 1959).

The perfect consistency in the voting of the justices in these double-jeopardy cases is evident in Table 25. By "consistency," we do not mean that a justice should always vote the same way (+ or −); but we do require that when he ceases to vote positively and begins to vote negatively, all of his positive votes (to the left of his break point) and all of his negative votes (to the right of his break point) should be consistent. Only Black, Warren, Brennan, and Whittaker show break points in the scalogram below; we assume that for the remaining justices, such points would be reached in the decision of more extreme cases (either pro or con) that did not actually confront the Court for decision during the defined period. Thus, the behavioral equivalent of the break point is the shift in a justice's attitude from sympathy to antipathy at a particular gradation in the questions concerning a policy (in this instance, double jeopardy) that are or might be evoked by cases the Court decides.[12]

The horizontal break line in Table 25 indicates that the separation of the justices into two groups is rather sharply and consistently defined. The libertarians were able to attract the essential fifth vote, needed to control decision, only in the Green case, which was decided shortly after Whittaker joined the Court; while in Abbate, the marginal libertarian justice, Brennan, was rewarded for his defection by Frankfurter (as the senior justice voting with the majority) by being chosen as the "instrument" for the expression of the opinion of the Court. (His acceptance of that role did not prevent him from appending an independent expression of his own concurring views, however.) The Williams case provoked three of the libertarians into voting against the petitioner's claims, leaving only Douglas to vote in behalf of the defendants in all seven cases. Three justices

[12] The number of cases is too few to meet conventional requirements for the computation of the coefficient of reproducibility, which is 1.0 when there are sufficient items and no inconsistent votes. The coefficient of reproducibility is simply the ratio of unity minus the number of inconsistent votes divided by the total number of votes (CR = $1 - \frac{\text{no. of inconsistent votes}}{\text{total votes}}$). It is conventional to disregard, in computing the CR, decisions in which fewer than two justices dissent, and it is also conventional to consider a CR of between .90–1.00 to be evidence of a high degree of consistency in the voting of the justices, assuming that the scale includes ten or more cases.

TABLE 25.

A Scalogram of Double-Jeopardy Decisions of the Warren Court (1957-1958 Terms)

SCALE SCORES	CASE	*Green*	*Hoag*	*Ciucci* [a]	*Gore*	*Bartkus*	*Abbate*	*Williams*	*Total Votes per Justice*	*Total Inconsistent Votes per Justice*
	SCALE POSITION	1	2	3	4	5	6	7		
7	Douglas	(+)	'+')	'+')	'+')	+)	+)	'+')	7	0
6	Black	('+')	+)	'+')	+)	'+')	'+')	(−)	7	0
6	Warren	(+)	'+')	+)	'+')	+)	+)	(−)	7	0
5	Brennan	(+)	NP	+)	'+')	'+')	('−')/('−'	(−)	6	0
1	Whittaker	(+)	(−)	(−)	(−)	(−)	(−)	('−')	7	0
0	Stewart	*	*	*	*	(−)	(−)	(−)	3	0
0	Burton	−)	(−)	(−)	(−)	*	*	*	4	0
0	Clark	−)	(−)	(−)	(−)	(−)	(−)	(−)	7	0
0	Harlan	−)	('−')	(−)	(−)	(−)	(−)	(−)	7	0
0	Frankfurter	'−')	(−)	(−)	('−')	('−')	(−)	(−)	7	0
	Voting Division	5-4 Pro	3-5 Con	4-5	4-5	4-5	3-6	1-8	62	
	Total Inconsistent	F	S	S	F	S	F	S		
	Votes per Case	0	0	0	0	0	0	0		0

LEGEND:

$+$ = a vote in favor of the defendant
$-$ = a vote against the defendant
* = not seated at the time of this decision
NP = seated but not participating in this decision
F = trial in a federal court
S = trial in a state court
' ' = wrote opinion
( ) = joined in the opinion of the Court
(= concurring opinion
) = dissenting opinion

a The decision in *Ciucci* v. *Illinois* was *per curiam.*

(Clark, Harlan, and Frankfurter) voted against all of the defendants, and presumably Burton would likewise have voted negatively in all cases if he had not retired. The disposition of the cases is in perfect accord with the voting of only one justice, Whittaker; and in a majority of four of the seven cases, Whittaker's vote was determinative, which made him the equipoise of the Court on this issue. Thus, the freshman justice of the 1956 Term became, in the decision of this set of cases, the most powerful justice on the Court.[13]

Federal and the state cases are interwoven throughout the scale. This raises the question whether the differences between the Fifth and the Fourteenth Amendments, and the reiterated issue of incorporation, really had very much to do with the outcome of these cases. At least during this brief but relatively homogeneous period, the attitudes of the justices toward the equity of double-jeopardy practices seemed to have a much more important bearing upon their decision-making than did the constitutional theories and concepts with which the opinions of the justices are concerned.

Rule-Making and the Fourth Amendment

It is the effect of the separation-of-powers and the federalism variables, which to the libertarians are usually—but not always—secondary to the cluster of civil-liberties values, that doubtless explains the Court's increasing reliance during the past two decades upon its "supervisory power" rather than upon the Bill of Rights as a basis for upholding civil-rights claims against the national government. There are two advantages to such a strategy from the point of view of nonlibertarians—i.e., justices who recognize the importance of other sociopolitical values. In the first place, the Court can establish its civil-rights policies on what is nominally a provisional, tentative basis, saying in effect (and frequently explicitly) that "we think this is a wise and proper standard for federal judicial administration, although if Congress should disagree with us and establish a different policy by statute, that would raise a quite different kind of question. . . ." Of course, the failure of the general public to discriminate and to comprehend the theoretical differences between the policies which the Court purports to establish by constitutional interpretation and those based upon its "supervisory power" over lower federal courts is a political factor which limits the effective scope of the congressional power of revision. Congress is not likely to overrule policies for judicial administration that the Court has announced, *irrespective of the attributed source of authority for the Court's action;* the debates and voting behavior of Congress regarding the Civil Rights Act of 1957 provide instructive reading on this point. Judicial administration, after all, falls within the core of the area in which the Supreme Court, not the Congress, is

---

13 We are defining "power" here in terms of the Shapley-Shubik index. See the Hugh-berts Game in Chapter 3.

supposed to be expert. Nevertheless, the theoretical distinction is apparently important to some of the justices, providing them with a rationale for upholding civil-liberties claims that they might be unwilling to support as "constitutional rights," and vice versa.

The second advantage is that policies established under the Court's supervisory power over the lower *federal* courts are considered to be beyond the scope of the full-incorporation argument.[14] Consequently, those justices (such as Holmes, Brandeis, Jackson, Harlan) who believe that the states ought to have broader discretion under the Constitution than the national government to abridge civil rights and liberties, can maximize the probability of achieving such a policy result by attributing civil-rights guarantees to the Court's residual powers rather than relating them to specific clauses of the Bill of Rights. This limits the protection of such a civil right to action of the national government, and leaves the states unencumbered by federal standards of justice. Moreover, each justice remains relatively free within the broad confines of the *stare decisis* convention to invoke either the Bill of Rights or the Court's residual powers as the policy base for civil rights that he is willing to support, in the context of the facts of individual cases as these are measured by the justice according to his own hierarchy of values.

Search-and-seizure claims provide an excellent example of such *selectivity* in the attitudes of the justices toward civil-liberties questions. Although Black, in general, votes much more consistently in support of civil-liberties claims than does Justice Frankfurter, this is not true of Fourth and Fourteenth Amendment cases in which the principal question relates to the reasonableness or legality of searches and seizures. In voting upon a group of 32 such cases decided over a twenty-one-year period (1939-1959), Frankfurter voted 25-6 in behalf of the defendants' claims, while Black voted only 17-15 in support of search-and-seizure claimants.[15] Frankfurter's over-all record of 25-6 is identical to that of Douglas. However, a breakdown of these data into federal and state cases shows that there were important differences, in addition to the time factor, in their voting behavior. Frankfurter was by far the Court's most consistent champion of Fourth Amendment rights: he voted in favor of all except one of twenty-four federal defendants over the period of two decades. Douglas, on the other hand, was the most consistent supporter of search-and-seizure claims based on the Fourteenth Amendment, voting in favor of all seven state defendants over the period of the decade 1949-1959. The breakdown of these data for Frankfurter, Black, and Douglas is:

---

[14] Recall, however, the bearing of *Hurd* v. *Hodge* upon *Barrows* v. *Jackson*, discussed in Chapter 9.

[15] Only since Warren became Chief Justice has Black supported search-and-seizure claims more strongly than Frankfurter, and at that only in state cases. (See Table 26, below.)

	Frankfurter		Black		Douglas	
	+	−	+	−	+	−
Federal	23	1	14	11	18	6
State	2	5	3	4	7	0

Having already and quite recently committed himself to a policy of "full incorporation" in *Adamson* v. *California* (above), Black found himself in 1949 faced with this dilemma: a state criminal defendant invoked a search-and-seizure claim that would unquestionably have required the reversal of his conviction in a federal court. Black solved his problem, however, and justified his vote *against* the claimant (i.e., Black voted to uphold the conviction of a defendant in a state court on the basis of evidence that was admittedly obtained as the result of an illegal search and seizure) by joining Frankfurter in *Wolf* v. *Colorado* (below) in the reinterpretation of an earlier precedent,[16] and discovering that the policy for which the precedent stood was based on the Court's residual powers, *not* on the Fourth Amendment. Frankfurter's exceptionally high degree of sympathy for *Fourth* Amendment claimants may help to account for his willingness to attribute at least an area of congruence between the core of the Fourth Amendment and the concept of ordered liberty; just as Black's relatively mild enthusiasm for search-and-seizure claims may have led him to contrive a nonconstitutional rationale which permitted him to vote against Wolf without retreating from the position argued in his Adamson dissent (only two years earlier).

On the other hand, Brennan voted in 1959 to *support* a search-and-seizure claim in a state case by drawing the same kind of distinction, and invoking (in dissent) the Court's supervisory powers in a case in which he was unwilling to join in the principal dissenting opinion of Black, Douglas, and Warren, which also supported the search-and-seizure claim, but upon constitutional grounds under the Fourth and Fourteenth Amendments.[17] It is therefore apparent that the distinction can cut both ways, sometimes inducing more and sometimes less support for civil-rights claims in state cases than would have been likely to have resulted from a "constitutional" basis of decision. And it is indisputable that the distinction broadens the discretion of the justices, both individually and collectively.

---

[16] *Weeks* v. *United States,* 232 U.S. 383 (1914).

[17] *Bartkus* v. *Illinois,* 359 U.S. 121, 164 (1959).

WOLF v. COLORADO

338 U.S. 25 (June 27, 1949)

Certiorari to the Supreme Court of Colorado.

Affirmed.

6-3

Frankfurter	('+')
Vinson, C.J.	(+)
Reed	(+)
Jackson	(+)
Burton	(+)
Black	('+'
Douglas	'—')
Murphy	'—')
Rutledge	'—')

Usually, when the opinion of the Court conspicuously neglects to mention the facts of a case, dissenters can be counted on to rush into the breach and provide a detailed recitation of the facts which the Court has omitted. (See, e.g., Ter-miniello v. Chicago, 337 U.S. 1 [1949], which was decided only six weeks earlier in the same term.) There is not even a hint in any of the five opinions in Wolf v. Colorado concerning what had happened in the real world to provoke such passionate disagreement among the justices. Wolf was a physician in Denver who was a key figure in an abortion ring. Local police officers entered Wolf's office at a time when he was present, arrested him, and seized his records containing the names and addresses of his patients. The police acted without either an arrest or a search warrant. Wolf's office records were used for leads to patients who were then induced to testify against him at his trial, at which he was convicted of the offense of aiding and abetting a criminal abortion. The state courts denied his motion to suppress the evidence obtained as the result of the illegal search and seizure of his office records.[18]

[18] For further details, see the opinions of the Supreme Court of Colorado in 117 Col. 279, 321 (1947).

MR. JUSTICE FRANKFURTER delivered the opinion of the Court.

The precise question for consideration is this: Does a conviction by a State court for a State offense deny the "due process of law" required by the Fourteenth Amendment, solely because evidence that was admitted at the trial was obtained under circumstances which would have rendered it inadmissible in a prosecution for violation of a federal law in a court of the United States because there deemed to be an infraction of the Fourth Amendment as applied in *Weeks* v. *United States,* 232 U.S. 383 [1914]? The Supreme Court of Colorado has sustained convictions in which such evidence was admitted, . . . and we brought the cases here. . . .

Unlike the specific requirements and restrictions placed by the Bill of Rights (Amendments I to VIII) upon the administration of criminal justice by federal authority, the Fourteenth Amendment did not subject criminal justice in the States to specific limitations. The notion that the "due process of law" guaranteed by the Fourteenth Amendment is shorthand for the first eight amendments of the Constitution and thereby incorporates them has been rejected by this Court again and again, after impressive consideration. See, *e.g., Hurtado* v. *California,* 110 U.S. 516; *Twining* v. *New Jersey,* 211 U.S. 78; *Brown* v. *Mississippi,* 297 U.S. 278; *Palko* v. *Connecticut,* 302 U.S. 319. Only the other day the Court reaffirmed this rejection after thorough reexamination of the scope and function of the Due Process Clause of the Fourteenth Amendment. *Adamson* v. *California,* 332 U.S. 46. The issue is closed.

For purposes of ascertaining the restrictions which the Due Process Clause imposed upon the States in the enforcement of their criminal law, we adhere to the views expressed in *Palko* v. *Connecticut, supra,* 302 U.S. 319. That decision speaks to us with the great weight of the authority, particularly in matters of civil liberty, of a court that included Mr. Chief Justice Hughes, Mr. Justice Brandeis, Mr. Justice Stone and Mr. Justice Cardozo, to speak only of the dead. In rejecting the suggestion that the Due Process Clause incorporated the original Bill of Rights, Mr. Justice Cardozo reaffirmed on behalf of that Court a different but deeper and more pervasive conception of the Due Process Clause. This Clause exacts from the States for the lowliest and the most outcast all that is "implicit in the concept of ordered liberty." 302 U.S. at 325.

Due process of law thus conveys neither formal nor fixed nor narrow requirements. It is the compendious expression for all those rights which the courts must enforce because they are basic to our free society. But basic rights do not become petrified as of any one time, even though, as a matter of human experience, some may not too rhetorically be called eternal verities. It is of the very nature of a free society to advance in its standards of what is deemed reasonable and right. Representing as it does a living principle, due process is not confined within a permanent catalogue of what may at a given time be deemed the limits or the essentials of fundamental rights.

To rely on a tidy formula for the easy determination of what is a fundamental right for purposes of legal enforcement may satisfy a longing for certainty but ignores the movements of a free society. It belittles the scale of the conception of due process. The real clue to the problem confronting the judiciary in the application of the Due Process Clause is not to ask where the line is once and for all to be drawn but to recognize that it is for the Court to draw it by the gradual and empiric process of "inclusion and exclusion." *Davidson* v. *New Orleans*, 96 U.S. 97, 104. This was the Court's insight when first called upon to consider the problem; to this insight the Court has on the whole been faithful as case after

case has come before it since *Davidson* v. *New Orleans* was decided.

The security of one's privacy against arbitrary intrusion by the police—which is at the core of the Fourth Amendment— is basic to a free society. It is therefore implicit in "the concept of ordered liberty" and as such enforceable against the States through the Due Process Clause. The knock at the door, whether by day or by night, as a prelude to a search, without authority of law but solely on the authority of the police, did not need the commentary of recent history to be condemned as inconsistent with the conception of human rights enshrined in the history and the basic constitutional documents of English-speaking peoples.

Accordingly, we have no hesitation in saying that were a State affirmatively to sanction such police incursion into privacy it would run counter to the guaranty of the Fourteenth Amendment.[19] But the ways of enforcing such a basic right raise questions of a different order. How such arbitrary conduct should be checked, what remedies against it should be afforded, the means by which the right should be made effective, are all questions that are not to be so dogmatically answered as to preclude the varying solutions which spring from an allowable range of judgment, for these are issues not susceptible of quantitative solutions.

In *Weeks* v. *United States, supra,* this Court held that in a federal prosecution the Fourth Amendment barred the use of evidence secured through an illegal search and seizure. This ruling was made for the first time in 1914. It was not derived from the explicit requirements of the Fourth Amendment; it was not based on legislation expressing Congressional policy in the enforcement of the Constitu-

[19] This promise was not kept. See Frankfurter's opinion for the Court, which divided 5-4 against the search-and-seizure claimant in *Frank* v. *Maryland*, 359 U.S. 360 (May 4, 1959). Black dissented in this later case. See also *Ohio ex rel. Eaton* v. *Price*, 360 U.S. 246 (June 8, 1959).

tion. The decision was a matter of judicial implication. Since then it has been frequently applied and we stoutly adhere to it. But the immediate question is whether the basic right to protection against arbitrary intrusion by the police demands the exclusion of logically relevant evidence obtained by an unreasonable search and seizure because, in a federal prosecution for a federal crime, it would be excluded. As a matter of inherent reason, one would suppose this to be an issue as to which men with complete devotion to the protection of the right of privacy might give different answers. When we find that in fact most of the English-speaking world does not regard as vital to such protection the exclusion of evidence thus obtained, we must hesitate to treat this remedy as an essential ingredient of the right. The contrariety of views of the States is particularly impressive in view of the careful reconsideration which they have given the problem in the light of the *Weeks* decision.

I. Before the *Weeks* decision 27 States had passed on the admissibility of evidence obtained by unlawful search and seizure.

   (a) Of these 26 States opposed the *Weeks* doctrine. . . .

   (b) Of these 1 State anticipated the *Weeks* doctrine. . . .

II. Since the *Weeks* decision 47 States all told have passed on the *Weeks* doctrine. . . .

   (a) Of these 20 passed on it for the first time.

      (1) Of the foregoing States 6 followed the *Weeks* doctrine. . . .

      (2) Of the foregoing States 14 rejected the *Weeks* doctrine. . . .

   (b) Of these 26 States reviewed prior decisions contrary to the *Weeks* doctrine.

      (1) Of these 10 States have followed *Weeks,* overruling or distinguishing their prior decisions. . . .

      (2) Of these 16 States adhered to their prior decisions against *Weeks.* . . .

   (c) Of these 1 State adhered to its prior formulation of the *Weeks* doctrine. . . .

III. As of today 30 States reject the *Weeks* doctrine, 17 States are in agreement with it. . . .

IV. Of 10 jurisdictions within the United Kingdom and the British Commonwealth of Nations which have passed on the question, none has held evidence obtained by illegal search and seizure inadmissible. . . .

The jurisdictions which have rejected the *Weeks* doctrine have not left the right to privacy without other means of protection.[20] Indeed, the exclusion of evidence is a remedy which directly serves only to protect those upon whose person or premises something incriminating has been found. We cannot, therefore, regard it as a departure from basic standards to remand such persons, together with those who emerge scatheless from a search, to the remedies of private action and such protection as the internal discipline of the police, under the eyes of an alert public opinion, may afford. Granting that in practice the exclusion of evidence may be an effective way of deterring unreasonable searches, it is not for this Court to condemn as falling below the minimal standards assured by the Due Process Clause a State's reliance upon other methods which, if consistently en-

[20] The common law provides actions for damages against the searching officer, . . . against one who procures the issuance of a warrant maliciously and without probable cause, . . . against a magistrate who has acted without jurisdiction in issuing a warrant, . . . against persons assisting in the execution of an illegal search. . . . One may also without liability use force to resist an unlawful search. . . . Statutory sanctions in the main provide for the punishment of one maliciously procuring a search warrant or willfully exceeding his authority in exercising it. . . . [Footnote by the Court.]

forced, would be equally effective. Weighty testimony against such an assertion of our own views is the opinion of Mr. Justice, then Judge, Cardozo in *People* v. *Defore,* 242 N.Y. 13, 150 N. E. 585.21 We cannot brush aside the experience of States which deem the incidence of such conduct by the police too slight to call for a deterent remedy not by way of disciplinary measures but by overriding the relevant rules of evidence. There are, moreover, reasons for excluding evidence unreasonably obtained by the federal police which are less compelling in the case of police under State or local authority. The public opinion of a community can far more effectively be exerted against oppressive conduct on the part of police directly responsible to the community itself than can local opinion, sporadically aroused, be brought to bear upon remote authority pervasively exerted throughout the country.

We hold, therefore, that in a prosecution in a State court for a State crime the Fourteenth Amendment does not forbid the admission of evidence obtained by an unreasonable search and seizure. And though we have interpreted the Fourth Amendment to forbid the admission of such evidence, a different question would be presented if Congress under its legislative powers were to pass a statute purporting to negate the *Weeks* doctrine. We would then be faced with the problem of the respect to be accorded the legislative judgment on an issue as to which, in default of that judgment, we have been forced to depend upon our own. Problems of a converse character, also not before us, would be presented should Congress under § 5 of the Fourteenth Amendment undertake to enforce

the rights there guaranteed by attempting to make the *Weeks* doctrine binding upon the States.

Affirmed.

MR. JUSTICE BLACK, concurring. . . .

For reasons stated in my dissenting opinion in *Adamson* v. *California,* 332 U.S. 46, 68, I agree with the conclusion of the Court that the Fourth Amendment's prohibition of "unreasonable searches and seizures" is enforceable against the states. Consequently, I should be for reversal of this case if I thought the Fourth Amendment not only prohibited "unreasonable searches and seizures," but also, of itself, barred the use of evidence so unlawfully obtained. But I agree with what appears to be a plain implication of the Court's opinion that the federal exclusionary rule is not a command of the Fourth Amendment but is a judicially created rule of evidence which Congress might negate. See *McNabb* v. *United States,* 318 U.S. 332. This leads me to concur in the Court's judgment of affirmance.

It is not amiss to repeat my belief that the Fourteenth Amendment was intended to make the Fourth Amendment in its entirety applicable to the states. The Fourth Amendment was designed to protect people against unrestrained searches and seizures by sheriffs, policemen and other law enforcement officers. Such protection is an essential in a free society. And I am unable to agree that the protection of people from over-zealous or ruthless state officers is any less essential in a country of "ordered liberty" than is the protection of people from over-zealous or ruthless federal officers. Certainly there are far more state than federal enforcement officers and their activities, up to now, have more frequently and closely touched the intimate daily lives of people than have the activities of federal officers. A state officer's "knock at the door . . . as a prelude to search, without authority of law," may be, as our experience shows,

21 "We hold, then, with the defendant that the evidence against him was the outcome of a trespass. The officer might have been resisted, or sued for damages, or even prosecuted for oppression. . . . He was subject to removal or other discipline at the hands of his superiors. These consequences are undisputed. . . ." [Footnote by the Court.]

just as ominous to "ordered liberty" as though the knock were made by a federal officer.

MR. JUSTICE MURPHY, with whom MR. JUSTICE RUTLEDGE joins, dissenting.

It is disheartening to find so much that is right in an opinion which seems to me so fundamentally wrong. Of course I agree with the Court that the Fourteenth Amendment prohibits activities which are proscribed by the search and seizure clause of the Fourth Amendment. See my dissenting views, and those of MR. JUSTICE BLACK, in *Adamson* v. *California*, 332 U.S. 46, 68, 123. Quite apart from the blanket application of the Bill of Rights to the States, a devotee of democracy would ill suit his name were he to suggest that his home's protection against unlicensed governmental invasion was not "of the very essence of a scheme of ordered liberty." *Palko* v. *Connecticut*, 302 U.S. 319, 325. It is difficult for me to understand how the Court can go this far and yet be unwilling to make the step which can give some meaning to the pronouncements it utters.

Imagination and zeal may invent a dozen methods to give content to the commands of the Fourth Amendment. But this Court is limited to the remedies currently available. It cannot legislate the ideal system. If we would attempt the enforcement of the search and seizure clause in the ordinary case today, we are limited to three devices: judicial exclusion of the illegally obtained evidence; criminal prosecution of violators; and civil action against violators in the action of trespass.

Alternatives are deceptive. Their very statement conveys the impression that one possibility is as effective as the next. In this case their statement is blinding. For there is but one alternative to the rule of exclusion. That is no sanction at all.

This has been perfectly clear since 1914, when a unanimous Court decided

Weeks v. *United States*, 232 U.S. 383, 393. . . .

Little need be said concerning the possibilities of criminal prosecution. Self-scrutiny is a lofty ideal, but its exaltation reaches new heights if we expect a District Attorney to prosecute himself or his associates for well-meaning violations of the search and seizure clause during a raid the District Attorney or his associates have ordered. But there is an appealing ring in another alternative. A trespass action for damages is a venerable means of securing reparation for unauthorized invasion of the home. Why not put the old writ to a new use? When the Court cites cases permitting the action, the remedy seems complete.

But what an illusory remedy this is, if by "remedy" we mean a positive deterrent to police and prosecutors tempted to violate the Fourth Amendment. The appealing ring softens when we recall that in a trespass action the measure of damages is simply the extent of the injury to physical property. If the officer searches with care, he can avoid all but nominal damages—a penny, or a dollar. Are punitive damages possible? Perhaps. But a few states permit none, whatever the circumstances. In those that do, the plaintiff must show the real ill will or malice of the defendant, and surely it is not unreasonable to assume that one in honest pursuit of crime bears no malice toward the search victim. If that burden is carried, recovery may yet be defeated by the rule that there must be physical damages before punitive damages may be awarded. In addition, some states limit punitive damages to the actual expenses of litigation. . . . Others demand some arbitrary ratio between actual and punitive damages before a verdict may stand. . . . Even assuming the ill will of the officer, his reasonable grounds for belief that the home he searched harbored evidence of crime is admissible in mitigation of punitive damages. . . . The bad reputation of the plaintiff is likewise admissible. . . . If the evidence seized was actually used at a trial, that fact has been held a complete justification of the search, and a defense against the trespass action. . . . And even if the plaintiff hurdles all these obstacles; and gains a substantial verdict, the individual officer's finances may well make the judgment useless—for the municipality, of course, is not liable without its consent. Is it surprising that there is so little in the books concerning trespass actions for violation of the search and seizure clause?

The conclusion is inescapable that but one remedy exists to deter violations of the search and seizure clause. That is the rule which excludes illegally obtained evidence. Only by exclusion can we impress upon the zealous prosecutor that violation of the Constitution will do him no good. And only when that point is driven home can the prosecutor be expected to emphasize the importance of observing constitutional demands in his instructions to the police.

If proof of the efficacy of the federal rule were needed, there is testimony in abundance in the recruit training programs and in-service courses provided the police in states which follow the federal rule. St. Louis, for example, demands extensive training in the rules of search and seizure, with emphasis upon the ease with which a case may collapse if it depends upon evidence obtained unlawfully. Current court decisions are digested and read at roll calls. The same general pattern prevails in Washington, D. C. . . .

But in New York City, we are informed simply that "copies of the State Penal Law and Code of Criminal Procedure" are given to officers, and that they are "kept advised" that illegally obtained evidence may be admitted in New York courts. In Baltimore, a "Digest of Laws" is distributed, and it is made clear that the statutory section excluding evidence "is limited in its applicaion to the trial of misdemeanors. . . . It would appear . . . that . . . evidence illegally ob-

tained may still be admissible in the trial of felonies." . . .

The contrast between states with the federal rule and those without it is . . . a positive demonstration of its efficacy. . . . But the examples cited above serve to ground an assumption that has motivated this Court since the *Weeks* case: that this is an area in which judicial action has positive effect upon the breach of law; and that without judicial action, there are simply no effective sanctions presently available.

I cannot believe that we should decide due process questions by simply taking a poll of the rules in various jurisdictions, even if we follow the *Palko* "test." Today's decision will do inestimable harm to the cause of fair police methods in our cities and states. Even more important, perhaps, it must have tragic effect upon public respect for our judiciary. For the Court now allows what is indeed shabby business: lawlessness by officers of the law.

Since the evidence admitted was secured in violation of the Fourth Amendment, the judgment should be reversed.

Mr. Justice Douglas, dissenting.

I believe for the reasons stated by Mr. Justice Black in his dissent in *Adamson v. California,* 332 U.S. 46, 68, that the Fourth Amendment is applicable to the States. I agree with Mr. Justice Murphy that the evidence obtained in violation of it *must* be excluded in state prosecutions as well as in federal prosecutions, since in absence of that rule of evidence the Amendment would have no effective sanction. I also agree with him that under that test this evidence was improperly admitted and that the judgments of conviction must be reversed.

Mr. Justice Rutledge, dissenting.

"Wisdom too often never comes, and so one ought not to reject it merely because it comes late." Similarly, one should not reject a piecemeal wisdom, merely because it hobbles toward the truth with backward glances. Accordingly, although I think that all "the specific guarantees of the Bill of Rights should be carried over intact into the first section of the Fourteenth Amendment," *Adamson* v. *California,* 332 U.S. 46, dissenting opinion at 124, I welcome the fact that the Court, in its slower progress toward this goal, today finds the substance of the Fourth Amendment "to be implicit in the concept of ordered liberty, and thus, through the Fourteenth Amendment, . . . valid as against the states." *Palko* v. *Connecticut,* 302 U.S. 319, 325.

But I reject the Court's simultaneous conclusion that the mandate embodied in the Fourth Amendment, although binding on the states, does not carry with it the one sanction—exclusion of evidence taken in violation of the Amendment's terms—failure to observe which means that "the protection of the Fourth Amendment . . . might as well be stricken from the Constitution." *Weeks* v. *United States,* 232 U.S. 383, 393. For I agree with my brother MURPHY's demonstration that the Amendment without the sanction is a dead letter.

. . . But the version of the Fourth Amendment today held applicable to the states hardly rises to the dignity of a form of words; at best it is a pale and frayed carbon copy of the original, bearing little resemblance to the Amendment the fulfillment of whose command I had heretofore thought to be "an indispensable need for a democratic society." . . .

I also reject any intimation that Congress could validly enact legislation permitting the introduction in federal courts of evidence seized in violation of the Fourth Amendment. . . . The view that the Fourth Amendment itself forbids the introduction of evidence illegally obtained in federal prosecutions is one of long standing and firmly established. . . . It is too late in my judgment to question it now. . . .

As Congress and this Court are, in my judgment, powerless to permit the admission in federal courts of evidence seized in defiance of the Fourth Amendment, so I think state legislators and judges—if subject to the Amendment, as I believe them to be—may not lend their offices to the admission in state courts of evidence thus seized. Compliance with the Bill of Rights betokens more than lip service.

The Court makes the illegality of this search and seizure its inarticulate premise of decision. I acquiesce in that premise and think the conviction should be reversed.

MR. JUSTICE MURPHY joins in this opinion.

Many commentators have cited the Wolf decision for the proposition that the Supreme Court has "incorporated" the Fourth Amendment, at least in part. Indeed, so much is suggested by the dissenting opinions of Murphy and Rutledge in this very case. Such inferences, however, must reflect either a complete lack of precision in using the concept "incorporation," or else excessive sanguinity on the part of libertarian observers. What Frankfurter says (above) is that "the security of one's privacy against arbitrary intrusion by the police" is so fundamental as to be *both* the "core" of the Fourth Amendment *and* implicit in "the concept of ordered liberty." After the lapse of a decade, the meaning of "the security of one's privacy against arbitrary intrusion by the police" had been revealed only by negative definition—that is, observers were able to learn what was *not* such an invasion, but the Court had no occasion to decide a case that would illustrate the kind of state police behavior that Justice Frankfurter may have had in mind.[22]

It should also be noted that Frankfurter, who wrote the opinion of the Court in the McNabb case (Chapter 4), does not say that the suppression, in the federal courts, of evidence obtained as the result of an illegal search or seizure reflected a policy that the Court had adopted under its supervisory authority over lower federal courts; to the contrary, Frankfurter says that the Weeks rule "was a matter of judicial implication"—i.e., the interpretation of the Fourth Amendment by the Supreme Court.[23] To Black, and to Black alone, Frankfurter's statement "appears to be a plain implication . . . that the federal exclusionary rule" is based upon the Court's supervisory powers, as McNabb had been, rather than upon the interpretation of the Fourth Amendment. Black's inference appears to be not only unique among the justices, and difficult to support by an examination of the opinion of the Court in any of the three relevant cases— Weeks, McNabb, and Wolf; his inference is also logically implausible, since it requires that the Court should have anticipated in Weeks in 1914 a theory of the Court's role and powers that was first articulated in the McNabb case in 1943, twenty-nine years later.

SEARCHES AND SEIZURES IN THE WARREN COURT

Wolf was the first major decision of the Court, at least during the modern period since World War I, to consider the question whether unreasonable searches and seizures are prohibited by the Fourteenth Amendment (i.e., whether the Supreme Court will uphold, as a matter of constitutional policy, state convictions based upon the use of evidence resulting from illegal searches and seizures). In the first decade after Wolf, there were half a dozen other state cases in which the Court reconsidered this question; all except one [24] were decided against the defendant. During this same ten-year period, the Court decided over twice as many federal cases "arising directly under the Fourth Amendment"; of these, eight were decided in favor of and six against the defendants. Since the deprivations suffered by the state defendants were, in four of the five state cases in which the Court *upheld* their convictions, greater than those visited upon half of the federal defendants whose convictions the Court *reversed,* it is clear that the Court

---

[22] Probably the best recent example of the arbitrary intrusion of the police is provided by *Miller* v. *United States,* 357 U.S. 301 (1958). This was a federal case in which the Court did uphold the defendant's claims, although at that two justices voted against "the core of the Fourth Amendment."

[23] The unanimous opinion of the Court stated: "If . . . a seizure under the authority of a warrant supposed to be legal, constitutes a violation of the constitutional protection, *a fortiori* does the attempt of an officer of the United States, the United States marshal, acting under color of his office,

without even the sanction of a warrant, constitute an invasion of the rights within the protection afforded *by the 4th Amendment.* . . . We therefore reach the conclusion that the letters in question were taken from the house of the accused by an official of the United States, acting under color of his office, *in direct violation of the constitutional rights of the defendant. . . .*" *Weeks* v. *United States,* 232 U.S. 383, 397-398 (1914). Emphasis added.

[24] *Rochin* v. *California,* 342 U.S. 165 (1952), and in Chapter 12 (below).

does indeed apply the Fourth Amendment more strictly in federal cases than the Fourteenth Amendment in state cases.[25] This finding supports Frankfurter's statement in Wolf and our own suggestion that it is quite misleading to speak of the "incorporation" of the Fourth Amendment.

On the other hand, it is entirely possible that the Court, although differentiating in the standards it applies to Fourth and to Fourteenth Amendment cases, nevertheless may apply both sets of norms *consistently* to the two types of cases. Table 26, on page 621, suggests that this is what happened during the first six terms of the Court under Chief Justice Warren.

The gradations in the attitudes of the justices toward the variations in the basic theme, presented by the different cases, is clearly evident in the table. Considering only the nine justices who participated in a majority or more of these decisions, the Court ranges from Douglas, who voted affirmatively in all cases, to Clark, who voted against nine of the eleven defendants (and who should have voted against Rea as well, if he had voted with perfect consistency). Black shows considerably more sympathy for search-and-seizure claimants during this six-year period than he manifested during the preceding fifteen years. It should also be noted that, although the Court upheld the defendants' claims in only half of these decisions, six of the nine federal cases were decided favorably to the defendants, while all three of the decisions in state cases were against the defendants. Again, this suggests that the requirements of natural law, civilized decency, and a system of "ordered liberty" are somewhat less restrictive than the old-fashioned concept of civil rights that the First Congress wrote into the Fourth Amendment.

Due Process and the Sixth Amendment

During a twenty-eight-year period beginning in 1932 and extending through 1959, the Supreme Court decided some thirty-six cases in which criminal defendants in state courts claimed that they had been denied the right to counsel, contrary to the requirements of the Fourteenth Amendment, and the Supreme Court considered this to be a primary issue in its disposition of the case. There have been only a handful of federal cases during the same period. The Sixth Amendment includes a specific right-to-counsel clause, which the Court has interpreted since 1938 to require representation by counsel of all federal defendants. (Prior to 1938, the Court had consistently interpreted an act of the First Congress in 1790, which imposed a statutory duty on federal courts to assign counsel to represent federal defendants charged with capital offenses, as implying that the Sixth Amendment's language meant that federal defendants in noncapital cases who could afford and obtain counsel must be allowed representation; but the federal trial courts had no obligation to assign counsel to indigent or unpopular

25 For a discussion of both the federal and state search and seizure decisions since 1937, see Glendon A. Schubert, *Quantitative Anal-* *ysis of Judicial Behavior* (Glencoe: The Free Press, 1959), pp. 341-361.

TABLE 26.

A Scalogram of Search-and-Seizure Decisions
of the Warren Court (1953-1958 Terms)

SCALE SCORES / CASE	Benanti v. United States, 355 U.S. 96 (1957)	Miller v. United States 357 U.S. 301 (1958)	Jones v. United States, 357 U.S. 493 (1958)	Giordenello v. United States, 357 U.S. 480 (1958)	Kremen v. United States 353 U.S. 346 (1957) a	Rea v. United States, 350 U.S. 214 (1956)	Irvine v. California, 347 U.S. 128 (1954)	Frank v. Maryland, 359 U.S. 360 (1959)	Breithaupt v. Abram, 352 U.S. 432 (1957)	Walder v. United States, 347 U.S. 62 (1954)	Rathbun v. United States, 355 U.S. 107 (1957)	Draper v. United States, 358 U.S. 307 (1959)	Total Votes per Justice	Total Inconsistent Votes per Justice
SCALE POSITION	1	2	3	4	5	6	7	8	9	10	11	12		
12 Douglas	(+)	(+)	(+)	(+)	(+)	('+')	+)	'+')	'+')	+	+	'+')	12	0
10 Black	(+)	(+)	+	(+)	(+)	(+)	'+')	+)	+)	+	(−)	(−)	12	0
9 Warren	('+')	(+)	(+)	(+)	(+)	(+)	(−)	+)	'+')	(−)	('−')	NP	11	1
8 Brennan	(+)	('+')	(+)	(+)	(+)	*	*	+)	(−)	*	(−)	(−)	9	0
7 Frankfurter	(+)	(+)	(+)	(+)	(+)	(+)	'+')	(−)	(−)	('−')	(+')	NP	11	1
5 Harlan	(+)	+	('+')	('+')	(+)	'−')	*	(−)	(−)	*	(−)	(−)	10	0
3 Whittaker	(+)	(+)	(+)	−)	NP	*	*	('−'	*	*	(−)	('−')	7	0
1 Burton	(+)	−)	−)	−)	'−')	−)	(+)	*	(−)	(−)	(−)	*	10	1
1 Clark	(+)	'−')	'−')	'−')	'−')	(+)	('−'	(−)	('−')	(−)	(−)	(−)	12	1
0 Stewart	*	*	*	*	*	*	*	(−)	*	*	*	(−)	2	0
0 Jackson	*	*	*	*	*	*	('−')	*	*	(−)	*	*	2	0
0 Minton	*	*	*	*	*	−)	(−)	*	*	(−)	*	*	3	0
0 Reed	*	*	*	*	*	−)	(−)	*	(−)	(−)	*	*	4	0
Voting Division	9-0	7-2	7-2	6-3	6-2	5-4 Pro	4-5 Con	4-5	3-6	2-7	2-7	1-6	105	
Total Inconsistent	F	F	F	F	F	F	S	S	S	F	F	F		
Votes per Case	0	0	0	0	0	1	2	0	0	0	1	0		4

LEGEND:
+ = a vote in favor of the defendant
− = a vote against the defendant
* = not seated at the time of this decision
NP = seated but not participating in this decision
F = trial in a federal court
S = trial in a state court
' ' = wrote opinion
( ) = joined in the opinion of the Court
(= concurring opinion
) = dissenting opinion
◯ = inconsistent vote

$$CR = 1 - \frac{4}{89} = .96$$

a The decision in *Kremen* v. *United States* was *per curiam.*

defendants unless they were charged with a capital offense.) But in the Fourteenth Amendment, there is no specific guarantee of the right to counsel; there is the due-process clause.

The Court first read a qualified right to counsel into the Fourteenth Amendment in the celebrated Scottsboro case, in which seven young Negro boys were sentenced to death for the rape of two white girls on a freight train in Alabama. Under circumstances of such popular frenzy that the presence of the state militia was considered necessary to prevent a lynching, the defendants were rushed to trial. The presiding judge appointed "all the members of the local bar" to represent the defendants at their arraignment; that which was every man's responsibility in general was perceived, naturally enough, as the obligation of no lawyer in particular. Two lawyers who were strangers to each other and to the defendants finally agreed to represent them moments before the actual trial began.

The Supreme Court reversed the ensuing convictions, but in ambiguous terms, remarking that

> . . . in a capital case, where the defendant is unable to employ counsel, *and* [emphasis added] is incapable adequately of making his own defense because of ignorance, feeble-mindedness, illiteracy, or the like, it is the duty of the court, whether requested or not, to assign counsel for him as a necessary requisite of due process of law; and that duty is not discharged by an assignment at such a time or under such circumstances as to preclude the giving of effective aid in the preparation and trial of the case.

The ambiguity is probably not the fault of Mr. Justice Sutherland, who wrote for the Court in *Powell* v. *Alabama,* 287 U.S. 45 (1932), because he seemed to state a policy that was a modification of the federal rule as the Sixth Amendment was still being interpreted at the time. Due process required appointment of counsel for an indigent defendant who labored under special disabilities *in a capital case.* But after the lapse of a decade, a later generation of Supreme Court justices had read Justice Sutherland's "and" to mean "or"; and thus two rules were excogitated: (1) due process requires the appointment of counsel for any state defendant charged with a capital offense (unless there is an understanding waiver of the right, etc.); *or* (2) in a noncapital case, due process requires the appointment of counsel if the defendant labors under special disabilities to such an extent that a fair trial would be impossible if he were left to argue his own defense. It is not irrelevant to note that the liberalization of the federal policy, and the consequent further liberalization of the policy applicable to the states, followed closely on the heels of the Court-packing episode of 1937.

Thus, by the early 1940's, the Court had developed three distinct policies concerning the right to counsel:

A. Appointment of counsel was mandatory in any federal criminal case. (A minority of the justices thought that this same policy ought to apply to the states, as a logical consequence of their stated belief that the Sixth Amendment had been incorporated into the Fourteenth.)

B. Appointment of counsel was mandatory in state cases involving a capital offense.

C. Appointment of counsel was *not* mandatory in state cases involving noncapital offenses, unless essential to a fair trial.

The Court decided only three cases in addition to Powell during the dozen years from 1932 to 1944; and of these, two were decided in favor of and two against the defendants. But during the four-year period 1945-1948, when the Libertarian Four were together and in a position to control the grant of certiorari, the Court decided nineteen state right-to-counsel cases, two-thirds of which were decided favorably to the claimants.

Typical of the decisions during the early period of the Vinson Court was *Uveges* v. *Pennsylvania,* 335 U.S. 437 (1948), in which the libertarian bloc succeeded in picking up two favorable votes—one more than was needed to control the decision on the merits. The Chief Justice, who was one of those coopted, was careful, however, to assign the writing of the opinion of the Court to Reed (who had been the spokesman of the majority in Adamson) rather than to any of the libertarians who favored the "incorporation" of the Sixth Amendment. Reed responded with an opinion which included an exceptionally candid statement of the underlying policy split which divided even the justices comprising the majority in this case as to the appropriate grounds for decision: [26]

Some members of the Court think that where serious offenses are charged, failure of a court to offer counsel in state criminal trials deprives an accused of rights under the Fourteenth Amendment. They are convinced that the services of counsel to protect the accused are guaranteed by the Constitution in every such instance. See *Bute* v. *Illinois,* 333 U.S. 640, dissent, 677-79.

It seems reasonably certain that the members of the Court who took this position, which we have specified above as policy "A," were the four libertarians: Rutledge, Murphy, Black, and Douglas.

Reed continued:

Others of us think that when a crime subject to capital punishment is not involved, each case depends on its own facts. See *Betts* v. *Brady,* 316 U.S. 455, 462. Where the gravity of the crime and other factors—such as the age and education of the defendant, the conduct of the court or the prosecuting officials, and the complicated nature of the offense charged and the possible

[26] Both groups agreed that the right to counsel could be waived by a defendant who understood the consequences of such an act.

defenses thereto—render criminal proceedings without counsel so apt to result in injustice as to be fundamentally unfair, the latter group holds that the accused must have legal assistance under the Amendment whether he pleads guilty or elects to stand trial, whether he requests counsel or not.

The "others of us" who adhered to what we have denoted as policies "B" and "C" (the "capital offense" and the "fair trial" rules) included not only Vinson and Reed; presumably they also included the three dissenters in this case. Although they disagreed with the application of the fair-trial rule to the facts in the Uveges case, Frankfurter, Jackson, and Burton all had invoked both the capital-offense and the fair-trial rules to support their votes in behalf of other right-to-counsel claimants during this same period.

THE RIGHT TO COUNSEL IN THE WARREN COURT

During the next eight years following the Uveges decision (1949-1956), the libertarians on the Court (Douglas and Black, and later Warren) were too few to control the grant of certiorari; and the number of state right-to-counsel decisions fell off to an average of less than one per term. But after Brennan joined the Court in the 1956 Term, the volume began to climb again; and as many cases were decided during the next three years as had been during the preceding eight. As Table 27, on page 625, shows, none of the four members of the present libertarian bloc has voted against a state right-to-counsel claimant since Warren took over as Chief Justice.

But the table also indicates that the other members of the Court have been just as cohesive in their voting behavior as the libertarians. With the single exception of Whittaker's decisive vote in *Moore* v. *Michigan*—which was decided only a few months after he joined the Court—the other justices also voted as a bloc. As a consequence, the other cases were decided either unanimously in favor of the claimant, or by five-man majorities over the dissents of the libertarians. The proportion of pro decisions by the Warren Court (64%) is about the same as the proportion of pro decisions for all thirty-six decisions beginning with Powell (61%); and this is also true of the nineteen decisions of the middle forties of which, as we have pointed out above, two-thirds were favorable to the claimants. This suggests that the primary effect that the libertarian bloc has had, during the relatively brief periods when the group has been large enough to control the grant of certiorari, has been to increase the number of the Court's favorable right-to-counsel decisions in absolute rather than in relative terms, by forcing more cases before the Court for decision.

CUMULATIVE FACTS AND JUDICIAL VALUES

The preceding discussion obviously has assumed that the behavior of the justices, both libertarian and otherwise, is political. In arguing for or against the

TABLE 27.

A Scalogram of the Right-to-Counsel Decisions of the Warren Court (1953-1958 Terms) [a]

SCALE SCORES	CASE	Chandler v. Fretag, 348 U.S. 3 (1954)	Massey v. Moore, 348 U.S. 105 (1954)	Reece v. Georgia, 350 U.S. 85 (1955)	Herman v. Claudy, 350 U.S. 116 (1956)	Cash v. Culver, 358 U.S. 633 (1959)	Spano v. New York, 360 U.S. 315 (1959)	Moore v. Michigan, 355 U.S. 155 (1957)	In re Groban, 352 U.S. 330 (1957)	Crooker v. California, 357 U.S. 433 (1958)	Anonymous Nos. 6 & 7 v. Baker, 360 U.S. 287 (1959)	Cicenia v. LaGay, 357 U.S. 504 (1958)	Total Votes per Justice	Total Inconsistent Votes per Justice
	SCALE POSITION	1	2	3	4	5	6	7	8	9	10	11		
11	Douglas	(+)	('+')	(+)	(+)	(+)	('+	(+)	+)	'+')	+)	'+')	11	0
11	Black	(+)	(+)	(+)	('+')	(+)	(+	(+)	'+')	+)	'+')	+)	11	0
11	Warren	('+')	(+)	(+)	(+)	(+)	('+')	(+)	+)	+)	+)	+)	11	0
10	Brennan	*	*	*	*	(+)	(+	('+')	+)	+)	+)	NP	6	0
7	Whittaker	*	*	*	*	(+)	(+)	(+)	*	(−)	(−)	(−)	6	0
6	Frankfurter	(+)	(+)	(+)	(+)	(+)	(+)	−)	('−'	(−)	(−)	(−)	11	0
6	Harlan	*	*	(+)	(+)	(+)	(+)	−)	(−	(−)	('−')	('−')	9	0
6	Clark	(+)	(+)	('+')	(+)	(+)	(+)	−)	(−)	('−')	(−)	(−)	11	0
6	Stewart	*	*	*	*	('+')	('+	*	*	*	(−)	*	3	0
4	Reed	(+)	(+)	(+)	(+)	*	*	*	('−')	*	*	*	5	0
4	Minton	(+)	(+)	(+)	(+)	*	*	*	*	*	*	*	4	0
4	Burton	(+)	(+)	(+)	(+)	*	*	'−')	(−)	(−)	*	(−)	8	0
Voting Division		8-0	8-0	9-0	9-0	9-0	9-0	5-4	4-5	4-5	4-5	3-5	96	
Total Inconsistent								Pro	Con					
Votes per Case		0	0	0	0	0	0	0	0	0	0	0		0 [b]

LEGEND:

+	=	a vote in favor of the defendant
−	=	a vote against the defendant
' '	=	wrote opinion
( )	=	joined in the opinion of the Court
(	=	concurring opinion
)	=	dissenting opinion
*	=	not seated at the time of this decision
NP	=	seated but not participating in this decision

a All of these decisions related to cases that originated as criminal trials in state courts.
b There are no inconsistent votes, but the number of cases (5) in which significant division occurred is too few to warrant any statement about the coefficient of reproducibility.

incorporation of the Sixth Amendment or the "fair trial" rule, we assume that the justices are taking a position on an issue of public policy that is of no little concern, not only to murderers, rapists, and burglars, but also to the communities in which crimes are committed and defendants stand trial in courts of law. It is possible to make diametrically opposed assumptions, however, and to interpret these same decisions from a point of view that casts the justices in the role of judicial robots who perform a function that could be done just as well, if not better, by an electronic calculator.

Introducing the Machine [27]

Although it is important to redress the emphasis in the study of decision processes toward "procedures" rather than exhaustive rules of "content," the time is approaching when machines will be sufficiently well developed to make it practicable for trial runs to be carried out in which human decision-makers and robots are pitted against one another. When machines are more perfect a bench of judicial robots, for example, can be constructed. The machine would apply a system of "weights" to allegations of fact made by parties to a controversy, and also to the justifications advanced in support of the claims put forward by participants. Litigation can proceed by counsel for the plaintiff and the defendant pressing buttons that translate their cases into the physical signs built into the machine. Many results would be "no decision." However, the machine could be designed to settle a controversy of this kind with a "random" operation (by lot). . . .

Preliminary try-outs of decision machines built according to various formal specifications can be made in relation to selected administrative or judicial tribunals. The Supreme Court might be chosen for the purpose. It is a challenging task for legal historians to assist in constructing a robot whose weights would give substantially the same result as those produced by the Court at various periods. The task would not be too difficult for some justices on some issues. But a robot facsimile of the less repetitive members of the Court would provide a genuine challenge to the engineers.

As a means of enabling the community to develop a rational consensus on whether to use robots or not, the machines could be tried out concurrently while the Court, for example, is making up its mind on contemporary controversies. Without giving publicity to the results in advance of decision the machine could be used to try the issue in advance and to predict the result. In this way the engineering problems in the creation of judicial robots could be kept up-to-date.

27 Harold D. Lasswell, "Current Studies in the Decision Process: Automation versus Creativity," *Western Political Quarterly*, Vol. 8, pp. 398-399 (1955).

Predicting Supreme Court Decisions Mathematically [28]

This study represents an attempt to apply quantitative methods to the prediction of human events that generally have been regarded as highly uncertain, namely, decisions by the Supreme Court of the United States. The study is designed to demonstrate that, in at least one area of judicial review, it is possible to take some decided cases, to identify factual elements that influenced the decisions, to derive numerical values for these elements by using a formula, and then to predict correctly the decisions of the remaining cases in the area specified. The analysis will be made independently of what the Court said by way of reasoning in these cases; it will rely only on the factual elements which have been emphasized by the justices in their opinions and on their votes to affirm or set aside convictions. Changes in Court personnel made no decisive difference in the pattern of judicial action in this area; so the analysis will not need to take into account the fact that twenty-five different justices have occupied the nine seats on the Court during the period covered, *i.e.*, the past quarter century. The cases are all those that involved the issue of "right to counsel" under the Fourteenth Amendment. Arranged in chronological order, the first half of the cases [is] used to determine the formula, to derive the numerical values, and to make the predictions; the second half [is] used to test the predictions.

The Supreme Court's decision in the first "Scottsboro Case" (*Powell* v. *Alabama*, 287 U.S. 45) in 1932 inaugurated an era of numerous, still continuing petitions for certiorari, asserting the invalidity of state criminal convictions on the ground that the defendants were effectively deprived of the aid of counsel in their trials, in violation of "due process of law." Undoubtedly, the majority opinion in *Powell* v. *Alabama* encouraged the expectation that the Court might, as it had done with free speech in the *Gitlow* case a few years earlier, incorporate the "right to counsel" provision in the Sixth Amendment into the "due process" clause of the Fourteenth Amendment as a mandatory obligation on the states. If this had happened, a clear and concise rule might have governed all subsequent cases. However, in actual experience the "incorporation" theory attracted the votes of only four justices, *i.e.*, Black, Douglas, Murphy, and Rutledge. The majority of the Court has adhered instead to the "fair trial" doctrine, holding in some cases that "due process" had been denied by the failure to provide the aid of counsel, and sustaining state convictions in other cases on the ground that the "very essence of a scheme of ordered liberty" had not been impaired. . . .

It is because of the difficulties of detecting a consistent pattern in these cases by conventional methods of qualitative appraisal that a quantitative method is used in this study; for such a pattern, concealed in qualitative evaluation, can nevertheless be identified in that way. To be sure, justices of the

28 Fred Kort, "Predicting Supreme Court Decisions Mathematically: A Quantitative Analysis of the 'Right to Counsel' Cases," *American Political Science Review*, Vol. 51, pp. 1-2, 11-12 (1957).

Supreme Court have said that "the due process clause is not susceptible of reduction to a mathematical formula," and ". . . whether a confession of a lad of fifteen is 'voluntary' and as such admissible, or 'coerced' and thus wanting in due process, is not a matter of mathematical determination." Notwithstanding this skepticism, the Supreme Court's own appraisal of its position in state "right to counsel" cases provides the basis for analysis here.

The author then proceeds to quote the paragraph that we have quoted, *supra,* from Reed's opinion in the Uveges case. We omit the author's formula and computations. Basically, what he did was to assign weights to factors that, in his opinion, the opinions of the Court had considered to be deprivational to the defendants in the cases. Of the twenty-six "pivotal factors" identified by the author, some dealt directly with the right to counsel (viz., "request for assigned counsel denied"), while other factors related to the severity of the punishment inflicted, or to other aspects of "fairness" (i.e., "limited contact with the prevailing culture pattern" or "accelerated trial.") Analyzing the first half of the cases systematically in terms of these pivotal factors that had been derived from the same cases, the author determined a composite weight for each case—the sum of the weights of the pivotal factors that had been identified in each case. By inspection, he then determined that all cases above a certain critical weight were decided in favor of the defendants' claims, and all cases with weights below the critical level were decided against the defendants. He then predicted that if he were to make a similar analysis of the second group of cases, using the same pivotal factor weights that had been derived from the first group, the same critical weight level should discriminate between the pro and the con cases of the second group of cases (i.e., cases with weights above the critical level should be decided pro, and those below it, con.) The prediction held. From this result, he concluded that:

> It appears that, in at least this area of judicial review, quantitative analysis discloses a consistency of Court action concealed in conventional qualitative interpretation. The results indicate that the Court has been willing to tolerate factors detrimental to the interests of the defendant in state criminal proceedings up to a certain critical point. . . . Beyond that critical point, the Court has invalidated the state criminal proceeding as deficient in the essentials of a "fair trial." It should not be inherently surprising that a gradually changing group of justices, acting over the years in an institutional as well as an intellectual tradition, should, when confronted with the necessity of saying yes or no in the presence of a complex body of competing considerations that are individually recurrent, behave according to statistical regularities of which they are unaware, and which they may . . . emphatically disavow.

Frankfurter, J., Concurring . . .[29]

"No single one of these circumstances alone would in my opinion justify a reversal. I cannot escape the conclusion, however, that in combination they bring the result below the Plimsoll line of 'due process.' " —Frankfurter, J., concurring, in *Fikes* v. *Alabama,* 352 U.S. 191, 199 (1957).

> Due process, once a slippery slope,[30]
>   Is now a Plimsoll line,
> Of rigid and invariant scope
>   And easy to define.
>
> The quickly curried horse [31] is gone—
>   Too late to lock that door—
> So let us concentrate upon
>   This latest metaphor.
>
> We don't decry the vivid phrase,
>   The erudite bravura,
> That gives judicial mayonnaise
>   A touch of Angostura.[32]

* * *

> But when his meaning's made obscure
>   By fancy verbal playing,
> 'Tis only fair that he be sure
>   He means just what he's saying.

* * *

> When Britain really ruled the waves
>   In good Queen Bess's reign,
> Her seamen oft found wat'ry graves
>   Through folly or chicane.
>
> When overloaded ships were wrecked,
>   The owners bore the onus;
> But nonetheless they would collect
>   A rich insurance bonus.

* * *

[29] Richard H. Field, "Frankfurter, J., Concurring . . . ," *Harvard Law Review,* Vol. 71, pp. 77-81 (November, 1957). Some of the verses in the original, and most of the footnotes, have been omitted here. The footnotes that have been retained have been renumbered as footnotes 30-37, below.

[30] "I have thus reached the slippery slope of due process." Frankfurter, "John Marshall and the Judicial Function," in *Government Under Law* 6, 18 (Sutherland ed. 1956). . . .

[31] Frankfurter, J., in *Olberding* v. *Illinois Cent. R. R.,* 346 U.S. 338, 340 (1953). The substitution of "quickly" for "soon" is dictated by the exigencies of the meter.

[32] Frankfurter, J., is not responsible for this figure of speech.

Sam Plimsoll [33] was the seaman's friend,
 A Liberal M.P.;
"The day of 'coffinships' must end,"
 He swore repeatedly.

"What boots it," old Sam Plimsoll said,
 "To see who'll pay the cost,
When British mariners are dead,
 And British cargoes lost?

"I'm sick to death of sophistry,
 In case-by-case decision,
I want responsibility,
 Determined with precision.

"We need a bright clear line to show
 The safety mark in loading,
So that a British tar can go
 To sea without foreboding." [34]

Sam Plimsoll was so eloquent
 That Parliament gave heed,
And sought this evil to prevent,
 With all deliberate speed.[35]

With fervent popular support
 It passed the law he urged,
Forbidding ships to sail from port
 With Plimsoll's line submerged.

   * * *

So if for metaphor you yearn,
 You'd better find a new one
To help your readers to discern
 The process that is due one.

A line that's etched upon the sand
 When tidal waters shrink?
Or one drawn by a palsied hand
 With disappearing ink?

An edict whispered in the dark
 Behind the Iron Curtain?

[33] Samuel Plimsoll (1824-1898) was born in Bristol and elected to Parliament in 1868 from Derby.

[34] It is to be understood that the quotation is fictive, but it fairly reflects Plimsoll's views. . . . [As for "fictive," see Frankfurter, J., in, e.g., *Keifer & Keifer* v. *R.F.C.*, 306 U.S. 381, 395 (1939).]

[35] In this case it was eight years. First proposed in 1868, Plimsoll's bill was enacted in 1876. The delay tactic of appointing a Royal Commission was resorted to in 1873. . . .

But not, oh not! a Plimsoll mark
So definite and certain.[36]

Words are the skin of living thought,
But here's an overstuffed one.
This time the mark you overshot;
Indeed, you simply muffed one.[37]

Unless perchance we find the key
In some sly Freudian twist:
A yearning for the certainty
You say cannot exist.

If with this though you disagree,
There is at least one other:
Is this a subtle parody
Of some more rigid brother?

* * *

But Burbank [38] is not brought to book
For one imperfect calyx;
So we're prepared to overlook
One metaphor *infelix*.

QUASI-DEFENDANTS AND THE RULE OF LAW

Although the question of the constitutional rights of persons whom we shall call "quasi-defendants" is not really a new one, its incidence as a critical issue of public policy is essentially a by-product of the Cold War. By "quasi-defendants," we refer to the situation of persons who are not technically defendants in a court on trial for offenses defined by law as crimes, consequent to the indictment of a grand jury or the filing of an information by a public prosecutor. Conspicuous examples (because of the widespread public notoriety that has focused upon them) are public employees threatened with suspension or dismissal from their employment in "loyalty" or "security" hearings, and witnesses before legislative investi-

---

36 The possibility has been explored that Frankfurter, J., was relying on the fact that a ship has two Plimsoll marks, one for summer and the other for winter. And a ship sailing on both salt and fresh water has a pair for each. On reflection, however, this appears merely to augment the difficulties.

37 It has been urged that in any case "above" rather than "below" the Plimsoll line would be the proper phraseology to indicate that due process was not satisfied, but Goddard, J., a distinguished admiralty judge, refers to a ship being loaded below

the Plimsoll mark when it is plain from the context that it was overloaded. . . . Both the Plimsoll statute and [that of New York State] use another wording: "to be so loaded as to submerge . . . the load line. . . ." Possibly resort to the language of the statute would eliminate the hazard of ambiguity. One might say that ". . . in combination they submerge the Plimsoll line of due process."

38 Luther Burbank (1849-1926), the American horticulturist and originator of new botanical varieties.

gating committees. Generally speaking, the direct sanction in the Executive loyalty proceedings is dismissal from public employment; [39] and in the cases of witnesses before legislative committees, it is subsequent trial in court for the crime of either contempt of or perjury before the committee.[40] The indirect sanctions include loss of government benefits or privileges; loss of private employment; loss of reputation and status in one's community; and a host of other ancillary deprivations.[41] It is not too great an exaggeration to draw the obvious parallel between these indirect sanctions and the old common-law punishment of outlawry.[42] Without being tried, as the Constitution requires, for the crime of treason, the quasi-defendant is frequently branded in the public eye and convicted in the public mind as being a traitor against his country.

This is not true of the ordinary criminals (i.e., big-time racketeers) who become quasi-defendants before legislative committees investigating organized crime; to the contrary, these hoodlums frequently enjoy a time of glory in which their fabulous exploits are recounted by the modern minstrels of the press, television, and the movies; their life stories are recorded for posterity on film and tape, and the legend of Robin Hood lives once again with labor racketeers and other thugs cast in the hero's role. But outlawry in modern garb is visited upon other quasi-defendants who are accused of having been Communists, or Communist sympathizers, or fellow-travelers, or persons who "fraternized" with suspected Communists. (Not infrequently, one who continues to maintain a social relationship with a son, or wife, or mother who is suspected of "subversion" becomes himself contaminated for having maintained, either knowingly or unwittingly, an association with a person suspected of being a part of the Communist conspiracy.)

Less conspicuous, but certainly of no less intrinsic importance, is the plight of the witness or attorney in court proceedings who suddenly discovers himself to be a defendant in a criminal proceeding in which the presiding judge is a man who wears many hats: that of the accuser, the grand jury, the petit jury, the trial judge, the probation officer for pre-sentence investigation and report, and the sentencing judge—all wrapped up in one enigmatic official personality. Such defendants, like ordinary criminals, are not usually subjected to the indirect or secondary sanctions that we have described; but they are subject to severe sanc-

---

[39] See, e.g., *Beilan* v. *Board of Education of Philadelphia*, 357 U.S. 399 (1958); *Cole* v. *Young*, 351 U.S. 536 (1956); *Peters* v. *Hobby*, 349 U.S. 331 (1955); *Wieman* v. *Updegraff*, 344 U.S. 183 (1952); *Adler* v. *Board of Education*, 342 U.S. 485 (1952); *Garner* v. *Board of Public Works*, 341 U.S. 716 (1951).

[40] See *Christoffel* v. *United States*, 338 U.S. 84 (1949), a perjury case, and *United States* v. *Bryan*, 339 U.S. 323 (1950), a contempt case, both of which are presented in Chapter 4.

[41] See, e.g., *Joint Anti-Fascist Refugee Committee* v. *McGrath*, 341 U.S. 123 (1951); *Sacher* v. *United States*, 347 U.S. 388 (1953); *Slochower* v. *Board of Higher Education*, 350 U.S. 551 (1956); *Peters* v. *New York City Housing Authority*, 128 N.Y.S. 2d 224 (1953) and 147 N.Y.S. 2d 859 (1955); *Greene* v. *McElroy*, 360 U.S. 474 (1959); and *In re Sawyer*, 360 U.S. 622 (1959).

[42] Cf. *Green* v. *United States*, 356 U.S. 165, 170-172 (1958).

tions imposed by grace of a summary process of trial that bears little superficial resemblance to what the Supreme Court has usually defined as the basic elements of a fair trial, even in a system of ordered liberty. These, too, are quasi-defendants.

In this section, we shall consider the question of the constitutional rights of witnesses before legislative investigative committees and of persons summarily tried for criminal contempt of court. We shall not deal further with the federal Executive loyalty defendants; the Court managed to avoid the constitutional issues explicit in those proceedings during the decade in which the federal Executive carried through its loyalty-security programs; and only after the program had substantially achieved the desired results did the Court begin to establish some limits to the scope of Executive discretion. At that, the Court based its decisions upon the interpretation of acts of Congress and Executive Orders of the President, by which authority was delegated to administrative subordinates, rather than upon the interpretation of the Constitution.[43] The Court has yet to rule upon the constitutional issues that it did consider in the comparable cases arising before the Legislative and Judicial branches, to which we now turn.

Legislative Investigators

In 1955, the Warren Court upheld the right of witnesses to invoke the Fifth Amendment privilege against self-incrimination before congressional investigating committees.[44] But the Court's broadest ruling in behalf of such quasi-defendants came two years later, in its decision in *Watkins* v. *United States*, 354 U.S. 178 (1957). Watkins was a union leader whose cooperation with the Communist Party during World War II was "exposed" by a subcommittee of the House Committee on Un-American Activities. He responded without apparent reservation to questions concerning his own past liaison with Communists, although denying that he ever had been a member of the Communist party; but he refused to discuss the political activities of his former associates who, to his "best knowledge and belief have long since removed themselves from the Communist movement." The quasi-defendants in the 1955 cases had invoked the self-incrimination clause in their own individual behalf; but Watkins claimed, in effect, a constitutional right not to be forced to become an informer or a "stool pigeon." He was, of course, cited by the House for his refusal to answer the questions put to him by the subcommittee; and he was subsequently tried and convicted in a federal district court for the crime of contempt of the Congress.

In a 6-1 decision, a majority of the Court reversed Watkins' conviction, on the grounds that neither Congress nor the Committee ever had defined "Un-

---

[43] See David Fellman, *The Defendant's Rights* (New York: Rinehart, 1958), chap. xii, esp. pp. 213-235; Glendon Schubert, *The Presidency in the Courts* (Minneapolis: University of Minnesota Press, 1957), pp. 21-33;

Greene v. *McElroy*, 360 U.S. 474 (1959).

[44] *Quinn* v. *United States*, 349 U.S. 155 (1955); *Emspak* v. *United States*, 349 U.S. 190 (1955); and *Bart* v. *United States*, 349 U.S. 219 (1955).

American Activities" with sufficient precision adequately to apprise the witness whether the questions that he refused to answer were "pertinent to the subject under inquiry." His conviction, therefore, was void for vagueness "under the Due Process Clause of the Fifth Amendment." Warren seized the occasion, however, to lecture the Congress in several flights of what obviously were *obiter dicta*:

> [The] constitutional rights of witnesses will be respected by the Congress as they are in a court of justice. The Bill of Rights is applicable to investigations as to all forms of governmental action. Witnesses cannot be compelled to give evidence against themselves. They cannot be subjected to unreasonable search and seizure. Nor can the First Amendment freedoms of speech, press, religion, or political belief and association be abridged. . . . The First Amendment may be invoked against infringement of the protected freedoms by law or by lawmaking. . . . We have no doubt that there is no congressional power to expose for the sake of exposure.

Whether the Chief Justice would be able, in future decisions, to hold together a majority that would live up to the promise of the dicta—or even the holding—seemed most doubtful, in the light of the Court's usual behavior in such matters. It was a beachhead that only a determined and majority libertarian bloc could hope to maintain; and Warren was at least one vote short of leading such a group. Harlan certainly could not be considered a member of the libertarian bloc; and Frankfurter was careful to state, in a concurring opinion, his own understanding of the Court's holding, which he defined narrowly (and doubtless properly) in terms of the vagueness of the offense, under Fifth Amendment due process, with which Watkins had been charged.

The Watkins decision was an exceptionally controversial one, and provoked sharp criticism of the Court from defenders, both in and outside of Congress, of the House Committee on Un-American Activities. In view of the motions that were introduced for the impeachment of the justices, it is understandable that the Court's announcement of a policy of constitutional rights for witnesses before investigating committees should have awaited the demise of Senator McCarthy and the denouement of the period of the "Grand Inquest" [45] that accompanied the sharp turn for the worse in American-Soviet relations, the shift to the left in the line of the Communist party in the United States, and the advent of the Cold War. The Watkins case came just a decade after it would have done the most good, assuming that the protection from testimonial compulsion of witnesses before legislative committees and the consequent frustration of the political careers of congressmen is a good thing.

---

[45] See, e.g., Telford Taylor, *Grand Inquest* (New York: Simon and Schuster, 1955). No doubt it is a coincidence, since the senator's effective power had been broken several years earlier, but it is a fact that Joseph McCarthy died on May 2, 1957, after argument had been held and six weeks before the announcement of the decision in the Watkins case. The conjuncture of the two events marked the end of an era.

The Vinson Court had approved policies pointing in the opposite direction in *United States* v. *Bryan,* 339 U.S. 323 (1950), and *Tenney* v. *Brandhove,* 341 U.S. 367 (1951). The shift in policy leading to Watkins began in the last year of Vinson's Chief Justiceship, with the Court's unanimous decision in *United States* v. *Rumely,* 345 U.S. 41 (1953). This case involved, not the investigation of crime or Communism, but rather the inquiries of the Select Committee of the House of Representatives (the Buchanan Committee) on Lobbying Activities—a query which came very close, at times, to becoming a form of self-analysis for the congressmen. Rumely was the executive secretary of the Committee for Constitutional Government, a right-wing organization which proselyted for public acceptance of something called "the American Way" in which laissez faire and the Constitution were inseparably merged in one entity. The Buchanan Committee wanted to know who made bulk purchases of C.C.G. publications. The Court, speaking through Frankfurter, avoided the constitutional questions that Rumely sought to raise by "interpreting" the authorizing resolution establishing and defining the responsibilities of the House Select Committee in such a narrow way that "lobbying" was construed to mean buttonholing congressmen in the corridors and open bribery, but nothing more sophisticated. Thus, any meaningful inquiry that the Buchanan Committee had made was branded as illegal; the reversal of Rumely's conviction for contempt of Congress was affirmed by the Court; and the question whether quasi-defendants before legislative investigating committees were protected by the First and Fifth Amendments (or the Fourteenth) was left open. Table 28, on page 637, presents the decisions of the Warren Court relating to this issue during the next half-dozen years following Rumely.

Sweezy v. *New Hampshire,* a companion case decided at the same time as Watkins, posited equivalent limitations under the Fourteenth Amendment for investigating committees of state legislatures. *Sacher* v. *United States* was a *per curiam* decision based upon the authority of Watkins and decided a year later.[46] As Table 28 indicates, the voting patterns for Watkins, Sweezy, and Sacher are identical, except for Burton's failure to participate in the decision of the federal cases and Whittaker's failure to participate in the two earlier decisions. In these decisions, neither the Court as a group nor the justices individually saw any difference between the requirements of the First and Fifth, and the Fourteenth Amendment, at least of sufficient dimension to affect their voting behavior. Only a year later, however, the Court swung back to the right in a pair of decisions that stringently modified, without formally overruling, the decisions of

---

[46] The defendant was the same lawyer who had been of counsel for the Communist party leaders in the Dennis case. His career as a quasi-defendant extended by now over the greater part of the decade, including his conviction for contempt of Judge Medina [*Sacher* v. *United States,* 343 U.S. 1 (1952)], the Supreme Court's reversal of his disbarment in New York on the same charges and evidence [*Sacher* v. *United States,* 347 U.S. 388 (1953)], and the Court's present reversal of his conviction for contempt of a two-man subcommittee of the Internal Security Subcommittee of the Senate Committee on the Judiciary [*Sacher* v. *United States,* 356 U.S. 576 (1958)].

the 1956 Term. Barenblatt, like Watkins, dealt with a claim of vagueness in the terms of reference of the House Committee on Un-American Activities; Uphaus, like Sweezy, involved an investigation into subversive activity by the New Hampshire Attorney General, who had been constituted as a "one-man legislative investigating committee" by joint resolution of the state legislature. As in Watkins and Sweezy, so in Barenblatt and Uphaus the justices made no distinction in their voting behavior between the federal and the state case.

Nevertheless, the 6-1 majority of 1957 had been changed into a 4-5 minority in only two years. How had this happened? There was no change in the positions of a majority of the justices: Warren, Black, Douglas, and Brennan voted to uphold the claims of the defendants, and Clark voted to uphold the authority of the committees, in all four cases. Burton was replaced by Stewart, but since both voted negatively in the cases in which they participated, this was no change, except that Burton's nonparticipation in Watkins artificially reduced the size of the real minority in that decision. Similarly, let us assume that Whittaker would have dissented if he had participated in Watkins and Sweezy, as he did dissent in Sacher. If both Burton and Whittaker had participated in Watkins and had voted as we have assumed, the decision still would have been 6-3 in Watkins' favor. In order for the Warren bloc to lose control over the Court's policies in this area, it was necessary for *both* of the two remaining justices to switch their votes, and this is precisely what Frankfurter and Harlan did. Having supported the civil rights of Watkins and Sweezy in 1957, and of Sacher in 1958, they voted against the similar claims of Barenblatt and Uphaus in 1959.

The critical factor explaining the difference in the outcome of the two sets of cases, therefore, is that two justices changed their minds. As a consequence, it might well be said that "the Court" also changed its mind on this issue, because all of the decisions from 1955 through 1958 were in support of the quasi-defendants; while all three of the negative decisions were announced in June, 1959. (Another 1959 decision, *Scull* v. *Virginia*, involved the enforcement of the Court's racial-integration policy, and, from a functional rather than a formal point of view, might well be considered not to belong to this universe of data.)

The Court's swing to the right might well be interpreted as a reaction to the heavy criticism that had been leveled against the Court, because of its allegedly overly libertarian bias, during recent years. It is certainly plausible that anyone who loved courts and judges as much as Mr. Justice Frankfurter might have profited from the experience of the Court-packing episode of the 1936 Term; and notwithstanding his express disclaimers—in behalf of another—to the contrary,[47] might have decided that the time had come to put out some fires before they got out of control. Such an example of judicial restraint not only would comport with the general tenor of Justice Frankfurter's expressed views concerning the proper relationship between the Court, on the one hand, and Congress and state legis-

47 See the section on "Roberts' Switch: An Inside View," at the end of Chapter 3.

TABLE 28.

A Scalogram of Decisions of the Warren Court Concerning the Rights of Quasi-Defendants Before Legislative Investigating Committees (1954-1958 Terms)

SCALE SCORES	CASE	Scull v. Virginia, 359 U.S. 344 (1959)	Raley et al. v. Ohio, 360 U.S. 423 (1959)	Quinn v. United States, 349 U.S. 155 (1955)	Emspak v. United States, 349 U.S. 190 (1955)	Bart v. United States, 349 U.S. 219 (1955)	Sacher v. United States, 356 U.S. 576 (1958) [a]	Watkins v. United States, 354 U.S. 178 (1957)	Sweezy v. New Hampshire, 354 U.S. 234 (1957)	Stern v. Ohio [see Raley v. Ohio]. (1959)	Barenblatt v. United States, 360 U.S. 109 (1959)	Uphaus v. Wyman, 360 U.S. 72 (1959)	Total Votes per Justice	Total Inconsistent Votes per Justice
	SCALE POSITION	1	2	3	4	5	6	7	8	9	10	11		
11	Warren	(+)	(+)	('+')	('+')	('+')	(+)	('+')	('+')	+)	+)	+)	11	0
11	Black	('+')	(+)	(+)	(+)	(+)	(+)	(+)	(+)	+)	'+')	+)	11	0
11	Douglas	(+)	(+)	(+)	(+)	(+)	(+)	(+)	(+)	+)	+)	+)	11·0	
11	Brennan	(+)	('+')	*	*	*	(+)	(+)	(+)	'+')	'+')	'+')	8·0	
8	Frankfurter	(+)	(+)	(+)	(+)	(+)	(+)	('+'	('+'	(−	(−)	(−)	11	0
8	Harlan	(+)	(+)	('+'	(−)	(−)	('+'	(+)	(+)	(−	('−')	(−)	11	2
5	Burton	*	*	(+)	(+)	(+)	NP	NP	−)	*	*	*	4	0
5	Clark	(│)	(+)	(+)	(+)	(+)	'−')	'−')	'−')	('−'	(−)	('−')	11	0
3	Minton	*	*	(+)	−)	−)	*	*	*	*	*	*	3	0
2	Whittaker	(+)	(+)	*	*	*	−)	NP	NP	(−	(−)	(−)	6	0
1	Stewart	(+)	NP	*	*	*	*	*	*	NP	(−)	(−)	3	0
0	Reed	*	*	'−')	'−')	'−')	*	*	*	*	*	*	3	0
	Voting Division	9-0	8-0	8-1	6-3	6-3	6-2	6-1	6-2 Pro	4-4 Con	4-5	4-5	93	
	Total Inconsistent Votes per Case	S 0	S 0	F 0	F 1	F 1	F 0	F 0	S 0	S 0	F 0	S 0		2

LEGEND:

- $+$ = a vote in favor of the defendant
- $-$ = a vote against the defendant
- * = not seated at the time of this decision
- NP = seated but not participating in this decision
- F = trial in a federal court
- S = trial in a state court
- ' ' = wrote opinion
- ( ) = joined in the opinion of the Court
- (= concurring opinion
-) = dissenting opinion
- ◯ = inconsistent vote

$$CR = 1 - \frac{2}{67} = .97$$

[a] The decision in *Sacher v. United States* was *per curiam*.

latures, on the other; it would also help to maintain the political power of the Court as an institution: "He who learns to run away, lives to fight another day." It is also notable, in this regard, that the only justice whose votes correspond precisely to the outcome of the cases in Table 28 is Justice Frankfurter. On this issue and for the period covered, it might not be too inaccurate to say that "As Frankfurter goes, so goes the Court."

Judge-Prosecutors

Since the School Segregation decision in 1954, there has been an unusual focusing of interest upon the exercise of contempt power, summary and otherwise, by the federal courts. Apart from normal usage as an adjunct to the enforcement of certain federal administrative orders, and to preserve order and decorum within courtrooms, the federal judicial contempt power has emerged as a primary weapon for assuring compliance with the Supreme Court's desegregation policy. This latent utility of the federal judicial-contempt power resulted in a quickening of congressional attention to a subject upon which a speaker could ordinarily expect to expound to an empty floor and galleries; out of the concern of Congress came a neat dilemma for liberals: whether to press for a "strong" bill, with effective enforcement power, or to uphold the right to a fair trial—including trial by jury—for violators of the proposed Civil Rights Act. Most liberals chose the former course and pressed for a strong bill (with a minimum of procedural guarantees for defendants); but they had to accept a mild and very watered-down version that applied only to the right to vote.[48] Among the more ironical touches in the enactment of the Civil Rights Act of 1957—the first statute of its kind since the days of Reconstruction—was the spectacle of the leading conservatives of the South insisting, and successfully, upon the right of jury trial for all except the most petty offenses defined by the statute. This right of trial by jury for defendants before federal judges on charges of contempt of court, granted by Congress for the narrow class of cases to which the statute applies, contrasts sharply with the lack of procedural rights to a fair trial that the Court, by interpretation of its own rules, has ordained for most other defendants in federal criminal contempt-of-court cases.

[48] Cf. Pritchett, *The American Constitution*, p. 630.

SACHER v. UNITED STATES
343 U.S. 1 (1952)

Certiorari to the United States Court of Appeals for the Second Circuit.

Affirmed.

5-3

Jackson	('+')
Vinson, C.J.	(+)
Reed	(+)
Burton	(+)
Minton	(+)
Black	'—')
Frankfurter	'—')
Douglas	'—')
Clark	NP

MR. JUSTICE JACKSON delivered the opinion of the Court.

After a turbulent nine months of trial, eleven Communist Party leaders were convicted of violating the Smith Act.[49] On receiving the verdict, the trial judge at once filed a certificate under Rule 42 (a), Fed Rules of Crim Proc, finding petitioners guilty of criminal contempt and imposing various jail terms up to six months. Those sentenced were defense counsel, with the exception of one defendant who had elected to conduct his own case.

The Court of Appeals reviewed the judge's action, both on facts and law, reversed some specifications of contempt, but affirmed the conviction and sentences. . . .

The actual effect of petitioners' conduct on the trial and on the burden of subsequent courts in reviewing an unnecessarily large record also was noted by a differently composed Court of Appeals when they sought reversal of their clients' conviction and assigned misconduct and bias of the trial judge as one of the grounds. The Court found that it could not consider the accusations against the judge separately from behavior of counsel. It unanimously found their charges against the trial judge "completely unconvincing," and of their own conduct said, "All was done that could contribute to make impossible an orderly and speedy dispatch of the case. . . ." The nature of this obstruction was thus described:

"The record discloses a judge, sorely tried for many months of turmoil, constantly provoked by useless bickering, exposed to offensive slights and insults, harried with interminable repetition, who, if at times he did not conduct himself with the imperturbability of a Rhadamanthus, showed considerably greater self-control and forbearance than it is given to most judges to possess."

. . . [The] importance of clarifying the permissible practice in such cases persuaded us to grant certiorari, limited to one question of procedure on which there was disagreement in the court below. Our order stated the issue for consideration:

". . . The sole question for review is: Was the charge of contempt, as and when certified, one which the accusing judge was authorized under Rule 42 (a) to determine and punish himself; or was it one to be adjudged and punished under Rule 42 (b) only by a judge other than the accusing one and after notice, hearing, and opportunity to defend?"

The certificate of contempt fills sixty pages of our record and incorporates, by reference, the 13,000 pages of trial record. The certificate in full and summary of relevant evidence have been reported below. Because our limited review does not require or permit reexamination of the facts, no purpose would be served by detailed recitals. It is relevant to the questions of law to observe that the behavior punished as a result of the Court of Appeals' judgment has these characteristics: It took place in the immediate presence of the trial judge; it consisted of breaches of decorum and disobedience in the presence of the jury of his orders and rulings

---

[49] *Dennis* v. *United States* 341 U.S. 494 [(1951). Footnote by the Court.]

upon the trial; the misconduct was professional in that it was that of lawyers, or of a layman acting as his own lawyer. In addition, conviction is not based on an isolated instance of hasty contumacious speech or behavior, but upon a course of conduct long-continued in the face of warnings that it was regarded by the court as contemptuous. The nature of the deportment was not such as merely to offend personal sensitivities of the judge, but it prejudiced the expeditious, orderly and dispassionate conduct of the trial. . . .

The issue we accepted for review is a narrow one. Petitioners do not deny that they might have been summarily punished for their conduct without hearing under Rule 42 (a) if the trial judge had acted at once upon occurrence of each incident. But it is contended that this power of summary punishment expired [because] the trial judge awaited completion of the trial, at which time its progress could no longer be obstructed, and hence, it is said, summary action had become unnecessary. . . .

Summary punishment always, and rightly, is regarded with disfavor and, if imposed in passion or pettiness, brings discredit to a court as certainly as the conduct it penalizes. But the very practical reasons which have led every system of law to vest a contempt power in one who presides over judicial proceedings also are the reasons which account for it being made summary. Our criminal processes are adversary in nature and rely upon the self-interest of the litigants and counsel for full and adequate development of their respective cases. The nature of the proceedings presupposes, or at least stimulates, zeal in the opposing lawyers. But their strife can pervert as well as aid the judicial process unless it is supervised and controlled by a neutral judge representing the overriding social interest in impartial justice and with power to curb both adversaries. The rights and immunities of accused persons would be exposed to serious and obvious abuse if the trial bench did not possess and frequently exert power to curb prejudicial and excessive zeal of prosecutors. The interests of society in the preservation of courtroom control by the judges are no more to be frustrated through unchecked improprieties by defenders. . . .

The Rule in question contemplates that occasions may arise when the trial judge must immediately arrest any conduct of such nature that its continuance would break up a trial, so it gives him power to do so summarily. But the petitioners here contend that the Rule not only permits but requires its instant exercise, so that once the emergency has been survived punishment may no longer be summary but can only be administered by the alternative method allowed by Rule 42 (b). We think "summary" as used in this Rule does not refer to the timing of the action with reference to the offense but refers to a procedure which dispenses with the formality, delay and digression that would result from the issuance of process, service of complaint and answer, holding hearings, taking evidence, listening to arguments, awaiting briefs, submission of findings, and all that goes with a conventional court trial. The purpose of that procedure is to inform the court of events not within its own knowledge. The Rule allows summary procedure only as to offenses within the knowledge of the judge because they occurred in his presence.

Reasons for permitting straightway exercise of summary power are not reasons for compelling or encouraging its immediate exercise. Forthwith judgment is not required by the text of the Rule. Still less is such construction appropriate as a safeguard against abuse of the power. If the conduct of these lawyers warranted immediate summary punishment on dozens of occasions, no possible prejudice to them can result from delaying it until the end of the trial if the circumstances permit such delay. The overriding consideration is the integrity and efficiency of the trial process, and if the judge deems immediate action inexpedient he should be allowed discretion to follow the procedure taken in this case. To summon a lawyer before the bench and pronounce him guilty of contempt is not unlikely to prejudice his client. It might be done out of the presence of the jury, but we have held that a contempt judgment must be public.[50] Only the naive and inexperienced would assume that news of such action will not reach the jurors. . . .

If we were to hold that summary punishment can be imposed only instantly upon the event, it would be an incentive to pronounce, while smarting under the irritation of the contemptuous act, what should be a well-considered judgment. We think it less likely that unfair condemnation of counsel will occur if the more deliberate course be permitted.

[50] *Re Oliver*, 333 U.S. 257 [(1948). Footnote by the Court.] There are interesting implications to the use of this decision in a state case, under the Fourteenth Amendment, as a precedent for a proposition relating to fair trials in the federal courts. Particularly is this so, since the Court's Rule 42(b) purports to be based upon the Court's "supervisory authority," not upon any requirements of the Fifth or Sixth or any other amendment. Does the Court's discussion imply that the substantive content of Rule 42 ought to be given an interpretation consistent with what the Court has held, or might in the future hold, that the *Fourteenth Amendment* requires? If so, it follows logically that Sacher should have been decided differently if Murchison (below) had been decided first. Moreover, the dissenters in Murchison explicitly point to the anomaly of that decision's having established a stricter policy for state judges than Sacher did for federal judges, who are presumably subject to the more restrictive restraints of the Supreme Court's "supervisory powers." As we observed in Chapter 9, *Shelley* v. *Kraemer* supplied the policy base for *Hurd* v. *Hodge;* and the only significant difference in this respect between the restrictive-covenant decisions and the use of Oliver implied by Jackson's footnote is that Rule 42 is a positive regulation, while the Court exercised its supervisory authority in *Hurd* v. *Hodge* to establish a policy for the federal courts by decisional law rather than through rule-making. Cf. Justice Stewart's concurring

We hold that Rule 42 allows the trial judge, upon the occurrence in his presence of a contempt, immediately and summarily to punish it, if, in his opinion, delay will prejudice the trial. We hold, on the other hand, that if he believes the exigencies of the trial require that he defer judgment until its completion he may do so without extinguishing his power. . . .

That contempt power over counsel, summary or otherwise, is capable of abuse is certain. Men who make their way to the bench sometimes exhibit vanity, irascibility, narrowness, arrogance, and other weaknesses to which human flesh is heir. Most judges, however, recognize and respect courageous, forthright lawyerly conduct. They rarely mistake overzeal or heated words of a man fired with a desire to win, for the contemptuous conduct which defies rulings and deserves punishment. They recognize that our profession necessarily is a contentious one and they respect the lawyer who makes a strenuous effort for his client.

The profession knows that no lawyer is at the mercy of a single federal trial judge. . . . These lawyers have not been condemned, as they claim, merely by the impulse of one lone and hostile judge. Their conduct has been condemned by every judge who has examined this record under a duty to review the facts. It is to be doubted whether the profession will be greatly terrorized by punishment of some of its members after such extended and detached consideration. Moreover, if power of contempt excites fear and terror in the bar, it would hardly be relieved by upholding petitioners' contention that the judge may proceed against a lawyer at the precise moment of maximum heat but may not do so if he awaits a cooler second thought. . . .

But that there may be no misunderstanding, we make clear that this Court,

opinion in *Spano* v. *New York,* 360 U.S. 315 (1959).

if its aid be needed, will unhesitatingly protect counsel in fearless, vigorous and effective performance of every duty pertaining to the office of the advocate on behalf of any person whatsoever. But it will not equate contempt with courage or insults with independence. It will also protect the processes of orderly trial, which is the supreme object of the lawyer's calling.

Affirmed.

MR. JUSTICE BLACK, dissenting.

I would reverse these convictions because of my belief that (1) the Judge should not have passed on the contempt charges he preferred; (2) whatever judge considered the charges, guilt should not have been summarily decided as it was—without notice, without a hearing and without an opportunity for petitioners to defend themselves; (3) petitioners were constitutionally entitled to have their guilt or innocence of criminal contempt decided by a jury.

After a nine months' trial of officials of the Communist Party a jury brought in a verdict of guilty and was discharged. Immediately, presiding Judge Medina asked all the defendants' lawyers to stand up, then read them a very minor part of a lengthy "contempt certificate" in which they were alleged to have committed many acts of contempt at various times during the protracted trial. Without affording any of them a chance to say a word before he acted, the presiding Judge held all of them guilty of contempt and sentenced each one to prison.

First. I think it was a grave error for the Judge to pass on the charges he brought. . . .

[*Second.*] . . . I think these cases should be reversed because Judge Medina denied petitioners a hearing. . . .

Third. Art. 3, § 2 of the Constitution provides that "The Trial of all Crimes . . . shall be by Jury." Not satisfied with this single protection for jury trial, the Founders reemphasized the guaranty by declaring in the Sixth Amendment that "In all criminal prosecutions, the accused shall enjoy the right to a speedy and public trial, by an impartial jury. . . ." And the Fifth Amendment provides that "No person shall be held to answer for a capital, or otherwise infamous crime, unless on a presentment or indictment of a grand jury. . . ." These contempt proceedings are "criminal prosecutions" brought to avenge an alleged public wrong. Petitioners were imprisoned for terms up to six months, but these terms could have been longer. . . . Certainly, petitioners have been sentenced for crimes. Consequently these lawyers have been wrongfully deprived of the jury benefits of the foregoing constitutional provisions unless they are inapplicable to the crime of contempt. . . .

A concurring judge in the Court of Appeals feared that it might bring about "demoralization of the court's authority" should any one other than Judge Medina try the case. The reason given was: "For instance, in all likelihood, at a trial of the lawyers, Sacher would introduce the testimony of himself and others in an effort to prove that he was not 'angrily shouting,' as charged in Specification VII, and did not speak 'in an insolent manner,' as charged in Specification VIII; Gladstein would similarly seek to prove that he did not 'angrily' advance 'toward the bench' or make remarks in a 'truculent manner,' as charged in Specification VIII, and did not speak to the judge 'in a sarcastic and impertinent manner' as charged in Specification XI, etc., etc." 182 F2d 416, 461. What would be wrong with this? Are defendants accused by judges of being offensive to them to be conclusively presumed guilty on the theory that judges' observations and inferences must be accepted as infallible? There is always a possibility that a judge may be honestly mistaken. Unfortunately history and the existence of our Bill of Rights indicate that judicial errors may be from worse causes. . . .

I believe these petitioners were entitled to a jury trial. I believe a jury is all the more necessary to obtain a fair trial when the alleged offense relates to conduct that has personally affronted a judge. . . . Preference for trial by a jury of laymen over trial by lawyer-judges lies behind the constitutional guarantee of trial by jury. I am among those who still believe in trial by jury as one of the indispensable safeguards of liberty.

MR. JUSTICE FRANKFURTER, dissenting. . . .

It is not for nothing that most of the provisions of our Bill of Rights are concerned with matters of procedure.

That is what this case is about—"procedural regularity." Not whether these petitioners have been guilty of conduct professionally inexcusable, but what tribunal should sit in judgment; not whether they should be punished, but who should mete out the appropriate punishment; not whether a Federal court has authority to prevent its proceedings from being subverted, but how that authority should be exercised so as to assure the rectitude of legal proceedings and at the same time not detract from the authority of law itself. . . .

I would not remotely minimize the gravity of the conduct of which the petitioners have been found guilty, let alone condone it. But their intrinsic guilt is not relevant to the issue before us. This Court brought the case here in order to consider whether the trial court followed the proper procedure in determining that the misconduct of the petitioners subjected them to punishment. . . . Time out of mind this Court has reversed convictions for the most heinous offenses, even though no doubt about the guilt of the defendant was entertained. It reversed because the mode by which guilt was established disregarded those standards of procedure which are so precious and so important for our society. So here, the only question for decision is whether, in the circumstances of this case, the trial judge himself should, without notice and hearing and after the successful termination of the trial, have summarily punished a series of contempts growing out of what he conceived to be a central mischievous design, committed over a period of nine months; or whether another judge, designated by the Chief Judge of the Court of Appeals or of the District Court of the Southern District of New York, should have heard, after due notice, the charges of contempt made by the trial judge. At the end of the trial the judge was not confronted with the alternatives of doing what he did or allowing the contemnors to go unpunished. The question was not punishment, but who should punish. It is in due regard for such procedural questions, too often misconceived as narrow and technical, that the truth of one of the great boasts of our democracy, the essential fairness in our judicial system, depends.

The particular circumstances of this case compel me to conclude that the trial judge should not have combined in himself the functions of accuser and judge. For his accusations were not impersonal. They concerned matters in which he personally was deeply engaged. Whatever occasion may have existed during the trial for sitting in judgment upon claims of personal victimization, it ceased after the trial had terminated. It falls to this Court as head of the Federal judicial system to correct such abuse of judicial power. . . .

Deeply as I believe in the importance of giving wide and not niggardly scope to the discretionary powers of trial judges and with a lifelong regard for the wisdom of the judge who, on behalf of the Court of Appeals, found that the discretion of the trial judge was not abused, I cannot escape the conviction that another district judge should have tried the contempt issue. And this, though one may well assume that any other judge would have been compelled to find contempt in this case and may have imposed even severer sentences. Preserving and enhancing the fair name of Law is always more important than sustaining the infliction of punishment in a particular case.

A reading of the fifteen volumes of testimony in the Dennis record leaves one with the strong feeling that the conduct found contemptuous was in the main directed against the trial judge personally and that the judge himself so regarded it. . . .

Not only were the contempts directed against the trial judge. The conduct of the lawyers had its reflex in the judge. At frequent intervals in the course of the trial his comments plainly reveal personal feeling against the lawyers, however much the course of the trial may have justified such feeling. On numerous occasions he expressed his belief that the lawyers were trying to wear him down, to injure his health, to provoke him into doing something that would show prejudice, or cause a mistrial or reversal on appeal. . . .

[An appendix to this opinion] indubitably establishe[s] that the judge felt deeply involved personally in the conduct for which he punished the defense lawyers. He was not merely a witness to an occurrence, as would be a judge who observed a fist fight in his courtroom or brutal badgering of a witness or an impropriety towards the jury. The judge acted as the prosecuting witness; he thought of himself as such. His self-concern pervades the record; it could not humanly have been excluded from his judgment of contempt. Judges are human, and it is not suggested that any other judge could have been impervious to the abuse had he been subjected to it. But precisely because a judge is human, and in common frailty or manliness would interpret such conduct of lawyers as an attack on himself personally, he should not subsequently sit in judgment on his assailants, barring only instances where such extraordinary procedure is compellingly necessary in order that the trial may proceed and not be aborted.

Summary punishment of contempt is concededly an exception to the requirements of Due Process. Necessity dictates the departure. Necessity must bound its limits. In this case the course of events to the very end of the trial shows that summary measures were not necessary to enable the trial to go on. . . . Despite the many incidents of contempt that were charged, the trial went to completion, nine months after the first incident, without a single occasion making it necessary to lay any one of the lawyers by the heel in order to assure that the trial proceed. The trial judge was able to keep order and to continue the court's business by occasional brief recesses calculated to cool passions and restore decorum, by periodic warnings to defense lawyers, and by shutting off obstructive arguments whenever rulings were concisely stated and firmly held to. . . .

Had the judge here found the petitioners guilty of contempt during the actual course of the trial a different problem would be presented. Even then, however, only compelling circumstances would justify a peremptory judgment of contempt. . . .

Truth compels the observation, painful as it is to make it, that the fifteen volumes of oral testimony in the principal trial record numerous episodes involving the judge and defense counsel that are more suggestive of an undisciplined debating society than of the hush and solemnity of a court of justice. Too often counsel were encouraged to vie with the court in dialectic, in repartee and banter, in talk so copious as inevitably to arrest the momentum of the trial and to weaken the restraints of respect that a judge should engender in lawyers. Counsel were not made to understand that in a criminal case not merely the liberty of individuals is at stake. Law itself is on trial as the "stern daughter of the voice of God." Throughout the proceedings, even after the trial judge had indicated that he thought defense counsel were in conspiracy against him and were seeking thereby to subvert the trial, he failed to exercise the moral authority of a court possessed of a great tradition. He indulged them, sometimes resignedly, sometimes playfully, in lengthy speeches. These incontinent wrangles between court and counsel were punctuated by occasional minatory intimations from the Bench. As in the case of parental warnings to children, feckless repetition deprived them of authority. . . .

Public respect for the federal judiciary is best enhanced by exacting high standards of judicial competence in the conduct of proceedings and by discouraging an assertion of power which is not restricted by the usual demands of Due Process and which too often manifests a failure of moral mastery.

APPENDIX

EXCERPTS FROM THE RECORD OF THE PRINCIPAL CASE, DENNIS V. UNITED STATES

* * *

Mr. Gladstein: I think Mr. Sacher was referring to the question of the hours that you want to sit today, the time. That is why he asked. I was getting a little hungry myself. And you look a little peaked I think.

The Court: If I felt any stronger than I do right now I would be sick. So don't worry about my looking peaked, I feel all right. (P. 88.)

* * *

The Court: . . . I think you have squeezed all the juice out of that particular orange.

Now, why don't you get on to the merits of your claim that the judges here should not try this issue.

Mr. Gladstein: If you would permit me, your Honor, to carry forward a little bit the allusion that you have just made, which happens to be closely identified with the State from which I come, from which the citrus fruits are a product—

The Court: No Californian ever misses the chance. (Pp. 208–209.)

* * *

Mr. Gladstein: . . . Now, although everybody, one would think, who did not prejudge the matter here—

The Court: Well I deny the motion to disqualify me.

Mr. Gladstein: Well, you were anticipating. I wasn't going to make one.

The Court: I am very quick to catch on, and I thought when you said "anybody who does not prejudge," it was just another way of telling me again what you have told me so many times, and your colleagues have told me so many times: that I have prejudged it all; that I am biased and prejudiced and unfit to sit here. Now, I am familiar with that, and if you think you are going to get me excited saying that over again, you are making a big mistake.

Mr. Gladstein: I wasn't going to say it over again, and if I were it would not be for the purpose of getting you excited. It is true I have a definite mind on the question of whether legally you are disqualified, whether you are biased, but I wasn't going to express it.

The Court: They went all the way up to the United States Supreme Court with it, and I suppose if there was any further you could go, you would do that.

Mr. Gladstein: They didn't pass on your Honor's bias. They did not say you were unbiased—

The Court: They denied the application for certiorari.

Mr. Gladstein: Yes, they refused to hear the question of whether or not you were biased, that is true, but that does not mean, your Honor, that they passed favorably on the contention of the Court. It does not mean, of course, that they held that you were biased, but neither does it mean that they held you were unbiased.

The Court: Well, you don't really need to keep rubbing it in and telling me every day that I am prejudiced, biased, corrupt, and all that sort of thing, because after a man has been called names a certain number of times they have no effect on him any more. (Pp. 1034–1035.)

* * *

Mr. Sacher: It is very strange that on the occasions when you scratched your head and pulled your ear, we were speaking and not Mr. McGohey.

The Court: Maybe you were not watching me.

Mr. Sacher: I just want to say that your conduct at all times—you see, you are doing it again.

The Court: I know, you are going to say I am corrupt and I am disqualified. You called me all those things before. Now you can run the catalogue again and I will listen patiently. Make it just as bad as you can.

Mr. Sacher: Your Honor, I am certainly aware of the fact that if I bear false witness against your Honor in anything I have said that I am subject to disciplinary measures and I am not inviting disciplinary measures by making false statements.

The Court: You mean that I will take disciplinary measures against you because you said I scratched my head? Don't be absurd, Mr. Sacher. Don't be absurd.

Mr. Sacher: The point I am making is that in every available means your Honor is conveying to the jury your lack of sympathy if not hostility to the defendants, their counsel's presentation of the case, and in these circumstances I want certainly to note on behalf of my clients a vigorous objection to your Honor's conduct and I wish to join Mr. Gladstein in the motion to declare a mistrial by the withdrawal of a juror.

The Court: Motion denied. (Pp. 3316–3317.)

* * *

Mr. Isserman: If the Court please, I would like to ask the Court to take judicial notice of the fact that the man Haym Solomon is dead some several years. He was a figure in the American Revolution.

The Court: This is the first time I ever have become acquainted with the gentleman. I don't see what that has got to do with it. You Communists have a way of taking all kinds of names.

Mr. Sacher: I object to that remark and ask your Honor to strike that remark and to direct the jury to disregard it.

The Court: I will deny the motion.

Mr. Gladstein: I wish to say that the remark was intended to be derogatory to the defendants and it couldn't have been intended any other way. I object to it.

The Court: You have done a lot of—

Mr. Gladstein: I would like an objection rather than an invitation to engage in repartee.

The Court: What is the objection that you want me to rule on?

Mr. Gladstein: The objection is that your Honor made a remark which is inappropriate, improper for a Judge sitting in a trial to make because it was intended to convey some kind of slur against the defendants.

The Court: Well, you see it is the old story. Mr. Isserman gets up and has his say and if I remain quiet and let you spread eagle all over the place everything is fine. But the minute I say something it is judicial misconduct. I thought the statement I made was well borne out by the record, you have objected to it, and there it is. Now that's that. (Pp. 4956–4957.)

* * *

Mr. Sacher: I object to this, your Honor—

The Court: Overruled. Mr. Sacher, I will not hear from you further.

Mr. Sacher: —unless the time and place are fixed, your Honor.

The Court: Overruled. You needn't smile and sneer at me that way either.

Mr. Sacher: I wish to state that I did not sneer or smile.

The Court: I am not going to have any more of that than I can help, I will tell you that. (P. 6118.)

* * *

Mr. Gladstein: . . . And I would say that your Honor should consider in determining the application of the law that Mr. Crockett has cited to this question the statement that this Court made in the course of this trial on this very question. Unwittingly your Honor has perhaps made a singular contribution to jurisprudence.

The Court: Thank you for that "unwittingly." You really are something, Mr. Gladstein. (P. 6331.)

* * *

Mr. McCabe: . . . I say that the reason counsel—I am speaking for myself now—the reason that I have perhaps not made similar utterances is simply because of my greater training to restrain myself under great provocation.

The Court: Well, you have been impudent enough to me on numerous occasions, and were it not for the fact that I have determined that this trial should not be disrupted by such things I should have taken action against you and against each of your colleagues long before this, but I shall not do it. *I shall leave that to the proper authorities to take care of in due course,*[51] and there it shall rest, but you need be under no misapprehension; I have been quite fully cognizant of your contemptuous conduct and your impudence.

Defendant Winter: Your Honor, may I—

Mr. McCabe: I deny the imputation of impudence or misconduct. I am perfectly willing to answer to any proper

[51] Emphasis added.

body for any actions of mine in this courtroom or out. [P. 6848.]

* * *

The Court: I wish you would stop talking about my nodding my head, scratching my head and pulling my ears. Why don't you leave that all out? What good does that do.

Mr. Isserman: Well, whether your Honor—

Mr. Crockett: Pardon me one minute. I think it is very important because there are some things that are not made a matter of record on the Court—

The Court: You haven't missed any of them.

Mr. Crockett: —so far as the transcript is concerned. Very frequently I notice in the course of testimony your Honor makes frequent glances over toward the jury or some facial expression that gives the impression, to me at least, that the Court—

The Court: Well, it is funny—

Mr. Crockett: Pardon me. I think that whenever it is so obvious, as it was a while ago, some mention of it should be made so that it will be carried in the record.

The Court: If there is something about my winking at the jury or something of that kind, I am surprised that you did not mention it at the time.

Mr. Crockett: No, I have not noticed a winking yet. If I had I would have mentioned it.

The Court: Well, there isn't much that you have missed, but you may just as well go ahead and get it all down and out of your system. [Pp. 7269-7270.]

* * *

MR. JUSTICE DOUGLAS, dissenting.

I agree with Mr. Justice Frankfurter that one who reads this record will have difficulty in determining whether members of the bar conspired to drive a judge from the bench or whether the judge used the authority of the bench to whipsaw the lawyers, to taunt and tempt them, and to create for himself the role of the persecuted. I have reluctantly concluded that neither is blameless, that there is fault on each side, that we have here the spectacle of the bench and the bar using the courtroom for an unseemly demonstration of garrulous discussion and of ill will and hot tempers.

I therefore agree with Mr. Justice Black and Mr. Justice Frankfurter that this is the classic case where the trial for contempt should be held before another judge. I also agree with Mr. Justice Black that petitioners were entitled by the Constitution to a trial by jury.

Seven years earlier, and four years before the Sacher case, the Court had decided *In re Oliver*, 333 U.S. 257 (1948). According to Black's opinion for the Court, Oliver "was called as a witness to testify in secret before a one-man grand jury conducting a grand jury investigation. In the midst of petitioner's testimony the proceedings abruptly changed. The investigation became a 'trial,' the grand jury became a judge, and the witness became an accused charged with contempt of court—all in secret. Following a charge, conviction and sentence, the petitioner was led away to prison—still without any break in the secrecy." The Court, by a vote of 7-2, reversed Oliver's conviction as having been in violation of due process under the Fourteenth Amendment, but the Court did not rule upon the constitutionality of the Michigan one-man grand jury statute. Although grand jury proceedings (one-man or otherwise) are traditionally secret, the Court ruled in Oliver that a *trial,* including a trial for criminal contempt of court, must be public, and must include such minimal procedural elements as the right to notice of the charges, the right to confront and to cross-examine witnesses against the defendant, and the right to counsel.

Many related questions were left open, however, such as the right of the judge to punish summarily contempts committed in his "presence" while he is sitting as a juror. Following the Oliver decision, the Michigan legislature amended the one-man grand jury statute to increase considerably the procedural guarantees for witnesses before such judge-jurors.[52] The Michigan Supreme Court declared unconstitutional, however, the provision of the revising statute which required a different judge than the one who sat as a juror to preside over trials of contempt of a one-man grand juror—a policy equivalent to that of Rule 42(b). It was this decision of the Michigan Supreme Court—which seemed to correspond with the United States Supreme Court's ruling in the Sacher case—that led to the decision below.

[52] See, generally, Robert G. Scigliano, *The Michigan One-Man Grand Jury* (East Lansing: Michigan State University Government-al Research Bureau, Political Research Studies No. 4, 1957).

In re MURCHISON

349 U.S. 133 (1955)

Certiorari to the Supreme Court of Michigan.

Reversed.

6-3

Black	('+')
Warren, C.J.	(+)
Frankfurter	(+)
Douglas	(+)
Clark	(+)
Harlan	(+)
Reed	'—')
Minton	'—')
Burton	—)

MR. JUSTICE BLACK delivered the opinion of the Court. . . .

[In] *In re Oliver*, 333 U.S. 257, [we] held that due process requires as a minimum that an accused be given a public trial after reasonable notice of the charges, have a right to examine witnesses against him, call witnesses on his own behalf, and be represented by counsel. The question now before us is whether a contempt proceeding conducted in accordance with these standards complies with the due process requirement of an impartial tribunal where the same judge presiding at the contempt hearing had also served as the "one-man grand jury" out of which the contempt charges arose. This does not involve, of course, the long-exercised power of courts summarily to punish certain conduct occurring in open court.[53]

The petitioners, Murchison and White, were called as witnesses before a "one-man judge-grand jury." Murchison, a Detroit policeman, was interrogated at length in the judge's secret hearings

where questions were asked him about suspected gambling in Detroit and bribery of policemen. His answers left the judge persuaded that he had committed perjury, particularly in view of other evidence before the "judge-grand jury." The judge then charged Murchison with perjury and ordered him to appear and show cause why he should not be punished for criminal contempt. White, the other petitioner, was also summoned to appear as a witness in the same "one-man grand jury" hearing. Asked numerous questions about gambling and bribery, he refused to answer on the ground that he was entitled under Michigan law to have counsel present with him. The "judge-grand jury" charged White with contempt and ordered him to appear and show cause. The judge who had been the "grand jury" then tried both petitioners in open court, convicted and sentenced them for contempt. Petitioners objected to being tried for contempt by this particular judge for a number of reasons including: (1) Michigan law expressly provides that a judge conducting a "one-man grand jury" inquiry will be disqualified from hearing or trying any case arising from his inquiry or from hearing any motion to dismiss or quash any complaint or indictment growing out of it, or from hearing any charge of contempt "except alleged contempt for neglect or refusal to appear in response to a summons or subpoena"; (2) trial before the judge who was at the same time the complainant, indicter and prosecutor, constituted a denial of the fair and impartial trial required by the Due Process Clause of the Fourteenth Amendment to the Constitution of the United States. The trial judge answered the first challenge by holding that the state statute barring him from trying the contempt cases violated the Michigan Constitution on the ground that it would deprive a judge of inherent power to punish contempt. This interpretation of the Michigan Constitution is binding here. As to the second challenge

---

[53] *Sacher* v. *United States*, 343 U.S. 1; *Cooke* v. *United States*, 267 U.S. 517, 539. . . . See also *In re Oliver*, 333 U.S. 257, 273-278. [Footnote by the Court.]

the trial judge held that due process did not forbid him to try the contempt charges. He also rejected other constitutional contentions made by petitioners. The State Supreme Court sustained all the trial judge's holdings and affirmed. . . .

A fair trial in a fair tribunal is a basic requirement of due process. Fairness of course requires an absence of actual bias in the trial of cases. But our system of law has always endeavored to prevent even the probability of unfairness. To this end no man can be a judge in his own case and no man is permitted to try cases where he has an interest in the outcome. . . .

It would be very strange if our system of law permitted a judge to act as a grand jury and then try the very persons accused as a result of his investigations. Perhaps no State has ever forced a defendant to accept grand jurors as proper trial jurors to pass on charges growing out of their hearings. A single "judge-grand jury" is even more a part of the accusatory process than an ordinary lay grand juror. Having been a part of that process a judge cannot be, in the very nature of things, wholly disinterested in the conviction or acquittal of those accused. While he would not likely have all the zeal of a prosecutor, it can certainly not be said that he would have none of that zeal.[54] Fair trials are too important a part of our free society to let prosecut-

[54] Apparently the trial judge here did consider himself a part of the prosecution. In passing on a request by Murchison's counsel for a two-day postponement of the contempt trial the judge said, "There are two points that suggest themselves to me.

"One is that if the respondent is going to claim that he was in Shrewsberry, Ontario, Canada, on March 9, 1954, that *we* ought to be furnished with information so that *we* could between now and two days from now, which I am going to give you, *we* could do some checking and investigating *ourselves*." (Emphasis supplied.)

Because of the judge's dual position the view he took of his function is not at all surprising. [Footnote by the Court.]

ing judges be trial judges of the charges they prefer. It is true that contempt committed in a trial courtroom can under some circumstances be punished summarily by the trial judge. See *Cooke* v. *United States,* 267 U.S. 517, 539. But adjudication by a trial judge of a contempt committed in his immediate presence in open court cannot be likened to the proceedings here. For we held in the *Oliver* case that a person charged with contempt before a "one-man grand jury" could not be summarily tried.

As a practical matter it is difficult if not impossible for a judge to free himself from the influence of what took place in his "grand-jury" secret session. His recollection of that is likely to weigh far more heavily with him than any testimony given in the open hearings. That it sometimes does is illustrated by an incident which occurred in White's case. In finding White guilty of contempt the trial judge said, "there is one thing the record does not show, and that was Mr. White's attitude, and I must say that his attitude was almost insolent in the manner in which he answered questions and his attitude upon the witness stand. . . . Not only was the personal attitude insolent, but it was defiant, and I want to put that on the record." In answer to defense counsel's motion to strike these statements because they were not part of the original record the judge said, "That is something . . . that wouldn't appear on the record, but it would be very evident to the court." Thus the judge whom due process requires to be impartial in weighing the evidence presented before him, called on his own personal knowledge and impression of what had occurred in the grand jury room and his judgment was based in part on this impression, the accuracy of which could not be tested by adequate cross-examination.

This incident also shows that the judge was doubtless more familiar with the facts and circumstances in which the charges were rooted than was any other witness. There were no public witnesses upon whom petitioners could call to give disinterested testimony concerning what took place in the secret chambers of the judge. If there had been they might have been able to refute the judge's statement about White's insolence. Moreover, as shown by the judge's statement here, a "judge-grand jury" might himself many times be a very material witness in a later trial for contempt. If the charge should be heard before that judge, the result would be either that the defendant must be deprived of examining or cross-examining him or else there would be the spectacle of the trial judge presenting testimony upon which he must finally pass in determining the guilt or innocence of the defendant. In either event the State would have the benefit of the judge's personal knowledge while the accused would be denied an effective opportunity to cross-examine. The right of a defendant to examine and cross-examine witnesses is too essential to a fair trial to have that right jeopardized in such way.

We hold that it was a violation of due process for the "judge-grand jury" to try these petitioners, and it was therefore error for the Supreme Court of Michigan to uphold the convictions. The cause is reversed and remanded for proceedings not inconsistent with this opinion.

Reversed.

MR. JUSTICE REED and MR. JUSTICE MINTON, dissenting, with whom MR. JUSTICE BURTON joins.

The Court holds that it is unconstitutional for a state judge to punish a contempt, previously committed before him while acting as a so-called one-man grand jury, after a full hearing in open court. It holds that White, in being so punished for his blanket refusal to answer any questions before the grand jury, and Murchison, in being so punished for perjury before the same body, were deprived

of their liberty without due process of law.

This conclusion is not rested on any irregularity in the proceedings before either the grand jury or the court. Under Michigan procedure a single state judge makes the grand jury investigation, not in secret, but with other public officials to aid him, and a transcript is made of the testimony. There is certainly nothing unconstitutional about this. A State may reduce the customary number of grand jurors to one, and impart the investigatory duty to a member of its judiciary if it so desires. Further, the accused is afforded a full hearing in open court, with a statement of charges, benefit of counsel, and a full opportunity to explain his conduct before the grand jury, before being held in contempt. Thus all the requirements set down in *In re Oliver,* 333 U.S. 257, are met.

The Court's determination is rested on the sole fact that the same judge first cited petitioners for contempt committed in his presence, and then presided over the proceedings leading to the final adjudication. It is neither shown nor alleged that the state judge was in any way biased. Nor is this required by the Court, for it holds, as a matter of law, that the judge's "interest" in a conviction makes the proceedings inherently prejudicial and thus constitutionally invalid. The fact that the "interest" of the state judge in this procedure is no different from that of other judges who have traditionally punished for contempt leads us to dissent.

In *Sacher* v. *United States,* 343 U.S. 1, we upheld the power of a federal district judge to summarily punish a contempt previously committed in his presence. In that case, after a trial which had extended for some nine months, the trial judge issued a certificate summarily holding defense counsel in contempt for their actions during the trial. There were no formalities, no hearings, no taking of evidence, no arguments and no briefs. We held that such a procedure was permitted by Rule 42 of the Federal Rules of Criminal Procedure which codified the "prevailing usages at law." The Court specifically rejected the contention that the judge who heard the contempt was disqualified from punishing it and should be required to assume the role of accuser or complaining witness before another judge. In *Offutt* v. *United States*, 348 U.S. 11, the Court simply stated an exception: when the trial judge becomes personally embroiled with the contemnor, he must step aside in favor of another judge. *That decision was rested upon our supervisory authority over the administration of criminal justice in the federal courts.*[55] The Court now holds, even though there is no showing or contention that the state judge became embroiled or personally exercised, or was in any way biased, that as a matter of constitutional law—of procedural due process—a state judge may not punish a contempt previously committed in his presence. This seems inconsistent with all that has gone before.

The Court, presumably referring to the situation in the federal courts, states that the "adjudication by a trial judge of a contempt committed in his immediate presence in open court cannot be likened to the proceedings here." The reason that it cannot, we are told, is because "we held in the *Oliver* case that a person charged with contempt before a 'one-man grand jury' could not be summarily tried." This is hardly explanatory, for the question of whether the hearing is to be summary or plenary has no bearing on the attitude or "interest" of the judges in the two situations, which is indistin-

guishable. The simple fact is that in the federal courts we allow the same judge who hears the contempt and issues the certificate to punish it subsequently and summarily, but in this case we do not allow such punishment even after a full court trial. The only factual difference between *Sacher* and this case is that the contempt in *Sacher* was committed at a public trial. When the contempt is not committed in open court, we require that the criminal conviction be in public and that the individual be given a full hearing, with an opportunity to defend himself against the charges proffered and to make a record from which to appeal. *In re Oliver*, 333 U.S. 257. Petitioners had all this. They are not entitled to more.

We do not see how it can be held that it violates fundamental concepts of fair play and justice for a state judge after a full court trial to punish a contempt previously observed when acting as a grand jury, when it has been held that it is perfectly proper for a federal judge to summarily punish a contempt previously observed in open court. It seems to us that the Court has imposed a more stringent requirement on state judges as a matter of due process than we have imposed on federal judges over whom we exercise supervisory power. . . .

The State of Michigan has decided that in the administration of its criminal law it is wise to have the investigating power in the hands of a judge. It has also decided that the judge who observes the contempt is to preside at the trial of the contemnor. It does not seem that there is here such a violation of accepted judicial standards as to justify this Court's determination of unconstitutionality.

We would affirm.

[55] Emphasis added.

In addition to the Oliver, Sacher, and Murchison cases, the Court has decided six other cases raising related questions during the dozen years ending with the 1958 Term. The results are shown in Table 29, on page 653.

Non-participation because of changes in personnel typically is high when

TABLE 29.

A Scalogram of Summary Criminal Contempt of Court Decisions of the Supreme Court (1947-1958 Terms)

SCALE SCORES	CASE / SCALE POSITION	In re Oliver, 333 U.S. 257 (1948)	In re Murchison, 349 U.S. 133 (1955)	Offutt v. United States, 348 U.S. 11 (1954)	Fisher v. Pace, 336 U.S. 155 (1949)	Nilva v. United States, 352 U.S. 385 (1957)	Green v. United States, 356 U.S. 165 (1958)	Brown v. United States, 359 U.S. 41 (1959)	Sacher v. United States, 343 U.S. 1 (1952)	Yates v. United States, 355 U.S. 66 (1957)	Total Votes per Justice	Total Inconsistent Votes per Justice
		1	2	3	4	5	6	7	8	9		
9	Black	('+')	('+')	('+'	+)	'+')	'+')	+)	'+')	+)	9	0
9	Douglas	(+)	(+)	('+'	'+')	+)	+)	+)	'+')	'+')	9	0
9	Warren	*	(+)	(+)	*	+)	+)	'+')	*	+)	6	0
7	Brennan	*	*	*	*	+)	'+')	+)	*	(—)	4	0
4	Rutledge	('+'	*	*	'+')	*	*	*	*	*	2	0
4	Murphy	(+)	*	*	'+')	*	*	*	*	*	2	0
3	Clark	*	(+)	(+)	*	(—)	(—)	(—)	NP	('—')	6	0
3	Frankfurter	(—')	(+)	('+')	(—)	(—)	('—'	(—)	(+')	(—)	9	2
2	Harlan	*	(+)	*	*	(—)	('—')	(—)	*	(—)	5	0
1	Vinson	(+)	*	*	(—)	*	*	*	(—)	*	3	0
1	Reed	(+)	'—')	—	('—')	(—)	*	*	(—)	*	6	0
1	Burton	(+)	—)	—	(—)	('—')	(—)	*	(—)	('—'	8	0
0	Stewart	*	*	*	*	*	*	('—')	*	*	1	0
0	Whittaker	*	*	*	*	*	(—)	(—)	*	(—)	3	0
0	Minton	*	'—')	'—')	*	*	*	*	(—)	*	3	0
0	Jackson	'—')	*	*	(—)	*	*	*	('—')	*	3	0
Voting Division		7-2	6-3	5-3	4-5	4-5	4-5	4-5	3-5	3-6	79	
				Pro	Con							
Total Inconsistent		S	S	F	S	F	F	F	F	F		
Votes per Case		1	0	0	0	0	0	0	1	0		2

LEGEND:

- $+$ = a vote in favor of the defendant
- $-$ = a vote against the defendant
- $*$ = not seated at the time of this decision
- NP = seated but not participating in this decision
- F = trial in a federal court
- S = trial in a state court
- ' ' = wrote opinion
- ( ) = joined in the opinion of the Court
- (= concurring opinion
-) = dissenting opinion
- ◯ = inconsistent vote

$$CR = 1 - \frac{2}{79} = .97$$

less than ten cases span a period of a dozen years, as in Table 29, in contrast to the concentration of a smaller number of cases within a shorter period of time, as in Table 25. Obviously, we should entertain higher confidence in the inferences concerning the behavior of the "Court" supported by Table 25 than by Table 29. Similarly, we should feel much more confidence in the placement on this scale of justices with full participation (such as Black and Douglas) and limited confidence in the necessarily tentative placement of justices with low participation (such as Stewart).

This scalogram also illustrates one of the weaknesses of any two-dimensional scheme as a tool for the analysis of judicial voting behavior: it fails to take into consideration the importance of time as a factor. If Sacher had been decided either three years earlier (when Murphy and Rutledge sat) or four years later (when both Warren and Brennan were on the Court), it is quite possible that it would have been decided differently—assuming that Frankfurter continued to vote affirmatively. Since his votes in both Sacher and Oliver appear on this scalogram as inconsistent votes,[56] it is difficult to say how Frankfurter might have voted if the Court had been differently composed at the time of decision,[57] or if the case had come up for decision at a different time. In the other two most similar cases, both of which also involved wrangling between the court and counsel to such an extent that it is difficult to say which engaged in the more reprehensible conduct, Frankfurter voted to uphold the lawyer in the federal case (Offutt) and to uphold the judge in the state case (Fisher). And yet, the point argued by the dissenters in Murchison seems well taken; the Court has announced a stricter policy for the states than for the national government: in the states, a different judge must try contempt charges brought by a judge-juror, while a federal judge may file his charges at the conclusion of a trial, when the need to preserve order and decorum has passed, and then summarily pronounce punishment, without a jury, without the taking of evidence, without formal notice, and without the semblance of adhering to the procedures associated with the concept of a trial. It is an incongruous situation, in the light of the Court's usual practice of establishing greater restraints upon criminal trials in the federal courts, either by interpretation of the "more specific" language of the Fourth through the Eighth Amendments or by exercising its supervisory powers over the administration of justice in the federal courts, and permitting the states to determine their own policies within the broad sweep of discretion permitted within the tolerant confines of a civilized system of ordered liberty.

---

56 Since he voted affirmatively in Murchison, Frankfurter clearly *did* vote inconsistently (entirely apart from the scalogram) in Oliver. In order for Frankfurter to have been "right" in his Oliver vote, in terms of the scalogram, Vinson, Reed, and Burton would all have had to be "wrong."

57 The scalogram shows that the opinion of the Court in Sacher was written by Jackson, the least sympathetic member of the Court during the eleven-year period to claims of some rights of due process in summary contempt of court cases. What would the effect have been upon the rest of the group if Jackson had not been on the Court at the time the Sacher case was decided?

12

The Implications of Ordered Liberty

"**G**IVE ME LIBERTY**," cried Patrick Henry, "or give me death!" [1] Almost a century later, the Fourteenth Amendment substituted for Henry's revolutionary ideal the less flamboyant decree that no state shall deprive any person of "life, liberty, or property, without due process of law." From a strictly logical point of view, one might infer from these words a constitutional policy of parity, of complete equality of intrinsic significance among the three factors—life, liberty, and property—to which the right of due process appertains. But as Justice Holmes pointed out long ago, the life of the law has not been logic, but experience. The hierarchy in which the Supreme Court has arranged these three values has varied in structure from time to time; in the first decade of the twentieth century, for instance, the Court's preferment seems clearly to have been: (1) property (= the pursuit of happiness), and (2) life or liberty. Since 1937, the Court seems to have preferred: (1) life, (2) liberty (= the pursuit of happiness), and (3) property.[2] It will be observed that in either period, the Court postulated some value other than personal liberty as a higher good to which the Court owed a primary duty of support.

We have considered various kinds of personal liberty in the preceding three chapters: the personal liberty to equality in the fulfillment of political obliga-

---

[1] In the ringing rhetoric of the eighteenth century, Henry preceded his exclamation with the question: "Is life so dear, or peace so sweet, as to be purchased at the price of chains and slavery?" (Both quotations are from Henry's speech before the House of Burgesses on March 23, 1775, on a resolution to put Virginia into a state of defense.)

[2] An example of the Court's preference of life over liberty is found in the "capital offense" and "fair trial" rules regarding the right to counsel in state courts; the so-called "preferred position" doctrine came very close, at least in some decisions, to equating "First Amendment freedoms" with the pursuit of happiness.

tions and in the enjoyment of political rights and services; the personal liberty to think and to believe, and to communicate and to share ideas and beliefs with other persons; and the personal liberty to receive fair treatment from an organized political society which tries and punishes deviants for infractions of the policy norms to which the majority (it is assumed) have in some manner given their consent. We are concerned in the present chapter, as in Chapter 11, with the rights of criminal defendants and quasi-defendants—but with an important difference. In Chapter 11, we focused upon *procedural* due process; in other words, upon the manner in which judgments are reached in judicial trials and in quasi-judicial hearings. In this chapter, our concern is with the *substantive* due process of personal liberty. Our question now is: are there limits to the authority of government, no matter what the process by which decisions are reached, to invade the bodies and the minds of individual human beings, even those who are accused of the most heinous crimes? To what extent are such limits recognized by the Supreme Court? If such exist, this substantive right to the due process of personal liberty is quite different from the concept of "substantive due process" that relates to the incorporation of the First Amendment into the Fourteenth.

PHYSIOLOGICAL PRIVACY

There are a variety of ways in which the personal physical privacy of human beings might be invaded "pursuant to law." Many ways that are recorded in legal history would today be considered to be in violation of the Eighth Amendment's prohibition of "cruel and unusual punishment," and of the Fourteenth Amendment's due-process clause. We can safely put to one side such methods of investigation as trial by ordeal or interrogation under the rack, and such methods of punishment as decapitation by battle axe; the Supreme Court would consider none of these to comport with the Constitution. (Such methods have been used in European countries within the last twenty years, however.) The third degree continues to be invoked as a method of police investigation in the United States; but again, the Court has condemned the rubber hose as unconstitutional whether wielded by state or federal police officers. Capital punishment, however, is carried out by a majority of the states and by the national government; and the execution of human beings, pursuant to the judgment of a court or a court-martial, is not unconstitutional. Execution by hanging, shooting, the gas chamber, and by electrocution (even when the chair is defective) [3] are neither cruel nor unusual, nor a violation of due process. Euthanasia—so-called "mercy killing"—remains controversial and would be considered a criminal offense—probably murder—by any of the American states today. But what of compulsory sterilization, or compulsory stomach-pumping, or compulsory blood tests? The difference, after all,

[3] *Louisiana ex rel Francis v. Resweber*, 329 U.S. 459 (1947).

between euthanasia and eugenic sterilization is simply the difference between the right to life and the right to personal liberty.

The Survival of the Fittest

When eugenic sterilization reached the Supreme Court as an issue of constitutional policy, over two decades had elapsed since the majority had embraced the theories of social Darwinism against which Holmes had protested so vigorously in his dissent in the Lochner case. In its first and leading decision dealing with compulsory sterilization, the Court once again made social Darwinism its major premise; but the spokesman for the majority who had seen the vision of the Brave New World that science could create was this time none other than the great dissenter himself. In a sense, Holmes' position in the two cases was quite consistent; in both Lochner and *Buck* v. *Bell,* Holmes voted—and with the support of Brandeis and Stone, among others, in the later case—to uphold socioeconomic experimentation by the legislative representatives of a majority of the people in the "cloistered laboratories" of the states. It is the more regrettable that, since the decision in *Buck* v. *Bell* purported to subserve the goals and the values of science, it appears to have been itself the fruit of a most unscientific process of decision-making, reflecting most proximately the insistent pressures of organized interest groups who sought and obtained the support of the Court in order to "get the law" on their side. Yet, it could not be said that science and society had not progressed during the preceding two centuries. In seventeenth-century Salem, the judges would most likely have decreed that moron Carrie Buck should be burned as a witch while mutilation would suffice for chicken-thief Skinner (both of whose cases are discussed below); in twentieth-century America, the judges agreed that mutilation was appropriate only in the case of the moron (and, although the point was not expressly decided, it seems fair to infer that the Court would have approved burning-at-the-stake in neither case). To this extent, at least, had a free society grown in wisdom.

BUCK v. BELL

274 U.S. 200 (1927)

Error to the Supreme Court of Appeals of Virginia.

Affirmed.

It certainly is relevant to know that the author of the opinion below was a disciple of Thomas Robert Malthus, whose Essay on the Principle of Population *(1798) enjoyed great popularity among the young intellectuals of Holmes' generation—i.e., those who attended college before the*

8-1

Holmes	('+')
Taft, C.J.	(+)
VanDevanter	(+)
McReynolds	(+)
Brandeis	(+)
Sutherland	(+)
Sanford	(+)
Stone	(+)
Butler	—

Civil War. Typical of views that Holmes had formed long before either Carrie Buck (the plaintiff-in-error in the case below) or her mother was—regrettably?—born are these sentiments, which Holmes expressed in 1919 in a letter to Brandeis: "Generally speaking, I agree with you in liking to see social experiments tried but I do so without enthusiasm because I believe it is merely shifting the pressure and that so long as we have free propagation Malthus is right in his general view." [4]

MR. JUSTICE HOLMES delivered the opinion of the Court.

This is a writ of error to review a judgment of the Supreme Court of Appeals of the State of Virginia, affirming a judgment of the Circuit Court of Amherst County, by which the defendant in error, the superintendent of the State Colony for Epileptics and Feeble Minded, was ordered to perform the operation of salpingectomy upon Carrie Buck, the plaintiff in error, for the purpose of making her sterile. . . . The case comes here upon the contention that the statute authorizing the judgment is void under the Fourteenth Amendment as denying to the plaintiff in error due process of law and the equal protection of the laws.

Carrie Buck is a feeble minded white woman who was committed to the State Colony above mentioned in due form. She is the daughter of a feeble minded mother in the same institution, and the mother of an illegitimate feeble minded child. She was eighteen years old at the time of the trial of her case in the Circuit Court, in the latter part of 1924. An Act of Virginia, approved March 20, 1924, recites that the health of the patient and the welfare of society may be promoted in certain cases by the sterilization of mental defectives, under careful safeguard, &c.;

[4] Alexander M. Bickel, *The Unpublished Opinions of Mr. Justice Brandeis* (Cambridge: Belknap Press 1957) of Harvard University Press, p. 221.

that the sterilization may be effected in males by vasectomy and in females by salpingectomy, without serious pain or substantial danger to life; that the Commonwealth is supporting in various institutions many defective persons who if now discharged would become a menace but if incapable of procreating might be discharged with safety and become self-supporting with benefit to themselves and to society; and that experience has shown that heredity plays an important part in the transmission of insanity, imbecility, &c. The statute then enacts that whenever the superintendent of certain institutions including the above named State Colony shall be of opinion that it is for the best interests of the patients and of society that an inmate under his care should be sexually sterilized, he may have the operation performed upon any patient afflicted with hereditary forms of insanity, imbecility, &c., on complying with the very careful provisions by which the act protects the patients from possible abuse.

The superintendent first presents a petition to the special board of directors of his hospital or colony, stating the facts and the grounds for his opinion, verified by affidavit. Notice of the petition and of the time and place of the hearing in the institution is to be served upon the inmate, and also upon his guardian, and if there is no guardian the superintendent is to apply to the Circuit Court of the County to appoint one. If the inmate is a minor notice also is to be given to his parents if any with a copy of the petition. The board is to see to it that the inmate may attend the hearings if desired by him or his guardian. The evidence is all to be reduced to writing, and after the board has made its order for or against the operation, the superintendent, or the inmate, or his guardian, may appeal to the Circuit Court of the County. The Circuit Court may consider the record of the board and the evidence before it and such other admissible evidence as may be offered, and may affirm, revise, or reverse the order of the board and enter such order as it deems just. Finally any party may apply to the Supreme Court of Appeals, which, if it grants the appeal, is to hear the case upon the record of the trial in the Circuit Court and may enter such order as it thinks the Circuit Court should have entered. There can be no doubt that so far as procedure is concerned the rights of the patient are most carefully considered, and as every step in this case was taken in scrupulous compliance with the statute and after months of observation, there is no doubt that in that respect the plaintiff in error has had due process of law.

The attack is not upon the procedure but upon the substantive law. It seems to be contended that in no circumstances could such an order be justified. It certainly is contended that the order cannot be justified upon the existing grounds. The judgment finds the facts that have been recited and that Carrie Buck "is the probable potential parent of socially inadequate offspring, likewise afflicted, that she may be sexually sterilized without detriment to her general health and that her welfare and that of society will be promoted by her sterilization," and thereupon makes the order. In view of the general declarations of the legislature and the specific findings of the Court, obviously we cannot say as matter of law that the grounds do not exist, and if they exist they justify the result. We have seen more than once that the public welfare may call upon the best citizens for their lives. It would be strange if it could not call upon those who already sap the strength of the State for these lesser sacrifices, often not felt to be such by those concerned, in order to prevent our being swamped with incompetence. It is better for all the world, if instead of waiting to execute degenerate offspring for crime, or to let them starve for their imbecility, society can prevent those who are manifestly unfit from continuing their kind. The principle that sustains compulsory vaccination is broad enough to cover cutting the Fallopian tubes. *Jacobson* v. *Massachusetts*, 197 U. S. 11 [1905]. Three generations of imbeciles are enough.

Affirmed.

THE ROOSEVELT COURT, *Dubitante*

Fifteen years later, Franklin Roosevelt's appointees disposed of the only other sterilization case that the Supreme Court has decided. The later case involved an actual criminal defendant, rather than a quasi-defendant like Carrie Buck. The petitioner in *Skinner* v. *Oklahoma*, 316 U.S. 535 (1942), challenged the state's compulsory sterilization statute, which was applicable to three-time losers in the state's penitentiaries who had been convicted of crimes amounting to felonies involving moral turpitude. One of the three offenses involving moral turpitude of which Skinner had been convicted was that of stealing chickens. Skinner was in the penitentiary for his third felony conviction at the time the Oklahoma Habitual Criminal Sterilization Act was passed; and it was adjudged that he "be rendered sexually sterile" after appropriate proceedings under the statute. There was no question that these proceedings provided Skinner with many of the basic elements of procedural due process; there was notice, hearing before a court, and the right to trial by jury.

Seven justices joined in an opinion by Douglas which declared the statute unconstitutional on equal-protection grounds. Conceivably (but not very likely), under this approach a statute which provided for the compulsory sterilization of *all* criminals would be constitutional. More realistically, the majority of the Court invoked the equal-protection clause to avoid the more controversial alternative— at a time when several of the justices were trying to eradicate substantive due process as a property right—of upholding the capacity to procreate as a substantive right of personal liberty, which would have necessitated the re-examination of *Buck* v. *Bell* and the constitutional policy for which it stood. Stone and Jackson wrote concurring opinions, although neither of them wanted to question the authority of *Buck* v. *Bell* as a precedent, either.

Chief Justice Stone, in his concurrence, looked beyond the issue of equal protection to that of *procedural* due process:

> I think the real question we have to consider is not one of equal protection, but whether the wholesale condemnation of a class to such an invasion of personal liberty, without opportunity to any individual to show that his is not the type of case which would justify resort to it, satisfies the demands of due process.
>
> There are limits to the extent to which the presumption of constitutionality can be pressed, especially where the liberty of the person is concerned (see *United States* v. *Carolene Products Co.,* 304 U.S. 144, 152, n. 4) and where the presumption is resorted to only to dispense with a procedure which the ordinary dictates of prudence would seem to demand for the protection of the individual from arbitrary action. Although petitioner here was given a hearing to ascertain whether sterilization would be detrimental to his health, he was given none to discover whether his criminal tendencies are of an inheritable type. Undoubtedly a state may, after appropriate inquiry, constitutionally interfere with the personal liberty of the individual to prevent the transmission by inheritance of his socially injurious tendencies. *Buck* v. *Bell,* 274 U.S. 200. But until now we have not been called upon to say that it may do so without giving him a hearing and opportunity to challenge the existence as to him of the only facts which could justify so drastic a measure.
>
> Science has found and the law has recognized that there are certain types of mental deficiency associated with delinquency which are inheritable. But the State does not contend—nor can there be any pretense—that either common knowledge or experience, or scientific investigation, has given assurance that the criminal tendencies of any class of habitual offenders are universally or even generally inheritable. In such circumstances, inquiry whether such is the fact in the case of any particular individual cannot rightly be dispensed with. Whether the procedure by which a statute carries its mandate into execution satisfies due process is a matter of judicial cognizance. A law which condemns, without hearing, all the individuals of a class to so harsh a measure as the present because some or even many merit condemnation, is lacking in the first principles of due process. . . . And so, while the state may protect itself from the demonstrably inheritable tendencies of the individual

which are injurious to society, the most elementary notions of due process would seem to require it to take appropriate steps to safeguard the liberty of the individual by affording him, before he is condemned to an irreparable injury in his person, some opportunity to show that he is without such inheritable tendencies. The state is called on to sacrifice no permissible end when it is required to reach its objective by a reasonable and just procedure adequate to safeguard rights of the individual which concededly the Constitution protects.

After paying his own respects to *Buck* v. *Bell,* Justice Jackson ventured the dictum that compulsory sterilization might, under appropriate circumstances, give rise to a question of *substantive* due process, saying:

> There are limits to the extent to which a legislatively represented majority may conduct biological experiments at the expense of the dignity and personality and natural powers of a minority—even those who have been guilty of what the majority define as crimes.

But Jackson did not think that it was necessary to consider such limits in the present case, since the statute obviously was invalid on both the ground of equal protection, as stated by the majority, and also the ground of procedural due process, as argued by the Chief Justice. Consequently, a Court which included such libertarians as Murphy, Douglas, and Black unanimously approved, by their refusal to reconsider *Buck* v. *Bell,* the policy that there is no denial of any substantive right of personal liberty in the compulsory sterilization of persons capable of "transmi[tting] by inheritance . . . socially injurious tendencies." But who are such persons? Surely, the Court's intimation that they do not necessarily include chicken thieves tells us very little. The Court did, it is true, suggest that there might be some problems of identification; but with the exception of Jackson, the justices seemed to consider such problems to be well within the fact-finding competence of judges and juries.

Some persons in the outside world shared the confidence of the Court that there were appropriate subjects for biological experimentation, whose deprivations would not constitute a denial of due process. For instance, the wire services early in March, 1959, carried reports of the efforts of a spinster obstetrician and freshman member of the North Carolina House of Delegates. Dr. Rachel Davis introduced legislation which would give the State Eugenics Board discretionary authority to order the sterilization of "grossly sexually delinquent persons," i.e., any female who gives birth to more than one child out of wedlock. Thus the bill respected the tradition of the common law that "every dog is entitled to one bite." There was also the pragmatic consideration that, according to Dr. Davis' statistics, slightly over half of North Carolina's unwed mothers did not repeat their crime. Second offenders were to be allowed procedural due process, and were required to run the gamut of (1) reference to local welfare agencies for psychiatric therapy; those who "cannot profit from that," according to Dr. Davis, would next proceed to (2) the State Eugenics Board, from whose sterilization verdicts appeal would lie to (3) Superior Court for jury trials. Presumably, the fact issue to be tried would be whether a woman had had the requisite number of illegitimate children to qualify her for corrective surgery; the issue whether or not a person was "grossly sexually delinquent" would appear to be a conclusion of law. But one nagging question still remains: what would be the "socially injurious tendencies" that such mothers could be assumed to transmit to their offspring? Is a tendency toward "gross sexual delinquency" an inheritable trait?

Buck v. Bell: *Due Process of Law?* [5]

I

A quarter of a century has passed since Justice Holmes provided the eugenical sterilization movement with a constitutional blessing and an epigrammatic battle cry. His opinion for the Court in *Buck* v. *Bell* was regarded by eugenicists as the herald of a new day, and was joined in by all his brethren except Justice Butler. Whether the latter believed three generations of imbeciles were *not* enough, or that the number of generations was immaterial, we do not know, for while he did not withhold his judgment, he kept his reasons for dissenting to himself. The eugenicists, on the other hand, were anything but silent. Holmes, the subject of so much adulation, was hailed by them as the new Prometheus, and excerpts from his opinion continue to this day to add spice to their literature.

Among political scientists concerned with constitutional law, the decision seems to have been implicitly accepted as a return to the "true" meaning of the due process clause. In his annual review of the Court's activities, Professor Cushman commented: "The Virginia act of 1924, which was attacked, had carefully safeguarded procedural rights of those subject to the law so that no want of due process was made out on that score. The substance of the law itself it upheld as a reasonable social protection, entirely compatible with due process of law. Mr. Justice Holmes' trenchant statement of this warrants quotation." He then proceeded to quote at length what is surely one of the most "totalitarian" statements in the history of the Court. The relevant part reads: "We have seen more than once that the public welfare may call upon the best citizens for their lives. It would be strange if it could not call upon those who already sap the strength of the State for these lesser sacrifices . . . in order to prevent our being swamped with incompetence."

If one accepts as a major premise that the state can demand of its citizens the supreme sacrifice, it is a simple matter for tyrants and logicians alike to reach the conclusion reached here by Holmes, that the state can then demand

5 Walter Berns, *"Buck* v. *Bell:* Due Process of Law?" *Western Political Quarterly,* Vol. 6, pp. 762-773 (1953).

every lesser sacrifice. But American government, and all non-tyrannical government, is based on the recognition that there are greater evils than death. . . .

Was the Court so convinced of the wisdom of the decision that it found no need for a qualifying word? What did Justice Brandeis, with his concern for the facts, think about compulsory sterilization? We know what Holmes thought. His mind on these matters was apparently made up long before the case of *Buck* v. *Bell* got to the Supreme Court. Writing in the *Illinois Law Review* in 1915, he said: "I believe that the wholesale social regeneration which so many now seem to expect, if it can be helped by conscious, co-ordinated human effort, cannot be affected appreciably by tinkering with the institutions of property, but only by taking in hand life and trying to build a race. That would be my starting point for an ideal for the law. . . ."

II

Prior to *Buck* v. *Bell*, the sterilization laws of seven states had been struck down by the courts, mostly for procedural reasons, but the Virginia statute under which Carrie Buck was to lose her ability to have children steered a prudent course around these reefs and arrived in Washington fairly glistening with safeguards for the individual: notice, hearing, counsel, and appeal by right to the courts. Such solicitude may have impressed Butler. Certainly it was not his habit to be overawed by Holmes, and if he had really believed that there was something inherently wrong in a law which com-pelled a person to be deprived of what can surely be numbered among the basic rights, he could have extrapolated something from her counsel's brief to support some kind of dissent. Certainly Holmes's argument that "The principle that sustains compulsory vaccination is broad enough to cover cut-ting the Fallopian tubes. . . ." should not have been permitted to escape at least examination. It is a broad principle indeed that sustains a needle's prick in the arm and an abdominal incision, if only in terms of the equip-ment used. It becomes something else again in terms of the results attained: no smallpox in the one case and no children in the other.

Perhaps the Court's position was not easy. The eugenicists had painted so lurid and so convincing a picture of an unsterilized America, with the Carrie Bucks and their offspring cluttering the scene like germs under the microscope in the Listerine advertisement, that even their opponents, how-ever few in number at the time, were disquieted. Furthermore, no one, not even her counsel, challenged the eugenical account; no civil liberties organi-zation sprang forward to defend Carrie, yet one would assume that children are as basic to the nation's needs as speech. Nor is it even necessary to elevate children to a "preferred position," or take an intransigent stand on natural rights, to disagree with this decision; a true pragmatist could have dissented just as well.

Holmes, however, was following his "ideal for the law" when he said, ". . . if they [the grounds for sterilization] exist they justify the result." But as one critic has written, "Justice Holmes assumes the efficacy of sterilization, a judgment on which would be worthy of a minor prophet." It would be more accurate to say that the Court assumed that the legislature possessed this gift of prophecy, which was an unwarranted assumption in this case. It was impossible to discover how intensive the hearings before the legislative com- mittee had been, but the record of the litigation shows that the state tri- bunal, the Virginia Supreme Court of Appeals, had probed no deeper into the substance of the eugenical argument than Holmes had; it merely accepted without question the evidence submitted by Bell, the superintendent of the state institution, and the testimony of his witnesses at the hearing of the special board. The court then said: "Carrie Buck, by the laws of heredity, is the probable potential parent of socially inadequate offspring likewise af- fected as she is."

To a considerable extent the court was able to escape the responsibility for examining these so-called "laws of heredity" because of the failure of Carrie Buck's counsel to force such an evaluation. Someone should have looked into the "probability of the potentiality of the inadequacy"; but at no time during the litigation, from the hearing before the special board to the brief he submitted to the Supreme Court of the United States, did Counsel Whitehead offer any evidence or produce any witness to question the validity of the eugenical basis of the statute. Perhaps there was no evidence available to him at the time, for, while Bell produced scientists, physicians, nurses, and other people who had known Carrie Buck, not one witness came forward on Carrie's behalf. It may be that only on the basis of knowledge available later could he have cast doubt on the relevance of Mendel's peas to the problem of human heredity, or attacked the deposition of Dr. H. H. Laughlin, one of the leaders of the sterilization movement, who pronounced Carrie feeble- minded without ever having seen her, or produced a witness to show that the "scientific evidence" was mere fabrication, or at most supposition; perhaps his ineffectual questions directed at subsidiary aspects of the case were the only ones available to him. It may be true that the case handed him was in- deed a hopeless one.

It was certainly a good one for Bell. Carrie was doubtless feeble-minded. R. G. Shelton, her "next friend," was actually a guardian appointed, under the terms of the statute, by the Circuit Court of Amherst County, Virginia. Her counsel was hired by the State. She had no relatives except her feeble- minded mother who, as a ward of the State, was under supervision; no friends came forward to protest at any stage of the proceedings; there was no one who was vitally concerned in her welfare. Her illegitimate child was ad- judged subnormal because it was not as "responsive" as the child of the woman who made the comparison! If ever the state of Virginia had a good case to push through the courts and a case likely to arouse the minimum of opposition, it was this case of friendless, feeble-minded Carrie Buck, who, in reply to this question put by Bell's counsel: "Do you care to say anything about having this operation performed on you?" said, "No, sir, I have not, it is up to my people"—whoever they were.

Bell's "people," on the other hand, were well known—at least in sterilization circles. Dr. Laughlin was out to rid the world of the Carrie Bucks, but also of the likes of Beethoven, Mozart, Milton, Poe, and Napoleon, to name only a few of the men who would have been sterilized under his "model law." [6] Arthur H. Estabrook, who also testified for Bell, was the man who had "proved" the applicability of Mendel's pea-findings to human beings by his studies of the Jukes and Nam families. A favorable decision from the Supreme Court was necessary for the fulfillment of their plans, and this case from Virginia was designed for that decision. As Dr. Laughlin put it, ". . . the Virginia statute is, in the main, one of the best laws thus far enacted in that it has avoided the principal eugenical and legal defects of previous statutes, and has incorporated into it the most effective eugenical features and the soundest legal principals of previous laws."

Although these litigants had technically adverse interests, this case, like so many others involving great constitutional issues, was probably a friendly one. Carrie Buck, to judge by the testimony in the hearing, had no quarrels with anyone; she simply was not very bright, which caused her to be a burden on the state and put her in a classification which Laughlin and Estabrook sought to eradicate from the American population. Holmes certified that such eradication was legal, but one is permitted to wonder if he would have been so cavalier in his certification if he had known the extent of the plans. Dr. Laughlin's plans called for the sterilization of 203,255 Americans annually by 1950, while estimating, according to a Mendelian thesis, that the number of "socially inadequate" persons, or persons capable of producing socially inadequate offspring, would total 11,891,700 in the same year! However the lines are drawn and the categories filled, this is a large section of the American people. Surely *Buck* v. *Bell* too raised the ". . . question . . . which [of] two powers or rights shall prevail—the power of the State to legislate or the right of the individual to liberty of person. . . . The mere assertion that the subject matter relates though but in a remote degree to the public health does not necessarily render the enactment valid." [7] Justice Holmes refused to subscribe to these words spoken "on behalf" of the bakers of New York, but they could have been used most appropriately against him by Butler here.

[6] This model law called for the sterilization, *regardless of etiology*, of the following inadequate classes: (1) feeble-minded; (2) insane (including the psychopathic); (3) criminalistic (including the delinquent and wayward); (4) epileptic; (5) inebriate (including drug habitues); (6) diseased (including the tuberculous, the syphilitic, the leprous, and others with chronic, infectious, and legally segregable diseases); (7) blind (including those with seriously impaired vision); (8) deaf (including those with seriously impaired hearing); (9) deformed (including the crippled); and (10) dependent (including orphans, ne'er-do-wells, the homeless, tramps, and paupers). H. H. Laughlin, *Eugenical Sterilization: 1926* (New York: The American Eugenics Society, 1925), p. 64. [Footnote in the original.]

[7] Justice Peckham for the Court in *Lochner* v. *New York*, 198 U.S. 45, 56-57 (1904). [Footnote in the original.]

III

What grievous conditions prevailed among the American people to justify the Laughlin program of hundreds of thousands of state-performed surgical operations annually? One woman, Mrs. E. H. Harriman, who apparently considered conditions grievous enough to warrant the gift of the Eugenics Record Office to doctors Laughlin and Davenport, once got up in a public meeting to shout, "What is the matter with the American people? 15,000,000 must be sterilized!" Not eleven, but fifteen million! But what were the symptoms, why must so many of us be sterilized? "The number of known mentally diseased persons is now three times as great in proportion to the total population, as it was in 1880." "America is breeding from the bottom." "Nature's plan is interfered with by human sympathy and modern charity." "Mentally deficient voters threaten democratic government." "Sterilization is a matter of national preservation." These are indeed grievous conditions, but what could be done about it? Just remove some "little bits of tubes." It is that simple. ". . . it is claimed that if sterilization laws could be enforced in the whole United States, less than four generations would eliminate nine-tenths of the feeble-mindedness, insanity and crime in the country." Even crime! O Brave New World! Can anyone protest its realization?

It should come as some relief to learn that these alarming conditions have been shown to be exaggerations, and it is therefore no surprise to learn that the claim that compulsory sterilization is a panacea has been refuted. . . . One critic of the program, basing his calculations on an estimate of 330,000 defectives in the country, not eleven or fifteen million, concluded: "It has been computed that if the proportion of feebleminded is one per thousand, to decrease that proportion to one per ten thousand will require about 68 generations, or two to three thousand years, if it is done merely by stopping the propagation of all feebleminded individuals. In the main, the eleven per cent reduction at the first generation is what is accomplished by this measure." . . .

Despite the fact, however, that compulsory sterilization is still being carried on in twenty states at the rate of about fourteen hundred a year, the assumption of most of the statutes under which these programs are carried on is now known to be false. "The essential point is that in the development of any individual all the thousand genes interact, work together. . . . To produce even any single feature or characteristic, this interaction must take place. It is not correct, as was at one time generally supposed to be the case, that each particular characteristic is represented by a single gene." The unit particle theory may be laid to rest with this epitaph: "The cerebral cortex is much more complicated than the eye, and it would not be surprising if it did not go wrong for a greater variety of causes. . . . And yet there are people who still claim to investigate the inheritance of mental defect as a well-defined character, and even to base eugenic programmes on their results."

Still another assumption in the argument for sterilization has become more and more dubious as research in genetics, neurology, and sociology has uncovered new facts: namely, that mental defects are caused in the vast majority of cases by factors inherited from parents. The evidence to support the antiheredity position can be cited from so many sources that to select the most authoritative is not easy, especially for a layman. But consider these statements by a neurologist, the late Abraham Myerson: ". . . the heredity mechanism by which they [schizophrenia and manic-depressive psychosis] are passed from one generation to another is unknown . . . what has been stated here of schizophrenia and manic-depressive psychosis is also true of the groups of conditions lumped together as feeble-mindedness."

One sentence from geneticist Haldane may be used to close this argument: "I think the following proposition would be accepted by most biologists: it is never possible, from a knowledge of a person's parents, to predict with certainty that he or she will be either a more or a less adequate member of society than the majority." . . .

The early diagnoses of feeble-mindedness did not take into account the variety of its causes and failed to comprehend the variety of its pathologies. By treating it as an easily defined malady, such as one caused by a particular kind of virus, and by oversimplifying the process of inheritance, the early Procrustean eugenicists, including those who testified against Carrie Buck, were led to propose action which could not materially effect the cure they sought. They were led to promise huge financial savings to the states which could not be fulfilled, both because the program will not eradicate mental deficiency or disease and because the sterilized patient cannot, except in a few cases, be released from state care. . . . Unhappily, the Supreme Court never had the opportunity to consider such evidence and this sort of juggling with the facts, and a position which might later have been successfully defended was surrendered without struggle, and to a group of shabby characters.

IV

. . . [Paul] Popenoe is only one of a group of people whose designs were much more ambitious than the mere eradication of mental defectives. Despite the change in tone which has occurred in the written statements of eugenicists since America's war with Hitler, and the modification of the aims of the one national organization devoted to the cause of sterilization, the Human Betterment Association of America, Inc., the present writer believes it important to reveal just what it was these men wanted.

It should be made clear that the men to be quoted in the following pages were not apostates but were the leaders of the sterilization movement in America; in fact, with no notable exceptions, they *were* the movement. They were the Cassandras whose dire prophecies frightened state legislators into voting for the bills they had composed and proposed. One of them had conducted the "research" which had led to the enthronement of three "royal families of feeble-mindedom," while others joined in the widespread lament for a soon-to-be-lost Anglo-Saxon world of their fathers. While joining the protest against the "new immigration," they were prepared to take harsher action if the quota system should prove inadequate. . . .

To begin with, were Laughlin and Davenport thinking of mental defectives when they penned this editorial?

"Within its own territory each race must, by all humanity, be granted the right to promote its own race integrity. The right to strive for race integrity is like the pursuit of happiness. . . .

"When the European emigration waves after the World War were about to overwhelm America, President Coolidge said 'American must remain American.' Similarly, each race, whether the French at home, the Germans at home, the Jews in their new homeland . . . has an inherent right to set its own racial standards and to regulate immigration and human reproduction in such a manner as to breed toward the attainment of these standards.

"It is the business of eugenics, both as a pure and as an applied science in each country, to collaborate with its national leadership in establishing the racial and family-stock ideals for the particular country, and in striving for the attainment of the established ideals."

"Race integrity" and "regulate human reproduction!" The copies of the *Eugenical News* published under the editorship of Laughlin and Davenport are filled with phrases similar to these. Another editorial in the same year reads: "One may condemn the Nazi policy generally, but specifically it remained for Germany in 1933 to lead the great nations of the world in recognition of the biological foundations of national character." Nor do they content themselves with editorials. In 1934 they reprinted an entire speech by Dr. Frick, Reichsminister of the Interior, entitled: "German Population and Race Politics"; and up until the time of the war the good news from Germany filled the pages of the magazine. The German law was reproduced, explained and, by a German here, interpreted:

"In the new Germany laws are made for the benefit of posterity, regardless of the approval or disapproval of present generations. . . .

"This [being swamped by degenerate stock] is the colossal danger Adolf Hitler wants to avert in Germany! A nation decays because its valuable germplasm disappears—that racial stock from which leaders emerge."

So that there can be no doubt where they stand, the editors, at the end of this article, write:

"Whether or not the critic agrees with current German ideas, real or reputed, the student of eugenics agrees that as practical statesmanship for effecting the announced ideals, Germany is the first of the great nations of the world to make direct use of eugenics. . . .

"To combat the rising tide of mental and physical defectives and to preserve the proper proportion of the Aryan elements in Germany the state is initiating many eugenic measures, including the sterilization law . . . and other measures *to eliminate the non-Aryan element from Germany."*

And in an unsigned book review in the same issue there appears this statement: "It appears that under the dictatorship Germany is moving more rapidly toward race purification than any other nation. Such race purification may be accompanied by hardships to the individual, but society follows nature's method in regarding the progress of the race as more important than that of the individual."

For anyone still in doubt as to what these eugenicists had in mind for the American people when they spoke of human betterment, the bound volumes of the *Eugenical News* will provide enlightenment, and especially recommended is the article "Patriotism and Racial Standards" in the issue of July-August, 1936, written by C. M. Goethe, one of the current sponsors of the Human Betterment Association; but here, one more quotation will suffice:

"It is unfortunate the anti-Nazi propaganda with which all countries have been flooded has gone far to obscure the correct understanding and the great importance of the German racial policy. . . . No earnest eugenicist can fail to give approbation to such a national policy."

Who was the man who wrote this? He was the honorary president of the Eugenics Research Association. He ended the article with these words:

"The Germans as a nation recognize that these obligations in the common interest go somewhat further, and they are quite happy and content to observe such further obligations in the feeling that their personal liberties are not unduly curtailed. The future will incontestably prove which nations have been the wiser."

Whether it was the advent of the war, the attacks on the American Bund, or the end of the editorial reign of Laughlin and Davenport, the tone of the magazine had changed by 1939, and while the Nazi racial policy apparently was never repudiated, the magazine printed an article in 1943 which, after a recitation of some of Hitler's crimes, contained this statement: "These almost unbelievable facts bring to our hearts a rush of pity for those victims of sadism, brutality and planned race extinction."

The elimination of the non-Aryan element had turned out to be race extinction! But how in the name of the English language could it have turned out to be anything else?

Conduct That Shocks the Conscience

As we observed in Chapter 11, only one of seven state court decisions adverse to search-and-seizure claimants has been reversed by the Supreme Court during the period of the 1948 through the 1958 Terms. The one favorable decision was made in the case reported below, which suggests the conceptual difficulty of fitting the techniques of modern science into the behavioral constructs of the eighteenth century.

ROCHIN v. CALIFORNIA

342 U.S. 165 (1952)

Certiorari to the California Second District Court of Appeal.

Reversed.

_____

8-0

Frankfurter	('+')
Vinson, C.J.	(+)
Reed	(+)
Jackson	(+)
Burton	(+)
Clark	(+)
Black	('+'
Douglas	('+'
Minton	NP

_____

Is the invasion of the physical privacy of a person, accomplished by the compulsory pumping out of his stomach, with the objective of obtaining evidence secreted inside his body, an illegal search and seizure? or does it force him to be a witness against himself, thus violating the so-called self-incrimination clause of the Fifth Amendment, to the extent (of course) that the core of the Fifth Amendment is also a part of the ordered liberty that is protected by the due-process clause of the Fourteenth Amendment?

In United States v. Willis, *85 F. Supp. 745 (1949), a federal district court in California ruled that the use of a stomach pump, under the direction of federal police officers, to extract heroin capsules from the stomach of a defendant, constituted an* illegal *search and seizure in violation of the Fourth Amendment; this judge refused to admit the heroin capsules as evidence and the defendant was acquitted. But the dissenting judges in*

the California Court of Appeal argued, in the Rochin case, that the pumping of Rochin's stomach violated his privilege against self-incrimination.

It will be observed that both Frankfurter (for the Court) and Douglas (in concurrence) analogize stomach-pumping to the Fifth Amendment by considering it to be a form of "coerced confession." [8] *This approach is not without its difficulties, however. The Court does not mention the fact that if the police had failed to administer the emetic, the amount of morphine that Rochin had ingested might well have been a fatal dose, taken orally as it was. Suppose the stomach-pumping was necessary to save his life: would the recovered capsules still be a "coerced confession"? Obviously, however, the Court could not call such evidence the fruit of an illegal search and seizure, and still reverse the California courts, unless a majority were prepared to overrule* Wolf v. Colorado; *and of the dissenters in the* Wolf *case, only Douglas remained on the Court.*

MR. JUSTICE FRANKFURTER delivered the opinion of the Court.

Having "some information that [the petitioner here] was selling narcotics," three deputy sheriffs of the County of Los Angeles, on the morning of July 1, 1949,

[8] It is also possible that some of the justices considered the events leading up to the pumping of Rochin's stomach to be just as "shocking" as what happened inside the hospital. The opinions here play down the details of the police brutality during the struggle in the Rochin bedroom. A more vivid account occurs in the opinions of the state court, 101 Cal. App. 2d 140-141 or 225 P. 2d 1 (1950); and for further details of the stomach-pumping technique, see *United States* v. *Willis,* 85 F. Supp. 745-746 (1949).

made for the two-story dwelling house in which Rochin lived with his mother, his common-law wife, brothers and sisters. Finding the outside door open, they entered and then forced open the door to Rochin's room on the second floor. Inside they found petitioner sitting partly dressed on the side of the bed, upon which his wife was lying. On a "night stand" beside the bed the deputies spied two capsules. When asked "Whose stuff is this?" Rochin seized the capsules and put them in his mouth. A struggle ensued, in the course of which the three officers "jumped upon him" and attempted to extract the capsules. The force they applied proved unavailing against Rochin's resistance. He was handcuffed and taken to a hospital. At the direction of one of the officers a doctor forced an emetic solution through a tube into Rochin's stomach against his will. This "stomach pumping" produced vomiting. In the vomited matter were found two capsules which proved to contain morphine.

Rochin was brought to trial before a California Superior Court, sitting without a jury, on the charge of possessing "a preparation of morphine" in violation of the California Health and Safety Code. . . . Rochin was convicted and sentenced to sixty days' imprisonment. The chief evidence against him was the two capsules. They were admitted over petitioner's objection, although the means of obtaining them was frankly set forth in the testimony by one of the deputies, substantially as here narrated.

On appeal, the District Court of Appeal affirmed the conviction, despite the finding that the officers "were guilty of unlawfully breaking into and entering defendant's room and were guilty of unlawfully assaulting and battering defendant while in the room," and "were guilty of unlawfully assaulting, battering, torturing and falsely imprisoning the defendant at the alleged hospital." . . . One of the three judges, while finding that "the record in this case reveals a shocking series of violations of constitutional rights," concurred only because he felt bound by decisions of his Supreme Court. These, he asserted, "have been looked upon by law enforcement officers as an encouragement, if not an invitation, to the commission of such lawless acts." Ibid. The Supreme Court of California denied without opinion Rochin's petition for a hearing. Two justices dissented from this denial, and in doing so expressed themselves thus: ". . . a conviction which rests upon evidence of incriminating objects obtained from the body of the accused by physical abuse is as invalid as a conviction which rests upon a verbal confession extracted from him by such abuse. . . . Had the evidence forced from the defendant's lips consisted of an oral confession that he illegally possessed a drug . . . he would have the protection of the rule of law which excludes coerced confessions from evidence. But because the evidence forced from his lips consisted of real objects the People of this state are permitted to base a conviction upon it. [We] find no valid ground of distinction between a verbal confession extracted by physical abuse and a confession wrested from defendant's body by physical abuse." . . .

This Court granted certiorari, 341 US 939, because a serious question is raised as to the limitations which the Due Process Clause of the Fourteenth Amendment imposes on the conduct of criminal proceedings by the States. . . .

The vague contours of the Due Process Clause do not leave judges at large. We may not draw on our merely personal and private notions and disregard the limits that bind judges in their judicial function. Even though the concept of due process of law is not final and fixed, these limits are derived from considerations that are fused in the whole nature of our judicial process. See Cardozo, The Nature of the Judicial Process; The Growth of the Law; The Paradoxes of Legal Science. These are considerations deeply rooted in reason and in the compelling traditions of the legal profession. The Due Process Clause places upon this Court the duty of exercising a judgment, within the narrow confines of judicial power in reviewing State convictions, upon interests of society pushing in opposite directions.

Due process of law thus conceived is not to be derided as resort to a revival of "natural law." To believe that this judicial exercise of judgment could be avoided by freezing "due process of law" at some fixed stage of time or thought is to suggest that the most important aspect of constitutional adjudication is a function for inanimate machines and not for judges, for whom the independence safeguarded by Article 3 of the Constitution was designed and who are presumably guided by established standards of judicial behavior. Even cybernetics has not yet made that haughty claim. To practice the requisite detachment and to achieve sufficient objectivity no doubt demands of judges the habit of self-discipline and self-criticism, incertitude that one's own views are incontestable and alert tolerance toward views not shared. But these are precisely the presuppositions of our judicial process. They are precisely the qualities society has a right to expect from those entrusted with ultimate judicial power.

Restraints on our jurisdiction are self-imposed only in the sense that there is from our decisions no immediate appeal short of impeachment or constitutional amendment. But that does not make due process of law a matter of judicial caprice. The faculties of the Due Process Clause may be indefinite and vague, but the mode of their ascertainment is not self-willed. In each case "due process of law" requires an evaluation based on a disinterested inquiry pursued in the spirit of science, on a balanced order of facts exactly and fairly stated, on the detached consideration of conflicting claims . . . on a judgment not ad hoc and episodic but duly mindful of reconciling the needs both of continuity and of change in a progressive society.

Applying these general considerations to the circumstances of the present case, we are compelled to conclude that the proceedings by which this conviction was obtained do more than offend some fastidious squeamishness or private sentimentalism about combatting crime too energetically. It is conduct that shocks the conscience. Illegally breaking into the privacy of the petitioner, the struggle to open his mouth and remove what was there, the forcible extraction of his stomach's contents—this course of proceeding by agents of government to obtain evidence is bound to offend even hardened sensibilities. They are methods too close to the rack and the screw to permit of constitutional differentiation.

It has long since ceased to be true that due process of law is heedless of the means by which otherwise relevant and credible evidence is obtained. Even before the series of recent cases enforced the constitutional principle the States could not base convictions upon confessions, however much verified, but obtained by coercion. These decisions are not arbitrary exceptions to the comprehensive right of States to fashion their own rules of evidence for criminal trials. They are not sports in our constitutional law but applications of a general principle. They are only instances of the general requirement that States in their prosecutions respect certain decencies of civilized conduct. Due process of law, as a historic and generative principle, precludes defining, and thereby confining, these standards of conduct more precisely than to say that convictions cannot be brought about by methods that offend "a sense of justice." . . . It would be a stultification of the responsibility which the course of constitutional history has cast upon this Court to hold that in order to convict a man the police cannot extract by force what is in his mind but can extract what is in his stomach.

To attempt in this case to distinguish what lawyers call "real evidence" from verbal evidence is to ignore the reasons for excluding coerced confessions. Use of involuntary verbal confessions in State criminal trials is constitutionally obnoxious not only because of their unreliability. They are inadmissable under the Due Process Clause even though statements contained in them may be independently established as true. Coerced confessions offend the community's sense of fair play and decency. So here, to sanction the brutal conduct which naturally enough was condemned by the court whose judgment is before us, would be to afford brutality the cloak of law. Nothing would be more calculated to discredit law and thereby to brutalize the temper of a society. . . .[9]   *Reversed.*

MR. JUSTICE BLACK, concurring. . . .

If the Due Process Clause does vest this Court with such unlimited power to invalidate laws, I am still in doubt as to why we should consider only the notions of English-speaking peoples to determine what are immutable and fundamental

[9] In view of Frankfurter's use of statistical polls in *Wolf* v. *Colorado* (and elsewhere), the question logically arises why there is no appendix presenting such data in his opinion for the Court in this case. Surely, it is just as relevant to know how the English-speaking peoples of the world, who are the heirs-at-law to the Anglo-Saxon legal system, feel about stomach-pumping, compulsory blood tests and involuntary urinalyses as it is to know how they react to the admission in court of evidence obtained as the result of an illegal search and seizure by the police. Yet, evidence bearing on the attitude of civilized society toward personal physiological privacy is available in the opinions in this case only in Douglas' concurrence, and then only in part. (We do not know, for instance, how New South Wales views the question, to say nothing of Mother England.) One would be loath to accept the inference that it is useful for the proponents of ordered liberty to count heads among the English-speaking peoples only when the results of the poll support the immutable commands of natural justice.

principles of justice. Moreover, one may well ask what avenues of investigation are open to discover "canons" of conduct so universally favored that this Court should write them into the Constitution? All we are told is that the discovery must be made by an "evaluation based on a disinterested inquiry pursued in the spirit of science on a balanced order of facts."

Some constitutional provisions are stated in absolute and unqualified language such, for illustration, as the First Amendment stating that no law shall be passed prohibiting the free exercise of religion or abridging the freedom of speech or press. Other constitutional provisions do require courts to choose between competing policies, such as the Fourth Amendment which, by its terms, necessitates a judicial decision as to what is an "unreasonable" search or seizure. There is, however, no express constitutional language granting judicial power to invalidate *every* state law of *every* kind deemed "unreasonable" or contrary to the Court's notion of civilized decencies; yet the constitutional philosophy used by the majority has, in the past, been used to deny a state the right to fix the price of gasoline, . . . and even the right to prevent bakers from palming off smaller for larger loaves of bread. . . . These cases, and others, show the extent to which the evanescent standards of the majority's philosophy have been used to nullify state legislative programs passed to suppress evil economic practices. What paralyzing role this same philosophy will play in the future economic affairs of this country is impossible to predict. Of even graver concern, however, is the use of the philosophy to nullify the Bill of Rights. I long ago concluded that the accordian-like qualities of this philosophy must inevitably imperil all the individual liberty safeguards specifically enumerated in the Bill of Rights. Reflection and recent decisions of this Court sanctioning abridgment of the freedom of speech and press have strengthened this conclusion.

MR. JUSTICE DOUGLAS, concurring.

The evidence obtained from this accused's stomach would be admissible in the majority of states where the question has been raised.[10] So far as the reported cases reveal, the only states which would probably exclude the evidence would be Arkansas, Iowa, Michigan, and Missouri. Yet the Court now says that the rule which the majority of the states have fashioned violates the "decencies of civilized conduct." To that I cannot agree. It is a rule formulated by responsible courts with judges as sensitive as we are to the proper standards for law administration.

As an original matter it might be debatable whether the provision in the Fifth Amendment that no person "shall be compelled in any criminal case to be a witness against himself" serves the ends of justice. Not all civilized legal procedures recognize it. But the choice was made by the Framers, a choice which sets a standard for legal trials in this country. The Framers made it a standard of due process for prosecutions by the Federal Government. If it is a requirement of due process for a trial in the federal court house, it is impossible for me to say it is not a re-

quirement of due process for a trial in the state court house. That was the issue recently surveyed in Adamson v. California, 332 U.S. 46. The Court rejected the view that compelled testimony should be excluded and held in substance that the accused in a state trial can be forced to testify against himself. I disagree. Of course an accused can be compelled to be present at the trial, to stand, to sit, to turn this way or that, and to try on a cap or a coat. . . . But I think that words taken from his lips, capsules taken from his stomach, blood taken from his veins are all inadmissible provided they are taken from him without his consent. They are inadmissible because of the command of the Fifth Amendment.

That is an unequivocal, definite and workable rule of evidence for state and federal courts. But we cannot in fairness free the state courts from that command and yet excoriate them for flouting the "decencies of civilized conduct" when they admit the evidence. That is to make the rule turn not on the Constitution but on the idiosyncrasies of the judges who sit here.

The damage of the view sponsored by the Court in this case may not be conspicuous here. But it is part of the same philosophy that produced Betts v. Brady, 316 U.S. 455, denying counsel to an accused in a state trial against the command of the Sixth Amendment and Wolf v. Colorado, 338 U.S. 25, allowing evidence obtained as a result of a search and seizure that is illegal under the Fourth Amendment to be introduced in a state trial. It is part of the process of erosion of civil rights of the citizen in recent years.

10 Mr. Justice Douglas cites the decisions of nine states: California, Idaho, Maryland, Nevada, New Hampshire, New Jersey, Ohio, Oregon, and Pennsylvania. The cited cases relate to: pumping of accused's stomach to recover swallowed narcotic; blood test to determine intoxication; blood typing to link accused with murder, or with assault; examination of accused for venereal disease; examination and urinalysis to determine intoxication, and commenting on refusal to submit to blood test or urinalysis to determine intoxication.

As we have noted, Rochin was the only state search-and-seizure case, during the decade following *Wolf* v. *Colorado,* that the Court decided in a claimant's favor; typical of the other half-dozen decisions of this period was the Court's negative decision in the Breithaupt case (below). But both Rochin and Breithaupt differed in one significant respect from the other cases in this group, which were concerned either with the physical invasion by state police of the privacy of the defendant's curtilage—his home or his office—or else with more sophisticated problems of electronic eavesdropping upon the defendant's speech in what were intended to be private conversations. Breithaupt, like Rochin, dealt with the question of privacy in its most pristine form: the sanctity of the human body against compulsory and corporal inquisition by teams of medicolegal investigators. If it were true (as the Court had said) that the involuntary stomach-pumping of a drug addict shocked the conscience of American society, what about the taking of an involuntary blood sample from a drunken driver who was party to a fatal highway "accident?" Are blood tests more—or less—constitutionally revolting than stomach pumps?

BREITHAUPT v. ABRAM

352 U.S. 432 (1957)

Certiorari to the Supreme Court of New Mexico.

Affirmed.

6-3

Clark	('+')
Reed	(+)
Frankfurter	(+)
Burton	(+)
Harlan	(+)
Brennan	(+)
Warren, C.J.	'−')
Black	−)
Douglas	'−')

MR. JUSTICE CLARK delivered the opinion of the Court.

Petitioner, while driving a pickup truck on the highways of New Mexico, was involved in a collision with a passenger car. Three occupants of the car were killed and petitioner was seriously injured. A pint whiskey bottle, almost empty, was found in the glove compartment of the pickup truck. Petitioner was taken to a hospital and while he was lying unconscious in the emergency room the smell of liquor was detected on his breath. A state patrolman requested that a sample of petitioner's blood be taken. An attending physician, while petitioner was unconscious, withdrew a sample of about 20 cubic centimeters of blood by use of a hypodermic needle. This sample was delivered to the patrolman and subsequent laboratory analysis showed this blood to contain about .17% alcohol.

Petitioner was thereafter charged with involuntary manslaughter. Testimony regarding the blood test and its result was admitted into evidence at trial over petitioner's objection. This included testimony of an expert that a person with .17% alcohol in his blood was under the influence of intoxicating liquor. Petitioner was convicted and sentenced for involuntary manslaughter. He did not appeal the conviction. Subsequently, however, he sought release from his imprisonment by a petition for a writ of habeas corpus to the Supreme Court of New Mexico. That court, after argument, denied the writ. . . . Petitioner contends that his conviction, based on the result of the involuntary blood test, deprived him of his liberty without that due process of law guaranteed him by the Fourteenth Amendment to the Constitution. . . .

It has been clear since *Weeks* v. *United States,* 232 U.S. 383 (1914), that evidence obtained in violation of rights protected by the Fourth Amendment to the Federal Constitution must be excluded in federal criminal prosecutions. There is argument on behalf of petitioner that the evidence used here, the result of the blood test, was obtained in violation of the Due Process

Clause of the Fourteenth Amendment in that the taking was the result of an unreasonable search and seizure violative of the Fourth Amendment. Likewise, he argues that by way of the Fourteenth Amendment there has been a violation of the Fifth Amendment in that introduction of the test result compelled him to be a witness against himself. Petitioner relies on the proposition that "the generative principles" of the Bill of Rights should extend the protections of the Fourth and Fifth Amendments to his case through the Due Process Clause of the Fourteenth Amendment. But *Wolf* v. *Colorado,* 338 U.S. 25 (1949), answers this contention in the negative. . . . New Mexico has rejected, as it may, the exclusionary rule set forth in *Weeks, supra. State* v. *Dillon,* 34 N.M. 366, 281 P. 474 (1929). Therefore, the rights petitioner claims afford no aid to him here for the fruits of the violations, if any, are admissible in the State's prosecution.

Petitioner's remaining and primary assault on his conviction is not so easily unhorsed. He urges that the conduct of the state officers here offends that "sense of justice" of which we spoke in *Rochin* v. *California,* 342 U.S. 165 (1952). . . . But we see nothing comparable here to the facts in *Rochin.*

Basically the distinction rests on the fact that there is nothing "brutal" or "offensive" in the taking of a sample of blood when done, as in this case, under the protective eye of a physician. To be sure, the driver here was unconscious when the blood was taken, but the absence of conscious consent, without more, does not necessarily render the taking a violation of a constitutional right; and certainly the test as administered here would not be considered offensive by even the most delicate. Furthermore, due process is not measured by the yardstick of personal reaction or the sphygmogram of the most sensitive person, but by that whole community sense of "decency and fairness" that has been woven by com-

mon experience into the fabric of acceptable conduct. It is on this bedrock that this Court has established the concept of due process. The blood test procedure has become routine in our everyday life. It is a ritual for those going into the military service as well as those applying for marriage licenses. Many colleges require such tests before permitting entrance and literally millions of us have voluntarily gone through the same, though a longer, routine in becoming blood donors. Likewise, we note that a majority of our States have either enacted statutes in some form authorizing tests of this nature or permit findings so obtained to be admitted in evidence.[11] We therefore conclude that a blood test taken by a skilled technician is not such "conduct that shocks the conscience," *Rochin, supra,* at 172, nor such a method of obtaining evidence that it offends a "sense of justice," *Brown* v. *Mississippi,* 297 U.S. 278, 285-286 (1936).[12] . . .

The test upheld here is not attacked on the ground of any basic deficiency or of

[11] Forty-seven States use chemical tests, including blood tests, to aid in the determination of intoxication in cases involving charges of driving while under the influence of alcohol. Twenty-three of these States sanction the use of the tests by statute. . . . Other States have accepted the use of chemical tests for intoxication without statutory but with court approval. [Eight states are listed.] . . . Still other States accept the practice of the use of chemical tests for intoxication though there does not appear to have been litigation on the problem. . . . The fact that so many States make use of the tests negatives the suggestion that there is anything offensive about them. For additional discussion of the use of these blood tests see, Inbau, Self-Incrimination (1950), 72-86. [Footnote by the Court.]

[12] Several States have considered the very problem here presented but none have found that the conduct of the state authorities was so offensive as to necessitate reversal of convictions based in part on blood tests. . . . The withdrawal of blood for use in blood-grouping tests in state criminal prosecutions is wide-spread. . . . Many States authorize blood tests in civil actions such as paternity proceedings. . . . [Footnote by the Court.]

injudicious application, but admittedly is a scientifically accurate method of detecting alcoholic content in the blood, thus furnishing an exact measure upon which to base a decision as to intoxication. Modern community living requires modern scientific methods of crime detection lest the public go unprotected. The increasing slaughter on our highways, most of which should be avoidable, now reaches the astounding figures only heard of on the battlefield. The States, through safety measures, modern scientific methods, and strict enforcement of traffic laws, are using all reasonable means to make automobile driving less dangerous.

As against the right of an individual that his person be held inviolable, even against so slight an intrusion as is involved in applying a blood test of the kind to which millions of Americans submit as a matter of course nearly every day, must be set the interests of society in the scientific determination of intoxication, one of the great causes of the mortal hazards of the road. And the more so since the test likewise may establish innocence, thus affording protection against the treachery of judgment based on one or more of the senses. Furthermore, since our criminal law is to no small extent justified by the assumption of deterrence, the individual's right to immunity from such invasion of the body as is involved in a properly safeguarded blood test is far outweighed by the value of its deterrent effect due to public realization that the issue of driving while under the influence of alcohol can often by this method be taken out of the confusion of conflicting contentions.

For these reasons the judgment is
Affirmed.

MR. CHIEF JUSTICE WARREN, with whom MR. JUSTICE BLACK and MR. JUSTICE DOUGLAS join, dissenting.

The judgment in this case should be reversed if *Rochin* v. *California,* 342 U. S. 165, is to retain its vitality and stand as

more than an instance of personal revulsion against particular police methods. I cannot agree with the Court when it says, "we see nothing comparable here to the facts in *Rochin.*" It seems to me the essential elements of the cases are the same and the same result should follow.

There is much in the Court's opinion concerning the hazards on our nation's highways, the efforts of the States to enforce the traffic laws and the necessity for the use of modern scientific methods in the detection of crime. Everybody can agree with these sentiments, and yet they do not help us particularly in determining whether this case can be distinguished from *Rochin.* That case grew out of police efforts to curb the narcotics traffic, in which there is surely a state interest of at least as great magnitude as the interest in highway law enforcement. Nor does the fact that many States sanction the use of blood test evidence differentiate the cases. At the time *Rochin* was decided illegally obtained evidence was admissible in the vast majority of States. In both *Rochin* and this case the officers had probable cause to suspect the defendant of the offense of which they sought evidence. In *Rochin* the defendant was known as a narcotics law violator, was arrested under suspicious circumstances and was seen by the officers to swallow narcotics. In neither case, of course, are we concerned with the defendant's guilt or innocence. The sole problem is whether the proceeding was tainted by a violation of the defendant's constitutional rights.

In reaching its conclusion that in this case, unlike *Rochin,* there is nothing "brutal" or "offensive" the Court has not kept separate the component parts of the problem. Essentially there are two: the character of the invasion of the body and the expression of the victim's will; the latter may be manifested by physical resistance. Of course, one may consent to having his blood extracted or his stomach pumped and thereby waive any due process objection. In that limited sense the expression of the will is significant. But where there is no affirmative consent, I cannot see that it should make any difference whether one states unequivocally that he objects or resorts to physical violence in protest or is in such condition that he is unable to protest. The Court, however, states that "the absence of conscious consent, without more, does not necessarily render the taking a violation of a constitutional right." This implies that a different result might follow if petitioner had been conscious and had voiced his objection. I reject the distinction.

Since there clearly was no consent to the blood test, it is the nature of the invasion of the body that should be determinative of the due process question here presented. The Court's opinion suggests that an invasion is "brutal" or "offensive" only if the police use force to overcome a suspect's resistance. By its recital of the facts in *Rochin*—the references to a "considerable struggle" and the fact that the stomach pump was "forcibly used"—the Court finds *Rochin* distinguishable from this case. I cannot accept an analysis that would make physical resistance by a prisoner a prerequisite to the existence of his constitutional rights.

Apart from the irrelevant factor of physical resistance, the techniques used in this case and in *Rochin* are comparable. In each the operation was performed by a doctor in a hospital. In each there was an extraction of body fluids. Neither operation normally causes any lasting ill effects. The Court denominates a blood test as a scientific method for detecting crime and cites the frequency of such tests in our everyday life. The stomach pump too is a common and accepted way of making tests and relieving distress. But it does not follow from the fact that a technique is a product of science or is in common, consensual use for other purposes that it can be used to extract evidence from a criminal defendant without his consent. Would the taking of spinal fluid from an unconscious person be condoned because such tests are commonly made and might be used as a scientific aid to law enforcement?

Only personal reaction to the stomach pump and the blood test can distinguish them. To base the restriction which the Due Process Clause imposes on state criminal procedures upon such reactions is to build on shifting sands. We should, in my opinion, hold that due process means at least that law-enforcement officers in their efforts to obtain evidence from persons suspected of crime must stop short of bruising the body, breaking skin, puncturing tissue or extracting body fluids, whether they contemplate doing it by force or by stealth.

Viewed according to this standard, the judgment should be reversed.

MR. JUSTICE DOUGLAS, with whom MR. JUSTICE BLACK joins, dissenting.

The Court seems to sanction in the name of law enforcement the assault made by the police on this unconscious man. If law enforcement were the chief value in our constitutional scheme, then due process would shrivel and become of little value in protecting the rights of the citizen. But those who fashioned the Constitution put certain rights out of the reach of the police and preferred other rights over law enforcement.

One source of protection of the citizen against state action is the Due Process Clause of the Fourteenth Amendment. Our decisions hold that the police violate due process when they use brutal methods to obtain evidence against a man and use it to convict him. *Rochin* v. *California,* 342 U.S. 165; *Chambers* v. *Florida,* 309 U.S. 227. But the conception of due process is not limited to a prohibition of the use of force and violence against an accused. In *Leyra* v. *Denno,* 347 U.S. 556, we set aside a conviction where subtle, nonviolent methods had been used to exact a confession from a prisoner. For it was obvious that coercion might be the product of subtlety as well as of violence. We should take the same libertarian approach here.

As I understand today's decision there would be a violation of due process if the blood had been withdrawn from the accused after a struggle with the police. But the sanctity of the person is equally violated and his body assaulted where the prisoner is incapable of offering resistance as it would be if force were used to overcome his resistance. In both cases evidence is used to convict a man which has been obtained from him on an involuntary basis. I would not draw a line between the use of force on the one hand and trickery, subterfuge, or any police technique which takes advantage of the inability of the prisoner to resist on the other. Nor would I draw a line between involuntary extraction of words from his lips, the involuntary extraction of the contents of his stomach, and the involuntary extraction of fluids of his body when the evidence obtained is used to convict him. Under our system of government, police cannot compel people to furnish the evidence necessary to send them to prison. Yet there is compulsion here, following the violation by the police of the sanctity of the body of an unconscious man.

And if the decencies of a civilized state are the test, it is repulsive to me for the police to insert needles into an unconscious person in order to get the evidence necessary to convict him, whether they find the person unconscious, give him a pill which puts him to sleep, or use force to subdue him. The indignity to the individual is the same in one case as in the other, for in each is his body invaded and assaulted by the police who are supposed to be the citizen's protector.

I would reverse this judgment of conviction.

Like the Wolf case, Breithaupt affords an interesting study in contrast to Rochin. In Rochin, reference to the Fourth Amendment is sublimated, and a case which, on its facts, seems to raise a search-and-seizure problem is analogized to Fifth Amendment sources. (The object of the search in Rochin never became assimilated as part of his body; if it had been, it would probably have killed him.) In Breithaupt, it would appear from a reading of the opinion of the Court that the only relevant criteria for assessing the constitutional validity of an involuntary blood test were provided by the Weeks rule and the Wolf decision. (The Fourth Amendment is now convenient for the majority to discuss; *Wolf* v. *Colorado* supports the affirmance of Breithaupt's conviction.) In Rochin, the statistics are in a separate concurring opinion; in Breithaupt, as in Wolf, the statistics are in the opinion of the Court. (The statistics failed to support the decision of the Court in Rochin, but did support it in Breithaupt and in Wolf.) It may be far-fetched, but perhaps not too far-fetched, to suggest the analogy of a shell game in attempting to reconcile, on logical grounds, the Court's opinion-writing behavior in these three cases. (It *is* difficult to keep track of which shell the pea is under, at any given time.)

The majority in Breithaupt claim that there is a constitutional difference between stomach pumps and blood tests; but the dissenters assert that the only basis for judicial discrimination between the two techniques is the personal reactions of the differentiating justices. A more objective criterion of judgment than the image of society's conscience entertained by a majority of the justices might obviate the necessity for Frankfurter's repeated disclaimers, as in Adamson and Rochin, that the sociological jurists do not draw upon their merely personal and private notions in defining the requisites of a system of ordered liberty.

In Breithaupt, the majority note that the blood sample was taken under "the protective eye of a physician"; but surely this is no basis for distinction. There are physicians in all three of these cases: Wolf was a doctor who cooperated with osteopathic and lay abortionists; Rochin's stomach was pumped by a physician; and both the taking of the blood sample and the stomach-pumping took place in hospitals, not in police interrogation rooms. In Breithaupt, the "absence of conscious consent" did not constitute a violation of the defendant's constitutional rights; does it follow that Rochin's stomach might have been pumped constitutionally if only he had been first rendered unconscious? If so, the lesson for the police is clear enough: they should have completed the beating that they began, before hauling Rochin off to the hospital. Then Rochin would have been assured the essence of a system of ordered liberty due him under the Fourteenth Amendment—wouldn't he?

PSYCHOLOGICAL PRIVACY

From the physical violence of Rochin and the laboratory analyses of the "skilled technicians" of Breithaupt, it is only a short step, as we learn from recent studies in psychosomatic medicine, to the problems evoked by the psychoanalysis and narcoanalysis of criminal suspects and defendants. In the cases above, the police invaded the bodies of defendants in order to obtain evidence of their criminal guilt; in the cases below, the police invade the minds of the defendants, for the same purpose and with a similar effect. From an empirical point of view, the principal difference between the two sets of police behaviors lies in their degree of sophistication. Most judges would probably agree that when a rural sheriff literally beats his prisoner to death in the public square in front of the county jail, he has violated the constitutional rights of the defendant.[13] The metropolitan police psychiatrist, who guides his patient to and through the catharsis by means of which he is relieved of his suppressed feelings of guilt, operates in another world—the world of today, rather than the world of the past. And the forensic scientist who skillfully depresses the cerebral cortex of a defendant, manipulating directly the subconscious mental processes that the psychiatrist must approach externally, operates in yet another world: is it the world of tomorrow? And if the Court holds that confessions coerced by brute force are invalid, what of those that are induced by anesthesia?

[13] Screws v. United States, 325 U.S. 91 (1945). For a good example of the third degree in action, complete with a tough private eye and permissive police ("just like on TV"), see Williams v. United States, 341 U.S. 97 (1951).

OEDIPUS IN BROOKLYN

As noted in the Douglas dissent in Breithaupt, the difference between medico-legal investigations of a suspect's body and of his mind are differences only in degree. From the stark brutality of Rochin to the sterile bloodletting of Breithaupt and thence to the psychoanalyst's couch in Leyra, we move along the gradations of the same continuum of deprivations of bodily privacy. (And as we shall observe soon, immediately following the Leyra case, beyond the analyst's couch there are other points on the continuum, such as the forensic-science operating room.)

But we can also relate the case below, from a somewhat different point of view, to *Buck* v. *Bell*. Both cases involve an element that does not appear, at least among the facts of record, in the other cases that we examine in this chapter: Carrie Buck and Buddy Leyra suffered from mental illnesses. Of course, there were also important differences between these two individuals and their problems, including their constitutional problems. Carrie's only real crime against society was that she was a happy moron; while Buddy was the protagonist in the plebian recreation of one of the oldest and most tragic dramas in Western culture: the Oedipus myth. Carrie did not, in all likelihood, even know her mother—much less her father; but Buddy Leyra knew both his mother and his father, too well.

LEYRA v. DENNO

347 U.S. 556 (1954)

Certiorari to the United States Court of Appeals for the Second Circuit.

Reversed.

5-3

Black	('+')
Warren, C.J.	(+)
Frankfurter	(+)
Douglas	(+)
Clark	(+)
Minton	'—')
Reed	—)
Burton	—)
Jackson	NP

MR. JUSTICE BLACK delivered the opinion of the Court.

Camilo Leyra, age 75, and his wife, age 80, were found dead in their Brooklyn apartment. Several days later petitioner, their son, age 50, was indicted in a state court charged with having murdered them with a hammer. He was convicted and sentenced to death, chiefly on several alleged confessions of guilt. The New York Court of Appeals reversed on the ground that one of the confessions, made to a state-employed psychiatrist, had been extorted from petitioner by coercion and promises of leniency in violation of the Due Process Clause of the Fourteenth Amendment. . . . Petitioner was then tried again. This time the invalidated confession was not used to convict him but several other confessions that followed it the same day were used. Petitioner objected to the admission of these other confessions on the ground that they were also coerced, but the trial court submitted to the jury the question of their "voluntariness." The jury convicted and the death sentence now before us was imposed. The New York Court of Appeals, holding that there was evidence to support a finding that the confessions used were free from the coercive influences of the one previously given the psychiatrist, affirmed, Judge Fuld and the late Chief Judge Loughran dissenting.... We denied certiorari. . . . Petitioner then filed this habeas corpus proceeding in a United States District Court, charging that the confessions used against him had been coerced, depriving him of due process of law. The District Court properly gave consideration to the petition, . . . but denied it. . . . The Court of Appeals for the Second Term affirmed, Judge Frank dissenting. . . . Petitioner then sought review in this Court, again urging that he was denied due process on the ground that his confessions to a police captain and to two assistant state prosecutors were forced. We granted certiorari because the constitutional question appeared substantial. . . .

The use in a state criminal trial of a defendant's confession obtained by coercion—whether physical or mental—is forbidden by the Fourteenth Amendment.[14] The question for our decision is therefore whether the present confessions were so coerced. This question can only be answered by reviewing the circumstances surrounding the confessions. We therefore examine the circumstances as shown by the undisputed facts of this case.

When the father failed to appear at his place of business on Tuesday, January 10, 1950, petitioner, his business partner, and others went to the father's apartment about 3 p. m. and found the bodies of the aged parents. Police were called.

14 See e.g., *Brown* v. *Mississippi*, 297 U.S. 278; *Chambers* v. *Florida*, 309 U.S. 227; *Lisenba* v. *California*, 314 U.S. 219; *Ashcraft* v. *Tennessee*, 322 U.S. 143; *Malinski* v. *New York*, 324 U.S. 401; *Haley* v. *Ohio*, 332 U.S. 596; *Watts* v. *Indiana*, 338 U.S. 49; *Stroble* v. *California*, 343 U.S. 181; *Stein* v. *New York*, 346 U.S. 156. The above cases illustrate the settled view of this Court that coerced confessions cannot be admitted as evidence in criminal trials. Some members of the Court reach this conclusion because of their belief that the Fourteenth Amendment makes applicable to the states the Fifth Amendment's ban against compulsory self-incrimination. [Footnote by the Court.]

Although they first suspected a prowling intruder, the presence on the couple's disarranged breakfast table of a third teacup led them to think that the killer was a welcome guest. This and other circumstances drew suspicion toward petitioner. He and others were questioned by the police until about 11 p. m. on the evening of the day the bodies were discovered. On Wednesday, police again questioned petitioner from about 10 in the morning to midnight. Once more, beginning about 9 Thursday morning petitioner was subjected to almost constant police questioning throughout the day and much of the night until about 8:30 Friday morning. At that time petitioner was taken by police to his parents' funeral. While petitioner was at the funeral and until he returned in the late afternoon, Captain Meenahan, his chief police questioner, went home to get some "rest." After the funeral petitioner himself was permitted to go to a hotel and sleep an hour and a half. He was returned to the police station about 5 p. m. on this Friday afternoon. During his absence a concealed microphone had been installed with wire connections to another room in which the state prosecutor, the police, and possibly some others were stationed to overhear what petitioner might say. Up to this time he had not confessed to the crime.

The petitioner had been suffering from an acutely painful attack of sinus and Captain Meenahan had promised to get a physician to help him. When petitioner returned to the questioning room after the funeral, Captain Meenahan introduced him to "Dr. Helfand," supposedly to give petitioner medical relief. Dr. Helfand, however, was not a general practitioner but a psychiatrist with considerable knowledge of hypnosis. Petitioner was left with Dr. Helfand while Captain Meenahan joined the state District Attorney in the nearby listening room. Instead of giving petitioner the medical advice and treatment he expected, the psychiatrist by subtle and suggestive questions simply continued the police effort of the past days and nights to induce petitioner to admit his guilt. For an hour and a half or more the techniques of a highly trained psychiatrist were used to break petitioner's will in order to get him to say he had murdered his parents. Time and time and time again the psychiatrist told petitioner how much he wanted to and could help him, how bad it would be for petitioner if he did not confess, and how much better he would feel, and how much lighter and easier it would be on him if he would just unbosom himself to the doctor. Yet the doctor was at that very time the paid representative of the state whose prosecuting officials were listening in on every threat made and every promise of leniency given.

A tape recording of the psychiatric examination was made and a transcription of the tape was read into the record of this case. To show exactly what transpired we attach rather lengthy excerpts from that transcription as an appendix. . . . The petitioner's answers indicate a mind dazed and bewildered. Time after time the petitioner complained about how tired and how sleepy he was and how he could not think. On occasion after occasion the doctor told petitioner either to open his eyes or to shut his eyes. Apparently many of petitioner's answers were barely audible. On occasions the doctor informed petitioner that his lips were moving but no sound could be heard. Many times petitioner was asked to speak louder. As time went on, the record indicates that petitioner began to accept suggestions of the psychiatrist. For instance, Dr. Helfand suggested that the petitioner had hit his parents with a hammer and after some minutes petitioner agreed that must have been the weapon.

Finally, after an hour and a half or longer, petitioner, encouraged by the doctor's assurances that he had done no moral wrong and would be let off easily, called for Captain Meenahan. The captain immediately appeared. It was then that the confession was given to him which was admitted against petitioner in this trial. Immediately following this confession to Captain Meenahan, petitioner's business partner was called from an adjoining room. The police had apparently brought the business partner there to have him talk to petitioner at an opportune moment. Petitioner repeated to his partner in a very brief way some of the things he had told the psychiatrist and the captain. Following this, petitioner was questioned by the two assistant state prosecutors. What purports to be his formal confession was taken down by their stenographer, with a notation that it was given at 10 p. m., several hours after the psychiatrist took petitioner in charge.

On the first appeal the New York Court of Appeals held that the admissions petitioner made to the psychiatrist were so clearly the product of "mental coercion" that their use as evidence was inconsistent with due process of law. On the second appeal, however, that court held that the subsequent confessions here challenged were properly admitted. The Court of Appeals for the Second Circuit held the same thing. With this holding we cannot agree. . . . [The] undisputed facts in this case are irreconcilable with petitioner's mental freedom "to confess to or deny a suspected participation in a crime," and the relation of the confessions made to the psychiatrist, the police captain and the state prosecutors is "so close that one must say the facts of one control the character of the other. . . ." All were simply parts of one continuous process. All were extracted in the same place within a period of about five hours as the climax of days and nights of intermittent, intensive police questioning. First, an already physically and emotionally exhausted suspect's ability to resist interrogation was broken to almost trance-like submission by use of the arts of a highly skilled psychiatrist. Then the confession petitioner began making to the psychiatrist was filled in and perfected by additional statements given in rapid succession to a police officer, a trusted friend, and two state prosecutors. We hold that use of confessions extracted in such a manner from a lone defendant unprotected by counsel is not consistent with due process of law as required by our Constitution.

It was error for the court below to affirm the District Court's denial of petitioner's application for habeas corpus.

Reversed.

APPENDIX TO OPINION OF THE COURT

Excerpts from the transcript of the questioning of petitioner by Dr. Max Helfand, a psychiatrist, at the 88th precinct on January 13, 1950

"Q. What do they call you for short? A. Buddy."

"Q. How old are you about? A. Fifty."

"Q. Are you married? A. Yes, sir."

"Q. Buddy, will you tell me something about yourself. I'll tell you what the purpose of my talk to you is. I want to see if I can help you. A. Yes, Doctor."

"Q. I know you are in a little trouble. We do sometimes things that are not right, but in a fit of temper or anger we sometimes do things that we aren't really responsible for. I want to see whether or not you did something but which you've done in a fit of temper or anger. Do you understand me? A. Yes."

* * *

"Q. I am going to put my hand on your forehead, and as I put my hand on your forehead, you are going to bring back all these thoughts that are coming to your mind. I am going to keep my hand on your forehead and I am going to ask you questions, and now you will be able to tell me. What happened Monday night? Where did you sleep? A. Last Monday night?"

"Q. That's right. A. I worked Monday night."

"Q. After you worked, where did you sleep? Where did you go to sleep? A. To the apartment on 10th Street."

"Q. What time did you sleep to, or get up in the morning? A. She got up about 6:30."

"Q. Well, after she left the house, then you couldn't sleep. Then you got dressed? Your thoughts are coming back to you. Answer me. Come on, you can answer me. You couldn't go back to bed. You didn't go back to bed. After she left, you got dressed, didn't you? A. Yes, I got dressed."

"Q. What did you do after you got dressed? Come on, now. Your thoughts are coming back to you. Come on. Come on, answer me. A. I went to Brooklyn."

"Q. You went to Brooklyn. Where did you go to Brooklyn? A. To my mother's house."

"Q. To your mother's house. When you came to your mother—now, all your thoughts are beginning to clear up. Now, everything is clear in your mind. You came to your mother. Who opened the door? A. My mother."

"Q. What did you say? A. I said, 'Hello, Teddy.'"

* * *

"Q. Now, you are back in your apartment, see. Your thoughts are clear now. What did you do after you took off your raincoat? A. She told me, 'Come and have some tea.'"

"Q. She told you what? A. 'Come and have a cup of tea. It will warm you up.'"

"Q. What did you do? A. Dad was having breakfast."

"Q. Where was Dad sitting? A. At the end of the table."

"Q. Where did you sit down? A. Between them."

"Q. Between whom? A. Mom and Pop."

"Q. Between Mom and Pop? A. That's right."

"Q. Where was Mom sitting? A. Next to the kitchen sink."

* * *

"Q. Your father went for the paper; then you hit your mother, didn't you? With what did you hit—with a hammer? Your thoughts are coming back to you. What did you use to hit your mother with? A. I loved my mother."

"Q. I know you did. You lost your temper. Don't be afraid. A lot of people do things that they are not responsible for while in a fit of temper. You see? A. My mother was the only thing in the world."

"Q. That's right. What did you hit her with? Come on, now. Speak up. A. I was so mad."

"Q. You were very mad. A. I said he's not going to treat my mother this way. He killed my brother."

"Q. Yes. He killed— A. My brother would have lived many years. The way my father made him work—"

"Q. That's right. A. I said he's not going to kill my mother and he's not going to kill me. The only way we can stop him. He's got to be stopped. He can't be the boss."

"Q. Go ahead. He's got to be stopped, you said. So? A. My mother always said she wanted to be with him."

"Q. Yes. A. Doc, I can't take it."

* * *

"Q. You know you hit your mother first. You hit your mother on the head. Speak up. What did you do? A. I don't know, Doctor."

"Q. Yes, you do. Speak up, now. Speak up. See, I can make you talk very truly. I can give you an injection now. It's much better if you tell me this way. Come on, now, speak up. A. I can't think, Doctor."

* * *

"Q. What then? A. I said, 'Mom, if he don't stop, I'll kill him.' "

"Q. I didn't hear that. What did you say? A. I told her, I said, 'Mom, if he don't stop the arguments with me, I'll kill him.' "

"Q. What did she say? A. So she said, 'Calm down. Here, take a drink of water.' So I said, 'Just wait until he comes back. We'll finish this once and for all.' "

* * *

"Q. So what did you do. Speak up. I'll positively help you if I can. I'm with you one hundred per cent. I'm going to help you. You're going to feel fine. Your conscience will be clear and everything will be fine. Don't hide anything. You did it in a fit of temper. Your mother went to the sink to give you some water. So you did what? You went up to her? A. I was standing there waiting for him to come back. I picked up the hammer."

"Q. You picked up the hammer? A. Yeah."

"Q. I didn't hear that. What did you say? A. I picked up the hammer."

"Q. Yes . . . say it. Say it. A. I said, 'He killed my brother, he'll kill my mother, and he'll kill me.' "

* * *

"Q. Did you have it in mind that your Mother would die with your Father because you always wanted it? A. She always said that."

"Q. She always said what? A. That she wanted to die with him."

"Q. You had it on your mind, didn't you? A. I don't know Doc."

"Q. Think and tell me; just think and tell me. A. She was just like a baby to me."

"Q. Just relax and your thoughts will come back to you because I have my hand on your forehead. Everything will be fine. If you tell us all the details we will know the whole story of what happened. You picked up the hammer and your Mother was sitting on the chair, you said, and you were standing at the sink? A. I was standing by the stove."

"Q. You were standing by the stove,

excuse me I made a mistake. What did you do with the hammer, you swung it? A. I must have Doc. Nobody else could have done it."

* * *

"A. I can't remember, Doctor."

"Q. Sure you can. A. I don't remember, Doctor."

"Q. Sure you can; try hard. A. I thought sometimes last night. I told the Captain last night I can't remember. That I would have to remember."

"Q. Why do you have to remember? A. Because if I can't remember these things here, my own children may not be safe. I can't remember what happened; I don't know what happened. I can't think."

"Q. What do you think will happen to the children? A. I don't know; it worries me."

"Q. What do you think might happen to the children? A. I was there with a hammer in my hand I know it. I remember having a hammer in my hand."

"Q. Take your time and relax. Now open your eyes and look at me, just open your eyes—look at me your thoughts will come back, look at me and concentrate. You said you were at the stove with the hammer in your right hand. You were very, very angry you said, right? A. I was never angry at my mother but my Father accused me."

"Q. Accuses you of what? A. That I was trying to put him out of business. The first day we went into the new business we gave him an equal share with us. (Noise) I knew for years that he killed my brother. My brother did the work of six men; he gave him a measly ten dollars a week. He'd sooner lose his son and stay in business so he could save the money and live with my mother."

"Q. I can understand how you feel about your Mother. (Noise) You were never so angry in all your life as you were at that time. You told your Mother that you were waiting to kill him. You were waiting for him to come back with the paper. That is what you told me. I can understand that the anger was sufficient to kill your Father? A. Why my mother?"

"Q. I don't know about your Mother but as far as your Father was concerned your thoughts were pretty clear, right? A. When he came back I said I was going to settle it once and for all."

* * *

"Q. Do you know you did it? A. I can't remember doing it. I know it happened. Look at my mother, the woman that I love most in the world. Look. How did it happen? I can't even remember. I can't remember him. I can't remember him coming back. Doctor, can anybody be this crazy?"

"Q. That is not crazy, my friend. That is not crazy."

* * *

"Q. These people are going to throw the book at you unless you can show that in a fit of temper, you got so angry that you did it. Otherwise they toss premeditation in and it's premeditation. See?"

"Q. Drink your coffee. Take your time. I got time. You got time. Just relax. Want some more coffee? A. I would like some hot coffee, doc. I would like to speak to the Captain." . . .

"Q. Well, we were getting along very nicely. I am trying to straighten him out with his troubles. He seemed a little mixed-up. His mind is clear now. I made him concentrate. His mind is much clearer. You can take my seat, Captain. [A.] Can I speak to the Captain?"

MR. JUSTICE MINTON, with whom MR. JUSTICE REED and MR. JUSTICE BURTON join, dissenting.

This petitioner was charged with murdering his parents by beating the life out of them with a hammer. No one claims that he has a defense to the charge. It is contended, however, that his conviction was not obtained in accordance with due process of law. . . .

The evidence shows an involuntary confession to Dr. Helfand. It was followed later by a confession to Captain Meenahan. Some half hour later petitioner confessed to a business associate, Herrschaft, saying, "Well, you know what it's all about; I did it." Herrschaft asked, "Do you mean that you killed your own mother and father?" and petitioner replied, "I did it." This confession was admitted in this Court to have been voluntarily made, and no complaint is made of its admission in evidence. Sandwiched in between the Meenahan confession and the confession to the assistant district attorneys some two and one-half hours later, the Herrschaft confession presents enough evidence in itself to go to the jury on whether these three confessions, one admitted to have been valid, were all given by petitioner voluntarily with the considered purpose of making a clean breast of the whole thing.

Nor was this the only evidence. Petitioner boldly examined Dr. Helfand, the State's witness, for the purpose, among others, of laying a foundation for the introduction of expert testimony by petitioner's psychiatrist that the effect of the coercion carried over to the later confes-

sions. Petitioner's expert testified as expected. The State then placed on the stand another psychiatrist who gave the opposite opinion, based on evidence that petitioner in his later confessions gave details of the crime known only to him and gave them freely without urging. If this disagreement between experts did not under New York law constitute a conflict in the evidence sufficient standing alone to go to the jury, there was other evidence, such as the Herrschaft confession, to be considered, together with the testimony of the assistant district attorneys that petitioner seemed quite normal and relaxed, and relieved to talk to them. As I said before, it is not our function to weigh the evidence. Whether there was any evidence to go to a jury is the question. In my opinion, there was a question of fact presented by the evidence. . . . I cannot say here that the subsequent confessions as a matter of law were so completely under the influence of the first confession that to let a jury pass upon that influence as it affected the voluntariness of the later confessions amounts to a denial of due process of law. To let the jury pass upon this question is not so unfair to petitioner as to violate the fundamental principles of justice.

1984 IN MINNEAPOLIS

The model of Supreme Court decision-making that we postulated in Chapter 11 for scalogram analysis assumed that the individual justices and the Court as a group respond in a systematic manner to a series of cases evoking questions that may appropriately be conceptualized as relating to the same underlying issue of constitutional policy; there is, in other words, a hierarchy of values for each justice and for the Court as a whole that is invoked for the decision of cases belonging to the same universe of data. For reasons that we have examined in Chapters 3 and 4, many cases are decided by lower courts, both state and federal, involving policy issues that are related to but not necessarily included among those that reach the Supreme Court for decision. Similarly, there are many other issues of constitutional policy that arise within American society but which are resolved, at least for the time being, by decision-making processes other than those of the judiciary. The latter two types of policy issues—those resolved in the lower courts and those which do not even reach the courts—may nevertheless have a significant bearing upon the cases that the Supreme Court does decide. Surely, the School Segregation Cases illustrate the fact that a social problem may be very real, and may continue as a focus of potential or actual controversy for over half a century, before the Supreme Court undertakes to deal with it openly as an articulate issue of constitutional policy.

The materials below relate to this kind of incipient issue which may or may not either proximately or ultimately be decided by the Court. Nevertheless, we can consider how the Court would be most likely to react to narcoanalysis as a technique for interrogating criminal suspects, both (1) by relating it to scaling theory and a scalogram of other cases that we have examined in this chapter (an exercise which we leave for the student to perform), and also (2) by an examination based upon the more traditional legal technique of *stare decisis* analysis. Does narcoanalysis raise questions, in addition to the obvious one of substantive due process, under the Fourteenth Amendment? And which of the correlates of "ordered liberty" does narcoanalysis most evidently involve: the search-and-seizure clause of the Fourth Amendment? the self-incrimination clause of the Fifth? the right to counsel of the Sixth? the cruel-and-unusual-punishment clause of the Eighth? Such an exercise is not academic, at least in the invidious sense of the word. It is true, of course, that *1984,* as depicted in George Orwell's novel, may never come to the United States. But some libertarian observers would argue that it is already here, in a modest sort of way, to the extent that forensic scientists are carrying out the biological experiments described below.

Narco Interrogation [15]

This is a PROSPECTUS: an analysis, and an accounting of the methods developed at the University of Minnesota for interrogation of criminal suspects during narcosis. Some of you will accept the challenge we offer, to try our methods, to duplicate, and to improve upon the results we have obtained. My missionary duties will be fulfilled if you only listen to the proposals which follow and recognize the tremendous usefulness this technique has in your criminological activities. The possibilities and potentialities we are to discuss are so broad and sweeping that just a brief review and summary are possible today.

Many of you are aware that the majority of my experience in the field of detecting deception has been with the polygraph. Frequently I have been asked about the limitations of this instrument and about the difficulties in interpretation of some of the recordings. At times we have been confronted

---

[15] C. B. Hanscom, "Narco Interrogation." Reprinted from *Journal of Forensic Sciences,* Vol. 1, No. 1, pp. 37-45 (January, 1956). [Annual Subscription Rate $20.00; published by Callaghan & Company, 6141 North Cicero Avenue, Chicago, Ill.] This article was earlier presented as a speech by Mr. Hanscom, Director of the Department of Protection and Investigation of the University of Minnesota, at the Annual Meeting of the American Academy of Forensic Sciences, February 17, 1955, Los Angeles, California.

with suspects with low mentality and with others who produce *"inconclusive charts,"* as they have been called.

But, on the 28th of September, 1948, I began one of the most interesting experiences in more than 25 years in the field of investigation. In essence, a young man with a long record of arrests and convictions was charged with the brutal murder of a boy and girl he surprised in unusual circumstances on a golf course. The conviction of this man finally depended upon locating the murder rifle. Our polygraph examinations disclosed his guilt, and he reacted to any possible location of the rifle which involved a body of water. We were at a loss to select the correct lake, river, or pond into which we could send divers.

In desperation we turned to the only other method of investigation we had not tried in this case—an interrogation of the suspect while he was influenced by anesthetic drugs! After three or four hours of questioning we had a complete confession of the crime, a description of the location of the gun, and the post-hypnotic suggestion that the suspect actually would lead us to the spot from which he threw the weapon into the pond! As promised, he helped us locate the rifle, and the case was prosecuted successfully.

More than thirty different tests under narcosis have followed this dramatic beginning. They have been concluded to our satisfaction and validated by the facts subsequently disclosed. We have no evidence of a failure in the series! Although this record is unusual, the Minnesota technique is based upon a firm historical background.

HISTORY. A study of more than 230 references to narco-analysis for criminal interrogation revealed that the evolution of our modern methods depended in every case, upon (1) the discovery of a drug which had narcotic or anesthetic properties; (2) upon the use of this drug in psychiatry where it was shown to produce changes in personality; and (3) upon the application of this combined knowledge in criminology. Recognizing this principle, those of us who were interested in improving the existing methods were obliged to continue testing newer drugs which have followed this pattern.

The process began as long ago as 1200 B.C. After the early explorations of opium, mandragora, the fumes of hemp, carbon dioxide, and potions of wine, there were few additions until after the Dark Ages. Later the Mexican Indians extracted a crude form of mescaline, called peyotl, from the cactus plant. They derived not only religious hallucinations from its use, but also used it as a means of obtaining confessions and social secrets. The priests who served these Indians reported these facts to the Old World in the 17th century. Psychiatrists of the 20th century rediscovered the modification of personality that mascaline could produce, and are now studying its effects on the accessibility of repressed information.

The Scientific Revolution of the 17th and 18th centuries discovered nitrous oxide, ether and chloroform for anesthetic purposes. In a short time there were discussions of "anesthetic revelations" and sporadic uses of the drugs in espionage, etc. In 1903 [Dr.] Wagner of New York used ether in the interrogation of a former police officer who was accused of murder. The technique he used in penetration of this officer's malingering was closely similar to the very method we use today. What a shame his reports were not studied by the forensic scientists long ago!

Throughout the first half of the 20th century there was a steady and rapid increase in our knowledge of anesthetic drugs, psychiatric principles, and forensic methods. Narco-analysis for criminal interrogation was tremendously improved by the experimental and factual results gained from the First and Second World wars. It was during this time that [Dr. R. E.] House [of Ferris, Texas] discovered that scopolamine was a powerful somnifacient and amnestic drug, which he claimed would produce the truth in more than 50 percent of his investigations of criminal suspects. His crusade attracted great publicity—during which the newspaper reporters coined the misleading term "truth serum"—and established Dr. House as the modern father of this field of interest.

During the wars our psychiatrists became proficient with sodium amytal and sodium pentothal in the exploration and treatment of mental illness. As we have been led to suspect, in a short time this information was brought into criminology where we find then the backbone of most pharmacological methods of interrogation. Thanks to the same teamwork and intensive effort, we also have derived plausible explanations and theories to explain the steps whereby we can elicit confessions and assay guilt or innocence during these examinations.

Lastly, the most recent advances have called for anesthesiological modification of the stages of narcosis required for proper interrogation. Perhaps the University of Minnesota is on the right path in this approach. Suffice it to say for this discussion, now various cerebral stimulants and mollifying agents have been introduced into the anesthetic mixtures. These and other changes allow the anesthesiologist to product wide fluctuations in the level of mental alterations with greater liberty, and in conformation with the decisions of the interrogators.

Research efforts presently call for the investigation of monitoring devices, such as the polyviso and electroencephalograph. These instruments gauge and direct the planes of anesthesia. They also allow us to continue our investigations of such new agents as thorazine, lysergic acid, mescaline, etc. in combination with the basic anesthetic drugs. Of course, newer methods of administration are also under investigation.

Although I am told the finite theory of narcosis is unexplained, clinical evidence of the anesthetic stages indicates that the various segments of the brain may be selectively depressed in a known order corresponding to their evolutional age, the more recently acquired cortex being depressed first. Psychiatrists generally believe that the cortex performs the discriminatory and integrative actions of the personality, while the diencephalon expresses the primitive emotional drives. Thus, in narco-analysis for criminal interrogation we are concerned only with depression of the cortex and diencephalon, which can be achieved in the first and second stages of general anesthesia. Now, by variation in the level of depression and selective stimulation, combined with proper interrogation techniques, we can modify the personality functions and lead the suspect into known confession mechanisms.

An untold degree of the success achieved by an interrogation team depends upon their thorough knowledge of the confession mechanisms available to the conscious (and thus, the unconscious) suspect. Most of you are aware that the more frequent admissions of guilt come from the criminal's inner desire to compromise with the community. Surely, a little persuasion from friends, relatives, attorneys, and skilled officers helps. Each of these associates helps to soften the emotional conflict of the subject and reduce his fear of punishment. This mechanism is produced easily under narcosis after the perceptive and integrative personality functions are depressed.

Besides this group of delinquents who confess readily, or with little assistance, are the informers and malingerers, the psychopaths, and the addicts, who welcome narco-analysis as an excuse to divulge their knowledge without fear of reprisal by their "friends." The knowledge that narco-analysis is available for the solution of cases involving these persons has been of immense value to our local officers.

Narcosis has been used to create, facilitate, or hasten, each of the above confession mechanisms by distorting the integrative functions along several pathways. Early in depression there is a reduction of the perceptive apparatus, which also diminishes the response to emotionally unpleasant stimuli, and produces a stage of heightened anxiety, or well-being, according to the ego efforts. At this drug level, skillful questioning may evade the discrimination of the subject and obtain sufficient facts to indicate culpability. Later the drugs attack integration directly, further depress the apprehensive ego, and allow the deepest inhibitions to be released painlessly.

Because this multitude of reactions is possible, some evidence of guilt usually escapes even the most hardened, repetitious, offenders who feel no remorse. These men have little knowledge of the successful record of the technique, and they consent to the examination because refusal might indicate complicity, or because they believe they can avoid detection and strengthen their case in court. This challenge has been met time and time again by careful manipulation of the psychological and pharmacological levers—by rapidly fluctuating the questioning and drugs to coincide with the mood—and by patient repetition of this process over and over through all the levels of personality and anesthesia! Application of these theories has helped us develop techniques and methods which extract the maximum from our tests.

TECHNIQUE. There are no "routines" that can be applied to narco-analysis for criminal interrogation, according to a standard which will insure optimum conditions every time. Each test is a problem in itself. It should be obvious also that one person cannot set himself up as an expert in *all* the phases of the test without limiting the result. Furthermore, until more research is possible in this field, the techniques we propose to discuss still must be manipulated by trial and error. The degree of precision achieved seems to depend largely upon the ability of the team members to adapt themselves, by enlargement and contraction of the knowledge applied to the problem, until they strike the proper balance in time and subject. However, certain practicalities have emerged as a result of accumulated experiences. Perhaps these can be described best by recounting the process we now follow in an ideal case—where all of our intentions can be translated into action!

When it becomes evident that narco-analysis for interrogation of a given suspect is possible, the proper team of consultants is drawn from the campus and the community. These individuals must be selected on the basis of (1) their scientific objectivity—for we do not have time under anesthesia to permit prejudice and lack of flexibility by the questioners to defeat the purpose— and (2) for whatever specific contribution they can lend to the actual interrogation. For example, on different occasions we have been benefited by the presence of lawyers for defense and prosecution, judges, psychiatrists, psychologists, foreign language experts, laboratory scientists, and various investigating officers. Those who are most familiar with the personality of the supect and the detail of the crime constitute the nucleus of the interrogation team. We always select an *anesthesiologist* for the drug administration because of his obvious knowledge of the pharmacology, limitations of the various agents required, and the levels of anesthesia sought during the test. His presence and the patient-physician relationship protects the patient medically and contributes something to the patient's emotional well-being.

In the initial interview the principal interrogator attempts to establish rapport with the suspect, convince him of our impartiality and fairness, and heighten his confidence in a fair examination. We usually conduct several preliminary psychological tests to establish a more scientific basis of our knowledge of his personality, intelligence, and emotional stability. The interview concludes when the suspect definitely understands his constitutional liberties, which allow him to refuse the examination or accept the possibility that its results might be used in subsequent investigations or prosecution.

The actual narco-analysis is conducted in an operating room suite. Although it is difficult to avoid the apprehension created by this location, the safety and convenience to the patient and physician are more important. Every effort is made to alter the furniture, etc., to create a better atmosphere. A thorough physical examination and medical history are evaluated by the anesthesiologist—just as he does for routine surgical anesthesia. The suspects seem to derive additional comfort from this precaution too!

Pre-anesthetic medication with intravenous barbiturates, scopolamine, and occasionally morphine, is just as essential for these examinations as it is for surgery. The dosage of scopolamine is increased slightly, but otherwise the quantities required for routine anesthetic premedication are used. Basal narcosis is accomplished with a 2½ percent concentration of sodium pentothal. All of the medication is given intravenously because of the rapid onset of effect and easy control achieved. The sodium pentothal is gradually injected as we converse with the suspect about anything *but* the crime. As the first stage of anesthesia is passed and the suspect finds it more and more difficult to hear and answer our questions, the conversation is changed to more critical events. At this stage he may repeat the same story he told before anesthesia. With some persuasion, as we described in the theoretical discussion, he may begin his confession. Usually it is first necessary to traverse the whole first and second stages of anesthesia before incriminating information is released. The interrogation is varied, just as the anesthesia is deepened and lightened, according to the decisions to attempt an emotional outburst, or to confuse the orderly thinking of the suspect.

Most of our confessions have followed reactions of fear, extreme anger, boasting, love, etc. Once the admission of guilt is begun, we attempt to hold the suspect on the same train of thought, and bring him slowly out of the anesthetic until we have a clear, intelligible record of the entire confession on a tape recorder. Occasionally picrotoxin, metrazol, benzedrine, and thorazine have been used to accentuate certain of the responses. More experience will be necessary with these drugs to outline the precise role they play in the interview.

The post-anesthetic interview offers the team an excellent opportunity to confront the suspect with recordings of his guilty knowledge. When properly presented to him, this surprise often produces an admissible extrajudicial confession. Reviews of the tape recordings also frequently suggest new avenues for police investigation.

Not all interviews end in confessions, of course. We are quite proud to say that *most* of our suspects were innocent. Their general conduct, eagerness to assist the interrogators explain their questionable actions, and their complete freedom from evasion helped persuade the referring officers to look elsewhere for their criminal.

Unsuccessful results probably come from a failure to apply the principles outlined here. Undoubtedly low intelligence contributes to the difficulties encountered and wears the patience of the team. Acts committed during profound alcoholic stupor and associated with severe head wounds probably are not accessible through this means. Prolonged incarceration and violent treatment or severe questioning reduce our ease of interrogation and may, at some future date, negate our efforts.

No reports have been discovered to the effect that narco-analysis for criminal interrogation has been used to force a suspect to confess a crime he did not commit! On the other hand, guilty suspects have maintained their lies during tests by methods other than we have described here. Perhaps our statistical group is still too small, and we may soon encounter a failure. Nevertheless, until the test is more fully developed, and more accurately measured, the suspects' drug influenced statements must be corroborated by fact before they can be admitted as evidence.

Whereas there is a great divergence of opinion about the need for legalizing these tests, we ought to conclude with a summary of our thoughts on this aspect:

1. We have shown that the test is capable of application to all types of cases—adaptable to all kinds of personalities.
2. Although the truth has been accessible in our limited experience, the suspects can still lie and thwart the examiners.
3. It, therefore, remains with sufficient inaccuracy to advise against admission as evidence on this basis alone.
4. The drug-induced statements must be corroborated by facts before they can serve defense or prosecution in court.

Therein lies the primary purpose of our tests. Ethically, it is far superior to third degree methods which employ physical or mental coercion. It frequently provides a rapid avenue to justice, which I am sure many can appreciate. The methods described are not intended to supplant accepted modes of investigation; rather, success seems proportioned to the quality of the investigation which precedes the narcosis! Lastly, narco-analysis is a delicate, prolonged operation, which should be available to any person who may benefit from it. But it should never be used without good reason.

I find it impossible to close without paying tribute to our anesthesiologist, Dr. James Matthews. Without his untiring efforts, knowledge and inspiration, our investigations of this technique would not have been possible. Those of you who are more interested in the precise details of both the drug and the interrogative process should consult the basic references outlined in the *Textbook of Legal Medicine,* edited by Dr. Gradwohl, wherein Dr. Matthews has summarized our findings.[16]

Narcoanalysis: A Service or An Assault? [17]

TO THE EDITOR:

The American Academy of Forensic Sciences invited one of its members, who is the director of the University's department of protection and investigation and the president of the American Academy of Scientific Interrogation, to discuss the University's program of narcoanalysis for criminal interrogation at their annual convention and seminar in Los Angeles on Feb. 17.

The Minneapolis and St. Paul newspapers carried full accounts of this scientific discussion the following day. The last issue of the Daily, March 13, published a "Campus Opinion" from an instructor in zoology who attacked

---

[16] Dr. James H. Matthews, "Narcoanalysis for Criminal Interrogation," pp. 945-979 (chap. xxxiii) in R. B. H. Gradwohl, *Legal Medicine* (St. Louis: C. V. Mosby Co., 1954).

[17] "Campus Opinion," The Minnesota Daily (University of Minnesota, Minneapolis), March 29, 1955.

the speaker, the research program and the University's policy of support to these studies.

The attack strongly implied the process was "brain-washing;" asked who had been victimized; if the tests were necessary for our protection; if they were in the interests of the University, and if they represented University policy. The spurious nature of the letter is attested by the manner in which certain items were carefully selected out of context to the exclusion of other basic references cited in the original news release. The author of that opinion and other readers who are not informed about present methods of criminological interrogation, and thus the nature of forensic science research, should consider the following statements.

Narcoanalysis for criminal interrogation is the phrase used on this campus to signify the administration of anesthetics (by a physician) to such a depth of unconsciousness that skilled interrogators (detectives, psychiatrists, psychologists, attorneys, etc.,) can ascertain more factual statements than could be obtained from the suspect in the conscious state. The process is ethically conducted only upon volunteers who are under arrest for heinous crimes.

The conclusions of the interrogation team are not admissible to court as evidence except when the drug-induced statements can be supported by facts ordinarily admissible under present rules of evidence. *The fact and not the manner of its ascertainment is more important to justice;* [18] but the process of interrogation must not, and in these instances, certainly does not, conflict with constitutional liberties.

We are informed that "brain-washing," on the other hand, is an attritious process involving complex psychiatric and phramacologic reorientation directed towards the total personality than toward isolated facts. The University's team is anxious that its test not supplant ordinary investigation and interrogation, but extend these means only when necessary.

We are equally convinced that the test must not be used as otherwise unsubstantiated evidence in court since our experience suggests that it does not have the accuracy required of such evidence. The test therefore is limited to volunteers by law, and further to a research status in our practices.

Since 1948 members of the medical school staff and the protection and investigation staff have responded to 31 requests from 15 law enforcement agencies in 5 states when ordinary methods of investigation were inadequate and the progress of these cases was halted. As a result 23 charges of murder, 3 cases of rape, and 5 other criminal charges of serious import have been solved or the suspects cleared. No other tests have been performed.

The record of 100 percent success with this type suspect is unique in forensic science experience and therefore deserves additional study. The University and many of the Daily's readers also will take pride in the fact that 16 of the 22 suspects subsequently *were declared innocent and were released* from suspicion and custody by the referring authorities primarily because

[18] Emphasis added.

of these activities. (These are the "victims" of "dubious practices" the zoologist challenges us to identify.)

Responsible officials of the University have encouraged continuation of the research program because our institution is adequately staffed and equipped to conduct this type test, because of the successful outcome of previous interrogations, and because the test is an obvious service to the individual and the community.

JAMES H. MATTHEWS, M.D.
Division of Anesthesiology, University Hospitals

C. B. HANSCOM
Director, Department of Protection and Investigation

Narcoanalysis: This Is the Technique [19]

(Ed. note [by Norman Larsen of *The Minnesota Daily*]: According to a chapter on "Narcoanalysis for Criminal Interrogation" by James H. Matthews of the University division of anesthesiology, in the book "Textbook of Legal Medicine," edited by Dr. R. B. H. Gradwohl, this is the technique generally used in narco interrogation. P and I director C. B. Hanscom cited the chapter in his narco-analysis speech at Los Angeles last February.)

The test is begun at the time of the initial scopolamine injection by showing the patient one or more common articles such as a bar of soap or a knife. He is instructed to remember these as long as possible.

The items are displayed periodically and additional injections of the drug are administered as soon as the subject no longer can recall the original items, usually after one or two hours. Then the "patient" is engaged in conversation on various irrelevant topics.

Following this period of light sleepiness, the patient may express symptoms of euphoria, hallucinations, intoxication, a "confident feeling" and additional evidences of mild disorientation and confusion.

As the narcosis deepens the patient may continue his conversation, but the substance becomes disconnected, the pauses longer and the vocabulary more and more inadequate.

Slurring, mumbling and thickening of speech become even more pronounced just before the last traces of consciousness are lost. This is the lowest kind of depression permissible with the scopolamine technique; any further indications of impending unconsciousness are considered early signs of poisoning.

Sodium pentothal and sodium amytal are then administered. ("The sodium pentothal is gradually injected as we converse about anything but crime," Hanscom said in his speech.) The patient now enters the level of superficial unconsciousness where verbal stimulus will arouse him.

When this state has been induced, "and the suspects finds it more and

---

[19] Norman Larsen, Daily News Editor, in "Campus Opinion," *loc. cit.,* March 30, 1955.

more difficult to hear and answer our questions," Hanscom said, the criminal interrogation should begin.

After the patient has been oriented to this new topic, his replies may indicate that he still is aware of his surroundings and desires to evade questions.

Depending upon the success and emotional show with which these initial replies are made, further anesthetization may or may not be given.

The last sign of the second stage of the sodium pentothal anesthesia consists of an exaggerated inappropriate movement of the arms and legs with the application of a very painful, surgical stimulus.

Just before this end point is reached, a mild to moderate stimulus will bring about a more or less automatic answer to loud, repeated questioning. These answers may be mumbled, thickened speech which is either barely audible or emotionally charged.

The "art" is to keep the patient in this state, and the plane just superficial, as long as the interrogator desires.

"Once the admission of guilt is begun," Hanscom said, "we attempt to hold the suspect on the same train of thought, and bring him slowly out of the anesthetic until we have a clear, intelligible record of the entire confession on a tape recorder."

However, Hanscom pointed out that "not all interviews end in confessions. In fact," he continued, "most of our suspects were innocent."

The Sense of Justice [20]

TO THE EDITOR:

Police methods raise moral and constitutional questions as well as issues concerning the efficiency of law enforcement. Both "the fact," and "the manner of its ascertainment," are essential to justice. "Due process," Mr. Justice Frankfurter teaches us, ". . . says that convictions cannot be brought about by methods that offend a 'sense of justice.' " [21] The use of some methods would, again in the words of the Justice, "be . . . calculated to discredit law and thereby to brutalize the temper of a society."

Apart from resorting to physical force, it is hard to imagine a method of interrogation more "brutalizing" than questioning an accused human being who has lost, by the injection of drugs, the use of those powers which are the distinguishing mark of his humanity.

The Matthews-Hanscom defense of employing drugs in criminal interrogation rests in part on the subject's "voluntary" submission to the technique. But "voluntary" after how much pressure? How "voluntary" will the surrender be if the failure to submit can be referred to in the prosecutor's summation? Is submission made only after the accused has consulted counsel?

More important, should a person be permitted, let alone encouraged, to put himself, impaired in his highest functions, into the hands of police

[20] "Campus Opinion," *loc. cit.*, March 31, 1955.

[21] *Rochin* v. *California*, 342 U.S. 165, 173 (1952), and *supra*, this chapter.

investigators? Once the subject is drugged, the scope of the questioning is controlled by the questioners. The accused can no longer refuse to talk of events foreign to the matter at hand or of persons toward whom he may have a duty of silence. Save for the professional discipline of the "police scientist" nothing stands in the way of a grand "fishing expedition."

The Matthews-Hanscom letters take pride in the fact that 16 suspects were declared innocent. I believe they would have been released, as well, by the ordinary processes of law, old fashioned, perhaps, but monuments to human dignity.

We need once more to listen to Mr. Justice Frankfurter: "Ours is the accusatorial as opposed to the inquisitorial system . . . Under our system society carries the burden of proving its charge against the accused not out of his own mouth. It must establish its case, not by interrogation of the accused even under judicial safeguards, but by evidence independently secured through a skillful investigation."

MONRAD PAULSEN
Professor of Law

Constitutional questions concerning the use as evidence of confessions induced by narcoanalysis have not as yet arisen before the Supreme Court. It is unlikely that questions concerning the direct use of such confessions will arise, because of the general assumpton that neither state courts nor the federal courts would condone the introduction of this kind of evidence in a criminal case. The obvious analogy is to the results of so-called "lie-detector tests," which are inadmissible in all courts, state and federal alike, in the United States.[22] The inadmissibility in court of polygraph results has not discouraged the extensive use of such tests in police investigations, however; nor is it unknown for news of the use of polygraph tests to reach the ears of jurors. Anyone who refuses to take a lie-detector test stands convicted before trial in the eyes of the press and public; and he immediately identifies himself to many prosecutors as a good suspect.

The polygraph yields a measure of the subject's emotional response to questions asked of him during the administration of the test. An analyst infers from the subject's response pattern whether his answers to key questions are truthful or not. But the results obtained from the use of the polygraph are quite different from the results obtained through narcoanalysis. Questions asked of a subject during narcoanalysis yield information of a quite different nature. The subject, having been deprived of the capacity to conceal information or to wish to avoid incriminating himself, reveals whether or not he committed the crime; where, how, when, and why he did it; the whereabouts of the *corpus delicti;* and so forth. Such responses may well lead to the recovery of physical evidence, such as the

[22] See the Annotation, "Physiological or psychological truth and deception tests," 23 A.L.R. 2d 1306-1311.

missing murder weapon; and the question then arises whether such physical evidence, corroborative of the suspect's guilt, can be introduced without violating the due-process clause of the Fourteenth Amendment. The suspect, if under the effects of posthypnotic suggestion, may even re-enact his crime for the benefit of the police. Of course, it may be said, a suspect cannot do such things unless he is guilty; and if he is guilty, isn't it better that he should be found out and punished? As for innocent suspects, they should be grateful that science has helped them to clear their good names.

It is by no means inconceivable that the fruits of narco-examinations may yet get into the state courts, and thence ultimately in a case brought before the Supreme Court, tomorrow if not today. And what would the Supreme Court be likely to do in such a case? There would be no police brutality, as in Rochin; just a nice, clean, hospital operating room, as in Breithaupt. The evidence, even if it were the result of an illegal search and seizure, would be admissible according to the Wolf rule. And, as the Breithaupt decision holds, "the absence of conscious consent [of a narco-subject to his confession?] does not necessarily render the taking a violation of a constitutional right." After all, people have operations, just as they undergo blood tests, every day; there is nothing particularly "brutal" or "offensive" about the administration of an anesthetic. And the actual administration of the narco-anesthetic requires only the injection of a needle in the arm, an invasion of bodily privacy that certainly is quite analogous to the prick of a pin or a needle necessary for a blood sample and test. Indeed, it is almost identical to the scratch in the arm required for vaccination, which is the type of "lesser sacrifice" that the good citizen must be prepared to make in the higher interests of the commonweal,[23] as Mr. Justice Holmes himself reminded us in Buck v. Bell.

The prediction problem is complicated, of course, by the uncertainty concerning how individual justices, sitting on the Court at the time such a case arose for decision, might react—whether personally and privately or through the mystical process by which some justices are able to excogitate the consensus of society toward questions whose existence and meaning are unknown to individual members of society, as the public-opinion polls constantly remind us. It is probably of slight help, but there are two or three utterances by Supreme Court justices—spoken, of course, in dissent—which seem to be somewhat in point. Mr. Justice Douglas has said that "Liberty in the constitutional sense must mean more than freedom from unlawful governmental restraint; it must include privacy as well, if it is to be a repository of freedom." [24] To this Justice Jackson has added, speaking of law and the citizen under our system, "I think we must let his mind alone." [25] But Jackson is dead and Douglas is only one of nine justices; so the

---

[23] See the senior Justice Harlan's opinion for the Court in *Jacobson* v. *Massachusetts*, 197 U.S. 11 (1905).

[24] Dissenting in *Public Utilities Commis-*

sion v. *Pollack*, 343 U.S. 451, 467 (1952).

[25] Dissenting in *American Communications Association* v. *Douds*, 339 U.S. 382, 444 (1950).

question remains: to what extent would the Court uphold what Justice Brandeis once described as "the right to be let alone—the most comprehensive of rights and the right most valued by civilized men"? [26]

[26] Dissenting in *Olmstead* v. *United States*, 277 U.S. 438, 478 (1928). Immediately preceding this oft-quoted statement by Brandeis is a sentence which is less well known: "The makers of our Constitution . . . sought to protect Americans in their beliefs, their thoughts, their emotions and their sensations."

APPENDIXES

APPENDIXES

The Publication of Reports
of the Supreme Court's Decisions

THE OPINIONS and decisions of the United States Supreme Court are reported in a variety of ways and formats. The most important of these are described below.

For almost a hundred years, the Court's opinions in cases decided formally (i.e., after oral argument and on the merits) were published, following the English and Colonial practice, under the name of the Court's reporter, although these same volumes also were retroactively assigned volume numbers in the continuous series of official *United States Reports* (U.S.), which supplanted the name of the reporter of the series after 1882. Beginning at the same time (October Term, 1882), a commercial publication of the Court's opinions and decisions, the *Supreme Court Reporter* (S.Ct.) was published by the West Publishing Company of St. Paul. In the preceding year, the first volume of the *Lawyers' Edition of the Opinions of the United States Supreme Court* (L.ed.) was published by The Lawyers Co-operative Publishing Company of Rochester; and unlike the *Supreme Court Reporter,* which extends only from the October Term, 1882, to the present, the *Lawyers' Edition* went back and reprinted all of the earlier volumes, so that the L.ed. series is complete from 1790 to the present. A collation of the volume numbers for these three series of reports appears on page 704.

There are advantages and disadvantages to the use of each of these three sets of the Court's reports (the *United States Reports* and those published under the names of reporters is really one series under varying titles). The official reports are printed in larger type and are therefore both easier to read and more bulky

United States Reports	Court Reporters	Lawyers' Edition	Supreme Court Reporter	Terms Included
2-4 [1]	2-4 Dallas	1	—	Feb., 1790-Aug., 1800
5-13	1-9 Cranch	2-3	—	Aug., 1801-Feb., 1815
14-25	1-12 Wheaton	4-6	—	Feb., 1816-Jan., 1827
26-41	1-16 Peters	7-10	—	Jan., 1828-Jan., 1842
42-65	1-24 Howard	11-16	—	Jan., 1843-Dec., 1860
66-67	1-2 Black	17	—	Dec., 1861-Dec., 1862
68-90	1-23 Wallace	17-23	—	Dec., 1863-Oct., 1874 [2]
91-107	1-17 Otto	23-27	1 [3]	Oct., 1875-Oct.. 1882
108-360	—	27-3L.ed.2d [4]	2-69	Oct., 1882-Oct., 1958

[1] Omitted from this list is Volume 1 U.S. (1 Dallas), which includes reports of the Pennsylvania state courts, largely during the period prior to the ratification of the Constitution and the establishment of the United States Supreme Court.

[2] The Court shifted to a system of annual October Terms beginning in 1873 (at 18 Wallace and 85 U.S.).

[3] Volume 1 S.Ct. includes 106-107 U.S. and part of the October Term of 1882. Volumes 2-4 S.Ct. cover the remainder of 1882 and the 1883 Terms; annual volumes, one for each term, begin with 5 S.Ct. and the October,

1884, Term.

[4] The volumes of the Lawyers' Edition preceding Volume 33 cover more than one term. Volume 100 L.ed. covered the 1955 Term. The set was then redesignated as the Lawyers' Edition, Second Series, and cited as "L.ed.2d," with 1 L.ed.2d covering the October, 1956, Term. (Actually, the coverage for both L.ed. and S.Ct. is from July 1–June 30, since the Court has convened in Special Terms during the summer vacation with increasing frequency during the decade of the 1950's.)

to handle. The *Supreme Court Reporter* (beginning with the 1884 Term) and *Lawyers' Edition* (beginning with the 1888 Term) offer the advantage of printing the decisions and opinions for an entire term in a single volume; the official reports required three volumes as long ago as the 1873 Term, and at present usually require three volumes per term. Together with the Court's opinions, L.ed. continues to report excerpts from the briefs filed by counsel (a practice discontinued in the official *United States Reports* by the advent of World War II), and also presents for many cases annotations which constitute useful introductions to and summaries of various legal questions. S.Ct. is tied in with the publisher's general indexing system (the Key Reporter System) for American case law; and the same publisher is the only publisher of a complete system of the reports of all of the highest courts of the states, as well as the only publisher of the decisions of the federal district courts and courts of appeals.[5]

[5] Selected lower federal court decisions are published, for the first century up to the 1880's, in a thirty-volume series of *Federal Cases* (Fed. Cas.), which is now out of print; this was followed by a three-hundred-volume series of the *Federal Reporter* (Fed.), in which both district court and circuit court of appeals decisions were included. The same practice was continued for a few years in a series called *Federal Supplement* (F.Supp.); but since approximately 1932, district court decisions have continued to be reported in *Federal Supplement*, while court of appeals decisions have been reported separately in a publication called *Federal Reporter, Second Series* (F.2d).

During the term and prior to the appearance of the bound volumes described above, there are at the present time six principal methods by which the Court's current decisions and opinions are reported. The official reporter distributes individual "slip opinions" of each case (and, more recently, of each set of miscellaneous orders plus the Court's *Journal*); these are generally received by libraries within a period of from a few days to a week or two after the announcement of the events to which they relate. The official reporter also distributes a paperback "Preliminary Print" of the *United States Reports;* there are usually four to six numbers (or parts) to each volume, and they appear from two to three months after the announcement of the decisions and opinions to which they relate. There are also advance paperback editions for both L.ed. and S.Ct.; these are issued approximately twice a month during the term, following each decision day, and are received from two to three weeks after the decisions and opinions they report.

Each of the three series of advance reports (U.S., L.ed., and S.Ct.) is paginated just as its respective bound volumes will later be. However, the advance opinions of L.ed. and S.Ct. obviously cannot include, as do the permanent bound volumes, the running key (for citational purposes) to the pagination of the official (U.S.) reports.

There are also two publishers of loose-leaf reporters, which generally provide the earliest issuance of the Court's decisions and opinions (except for the official slip opinions). *United States Law Week (Supreme Court Section),* cited as L.W. and published by The Bureau of National Affairs, Inc. of Washington, D.C., reports excerpts of oral argument in what the publishers consider to be the more important cases heard by the Court, together with information on the status of the Court's docket and a cumulative index; the Court's opinions are published and mailed to subscribers the day after they are announced, and are generally available within a week after the Court's decision days. L.W. began publication (Volume I) with the October Term, 1932; the 1958 Term is reported in Volume 27. The *Supreme Court Bulletin* is a loose-leaf reporter published by Commerce Clearing House Inc., of Chicago, beginning in the 1939 Term; Volume 19 covers the 1958 Term. C.C.H. publishes advance opinions in facsimile from the official copies, and its reports are normally mailed from Washington on decision day. The *Supreme Court Bulletin* also covers the docket and digests the issues in pending appeals, but it does not report oral argument before the Supreme Court. There are also some newspapers, such as the *New York Times,* which summarize the Court's decisions and occasionally (but not systematically) quote from oral argument before the Court or the opinions of the justices.

The *New York Times,* of course, is indexed. There are individual volume indexes and tables of cases to all of the series described above (except the slip opinions), but for general use, indexes covering a longer period of time are required. Probably the most useful of these are the *U.S. Supreme Court Digest,* published by the publisher of S.Ct.; *U.S. Supreme Court Digest, Annotated,* published by the publisher of L.ed.; and *Shepard's Citator* (Supreme Court Edition). All three of these include parallel references to U.S., S.Ct., and L.ed. reports.

B]

Tenure of Supreme Court Justices (1789-1959)

T HE NAME of each justice is entered in the year of his appointment, under the number of the position to which he was appointed. Position 1 is that of the Chief Justice. If a justice left the Court during the same year in which his successor was seated, this is indicated by the entry of the successor's appointment. If a justice left the Court in a year prior to the seating of his successor, the word *"Vacated"* indicates the year in which the justice vacated his office. The usual abbreviations indicate the state to which residence was credited at the time of appointment. The political-party affiliation, at the time of appointment, is indicated by F (Federalist), DR (Democratic Republican), D (Democrat), W (Whig), R (Republican), or I (Independent).

Date	Positions									
	1	2	3	4	5	6	7	8	9	10
1789	Jay F/N.Y.	J. Rutledge a F/S.C.	Cushing F/Mass.	Wilson F/Pa.	Blair F/Va.					
1790						Iredell F/N.C.				

a Rutledge was confirmed and commissioned as an associate justice of the original Court; he served on circuit duty but never sat with the Supreme Court during the twenty-one months before he resigned to become Chief Justice of the highest court of the State of South Carolina.

Date   Positions

	1	2	3	4	5	6	7	8	9	10
1791		T. Johnson F/Md.								
1793		Paterson F/N.J.								
1795	J. Rutledge b F/S.C.									
1796	Ellsworth F/Conn.				Chase F/Md.					
1798				Washington F/Va.						
1799						Moore F/N.C.				
1800	*Vacated*									
1801	Marshall F/Va.									
1804						W. Johnson DR/S.C.				
1806		Livingston DR/N.Y.								
1807							Todd DR/Ky.			
1810			*Vacated*							
1811			Story DR/Mass.	Duval DR/Md.						
1823		*Vacated*								
1824		Thompson DR/N.Y.								
1826							Trimble DR/Ky.			
1828							*Vacated*			
1829				*Vacated*		McLean D/Ohio				
1830			Baldwin D/Pa.							
1834						*Vacated*				

b Rutledge sat briefly as Chief Justice on an interim appointment, but the Senate failed to confirm his permanent appointment.

Date	Positions									
	1	2	3	4	5	6	7	8	9	10
1835	*Vacated*				*Vacated*	Wayne D/Ga.				
1836	Taney D/Md.				Barbour D/Va.					
1837								Catron D/Tenn.	McKinley D/Ky.	
1841					Daniel D/Va.					
1843		*Vacated*								
1844				*Vacated*						
1845		Nelson D/N.Y.	Woodbury D/N.H.							
1846				Grier D/Pa.						
1851			Curtis W/Mass.							
1852									*Vacated*	
1853									Campbell D/Ala.	
1857			*Vacated*							
1858			Clifford D/Me.							
1860					*Vacated*					
1861							*Vacated*		*Vacated*	
1862					Miller R/Iowa		Swayne R/Ohio		Davis R/Ill.	
1863										Field D/Cal.
1864	Chase R/Ohio									
1865								*Vacated*		

Date	Positions									
	1	2	3	4	5	6	7	8	9	10
1867						*Vacated*				
1870				Strong R/Pa.		Bradley R/N.J.				
1872		Hunt R/N.Y.								
1873	*Vacated*									
1874	Waite R/Ohio									
1877									Harlan R/Ky.	
1880				*Vacated*						
1881			*Vacated*	Woods R/Ga.		Matthews R/Ohio				
1882		Blatch- ford	Gray R/Mass.							
1887		R/N.Y.		*Vacated*						
1888	Fuller D/Ill.			L. Lamar D/Miss.						
1889						*Vacated*				
1890					*Vacated*	Brewer R/Kan.				
1891					Brown R/Mich.					
1892						Shiras R/Pa.				
1893		*Vacated*		H. Jackson D/Tenn.						
1894		White D/La.								
1895				*Vacated*						
1896				Peckham D/N.Y.						
1897										*Vacated*

Date	Positions									
	1	2	3	4	5	6	7	8	9	10
1898										McKenna [c] R/Cal.
1902			Holmes R/Mass.							
1903						Day R/Ohio				
1906					Moody R/Mass.					
1909				Vacated						
1910	White [d] D/La.	Vacated		Lurton D/Tenn.	Vacated		Hughes R/N.Y.			
1911		Van Devanter R/Wyo.			J. Lamar D/Ga.				Vacated	
1912									Pitney R/N.J.	
1914				McReynolds D/Tenn.						
1916					Brandeis D/Mass.		Clarke D/Ohio			
1921	Taft R/Conn.									
1922						Vacated	Suther- land		Vacated	
1923						Butler D/Minn.	R/Utah		Sanford R/Tenn.	
1925								Stone [e] R/NY		Vacated [e]
1930	Hughes R/N.Y.								Roberts R/Pa.	
1932			Cardozo D/N.Y.							

[c] After having increased the size of the Court to ten positions in 1863, Congress reduced the number to seven in 1866 (in order to prevent President Johnson from making any appointments) and then raised it back to nine in 1869 after Grant's election. The Catron vacancy in position 8, which occurred in 1865, was never filled. Field, who was appointed to position 10 when it was created in 1863, did not retire until 1897, and McKenna replaced him in the following year. But there have been only nine positions on the Court since 1869.

[d] White was promoted to the Chief Justiceship, which required, of course, a new appointment and confirmation.

[e] Stone replaced McKenna, who appears to have occupied what was originally position 10. However, it seems less confusing to show Stone in position 8, in place of the dropped position which was occupied by only one justice, Catron (1837-1865). See note c, above.

Date	Positions									
	1	2	3	4	5	6	7	8	9	10
1937		Black D/Ala.								
1938		*Vacated*					Reed D/Ky.			
1939			Frankfurter I/Mass.	Douglas D/Conn.	*Vacated*					
1940					Murphy D/Mich.					
1941	Stone[f] R/N.Y.			Byrnes D/S.C.				R. Jackson D/N.Y.		
1942				*Vacated*						
1943				W. Rutledge D/Iowa						
1945									Burton R/Ohio	
1946	Vinson D/Ky.									
1949				Minton D/Ind.	Clark D/Tex.					
1953	Warren R/Cal.									
1954									*Vacated*	
1955									Harlan R/N.Y.	
1956				Brennan D/N.J.						
1957							Whittaker R/Mo.			
1958									Stewart R/Ohio	

Composition of the Court at the End of the October, 1958, Term

Warren R/Cal.	Black D/Ala.	Frankfurter I/Mass.	Brennan D/N.J.	Douglas D/Conn.	Clark D/Tex.	Whittaker R/Mo.	Harlan R/N.Y.	Stewart R/Ohio

[f] Stone was promoted to the position of Chief Justice.

Political-Party Domination over Appointments to the Supreme Court (1789-1959)

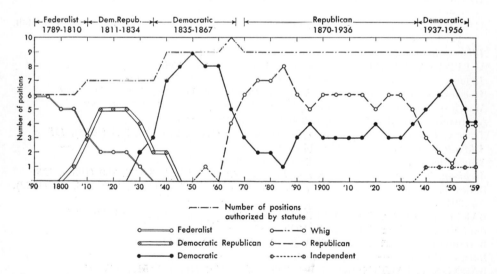

The curve has been rounded at five-year intervals. The exact data for each year can be derived from Appendix B. Party identification is that as of the time of appointment; in other words, the data do not take into consideration the fact that McLean, who was appointed as a Democrat, later became a Republican (or that Davis changed in the opposite direction).

Table of Cases

Case titles printed in CAPITALS designate the major cases that are reprinted in this volume; and boldface numbers (**000**) are used to cite the first page of such reprinting, in each case. Cases that are discussed in the text, or in the (italicized) case introductions or in footnotes written by the author, have titles printed below in ordinary (or roman) type. Case titles printed in *italics* designate cases which are only cited by the author, or which are discussed only in judicial opinions or other quoted selections. Page citations to discussions of cases in the text, or in case introductions or footnotes written by the author, are set in ordinary (or roman) numbers (000). Other page references to cases (i.e., cited but not discussed by the author, or discussed in judicial opinion or other quoted selection) are set in italic numbers (*000*).

Index